Cases and Materials on TORTS

EDITORIAL ADVISORY BOARD

Cases and Materials on TORTS

Sixth Edition

Richard A. Epstein

James Parker Hall
Distinguished Service Professor of Law
The University of Chicago

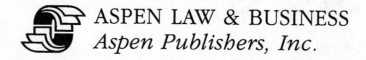
ASPEN LAW & BUSINESS
Aspen Publishers, Inc.

Library of Congress Catalog Card No. 94-73115

ISBN 0-316-24587-9

Sixth Edition

Third Printing

KP

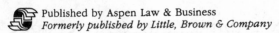 Published by Aspen Law & Business
Formerly published by Little, Brown & Company

Printed in the United States of America

To the memory of two great men,
and great men of torts:

Charles O. Gregory
Harry Kalven, Jr.

Summary of Contents

Table of Contents

PART TWO.   NON-PHYSICAL INTERESTS

Preface

This is now the sixth edition of this casebook, and the fourth one I have undertaken myself. Its origins go back to the 1950s, when Charles O. Gregory and Harry Kalven, Jr. prepared the first edition, which appeared in 1959. A second edition followed some ten years later, and was in fact the book from which I first taught torts at the University of Southern California in 1969. In 1972 I came to the University of Chicago. In January 1974, with Gregory in retirement, my colleague, Professor Kalven, asked me to collaborate with him on the third edition of Gregory and Kalven, Cases and Materials on Torts. Kalven's tragic death in October 1974 cut short our brief collaboration just as we were beginning work. Thereafter Professor Charles O. Gregory was kind enough to reenter the lists and to read and comment on the drafts of the third edition, which appeared in 1977. The work on the fourth edition of Epstein, Gregory and Kalven, which appeared in 1984, I did alone. Gregory died in April 1987, after a rich and full life. The fifth edition (1990) and this sixth edition both bear my name alone, for the change of the guard between generations is now complete. Even so, the case selection and organization of this book continue to owe much to Gregory and Kalven, who brought a pioneering spirit and rich imagination to the study of torts. I shall always be in their debt.

The sixth edition blends new with old elements. There are two major changes in overall design. First, I have dismantled the old chapter on nervous shock and emotional distress that used to begin the second half of the book on nonphysical injuries. The increased importance of these cases in ordinary tort litigation has made it advisable to bring these questions to the attention of the student earlier in the course, so they are now paired with physical injuries in the treatment of both intentional and accidental torts. Second, I have created a new chapter on multiple parties, which brings together the materials on joint and several liability, joint causation, and vicarious liability. But even with these organizational changes I have worked hard to preserve the continuity between the sixth edition and its predecessors. I have thus retained those great older cases, both English and American, that have proved themselves time and again in the classroom while incorporating the most important recent developments on both the judicial and legislative fronts.

In their preface to the second edition, Gregory and Kalven wrote that "the study of the tort law emerges as the great opportunity to watch the common law at work." These words remain as true today as they were when written over a quarter of a century ago.

Richard A. Epstein

Chicago
February 1995

Acknowledgments

In preparing the sixth edition of this casebook I have been fortunate enough to be able to draw on the comments of many teachers and students who have used the book. Although in many cases the source of a casual comment has long been forgotten, the point has usually been retained. To all these students and teachers, my thanks. In particular, I should like to thank Stanton Krauss, Kenneth Simon, and Jerry Wiley for their detailed written comments on the first part of the casebook, which I used as a guide for much of the revision. In addition, I profited from suggestions and comments by Jennifer Arlen, Richard Craswell, Michael Corrado, Stephen Gilles, Gail Heriot, William Landes, Mark Miller, Malla Pollock, Gary Schwartz, and Alan Sykes. The valuable comments on earlier editions from Kenneth Abraham, Vincent Blasi, William Cohen, Theodore Eisenberg, Robert Ellickson, James Henderson, Morton Horwitz, Jason Johnston, Spencer Kimball, Alvin Klevorick, Cornelius Peck, Richard Posner, Glen Robinson, Howard Sacks, Geoffrey Stone, Perry Sentell, Aaron Twerski, and Ernest Weinrib are still evident in the sixth edition.

I should also like to thank Isaac Barchas, Donna Côte, and Jay Wright for their assistance in preparing this edition. And a special note of thanks goes to omnipresent P. J. Karafiol who, with good cheer and great enthusiasm, reviewed and corrected virtually the entire manuscript, and whose work makes him a causa sine qua non of this book. Once again my secretary Katheryn Kepchar proved herself equal to putting the manuscript into final form notwithstanding the best efforts of its author to frustrate her endeavors.

I should also like to thank the authors and copyright holders of the following works for permitting their inclusion in this book:

Abraham, Individual Action and Collective Responsibility: The Dilemma of Mass Tort Reform, 73 Va. L. Rev. 845, 860, 867-868 (1987). Reprinted with permission.

Abraham and Jeffries, Punitive Damages and the Rule of Law: The Role of Defendant's Wealth, 18 J. Legal Stud. 415, 417, 418 (1989). Reprinted with permission.

American Bar Association, Special Committee on Automobile Insurance Legislation, Automobile No-Fault Insurance (1978). Reprinted with permission.

American Law Institute, Restatement (Second) of the Law of Torts §§18, 46, 46(2),315,323,324,324A,332,339,402A,431,478,480,494. Copyright © 1965 by the American Law Institute. Reprinted with permission of the American Law Institute.

American Law Institute, Restatement (Second) of the Law of Torts §§504, 519, 520, 520A, 522, 523, 524, 524A, 525, 538, 549, 559, 560(3), 575C, 577, 577A, 652B-E. Copyright © 1977 by the American Law Institute. Reprinted with permission of the American Law Institute.

American Law Institute, Restatement (Second) of the Law of Torts §826. Copyright © 1979 by the American Law Institute. Reprinted with permission of the American Law Institute.

Arnold, Accident, Mistake and Rules of Liability in the Fourteenth Century Law of Torts, 128 U. Pa. L. Rev. 361 (1979). Reprinted with permission.

Bender, A Lawyer's Primer on Feminist Theory and Tort, 38 J. Legal Education 34-35 (1988).

Bovbjerg, Sloan and Blumstein, Valuing Life and Limb in Tort: Scheduling "Pain and Suffering," 83 Nw. U.L. Rev. 908, 923-924 (1989).

Calabresi and Hirschoff, Toward a Test for Strict Liability in Tort, 81 Yale L.J. 1055 (1972). Reprinted by permission of the Yale Law Journal Company and Fred B. Rothman & Company from the Yale Law Journal, Vol. 81, pp. 1055, 1059, 1060-1061.

Calabresi and Melamed, Property Rules, Liability Rules and Inalienability: One View of the Cathedral, 85 Harv. L. Rev. 1089 (1972). Copyright © 1972 by the Harvard Law Review Association. Reprinted with permission.

Epstein, Automobile No-Fault Plans: A Second Look at First Principles, 13 Creighton L. Rev. 769 (1980). Reprinted with permission.

Fletcher, Fairness and Utility in Tort Theory, 85 Harv. L. Rev. 537 (1972). Copyright © 1972 by the Harvard Law Review Association. Reprinted with permission.

Jaffe, Damages for Personal Injury: The Impact of Insurance, 18 Law & Contemp. Probs. 219 (1953). Reprinted with permission from a symposium on the Federal Employers' Liability Act appearing in Law and Contemporary Problems, Vol. 18, No. 2, published by the Duke University School of Law. Copyright © 1953 by Duke University.

James, The Qualities of the Reasonable Man in Negligence Cases, 16 Mo. L. Rev. 1 (1951). Copyright © 1951 by the Curators of the University of Missouri. Reprinted with permission.

Kronman, Mistake, Disclosure, Information and the Law of Contracts, 7 J. Legal Stud. 1 (1978). Copyright © 1978 by the University of Chicago Press. Reprinted with permission.

Posner, Economic Analysis of Law 192 (Little, Brown and Company, 4th ed. 1992). Copyright © 1992 by Richard A. Posner. Reprinted with permission.

Posner, Epstein's Tort Theory: A Critique, 8 J. Legal Stud. 457 (1979). Copyright © 1979 by the University of Chicago Press. Reprinted with permission.

Schuck, Rethinking Informed Consent, 103 Yale L.J. 899, 957-958 (1994).

Schwartz, Tort Law and the Economy in Nineteenth-Century America: A Reinterpretation, 90 Yale L.J. 1717 (1981). Reprinted with permission of the Yale Law Journal and Fred B. Rothman & Company from the Yale Law Journal, Vol. 90, pp. 1717, 1759-1762.

Seavey, Negligence — Subjective or Objective? 41 Harv. L. Rev. 1 (1927). Copyright © 1927 by the Harvard Law Review Association. Reprinted with permission.

Seavey, Reliance upon Gratuitous Promises or Other Conduct, 64 Harv. L. Rev. 913 (1951). Copyright © 1951 by the Harvard Law Review Association. Reprinted with permission.

Shavell, Suit, Settlement and Trial: A Theoretical Analysis under Alternative Methods for the Allocation of Legal Costs, 11 J. Legal Stud. 35, 58-60 (1981). Reprinted with permission.

Shukaitis, A Market in Personal Injury Tort Claims, 16 J. Legal Stud. 329, 329-330, 339-340 (1987). Reprinted with permission.

Sloan, Suing for Medical Malpractice 9-10 (1993).

Thomson, The Trolley Problem, 94 Yale L.J. 1395, 1395-96 (1985).

Viscusi, Risk by Choice 43-44 (Harvard University Press, 1983). Reprinted with permission.

Weiler, The Case for No-Fault Medical Liability, 52 Md. L. Rev. 908, 919, 928-929, 931 (1993).

Introduction

The sixth edition of this casebook appears 5 years after the fifth edition and some 36 years after the publication of the original Gregory and Kalven casebook. That period of over nearly four decades has been marked by both continuity and change in the law. Until the late 1980s, these changes tended to be largely in one direction. With the exception of the law of defamation and privacy, tort liability had been expanding on all fronts. Today, however, the picture is far more clouded. In the traditional areas of physical injuries, tort liability appears to have reached its high water mark, and in some jurisdictions — California and perhaps New York — the tides have been receding. Ironically, at the same time the law of defamation and privacy seems to have expanded, if not doctrinally, then surely in the frequency and intensity of suits.

In the midst of these ebbs and flows in tort liability, certain questions have remained with us in more or less the same form in which they were faced by the earliest of common-law lawyers. The tension between the principles of negligence and strict liability in stranger cases surely falls into this class. The debates framed in the nineteenth-century cases have largely dictated the subsequent analysis in such important areas of the law as the rules dealing with abnormally dangerous activities and with ordinary nuisances, both of which have assumed greater importance in an age which shows greater concern with environmental harms and toxic torts.

Yet in other areas we have witnessed major transformations, both in the types of cases brought to litigation, and in the choice of legal theories used to decide them. In 1959 — the year of the first edition — the paradigm tort action was still the automobile collision. Torts against institutional defendants — products liability and medical malpractice cases most readily leap to mind — were, when viewed with the benefit of hindsight, still in their infancy, while mass torts and toxic torts (the two often go together) still lay in the future.

The emergence of new types of litigation has taken its toll on traditional tort theory. The question of "proximate cause" — could this remote consequence be properly attributed to the wrongful conduct of the defendant? — was the dominant issue of causation in 1959 and the major source of contention among academic writers. That is no longer true today. Increasingly, modern tort litigation concentrates on two other problems. The first involves the difficult questions of evidence and statistics necessary to establish the factual connection between, say, the defendant's drug or waste discharge and the medical injuries of the plaintiff. The second involves the rules designed to deal with multiple causation when two or more parties are charged with responsibility for all or part of the same harms. Both these shifts in emphasis are duly taken into account in this edition.

Notwithstanding the enormous substantive changes, the educational aims of this casebook are much the same as those of the previous five editions. The primary goal remains one of giving to the student an accurate sense of the current legal position in this, one of the most active and important branches of the law. But this casebook would fail in its essential mission if it did not accomplish two other tasks. First, it should provide the student with an opportunity to examine the processes of legal method, legal reasoning, and the impact of legal rules on social institutions. Second, it should give the student some sense of the different systematic and intellectual approaches that have been taken to the law of torts over the years.

The importance of method cannot be underestimated in legal education. A casebook — certainly this casebook — is not a reference book, much less a treatise. The standard legal curriculum, of necessity, touches on only a small fraction of the huge and ever-growing body of substantive rules, and even many of those will change with time. The education of the lawyer of the future therefore rests on an ability to deal with a mass of legal materials, to identify the underlying assumptions, to determine possible implications for analogous cases, and, above all, to deal with the persistent uncertainty, ambiguity, and at times downright confusion in the law. To help with these tasks it is essential to deal with the development of a legal principle over time, through a line of cases that illustrates its application and tests its limits. To that end this casebook contains many cases from the nineteenth century and before, even some that have long ceased to represent the current law. Likewise, in order to capture the nature of legal debate, in many principal cases I have reprinted not only the opinion of the court but those of concurring or dissenting judges. With Fletcher v. Rylands, at page 120 infra, for example, five separate opinions from three different courts are reproduced, because each adds something to the total picture.

A sound legal education requires more than attention to analytical skills. The law of torts in particular is one of the richest bodies of law, and it has been examined and explored from historical, philosophical, and institutional perspectives not only by the common-law judges, but also by generations of academic writers. It is essential for all students to gain some sense of the diverse possible approaches to tort law, lest the constant probings of the Socratic method lead to an unhappy form of intellectual nihilism. The materials selected are designed, wherever possible, to allow torts to be confronted not only as a collection of discrete rules but also as a systematic intellectual discipline.

There is in the tort law today fundamental disagreement about the proper orientation toward its subject matter and about the proper choice of its key substantive rules. Speaking first to the question of general orientation, it is possible to identify three major positions. The traditional view — which had unspoken dominance at the time of the first two editions — was to look at the law of torts as a study in corrective justice, as an effort to develop a coherent set of principles to decide whether *this* plaintiff was entitled to compensation from *this* defendant as a matter of fairness between the parties. Issues of public policy and social control were of course not absent, but they did not dominate judicial or academic attitudes toward either particular cases or general theory.

Today the traditional approach is under attack from two flanks. On the one hand there is renewed insistence, which today is often expressly articulated in the cases, that the compensation of injured parties is in itself a valid end of the tort law and that the doctrines of tort law that frustrate that objective must be hedged with limitations or totally eliminated unless strong justification is given for their retention. The older presumption that the plaintiff had to show "good cause" to hold a defendant liable (roughly speaking) has yielded in some quarters to a new presumption that the defendant who has demonstrably caused harm must show why liability should not be imposed. That shift in presumptions, if accepted, has two major implications. First, the class of "inevitable accidents" that usually fell outside the tort law under the older view is more likely to be brought within it under the new. The defendant charged with tort liability, it is said, can shift the loss to society at large, either by altering the nature and type of products sold and services provided, or by spreading the risk by way of liability insurance. Second, defenses based on plaintiff's conduct — notably contributory negligence and assumption of risk — receive a narrower interpretation and no longer bar, but at most reduce, the plaintiff's recovery.

The second critique of the traditional approach comes from a different quarter, that of economic theory. Looking first at the tort law as a system of social control, advocates of the economic approach have generally argued that the proper function of the tort law is to lay down workable liability rules which create incentives for both individuals and firms to minimize (the sum of) the costs of accidents and the costs of their prevention. In this view of the subject, the compensation of individual parties is not an end in itself, but only a means to enlist private parties to help police the harmful activities of others. The economic approach tends to downplay the importance of corrective justice in the individual case and compensation for individual victims of accidents, treating the first as largely question-begging and the second as better achieved through voluntary insurance arrangements. Until very recently its importance was largely academic, but today its influence in the decided cases is increasing.

The diversity of opinions on the proper approach to the tort law carries over to disputes about the proper substantive basis of tort liability. From the earliest times until today courts have entertained three main theories — each subject to many variants — for recovery in tort. There is, first, recovery for harms intentionally inflicted by defendant on plaintiff. Second, there is recovery for harms negligently inflicted, that is, through the want of reasonable or ordinary care. Last, there is recovery under a theory of strict liability, that is, for harms inflicted on the plaintiff by a defendant who acts without negligence and without any intention to harm.

In dealing with these three theories it is important to keep in mind several important themes that reassert themselves throughout the law of torts. One set of issues concerns the relationships between the general approach to the law of torts and the choice of specific theories of liability in particular cases. When does a concern for corrective justice require the use of a strict liability principle, a negligence principle, or an intentional tort principle? What about theories based on the need for individual compensation or on the use of the tort law as a device for minimizing accident costs by channelling scarce resources to their most efficient use? Conversely, it is important to ask which *limitations* on recovery are consistent with the basic theories of liability and with their basic orientation to the subject matter. In this connection it is important to ask the extent to which recovery should be denied because of (to use the standard classification) plaintiff's own conduct — be it called contributory negligence or assumption of risk — the conduct of a third party, or an act of God when plaintiff has otherwise made out a good cause of action.

Finally, it is crucial to consider what might conveniently be termed the "boundary" questions in the law of torts. As stated, any of the three theories of liability — strict liability, negligence liability, or liability for intentional harms — could apply to any case involving harm. How do these different theories coexist across the full range of tort cases? To anticipate for a moment, does, for example, the commitment to a theory of strict liability in classical trespass cases — those involving the di-

rect application of force on the person or property of another —
require (or allow) the use of a similar theory in cases involving slips
and falls on business or residential premises or for the harm caused
by those engaged in ultrahazardous activities or the manufacture of
dangerous products? Similarly, it must be asked whether the choice of
a negligence theory in medical malpractice cases commits us to that
theory for routine traffic accidents or whether a theory of intentional
harms in assault cases commits us to that theory in defamation cases.

With our major conceptual dimensions identified, it is perhaps desirable to close this introduction with a word about the organization of
this book. The subject matter of the law of torts can be approached
from a large number of different perspectives, and the order of organization is by no means "neutral," since instructors with one outlook are
apt to use certain materials in one order while those with a different
outlook are apt to use somewhat different materials in yet another order. Here I have tried to adhere to traditional modes of presentation
that can, it is hoped, be varied with minimum confusion to suit the
tastes of different instructors.

Chapter 1 begins with an exploration of the principles of intentional
harms that can be conveniently concluded before turning to the bulk
of the materials, which deal with accidentally caused physical harm.
The chapter covers not only the cases of physical injuries but also the
closely associated harm associated with wrongful imprisonment and the
intentional infliction of emotional distress. The material here also considers the full range of justifications for such conduct, including consent, self-defense, and necessity. Chapter 2 introduces the recurrent
tension between negligence and strict liability in the context of accidental physical injuries by examining the two alternatives in both their historical and analytical aspects. Chapter 3 then undertakes a detailed
analysis of the negligence principle, which addresses not only the different interpretations that can be attached to the idea of unreasonable
conduct, but also to the issues of how these cases are litigated before
juries. Chapter 4 turns to plaintiff's conduct, including contributory
negligence, assumption of risk, and comparative negligence. Chapter 5
deals with the many hard questions that arise when two or more parties
may be held responsible for a single harm, and thus addresses questions
of joint and several liability, joint causation, and vicarious liability.
Chapter 6 then turns to two of the major issues of causation, cause
in-fact and proximate cause. Chapter 7 addresses affirmative duties to
strangers and to persons with whom the defendant stands in some special relationship. Chapter 8 then deals with the traditional strict liability
torts: conversion, animals, ultrahazardous activities, and nuisance.
Chapter 9 examines products liability from its nineteenth-century origins to its modern applications. Chapter 10 completes the exposition of
the elements of the basic tort with an analysis of the rules for governing

damages, both compensatory and punitive. Chapter 11 deals with immunities, both for private persons and for public bodies and officials. Chapter 12 goes beyond the tort system narrowly defined and deals with the role of insurance in dealing with tort cases, including the major coverage disputes that have arisen in connection with toxic and mass torts. Chapter 13 examines two alternatives to the tort system, workers' compensation and the various forms of no-fault insurance for automobiles, products, and medical accidents, as well as the comprehensive no-fault scheme now in place in New Zealand.

The last four chapters of this book are concerned primarily with nonphysical injuries. Chapter 14 covers defamation from its common-law origins to its constitutional complications. Chapter 15 then takes up the closely related issue of rights of privacy, both as they relate to the right of individuals to control the use of their name and likeness, and to resist the intrusions from the external world. The last two chapters of the book deal with more traditional economic relationships: Chapter 16 is devoted to the law of misrepresentation (with a peek at modern securities law) and Chapter 17 is directed to the general subject of economic harms, here defined as those harms that do not flow from either bodily injury or property damage to the plaintiff.

I have edited the materials with an eye toward smoother reading. The male pronoun has generally been used to include both genders. Citations to cases (and to cases within cases), footnotes, and other quoted material have been eliminated or simplified without any special indication in order to remove clutter and preserve readability. Those footnotes that have been retained have their original numbering. The editor's footnotes are indicated by an asterisk.

References to W. Prosser and W. Keeton on Torts (5th ed. 1984) are simply to Prosser and Keeton on Torts. References to F. Harper, F. James, and O. Gray, The Law of Torts (2d ed. 1986) are simply to Harper, James and Gray, Torts.

Cases and Materials on TORTS

PART ONE
PHYSICAL AND
MENTAL HARMS

Chapter One
Intentionally Inflicted Harm: The Prima Facie Case and Defenses

A. INTRODUCTION

It is best to begin our study of the law of torts with an examination of the rules that govern liability for the intentional infliction of harm. At first blush these intentional torts are the easiest to understand and comprehend. More than one torts teacher has observed that everyone understands a punch in the nose. But as these materials will reveal, however, there are, so to speak, punches in the nose and punches in the nose. Our intuitive sense that compensation and redress are required must be refined to systematically take into account the variety of excuses or justifications that may be offered for deliberately inflicted harms. In organizing our study, it is important to keep two recurrent themes in mind. First, the law often distinguishes between the intention to do some act that causes harm and the intention to cause the harm itself. Why is that distinction important, and how should it be taken into account? And how does it differ from the concept of mens rea (the guilty mind) found in the criminal law? Second, once the plaintiff's prima facie case is made, how does one decide on the types of permissible excuses and justifications and the limitations that may be imposed upon them?

The law covering the intentional infliction of harm has traditionally offered a curious blend of protection. Most obviously the law guards against obvious physical harm to person or property, but it also extends, somewhat more haltingly, its protection against affronts to personal dig-

3

nity and emotional tranquillity. Both forms of harm are covered in this chapter, which begins with physical harms and then veers off to both dignitary and emotional harms. The first part of the chapter concentrates on physical harms and covers the torts of battery (or trespass to the person), trespass to real and personal property, and the full range of defenses based on consent, insanity, defense of person and property, and necessity. The second half of the chapter examines the interplay between the plaintiff's basic case and the available defenses for torts designed to protect dignitary or emotional interests: assault and offensive battery, false imprisonment, and the intentional infliction of emotional distress.

B. PHYSICAL HARMS

1. Battery and Consent

Vosburg v. Putney
50 N.W. 403 (Wis. 1891)

The action was brought to recover damages for an assault and battery, alleged to have been committed by the defendant upon the plaintiff on February 20, 1889. The answer is a general denial. At the date of the alleged assault the plaintiff was a little more than fourteen years of age, and the defendant a little less than twelve years of age.

The injury complained of was caused by a kick inflicted by defendant upon the leg of the plaintiff, a little below the knee. The transaction occurred in a schoolroom in Waukesha, during school hours, both parties being pupils in the school. A former trial of the cause resulted in a verdict and judgment for the plaintiff for $2,800. The defendant appealed from such judgment to this court, and the same was reversed for error, and a new trial awarded.

[A more complete statement of the facts is found in the opinion by Orton, J., 47 N.W. 99, 99 (1890), when the case was first brought before the Wisconsin Supreme Court on appeal: "The plaintiff was about 14 years of age, and the defendant about 11 years of age. On the 20th day of February, 1889, they were sitting opposite to each other across an aisle in the high school of the village of Waukesha. The defendant reached across the aisle with his foot, and hit with his toe the shin of the right leg of the plaintiff. The touch was slight. The plaintiff did not feel it, either on account of its being so slight or of loss of sensation produced by the shock. In a few moments he felt a violent pain in that place, which caused him to cry out loudly. The next day he was sick, and had to be helped to school. On the fourth day he was vomiting, and Dr. Bacon was sent for, but could not come, and he sent medicine to stop the vomiting, and came to see him the next day, on the 25th. There was a slight discoloration of the skin entirely over the inner surface of the tibia an inch below the bend of the knee. The doctor applied fomentations, and gave him anodynes to quiet the pain. This treatment was continued, and the swelling so increased by the 5th day of March that counsel was called, and on the 8th of March an operation was performed on the limb by making an incision, and a moderate amount of pus escaped. A drainage tube was inserted, and an iodoform dressing put on. On the sixth day after this, another incision was made to the bone, and it was found that destruction was going on in the bone, and so it has continued exfoliating pieces of bone. He will never recover the use of his limb. There were black and blue spots on the shin bone, indicating that there had been a blow. On the 1st day of January before, the plaintiff received an injury just above the knee of the same leg by coasting, which appeared to be healing up and drying down at the time of the last injury. The theory of at least one of the medical witnesses was that the limb was in a diseased condition when this touch or kick was given, caused by microbes entering in through the wound above the knee, and which were revivified by the touch, and that the touch was the exciting or remote cause of the destruction of the bone, or of the plaintiff's injury. It does not appear that there was any visible mark made or left by this touch or kick of the defendant's foot, or any appearance of injury until the black and blue spots were discovered by the physician several days afterwards, and then there were more spots than one. There was no proof of any other hurt, and the medical testimony seems to have been agreed that this touch or kick was the exciting cause of the injury to the plaintiff. The jury rendered a verdict for the plaintiff of $2,800. The learned circuit judge said to the jury: 'It is a peculiar case, an unfortunate case, a case, I think I am at liberty to say that ought not to have come into court. The parents of these children ought, in some way, if possible, to have adjusted it between themselves.' We have much of the same feeling about the case."]

The case has been again tried in the circuit court, and the trial resulted in a verdict for plaintiff for $2,500. . . .

On the last trial the jury found a special verdict, as follows: "(1) Had the plaintiff during the month of January, 1889, received an injury just above the knee, which became inflamed, and produced pus? *Answer.* Yes. (2) Had such injury on the 20th day of February, 1889, nearly healed at the point of the injury? *A.* Yes. (3) Was the plaintiff, before said 20th of February, lame, as the result of such injury? *A.* No. (4) Had the tibia in the plaintiff's right leg become inflamed or diseased to some extent before he received the blow or kick from the defendant? *A.* No. (5) What was the exciting cause of the injury to the plaintiff's leg? *A*. Kick. (6) Did the defendant, in touching the plaintiff with his foot, intend to do him any harm? *A*. No. (7) At what sum do you assess the damages of the plaintiff? *A*. $2,500."

The defendant moved for judgment in his favor on the verdict, and also for a new trial. The plaintiff moved for judgment on the verdict in his favor. The motions of defendant were overruled, and that of the plaintiff granted. Thereupon judgment for plaintiff for $2,500 damages and costs of suit was duly entered. The defendant appeals from the judgment.

LYON, J. The jury having found that the defendant, in touching the plaintiff with his foot, did not intend to do him any harm, counsel for defendant maintain that the plaintiff has no cause of action, and that defendant's motion for judgment on the special verdict should have been granted. In support of this proposition counsel quote from 2 Greenl. Ev. §83, the rule that "the intention to do harm is of the essence of an assault." Such is the rule, no doubt, in actions or prosecutions for mere assaults. But this is an action to recover damages for an alleged assault and battery. In such case the rule is correctly stated, in many of the authorities cited by counsel, that plaintiff must show either that the intention was unlawful, or that the defendant is in fault. If the intended act is unlawful, the intention to commit it must necessarily be unlawful. Hence, as applied to this case, if the kicking of the plaintiff by the defendant was an unlawful act, the intention of defendant to kick him was also unlawful.

Had the parties been upon the play-grounds of the school, engaged in the usual boyish sports, the defendant being free from malice, wantonness, or negligence, and intending no harm to plaintiff in what he did, we should hesitate to hold the act of the defendant unlawful, or that he could be held liable in this action. Some consideration is due to the implied license of the play-grounds. But it appears that the injury was inflicted in the school, after it had been called to order by the teacher, and after the regular exercises of the school had commenced. Under these circumstances, no implied license to do the act complained of existed, and such act was a violation of the order and decorum of the school, and necessarily unlawful. Hence we are of the opinion that, under the evidence and verdict, the action may be sustained.

Certain questions were proposed on behalf of defendant to be submitted to the jury, founded upon the theory that only such damages could be recovered as the defendant might reasonably be supposed to have contemplated as likely to result from his kicking the plaintiff. The court refused to submit such questions to the jury. The ruling was correct. The rule of damages in actions for torts was held . . . to be that the wrong-doer is liable for all injuries resulting directly from the wrongful act, whether they could or could not have been foreseen by him. The chief justice and the writer of this opinion dissented from the judgment in that case, chiefly because we were of the opinion that the complaint stated a cause of action ex contractu, and not ex delicto, and hence that a different rule of damages — the rule here contended for — was applicable. We did not question that the rule in actions for tort was correctly stated. That case rules this on the question of damages.

[Judgment was reversed and the case was remanded for a new trial because of error in a ruling on an objection to certain testimony.]

NOTES

1. Centennial celebrity. The interest in *Vosburg* on the occasion of its 100th anniversary continues to be great. The case has been subject to an exhaustive analysis in Zile, *Vosburg v. Putney:* A Centennial Story, 1992 Wis. L. Rev. 877, which probes every aspect of the social setting, legal proceedings, and aftermath of what has become one of the most storied cases in American legal history. The case itself has a rich social history. Zile relates the newspaper publicity, the spate of low-level criminal proceedings in justice court brought against the defendant, the possible medical malpractice action lurking in the background, and the political overtones and the incessant glare of newspaper publicity. The story received much of its local prominence at the time because the plaintiff Andrew Vosburg was a sickly boy from an ordinary farming background while the defendant George Putney was the scion of a wealthy and prominent Wisconsin family whose ancestors arrived in Massachusetts in 1637. The Wisconsin volume also features shorter pieces by Henderson (at 853), Rabin (at 863), and Hurst (at 875).

2. Defendant's intention and plaintiff's conduct. Given the jury's response to the sixth question, should defendant's act be regarded as an intentional tort? Does it make a difference that the teacher had already called the class to order? If the kick had landed a moment before order had been called, could plaintiff have recovered? If so, on what theory? Why might the plaintiff be required to demonstrate defendant's actual malice or wantonness on the part of the defendant if the incident had taken place on the playground? If the pupils typically tapped each other on the leg under the desk to get each other's attention after the class had been called to order, should plaintiff's act be excused by the "implied license of the classroom?"

Should plaintiff have worn a shin guard in order to protect his leg from further injury? Stayed home from school? If a shin guard had been worn and the damage had still been caused by the kick, would plaintiff necessarily be entitled to recover?

3. Whither "unlawful" intent? In Garratt v. Dailey, 279 P.2d 1091 (Wash. 1955), and 304 P.2d 681 (Wash. 1956), the plaintiff, an adult woman, brought an action for battery against Brian Dailey, a boy five years and nine months old, for her fractured hip caused when Dailey was a guest in her backyard. The case is complicated because there were two trials and two appellate decisions, which at all times revealed sharp factual disputes. The defendant contended that he had tried to help the plaintiff by placing a chair under her as she was about to fall, but that he was too small to move it into place. His version was accepted by the trial judge at the first trial. The second account of the incident, offered by the plaintiff's sister, who was present at the occasion, was that the plaintiff, an "arthritic woman had begun the slow process of being seated when the defendant quickly removed the chair and seated himself upon it, and that he knew, with substantial certainty at the time, that she would attempt to sit in the place where the chair had been."

On appeal from the first judgment, 279 P.2d 1091, 1093-1094, the Washington Supreme Court addressed the issue of intent in the tort of battery:

> It is urged that Brian's action in moving the chair constituted a battery. A definition (not all-inclusive but sufficient for our purpose) of a battery is the intentional infliction of a harmful bodily contact upon another. . . .
>
> We have here the conceded volitional act of Brian, i.e., the moving of a chair. Had the plaintiff proved to the satisfaction of the trial court that Brian moved the chair while she was in the act of sitting down, Brian's action would patently have been for the purpose or with the intent of causing the plaintiff's bodily contact with the ground, and she would be entitled to a judgment against him for the resulting damages. Vosburg v. Putney . . . .
>
> A battery would be established if, in addition to plaintiff's fall, it was proved that, when Brian moved the chair, he knew with substantial certainty that the plaintiff would attempt to sit down where the chair had been. . . .
>
> The mere absence of any intent to injure the plaintiff or to play a prank on her or to embarrass her, or to commit an assault and battery on her would not absolve him from liability if in fact he had such knowledge. Without such knowledge, there would be nothing wrongful about Brian's act in moving the chair and, there being no wrongful act, there would be no liability.

The case was remanded for clarification. The trial judge then reconsidered the evidence, accepted the testimony of the plaintiff's sister, and awarded an $11,000 judgment for the plaintiff, which was upheld on the second appeal. Is removing a chair tantamount to striking the plaintiff?

4. The Restatement account of intention. The common law of torts has been "codified" in the Restatement of Torts. The original version of this influential work was published in 1934 by the American Law Institute, where it was prepared by a large and distinguished team of judges, practicing lawyers, and academics, with Professor Francis H. Bohlen as its chief reporter. The Restatement (Second) of Torts appeared in four volumes, published between 1965 and 1979. The Restatement, as its name implies, emphasizes "restating" not "reforming" the law, but some interstitial reform takes place whenever the path of the law is uncertain or some conflict persists among the various states. The first 280 sections of the Second Restatement are devoted to the intentional torts. Its account of "intention" parallels the definition offered in *Garratt.* Thus the Restatement definition uses the term "to denote that the actor desires to cause consequences of his act, or that he believes that the consequences are substantially certain to result from it." Restatement (Second) of Torts §8A. Does this definition work well in the context of a large construction project where the general contractor knows that it is highly likely that some worker will be killed or injured during the work? If he knows that some jobs are substantially more dangerous than others? For the various senses of intention, see W. Landes and R. Posner, The Economic Structure of Tort Law 149-150 (1987).

Note also that the Restatement approves the result in *Vosburg,* which it describes as follows: "Intending an offensive contact, A lightly kicks B on the shin." §16, comment *a,* Illustration 1. Did the court in *Vosburg* treat it as a case of offensive battery?

5. *Transferred intent.* In Talmage v. Smith, 59 N.W. 656 (Mich. 1894), the plaintiff was struck in the eye by a stick that the defendant threw at two of the plaintiff's companions who were trespassing upon the defendant's property. In an effort to defeat the plaintiff's action for trespass to the person, the defendant urged that he did not see the plaintiff, much less intend to hurt him. The court held the circumstances immaterial: "The right of the plaintiff to recover was made to depend upon an intention on the part of the defendant to hit somebody, and to inflict an unwarranted injury upon someone. Under these circumstances, the fact that the injury resulted to another than was intended does not relieve the defendant from responsibility." Does it make a difference whether the injured plaintiff was trespassing on defendant's property?

See generally Prosser, Transferred Intent, 45 Tex. L. Rev. 650 (1967).

6. *Intent to harm and trespass to real property.* The action for trespass to real property is designed to protect the plaintiff's interest in the exclusive possession of land and its improvements. Like battery, it does not even require a showing of minimal harm. The ordinary requirement for the action was the defendant's entry onto the plaintiff's land, on, above, or below the surface. "It is an elementary principle, that every unauthorized, and therefore unlawful entry, into the close of another,

is a trespass. From every such entry against the will of the possessor, the law infers some damage if nothing more, the treading down the grass or the herbage, or as here, the shrubbery." Dougherty v. Stepp, 18 N.C. 371 (1835). The traditional formula for the action was known as quare clausum fregit — wherefore does the defendant break into the plaintiff's close — or "trespass qcf." Nonetheless it has been long settled that an action of trespass qcf may lie for an intrusion above or below the surface of the land. In Smith v. Smith, 110 Mass. 302 (1872), the defendant was adjudged a trespasser when the eaves of his barn overhung the plaintiff's land, and in Neiswonger v. Goodyear Tire and Rubber Co., 35 F.2d 761 (N.D. Ohio 1929), airplane overflights within 500 feet of the ground, in violation of air traffic rules established by the Department of Commerce, were also treated as a common-law trespass.

7. *Actual damages in trespass.* In Brown v. Dellinger, 355 S.W.2d 742 (Tex. Civ. App. 1962), an action against two children, aged 7 and 8, where the plaintiff's $28,000 home was destroyed by fire, for which loss the defendants were held liable, the court observed: "The acts of the minor defendants in bringing matches onto the premises of [plaintiff] and igniting the fire in the charcoal burner in appellee's garage were all voluntary and purposeful and were acts which they even at their tender years had sufficient capacity to do, as evidenced by the fact that they did do such acts. Undoubtedly they did not intend for the fire to escape from the grill and spread to the curtain canvas and burn and damage the garage, house and contents thereof. However their acts of igniting an unauthorized fire on [plaintiff's] premises made them trespassers, and they must be held civilly liable for the consequences which directly flowed from their unauthorized acts of igniting the fire in question."

If the plaintiff's charcoal burner had been defective and the defendants had used it with all possible care, should the plaintiff still recover? If the defendants had been burned while using the defective burner, could they have recovered from the plaintiff for their personal injuries? If the defendants had started the fire in their own burner located on their own property, could the plaintiff have recovered under the rationale in Brown v. Dellinger if the fire had spread to his premises?

In Cleveland Park Club v. Perry, 165 A.2d 485 (D.C. 1960), the plaintiff operated a social club for the benefit of its members. One day while the defendant, a 9-year-old boy, was using the pool, he dove down to a depth of seven feet, "and thinking there was no suction at the time," removed the drain cover and inserted a rubber ball. The ball then passed into a critical portion of a pipe where it caused extensive damage, requiring that the pool be closed for repairs. The judgment for the defendant at trial was reversed on appeal, and a new trial ordered. In passing on the intent requirement in trespass cases, the court stressed "that the intent controlling is the intent to complete the physical act and not the intent to cause injurious consequences." Did the defendant intend to place the ball in the mouth of the drain, or in the middle of the pipe? What weight should be given to his mistaken belief that there was no suction? Should it make a difference if the defendant was on the premises with the plaintiff's permission? Or was the act done outside the scope of the permission granted? Could the defendants in *Garratt, Brown,* and *Cleveland Park* be held liable on a negligence theory? See infra Chapter 3, Section A for a discussion of the liability of infants in negligence.

Prosser notes that intention under the tort law "is not necessarily a hostile intent, or a desire to do any harm. Rather it is an intent to bring about a result which will invade the interests of another in a way that the law will not sanction." Prosser and Keeton, Torts at 36. What role does intention, as defined by Prosser, play in these cases? Does the judge or jury decide whether an invasion is one that the "law will not sanction"? See generally Epstein, Intentional Harms, 4 J. Legal Stud. 391 (1975).

8. Innocent conversion of property. If the defendant enters upon the plaintiff's land and there cuts down trees belonging to the plaintiff, is this an intentional tort if the defendant has an honest belief that he owns both the land and the trees? In cases of this sort the plaintiff is uniformly held to have an action for damages. In Maye v. Tappan, 23 Cal. 306, 307-308 (1863), the defendant dug up gold-bearing earth from the plaintiffs' land, after the plaintiffs mistakenly but honestly told the defendant that he, the defendant, owned the land. The court allowed the plaintiffs to recover damages equal to the value of the gold, less the cost of its extraction and refinement.

> The plaintiffs, in this action, were not entitled to vindictive or exemplary damages, but could only recover the damages they had actually sustained by being deprived of the gold or gold-bearing earth taken by the defendants from their mining ground. It follows, that the question whether the defendants acted willfully and maliciously, or ignorantly and innocently, in digging up and taking away the gold-bearing earth, is entirely immaterial. The defendants took property belonging to the plaintiffs, and have thereby injured them to a certain amount; and that amount is made no greater nor less by the fact that the act was done without any malicious intent. The right of the plaintiffs to recover damages, or the amount of the damages to which they may be entitled, is not affected by the fact that the trespass was not willful in its character.

A defense of that result is given by Oliver Wendell Holmes in his classic book, The Common Law 97(1881):

> Take first the case of trespass upon land attended by actual damage. When a man goes upon his neighbor's land, thinking it is his own, he intends the very act or consequence complained of. He means to inter-

meddle with a certain thing in a certain way, and it is just that intended intermeddling for which he is sued. It might be answered, to be sure, that it is not for intermeddling with property, but for intermeddling with the plaintiff's property, that a man is sued and that in the supposed cases the defendant is ignorant of one of the facts making up the total environment, and which must be present to make his action wrong. He is ignorant, that is to say, that the true owner either has or claims any interest in the property in question, and therefore he does not intend a wrongful act, because he does not mean to deal with his neighbor's property. But the answer to this is, that he does intend to do the damage complained of. One who diminishes the value of property by intentional damage knows it belongs to somebody. If he thinks it belongs to himself, he expects whatever harm he may do to come out of his own pocket. It would be odd if he were to get rid of the burden by discovering that it belonged to his neighbor. It is a very different thing to say he who intentionally does harm must bear the loss, from saying that one from whose acts harm follows accidentally, as a consequence which could not have been foreseen, must bear it.

The question of damages bears some special attention in these cases. When the defendant mines gold ore or cuts trees in good faith, then the plaintiff is allowed to recover the value of the property taken but must allow the defendant a setoff for the value that his labor has added to the thing converted. In effect the defendant is not treated as having made a gift of services to the plaintiff. But when the ore is taken, or the trees cut, in bad faith (that is, with knowledge that they belong to another) the set-off for labor expended is not allowed, in order to discourage the conscious violation of property rights in the first place.

Mohr v. Williams
104 N.W. 12 (Minn. 1905)

BROWN, J.R. Defendant is a physician and surgeon of standing and character, making disorders of the ear a specialty, and having an extensive practice in the city of St. Paul. He was consulted by plaintiff, who complained to him of trouble with her right ear, and, at her request, made an examination of that organ for the purpose of ascertaining its condition. He also at the same time examined her left ear, but, owing to foreign substances therein, was unable to make a full and complete diagnosis at that time. The examination of her right ear disclosed a large perforation in the lower portion of the drum membrane, and a large polyp in the middle ear, which indicated that some of the small bones of the middle ear (ossicles) were probably diseased. He informed plaintiff of the result of his examination, and advised an operation for the purpose of removing the polyp and diseased ossicles. After consultation with her family physician, and one or two further consultations with defendant, plaintiff decided to submit to the proposed operation.

She was not informed that her left ear was in any way diseased, and understood that the necessity for an operation applied to her right ear only. She repaired to the hospital, and was placed under the influence of anaesthetics; and, after being made unconscious, defendant made a thorough examination of her left ear, and found it in a more serious condition than her right one. A small perforation was discovered high up in the drum membrane, hooded, and with granulated edges, and the bone of the inner wall of the middle ear was diseased and dead. He called this discovery to the attention of Dr. Davis — plaintiff's family physician, who attended the operation at her request — who also examined the ear and confirmed defendant in his diagnosis. Defendant also further examined the right ear, and found its condition less serious than expected, and finally concluded that the left, instead of the right, should be operated upon; devoting to the right ear other treatment. He then performed the operation of ossiculectomy on plaintiff's left ear; removing a portion of the drum membrane, and scraping away the diseased portion of the inner wall of the ear. The operation was in every way successful and skilfully performed. It is claimed by plaintiff that the operation greatly impaired her hearing, seriously injured her person, and, not having been consented to by her, was wrongful and unlawful, constituting an assault and battery; and she brought this action to recover damages therefor.

The trial in the court below resulted in a verdict for plaintiff for $14,322.50. [The trial court set aside the verdict as excessive and ordered a new trial. This is an appeal by both parties from those orders. On appeal Brown, J., refused to overturn the jury's finding that there had been no emergency. He therefore held that plaintiff's consent to the operation could not be implied, and said in part:]

The last contention of defendant is that the act complained of did not amount to an assault and battery. This is based upon the theory that, as plaintiff's left ear was in fact diseased, in a condition dangerous and threatening to her health, the operation was necessary, and, having been skillfully performed at a time when plaintiff had requested a like operation on the other ear, the charge of assault and battery cannot be sustained; that, in view of these conditions, and the claim that there was no negligence on the part of defendant, and an entire absence of any evidence tending to show an evil intent, the court should say, as a matter of law, that no assault and battery was committed, even though she did not consent to the operation. In other words, that the absence of a showing that defendant was actuated by a wrongful intent, or guilty of negligence, relieves the act of defendant from the charge of an unlawful assault and battery.

We are unable to reach that conclusion, though the contention is not without merit. It would seem to follow from what has been said on the other features of the case that the act of defendant amounted at least to a technical assault and battery. If the operation was performed without plaintiff's consent, and the circumstances were not such as to justify its performance without, it was wrongful; and, if it was wrongful, it was unlawful. As remarked in 1 Jaggard, Torts, 437, every person has a right to complete immunity of his person from physical interference of others, except in so far as contact may be necessary under the general doctrine of privilege; and any unlawful or unauthorized touching of the person of another, except it be in the spirit of pleasantry, constitutes an assault and battery. In the case at bar, as we have already seen, the question whether defendant's act in performing the operation upon plaintiff was authorized was a question for the jury to determine. If it was unauthorized, then it was, within what we have said, unlawful. It was a violent assault, not a mere pleasantry; and, even though no negligence is shown, it was wrongful and unlawful. The case is unlike a criminal prosecution for assault and battery, for there an unlawful intent must be shown. But that rule does not apply to a civil action, to maintain which it is sufficient to show that the assault complained of was wrongful and unlawful or the result of negligence. . . . Vosburg v. Putney, 80 Wis. 523, 50 N.W. 403.

The amount of plaintiff's recovery, if she is entitled to recover at all, must depend upon the character and extent of the injury inflicted upon her, in determining which the nature of the malady intended to be healed and the beneficial nature of the operation should be taken into consideration, as well as the good faith of the defendant.

Orders affirmed.

NOTES

1. *Scope of Mohr v. Williams.* Did the defendant in Mohr v. Williams make a violent assault upon the plaintiff solely because he had not received the requisite consent to perform the operation? Indeed, in the recovery of actual damages, what reasons do you suppose might be given to support the determination of the trial court that the damages awarded were excessive? (On remand, the jury awarded only nominal damages.) Is *Mohr* distinguishable from Vosburg v. Putney, upon which the court relies?

How do doctors today usually avoid the dilemma of Mohr v. Williams? See the form on page 16, taken from R. Morris and A. Moritz, Doctor and Patient and the Law (5th ed. 1971).

Will the use of the standard form eliminate all litigation over the question of consent? In Beck v. Lovell, 361 So. 2d 245 (La. App. 1978), the court held that permission to perform a tubal ligation after the delivery of the plaintiff's third child could not be inferred from her husband's signature on the consent form and that it was a jury question whether the plaintiff herself had expressly or impliedly authorized the procedure when she had never signed the consent form. Should the plaintiff be required to prove the lack of consent by expert witnesses? See Meretsky v. Ellenby, 370 So. 2d 1222 (Fla. App. 1979), holding that experts were required only in informed consent cases. Why the difference? See infra Chapter 3, Section C.

2. *Consent to what?* Mohr v. Williams is but one of many cases in which the consent given was ineffective because it was not consent to the act actually performed. In Bang v. Charles T. Miller Hospital, 88 N.W.2d 186 (Minn. 1958), it was held to be a jury question whether consent for removal of a prostate gland was tantamount to consent to cut the plaintiff's spermatic cords. If the plaintiff had told the physician to do whatever was necessary to insure the safety of the operation, what result? If there was only a probability that the cords would be cut inadvertently in the operation, could the plaintiff still maintain his cause of action? On the entire question, see generally McCoid, A Reappraisal of Liability for Unauthorized Medical Treatment, 41 Minn. L. Rev. 381 (1957).

3. *Emergency rule.* The issue of consent arises in the ordinary medical case because the patient normally has the right to accept or reject the proffered treatment, making an unauthorized operation a technical assault and battery even if no damage ensues. See Schloendorff v. Society of New York Hospital, 105 N.E. 92 (N.Y. 1914); Franklyn v. Peabody, 228 N.W. 681 (Mich. 1930). But it seems equally well established that in the case of an emergency that endangers the life or health of the plaintiff, an unauthorized operation is justified under consent implied from the circumstances. See McGuire v. Rix, 225 N.W. 120 (Neb. 1929); Jackovach v. Yocom, 237 N.W. 444 (Iowa 1931). Such implied consent is, of course, a pure fiction, and the customary justification for the position is that the plaintiff would have consented to the operation if she had been in a position to ask to do so. One important purpose of this rule therefore is to protect persons in the position of plaintiff by encouraging others to go to their assistance in time of need. Should compensation be awarded to the bystander whose quick intervention saves the plaintiff's life? To the surgeon who operates, even if the results are unsuccessful? See Cotnam v. Wisdom, 104 S.W. 164 (Ark. 1907), allowing the action, but preventing any collection of higher fees based on special knowledge of the defendant's wealth.

In Kennedy v. Parrott, 90 S.E.2d 754, 759 (N.C. 1956), the defendant was hired to perform the plaintiff's appendectomy. During the course of the operation he discovered that the plaintiff had several large cysts on her left ovary, and he punctured the cysts without negligence. Unfortunately, the puncture cut one of plaintiff's blood vessels, and led to her developing a painful phlebitis in her leg. The court refused to allow

Consent to Operation, Anesthetics, and other Medical Services*

Date _____ Time _____ A.M.
P.M.

1. I authorize the performance upon _____ of
(myself or name of patient)
the following operation _____, to be
(state nature and extent of operation)
performed under the direction of Dr. _____.

2. I consent to the performance of operations and procedures in addition to or different from those now contemplated, whether or not arising from presently unforeseen conditions, which the above-named doctor or his associates or assistants may consider necessary or advisable in the course of the operation.

3. I consent to the administration of such anesthetics as may be considered necessary or advisable by the physician responsible for this service, with the exception of _____.
(state "none," "spinal anesthesia," etc.)

4. I consent to the photographing or televising of the operations or procedures to be performed, including appropriate portions of my body, for medical, scientific, or educational purposes, provided my identity is not revealed by the pictures or by descriptive texts accompanying them.

5. For the purpose of advancing medical education, I consent to the admittance of observers to the operating room.

6. I consent to the disposal by hospital authorities of any tissues or parts that may be removed.

7. I am aware that sterility may result from this operation. I know that a sterile person is incapable of becoming a parent.

8. The nature and purpose of the operation, possible alternative methods of treatment, the risks involved, and the possibility of complications have been fully explained to me. No guarantee or assurance has been given by anyone as to the results that may be obtained.

(cross out any paragraphs above which do not apply)

Signed _____
*(patient or person authorized to
consent for patient)*

Witness_____

*This is a general form of consent that will apply to various procedures by striking out the portions that are inapplicable.

an action for trespass to the person even though she did not consent to the puncturing of the cysts. It noted first that in earlier and simpler times operations were often performed at home, with the patient conscious and family members nearby. Under those circumstances consent could be easily obtained by the patient or family members. But with the rise of hospital-based operations, conditions radically changed, and with it the justification for the earlier strict rule at common law eroded. It therefore concluded:

> In major internal operations, both the patient and the surgeon know that the exact condition of the patient cannot be finally and definitely diagnosed until after the patient is completely anesthetized and the incision has been made. In such case the consent — in the absence of proof to the contrary — will be construed as general in nature and the surgeon may extend the operation to remedy any abnormal or diseased condition in the area of the original incision whenever he, in the exercise of his sound professional judgment, determines that correct surgical procedure dictates and requires such an extension of the operation originally contemplated. This rule applies when the patient is at the time incapable of giving consent, and no one with authority to consent for him is immediately available.

4. Consent implied in fact. Consent is normally manifested by language, but there is no reason why it cannot be inferred from conduct. In O'Brien v. Cunard Steamship Co., 28 N.E. 266 (Mass 1891), the plaintiff was an immigrant to the United States who required vaccination against smallpox as a condition of entry into this country. She entered the line with many other women passengers, held out her arm to the defendant's surgeon, who inspected it and noted that there was no mark on it (as is routinely found after smallpox vaccinations). Thereafter he told her that she should be vaccinated, and she answered that she had been vaccinated before and that the shot had left no mark. The physician did not respond further, and plaintiff held up her arm and allowed the vaccination to take place, after which she received her entry ticket. The alternative to vaccination was detainment and quarantine. The court held that her consent barred her cause of action. "If the plaintiff's behavior was such as to indicate consent on her part, the surgeon was justified in his act, whatever her unexpressed feelings may have been. In determining whether she consented, he could be guided only by her overt acts and the manifestations of her feelings." Plaintiff "was one of a large number of who were vaccinated on that occasion, without, so far as appears, a word of objection from any of them. They all indicated by their conduct that they desired to avail themselves of the provisions made for their benefit. There was nothing in the conduct of the plaintiff to indicate to the surgeon that she did not wish to obtain a card which would save her from detention at quarantine, and to be vaccinated, if necessary for that purpose." The court's decision did not state the damages claimed by the plaintiff. What might they be?

5. *Minors, incompetents, and "substituted judgment."* How ought one to proceed in the treatment of individuals who are unable to give their consent? If the consent requirement were not routinely relaxed for minors and incompetents, then all surgeries on members of these groups could constitute batteries, which would place physicians in the intolerable position of operating at their peril. Yet their refusal to provide services could only make the position of the minor or incompetent who might be easily cured more precarious. Instead of having the physician make the decision on his or her own initiative, the guardian is asked to make the decision for the benefit of the minor or incompetent. "[T]he general rule is that the consent of the parent is necessary for an operation on a child." Bonner v. Moran, 126 F.2d 121, 122 (D.C. Cir. 1941). Should the rule be applied to teenagers? What result if the parent consents to the operation but the child does not?

6. *Substituted consent in end-of-life situations.* Substituted consent becomes even more ambiguous with adult incompetents who lack any capacity to make decisions on their own behalf. In this situation, the law generally protects the guardian's good faith decision from any judicial challenge or review. Courts cannot develop the standards needed to review these determinations and often are unable to intervene in time even if they could. Recently, however, some courts, often on the initiative of treating physicians, have been drawn into the area. In Matter of Quinlan, 355 A.2d 647 (N.J. 1976), the New Jersey Supreme Court affirmed the right of the parents of a comatose 21-year-old woman to cease all extraordinary efforts to keep her alive and specifically permitted them to order the attending physicians to disconnect her respirator. But in Superintendent of Belchertown State School v. Saikewicz, 370 N.E.2d 417, 435 (Mass. 1977), the court decided on the merits that it was appropriate *not* to embark upon a painful and uncertain course of chemotherapy to prolong the life of a 67-year-old man with an I.Q. of 10 and the intelligence of a child 2 years and 8 months of age. But it insisted that it, and not the incompetent's family, guardian, or physicians, should make the ultimate decision, even though a court could take into account the views of the more immediate parties, or, for that matter, those of ethical experts.

> We do not view the judicial resolution of this most difficult and awesome question — whether potentially life-prolonging treatment should be withheld from a person incapable of making his own decision — as constituting a "gratuitous encroachment" on the domain of medical expertise. Rather, such questions of life and death seem to us to require the process of detached but passionate investigation and decision that forms the ideal on which the judicial branch of government was created. Achieving this ideal is our responsibility and that of the lower court, and is not to be entrusted to any other group purporting to represent the

"morality and conscience of our society," no matter how highly motivated or impressively constituted.

The *Saikewicz* approach placed enormous burdens on everyone concerned with end-of-life decisions, for it left unclear the circumstances under which physicians or guardians would have to seek guidance from the courts or how matters should have been decided. See Curran, The *Saikewicz* Decision: Judges as Physicians, 298 New Eng. J. Med. 508 (1978). The retreat from *Saikewicz* in Massachusetts took place in two stages. In Matter of Spring, 405 N.E.2d 115 (Mass. 1980), the court rejected the implication that *Saikewicz* "required prior judicial approval" in prolongation-of-life cases. Then in Brophy v. New England Sinai Hospital Inc., 497 N.E.2d 626 (Mass. 1986), the court allowed the wife and family of a man left in a permanent vegetative state from an aneurysm (rupture of an artery at the base of his brain) to cut off all nutrition and hydration, even over the objections of his treating physicians. It was agreed on all sides that, had he been competent, he would have consented to the removal of his feeding tubes, and the evidence suggested that he would experience no pain when allowed slowly to die. The court rested its decision on the need for "honoring the privacy and dignity of the individual," and ordered the incompetent transferred to another hospital where the tubes could be removed. If a physician inserts the tubes when there is reason to believe that the patient would reject them, is he liable for assault and battery? If it is believed that the incompetent person would have requested a lethal injection, should that request be honored? If a competent, but terminal, cancer patient requests that injection, should that request be honored? In *Brophy*, the court held that the state's interest in preventing suicide was strong enough to override these requests. Does the autonomy principle compel the acceptance of the right to voluntary euthanasia? Protect a physician who assists in allowing competent persons to engage in suicide? See Michigan v. Kevorkian, 517 N.W.2d 293 (Mich. 1993).

7. *Substituted consent for the benefit of others.* The matter of substituted judgment is also difficult when the treatment or operation is for the benefit of another. In Lausier v. Pescinski, 226 N.W.2d 180 (Wis. 1975), the court held that it did not have the power to permit the removal of one of the incompetent's kidneys, necessary to save the life of his brother, even though the risk of harm to the incompetent was slight. In this case, the incompetent's guardian, his sister, opposed the operation because it "brought back memories of the Dachau concentration camp in Nazi Germany and of medical experiments on unwilling subjects." Compare Strunk v. Strunk, 445 S.W.2d 145 (Ky. App. 1969), where the court applied the doctrine of "substituted judgment," and allowed a kidney transplant in a similar case, when the application was supported by the incompetent's guardian. The court believed that the incompe-

tent "would have" consented to the operation if he had been able. Should the consent of the incompetent's guardian make a difference? How persuasive is the argument that the incompetent will benefit by the survival of his brother? Is the result here consistent with that reached in the emergency cases?

8. Substituted consent in parent/fetus conflict situations. Something of a return to the attitude of *Saikewicz* is found In Re A.C., 573 A.2d 1235, 1248, 1249, 1252 (D.C. 1990). There a terminally ill pregnant woman had to decide whether to consent to a caesarean section which would materially increase the likelihood of survival for the 26-week-old fetus, whose condition was otherwise likely to deteriorate markedly, even though she bore a substantial risk of dying in surgery. Her alternative was to hold off on the operation in the hopes of living long enough so that she could hold her baby in her arms before she died. Terry, J., first held that when competence is found "that in virtually all cases the question of what is to be done is to be decided by the patient — the pregnant woman — on behalf of herself and the fetus." His opinion also instructed the trial judge, when possible, to "personally attempt to speak with the patient and ascertain her wishes directly, rather than relying on hearsay evidence, even from doctors." He recognized that this procedure allowed the mother to decide the fate of the child; he defended that decision as follows:

> There are two additional arguments against overriding A.C.'s objections to caesarean surgery. First, as the American Public Health Association cogently states in its *amicus curiae* brief:
>
>> Rather than protecting the health of women and children, court-ordered caesareans erode the element of trust that permits a pregnant woman to communicate to her physician — without fear of reprisal — all information relevant to her proper diagnosis and treatment. An even more serious consequence of court-ordered intervention is that it drives women at high risk of complications during pregnancy and childbirth out of the health system to avoid coerced treatment. Second, and even more compellingly, any judicial proceeding in a case such as this will ordinarily take place — like the one before us here — under time constraints so pressing that it is difficult or impossible for the mother to communicate adequately with counsel, or for counsel to organize an effective factual and legal presentation in defense of her liberty and privacy interests and bodily integrity.

Terry, J., then held that where the patient is incompetent or otherwise unable to give her judgment, the procedures of substitute consent should kick in. "[T]he substituted judgment inquiry is primarily a subjective one: as nearly as possible, the court must ascertain what the patient would do if competent," taking into account previously expressed opinions on medical matters or previous decisions on medical issues that she had faced in the search for "a discernibly consistent pattern of conduct or of thought." Whatever the limitations on this process it clearly *excludes* doing what an independent third party would decide, balancing the interests of mother and fetus, even where an early caesarean would assure normal life for a fetus with virtual certainty. The court then concluded that, in its view, the procedures involving consent and substituted judgment could only be displaced in "truly extraordinary cases" but declined to speculate as to what conditions might justify the "massive intrusion" of a caesarean section, noting that "this case is difficult enough as it is." If you were a family member or friend of the terminally ill pregnant woman, what would you advise her to do and why?

In re A.C. was followed in Doe v. Doe, 632 N.E.2d 326, 333-334 (Ill. App. 1994), which held that a competent pregnant woman had an absolute right to refuse a caesarean section even if her decision might prove harmful to the fetus. *Doe* also relied on Curran v. Bosze, 566 N.E.2d 1319, 1326 (Ill. 1990), where the court upheld the right of a mother of two 3½-year-old twins to refuse to have her children tested to see if they could make bone marrow transplants to their 12-year-old half-brother who was dying of leukemia. The twins and their half-sibling had a common father but different mothers, and neither the test nor the bone marrow transplant itself posed more than a tiny risk to the twins. In *Curran* the court refused to use the doctrine of substituted consent because the preferences of the twins were so ill-formed "that it is not possible to determine the intent of a 3½-year-old child with regard to consenting to a bone marrow harvesting procedure by examining the child's personal value system." In *Doe* the court took the argument a step further: "If a sibling cannot be forced to donate bone marrow to save a sibling's life, if an incompetent brother cannot be forced to donate a kidney to save the life of his dying sister, then surely a mother cannot be forced to undergo a caesarean section to benefit her viable fetus."

See generally Johnsen, The Creation of Fetal Rights: Conflicts with Woman's Constitutional Rights to Liberty, Privacy, and Equal Protection, 95 Yale L.J. 599 (1986).

9. Constitutional overtones for substituted judgment. In Cruzan v. Director, Missouri Department of Health, 487 U.S. 261 (1990), Missouri allowed a comatose patient to be disconnected from a life support system only on proof by "clear and convincing evidence" that she would have adopted that course of action if presented with the choice while still competent. The Court rebuffed that constitutional claim (brought under the due process clause). Its analysis proceeded in two stages. Speaking through Rehnquist, C.J., the Court first noted not only the sacredness of life under the law of homicide, but also that

> the majority of States in this country have laws imposing criminal penalties on one who assists another to commit suicide. We do not think that the state is required to remain neutral in the face of an informed and voluntary decision by a physically-able adult to starve to death.

But in the context presented here, a State has more particular interests at stake. The choice between life and death is a deeply personal decision of obvious and overwhelming finality. We believe Missouri may legitimately seek to safeguard the personal element of this choice through the imposition of heightened evidentiary requirements. It cannot be disputed that the Due Process Clause protects an interest in life as well as an interest in refusing life-sustaining medical treatment. Not all incompetent patients will have loved ones available to serve as surrogate decisionmakers. And even where family members are present, "[t]here will, of course, be some unfortunate situations in which family members will not act to protect a patient." A State is entitled to guard against potential abuses in such situations. . . . Finally, we think that a State may properly decline to make judgments about the "quality" of life that a particular individual may enjoy, and simply assert an unqualified interest in the preservation of human life to be weighed against the constitutionally protected interests of the individual.

Does this last statement suggest that there is no constitutionally protected right to voluntary euthanasia? Justice Brennan dissented on the ground that "improperly biased procedural obstacles" imposed under Missouri law "impermissibly burdened" the right of Nancy Cruzan "to choose to die with dignity."

10. *Consent, nondisclosure, and the sexual transmission of diseases.* Normally, the defense of consent to physical contact can be overridden if it is shown that the consent was induced by fraud or even by nondisclosure of some material fact. The problem often arises in connection with venereal diseases communicated by sexual intercourse. Thus in Maharam v. Maharam, 510 N.Y.S.2d 104 (1986), the plaintiff's husband infected her with an incurable case of genital herpes which he had contracted "through sexual relations with third parties other than his wife." The court held that the defendant's conduct was actionable if he intentionally misrepresented his condition to his wife, or if he failed to affirmatively disclose it, in light of their 31 years of marriage. What implications do decisions like *Maharam* have for the sexual transmission of AIDS? What role should be accorded to section 2307 of the New York Public Health Law, which provides that "[a]ny person who, knowing himself or herself to be infected with an infectious venereal disease, has sexual intercourse with another shall be guilty of a misdemeanor." See generally Fischer, Fraudulently Induced Consent to Intentional Torts, 46 U. Cin. L. Rev. 71 (1977).

Canterbury v. Spence
464 F.2d 772 (D.C. Cir. 1972)

[The text of the opinion and notes thereto are found beginning on page 233.]

Hudson v. Craft
204 P.2d 1 (Cal. 1949)

CARTER, J. Plaintiffs appeal from a judgment of dismissal, because of
their failure to amend their complaint, after a demurrer thereto was
sustained with leave to amend.

Plaintiff (the reference herein will be to the one plaintiff, the other
one being his father who makes a claim for hospital and medical expenses) alleges that he is 18 years of age; that defendants were conducting a carnival where one of the concessions, for which a separate
admission fee was charged, consisted of boxing exhibitions; that such
concession was conducted in violation of section 412 of the Penal Code,
and the Business & Professions Code (chap. 2 of div. 8) in that prizes
and prize money were given to contestants and no license to conduct
the same had been obtained from the State Athletic Commission, and
they were not conducted in accordance with the rules of the commission; that plaintiff, on the solicitation of defendants, and a promise of
receiving $5.00, engaged in a boxing match and suffered personal in-
juries as the result of being struck by his opponent. Plaintiff's opponent
in the match was also made a party defendant but was not served with
process.

The basis and theory of liability, if any, in mutual combat cases has
been the subject of considerable controversy. Proceeding from the
premise that, as between the combatants, the tort involved is that of
assault and battery, many courts have held that, inasmuch as each contestant has committed a battery on the other, each may hold the other
liable for any injury inflicted although both consented to the contest.
[The court cited many cases, including Teeters v. Frost, 292 P. 356
(Okla. 1930).] Being contrary to the maxim volenti non fit injuria, the
courts have endeavored to rationalize the rule by reasoning that the
state is a party where there is a breach of the peace, such as occurs in a
combat, and that no one may consent to such breach. There are cases
expressing a minority view and severe criticism has been leveled at the
majority rule, such as, that it ignores the principle of pari delicto and
encourages rather than deters mutual combat. See Hart v. Geysel, 159
Wash. 632 [294 P. 570]; 22 Minn. L. Rev. 546; Bohlen, Consent as Affecting Civil Liability for Breaches of the Peace, 24 Col. L. Rev. 819; 79
U. Pa. L. Rev. 509; 17 Va. L. Rev. 374. . . . The Restatement adopts the
minority view. An assent which satisfies the rules stated "prevents an
invasion from being tortious and, therefore, actionable, although the
invasion assented to constitutes a crime." (Rest., Torts, §60.) An example given thereunder is a boxing match where no license was had as
required by law. The only case discovered involving the liability of a
third-party promoter of the combat such as we have in the case at bar,
is Teeters v. Frost, supra, where the court, following the majority posi-

tion as to the liability of the participants as between themselves, was not confronted with any difficulty in deciding that the instigator was liable as an aider and abetter.

There is an exception to the rule stated in the Restatements, reading: "Where it is a crime to inflict a particular invasion of an interest of personality upon a particular class of persons, irrespective of their assent, and the policy of the law is primarily to protect the interests of such a class of persons from their inability to appreciate the consequences of such an invasion, and it is not solely to protect the interests of the public, the assent of such a person to such an invasion is not a consent thereto." (Rest., Torts, §61.) (See also Prosser on Torts, pp. 124-125, and cases cited.) It is evident that the so-called exception and the foregoing discussion has to do only with consent as refuting liability, not with the basic tort upon which the liability is rested, assault and battery. Concerning the bearing of the factor of consent or assumption of risk on liability, the instant case, as will more fully appear from the later discussion herein, clearly falls within the exception stated in section 61 (supra) by reason of the declared public policy of the state.

If liability is predicated on the tort of battery, it might seem to follow that in order to hold the promoter liable, it would be necessary to impose responsibility upon the combatants as to each other on the theory that they are the principals while the instigator is only the aider and abetter. In view of the public policy of this state as expressed by initiative, legislation, rules of the Athletic Commission, and the Constitution, the promoter must be held liable as a principal regardless of what the rule may be as between the combatants.

From the beginning, this state has taken an uncompromising stand against uncontrolled prize fights and boxing matches.

[The court then reviewed this history of boxing regulation in California, and noted that in 1850 prize fighting had been made a felony, but that several subsequent statutes from 1893 to 1903 had allowed sparring matches under certain restricted conditions. In 1924 a popular initiative was passed regulating prize-fighting, and in 1942 a constitutional amendment vested in the legislature extensive powers to regulate prize fights and to amend where necessary the 1924 initiative. When this fight took place, the law forbade any person under 18 from participating in a fight, required all fighters to undergo physical examinations before fighting, prescribed a maximum number of rounds and a minimum weight for gloves, required a physician to be in attendance at the fight, and required that a referee supervise the match and stop the fight if there were "too great a disparity between the boxers." The statute also authorized the boxing commission to adopt rules to set weight classes for fighters, define fouls in the ring, and provide for inspection and physical examination of the premises. It was clear that many, if not all, of these requirements were violated in the instant case.]

The foregoing declarations by the people, the Legislature, and the commission evince an unusually strong policy, obviously resting upon a detailed study of the problems relative to boxing matches. While there are other purposes underlying that policy, it is manifest that one of the chief goals is to provide safeguards for the protection of persons engaging in the activity. It may be that the actual participants, as well as the promoter, are liable criminally for a violation of the provisions, but insofar as the purpose is protection from physical harm, the chief offender would be the promoter — the activating force in procuring the occurrence of such exhibitions. It is from his uncontrolled conduct that the combatants are protected. Secondarily, the contestants are protected against their own ill-advised participation in an unregulated match. This is especially true in the case at bar where plaintiff is a lad of 18 years.

The foregoing policy compels the conclusion that the promoter is liable where he conducts boxing matches or prize fights without a license and in violation of the statutory provisions above discussed, regardless of the rights as between the contestants, and that the consent of the combatants does not relieve him of that liability. Manifestly the doctrine of pari delicto is not pertinent inasmuch as one of the main purposes of the statutes is to protect a class (combatants) of which plaintiff is a member. It may be observed that the basis of such liability finds some support in principle in the doctrine of negligence per se . . . , and strict liability arising from the nature of the conduct and its consequences . . . , the seriousness of which is here established by a statute with comprehensive regulatory features aimed at the goal of especial protection for a certain class. The end result is the same and the controlling factor is whether or not the expressed public policy is sufficiently urgent, explicit and comprehensive.

It is not necessary in the instant case to state a general rule inasmuch as each situation must have individual consideration. The nature and scope of the legislation here involved and above shown requires liability, especially when we consider that it calls for continuous and "on the spot" supervision of boxing matches. That feature alone is sufficient to distinguish it from such cases as a person operating a car without an operator's license and the like. Moreover, we have more here than the mere failure to obtain a license. While it could have been more accurately pleaded, it may be inferred that the defendants did not comply with the statutes from the allegation that they failed to so comply therewith in that they did not obtain a license and did not observe the rules and regulations of the Athletic Commission.

For the foregoing reasons, the judgment is reversed.

NOTES

1. Minority view on consent to illegal acts. *Hudson* is an unusual case because the direct action was brought against the promoter who did not participate in the fight and could not therefore be charged with a personal assault and battery. On what grounds is it possible to hold him responsible for blows inflicted by a third party, and should the action be allowed if the other combatant is entitled to a defense of consent?

In Hart v. Geysel, 294 P. 570, 572 (Wash. 1930), referred to in *Hudson,* the plaintiff's husband was killed as the result of a blow struck in an illegal prizefight, in which he consented to participate. In adopting the minority and Restatement view, the court in *Hart,* over vigorous dissent, took the position that the illegal conduct could still be regulated by criminal prosecution of either or both fighters. The court noted that to "enforce the criminal statute against prizefighting, it is not necessary to reward the one that got the worst of the encounter at the expense of his more fortunate opponent." *Hart* seeks to give effect to two basic legal policies that the majority view overrides: (1) volenti non fit injuria, or the volunteer suffers no wrong, and (2) ex turpi causa non oritur actio, or no action shall arise out of an improper or immoral cause. Why is not the private action for damages an aid to criminal enforcement? Again, does the denial of a private action encourage or discourage participation in illegal prizefights? Does the action against the promoter discourage prizefighting? Reduce the size of the purses? Both? For an excellent defense of the Restatement's adoption of the minority rule see F. Bohlen, Studies in the Law of Torts 577 (1926).

2. Private rights of action for statutory rape. In Barton v. Bee Line, Inc., 265 N.Y.S. 284 (1933), the Court addressed the question of whether an underaged plaintiff — 18 was the legal age of consent — could bring an action for damages even if she had fully consented to sexual intercourse with the defendant's servant. Because of her age, his conduct made him guilty of statutory rape, a crime then punishable by up to ten years of imprisonment. The court refused to allow her private action:

> Should a consenting female under the age of eighteen have a cause of action if she has full understanding of the nature of her act? It is one thing to say that society will protect itself by punishing those who consort with females under the age of consent; it is another to hold that knowing the nature of her act, such female shall be rewarded for her indiscretion. Surely public policy — to serve which the statute was adopted — will not be vindicated by recompensing her for willing participation in that against which the law sought to protect her. The very object of the statute will be frustrated if by a material return for her fall we should unwarily put it in the power of the female sex to become seducers in their turn.

Distinguishable from the illegal boxing cases?

3. Athletic injuries: formal settings. The question of whether actions for damages lie to persons deliberately or recklessly injured in professional athletic contests has also been the subject of recent litigation. In these cases it is understood that plaintiffs consent to injury from blows that are administered under the rules of the game. But matters are quite different when deliberately illegal blows are struck. In Hackbart v. Cincinnati Bengals, Inc., 601 F.2d 516, 520-521 (10th Cir. 1979), Dale Hackbart, then a defensive back for the Denver Broncos, was injured by a blow struck by Charles "Booby" Clark, then an offensive halfback for the Bengals. As the play began, the Bengals were on the offensive; the pass thrown was intercepted and run back by another player, with Hackbart becoming a blocker and Clark a tackler. After the play was over Clark, "acting out of anger and frustration, but without a specific intent to injure . . . stepped forward and struck a blow with his right forearm to the back of the kneeling plaintiff's head and neck with sufficient force to cause both players to fall forward to the ground." Although Hackbart suffered no immediate ill effects from the blow, shortly thereafter he experienced severe pains which, after two more brief game appearances, forced him to retire, ending a successful 13-year career. The trial court dismissed the action, chiefly on the ground that it was inappropriate to impose upon one professional football player the duty of care for the safety of another. The decision was reversed and remanded by the 10th Circuit, which wrote as follows:

> The evidence at the trial uniformly supported the proposition that the intentional striking of a player in the head from the rear is not an accepted part of either the playing rules or the general customs of the game of professional football. The trial court, however, believed that the unusual nature of the case called for the consideration of underlying policy which it defined as common law principles which have evolved as a result of the case to case process and which necessarily affect behavior in various contexts. From these considerations the belief was expressed that even *intentional* injuries incurred in football games should be outside the framework of the law. The court recognized that the potential threat of legal liability has a significant deterrent effect, and further said that private civil actions constitute an important mechanism for societal control of human conduct. Due to the increase in severity of human conflicts, a need existed to expand the body of governing law more rapidly and with more certainty, but that this had to be accomplished by legislation and administrative regulation. The judge compared football to coal mining and railroading insofar as all are inherently hazardous. Judge Matsch said that in the case of football it was questionable whether social values would be improved by limiting the violence. . . .
>
> Contrary to the position of the court then, there are no principles of law which allow a court to rule out certain tortious conduct by reason of general roughness of the game or difficulty of administering it.
>
> Indeed, the evidence shows that there are rules of the game which prohibit the intentional striking of blows. Thus, Article 1, Item 1, Subsection C, provides that: "All players are prohibited from striking on the

head, face or neck with the heel, back or side of the hand, wrist, forearm, elbow or clasped hands." Thus the very conduct which was present here is expressly prohibited by the rule which is quoted above. . . . There-fore, the notion is not correct that all reason has been abandoned, whereby the only possible remedy for the person who has been the victim of an unlawful blow is retaliation.

What should be the result in the absence of a specific rule such as that referred to in the opinion? If there is a general agreement among the owners of all teams that no actions should lie for injuries suffered on the playing field? What about an agreement among the players to the same effect? After *Hackbart,* can one professional boxer sue another for harm caused by a deliberate low blow? See Note, Compensating Injured Professional Athletes: The Mystique of Sport Versus Traditional Tort Principles, 55 N.Y.U. L. Rev. 971 (1980).

Similar principles have been applied to athletic contests at the high school and college level. In Nabozny v. Barnhill, 334 N.E.2d 258, 260-261 (Ill. App. 1975), the plaintiff goalie sustained severe and perma-nent head injuries when kicked in the head inside the penalty area, even though the defendant had an easy opportunity to avoid contact. The game was played under football association rules, under which "any contact with a goalkeeper in possession in the penalty area is an infraction of the rules, even if such contact is unintentional." The court, while concerned with the impact that tort suits might have on legiti-mate athletic activities, announced the following rule, foreshadowing the result in *Hackbart:*

> [T]his court believes that when athletes are engaged in an athletic competition all teams involved are trained and coached by knowledge-able personnel; a recognized set of rules governs the conduct of the com-petition; and a safety rule is contained therein which is primarily designed to protect players from serious injury, a player is then charged with a legal duty to every other player on the field to refrain from con-duct proscribed by a safety rule. A reckless disregard for the safety of other players cannot be excused. To engage in such conduct is to create an intolerable and unreasonable risk of serious injury to other partici-pants. We have carefully drawn the rule announced herein in order to control a new field of personal injury litigation.
>   It is our opinion that a player is liable for injury in a tort action if his conduct is such that it is either deliberate, wilful or with a reckless disre-gard for the safety of the other player so as to cause injury to that player, the same being a question of fact to be decided by a jury.

In Turcotte v. Fell, 502 N.E.2d 964, 969-970 (N.Y. 1986), the plaintiff, a professional jockey, sued for damages when injured in a race by the defendant, who had violated track rules. The court refused to allow the action, contrasting this case with *Hackbart* and *Nabozny* as follows.

The rules of the sport, however, do not necessarily limit the scope of the professional's consent. Although the foul riding rule is a safety measure, it is not by its terms absolute for it establishes a spectrum of conduct and penalties, depending on whether the violation is careless or willful and whether the contact was the result of mutual fault. As the rule recognizes, bumping and jostling are normal incidents of the sport. They are not, as were the blows in *Nabozny* and *Hackbart*, flagrant infractions unrelated to the normal method of playing the game and done without any competitive purpose. Plaintiff does not claim that Fell intentionally or recklessly bumped him; he claims only that as a result of carelessness, Fell failed to control his mount as the horses raced for the lead and a preferred position on the track. While a participant's "consent" to join in a sporting activity is not a waiver of all rules infractions, nonetheless a professional clearly understands the usual incidents of competition resulting from carelessness, particularly those which result from the customarily accepted method of playing the sport, and accepts them. They are within the known, apparent and foreseeable dangers of the sport and not actionable and thus plaintiff's complaint against defendant Fell was properly dismissed.

Hackbart and *Nabozny* received a narrow interpretation in Gauvin v. Clark, 537 N.E.2d 94, 97 (Mass. 1989), where the defendant "butted-ended" plaintiff (that is, hit him with the nonblade end of the hockey stick) in his mid-section causing serious internal injuries. The blow in question was deliberate and resulted in a major penalty and expulsion from the game under a rule enacted for the protection of the players. Nonetheless the court upheld a directed verdict for the defendant on the ground that there was no evidence that he had acted "wilfully, wantonly or recklessly." The court noted that "personal injury cases arising out of an athletic event must be predicated on reckless disregard for safety . . . Allowing the imposition of liability in cases of reckless disregard of safety diminishes the need for players to seek retaliation during the game or future games. Precluding the imposition of liability in case of negligence without reckless misconduct furthers the policy that '[v]igorous and active participation in sporting events should not be chilled by the threat of litigation.' " Why isn't this flagrant foul evidence of reckless misconduct notwithstanding the jury's finding?

4. *Athletic injuries: informal settings.* In Marchetti v. Kalish, 559 N.E.2d 699 (Ohio 1990), plaintiff and defendant were engaged in a backyard game called "kick the can." In this game, one party is designated as "it." The players run and hide, and then attempt to sneak up and kick the can undetected by "it." When "it" spots another player, he runs to the can, places his foot on it, and calls out the player's name and then cries out "kick the can — one, two, three" after which the spotted player is considered captured and must stay by the home base until another player reaches the can undetected and frees him. (The rules of the game were sufficiently well articulated that the parties were able to set them out in a joint appendix that appeared at the end of the opinion.)

On the day in question plaintiff, a 13-year-old girl, and defendant, a 15-year-old boy, played a variation of the basic game with a ball whereby the first player captured immediately becomes the new "it." Plaintiff then placed her foot on the ball and announced that the defendant was "it." "[Defendant], however, continued to run towards [plaintiff], colliding with her and kicking the ball out from under her foot. [Plaintiff] fell to the ground, and her right leg was broken in two places."

Plaintiff conceded that the injuries in question were not intentionally or recklessly inflicted. The Ohio Supreme Court entered a summary judgment for defendant, relying on, among other cases, *Nabozny* and *Hackbart*. "[Plaintiff] argues that these cases from other jurisdictions are distinguishable from the present case because we are dealing with children involved in a simple neighborhood game rather than an organized contact sport." It then held the distinction was immaterial so long as the children "were engaging in some type of recreational or sports activity. Whether the activity is organized, unorganized, supervised or unsupervised, is immaterial to the standard of liability." "[B]efore a party may proceed with a cause of action involving injury resulted from a recreational or sports activity, reckless or intentional conduct must exist." How far has the law moved from *Vosburg*?

The rule requiring reckless or negligent infliction of harm has been extended to cooperative as well as competitive athletic events in Ford v. Gouin, 834 P.2d 724, 728 (Cal. 1992). There plaintiff alleged that the defendant had negligently steered his powerboat through a narrow cut while pulling the plaintiff, waterskiing barefooted, who was trying to execute difficult maneuvers. Plaintiff struck the back of his head against an overhanging tree. Arabian, J., granted defendant a summary judgment stating:

> Even when a water skier is not involved in a "competitive" event, the skier has undertaken vigorous, athletic activity, and the ski boat driver operates the boat in a manner that is consistent with, and enhances, the excitement and challenge of the active conduct of the sport. Imposition of legal liability on a ski boat driver for ordinary negligence in making too sharp a turn, for example, or in pulling the skier too rapidly or too slowly, likely would have the same kind of undesirable chilling effect on the driver's conduct that courts in other cases feared would inhibit ordinary conduct in various sports. As a result, holding ski boat drivers liable for their ordinary negligence might well have a generally deleterious effect on the nature of the sport of water skiing as a whole. Additionally, imposing such liability might well deter friends from voluntarily assisting one another in such potentially risky sports. Accordingly, the general rule limiting the duty of care of a coparticipant in active sports to the avoidance of intentional and reckless misconduct, applies to participants engaged in noncompetitive but active sports activity, such as a ski boat driver towing a water skier.

Is it bad to deter friends from undertaking these risky tasks if they are unable to discharge them effectively?

2.   Nonconsensual Defenses

a.   Insanity

McGuire v. Almy
8 N.E.2d 760 (Mass. 1937)

QUA, J. This is an action of tort for assault and battery. The only question of law reported is whether the judge should have directed a verdict for the defendant.

The following facts are established by the plaintiff's own evidence: In August, 1930, the plaintiff was employed to take care of the defendant. The plaintiff was a registered nurse and was a graduate of a training school for nurses. The defendant was an insane person. Before the plaintiff was hired she learned that the defendant was a "mental case and was in good physical condition," and that for some time two nurses had been taking care of her. The plaintiff was on "twenty-four hour duty." The plaintiff slept in the room next to the defendant's room. Except when the plaintiff was with the defendant, the plaintiff kept the defendant locked in the defendant's room. There was a wire grating over the outside of the window of that room. During the period of "fourteen months or so" while the plaintiff cared for the defendant, the defendant "had a few odd spells," when she showed some hostility to the plaintiff and said that "she would like to try and do something to her." The defendant had been violent at times and had broken dishes "and things like that," and on one or two occasions the plaintiff had to have help to subdue the defendant.

On April 19, 1932, the defendant, while locked in her room, had a violent attack. The plaintiff heard a crashing of furniture and then knew that the defendant was ugly, violent and dangerous. The defendant told the plaintiff and a Miss Maroney, "the maid," who was with the plaintiff in the adjoining room, that if they came into the defendant's room, she would kill them. The plaintiff and Miss Maroney looked into the defendant's room, "saw what the defendant had done," and "thought it best to take the broken stuff away before she did any harm to herself with it." They sent for one Emerton, the defendant's brother-in-law. When he arrived the defendant was in the middle of her room about ten feet from the door, holding upraised the leg of a low-boy as if she were going to strike. The plaintiff stepped into the room and walked toward the defendant, while Emerton and Miss Maroney remained in the doorway. As the plaintiff approached the defendant and tried to take hold of the defendant's hand which held the leg, the defendant struck the plaintiff's head with it, causing the injuries for which the action was brought. [After discussing the Massachusetts precedents on the liability of an insane person for his tortious conduct and finding the point not fully settled, the court continued:]

Turning to authorities elsewhere, we find that courts in this country almost invariably say in the broadest terms that an insane person is liable for his torts. As a rule no distinction is made between those torts which would ordinarily be classed as intentional and those which would ordinarily be classed as negligent, nor do the courts discuss the effect of different kinds of insanity or of varying degrees of capacity as bearing upon the ability of the defendant to understand the particular act in question or to make a reasoned decision with respect to it, although it is sometimes said that an insane person is not liable for torts requiring malice of which he is incapable. Defamation and malicious prosecution are the torts more commonly mentioned in this connection. A number of illustrative cases appear in the footnote. These decisions are rested more upon grounds of public policy and upon what might be called a popular view of the requirements of essential justice than upon any attempt to apply logically the underlying principles of civil liability to the special instance of the mentally deranged. Thus it is said that a rule imposing liability tends to make more watchful those persons who have charge of the defendant and who may be supposed to have some interest in preserving his property; that as an insane person must pay for his support, if he is financially able, so he ought also to pay for the damage which he does; that an insane person with abundant wealth ought not to continue in unimpaired enjoyment of the comfort which it brings while his victim bears the burden unaided; and there is also a suggestion that courts are loath to introduce into the great body of civil litigation the difficulties in determining mental capacity which it has been found impossible to avoid in the criminal field.

The rule established in these cases has been criticized severely by certain eminent text writers both in this country and in England, principally on the ground that it is an archaic survival of the rigid and formal medieval conception of liability for acts done, without regard to fault, as opposed to what is said to be the general modern theory that liability in tort should rest upon fault. Notwithstanding these criticisms, we think that as a practical matter there is strong force in the reasons underlying these decisions. They are consistent with the general statements found in the cases dealing with the liability of infants for torts. Fault is by no means at the present day a universal prerequisite to liability, and the theory that it should be such has been obliged very recently to yield at several points to what have been thought to be paramount considerations of public good. Finally, it would be difficult not to recognize the persuasive weight of so much authority so widely extended.

But the present occasion does not require us either to accept or to reject the prevailing doctrine in its entirety. For this case it is enough to say that where an insane person by his act does intentional damage to the person or property of another he is liable for that damage in the same circumstances in which a normal person would be liable. This means that in so far as a particular intent would be necessary in order to render a normal person liable, the insane person, in order to be liable, must have been capable of entertaining that same intent and must have entertained it in fact. But the law will not inquire further into his peculiar mental condition with a view to excusing him if it should appear that delusion or other consequence of his affliction has caused him to entertain that intent or that a normal person would not have entertained it.

We do not suggest that this is necessarily a logical stopping point. If public policy demands that a mentally affected person be subjected to the external standard for intentional wrongs, it may well be that public policy also demands that he should be subjected to the external standard for wrongs which are commonly classified as negligent, in accordance with what now seems to be the prevailing view. We stop here for the present, because we are not required to go further in order to decide this case, because of deference to the difficulty of the subject, because full and adequate discussion is lacking in most of the cases decided up to the present time, and because by far the greater number of those cases, however broad their statement of the principle, are in fact cases of intentional rather than of negligent injury.

Coming now to the application of the rule to the facts of this case, it is apparent that the jury could find that the defendant was capable of entertaining and that she did entertain an intent to strike and to injure the plaintiff and that she acted upon that intent. See Am. Law Inst. Restatement: Torts §§13, 14. We think this was enough. [The court then rejected the argument that the plaintiff had consented to or assumed the risk as a matter of law. In its view the risk became "plain and obvious" only after she entered the room, just before the assault, when an emergency sufficient to deny voluntary consent had already been created.]

Judgment for the plaintiff on the verdict.

NOTE

Intention and insanity. One issue that arises with the insanity defense concerns the mental state which the defendant has formed toward her victim. What result if Almy had thought she was striking a creature from outer space? That her actions were in self-defense because of an imagined assault by McGuire? Looking at the other side of the case, was the court right to reject defendant's assumption-of-risk defense in light of the elaborate preparations plaintiff took before entering the defendant's room?

The bulk of the decisions on the insanity defense have hewed to the uncompromising line set out in McGuire v. Almy. See, e.g., Seals v. Snow, 254 P. 348 (Kan. 1927), noting that "where one of two innocent persons must suffer a loss, it should be borne by the one who occasioned it." In Polmatier v. Russ, 537 A.2d 468, 472 (Conn. 1988), the court showed a manifest impatience with the defendant's effort to demonstrate that he did not have the requisite intention to support civil liability for the killing of his father-in-law. Defendant Russ and his 2-year-old daughter visited the house of his father-in-law. The defendant then sat astride the decedent, beating him over the head with a beer bottle. Shortly thereafter the defendant got up, searched two bedrooms in the house, found 30-30 ammunition and a Winchester rifle, and returned to the living room where he killed his father-in-law with two shots. Thereafter the defendant was found naked, sitting on a stump in a wooded area about two miles from the decedent's home, carrying his blood-soaked clothing and cradling his daughter in his arms. He was diagnosed as "suffering from a severe case of paranoid schizophrenia that involved delusions of persecution, grandeur, influence and reference, and also involved auditory hallucinations." The defendant was found unfit to stand for a criminal trial, but was held responsible for an intentional tort.

> We note that we have not been referred to any evidence indicating that the defendant's acts were reflexive, convulsive or epileptic. Furthermore, under the Restatement (Second) of Torts §2, "act" is used "to denote an external manifestation of the actor's will and does not include any of its results, even the most direct, immediate, and intended." Comment b to this section provides in pertinent part: "A muscular reaction is always an act unless it is a purely reflexive reaction in which the mind and will have no share." Although the trial court found that the defendant could not form a rational choice, it did find that he could make a schizophrenic or crazy choice. Moreover, a rational choice is not required since "[a]n insane person may have an intent to invade the interests of another, even though his reasons and motives for forming that intention may be entirely irrational." Restatement (Second) of Torts §895J, comment c. The following example is given in the Restatement to illustrate the application of comment c: "A, who is insane believes that he is Napoleon Bonaparte, and that B, his nurse, who confines him in his room, is an agent of the Duke of Wellington, who is endeavoring to prevent his arrival on the field of Waterloo in time to win the battle. Seeking to escape, he breaks off the leg of a chair, attacks B with it and fractures her skull. A is subject to liability to B for battery."

The court then rejected the further argument that the defendant must have been shown to have "acted for the *purpose* of causing," or with a "desire to cause the resulting injury," in line with the Restatement definitions of intention.

The English cases have also shown a strong reluctance to allow the insanity defense. In Morriss v. Marsden, [1952] 1 All E.R. 925 (Q.B.), the court held the defendant liable, though insane, for the harm he caused to the plaintiff, the manager of a hotel in which the defendant had a room, by striking him over the head with a blunt instrument. In the course of his opinion, Stable, J., ruled:

> I cannot think that, if a person of unsound mind converts my property under a delusion that he is entitled to do it or that it was not property at all, that affords a defence. I can bring an action against him for the recovery of my property, or, if it has been converted and destroyed, for its value. Against that it may be said: "There all you are seeking is restitution, either the return of your property or the equivalent. In this case what is being asked for is damages, which is compensation and involves in a sense some punitive element." On the whole, I accept the view that an intention — i.e., a voluntary act, the mind prompting and directing the act which is relied on, as in this case, as the tortious act — must be averred and proved. For example, I think that, if a person in a condition of complete automatism inflicted grievous injury, that would not be actionable.

What should be done in cases of automatism, where the claim is that the sleepwalking defendant has done *no act* at all and thus cannot have committed any tort, intentional or otherwise? See generally Bohlen, Liability in Torts of Infants and Insane Persons, 23 Mich. L. Rev. 9 (1924), reprinted in his Studies at 543 (1926).

b. Self-defense

Courvoisier v. Raymond
47 P. 284 (Colo. 1896)

HAYT, C.J. It is admitted or proven beyond controversy that appellee received a gunshot wound at the hands of the appellant at the time and place designated in the complaint, and that as the result of such wound the appellee was seriously injured. It is further shown that the shooting occurred under the following circumstances:

That Mr. Courvoisier, on the night in question, was asleep in his bed in the second story of a brick building, situate at the corner of South Broadway and Dakota streets in South Denver; that he occupied a portion of the lower floor of this building as a jewelry store. He was aroused from his bed shortly after midnight by parties shaking or trying to open the door of the jewelry store. These parties, when asked by him as to what they wanted, insisted upon being admitted, and upon his refusal to comply with this request, they used profane and abusive epithets toward him. Being unable to gain admission, they broke some signs upon the front of the building, and then entered the building by another entrance, and passing upstairs commenced knocking upon the door of a room where defendant's sister was sleeping. Courvoisier partly dressed himself, and, taking his revolver, went upstairs and expelled the intruders from the building. In doing this he passed downstairs and out on the sidewalk as far as the entrance to his store, which was at the corner of the building. The parties expelled from the building, upon reaching the rear of the store, were joined by two or three others. In order to frighten these parties away, the defendant fired a shot in the air, but instead of retreating they passed around to the street in front, throwing stones and brickbats at the defendant, whereupon he fired a second and perhaps a third shot. The first shot fired attracted the attention of plaintiff Raymond and two deputy sheriffs, who were at the Tramway depot, across the street. These officers started toward Mr. Courvoisier, who still continued to shoot, but two of them stopped when they reached the men in the street, for the purpose of arresting them, Mr. Raymond alone proceeding towards the defendant, calling out to him that he was an officer and to stop shooting. Although the night was dark, the street was well lighted by electricity, and when the officer approached him defendant shaded his eyes, and, taking deliberate aim, fired, causing the injury complained of.

The plaintiff's theory of the case is that he was a duly authorized police officer, and in the discharge of his duties at the time that the defendant was committing a breach of the peace, and that the defendant, knowing him to be a police officer, recklessly fired the shot in question.

The defendant claims that the plaintiff was approaching him at the time in a threatening attitude, and that the surrounding circumstances were such as to cause a reasonable man to believe that his life was in danger, and that it was necessary to shoot in self-defense, and that defendant did so believe at the time of firing the shot. . . .

The next error assigned relates to the instructions given by the court to the jury and to those requested by the defendant and refused by the court. The second instruction given by the court was clearly erroneous. The instruction is as follows: "The court instructs you that if you believe from the evidence, that, at the time the defendant shot the plaintiff, the plaintiff was not assaulting the defendant, then your verdict should be for the plaintiff."

The vice of this instruction is that it excluded from the jury a full consideration of the justification claimed by the defendant. The evidence for the plaintiff tends to show that the shooting, if not malicious, was wanton and reckless, but the evidence for the defendant tends to show that the circumstances surrounding him at the time of the shooting were such as to lead a reasonable man to believe that his life was in danger, or that he was in danger of receiving great bodily harm at the hands of the plaintiff, and the defendant testified that he did so believe. [The court then reviewed the injured plaintiff's sworn version of the facts of the case and continued:]

. . . He then adds: "I saw a man come away from the bunch of men and come up towards me, and as I looked around I saw this man put his hand to his hip pocket. I didn't think I had time to jump aside, and therefore turned around and fired at him. I had no doubts but it was somebody that had come to rob me, because some weeks before Mr. Wilson's store was robbed. It is next door to mine."

By this evidence two phases of the transaction are presented for consideration: *First,* was the plaintiff assaulting the defendant at the time plaintiff was shot? *Second,* if not, was there sufficient evidence of justification for the consideration of the jury? The first question was properly submitted, but the second was excluded by the instruction under review. The defendant's justification did not rest entirely upon the proof of assault by the plaintiff. A riot was in progress, and the defendant swears that he was attacked with missiles, hit with stones, brickbats, etc.; that he shot plaintiff, supposing him to be one of the rioters. We must assume these facts as established in reviewing the instruction, as we cannot say what the jury might have found had this evidence been submitted to them under a proper charge.

By the second instruction the conduct of those who started the fracas was eliminated from the consideration of the jury. If the jury believed from the evidence that the defendant would have been justified in shooting one of the rioters had such person advanced towards him as did the plaintiff, then it became important to determine whether the defendant mistook plaintiff for one of the rioters, and if such a mistake was in fact made, was it excusable in the light of all the circumstances leading up to and surrounding the commission of the act? If these issues had been resolved by the jury in favor of the defendant, he would have been entitled to a judgment. Morris v. Platt, 32 Conn. 75.

[Judgment was reversed.]

NOTES

1. *Self-defense against the innocent attacker.* While self-defense is universally recognized as a justification for an intentionally inflicted harm, there is a persistent debate over the circumstances that limit its use. May a social outcast use force to protect himself from attack by a prominent businessman or scientist, temporarily gone mad, if, say, both are

trapped together in an elevator? If he can, how does one measure the claims to personal integrity against those of social welfare? The Restatement (Second) takes a discreet pass: "The Institute expresses no opinion as to whether there is a similar privilege of self-defense against conduct which the actor recognizes, or should recognize, to be entirely innocent." How ought the question be resolved?

For the complex rules governing self-defense, see Restatement (Second) of Torts §§63-76. For an excellent discussion of the problem see Fletcher, Proportionality and the Psychotic Aggressor: A Vignette in Comparative Criminal Theory, 8 Israel L. Rev. 367 (1973).

2. *Self-defense and the innocent bystander.* In Morris v. Platt, 32 Conn. 75 (1864), the court held that the accidental harming of an innocent bystander by force reasonably intended in self-defense to repel an attack by a third party is not actionable. On this issue the Restatement concurs, noting that the defendant is liable to the innocent third party "only if the actor realizes or should realize that his act creates an unreasonable risk of causing such harm." Restatement (Second) of Torts §75. Is that decision consistent with the trial judge's approach in *Courvoisier?* The appellate court's? Does the plaintiff in Morris v. Platt have a cause of action against the defendant's assailant?

With Morris v. Platt, contrast the Roman law approach. "Persons who do damage because they cannot otherwise defend themselves are innocent; for all statutes and legal systems allow one to repel force by force. But if in order to defend myself I throw a stone at my adversary, but hit, not him but a passer-by, I shall be liable under the Lex Aquilia [the general tort statute for wrongful damage]; for one is allowed to strike only the person who uses force, and then only when it is done for the purpose of protection and not revenge as well." Digest 9.2.45.4.

3. *Limitations on self-defense.* The most recurrent issues in self-defense cases are more prosaic: who struck the first blow, and was the force excessive under the circumstances? In Boston v. Muncy, 233 P.2d 300, 301, 303 (Okla. 1951), the defendant encountered the plaintiff in a domino parlor after work and asked him what had happened to the automobile heater — difficult to obtain because of post-World War II rationing — that he had promised to put aside for the defendant. The plaintiff denied having promised to put aside the heater. According to the plaintiff's version, the defendant then called plaintiff a liar and, without provocation, struck him over the right eye, causing serious damage. According to the defendant, "when he reminded plaintiff that he had promised to save a heater for him plaintiff called him a liar and made an attempt to hit him with his fist; that he then struck the plaintiff in self-defense." Plaintiff and defendant each had witnesses to support his version of the facts. The defendant then asked for instructions that said "the defendant had the right to exercise and use such reasonable

force as may have reasonably appeared to him in good faith to be necessary to protect himself from bodily harm, even though he may not have been actually in danger." But the trial court, in instruction No. 8, said:

> . . . if at the time the defendant is alleged to have assaulted and struck the plaintiff the defendant in doing what he did was acting in an effort to protect his own person or life, and the circumstances then surrounding the defendant were such [that] the exercise of reasonable judgment would justify or induce in his mind an honest belief that he was in danger of receiving some great bodily harm, judging from the standpoint of the defendant, then the defendant would be justified in doing what he did, and your verdict should be for the defendant.

The Oklahoma court held that the instructions created prejudicial error, and remanded the case for a new trial:

> It is further contended by plaintiff that the error, if any, in giving instruction No. 8 could in no manner have misled the jury and the error in giving the instruction is therefore harmless. We do not agree. The instruction too narrowly limits defendant's right of self-defense.
> The evidence is highly conflicting as to who was the aggressor. The jury might have found that plaintiff was the aggressor, but it also might have further found that defendant was not justified in apprehending or believing that plaintiff intended to inflict upon him some great bodily harm, and under the instruction it might have concluded that the defendant therefore had no right to stand his ground and defend himself against the attack and it was therefore its duty to render a verdict for plaintiff.

Does elimination of the word "great" from the trial judge's instructions entitle the defendant to use the minimum force that is in fact necessary to protect himself, even from trivial harm? If the defendant had been a squeamish and nervous little man, is he held to a standard of "ordinary firmness and courage," even if unable to meet it in practice? If he is carrying a gun, may he use it when an ordinary man could not? See Restatement (Second) of Torts §63 comments *i* and *j*.

4. *Defense of third parties.* Under what circumstances is a person allowed to act in defense of a third party? Does a person have a good defense if he hurts a plaintiff in the mistaken, but reasonable, belief that a third party is in need of assistance? See Restatement (Second) of Torts §76, which notes that a person is privileged to defend a third party "under the same conditions and by the same means as those under and by which he is privileged to defend himself if the actor correctly or reasonably believes" that the third party is entitled to use force in self-defense and that his own intervention is necessary to protect that party. How can one argue from *Courvoisier, Morris,* and Digest 9.2.45.4?

c. Defense of property

M'Ilvoy v. Cockran
2 A. K. Marsh. 271 (Ky. 1820)

[Cockran sued M'Ilvoy for damages arising out of an assault and battery committed by the latter in defense of his real property. It appears that Cockran was tearing down a fence on M'Ilvoy's land and M'Ilvoy used sufficient force in repelling Cockran to wound him severely. The court refused to instruct the jury that if the truth of the defendant's second plea, dealing with the defense of real property, were established, the verdict should be for defendant. After verdict for the plaintiff, defendant moved for a new trial. This motion was overruled and judgment was entered for the plaintiff. Affirmed.]

OWSLEY, J. [I]t must be borne in mind that the declaration contains a charge of assault, battery and wounding and the plea alledges the injury to have been occasioned by M'Ilvoy (the defendant in the circuit court) in defence of a close of which he was possessed, and in resisting the attempt of Cockran *forcibly* to enter and demolish the fence thereto appertaining.

It is not denied but that an assault and battery may be justified in the defence of the possession of either real or personal property; but it is contended that previous to the use of force there should be a request to depart, and that the injury should not be justified in the mode adopted by M'Ilvoy, but that he ought to have pleaded by way of moliter manus imposuit. [He gently laid his hands (upon the plaintiff).]

That moliter manus is the proper mode of pleading to many actions brought for injuries arising in defence of the possession of property, will not be controverted; but that it is the only admissible mode in every possible case, we apprehend, cannot be maintained.

There are certainly cases where force may be employed in defence of possession without a previous request to depart. Thus in the case of Green v. Godard, 2 Salk. 641, the court said, in cases of *actual force,* as breaking open a gate or door, it is lawful to oppose force with force; and if one breaks down a gate, or comes into a close with force and arms, the possessor need not request him to depart, but may lay hands upon him immediately, for it is but returning violence with violence: so if one comes forcibly and takes away my goods, he may be opposed immediately, for there is no time to make a request: but, say the court, where one enters the close without actual force, although his entry will be construed a *force in law,* there must be a request to depart before the possessor can lay hands upon him and turn him out.

This case from Salkeld, whilst it discriminates between those cases where force may or may not be employed without a request to depart, illustrates conclusively the cases where moliter manus should properly be pleaded, as well as those where such a plea as that adopted by M'Il-voy may be adopted. It shows that where possession has been invaded by *implied force* only, injuries in defence of the possession ought to be justified by way of moliter manus; but where the possession is attacked by actual force, as no request to desist is necessary, the injury may be justified by pleading the facts which authorise the employment of force in defence of the possession.

We are aware that, in some reported cases, judges are said to have used expressions negativing the idea of any justification in defence of possession, other than by a plea of moliter manus; but, in using those expressions, we apprehend, the court must have had in view injuries resulting in the defence of possession invaded, not by actual, but by constructive force.

It is upon this distinction between *actual* and *constructive* force, and this only, and by applying the plea of moliter manus to the latter, and not the former, that the reported cases can be reconciled with each other; and, understanding the court, when speaking on the subject of that plea, to have had in mind the cases of constructive force, there is no difficulty in reconciling the authorities.

But whilst each plea is admissible when applied to its appropriate case, in neither mode can every species of injuries be justified, exclusively in defence of possession. Where the possession is invaded by force in law, and the intruder refuses to depart, or where it is invaded by actual force, force may be employed by the possessor and as every forcible laying of hands upon another is, in legal contemplation, a battery, it follows that, in either mode of pleading, an assault and battery may be justified.

Notwithstanding, however, an assault and battery may be justified in either mode of pleading, we apprehend a wounding cannot be: for it is well settled that in defence of possession a wounding cannot be justified. But although a wounding cannot be justified barely in defence of possession, yet if, in attempting to remove the intruder, or prevent his forcible entry, he should commit an assault upon the person of the possessor, or his family, and the owner should, in defence of himself or family, wound him, the wounding may, no doubt, be justified; but then, as the personal assault would form the grounds of justification, the plea should set out, specifically, the assault in justification.

From what has been said, it will be perceived that the plea of M'Ilvoy, as it contains allegations of actual force on the part of Cockran, imports a defence to the assault and battery charged in the declaration; but as it contains no allegation of a personal assault by Cockran, it furnishes no justification to the wounding stated in the declaration. It results, therefore, that if the plea was proven to be true, the jury, sworn to try also on other issues going to the whole cause of action, could not regularly have found a general verdict for M'Ilvoy, and, consequently, the court properly refused the instructions to the jury asked by M'Ilvoy.

Bird v. Holbrook
130 Eng. Rep. 911 (C.P. 1825)

The following were the facts of the case: —

Before, and at the time of the Plaintiff's sustaining the injury complained of, the Defendant rented and occupied a walled garden in the parish of St. Phillip and Jacob, in the county of Gloucester, in which the Defendant grew valuable flower-roots, and particularly tulips, of the choicest and most expensive description. The garden was at the distance of near a mile from the Defendant's dwelling-house, and above one hundred yards from the road. In it there was a summer-house, consisting of a single room, in which the defendant and his wife had some considerable time before slept, and intended in a few days after the accident again to have slept, for the greater protection of their property. The garden was surrounded by a wall, by which it was separated on the south from a footway up to some houses, on the east and west from other gardens, and on the north from a field which had no path through it, and was itself fenced against the highway, at a considerable distance from the garden, by a wall. On the north side of the garden the wall adjoining the field was seven or eight feet high. The other walls were somewhat lower. The garden was entered by a door in the wall. The Defendant had been, shortly before the accident, robbed of flowers and roots from his garden to the value of £20 and upwards: in consequence of which, for the protection of his property, with the assistance of another man, he placed in the garden a spring gun, the wires connected with which were made to pass from the door-way of the summer-house to some tulip beds, at the height of about fifteen inches from the ground, and across three or four of the garden paths, which wires were visible from all parts of the garden or the garden wall; but it was admitted by the Defendant, that the Plaintiff had not seen them, and that he had no notice of the spring gun and the wires being there; and that the Plaintiff had gone into the garden for an innocent purpose, to get back a pea-fowl that had strayed.

A witness to whom the Defendant mentioned the fact of his having been robbed, and of having set a spring gun, proved that he had asked the Defendant if he had put up a notice of such gun being set, to which the Defendant answered, that "he did not conceive that there was any law to oblige him to do so," and the Defendant desired such person not to mention to any one that the gun was set, "lest the villain should not be detected." The Defendant stated to the same person that the garden was very secure, and that he and his wife were going to sleep in the summer-house in a few days. . . .

On the 21st March 1825, between the hours of six and seven in the afternoon, it being then light, a pea-hen belonging to the occupier of a house in the neighbourhood had escaped, and, after flying across the field above mentioned, alighted in the Defendant's garden. A female servant of the owner of the bird was in pursuit of it, and the Plaintiff (a youth of the age of nineteen years), seeing her in distress from the fear of losing the bird, said he would go after it for her: he accordingly got upon the wall at the back of the garden, next to the field, and having called out two or three times to ascertain whether any person was in the garden, and waiting a short space of time without receiving any answer, jumped down into the garden.

The bird took shelter near the summer-house, and the boy's foot coming in contact with one of the wires, close to the spot where the gun was set, it was thereby discharged, and a great part of its contents, consisting of large swan shot, were lodged in and about his knee-joint, and caused a severe wound.

The question for the opinion of the Court was, Whether Plaintiff was entitled to recover: if so, the verdict was to stand; otherwise a nonsuit was to be entered.

Merewether, Serjt. for the defendant. . . . The main ground of the defence, however, is, that the Plaintiff cannot recover for an injury occasioned to him by his own wrongful act. Commodum ex injuria non oritur and it is equally the principle of our law, that jus ex injuria non oritur. If a man place broken glass on a wall, or spikes behind a carriage, one who wilfully encounters them, and is wounded, even though it were by night, when he could have no notice, has no claim for compensation. Volenti non fit injuria. The Defendant lawfully places a gun on his own property; he leaves the wires visible; he builds a high wall, expressly to keep off intruders; and if, under those circumstances, they are permitted to recover for an injury resulting from their scaling the wall, no man can protect his property at a distance.

Wilde in reply. . . . No illustration can be drawn from the use of spikes and broken glass on walls, &c. These are mere preventives, obvious to the sight, — unless the trespasser *chooses* a time of darkness, when no notice could be available, — mere preventives, injurious only to the persevering and determined trespasser, who can calculate at the moment of incurring the danger the amount of suffering he is about to endure, and who will, consequently, desist from his enterprise whenever the anticipated advantage is outweighed by the pain which he must endure to obtain it.

BEST, C.J. I am of opinion that this action is maintainable. . . .

It has been argued that the law does not compel every line of conduct which humanity or religion may require; but there is no act which Christianity forbids, that the law will not reach: if it were otherwise, Christianity would not be, as it has always been held to be, part of the law of England. I am, therefore, clearly of opinion that he who sets spring guns, without giving notice, is guilty of an inhuman act, and that, if injurious consequences ensue, he is liable to yield redress to the sufferer. But this case stands on grounds distinct from any that have preceded it. In general, spring guns have been set for the purpose of deterring; the Defendant placed his for the express purpose of doing injury; for, when called on to give notice, he said, "If I give notice, I shall not catch him." He intended, therefore, that the gun should be discharged, and that the contents should be lodged in the body of his victim, for he could not be caught in any other way. On these principles the action is clearly maintainable, and particularly on the latter ground. The only thing which raised any doubt in my mind was the recent act of parliament; and if that had been purely prohibitory, there would be great weight in the argument which has been raised on it; because in a new prohibitory law we have the testimony of the legislature that there was no previous law against the thing prohibited. But the act is declaratory as to part, and prohibitory as to part; declaratory as to the setting of spring guns without notice, and the word "declared" is expressly introduced; prohibitory as to setting spring guns, even with notice, except in dwelling-houses by night. As to the case of Brock v. Copeland, Lord Kenyon proceeded on the ground that the Defendant had a right to keep a dog for the preservation of his house, and the Plaintiff, who was his foreman, knew where the dog was stationed. The case of the furious bull is altogether different; for if a man places such an animal where there is a public footpath, he interferes with the rights of the public. What would be the determination of the court if the bull were placed in a field where there is no footpath, we need not now decide; but it may be observed, that he must be placed somewhere, and is kept, not for mischief, but to renew his species; while the gun in the present case was placed purely for mischief. The case of the pit dug on a common has been distinguished, on the ground that the owner had a right to do what he pleased with his own land, and the Plaintiff could shew no right for the horse to be there.

. . . But we want no authority in a case like the present; we put it on the principle that it is inhuman to catch a man by means which may maim him or endanger his life, and, as far as human means can go, it is the object of English law to uphold humanity and the sanctions of religion. It would be, indeed, a subject of regret, if a party were not liable in damages, who, instead of giving notice of the employment of a destructive engine, or removing it, at least, during the day, expressed a resolution to withhold notice, lest, by affording it, he should fail to entrap his victim.

BURROUGH, J. The common understanding of mankind shews, that notice ought to be given when these means of protection are resorted to; and it was formerly the practice upon such occasions to give public notice in market towns. But the present case is of a worse complexion than those which have preceded it; for if the Defendant had proposed merely to protect his property from thieves, he would have set the spring guns only by night. The Plaintiff was only a trespasser: if the Defendant had been present, he would not have been authorised even in taking him into custody, and no man can do indirectly that which he is forbidden to do directly.

NOTES

1. *Spring guns and poachers.* The spring gun was at one time a cele-brated issue in England when large landowners sought to protect their game from poachers eager to supply the urban markets. Consider the following passage from a famous speech by Sidney Smith in the House of Commons:

> If a man be not mad, he must be presumed to foresee common conse-quences if he puts a bullet into a spring gun — he must be supposed to foresee that it will kill any poacher who touches the wire — and to that consequence he must stand. We do not suppose all preservers of game to be so bloodily inclined that they would prefer the death of a poacher to his staying away. Their object is to preserve game; they have no objec-tion to preserve the lives of their fellow-creatures also, if both can exist at the same time; if not, the least worthy of God's creatures must fall — the rustic without a soul, — not the Christian partridge — not the immortal pheasant — not the rational woodcock, or the accountable hare. [The Selected Writings of Sidney Smith 230-231 (Auden ed. 1956).]

2. *The statutory response to the spring gun question.* As noted in Bird v. Holbrook, the use of spring guns had been regulated by Parliamentary enactment shortly before the case was decided. The statute itself (7 & 8 Geo. 4, c. 18 §§1-5 (1826)) was passed in response to the earlier deci-sion of Ilott v. Wilkes, 106 Eng. Rep. 674 (K.B. 1820), where it was held: "A trespasser, having knowledge that there are spring-guns in a wood, although he may be ignorant of the particular spots where they are placed, cannot maintain an action for an injury received in conse-quence of his accidentally treading on the latent wire communicating with the gun, and thereby letting it off." The central provisions of the statute read as follows:

> Whereas it is expedient to prohibit the setting of Spring Guns and Man Traps, and other Engines calculated to destroy human Life, or inflict grievous bodily harm; Be it therefore enacted and declared . . .
> That from and after the passing of this Act, if any Person shall set or place or cause to be set or placed, any Spring Gun, Man Trap, or other Engine calculated to destroy human Life, or inflict grievous bodily Harm, with the Intent that the same or whereby the same may destroy or inflict grievous bodily Harm upon a Trespasser or other Person coming in con-

tact therewith, the Person so setting or placing, or causing to be so set or placed, such Gun, Trap, or Engine as aforesaid, shall be guilty of a Misdemeanor. . . .

IV. Provided always, and be it further enacted, That nothing in this Act shall be deemed or construed to make it a Misdemeanor, within the Meaning of this Act, to set or cause to be set, or to be continued set, from Sunset to Sunrise, any Spring Gun, Man Trap, or other Engine which shall be set, or caused or continued to be set, in a Dwelling House for the Protection thereof.

V. Provided always, and it is hereby further enacted and declared, That nothing in this Act contained shall in any Manner affect or authorize any Proceedings in any Civil or Criminal Court touching any Matter or Thing done or committed previous to the passing of this Act.

A move by English truck farmers to carve out a further exception from the statute to protect their own interests was defeated. Did Best, C.J., give an accurate reading of the statute, especially on the question of notice? Suppose a person sets a spring gun in violation of the statute. If the gun is triggered by an individual against whom the application of direct force is warranted (e.g., a would-be assailant who enters a home during the day), does the statute override any defense the homeowner has to the intruder's cause of action for personal injuries? Should it excuse the payment of the statutory fine? Note that the statute was repealed in its entirety, 24 & 25 Vict. c. 95 §1 (1861).

3. An economic interpretation of Bird v. Holbrook. Writing from an economic perspective, Judge Posner has analyzed *Bird* as follows:

> The issue in the case, as an economist would frame it, was the proper accommodation of two legitimate activities, growing tulips and raising peacocks. The defendant had a substantial investment in the tulip garden; he lived at a distance; and the wall had not proved effective against thieves. In an era of negligible police protection, a spring gun may have been the most cost-effective means of protection for the tulips. But since spring guns do not discriminate between the thief and the innocent trespasser, they deter owners of domestic animals from pursuing their animals onto other people's property and so increase the costs (enclosure costs or straying losses) of keeping animals. The court in the *Bird* case implied an ingenious accommodation: One who sets a spring gun must post notices that he has done so. Then owners of animals will not be reluctant to pursue their animals onto property not so posted. A notice will be of no avail at night, but animals are more likely to be secured then and in any event few owners would chase their straying animals after dark.

R. Posner, Economic Analysis of Law 207 (4th ed. 1992). For his more extensive analysis see Posner, Killing or Wounding to Protect a Property Interest, 14 J.L. & Econ. 201, 208-211 (1971).

What result in the case if the injured person is a child who cannot read English? Is it ever proper to use spring guns for property that is not surrounded by a fence or protective wall? Should a landowner be entitled to set spring guns to protect a warehouse as well as a dwelling house? For an affirmative answer see Scheurman v. Scharfenberg, 50 So. 335 (Ala. 1909).

KATKO v. BRINEY, 183 N.W.2d 657, 659, 663 (Iowa 1971). The defendants owned an old, boarded-up house, located several miles from their home, in which they stored various old bottles, fruit jars and the like, which they considered to be antiques. Several times during the previous several years the windows in the house had been broken and the entire place "messed up." The defendants first posted "no trespass" signs to keep off intruders, but the break-ins continued. Shortly before the injury to the plaintiff, the defendants placed a "shotgun trap" in one of the bedrooms. The gun was first positioned so as to hit an intruder in the stomach, but Mr. Briney, at his wife's insistence, lowered it to hit at the legs. He said that he set the gun "because I was mad and tired of being tormented," but insisted that "he did not intend to injure anyone."

The plaintiff was shot in the legs and permanently injured when he entered the defendant's bedroom shortly after the gun was set. He had been to the place several times before, and had intended upon this occasion to steal some of the defendant's possessions. The plaintiff pleaded guilty to a charge of larceny and paid a fine of $50. He also sued the defendant for personal injuries and was awarded $20,000 in actual damages and $10,000 in punitive damages.

At trial the jury was instructed as follows:

> Instruction 5 stated: "You are hereby instructed that one may use reasonable force in the protection of his property, but such right is subject to the qualification that one may not use such means of force as will take human life or inflict great bodily injury. Such is the rule even though the injured party is a trespasser and is in violation of the law himself."
>
> Instruction 6 stated: "An owner of premises is prohibited from willfully or intentionally injuring a trespasser by means of force that either takes life or inflicts great bodily injury and therefore a person owning a premise is prohibited from setting out 'spring guns' and like dangerous devices which will likely take life or inflict great bodily injury, for the purpose of harming trespassers. The fact that the trespasser may be acting in violation of the law does not change the rule. The only time when such conduct of setting a 'spring gun' or a like dangerous device is justified would be when the trespasser was committing a felony of violence or a felony punishable by death, or where the trespasser was endangering human life by his act."

The Iowa Supreme Court approved these instructions on appeal and affirmed the judgment for the plaintiff below. The court expressly noted that it did not pass on the question of punitive damages, since that issue was not raised by counsel at trial.

There was a dissent in the case by Larson, J., who argued:

> I would hold there is no absolute liability for injury to a criminal intruder by setting up such a device on his property, and, unless done with an intent to kill or seriously injure the intruder, I would absolve the owner from liability other than for negligence. I would also hold the court had no jurisdiction to allow punitive damages when the intruder was engaged in a serious criminal offense such as breaking and entering with intent to steal. . . .
>
> Although I am aware of the often-repeated statement that personal rights are more important than property rights, where the owner has stored his valuables representing his life's accumulations, his livelihood business, his tools and implements, and his treasured antiques as appears in the case at bar, and where the evidence is sufficient to sustain a finding that the installation was intended only as a warning to ward off thieves and criminals, I can see no compelling reason why the use of such a device alone would create liability as a matter of law. . . .
>
> In the case at bar the plaintiff was guilty of serious criminal conduct, which event gave rise to his claim against defendants. Even so, he may be eligible for an award of compensatory damages which so far as the law is concerned redresses him and places him in the position he was prior to sustaining the injury. The windfall he would receive in the form of punitive damages is bothersome to the principle of damages, because it is a response to the conduct of the defendants rather than any reaction to the loss suffered by plaintiff or any measurement of his worthiness for the award.
>
> When such a windfall comes to a criminal as a result of his indulgence in serious criminal conduct, the result is intolerable and indeed shocks the conscience. If we find the law upholds such a result, the criminal would be permitted by operation of law to profit from his own crime.
>
> Furthermore, if our civil courts are to sustain such a result, it would in principle interfere with the purposes and policies of the criminal law. This would certainly be ironic since punitive damages have been thought to assist and promote those purposes, at least so far as the conduct of the defendant is concerned.

NOTES

1. Aftermath of Katko v. Briney. The decision for the plaintiff in the case stirred up great protest in Iowa and throughout the nation. After the judgment was handed down by the state supreme court, checks and cash amounting to more than $10,000 were sent to the Brineys by hundreds of persons, including prison inmates. Some of their Iowa neighbors also took up the Brineys' cause in a very special way. When Katko moved to auction the Brineys' land in order to satisfy his judgment, the neighborhood "defense committee," organized to help the Brineys, "purchased" the land for $10,000 and agreed to lease it back to the Brineys for a rent that covered interest on the $10,000 and the real estate taxes. The land appreciated in value, however, and the neighbors evenutally forced the Brineys off the property, which they then sold to one of the original purchasers at a profit of $6,500. Briney and Katko then joined forces to sue the neighbors, claiming in effect that the land transaction with them was a mortgage and not a sale. As to the original incident, Briney remained unrepentant: "They used booby traps in Viet Nam, didn't they? Why can't we use them here to protect our property in this country?" Asked if he would do it again, Briney replied, "There's one thing I'd do different, though, I'd have aimed that gun a few feet higher." See a fuller account in the Chicago Tribune of April 25, 1975, at 1, col. 1.

2. *Restatement position on the use of force.* The Restatement (Second) of Torts in general takes a fairly permissive approach toward the use of force in defense of property.

> §85. USE OF MECHANICAL DEVICE THREATENING DEATH OR SERIOUS BODILY INJURY
> The actor is so far privileged to use a device intended or likely to cause serious bodily harm or death for the purpose of protecting his land or chattels from intrusion that he is not liable for the serious bodily harm or death thereby caused to an intruder whose intrusion is, in fact, such that the actor, were he present, would be privileged to prevent or terminate it by the intentional infliction of such harm.

In addition, section 143 provides for a two-tiered privilege for the use of force (or "impose confinement") to prevent the commission of a felony. Thus, for felonies generally any "peace officer or private person" may use force "which is not intended or likely to cause death or serious bodily harm," as long as lesser force cannot achieve the same end. But when the felony threatens either death or serious bodily harm, or involves breaking and entering a dwelling place, then the actor may use force or impose confinement "intended or likely to cause death or serious bodily harm," again if lesser means to prevent the crime are not available.

To what extent does *Katko* deviate from the Restatement's requirements? Note that People v. Caballos, 526 P.2d 241, (Cal. 1974), relying in part on the Model Penal Code, refused to carry over the logic of section 85 to the criminal context. "It seems clear that the use of such [mechanical] devices should not be encouraged. Moreover, whatever may be thought in torts, the [Restatement] rule setting forth an exception to liability for death or injuries inflicted by such devices 'is inappropriate in penal law for it is obvious that it does not prescribe a workable standard of conduct; liability depends upon fortuitous results.' " In a jurisdiction that has abolished capital punishment, is killing in defense of property ever privileged? In self-defense?

d. Recapture of chattels

Kirby v. Foster
22 A. 1111 (R.I. 1891)

STINESS, J. The plaintiff was in the employ of the Providence Warehouse Co., of which the defendant, Samuel J. Foster, was the agent, and his son, the other defendant, an employee. A sum of fifty dollars belonging to the corporation had been lost, for which the plaintiff, a bookkeeper, was held responsible, and the amount was deducted from his pay. On January 20, 1888, Mr. Foster handed the plaintiff some money to pay the help. The plaintiff, acting under the advice of counsel, took from this money the amount due him at the time, including what had been deducted from his pay, put it into his pocket, and returned the balance to Mr. Foster, saying he had received his pay and was going to leave, and that he did this under advice of counsel. The defendants then seized the plaintiff and attempted to take the money from him. A struggle ensued, in which the plaintiff claims to have received injury, for which this suit is brought. The jury having returned a verdict for the plaintiff, the defendants petition for a new trial on exceptions to the rulings and refusals to rule of the presiding justice. It is unnecessary to repeat the several exceptions, since they involve substantially but one question, viz.: whether the defendants were justified in the use of force upon the plaintiff to retake the money from him. As the defendants only pleaded the general issue, all requests relating to justification might properly have been refused on that ground. 1 Chitty on Pleading, 501; 2 Greenleaf on Evidence, §92. This case, however, having been tried upon the defence of justification, we will consider the exceptions as though that defence had been pleaded.

The defendants contend that the relation of master and servant subsisted between the plaintiff and Samuel J. Foster, the manager of the warehouse, whereby possession of money by the plaintiff was constructively possession by the manager, acting in behalf of the company and that the money having been delivered to the plaintiff for the specific purpose of paying the help, his conversion of it to his own use was a wrongful conversion amounting to embezzlement, which justified the defendants in using force in defence of the property under their charge. Unquestionably, if one takes another's property from his possession without right and against his will, the owner or person in charge may protect his possession, or retake the property, by the use of necessary force. He is not bound to stand by and submit to wrongful dispossession or larceny when he can stop it, and he is not guilty of assault in thus defending his right, by using force to prevent his property from being carried away. But this right of defence and recapture involves two things: first, possession by the owner, and, second, a purely wrongful taking or conversion, without a claim of right. If one has entrusted his property to another, who afterwards, honestly though erroneously, claims it as his own, the owner has no right to retake it by personal force. If he has, the actions of replevin and trover in many cases are of little use. The law does not permit parties to take the settlement of conflicting claims into their own hands. It gives the right of defence, but not of redress. The circumstances may be exasperating; the remedy at law may seem to be inadequate; but still the injured party cannot be arbiter of his own claim. Public order and the public peace are of greater consequence than a private right or an occasional hardship. Inadequacy of remedy is of frequent occurrence, but it cannot find its complement in personal violence. Upon these grounds the doctrine contended for by the defendants is limited to the defence of one's possession and the right of recapture as against a mere wrong-doer. It is therefore to be noted in this case that the money was in the actual possession of the plaintiff, to whom it had been entrusted for the purpose of paying help, who thereupon claimed the right to appropriate it to his own payment, supposing he might lawfully do so. Conceding that the advice was bad, nevertheless, upon such appropriation the plaintiff held the money adversely, as his own, and not as the servant or agent of the company. If his possession was the company's possession, then the company was not deprived of its property, and there could be neither occasion nor justification for violence. Possession by the company would be constructive merely, which would cease when the plaintiff exercised dominion and control on his own behalf under an honest claim of right. It is only in this way, in many cases, that conversion is established. Having thus appropriated the money to himself, it is urged that the act amounted to embezzlement, which justified the intervention of the defendants to prevent the consummation of the crime. We do not think this is so. The plaintiff stated what he had done, and the grounds upon which he claimed the right to do it, handing back the balance above what was due him. A controversy followed; he started to go out, but was stopped by the defendants, and then the assault took place. The sincerity of the plaintiff's belief that he had a right to retain the money is unquestionable. . . .

In the most favorable view of the case for the defendants, the plaintiff having obtained the money by no crime, misrepresentation, or violence, nor against the will of its owner, retained it wrongfully. In such cases the rule is clearly stated in Bliss v. Johnson, 73 N.Y. 529: "The general rule is, that a right of property merely, not joined with the possession, will not justify the owner in committing an assault and battery upon the person in possession, for the purpose of regaining possession, although the possession is wrongfully withheld." . . .

But, it is said, the plaintiff was about to carry away the money against the will of the owner. Undoubtedly this was so but this is true in every case of wrongful conversion of property. If it be not taken against the will of the owner, it cannot be retaken by force, but only by the usual civil remedy.

The defendants cite the following cases, which, it will be seen, are plainly distinguishable from the case at bar . . .

The defendants object to the charge of the court, that where a person has come into the peaceable possession of a chattel from another, the latter has no right to retake it by violence, whether the possession is lawful or unlawful, upon the ground that this rule would prevent the recapture of property obtained by trickery or fraud. The instruction must be considered not as an abstract proposition, but with reference to the case before the jury. Nothing appeared to show that the money has been procured by misrepresentation, trickery, or fraud. It was delivered to the plaintiff voluntarily, in the usual course of business. True, under the advice of a lawyer whom he had consulted, the plaintiff had previously determined to apply the money to his own payment when he should receive it; but this did not make the delivery itself fraudulent, nor did his intent to assert what he believed to be his right make that intent criminal. We think, therefore, with reference to the case as it stood, there was no error in the charge as given, nor in the refusals to charge as requested.

Exceptions overruled.

NOTES

1. Recapture of chattels. The general rules on recapture allow the privilege in situations in which the defendant wrongfully obtained possession of the chattel by either force, fraud, or without claim of right. See Restatement (Second) of Torts §101. The words here are broad, but they are not unlimited, for in addition to the voluntary transfer found in Kirby v. Foster, the rule denies the privilege of forcible recapture in a number of important commercial situations, most notably cases where the buyer or lessor of chattels has fallen behind in installment payments on property voluntarily delivered over to him. Many of these transactions are today governed by the Uniform Commercial Code, which permits a secured party to repossess collateral in the event of default without a judicial proceeding "if this can be done without breach of the peace." See U.C.C. §9-503. In addition, the privilege of recapture must be exercised promptly — the so-called hot pursuit requirement — or it will otherwise be lost. The restrictions with respect to the recapture of chattels thus follow in some important ways the restrictions on the use of force to protect real property. The constant tradeoff is between the virtues of self-help, which tend to deter the unlawful takings in the first instance, and the dangers of self-help, whose escalating violence may engulf bystanders. For a general discussion of these rules see 1 Harper, James and Gray, Torts §3.16.

2. *"Recapture of land."* Landlords have often been sued for assault and battery when they have used force against tenants who have refused to vacate the premises after the expiration of a lease. In many jurisdictions, the landlord's rights are determined by statutes modeled on The Forcible Entry Act, 1381, 5 Rich. 2, c. 7., which makes it an indictable offense to enter upon land except where an entry is given by law, and then "not with a strong hand but in a peaceable and easy fashion." After years of uncertainty, the Court of Appeal in England finally held that although the offender may be subject to an indictment, the aggrieved tenant, being in the wrong, has no private right of action. See Hemmings v. Stoke Poges Golf Club, Ltd., [1920] 1 K.B. 720, reviewing all the cases in England on this subject.

In the United States, the early common-law cases generally followed the English approach and allowed peaceable entry when the landlord was entitled to evict the tenant. Under this system, the tenant has a remedy only when in fact entitled to remain on the premises, or when the eviction was forceful. See, e.g., Poppen v. Wadleigh, 51 N.W.2d 75 (Minn. 1952). With the rise of modern summary eviction statutes, designed to expedite the landlord's ability to obtain legal assistance in securing an eviction, the judicial mood has changed. Thus in Berg v. Wiley, 264 N.W.2d 145 (Minn. 1978) the Minnesota court modified its earlier decisions, and held that the landlord had committed a tort when he changed the locks on the restaurant leased by the plaintiff while she was away. The court refused to find the defendant's conduct "peaceable" under the common-law rule, and concluded "the singular reason why actual violence did not erupt" when the locks were changed was the tenant's "absence and her subsequent self-restraint and resort to the judicial process." The *Berg* decision changes the older rule in the guise of applying it, for it rules out the possibility that entry can ever be peaceable if not consented to by the tenant. Why force the landlord to resort to the judicial process rather than allowing the tenant a remedy (perhaps for treble or punitive damages) if the landlord's repossession falls outside the traditional common-law justifications? See generally Comment, Landlord Eviction Remedies Act — Legislative Overreaction to Landlord Self-Help, 18 Wake Forest L. Rev. 25 (1982).

e. *Necessity*

Ploof v. Putnam
71 A. 188 (Vt. 1908)

MUNSON, J. It is alleged as the ground of recovery that on the 13th day of November, 1904, the defendant was the owner of a certain island in Lake Champlain, and of a certain dock attached thereto, which island and dock were then in charge of the defendant's servant; that the plaintiff was then possessed of and sailing upon said lake a certain loaded sloop, on which were the plaintiff and his wife and two minor children; that there then arose a sudden and violent tempest, whereby the sloop and the property and persons therein were placed in great danger of destruction; that to save these from destruction or injury the plaintiff was compelled to, and did, moor the sloop to defendant's dock; that the defendant by his servant unmoored the sloop, whereupon it was driven upon the shore by the tempest, without the plaintiff's fault; and that the sloop and its contents were thereby destroyed, and the plaintiff and his wife and children cast into the lake and upon the shore, receiving injuries.

This claim is set forth in two counts: one in trespass, charging that the defendant by his servant with force and arms wilfully and designedly unmoored the sloop; the other in case, alleging that it was the duty of the defendant by his servant to permit the plaintiff to moor his sloop to the dock, and to permit it to remain so moored during the continuance of the tempest, but that the defendant by his servant, in disregard of this duty, negligently, carelessly and wrongfully unmoored the sloop. Both counts are demurred to generally.

There are many cases in the books which hold that necessity, and an inability to control movements inaugurated in the proper exercise of a strict right, will justify entries upon land and interferences with personal property that would otherwise have been trespasses. A reference to a few of these will be sufficient to illustrate the doctrine.

In Miller v. Fandrye, Poph. 161, trespass was brought for chasing sheep, and the defendant pleaded that the sheep were trespassing upon his land, and that he with a little dog chased them out, and that as soon as the sheep were off his land he called in the dog. It was argued that, although the defendant might lawfully drive the sheep from his own ground with a dog, he had no right to pursue them into the next ground. But the court considered that the defendant might drive the sheep from his land with a dog, and that the nature of a dog is such that he cannot be withdrawn in an instant, and that as the defendant had done his best to recall the dog trespass would not lie.

In trespass of cattle taken in A, defendant pleaded that he was seized of C, and found the cattle there damage feasant, and chased them toward the pound, and that they escaped from him and went into A, and he presently retook them and this was held a good plea. 21 Edw. IV, 64 Vin. Ab. Trespass, H. a. 4 pl. 19. If one have a way over the land of another for his beasts to pass, and the beasts, being properly driven, feed the grass by morsels in passing, or run out of the way and are promptly pursued and brought back, trespass will not lie. See Vin. Ab. Trespass, K. a. pl. 1.

A traveller on a highway, who finds it obstructed from a sudden and temporary cause, may pass upon the adjoining land without becoming a trespasser, because of the necessity.

An entry upon land to save goods which are in danger of being lost or destroyed by water or fire is not a trespass. 21 Hen. VII, 27 Vin. Ab. Trespass, H. a. 4, pl. 24, K. a. pl. 3. In Proctor v. Adams, 113 Mass. 376, the defendant went upon the plaintiff's beach for the purpose of saving and restoring to the lawful owner a boat which had been driven ashore and was in danger of being carried off by the sea and it was held no trespass.

This doctrine of necessity applies with special force to the preservation of human life. One assaulted and in peril of his life may run through the close of another to escape from his assailant. 37 Hen. VII, pl. 26. One may sacrifice the personal property of another to save his life or the lives of his fellows. In Mouse's Case, 12 Co. 63, the defendant was sued for taking and carrying away the plaintiff's casket and its contents. It appeared that the ferryman of Gravesend took forty-seven passengers into his barge to pass to London, among whom were the plaintiff and defendant; and the barge being upon the water a great tempest happened, and a strong wind, so that the barge and all the passengers were in danger of being lost if certain ponderous things were not cast out, and the defendant thereupon cast out the plaintiff's casket. It was resolved that in case of necessity, to save the lives of the passengers, it was lawful for the defendant, being a passenger, to cast the plaintiff's casket out of the barge; that if the ferryman surcharge the barge the owner shall have his remedy upon the surcharge against the ferryman, but that if there be no surcharge, and the danger accrue only by the act of God, as by tempest, without fault of the ferryman, every one ought to bear this loss, to safeguard the life of a man.

It is clear that an entry upon the land of another may be justified by necessity, and that the declaration before us discloses a necessity for mooring the sloop. But the defendant questions the sufficiency of the counts because they do not negative the existence of natural objects to which the plaintiff could have moored with equal safety. The allegations are, in substance, that the stress of a sudden and violent tempest compelled the plaintiff to moor to defendant's dock to save his sloop and the people in it. The averment of necessity is complete, for it covers not only the necessity of mooring, but the necessity of mooring to the dock; and the details of the situation which created this necessity, whatever the legal requirements regarding them, are matters of proof and need not be alleged. It is certain that the rule suggested cannot be held applicable irrespective of circumstance, and the question must be left for adjudication upon proceedings had with reference to the evidence or the charge. . . .

Judgment affirmed and cause remanded.

NOTES

1. Necessity and self-help. While they were still at sea, were the plaintiffs entitled to use force to land on the dock if the defendant's servant had resisted them? To keep their boat moored to the dock? Note that under the general common-law rules, the defendant's servants, while they may not resist plaintiff's entry to dock in conditions of necessity, are not obliged to lend a helping hand. See Chapter 7. Why the difference?

2. General average contribution. Mouse's Case, 66 Eng. Rep. 1341 (K.B. 1609), discussed in cryptic form in *Ploof,* held "that in a case of necessity, for the saving of the lives of the passengers, it was lawful to the defendant, being a passenger, to cast the casket of the plaintiff out of the barge, with other things in it." The general problem discussed in *Mouse's Case* has been the subject of extensive treatment in the law of admiralty under the rubric of general average contribution. Suppose a vessel is carrying cargo owned by a number of different parties when its master is confronted with a sudden emergency that jeopardizes the safety of the ship and its cargo. Under the law of general average contribution, the master can choose to jettison some of the cargo in order to save the ship and the cargo that remains. In order to insure that some persons are not relatively disadvantaged by the loss of their cargo, they receive pro rata compensation from other interested parties, including the owner of the hull, such that the economic loss is borne equally by all interested parties. In effect, at the time of emergency all are treated as joint owners of all the property in question. Note that this rule creates the desirable incentive upon the master to minimize the aggregate loss to all concerned, for having been placed, as it were, behind a veil of ignorance, he can do best by himself only if he does best by all owners of hull and cargo alike. On the complexities of the law of general average contribution see G. Gilmore and C. Black, The Law of Admiralty §§5.1, 5.2 (2d ed. 1975). See also Landes and Posner, Salvors, Finders, Good Samaritans, and Other Rescuers: An Economic Study of Law and Altruism, 7 J. Legal Stud. 83 (1978).

Vincent v. Lake Erie Transportation Co.
124 N.W. 221 (Minn. 1910)

O'BRIEN, J. The steamship Reynolds, owned by the defendant, was for the purpose of discharging her cargo on November 27, 1905, moored to plaintiff's dock in Duluth. While the unloading of the boat was taking place a storm from the northeast developed, which at about ten o'clock P.M., when the unloading was completed, had so grown in violence that the wind was then moving at fifty miles per hour and continued to increase during the night. There is some evidence that one, and perhaps two, boats were able to enter the harbor that night, but it is plain that navigation was practically suspended from the hour mentioned until the morning of the twenty-ninth, when the storm abated, and during that time no master would have been justified in attempting to navigate his vessel, if he could avoid doing so. After the discharge of the cargo the Reynolds signaled for a tug to tow her from the dock, but none could be obtained because of the severity of the storm. If the lines holding the ship to the dock had been cast off, she would doubtless have drifted away; but, instead, the lines were kept fast, and as soon as one parted or chafed it was replaced, sometimes with a larger one. The vessel lay upon the outside of the dock, her bow to the east, the wind and waves striking her starboard quarter with such force that she was constantly being lifted and thrown against the dock, resulting in its damage, as found by the jury, to the amount of $500.

We are satisfied that the character of this storm was such that it would have been highly imprudent for the master of the Reynolds to have attempted to leave the dock or to have permitted his vessel to drift away from it. One witness testified upon the trial that the vessel could have been warped into a slip, and that, if the attempt to bring the ship into the slip had failed, the worst that could have happened would be that the vessel would have been blown ashore upon a soft and muddy bank. The witness was not present in Duluth at the time of the storm, and, while he may have been right in his conclusions, those in charge of the dock and the vessel at the time of the storm were not required to use the highest human intelligence, nor were they required to resort to every possible experiment which could be suggested for the preservation of their property. Nothing more was demanded of them than ordinary prudence and care, and the record in this case fully sustains the contention of the appellant that, in holding the vessel fast to the dock, those in charge of her exercised good judgment and prudent seamanship.

It is claimed by the respondent that it was negligence to moor the boat at an exposed part of the wharf, and to continue in that position after it became apparent that the storm was to be more than usually severe. We do not agree with this position. The part of the wharf where the vessel was moored appears to have been commonly used for that purpose. It was situated within the harbor at Duluth, and must, we think, be considered a proper and safe place, and would undoubtedly have been such during what would be considered a very severe storm. The storm which made it unsafe was one which surpassed in violence any which might have reasonably been anticipated.

The appellant contends by ample assignments of error that, because its conduct during the storm was rendered necessary by prudence and good seamanship under conditions over which it had no control, it cannot be held liable for any injury resulting to the property of others, and claims that the jury should have been so instructed. An analysis of the charge given by the trial court is not necessary, as in our opinion the only question for the jury was the amount of damages which the plaintiffs were entitled to recover, and no complaint is made upon that score.

The situation was one in which the ordinary rules regulating property rights were suspended by forces beyond human control, and if, without the direct intervention of some act by the one sought to be held liable, the property of another was injured, such injury must be attributed to the act of God, and not to the wrongful act of the person sought to be charged. If during the storm the Reynolds had entered the harbor, and while there had become disabled and been thrown against the plaintiffs' dock, the plaintiffs could not have recovered. Again, if while attempting to hold fast to the dock the lines had parted, without any negligence, and the vessel carried against some other boat or dock in the harbor, there would be no liability upon her owner. But here those in charge of the vessel deliberately and by their direct efforts held her in such a position that the damage to the dock resulted, and, having thus preserved the ship at the expense of the dock, it seems to us that her owners are responsible to the dock owners to the extent of the injury inflicted.

In Depue v. Flatau, 111 N.W. 1, this court held that where the plaintiff, while lawfully in the defendants' house, became so ill that he was incapable of traveling with safety, the defendants were responsible to him in damages for compelling him to leave the premises. If, however, the owner of the premises had furnished the traveler with proper accommodations and medical attendance, would he have been able to defeat an action brought against him for their reasonable worth?

In Ploof v. Putnam (Vt.) 71 Atl. 188, the supreme court of Vermont held that where, under stress of weather, a vessel was without permission moored to a private dock at an island in Lake Champlain owned by the defendant, the plaintiff was not guilty of trespass, and that the defendant was responsible in damages because his representative upon the island unmoored the vessel, permitting it to drift upon the shore, with resultant injuries to it. If, in that case, the vessel had been permitted to remain, and the dock had suffered an injury, we believe the shipowner would have been held liable for the injury done.

Theologians hold that a starving man may, without moral guilt, take what is necessary to sustain life but it could hardly be said that the obligation would not be upon such person to pay the value of the property so taken when he became able to do so. And so public necessity, in times of war or peace, may require the taking of private property for public purposes; but under our system of jurisprudence compensation must be made.

Let us imagine in this case that for the better mooring of the vessel those in charge of her had appropriated a valuable cable lying upon the dock. No matter how justifiable such appropriation might have been, it would not be claimed that, because of the overwhelming necessity of the situation, the owner of the cable could not recover its value.

This is not a case where life or property was menaced by any object or thing belonging to the plaintiffs, the destruction of which became necessary to prevent the threatened disaster. Nor is it a case where, because of the act of God, or unavoidable accident, the infliction of the injury was beyond the control of the defendant, but is one where the defendant prudently and advisedly availed itself of the plaintiffs' property for the purpose of preserving its own more valuable property, and the plaintiffs are entitled to compensation for the injury done.

Order affirmed.

LEWIS, J. I dissent. It was assumed on the trial before the lower court that appellant's liability depended on whether the master of the ship might, in the exercise of reasonable care, have sought a place of safety before the storm made it impossible to leave the dock. The majority opinion assumes that the evidence is conclusive that appellant moored its boat at respondents' dock pursuant to contract, and that the vessel was lawfully in position at the time the additional cables were fastened to the dock, and the reasoning of the opinion is that, because appellant made use of the stronger cables to hold the boat in position, it became liable under the rule that it had voluntarily made use of the property of another for the purpose of saving its own.

In my judgment, if the boat was lawfully in position at the time the storm broke, and the master could not, in the exercise of due care, have left that position without subjecting his vessel to the hazards of the storm, then the damage to the dock, caused by the pounding of the boat, was the result of an inevitable accident. If the master was in the exercise of due care, he was not at fault. The reasoning of the opinion admits that if the ropes, or cables, first attached to the dock had not parted, or if, in the first instance, the master had used the stronger cables, there would be no liability. If the master could not, in the exercise of reasonable care, have anticipated the severity of the storm and sought a place of safety before it became impossible, why should he be required to anticipate the severity of the storm, and, in the first instance, use the stronger cables?

I am of the opinion that one who constructs a dock to the navigable line of waters, and enters into contractual relations with the owner of a vessel to moor the same, takes the risk of damage to his dock by a boat caught there by a storm, which event could not have been avoided in the exercise of due care, and further, that the legal status of the parties in such a case is not changed by renewal of cables to keep the boat from being cast adrift at the mercy of the tempest.

JAGGARD, J.: I concur with LEWIS, J.

NOTES

1. *Private necessity, assumption of risk, and unjust enrichment.* Under traditional law, *Vincent* is said to represent a case of "conditional" or "incomplete" privilege. The defendant is entitled to use, or damage, the plaintiff's dock in ways that he could not do in the absence of necessity, but, unlike the case of self-defense, he must pay for the privilege, by paying reasonable rental value or making compensation for lost or damaged property, as the case may be. See Restatement (Second) of Torts §197. The usual case of incomplete privilege arises between two strangers, but also covers cases where the defendant remains on plaintiff's property to avoid the necessity. Does the majority opinion ever come to grips with the dissent's contention that the case turns on how the mooring contract allocated the risk of damages? How does one decide which risks the shipowner assumed when the contract does not expressly cover the problem? See generally Bohlen, Incomplete Privilege to Inflict Intentional Invasions of Interests of Property and Personalty, 39 Harv. L. Rev. 307 (1926), reprinted in his Studies in the Law of Torts 614 (1926). See also Epstein, A Theory of Strict Liability, 2 J. Legal Stud. 151, 157-160 (1973); Weinrib, Causation and Wrongdoing, 63 Chi.-Kent L. Rev. 407, 425-429 (1987).

Another justification for the result in *Vincent* appeals to a theory of "unjust enrichment," which in effect requires the boat owner to compensate the dock owner for the benefit that he received from the use of the dock. How does that theory work if the shipowner's benefit is $10,000, and the harm to the dock $500? When the figures are reversed? Where the ship is lost and the dock damaged? See generally, on the theory of unjust enrichment, Keeton, Conditional Fault in the Law of Torts, 72 Harv. L. Rev. 401, 410 et seq. (1959).

2. *Necessity and bilateral monopoly.* The private necessity issue also has an important contractual dimension. Suppose, for example, that a vessel in distress at sea seeks to put in at a dock whose normal mooring fee is $100. In a world without any restrictions on contract, the dock owner is not limited to that normal fee but may "hold out" for a larger fee, perhaps one approaching the value of the boat and cargo. If the boat owner complies with the demand, should he be held to the contractual price when the dock owner practiced neither fraud nor duress? The standard response, both in admiralty and common law, is to set aside

the contract, and to restrict the dock owner's recovery to a reasonable fee. The point has been made most forcefully in connection with contracts for salvage, or rescue at sea by professional salvors:

> Courts of admiralty will enforce contracts made for salvage service and salvage compensation, where the salvor has not taken advantage of his power to make an unreasonable bargain; but they will not tolerate the doctrine that a salvor can take advantage of his situation, and avail himself of the calamities of others to drive a bargain; nor will they permit the performance of a public duty to be turned into a traffic of profit. The general interests of commerce will be much better promoted by requiring the salvor to trust for compensation to the liberal recompense usually awarded by the courts for such services.

Post v. Jones, 60 U.S. 150, 160 (1856). In practice, the "liberal" compensation practices of courts take into account the riskiness of cure and the value of the cargo and hull saved from the perils of the sea. Salvage contracts all proceed on a "no rescue, no pay" basis in order to give the salvor the strongest incentive to save the ship. The risk premium awarded is intended to compensate the salvor for those rescue attempts that have failed, much as the generous returns on wells that strike oil compensate for dry holes. In practice the holdout problem at sea is often averted by the common practice of referring salvage awards to arbitration, often through Lloyd's of London, where they are resolved in accordance with standard industry practice. The traditional salvage contract has been limited to the rescue of hull and cargo. Today, liability for pollution has become a major economic risk, so that salvage arrangements now provide for "liability salvage" arrangements to provide that the salvor receives some award for preventing spillage, notwithstanding the obvious measurement problems involved. See Brough, Liability Salvage — By Private Ordering, 19 J. Legal Stud. 95 (1990).

3. *Public necessity.* What is the scope of the privilege, for either private or government agents, to destroy private property in order to protect the interests of the community at large? The problem has arisen chiefly in two contexts: first, where the property is destroyed in order to prevent the destruction of a city by fire, and second, where it is destroyed in order to keep it from falling into enemy hands in time of war. Although authority on the question is scant, the general view is that, unlike that of private necessity, the privilege is complete in that no action will lie against either the private or governmental parties whose conduct is justified by a public necessity. In the words of Bohlen, "since the benefit is solely social, there is no reason why one who acts as a champion of the public should be required to pay for the privilege of so doing." Bohlen, Incomplete Privilege, 39 Harv. L. Rev. at 317-318, Studies in the Law of Torts at 627. Is there any reason why the person whose

property is so converted to the public use should, as against the defendant, be required against his will to become the champion of the public?

In order to keep the defense of public necessity in its proper perspective, it is helpful to distinguish between two situations. In the first, the property destroyed would have been destroyed even if there had been no intervention. The existing fire would have consumed the homes demolished in order to prevent its spread; the industrial installations blown up would have been destroyed in any event by the enemy. In this case the plaintiff loses not because the privilege is complete, but because virtually all the loss is caused by a third party.

The second situation raises squarely the issue of privilege, for the property would *not* have been destroyed without the defendant's intervention. The fire died out before it reached the demolished homes; the enemy was unable to capture the installations. The justification for the complete privilege in this context was offered by Pennsylvania Supreme Court in Respublica v. Sparhawk, 1 U.S. 357, 362 (Pa. 1788): "We find, indeed, a memorable instance of folly recorded in the 3 Vol. of Clarendon's History, where it is mentioned, that the Lord Mayor of London, in 1666, when that city was on fire, would not give directions for, or consent to, the pulling down forty wooden houses, or to the removing the furniture, &c. belonging to the Lawyers of the Temple, then on the Circuit, for fear he should be answerable for a trespass; and in consequence of this conduct half that great city was burnt."

Sparhawk reveals the problem of asymmetrical incentives in cases of public necessity, to which the complete privilege responds. The public official who wrongly orders the destruction of property bears all loss if his prediction proves false, but captures none of the gain if his prediction proves correct. Why then should he act at all? As it seems quite impossible to allow the official to recoup the value of the property spared in a personal action against its owners, the only way to balance the incentives under which he labors is to insulate him from liability, at least in those cases in which he acts reasonably and in good faith. But this approach, taken alone, affords no compensation to the individual owners made to suffer enormous private losses for the benefit of the community at large. Is it best to handle this aspect of the situation by allowing the aggrieved landowner an action for restitution against the benefited landowners? Or should the government, but not the official, be required to make good the loss? If so, should it pay out of general revenues, or from special assessments levied against the parties benefited? On the general merits of personal and official immunity, see the symposium, Civil Liability for Government Officials, 42 Law & Contemp. Probs. 12 (1978), and infra at Chapter 11.

The privilege of public necessity is often relatively straightforward. The state may kill diseased or infected elk, without compensation,

South Dakota Department of Health v. Heim, 357 N.W.2d 522 (S.D. 1984). But other cases are more complex: should the public necessity defense be complete for the California Department of Agriculture's Medfly extermination program whose "wide scale aerial spraying caused erosion of the painted surface of automobiles," thereby requiring the plaintiff insurance companies to pay out numerous claims? See Farmers Insurance Exchange v. State, 221 Cal. Rptr. 225 (Cal. App. 1985).

4. Public necessity and just compensation. The complete privilege in cases of public necessity is in constant tension with the basic constitutional principle that the government may take private property, even for public use, only upon payment of just compensation. For a vivid example of how close the line between the two doctrines can be during wartime, see United States v. Caltex, Inc., 344 U.S. 149 (1952), where the Court refused to order compensation for the demolition of an oil company's terminal facilities in Manila before the Japanese takeover, Black and Douglas, JJ., dissenting. Likewise, in National Board of Y.M.C.A.s v. United States, 395 U.S. 85 (1969), the Court also found no compensable taking when United States army troops occupied the plaintiff's buildings located in the Panama Canal Zone after they had been placed under siege by rioting Panamanians, who had already caused substantial damage to the structures. See Broeder, Torts and Just Compensation: Some Personal Reflections, 17 Hastings L.J. 217 (1965).

The issue of public necessity is also obliquely raised in Scheuer v. Rhodes, 416 U.S. 232, 246-248 (1974), which arose out of the dramatic events at Kent State, when many protesting students were either killed or injured by the National Guardsmen sent to the campus by the then governor of Ohio, James Rhodes. The opinion of Chief Justice Burger's opinion addressed the question of whether the plaintiff could have a jury trial on the issue of Rhodes' liability, and was mainly concerned with the various immunities available to state officials acting in the course of their duties, but some of his remarks bear on the question of public necessity:

> When a condition of civil disorder in fact exists, there is obvious need for prompt action, and decisions must be made in reliance on factual information supplied by others. While both federal and state laws plainly contemplate the use of force when the necessity arises, the decision to invoke military power has traditionally been viewed with suspicion and skepticism since it often involves the temporary suspension of some of our most cherished rights — government by elected civilian leaders, freedom of expression, of assembly, and of association. Decisions in such situations are more likely than not to arise in an atmosphere of confusion, ambiguity, and swiftly moving events and when, by the very existence of some degree of civil disorder, there is often no consensus as to the appropriate remedy. In short, since the options which a chief executive and his principal subordinates must consider are far broader and far

more subtle than those made by officials with less responsibility, the range of discretion must be comparably broad. . . .

These considerations suggest that, in varying scope, a qualified immunity is available to officers of the executive branch of government, the variation being dependent upon the scope of discretion and responsibilities of the office and all the circumstances as they reasonably appeared at the time of the action on which liability is sought to be based. It is the existence of reasonable grounds for the belief formed at the time and in light of all the circumstances, coupled with good-faith belief, that affords a basis for qualified immunity of executive officers for acts performed in the course of official conduct. Mr. Justice Holmes spoke of this, stating:

> No doubt there are cases where the expert on the spot may be called upon to justify his conduct later in court, notwithstanding the fact that he had sole command at the time and acted to the best of his knowledge. That is the position of the captain of a ship. But even in that case great weight is given to his determination and the matter is to be judged on the facts as they appeared then and not merely in the light of the event.

Moyer v. Peabody, 212 U.S. 78, 85 (1909).

At trial the jury verdict was for all defendants, including Rhodes. The case was later reversed on grounds of jury tampering, see Krause v. Rhodes, 570 F.2d 563 (6th Cir. 1977), and was settled thereafter.

Judith Jarvis Thomson, The Trolley Problem
94 Yale L.J. 1395 (1985)

I

Some years ago, Philippa Foot drew attention to an extraordinarily interesting problem. Suppose you are the driver of a trolley. The trolley rounds a bend, and there come into view ahead five track workmen, who have been repairing the track. The track goes through a bit of a valley at that point, and the sides are steep, so you must stop the trolley if you are to avoid running the five men down. You step on the brakes, but alas they don't work. Now you suddenly see a spur of track leading off to the right. You can turn the trolley onto it, and thus save the five men on the straight trace ahead. Unfortunately, Mrs. Foot has arranged that there is one track workman on that spur of track. He can no more get off the track in time than the five can, so you will kill him if you turn the trolley onto him. Is it morally permissible for you to turn the trolley?

Everybody to whom I have put this hypothetical case says, Yes, it is. Some people say something stronger than that it is morally *permissible* for you to turn the trolley: They say that morally speaking, you *must* turn it — that morality requires you to do so. Others do not agree that morality requires you to turn the trolley, and even feel a certain discomfort at the idea of turning it. But everybody says that it is true, at a minimum, that you *may* turn it — that it would not be morally wrong in you to do so.

Now consider a second hypothetical case. This time you are to imagine yourself to be a surgeon, a truly great surgeon. Among other things you do, you transplant organs, and you are such a great surgeon that the organs you transplant always take. At the moment you have five patients who need organs. Two need one lung each, two need a kidney each, and the fifth needs a heart. If they do not get those organs today, they will all die; if you find organs for them today you can transplant the organs and they will all live. But where to find the lungs, the kidneys, and the heart? The time is almost up when a report is brought to you that a young man who has just come into your clinic for his yearly check-up has exactly the right blood-type, and is in excellent health. Lo, you have your possible donor. All you need do is cut him up and distribute *his* parts among the five who need them. You ask, but he says, "Sorry. I deeply sympathize, but no." Would it be morally permissible for you to operate anyway? Everybody to whom I have put this second hypothetical says, No, it would not be morally permissible for you to proceed.

Here then is Mrs. Foot's problem: *Why* is it that the trolley driver may turn his trolley, though the surgeon may not remove the young man's lungs, kidneys, and heart? In both cases, one will die if the agent acts, but five will live who would otherwise die — net saving of four lives. What difference in the other facts of these cases explains the moral difference between them? I fancy that the theorists of tort and criminal law will find this problem as interesting as the moral theorist does.

NOTE

Moral and legal theories. What responses might a legal theorist make to Professor Thomson's challenge? Wholly apart from the question of whether you as trolley driver should turn the wheel, is there any question of liability for death? If you do not decide to turn the wheel are you subject to punitive damages? What result if the trolley driver can save himself by turning the wheel but will perish if he continues straight on?

Having restated Foot's problem, Professor Thomson then explores some possible answers to it. One possible solution is that morally it is worse to kill than to let die, so that the surgeon should not act while the trolley driver can turn the wheel because his only choice is between killing one and killing five. But what result should then happen if, as Professor Thomson next suggests, a bystander is able to throw a switch that will divert the trolley from its original track, but can choose to do nothing, in which case the trolley will kill five? Is the bystander not justified in doing what the trolley driver may do?

Another possible way to look at the problem is to ask about the long-term effects of adopting one rule or the other. So long as the trolley driver is held responsible whether he kills one or five, he faces two separate incentives: the first, which is the subject of the Thomson inquiry, is to minimize the number of deaths *once* the emergency occurs. The second is to check the brakes to see that the emergency does not arise in the first place — an incentive that remains in place so long as the liability rule remains fixed. But the effects in the prior period on the famous surgeon are quite different, for she will never be able to attract patients in the first place if she is intent on cutting them up for the benefit of others. Yet given the long time frame, it could well be possible to organize a voluntary market for the sale of organs either during life or after death, which has none of the downside of coerced transfers. Yet while organ donations are legal today, their sale is flatly prohibited by federal law. For a critique, see generally Cohen, Increasing the Supply of Transplant Organs: The Virtues of a Future Market, 58 Geo. Wash. L. Rev. 1 (1989).

C.   EMOTIONAL AND DIGNITARY HARMS

1.   Assault

I. de S. and Wife v. W. de S.
At the Assizes, coram Thorpe, C.J., 1348 [or 1349] Year Book,
Liber Assisarum, folio 99, placitum 60

I. de S. & M. uxor ejus querunt de W. de S. de eo quod idem W. anno, & c., vi et armis, & c., apud S., in ipsam M. insultum fecit, et ipsam verberavit, & c. [I. de S. and his wife, M., sue W. de S. concerning that which in the year, etc., by force and arms, etc., at S. has made insults of the aforesaid M., and has beat her.] And W. pleaded not guilty. And it was found by verdict of the inquest that the said W. came in the night to the house of the said I., and would have bought some wine, but the door of the tavern was closed; and he struck on the door with a hatchet, which he had in his hand, and the woman plaintiff put her head out at a window and ordered him to stop; and he perceived her and struck with the hatchet, but did not touch the woman. Whereupon the inquest said that it seemed to them that there was no trespass, since there was no harm done.

THORPE, C.J. There is harm, and a trespass for which they shall recover damages, since he made an assault upon the woman, as it is found, although he did no other harm. Wherefore tax his damages, & c. And they taxed the damages at half a mark.

Thorpe, C.J., awarded that they should recover their damages, & c., and that the other should be taken. Et sic nota, [And thus it was noted] that for an assault one shall recover damages, & c.

Tuberville v. Savage
86 Eng. Rep. 684 (K.B. 1669)

Action of *assault, battery,* and *wounding.* The evidence to prove a provocation was, that the plaintiff put his hand upon his sword and said, "If *it were not assize-time, I would not take such language from you.*" — The question was, If that were an assault? — The Court agreed that it was not; for the declaration of the plaintiff was, that he would not assault him, the Judges being in town; and *the intention* as well as *the act* makes an assault. Therefore if one strike another upon the hand, or arm, or breast in discourse, it is no assault, there being no *intention* to assault; but if one intending to assault, strike *at* another and miss him, this is an assault: so if he hold up his hand against another in a threatening manner and say nothing, it is an assault. — In the principal case the plaintiff had judgment.

W. Blackstone, Commentaries
Vol. 3, p. 120 (1790)

[A]ssault [is] an attempt to offer to beat another, without touching him: as if one lifts up his cane, or his fist, in a threatening manner at another; or strikes at him, but misses him; this is an assault, insultus, which Finch describes to be "an unlawful setting upon one's person." This also is an inchoate violence, amounting considerably higher than bare threats; and therefore, though no actual suffering is proved, yet the party injured may have redress by action of trespass vi et armis; wherein he shall recover damages as compensation for the injury.

NOTES

1. The social interest against assaults. Does *I. de S.* give uniform protection against mental distress from the threat of assault? Should the defendant be held for committing an assault when he first struck the door with the hatchet if he knew that the plaintiff was inside? If he thought there was a good chance she was inside? Should it matter that the defendant struck the second blow — where?, why?, how? — only after he "perceived" the plaintiff?

The dangers to the social fabric from demonstrations of force have been forcefully stated in Allen v. Hannaford, 244 P. 700 (Wash. 1926). There the plaintiff had hired moving men to take her furniture from an apartment she had rented from the defendant. The defendant had claimed a lien on the plaintiff's furniture (that is, a right to seize the furniture, sell it, and apply the proceeds to unpaid back rent). When the defendant discovered that the furniture was being removed, she appeared with a pistol and threatened to shoot the moving men "full of holes" if they took a single piece of the plaintiff's furniture. Then "standing only a few feet from [plaintiff], she pointed the pistol at her face and threatened to shoot her." The defendant denied pointing the gun at the plaintiff, but evidence in the record allowed the jury to find that she did. The defendant argued that she could not in any event be guilty of an assault because the gun she held was unloaded. The court affirmed a $750 verdict to the plaintiff, saying,

> So far as the [plaintiff] was concerned, the [defendant] had the apparent ability to make her threat good. In Beach v. Hancock, 27 N.H. 223 (1853), it was said:
>
>> One of the most important objects to be attained by the enactment of laws and the institutions of civilized society is, each of us shall feel secure against unlawful assaults. Without such security society loses most of its value. Peace and order and domestic happiness, inexpressibly more precious than mere forms of government, cannot be enjoyed without the sense of perfect security. We have a right to live in society without being put in fear of personal harm. But it must be a reasonable fear of which we complain. And it surely is not unreasonable for a person to entertain a fear of personal injury, when a pistol is pointed at him in a threatening manner, when, for aught he knows, it may be loaded, and may occasion his immediate death. The business of the world could not be carried on with comfort, if such things could be done with impunity.
>
> Whether there is an assault in a given case depends more upon the apprehensions created in the mind of the person assaulted than upon what may be the secret intentions of the person committing the assault. . . .
>
> If the appellant pointed the pistol at the [plaintiff] and threatened to shoot this would constitute an assault, even though the [plaintiff] may not have known whether it was loaded.

If the gun was not pointed toward the plaintiff, did the defendant only make, to use Blackstone's distinction, a "mere threat" or did she commit an act of "inchoate violence"? Is there an assault if the plaintiff knows that the gun is not loaded when a defendant points it at her? See infra at notes to Kirby v. Foster.

2. *Mere words and conditional threats and the use of force.* One time-honored maxim is that "mere words do not amount to an assault." The

maxim applies to strong words that are used in the course of an argument. It has been criticized as not taking into account the subtle (and not-so-subtle) ways in which the voice alone can convey threats of the immediate or future use of force. Undoubtedly such a formula is meant to preclude liability in the great variety of instances where intemperate or insulting speech injures feelings or arouses apprehension. In Tuberville v. Savage, the defendant claimed that the plaintiff's words constituted the assault that justified the defendant's wounding the plaintiff. In rejecting the claim, why should the court assume that the plaintiff's words gave an accurate reading of his intention, instead of being an attempt to catch the defendant off guard? What result if it had not been "assize-time" (that is, if the judge were not in town), and the plaintiff had said, "If it were not for my generous nature, I would not take such language from you"? Is there an assault if the defendant says: "I've half a mind to knock your block off"? If he says, "If you do not pay me money, I will have your life"?

The limits of the common-law action for assault are also clearly revealed when the defendant makes a threat at a distance. In Brooker v. Silverthorne, 199 S.E. 350 (S.C. 1918), the jury had awarded the plaintiff, the night operator of a telephone exchange, $2,000 for mental anguish and nervous shock alleged to have been caused when the defendant abused her when she was unable to get his connection. The defendant first said, "You God damned woman. None of you attend your business." After her protests, he continued, "You are a God damned liar. If I were there, I would break your God damned neck." The plaintiff feared that the defendant would come to the exchange and either insult or hurt her. The court agreed that the defendant's conduct "merits severest condemnation," but refused to uphold the jury's award because "the words used did not amount to a threat. Defendant said: 'If I were there I would break your . . . . neck.' But he was not there and plaintiff knew it; and there is nothing in what he said expressive of an intention to go there and injure plaintiff. . . . As Judge Cooley says, 'a threat only promises a future injury.' Here there was no expression of an intention to injure in the future, and therefore no threat."

3. The Restatement definition.

§21. ASSAULT
(1) An actor is subject to liability to another for assault if
    (a) he acts intending to cause a harmful or offensive contact with the person of the other or a third person, or an imminent apprehension of such a contact, and
    (b) the other is thereby put in such imminent apprehension.

The Restatement then refines its use of the term "apprehension" in §24, comment *b:*

b. Distinction between apprehension and fright. It is not necessary that the other believe that the act done by the actor will be effective in inflicting the intended contact upon him. It is enough that he believes that the act is capable of immediately inflicting the contact upon him unless something further occurs. Therefore, the mere fact that he can easily prevent the threatened contact by self-defensive measures which he feels amply capable of taking does not prevent the actor's attempt to inflict the contact upon him from being an actionable assault. So too, he may have every reason to believe that bystanders will interfere in time to prevent the blow threatened by the actor from taking effect and his belief may be justified by the event. Bystanders may intervene and prevent the actor from striking him. None the less, the actor's blow thus prevented from taking effect is an actionable assault. The apprehension which is sufficient to make the actor liable may have no relation to fear, which at least implies a doubt as to whether the actor's attempt is capable of certain frustration.

In ordinary English, apprehension and fear are regarded as synonyms and not as distinct terms. The Restatement, therefore, deviates from common usage in order to make a point that the plaintiff has suffered a compensable injury from a threat of attack that is easily warded off.

2.   Offensive Battery

Alcorn v. Mitchell
63 Ill. 553 (1872)

SHELDON, J. The ground mainly relied on for the reversal of the judgment in this case is, that the damages are excessive, being $1000.

The case presented is this: There was a trial of an action of trespass between the parties, wherein the appellee was defendant, in the circuit court of Jasper county. At the close of the trial the court adjourned, and, immediately upon the adjournment, in the court room, in the presence of a large number of persons, the appellant deliberately spat in the face of the appellee.

So long as damages are allowable in any civil case, by way of punishment or for the sake of example, the present, of all cases, would seem to be a most fit one for the award of such damages.

The act in question was one of the greatest indignity, highly provocative of retaliation by force, and the law, as far as it may, should afford substantial protection against such outrages, in the way of liberal damages, that the public tranquillity may be preserved by saving the necessity of resort to personal violence as the only means of redress.

Suitors, in the assertion of their rights, should be allowed approach to the temple of justice without incurring there exposure to such disgraceful indignities, in the very presence of its ministers.

It is customary to instruct juries that they may give vindictive damages where there are circumstances of malice, wilfulness, wantonness, outrage and indignity attending the wrong complained of. The act in question was wholly made up of such qualities. It was one of pure malignity, done for the mere purpose of insult and indignity.

An exasperated suitor has indulged the gratification of his malignant feelings in this despicable mode. The act was the very refinement of malice. The defendant appears to be a man of wealth; we can not say that he has been made to pay too dearly for the indulgence. . . .

The judgment must be affirmed.

NOTE

Basis of liability for offensive battery. What result in Alcorn v. Mitchell if the appellee spat at the appellant but missed? Does it make a difference whether the appellant knew that the appellee spat at him? That others in the courtroom knew?

The Restatement (Second) of Torts §18 defines an offensive battery as follows:

§18. BATTERY: OFFENSIVE CONTACT
  (1) An actor is subject to liability to another for battery if
    (a) he acts intending to cause a harmful or offensive contact with the person of the other or a third person, or an imminent apprehension of such a contact, and
    (b) an offensive contact with the person of the other directly or indirectly results.
(2) An act which is not done with the intention stated in Subsection (1)(a) does not make the actor liable to the other for a mere offensive contact with the other's person although the act involves an unreasonable risk of inflicting it and, therefore, would be negligent or reckless if the risk threatened bodily harm.

There are many reported cases of nonharmful offensive batteries. In Respublica v. De Longchamps, 1 Dall. 111 (Pa. 1784), defendant struck the cane of the French ambassador and was prosecuted under the law of nations. The court remarked: "As to the assault, this is, perhaps, one of that kind, in which the insult is more to be considered than the actual damage; for, though no great bodily pain is suffered by a blow on the palm of the hand, or the skirt of the coat, yet these are clearly within the definition of assault and battery, and among gentlemen too often induce duelling and terminate in murder." The court in Richmond v. Fiske, 35 N.E. 103 (Mass. 1893), also found a battery when a milkman entered the bedroom of the plaintiff-customer, shook him to awaken him, and then presented him with the milk bill. The Restatement notes that knowledge that unpermitted conduct has taken place is not necessary to establish the battery. "A kisses B while asleep but does not waken or harm her. A is subject to liability to B." Restatement (Second) of Torts §18 comment *d*, illustration 2.

The protection afforded against offensive battery does not extend only to cases of direct contact with the plaintiff's person. It also covers contact with "anything so closely attached [to the plaintiff's person] that it is customarily regarded as a part thereof and which is offensive to a reasonable sense of personal dignity." Restatement (Second) of Torts §18 comment *c*. An example is the striking of the plaintiff's cane in the *Longchamps* case, supra; for other such acts see Clark v. Downing, 55 Vt. 259 (1882) (striking the horse that plaintiff was riding); Morgan v. Loyacomo, 1 So. 2d 510 (Miss. 1941) (seizing an object from plaintiff's hand); and Fisher v. Carrousel Motor Hotel, 424 S.W.2d 62 (Tex. 1967) (grabbing at plaintiff's plate).

Why the reference to "indirect" offensive contact in section 18(1)(b) of the Restatement (Second)?

3.   False Imprisonment

Bird v. Jones
115 Eng. Rep. 688 (K.B. 1845)

COLERIDGE, J. . . . . This point is, whether certain facts, which may be taken as clear upon the evidence, amount to an imprisonment. These facts, stated shortly, and as I understand them, are in effect as follows.

A part of a public highway was inclosed, and appropriated for spectators of a boat race, paying a price for their seats. The plaintiff was desirous of entering this part, and was opposed by the defendant: but, after a struggle, during which no momentary detention of his person took place, he succeeded in climbing over the inclosure. Two policemen were then stationed by the defendant to prevent, and they did prevent, him from passing onwards in the direction in which he declared his wish to go: but he was allowed to remain unmolested where he was, and was at liberty to go, and was told that he was so, in the only other direction by which he could pass. This he refused for some time, and, during that time, remained where he had thus placed himself.

These are the facts: and, setting aside those which do not properly bear on the question now at issue, there will remain these: that the plaintiff, being in a public highway and desirous of passing along it, in a particular direction, is prevented from doing so by the orders of the defendant, and that the defendant's agents for the purpose are policemen, from whom, indeed, no unnecessary violence was to be anticipated, or such as they believed unlawful, yet who might be expected to execute such commands as they deemed lawful with all necessary force, however resisted. But, although thus obstructed, the plaintiff was at liberty to move his person and go in any other direction, at his free will and pleasure: and no actual force or restraint on his person was used, unless the obstruction before mentioned amounts to so much.

I lay out of consideration the question of right or wrong between these parties. The acts will amount to imprisonment neither more nor less from their being wrongful or capable of justification.

And I am of opinion that there was no imprisonment. To call it so appears to me to confound partial obstruction and disturbance with total obstruction and detention. A prison may have its boundary large or narrow, visible and tangible, or, though real, still in the conception only; it may itself be moveable or fixed: but a boundary it must have; and that boundary the party imprisoned must be prevented from passing; he must be prevented from leaving that place, within the ambit of which the party imprisoning would confine him, except by prison-breach. Some confusion seems to me to arise from confounding imprisonment of the body with mere loss of freedom: it is one part of the definition of freedom to be able to go whithersoever one pleases; but imprisonment is something more than the mere loss of this power; it includes the notion of restraint within some limits defined by a will or power exterior to our own.

. . . If it be said that to hold the present case to amount to an imprisonment would turn every obstruction of the exercise of a right of way into an imprisonment, the answer is, that there must be something like personal menace or force accompanying the act of obstruction, and that, with this, it will amount to imprisonment. I apprehend that is not so. If, in the course of a night, both ends of a street were walled up, and there was no egress from the house but into the street, I should have no difficulty in saying that the inhabitants were thereby imprisoned; but, if only one end were walled up, and an armed force stationed outside to prevent any scaling of the wall or passage that way, I should feel equally clear that there was no imprisonment. If there were, the street would obviously be the prison; and yet, as obviously, none would be confined to it.

[Defendant's request for a new trial was granted. The concurring opinion of Williams, J., is omitted.]

LORD DENMAN, C.J. [dissenting]. . . . A Company unlawfully obstructed a public way for their own profit, extorting money from passengers, and hiring policemen to effect this purpose. The plaintiff, wishing to exercise his right of way, is stopped by force, and ordered to move in a direction which he wished not to take. He is told at the same time that a force is at hand ready to compel his submission. That proceeding appears to me equivalent to being pulled by the collar out of the one line and into the other.

There is some difficulty perhaps in defining imprisonment in the abstract without reference to its illegality; nor is it necessary for me to do so, because I consider these acts as amounting to imprisonment. That word I understand to mean any restraint of the person by force. . . .

I had no idea that any person in these times supposed any particular boundary to be necessary to constitute imprisonment, or that the restraint of a man's person from doing what he desires ceases to be an imprisonment because he may find some means of escape.

It is said that the party here was at liberty to go in another direction. I am not sure that in fact he was, because the same unlawful power which prevented him from taking one course might, in case of acquiescence, have refused him any other. But this liberty to do something else does not appear to me to affect the question of imprisonment. As long as I am prevented from doing what I have a right to do, of what importance is it that I am permitted to do something else? How does the imposition of an unlawful condition show that I am not restrained? If I am locked in a room, am I not imprisoned because I might effect my escape through a window, or because I might find an exit dangerous or inconvenient to myself, as by wading through water or by taking a route so circuitous that my necessary affairs would suffer by delay?

It is said that, if any damage arises from such obstruction, a special action on the case may be brought. Must I then sue out a new writ stating that the defendant employed direct force to prevent my going where my business called me, whereby I sustained loss? And, if I do, is it certain that I shall not be told that I have misconceived my remedy, for all flows from the false imprisonment, and that should have been the subject of an action of trespass and assault? For the jury properly found that the whole of the defendant's conduct was continuous: it commenced in illegality; and the plaintiff did right to resist it as an outrageous violation of the liberty of the subject from the very first.

NOTES

1. Stone walls do not a prison make. As Bird v. Jones illustrates, one of the major problems in an action for false (i.e., wrongful) imprisonment is the nature of the confinement required for liability. In Whittaker v. Sandford, 85 A. 399, 402-403 (Me. 1912), a woman was given complete freedom of movement on defendant's palatial yacht but, when she went on shore occasionally, was not given liberty to roam or to remain there; she was held to have been imprisoned while on the boat so long as she was not given access to shore by a boat. But her damages were reduced from $1,100 to $500 dollars because she was not kept in "close confinement." "She was afforded all the liberties of the yacht. She was taken on shore by her husband to do shopping and transact business at a bank. She visited neighboring islands with her husband and children, on one of which they enjoyed a family picnic. The case lacks the elements of humiliation and disgrace that frequently attend false imprisonment. She was respectfully treated as a guest in every way, except that she was restrained from quitting the yacht for good and all." . . .

Section 36 comment *b*, of the Restatement of Torts reads: "The area within which another is completely confined may be large and need not be stationary. Whether the area from which the actor prevents the other from going is so large that it ceases to be a confinement within the area and becomes an exclusion from some other area may depend upon the circumstances of the particular case and be a matter for the judgment of the court and jury." Illustration 6 under this comment reads: "*A* by an invalid process restrains *B* within prison limits which are coterminous with the boundaries of a considerable town. *A* has confined *B*." The Restatement then goes on to suggest that if the plaintiff was wrongfully excluded from the United States by the defendant's conduct, this would not amount to false imprisonment even though, in a sense, the plaintiff "may be said to be confined within the residue of the habitable world."

2. Containment and coercion. How much coercion must be exercised to make out a tortious confinement? Undoubtedly the defendant will be held to have confined the plaintiff if the circumstances made it physically impossible to leave. Though it is not false imprisonment to lock an athletic young man in a first-floor room with an open window, it would be if he were undressed at the time and had been deprived of his clothing.

The doctrine of confinement also has been extended to cover situations where the plaintiff, while free to go as she pleases, accepts confinement in order to protect her property from wrongful appropriation by the defendant. In Griffin v. Clark, 42 P.2d 297 (Idaho 1935), the defendants and one North, in a burst of aggressive hospitality, stashed the plaintiff's suitcase in their car in order to make her join them in the trip to their common destination, even though she preferred to travel by train. While they were talking her train pulled out of the station. In the course of the trip, the plaintiff was injured in a collision that also killed North, the driver. The court sustained her action against the two Clarks, brother and sister, for false imprisonment, given that they jointly restrained her "in her right of freedom of locomotion." What result if the collision was in no way attributable to North's negligence in the operation of the vehicle?

3. Basis of liability for false imprisonment. There is some confusion regarding the basis of liability for false imprisonment. Usually the defendant must intend to confine the plaintiff, there being no liability for negligently caused imprisonments. See Restatement (Second) of Torts

§35. The result seems appropriate in case of minor harms, where the concern with dignity is paramount. Yet where the plaintiff suffers major physical harm from the defendant's imprisonment, negligence principles are used, for here the compensatory concern looms larger. Thus, to use the Restatement illustration (section 35, illustration 2), suppose that defendant mistakenly has locked plaintiff in a walk-in cold storage vault that he had permitted plaintiff to enter. If defendant discovers his mistake in time to release the plaintiff before serious injury results, the Restatement holds he will not be held liable for the unpleasant consequences of the "momentary confinement." Where, however, the defendant discovers his mistake only hours later, the Restatement holds that the defendant can be held subject to liability for negligence if, for example, pneumonia follows as a result of that confinement.

4. *Consciousness of confinement.* Must plaintiff be aware of the external restraint in order to maintain an action for false imprisonment? In Herring v. Boyle, 149 Eng. Rep. 1126 (Ex. 1834), "the plaintiff had been placed by his mother at the school kept by the defendant, and it appeared that she had applied to take him away. The schoolmaster very improperly refused to give him up to the mother, unless she paid an amount which he claimed to be due." The court did not allow the action for false imprisonment because the plaintiff could not show that he was subjected to any special supervision or that he was conscious of restraint.

On the other hand, in Meering v. Grahame-White Aviation Co., Ltd., 122 L.T. 44 (C.A. 1920), Atkin, L.J., noted that a person could be imprisoned while drunk, asleep, or insane, and that the question of his mental state at the time of the imprisonment should go only to the issue of damages, not to liability. Should plaintiff be allowed damages for emotional distress if he became indignant about an imprisonment only long afterwards, when he discovered that it had occurred? If the defendant boasted of the imprisonment to third persons? For a review of the few cases that deal with this problem and for a criticism of the Restatement's position see Prosser, False Imprisonment: Consciousness of Confinement, 55 Colum. L. Rev. 847 (1955).

Coblyn v. Kennedy's, Inc.
268 N.E.2d 860 (Mass. 1971)

[The plaintiff, a man 70-years-old, five feet four inches tall, and dressed in a woolen shirt, topcoat, and hat, was shopping in defendant's store. Around his neck plaintiff wore an ascot he had previously purchased in Filene's, another department store. While trying on a sportscoat, the plaintiff took off his ascot and put it into his pocket. He purchased the coat, left it downstairs for alterations, and, as he was leaving the store, took the ascot out of his pocket and put it on again. At that moment the defendant Goss, an employee of Kennedy's, "loomed up" in front of the plaintiff and demanded that he stop and explain where he had gotten the ascot. As approximately eight to ten people looked on, the plaintiff agreed to return with Goss to the store. On the way up the stairs, the plaintiff experienced chest and back pains and had to stop several times. When they reached the second floor, the salesman who had sold plaintiff the sportscoat told Goss that the ascot was indeed the plaintiff's. The plaintiff was so upset by the incident that he required the attention of the store's nurse and was consequently hospitalized and treated for a "myocardial infarct." The jury awarded plaintiff $12,500 for false imprisonment. The defendant appealed.]

SPIEGEL, J. Initially, the defendants contend that as a matter of law the plaintiff was not falsely imprisoned. They argue that no unlawful restraint was imposed by either force or threat upon the plaintiff's freedom of movement. However, "[t]he law is well settled that '[a]ny general restraint is sufficient to constitute an imprisonment . . .' and '[a]ny demonstration of physical power which, to all appearances, can be avoided only by submission, operates as effectually to constitute an imprisonment, if submitted to, as if any amount of force had been exercised.' 'If a man is restrained of his personal liberty by fear of a personal difficulty, that amounts to a false imprisonment' within the legal meaning of such term."

We think it is clear that there was sufficient evidence of unlawful restraint to submit this question to the jury. Just as the plaintiff had stepped out of the door of the store, the defendant Goss stopped him, firmly grasped his arm and told him that he had "better go back and see the manager." There was another employee at his side. The plaintiff was an elderly man and there were other people standing around staring at him. Considering the plaintiff's age and his heart condition, it is hardly to be expected that with one employee in front of him firmly grasping his arm and another at his side the plaintiff could do other than comply with Goss's "request" that he go back and see the manager. . . .

In addition, as this court observed . . . the "honesty and veracity [of the plaintiff] had been openly . . . challenged. If he had gone out before . . . [exonerating himself], his departure well might have been interpreted by the lookers on as an admission of guilt, or of circumstances from which guilt might be inferred. The situation was in the control of the defendant. The restraint or duress imposed by the mode of investigation . . . the jury could say was for the accomplishment of the defendant's purpose, even if no threats of public exposure or of arrest were made, and no physical restraint of . . . [the plaintiff] was attempted." . . .

The defendants next contend that the detention of the plaintiff was sanctioned by G. L. c. 231, §94B, inserted by St. 1958, c. 337. This statute provides as follows: "In an action for false arrest or false imprisonment brought by any person by reason of having been detained for questioning on or in the immediate vicinity of the premises of a merchant, if such person was detained in a reasonable manner and for not more than a reasonable length of time by a person authorized to make arrests or by the merchant or his agent or servant authorized for such purpose and if there were reasonable grounds to believe that the person so detained was committing or attempting to commit larceny of goods for sale on such premises, it shall be a defence to such action. If such goods had not been purchased and were concealed on or amongst the belongings of a person so detained it shall be presumed that there were reasonable grounds for such belief."

The defendants argue in accordance with the conditions imposed in the statute that the plaintiff was detained in a reasonable manner for a reasonable length of time and that Goss had reasonable grounds for believing that the plaintiff was attempting to commit larceny of goods held for sale.

It is conceded that the detention was for a reasonable length of time. We need not decide whether the detention was effected in a reasonable manner for we are of opinion that there were no reasonable grounds for believing that the plaintiff was committing larceny and, therefore, he should not have been detained at all. However, we observe that Goss's failure to identify himself as an employee of Kennedy's and to disclose the reasons for his inquiry and actions, coupled with the physical restraint in a public place imposed upon the plaintiff, an elderly man, who had exhibited no aggressive intention to depart, could be said to constitute an unreasonable method by which to effect detention.

The pivotal question before us as in most cases of this character is whether the evidence shows that there were reasonable grounds for the detention. At common law in an action for false imprisonment, the defence of probable cause, as measured by the prudent and cautious man standard, was available to a merchant. In enacting G. L. c. 231, §94B, the Legislature inserted the words, "reasonable grounds." Historically, the words "reasonable grounds" and "probable cause" have been given the same meaning by the courts. In the case of United States v. Walker, 246 F.2d 519, 526 (7th Cir.) it was said: " 'Probable cause' and 'reasonable grounds' are concepts having virtually the same meaning." . . .

The defendants assert that the judge improperly instructed the jury in stating that "grounds are reasonable when there is a basis which would appear to the reasonably prudent, cautious, intelligent person." In their brief, they argue that the "prudent and cautious man rule" is an objective standard and requires a more rigorous and restrictive standard of conduct than is contemplated by G. L. c. 231, §94B. The defendants' requests for instructions, in effect, state that the proper test is a subjective one, viz., whether the defendant Goss had an honest and strong suspicion that the plaintiff was committing or attempting to commit larceny. . . .

If we adopt the subjective test as suggested by the defendants, the individual's right to liberty and freedom of movement would become subject to the "honest . . . suspicion" of a shopkeeper based on his own "inarticulate hunches" without regard to any discernible facts. In effect, the result would be to afford the merchant even greater authority than that given to a police officer. In view of the well established meaning of the words "reasonable grounds" we believe that the Legislature intended to give these words their traditional meaning. This seems to us a valid conclusion since the Legislature has permitted an individual to be detained for a "reasonable length of time."

We also note that an objective standard is the criterion for determining probable cause or reasonable grounds in malicious prosecution and false arrest cases. . . .

Applying the standard of reasonable grounds as measured by the reasonably prudent man test to the evidence in the instant case, we are of opinion that the evidence warranted the conclusion that Goss was not reasonably justified in believing that the plaintiff was engaged in shoplifting. There was no error in denying the motion for directed verdicts and in the refusal to give the requested instructions.

Exceptions overruled.

NOTES

1. Protection of person and property. In *Coblyn* what justification is there for making an innocent plaintiff bear the costs of the defendant's error in apprehension, even if the defendant's mistake is entirely reasonable? For a discussion of common-law approaches to shoplifting see Note, The Protection and Recapture of Merchandise from Shoplifters, 46 Ill. L. Rev. 887 (1952), continued in 47 Nw. U. L. Rev. 82 (1952).

As with other intentional harms, actions of imprisonment may in principle be justified by showing that these are necessary for the protection of person and property. In Sindle v. New York City Transit Authority, 307 N.E.2d 245, 248 (N.Y. 1973), the defendant operated a school bus carrying between 65 and 70 junior high school students, including the plaintiff. Some of the other students became rowdy, committed acts of vandalism, and remained abusive even when warned by the driver. The driver then abandoned his ordinary route, passed several stops, and drove to the police station. On the way, the plaintiff, who had not behaved improperly, jumped out of a side window, only to be run over by the bus's back wheels. The plaintiff abandoned any action for negligence (why?) and pitched the case solely on a false imprisonment theory. The trial judge refused to allow the defendants to introduce any evidence to justify the imprisonment. The Court of Appeals held that this exclusion was improper:

> In view of our determination, it would be well to outline some of the considerations relevant to the issue of justification. In this regard, we note that, generally, restraint or detention, reasonable under the circumstances and in time and manner, imposed for the purpose of preventing another from inflicting personal injuries or interfering with or damaging real or personal property in one's lawful possession or custody is not unlawful. (Cf. Penal Law, §§35.20, 35.25; see, also, General Business Law, §218, which affords a retail merchant a defense to an action for false arrest and false imprisonment where a suspected shoplifter is reasonably detained for investigation or questioning.) Also, a parent, guardian or teacher entrusted with the care or supervision of a child may use physical force reasonably necessary to maintain discipline or promote the welfare of the child. (Penal Law, §35.10)
>
> Similarly, a school bus driver, entrusted with the care of his student-passengers and the custody of public property, has the duty to take reasonable measures for the safety and protection of both — the passengers and the property. In this regard, the reasonableness of his actions — as bearing on the defense of justification — is to be determined from a consideration of all the circumstances. At a minimum, this would seem to import, a consideration of the need to protect the persons and property in his charge, the duty to aid the investigation and apprehension of those inflicting damage, the manner and place of the occurrence, and the feasibility and practicality of other alternative courses of action.

2. *Consent.* Yet another defense available in false imprisonment cases is consent. The most difficult issues in this regard often arise when the plaintiff seeks to retract a consent to confinement that was previously given. In Herd v. Weardale Steel, Coal & Coke Co., [1913] 3 K.B. 771, [1915] A.C. 67, plaintiff, a miner, entered defendant's mine for a shift that normally ended at 4:00 P.M. At 11:00 A.M. plaintiff expressed a desire to leave the mine, claiming that he was being required by the defendant to do unsafe work in violation of his employment contract and the applicable statutory provisions. Twenty-nine of the plaintiff's fellow workers joined with the plaintiff and also demanded to be taken to the surface. An empty elevator was available to take the men up at 1:00 P.M., but it was not until about 1:30 P.M. that plaintiff was permitted to use the elevator and ascend to the surface. The trial court held that the detention from 1:00 to 1:30 constituted a false imprisonment. This decision was reversed on appeal by a divided court. The House of Lords affirmed the decision of the appellate court; Haldane, L.C., said: "The man chose to go to the bottom of the mine under these conditions, — conditions which he accepted. He had no right to call upon the em-

ployers to make use of special machinery put there at their cost, and involving cost in its working, to bring him to the surface just when he pleased." Is there a false imprisonment if the plaintiff had a legitimate safety grievance?

3. *Deprogramming.* As noted in *Sindle,* parental control and discipline is generally regarded as a defense in false imprisonment cases, just as it is in actions for assault and battery. The full limits of this defense have been sorely tested in the recent actions against parents brought by children who have been seized by force in efforts to counteract "cult" allegiances and control. One of the most vivid suits of this sort is Peterson v. Sorlien, 299 N.W.2d 123, 129, 136 (Minn. 1980), where the plaintiff, a college student, fell under the influence of "The Way Ministry" a religious organization, after which her schoolwork subsequently deteriorated, and she became "overly tired, unusually pale, distraught and irritable." After her junior year, her parents concluded that she had been a victim of "coercive persuasion" and brought her to a "deprogrammer" who after several days of intensive treatment was able to restore her to her former sunny disposition. Plaintiff thereafter sought to persuade her fiancé to leave the cult, but he in turn urged her to return, which she did. Afterwards she brought an action for false imprisonment and intentional infliction of emotional distress against her parents and her deprogrammer. The jury found for the parents and against the deprogrammer, and the Minnesota Supreme Court gave its *Subjective test* cautious vindication of the parent's position: "we <u>hold that when par</u>ents, or their agents, <u>acting under the conviction</u> that the judgmental capacity of their adult child is impaired, seek to extricate that child from what they reasonably believe to be a religious or pseudo-religious cult, and the child at some juncture assents to the actions in question, limitations upon the child's mobility do not constitute meaningful deprivations of personal liberty sufficient to support a judgment for false imprisonment. But owing to the threat that deprogramming poses to public order, we do not endorse self-help as a preferred alternative."

An uneasy dissent took the opposite view: "to hold that for seeking companionship and identity in a group whose proselytizing tactics may well be suspect, she must endure without a remedy the degrading and humiliating treatment she received at the hands of her parents, is, in my opinion, totally at odds with the basic rights of young people to think unorthodox thoughts, join unorthodox groups, and proclaim unorthodox views. I would reverse the denial of recovery as to that cause of action."

What result if the plaintiff had been a minor when she first joined the cult, but over 18 when she returned? If plaintiff had decided to cast her lot with her parents, could she have maintained an action against the cult for false imprisonment or intentional infliction of emotional distress?

4.   The Intentional Infliction of Emotional Distress: Extreme and Outrageous Conduct

Wilkinson v. Downton
[1897] 2 Q.B. 57

[The facts are set forth in the court's opinion. The jury gave a verdict of 1*s*. 10 1/2*d*. for transportation money given by plaintiff to friends to fetch her husband home and £100 for injuries caused by nervous shock. Defendant contended that the damage caused by nervous shock was not actionable.]

WRIGHT, J. In this case the defendant, in the execution of what he seems to have regarded as a practical joke, represented to the plaintiff that he was charged by her husband with a message to her to the effect that her husband was smashed up in an accident, and was lying at The Elms at Leytonstone with both legs broken, and that she was to go at once in a cab with two pillows to fetch him home. All this was false. The effect of the statement on the plaintiff was a violent shock to her nervous system, producing vomiting and other more serious and permanent physical consequences at one time threatening her reason, and entailing weeks of suffering and incapacity to her as well as expense to her husband for medical attendance. These consequences were not in any way the result of previous ill-health or weakness of constitution; nor was there any evidence of predisposition to nervous shock or any other idiosyncrasy. . . .

[The court then stated that while the 1*s*. 10 1/2*d*. was recoverable in fraud and deceit, the substantial damages could not be allowed on that theory since they were not appropriate damages for fraud and deceit, thus refusing to treat this as a case of damages that were parasitic on some other tort.]

I think, however, that the verdict may be supported upon another ground. The defendant has, as I assume for the moment, wilfully done an act calculated to cause physical harm to the plaintiff — that is to say, to infringe her legal right to personal safety, and has in fact thereby caused physical harm to her. That proposition without more appears to me to state a good cause of action, there being no justification alleged for the act. This wilful *injuria* is in law malicious, although no malicious purpose to cause the harm which was caused nor any motive of spite is imputed to the defendant.

It remains to consider whether the assumptions involved in the proposition are made out. One question is whether the defendant's act was so plainly calculated to produce some effect of the kind which was produced that an intention to produce it ought to be imputed to the defendant, regard being had to the fact that the effect was produced on a person proved to be in an ordinary state of health and mind. I think that it was. It is difficult to imagine that such a statement, made suddenly and with apparent seriousness, could fail to produce grave effects under the circumstances upon any but an exceptionally indifferent person, and therefore an intention to produce such an effect must be imputed, and it is no answer in law to say that more harm was done than was anticipated, for that is commonly the case with all wrongs. The other question is whether the effect was, to use the ordinary phrase, too remote to be in law regarded as a consequence for which the defendant is answerable. Apart from authority, I should give the same answer and on the same ground as the last question, and say that it was not too remote. . . .

[The court went on to discuss prior authorities dealing mainly with cases involving damages caused by emotional disturbance resulting from negligence and the relevance of damages caused by emotional disturbance in slander actions.] That case [a slander case], however, appears to have been decided on the ground that in all the innumerable actions for slander there were no precedents for alleging illness to be sufficient special damage, and that it would be of evil consequence to treat it as sufficient, because such a rule might lead to an infinity of trumpery or groundless actions. Neither of these reasons is applicable to the present case. Nor could such a rule be adopted as of general application without results which it would be difficult or impossible to defend. Suppose that a person is in a precarious and dangerous condition, and another person tells him that his physician has said that he has but a day to live. In such a case, if death ensued from the shock caused by the false statement, I cannot doubt that at this day the case might be one of criminal homicide, or that if a serious aggravation of illness ensued damages might be recovered. I think, however, that it must be admitted that the present case is without precedent. . . .

There must be judgment for plaintiff for £100 1s. 10 1/2d.

NOTE

Parasitic damages. In Bouillon v. Laclede Gaslight Co., 129 S.W. 401, 402 (Mo. App. 1910), the defendant's meter reader tried to force his way in through the front door of the plaintiff's apartment while the plaintiff was pregnant and at risk for a miscarriage. He had several nasty exchanges with the plaintiff's nurse which were overheard by the plaintiff through the open front door, which also let in the cold air. That evening the plaintiff suffered chills, and the next day had a miscarriage which her physician attributed to the events of the prior day. Plaintiff was sick for an extended period of time after the incident, and suffered permanent impairments to her health. Nortoni, J., allowed plaintiff's cause of action.

> Defendant insists the facts relied upon present no cause of action known under the various heads of tort, unless it be for an assault, and then proceeds to point out why no assault on plaintiff is shown by the proof. No one can doubt that the case fails to disclose an assault on plaintiff as the controversy was principally had with, and all the insulting language directed against, another, the nurse. However this may be, the facts reveal a valid ground of liability on the score of trespass, and this is true notwithstanding the damages laid are not for the commission of the initial act of trespass, but relate instead to its consequence alone. Although defendant's agent had a right to enter the basement beneath plaintiff's apartment for the purpose of reading the gas meter, it is entirely clear that he had no authority to enter or pass through plaintiff's flat for that purpose. She was not a consumer of gas and the gas meter was in no sense connected with her household. Plaintiff is assured peaceful repose of her home against unwarranted intrusion from others. A trespasser is liable to respond in damages for such injuries as may result naturally, necessarily, directly, and proximately in consequence of his wrong. This is true for the reason the original act involved in the trespass is unlawful. . . . The doctrine is that though a mere mental disturbance of itself may not be a cause of action in the first instance, fright and mental anguish are competent elements of damage if they arise out of a trespass upon the plaintiff's person or possession and may be included in a suit for the trespass if plaintiff chooses so to do, or, if a physical injury results from such fright, a cause of action accrues from the trespass for compensation as to the physical injury and its consequences alone, which may be pursued even though plaintiff seeks no compensation for the original wrong.

In both *Wilkinson* and *Bouillon*, the defendant committed independent torts, namely, deceit and trespass. Is there any need for a new head of liability given the commission of admitted wrongs when the damages complained of are "parasitic" on an existing wrong? In 1 Street, Foundations of Legal Liability 466, 470 (1906), the author, in commenting on legal protection against mental distress observes:

> The reader will rightly anticipate that if this element of damage is recognized at all it must first appear in the role of a parasite; that is to say, a cause of action being shown apart from mental distress, the court may allow such factor to be taken into consideration in fixing the amount to be recovered, but not otherwise. . . .
> The treatment of any element of damage as a parasitic factor belongs essentially to a transitory stage of legal evolution. A factor which is today recognized as parasitic will, forsooth, tomorrow be recognized as an independent basis of liability. It is merely a question of social, economic, and industrial needs as those needs are reflected in the organic law.

American Law Institute, Restatement (Second) of Torts
(1966)

§46. OUTRAGEOUS CONDUCT CAUSING SEVERE EMOTIONAL DISTRESS

(1) One who by extreme and outrageous conduct intentionally or recklessly causes severe emotional distress to another is subject to liability for such emotional distress, and if bodily harm to the other results from it, for such bodily harm.

(2) Where such conduct is directed at a third person, the actor is subject to liability if he intentionally or recklessly causes severe emotional distress

(a) to a member of such person's immediate family who is present at the time, whether or not such distress results in bodily harm, or

(b) to any other person who is present at the time, if such distress results in bodily harm.

Caveat:

The Institute expresses no opinion as to whether there may not be other circumstances under which the actor may be subject to liability for the intentional or reckless infliction of emotional distress.

Comment . . .

d. Extreme and outrageous conduct. The cases thus far decided have found liability only where the defendant's conduct has been extreme and outrageous. It has not been enough that the defendant has acted with an intent which is tortious or even criminal, or that he has intended to inflict emotional distress, or even that his conduct has been characterized by "malice," or a degree of aggravation which would entitle the plaintiff to punitive damages for another tort. Liability has been found only where the conduct has been so outrageous in character, and so extreme in degree, as to go beyond all possible bounds of decency, and to be regarded as atrocious, and utterly intolerable in a civilized community. Generally, the case is one in which the recitation of the facts to an average member of the community would arouse his resentment against the actor, and lead him to exclaim, "Outrageous!"

The liability clearly does not extend to mere insults, indignities, threats, annoyances, petty oppressions, or other trivialities. The rough edges of our society are still in need of a good deal of filing down, and in the meantime plaintiffs must necessarily be expected and required to be hardened to a certain amount of rough language, and to occasional acts that are definitely inconsiderate and unkind. There is no occasion for the law to intervene in every case where someone's feelings are hurt. There must still be freedom to express an unflattering opinion, and some safety valve must be left through which irascible tempers may blow off relatively harmless steam. See Magruder, Mental and Emotional Disturbance in the Law of Torts, 47 Harv. Law Rev. 1033, 1053 (1936). It is only where there is a special relation between the parties, as stated in §48, that there may be recovery for insults not amounting to extreme outrage. . . .

f. The extreme and outrageous character of the conduct may arise from the actor's knowledge that the other is peculiarly susceptible to emotional distress, by reason of some physical or mental condition or peculiarity. The conduct may become heartless, flagrant, and outrageous when the actor proceeds in the face of such knowledge, where it would not be so if he did not know. It must be emphasized again, however, that major outrage is essential to the tort; and the mere fact that the actor knows that the other will regard the conduct as insulting, or will have his feelings hurt, is not enough.

§48. SPECIAL LIABILITY OF PUBLIC UTILITY FOR INSULTS BY SERVANTS

A common carrier or other public utility is subject to liability to patrons utilizing its facilities for gross insults which reasonably offend them, inflicted by the utility's servants while otherwise acting within the scope of their employment.

NOTES

1. Extreme and outrageous conduct. To what extent does the Restatement formulation represent an advance over the prior state of the law? As stated, the Restatement allows the liability to rest on the intention of the defendant alone, without proof of any other tort such as trespass or deceit. There is, of course, always some hesitation against extending the protection of interests that are so fragile in nature, and over the years the observation of the late Judge (then Professor) Magruder has often been quoted: "Against a large part of the frictions and irritations and clashing of temperaments incident to participation in a community life, a certain toughening of the mental hide is a better protection than the law could ever be." Magruder, Mental and Emotional Disturbance in the Law of Torts, 49 Harv. L. Rev. 1033, 1035 (1936). But although Magruder's point is well taken, it is also incomplete. Even if certain forms of offensive behavior are regarded as beneath the threshold appropriate to the tort law, a wide set of social sanctions, including those imposed by social groups and employers may be brought into play to check various forms of misconduct. And when the level of harm increases, there has been for the past several generations a wide agreement on the need for tort sanctions that has grown more powerful in recent years. On the emergence of the new consensus, see Prosser, Insult and Outrage, 44 Cal. L. Rev. 40 (1956).

2. *Modern developments: a case sampler.* Today, virtually all states apply the tort of extreme and outrageous conduct in a wide range of social settings.

(a) Strong arm tactics. In State Rubbish Collectors Association v. Siliznoff, 240 P.2d 282, 286 (Cal. 1952), the Acme Brewing company switched its account for the collection of garbage from Abramoff to Kosoff, who in turn assigned the account to Siliznoff. At a meeting with representatives of the State Rubbish Collectors Association, members of the association threatened to beat up Siliznoff, to destroy his property, and to put him out of business unless he agreed to pay over to the association part of the proceeds from the Acme account. Siliznoff then agreed to pay Abramoff $1,850 for the contract and gave the association a series of notes for that sum.

The association brought its action on the notes a year later. The defendant Siliznoff asked that the notes be canceled because of duress and lack of consideration; he also filed a cross-complaint praying for "general and exemplary damages because of assaults made by plaintiff and its agents to compel him to join the association and pay Abramoff for the Acme account." Siliznoff recovered $1,250 general and special damages and $4,000 exemplary damages. On appeal the association contended that "the evidence does not establish an assault against defendant because the threats made all related to action that might take place in the future," and that there was no threat of "immediate physical harm." But the unanimous court, through Traynor, J., concluded that a cause of action was established "when it is shown that one, in the absence of any privilege, intentionally subjects another to mental suffering incident to serious threats to his physical well-being, whether or not the threats are made under such circumstances as to constitute a technical assault."

(b) Bill collection. In George v. Jordan Marsh Co., 268 N.E.2d 915, 921 (Mass. 1971), the plaintiff's complaint alleged that the defendant bill collectors badgered the plaintiff with phone calls during the late evening hours, sent her letters marked "account referred to law and collection department," wrote her that her credit was revoked and that she was liable for late charges, and engaged in other dunning tactics. The plaintiff further claimed that she did not owe the money which the defendants sought to collect from her because she had never guaranteed her son's unpaid debts. As a result of the calls, the plaintiff suffered a heart attack. Her attorney then protested defendant's "harassing" tactics, but the onslaught still continued until the plaintiff suffered a second heart attack. After an exhaustive review of the earlier Massachusetts precedents, the court upheld the sufficiency of her complaint:

> Considering the weight of judicial authority as reflected in the most recent statement of the law in Restatement 2d: Torts, §46, and limiting ourselves to the allegations contained in the declaration before us, we hold that the law of this Commonwealth should be, and is, that one who, without a privilege to do so, by extreme and outrageous conduct intentionally causes severe emotional distress to another, with bodily harm resulting from such distress, is subject to liability for such emotional distress and bodily harm even though he has committed no heretofore recognized common law tort. Because of the allegations in the declaration before us, we are not required to rule, and do not rule, on the legal sufficiency of allegations of negligent, grossly negligent, wanton or reckless conduct causing severe emotional distress resulting in bodily injury, or on the legal sufficiency of allegations of distress without resulting bodily injury. . . .

(c) Outrageous professional conduct. In Rockhill v. Pollard, 485 P.2d 28 (Ore. 1971), the plaintiff, her mother-in-law, and her 10-month-old daughter, Marla, were all seriously injured in an automobile accident. Both women had serious cuts and bruises, and the daughter was apparently lifeless, with a ghostly pallor to her skin. A passing motorist took them to the office of the defendant physician, who, when summoned, did not examine either of the women and gave Marla only a brief examination. When Marla starting vomiting the defendant said it was a result of overeating. He then ordered the women to wait outside in the freezing rain until the plaintiff's husband arrived. The three were then taken to a hospital, where Marla was successfully operated on for a depressed skull fracture.

McAllister, J., first quoted extensively from comment *d* to Restatement §46, and then concluded that the evidence supported a finding of conduct outrageous in the extreme, noting that it was appropriate to factor into the equation the special duties that physicians owed their patients. "Certainly a physician who is consulted in an emergency has a duty to respect that interest, at least to the extent of making a good-faith attempt to provide adequate treatment or advice. We think a jury could infer from the evidence that defendant wilfully or recklessly failed to perform that duty."

Why does plaintiff have no action for medical malpractice or breach of contract?

(d) Racial insults. A claim for extreme and outrageous misconduct fared poorly in Patterson v. McLean Credit Union, 805 F.2d 1143 (4th Cir. 1986), where the plaintiff alleged that her supervisor engaged in racially motivated harassment by "staring" at her for several minutes at a time, by assigning her too many tasks, by making her do sweeping and dusting jobs not assigned to whites, and by telling her that blacks were known to work "slower than" whites. Phillips, J., rejected the tort suit, noting that the allegations fell "far short" of the stringent requirements of North Carolina law. In so doing he distinguished Patterson's case from Hogan v. Forsyth Country Club Co., 340 S.E.2d 116 (N.C. App. 1986), which Judge Phillips described as allowing a claim "when a fellow employee of her employer-defendant screamed and shouted at her, engaging in non-consensual and intimate sexual touchings, made sexual remarks, and threatened her with a knife. Significantly, the two other plaintiffs were denied recovery though the same fellow employee had screamed, shouted, and thrown a menu at one of them and had given strenuous work to and denied the request of another, who was pregnant, to leave work when she was in labor." *Patterson* also raised claims under the civil rights law, which were rebuffed by the Supreme Court. The case is far more important for its relatively narrow construction of the scope of the protection afforded the plaintiff under 42 U.S.C. §1981, in Patterson v. McLean Credit Union, 491 U.S. 164 (1989).

(e) Sexual harassment. The bypass of the tort law is evidenced in that many cases of sexual harassment are today couched as actions for wrongful discrimination brought under Title VII of the Civil Rights Act of 1964, §§701 et seq., 42 U.S.C.A. §§2000e et seq. Thus in Harris v. Forklift Systems, Inc., — U.S. —, 114 S. Ct. 367, 370-371 (1993), Charles Hardy, the defendant's president "often insulted [plaintiff, Teresa Harris] because of her gender and often made her the target of unwanted sexual innuendoes." These included impugning her ability to run a rental operation because she was a woman, calling her a "dumb ass woman," asking her and other female employees to take coins from his front pants pocket, and suggesting that they negotiate Harris's raise at the local Holiday Inn. When she first pointed this out to him, he apologized and promised to stop, but several months later, when Harris was arranging a deal with another customer, Hardy "asked her, again in front of other employees, 'What did you do, promise the guy . . . some [sex] Saturday night?' " She took her paycheck and quit.

The lower courts denied relief on the ground that the employer's loutish conduct was not so severe as to affect the plaintiff's "psychological well-being," but the Supreme Court unanimously remanded the case for trial, saying:

> But Title VII comes into play before the harassing conduct leads to a nervous breakdown. A discriminatorily abusive work environment, even one that does not seriously affect employees' psychological well-being, can and often will detract from employees' job performance, discourage employees from remaining on the job, or keep them from advancing in their careers. Moreover, even without regard to these tangible effects, the very fact that the discriminatory conduct was so severe or pervasive

that it created a work environment abusive to employees because of their race, gender, religion, or national origin offends Title VII's broad rule of workplace equality. The appalling conduct alleged in *Meritor [Savings Bank v. Vinson]*, 477 U.S. 57 (1986), and the reference in that case to environments "so heavily polluted with discrimination as to destroy completely the emotional and psychological stability of minority group workers," merely present some especially egregious examples of harassment. They do not mark the boundary of what is actionable. . . .

So long as the environment would reasonably be perceived, and is perceived, as hostile or abusive, there is no need for it also to be psychologically injurious.

Why should the normal safeguards of the tort of extreme and outrageous conduct be lifted only in discrimination cases, and then only with employees? In sexual harassment cases, should the standard of reasonableness be set by the reasonable person or by the reasonable woman?

3. Constitutional overtones. It is commonplace today for common-law tort rules to be subject to constitutional scrutiny in the United States Supreme Court. Just that has happened in the intersection between the tort of intentional infliction of emotional distress and the protection of freedom of speech. The most notable case in this regard is Hustler Magazine v. Falwell, 485 U.S. 46 (1988). The Supreme Court summarized its lurid facts as follows:

> The inside front cover of the November 1983 issue of Hustler Magazine featured a "parody" of an advertisement for Campari Liqueur that contained the name and picture of respondent and was entitled "Jerry Falwell talks about his first time." This parody was modeled after actual Campari ads that included interviews with various celebrities about their "first times." . . . Copying the form and layout of these Campari ads, Hustler's editors chose respondent as the featured celebrity and drafted an alleged "interview" with him in which he states that his "first time" was during a drunken incestuous rendezvous with his mother in an outhouse. The Hustler parody portrays respondent and his mother as drunk and immoral, and suggests that respondent is a hypocrite who preaches only when he is drunk. In small print at the bottom of the page, the ad contains the disclaimer, "ad parody — not to be taken seriously." The magazine's table of contents also lists the ad as "Fiction; Ad and Personality Parody."

The jury awarded Falwell $100,000 in actual damages and $50,000 in punitive damages against both Hustler and its publisher, Larry Flynt, for the intentional infliction of emotional distress under state law. The court overturned that award on constitutional grounds. Rehnquist, C.J., first stressed the need for "breathing room" under the First Amendment, and continued:

Generally speaking the law does not regard the intent to inflict emotional distress as one which should receive much solicitude, and it is quite understandable that most if not all jurisdictions have chosen to make it civilly culpable where the conduct in question is sufficiently "outrageous." But in the world of debate about public affairs, many things done with motives that are less than admirable are protected by the First Amendment. . . .

Were we to hold otherwise, there can be little doubt that political cartoonists and satirists would be subjected to damages awards without any showing that their work falsely defamed its subject. . . . The appeal of the political cartoon or caricature is often based on exploration of unfortunate physical traits or politically embarrassing events — an exploration often calculated to injure the feelings of the subject of the portrayal. The art of the cartoonist is often not reasoned or evenhanded, but slashing and one-sided. . . .

Several famous examples of this type of intentionally injurious speech were drawn by Thomas Nast, probably the greatest American cartoonist to date, who was associated for many years during the post-Civil War era with Harper's Weekly. In the pages of that publication Nast conducted a graphic vendetta against William M. "Boss" Tweed and his corrupt associates in New York City's "Tweed Ring." . . .

Despite their sometimes caustic nature, from the early cartoon portraying George Washington as an ass down to the present day, graphic depictions and satirical cartoons have played a prominent role in public and political debate. Nast's castigation of the Tweed Ring, Walt McDougall's characterization of presidential candidate James G. Blaine's banquet with the millionaires at Delmonico's as "The Royal Feast of Belshazzar," and numerous other efforts have undoubtedly had an effect on the course and outcome of contemporaneous debate. Lincoln's tall, gangling posture, Teddy Roosevelt's glasses and teeth, and Franklin D. Roosevelt's jutting jaw and cigarette holder have been memorialized by political cartoons with an effect that could not have been obtained by the photographer or the portrait artist. From the viewpoint of history it is clear that our political discourse would have been considerably poorer without them.

Is there a slippery slope from Nast to Flynt? Why no action for defamation?

Chapter Two
Strict Liability and Negligence: Historic and Analytic Foundations

A. INTRODUCTION

We now turn our attention to the central issue of tort theory: when is a defendant liable for the physical harm he accidentally or inadvertently causes? The question appears to admit of a simple answer, complete with reasons, given once and for all in a few quick sentences. Yet over the years this question in its various forms has generated more debate and less consensus in the tort literature than any other. One approach — the traditional view of strict liability — holds that the defendant is prima facie liable for any harm that he causes to the plaintiff's person or property. The opposing position holds that the plaintiff's prima facie case is established only if, intentional harms aside, the defendant acted with insufficient care.

When these approaches are juxtaposed several inquiries emerge, all of which must be pursued throughout the law of torts. Must one theory be accepted in toto to the exclusion of the other, or is it possible to define appropriate areas for each? If the latter, has the law drawn the lines in their proper places? Note, too, that the element of causation appears to be a common bond between the two theories. Yet how should "causation" be interpreted? Does its meaning shift as we move from theories of strict liability to those of negligence? And, if so, how? Again, what is meant by "negligence"? Is it a technical term or one of ordinary language? Is it enough that the defendant was careless in the manner in which he conducted his affairs, or is it also necessary that he owe some duty of care to the plaintiff which makes his carelessness not only morally blameworthy but legally culpable as well? Finally, note that the opposition between the two theories is stated solely with reference to the prima facie case. But the defenses for accidental injuries may well narrow the gap between them, especially if the defendant is allowed to argue that he has conducted himself both carefully and honorably.

The ongoing debate among the common-law judges necessarily took place in historical sequence, and judges both in England and the United States have placed heavy emphasis on the early English cases. It is therefore both useful and instructive to retrace their lengthy journey here. Section B of this chapter therefore examines the tension between negligence and strict liability in the early English cases. Section C traces the influence of the forms of action on the choice of liability rules. Section D follows the debate over the principle of liability in nineteenth-century law in both England and the United States, after the abolition of the forms of action. Section E examines the same conflict in the twentieth century. The law in each period builds heavily on what has gone before, so it is important to observe how earlier precedents are followed, reshaped, expanded, or abandoned in the course of their application and elaboration.

B. THE EARLY CASES

The Thorns Case
Y.B. Mich. 6 Ed. 4, f. 7, pl. 18 (1466)

A man brought a writ of Trespass quare vi et armis clausum fregit, etc. et herbam suam pedibus conculcando consumpsit, [Roughly: why by force and arms he broke into the plaintiff's close, and consumed his crops by trampling them with his feet] and alleged the trespass in 5 acres and the defendant said, as to the coming, etc. and as to the trespass in the 5 acres, not guilty and, as to the trespass in the 5 acres, that the plaintiff ought not to have an action for he says that he [the defendant] has an acre of land on which a thorn hedge grows, adjoining the said 5 acres, and that he [the defendant], at the time of the supposed trespass, came and cut the thorns, and that they, against his will, fell on the said acres of the plaintiff, and that he [the defendant] came freshly on to the said acres and took them, which is the same trespass for which he has conceived this action. And on this they demurred and it was well argued, and was adjourned.

And now Catesby says: Sir, it has been said that, if a man does some act, even if it be lawful, and by this act tort and damage are done to another against his will, yet, if he could by any means have eschewed the damage, he shall be punished for this act. Sir, it seems to me that the contrary is true, and, as I understand, if a man does a lawful act and thereby damage comes to another against his will, he shall not be punished. Thus, I put the case that I drive my cattle along the highway, and you have an acre of land lying next the highway, and my beasts enter your land and eat your grass, and I come freshly and chase them out of your land; now here, because the chasing out was lawful and the entry on the land was against my will, you shall not have an action against me. No more shall you have an action here, for the cutting was lawful and the falling on your land was against my will, and so the re-taking was good and lawful. And, Sir, I put the case that I cut my trees and the boughs fall on a man and kill him; in this case I shall not be attainted as of felony, for my cutting was lawful and the falling on the man was against my will. No more here, therefore, etc.

Fairfax: It seems to me that the contrary is true and I say that there is a difference where a man does a thing from which felony ensues and one from which trespass ensues; for in the case which Catesby puts there was no felony, since felony is of malice prepense and, as the act was against his will, it was not animo felonico. But if one cuts his trees and the boughs fall on a man and hurt him, in this case he shall have an action of Trespass. So, too, Sir, if a man shoots at the butts and his bow trembles in his hands and he kills a man ipso invito, this is no felony, as has been said. But if he wounds a man by his shooting, he shall have a good action of Trespass against him, and yet the shooting was lawful and the tort that the other had was against his will. And so here.

Pigot: To the same intent. I put the case that I have a mill and the water which comes to my mill runs past your land, and you have willows growing by the water, and you cut your willows and against your will they fall in the water and stop the water so that I have not sufficient water for my mill, in this case I shall have an action of Trespass, and yet the cutting was lawful and the falling was against my will. And so if a man has a fish-pond in his manor and he empties the water out of the pond to take the fishes and the water floods my land, I shall have a good action, and yet the act was lawful.

Yonge: The contrary seems to me to be true; and in such a case, where a man has dampnum absque injuria, he shall have no action, for if he has no tort he has no reason to recover damages. So in this case, when he came on to his close to take the thorns which had fallen on to it, this entry was not tortious, for when he cut them and they fell on his close ipso invito, the property in them was in him and thus it was lawful for him to take them out of his close; wherefore, notwithstanding that he has done damage, he has done no tort.

Brian: I think the contrary. To my intent, when any man does an act, he is bound to do it in such manner that by his act no prejudice or damage is done to others. Thus, in a case where I am building a house and, while the timber is being put up, a piece of it falls on my neighbour's house and damages it, he shall have a good action, and yet the building of the house was lawful and the timber fell me invito. So, too, if a man makes an assault upon me and I cannot avoid him, and in my own defence I raise my stick to strike him, and a man is behind me and in raising my stick I wound him, in this case he shall have an action against me, and yet the raising of my stick to defend myself was lawful and I wounded him me invito. So in this case.

LITTLETON, J.: To the same intent. If a man suffers damage, it is right that he be recompensed; and to my intent the case which Catesby has put is not law; for if your cattle come on to my land and eat my grass, notwithstanding you come freshly and drive them out, it is proper for you to make amends for what your cattle have done, be it more or less. . . . And, Sir, if it were law that he could enter and take the thorns, by the same reasoning, if he cut a great tree, he could come with his carts and horses to carry off the tree, which is not reason, for peradventure he has corn or other crops growing, etc. No more here may he do it, for the law is all one in great things and in small and so, according to the amount of the trespass, it is proper that he should make amends.

CHOKE, C.J.: I think the same; for when the principal thing is not lawful, then the thing which depends upon it is not lawful. For when he cut the thorns and they fell on to my land, this falling was not lawful, and then his coming to take them away was not lawful. As to what has been said that they fell ipso invito, this is not a good plea; but he should have said that he could not do it in any other manner or that he did all that was in his power to keep them out; otherwise he shall pay damages. And, Sir, if the thorns or a great tree had fallen on his land by the blowing of the wind, in this case he might have come on to the land to take them, since the falling had then been not his act, but that of the wind.

NOTES

1. *Basis for liability in tort.* The *Thorns Case* is one of the earliest English cases to discuss in general terms the basis for liability in tort. It is first debated by five lawyers, after which the two judges, Littleton and Choke, give their opinions. Note that Catesby, as a lawyer for the defendant, tries to establish as the initial premise of the tort law the proposition that there can be a tort only where there is a crime. Does Fairfax, as a lawyer for the plaintiff, adequately respond to that contention? Or give any explanation why it is in general false?

The major historical controversy over the *Thorns Case* is whether it adopts the theory of strict liability in tort. The case's connection to the negligence/strict liability debate, however, seems attenuated at first glance since the defendant's entry upon the plaintiff's land was deliberate. The sticking point in the case, reminiscent of the materials on necessity in Chapter 1, concerns the scope of the defendant's privilege to retake his thorns from the defendant's property, even if he caused damage thereby. Nonetheless, the language and the examples discussed in the case range far beyond its particular circumstances, for the judges and lawyers alike agree that the defendant has some privilege to enter and retake the thorns so long as the original cutting was not tortious. The choice between strict liability and negligence thus sets the appropriate boundaries for the privilege. What passages in the arguments of counsel and in the opinions of the judges point to the strict liability rule? What passages point in the opposite direction?

The historical basis of tort liability has been reviewed in Arnold, Accident, Mistake, and Rules of Liability in The Fourteenth Century Law of Torts, 128 U. Pa. L. Rev. 361, 374-375 (1979), where Arnold concludes that "the inference to be drawn from all the available evidence is that in fourteenth-century tort actions civil liability was strict." In the course of the article, Arnold identifies a number of grounds on which a defendant could escape liability. Thus it was "a familiar principle in the law of torts that no one was liable to make compensation for injuries that were attributable to some entirely providential cause," such as harms brought about by tempests, earthquakes, or fires of spontaneous origin. And the plaintiff's own contributory negligence was also regarded a good defense because "it is the plaintiff, not the defendant, who is perceived as having 'done' the act resulting in injury." Within the framework of these settled principles, Arnold found only a few cases where the plaintiff alleged the defendant's negligence in his complaint, and fewer still where the defendant sought to raise his own lack of negligence as a defense. For Arnold, the explanation lies as much in the structure of the standard rules of pleading as it does in the substantive issues:

> The most telling difficulty is that the absence of pleas of this sort may simply be attributable not to any abstract liability rule but rather to a pleading rule that barred the defendant from asserting such facts purely as a technical matter. To simplify somewhat, a defendant in a writ of trespass was obligated to choose between two kinds of answer: He either had to deny the physical acts he was alleged to have done, or he had to admit them and assign a cause for them. In the case of an assault and battery, for instance, an acceptable "cause" would have been self-defense. Now if a defendant wanted to say that he had hit the plaintiff accidentally (that is, nonnegligently), his story would not technically have fit either of the two modes of responding to complaints. He had, in fact, hit the plaintiff, so a denial was obviously of no use; moreover, he had had no cause,

no justification, for hitting him because "cause," as we have seen, was thought of in motivational terms. Here, the defendant's case was that he had had no motive at all in hitting the plaintiff, for the act of hitting him had been unintentional.

How do the justifications considered in the following cases tie into Arnold's theory?

2. *"Best efforts" and the law of torts.* In Millen v. Fandrye, 79 Eng. Rep. 1259 (K.B. 1626), plaintiff brought an action for the damage caused to his sheep when defendant's dog chased the sheep off defendant's land, where they had been trespassing. The dog had, moreover, continued the chase even after the sheep had entered a neighbor's land. In giving judgment for the defendant after the plaintiff had demurred to his plea, Crew, C.J., noted, "It seems to me that he might drive the sheep out with the dog, and he could not withdraw his dog when he would in an instant. . . . [A] man cuts thorns and they fall into another man's land, and in trespass he justified for it; and the opinion was, that notwithstanding this justification trespass lies, because he did not plead that he did his best endeavour to hinder their falling there, yet this was a hard case; but this case is not like to [the instant case], for here it was lawful to chase them [the sheep] out of his own land, and he did his best endeavour to recall the dog, and therefore trespass does not lie."

The decision in *Millen* endorses the view taken by Choke in the *Thorns Case,* but the result in *Millen* is also consistent with Littleton's earlier preference for stricter liability. The main point is that the "best efforts" defense in *Millen* arose in a context in which the defendant was defending his property against the wrongful incursions of the plaintiff's sheep. The law in these cases frowns on the use of excessive force, but tolerates it when the defendant tried in good faith to minimize that excess. As a variation on a familiar theme, the aggressor takes his victim as he finds him. In contrast, the defendant's cutting in the *Thorns Case* was in no sense justified or excused by any prior wrong of the plaintiff, so the defendant in the *Thorns Case* does not have the latitude afforded by the self-defense issue. The hard case suggested by the facts in *Millen* is one where a third person sues after the defendant's dog drives the sheep not only off the defendant's land but onto the third person's property, even though the dog's owner tried to call him off. Should the defense of "best efforts" be available to the landowner in a suit by that third party? See the discussion of Morris v. Platt, supra at page 38.

3. *Justification in trespass.* In the *Tithe Case,* Y.B. Trin., 21 Hen. 7, f. 26, 27, 28, pl. 5 (1506), plaintiff, a local parson, brought an action for the loss of corn tithed to him. The corn in question had been cut by a local farmer, who had placed it in a separate part of his field for the parson. The defendant placed the corn in plaintiff's barn, where it perished

from causes not specified in the opinion. Defendant justified his action on the ground that plaintiff was in danger of losing the corn to beasts that were straying in the field. The courts disallowed the justification:

KINGSMILL, J.: Where the goods of another are taken against his will, it must be justified either as a thing necessary for the Commonwealth or through a condition recognized by the law. First, as a thing concerning the Commonwealth, one may justify for goods taken out of a house when it is purely to safeguard the goods, or for breaking down a house to safeguard others; and so in time of war one may justify the entry into another's land to make a bulwark in defence of King and Country; and these things are justifiable and lawful for the maintenance of the Commonwealth. The other cause of justification is where one distrains [i.e., seizes to hold as security] my horse for his rent, and that is justifiable because the land was bound by such a condition of distress; and so in the case of other such conditions. Thus for these two reasons one may justify the taking of a thing against the will of its owner. But in this case here we are outside these reasons, for we are not within the cases of the Commonwealth nor in those of a condition; and, although it is pleaded that this corn was in danger of being lost, yet it was not in such danger but that the party could have had his remedy. Thus, if I have beasts damage feasant, [causing damage] I shall not justify my entry to chase them out unless I first tender all amends. So here, when the defendant took the plaintiff's corn that it might not be destroyed, yet this is not justifiable. For if it had been destroyed, the plaintiff would have his remedy against those who destroyed it. And as for his having put it into the plaintiff's barn, yet he must keep it safe against any other mischance; and so no advantage thereby comes to the plaintiff. So this plea is not good.

REDE, C.J.: Although the defendant's intent here was good, yet the intent is not to be construed, though in felony it shall be; as where one shoots at the butts and kills a man, this is not felony, since he had no intent to kill him; and so of a tiler on a house where against his knowledge a stone kills a man, it is not felony. But where one shoots at the butts and wounds a man, although it be against his will, yet he shall be called a trespasser against his will. So it is necessary always to have a good case to justify; as in Trespass, a license is good justification. . . . But, to return to the case here, when he took the corn, although this was a good deed as regards the damage which cattle or a stranger might do to it, yet this is not a good deed and no manner of justification as regards the owner of the corn; for the latter would have his remedy by action against him who destroyed the corn, if it had been destroyed. Thus, if my beasts are damage feasant in another's land, I cannot enter to chase them out; and yet it would be a good deed to chase them out, to save them doing more damage. But it is otherwise where a stranger drives my horses into another's land, where they do damage; for here I may justify my entry to drive them out, since this tort has its beginning in the tort of another. But here, because the plaintiff could have his remedy if the corn had been destroyed, it was not lawful to take them; and it is not like the cases where things are in jeopardy of loss through water or fire and the like, for there the plaintiff has no remedy for the destruction against anyone. So the plea is not good.

The *Tithe Case* raises a variation on the necessity issue already encountered in *Vincent*. One critical difference, however, is that the defendant in *Vincent* acted to preserve his own property, whereas the defendant in the *Tithe Case* acted to preserve the plaintiff's property. Both Kingsmill and Rede allow the necessity defense where corn is moved to protect it against natural losses, but neither allows it where third parties threaten its destruction, on the assumption that the owner faces no loss because he still has a cause of action against the third party. With third-party threats, therefore, the *Tithe Case* presents the same problem of asymmetrical incentives encountered in the public necessity cases, supra at page 63. Why should anyone act to benefit a stranger if he must bear the risk of loss? One way to offset that risk is to allow the defendant an action for restitution in the event that he saves the corn; but if that remedy is limited to a recovery of out-of-pocket expenses, then there will still be no compensation for the extra risk voluntarily assumed. Should the privilege cover the risk of loss from third parties as well as from natural events? Should a system of rewards be introduced? For discussion see Epstein, Holdouts, Externalities and The Single Owner: Another Tribute to Ronald Coase 36 J.L. & Econ. 553, 579-81 (1993).

Weaver v. Ward
80 Eng. Rep. 284 (K.B. 1616)

Weaver brought an action of trespass of assault and battery against Ward. The defendant pleaded, that he was amongst others by the commandment of the Lords of the Council a trained soldier in London, of the band of one Andrews captain; and so was the plaintiff, and that they were skirmishing with their musquets charged with powder for their exercise in re militari, [on matters military] against another captain and his band; and as they were so skirmishing, the defendant casualiter & per infortunium & contra voluntatem suam, [accidentally, and by bad fortune, and against his own will] in discharging of his piece did hurt and wound the plaintiff. And upon demurrer by the plaintiff, judgment was given for him; for though it were agreed, that if men tilt or turney in the presence of the King, or if two masters of defence playing their prizes kill one another, that this shall be no felony; or if a lunatick kill a man, or the like, because felony must be done animo felonico [with felonious intent]: yet in trespass, which tends only to give damages according to hurt or loss, it is not so; and therefore if a lunatick hurt a man, he shall be answerable in trespass: and therefore no man shall be excused of a trespass (for this is the nature of an excuse, and not of a justification, prout ei bene licuit) [as it well appeared to him] except it may be judged utterly without his fault.

As if a man by force take my hand and strike you, or if here the defendant had said, that the plaintiff ran cross his piece when it was discharging, or had set forth the case with the circumstances, so as it had appeared to the Court that it had been inevitable, and that the defendant had committed no negligence to give occasion to the hurt.

NOTES

1. Inevitable accident: conceptual difficulties. In Weaver v. Ward, the court offers neither a definition of inevitable accident nor examples of its application. The modern cases and commentators have tended to regard "inevitable accident" as a backhanded way of saying that the defendant acted neither negligently nor with an intention to harm. See, e.g., Brown v. Kendall infra at page 115; Holmes, The Common Law, infra at page 140. This argument is, however, inconsistent with the procedural posture of the earlier cases, see supra page 97 at note 1, and in any event seems odd on textual grounds because it renders the last clause (referring to antecedent negligence) wholly superfluous.

In order to reject this reading, however, it is necessary to propose another. One recent suggestion is that inevitable accident occupies a niche midway between strict liability and ordinary negligence. Gilles, Inevitable Accident in Classical English Tort Law, 43 Emory L. J. 575, 577 (1994) states the position as follows:

> The pre-nineteenth-century test for determining whether an accident was inevitable was typically described in terms such as "utterly without his fault," "did all that was in his power," "unavoidable necessity," and the like. To escape liability, defendants who had *prima facie* caused harm had to establish that they should not be viewed as responsible for the accident because some other cause had made it impossible, as a practical matter, to avoid injuring the plaintiff. Under this approach, the question was not whether the actors had behaved unreasonably — whether they *should* have avoided the accident — but whether they *could* have avoided it by greater practical care.

Still another interpretation gives the term inevitable accident a literal reading, so that it only refers to those accidents that "had to happen," whether or not the defendant acted as he did. The defendant may have caused the harm, but the harm would have occurred from some other cause even if he had not acted at all. Within this narrower definition the damage to the dock in *Vincent* is inevitable if it would have occurred whether or not the defendant made efforts to keep its ship fast to the dock during the storm. Is there a case of inevitable accident in the last case put by Choke, J., where the defendant enters the plaintiff's lands to recover a tree blown there by a great wind? Is there a case of private necessity?

2. *Inevitable accident: historical treatment.* The full report of Smith v. Stone, 82 Eng. Rep. 533 (K.B. 1647), is as follows:

> Smith brought an action of trespasse against Stone pedibus ambulando [walking by his feet], the defendant pleads this speciall plea in justification, viz. that he was carryed upon the land of the plaintiff by force, and violence of others, and was not there voluntarily, which is the same trespasse, for which the plaintiff brings his action. The plaintiff demurs to this plea: in this case Roll Iustice said, that it is the trespasse of the party that carryed the defendant upon the land, and not the trespasse of the defendant: as he that drives my cattel into another mans land is the trespassor against him, and not I who am owner of the cattell.

Does the defendant need to plead specially as he did in Weaver v. Ward, or is a general denial — it was not my act — sufficient to allow him to introduce at trial the evidence needed to escape liability?

With Smith v. Stone, contrast Gilbert v. Stone, 82 Eng. Rep. 539 (K.B. 1647):

> Gilbert brought an action of trespasse quare clausum fregit, and taking of a gelding, against Stone. The defendant pleads that he for fear of his life, and wounding of twelve armed men, who threatened to kill him if he did not [do the act] went into the house of the plaintiff, and took the gelding. The plaintiff demurred to this plea; Roll Iustice, This is no plea to justifie the defendant; for I may not do a trespasse to one for fear of threatnings of another, for by this means the party injured shall have no satisfaction, for he cannot have it of the party that threatned. Therefore let the plaintiff have his judgement.

Other early English cases also gave a narrow construction to the defense of inevitable accident. Thus in Dickenson v. Watson, Jones T., 84 Eng. Rep. 1218 (K.B. 1682), the defendant (a tax collector of "hearth-money") discharged his firearm when no one was in view without intending to harm anyone, but shot the plaintiff while the latter was walking along his own way, minding his own business. On defendant's demurrer, the judgment for the plaintiff was upheld, "for in trespass the defendant shall not be excused without unavoidable necessity which is not shewn here. . . ."

Finally in Gibbons v. Pepper, 91 Eng. Rep. 922 (K.B. 1695), the defendant was riding a horse on the highway. The horse, being frightened, bolted, carrying the defendant along until it struck and injured the plaintiff. The defendant also claimed that he called out to the plaintiff to take care, "but that notwithstanding the plaintiff did not go out of the way, but continued there." The defendant pleaded as his justification "that the accident was inevitable, and that the negligence of the defendant did not cause it." Again on demurrer, judgment was given for the plaintiff, "[o]f which opinion was the whole court. For if I ride upon a horse, and J. S. whips the horse so that he runs away with me and runs over any other person, he who whipped the horse is guilty of the battery, and not me. But if I by spurring was the cause of such accident, then I am guilty. In the same manner, if *A*. takes the hand of *B*. and with it strikes *C*., *A*. is the trespasser and not *B*. And, per Curiam, the defendant might have given this justification in evidence upon the general issue pleaded. And therefore judgment was given for the plaintiff." Should the issue of plaintiff's conduct have been considered in light of Weaver v. Ward?

Gibbon rests on the assumption that the defendant's animal should be treated as the passive instrument of any third party who causes it to hurt the plaintiff or his property. Yet this equation between animal and inanimate object is far from evident, for animals have wills of their own. Another approach is to hold the owner (vicariously) responsible for the harms caused by his animals, but to allow him an action over against any third party who rode, spurred or otherwise caused the animal to do damage. In order to decide between these two approaches, it is instructive to ask, who should bear the risk of insolvency of the third party, the owner of the animal or the victim? How should that question be answered if *A* picks *B*'s stick off the ground and uses it to strike *C*? For further elaboration of these examples, see Scott v. Shepherd, infra at page 107; Chapter 8 on animals.

3. Inevitable accident: modern response. From time to time, the inevitable accident instruction has been proffered in modern cases, where it has been ruled out of order. In Butigan v. Yellow Cab Co., 320 P.2d 500, 504 (Cal. 1958), the court repudiated its earlier view that the inevitable accident defense was a holdover in intersection cases. For these purposes, it noted that "an accident may be 'unavoidable or inevitable' where it is caused by a superior or irresistible force or by an absence of exceptional care which the law does not expect of the ordinary prudent man," and held that no defendant should be held to so high a standard of care: "In reality, the so-called defense of unavoidable accident has no legitimate place in our pleading. It appears to be an obsolete remnant from a time when damages for injuries to person or property directly caused by a voluntary act of the defendant could be recovered in an action of trespass and when strict liability would be imposed unless the defendant proved that the injury was caused through 'inevitable accident.' " In its place, ordinary negligence principles were held to govern so that "the defendant under a general denial may show any circumstance which militates against his negligence or its causal effect."

C. THE FORMS OF ACTION

1. The Significance of the Forms

The historical materials that we have just examined show the close interplay between substantive and procedural issues. In this section we turn to a study of the early forms of action, which also exerted a strong, if unintended, influence upon the growth of the substantive tort law. In the well-known phrase of Henry Maine, "So great is the ascendancy of the Law of Actions in the infancy of Courts of Justice, that substantive law has at first the look of being gradually secreted in the interstices of procedure." H. Maine, Early Law and Custom 389 (1907). The most distinctive feature of the forms of action was their jurisdictional significance. Under the old systems, the plaintiff could not simply state in his complaint the facts sufficient to get relief. See Federal Rules of Civil Procedure, Rule 8(a). He had to show in addition that his cause of action fell within one of the writs (royal orders used to commence civil actions) recognized at that time.

The consequences of the choice of writs were important in the law. As Frederick W. Maitland observed in his masterly essay The Forms of Action at Common Law 4-5 (1936 ed.):

> [T]o a very considerable degree the substantive law administered in a given form of action has grown up independently of the law administered in other forms. Each procedural pigeon-hole contains its own rules of substantive law, and it is with great caution that we may argue from what is found in one to what will probably be found in another; each has its own precedents. It is quite possible that a litigant will find that his case will fit some two or three of these pigeon-holes. If that be so he will have a choice, which will often be a choice between the old, cumbrous, costly, on the one hand, the modern, rapid, cheap, on the other. Or again he may make a bad choice, fail in his action, and take such comfort as he can from the hints of the judges that another form of action might have been more successful. The plaintiff's choice is irrevocable; he must play the rules of the game that he has chosen. Lastly he may find that, plausible as his case may seem, it just will not fit any one of the receptacles provided by the courts and he may take to himself the lesson that where there is no remedy there is no wrong.

2. Trespass and Case

Of immediate relevance to the history of tort law are two writs — trespass and trespass on the case (or more simply "case") — which between them covered most of the harms actionable at common law. By the final stages of the writ system, it was generally settled that trespass lay for the redress of harm caused by the defendant's direct and immediate application of force against the person or property of the plaintiff. Case, on the other hand, covered all those "indirect" harms, not involving the use of force, that were actionable at common law. The classic illustration of the difference was given by Fortescue, J., in Reynolds v. Clarke: "[I]f a man throws a log into the highway, and in that act it hits me, I may maintain trespass, because it is an immediate wrong; but if as it lies there I tumble over it, and receive an injury, I must bring an action upon the case; because it is only prejudicial in consequence, for which originally I could have no action at all." 92 Eng. Rep. 410 (K.B. 1726). Is there an intelligible distinction between "slip and fall" cases and collision cases? If so, what is its significance?

The last sentence of Fortescue's opinion hints at the traditional view of the early development of the substantive rules of tort law. Under that view, royal recognition of the action of trespass came first because of the vital protection against the direct use of force. Telltale signs of the early history of the trespass writ are found in two of its Latin phrases: vi et armis, by force and arms, and contra pacem regis, against the peace of the king. According to the traditional view, the action on the case was a much later development, one that took place well after the Norman Conquest, toward the middle of the fourteenth century, when the royal courts completed a silent revolution by finally allowing novel actions in tort to plaintiffs who were not the victims of direct and immediate force. C. H. S. Fifoot, History and Sources of the Common Law, Tort and Contract, ch. 4 (1949).

Subsequently, however, this view has been effectively, indeed decisively, challenged by Professor Milsom, who has demonstrated that the emergence of the action on the case as a distinct writ in the fourteenth century did not signal a transformation of the substantive law. S. F. C. Milsom, Historical Foundations of the Common Law ch. 11 (2d ed. 1981). Like the Latin "transgressio," trespass originally meant simply "wrong," and cases brought under that writ in royal courts covered not only the particular species of wrong involving the use of force, but all manner of other actionable harms as well. "If we identify trespass not with a narrow category of wrongs but with wrong generally, with the category of tort rather than a particular tort, we are good deal closer to thinking fourteenth-century thoughts than we previously were." M. Arnold, Select Cases of Trespass from the King's Courts — 1307-1399, at ix (Selden Society, vol. 100 (1984)). The radical change in subsequent centuries, far from altering the underlying substantive principles, came about for procedural reasons. The courts no longer required the use of the magic words, vi et armis and contra pacem regis, to describe situations to which they could by no extension of their ordinary meanings apply. As evidence for his thesis, Milsom thus collected from the old legal records a large number of writs framed in trespass where the phrases vi et armis and contra pacem regis were included solely by way of legal fiction to secure the jurisdiction of the royal courts. The writ of trespass was, for example, broad enough to encompass suits brought by lower riparians who suffered flooding because upper riparians had not made the required repairs to their river walls. Similarly, early trespass actions could be brought to stop unfair competition by, for example, the owner of a fair against persons who had sold goods in violation of his exclusive franchise granted by the king. In neither case did the words vi et armis or contra pacem regis describe the event for which redress was sought.

Perhaps the most interesting case discussed by Milsom, however, was the action for professional malpractice (to use the modern term) brought by the owner of a horse against a smith to whom he had entrusted the care of his animal. The plaintiff could not state his cause of action in simple and direct terms and still allege that the defendant's use of force and arms was in violation of the king's peace, necessary to attract royal jurisdiction. To speak of force and arms made the complaint internally inconsistent, for if the plaintiff entrusted the defendant with the care of his horse, he could not simultaneously insist that the defendant's conduct amounted to a breach of the king's peace. What could be done in order to escape from this dilemma? Milsom explains:

> To excise the *vi et armis* and *contra pacem* left the perfectly good complaint from which the plaintiff had started: but it was not even technically a plea of the crown, and so was not within the jurisdiction of a royal court. To bring the matter to a royal court, therefore, he had to excise the other allegation, that which showed that the object was lawfully in the defendant's possession. Instead of complaining that the smith did his work so badly that the horse died, his writ would run something like this: why with force and arms the defendant killed the plaintiff's horse, to his damage and against the king's peace. The count would follow the writ, the defendant would plead Not Guilty, the jury would find him guilty or not guilty, and the record would look like that of an action for malicious injury by a stranger. Knowledge of what happened in later times might make us suspect that it was really a road accident or the like. But were it not for the chinks of a few unusual cases, there would be nothing to make us suspect the truth, except this: the defendants in many such actions for killing horses are named or described as smiths. [S. F. C. Milsom, Historical Foundations of the Common Law 289 (2d ed. 1981)].

The royal judges eventually tired of these elaborate fictions, and in the Farrier's Case of 1372 they allowed the plaintiff to sue in royal court without having to plead either vi et armis or contra pacem regis. The emergence of the action on the case was a triumph for judicial candor, but it did not mark the creation of any new kind of liability in the royal courts. This development did, however, make it necessary to determine when each of the two distinct writs — trespass and case — were appropriate. Part of the impulse for clarifying the boundaries between the two writs was procedural. With trespass, the plaintiff was allowed to begin his action with the stringent process of capias, whereby he could seize the defendant's personal property. With case, however, the plaintiff had to rest content with commencing his action with the less coercive summons and complaint. That distinction was eliminated by statute in 1504. Yet by a statute of 1677 (16 & 17 Car. 2), a further procedural point again separated the two writs. In the words of Lord Kenyon in Savignac v. Roome, 101 Eng. Rep. 470 (K.B. 1794): "if in an action of trespass the plaintiff recover less than 40 s., he is entitled to no more costs than damages; whereas a verdict with nominal damages only in an action on the case carries all the costs."

The division in the writs between trespass and case raised substantive problems as well. To get a flavor of the common-law disputes, we can do no better than an examination of the famous *Squib Case*.

Scott v. Shepherd
96 Eng. Rep. 525 (K.B. 1773)

Trespass and assault for throwing, casting, and tossing a lighted squib at and against the plaintiff, and striking him therewith on the face, and so burning one of his eyes, that he lost the sight of it, whereby, &c. On Not Guilty pleaded, the cause came on to be tried before Nares, J., last Summer Assizes, at Bridgwater, when the jury found a verdict for the plaintiff with £100 damages, subject to the opinion of the Court on this case: — On the evening of the fair-day at Milborne Port, 28th October, 1770, the defendant threw a *lighted squib*, made of gun powder, &c. from the street into the market-house, which is a covered building, supported by arches, and enclosed at one end, but open at the other and both the sides, where a large concourse of people were assembled; which lighted squib, so thrown by the defendant, fell upon the standing of one Yates, who sold gingerbread, &c. That one Willis instantly, and to prevent injury to himself and the said wares of the said Yates, took up the said lighted squib from off the said standing, and then threw it across the said market-house, when it fell upon another standing there of one Ryal, who sold the same sort of wares, who instantly, and to save his own goods from being injured, took up the said lighted squib from off the said standing, and then threw it to another part of the said market-house, and, in so throwing it, struck the plaintiff then in the said market-house in the face therewith, and the combustible matter then bursting, put out one of the plaintiff's eyes. *Qu.* If this action be maintainable? . . .

NARES, J., was of opinion, that trespass would well lie in the present case. That the natural and probable consequence of the act done by the defendant was injury to somebody, and therefore the act was illegal at common law. And the throwing of squibs has by statute W.3, been since made a nuisance. Being therefore unlawful, the defendant was liable to answer for the consequences, be the injury mediate or immediate. 21 Hen. 7, 28, is express that malus animus is not necessary to constitute a trespass. . . .

BLACKSTONE, J., was of opinion, that an action of trespass did not lie for Scott against Shepherd upon this case. He took the settled distinction to be, that where the injury is *immediate,* an action of trespass will lie; where it is only *consequential,* it must be an action on the case: Reynolds and Clarke, Lord Raym. 1401, Stra. 634; . . . The lawfulness or unlawfulness of the original act is not the criterion; though something of that sort is put into Lord Raymond's mouth in Stra. 635, . . . [L]awful or unlawful is quite out of the case; the solid distinction is between direct or immediate injuries on the one hand, and mediate or consequential on the other. And trespass never lay for the latter. If this be so, the only question will be, whether the injury which the plaintiff suffered was immediate, or consequential only; and I hold it to be the latter. The original act was, as against Yates, a trespass; not as against Ryal, or Scott. The tortious act was complete when the squib lay at rest upon Yates's stall. He, or any bystander, had, I allow, a right to protect themselves by removing the squib, but should have taken care to do it in such a manner as not to endamage others. But Shepherd, I think, is not answerable in an action of trespass and assault for the mischief done by the squib in the new motion impressed upon it, and the new direction given it, by either Willis or Ryal; who both were free agents, and acted upon their own judgment. This differs it from the cases put of turning loose a wild beast or a madman. They are only instruments in the hand of the first agent. Nor is it like diverting the course of an enraged ox, or of a stone thrown, or an arrow glancing against a tree; because there the original motion, the vis impressa, is continued, though diverted. Here the instrument of mischief was at rest, till a new impetus and a new direction are given it, not once only, but by two successive rational agents. But it is said that the act is not complete, nor the squib at rest, till after it is spent or exploded. It certainly has a power of doing fresh mischief, and so has a stone that has been thrown against my windows, and now lies still. Yet if any person gives that stone a new motion, and does farther mischief with it, trespass will not lie for that against the original thrower. No doubt but Yates may maintain trespass against Shepherd. And, according to the doctrine contended for, so may Ryal and Scott. Three actions for one single act! nay, it may be extended in infinitum. If a man tosses a football into the street, and, after being kicked about by one hundred people, it at last breaks a tradesman's windows; shall he have trespass against the man who first produced it? Surely only against the man who gave it that mischievous direction. But it is said, if Scott has no action against Shepherd, against whom must he seek his remedy? I give no opinion whether case would lie against Shepherd for the consequential damage; though, as at present advised, I think, upon the circumstances, it would. But I think, in strictness of law, trespass would lie against Ryal, the immediate actor in this unhappy business. Both he and Willis have exceeded the bounds of self-defence, and not used sufficient circumspection in removing the danger from themselves. The throwing it across the market-house, instead of brushing it down, or throwing [it] out of the open sides into the street, (if it was not meant to continue the sport, as it is called), was at least an unnecessary and incautious act. Not even menaces from others are sufficient to justify a trespass against a third person; much less a fear of danger to either his goods or his person — nothing but inevitable necessity; Weaver and Ward, Hob. 134; Dickenson and Watson, T. Jones, 205; Gilbert and Stone, Al. 35, Styl. 72. . . . And I admit that the defendant is answerable in trespass for all the direct and inevitable effects caused by his own immediate act. — But what is his own immediate act? The throwing the squib to Yates's stall. Had Yates's goods been burnt, or his person injured, Shepherd must have been responsible in trespass. But he is not responsible for the acts of other men. The subsequent throwing across the market-house by Willis, is neither the act of Shepherd, nor the inevitable effect of it; much less the subsequent throwing by Ryal. . . . It is said by Lord Raymond, and very justly, in Reynolds and Clarke, "We must keep up the boundaries of actions, otherwise we shall introduce the utmost confusion." As I therefore think no immediate injury passed from the defendant to the plaintiff (and without such immediate injury no action of trespass can be maintained), I am of opinion, that in this action judgment ought to be for the defendant.

De Grey, C.J. This case is one of those wherein the line drawn by the law between actions on the case and actions of trespass is very nice and delicate. Trespass is an injury accompanied with force, for which an action of trespass vi et armis lies against the person from whom it is received. The question here is, whether the injury received by the plaintiff arises from the force of the original act of the defendant, or from a new force by a third person. I agree with my Brother Blackstone as to the principles he has laid down, but not in his application of those principles to the present case. . . . [T]he true question is, whether the injury is the direct and immediate act of the defendant; and I am of opinion, that in this case it is. The throwing the squib was an act unlawful and tending to affright the bystanders. So far, mischief was originally intended; not any particular mischief, but mischief indiscriminate and wanton. Whatever mischief therefore follows, he is the author of it; — Egreditur personam, as the phrase is in criminal cases. And though criminal cases are no rule for civil ones, yet in trespass I think there is an analogy. Every one who does an unlawful act is considered as the doer of all that follows; if done with a deliberate intent, the consequence may amount to murder; if incautiously, to manslaughter; Fost. 261. So too, in 1 Ventr. 295, a person breaking a horse in Lincoln's Inn Fields hurt a man; held, that trespass lay: and, 2 Lev. 172, that it need not be laid scienter. I look upon all that was done subsequent to the original throwing as a continuation of the first force and first act, which will continue till the squib was spent by bursting. And I think that any innocent person removing the danger from himself to another is justifiable; the blame lights upon the first thrower. The new direction and new force flow out of the first force, and are not a new trespass. . . . It has been urged, that the intervention of a free agent will make a difference: but I do not consider Willis and Ryal as free agents in the present case, but acting under a compulsive necessity for their own safety and self-preservation. On these reasons I concur with Brothers Gould and Nares, that the present action is maintainable.

NOTE

Under which writ lies the cause of action? Two complementary ways to determine the boundary line between trespass and case are evident in *Scott*. One method was to hold that trespass lay where the harm was direct, and case where it was consequential. A second method, championed by Nares, J., in *Scott* was to insist that trespass also lies for all harm, direct or consequential, where the defendant's action is unlawful by statute, including one that declares the throwing of a lighted squib a public nuisance. Nares here picked up on similar language that had been adopted by Chief Justice Raymond in Reynolds v. Clarke (the very case in which Fortescue, J., supra at page 110 made his classic distinction. "We must," he warned, "keep up the boundaries of actions, otherwise we shall introduce the utmost confusion: if the act in the first instance be unlawful, trespass will lie but if the act is *prima facie* lawful and the prejudice to another is *not* immediate, but consequential, it must be an action on the case." Reynolds v. Clarke, 92 Eng. Rep. 410 (K.B. 1726). With those words, the plaintiff's action for trespass was dismissed when the defendant fixed a spout in plaintiff's yard from which water leaked, thereby rotting the walls of plaintiff's house. Where the invasion is direct, and the harm is consequential, which action should prevail?

A similar difficulty in choosing the right form arose in the celebrated case of Guille v. Swan, 19 Johns. (N.Y.) 381 (1822). There the defendant Guille flew in a balloon which landed in the garden of the plaintiff Swan. When the balloon landed it dragged for about 30 feet causing damage to Swan's potatoes and radishes. Guille was in a perilous position, and he called out to a workman in Swan's field for help in a voice that could be heard by the crowd assembled at the boundary line. About 200 people came tearing across plaintiff's land causing damage to his vegetables and flowers, for which Swan sued Guille in trespass. Guille defended himself on the ground that he could only be held responsible for the damage that he had caused, not that of the crowd. But Spencer, C.J., was unimpressed with the argument and upheld a jury verdict against Guille for the full $90 in damages.

> The *intent* with which an act is done, is by no means the test of liability of a party to an action of trespass. If the act causes the immediate injury, whether it was intentional or unintentional, trespass is the proper action to redress the wrong. [The court discusses Scott v. Shepherd among other cases, and continues.]
>
> I will not say that ascending in a balloon is an unlawful act, for it is not so; but, it is certain, that the *Aeronaut* has no control over its motion horizontally; he is at the sport of the winds, and is to descend when and how he can; his reach the earth is a matter of hazard. He did descend on the premises of the plaintiff below, at a short distance from the place where he ascended. Now, if his descent, under such circumstances, would, ordinarily and naturally, draw a crowd of people about him, either from curiosity, or for the purpose of rescuing him from a perilous situation; all this he ought to have foreseen, and must be responsible for. Whether the crowd heard him call for help, or not, is immaterial; he had put himself in a situation to invite help, and they rushed forward, impelled, perhaps, by the double motive of rendering aid, and gratifying a curiosity which he had excited. Can it be doubted, that if the plaintiff in error [i.e. defendant-appellant] had beckoned to the crowd to come to his assistance, that he would be liable for their trespass in entering the enclosure? I think not. In that case, they would have been co-trespassers, and we must consider the situation in which he placed himself, voluntarily and designedly, as equivalent to a direct request to the crowd to follow him. In the present case, he did call for help and may have been heard by the crowd; he is, therefore, undoubtedly, liable for all the injury sustained.

In trespass?

3.   The Breakdown of the Forms

The lighted squib in Scott v. Shepherd, and the descending balloon in Guille v. Swan present novel ways to test the theoretical line between trespass and case. Yet their importance for the administration of justice was not likely very great, for it is quite doubtful that the English courts were required to dispose of many cases of lighted squibs or falling balloons. The division between the writs, however, was of crucial importance in the frequent cases involving accidents on the highway or on the high seas that started to come to the courts in great numbers by the 1790s. With respect to these cases, it was impossible as a matter of principle to give any firm or general answer to the question: which writ, trespass or case? The root question was as much practical as theoretical. Even if it were possible to define the line between trespass and case in the abstract, it was never clear to the plaintiff in advance of trial whether his particular cause of action fell on one side of the line or the other. If the plaintiff brought an action in trespass, the defendant could prevail by showing that his horse, which he had outfitted with too-weak reins, had bolted out of control. If the action were in case, the defendant could still prevail, by showing that he had indeed run right over the plaintiff. If running-down accidents were complicated, collisions at sea were even more so. It was always a very delicate question to determine whether a captain had rammed his ship into another ship, or whether the wind or the sea (an act of God) had carried it into the other ship after the defendant had allowed it to become disabled. See, e.g., Ogle v. Barnes, 101 Eng. Reg. 1338 (K.B. 1799).

The situation was further complicated by the twin problems of vicarious liability and joinder of actions. If the plaintiff was run down by a carriage owned by the defendant, should his action be brought in trespass or in case? If it turned out that the carriage was driven by the defendant's servant, it was settled that trespass against the master was not the appropriate action, no matter what action lay against the servant. McManus v. Crickett, 102 Eng. Rep. 580 (K.B. 1800); Sharrod v. London & N.W. Ry., 154 Eng. Rep. 1345 (Ex. 1849). There was no direct and immediate application of force by the defendant; and even if trespass lay against the servant, it could not by any stretch of the imagination lie against the master, who was held accountable, if at all, on principles of vicarious liability. Yet, suppose the original action were brought in case, in order to cover the possibility that the coach had been driven by a servant in the defendant's employ. The plaintiff then ran the risk of nonsuit if the defendant himself had driven the coach. Equally important, the rules governing the joinder of actions prohibited the plaintiff in an accident involving direct harm from suing both the owner and his servant under the same writ: trespass required one form of action and case required quite another. The multiplicity of writs forced the plaintiffs and courts to play an uncertain shell game for the defendant's benefit, since several separate and expensive actions were necessary to guard against all the unhappy possibilities that might emerge at trial.

How could the courts break the logjam? The most obvious proposal was to ignore tradition by allowing a plaintiff to include separate counts of trespass and case within a single writ. That result was achieved by statute by the middle of the nineteenth century (Common Law Procedure Act 15 & 16 Vict., c. 76, §41 (1852)), but the early nineteenth-century English courts were not prepared to introduce so bold a reform by themselves. A second possibility was to bend the rules by allowing the plaintiff to use trespass against the master when the servant caused immediate and direct harm, a proposal that would have eliminated the gamesmanship involved in the joinder of actions. Yet here too the writ tradition resisted judicial innovation.

In the end the courts adopted a third solution. In the watershed case of Williams v. Holland, 131 Eng. Rep. 848 (C.P. 1833), the Court of Common Pleas held that the plaintiff could sue in case, no matter whether the harm was immediate or consequential, as long as the plaintiff could establish that the harm occurred as a result of the defendant's negligence. The writ of trespass could be maintained for all immediate harms, whether willful or negligent, and only trespass would lie in cases of willful and immediate harm. Harms directly and negligently caused could under this rule be remedied in either trespass or case. Under the rule in Williams v. Holland the plaintiff in all but a very few running-down cases would prefer case to trespass because that writ allowed him, first, to avoid having to guess whether harm was immediate or consequential and, second, to join both master and servant in a single suit. Joinder of claims was not possible under the system in Williams v. Holland when the injury inflicted by the servant was both willful and direct, but that limitation was of little consequence since there were few road incidents of that sort. And when these cases did occur, the master was probably not liable. He could defend himself under an early version of the "frolic and detour" doctrine, an exception to the general rule of vicarious liability, applicable to cases of willful wrongs of servants committed outside the course of employment.

The rule in Williams v. Holland was not only important for its procedural consequences; it also had a great bearing on the strict liability/ negligence controversy. In the earlier cases, of which Scott v. Shepherd is but one clear example, there were many intimations that trespass would lie for direct harm caused by the defendant even in the absence of negligence or intent. The system in effect allowed, or so it appeared, actions to be maintained on causal theories alone: You struck my wagon. With the decision in Williams v. Holland, the element of negligence assumed a much more prominent role within the system: it became an essential element for recovery in all highway accident cases, no matter whether direct or consequential damages were involved. The English position was summed up by Bramwell, B., in Holmes v. Mather, L.R. 10 Ex. 261, 268-269 (1875), where, in giving judgment for the defendant, he reviewed the old cases and observed:

> As to the cases cited, most of them are really decisions on the form of action, whether case or trespass. The result of them is this, and it is intelligible enough: if the act that does an injury is an act of direct force vi et armis, trespass is the proper remedy (if there is any remedy) where the act is wrongful, either as being wilful or as being the result of negligence. Where the act is not wrongful for either of these reasons, no action is

maintainable, though trespass would be the proper form of action if it were wrongful.

Even after the general substantive principles were settled in England, some procedural consequences could still be traced to the writ system. In actions framed in trespass the issue of negligence originally came into the lawsuit through the back door via the defense of "inevitable accident." On the other hand, negligence had to be raised by the plaintiff when a case lay under the old forms of action. Under the general rule requiring each party to prove what he pleads, the plaintiff was required to demonstrate the defendant's negligence in cases of indirect harm, but could require the defendant to show that he was free of all fault in cases of direct harm. Stanley v. Powell, [1891] 1 Q.B. 86. Indeed, in England it was only settled in 1959 that the plaintiff must both plead and prove negligence in all actions for unintended personal injury. Fowler v. Lanning, [1959] 1 Q.B. 426. The procedural problems left by the division between the two writs carried over to other areas as well. To give but one example, it took until 1965 to decide that the same three-year statute of limitations applied to all personal injury actions, whether the action was framed in trespass or negligence. Letang v. Cooper, [1965] 1 Q.B. 232.

The story of trespass and case in England is given here in much abbreviated form. For further materials see M. Arnold, Select Cases of Trespass from the King's Courts: 1307-1399 (Seldon Society, vol. 100, 1985); C. H. S. Fifoot, History and Sources of the Common Law, Tort and Contract ch. 9 (1949); A. Harari, The Place of Negligence in the Law of Torts ch. 11 and app. (1962); S. F. C. Milsom, Historical Foundations of the Common Law chs. 11, 13 (2d ed. 1981); M. J. Prichard, Trespass, Case and The Rule in Williams v. Holland, 22 Cambridge L.J. 234 (1964), an excellent article from which much of the account given here is drawn; Gregory, Trespass to Negligence to Absolute Liability, 37 Va. L. Rev. 359 (1951).

D.   STRICT LIABILITY AND NEGLIGENCE IN THE LAST HALF OF THE NINETEENTH CENTURY

Toward the middle of the nineteenth century, the forms of action fell by the wayside in both England and the United States. Just before the English Common Law Procedure Acts of 1852 removed the last vestiges of the forms of action from English law, the widespread adoption of the so-called Field Codes — named after the reformer David Dudley Field, who championed the adoption of "code pleading" in New

York — did the same thing in the United States. See New York, First Report of Commissioners on Practice and Pleading (1848). The purpose of these procedural reforms was simply to abolish the forms of action as procedural devices. "No rule of law, by which rights and wrongs are measured, will be touched, the object and effect of the change being only the removal of old obstructions, in the way of enforcing the rights, and redressing the wrongs." Id. at 146-147. It followed therefore that the legal precedents in tort, both in England and the United States, survived the reformation of the procedural system. With the removal of the forms, the choice between negligence and strict liability was thus inescapably presented in its most general form. See generally C. Clark, Code Pleading (2d ed. 1947).

The emergence of negligence as the dominant standard of civil liability in tort within American law during the first half of the nineteenth century parallels in many important ways the English experience we have already reviewed. At the beginning of the nineteenth century the writ system, with its distinction between trespass and case, was in general use in the United States, and American lawyers had many of the same problems as their English brethren in deciding whether a given action should be brought under one writ or another, as in *Guille*, supra at page 110. Furthermore, negligence was a shadowy concept, with but a secondary position in the tort law. In its primary sense the negligence concept applied to the *nonfeasance* of individuals charged either by contract or statute with a duty of care. Smiths and surgeons were, for example, required by contract to conduct their professions carefully, while jailors and those charged with the maintenance of the public highways were persons on whom statutes placed the duty of care. Negligence, in the sense of carelessness in the performance of some affirmative act which causes harm to a stranger, was not the prevalent conception.

Yet by 1830, with the increase in collision cases, this second concept of negligence received greater attention in the courts; and it was clear that the substantive principles of liability at work would have, one way or another, to be clarified. For the case law of this period see Harvey v. Dunlop (Hill & Den.) 193 (N.Y. 1843); Bridge Co. v. Lehigh Coal & Navigation Co., 4 Rawle 8 (Pa. 1833); Sullivan v. Murphy, 2 Miles 298, 2 Law Rep. 246 (1839). See generally for the account M. Horwitz, The Transformation of American Law: 1780 to 1860, 89-94 (1977).

Brown v. Kendall
60 Mass. 292 (1850)

It appeared in evidence, on the trial, which was before Wells, C.J., in the court of common pleas, that two dogs, belonging to the plaintiff and the defendant, respectively, were fighting in the presence of their masters; that the defendant took a stick about four feet long, and commenced beating the dogs in order to separate them; that the plaintiff was looking on, at the distance of about a rod, and that he advanced a step or two towards the dogs. In their struggle, the dogs approached the place where the plaintiff was standing. The defendant retreated backwards from before the dogs, striking them as he retreated; and as he approached the plaintiff, with his back towards him, in raising his stick over his shoulder, in order to strike the dogs, he accidentally hit the plaintiff in the eye, inflicting upon him a severe injury. . . .

SHAW, C.J. This is an action of trespass, vi et armis, brought by George Brown against George K. Kendall, for an assault and battery; and the original defendant having died pending the action, his executrix has been summoned in. The rule of the common law, by which this action would abate by the death of either party, is reversed in this commonwealth by statute, which provides that actions of trespass for assault and battery shall survive. Rev. Sts. c. 93, §7.

The facts set forth in the bill of exceptions preclude the supposition, that the blow, inflicted by the hand of the defendant upon the person of the plaintiff, was intentional. The whole case proceeds on the assumption, that the damage sustained by the plaintiff, from the stick held by the defendant, was inadvertent and unintentional; and the case involves the question how far, and under what qualifications, the party by whose unconscious act the damage was done is responsible for it. We use the term "unintentional" rather than involuntary, because in some of the cases, it is stated, that the act of holding and using a weapon or instrument, the movement of which is the immediate cause of hurt to another, is a voluntary act, although its particular effect in hitting and hurting another is not within the purpose or intention of the party doing the act.

It appears to us, that some of the confusion in the cases on this subject has grown out of the long-vexed question, under the rule of the common law, whether a party's remedy, where he has one, should be sought in an action of the case, or of trespass. This is very distinguishable from the question, whether in a given case, any action will lie. The result of these cases is, that if the damage complained of is the immediate effect of the act of the defendant, trespass vi et armis lies; if consequential only, and not immediate, case is the proper remedy. . . .

In these discussions, it is frequently stated by judges, that when one receives injury from the direct act of another, trespass will lie. But we think this is said in reference to the question, whether trespass and not case will lie, assuming that the facts are such, that some action will lie. These dicta are no authority, we think, for holding, that damage received by a direct act of force from another will be sufficient to maintain an action of trespass, whether the act was lawful or unlawful, and neither wilful, intentional, nor careless. . . .

We think, as the result of all the authorities, the rule is correctly stated by Mr. Greenleaf, that the plaintiff must come prepared with evidence to show either that the *intention* was unlawful, or that the defendant was *in fault;* for if the injury was unavoidable, and the conduct of the defendant was free from blame, he will not be liable. 2 Greenl. Ev. §§85 to 92; Wakeman v. Robinson, 1 Bing. 213. If, in the prosecution of a lawful act, a casualty purely accidental arises, no action can be supported for an injury arising therefrom. . . . In applying these rules to the present case, we can perceive no reason why the instructions asked for by the defendant ought not to have been given; to this effect, that if both plaintiff and defendant at the time of the blow were using ordinary care, or if at that time the defendant was using ordinary care, and the plaintiff was not, or if at that time, both the plaintiff and defendant were not using ordinary care, then the plaintiff could not recover.

In using this term, ordinary care, it may be proper to state, that what constitutes ordinary care will vary with the circumstances of cases. In general, it means that kind and degree of care, which prudent and cautious men would use, such as is required by the exigency of the case, and such as is necessary to guard against probable danger. A man, who should have occasion to discharge a gun, on an open and extensive marsh, or in a forest, would be required to use less circumspection and care, than if he were to do the same thing in an inhabited town, village, or city. To make an accident, or casualty, or as the law sometimes states it, inevitable accident, it must be such an accident as the defendant could not have avoided by the use of the kind and degree of care necessary to the exigency, and in the circumstances in which he was placed.

We are not aware of any circumstances in this case, requiring a distinction between acts which it was lawful and proper to do, and acts of legal duty. There are cases, undoubtedly, in which officers are bound to act under process, for the legality of which they are not responsible, and perhaps some others in which this distinction would be important. We can have no doubt that the act of the defendant in attempting to part the fighting dogs, one of which was his own, and for the injurious acts of which he might be responsible, was a lawful and proper act, which he might do by proper and safe means. If, then, in doing this act, using due care and all proper precautions necessary to the exigency of the case, to avoid hurt to others, in raising his stick for that purpose, he accidentally hit the plaintiff in his eye, and wounded him, this was the result of pure accident, or was involuntary and unavoidable, and therefore the action would not lie. Or if the defendant was chargeable with some negligence, and if the plaintiff was also chargeable with negligence, we think the plaintiff cannot recover without showing that the damage was caused wholly by the act of the defendant, and that the plaintiff's own negligence did not contribute as an efficient cause to produce it.

The court instructed the jury, that if it was not a necessary act, and the defendant was not in duty bound to part the dogs, but might with propriety interfere or not as he chose, the defendant was responsible for the consequences of the blow, unless it appeared that he was in the exercise of extraordinary care, so that the accident was inevitable, using the word not in a strict but a popular sense. This is to be taken in connection with the charge afterwards given, that if the jury believed, that the act of interference in the fight was unnecessary, (that is, as before explained, not a duty incumbent on the defendant,) then the burden of proving extraordinary care on the part of the defendant, or want of ordinary care on the part of plaintiff, was on the defendant.

The court is of opinion that these directions were not conformable to law. If the act of hitting the plaintiff was unintentional, on the part of the defendant, and done in the doing of a lawful act, then the defendant was not liable, unless it was done in the want of exercise of due care, adapted to the exigency of the case, and therefore such want of due care became part of the plaintiff's case, and the burden of proof was on the plaintiff to establish it. . . .

Perhaps the learned judge, by the use of the term extraordinary care, in the above charge, explained as it is by the context, may have intended nothing more than that increased degree of care and diligence, which the exigency of particular circumstances might require, and which men of ordinary care and prudence would use under like circumstances, to guard against danger. If such was the meaning of this part of the charge, then it does not differ from our views, as above explained. But we are of opinion, that the other part of the charge, that the burden of proof was on the defendant, was incorrect. Those facts which are essential to enable the plaintiff to recover, he takes the burden of proving. The evidence may be offered by the plaintiff or by the defendant; the question of due care, or want of care, may be essentially connected with the main facts, and arise from the same proof; but the effect of the rule, as to the burden of proof, is this, that when the proof is all in, and before the jury, from whatever side it comes, and whether directly proved, or inferred from circumstances, if it appears that the defendant was doing a lawful act, and unintentionally hit and hurt the plaintiff, then unless it also appears to the satisfaction of the jury, that the defendant is chargeable with some fault, negligence, carelessness, or want of prudence, the plaintiff fails to sustain the burden of proof, and is not entitled to recover.

New trial ordered.

NOTE

Negligence and economic growth. The acceptance of the negligence standard in American tort law has been often viewed as a subsidy for the protection of infant industries. See, e.g., Gregory, Trespass, to Negligence, to Absolute Liability, 37 Va. L. Rev. 359 (1951). In recent years the thesis has been advanced by Professor Morton Horwitz in his influential work, The Transformation of American Law, 1780-1860, 99-101 (1977): "One of the most striking aspects of legal change during the antebellum period is the extent to which common law doctrines were transformed to create immunities from legal liability and thereby to provide substantial subsidies for those who undertook schemes of economic development." In his view the efforts to obtain subsidies through legal doctrine instead of through the tax system were designed to "more easily disguise underlying political choices. Subsidy through the tax system by contrast, inevitably involves greater danger of political conflict." In Horwitz's view, more empirical research is needed to compare the effects of taxation (typically low in the nineteenth century) with those attributable to changes in common law rules. "Nevertheless, it does seem fairly clear that the tendency of subsidy through legal change during this period was dramatically to throw the burden of economic development on the weakest and least active elements in the population."

The subsidy thesis itself has been challenged on several counts. Thus it has been observed that "Brown [v. Kendall] itself, after all, did not involve industry; it involved private persons and a dog fight. Rather than simply promoting 'General Motors,' is it not more accurate to say that Chief Judge Shaw saw the change in moral terms as well, as a sound social policy not only for business but for every man?" Roberts, Negligence: Blackstone to Shaw to ?: An Intellectual Escapade in a Tory Vein, 50 Cornell L.Q. 191, 205 (1965). Is it a fair reply to say that Shaw well understood the implications of his decision upon the growth of industry and trade?

More recently, Professor Gary Schwartz has challenged the Horwitz thesis in his article Tort Law and the Economy in Nineteenth-Century America: A Reinterpretation, 90 Yale L.J. 1717 (1981). Schwartz's own reading of the earlier English cases, and particularly the American cases around 1800, indicates that the negligence principle was then operative in many, if not most, instances, so that the widespread adoption of negligence toward the middle of the nineteenth century cannot count as a legal transformation. In addition, Schwartz read and analyzed every nineteenth-century tort case decided in both California and New Hampshire and found no support for the subsidy thesis and no effort by the courts to engage in the "dynamic, utilitarian" calculations that Horwitz attributes to them. Schwartz also noted that it was unlikely that the subsidy question could be kept silent in the face of explicit legislative debate over subsidies to both railroads and canals.

How should the subsidy question be evaluated from a theoretical perspective? Is it possible that some industries were hurt by the rule because they were unable to recover as plaintiffs for the harms inflicted upon them by firms in other industries? For the argument that the manipulation of general common-law tort rules is a poor way to create interest group subsidies, see Epstein, The Social Consequences of Common Law Rules, 95 Harv. L. Rev. 1717 (1982). See also Schwartz, The Character of Early American Tort Law, 36 U.C.L.A. L. Rev. 641 (1989).

The same debate over negligence and strict liability also surfaced in the English cases shortly after *Brown.*

Fletcher v. Rylands
159 Eng. Rep. 737 (Ex. 1865)

[The following statement of facts is taken from the opinion of Blackburn, J., in the intermediate appellate court:

"It appears from the statement in the case, that the plaintiff was damaged by his property being flooded by water, which, without any fault on his part, broke out of a reservoir constructed on the defendants' land by the defendants' orders, and maintained by the defendants.

It appears from the statement in the case, that the coal under the defendants' land had, at some remote period, been worked out; but this was unknown at the time when the defendants gave directions to erect the reservoir, and the water in the reservoir would not have escaped from the defendants' land, and no mischief would have been done to the plaintiff, but for this latent defect in the defendants' subsoil. And it further appears, that the defendants selected competent engineers and contractors to make their reservoir, and themselves personally continued in total ignorance of what we have called the latent defect in the subsoil; but that these persons employed by them in the course of the work became aware of the existence of the ancient shafts filled up with soil, though they did not know or suspect that they were shafts communicating with old workings.

It is found that the defendants, personally, were free from all blame, but that in fact proper care and skill was not used by the persons employed by them, to provide for the sufficiency of the reservoir with reference to these shafts. The consequence was, that the reservoir when filled with water burst into the shafts, the water flowed down through them into the old workings, and thence into the plaintiff's mine, and there did the mischief."

The above statement of facts should be supplemented by a few additional facts drawn from the opinion of Lord Cairns when the case reached the House of Lords. Thus it appeared that (1) the plaintiff had leased his coal mines from the Earl of Wilton; (2) the defendants had constructed their new reservoir upon other land of the Earl of Wilton, with his permission; (3) the reservoir in question was to be used to collect water for the defendants' mill; (4) the defendants had already placed, on their own nearby land, a small reservoir and a mill; (5) the plaintiff in the course of working his mines came across some abandoned shafts and mine passages of unknown origin; and (6) the reservoir burst when it was partially filled with water when one of the vertical shafts beneath it gave way.]

BRAMWELL, B. . . . Now, what is the plaintiff's right? He had the right to work his mines to their extent, leaving no boundary between himself and the next owner. By so doing he subjected himself to all consequences resulting from natural causes, among others, to the influx of all water naturally flowing in. But he had a right to be free from what has been called "foreign" water, that is, water artificially brought or sent to him directly, or indirectly by its being sent to where it would flow to him. The defendants had no right to pour or send water onto the plaintiff's works. Had they done so knowingly it is admitted an action would lie; and that it would if they did it again. That is also proved by the case of Hodgkinson v. Ennor, 4 B. & S. 229 (E.C.L.R. vol. 116). The plaintiff's right then has been infringed; the defendants in causing water to flow to the plaintiff have done that which they had no right to do; what difference in point of law does it make that they have done it unwittingly? I think none, and consequently that the action is maintainable. The plaintiff's case is, you have violated my rights, you have done what you had no right to do, and have done me damage. If the plaintiff has the right I mention, the action is maintainable. If he has it not, it is because his right is only to have his mines free from foreign water by the act of those who know what they are doing. I think this is not so. I know no case of a right so limited. As a rule the knowledge or ignorance of the damage done is immaterial. The burden of proof of this proposition is not on the plaintiff.

I proceed to deal with the arguments the other way. It is said there must be a trespass, a nuisance or negligence. I do not agree. . . . But why is this not a trespass? Wilfulness is not material. . . . Why is it not a nuisance? The nuisance is not in the reservoir, but in the water escaping. . . . [T]he act was lawful, the mischievous consequence is a wrong. Where two carriages come in collision, if there is no negligence in either it is as much the act of the one driver as of the other that they meet. The cases of carriers and innkeepers are really cases of contract, and, though exceptional, furnish no evidence that the general law in matters wholly independent of contract is not what I have stated. The old common law liability for fire, created a liability beyond what I contend for here. . . .

I think, therefore, on the plain ground that the defendants have caused water to flow into the plaintiff's mines which but for their, the defendants', act would not have gone there, this action is maintainable. I think that the defendants' innocence, whatever may be its moral bearing on the case, is immaterial in point of law. But I may as well add, that if the defendants did not know what would happen their agents knew that there were old shafts on their land — knew therefore that they must lead to old workings — knew that those old workings *might* extend in any direction, and consequently knew damage might happen. The defendants surely are as liable as their agents would be — why should not they and the defendants be held to act at their peril? But I own this seems to me rather to enforce the rule, that knowledge and wilfulness are not necessary to make the defendants liable, than to give the plaintiff a separate ground of action.

MARTIN, B. . . . First, I think there was no trespass. In the judgment of my brother Bramwell, to which I shall hereafter refer, he seems to think the act of the defendants was a trespass, but I cannot concur, and I own it seems to me that the cases cited by him, viz., Leame v. Bray, 3 East 593, and Gregory v. Piper, 9 B. & C. 591 (E.C.L.R. vol. 17), prove the contrary. I think the true criterion of trespass is laid down in the judgments in the former case, viz., that to constitute trespass the act doing the damage must be immediate, and that if the damage be mediate or consequential (which I think the present was) it is not a trespass. Secondly, I think there was no nuisance in the ordinary and generally understood meaning of that word, that is to say, something hurtful or injurious to the senses. The making a pond for holding water is a nuisance to no one. The digging a reservoir in a man's own land is a lawful act. It does not appear that there was any embankment, or that the water in the reservoir was ever above the level of the natural surface of the land, and the water escaped from the bottom of the reservoir, and in ordinary course would descend by gravitation into the defendants' own land, and they did not know of the existence of the old workings. To hold the defendants liable would therefore make them insurers against the consequence of a lawful act upon their own land when they had no reason to believe or suspect that any damage was likely to ensue.

No case was cited in which the question has arisen as to real property; but as to personal property the question arises every day, and there is no better established rule of law than that when damage is done to personal property, and even to the person, by collision either upon the road or at sea, there must be negligence in the party doing the damage to render him legally responsible, and if there be no negligence the party sustaining the damage must bear with it. The existence of this rule is proved by the exceptions to it, viz., the cases of the innkeeper and common carrier of goods for hire, who are quasi insurers. These cases are said to be by the custom of the realm, treating them as exceptions from the ordinary rule of law. In the absence of authority to the contrary, I can see no reason why damage to real property should be governed by a different rule or principle than damage to personal property. There is an instance also of damage to real property, when the party causing it was at common law liable upon the custom of the realm as a quasi insurer, viz., the master of a house if a fire had kindled there and consumed the house of another. In such case the master of the house was liable at common law without proof of negligence on his part. This seems to be an exception from the ordinary rule of law, and in my opinion affords an argument that in other cases such as the present there must be negligence to create a liability. For these reasons I think the first question ought to be answered in favour of the defendants. . . .

I have already referred to the judgment of my brother Bramwell, which I have carefully read and considered, but cannot concur in it. I entertain no doubt that if the defendants directly and by their immediate act cast water upon the plaintiff's land it would have been a trespass, and that they would be liable to an action for it. But this they did not do. What they did was this, they dug a reservoir in their own land and put water in it, which, by underground openings of which they were ignorant, escaped into the plaintiff's land. I think this a very different thing from a direct casting of water upon the land, and that the legal liabilities consequent upon it are governed by a different principle. . . .

I still retain the opinion I originally formed. I think . . . that to hold the defendant liable without negligence would be to constitute him an insurer, which, in my opinion, would be contrary to legal analogy and principle.

[Pollock, C.B., after stating that the issue was "one of great difficulty, and therefore of much doubt," wrote a brief opinion agreeing with Martin, B.]

Fletcher v. Rylands
L.R. 1 Ex. 265 (1866)

BLACKBURN, J. . . . The plaintiff, though free from all blame on his part, must bear the loss, unless he can establish that it was the consequence of some default for which the defendants are responsible. The question of law therefore arises, what is the obligation which the law casts on a person who, like the defendants, lawfully brings on his land something which, though harmless whilst it remains there, will naturally do mischief if it escape out of his land. It is agreed on all hands that he must take care to keep in that which he has brought on the land and keeps there, in order that it may not escape and damage his neighbours, but the question arises whether the duty which the law casts upon him, under such circumstances, is an absolute duty to keep it in at his peril, or is, as the majority of the Court of Exchequer have thought, merely a duty to take all reasonable and prudent precautions, in order to keep it in, but no more. If the first be the law, the person who has brought on his land and kept there something dangerous, and failed to keep it in, is responsible for all the natural consequences of its escape. If the second be the limit of his duty, he would not be answerable except on proof of negligence, and consequently would not be answerable for escape arising from any latent defect which ordinary prudence and skill could not detect.

Supposing the second to be the correct view of the law, a further question arises subsidiary to the first, viz., whether the defendants are not so far identified with the contractors whom they employed, as to be responsible for the consequences of their want of care and skill in making the reservoir in fact insufficient with reference to the old shafts, of the existence of which they were aware, though they had not ascertained where the shafts went to.

We think that the true rule of law is, that the person who for his own purposes brings on his lands and collects and keeps there anything likely to do mischief if it escapes, must keep it in at his peril, and, if he does not do so, is prima facie answerable for all the damage which is the natural consequence of its escape. He can excuse himself by shewing that the escape was owing to the plaintiff's default; or perhaps that the escape was the consequence of vis major, or the act of God; but as nothing of this sort exists here, it is unnecessary to inquire what excuse would be sufficient. The general rule, as above stated, seems on principle just. The person whose grass or corn is eaten down by the escaping cattle of his neighbour, or whose mine is flooded by the water from his neighbour's reservoir, or whose cellar is invaded by the filth of his neighbour's privy, or whose habitation is made unhealthy by the fumes and noisome vapours of his neighbour's alkali works, is damnified without any fault of his own; and it seems but reasonable and just that the neighbour, who has brought something on his own property which was not naturally there, harmless to others so long as it is confined to his own property, but which he knows to be mischievous if it gets on his neighbour's, should be obliged to make good the damage which ensues if he does not succeed in confining it to his own property. But for his act in bringing it there no mischief could have accrued, and it seems but just that he should at his peril keep it there so that no mischief may accrue, or answer for the natural and anticipated consequences. And upon authority, this we think is established to be the law whether the things so brought be beasts, or water, or filth, or stenches.

The case that has most commonly occurred, and which is most frequently to be found in the books, is as to the obligation of the owner of cattle which he has brought on his land, to prevent their escaping and doing mischief. The law as to them seems to be perfectly settled from early times; the owner must keep them in at his peril, or he will be answerable for the natural consequences of their escape; that is with regard to tame beasts, for the grass they eat and trample upon, though not for any injury to the person of others, for our ancestors have settled that it is not the general nature of horses to kick, or bulls to gore; but if the owner knows that the beast has a vicious propensity to attack man, he will be answerable for that too. [The opinion then conducts an exhaustive examination of the earlier cases in support of the general proposition, and continues:]

. . . But it was further said by Martin, B., that when damage is done to personal property, or even to the person, by collision, either upon land or at sea, there must be negligence in the party doing the damage to render him legally responsible; and this is no doubt true, and as was pointed out by Mr. Mellish during his argument before us, this is not confined to cases of collision, for there are many cases in which proof of negligence is essential, as for instance, where an unruly horse gets on the footpath of a public street and kills a passenger . . . ; or where a person in a dock is struck by the falling of a bale of cotton which the defendant's servants are lowering . . . ; and many other similar cases may be found. But we think these cases distinguishable from the present. Traffic on the highways, whether by land or sea, cannot be conducted without exposing those whose persons or property are near it to some inevitable risk; and that being so, those who go on the highway, or have their property adjacent to it, may well be held to do so subject to their taking upon themselves the risk of injury from that inevitable danger; and persons who by the licence of the owner pass near the warehouses where goods are being raised or lowered, certainly do so subject to the inevitable risk of accident. In neither case, therefore, can they recover without proof of want of care or skill occasioning the accident; and it is believed that all the cases in which inevitable accident has been held an excuse for what prima facie was a trespass, can be explained on the same principle, viz., that the circumstances were such as to shew that the plaintiff had taken that risk upon himself. But there is no ground for saying that the plaintiff here took upon himself any risk arising from the uses to which the defendants should choose to apply their land. He neither knew what these might be, nor could he in any way control the defendants, or hinder their building what reservoirs they liked, and storing up in them what water they pleased, so long as the defendants succeeded in preventing the water which they there brought from interfering with the plaintiff's property.

The view which we take of the first point renders it unnecessary to consider whether the defendants would or would not be responsible for the want of care and skill in the persons employed by them, under the circumstances stated in the case.

Rylands v. Fletcher
L.R. 3 H.L. 330 (1868)

CAIRNS, L. C. . . . My Lords, the principles on which this case must be determined appear to me to be extremely simple. The Defendants, treating them as the owners or occupiers of the close on which the reservoir was constructed, might lawfully have used that close for any purpose for which it might in the ordinary course of the enjoyment of land be used, and if, in what I may term the natural use of that land, there had been any accumulation of water, either on the surface or underground, and if, by the operation of the laws of nature, that accumulation of water had passed off into the close occupied by the Plaintiff, the Plaintiff could not have complained that that result had taken place. If he had desired to guard himself against it, it would have lain upon him to have done so, by leaving, or by interposing, some barrier between his close and the close of the Defendants in order to have prevented the operation of the law of nature. . . .

On the other hand if the Defendants, not stopping at the natural use of their close, had desired to use it for any purpose which I may term a non-natural use, for the purpose of introducing into the close that which in its natural condition was not in or upon it, for the purpose of introducing water either above or below ground in quantities and in a manner not the result of any work or operation on or under the land, — and if in consequence of their doing so, or in consequence of any imperfection in the mode of their doing so, the water came to escape and to pass off into the close of the Plaintiff, then it appears to me that that which the Defendants were doing they were doing at their own peril and, if in the course of their doing it, the evil arose to which I have referred, the evil, namely, of the escape of the water and its passing away to the close of the Plaintiff and injuring the Plaintiff, then for the consequence of that, in my opinion, the Defendants would be liable. . . .

LORD CRANWORTH. My Lords, I concur with my noble and learned friend in thinking that the rule of law was correctly stated by Mr. Justice Blackburn in delivering the opinion of the Exchequer Chamber. If a person brings, or accumulates, on his land anything which, if it should escape, may cause damage to his neighbour, he does so at his peril. If it does escape, and cause damage, he is responsible, however careful he may have been, and whatever precautions he may have taken to prevent the damage.

In considering whether a Defendant is liable to a Plaintiff for damage which the Plaintiff may have sustained, the question in general is not whether the Defendant has acted with due care and caution, but whether his acts have occasioned the damage. . . . And the doctrine is founded on good sense. For when one person, in managing his own affairs, causes, however innocently, damage to another, it is obviously only just that he should be the party to suffer. He is bound sic uti suo ut non laedat alienum. This is the principle of law applicable to cases like the present, and I do not discover in the authorities which were cited anything conflicting with it.

The doctrine appears to me to be well illustrated by the two modern cases in the Court of Common Pleas. . . . I allude to the two cases of Smith v. Kenrick [137 Eng. Rep. 205 (C.P. 1849)], and Baird v. Williamson [143 Eng. Rep. 831 (C.P. 1863)]. In the former the owner of a coal mine on the higher level worked out the whole of his coal, leaving no barrier between his mine and the mine on the lower level, so that the water percolating through the upper mine flowed into the lower mine, and obstructed the owner of it in getting his coal. It was held that the owner of the lower mine had no ground of complaint. The Defendant, the owner of the upper mine, had a right to remove all his coal. The damage sustained by the Plaintiff was occasioned by the natural flow or percolation of water from the upper strata. There was no obligation on the Defendant to protect the Plaintiff against this. It was his business to erect or leave a sufficient barrier to keep out the water, or to adopt proper means for so conducting the water as that it should not impede him in his workings. The water, in that case, was only left by the Defendant to flow in its natural course.

But in the later case of Baird v. Williamson the Defendant, the owner of the upper mine, did not merely suffer the water to flow through his mine without leaving a barrier between it and the mine below, but in order to work his own mine beneficially he pumped up quantities of water which passed into the Plaintiff's mine in addition to that which would have naturally reached it, and so occasioned him damage. Though this was done without negligence, and in the due working of his own mine, yet he was held to be responsible for the damage so occasioned. It was in consequence of his act, whether skilfully or unskilfully performed, that the Plaintiff had been damaged, and he was therefore held liable for the consequences. The damage in the former case may be treated as having arisen from the act of God; in the latter, from the act of the Defendant.

Applying the principle of these decisions to the case now before the House, I come without hesitation to the conclusion that the judgment of the Exchequer Chamber was right. . . . The Defendants, in order to effect an object of their own, brought on to their land, or on to land which for this purpose may be treated as being theirs, a large accumulated mass of water, and stored it up in a reservoir. The consequence of this was damage to the Plaintiff, and for that damage, however skilfully and carefully the accumulation was made, the Defendants, according to the principles and authorities to which I have adverted, were certainly responsible.

Judgment of the Court of Exchequer Chamber affirmed.

NOTES

1. Rylands v. Fletcher, the forms of action, and common-law precedent. The initial debate between Martin and Bramwell harkens back to the forms of action when it asks whether the harm was immediate or consequential. For them the categorization of the loss was critical to deciding whether proof of negligence was required, as was necessary with actions that formerly would have been on the case. On this question, does it make a difference that the reservoir was not in fact completely filled when its floor gave way? Blackburn, J., sidesteps the disagreement below by treating the harm as consequential, and then applies a strict liability rule to the situation as he describes. Do the earlier precedents on cattle trespass, fire, nuisance, and filth escaping from privies support his decision, or were these all instances of "direct harm"?

The extent to which *Rylands* marks a departure from the earlier law has given rise to a spirited debate. Wigmore's view was that the case was soundly reasoned from its precedents: "Briefly, the [scattered classes of cases] wandered about, unhoused and unshepherded, except for casual attention, in the pathless fields of jurisprudence, until they were met, some thirty years ago, by the master-mind of Mr. Justice Blackburn, who guided them to the safe fold where they have since rested." Wigmore, Responsibility for Tortious Acts: Its History — III, 7 Harv. L. Rev. 441, 454 (1894).

Other writers have been less sure that *Rylands* fit in harmoniously with the overall historical and intellectual structure of the common law. The noted English torts scholar Frederick Pollock wrote of the decision that "carefully prepared as it evidently was, [it] hardly seems to make such grounds clear enough for universal acceptance." See Pollock, Torts 398 (1st ed. 1887). He then continued:

> In part the case is assimilated to that of a nuisance, and in part also, traces are apparent of the formerly prevalent theory that a man's voluntary acts, even when lawful and free of negligence, are prima facie done at his peril, a theory which modern authorities have explicitly rejected. Putting that question aside, one does not see why the policy of the law might not have been satisfied by requiring the defendant to insure diligence in proportion to the manifest risk . . . Id. at 398-99.

Pollock subsequently adopted the suggestion in Thayer, Liability Without Fault, 29 Harv. L. Rev. 801 (1916) that the principle of res ipsa loquitur (infra at Chapter 3. G. 2) "which was hardly developed at the date of Rylands v. Fletcher, would suffice to cover the ground for all useful purposes in a simpler and more rational manner." See F. Pollock, Torts 507 (13th ed. 1929). Holmes, for his part, devoted relatively little attention to Rylands v. Fletcher, which he treated gingerly: "It may even be very much for the public good that the dangerous accumulation should be made (a consideration which might influence the decision in some instances, and differently in others): but as there is a limit to the nicety of an inquiry which is possible in a trial, it may be considered that the safest way to secure care is to throw the risk upon the person who decides what precautions shall be taken." Holmes, The Common Law 117 (1881). Is this point universally true in all negligence cases?

2. Rylands v. Fletcher in historical context. For an exhaustive account of the historical setting of *Rylands,* see Simpson, Legal Liability for Bursting Reservoirs, 13 J. Legal Stud. 209, 244 (1984). Simpson notes that during the nineteenth century dam failures were regarded as major disasters, perhaps as airplane crashes are today. *Rylands* itself followed several major dam failures in England, each of which had resulted in a massive loss of life and property and had prompted major campaigns of private relief to aid accident victims. Simpson also observed the following about nineteenth-century England: "Most large reservoirs (indeed, almost all) had been constructed under special statutory powers, conferred by private and local acts, and it would have been normal to turn to the legislation to determine what Parliament had laid down as to the legal liability of those responsible for them."

The decision in *Rylands* offered an opportunity to impose universal standards on what was a very pressing problem. The opportunity was ignored in practice, however, as the subsequent decisions on tort liability vacillated between negligence and strict liability rules. Simpson's overall evaluation of the situation stresses the point:

> Since 1930 there have been no serious reservoir disasters in Britain, though there exist many ancient dams, some very ill maintained, and in the whole long curious story the only individual in Britain who ever seems actually to have employed the rule in Rylands v. Fletcher to recover damages for a burst reservoir is Thomas Fletcher himself. Where this leaves the great cases of the common law, I leave to the reader. But insofar as the whole story is relevant to the general and much-discussed question of the relationship between the state of the law and economic development, there is perhaps one general moral. To an extent generally underestimated, the mechanism used to regulate enterprises and cope with the problems of rapid industrial and agricultural change was not the common law but the private act of Parliament, and the judges played only a peripheral role in interpreting such legislation. Id. at 263-64.

At one time the decision in *Rylands* was thought to reflect a bias for the landed as against the commercial classes, sort of the reverse story of the Horwitz thesis considered above at page 119. Thus Bohlen wrote: "To such a [landed] class it was inevitable that the right of exclusive possession should appear paramount to its commercial utilitization; to them commerce and manufacture in which they had little or no direct interest, appeared comparatively unimportant." Bohlen, The Rule in Rylands v. Fletcher (pts. 1-3), 59 U. Pa. L. Rev. 298, 373, 423 (1911), reprinted in his Studies on the Law of Tort 369. But his view is generally rejected today, largely after the detailed examination of the backgrounds of the judges revealed that they had no such bias. See Malloy, *Fletcher v. Rylands* — A Reexamination of Juristic Origins, 9 U. Chi. L. Rev. 266 (1941).

3. *"Non-natural use" and acts of third parties.* What importance should be attached to the qualification of "non-natural use" mentioned by Lord Cairns, but not by the other judges in the case? One way to read the term "natural" is in opposition to "artificial" or "man-made." Yet a second way to read it is in opposition to "unreasonable or inappropriate." The second reading appears to have been adopted in Rickards v. Lothian, [1913] A.C. 263, where the defendant owned a business building in which he had installed a lavatory on the fourth floor. One night, after the defendant's caretaker had made his usual tour of inspection, an unknown person entered the building, stuffed the lavatory with "various articles such as nails, penholders, string and soap," and then turned the faucet on all the way. The next morning, the plaintiff discovered that his stock in trade had been damaged, and sued the defendant for his losses. The House of Lords decided the case for the defendant, holding that it did not come within the scope of Rylands v. Fletcher because "the provision of a proper supply of water to the various parts of a house is not only reasonable, but has become, in accordance with modern sanitary views, an almost necessary feature of town life. . . . It would be unreasonable for the law to regard those who install and maintain such a system of supply as doing so at their own peril." Given the condition of the privy before the act of the third party, is it possible to find for the defendant on causal grounds — the independent act of a third party — even if it is decided that this use of a lavatory was in Lord Cairns' sense a non-natural use? Suppose that water had leaked into the plaintiff's premises even though the lavatory had been used in an ordinary manner. Is the defendant liable under the rule of Rylands v. Fletcher? As interpreted in Rickards v. Lothian? Would it make a difference if the defendant had hired competent plumbers to repair the lavatory before the flooding took place? For an excellent critique of the non-natural use requirement of Rylands v. Fletcher see A. Harari, The Place of Negligence in the Law of Torts 157-167 (1962).

4. *Acts of God and the rule in Rylands v. Fletcher.* If the defendant did not pour the water into the plaintiff's mine, how did it get there if not by an act of God? And if there was indeed an act of God, how can

Blackburn avoid passing on the effects of acts of God in his statement of the general rule?

In Nichols v. Marsland, 2 Ex. D. 1 (1876), the plaintiff's land was flooded when the defendant's "ornamental pools" containing large amounts of water broke their banks during an extraordinary rainfall of unanticipated severity. Bramwell, B., found this storm to be an act of God, thus within the exception to Rylands v. Fletcher, and accordingly it affirmed a judgment for the defendant. The court also found that there was no negligence in the construction or maintenance of the pools. And in Carstairs v. Taylor, L.R. 6 Ex. 217 (1871), the plaintiff, a tenant in the defendant's building, was unable to recover when rats ate through a box containing water that was collected by gutters from the roof of the building. Bramwell, B., also noted that, since the box and gutters had been installed for the mutual benefit of both parties, the rule in Rylands v. Fletcher did not apply because the defendant did not bring the water into the structure for his purposes alone.

5. *Rylands v. Fletcher and highway cases.* One of the most pressing issues faced by the judges in Rylands v. Fletcher was to distinguish the question of harms occurring on the highway from those between neighboring landowners. Does either Bramwell or Blackburn explain why the negligence principle does not carry over from highway cases to neighbor or stranger cases? What rule should govern where conduct on the highway causes danger to landowners whose property is adjacent to the public way? Is it possible to say that people assume the risk of accidental injuries while traveling on the highways, but not when they live nearby?

6. *Personal injuries under the rule in Rylands v. Fletcher.* As late as 1947, the House of Lords expressed grave doubts about whether the rule in Rylands v. Fletcher applied to personal injuries. In Read v. J. Lyons & Co., [1947] A.C. 156, Lord MacMillan noted, "Whatever may have been the law of England in early times I am of opinion that, as the law now stands an allegation of negligence is in general essential to the relevancy of an action of reparation for personal injuries." In *Read,* the House of Lords also decided that the plaintiff, who was a government inspector of munitions, could not recover when injured by an explosion in the defendant's plant because there had been no "escape" from defendant's premises as required by the rule in Rylands v. Fletcher. Is this a sensible result? Should the defendant be given judgment on the grounds of assumption of risk? See E. I. du Pont de Nemours & Co. v. Cudd, 176 F.2d 855 (10th Cir. 1949).

7. *Default of plaintiff.* What sorts of conduct might constitute "a default of the plaintiff" to which Blackburn referred in his articulation of the rule? Note that it is a fair implication from Smith v. Kenrick that a plaintiff who removes all the coal up to the boundary of his mine is not in default within the meaning of the rule in Rylands v. Fletcher, even if the coal removed served as a barrier between his own land and that of

the defendant. In Holgate v. Bleazard, [1917] 1 K.B. 443, it was held that the plaintiff was not in default in a case of horse trespass when he had not repaired the fence around his own land as he had covenanted to do with his own landlord. How would the case be decided if the covenant to fence had been made with the defendant? Note too that while cases of plaintiff's default are likely to be unimportant in *Rylands,* the defense could prove relevant if the plaintiff's operation on his own land had removed the support for the defendant's operations.

Brown v. Collins
53 N.H. 442 (1873)

Doe, J. It is agreed that the defendant was in the use of ordinary care and skill in managing his horses, until they were frightened; and that they then became unmanageable, and ran against and broke a post on the plaintiff's land. It is not explicitly stated that the defendant was without actual fault, — that he was not guilty of any malice, or unreasonable unskilfulness or negligence; but it is to be inferred that the fact was so: and we decide the case on that ground. We take the case as one where, without actual fault in the defendant, his horses broke from his control, ran away with him, went upon the plaintiff's land, and did damage there, against the will, intent, and desire of the defendant.

[In the course of its opinion the court discusses the rule in Rylands v. Fletcher, continuing:]

. . . The rule of such cases is applied, by Blackburn, to everything which a man brings on his land, which will, if it escapes, naturally do damage. One result of such a doctrine is, that every one building a fire on his own hearth, for necessary purposes, with the utmost care, does so at the peril, not only of losing his own house, but of being irretrievably ruined if a spark from his chimney starts a conflagration which lays waste the neighborhood. "In conflict with the rule, as laid down in the English cases, is a class of cases in reference to damage from fire communicated from the adjoining premises. Fire, like water or steam, is likely to produce mischief if it escapes and goes beyond control; and yet it has never been held in this country that one building a fire upon his own premises can be made liable if it escapes upon his neighbor's premises, and does him damage without proof of negligence." Losee v. Buchanan, 51 N.Y. 476, 487 (1873).

Everything that a man can bring on his land is capable of escaping, — against his will, and without his fault, with or without assistance, in some form, solid, liquid, or gaseous, changed or unchanged by the transforming processes of nature or art, — and of doing damage after its escape. Moreover, if there is a legal principle that makes a man liable for the natural consequences of the escape of things which he brings on his land, the application of such a principle cannot be limited to those things: it must be applied to all his acts that disturb the original order of creation or, at least, to all things which he undertakes to possess or control anywhere, and which were not used and enjoyed in what is called the natural or primitive condition of mankind, whatever that may have been. This is going back a long way for a standard of legal rights, and adopting an arbitrary test of responsibility that confounds all degrees of danger, pays no heed to the essential elements of actual fault, puts a clog upon natural and reasonably necessary uses of matter, and tends to embarrass and obstruct much of the work which it seems to be man's duty carefully to do. The distinction made by Lord Cairns — Rylands v. Fletcher, L.R. 3 H.L. 330 — between a natural and non-natural use of land, if he meant anything more than the difference between a reasonable use and an unreasonable one, is not established in the law. Even if the arbitrary test were applied only to things which a man brings on his land, it would still recognize the peculiar rights of savage life in a wilderness, ignore the rights growing out of a civilized state of society, and make a distinction not warranted by the enlightened spirit of the common law: it would impose a penalty upon efforts, made in a reasonable, skillful, and careful manner, to rise above a condition of barbarism. It is impossible that legal principle can throw so serious an obstacle in the way of progress and improvement. Natural rights are, in general, legal rights; and the rights of civilization are, in a legal sense, as natural as any others. "Most of the rights of property, as well as of person, in the social state, are not absolute but relative" — Losee v. Buchanan, 51 N.Y. 485; and, if men ever were in any other than the social state, it is neither necessary nor expedient that they should now govern themselves on the theory that they ought to live in some other state. The common law does not usually establish tests of responsibility on any other basis than the propriety of their living in the social state, and the relative and qualified character of the rights incident to that state. . . .

It is not improbable that the rules of liability for damage done by brutes or by fire, found in the early English cases, were introduced, by sacerdotal influence, from what was supposed to be the Roman or the Hebrew law. 7 Am. L. Rev. 652, note; 1 Domat Civil Law (Strahan's translation, 2d ed.) 304, 305, 306, 312, 313; Exodus xxi:28-32, 36; xxii:5, 6, 9. It would not be singular if these rules should be spontaneously produced at a certain period in the life of any community. Where they first appeared is of little consequence in the present inquiry. They were certainly introduced in England at an immature stage of English jurisprudence, and an undeveloped state of agriculture, manufactures, and commerce, when the nation had not settled down to these modern, progressive, industrial pursuits which the spirit of the common law, adapted to all conditions of society, encourages and defends. They were introduced when the development of many of the rational rules now universally recognized as principles of the common law had not been demanded by the growth of intelligence, trade, and productive enterprise, — when the common law had not been set forth in the precedents, as a coherent and logical system on many subjects other than the tenures of real estate. At all events, whatever may be said of the origin of those rules, to extend them, as they were extended in Rylands v. Fletcher, seems to us contrary to the analogies and the general principles of the common law, as now established. To extend them to the present case would be contrary to American authority, as well as to our understanding of legal principles. . . .

Upon the facts stated, taken in the sense in which we understand them, the defendant is entitled to judgment.

NOTE

The reception of Rylands v. Fletcher into American common law. As Brown v. Collins illustrates, initially *Rylands* received a frosty reception in the United States as both Brown v. Collins and Losee v. Buchanan, 51 N.Y. 483, 484-485 (1873) explicitly repudiated *Rylands*. In *Losee* the plaintiff sued for damages that resulted when the defendant's boiler, while being operated with all care and skill, exploded, whereby "it was projected and thrown onto the plaintiff's premises," where it caused damage to the buildings located thereon. The action was denied for the following reasons:

> By becoming a member of civilized society, I am compelled to give up many of my natural rights, but I receive more than a compensation from the surrender by every other man of the same rights, and the security, advantage and protection which the laws give me. So, too, the general rules that I may have the exclusive and undisturbed use and possession of my real estate, and that I must so use my real estate as not to injure my neighbor, are much modified by the exigencies of the social state. We must have factories, machinery, dams, canals and railroads. They are demanded by the manifold wants of mankind, and lay at the basis of all our civilization. If I have any of these upon my lands, and they are not a nuisance and are not so managed as to become such, I am not responsible for any damage they accidentally and unavoidably do my neighbor. He receives his compensation for such damage by the general good, in which he shares, and the right which he has to place the same things upon his lands.

Why does the argument of implicit compensation work only in one direction? Is it a fair response to argue that the greater security that is obtained by a uniform rule of strict liability is the compensation afforded to the defendant which justifies liability in the instant case? For a further expansion of this theme of "reciprocity" see Fletcher, Fairness and Utility in Tort Law, 85 Harv. L. Rev. 537 (1972), at Chapter 8 infra. For its constitutional application when private property is taken by the state for public use, see R. Epstein, Takings ch. 14 (1985). If the argument for reciprocity only argues for consistency of treatment between cases, then how should one choose between the consistent application of the negligence and strict liability rules in disputes between neighbors? On the fate of *Losee* see Spano v. Perini infra at Chapter 8.

In Turner v. Big Lake Oil Co., 96 S.W. 2d 221, 226 (Tex. 1936), the supreme court of Texas rejected the rule of Rylands v. Fletcher on the grounds that its rationale did not apply in Texas, where the storage of water in large cisterns was a "natural" use of the land:

> In Texas we have conditions very different from those which obtain in England. A large portion of Texas is an arid or semi-arid region. West of the 98th meridian of longitude, where the rainfall is approximately 30 inches, the rainfall decreases until finally, in the extreme western part of the State, it is only about 10 inches. This land of decreasing rainfall is the great ranch or livestock region of the state, water for which is stored in thousands of ponds, tanks, and lakes on the surface of the ground. The country is almost without streams and without the storage of water from rainfall in basins constructed for the purpose, or to hold waters pumped from the earth, the great livestock industry of West Texas must perish. No such condition obtains in England. With us the storage of water is a natural or necessary and common use of the land, necessarily within the contemplation of the State and its grantees when grants were made, and obviously the rule announced in Rylands v. Fletcher, predicated upon different conditions, can have no application here.
>
> Again, in England there are no oil wells, no necessity for using surface storage facilities for impounding and evaporating salt waters therefrom. In Texas the situation is different. Texas has many great oil fields, tens of thousands of wells in almost every part of the State. Producing oil is one of our major industries. One of the by-products of oil production is salt water, which must be disposed of without injury to property or the pollution of streams. The construction of basins or ponds to hold this salt water is a necessary part of the oil business.

One way to look at the situation is to ask whether the need for water in Texas should go to the issue of liability for damages caused or to the question of whether the use of water should be regulated or banned by statute or private injunction. Clearly the latter course of action would be disastrous if it required shutting down the operation of the entire oil industry, but it is far from clear that the industry would suffer any major dislocations if the use of water were allowed under a strict liability scheme, so long as the operators of oil rigs are allowed to choose the conditions under which it was stored. See Powell v. Fall, infra at page 136.

In spite of the judicial concerns with the reach of *Rylands,* the case made substantial inroads in the first half of the twentieth century. Writing in 1953, Prosser reviewed the American reception of the rule of Rylands v. Fletcher. He concluded that it had been repudiated by name in 10 to 12 states and adopted in at least 18 to 20. He argued that in general the cases in the states that have refused to apply it have been cases to which the doctrine was not properly applicable. "In other words, the rule of the case was misstated, and as misstated was rejected, in cases in which it had no proper application in the first place." See Prosser, The Principle of *Rylands v. Fletcher,* in Selected Topics on the Law of Torts 135, 149 et seq. (1953).

The recent reception of *Rylands* has been more favorable. The count taken by Prosser and Keeton in 1984 (Torts at 549) reports that only 7 states reject the *Rylands* principle and that 30 now accept it; that balance continues to swing in favor of the decision. Similar results are reported in 3 Harper, James and Gray §14.4. Representative of the recent cases is Clark-Aiken Co. v. Cromwell-Wright Co., 323 N.E.2d 876 (Mass. 1975), where the Supreme Judicial Court of Massachusetts unanimously held, after exhaustive discussion, that the rule of Rylands v. Fletcher applied when the plaintiff's land was flooded by waters that the defendant had stored behind an upstream dam that failed. In his complaint, the plaintiff alleged that "the waters held back by the said dam were dangerous and created a risk of harm to the land and property of the plaintiff."

Powell v. Fall
5 Q.B. 597 (1880)

MELLOR, J. This was an action tried before me at Devizes without a jury. It was brought by the plaintiffs to recover a sum of £53 6s. 8d., in respect of injury done to a rick of hay upon a farm of the plaintiff, John Thomas Powell, adjoining a public highway, and which injury was caused by sparks escaping from the fire of a traction engine belonging to the defendant, which was then being propelled by steam power along the highway. The engine was constructed in conformity with the provisions of 24 & 25 Vict. c.70, and of 28 & 29 Vict. c.83, being the Acts then in force for regulating the use of locomotives on turnpike and other roads.

At the time when the injury was occasioned to the hay stack by the sparks of fire issuing from the defendant's engine, it was not travelling at a greater speed than that prescribed by the Acts referred to, nor was the injury occasioned by any negligence on the part of the defendant's servants conducting or managing the same. . . .

The 13th section of 24 & 25 Vict. c.70, is as follows: "Nothing in this Act contained shall authorize any person to use upon a highway a locomotive engine, which shall be so constructed or used as to cause a public or private nuisance, and every such person so using such engine shall notwithstanding this Act be liable to an indictment or action as the case may be, for such use where, but for the passing of this Act, such indictment or action could be maintained:" and by s.12 of 28 & 29 Vict. c.83, it is enacted that "Nothing in this Act contained shall authorize any person to use a locomotive which may be so constructed or used as to be a public nuisance at common law, and nothing herein contained shall affect the right of any person to recover damages in respect of any injury he may have sustained in consequence of the use of a locomotive." And it was further contended on the part of the plaintiffs that whilst the Acts entitled the defendant to use a locomotive properly constructed on the public highway, yet it never was intended by the legislature to exempt him from liability to damages in respect of any injury sustained by third persons in consequence of the use by him of a locomotive, and that it was wholly immaterial to the result that such injury arose from no want of care or negligence on the part of the defendant's servants in the management and use of the same. On the part of the defendant it was contended that the effect of the several statutes being to authorize the use of locomotives on public highways, if constructed and managed according to the provisions of such statutes, was to exempt the owners from liability to make good any injury arising from the use of locomotives, unless some improper construction of the engine, or some act of negligence in the use of it, could be imputed to such owners or their servants. I am of opinion that the contention on the part of the plaintiffs must prevail.

The principle which governs this case is that established by Fletcher v. Rylands, and affirmed in the House of Lords: Rylands v. Fletcher, which overruled the decision of the majority of the Court of Exchequer, and supported the view taken by Bramwell, B., in that Court. That case, which settled, as I think, the principle, upon which the result of this case depends, is "that when a man brings or uses a thing of a dangerous character on his own land, he must keep it in at his own peril and is liable to the consequences, if it escapes and does injury to his neighbour." . . .

The defendant appealed. . . .

BRAMWELL, L.J. I think that the judgment of Mellor, J., ought to be affirmed. The passing of the engine along the road is confessedly dangerous, inasmuch as sparks cannot be prevented from flying from it. It is conceded that at common law an action may be maintained for the injury suffered by the plaintiffs. The Locomotive Acts are relied upon as affording a defence, but instead of helping the defendant they shew not only that an action would have been maintainable at common law, but also that the right to sue for an injury is carefully preserved. It is just and reasonable that if a person uses a dangerous machine, he should pay for the damage which it occasions; if the reward which he gains for the use of the machine will not pay for the damage, it is mischievous to the public and ought to be suppressed, for the loss ought not to be borne by the community or the injured person. If the use of the machine is profitable, the owner ought to pay compensation for the damage. The plaintiffs are protected by the common law, and nothing adverse to their right to sue can be drawn from the statutes: the statutes do not make it lawful to damage property without paying for the injury. A great deal has been said about the liability of persons who have stored water which has subsequently escaped and done injury, and it has been urged that the emission of sparks from an engine is not so mischievous as the overflow of a large body of water. The arguments which we have heard are ingenious; but I need only say in reply to them that they have hardened my conviction that Rex v. Pease (4 B. & Ad. 30) and Vaughan v. Taff Vale Ry. Co. (5 H. & N. 679 29 L. J. (Ex.) 247) were wrongly decided.

NOTES

1. The impact of statute on common-law liability. Powell v. Fall stands in sharp contrast with the earlier decision in Vaughn v. Taff Vale Ry. Co., 157 Eng. Rep. 1351, 1354 (Ex.1860), disapproved by Bramwell, in which Cockburn, C.J., held that since the defendant operated the railroad under statutory authorization, proof of negligence was required to hold it liable in damages:

> Although it may be true, that if a person keeps an animal of known dangerous propensities, or a dangerous instrument, he will be responsible to those who are thereby injured, independently of any negligence in the mode of dealing with the animal or using the instrument; yet when the legislature has sanctioned and authorized the use of a particular thing, and it is used for the purpose for which it was authorized, and every precaution has been observed to prevent injury, the sanction of the legislature carries with it this consequence, that if damage results from the use of such thing independently of negligence, the party using it is not responsible. . . . It is admitted that the defendants used fire for the purpose of propelling locomotive engines, and no doubt they were bound to take proper precaution to prevent injury to persons through whose lands they passed; but the mere use of fire in such engines does not make them liable for injury resulting from such use without any negligence on their part.

The consequences of a statute upon a private cause of action were also in issue in River Wear Commissioners v. Adamson, L.R. 2 App. Cas.

743, 767 (H.L.(E.) 1877), where the applicable statute provided that "the owner of every vessel . . . shall be answerable to the undertakers [plaintiffs] for any damage done by such vessel . . . and the master or person having charge of such vessel through whose wilful act or negligence any such damage is done, shall also be liable to make good the same." In *Adamson*, the defendant's boat was wrecked in a storm. After the crew abandoned it, it crashed into the plaintiff's dock. An action under the statute was then brought against the owners of the ship. It was held that the owners were not liable without proof of negligence. Lord Blackburn, who wrote Rylands v. Fletcher, concurred saying:

> My Lords, the Common Law is, I think, as follows: — Property adjoining to a spot on which the public have a right to carry on traffic is liable to be injured by that traffic. In this respect there is no difference between a shop, the railings or windows of which may be broken by a carriage on the road, and a pier adjoining to a harbour or a navigable river or the sea, which is liable to be injured by a ship. In either case the owner of the injured property must bear his own loss, unless he can establish that some other person is in fault, and liable to make it good. And he does not establish this against a person merely by shewing that he is owner of the carriage or ship which did the mischief, for the owner incurs no liability merely because he is owner.
>
> But he does establish such a liability against any person who either wilfully did the damage, or neglected that duty which the law casts upon those in charge of a carriage on land, and a ship or a float of timber on water, to take reasonable care and use reasonable skill to prevent it from doing injury, and that this wilfulness or neglect caused the damage.

Is the result consistent with the statute? At common law would the act of God exception under Rylands v. Fletcher apply?

2. *The subsequent history of Powell v. Fall.* "Over the next forty years, Powell v. Fall was repeatedly followed in cases involving traction-engines and steam-rollers which, though driven with due care, had scared horses, crushed water-mains, or started fires." Spencer, Motor-Cars and the Rule in *Rylands v. Fletcher:* A Chapter of Accidents in the History of Law and Motoring, [1983] Cambridge L.J. 65, 70. Spencer nonetheless reports that the decision did not have enough influence to introduce a regime of strict liability back into the law of ordinary highway accidents. Early buses and cars in England were dangerous affairs, with hard rubber tires and thin wheels which made them prone to skidding. Nonetheless the strict liability approach was rejected for skidding buses in Wing v. L.G.O.C., 25 Times L. Rep. 14 (1908), and for ordinary cars in Park v. L.G.O.C., 73 J.P. 283 (1909), even though the early buses and autos were greeted with much public hostility. In part the rationale for these later cases was that cars (but not buses) are not run for profit within the rationale of *Powell.* Id. at 76-77.

Holmes, The Common Law
77-84, 88-96 (1881)

The object of the next two Lectures is to discover whether there is any common ground at the bottom of all liability in tort, and if so, what that ground is. Supposing the attempt to succeed, it will reveal the general principle of civil liability at common law. The liabilities incurred by way of contract are more or less expressly fixed by the agreement of the parties concerned, but those arising from a tort are independent of any previous consent of the wrong-doer to bear the loss occasioned by his act. If A fails to pay a certain sum on a certain day, or to deliver a lecture on a certain night, after having made a binding promise to do so, the damages which he has to pay are recovered in accordance with his consent that some or all of the harms which may be caused by his failure shall fall upon him. But when A assaults or slanders his neighbor, or converts his neighbor's property, he does a harm which he has never consented to bear, and if the law makes him pay for it, the reason for doing so must be found in some general view of the conduct which every one may fairly expect and demand from every other, whether that other has agreed to it or not.

Such a general view is very hard to find. The law did not begin with a theory. It has never worked one out. The point from which it started and that at which I shall try to show that it has arrived, are on different planes. In the progress from one to the other, it is to be expected that its course should not be straight and its direction not always visible. All that can be done is to point out a tendency, and to justify it. The tendency, which is our main concern, is a matter of fact to be gathered from the cases. But the difficulty of showing it is much enhanced by the circumstances that, until lately, the substantive law has been approached only through the categories of the forms of action. Discussions of legislative principle have been darkened by arguments on the limits between trespass and case, or on the scope of a general issue. In place of a theory of tort, we have a theory of trespass. And even within that narrower limit, precedents of the time of the assize and jurata have been applied without a thought of their connection with a long forgotten procedure.

Since the ancient forms of action have disappeared, a broader treatment of the subject ought to be possible. Ignorance is the best of law reformers. People are glad to discuss a question on general principles, when they have forgotten the special knowledge necessary for technical reasoning. But the present willingness to generalize is founded on more than merely negative grounds. The philosophical habit of the day, the frequency of legislation, and the ease with which the law may be changed to meet the opinions and wishes of the public, all make it natural and unavoidable that judges as well as others should openly discuss the legislative principles upon which their decisions must always rest in the end, and should base their judgments upon broad considerations of policy to which the traditions of the bench would hardly have tolerated a reference fifty years ago.

The business of the law of torts is to fix the dividing lines between those cases in which a man is liable for harm which he has done, and those in which he is not. But it cannot enable him to predict with certainty whether a given act under given circumstances will make him liable, because an act will rarely have that effect unless followed by damage, and for the most part, if not always, the consequences of an act are not known, but only guessed at as more or less probable. All the rules that the law can lay down beforehand are rules for determining the conduct which will be followed by liability if it is followed by harm, — that is, the conduct which a man pursues at his peril. The only guide for the future to be drawn from a decision against a defendant in an action of tort is that similar acts, under circumstances which cannot be distinguished except by the result from those of the defendant, are done at the peril of the actor; that if he escapes liability, it is simply because by good fortune no harm comes of his conduct in the particular event.

If, therefore, there is any common ground for all liability in tort, we shall best find it by eliminating the event as it actually turns out, and by considering only the principles on which the peril of his conduct is thrown upon the actor. We are to ask what are the elements, on the defendant's side, which must all be present before liability is possible, and the presence of which will commonly make him liable if damage follows.

The law of torts abounds in moral phraseology. It has much to say of wrongs, of malice, fraud, intent, and negligence. Hence it may naturally be supposed that the risk of a man's conduct is thrown upon him as the result of some moral shortcoming. But while this notion has been entertained, the extreme opposite will be found to have been a far more popular opinion — I mean the notion that a man is answerable for all the consequences of his acts, or, in other words, that he acts at his peril always, and wholly irrespective of the state of his consciousness upon the matter. . . .

As has just been hinted, there are two theories of the common-law liability for unintentional harm. Both of them seem to receive the implied assent of popular textbooks, and neither of them is wanting in plausibility and the semblance of authority.

The first is that of Austin, which is essentially the theory of a criminalist. According to him, the characteristic feature of law, properly so called, is a sanction or detriment threatened and imposed by the sovereign for disobedience to the sovereign's commands. As the greater part of the law only makes a man civilly answerable for breaking it, Austin is compelled to regard the liability to an action as a sanction, or, in other words, as a penalty for disobedience. It follows from this, according to the prevailing views of penal law, that such liability ought only to be based upon personal fault; and Austin accepts that conclusion, with its corollaries, one of which is that negligence means a state of the party's mind. These doctrines will be referred to later, so far as necessary.

The other theory is directly opposed to the foregoing. It seems to be adopted by some of the greatest common-law authorities, and requires serious discussion before it can be set aside in favor of any third opinion which may be maintained. According to this view, broadly stated, under the common law a man *acts* at his peril. It may be held as a sort of setoff, that he is never liable for omissions except in consequence of some duty voluntarily undertaken. But the whole and sufficient ground for such liabilities as he does incur outside the last class is supposed to be that he has voluntarily acted, and that damage has ensued. If the act was voluntary, it is totally immaterial that the detriment which followed from it was neither intended nor due to the negligence of the actor.

In order to do justice to this way of looking at the subject, we must remember that the abolition of the common-law forms of pleading has not changed the rules of substantive law. Hence, although pleaders now generally allege intent or negligence, anything which would formerly have been sufficient to charge a defendant in trespass is still sufficient, notwithstanding the fact that the ancient form of action and declaration has disappeared.

In the first place, it is said, consider generally the protection given by the law to property, both within and outside the limits of the last-named action. If a man crosses his neighbor's boundary by however innocent a mistake, or if his cattle escape into his neighbor's field, he is said to be liable in trespass quare clausum fregit. . . .

Now suppose that, instead of a dealing with the plaintiff's property, the case is that force has proceeded directly from the defendant's body to the plaintiff's body, it is urged that, as the law cannot be less careful of the persons than of the property of its subjects, the only defences possible are similar to those which would have been open to an alleged trespass on land. You may show that there was no trespass by showing that the defendant did no act; as where he was thrown from his horse upon the plaintiff, or where a third person took his hand and struck the plaintiff with it. In such cases the defendant's body is the passive instrument of an external force, and the bodily motion relied on by the plaintiff is not his act at all. So you may show a justification or excuse in the conduct of the plaintiff himself. But if no such excuse is shown, and the defendant has voluntarily acted, he must answer for the consequences, however little intended and however unforeseen. If, for instance, being assaulted by a third person, the defendant lifted his stick and accidentally hit the plaintiff, who was standing behind him, according to this view he is liable, irrespective of any negligence toward the party injured.

The arguments for the doctrine under consideration are, for the most part, drawn from precedent, but it is sometimes supposed to be defensible as theoretically sound. Every man, it is said, has an absolute right to his person, and so forth, free from detriment at the hands of his neighbors. In the cases put, the plaintiff has done nothing; the defendant, on the other hand, has chosen to act. As between the two, the party whose voluntary conduct has caused the damage should suffer, rather than one who has had no share in producing it. . . .

[Holmes then reviews the historical precedents set out in section A and continues.]

In spite, however, of all the arguments which may be urged for the rule that a man acts at his peril, it has been rejected by very eminent courts, even under the old forms of action. In view of this fact, and of the further circumstance that, since the old forms have been abolished, the allegation of negligence has spread from the action on the case to all ordinary declarations in tort which do not allege intent, probably many lawyers would be surprised that any one should think it worth while to go into the present discussion. Such is the natural impression to be derived from daily practice. But even if the doctrine under consideration had no longer any followers, which is not the case, it would be well to have something more than daily practice to sustain our views upon so fundamental a question; as it seems to me at least, the true principle is far from being articulately grasped by all who are interested in it, and can only be arrived at after a careful analysis of what has been thought hitherto. It might be thought enough to cite the decisions opposed to the rule of absolute responsibility, and to show that such a rule is inconsistent with admitted doctrines and sound policy. But we may go further with profit, and inquire whether there are not strong grounds for thinking that the common law has never known such a rule, unless in that period of dry precedent which is so often to be found midway between a creative epoch and a period of solvent philosophical reaction. Conciliating the attention of those who, contrary to most modern practitioners, still adhere to the strict doctrine, by reminding them once more that there are weighty decisions to be cited adverse to it, and that, if they have involved an innovation, the fact that it has been made by such magistrates as Chief Justice Shaw goes far to prove that the change was politic, I think I may assert that a little reflection will show that it was required not only by policy, but by consistency. I will begin with the latter.

The same reasoning which would make a man answerable in trespass for all damage to another by force directly resulting from his own act, irrespective of negligence or intent, would make him answerable in case for the like damage similarly resulting from the act of his servant, in the course of the latter's employment. The discussions of the company's negligence in many railway cases would therefore be wholly out of place, for although, to be sure, there is a contract which would make the company liable for negligence, that contract cannot be taken to diminish any liability which would otherwise exist for a trespass on the part of its employees.

More than this, the same reasoning would make a defendant responsible for all damage, however remote, of which his act could be called the cause. So long, at least, as only physical or irresponsible agencies, however unforeseen, cooperated with the act complained of to produce the result, the argument which would resolve the case of accidentally striking the plaintiff, when lifting a stick in necessary self-defence, adversely to the defendant, would require a decision against him in every case where his act was a factor in the result complained of. The distinction between a direct application of force, and causing damage indirectly, or as a more remote consequence of one's act, although it may determine whether the form of action should be trespass or case, does not touch the theory of responsibility, if that theory be that a man acts at his peril. As was said at the outset, if the strict liability is to be maintained at all, it must be maintained throughout. A principle cannot be stated which would retain the strict liability in trespass while abandoning it in case. It cannot be said that trespass is for acts alone, and case for consequences of those acts. All actions of trespass are for consequences of acts, not for the acts themselves. And some actions of trespass are for consequences more remote from the defendant's act than in other instances where the remedy would be case.

An act is always a voluntary muscular contraction, and nothing else. The chain of physical sequences which it sets in motion or directs to the plaintiff's harm is no part of it, and very generally a long train of such sequences intervenes. An example or two will make this extremely clear.

When a man commits an assault and battery with a pistol, his only act is to contract the muscles of his arm and forefinger in a certain way, but it is the delight of elementary writers to point out what a vast series of physical changes must take place before the harm is done. Suppose that, instead of firing a pistol, he takes up a hose which is discharging water on the sidewalk, and directs it at the plaintiff, he does not even set in motion the physical causes which must cooperate with his act to make a battery. Not only natural causes, but a living being, may intervene between the act and its effect. Gibbons v. Pepper [91 Eng. Rep. 922 (K.B. 1695)], which decided that there was no battery when a man's horse was frightened by accident or a third person and ran away with him, and ran over the plaintiff, takes the distinction that, if the rider by spurring is the cause of the accident, then he is guilty. In Scott v. Shepherd [96 Eng. Rep. 525 (K.B. 1773)], already mentioned, trespass was maintained against one who had thrown a squib into a crowd, where it was tossed from hand to hand in self-defence until it burst and injured the plaintiff. Here even human agencies were a part of the chain between the defendant's act and the result, although they were treated as more or less nearly automatic, in order to arrive at the decision.

Now I repeat, that, if principle requires us to charge a man in trespass when his act has brought force to bear on another through a comparatively short train of intervening causes, in spite of his having used all possible care, it requires the same liability, however numerous and unexpected the events between the act and the result. If running a man down is a trespass when the accident can be referred to the rider's act of spurring, why is it not a tort in every case, as was argued in Vincent v. Stinehour [7 Vt. 62 (1835)], seeing that it can always be referred more remotely to his act of mounting and taking the horse out?

Why is a man not responsible for the consequences of an act innocent in its direct and obvious effects, when those consequences would not have followed but for the intervention of a series of extraordinary, although natural, events? The reason is, that, if the intervening events are of such a kind that no foresight could have been expected to look out for them, the defendant is not to blame for having failed to do so. . . .

But there is no difference in principle between the case where a natural cause or physical factor intervenes after the act in some way not to be foreseen, and turns what seemed innocent to harm, and the case where such a cause or factor intervenes, unknown, at the time; as for the matter of that, it did in the English cases cited. If a man is excused in the one case because he is not to blame, he must be in the other. The difference taken in Gibbons v. Pepper, cited above, is not between results which are and those which are not the consequences of the defendant's acts: it is between consequences which he was bound as a reasonable man to contemplate, and those which he was not. Hard spurring is just so much more likely to lead to harm than merely riding a horse in the street, that the court thought that the defendant would be bound to look out for the consequences of the one, while it would not hold him liable for those resulting merely from the other; because the possibility of being run away with when riding quietly, though familiar, is comparatively slight. If, however, the horse had been unruly, and had been taken into a frequented place for the purpose of being broken, the owner might have been liable, because "it was his fault to bring a wild horse into a place where mischief might probably be done."

To return to the example of the accidental blow with a stick lifted in self-defence, there is no difference between hitting a person standing in one's rear and hitting one who was pushed by a horse within range of the stick just as it was lifted, provided that it was not possible, under the circumstances, in the one case to have known, in the other to have anticipated, the proximity. In either case there is wanting the only element which distinguishes voluntary acts from spasmodic muscular contractions as a ground of liability. In neither of them, that is to say, has there been an opportunity of choice with reference to the consequence complained of, — a chance to guard against the result which has come to pass. A choice which entails a concealed consequence is as to that consequence no choice.

The general principle of our law is that loss from accident must lie where it falls, and this principle is not affected by the fact that a human being is the instrument of misfortune. But relatively to a given human being anything is accident which he could not fairly have been expected to contemplate as possible, and therefore to avoid. In the language of the late Chief Justice Nelson of New York: "No case or principle can be found, or if found can be maintained, subjecting an individual to liability for an act done without fault on his part. . . . All the cases concede that an injury arising from inevitable accident, or, which in law or reason is the same thing, from an act that ordinary human care and foresight are unable to guard against, is but the misfortune of the sufferer, and lays no foundation for legal responsibility." [Harvey v. Dunlop, Lalor 193 (N.Y. Sup. Ct. 1843).] If this were not so, any act would be sufficient, however remote, which set in motion or opened the door for a series of physical sequences ending in damage such as riding the horse, in the case of the runaway, or even coming to a place where one is seized with a fit and strikes the plaintiff in an unconscious spasm. Nay, why need the defendant have acted at all, and why is it not enough that his existence has been at the expense of the plaintiff? The requirement of an act is the requirement that the defendant should have made a choice. But the only possible purpose of introducing this moral element is to make the power of avoiding the evil complained of a condition of liability. There is no such power where the evil cannot be foreseen. Here we reach the argument from policy, and I shall accordingly postpone for a moment the discussion of trespasses upon land, and of conversions, and will take up the liability for cattle separately at a later stage.

A man need not, it is true, do this or that act, — the term *act* implies a choice, — but he must act somehow. Furthermore, the public generally profits by individual activity. As action cannot be avoided, and tends to the public good, there is obviously no policy in throwing the hazard of what is at once desirable and inevitable upon the actor.

The state might conceivably make itself a mutual insurance company against accidents, and distribute the burden of its citizens' mishaps among all its members. There might be a pension for paralytics, and state aid for those who suffered in person or estate from tempest or wild beasts. As between individuals it might adopt the mutual insurance principle *pro tanto,* and divide damages when both were in fault, as in the *rusticum judicium* of the admiralty, or it might throw all loss upon the actor irrespective of fault. The state does none of those things, however, and the prevailing view is that its cumbrous and expensive machinery ought not to be set in motion unless some clear benefit is to be derived from disturbing the status quo. State interference is an evil, where it cannot be shown to be a good. Universal insurance, if desired, can be better and more cheaply accomplished by private enterprise. The undertaking to redistribute losses simply on the ground that they resulted from the defendant's act would not only be open to these objections, but, as it is hoped the preceding discussion has shown, to the still graver one of offending the sense of justice. Unless my act is of a nature to threaten others, unless under the circumstances a prudent man would have foreseen the possibility of harm, it is no more justifiable to make me indemnify my neighbor against the consequences, than to make me do the same thing if I had fallen upon him in a fit, or to compel me to insure him against lightning.

Louisville Ry. Co. v. Sweeney, 163 S.W. 739, 740 (Ky. 1914). The plaintiff was standing in her front yard when she was struck by a gate that had been hit by a telephone pole that had been knocked over by one of defendant's trolley cars, which had jumped the track at a curve on a downgrade. The trial court instructed the jury that the plaintiff was entitled to recover for her injuries even if the defendant had not been negligent. The decision was affirmed on appeal. The court first noted that the principles in the *Squib Case* supra at page 107 governed. It treated the case exactly as if the street car "had itself run against her and had inflicted injury to her upon her own property." It then continued:

> The plaintiff as the owner of her property was entitled to the undisputed possession of it. The entry of the defendant upon it, either by its street car or by the pole which it set in motion, was a trespass. One who trespasses upon another and inflicts an injury, is liable for the injury unless caused by the act of God or produced by causes beyond his control. We have held that one who in blasting throws rocks or other debris upon the land of another, is liable for the injury done irrespective of whether the blasting was negligently done or not, as there is in such a case an actual invasion of another's premises and the act itself is a nuisance. The same principle has been applied to the pollution of air or the abstraction of any portion of the soil, or the casting of anything upon the land in other ways. The same principle must apply here. The plaintiff while standing on her own premises was struck and injured by a force put in motion by the defendant which knocked over the telephone pole and threw it upon her gate, causing the gate to inflict a serious injury upon her. The act was a trespass. The defendant had a right to run its cars in the street, but it had no right to run them upon the plaintiff's property or to throw things out of the street on her property. The doctrine of res ipsa loquitur in case of negligence has no application. The

defendant introduced no evidence to show that the occurrence happened from causes beyond its control or by the act of God. In fact it did
not undertake to explain the occurrence in any way. The court, therefore, properly instructed the jury to find for the plaintiff as above indicated.

NOTE

Trespass to the person and trespass to property. Does *Sweeney* present the
causal complications of the sort envisioned by Holmes in his attack on
strict liability in The Common Law? Note that the decision was overruled in Randall v. Shelton, 293 S.W.2d 559 (Ky. 1956), in favor of the
regime, advocated by Pollock and Thayer, that made negligence part
of the plaintiff's case, but then allowed the plaintiff to use of the doctrine of res ipsa loquitur previously disavowed in *Sweeney.*

The Restatement (Second) of Torts §166 takes the position that accidental entries into land are not actionable except in conjunction with
"abnormally dangerous activities." See also Prosser and Keeton 68,
where it is noted (in support of the negligence rule) that "There is no
great triumph of reason in a rule which makes a street railway, whose
car jumps the track, liable only for negligence to a pedestrian on the
sidewalk, but absolutely liable to the owner of the plate-glass window
behind him." Why did trespass to real property remain a tort of strict
liability after trespass to the person was converted to a tort of negligence?

E.   STRICT LIABILITY AND NEGLIGENCE IN
MODERN TIMES

Stone v. Bolton
[1950] 1 K.B. 201 (C.A.)

[The plaintiff, Bessie Stone, lived on Beckenham Road, a side street
next to a cricket ground. One day, as she had just passed outside the
gate in front of her house, she was struck on the head by a cricket ball
that had been hit from the grounds. The ball was hit by a player on the
visiting team, and by all accounts, was one of the longest balls — travelling about 100 yards before it struck the plaintiff — that had ever been
hit at the grounds during the last 40 years. The cricket ground was
found at trial to be "quite large enough for all practical purposes," even
after it was remodeled in 1910 or 1911 to allow for construction of
Beckenham Road. The field itself was surrounded by a twelve-foot-high

fence or hoarding which, owing to a rise in the ground, was about seventeen feet above the street on the Beckenham Road side. The southern wicket from which the ball was struck was about 78 yards from Beckenham Road fence. Witnesses testified that over a 30-year period about six to ten balls had been hit onto Beckenham Road, and that several others had landed in the garden of one Brownson, whose house was the closest to the cricket grounds of all the houses in the neighborhood. The plaintiff did not sue the batsman or his club but she did sue the home cricket club and all of its members, alleging first that the grounds constituted a public nuisance. A second and separate count was based on common law negligence. The particulars of negligence were that the defendants had placed the cricket pitch too close to Beckenham Road, that they had failed to erect a fence of sufficient height to prevent balls from being hit onto the road, and that they had otherwise failed to insure that cricket balls would not be hit into said road. At trial, Oliver, J., gave judgment to the defendants on both the public nuisance and negligence counts. That judgment was reversed by a two-to-one vote in the Court of Appeal, which held for the plaintiff on the negligence question.]

JENKINS, L.J. . . . The case as regards negligence, therefore, seems to me to resolve itself into the question whether, with the wickets sited as they were, and the fence at the Beckenham Road end as it was, on August 9, 1947, the hitting into Beckenham Road of the ball which struck and injured the plaintiff was the realization of a reasonably foreseeable risk, or was in the nature of an unprecedented occurrence which the defendants could not reasonably have foreseen.

On the evidence this question seems to me to admit of only one answer. Balls had been hit into Beckenham Road before. It is true this had happened only at rare intervals, perhaps no more than six times in thirty seasons. But it was known from practical experience to be an actual possibility in the conditions in which matches were customarily played on the ground from about 1910 onwards, that is to say, with the wickets sited substantially as they were, and the fence at the Beckenham Road end, I gather, exactly as it was as regards height and position on August 9, 1947. What had happened several times before could, as it seems to me, reasonably be expected to happen again sooner or later. It was not likely to happen often, but it was certainly likely to happen again in time. When or how often it would happen again no one could tell, as this would depend on the strength of the batsmen playing on the ground (including visitors about whose capacity the defendants might know nothing) and the efficiency or otherwise of the bowlers. In my opinion, therefore, the hitting out of the ground of the ball which struck and injured the plaintiff was a realization of a reasonably foreseeable risk, which because it could reasonably be foreseen, the defendants were under a duty to prevent.

The defendants had, in fact, done nothing since the rearrangement of the ground on the making of Beckenham Road in or about 1910, whether by heightening the fence (e.g., by means of a screen of wire netting on poles) or by altering the position of the pitch, to guard against the known possibility of balls being hit into Beckenham Road. It follows that, if I have rightly defined the extent of the defendants' duty in this matter, the hitting out of the ground of the ball which injured the plaintiff did involve a breach of that duty for the consequences of which the defendants must be held liable to the plaintiff in damages. . . .

It was also, I think, suggested that no possible precaution would have arrested the flight of this particular ball, so high did it pass over the fence. This seems to me an irrelevant consideration. If cricket cannot be played on a given ground without foreseeable risk of injury to persons outside it, then it is always possible in the last resort to stop using that ground for cricket. The plaintiff in this case might, I apprehend, quite possibly have been killed. I ask myself whether in that event the defendants would have claimed the right to go on as before, because such a thing was unlikely to happen again for several years, though it might happen again on any day on which one of the teams in the match included a strong hitter. No doubt as a practical matter the defendants might decide that the double chance of a ball being hit into the road and finding a human target there was so remote that, rather than go to expense in the way of a wire screen or the like, or worse still abandon the ground, they would run the risk of such an occurrence and meet any ensuing claim for damages if and when it arose. But I fail to see on what principle they can be entitled to require people in Beckenham Road to accept the risk, and, if hit by a ball, put up with the possibly very serious harm done to them as damnum sine injuria, unless able to identify, trace, and successfully sue the particular batsman who made the hit.

Bolton v. Stone
[1951] A.C. 850

[After judgment went against the defendants in the Court of Appeal, they took the case to the House of Lords, which unanimously decided the case in favor of the defendants.]

LORD REID. . . . This case, therefore raises sharply the question what is the nature and extent of the duty of a person who promotes on his land operations which may cause damage to persons on an adjoining highway. Is it that he must not carry out or permit an operation which he knows or ought to know clearly can cause such damage, however improbable that result may be, or is it that he is only bound to take into account the possibility of such damage if such damage is a likely or probable consequence of what he does or permits, or if the risk of damage is such that a reasonable man, careful of the safety of his neighbor, would regard that risk as material? . . .

Counsel for the respondent in this case had to put his case so high as to say that, at least as soon as one ball had been driven into the road in the ordinary course of a match, the appellants could and should have realized that that might happen again and that, if it did, someone might be injured; and that that was enough to put on the appellants a duty to take steps to prevent such an occurrence. If the true test is foreseeability alone I think that must be so. Once a ball has been driven on to a road without there being anything extraordinary to account for the fact, there is clearly a risk that another will follow, and if it does there is clearly a chance, small though it may be, that someone may be injured. On the theory that it is foreseeability alone that matters it would be irrelevant to consider how often a ball might be expected to land in the road and it would not matter whether the road was the busiest street, or the quietest country lane; the only difference between these cases is in the degree of risk.

It would take a good deal to make me believe that the law has departed so far from the standards which guide ordinary careful people in ordinary life. In the crowded conditions of modern life even the most careful person cannot avoid creating some risks and accepting others. What a man must not do, and what I think a careful man tries not to do, is to create a risk which is substantial. Of course there are numerous cases where special circumstances require that a higher standard shall be observed and where that is recognized by the law. But I do not think that this case comes within any such special category. It was argued that this case comes within the principle in Rylands v. Fletcher, but I agree with your Lordships that there is no substance in this argument. In my judgment the test to be applied here is whether the risk of damage to a person on the road was so small that a reasonable man in the position of the appellants, considering the matter from the point of view of safety, would have thought it right to refrain from taking steps to prevent the danger.

In considering that matter I think that it would be right to take into account not only how remote is the chance that a person might be struck but also how serious the consequences are likely to be if a person is struck; but I do not think that it would be right to take into account the difficulty of remedial measures. If cricket cannot be played on a ground without creating a substantial risk, then it should not be played there *at all*. I think that this is in substance the test which Oliver, J., applied in this case. He considered whether the appellants' ground was large enough to be safe for all practical purposes and held that it was. This is a question not of law but of fact and degree. It is not an easy question and it is one on which opinions may well differ. I can only say that having given the whole matter repeated and anxious consideration I find myself unable to decide this question in favour of the respondent. But I think that this case is not far from the borderline. If this appeal is allowed, that does not in my judgment mean that in every case where cricket has been played on a ground for a number of years without accident or complaint those who organize matches there are safe to go on in reliance on past immunity. I would have reached a different conclusion if I had thought that the risk here had been other than extremely small, because I do not think that a reasonable man considering the matter from the point of view of safety would or should disregard any risk unless it is extremely small.

LORD RADCLIFFE. My Lords, I agree that this appeal must be allowed. I agree with regret, because I have much sympathy with the decision that commended itself to the majority of the members of the Court of Appeal. I can see nothing unfair in the appellants being required to compensate the respondent for the serious injury that she has received as a result of the sport that they have organized on their cricket ground at Cheetham Hill. But the law of negligence is concerned less with what is fair than with what is culpable, and I cannot persuade myself that the appellants have been guilty of any culpable act or omission in this case.

. . . [A] breach of duty has taken place if they show the appellants guilty of a failure to take reasonable care to prevent the accident. One may phrase it as "reasonable care" or "ordinary care" or "proper care" — all these phrases are to be found in decisions of authority — but the fact remains that, unless there has been something which a reasonable man would blame as falling beneath the standard of conduct that he would set for himself and require of his neighbour, there has been no breach of legal duty. And here, I think, the respondent's case breaks down. It seems to me that a reasonable man, taking account of the chances against an accident happening, would not have felt himself called upon either to abandon the use of the ground for cricket or to increase the height of his surrounding fences. He would have done what the appellants did: in other words, he would have done nothing. Whether, if the unlikely event of an accident did occur and his play turn to another's hurt, he would have thought it equally proper to offer no more consolation to his victim than the reflection that a social being is not immune from social risks, I do not say, for I do not think that that is a consideration which is relevant to legal liability.

NOTES

1. Negligence, strict and vicarious liability in Bolton v. Stone. The plaintiff in Bolton v. Stone had a choice of suing three possible defendants: the batsman from the visiting team, the visiting team, or the owner of the home team. Should an action lie against the batsman on a theory of strict liability? If so, is the visiting team vicariously liable for the torts of its servants? See infra Chapter 5. Could vicarious liability also be used against the owners of the cricket field, or is it limited to employers? Note that at common law the owner of property was held responsible for fires set on his land by his guests, but not those set by strangers. See the opinion of Markham, J., in Beaulieu v. Finglam infra at page 171.

In the alternative, how should the negligence action against the defendant be evaluated? What is the relevance to this action of the location of the cricket field? The shape of the pitch? The efforts of the home team to get the batsman out? The balls that landed in Brownson's garden? In dealing with the negligence side of this case it is useful to know something about the dominant offensive strategy in cricket, a game in which, unlike baseball, runs are plentiful (a batsman hitting for a century is not uncommon) while outs (of which there are ten per innings) represent major misfortunes for the batting team. The astute batsman therefore will normally try to keep the ball on the ground, knowing that if it crosses the boundary at the edge of the field, he will get four runs. Hitting the ball out of the field on a fly is worth only six runs, and carries with it a substantial risk of being caught, which is why skilled batsmen learn to keep the ball on the ground. How does knowledge of the game influence the analysis of the negligence issue?

2. *Aftermath of Bolton v. Stone.* Bolton v. Stone is one of those rare torts cases that received a good deal of public attention after its adjudication. When the defendants prevailed in the House of Lords, it was thought by some that strict legal principle had yielded to the love of cricket in the House of Lords. Professor Goodhart's note on the case was entitled "Is It Cricket?" 67 Law Q. Rev. 460 (1951), while Dennis Lloyd, a legal commentator on the case, doubted whether the outcome would have been the same "[i]f it had not involved an accident arising out of . . . a highly meritorious national pastime." Case note, 14 Mod. L. Rev. 499, 499-500 (1951). Perhaps in response to the public concern with the case ("outrage" is too strong a term), the Cricket Clubs in England that supported defendants' appeal to the House of Lords wrote to the editor of the Law Quarterly Review that they "have done everything that they can to see that Stone does not suffer financially. In fact, so far as they are concerned, she has been left in possession of the damages originally awarded." Note, 68 Law Q. Rev. 3 (1952). Indeed, the defendants did not even demand that Stone pay their costs of £3,000, as she was obliged to do under the English system of costs.

In an effort to explain the dissonance between the legal rule and the social practice, resort has been made to the notion of "ethical compensation," first advanced by Glanville Williams in The Aims of the Law of Tort, 4 Current Legal Probs. 137 (1951). Thus Salmond on Torts 30

(13th ed. 1961) notes that "one who is under no legal liability for damage caused to another may yet think it right and proper to offer some measure of compensation." Is there any need for the principle of ethical compensation under a theory of strict liability? Any way to account for the divergence between the legal and the moral duty? For an excellent criticism of Bolton v. Stone see A. Harari, The Place of Negligence in the Law of Torts 170-179 (1962).

3. *Corrective justice and Bolton v. Stone.* Bolton v. Stone raises important questions about the proper theoretical orientation to tort law. One possible way to look at cases is to determine the original entitlements of both parties to a dispute and then ask whether the actions of the defendant are such as to demand *rectification* or *redress* by the legal system. This approach — which often goes under the name "corrective justice" — presupposes that there is a preexisting set of entitlements, the violations of which the law must undo solely as a matter of fairness between the parties to the case. That set of entitlements is usually thought to include exclusive control over a person's own body (as the references to personal integrity in Mohr v. Williams, supra page 12 suggest), and the exclusive control over external things, which, at least at common law, are acquired by original (i.e., first) possession of previously unowned things or voluntary transfer of things already reduced to ownership. See Epstein, Possession as the Root of Title, 13 Ga. L. Rev. 1221 (1979), and for a theoretical account, R. Nozick, Anarchy, State, and Utopia ch. 7 (1974).

Violations of the rights so acquired are usually (but not exclusively) understood in terms of physical invasions. In Bolton v. Stone, the prima facie causal case against the batsman is simply "he hit me." The significance of this causal paradigm has been defended in Epstein, A Theory of Strict Liability, 2 J. Legal Stud. 151, 168-169 (1973):

> Once this simple causal paradigm is accepted, its relationship to the question of responsibility for the harm so caused must be clarified. Briefly put, the argument is that proof of the proposition *A hit B* should be sufficient to establish a prima facie case of liability. I do not argue that proof of causation is equivalent to a conclusive demonstration of responsibility. Both the modern and classical systems of law are based upon the development of prima facie cases and defenses thereto. They differ not in their use of presumptions but in the elements needed to create the initial presumption in favor of the plaintiff. The doctrine of strict liability holds that proof that the defendant caused harm creates that presumption because proof of the non-reciprocal source of the harm is sufficient to upset the balance where one person must win and the other must lose. There is no room to consider, as part of the prima facie case, allegations that the defendant intended to harm the plaintiff, or could have avoided the harm he caused by the use of reasonable care. The choice is plaintiff or defendant, and the analysis of causation is the tool which, prima facie, fastens responsibility upon the defendant. Indeed for most persons, the difficult question is often not whether these causal assertions create the presumption, but whether there are in fact

any means to distinguish between causation and responsibility, so close is the connection between what a man does and what he is answerable for.

The corrective justice principle has also been invoked to support the principle of negligence. In this context, the argument is usually that the plaintiff cannot expect the defendant to conform to any higher standard of conduct than the plaintiff could demand of himself. If, therefore, the plaintiff cannot identify any flaw in the defendant's conduct, he cannot characterize that conduct as *wrongful* and therefore cannot be entitled to recovery. Thus it is said "corrective justice requires annulling a departure from the preexisting distribution of money or honors in accordance with merit, but only when the departure is the result of *an act of injustice,* causing injury." Posner, The Concept of Corrective Justice in Recent Theories of Tort Law, 10 J. Legal Stud. 187, 200 (1981). The same idea is expressed by Glanville Williams in The Aims of the Law of Tort, 4 Current Legal Probs. 137, 151 (1951):

> Finally there is the compensatory or reparative theory, according to which one who has caused injury to another must make good the damage whether he was at fault or not. This is the same as the theory of ethical compensation except that it does not require culpability on the part of the defendant. If valid, it justifies strict liability, which the theory of ethical compensation does not. The difficulty is, however, to state it in such a form as to make it acceptable. If it is said that a person who has been damaged by another ought to be compensated, we readily assent, moved as we are by sympathy for the victim's loss. But what has to be shown is not merely that the sufferer ought to be compensated, but that he ought to be compensated by the defendant. In the absence of any moral blame of the defendant, how is this demonstration possible?

There is an alternative account of wrongful conduct which ties into the system of pleadings outlined by Arnold supra at 97, and which stresses the difference between a system of strict and absolute liability. For these purposes, absolute liability refers to a legal system that treats causation of plaintiff's harm by defendant's acts as the *only* question relevant to liability. Once causation is established, a system of absolute liability has no room for any excuses or justifications. Strict liability starts with the same prima facie case, and rules out all defenses based on defendant's having taken due care, but it still allows other defenses based, for example, on plaintiff's misconduct or inevitable accident, narrowly construed. A system of absolute liability may be inconsistent with the norms of corrective justice, but a system of strict liability allows the element of wrongfulness to be explicated, not in terms of negligence or intention, but in terms of these other substantive defenses.

The debate on corrective justice continues apace. One important variation of the question is whether the principle of corrective justice requires that the compensation for the plaintiff's injury be made by the defendant, or whether it is an obligation that might be discharged by payments from some social fund? For a look at this view of the world see Jules Coleman, Risks and Wrongs (1992). For an overview of the recent literature on corrective justice see Symposium: Corrective Justice and Formalism: The Care One Owes One's Neighbors, 77 Iowa L. Rev. 403-865 (1992), with articles by Ernest J. Weinrib, Jules L. Coleman, Stephen R. Perry, Peter Benson, and Richard W. Wright.

4. *Economic efficiency as an alternative to corrective justice.* Not all accounts of modern tort law regard corrective justice as the touchstone of liability, and much of modern tort scholarship has sought to develop alternative economic accounts of the tort system. One early notable explication of an economic approach is contained in Calabresi and Melamed, Property Rules, Liability Rules and Inalienability: One View of the Cathedral, 85 Harv. L. Rev. 1089, 1093-1094 (1972):

> Perhaps the simplest reason for a particular entitlement is to minimize the administrative costs of enforcement. This was the reason Holmes gave for letting the costs lie where they fall in accidents unless some clear societal benefit is achieved by shifting them. By itself this reason will never justify any result except that of letting the stronger win, for obviously that result minimizes enforcement costs. Nevertheless, administrative efficiency may be relevant to choosing entitlements when other reasons are taken into account. This may occur when the reasons accepted are indifferent between conflicting entitlements and one entitlement is cheaper to enforce than the others. It may also occur when the reasons are not indifferent but lead us only slightly to prefer one over another and the first is considerably more expensive to enforce than the second.
>
> But administrative efficiency is just one aspect of the broader concept of economic efficiency. Economic efficiency asks that we choose the set of entitlements which would lead to that allocation of resources which could not be improved in the sense that a further change would not so improve the condition of those who gained by it that they could compensate those who lost from it and still be better off than before. This is often called Pareto optimality. To give two examples, economic efficiency asks for that combination of entitlements to engage in risky activities and to be free from harm from risky activities which will most likely lead to the lowest sum of accident costs and of costs of avoiding accidents. It asks for that form of property, private or communal, which leads to the highest product for the effort of producing.

Transaction costs, i.e., the costs involved in establishing and enforcing both property rights and contractual arrangements, are critical to the economic analysis. If these could be held to zero, the initial distribution of rights would be of little economic consequence, as private parties could, through repeated, costless, and instantaneous transactions, move resources to their highest value use. The end use of any resource would be the same regardless of who was its original owner, so that decisions about property rights would only effect their initial distribution, but not their final allocation. See Coase, The Problem of Social Cost, 3 J.L. & Econ. 1 (1960), for the initial elaboration of what is today known as the Coase theorem. In all real world situations, however, transaction costs are positive, if not prohibitive. In consensual situations the high costs of transacting can be reduced when either courts or legislatures announce standard "gap-filling" terms for matters on which the parties are silent. In tort cases between strangers, however, voluntary transactions are typically unattainable. The tort rule therefore cannot be displaced before harm occurs, and will therefore govern liability afterwards. What factors should be taken into account in order to fashion the ideal liability rule where there are high transaction costs? The response given by Calabresi and Melamed, supra at 1096-1097, drawing heavily upon Calabresi's book The Costs of Accidents (1970), was summarized as follows:

> (1) that economic efficiency standing alone would dictate that set of entitlements which favors knowledgeable choices between social benefits and the social costs of obtaining them, and between social costs and the social costs of avoiding them; (2) that this implies, in the absence of certainty as to whether a benefit is worth its costs to society, that the cost should be put on the party or activity best located to make such a cost-benefit analysis; (3) that in particular contexts like accidents or pollution this suggests putting costs on the party or activity which can most cheaply avoid them; (4) that in the absence of certainty as to who that party or activity is, the costs should be put on the party or activity which can with the lowest transaction costs act in the market to correct an error in entitlements by inducing the party who can avoid social costs most cheaply to do so; and (5) that since we are in an area where by hypothesis markets do not work perfectly — there are transaction costs — a decision will often have to be made on whether market transactions or collective fiat is most likely to bring us closer to the Pareto optimal result the "perfect" market would reach.

How does one determine which party is "best located to make a cost-benefit analysis" if the parties to the accident are not identified before the accident occurs? What should be done if the defendant has greater information about the possibility of harm being caused to another, but the plaintiff has greater information about the likely extent of the harm? What result does the Calabresian analysis suggest for the case of the extrasensitive plaintiff? For Bolton v. Stone? For the other cases in this chapter?

Hammontree v. Jenner
97 Cal. Rptr. 739 (Cal. App. 1971)

LILLIE, J. Plaintiffs Maxine Hammontree and her husband sued defendant for personal injuries and property damage arising out of an automobile accident. The cause was tried to a jury. Plaintiffs appeal from judgment entered on a jury verdict returned against them and in favor of defendant.

The evidence shows that on the afternoon of April 25, 1967, defendant was driving his 1959 Chevrolet home from work; at the same time plaintiff Maxine Hammontree was working in a bicycle shop owned and operated by her and her husband; without warning defendant's car crashed through the wall of the shop, struck Maxine and caused personal injuries and damage to the shop.

Defendant claimed he became unconscious during an epileptic seizure losing control of his car. He did not recall the accident but his last recollection before it, was leaving a stop light after his last stop, and his first recollection after the accident was being taken out of his car in plaintiffs' shop. Defendant testified he has a medical history of epilepsy and knows of no other reason for his loss of consciousness except an epileptic seizure. [The defendant first learned of his epileptic condition in 1952 and from that time until his accident, he was under the constant care of a neurologist who treated him first with dilantin and then with phelantin. The defendant's last seizure was in 1953, and from that time forward he had no trouble at all. His physician testified that he had seen the defendant on a regular basis over the years and that at all times he was "doing normally." He further testified that he believed that it was "safe" for the defendant to drive with the medication, even though it was impossible for the defendant to drive during a seizure.]

In 1955 or 1956 the Department of Motor Vehicles was advised that defendant was an epileptic and placed him on probation under which every six months he had to report to the doctor who was required to advise it in writing of defendant's condition. In 1960 his probation was changed to a once-a-year report. . . .

Appellants' contentions that the trial court erred in refusing to grant their motion for summary judgment on the issue of liability and their motion for directed verdict on the pleadings and counsel's opening argument are answered by the disposition of their third claim that the trial court committed prejudicial error in refusing to give their jury instruction on absolute liability.[1]

Under the present state of the law found in appellate authorities beginning with Waters v. Pacific Coast Dairy, Inc., [131 P.2d 588]

---

1. "When the evidence shows that a driver of a motor vehicle on a public street or highway loses his ability to safely operate and control such vehicle because of some seizure or health failure, that driver is nevertheless legally liable for all injuries and property damage which an innocent person may suffer as a proximate result of the defendant's inability to so control or operate his motor vehicle.

"This is true even if you find the defendant driver had no warning of any such impending seizure or health failure."

(driver rendered unconscious from sharp pain in left arm and shoulder) through Ford v. Carew & English, [200 P.2d 828] (fainting spells from strained heart muscles), Zabunoff v. Walker, [13 Cal. Rptr. 463] (sudden sneeze), and Tannyhill v. Pacific Motor Trans. Co., [38 Cal. Rptr. 774] (heart attack), the trial judge properly refused the instruction. The foregoing cases generally hold that liability of a driver, suddenly stricken by an illness rendering him unconscious, for injury resulting from an accident occurring during that time rests on principles of negligence. However, herein during the trial plaintiffs withdrew their claim of negligence and, after both parties rested and before jury argument, objected to the giving of any instructions on negligence electing to stand solely on the theory of absolute liability. The objection was overruled and the court refused plaintiffs' requested instruction after which plaintiffs waived both opening and closing jury arguments. Defendant argued the cause to the jury after which the judge read a series of negligence instructions and, on his own motion, BAJI [Book of Approved Jury Instructions] 4.02 (res ipsa loquitur).

Appellants seek to have this court override the established law of this state which is dispositive of the issue before us as outmoded in today's social and economic structure, particularly in the light of the now recognized principles imposing liability upon the manufacturer, retailer and all distributive and vending elements and activities which bring a product to the consumer to his injury, on the basis of strict liability in tort expressed first in Justice Traynor's concurring opinion in Escola v. Coca Cola Bottling Co., [150 P.2d 436 (Cal. 1944)]; and then in Greenman v. Yuba Power Products, Inc., [377 P.2d 897 (Cal. 1963)]; Vandermark v. Ford Motor Co., [391 P.2d 168 (Cal. 1964)]; and Elmore v. American Motors Corp., [451 P.2d 84 (Cal. 1969)]. These authorities hold that "A manufacturer [or retailer] is strictly liable in tort when an article he places on the market, knowing that it is to be used without inspection for defects, proves to have a defect that causes injury to a human being." (Greenman v. Yuba Power Products, Inc., supra) Drawing a parallel with these products liability cases, appellants argue, with some degree of logic, that only the driver affected by a physical condition which could suddenly render him unconscious and who is aware of that condition can anticipate the hazards and foresee the dangers involved in his operation of a motor vehicle, and that the liability of those who by reason of seizure or heart failure or some other physical condition lose the ability to safely operate and control a motor vehicle resulting in injury to an innocent person should be predicated on strict liability.

We decline to superimpose the absolute liability of products liability cases upon drivers under the circumstances here. The theory on which those cases are predicated is that manufacturers, retailers and distributors of products are engaged in the business of distributing goods to the public and are an integral part of the over-all producing and marketing enterprise that should bear the cost of injuries from defective parts. . . . This policy hardly applies here and it is not enough to simply say, as do appellants, that the insurance carriers should be the ones to bear the cost of injuries to innocent victims on a strict liability basis. In Maloney v. Rath, [445 P.2d 513 (Cal. 1968)], followed by Clark v. Dziabas, [445 P.2d 517 (Cal. 1968)], appellant urged that defendant's violation of a safety provision (defective brakes) of the Vehicle Code makes the violator strictly liable for damages caused by the violation. While reversing the judgment for defendant upon another ground, the California Supreme Court refused to apply the doctrine of strict liability to automobile drivers. The situation involved two users of the highway but the problems of fixing responsibility under a system of strict liability are as complicated in the instant case as those in Maloney v. Rath, and could only create uncertainty in the area of its concern. As stated in *Maloney*, at page 446: "To invoke a rule of strict liability on users of the streets and highways, however, without also establishing in substantial detail how the new rule should operate would only contribute confusion to the automobile accident problem. Settlement and claims adjustment procedures would become chaotic until the new rules were worked out on a case-by-case basis, and the hardships of delayed compensation would be seriously intensified. Only the Legislature, if it deems it wise to do so, can avoid such difficulties by enacting a comprehensive plan for the compensation of automobile accident victims in place of or in addition to the law of negligence."

The instruction tendered by appellants was properly refused for still another reason. Even assuming the merit of appellants' position under the facts of this case in which defendant knew he had a history of epilepsy, previously had suffered seizures and at the time of the accident was attempting to control the condition by medication, the instruction does not except from its ambit the driver who suddenly is stricken by an illness or physical condition which he had no reason whatever to anticipate and of which he had no prior knowledge.

The judgment is affirmed.

Wood, P.J., and Thompson, J. concurred.

Appellants' petition for a hearing by the Supreme Court was denied December 16, 1971.

Helling v. Carey
519 P.2d 981 (Wash. 1974)

[See text of opinions at page 225 infra.]

R. Keeton and J. O'Connell, Basic Protection
for the Traffic Victim
242 (1965)

It is often stated that the principal objective of tort law, and of any automobile claims system, is to compensate for loss. More precisely, however, the objective is to determine whether to compensate, and if so, how. Tort law prescribes the negative of compensation — the circumstances under which compensation will not be awarded — as well as the affirmative. Underlying the whole body of tort law is an awareness that the need for compensation, alone, is not a sufficient basis for an award. When a plaintiff receives a defendant's payment in satisfaction of a judgment obtained in court, loss is not compensated in the sense that it is somehow made to disappear. It is only shifted: To the extent that the plaintiff gains, the defendant loses. Moreover, the machinery for adjudicating whether and how loss is to be shifted is provided at considerable economic cost to the community and to the parties. To the costs of courts to society and the costs of lawyers to the parties must be added others less tangible and direct; for example, the costs of missing work to testify in court, the discomfiture and even agony of recreating the accident at the trial, and the anger and frustration of a courtroom fight. When loss is shifted by way of an award, these costs of adjudication, tangible and intangible, produce a net loss from an overall point of view unless advantages outweighing them are realized.

From a recognition of this truth emerges a basic principle underlying both tort law generally and that segment of tort law concerned with automobile cases: An award is not to be made unless there exists some reason other than the mere need of the victim for compensation. Otherwise, the award will be an arbitrary shifting of loss from one person to another at a net loss to society due to the economic and sociological costs of adjudication.

NOTE

Why the choice between negligence and strict liability is so difficult. The excerpt from Keeton and O'Connell suggests one set of reasons why the common-law courts have struggled with such enormous difficulty in deciding whether to adopt a rule of negligence or strict liability. Their major point is that all litigation is expensive, so that there must be some social gain to justify the manifest social cost incurred. Compensation of the plaintiff, taken alone, fails to achieve that goal, as long as first-party insurance is available in some ready market. Each person can then choose the level of coverage that he or she desires, based upon an intimate knowledge of personal needs and circumstances that no tort defendant could ever obtain. The natural bias for first-party coverage therefore must be overcome by some powerful justification. What is it?

Since compensation as such cannot supply that justification, the arguments for tort liability tend to rest on the need to fashion incentives that reduce the costs of accidents, given the costs of their prevention. Those liability rules seem unproblematic when the defendant's conduct is negligent, for a tort damage rule appears to work unambiguously to create incentives to avoid costs that exceed the benefits that they generate. But the correct incentive arguments are not so evident where the defendant has taken all the steps needed to satisfy the optimum level of care. To see why, it is useful to regard the optimal level of care as the same amount of care that he would have taken if he himself were the only person at risk for property damage or bodily injury. At this point single individuals would prefer suffering the consequences of some accidents to bearing the greater costs of avoiding them.

A liability suit only arises because the plaintiff and defendant are separate parties. At this point intuitions run in two contrary directions. One impulse is that liability should be imposed to make the defendant internalize the costs imposed upon others. The stress is on making the actor bear the costs that he would incur if he were the sole owner. The rival impulse is to dismiss plaintiff's suit because the defendant has acted just as the plaintiff would (and should) have under the same circumstances. The objective is now to make the defendant take the same level of precaution that he or she would have taken as a sole owner. The strict liability theory is preoccupied by making defendant bear losses inflicted on others; the negligence theory, with imposing liability only when needed to alter basic behavior. How then to choose between them?

One approach rests on considerations of reciprocity of the sort advanced in *Losee* supra at page 134. But these arguments cut with equal force in both directions, for the norm of reciprocity is consistent with any general system, whether of negligence or strict liability. The incentive effects of the two rules are the same when viewed from the "ex ante" perspective (that is, before the harm) and it is difficult to identify any systematic distributional consequences that flow from the choice of liability rules. This stalemate tends to make administrative costs the deciding factor in the debate. Yet again the relevant considerations tug in both directions. The strict liability rule eliminates the need to make a nice determination of the standard of care. But the negligence rule generates fewer suits (since plaintiff must do more to win), albeit of greater complexity. The trade-off between these two effects rests on empirical judgments about their relative magnitude. This inquiry takes us a long way from principles of fundamental fairness that have been invoked *both* ways to resolve the controversy. Yet if this trade-off shapes the strict liability/negligence debate, then it is easy to see why a consensus has been so slow in developing. While the choice of rule could have enormous impact in deciding specific cases, the overall social consequences of the choice are less important than first meet the eye. And if this is so, then there is good reason why both rules provide workable foundations for the tort law.

Chapter Three
The Negligence Issue

Thayer, Public Wrong and Private Action
27 Harv. L. Rev. 317, 318 (1914)

In the law of negligence no doctrine is useful or appropriate which cannot be plainly and simply stated, and which, when so stated, does not respond to the test of common sense.

L. Green, Judge and Jury
185 (1930)

In other words, we may have a process for passing judgment in negligence cases, but practically no "law of negligence" beyond the process itself.

A. INTRODUCTION

The long debate between negligence and strict liability, which was the subject of the last chapter, has not yet come to its final resting place. It is clear, however, that the negligence principle has an important — many would say dominant — place to play in the law governing unintentional torts. It is therefore necessary to explore how the negligence principle operates as a *limitation* on a defendant's liability in both theory and practice. This chapter begins with a detailed examination of the negligence standard and the problems of proof that it presents. But before beginning that inquiry, it is useful to draw an important distinction between simple negligence, the failure to take reasonable care, and legal negligence, a tort that generates civil liability. In its modern elaboration, the tort of negligence contains four distinct elements: duty, breach, causation and damage. Thus stated a plaintiff must be able to answer four questions in the affirmative in order to prevail.

First, *duty:* did the defendant owe the plaintiff a duty to conform his conduct to a standard necessary to avoid an unreasonable risk of harm to others?

Second, *breach:* did the defendant's conduct, whether by way of act or omission, fall below the applicable standard of care set by law?

Third, *causation:* was the defendant's failure to meet the applicable standard of care causally connected to the plaintiff's harm? Often this inquiry is divided into two parts: causation in fact, and proximate causation.

Fourth, *damages:* did the plaintiff suffer harm?

This chapter concentrates on the second of these questions — whether the defendant was negligent, that is, did the defendant engage in "conduct which falls below the standard established by law for the protection of others against unreasonable risk of harm." Restatement (Second) of Torts §282. The issues of causation and duty are treated together in Chapter 6, while the discussion of damages is postponed to Chapter 10.

The question of negligence is one that runs across the length and breadth of the tort law. So long as negligence is treated as a general test of civil liability, then its dictates must be applied not only to the conduct of ordinary individuals, with the full range of strengths and frailties, but also to a wide variety of social organizations, including small businesses, large corporations, government entities, unions, and nonprofit associations. This chapter is designed to give some sense of the reach and application of the negligence principle to these different types of parties in different institutional settings. Accordingly, Section B begins with a study of the commonsense interpretation of negligence and the efforts to breathe life into the abstract concept of the reasonable person. The key inquiry here is what allowances, if any, the law should make for the character weaknesses of those individuals who are not blessed with the knowledge, skill, or ability of that durable but hypothetical construct of the law of negligence — the reasonable person.

Section C puts aside the study of these individual differences and traces the development of the general conception of negligence as applied to all reasonable persons. That test is commonly said to require a "balancing of interests" to determine whether the risks taken by the defendant are justified by the ends sought. At one level this inquiry delves into the uses and limitations of the various economic, or cost-benefit, interpretations of the negligence principle. But while these theoretical notions set the stage for evaluating any case, standing by themselves they are usually insufficient to complete the job. In addition, the skillful lawyer typically must supplement an appeal to general negligence principles by pointing to some specific "untaken precaution" which could have prevented the accident that actually occurred. See Grady, Untaken Precautions, 18 J. Legal Stud. 139 (1989). Throughout a trial the plaintiff tries to show that some inexpensive precaution (a railing, a warning, an inspection) could have prevented a serious injury that was likely to occur, while the defendant tries to show that the precaution was excessively costly, redundant, ineffective, or downright counterproductive. In hotly contested cases, there is no shortcut for a complete mastery of the relevant social and technical facts of every aspect of the situation. Of necessity, skilled negligence lawyers become their own experts on printing presses and toxic chemicals, on warnings and complex surgery. Indeed within law firms, the field is often organized by subject matter — medical malpractice, machine tools, chemicals, or hunting accidents and not by abstract doctrinal category.

Sometimes, however, we do have guideposts in the featureless landscape generated by a direct engagement with the concept of an unreasonable risk. Once our analysis of negligence in its most general form is complete, we shall examine in Section D the relationship between customary practice and negligence. Section E extends the same inquiry to the criminal statutes, and asks whether safety regulations are used to determine whether the parties have acted negligently.

The last two sections of the chapter deal with the trial of a negligence action. Section F examines the division of responsibility between judge and jury and, in that connection, the success of judicial efforts to create uniform standards of conduct as a matter of law. Section G then examines the principles governing the proof of negligence at trial, especially the doctrine of res ipsa loquitur — the thing speaks for itself (but usually not as clearly as we would like).

B. THE REASONABLE PERSON

It is sometimes said that the study of negligence is the study of the mistakes a reasonable man might make (Harry Kalven, Jr.).

Vaughan v. Menlove
132 Eng. Rep. 490 (C.P. 1837)

[The plaintiff owned two cottages in the County of Salop, which he rented out to two tenants. The defendant was a neighbor who had placed certain buildings and a hay stack, or rick, on his own property, near the plaintiff's two cottages.]

At the trial it appeared that the rick in question had been made by the Defendant near the boundary of his own premises; that the hay was in such a state when put together, as to give rise to discussions on the probability of fire: that though there were conflicting opinions on the subject, yet during a period of five weeks, the Defendant was repeatedly warned of his peril; that his stock was insured; and that upon one occasion, being advised to take the rick down to avoid all danger, he said "he would chance it." He made an aperture or chimney through the rick; but in spite, or perhaps in consequence of this precaution, the rick at length burst into flames from the spontaneous heating of its materials; the flames communicated to the Defendant's barn and stables, and thence to the Plaintiff's cottages, which were entirely destroyed.

PATTESON, J. before whom the cause was tried, told the jury that the question for them to consider, was, whether the fire had been occasioned by gross negligence on the part of the Defendant; adding, that he was bound to proceed with such reasonable caution as a prudent man would have exercised under such circumstances.

A verdict having been found for the Plaintiff, a rule nisi for a new trial was obtained, on the ground that the jury should have been directed to consider, not, whether the Defendant had been guilty of gross negligence with reference to the standard of ordinary prudence, a standard too uncertain to afford any criterion; but whether he had acted bona fide to the best of his judgment; if he had, he ought not to be responsible for the misfortune of not possessing the highest order of intelligence. The action under such circumstances, was of the first impression. . . .

Talfourd Serjt. and Whately, shewed cause [for plaintiff].

The pleas having expressly raised issues on the negligence of the Defendant, the learned Judge could not do otherwise than leave that question to the jury. . . . And the action, though new in specie, is founded on a principle fully established, that a man must so use his own property as not to injure that of others. On the same circuit a defendant was sued a few years ago, for burning weeds so near the extremity of his own land as to set fire to and destroy his neighbours' wood. The plaintiff recovered damages, and no motion was made to set aside the verdict. Then, there were no means of estimating the defendant's negligence, except by taking as a standard, the conduct of a man of ordinary prudence: that has been the rule always laid down, and there is no other that would not be open to much greater uncertainties.

R. V. Richards, in support of the rule [for defendant].

First, there was no duty imposed on the Defendant, as there is on carriers or other bailees, under an implied contract, to be responsible for the exercise of any given degree of prudence: the Defendant had a right to place his stack as near to the extremity of his own land as he pleased . . .: under that right, and subject to no contract, he can only be called on to act bona fide to the best of his judgment: if he has done that, it is a contradiction in terms, to inquire whether or not he has been guilty of gross negligence. At all events what would have been gross negligence ought to be estimated by the faculties of the individual, and not by those of other men. The measure of prudence varies so with the varying faculties of men, that it is impossible to say what is gross negligence with reference to the standard of what is called ordinary prudence. . . .

TINDAL, C.J. I agree that this is a case primae impressionis; but I feel no difficulty in applying to it the principles of law as laid down in other cases of a similar kind. Undoubtedly this is not a case of contract, such as a bailment or the like where the bailee is responsible in consequence of the remuneration he is to receive: but there is a rule of law which says you must so enjoy your own property as not to injure that of another; and according to that rule the Defendant is liable for the consequence of his own neglect: and though the Defendant did not himself light the fire, yet mediately, he is as much the cause of it as if he had himself put a candle to the rick; for it is well known that hay will ferment and take fire if it be not carefully stacked. It has been decided that if an occupier burns weeds so near the boundary of his own land that damage ensues to the property of his neighbour, he is liable to an action for the amount of injury done, unless the accident were occasioned by a sudden blast which he could not foresee: Turberville v. Stamp (1 Salk. 13). But put the case of a chemist making experiments with ingredients, singly innocent, but when combined, liable to ignite if he leaves them together, and injury is thereby occasioned to the property of his neighbour, can any one doubt that an action on the case would lie?

It is contended, however, that the learned Judge was wrong in leaving this to the jury as a case of gross negligence, and that the question of negligence was so mixed up with reference to what would be the conduct of a man of ordinary prudence that the jury might have thought the latter the rule by which they were to decide; that such a rule would be too uncertain to act upon; and that the question ought to have been whether the Defendant had acted honestly and bona fide to the best of his own judgment. That, however, would leave so vague a line as to afford no rule at all, the degree of judgment belonging to each individ-

ual being infinitely various: and though it has been urged that the care
which a prudent man would take, is not an intelligible proposition as a
rule of law, yet such has always been the rule adopted in cases of bailment, as laid down in Coggs v. Bernard (2 Ld. Raym. 909). Though in
some cases a greater degree of care is exacted than in others, yet in
"the second sort of bailment, viz. commodatum or lending gratis, the
borrower is bound to the strictest care and diligence to keep the goods
so as to restore them back again to the lender; because the bailee has a
benefit by the use of them, so as if the bailee be guilty of the least
neglect he will be answerable; as if a man should lend another a horse
to go westward, or for a month; if the bailee put this horse in his stable,
and he were stolen from thence, the bailee shall not be answerable for
him: but if he or his servant leave the house or stable doors open, and
the thieves take the opportunity of that, and steal the horse, he will be
chargeable, because the neglect gave the thieves the occasion to steal
the horse." The care taken by a prudent man has always been the rule
laid down; and as to the supposed difficulty of applying it, a jury has
always been able to say, whether, taking that rule as their guide, there
has been negligence on the occasion in question.

Instead, therefore, of saying that the liability for negligence should
be co-extensive with the judgment of each individual, which would be
as variable as the length of the foot of each individual, we ought rather
to adhere to the rule which requires in all cases a regard to caution
such as a man of ordinary prudence would observe. That was in substance the criterion presented to the jury in this case, and therefore the
present rule must be discharged.

PARK, J.: I entirely concur in what has fallen from his lordship. Although the facts in this case are new in specie, they fall within a principle long established, that a man must so use his own property as not to
injure that of others. [Park, J., then recited extensively from Tuberville
v. Stamp, infra at note 1, and concluded:]

As to the direction of the learned judge, it was perfectly correct. Under the circumstances of the case it was proper to leave it to the jury
whether with reference to the caution which would have been observed
by a man of ordinary prudence, the Defendant had not been guilty of
gross negligence. After he had been warned repeatedly during the five
weeks as to the consequences likely to happen, there is no colour for
altering the verdict, unless it were to increase the damages.

VAUGHAN, J.: The principle on which this action proceeds, is by no
means new. It has been urged that the Defendant in such a case takes
no duty on himself; but I do not agree in that position: every one takes
upon himself the duty of so dealing with his own property as not to
injure the property of others. It was, if any thing, too favourable to the
Defendant to leave it to the jury whether he had been guilty of gross
negligence; for when the Defendant upon being warned as to the

consequences likely to ensue from the condition of the rick, said, "he would chance it," it was manifest he adverted to his interest in the insurance office. The conduct of a prudent man has always been the criterion for the jury in such cases: but it is by no means confined to them. . . . Here, there was not a single witness whose testimony did not go to establish gross negligence in the Defendant. He had repeated warnings of what was likely to occur, and the whole calamity was occasioned by his procrastination.

Rule discharged.

NOTES

1. Liability for fire at common law. Vaughan is scarcely the first common-law decision that has addressed liability for fire at common law. In Beaulieu v. Finglam, Y.B. 2 Hen. 4, f. 18, pl. 6 (1401), plaintiff alleged that his house and furniture had been destroyed by a fire, carelessly watched, that had been set by one of the defendant's servants in the course of his duties. The court held for plaintiff.

> MARKHAM, J. I shall answer to my neighbour for each person who enters my house by my leave or my knowledge, or is my guest through me or through my servant, if he does any act, as with a candle or aught else, whereby my neighbour's house is burnt. But if a man from outside my house and against my will starts a fire in the thatch of my house or elsewhere, whereby my house is burned and my neighbours' houses are burned as well, for this I shall not be held bound to them; for this cannot be said to be done by wrong on my part, but is against my will.
>
> HORNBY. This defendant will be undone and impoverished all his days if this action is to be maintained against him; for then twenty other such suits will be brought against him for the same matter.
>
> THIRNING, C.J. What is that to us? It is better that he should be utterly undone than that the law be changed for him.
>
> And then they joined issue that the plaintiff's house was not burned by the fire of the defendant.

In Tuberville v. Stamp, 1 Ld. Raym. 264, 91 Eng. Rep. 1072 (1697), the defendant "tam improvide . . . custodivit ignem suum [so improvidently guarded his fire] in his field that it burnt the plaintiff's heath in his field." The judgments of the court were as follows:

> TURTON, J. There is difference between fire in a man's house and in the fields. In some countries it is a necessary part of husbandry to make fire on the ground, and some unavoidable accident may carry it into a neighbour's ground and do injury there; and this fire, not being so properly in his custody as the fire in his house, I think is not actionable, as it is laid.

But by HOLT, C.J., ROKEBY and EYRE, JJ. Every man must so use his own as not to injure another. The law is general. The fire which a man makes in the fields is as much his fire as his fire in his house; it is made on his ground with his materials and by his order, and he must at his peril take care that it does not, through his neglect, injure his neighbour. If he kindle it at a proper time and place, and the violence of the wind carry it into his neighbour's ground and prejudice him, this is fit to be given in evidence. But now here it is found to have been by his negligence; and it is the same as if it had been in his house.

Judgment was given for the Plaintiff.

Why don't *Beaulieu* and *Tuberville* require the use of a strict liability standard in *Vaughan*?

2. The standard of care for bailments. While the judges in *Vaughan* did not rely on the early fire cases (why?), they did examine the traditional common-law rules of liability as they applied to bailments (i.e., consensual arrangements under which goods are delivered to another with the intention that they be redelivered at some future time). Under the leading case of Coggs v. Bernard, 92 Eng. Rep. 107 (Q.B. 1704), Holt, C.J., explicitly relied on principles of Roman law to distinguish among six types of bailment, each with a distinct standard of care. He categorized them as: (1) gratuitous bailment for safekeeping (depositum); (2) bailment for the bailee's use (commodatum); (3) a simple pawn (vadium); (4) bailment for hire (locatio rei); (5) bailment whereby the bailee agrees for a fee to operate or manage the thing bailed (locatio operis faciendi); and (6) the bailment of a thing to be managed (not merely stored) by the bailee without compensation (mandatum). The underlying principle is that the bailee is subject to a standard of care varying in proportion to the benefit that he derives from the bailment; he is held for the "slightest negligence" where the loan is for his own benefit or use, but for gross neglect only when he undertakes safekeeping for the bailor. Where both parties benefit, the usual standard is that of ordinary care. And in all cases it is, of course, possible to vary the standard of care by private agreement. How successful is defendant's implicit argument that the law of bailment authorizes the use of a good faith standard in disputes between neighbors?

3. Guest statutes. The different level of care required at common law for gratuitous and commercial bailments at one time influenced the standard of care owed by automobile drivers to their guests. During the 1920s and 1930s a large number of states passed statutes that provided that the driver of a car could be liable to a nonpaying guest, in somewhat varying formulations, only if willful misconduct, recklessness, or gross negligence were established. The rules here all rested on the perception that persons who do not pay for protection are entitled only to a lower level of care. Massaletti v. Fitzroy, 118 N.E. 168 (Mass. 1917);

Note, The Common Law Basis of Automobile Guest Statutes, 43 U. Chi. L. Rev. 798 (1976).

In practice, litigation over guest statutes has often placed a far heavier burden on plaintiffs than they bear in ordinary negligence cases. Some judges have been skeptical that any distinction could be drawn between different degrees of negligence. In a famous bon mot, Baron Rolfe once described gross negligence as the same thing as ordinary negligence "with the addition of a vituperative epithet" (Wilson v. Brett, 152 Eng. Rep. 737 (Ex. 1843)). But when the guest statutes have protected defendants from liability from ordinary negligence, the judges dutifully followed the statutory command and barred suits that did not meet the more exacting standard of liability. Conway v. O'Brien, 111 F.2d 611 (2d Cir. 1940), involved the Vermont guest statute that permitted a passenger to recover from his host only for "gross negligence." Accordingly, Judge Learned Hand held that the plaintiff could not reach the jury when the defendant was driving at 15 miles per hour on the wrong side of a narrow highway while coming around a sharp curve. "Had he been driving twice as fast, or on a much travelled highway, we might think otherwise; but on that road and at that speed it seems to us that his fault was only a routine dereliction, not grave enough to fall within the statute. It is plain from the Vermont decisions that we cannot properly devolve the entire responsibility for a decision upon a jury. . . ."

The first round of guest statutes was passed in the 1920s, and were promptly attacked constitutionally for violating the equal protection clause of the Fourteenth Amendment. In Silver v. Silver, 280 U.S. 117 (1928), the Supreme Court rejected that challenge on the ground that the risk of collusive suits between passengers and drivers was sufficiently great to warrant the legislature's separating guest cases out for special attention. A second wave of constitutional challenges at the state level, beginning with Brown v. Merlo, 506 P.2d 212 (Cal. 1973), proved successful in about half the states that had these statutes. In recent years the constitutional debate has ebbed as most state legislatures have repealed their guest statutes. For the current constitutional tally see 3 Harper, James and Gray, Torts §16.15 n.4.

Holmes, The Common Law
107-109 (1881)

Supposing it now to be conceded that the general notion upon which liability to an action is founded is fault or blameworthiness in some sense, the question arises, whether it is so in the sense of personal moral shortcoming, as would practically result from Austin's teaching. The language of Rede, J., which has been quoted from the Year Book, gives a sufficient answer. "In trespass the intent" (we may say more broadly, the defendant's state of mind) "cannot be construed." Suppose that a defendant were allowed to testify that, before acting, he considered carefully what would be the conduct of a prudent man under the circumstances, and, having formed the best judgment he could, acted accordingly. If the story was believed, it would be conclusive against the defendant's negligence judged by a moral standard which would take his personal characteristics into account. But supposing any such evidence to have got before the jury, it is very clear that the court would say, Gentlemen, the question is not whether the defendant thought his conduct was that of a prudent man, but whether you think it was.

Some middle point must be found between the horns of this dilemma.

The standards of the law are standards of general application. The law takes no account of the infinite varieties of temperament, intellect, and education which make the internal character of a given act so different in different men. It does not attempt to see men as God sees them, for more than one sufficient reason. In the first place, the impossibility of nicely measuring a man's powers and limitations is far clearer than that of ascertaining his knowledge of law, which has been thought to account for what is called the presumption that every man knows the law. But a more satisfactory explanation is, that, when men live in society, a certain average of conduct, a sacrifice of individual peculiarities going beyond a certain point, is necessary to the general welfare. If, for instance, a man is born hasty and awkward, is always having accidents and hurting himself or his neighbors, no doubt his congenital defects will be allowed for in the courts of Heaven, but his slips are no less troublesome to his neighbors than if they sprang from guilty neglect. His neighbors accordingly require him, at his proper peril, to come up to their standard, and the courts which they establish decline to take his personal equation into account.

The rule that the law does, in general, determine liability by blameworthiness, is subject to the limitation that minute differences of character are not allowed for. The law considers, in other words, what would be blameworthy in the average man, the man of ordinary intelligence and prudence, and determines liability by that. If we fall below the level in those gifts, it is our misfortune so much as that we must have at our peril, for the reasons just given. But he who is intelligent and prudent does not act at his peril, in theory of law. On the contrary, it is only when he fails to exercise the foresight of which he is capable, or exercises it with evil intent, that he is answerable for the consequences.

There are exceptions to the principle that every man is presumed to possess ordinary capacity to avoid harm to his neighbors, which illustrate the rule, and also the moral basis of liability in general. When a man has a distinct defect of such a nature that all can recognize it as making certain precautions impossible, he will not be held answerable for not taking them. A blind man is not required to see at his peril; and although he is, no doubt, bound to consider his infirmity in regulating his actions, yet if he properly finds himself in a certain situation, the neglect of precautions requiring eyesight would not prevent his recovering for an injury to himself, and, it may be presumed, would not make him liable for injuring another. So it is held that, in cases where he is the plaintiff, an infant of very tender years is only bound to take the precautions of which an infant is capable; the same principle may be cautiously applied where he is defendant. Insanity is a more difficult matter to deal with, and no general rule can be laid down about it. There is no doubt that in many cases a man may be insane, and yet perfectly capable of taking the precautions, and of being influenced by the motives, which the circumstances demand. But if insanity of a pronounced type exists, manifestly incapacitating the sufferer from complying with the rule which he has broken, good sense would require it to be admitted as an excuse.

Roberts v. Ring
173 N.W. 437 (Minn. 1919)

HALLAM, J.: Plaintiff brings this action on behalf of his minor son, John B. Roberts, seven years old, to recover damages for injury from collision with defendant's automobile. The jury found for defendant. Plaintiff appeals. Defendant assigns as error certain portions of the charge. Defendant contends that the charge was without error and further contends that as a matter of law, defendant was without negligence and that the boy was negligent.

1. Defendant was driving south on a much traveled street in Owatonna. He was seventy-seven years old. His sight and hearing were defective. A buggy was approaching him from the south. There were other conveyances on the street. The travel was practically blocked. The boy ran from behind the buggy across the street to the west and in front of defendant's automobile. There is evidence that he had been riding on the rear of the buggy. He himself testified that he was crossing the street. As he passed in front of defendant's automobile he was struck and injured.

The question of defendant's negligence was a proper one to be submitted to the jury. Defendant was driving from four to five miles an hour, not a negligent rate of speed. If he was negligent, it was in failing to keep a proper lookout and in failing to promptly stop his car. He testified that he saw the boy when he was four or five feet from the automobile. It is a matter of common knowledge that an automobile traveling four or five miles an hour can be stopped within a very few

feet, yet defendant knocked the boy down and his car passed clear over
him. If defendant saw the boy, as he now claims, he was not alert in
stopping his car. If he did not see him as he is alleged to have stated to
others he was not keeping a sharp lookout in this crowded street. We
are of the opinion that the evidence was such as to raise an issue of fact
as to his negligence.

2. The question of the boy's negligence was likewise for the jury.
Had a mature man acted as did this boy he might have been chargeable
with negligence as a matter of law. But a boy of seven is not held to the
same standard of care in self-protection. In considering his contributory negligence the standard is the degree of care commonly exercised
by the ordinary boy of his age and maturity. It would be different if he
had caused injury to another. In such a case he could not take advantage of his age or infirmities.

3. The case being a proper one for submission to the jury the question is was it properly submitted.

[A discussion of the charge on contributory negligence is omitted.]

As to the negligence of defendant the court charged:

> In determining whether the defendant was guilty of negligence you
> may take into consideration . . . the age of the defendant . . . and
> whether or not the defendant had any physical infirmities.

. . . . As above indicated, defendant's infirmities did not tend to relieve him from the charge of negligence. On the contrary they weighed
against him. Such infirmities, to the extent that they were proper to be
considered at all, presented only a reason why defendant should refrain
from operating an automobile on a crowded street where care was required to avoid injuring other travelers. When one, by his acts or omissions causes injury to others, his negligence is to be judged by the
standard of care usually exercised by the ordinarily prudent normal
man.

Order reversed.

NOTES

1. The reasonable retiree: With *Roberts* contrast Johnson v. St. Paul City
Ry. Co., 69 N.W. 900 (Minn. 1897). The plaintiff was an elderly woman
who was in the back seat of a buggy being driven by her daughter-in-
law. The buggy, the last vehicle in a funeral procession, was struck by a
streetcar driven by defendant's servant. The plaintiff, while familiar
with the locale, "she did not look or listen for approaching cars, but sat
in a deep study with her eyes cast down, feeling entirely safe, as she was

riding in a funeral procession." Mitchell, J., held that her conduct raised no issue of contributory negligence to be left to the jury. He noted first that the plaintiff was entitled to assume that others would not interrupt the funeral procession, and then noted that some allowance should be made for the plaintiff's age and condition: "The age of the plaintiff is also to be kept in mind. All that the law requires of an infant is a degree of care commensurate with its age and discretion. We think the same rule should apply to old people, whose senses are blunted, and mental faculties impaired, by age. Like children, they are accustomed to intrust their safety to those who are younger and stronger mentally and physically than themselves and within reasonable limits they may do so without being guilty of negligence."

2. *Beginners and experts.* Another problem faced by the law of negligence concerns the adjustments in the standard of care appropriate for beginners and experts in certain lines of endeavor. The use of a lower standard of care for a beginner provides an encouragement to undertake activities that might not otherwise be attempted, but exacts that subsidy from the person unfortunate enough to be hurt, and not from the public at large. The general rule therefore has been to hold the beginner to the standard of care expected of those who are reasonably skilled and practiced in the art. See, for example, Hughey v. Lennox, 219 S.W. 323 (Ark. 1920). There is an exception to the rule that covers those cases in which the plaintiff has assumed the risk that the defendant will exercise a lower standard of care, as happens when an experienced driver agrees to teach a novice how to drive. Holland v. Pitocchelli, 13 N.E.2d 390 (Mass. 1938). See generally Restatement (Second) of Torts §299 comment *d*, basically endorsing the rule requiring a defendant meet the objective standard of care.

The converse problem arises when a defendant has greater skills than most people in that line of endeavor. On this issue the Restatement position is that the defendant is "required to exercise the skill and knowledge normally possessed by members of that profession or trade in good standing in similar communities," but that standard is subject to an important caveat — "unless he represents that he has greater or less skill" than the average. Restatement (Second) of Torts §299A. Is there any minimum standard of care that a defendant must exercise in order to remain a member of a profession in good standing?

Daniels v. Evans
224 A.2d 63 (N.H. 1966)

[Plaintiff's deceased, a youth 19-years-old, was killed when the motorcycle he was driving collided with defendant's automobile. A trial by jury resulted in a verdict for plaintiff, and the only alleged error argued on appeal was the trial court's charge pertaining to the standard of care required of plaintiff's deceased.]

LAMPRON, J. As to the standard of care to be applied to the conduct of the decedent Robert E. Daniels, 19 years of age, the Trial Court charged the jury in part as follows:

"Now, he is considered a minor, being under the age of twenty-one, and a minor child must exercise the care of the average child of his or her age, experience and stage of mental development. In other words, he is not held to the same degree of care as an adult."

Concededly these instructions substantially reflect the rule by which the care of a minor has been judged heretofore in the courts of our State. Charbonneau v. MacRury, 84 N.H. 501. However an examination of the cases will reveal that in most the minors therein were engaged in activities appropriate to their age, experience and wisdom. These included being a pedestrian, riding a bicycle, riding a horse, [and] coasting.

We agree that minors are entitled to be judged by standards commensurate with their age, experience, and wisdom when engaged in activities appropriate to their age, experience, and wisdom. Hence when children are walking, running, playing with toys, throwing balls, operating bicycles, sliding or engaged in other childhood activities their conduct should be judged by the rule of what is reasonable conduct under the circumstances among which are the age, experience, and stage of mental development of the minor involved. Charbonneau v. MacRury, 84 N.H. 501, 507.

However, the question is raised by the defendant in this case whether the standard of care applied to minors in such cases should prevail when the minor is engaged in activities normally undertaken by adults. In other words, when a minor undertakes an adult activity which can result in grave danger to others and to the minor himself if the care used in the course of the activity drops below that care which the reasonable and prudent adult would use, the defendant maintains that the minor's conduct in that instance should meet the same standards as that of an adult.

Many recent cases have held that "when a minor assumes responsibility for the operation of so potentially dangerous an instrument as an automobile, he should . . . assume responsibility for its careful and safe operation in the light of adult standards." 2 Idaho L. Rev., 103, 111 (1965); Dellwo v. Pearson, 107 N.W.2d 859 (Minn. 1961). The rule has been recognized in Restatement (Second), Torts, s. 283 A, comment c, in 2 Harper and James, The Law of Torts, s. 16.8, p. 926, and in Prosser, Torts (3rd ed.), s. 19, p. 159. In an annotation in 97 A.L.R.2d 872 at page 875 it is said that recent decisions "hold that when a minor engages in such activities as the operation of an automobile or similar power driven device, he forfeits his rights to have the reasonableness of his conduct measured by a standard commensurate with his age and is thenceforth held to the same standard as all other persons."

One of the reasons for such a rule has been stated thusly in Dellwo v. Pearson, supra: "To give legal sanction to the operation of automobiles by teen-agers with less than ordinary care for the safety of others is impractical today, to say the least. We may take judicial notice of the hazards of automobile traffic, the frequency of accidents, the often catastrophic results of accidents, and the fact that immature individuals are no less prone to accidents than adults. . . . [I]t would be unfair to the public to permit a minor in the operation of a motor vehicle to observe any other standards of care and conduct than those expected of all others. A person observing children at play . . . may anticipate conduct that does not reach an adult standard of care or prudence. However, one cannot know whether the operator of an approaching automobile . . . is a minor or an adult, and usually cannot protect himself against youthful imprudence even if warned." . . .

RSA 262-A:2 which establishes rules of the road for the operation of motor vehicles on our highways reads as follows: "Required Obedience to Traffic Laws. It is unlawful and . . . a misdemeanor for *any person* to do any act forbidden or fail to perform any act required in this chapter." (Emphasis supplied.) This is some indication of an intent on the part of our Legislature that all drivers must, and have the right to expect that others using the highways, regardless of their age and experience, will, obey the traffic laws and thus exercise the adult standard of ordinary care. . . .

The rule charged by the Trial Court pertaining to the standard of care to be applied by the jury to the conduct of the minor plaintiff Robert E. Daniels in the operation of the motorcycle was proper in "the bygone days" when children were using relatively innocent contrivances. However in the circumstances of to-day's modern life, where vehicles moved by powerful motors are readily available and used by many minors, we question the propriety of a rule which would allow such vehicles to be operated to the hazard of the public, and to the driver himself, with less than the degree of care required of an adult.

We are of the opinion that to apply to minors a more lenient standard in the operation of motor vehicles, whether an automobile or a motorcycle, than that applied to adults is unrealistic, contrary to the expressed legislative policy, and inimical to public safety. Furthermore when a minor is operating a motor vehicle there is no reason for making a distinction based on whether he is charged with primary negligence, contributory negligence, or a causal violation of a statute and we so hold. Charbonneau v. MacRury.

We hold therefore that a minor operating a motor vehicle, whether an automobile or a motorcycle, must be judged by the same standard of care as an adult and the defendant's objection to the Trial Court's charge applying a different standard to the conduct of plaintiff's intestate was valid. . . .

Exception sustained.

NOTES

1. Adult and infant activities. In Charbonneau v. MacRury, 153 A. 457, 462-463 (N.H. 1931), overruled by Daniels v. Evans, the court justified the adoption of a variable standard of care for infants as follows:

> Unless infants are to be denied the environment and association of their elders until they have acquired maturity, there must be a living relationship between them on terms which permit the child to act as a child in his stage of development. As well expect a boy to learn to swim without experience in the water as to expect him to learn to function as an adult without contact with his superiors. For the law to hold children to the exercise of the care of adults "would be to shut its eyes, ostrich-like to the facts of life and to burden unduly the child's growth to majority." [Shulman, The Standard of Care Required of Children,] 37 Yale L.J. 618. During the period of his development he must participate in human activities on some basis of reason. Reason requires that indulgence be shown him commensurate with his want of development as indicated by his age and experience. Id. 621. Though strictly speaking it is the resultant qualities reasonably attributable to these factors that measure his capacity (1 Shearman & Redfield, Neg. (6th ed.) 72a) it is sufficient, as a practical matter, to speak of age and experience as inclusive of these qualities. . . .

In Goss v. Allen, 360 A.2d 388 (N.J. 1976), the supreme court affirmed a jury instruction that a 17-year-old beginning skier be held, not to the adult standard of care, but to a standard appropriate to youths of the same age. In distinguishing the case from other adult activities — driving a car or motorcycle or hunting — the court noted that no license was required for youths to engage in skiing.

There was a sharp dissent insisting that the loss of an eye "resulting from a carelessly thrown dart, or stone, or firecracker, the death caused by a bicycle, or an individual seriously maimed due to an errant skier — all are indisputable proof of 'potentially hazardous' activity — even when the activity was not subject to government licensing. The court then noted in a footnote: "No license is required for a motorized bike, but a ten-speed bike can be pedaled at 25 miles per hour on a flat road. The U.S. Consumer Product Safety Commission reports that there are 500 to 1000 fatalities and about 500,000 permanently crippled each year from bicycle mishaps."

Goss v. Allen is but one of the many cases that test the line between infant and adult activities. In Dellwo v. Pearson, 107 N.W.2d 859 (Minn.

1961), a 12-year-old defendant was held to the adult standard of care in the operation of a speed boat, even though there was apparently no licensing statute for such boats. In Harrelson v. Whitehead, 365 S.W.2d 868 (Ark. 1963), a 15-year-old plaintiff operating a motorcycle was held to the adult standard of care on the issue of contributory negligence. Jackson v. McCuiston, 448 S.W.2d 33 (Ark. 1969), held that a 13-year-old farm boy should be judged by the adult standard of care in operating a tractor-propelled stalk cutter, a large piece of machinery with a dangerous cutting blade. In Purtle v. Shelton, 474 S.W.2d 123 (Ark. 1971), the Arkansas court cut back on its decision in *Jackson*, holding that a 17-year-old boy was not subject to the adult standard of care in the use of dangerous firearms. It argued that a lower standard for minors was appropriate because deer hunting was not exclusively an adult activity. One dissenting justice argued: "Because a bullet fired from the gun by a minor is just as deadly as a bullet fired by an adult, I'm at a loss to understand why one with 'buck fever' because of his minority is entitled to exercise any less care than anyone else deer hunting. One killed by a bullet so fired would be just as dead in one instance as the other and without any more warning."

Suppose plaintiff is struck by a batted ball hit by a child plaintiff does not see? Suppose plaintiff is hit from behind by a child on a bicycle? Or suppose a child wrecks an automobile lent her by the owner. What standard should be applied if the owner sues?

2. *Reasonable plaintiff versus reasonable defendant.* In Daniels v. Evans, the court held that the same standard of care was required of infants whether they were cast in the role of plaintiffs or defendants. The dual standard (also accepted in *Roberts*) was also rejected in Miller v. Minnesota, 306 N.W.2d 554, 554-555 (Minn. 1981), where the court, following its earlier decision in Dellwo v. Pearson, supra, granted defendant's motion for a new trial when the jury was instructed "in part that when determining whether Kim Miller was negligent 'reasonable care is that care which a reasonable child of the same age, that is, sixteen, the same intelligence, training and experience as Kim Miller at the time of the accident would have used under the circumstances.' " The court held that the lower standard of care was applicable only when minors were engaged in activities uniquely appropriate to children.

While the case law has moved toward the single ordinary standard of care for youthful drivers, both as plaintiff and defendant, the case for a general dual standard has been advanced in James, The Qualities of the Reasonable Man in Negligence Cases, 16 Mo. L. Rev. 1, 1-2 (1951):

By and large the law has chosen external, objective standards of conduct. The reasonably prudent man is, to be sure, endowed with some of the qualities of the person whose conduct is being judged, especially where the latter has greater knowledge, skill, or the like, than people generally. But many of the actor's shortcomings such as awkwardness, faulty perception, or poor judgment, are not taken into account if they fall below the general level of the community. This means that individuals are often held guilty of legal fault for failing to live up to a standard which as a matter of fact they cannot meet. Such a result shocks people who believe in refining the fault principle so as to make legal liability correspond more closely to personal moral shortcoming. There has, therefore, been some pressure towards the adoption of a more subjective test. But if the standard of conduct is relaxed for *defendants* who cannot meet a normal standard, then the burden of accident loss resulting from the extra hazards created by society's most dangerous groups (e.g. the young, the novice, the accident prone) will be thrown on the innocent victims of substandard behavior. Such a conclusion shocks people who believe that the compensation of accident victims is a more important objective of modern tort law than a further refinement of the tort principle, and that compensation should prevail when the two objectives conflict. The application of a relaxed subjective standard to the issue of *plaintiff's* contributory negligence, however, involves no such conflict. On this issue the forces of the two objectives combine to demand a subjective test: the refinement of the fault principle furthers the compensation of accident victims by cutting down a defense that would stand in its way. For this reason the writer has elsewhere developed the thesis that there should be an explicit double standard of conduct, namely, an external standard for a defendant's negligence, and a (relaxed) subjective standard for contributory negligence. Even if this thesis is rejected, the same result probably prevails anyhow, because the application of the legal standard is largely left to the jury, and juries, by and large, tend to resolve doubts on both issues in favor of plaintiffs.

The explicit adoption of separate standards for negligence and contributory negligence raises a number of important questions. What should be done when both parties are infants and both are injured? Should the result depend on whether either or both the parties are insured? Note that the use of the double standard necessarily works to increase the administrative costs of both settlement and litigation. Are those costs justified by the greater efficiency, or equity, that it generates?

Breunig v. American Family Insurance Co.
173 N.W.2d 619 (Wis. 1970)

[Plaintiff brought this action for personal injuries sustained when his car was struck by a car driven by Erma Veith, an insured of the defendant. The accident occurred when Mrs. Veith's car veered across the center of the road into the lane in which plaintiff was traveling. Defendant argued that Mrs. Veith "was not negligent because just prior to the collision she suddenly and without warning was seized with a mental aberration or delusion which rendered her unable to operate the automobile with her conscious mind." The jury returned a verdict finding

her causally negligent on the theory she "had knowledge or forewarning of her mental delusions or disability." From the award of $7,000
damages, defendant appeals.]

HALLOWS, C.J. There is no question that Erma Veith was subject at
the time of the accident to an insane delusion which directly affected
her ability to operate her car in an ordinarily prudent manner and
caused the accident. The specific question considered by the jury under
the negligence inquiry was whether she had such foreknowledge of her
susceptibility to such a mental aberration, delusion or hallucination as
to make her negligent in driving a car at all under such conditions.

. . . The evidence established that Mrs. Veith, while returning home
after taking her husband to work, saw a white light on the back of a car
ahead of her. She followed this light for three or four blocks. Mrs. Veith
did not remember anything else except landing in a field, lying in the
side of the road and people talking. She recalled awaking in the hospital.

The psychiatrist testified Mrs. Veith told him she was driving on a
road when she believed that God was taking ahold of the steering wheel
and was directing her car. She saw the truck coming and stepped on
the gas in order to become airborne because she knew she could fly
because Batman does it. To her surprise she was not airborne before
striking the truck but after the impact she was flying. . . .

The insurance company argues Erma Veith was not negligent as a
matter of law because there is no evidence upon which the jury could
find that she had knowledge or warning or should have reasonably foreseen that she might be subject to a mental delusion which would suddenly cause her to lose control of the car. Plaintiff argues there was
such evidence of forewarning and also suggests Erma Veith should be
liable because insanity should not be a defense in negligence cases.

The case was tried on the theory that some forms of insanity are a
defense to and preclude liability for negligence under the doctrine of
Theisen v. Milwaukee Automobile Mut. Ins. Co. (1962), 18 Wis. 2d 91.
We agree. Not all types of insanity vitiate responsibility for a negligent
tort. The question of liability in every case must depend upon the kind
and nature of the insanity. The effect of the mental illness or mental
hallucinations or disorder must be such as to affect the person's ability
to understand and appreciate the duty which rests upon him to drive
his car with ordinary care, or if the insanity does not affect such understanding and appreciation, it must affect his ability to control his car in
an ordinarily prudent manner. And in addition, there must be an absence of notice or forewarning to the person that he may be suddenly
subject to such a type of insanity or mental illness.

In *Theisen* we recognized one was not negligent if he was unable to
conform his conduct through no fault of his own but held a sleeping
driver negligent as a matter of law because one is always given conscious
warnings of drowsiness and if a person does not heed such warnings

and continues to drive his car, he is negligent for continuing to drive under such conditions. But we distinguished those exceptional cases of loss of consciousness resulting from injury inflicted by an outside force, or fainting, or heart attack, or epileptic seizure, or other illness which suddenly incapacitates the driver of an automobile when the occurrence of such disability is not attended with sufficient warning or should not have been reasonably foreseen. . . .

There are authorities which generally hold insanity is not a defense in tort cases except for intentional torts. Restatement, 2 Torts, 2d, p. 16, sec. 283 B, and appendix (1966) and cases cited therein. These cases rest on the historical view of strict liability without regard to the fault of the individual. Prosser, in his Law of Torts (3d ed.), p. 1028, states this view is a historical survival which originated in the dictum in Weaver v. Ward (1616), Hob. 134, 80 English Reports 284, when the action of trespass still rested upon strict liability. He points out that when the modern law developed to the point of holding the defendant liable for negligence, the dictum was repeated in some cases.

The policy basis of holding a permanently insane person liable for his tort is: (1) Where one of two innocent persons must suffer a loss it should be borne by the one who occasioned it; (2) to induce those interested in the estate of the insane person (if he has one) to restrain and control him and; (3) the fear an insanity defense would lead to false claims of insanity to avoid liability. . . .

We think the statement that insanity is no defense is too broad when it is applied to a negligence case where the driver is suddenly overcome without forewarning by a mental disability or disorder which incapacitates him from conforming his conduct to the standards of a reasonable man under like circumstances. These are rare cases indeed, but their rarity is no reason for overlooking their existence and the justification which is the basis of the whole doctrine of liability for negligence, i.e., that it is unjust to hold a man responsible for his conduct which he is incapable of avoiding and which incapability was unknown to him prior to the accident.

We need not reach the question of contributory negligence of an insane person or the question of comparative negligence as those problems are not now presented. All we hold is that a sudden mental incapacity equivalent in its effect to such physical causes as a sudden heart attack, epileptic seizure, stroke, or fainting should be treated alike and not under the general rule of insanity.

An interesting case holding this view in Canada is Buckley & Toronto Transportation Comm. v. Smith Transport, 1946 Ont. Rep. 798, 4 Dom. L. Rep. 721, which is almost identical on the facts with the case at bar. There, the court found no negligence when a truck driver was overcome by a sudden insane delusion that his truck was being operated by remote control of his employer and as a result he was in fact helpless to avert a collision.

The insurance company argues that since the psychiatrist was the only expert witness who testified concerning the mental disability of Mrs. Veith and the lack of forewarning that as a matter of law there was no forewarning and she could not be held negligent and the trial court should have so held. While there was testimony of friends indicating she was normal for some months prior to the accident, the psychiatrist testified the origin of her mental illness appeared in August, 1965, prior to the accident. In that month Mrs. Veith visited the Necedah Shrine where she was told the Blessed Virgin had sent her to the shrine. She was told to pray for survival. Since that time she felt it had been revealed to her the end of the world was coming and that she was picked by God to survive. Later she had visions of God judging people and sentencing them to Heaven or Hell; she thought Batman was good and was trying to help save the world and her husband was possessed of the devil. Mrs. Veith told her daughter about her visions.

The question is whether she had warning or knowledge which would reasonably lead her to believe that hallucinations would occur and be such as to affect her driving an automobile. Even though the doctor's testimony is uncontradicted, it need not be accepted by the jury. It is an expert's opinion but it is not conclusive. It is for the jury to decide whether the facts underpinning an expert opinion are true. . . . The jury could find that a woman, who believed she had a special relationship to God and was the chosen one to survive the end of the world, could believe that God would take over the direction of her life to the extent of driving her car. Since these mental aberrations were not constant, the jury could infer she had knowledge of her condition and the likelihood of a hallucination just as one who has knowledge of a heart condition knows the possibility of an attack. While the evidence may not be strong upon which to base an inference, especially in view of the fact that two jurors dissented on this verdict and expressly stated they could find no evidence of forewarning, nevertheless, the evidence to sustain the verdict of the jury need not constitute the great weight and clear preponderance.

The insurance company claims the jury was perverse because the verdict is contrary both to the evidence and to the law. We think this argument is without merit.

Fletcher v. City of Aberdeen
338 P.2d 743 (Wash. 1959)

FOSTER, J. . . . For the purpose of placing electric wires underground, the city dug a ditch in the parking strip adjacent to the sidewalk at the intersection of Broadway and Fourth streets in the city of Aberdeen. Suitable barricades were erected to protect pedestrians from falling into the excavation, but, unfortunately, at the time of the mishap in question, one of the city's employees had removed the barriers to facilitate his work in the excavation. When he went elsewhere to work, he negligently failed to replace the barricades, which left the excavation unprotected. In approaching the intersection, the respondent husband, who had been blind since his eighth year, had his kit of piano-tuning tools in his left hand and his cane in his right. With the cane he was cautiously feeling his way. Because the protective barriers had been removed, the existence of the excavation was unknown to the respondent. By the use of the cane, the barriers would have protected the respondent if they had been in place. The jury was entitled to find that the city was negligent in removing the barriers without providing other warning.

. . . The city's argument is that it had discharged its duty by the erection of barricades. It may be assumed for present purposes, that the barriers originally erected were sufficient to discharge the city's duty of maintaining its streets and adjacent parking strips in a reasonably safe condition for pedestrian use. However, the city's argument completely ignores the undisputed evidence that its workman had removed the barricades and that the accident in question occurred during this interval. The duty of maintaining the sidewalks and adjacent parking strips is a continuing one. . . .

The city assigns error upon the giving of instruction No. 9.[1] The city contends that this instruction places a higher degree of care upon it with reference to the parking strips than the degree of care required as to sidewalks. This argument overlooks instructions Nos. 7 and 7A in which the jury was told that the city was not an insurer and was required only to keep the streets and sidewalks in a reasonably safe condition, that this duty did not require a complete barricade but that only reasonable warning was required, and that it was a question of fact whether the city discharged this duty. . . .

The city assigns error upon the refusal to instruct as requested that "The fact that the plaintiff is blind does not impose on the City any higher degree of care." . . . The supreme court of Oregon recently commented:

". . . Public thoroughfares are for the beggar on his crutches as well as the millionaire in his limousine. Neither is it the policy of the law to discriminate against those who suffer physical infirmity. The blind and the halt may use the streets without being guilty of negligence if, in so doing, they exercise that degree of care which an ordinarily prudent

---

1. "You are instructed that that portion of a city street lying between the sidewalk and the curb, commonly referred to as the parking strip, is as much a part of the public street as any other portion. It is not unlawful for a person to step upon or walk across a parking strip. It is the duty of the municipality to keep its parking strips in a reasonably safe condition so that persons traveling thereon, exercising ordinary prudence and caution, may do so with safety."

person similarly afflicted would exercise under the same circumstances. . . ." Weinstein v. Wheeler, 127 Or. 406. . . .

Dean Prosser declares that a blind person, or one with physical infirmities, is entitled to live in the world, and that his conduct must be reasonable in the light of knowledge of his infirmity. . . .

The city is charged with knowledge that its streets will be used by those who are physically infirm as well as those in perfect physical condition. . . . The obligations are correlative. The person under a physical disability is obliged to use the care which a reasonable person under the same or similar disability would exercise under the circumstances. The city, on the other hand, is obliged to afford that degree of protection which would bring to the notice of the person so afflicted the danger to be encountered. There was no error, therefore, in the denial of the appellant's requested instruction No. 13. . . .

The judgment is, therefore, affirmed.

WEAVER, C.J., and DONWORTH, OTT and HUNTER, JJ., concur.

Robinson v. Pioche, Bayerque & Co.
5 Cal. 460 (1855)

Appeal from the Superior Court of the City of San Francisco.

Action for damages sustained by the plaintiff in falling into an uncovered hole, dug in the sidewalk in front of defendants' premises. . . .

HEYDENFELDT, J. . . . If the defendants were at fault in leaving an uncovered hole in the sidewalk of a public street, the intoxication of the plaintiff cannot excuse such gross negligence. A drunken man is as much entitled to a safe street, as a sober one, and much more in need of it.

The judgment is reversed and the cause remanded.

Denver & Rio Grande R.R. v. Peterson
69 P. 578 (Colo. 1902)

CAMPBELL, C.J. The care required of a warehouseman is the same, whether he be rich or poor. For, if the fact that he is rich requires of him greater care than if he possessed only moderate means or is poor, then, if he were extremely poor, the care required might be such as practically to amount to nothing; and no one would claim that such an uncertain and sliding rule should be the measure of his liability. . . .

NOTE

The relevance of wealth to negligence liability. The decision in *Peterson* suggests that the level of care required of a defendant is constant regardless of its wealth. A justification for that result has been offered by Professors Abraham and Jeffries in Punitive Damages and the Rule of Law: The Role of Defendant's Wealth, 18 J. Legal Stud. 415, 416-418 (1989):

> The two major purposes for awarding compensatory tort damages are deterrence of socially undesirable conduct and compensation of the victims of such misconduct.
>
> First, and most importantly, the defendant's wealth is irrelevant to deterrence. Whether the defendant is rich or not simply has no logical bearing on the inhibitory role of the threat of tort liability. Deterrence theory is based on the (usually and to one or another extent plausible) assumption that actors weigh the expected costs and benefits of their future actions. Specifically, a potentially liable defendant will compare the benefits it will derive from an action that risks tort liability against the discounted present expected value of the liability that will be imposed if the risk occurs. Whether a defendant is wealthy or poor, this cost-benefit calculation is the same. If, as is likely, a wealthy defendant derives no greater benefit from a given action than a poor defendant, then both will be equally deterred (or equally undeterred) by the threat of tort liability. A defendant's existing assets do not increase the expected value of a given future action. Therefore they do not require any adjustment in the level of sanction needed to offset that expected value. The defendant's wealth or lack of it is thus irrelevant to the deterrence of socially undesirable conduct, and evidence on the subject is inadmissible in the typical tort action claiming compensatory damages. . . .
>
> Defendant's wealth is also irrelevant to the compensation aims of conventional tort liability. The successful tort plaintiff is entitled to recover in full for all losses proximately resulting from the action for which the defendant is held liable. The wealth available to the defendant to satisfy this obligation may be an important practical concern in settlement negotiations, but it is irrelevant to plaintiff's right of recovery. If evidence of the defendant's wealth were admissible, and if the jury took such considerations into account, the plaintiff's right to recover and the magnitude of the defendant's liability would depend on the identity of the defendant, rather than on the nature of the defendant's action and the extent of the plaintiff's loss. Although juries sometimes act as if they knew the extent of the defendant's wealth — to the point that commentators have coined the term "deep pocket" to explain the phenomenon — the law governing recovery of compensatory damages excludes such considerations as best it can.

The position taken by Abraham and Jeffries has been challenged in Arlen, Should Defendants' Wealth Matter?, 21 J. Legal Stud. 413, 422 (1992). Professor Arlen first notes that all individuals are risk averse (that is, they will pay a premium in order to avoid uncertainty) and then concludes that wealthier persons should be subjected to a higher standard of care. She writes: "If individuals are risk averse, then, all other things being equal, a wealthier potential defendant has a lower marginal utility of wealth than does a poorer potential defendant: he is, in other words, less adversely affected by a given expenditure on care than is a poorer person." The richer person thus sacrifices less utility for any given unit of wealth than does the poor person. This conclusion holds whether or not a defendant is able to purchase liability insurance. In principle Arlen's argument calls not for a simple division of defendants into rich and poor persons, but for an infinite gradation of defendants in accordance with their wealth. How is such a system to be administered? In determining this question does it make a difference how pronounced risk aversion is likely to be? What standard should be applied to corporate defendants with both rich and poor shareholders? Note that at present evidence that the defendant is insured is not admissible into evidence in most states and under the Federal Rules of Evidence, R. 411. It is, however, discoverable, Fed. R. Civ. P. 26(b)(2).

C. CALCULUS OF RISK

In this section we continue our examination of the judicial efforts to fashion and apply a standard of reasonable care. Our discussion proceeds on two levels. The first level deals with the creation of a theory of negligence applicable to ordinary individuals as well as to corporate or business entities. In some cases, negligence is given a commonsense, intuitive interpretation. In other cases courts, dissatisfied with the vagueness of the commonsense interpretation, seek to impart a more precise economic meaning to the term, adopting the language of costs and benefits — the "calculus" of risk. Both of these approaches are part of the law today, and both are examined here.

Blyth v. Birmingham Water Works
156 Eng. Rep. 1047 (Ex. 1856)

[The defendants were owners of a nonprofit waterworks charged by statute with the laying of water mains and fire plugs in the city streets, which pipes were to be 18 inches under ground. The fireplug in the instant case was built "according to the best known system, and the materials of it were at the time of the accident sound and in good order."]

On the 24th of February, a large quantity of water, escaping from the neck of the main, forced its way through the ground into the plaintiff's house. The apparatus had been laid down 25 years, and had worked well during that time. The defendants' engineer stated, that the water might have forced its way through the brickwork round the neck of the main, and that the accident might have been caused by the frost, inasmuch as the expansion of the water would force up the plug out of the neck, and the stopper being encrusted with ice would not suffer the plug to ascend. One of the severest frosts on record set in on the 15th of January, 1855, and continued until after the accident in question. An incrustation of ice and snow had gathered about the stopper, and in the street all round, and also for some inches between the stopper and the plug. The ice had been observed on the surface of the ground for a considerable time before the accident. A short time after the accident, the company's turncock removed the ice from the stopper, took out the plug, and replaced it.

The judge left it to the jury to consider whether the company had used proper care to prevent the accident. He thought that, if the defendants had taken out the ice adhering to the plug, the accident would not have happened, and left it to the jury to say whether they ought to have removed the ice. The jury found a verdict for the plaintiff for the sum claimed. . . .

ALDERSON, B. I am of opinion that there was no evidence to be left to the jury. The case turns upon the question, whether the facts proved shew that the defendants were guilty of negligence. Negligence is the omission to do something which a reasonable man, guided upon those considerations which ordinarily regulate the conduct of human affairs, would do, or doing something which a prudent and reasonable man would not do. The defendants might have been liable for negligence, if, unintentionally, they omitted to do that which a reasonable person would have done, or did that which a person taking reasonable precautions would not have done. A reasonable man would act with reference to the average circumstances of the temperature in ordinary years. The defendants had provided against such frosts as experience would have led men, acting prudently, to provide against; and they are not guilty of negligence, because their precautions proved insufficient against the effects of the extreme severity of the frost of 1855, which penetrated to a greater depth than any which ordinarily occurs south of the polar regions. Such a state of circumstances constitutes a contingency against which no reasonable man can provide. The result was an accident, for which the defendants cannot be held liable.

BRAMWELL, B. The Act of Parliament directed the defendants to lay down pipes, with plugs in them, as safety-valves, to prevent the bursting of the pipes. The plugs were properly made, and of proper material; but there was an accumulation of ice about this plug, which prevented it from acting properly. The defendants were not bound to keep the plugs clear. It appears to me that the plaintiff was under quite as much obligation to remove the ice and snow which had accumulated, as the defendants. However that may be, it appears to me that it would be monstrous to hold the defendants responsible because they did not foresee and prevent an accident, the cause of which was so obscure, that it was not discovered until many months after the accident had happened.

Verdict to be entered for the defendants.

Eckert v. Long Island R.R.
43 N.Y. 502 (1871)

. . . The case, as made by the plaintiff, was, that the deceased received an injury from a locomotive engine of the defendant, which resulted in his death, on the 26th day of November, 1867, under the following circumstances:

He was standing in the afternoon of the day named, in conversation with another person about fifty feet from the defendant's track, in East New York, as a train of cars was coming in from Jamaica, at a rate of speed estimated by the plaintiff's witnesses of from twelve to twenty miles per hour. The plaintiff's witnesses heard no signal either from the whistle or the bell upon the engine. The engine was constructed to run either way without turning, and it was then running backward with the cow-catcher next [to] the train it was drawing, and nothing in front to remove obstacles from the track. The claim of the plaintiff was that the evidence authorized the jury to find that the speed of the train was improper and negligent in that particular place, it being a thickly populated neighborhood, and one of the stations of the road.

The evidence on the part of the plaintiff, also showed, that a child three or four years old, was sitting or standing upon the track of the defendant's road as the train of cars was approaching, and was liable to be run over, if not removed; and the deceased, seeing the danger of the child, ran to it, and seizing it, threw it clear of the track on the side opposite to that from which he came; but continuing across the track himself, was struck by the step or some part of the locomotive or tender, thrown down, and received injuries from which he died the same night.

The evidence on the part of defendant, tended to prove that the cars were being run at a very moderate speed, not over seven or eight miles per hour, that the signals required by law were given, and that the child was not on the track over which the cars were passing, but on a side track near the main track.

So far as there was any conflict of evidence or question of fact, the questions were submitted to the jury. At the close of the plaintiff's case, the counsel for the defendant moved for a nonsuit upon the ground that it appeared that the deceased's negligence contributed to the injury, and the motion was denied and an exception taken. After the evidence was all in, the judge was requested by the counsel for the defendant to charge the jury, in different forms, that if the deceased voluntarily placed himself in peril from which he received the injury, to save the child, whether the child was or was not in danger, the plaintiff could not recover, and all the requests were refused and exceptions taken, and the question whether the negligence of the intestate contributed to the accident was submitted to the jury. The jury found a verdict for the plaintiff, and the judgment entered thereon was affirmed, on appeal, by the Supreme Court, and from the latter judgment the defendant has appealed to this court.

GROVER, J. The important question in this case arises upon the exception taken by the defendant's counsel to the denial of his motion for a nonsuit, made upon the ground that the negligence of the plaintiff's intestate contributed to the injury that caused his death. The evidence showed that the train was approaching in plain view of the deceased, and had he for his own purposes attempted to cross the track, or with a view to save property placed himself voluntarily in a position where he might have received an injury from a collision with the train, his conduct would have been grossly negligent, and no recovery could have been had for such injury. But the evidence further showed that there was a small child upon the track who, if not rescued, must have been inevitably crushed by the rapidly approaching train. This the deceased saw, and he owed a duty of important obligation to this child to rescue it from its extreme peril, if he could do so without incurring great danger to himself. Negligence implies some act of commission or omission wrongful in itself. Under the circumstances in which the deceased was placed, it was not wrongful in him to make every effort in his power to rescue the child, compatible with a reasonable regard for his own safety. It was his duty to exercise his judgment as to whether he could probably save the child without serious injury to himself. If, from the appearances, he believed that he could, it was not negligence to make an attempt so to do, although believing that possibly he might fail and receive an injury himself. He had no time for deliberation. He must act instantly, if at all, as a moment's delay would have been fatal to the child. The law has so high a regard for human life that it will not impute negligence to an effort to preserve it, unless made under such circumstances as to constitute rashness in the judgment of prudent persons. For a person engaged in his ordinary affairs, or in the mere protection of property, knowingly and voluntarily to place himself in a position where he is liable to receive a serious injury, is negligence, which will preclude a recovery for an injury so received; but when the exposure is for the purpose of saving life, it is not wrongful, and therefore not negligent unless such as to be regarded either rash or reckless. The jury were warranted in finding the deceased free from negligence under the rule as above stated. . . .

ALLEN, J., dissenting. The plaintiff's intestate was not placed in the peril from which he received the injury resulting in his death, by any act or omission of duty of the defendants, its servants, or agents. He went upon the track of the defendant's road in front of an approaching train, voluntarily, in the exercise of his free will, and while in the full possession of all his faculties, and with capacity to judge of the danger. His action was the result of his own choice, and such choice not compulsory. He was not compelled, or apparently compelled, to take any action to avoid a peril, and harm to himself, from the negligent or wrongful act of the defendant, or the agents in charge of the train. The plaintiff's rights are the same as those of the intestate would have been, had he survived the injury and brought the action, and must be tested by the same rules; and to him and consequently to the plaintiff, the maxim volenti non fit injuria applies. It is a well established rule, that no one can maintain an action for a wrong, when he consents or contributes to the act which occasions his loss. One who with liberty of choice, and knowledge of the hazard of injury, places himself in a position of danger, does so at his own peril, and must take the consequences of his act.

Terry, Negligence
29 Harv. L. Rev. 40, 42-44 (1915)

To make conduct negligent the risk involved in it must be unreasonably great; some injurious consequences of it must be not only possible or in a sense probable, but unreasonably probable. It is quite impossible in the business of life to avoid taking risks of injury to one's self or others, and the law does not forbid doing so; what it requires is that the risk be not unreasonably great. The essence of negligence is unreasonableness; due care is simply reasonable conduct. There is no mathematical rule of percentage of probabilities to be followed here. A risk is not necessarily unreasonable because the harmful consequence is more likely than not to follow the conduct, nor reasonable because the chances are against that. A very large risk may be reasonable in some circumstances, and a small risk unreasonable in other circumstances. When due care consists in taking precautions against harm, only reasonable precautions need be taken, not every conceivable or possible precaution. And precautions need not be taken against every conceivable or foreseeable danger, but only against probable dangers. The books are full of cases where persons have been held not negligent for not guarding against a certain harmful event, on the ground that they need not reasonably have expected it to happen. . . .

The reasonableness of a given risk may depend upon the following five factors:

(1) The magnitude of the risk. A risk is more likely to be unreasonable the greater it is.

(2) The value or importance of that which is exposed to the risk, which is the object that the law desires to protect, and may be called the principal object. The reasonableness of a risk means its reasonableness with respect to the principal object.

(3) A person who takes a risk of injuring the principal object usually does so because he has some reason of his own for such conduct, — is pursuing some object of his own. This may be called the collateral object. In some cases, at least, the value or importance of the collateral object is properly to be considered in deciding upon the reasonableness of the risk.

(4) The probability that the collateral object will be attained by the conduct which involves risk to the principal; the utility of the risk.

(5) The probability that the collateral object would not have been attained without taking the risk; the necessity of the risk. The following case will serve as an illustration.

The plaintiff's intestate, seeing a child on a railroad track just in front of a rapidly approaching train, went upon the track to save him. He did save him, but was himself killed by the train. The jury were allowed to find that he had not been guilty of contributory negligence. The question was of course whether he had exposed himself to an unreasonably great risk. Here the above-mentioned elements of reasonableness were as follows:

(1) The magnitude of the risk was the probability that he would be killed or hurt. That was very great.

(2) The principal object was his own life, which was very valuable.

(3) The collateral object was the child's life, which was also very valuable.

(4) The utility of the risk was the probability that he could save the child. That must have been fairly great, since he in fact succeeded. Had there been no fair chance of saving the child, the conduct would have been unreasonable and negligent.

(5) The necessity of the risk was the probability that the child would not have saved himself by getting off the track in time.

Here, although the magnitude of the risk was very great and the principal object very valuable, yet the value of the collateral object and the great utility and necessity of the risk counterbalanced those considerations, and made the risk reasonable. The same risk would have been unreasonable, had the creature on the track been a kitten, because the value of the collateral object would have been small. There is no general rule that human life may not be put at risk in order to save property; but since life is more valuable than property, such a risk has often been held unreasonable in particular cases, which has given rise to dicta to the effect that it is always so. But in the circumstances of other cases a risk of that sort has been held reasonable.

Seavey, Negligence — Subjective or Objective?
41 Harv. L. Rev. 1, 8, n.7 (1927)

We must not assume that we can rely upon any formula in regard to "balancing interests" to solve negligence cases. The phrase is only a convenient one to indicate factors which may be considered and should not connote any mathematical correspondence. Thus I would assume that an actor is liable if, to save his own horse of equal value with the plaintiff's, he were to take a fifty per cent chance of killing the plaintiff's horse, while it would at least be more doubtful whether he might not take a fifty per cent chance of killing another to save his own life. In either event, if the plaintiff's and the defendant's interests are considered of equal value, the defendant would not be liable upon the theory of balancing interests. Upon the same theory one doing an unlawful act or an act in preparation for one, would be liable to any one injured as a consequence, since, by hypothesis, his act has no social value. In the field of negligence, interests are balanced only in the sense that the purposes of the actor, the nature of his act and the harm that may result from action or inaction are elements to be considered. Some of these elements are not considered when the actor knows or desires that his conduct will result in interference with the plaintiff or his property. Thus if, to save his life, A intentionally destroys ten cents worth of B's property, A must pay; if, however, he takes a ten per cent chance of killing B in an effort to save his own life, his conduct might not be found to be wrongful, although obviously B would much prefer, antecedently, to lose ten cents worth of property than to submit to a ten per cent chance of being killed.

Osborne v. Montgomery
234 N.W. 372 (Wis. 1931)

On August 30, 1928, the plaintiff Lester Osborne, then a boy of thirteen years of age, was employed by the Wisconsin State Journal in running errands. He was returning to his place of employment on a bicycle.

Traveling westerly on East Washington Street, he turned northerly on Pinckney street and as he proceeded north on Pinckney street he followed a car driven by the defendant. The defendant stopped his car for the purpose of leaving some clothing at a cleaner's. The defendant opened the door to his car intending to step from it on the left-hand side. The defendant's car at the time of the accident stood between a line of cars parked at the curb and the easterly rail of the street car tracks. As the defendant's car stopped and the door opened, and the plaintiff endeavored to pass, the right handle bar of his bicycle came in contact with the outside edge of the door, tipping the bicycle and throwing the plaintiff to the ground, causing the injuries complained of.

There was a jury trial, the jury found the defendant negligent as to lookout and the opening of his car door, but that he was not negligent in stopping his car where he did; that defendant's negligence was the cause of the injury; that the plaintiff was not guilty of contributory negligence; and assessed plaintiff's damages at $2,500. . . .

ROSENBERRY, C.J. Manifestly, not every want of care results in liability. In order to measure care some standards must be adopted. Human beings must live in association with each other, as a consequence of which their rights, duties, and obligations are relative, not absolute. We apply the standards which guide the great mass of mankind in determining what is proper conduct of an individual under all the circumstances and say that he was or was not justified in doing the act in question. While it is true that the standard thus set up is varying and indefinite, it is nevertheless one which may be fairly and justly applied to human conduct. Such a standard is usually spoken of as ordinary care, being that degree of care which under the same or similar circumstances the great mass of mankind would ordinarily exercise.

In a consideration of this subject it is easy to get lost in a maze of metaphysical distinctions, or perhaps it may better be said it is difficult not to be so lost. The defect in the instruction is that it indicates no standard by which the conduct of the defendant is to be measured. In support of the instruction it is argued that the great mass of mankind do not indulge in conduct which results in harm to others; and therefore it must follow that if one does an act which results in injury to another, he departs from the standards which are followed by the great mass of mankind. The argument is based upon an inference not readily drawn, and, in addition to that, the premise is not sound. We are constantly doing acts which result in injury to others which are not negligent and do not result in liability. Many of the cases classified as those damnum absque injuria and cases where the damages are said to be consequential and remote are illustrations of this. While the acts result in injury to others, they are held to be not negligent because they are in conformity to what the great mass of mankind would do under the same or similar circumstances. The statement is true in all situations where liability exists, but it does not exclude situations where liability does not exist.

The fundamental idea of liability for wrongful acts is that upon a balancing of the social interests involved in each case, the law determines that under the circumstances of a particular case an actor should or should not become liable for the natural consequences of his conduct. One driving a car in a thickly populated district on a rainy day, slowly and in the most careful manner, may do injury to the person of another by throwing muddy or infected water upon that person. Society does not hold the actor responsible because the benefit of allowing people to travel under such circumstances so far outweighs the probable injury to bystanders that such conduct is not disapproved. Circumstances may require the driver of a fire truck to take his truck through a thickly populated district at a high rate of speed, but if he exercises that degree of care which such drivers ordinarily exercise under the same or similar circumstances, society, weighing the benefits against the probabilities of damage, in spite of the fact that as a reasonably prudent and intelligent man he should foresee that harm may result, justifies the risk and holds him not liable.

Cooley v. Public Service Co.
10 A.2d 673 (N.H. 1940)

[Defendant power company maintained uninsulated electric lines crossing the telephone company's wires about 8 or 10 feet above them at right angles. During a severe winter storm a power line broke and, before it was grounded and rendered harmless, it hit a telephone cable, burning through its cover and causing the incident which led to the harm complained of. Plaintiff was using the telephone when suddenly a terrifically loud noise came through the diaphragm into her ear, and she fell to the floor in a faint. She sustained a very rare neurosis, with fairly severe physical consequences.

Plaintiff sued the power company and the telephone company. At the trial the jury found for the telephone company but against the power company. The power company appealed, and the judgment was reversed.]

PAGE, J. Apparently there is no claim that the negligence of the defendant caused the wires to fall. The plaintiff's sole claim is that the defendant could have anticipated (1) that its wire might fall for a variety of reasons, which is true; (2) that a telephone subscriber in such case might hear a great noise, which also is true; (3) that as a result of fright thereby induced the user of the telephone would suffer physical injuries, which, as we have seen, is a rare contingency, though it may be anticipated. It is urged that the defendant's consequent duty was to maintain such devices at cross-overs as would prevent one of its falling wires from coming into contact with a telephone wire.

The devices suggested are two. The first is a wire-mesh basket suspended from the poles of the defendant at the point of cross-over, above the cable and below the defendant's wires. Two forms were suggested. One would be about six by eight feet. The other would be of an unassigned width and would stretch the full distance between defendant's poles. In either case the basket would be insulated. The theory is that falling wires, though alive, would remain harmless in the basket.

[The court, after detailed examination of these proposals, concluded that each of these suggested devices would have entailed a greater risk of electrocution to people passing on the street, even assuming that they might have reduced the risk of loud noises to those using the telephone. The court then continued, in part:]

In the case before us, there was danger of electrocution in the street. As long as the telephone company's safety devices are properly installed and maintained, there is no danger of electrocution in the house. The only foreseeable danger to the telephone subscriber is from noise — fright and neuroses. Balancing the two, the danger to those such as the plaintiff is remote, that to those on the ground near the broken wires is obvious and immediate. The balance would not be improved by taking a chance to avoid traumatic neurosis of the plaintiff at the expense of greater risk to the lives of others. To the extent that the duty to use care depends upon relationship, the defendant's duty of care towards the plaintiff is obviously weaker than that towards the man in the street.

The defendant's duty cannot, in the circumstances, be to both. If that were so, performance of one duty would mean non-performance of the other. If it be negligent to save the life of the highway traveler at the expense of bodily injury resulting from the fright and neurosis of a telephone subscriber, it must be equally negligent to avoid the fright at the risk of another's life. The law could tolerate no such theory of "be liable if you do and liable if you don't." The law does not contemplate a shifting duty that requires care towards A and then discovers a duty to avoid injury incidentally suffered by B because there was due care with respect to A. Such a shifting is entirely inconsistent with the fundamental conception that the duty of due care requires precisely the measure of care that is reasonable under all the circumstances. 2 Restatement Torts, §§291-295. . . .

It is not doubted that due care might require the defendant to adopt some device that would afford protection against emotional disturbances in telephone-users without depriving the traveling public of reasonable protection from live wires immediately dangerous to life. Such a device, if it exists, is not disclosed by the record. The burden was upon the plaintiff to show its practicability. Since the burden was not sustained a verdict should have been directed for the defendant.

Other exceptions therefore require no consideration.
Judgment for the defendant. All concurred.

NOTE

Activity level versus care level. The plaintiff in *Cooley* tried to find fault
with the way in which the power company maintained its wires above
ground. Yet nowhere did the decision ask whether the company made
a sound decision to place the wires above ground in the first place.
Stated more generally, the issue is whether a system of tort law should
examine only the level of care undertaken once the defendant has decided to undertake a given activity or whether it should also examine
the type or level of activity that the defendant is prepared to engage in.
   The theoretical point is raised in Shavell, Strict Liability versus Negligence, 9 J. Legal Stud. 1, 2-3 (1980). There Shavell discusses the "unilateral case," "by which it is meant the actions of injurers but not of victims
are assumed to affect the probability or severity of losses."

> By definition, under the negligence rule all that an injurer needs to
> do to avoid the possibility of liability is to make sure to exercise due care
> if he engages in his activity. Consequently *he will not be motivated to consider
> the effect on accident losses of his choice of whether to engage in his activity or,
> more generally, of the level at which to engage in his activity*; he will choose his
> level of activity in accordance only with the personal benefits so derived.
> But surely any increase in his level of activity will typically raise expected
> accident losses (holding constant the level of care). Thus he will be led
> to choose too high a level of activity; the negligence rule is not "efficient."
>   Consider by way of illustration the problem of pedestrian-automobile
> accidents (and, as we are now discussing the unilateral case, let us imag-
> ine the behavior of pedestrians to be fixed). Suppose that drivers of auto-
> mobiles find it in their interest to adhere to the standard of due care but
> that the possibility of accidents is not thereby eliminated. Then, in decid-
> ing how much to drive, they will contemplate only the enjoyment they
> get from doing so. Because (as they exercise due care) they will not be
> liable for harm suffered by pedestrians, drivers will not take into account
> that going more miles will mean a higher expected number of accidents.
> Hence, there will be too much driving; an individual will, for example,
> decide to go for a drive on a mere whim despite the imposition of a
> positive expected cost to pedestrians.
>   However, under a rule of strict liability, the situation is different. Be-
> cause an injurer must pay for losses whenever he is involved in an acci-
> dent, he will be induced to consider the effect on accident losses of both
> his level of care *and* his level of activity. His decisions will therefore be
> efficient. Because drivers will be liable for losses sustained by pedestrians,
> they will decide not only to exercise due care in driving but also to drive
> only when the utility gained from it outweighs expected liability pay-
> ments to pedestrians.

Does it follow as a matter of definition that choices of activity level are outside judicial review under a negligence decision? Recall in this context the suggestion made in Bolton v. Stone, supra at page 150, that it might have been negligent to play cricket *at all* on the field. Is a jury as competent in making decisions on activity levels as it is on care levels? Should it examine the pedestrian's care level?

United States v. Carroll Towing Co.
159 F.2d 169 (2d Cir. 1947)

[The defendant tug was moving a line of barges in and out of New York Harbor, including the *Anna C,* owned by the Connors Company. The *Anna C* broke away from the line of barges being moved and was carried by the wind and tide into a tanker, whose propeller broke through the *Anna C's* hull, after which the barge started to leak. One question before the court was the contributory negligence of the barge owner: should a bargee have been kept on board the barge? If a bargee had been on board it might have been possible to save the barge by an early discovery of the damage to the hull.]

L. HAND, C.J. . . . It appears from the foregoing review that there is no general rule to determine when the absence of a bargee or other attendant will make the owner of the barge liable for injuries to other vessels if she breaks away from her moorings. However, in any cases where he would be so liable for injuries to others, obviously he must reduce his damages proportionately, if the injury is to his own barge. It becomes apparent why there can be no such general rule, when we consider the grounds for such a liability. Since there are occasions when every vessel will break from her moorings, and since, if she does, she becomes a menace to those about her, the owner's duty, as in other similar situations, to provide against resulting injuries is a function of three variables: (1) The probability that she will break away; (2) the gravity of the resulting injury, if she does; (3) the burden of adequate precautions. Possibly it serves to bring this notion into relief to state it in algebraic terms: if the probability be called P; the injury, L; and the burden, B; liability depends upon whether B is less than L multiplied by P: i.e., whether B [is less than] PL. Applied to the situation at bar, the likelihood that a barge will break from her fasts and the damage she will do, vary with the place and time; for example, if a storm threatens, the danger is greater; so it is, if she is in a crowded harbor where moored barges are constantly being shifted about. On the other hand, the barge must not be the bargee's prison, even though he lives aboard; he must go ashore at times. We need not say whether, even in such crowded waters as New York Harbor a bargee must be aboard at night at all; it may be that the custom is otherwise, as Ward, J., supposed in

The Kathryn B. Guinan, 176 F. 301 [2d Cir. 1910]; and that, if so, the situation is one where custom should control. We leave that question open; but we hold that it is not in all cases a sufficient answer to a bargee's absence without excuse, during working hours, that he has properly made fast his barge to a pier, when he leaves her. In the case at bar the bargee left at five o'clock in the afternoon of January 3rd, and the flotilla broke away at about two o'clock in the afternoon of the following day, twenty-one hours afterwards. The bargee had been away all the time, and we hold that his fabricated story was affirmative evidence that he had no excuse for his absence. At the locus in quo — especially during the short January days and in the full tide of war activity — barges were being constantly "drilled" in and out. Certainly it was not beyond reasonable expectation, that with the inevitable haste and bustle, the work might not be done with adequate care. In such circumstances we hold — and it is all that we do hold — that it was a fair requirement that the Connors Company should have a bargee aboard (unless he had some excuse for his absence), during the working hours of daylight.

NOTES

1. *An economic interpretation of negligence?* Within the law and economics movement, Learned Hand's opinion in *Carroll Towing* has spawned a burgeoning academic literature on the economic interpretation of negligence and, by implication, the entire tort law. Thus Judge Posner, A Theory of Negligence, 1 J. Legal Stud. 29, 32-33 (1972), opened the debate by arguing that the Hand formula provides an operational definition of unreasonable risk under the negligence law:

> Hand was adumbrating, perhaps unwittingly, an economic meaning of negligence. Discounting (multiplying) the cost of an accident if it occurs by the probability of occurrence yields a measure of the economic benefit to be anticipated from incurring the costs necessary to prevent the accident. The cost of prevention is what Hand meant by the burden of taking precautions against the accident. It may be the cost of installing safety equipment or otherwise making the activity safer, or the benefit forgone by curtailing or eliminating the activity. If the cost of safety measures or of curtailment — whichever cost is lower — exceeds the benefit in accident avoidance to be gained by incurring that cost, society would be better off, in economic terms, to forgo accident prevention. A rule making the enterprise liable for the accidents that occur in such cases cannot be justified on the ground that it will induce the enterprise to increase the safety of its operations. When the cost of accidents is less than the cost of prevention, a rational profit-maximizing enterprise will pay tort judgments to the accident victims rather than incur the larger cost of avoiding liability. Furthermore, overall economic value or welfare

would be diminished rather than increased by incurring a higher accident-prevention cost in order to avoid a lower accident cost. If, on the other hand, the benefits in accident avoidance exceed the costs of prevention, society is better off if those costs are incurred and the accident averted, and so in this case the enterprise is made liable, in the expectation that self-interest will lead it to adopt the precautions in order to avoid a greater cost in tort judgments.

2. *Measurement problems under the Hand formula.* How does a court or jury find the information needed to apply the Hand formula? Hand himself was sensitive to the problem. In Moisan v. Loftus, 178 F.2d 148, 149 (2d Cir. 1949), he wrote:

> The difficulties are in applying the rule, . . . they arise from the necessity of applying a quantitative test to an incommensurable subject-matter and the same difficulties inhere in the concept of "ordinary" negligence. It is indeed possible to state an equation for negligence in the form, $C = P \times D$ [in] which the C is the care required to avoid risk, D, the possible injuries, and P, the probability that the injuries will occur, if the requisite care is not taken. But of these factors care is the only one ever susceptible of quantitative estimate, and often that is not. The injuries are always a variable within limits, which do not admit of even approximate ascertainment and, although probability might theoretically be estimated, if any statistics were available, they never are and, besides, probability varies with the severity of the injuries. It follows that all such attempts are illusory, and, if serviceable at all, are so only to center attention upon which one of the factors may be determinative in any given situation.

Does the Hand formula apply any effective constraint upon the negligence determination made by a jury? What should be done if the estimates of B, P, and L can each vary independently by a factor of 10? Does it make a difference if human life (unlike property damage) has no estimable market value?

Thus far the analysis presupposes that both the probability and expected severity of harm have equal weight in the calculations. Need this be so? In Paris v. Stepney Borough Council, [1951] A.C. 367, the defendant employer did not provide plaintiff with a pair of goggles. Plaintiff was a one-eyed workman who in the course of his duties was required to hammer metal in such a manner that chips would fly about. One of those chips struck plaintiff in his eye and blinded him. It was agreed by all parties that defendant was not obligated to provide goggles to two-eyed employees. Defendant argued that likewise it was not obligated to provide them to plaintiff. The House of Lords, by a vote of three to two, restored a verdict in favor of plaintiff, noting that even though the risk of harm was the same for both one- and two-eyed men, the consequences of the loss of an eye were far more serious in the latter case. The decision reversed the judgment in the Court of Appeal, where Asquith, L.J., had argued: " . . . The plaintiff's disability could only be relevant to the stringency of the duty owed to him if it increased the risk to which he was exposed. A one-eyed man is no more likely to get a splinter or a chip in his eye than is a two-eyed man. The risk is no greater although the damage may be to a man with only one good eye than to a man with two good eyes. But the quantum of damage is one thing and the scope of duty is another. A greater risk of injury is not the same thing as a risk of greater injury; the first alone is relevant to liability."

3. *Marginal precautions and the Hand formula.* One important conceptual problem involves choosing the correct interval over which to assess defendant's conduct. Suppose that it is possible for the defendant to take an extra $100 in precautions which yield, say, $150 in additional benefits. At first blush, it appears that the precautions should be taken given that *in aggregate* the expected benefits exceed the expected costs. Nonetheless a closer analysis reveals that too much care may be required under this approach. The key point is that in economic terms, additional precautions are desirable *at the margin* only as long as an additional dollar of precautions reduces the expected costs of injury by a dollar. Thus, in the example above, suppose that the first $60 in precautions yield $120 in benefits, while the next $40 in precautions yielded only $30 in benefits. In principle the lesser precaution is more desirable because it generates $60 in *net* benefits ($120-$60), while the next $40 in precautions generates *minus* $10 in net benefits ($30-$40). The lesser precaution therefore generates the greater social benefit. On this analysis, therefore, the plaintiff does not make out a conclusive case of negligence by showing only a net social gain from taking the proposed precautions. In principle the defendant should be allowed to show that some lower level of precaution would have generated a higher net social return. Assuming this issue can be litigated, how should the burdens of proof be distributed on the question of marginal precautions?

4. *Risk neutrality.* On its face, the Hand formula appears to presuppose that all individuals are risk-neutral in their attitude and behavior. A risk-neutral actor, in dealing with the expected gains or losses of a future uncertain event, simply multiplies the probability of its occurrence by its magnitude, as in the Hand formula itself. It is, however, recognized that some people prefer risk and others are averse to it. In essence, the first class of individuals gains some positive satisfaction from taking chances, while persons in the second class are prepared to pay in order to avoid having to confront risks. Thus a risk preferrer would prefer a 10 percent chance of receiving $100 to a certainty of receiving $10. Conversely, the risk-averse person prefers the certainty of receiving $10 to a 10 percent chance of receiving $100. Risk preference and risk aversion are both matters of degree; it is quite possible

that some would pay only $11 to avoid the 10 percent chance of a $100 loss while someone else might pay as much as $20. For a defense of the risk neutrality assumption in the Hand formula see W. Landes and R. Posner, The Economic Structure of Tort Law 55-57 (1987). Should it be followed if most individuals and most corporations are risk averse?

5. *Does efficiency require negligence?* Under the orthodox economic accounts of the tort law, the Hand formula is not the only rule that leads to social efficiency. A system of strict liability with contributory negligence, or even a system of negligence without contributory negligence, should also induce (as a first approximation) optimal behavior by both parties. The proposition was demonstrated in Brown, Toward an Economic Theory of Liability, 2 J. Legal Stud. 323 (1973), and more complete expositions can be found in W. Landes and R. Posner, The Economic Structure of Tort Law ch. 3 (1987), and S. Shavell, Economic Analysis of Accident Law 26-46 (1987).

The basic intuition behind the position is as follows. Let us assume that each (rationally self-interested) party wishes to minimize the sum of its precaution and accident costs. In the legal regime that predicates liability on proof of defendant's negligence alone, the defendant will take care, even *without* the defense of contributory negligence: the cost of precautions is below that of the anticipated liability. Once the plaintiff knows that the defendant will take care, the plaintiff also knows that all prospect of recovery is thereby precluded. The plaintiff therefore now has (wholly without regard to the contributory negligence defense) an incentive to take the optimal level of care as well. Both parties will behave optimally without the contributory negligence defense.

Similarly, under the strict liability system, the plaintiff will recover unless barred by contributory negligence. Yet so long as precautions are cheaper than expected accidents, it will pay the plaintiff to take care in order to preserve the right of action. Once the defendant knows that the plaintiff will not misbehave, then, even with the strict liability rule, he has an incentive to choose the optimal level of care to minimize his own costs. Again both sides will take proper care, although one party has a duty of care.

Brown's proofs generate a certain paradoxical result: since all persons are rational, no one can ever be negligent. Yet negligence is commonplace, and so the question is, why? The most obvious explanation is that error pervades the behavior of both the judges and juries who operate the legal system, making every trial something of a rational gamble. Similar types of error are likely to influence the conduct of the private actors who are ignorant of the rules, and even those who struggle to comply with them. In addition, private actors may have all sorts of reason for not complying with the law because they are broke, stressed, demoralized, bored, or fatigued. Finally, the increased possibilities for taking care may simply increase the number of ways in which it is possible to be negligent. The physician who could do nothing to help a patient in 1900 could be negligent in a thousand ways in 1995. See generally Grady, Why Are People Negligent? Technology, Nondurable Precautions, and the Medical Malpractice Explosion, 82 Nw. U. L. Rev. 293 (1988).

6. *Discontinuities and the choice between negligence and strict liability.* The first round of theory about the negligence standard assumed that if both courts and litigants could determine the optimal standard of care then any negligence system was efficient. But suppose that the standard of negligence, so fluid in its formulation, cannot be perfectly ascertained beforehand. To make the model manageable assume that judges and juries after the fact are able to apply the negligence standard perfectly, while potential defendants are not.

Under these circumstances it is possible to make the somewhat counterintuitive argument that the negligence standard induces a somewhat higher level of care than the strict liability rule. See Grady, A New Positive Economic Theory of Negligence, 92 Yale L.J. 799 (1983). Grady's argument rests on the assumption that the tort defendant knows that in searching for the appropriate care level it may take too little or too much care. Under a strict liability system, the consequences of error in either direction are relatively small and evenly balanced. Taking too much care results in some small increase in the total costs of prevention, suit, and damage payments because too much is spent on prevention. Taking too little care has the same effect because now too much is paid in damages. Under a negligence system, however, the two types of error have dramatically different error costs. Taking too much care has, as before, the effect of imposing some small increases on the defendant's total costs. Taking too little care, however, immediately exposes the defendant to onerous tort liabilities. Under strict liability, a defendant has no incentive to prefer one type of error to the other. In contrast, under negligence the defendant has the incentive to take some additional care to avoid heavy liabilities.

Grady's analysis of error has in turn been challenged in Calfee and Craswell, Some Effects of Uncertainty on Compliance with Legal Standards, 70 Va. L. Rev. 965, 982, n.36 (1984) who conclude that it is unclear whether the use of a negligence standard will induce too much or too little care by defendants, and may under different circumstances do some of each.

> Professor Grady has recently argued that defendants facing an uncertain negligence standard (who are made to pay the full accident costs if they are found negligent) will *always* overcomply as long as the uncertainty is symmetrical. However, Grady compares the costs and benefits facing defendants who take too little care without taking into account that the benefits of too little care (reduced expenditures on care) accrue to the defendant with absolute certainty, whereas the costs of too little

care (liability for tort damages) may not have to be paid if the defendant is fortuitously found not liable. In other words, Grady's analysis of uncertainty omits the effect of the chance that the defendant might not "get caught," which is precisely the factor that creates the incentive to undercomply.

7. *Application of the Hand formula: public or private function.* The Hand formula imposes an explicit demand on the trier of fact to the relevant cost-benefit analysis. In order to place that function on private parties, Calabresi and Hirschoff have advocated a version of strict liability in Toward a Test for Strict Liability in Torts, 81 Yale L.J. 1055, 1060-1061 (1972):

> The strict liability test we suggest does not require that a governmental institution make such a cost-benefit analysis. It requires of such an institution only a decision as to which of the parties to the accident *is in the best position to make the cost-benefit analysis between accident costs and accident avoidance costs and to act on that decision once it is made.* The question for the court reduces to a search for the cheapest cost avoider.
>
> So stated, the strict liability test sounds deceptively simple to apply. Instead of requiring a judgment as to whether an injurer *should* have avoided the accident costs because the costs of avoidance were less than the foreseeable accident costs as the Learned Hand test does, the strict liability test would simply require a decision as to whether the injurer or the victim was in the better position both to judge whether avoidance costs would exceed foreseeable accident costs and to act on that judgment. The issue becomes not *whether* avoidance is worth it, but which of the parties is relatively more likely to find out whether avoidance is worth it. This judgment is by no means an easy one, but we would suggest that in practice it is usually easier to make correctly than is the judgment required under either the Learned Hand test or its reverse. It also implies a lesser degree of governmental intervention than does either of the Hand type tests.

Elsewhere in their article Calabresi and Hirschoff (Id. at 1059) introduce their "reverse Hand" formula in order to show how the Hand formula can be applied to the plaintiff's conduct.

> Under such a "reverse Learned Hand test," the costs of an accident would be borne by the *injurer* unless accident avoidance on the part of the victim would have cost less than the accident. If a reverse contributory negligence test were added, the victim would bear the accident costs only if the injurer could not also have avoided the accident at less cost than the accident entailed. A reverse Learned Hand test, in other words, which always made the injurer liable without fault unless the victim were negligent, and even then held the injurer liable if he also were negligent, would do for primary accident cost avoidance just what the actual Learned Hand test with contributory negligence is said to do. The only difference between the tests is distributional. Under the Learned Hand test, the costs of all accidents *not* worth avoiding are borne by victims,

whereas under the reverse Learned Hand test they would be borne by injurers.

How does a court identify the cheaper cost avoider when one party is better able to assess the magnitude of the risk while the other party is better able to control damages in the event the harm materializes?

For criticism of Calabresi's test of strict liability see Posner, Strict Liability: A Comment, 2 J. Legal Stud. 205, 213-215 (1973). For an elaboration of his earlier work with Hirschoff see Calabresi and Klevorick, Four Tests for Liability in Tort, 14 J. Legal Stud. 585 (1985), with comments thereon by Brown and Rabin.

To what extent are these various accounts of negligence and strict liability reflected in the following materials?

H. Laurence Ross, Settled Out of Court
The Social Process of Insurance Claims Adjustment 98-99 (1970)

The formal law of negligence liability, as stated in casebooks from the opinions of appellate courts, is not easily applied to the accident at Second and Main. It deals with the violation of a duty of care owed by the insured to the claimant and is based on a very complex and perplexing model of the "reasonable man," in this case the reasonable driver. . . . In their day-to-day work, the concern with liability is reduced to the question of whether either or both parties violated the rules of the road as expressed in common traffic laws. Taking the doctrine of negligence per se to an extreme doubtless unforeseen by the makers of the formal law, adjusters tend to define a claim as one of liability or of no liability depending only on whether a rule was violated, regardless of intention, knowledge, necessity, and other such qualifications that might receive sympathetic attention even from a traffic court judge. Such a determination is far easier than the task proposed in theory by the formal law of negligence.

To illustrate, if Car A strikes Car B from the rear, the driver of A is assumed to be liable and B is not. In the ordinary course of events, particularly where damages are routine, the adjuster is not concerned with *why* A struck B, or with whether A violated a duty of care to B, or with whether A was unreasonable or not. These questions are avoided, not only because they may be impossible to answer, but also because the fact that A struck B from the rear will satisfy all supervisory levels that a payment is in order, without further explanation. Likewise, in the routine case, the fact that A was emerging from a street governed by a stop sign will justify treating this as a case of liability, without concern for whether the sign was seen or not, whether there was adequate reason for not seeing the sign, etc. In short, in the ordinary case the physical facts of the accident are normally sufficient to allocate liability between the drivers. Inasmuch as the basic physical facts of the accident are easily known — and they are frequently ascertainable from the first notice — the issue of liability is usually relatively easy to dispose of.

Rinaldo v. McGovern
587 N.E. 2d 264 (N.Y. 1991)

TITONE, J. The issue in this appeal is whether a golfer who accidentally misses the fairway and instead sends the ball soaring off the golf course onto an adjacent roadway can be held liable in negligence for the resulting injury. Under the circumstances of this case, we hold that the defendant golfer incurred no tort liability for what amounted to nothing more than his poorly hit tee shot.

The present action arises out of an accident in which a golf ball driven by one of the two individual defendants soared off the golf course on which they were playing, traveled through (or over) a screen of trees and landed on an adjacent public road, where plaintiffs happened to be driving their automobile. The ball struck and shattered plaintiffs' windshield, with the result that plaintiff Roberta Rinaldo was injured. It is undisputed that both defendants, who were teeing off at the eleventh hole of the golf course, intended to drive their balls straight down the fairway and not in the direction of the trees. However, each defendant "sliced" his ball, causing it to veer off to the right. There is no evidence that either defendant was careless or guilty of anything other than making an inept tee shot.

Plaintiffs commenced the present action charging the individual defendants with negligence and failure to warn. On defendants' motion for summary judgment, the Supreme Court, Erie County, dismissed both causes of action, holding that defendants had no duty to warn plaintiffs of their impending tee shots and that defendants' conduct in mishitting their golf balls did not, without more, constitute actionable negligence. The Appellate Division affirmed with two Justices dissenting. This appeal ensued. Plaintiffs also sued the operator of the golf course, Springville Country Club, Inc. By consent order dated May 6, 1991, plaintiffs' appeal with respect to this defendant, as well as to the individual defendant Donald Vogel, was discontinued. Accordingly, the only question before us now is the liability of the other individual defendant, Arthur McGovern.

In general, a golfer preparing to drive a ball has no duty to warn persons "not in the intended line of flight on another tee or fairway." Even more to the point, whatever the extent of a golfer's duty to other players in the immediate vicinity on the golf course, a golfer ordinarily may not be held liable to individuals located entirely outside of the boundaries of the golf course who happen to be hit by a stray, mishit ball (see, Nussbaum v. Lacopo, 265 N.E.2d 762 (N.Y. 1970)).

In Nussbaum v. Lacopo, we considered the liability of a golfer for failing to warn the occupant of a nearby residence before driving his golf ball. In rejecting the injured resident's claim, we noted that the duty to warn "is imposed to prevent accidents" and that no such duty should be imposed where "the relationship between the failure to warn and [the] plaintiff's injuries is tenuous." We concluded that imposing a duty to warn would be futile under the circumstances presented in *Nussbaum* because "[l]iving so close to a golf course, plaintiff would necessarily hear numerous warning shouts each day . . . [and, consequently,] could be expected to ignore them."

Plaintiffs contend that the analysis in *Nussbaum* is inapplicable to this case because the *Nussbaum* Court specifically stated that "one who chooses to reside on property abutting a golf course is not entitled to the same protection as the traveler on the public highway," thereby suggesting that individuals in the latter class are entitled to special protection. Although plaintiffs, who were innocent travelers, hope to benefit from this distinction, their argument on this point is meritless. The dictum on which plaintiffs rely appears in the section of the Court's opinion dealing with the liability of the golf course for nuisance and negligent design. Whatever its legal significance in that category of cases, this dictum has no bearing on the viability of a claim such as this one, which was brought against an individual golfer on the basis of an alleged failure to warn.

Instead, the pertinent question here, as in *Nussbaum,* is whether a warning, if given, would have been effective in preventing the accident. We conclude that, under the circumstances of this case, a warning would have been all but futile, albeit for a somewhat different reason than in *Nussbaum.* Even if defendant had shouted "fore," the traditional golfer's warning, it is unlikely that plaintiffs, who were driving in a vehicle on a nearby roadway, would have heard, much less had the opportunity to act upon, the shouted warning. Accordingly, just as was true in *Nussbaum,* the possibility that a warning would have been effective here to prevent the accident was simply too "remote" to justify submission of the case to the jury.

Plaintiffs' cause of action based on the claimed negligence of the defendant golfer is similarly untenable. Although the object of the game of golf is to drive the ball as cleanly and directly as possible toward its ultimate intended goal (the hole), the possibility that the ball will fly off in another direction is a risk inherent in the game. Contrary to the view of the dissenters below, the presence of such a risk does not, by itself, import tort liability. The essence of tort liability is the failure to take reasonable steps, where possible, to minimize the chance of harm. Thus, to establish liability in tort, there must be both the existence of a recognizable risk and some basis for concluding that the harm flowing from the consummation of that risk was reasonably preventable.

Since "even the best professional golfers cannot avoid an occasional 'hook' or 'slice,' " it cannot be said that the risk of a mishit golf ball is a fully preventable occurrence. To the contrary, even with the utmost concentration and the "tedious preparation" that often accompanies a golfer's shot, there is no guarantee that the ball will be lofted onto the correct path. For that reason, we have held that the mere fact that a golf ball did not travel in the intended direction does not establish a viable negligence claim. To provide an actionable theory of liability, a person injured by a mishit golf ball must affirmatively show that the golfer failed to exercise due care by adducing proof, for example, that the golfer "aimed so inaccurately as to unreasonably increase the risk of harm."

No such proof was adduced here. In response to defendants' motion for summary judgment, plaintiffs submitted nothing more than the affidavit of a golf pro explaining that "slicing" is a common problem among inexperienced and experienced golfers alike and a deposition statement by defendant Vogel to the effect that his codefendant, McGovern, had such a problem. At most, this evidence, if ultimately proven to be true, would establish only what is obvious — that if one or both defendants teed off from the eleventh hole, there was a risk that one or both of their golf balls would travel off to the right in the direction of the road rather than the direction of the fairway. Plaintiffs' evidence did not, however, support the other element of the cause of action essential to plaintiffs' recovery, i.e., that defendant's actions with respect to this risk were negligent. Hence, plaintiffs' cause of action based on defendants' purported lack of due care was properly dismissed.

Accordingly, the order of the Appellate Division should be affirmed, with costs.

D. CUSTOM

The general principles of negligence law give judges and juries a great deal of latitude. In some cases that latitude can be taken as a sign of the strength of the system, for with latitude comes the flexibility necessary to apply traditional standards to new situations without having to fundamentally remake the substantive law. But there are costs associated with the "featureless generality" of reasonable care, for it introduces a large element of uncertainty even into what are, at least on their face, routine cases. The appeal to custom as a source of the standard of care represents one effort to reduce this uncertainty. Customs lack the generality of the basic reasonable care standard, but within their specific area of application they promise greater direction than any broader standard can provide.

This section deals with the role of custom in negligence cases. Should custom be given the same deference in actions between strangers as in actions that arise out of consensual relations (employer-employee, physician-patient)? Should custom be given the same respect when a defendant argues that he is not negligent because his conduct conforms to custom, as it is given when the plaintiff argues that the defendant is negligent because his conduct fails to conform to custom?

Titus v. Bradford, B. & K. R. Co.
20 A. 517 (Pa. 1890)

[The defendant railroad operated a narrow gauge railroad track between Bradford and Smethport. This line was connected with the standard-gauge tracks of major lines, and part of the defendant's business was to transfer over its tracks the loaded and unloaded freight cars of major carriers. The transfers were accomplished by means of a "hoist" which lifted car bodies from the standard trucks (bases) used on the major lines and set them down on the narrow trucks that were used on the defendant's lines. Most of the car bodies from the major lines were designed with flat bottoms, which could be set down relatively easily on the flat trucks in use on the narrow-gauge rails. A substantial portion of the defendant's business, however, involved the transfer of cars from the New York, Pennsylvania and Ohio Railroad. These "Nypano" cars had slightly rounded bottoms, "shaped somewhat like the bottom of a common saucer," which fit into correspondingly shaped trucks when in use on the Nypano lines. When transferred to the defendant's tracks, however, this car body did not sit securely on its truck, since its bottom was about three inches higher at its edges than at its center. In order to prevent the car bodies from wobbling and toppling when the defendant's train was in motion, the defendant's employees secured them with blocks of hard wood which were either bolted in place or tied in place with telegraph wire.

The decedent had worked on the defendant's railroad with the Nypano cars for nearly two years and was quite familiar with the methods used to secure them to the flat trucks. In the spring of 1888 he became a brakeman on the line. On June 7, 1888, in that capacity, he was riding atop a loaded Nypano freight car. Before setting off, the train's conductor had visually inspected the blocks and found that they had been tied in place with telegraph wire and all appeared to be in order. As the train rounded a curve at a speed of between 7 and 10 miles per hour, it started to sway from side to side. The decedent, who was sitting by the brake wheel on the top rear of the car, tried to run forward over the load to the car in front of him, but could not reach the safety of the next car before his car tipped over. He jumped off onto the track and was killed when struck by the car immediately behind him. A subsequent investigation showed that some of the wire fastening around the blocks of his car had come loose, which allowed the block to become dislodged and the car to wobble and tumble.

"The contention of the plaintiff in this case is, that the company was negligent in using on this narrow-gauge road these standard car bodies," this "on account of the ill-adoption of this car body to the truck." The jury returned a verdict for the plaintiff in the amount of $5,325 and the defendant appealed.]

MITCHELL, J. We have examined all the testimony carefully, and fail to find any evidence of defendant's negligence. The negligence declared upon is the placing of a broad-gauge car upon a narrow-gauge truck, and the use of "an unsafe, and not the best appliance, to wit, the flat centre plate"; or, as expressed by the learned judge in his charge, in using on the narrow-gauge road the standard car bodies, and particularly the New York, Pennsylvania & Ohio car body described by the witnesses. But the whole evidence, of plaintiff's witnesses as well as of defendant's, shows that the shifting of broad-gauge or standard car bodies on to narrow-gauge trucks for transportation, is a regular part of the business of narrow-gauge railroads, and the plaintiff's evidence makes no attempt to show that the way in which it was done here was either dangerous or unusual. . . . Cazely and Richmond say it was the custom to haul these broad-gauge cars on the narrow-gauge trucks, though most of the broad-gauge were Erie cars, of a somewhat different construction; and Morris says the car in question was put on a Hays truck, fitted for carrying standard-gauge cars on a narrow-gauge road, and that this particular kind of "Nypano" car was so hauled quite often. These are plaintiff's own witnesses, and none of them say the practice was dangerous. The nearest approach to such testimony is by Morris, who says he "had his doubts."

But, even if the practice had been shown to be dangerous, that would not show it to be negligent. Some employments are essentially hazardous, as said by our Brother Green, in North. C. Ry. Co. v. Husson, 101 Pa. 1, of coupling railway cars; and it by no means follows that an employer is liable "because a particular accident might have been prevented by some special device or precaution not in common use." All the cases agree that the master is not bound to use the newest and best appliances. He performs his duty when he furnishes those of ordinary character and reasonable safety, and the former is the test of the latter; for, in regard to the style of implement or nature of the mode of performance of any work, "reasonably safe" means safe according to the usages, habits, and ordinary risks of the business. Absolute safety is unattainable, and employers are not insurers. They are liable for the consequences, not of danger but of negligence; and the unbending test of negligence in methods, machinery, and appliances is the ordinary usage of the business. No man is held by law to a higher degree of skill than the fair average of his profession or trade, and the standard of due care is the conduct of the average prudent man. The test of negligence in employers is the same, and however strongly they may be convinced that there is a better or less dangerous way, no jury can be permitted to say that the usual and ordinary way, commonly adopted by those in the same business, is a negligent way for which liability shall be imposed. Juries must necessarily determine the responsibility of individual conduct, but they cannot be allowed to set up a standard which shall, in effect, dictate the customs or control the business of the community. . . .

It is also entirely clear that defendant's third point should have been affirmed. The deceased had been a brakeman on this train for five or six months, during which this mode of carrying broad-gauge cars had been used; cars similar to the one on which the accident occurred had been frequently carried, and that very car at least once, about ten days before. He not only thus had ample opportunity to know the risks of such trains, but he had his attention specially called to the alleged source of the accident, by having worked, just before becoming a brakeman, on the hoist by which the car bodies were transferred to the trucks. It was a perfectly plain case of acceptance of an employment, with full knowledge of the risks.

Judgment reversed.

Mayhew v. Sullivan Mining Co.
76 Me. 100 (1884)

[The plaintiff, an independent contractor, was hired by the defendant to trace veins of new ore. During the course of his duties the plaintiff worked on a platform in a mine shaft some 270 feet below ground. Near one corner of the platform was a "bucket-hole" which the plaintiff used in his work. The plaintiff alleged that on the day of the accident the defendant "carelessly and negligently caused a hole three feet in length by twenty-six inches in breadth to be cut for a ladder-hole in the platform near the centre of it directly back of the bucket-hole and twenty inches distant therefrom, without placing any rail or barrier about it, or any light or other warning there, and without giving plaintiff notice that any such dangerous change had been made in the platform; and that without any knowledge of its existence or fault on his part, the plaintiff, in the ordinary course of his business having occasion to go upon the platform fell through this new hole a distance of thirty-five feet, and received serious injury." The ladder-hole was made by one Stanley under the direction of the superintendent. The defendant sought to ask Stanley at trial whether he had "ever known ladder holes at a low level to be railed or fenced around," whether "as a miner" he thought it was "feasible" to use a ladder-hole with a railing around it, or whether he had "ever seen a ladder-hole in a mine, below the surface, with a railing around it." The court refused to allow the questions to be asked. Thereafter the jury found negligence and returned a verdict for the plaintiff of $2,500.]

BARROWS, J. Defendants' counsel claim that the favorable answers to these questions which they had a right to expect would have tended to show that there was no want of "average ordinary care" on the part of the defendants. We think the questions were properly excluded. The nature of the act in which the defendants' negligence was asserted to consist, with all the circumstances of time and place, whether of commission or omission, and its connection with the plaintiff's injury, presented a case as to which the jury were as well qualified to judge as any expert could be. It was not a case where the opinion of experts could be necessary or useful. . . . If the defendants had proved that in every mining establishment that has existed since the days of Tubal-Cain, it has been the practice to cut ladder-holes in their platforms, situated as this was while in daily use for mining operations, without guarding or lighting them, and without notice to contractors or workmen, it would have no tendency to show that the act was consistent with ordinary prudence or a due regard for the safety of those who were using their premises by their invitation. The gross carelessness of the act appears conclusively upon its recital. Defendants' counsel argue that "if it should appear that they rarely had railings, then it tends to show no want of ordinary care in that respect," that "if one conforms to custom he is so far exercising average ordinary care." The argument proceeds upon an erroneous idea of what constitutes ordinary care. "Custom" and "average" have no proper place in its definition.

It would be no excuse for a want of ordinary care that carelessness was universal about the matter involved, or at the place of the accident, or in the business generally. . . .

The T.J. Hooper
53 F.2d 107 (S.D.N.Y. 1931)

[The operator of the tugboats *The T.J. Hooper* and the *Montrose* was sued under a towing contract when two barges and their cargo of coal were lost in a gale off the coast of New Jersey while in transit from

Virginia to New York. The gist of the negligence charges was that neither tug was equipped with reliable radios that would have allowed them to receive the storm warnings that had been broadcast in both the morning and the afternoon of March 8, 1928, by the naval station at Arlington. Four other tugs, the *Mars,* the *Menominee, The A.L. Walker,* and the *Waltham,* were on the same northbound route as *The T.J. Hooper.* They had received the messages and put safely into the Delaware breakwater.]

COXE, DISTRICT JUDGE: This raises the question whether the *Hooper* and *Montrose* were required to have effective radio sets to pick up weather reports broadcast along the coast. Concededly, there is no statutory law on the subject applicable to tugs of that type, the radio statute applying only to steamers "licensed to carry, or carrying, fifty or more persons"; and excepting by its terms "steamers plying between ports, or places, less than two hundred miles apart." U.S. Code Annotated, title 46, §484. The standard of seaworthiness is not, however, dependent on statutory enactment, or condemned to inertia or rigidity, but changes "with advancing knowledge, experience, and the changed appliances of navigation." It is particularly affected by new devices of demonstrated worth, which have become recognized as regular equipment by common usage.

Radio broadcasting was no new or untried thing in March, 1928. Everywhere, and in almost every field of activity, it was being utilized as an aid to communication, and for the dissemination of information. And that radio sets were in widespread use on vessels of all kinds is clearly indicated by the testimony in this case. Twice a day the government broadcast from Arlington weather reports forecasting weather conditions. Clearly this was important information which navigators could not afford to ignore.

Captain Powell, master of the *Menominee,* who was a witness for the tugs, testified that prior to March, 1928, his tug, and all other seagoing tugs of his company, were equipped by the owner with efficient radio sets, and that he regarded a radio as part "of the necessary equipment" of every reasonably well-equipped tug in the coastwise service. He further testified that 90 per cent of the coastwise tugs operating along the coast were so equipped. It is, of course, true that many of these radio sets were the personal property of the tug master, and not supplied by the owner. This was so with the *Mars, Waltham,* and *Menominee;* but, notwithstanding that fact, the use of the radio was shown to be so extensive as to amount almost to a universal practice in the navigation of coastwise tugs along the coast. I think therefore there was a duty on the part of the tug owner to supply effective receiving sets.

How have the tugs met this requirement? The Hooper had a radio set which belonged to her master, but was practically useless even before the tug left Hampton Roads, and was generally out of order. . . .

I hold therefore . . . (2) that the tugs *T.J. Hooper* and *Montrose* were unseaworthy in failing to have effective radio sets, capable of receiving weather reports on March 8th, . . . (3) that the claims of the cargo owners against the tugs should be allowed; . . .

The T.J. Hooper
60 F.2d 737 (2d Cir. 1932)

[On appeal from the decision below. The court first noted that the evidence supported the claim that *The T.J. Hooper* would have taken shelter if its captain had received the naval broadcasts.]

L. HAND, J. They did not, because their private radio receiving sets, which were on board, were not in working order. These belonged to them personally, and were partly a toy, partly a part of the equipment, but neither furnished by the owner, nor supervised by it. It is not fair to say that there was a general custom among coastwise carriers so to equip their tugs. One line alone did it; as for the rest, they relied upon their crews, so far as they can be said to have relied at all. An adequate receiving set suitable for a coastwise tug can now be got at small cost and is reasonably reliable if kept up; obviously it is a source of great protection to their tows. Twice every day they can receive these predictions, based upon the widest possible information, available to every vessel within two or three hundred miles and more. Such a set is the ears of the tug to catch the spoken word, just as the master's binoculars are her eyes to see a storm signal ashore. Whatever may be said as to other vessels, tugs towing heavy coal laden barges, strung out for half a mile, have little power to manoeuvre, and do not, as this case proves, expose themselves to weather which would not turn back stauncher craft. They can have at hand protection against dangers of which they can learn in no other way.

Is it then a final answer that the business had not yet generally adopted receiving sets? There are, no doubt, cases where courts seem to make the general practice of the calling the standard of proper diligence; we have indeed given some currency to the notion ourselves. Indeed in most cases reasonable prudence is in fact common prudence; but strictly it is never its measure; a whole calling may have unduly lagged in the adoption of new and available devices. It never may set its own tests, however persuasive be its usages. Courts must in the end say what is required; there are precautions so imperative that even their universal disregard will not excuse their omission. But here there was no custom at all as to receiving sets; some had them, some did not; the most that can be urged is that they had not yet become general. Certainly in such a case we need not pause; when some have thought a device necessary, at least we may say that they were right, and the others too slack. The statute [46 USCA §484] does not bear on this situation at all. It prescribes not a receiving, but a transmitting set, and for a very different purpose; to call for help, not to get news. We hold the tugs therefore because had they been properly equipped, they would have got the Arlington reports. The injury was a direct consequence of this unseaworthiness.

Decree affirmed.

NOTES

short response

1. *The relation between custom and negligence.* The three previous opinions all express different relationships between custom and negligence. The decision in *Mayhew* has received little following, either in its own time or today. *Titus* had received a considerable following, especially in the context of industrial accidents, although the balance of authority was probably against it even during the nineteenth century. See, e.g., Maynard v. Buck, 100 Mass. 40 (1868). And the United States Supreme Court chimed in with a similar view in Wabash Railway Co. v. McDaniels, 107 U.S. 454 (1882). The attack on *Titus* was often quite severe, and often took a strong theoretical turn. Thus Miller, The So-Called Unbending Test of Negligence, 3 Va. L. Rev. 537, 543 (1916), argued that the *Titus* rule would deter new innovations by firms that might otherwise be prepared to make them, since "the rule of the 'unbending test' constrains him to adopt the unsafe method in order to bring himself within the rule and escape the charge of negligence." Sound?

The T.J. Hooper did not therefore mark a radical break from tradition, although its allusion that "a whole calling may have unduly lagged in the adoption of new and available devices," has allowed wholesale attacks on standard industry policy, not only in admiralty cases but in other areas as well. Some sense of this approach is found in Bimberg v. Northern Pacific Ry., 14 N.W.2d 410, 413 (Minn. 1944), a wrongful death action brought under the Federal Employers' Liability Act. The defendant argued that designing a trestle was "an engineering problem for solution by the railroads and not by the courts" but the court took a different view of the subject:

> Local usage and general custom, either singly or in combination, will not justify or excuse negligence. They are merely foxholes in one of the battlefields of law, providing shelter, but not complete protection against charges of negligence. The generality of its plan of construction for trestles or bridges cannot excuse a railroad company from responsibility for negligence in its construction. Such plan of construction, commonly followed and "fortified," as defendant insists, "by many years of successful railroad operation," may be evidence of due care, but it cannot avail to establish as safe in law that which is dangerous in fact.

Even after these decisions, the precise relationship between custom and negligence still remains controversial. Should compliance with custom establish a prima facie case of due care? Or should it only be evidence tending to show that the defendant did not take unreasonable risks of harm to others?

2. *Custom and cost-benefit analysis.* Hand's decision in *The T.J. Hooper* complements his analysis in *Carroll Towing,* supra at 200, for while the latter opinion articulates his use of a cost-benefit formula, *The T.J. Hooper* denies any conclusive weight to custom — its major rival in setting the standard of care. Hand's view has received overwhelming acceptance in the courts and among the commentators. For a dissenting view on the subject, see Epstein, The Path to *The T.J. Hooper:* The Theory and History of Custom in the Law of Tort, 21 J. Legal Stud. 1, 4-5 (1992), which argues as follows:

> [G]iven the imperfections of the legal system, the conventional wisdom that places cost-benefit analysis first and custom second is incorrect in at least two ways. First, in cases that arise out of a consensual arrangement, negligence is often the appropriate standard for liability, and, where it is so, custom should be regarded as conclusive evidence of due care in the absence of any contractual stipulation to the contrary. It is quite possible in some consensual settings no custom will emerge, at which point the negligence inquiry will be inescapably ad hoc. But where consistent custom emerges, regardless of its origins, it should be followed. Second, in stranger cases — that is, those where the harm does not fall on a contracting party or someone with whom the defendant has a special relationship — negligence should normally not be the appropriate standard of care, so that reliance on custom is as irrelevant as the negligence issue to which custom alone is properly directed. But where negligence is adopted in these stranger cases, then custom is normally *not* the appropriate standard because it registers the preferences of the parties to the custom, not those who are victimized by it. It should be taken into account, but given no dispositive weight . . . .
>
> Much, if not most of the litigation over custom comes in consensual situations, so the choice between custom and cost-benefit formulas lies at the heart of understanding the distribution of power between the market and the courts in setting the standards of conduct for defendants in all lines of business and endeavors. Although championed by Landes and Posner, Steven Shavell, and other conservative economists, the cost-benefit formula is, when generally applied, far more *interventionist* than the standard of care based on custom. These cost-benefit tests are used to challenge the rationality of markets, while formulas based on custom accept and rely on some level of implicit rationality in market behavior.

How do customs emerge? Should it make any difference whether we deal with customs in a closely knit industry or with those that reach a broad commercial market? Whether we deal with parties who have overlapping roles (that is, transactions between merchants in the same

line of business) or with parties having specialized distinctive relationships (e.g. physician/patient, or landlord/tenant)?

3. *Custom and private rules of conduct.* Can plaintiff use the rules that
the defendant establishes for governing the conduct of his employees
as evidence of negligence? Such rules were held inadmissible in Fonda
v. St. Paul City Ry., 74 N.W. 166 (Minn. 1898), at least in instances in
which the plaintiff's "conduct could not have been in any way affected
or influenced" by rules of which he had no knowledge.

> Private rules of a master regulating the conduct of his servants in the
> management of his own business, although designed for the protection
> of others, stand on an entirely different footing from statutes and munici-
> pal ordinances designed for the protection of the public. The latter, as
> far as they go, fix the standard of duty towards those whom they were
> intended to protect, and a violation of them is negligence in law or per
> se. But a person cannot, by the adoption of private rules, fix the standard
> of his duty to others. That is fixed by law, either statutory or common.
> Such rules may require more, or they may require less, than the law re-
> quires; and whether a certain course of conduct is negligent, or the exer-
> cise of reasonable care, must be determined by the standard fixed by law,
> without regard to any private rules of the party. . . .
>
> The fallaciousness and unfairness of any such doctrine ought to be
> apparent on a moment's reflection. The effect of it is that, the more
> cautious and careful a man is in the adoption of rules in the management
> of his business in order to protect others, the worse he is off, and the
> higher the degree of care he is bound to exercise. A person may, out of
> abundant caution, adopt rules requiring of his employees a much higher
> degree of care than the law imposes. This is a practice that ought to be
> encouraged, and not discouraged. But, if the adoption of such a course
> is to be used against him as an admission, he would naturally find it to
> his interest not to adopt any rules at all.

More recent cases have shown a willingness to allow the plaintiff to
introduce the defendant's own internal rules on the standard of care
question. Thus in Lucy Webb Hayes National Training School v. Perotti, 419 F.2d 704, 710 (D.C. Cir. 1969), the plaintiff's decedent had
been admitted into the defendant's hospital as a mental patient for
observation and treatment of his mental condition. Shortly after being
admitted, the decedent slipped past the nurses' station that separated
the secured portion of the floor, Ward 7-W, into the unsecured area on
the same floor. While the defendant's attendant was leading the decedent back to Ward 7-W, he bolted away and killed himself by jumping
through a window and plunging to his death. The plaintiff argued that
the hospital fell short of its own internal standard when it allowed the
decedent to wander from the closed to the open ward.

> We think the jury could find negligence upon the part of the hospital
> from this evidence without the assistance of expert testimony. The jurors

might not be able to determine the necessity for a closed ward for mental patients of the type admitted to Ward 7-W, nor to evaluate the need for restrictions upon the movement of patients into and out of the closed ward. But the hospital itself had made these decisions. It could, of course, have presented evidence that the limitations upon patient movement constituted more than due care, or were unrelated to patient safety. Indeed, witnesses did testify for the hospital that the open and closed wards were separated by a locked door chiefly, or only, to isolate the more disturbed patients from those not so acutely ill. On the basis of all the evidence, however, the jury could reasonably conclude that the hospital's failure to observe the standards it had itself established represented negligence.

4. *Updating custom.* In Trimarco v. Klein, 436 N.E.2d 502 (N.Y. 1982), the plaintiff was injured in 1976 when he slipped in his bathroom and received serious lacerations from crashing against a shower door made of ordinary glass estimated to be between 1/16 and 1/4 of an inch thick. The shower door had been installed in the 1950s, when the use of ordinary glass was standard practice. Since the mid-1960s, the common practice in New York City had been to use safer tempered glass "whether to replace broken glass or to comply with the request of a tenant." The plaintiff in this instance did not know that ordinary glass was used in his shower door. Reversing a decision of the Appellate Division, the New York Court of Appeals allowed the plaintiff to reach the jury. The court first noted that evidence of custom was admissible because "it reflects the judgment and experience and conduct of many," and because "its relevancy and reliability comes too from the direct bearing it has on feasibility, for its focusing is on the practicability of a precaution in actual operation and the readiness with which it can be employed." Nonetheless the court refused to give the custom conclusive weight, noting "[a]fter all, customs and usages run the gamut of merit like anything else." The court then concluded that "it was also for the jury to decide whether, at the point in time when the accident occurred, the modest cost and ready availability of safety glass and the dynamics of the growing custom to use it for shower enclosures had transformed what once may have been considered a reasonably safe part of the apartment into one which, in light of later developments, no longer could be so regarded."

Must all old shower doors be replaced? Sprinklers and burglar alarms retrofitted into old buildings?

Brune v. Belinkoff
235 N.E.2d 793 (Mass. 1968)

SPAULDING, J. In this action of tort for malpractice Theresa Brune (plaintiff) seeks to recover from the defendant because of alleged negligence in administering a spinal anesthetic. . . . The jury returned verdicts for the defendant on each count. The case comes here on the plaintiffs' exceptions to the judge's refusal to grant certain requests for instructions, to portions of the charge, and to the denial of the plaintiffs' motion for a new trial.

[During the delivery of plaintiff's baby in October, 1958, the defendant anesthesiologist, practicing in New Bedford, Massachusetts, gave plaintiff an eight-milligram dosage of pontocaine. Eleven hours later plaintiff attempted to climb out of bed, but slipped and fell, suffering injuries that persisted until the time of trial. Sufficient evidence was introduced at trial to establish that her fall was due to an excessive dosage of pontocaine. Some medical evidence was introduced to show that good medical practice required a dosage of less than five milligrams. Other evidence, including that of defendant, tended to show that the dosage given was customary in New Bedford, and that the smaller dosages given in New York and Boston were required because of the different obstetrical procedures used in those two cities. "The New Bedford obstetricians use supra fundi pressure (pressure applied to the uterus during delivery) which 'requires a higher level of anesthesia.' "]

The plaintiffs' exception to the refusal to give their first request for instruction and their exception to a portion of the charge present substantially the same question and will be considered together. The request reads: "As a specialist, the defendant owed the plaintiff the duty to have and use the care and skill commonly possessed and used by similar specialist[s] in like circumstances." The relevant portion of the charge excepted to was as follows: "[The defendant] must measure up to the standard of professional care and skill ordinarily possessed by others in his profession in the community, which is New Bedford, and its environs, of course, where he practices, having regard to the current state of advance of the profession. If, in a given case, it were determined by a jury that the ability and skill of the physician in New Bedford were fifty percent inferior to that which existed in Boston, a defendant in New Bedford would be required to measure up to the standard of skill and competence and ability that is ordinarily found by physicians in New Bedford."

The basic issue raised by the exceptions to the charge and to the refused request is whether the defendant was to be judged by the standard of doctors practising in New Bedford.

The instruction given to the jury was based on the rule, often called the "community" or "locality" rule first enunciated in Small v. Howard, 128 Mass. 131, a case decided in 1880. There the defendant, a general practitioner in a country town with a population of 2,500, was consulted by the plaintiff to treat a severe wound which required a considerable degree of surgical skill. In an action against the defendant for malpractice this court defined his duty as follows: "It is a matter of common knowledge that a physician in a small country village does not usually make a specialty of surgery, and, however well informed he may be in the theory of all parts of his profession, he would, generally speaking, be but seldom called upon as a surgeon to perform difficult operations. He would have but few opportunities of observation and practice in that line such as public hospitals or large cities would afford. The defendant was applied to, being the practitioner in a small village, and we think it was correct to rule that 'he was bound to possess that skill only which physicians and surgeons of ordinary ability and skill, practising in similar localities, with opportunities for no larger experience, ordinarily possess; and he was not bound to possess that high degree of art and skill possessed by eminent surgeons practising in large cities, and making a specialty of the practice of surgery.' " The rule in Small v. Howard has been followed and applied in a long line of cases, some of which are quite recent. Although in some of the later decisions the court has said that the doctor must exercise the care prevailing in "the locality where he practiced" it is doubtful if the court intended to narrow the rule in Small v. Howard where the expression "similar localities" was used.

The rationale of the rule of Small v. Howard is that a physician in a small or rural community will lack opportunities to keep abreast with the advances in the profession and that he will not have the most modern facilities for treating his patients. Thus, it is unfair to hold the country doctor to the standard of doctors practising in large cities. The plaintiffs earnestly contend that distinctions based on geography are no longer valid in view of modern developments in transportation, communication and medical education, all of which tend to promote a certain degree of standardization within the profession. Hence, the plaintiffs urge that the rule laid down in Small v. Howard almost ninety years ago now be re-examined in the light of contemporary conditions.

The "community" or "locality" rule has been modified in several jurisdictions and has been subject to critical comment in legal periodicals.

One approach, in jurisdictions where the "same community rule" obtains, has been to extend the geographical area which constitutes the community. The question arises not only in situations involving the standard of care and skill to be exercised by the doctor who is being sued for malpractice, but also in the somewhat analogous situations concerning the qualifications of a medical expert to testify. See Sampson v. Veenboer, 252 Mich. 660 (expert from another State permitted to testify as to standards in Grand Rapids, in view of evidence that he was familiar with standards in similar localities). . . .

And in Cavallaro v. Sharp, 84 R.I. 67, a medical expert formerly of Philadelphia was allowed to testify as to required degree of care in Providence, the court saying at page 72: "The two localities cannot be deemed so dissimilar as to preclude an assumption that mastoidectomies are performed by otologists in Providence with the same average degree of careful and skillful technique as in Philadelphia. It is to be remembered in this connection that Providence is not a small city but is the metropolitan center of upwards of a million people, and moreover is in reasonable proximity to Boston, one of the principal medical centers of the country."

Other decisions have adopted a standard of reasonable care and allow the locality to be taken into account as one of the circumstances, but not as an absolute limit upon the skill required. "Frequent meetings of medical societies, articles in the medical journals, books by acknowledged authorities, and extensive experience in hospital work put the country doctor on more equal terms with his city brother. . . . [W]e are unwilling to hold that he is to be judged only by the qualifications that others in the same village or similar villages possess." . . .

We are of opinion that the "locality" rule of Small v. Howard which measures a physician's conduct by the standards of other doctors in similar communities is unsuited to present day conditions. The time has come when the medical profession should no longer be Balkanized by the application of varying geographic standards in malpractice cases. Accordingly, Small v. Howard is hereby overruled. The present case affords a good illustration of the inappropriateness of the "locality" rule to existing conditions. The defendant was a specialist practising in New Bedford, a city of 100,000, which is slightly more than fifty miles from Boston, one of the medical centers of the nation, if not the world. This is a far cry from the country doctor in Small v. Howard, who ninety years ago was called upon to perform difficult surgery. Yet the trial judge told the jury that if the skill and ability of New Bedford physicians were "fifty percent inferior" to those obtaining in Boston the defendant should be judged by New Bedford standards, "having regard to the current state of advance of the profession." This may well be carrying the rule of Small v. Howard to its logical conclusion, but it is, we submit, a reductio ad absurdum of the rule.

The proper standard is whether the physician, if a general practitioner, has exercised the degree of care and skill of the average qualified practitioner, taking into account the advances in the profession. In applying this standard it is permissible to consider the medical resources available to the physician as *one* circumstance in determining the skill and care required. Under this standard some allowance is thus made for the type of community in which the physician carries on his practice. . . .

One holding himself out as a specialist should be held to the standard of care and skill of the average member of the profession practising the specialty, taking into account the advances in the profession.

And, as in the case of the general practitioner, it is permissible to consider the medical resources available to him.

Because the instructions permitted the jury to judge the defendant's conduct against a standard that has now been determined to be incorrect, the plaintiffs' exceptions to the charge and to the refusal of his request must be sustained. . . .

Exceptions sustained.

NOTES

1. The rise of the national market. Although a few cases continue to adhere to the traditional locality rule, the rise of national standards in board-certified specialties has induced state after state to abridge or jettison its traditional locality rule. In Buck v. St. Clair, 702 P.2d 781, 783 (Idaho 1985), the court overturned a directed verdict granted the defendant below, stating:

> The ruling by the trial court suggests that the local standard of care for board-certified obstetrician-gynecologists differs from the national standard. We believe that for board-certified specialists, the local standard of care is equivalent to the national standard of care. Our reasons for this decision are simple: board-certified medical specialists are highly-trained individuals who become certified after completing a rigorous training program. Medical schools are accredited by a national team of physicians and administrators. The residency training programs are approved by a single board of specialists, and a physician is certified as a specialist only after passing a nationally administered exam consisting of both oral and written components. The board-certified specialists practicing within the state are the product of nationally designed education programs. The standard of care familiar to any board-certified physician in this state is a national standard of care. We see no reason to believe there is a local standard of care which deviates from the national standard of care for board-certified physicians. Our ruling today is limited to board-certified doctors practicing in the same area of specialty. Hence, a board-certified physician can testify only against another board-certified physician practicing in the same area of medicine: surgeons against surgeons, obstetrician-gynecologists against obstetrician-gynecologists, anesthesiologists against anesthesiologists, and so forth.

Should the defendant be allowed to introduce local experts who will testify that differences in the standard of care remain? Even after the passing of the locality rule, should a rural clinic be required to have the same equipment as a state-of-the-art university hospital? See Morreim, Cost Containment and the Standard of Medical Care, 75 Cal. L. Rev. 1719 (1987).

2. Variations of levels of care within institutions. The movement toward national standards does not necessarily point to uniform standards for all physicians regardless of their level of training. A Connecticut statute (C.G.S.A. §2-184c(c)(1994), for example, draws a distinction between those physicians who do, and do not, hold themselves out as board-certified specialists. Roughly speaking, its general scheme allows a board-certified specialist with five years' training to testify in any case within his sphere of competence, and allows non-board-certified physicians to testify only in suits brought against non-board-certified doctors, but not against board-certified doctors. There is no requirement that the physicians in either class be licensed in Connecticut.

At the other end of the system, some early cases have suggested that a lower standard of care is appropriate for interns and residents. Thus, the court in Rush v. Akron General Hospital, 171 N.E.2d 378, 381 (Ohio App. 1957), held that

> It would be unreasonable to exact from an intern, doing emergency work in a hospital, that high degree of skill which is impliedly possessed by a physician or surgeon in the general practice of his profession, with an extensive and constant practice in the hospitals and the community.
>
> What is required in the case of an intern is that he shall possess such skill and use such care and diligence in handling of emergency cases as capable medical college graduates serving hospitals as interns ordinarily possess under similar circumstances.

Subsequent cases have inclined toward a uniform standard of care. In McBride v. United States, 462 F.2d 72, 74 (9th Cir. 1972), an intern working in the emergency room of a military hospital sent a patient home after he incorrectly interpreted the patient's electrocardiogram as normal. While most interns and residents would have missed the diagnosis, a more experienced physician would have detected the abnormality. The court stated the standard of care as follows:

> [The patient] had the right to expect the quality of care usually found in the medical community and the hospital was obliged to provide physicians who could meet that standard. If the hospital staff had reason to believe its interns and residents could not reasonably be expected to discern subtle abnormalities in electrocardiogram tracings, it should not have permitted them to make unaided electrocardiogram analyses.

Helling v. Carey
519 P.2d 981 (Wash. 1974)

[The plaintiff first consulted defendant in 1959 and visited his offices over a nine-year period, largely for treatment for the irritation caused to her eyes by the use of contact lenses. By the end of 1968, when plaintiff was 32, defendant suspected that she had glaucoma — a disease of the eye caused by pressure on the optic nerve — after she complained of impaired peripheral vision. He then administered a pressure test which confirmed the diagnosis. The plaintiff suffered a permanent impairment of her vision.]

. . . During trial, the testimony of the medical experts for both the plaintiff and the defendants established that the standards of the profession for that specialty in the same or similar circumstances do not require routine pressure tests for glaucoma upon patients under 40 years of age. The reason the pressure test for glaucoma is not given as a regular practice to patients under the age of 40 is that the disease rarely occurs in this age group. Testimony indicated, however, that the standards of the profession do require pressure tests if the patient's complaints and symptoms reveal to the physician that glaucoma should be suspected.

The trial court entered judgment for the defendants following a defense verdict. The plaintiff thereupon appealed to the Court of Appeals, which affirmed the judgment of the trial court. . . . The plaintiff then petitioned this Court for review, which we granted.

HUNTER, J. We find this to be a unique case. The testimony of the medical experts is undisputed concerning the standards of the profession for the specialty of ophthalmology. It is not a question in this case of the defendants having any greater special ability, knowledge and information than other ophthalmologists which would require the defendants to comply with a higher duty of care than that "degree of care and skill which is expected of the average practitioner in the class to which he belongs, acting in the same or similar circumstances." Pederson v. Dumouchel, 72 Wash. 2d 73, 79 (1967). The issue is whether the defendants' compliance with the standard of the profession of ophthalmology, which does not require the giving of a routine pressure test to persons under 40 years of age, should insulate them from liability under the facts in this case where the plaintiff has lost a substantial amount of her vision due to the failure of the defendants to timely give the pressure test to the plaintiff.

The defendants argue that the standard of the profession, which does not require the giving of a routine pressure test to persons under the age of 40, is adequate to insulate the defendants from liability for negligence because the risk of glaucoma is so rare in this age group. . . .

The incidence of glaucoma in one out of 25,000 persons under the age of 40 may appear quite minimal. However, that one person, the plaintiff in this instance, is entitled to the same protection, as afforded persons over 40, essential for timely detection of the evidence of glaucoma where it can be arrested to avoid the grave and devastating result of this disease. The test is a simple pressure test, relatively inexpensive. There is no judgment factor involved, and there is no doubt that by giving the test the evidence of glaucoma can be detected. The giving of the test is harmless if the physical condition of the eye permits. The testimony indicates that although the condition of the plaintiff's eyes might have at times prevented the defendants from administering the pressure test, there is an absence of evidence in the record that the test could not have been timely given.

Justice Holmes stated in Texas & Pac. Ry. v. Behymer, 189 U.S. 468, 470 (1903): "What usually is done may be evidence of what ought to be done, but what ought to be done is fixed by a standard of reasonable prudence, whether it usually is complied with or not."

In *The T.J. Hooper,* Justice Hand stated: "[I]n most cases reasonable prudence is in fact common prudence but strictly it is never its measure; a whole calling may have unduly lagged in the adoption of new and available devices. It never may set its own tests, however persuasive be its usages. *Courts must in the end say what is required; there are precautions so imperative that even their universal disregard will not excuse their omission.*" (Italics ours.)

Under the facts of this case reasonable prudence required the timely giving of the pressure test to this plaintiff. The precaution of giving this test to detect the incidence of glaucoma to patients under 40 years of age is so imperative that irrespective of its disregard by the standards of the ophthalmology profession, it is the duty of the courts to say what is required to protect patients under 40 from the damaging results of glaucoma.

We therefore hold, as a matter of law, that the reasonable standard that should have been followed under the undisputed facts of this case was the timely giving of this simple, harmless pressure test to this plaintiff and that, in failing to do so, the defendants were negligent, which proximately resulted in the blindness sustained by the plaintiff for which the defendants are liable. . . .

The judgment of the trial court and the decision of the Court of Appeals is reversed, and the case is remanded for a new trial on the issue of damages only.

HALE, C.J., and ROSELLINI, STAFFORD, WRIGHT and BRACHTENBACH, JJ., concur.

UTTER, J., concurring. I concur in the result reached by the majority. . . .

The difficulty with [the court's] approach is that we as judges, by using a negligence analysis, seem to be imposing a stigma of moral blame upon the doctors who, in this case, used all the precautions commonly prescribed by their profession in diagnosis and treatment. Lacking their training in this highly sophisticated profession, it seems illogical for this court to say they failed to exercise a reasonable standard of care. It seems to me we are, in reality, imposing liability, because, in choosing between an innocent plaintiff and a doctor, who acted reasonably according to his specialty but who could have prevented the full effects of this disease by administering a simple, harmless test and treatment, the plaintiff should not have to bear the risk of loss. As such, imposition of liability approaches that of strict liability.

Strict liability or liability without fault is not new to the law. Historically, it predates our concepts of fault or moral responsibility as a basis of the remedy.

When types of problems rather than numbers of cases are examined, strict liability is applied more often than negligence as a principle which determines liability. Peck, Negligence and Liability Without Fault in Tort Law, 46 Wash. L. Rev. 225, 239 (1971). There are many similarities in this case to other cases of strict liability. Problems of proof have been a common feature in situations where strict liability is applied. Where events are not matters of common experience, a juror's ability to comprehend whether reasonable care has been followed diminishes. There are few areas as difficult for jurors to intelligently comprehend as the intricate questions of proof and standards in medical malpractice cases.

In applying strict liability there are many situations where it is imposed for conduct which can be defined with sufficient precision to insure that application of a strict liability principle will not produce miscarriages of justice in a substantial number of cases. If the activity involved is one which can be defined with sufficient precision, that definition can serve as an accounting unit to which the costs of the activity may be allocated with some certainty and precision. With this possible, strict liability serves a compensatory function in situations where the defendant is, through the use of insurance, the financially more responsible person. . . .

If the standard of a reasonably prudent specialist is, in fact, inadequate to offer reasonable protection to the plaintiff, then liability can be imposed without fault. To do so under the narrow facts of this case does not offend my sense of justice. The pressure test to measure intraocular pressure with the Schiotz tonometer and the Goldman applanometer takes a short time, involves no damage to the patient, and consists of placing the instrument against the eyeball. An abnormally high pressure requires other tests which would either confirm or deny the existence of glaucoma. It is generally believed that from 5 to 10 years of detectable increased pressure must exist before there is permanent damage to the optic nerves.

Although the incidence of glaucoma in the age range of the plaintiff is approximately one in 25,000, this alone should not be enough to deny her a claim. Where its presence can be detected by a simple, well-known harmless test, where the results of the test are definitive, where the disease can be successfully arrested by early detection and where its effects are irreversible if undetected over a substantial period of time, liability should be imposed upon defendants even though they did not violate the standard existing within the profession of ophthalmology. . . .

NOTES

1. Reaction to Helling v. Carey. What factors should be relevant to the cost-benefit analysis in *Helling*? Note that 96 percent of the patients diagnosed as glaucoma cases by the pressure tests do not have the disease. See Wiley, The Impact of Judicial Decisions on Professional Conduct: An Empirical Study, 55 S. Cal. L. Rev. 345, 388 n.143 (1982), which also argues that once the costs of these false positives are taken into account the test is not cost-justified even under the Hand formula, at least if the damage awards at the time of the treatment are regarded as an accurate measure of the plaintiff's loss.

Helling provoked a swift statutory response. Washington Revised Code, Section 4.24.290, now provides:

> In any civil action for damages based on professional negligence against a hospital which is licensed by the state of Washington or against the personnel of any such hospital, or against a member of the healing arts including, but not limited to, a physician . . . a chiropractor . . . a dentist . . . a podiatrist . . . or a nurse . . . the plaintiff in order to prevail shall be required to prove by a preponderance of the evidence that the defendant or defendants failed to exercise that degree of skill, care and learning possessed by other persons in the same profession and that as a proximate result of such failure the plaintiff suffered damages, but in no event shall the provisions of this section apply to an action based on the failure to obtain the informed consent of a patient.

Similarly, *Helling* has had a rough judicial reception. In Barton v. Owen, 139 Cal. Rptr. 494 (Cal. App. 1977), the California Court of Appeal "disapproved" of *Helling*, noting that it "does not state the law in California." *Helling* was also given a narrow reading in Meeks v. Marx, 550 P.2d 1158 (Wash. App. 1976), where the court concluded that "[a] thorough analysis of that decision leads us to conclude the holding there was intended to be restricted solely to its own 'unique' facts, i.e., cases in which an ophthalmologist is alleged to have failed to test for glaucoma under the same or similar circumstances."

Today the typical standards for medical malpractice actions require that "a doctor must use that degree of skill and learning which is normally possessed and used by doctors in good standing in a similar practice in similar communities and under like circumstances," approved in Kalsbeck v. Westview Clinic, P.A., 375 N.W.2d 861, 868 (Minn. App.

1985), or that "[a] physician who undertakes a mode or form of treatment which a reasonable and prudent member of the medical profession would undertake under the same or similar circumstances shall not be subject to liability for harm caused thereby to the patient." Hood v. Phillips, 554 S.W.2d 160, 165 (Tex. 1977).

Often, no single custom covers a given issue. In Jones v. Chidester, 610 A.2d 964, 965 (Pa. 1992), the court set up the "two schools" problem as follows:

> A medical practitioner has an absolute defense to a claim of negligence when it is determined that the prescribed treatment or procedure has been approved by one group of medical experts even though an alternate school of thought recommends another approach, or it is agreed among experts that alternative treatments and practices are acceptable. The doctrine is applicable only where there is more than one method of accepted treatment or procedure. In specific terms, however, we are called upon in this case to decide once again whether a school of thought qualifies as such when it is advocated by a "considerable number" of medical experts or when it commands acceptance by "respective, reputable and reasonable" practitioners. The former test calls for a quantitative analysis, while the latter is premised on qualitative grounds.

The court then noted that its exhaustive review of the precedents gave an unclear answer to the question, and continued:

> It is incumbent upon us to settle this confusion. The "two schools of thought doctrine" provides a complete defense to malpractice. It is therefore insufficient to show that there exists a "small minority" of physicians who agree with the defendant's questioned practice. Thus, the Superior Court's "reputable and respected by reasonable medical experts" test is improper. Rather, there must be a considerable number of physicians, recognized and respected in their field, sufficient to create another "school of thought."

What result should apply if the physician discloses that the proposed treatment is experimental? If the treatment has been adopted by only a tiny fraction of the profession?

2. *Conflict with The T.J. Hooper.* The current view that custom is conclusive on the standard of medical care is a significant exception to the general rule in *The T.J. Hooper.* For one justification of this position see Morris, Custom and Negligence, 42 Colum. L. Rev. 1147, 1164-1165 (1942):

> Why should conformity to the practice protect a physician from liability? Drovers, railroads, merchants, etc., are not so protected. The doctor escapes liability even though he conforms only to the practice in his locality or the practice in similar localities. And treatment need not conform to a general usage, it need only be like that used by some reputable doc-

tors. If all doctors reasonably developed and applied their skill and knowledge, the conformity test might be the equivalent of reasonable care under the circumstances. Doctors as a class may be more likely to exert their best efforts than drovers, railroads, and merchants but they are human and subject to the temptations of laziness and unthinking acceptance of traditions. The rationale is: no other standard is practical. Our judges and juries are usually not competent to judge whether or not a doctor has acted reasonably. The conformity test is probably the only workable test available. . . .

The patient who has endured suffering is an appealing plaintiff. Juries are likely to favor him. And it is widely known that doctors usually carry liability insurance. But a doctor who loses a malpractice case stands to lose more than the amount of the judgment — he may also lose his professional reputation and his livelihood. These considerations heighten the need for a test of malpractice that will protect doctors against undeserved liability. The law may be academically deficient in countenancing an excuse that may occasionally be based on the negligence of the other doctors. But the grossly incompetent practitioner will find little comfort in the tests of malpractice. A few negligent doctors may escape, but the quack will not. The reasonably prudent man "test" would enable the ambulance chaser to make a law suit out of any protracted illness.

See also Epstein, Medical Malpractice: The Case for Contract, 1 Am. B. Found. Res. J. 87, 108-113 (1976); King, In Search of a Standard of Care for the Medical Profession: The "Accepted Practice" Formula, 28 Vand. L. Rev. 1213 (1975).

3. *How is the standard of care determined?* In ordinary medical malpractice actions, the plaintiff uses expert testimony to prove the deviation from the legal standard of care. The case law, however, is largely silent on what should be done when the testimony offered differs from the practice as it actually takes place, as evidenced, for example, by systematic data collection. The differences between the two approaches can be quite dramatic. Meadow, Lantos et al., Ought 'Standard Care' Be the 'Standard of Care'?, 147 Am. J. Diseases of Children 40 (1993), note that their "investigations were prompted by the testimony of a single medical expert witness who stated that the standard of care for the time from presentation to administration of antibiotics with meningitis was 30 minutes or less." Their own study of the clinical records of some 93 children admitted with meningitis showed that only one patient received antibiotics within that 30-minute period, and that the median time was in fact 2 hours, with three-fourths of the cases being treated between 1.25 and 3.33 hours after presentation, data that conformed closely to that found in other surveys. The authors also polled physicians independently and found that they overestimated the promptness of the response as well, thinking on average the first response was 0.93 hours for emergency cases and 1.45 hours for other treatment. When the practice in the books and the practice in the clinics diverge, which

should prevail? Meadow and his colleagues propose that this Gordian knot be cut as follows: "When expert witnesses present unsupported beliefs, or when their expert testimony is contradicted by documented medical practice, witnesses should be obliged to articulate the rationale for preferring their idiosyncratic opinions to data depicting the care physicians actually provide."

What should be done if the delay in responding to the risk in meningitis has occurred because of cutbacks in Medicaid support for physicians?

4. *Contract for cure.* In Sullivan v. O'Connor, 296 N.E.2d 183, 186 (Mass. 1973), plaintiff, an entertainer by profession, alleged that defendant, a plastic surgeon, orally promised to improve the appearance of her nose, but failed to achieve the intended result. On the question of whether there could be a contract for specific results, Kaplan, J., observed:

> It is not hard to see why the courts should be unenthusiastic or skeptical about the contract theory. Considering the uncertainties of medical science and the variations in the physical and psychological conditions of individual patients, doctors can seldom in good faith promise specific results. Therefore it is unlikely that physicians of even average integrity will in fact make such promises. Statements of opinion by the physician with some optimistic coloring are a different thing, and may indeed have therapeutic value. But patients may transform such statements into firm promises in their own minds, especially when they have been disappointed in the event, and testify in that sense to sympathetic juries. If actions for breach of promise can be readily maintained, doctors, so it is said, will be frightened into practising "defensive medicine." On the other hand, if these actions were outlawed, leaving only the possibility of suits for malpractice, there is fear that the public might be exposed to the enticements of charlatans, and confidence in the profession might ultimately be shaken. See Miller, The Contractual Liability of Physicians and Surgeons, 1953 Wash. L.Q. 413, 416-423. The law has taken the middle of the road position of allowing actions based on alleged contract, but insisting on clear proof. Instructions to the jury may well stress this requirement and point to tests of truth, such as the complexity or difficulty of an operation as bearing on the probability that a given result was promised.

If the parties by agreement are allowed to contract for cure, why are they not allowed to contract for care in accordance with the general standards of the profession? In accordance with the physician's own best efforts?

Sullivan was followed in Clevenger v. Haling, 394 N.E.2d 1119 (Mass. 1979), where a majority of the court refused to allow the plaintiff to reach the jury for the birth of an unwanted child after she had been given a tubal ligation, when the physician had said the ligation was "a permanent thing" and that "you are not going to have any more children after this operation."

Canterbury v. Spence
464 F.2d 772 (D.C. Cir. 1972)

[The plaintiff-appellant first consulted Dr. Spence, the defendant-appellee, after experiencing severe back pain in December 1958. After a preliminary examination, Dr. Spence had the appellant undergo a myelogram — a procedure in which dye is injected into the spinal column which is then examined for disease or other disorder — that revealed that the appellant suffered from a "filling defect" in the region of his fourth thoracic vertebra. Dr. Spence then told the appellant that he needed to undergo a laminectomy — an operation on the posterior arch of the vertebra — to correct what he suspected was a ruptured disc. He did not tell the appellant the details of the proposed operation, nor did the appellant inquire about them. Dr. Spence then contacted the appellant's mother and told her, when asked, that the operation he proposed was a serious one, but "not any more than any other operation." The appellee performed the operation on February 11, 1959, only to discover that the appellant's spinal cord was swollen and in very poor condition. He then did what he could to relieve the pressure on the appellant's spinal cord and left the appellant in bed to recuperate.

For the first day or so, the appellant's recuperation proceeded normally. Then, at least according to appellant's testimony, he was allowed, contrary to the appellee's original instructions, to void unattended. While doing so, he slipped off the side of the bed, there being no one there to assist and no side rail to break his fall. Several hours later the appellant had difficulty breathing and suffered near-complete paralysis from the waist down. The appellee performed another emergency operation that night, and the appellant's condition improved thereafter. "Despite extensive medical care, he [the appellant] has never been what he was before. Instead of the back pain, even years later, he hobbled about on crutches, a victim of paralysis of the bowels and urinary incontinence. In a very real sense this lawsuit is an understandable search for reasons."]

ROBINSON, J. Appellant filed suit in the District Court on March 7, 1963, four years after the laminectomy and approximately two years after he attained his majority. The complaint stated several causes of action against each defendant. Against Dr. Spence it alleged, among other things, negligence in the performance of the laminectomy and failure to inform him beforehand of the risk involved. Against the hos-

pital the complaint charged negligent post-operative care in permitting
appellant to remain unattended after the laminectomy, in failing to
provide a nurse or orderly to assist him at the time of his fall, and in
failing to maintain a side rail on his bed. The answers denied the allegations of negligence and defended on the ground that the suit was
barred by the statute of limitations.

Pretrial discovery — including depositions by appellant, his mother
and Dr. Spence — continuances and other delays consumed five years.
At trial, disposition of the threshold question whether the statute of
limitations had run was held in abeyance until the relevant facts developed. Appellant introduced no evidence to show medical and hospital
practices, if any, customarily pursued in regard to the critical aspects of
the case, and only Dr. Spence, called as an adverse witness, testified on
the issue of causality. Dr. Spence described the surgical procedures he
utilized in the two operations and expressed his opinion that appellant's disabilities stemmed from his pre-operative condition as symp-
tomized by the swollen, nonpulsating spinal cord. He stated, however,
that neither he nor any of the other physicians with whom he consulted
was certain as to what that condition was, and he admitted that trauma
can be a cause of paralysis. Dr. Spence further testified that even without trauma paralysis can be anticipated "somewhere in the nature of
one percent" of the laminectomies performed, a risk he termed "a very
slight possibility." He felt that communication of that risk to the patient
is not good medical practice because it might deter patients from undergoing needed surgery and might produce adverse psychological reactions which could preclude the success of the operation.

At the close of appellant's case in chief, each defendant moved for a
directed verdict and the trial judge granted both motions. The basis of
the ruling, he explained, was that appellant had failed to produce any
medical evidence indicating negligence on Dr. Spence's part in diag-
nosing appellant's malady or in performing the laminectomy; that
there was no proof that Dr. Spence's treatment was responsible for appellant's disabilities; and that notwithstanding some evidence to show
negligent post-operative care, an absence of medical testimony to show
causality precluded submission of the case against the hospital to the
jury. The judge did not allude specifically to the alleged breach of duty
by Dr. Spence to divulge the possible consequences of the laminectomy.

We reverse. The testimony of appellant and his mother that Dr.
Spence did not reveal the risk of paralysis from the laminectomy made
out a prima facie case of violation of the physician's duty to disclose
which Dr. Spence's explanation did not negate as a matter of law.
There was also testimony from which the jury could have found that
the laminectomy was negligently performed by Dr. Spence, and that
appellant's fall was the consequence of negligence on the part of the

hospital. The record, moreover, contains evidence of sufficient quantity and quality to tender jury issues as to whether and to what extent any such negligence was causally related to appellant's post-laminectomy condition. These considerations entitled appellant to a new trial.

Suits charging failure by a physician adequately to disclose the risks and alternatives of proposed treatment are not innovations in American law. They date back a good half-century, and in the last decade they have multiplied rapidly. There is, nonetheless, disagreement among the courts and the commentators on many major questions, and there is no precedent of our own directly in point. For the tools enabling resolution of the issues on this appeal, we are forced to begin at first principles.

The root premise is the concept, fundamental in American jurisprudence, that "[e]very human being of adult years and sound mind has a right to determine what shall be done with his own body. . . ." True consent to what happens to one's self is the informed exercise of a choice, and that entails an opportunity to evaluate knowledgeably the options available and the risks attendant upon each. The average patient has little or no understanding of the medical arts, and ordinarily has only his physician to whom he can look for enlightenment with which to reach an intelligent decision. From these almost axiomatic considerations springs the need, and in turn the requirement, of a reasonable divulgence by physician to patient to make such a decision possible. . . .[15]

A reasonable revelation in these respects is not only a necessity but, as we see it, is as much a matter of the physician's duty. It is a duty to warn of the dangers lurking in the proposed treatment, and that is surely a facet of due care. It is, too, a duty to impart information which the patient has every right to expect.[27] The patient's reliance upon the physician is a trust of the kind which traditionally has exacted obliga-

15. In duty-to-disclose cases, the focus of attention is more properly upon the nature and content of the physician's divulgence than the patient's understanding or consent. Adequate disclosure and informed consent are, of course, two sides of the same coin — the former a sine qua non of the latter. But the vital inquiry on duty to disclose relates to the physician's performance of an obligation, while one of the difficulties with analysis in terms of "informed consent" is its tendency to imply that what is decisive is the degree of the patient's comprehension. As we later emphasize, the physician discharges the duty when he makes a reasonable effort to convey sufficient information although the patient, without fault of the physician, may not fully grasp it.

27. Some doubt has been expressed as to [the] ability of physicians to suitably communicate their evaluations of risks and the advantages of optional treatment, and as to the lay patient's ability to understand what the physician tells him. Karchmer, Informed Consent: A Plaintiff's Medical Malpractice "Wonder Drug," 31 Mo. L. Rev. 29, 41 (1966). We do not share these apprehensions. The discussion need not be a disquisition, and surely the physician is not compelled to give his patient a short medical education; the disclosure rule summons the physician only to a reasonable explanation. That means generally informing the patient in nontechnical terms as to what is at stake: the therapy alternatives open to him, the goals expectably to be achieved, and the risks that may ensue from particular treatment and no treatment. . . . So informing the patient

tions beyond those associated with arms-length transactions. His dependence upon the physician for information affecting his well-being, in
terms of contemplated treatment, is well-nigh abject. . . .

Thus the physician has long borne a duty, on pain of liability for
unauthorized treatment, to make adequate disclosure to the patient.
The evolution of the obligation to communicate for the patient's benefit as well as the physician's protection has hardly involved an extraordinary restructuring of the law.

Duty to disclose has gained recognition in a large number of American jurisdictions, but more largely on a different rationale. The majority of courts dealing with the problem have made the duty depend on
whether it was the custom of physicians practicing in the community to
make the particular disclosure to the patient. If so, the physician may
be held liable for an unreasonable and injurious failure to divulge, but
there can be no recovery unless the omission forsakes a practice prevalent in the profession. We agree that the physician's noncompliance
with a professional custom to reveal, like any other departure from
prevailing medical practice, may give rise to liability to the patient. We
do not agree that the patient's cause of action is dependent upon the
existence and nonperformance of a relevant professional tradition.

There are, in our view, formidable obstacles to acceptance of the
notion that the physician's obligation to disclose is either germinated
or limited by medical practice. To begin with, the reality of any discernible custom reflecting a professional consensus on communication of
option and risk information to patients is open to serious doubt. We
sense the danger that what in fact is no custom at all may be taken as
an affirmative custom to maintain silence, and that physician-witnesses
to the so-called custom may state merely their personal opinions as to
what they or others would do under given conditions. We cannot gloss
over the inconsistency between reliance on a general practice respecting divulgence and, on the other hand, realization that the myriad of
variables among patients makes each case so different that its omission
can rationally be justified only by the effect of its individual circumstances. Nor can we ignore the fact that to bind the disclosure obligation to medical usage is to arrogate the decision on revelation to the

---

hardly taxes the physician, and it must be the exceptional patient who cannot comprehend such an explanation at least in a rough way. We discard the thought that the
patient should ask for information before the physician is required to disclose. Caveat
emptor is not the norm for the consumer of medical services. Duty to disclose is more
than a call to speak merely on the patient's request, or merely to answer the patient's
questions; it is a duty to volunteer, if necessary, the information the patient needs for
intelligent decision. The patient may be ignorant, confused, overawed by the physician
or frightened by the hospital, or even ashamed to inquire. . . . Perhaps relatively few
patients could in any event identify the relevant questions in the absence of prior explanation by the physician. Physicians and hospitals have patients of widely divergent socio-
economic backgrounds, and a rule which presumes a degree of sophistication which
many members of society lack is likely to breed gross inequities.

physician alone. Respect for the patient's right of self-determination on particular therapy demands a standard set by law for physicians rather than one which physicians may or may not impose upon themselves. . . .

The majority rule, moreover, is at war with our prior holdings that a showing of medical practice, however probative, does not fix the standard governing recovery for medical malpractice. Prevailing medical practice, we have maintained, has evidentiary value in determinations as to what the specific criteria measuring challenged professional conduct are and whether they have been met, but does not itself define the standard. That has been our position in treatment cases, where the physician's performance is ordinarily to be adjudicated by the special medical standard of due care. We see no logic in a different rule for nondisclosure cases, where the governing standard is much more largely divorced from professional considerations. And surely in nondisclosure cases the fact-finder is not invariably functioning in an area of such technical complexity that it must be bound to medical custom as an inexorable application of the community standard of reasonable care.

. . . We hold that the standard measuring performance of that duty [to disclose] by physicians, as by others, is conduct which is reasonable under the circumstances.

Once the circumstances give rise to a duty on the physician's part to inform his patient, the next inquiry is the scope of the disclosure the physician is legally obliged to make. The courts have frequently confronted this problem but no uniform standard defining the adequacy of the divulgence emerges from the decisions. Some have said "full" disclosure, a norm we are unwilling to adopt literally. It seems obviously prohibitive and unrealistic to expect physicians to discuss with their patients every risk of proposed treatment — no matter how small or remote and generally unnecessary from the patient's viewpoint as well. Indeed, the cases speaking in terms of "full" disclosure appear to envision something less than total disclosure, leaving unanswered the question of just how much.

The larger number of courts, as might be expected, have applied tests framed with reference to prevailing fashion within the medical profession. Some have measured the disclosure by "good medical practice," others by what a reasonable practitioner would have bared under the circumstances, and still others by what medical custom in the community would demand. We have explored this rather considerable body of law but are unprepared to follow it. . . .

In our view, the patient's right of self-decision shapes the boundaries of the duty to reveal. That right can be effectively exercised only if the patient possesses enough information to enable an intelligent choice. The scope of the physician's communications to the patient, then, must be measured by the patient's need, and that need is the information material to the decision. Thus the test for determining whether a particular peril must be divulged is its materiality to the patient's decision: all risks potentially affecting the decision must be unmasked. And to safeguard the patient's interest in achieving his own determination on treatment, the law must itself set the standard for adequate disclosure.

Optimally for the patient, exposure of a risk would be mandatory whenever the patient would deem it significant to his decision, either singly or in combination with other risks. Such a requirement, however, would summon the physician to second-guess the patient, whose ideas on materiality could hardly be known to the physician. That would make an undue demand upon medical practitioners, whose conduct, like that of others, is to be measured in terms of reasonableness. Consonantly with orthodox negligence doctrine, the physician's liability for nondisclosure is to be determined on the basis of foresight, not hindsight; no less than any other aspect of negligence, the issue on nondisclosure must be approached from the viewpoint of the reasonableness of the physician's divulgence in terms of what he knows or should know to be the patient's informational needs. If, but only if, the fact-finder can say that the physician's communication was unreasonably inadequate is an imposition of liability legally or morally justified. . . .

From these considerations we derive the breadth of the disclosure of risks legally to be required. The scope of the standard is not subjective as to either the physician or the patient; it remains objective with due regard for the patient's informational needs and with suitable leeway for the physician's situation. In broad outline, we agree that "[a] risk is thus material when a reasonable person, in what the physician knows or should know to be the patient's position, would be likely to attach significance to the risk or cluster of risks in deciding whether or not to forego the proposed therapy."

The topics importantly demanding a communication of information are the inherent and potential hazards of the proposed treatment, the alternatives to that treatment, if any, and the results likely if the patient remains untreated. The factors contributing significance to the dangerousness of a medical technique are, of course, the incidence of injury and the degree of the harm threatened. A very small chance of death or serious disablement may well be significant; a potential disability which dramatically outweighs the potential benefit of the therapy or the detriments of the existing malady may summon discussion with the patient.[86]

86. See Bowers v. Talmage, 159 So. 2d 888 (Fla. App. 1963) (3% chance of death, paralysis or other injury, disclosure required); Scott v. Wilson, 396 S.W.2d 532 (Tex. Civ. App. 1965) (1% chance of loss of hearing, disclosure required). Compare cases in which the physician was held not liable: Stottlemire v. Cawood, 213 F. Supp. 897 (D.D.C. 1963) (1/8,000,000 chance of aplastic anemia); Yeates v. Harms, 193 Kan. 320, 393 P. 2d 982 (1964) (1.5% chance of loss of eye); Starnes v. Taylor, 272 N.C. 386, 158 S.E.2d 339, 344 (1968) (1/250 to 1/500 chance of perforation of esophagus).

There is no bright line separating the significant from the insignificant; the answer in any case must abide a rule of reason. Some dangers — infection, for example — are inherent in any operation; there is no obligation to communicate those of which persons of average sophistication are aware. Even more clearly, the physician bears no responsibility for discussion of hazards the patient has already discovered, or those having no apparent materiality to patients' decision on therapy. The disclosure doctrine, like others marking lines between permissible and impermissible behavior in medical practice, is in essence a requirement of conduct prudent under the circumstances. Whenever nondisclosure of particular risk information is open to debate by reasonable-minded men, the issue is for the finder of the facts.

Two exceptions to the general rule of disclosure have been noted by the courts. Each is in the nature of a physician's privilege not to disclose, and the reasoning underlying them is appealing. . . . The first comes into play when the patient is unconscious or otherwise incapable of consenting, and harm from a failure to treat is imminent and outweighs any harm threatened by the proposed treatment. When a genuine emergency of that sort arises, it is settled that the impracticality of conferring with the patient dispenses with need for it. Even in situations of that character the physician should, as current law requires, attempt to secure a relative's consent if possible. But if time is too short to accommodate discussion, obviously the physician should proceed with the treatment.

The second exception obtains when risk-disclosure poses such a threat of detriment to the patient as to become unfeasible or contraindicated from a medical point of view. It is recognized that patients occasionally become so ill or emotionally distraught on disclosure as to foreclose a rational decision, or complicate or hinder the treatment, or perhaps even pose psychological damage to the patient. Where that is so, the cases have generally held that the physician is armed with a privilege to keep the information from the patient, and we think it clear that portents of that type may justify the physician in action he deems medically warranted. The critical inquiry is whether the physician responded to a sound medical judgment that communication of the risk information would present a threat to the patient's well-being.

The physician's privilege to withhold information for therapeutic reasons must be carefully circumscribed, however, for otherwise it might devour the disclosure rule itself. The privilege does not accept the paternalistic notion that the physician may remain silent simply because divulgence might prompt the patient to forego therapy the physician feels the patient really needs. That attitude presumes instability or perversity for even the normal patient, and runs counter to the foundation principle that the patient should and ordinarily can make the choice for himself.

No more than breach of any other legal duty does nonfulfillment of the physician's obligation to disclose alone establish liability to the patient. . . . [A]s in malpractice actions generally, there must be a causal relationship between the physician's failure to adequately divulge and damage to the patient.

A causal connection exists when, but only when, disclosure of significant risks incidental to treatment would have resulted in a decision against it. The patient obviously has no complaint if he would have submitted to the therapy notwithstanding awareness that the risk was one of its perils. On the other hand, the very purpose of the disclosure rule is to protect the patient against consequences which, if known, he would have avoided by foregoing the treatment. The more difficult question is whether the factual issue on causality calls for an objective or a subjective determination.

It has been assumed that the issue is to be resolved according to whether the fact-finder believes the patient's testimony that he would not have agreed to the treatment if he had known of the danger which later ripened into injury. We think a technique which ties the factual conclusion on causation simply to the assessment of the patient's credibility is unsatisfactory. To be sure, the objective of risk-disclosure is preservation of the patient's interest in intelligent self-choice on proposed treatment, a matter the patient is free to decide for any reason that appeals to him. When, prior to commencement of therapy, the patient is sufficiently informed on risks and he exercises his choice, it may truly be said that he did exactly what he wanted to do. But when causality is explored at a post-injury trial with a professedly uninformed patient, the question whether he actually would have turned the treatment down if he had known the risks is purely hypothetical: "Viewed from the point at which he had to decide, would the patient have decided differently had he known something he did not know?" And the answer which the patient supplies hardly represents more than a guess, perhaps tinged by the circumstance that the uncommunicated hazard has in fact materialized.

In our view, this method of dealing with the issue on causation comes in second-best. It places the physician in jeopardy of the patient's hindsight and bitterness. It places the factfinder in the position of deciding whether a speculative answer to a hypothetical question is to be credited. It calls for a subjective determination solely on testimony of a patient-witness shadowed by the occurrence of the undisclosed risk.

Better it is, we believe, to resolve the causality issue on an objective basis: in terms of what a prudent person in the patient's position would have decided if suitably informed of all perils bearing significance. If adequate disclosure could reasonably be expected to have caused that person to decline the treatment because of the revelation of the kind of risk or danger that resulted in harm, causation is shown, but otherwise not. The patient's testimony is relevant on that score of course but it would not threaten to dominate the findings. . . .

We now delineate our view on the need for expert testimony in non-disclosure cases. [The court then held that "lay witness testimony can competently establish a physician's failure to disclose particular risk information, the patient's lack of knowledge of the risk, and the adverse consequences following the treatment. Experts are unnecessary to a showing of the materiality of a risk to a patient's decision on treatment, or to the reasonably expectable effect of risk disclosure on the decision."

The court then held that plaintiff's cause of action for breach of the duty to disclose was governed by the negligence statute with its three-year period of limitation, and consequently was not barred by the one-year battery statute.]

This brings us to the remaining question, common to all three causes of action: whether appellant's evidence was of such caliber as to require a submission to the jury.

[The court then ordered a new trial because: (1) the appellant testified that he was not told of the hazards of the operation; (2) his mother was told that the laminectomy was no more serious than any other operation; (3) Dr. Spence himself testified about the one-percent risk of paralysis; and (4) there was no evidence that appellant's "emotional makeup was such that concealment of the risk of paralysis was medically sound."[138]

NOTES

1. *The case on remand.* What issues were left to be resolved in *Canterbury* on remand? If the risk of paralysis from falling out of bed is common knowledge, does it make a difference that the defendant did not disclose the risk of paralysis from the operation itself? How ought Canterbury's prior condition be taken into account in the assessment of damages? Is it correct to argue that Canterbury only suffered back pain before the operation?

Upon remand the case was retried, with the jury finding for the de-

---

138. Dr. Spence's opinion — that disclosure is medically unwise — was expressed as to patients generally, and not with reference to traits possessed by appellant. His explanation was:

> I think that I always explain to patients the operations are serious, and I feel that any operation is serious. I think that I would not tell patients that they might be paralyzed because of the small percentage, one per cent, that exists. There would be a tremendous percentage of people that would not have surgery and would not therefore be benefited by it, the tremendous percentage that get along very well, 99 per cent.

fendant. The decision was affirmed on appeal, without opinion. 509 F.2d 537 (D.C. Cir. 1975).

2. *The British repudiation of the duty of full disclosure.* The duty to disclose has received a far narrower construction in the British cases than it received in *Canterbury.* In the early case of Hatcher v. Black, The Times (London), 2 July (1954), the defendant physician advised the plaintiff that a proposed operation posed no risk to her vocal cords when he in fact knew that it did. Denning, L.J., first observed that "an action for negligence against a doctor was like a dagger, which could wound his reputation as severely as it could his body," and then concluded that no action would lie. "He had told a lie which in the circumstances was justifiable. It was a matter which in law was left to the conscience of the doctor himself."

More recently, in Sidaway v. Bethlem Royal Hospital, [1984] All Eng. Rep. 1018, 1030, 1031, the English Court of Appeal explicitly rejected *Canterbury* on a case with surprisingly similar facts. The plaintiff had suffered adverse consequences from a laminectomy performed by one of the defendant's neurosurgeons, Mr. Falconer, since deceased. It was found that "(a) Mr. Falconer did not tell the plaintiff that this was an operation of choice or an 'elective operation,' meaning thereby that it could be postponed or even refused at the price of enduring pain and possibly increasing pain meanwhile, and (b) while Mr. Falconer 'did not make a full disclosure to the plaintiff of all the risks involved in the operation she was about to undergo so that she was in a position to make a fully informed decision whether to agree to it.'" More concretely, he told her of the risk of minor damage to the nerve root, which was in the nature of one to two percent, but did not inform her of the far more severe consequence of permanent injury to the spinal cord, which was a "remote" risk of "less than 1%."

The court affirmed the decision of the trial judge below, dismissing the plaintiff's cause of action. Dunn, L.J., observed:

> I confess that I reach this conclusion with no regret. The evidence in this case showed that a contrary result would be damaging to the relationship of trust and confidence between doctor and patient, and might well have an adverse effect on the practice of medicine. It is doubtful whether it would be of any significant benefit to patients, most of whom prefer to put themselves unreservedly in the hands of their doctors. This is not in my view 'paternalism', to repeat an evocative word used in argument. It is simply an acceptance of the doctor/patient relationship as it has developed in this country. The principal effect of accepting the proposition advanced by the plaintiff would be likely to be an increase in the number of claims for professional negligence against doctors. This would be likely to have an adverse effect on the general standard of medical care, since doctors would inevitably be concerned to safeguard themselves against such claims, rather than to concentrate on their primary duty of treating their patients.

3. Informed consent: negligence or battery? As *Canterbury* indicates, nearly all modern informed consent cases are brought upon negligence theories. There are, however, occasional situations in which plaintiffs resort to the older battery theory. In Mink v. University of Chicago, 460 F. Supp. 713, 716-717 (N.D. Ill. 1978), the named plaintiffs brought a class action on behalf of themselves and other women who were administered DES during pregnancy. The women were not told that they were part of a double blind experiment conducted at the University to determine the effectiveness of DES in preventing miscarriages. The plaintiffs sued *in battery* not for injuries to themselves, but for their concern over the possible reproductive injury to their offspring, both male and female. The defendants countered that the proper cause of action was for failure to obtain informed consent, which, unlike battery, did not lie without an allegation of physical injury to the plaintiffs themselves. The court held that the battery claim was proper:

> True "informed consent" cases concern the duty of the physician to inform his patient of risks inherent in the surgery or treatment to which he has consented. While early cases treated lack of informed consent as vitiating the consent to treatment so there was liability for battery, the modern view "is that the action . . . is in reality one for negligence in failing to conform to the proper standard, to be determined on the basis of expert testimony as to what disclosure should be made." W. Prosser, Law of Torts §32, at 165 (4th ed. 1971). Nonetheless, a battery action may still be appropriate in certain circumstances. Where the patient has not consented to the treatment, it is meaningless to ask whether the doctor should have revealed certain risks necessary to make the consent an "informed" one. . . .
>
> The question thus becomes whether the instant case is more akin to the performance of an unauthorized operation than to the failure to disclose the potential ramifications of an agreed to treatment. We think the situation is closer to the former. The plaintiffs did not consent to DES treatment; they were not even aware that the drug was being administered to them. They were the subjects of an experiment whereby nonemergency treatment was performed upon them without their consent or knowledge.

Is *Mink* distinguishable from Mohr v. Williams, supra at page 12? If the plaintiffs knew that the program was experimental, and that the drug was DES, is an informed consent theory proper? Required? Note that *Mink* was settled before trial with payments to the named members of the class.

4. Materiality of risk. One source of constant litigation under *Canterbury* has been the level of risk sufficiently great to trigger the duty to disclose. In Kozup v. Georgetown University, 663 F. Supp. 1048, 1053-1054 (1987), the parents of the decedent, Matthew Kozup, brought an informed consent claim against the defendant hospital, which gave a transfusion to Matthew at birth in 1983. The blood provided was contaminated with the AIDS virus and Matthew died three years afterward. The district court judge held that a suit against the hospital was inappropriate because the risk was not material in 1983:

> No reasonable jury could find that the possibility of contracting AIDS from a blood transfusion was a material risk at the time Matthew Kozup received his three transfusions. As of January, 1983, only a single case of possible transfusion-related AIDS had been diagnosed, and that only weeks before Matthew received the contaminated blood. This single case stands in contrast to the approximately 3.5 million blood donations annually. A risk of one in 3.5 million cannot be said to be material to a reasonable patient in Matthew Kozup's situation. *Canterbury*, . . . Indeed, plaintiffs' own expert, Dr. Donald Armstrong, Chief of Infectious Diseases at Memorial Sloan Kettering Cancer Center, admitted that he did not warn his patients prior [to] transfusion in late 1982 or early 1983. Without some evidence to oppose defendants' strong showing of lack of materiality of the risk, plaintiffs cannot prevail.
>
> In addition, as of January, 1983, there was still no consensus in the medical or blood banking communities that AIDS was transmitted by a blood-borne agent. The viral agent HTLV-III would not be identified for another 15 months. Thus, what doctors "knew or should have known" about the risk of AIDS in blood transfusion therapy was virtually nothing: this remote possibility cannot, as a matter of law, have amounted to a "material risk" within the meaning of that term as set forth in *Canterbury*. Thus, plaintiffs' cause of action under the theory of lack of informed consent must fail on this basis alone.
>
> However, in addition to this flaw in plaintiffs' theory, a second equally fatal problem remains. Even if plaintiffs could show that the risk of AIDS would have been material to their decision regarding Matthew's transfusions, plaintiffs must also show that the hospital's failure to warn of that risk *caused* the injury involved. That is, plaintiffs must show that "disclosure of significant risks incidental to treatment would have resulted in a decision against it." *Canterbury*. No reasonable jury could conclude on the facts of this case that, had the Kozups been informed of a one in 3.5 million possibility of contracting AIDS, they would have declined to permit Georgetown's physicians to transfuse blood into their son. Matthew was premature and his birth was accompanied by many complications including hypovolemia. The transfusions were absolutely necessary to save his life.

The case was remanded for a new trial on appeal, Kozup v. Georgetown University, 851 F.2d 437 (D.C. Cir. 1988). There the court held that it was improper for the trial judge to blend the informed consent with the battery count, as the plaintiffs did in their complaint. The court held that the trial court was correct in its assessment of materiality in informed consent but remanded the case for a new trial on the battery count, noting that no parental consent had been obtained at all. It rejected, at least for summary judgment purposes, the hospital's theory that "there is no necessity to obtain parent consent for life-saving treatment."

In subsequent cases, expert evidence has been allowed to establish that blood banks have been negligent in failing to perceive material transfusion risks of AIDS in early 1983. See, e.g., United Blood Services v. Quintana, 827 P.2d 509 (Colo. 1992). It is worth noting that matters had moved sufficiently between January and May of 1983 so that the legal issues at the latter time were concerned less with informed consent, and more with the development of effective institutional safeguards against the transmission of AIDS. Note that conformity with professional blood bank testing standards is not an absolute defense after *The T.J. Hooper.* What safeguards, if any, should be introduced to deal with the question of 20/20 hindsight? For a sharp criticism of blood bank practices in the critical 1983 period, see Eckert, The AIDS Blood-Transfusion Cases: A Legal and Economic Analysis of Liability, 29 San Diego L. Rev. 203, 294 (1992), calling for a general regime of strict liability for blood banks to "encourage them to solicit donors in low-risk areas and to screen them more carefully."

5. *On the edges of disclosure.* In Truman v. Thomas, 611 P.2d 902, 906 (Cal. 1980), the doctrine of informed consent received a novel twist. The decedent had died of cervical cancer at age 30. The plaintiff contended that the defendant physician was guilty of medical malpractice because he did not inform the decedent of the risks of cervical cancer, which might have been detected by a Pap smear, a procedure which he had from time to time urged her to undergo. The court held that the jury could find that the defendant had breached his duty to disclose by his failure to make clear the necessity for the Pap smear.

> If a patient indicates that he or she is going to *decline* the risk-free test or treatment, then the doctor has the additional duty of advising of all material risks of which a reasonable person would want to be informed before deciding not to undergo the procedure. On the other hand, if the recommended test or treatment is itself risky, then the physician should always explain the potential consequences of declining to follow the recommended course of action.

The dissent argued that this extension of the doctrine of informed consent to routine cases would "impose upon doctors the intolerable burden of having to explain diagnostic tests to healthy patients." In *Truman* the patient had repeated contact with the defendant for different ailments during the five-year period in which he treated her. Does the court's decision mean that a physician must explain every routine test to every patient? If so, must the explanation be given during every visit?

The California court arguably took a more restrained view of informed consent in Arato v. Avedon, 858 P.2d 598 (Cal. 1993), where the decedent died of pancreatic cancer after a long bout of chemotherapy and radiation therapy. The plaintiff sued on the ground that her husband would have refused this treatment, in order to live out his last days in comfort, and put his business and personal affairs in order. But instead he endured 70 or more visits to his oncologist because he had never been given explicit statement of the relevant life expectancy probabilities, which showed at most a five to ten percent five-year survival rate for persons in decedent's position. The defendant believed that this cancer was more curable than most because it was diagnosed before it metastasized, and was cleanly excised. But the patient had also indicated that he wanted to be "told the truth" rather than have his doctors "bear the burden" for him. Overruling an appellate court decision that called for "mandatory" disclosure of this information, the court adhered to its earlier view (see Cobbs v. Grant, 502 P.2 1 (Cal. 1972)) which, consistent with *Canterbury*, calls for a generalized jury instruction that requires "a physician to disclose to the patient all material information to enable the patient to make an informed decision regarding the proposed operation or treatment." It then unanimously reinstated a jury verdict that found the defendants had made sufficient disclosures prior to treatment.

> There was testimony that Mr. and Mrs. Arato were informed that cancer of the pancreas is usually fatal; of the substantial risk of recurrence, an event that would mean his illness was incurable; of the unproven nature of the F.A.M. [a chemotherapy regimen] treatments and their principal side effects; and of the option of foregoing such treatments. Mr. Arato's doctors also testified that they could not with confidence predict how long the patient might live, notwithstanding statistical mortality tables.

6. Expert testimony in informed consent cases. One decision that broke with Canterbury v. Spence on a number of important points is Bly v. Rhoads, 222 S.E.2d 783, 787-788 (Va. 1976), where the plaintiff sued under an informed consent theory after she suffered adverse consequences from a hysterectomy. The court agreed with the position taken in *Canterbury* insofar as it allowed the plaintiff "to establish by lay evidence that his physician did not disclose particular risk information and that he, the patient, had no knowledge of the risk." It also agreed that lay evidence could be used in some cases "to show the adverse consequences following treatment" and it left open the possibility that in some infrequent cases "the duty of disclosure is so obvious that expert testimony should not be required." But the court then noted that expert evidence was required on the full range of complex issues raised by the disclosure question. It then concluded:

> We believe the better rule, which we now adopt, is to require a patient-plaintiff to show by qualified medical experts whether and to what extent information should be disclosed by the physician to his patient. This rule would not, contrary to what *Canterbury* suggests, impose an undue burden

upon the patient-plaintiff. After all, in the usual case, the patient unquestionably will have obtained experts to establish the negligent treatment phase of his malpractice action.

7. *Objective and subjective causation.* The "objective" causation standards of *Canterbury* were also adopted in Cobbs v. Grant, 502 P.2d 1 (Cal. 1972). The court recognized the tension between the autonomy principle and the objective standard, but adopted it nonetheless because it declined to place the "physician in jeopardy of the patient's bitterness and disillusionment" resulting with "20/20 hindsight." The objective standard was also followed in Largey v. Rothman, 540 A.2d 504 (N.J. 1988), which relied explicitly on *Canterbury.* The opposite position was taken in Arena v. Gingrich, 748 P.2d 547 (Or. 1988), construing Oregon's informed consent statute (ORS 677.097), which provided that informed consent could be obtained only if the physician explained "[i]n general terms the treatment to be undertaken," the "alternative procedures or methods of treatment, if any," and the "risks, if any, to the procedure or treatment." Thereafter the physician had to ask the patient if he or she desired a fuller explanation. In light of this statute Linde, J., held that the objective standard was inappropriate: "The statute having defined the standard of disclosure without required reference to what a prudent patient reasonably would want to know, we shall not reintroduce that hypothetical prudent patient by the back door of 'causation.' "

8. *Legislative response to informed consent.* In the wake of Canterbury v. Spence, the question of informed consent, along with the rest of the medical malpractice situation, has received legislative attention, often at the request of insurance companies and medical organizations. Consider the impact and worth of the New York legislation. (New York Public Health Law §2805-d (1994)).

> 1. Lack of informed consent means the failure of the person providing the professional treatment or diagnosis to disclose to the patient such alternatives thereto and the reasonably foreseeable risks and benefits involved as a reasonable medical . . . practitioner under similar circumstances would have disclosed, in a manner permitting the patient to make a knowledgeable evaluation.
> 2. The right of action to recover for medical malpractice based on a lack of informed consent is limited to those cases involving either (a) non-emergency treatment, procedure or surgery, or (b) a diagnostic procedure which involved invasion or disruption of the integrity of the body.
> 3. For a cause of action therefor it must also be established that a reasonably prudent person in the patient's position would not have undergone the treatment or diagnosis if he had been fully informed and that the lack of informed consent is a proximate cause of the injury or condition for which recovery is sought.
> 4. It shall be a defense to any action for medical malpractice based upon an alleged failure to obtain such an informed consent that:

(a) the risk not disclosed is too commonly known to warrant disclosure; or

(b) the patient assured the medical . . . practitioner he would undergo the treatment, procedure or diagnosis regardless of the risk involved, or the patient assured the medical practitioner that he did not want to be informed of the matters to which he would be entitled to be informed; or

(c) consent by or on behalf of the patient was not reasonably possible; or

(d) the medical . . . practitioner, after considering all of the attendant facts and circumstances, used reasonable discretion as to the manner and extent to which such alternatives or risks were disclosed to the patient because he reasonably believed that the manner and extent of such disclosure could reasonably be expected to adversely and substantially affect the patient's condition.

How do the rules of this statute differ from those under Canterbury v. Spence, and what influence, if any, might the adoption of the New York statute have in the trial of cases like *Canterbury*? Is the statute preferable to a general good faith standard whereby doctors make whatever disclosures they regard as fit under the circumstances?

9. *A contract solution to informed consent.* A more radical approach to the informed consent would allow physicians and patients to alter the scope of the legal rule by private contract. Arguments supporting that conclusion are found in Epstein, Medical Malpractice, The Case for Contract, 1 Am. B. Found. Res. J. 87, 119-128 (1976). A more bittersweet conclusion on that question was reached recently in Schuck, Rethinking Informed Consent, 103 Yale L.J. 899, 957-958 (1994):

> With some relatively narrow exceptions, the law treats all patients and physicians the same; it posits an abstracted, objectively defined "prudent patient" as the consumer of information and the maker of choices, and conforms all physicians' legal obligations to this uniform abstraction. For these reasons, current law might not enforce contract terms providing for an informed consent standard less demanding than that which the law now imposes. In rejecting such terms, a court would probably argue categorically that a patient's pre-illness decision to forgo information must be even less well-informed than a decision about treatment made by the patient after illness strikes.
>
> Like the "reasonable person" standard and other objective standards in tort law, the existing uniform approach to informed consent has two virtues: it is cheaper to know and administer, and it seeks to protect patients against gross inequalities of bargaining power vis-à-vis providers. But a doctrine that treats all patients and physician-patient relationships as essentially homogenous when in fact they are not exacts a price. Specifically, the law requires a level of informed consent that is different from the level that many consumers or groups of consumers want and for which they would be willing to pay if the choice were presented to them. The existing doctrine, then suffers from an ironic, if endemic vice: it deprives patients of choice in the name of choice.

See also, on informed consent generally, Shultz, From Informed Consent to Patient Choice: A New Protected Interest, 95 Yale L.J. 219 (1985); Twerski and Cohen, Informed Decision Making and the Law of Torts: The Myth of Justiciable Causation, [1988] U. Ill. L. Rev. 607.

10. Overall assessment of the medical malpractice system. At this point it is perhaps appropriate to take stock of the effectiveness of the malpractice system as a method for accident prevention and compensation. The most recent comprehensive book on the subject is Paul C. Weiler, Medical Malpractice On Trial 14 (1991), which reports that two major studies, one in California from the 1970s, and a New York study from the late 1980s, together reviewed the patient records of some 50,000 hospitalizations (some 20,000 in California and 30,000 in New York). These studies concluded that in both states the instances of negligence resulting in patient harm was far greater than the number of malpractice actions filed, and greater still than the number of cases in which recovery was made. The New York investigation (in which Weiler took part), for example, estimated that about 1 in 100 patients suffered serious injury or death attributable to negligent medical treatment; yet that suit was filed for only one of each eight valid claims, with compensation paid in only half those claims. Worse still, further investigation of the claims filed revealed that "a substantial proportion of the claims actually filed were for cases in which we had concluded on the basis of hospital records that no medical injury at all had occurred, much less one caused by medical negligence." It was not possible to conclude whether or not the compensation was paid in the meritorious cases. Stated otherwise, these studies suggest that the liability system picks out the wrong cases for suit, and thus produces a higher error rate than if *no* suits had been filed at all.

For a more optimistic study see Frank Sloan, Suing for Medical Malpractice 9-10 (1993), based on a detailed examination of the obstetrical and emergency room claims filed in Florida, one of the most active malpractice states, between 1986 and 1989.

> If the system of liability determination and compensation is indeed "broken," this should be most obvious in a state like Florida. . . . Yet in spite of some weaknesses, we find that the system works better than media accounts and frequent complaints from the health care community would lead one to expect. Overall, claimants appear to be satisfied with the process even when they do not receive compensation. Claimants, not their lawyers, tend to initiate the process. Injured parties find lawyers, not the reverse. Liability determination is not capricious. There is overall agreement between the independent evaluations of our study's physician panelists and the outcomes of the cases. Compensation was much more likely to have been paid when the panelists found evidence of physician liability than when they did not. On the whole, claimants did not even

recover their total past and future economic losses, after when we accounted for funds they obtained from collateral sources, such as health and disability insurance.

Finally, to round out the picture, a comprehensive review of all tort systems, Dewees & Trebilcock, The Efficacy of the Tort System and Its Alternatives: A Review of the Empirical Evidence, 30 Osgoode Hall L. J. 57 (1992), concludes that it is exceedingly difficult to find any empirical evidence of a strong deterrent effect of the system of medical malpractice liability. It cites work by the Weiler group which suggests that a ten percent increase in malpractice claims should lead to a four percent reduction in the level of medical accidents, and then notes that while Canadian doctors are only twenty percent as likely to be sued as U.S. doctors, and pay insurance premiums around ten percent of those paid by U.S. doctors, yet "there appears to be no evidence that Canadian physicians are more careless than their U.S. counterparts." Dewees and Trebilcock then conclude that the medical malpractice system fares badly, both in absolute terms and in comparison with automobile insurance, in providing compensation to injured parties and in meeting the concerns of corrective justice.

E.   CRIMINAL STATUTES

This section explores another approach to the task of supplying specific content to the reasonable care standard: the use of criminal statutes, and for that matter, local ordinances or administrative regulations. Typically, a statute involved in a negligence case provides for some penalty to be administered by the state, usually a fine, but sometimes incarceration or, on occasion, injunctive relief.

The first question is how these statutes come to be a source of private rights. When the statute expressly creates a private remedy for one injured through its violation, it is a matter of following the explicit statutory command. When the statute is silent on the question of private enforcement, however, the question becomes one of statutory construction. Some courts assume that private action is authorized by some "overriding" legislative intention. Yet such an intention is fictional, since the statutory silence is compatible with the opposite position that only direct criminal penalties should be imposed for violations. Given the wide variety of criminal statutes on the books, it is doubtful that either of these two positions (automatic creation or automatic denial of a private action) represents the best that the courts can do in the absence of more specific legislative guidance. The central task is to develop a set of principles to help determine in which cases private rights of action are created.

Anon.
87 Eng. Rep. 791 (K.B. 1703)

HOLT, C.J. For wherever a statute enacts anything, or prohibits anything, for the advantage of any person, that person shall have remedy to recover the advantage given him, or to have satisfaction for the injury done him contrary to law by the same statute; for it would be a fine thing to make a law by which one has a right, but no remedy but in equity. . . .

Thayer, Public Wrong and Private Action
27 Harv. L. Rev. 317, 321-323 (1914), Reprinted in Selected Essays on the Law of Torts 276, 280-281 (1924)

Before the ordinance the plaintiff, injured by the runaway horse, must have based his action on negligence. Whether the defendant was negligent in leaving the horse unhitched would have been for the jury to say, unless this was so clear one way or the other that the court must deal with it as a "question of law" (so-called); i.e., as a point on which fair minds could reach but one conclusion. In any situation less extreme the whole matter would have been within the jury's province. And the jury was bound in deciding it to use the test of the "ordinary prudent man." They could not acquit the defendant of negligence without saying that an ordinary prudent man would have left his horse unhitched under these circumstances; that with such a horse as this, and in such a place, the prudent man would have foreseen no danger to others —for the foresight of the prudent man in the defendant's position (in other words, the probability of danger from his standpoint) is the test of negligence. The jury was justified either in accepting or rejecting the theory that he was negligent, for the mere fact of submitting the issue of negligence to them means that a finding either way is warranted by the evidence. The reasonableness of the defendant's conduct was thus in the eye of the law an open question, depending on the circumstances and the inferences fairly to be drawn from them.

Suppose now the situation to be changed by the single circumstance of the ordinance, all other facts remaining the same. Can the issue of negligence any longer be left to the jury? Not unless they would be justified in finding for either party; and what must a finding for the defendant on this issue mean? That an ordinary prudent man, knowing the ordinance —for upon familiar principles he can claim no benefit from his ignorance of the law —would have chosen to break it, "reasonably" believing that damage would not result from his action. It must then, upon this view, be deemed consistent with ordinary prudence for an individual to set his own opinion against the judgment authoritatively pronounced by constituted public authority, for the ordinance has prohibited leaving *all* horses unhitched, without exception, and has done this in order to prevent just such consequences as have occurred. It has thus declared the danger to be so serious and constant that a less sweeping prohibition would be inadequate. And when eminent courts, using familiar phraseology, state that the breach of the ordinance is not "negligence per se," but only "evidence of negligence," and leave the question of negligence as a fact to the jury, they are doing nothing less than informing that body that it may properly stamp with approval, as reasonable conduct, the action of one who has assumed to place his own foresight above that of the legislature in respect of the very danger which it was legislating to prevent.

Osborne v. McMasters
41 N.W. 543 (Minn. 1889)

MITCHELL, J. Upon the record in this case it must be taken as the facts that defendant's clerk in his drug-store, in the course of his employment as such, sold to plaintiff's intestate a deadly poison without labelling it "Poison," as required by statute; that she, in ignorance of its deadly qualities, partook of the poison, which caused her death. Except for the ability of counsel and the earnestness with which they have argued the case, we would not have supposed that there could be any serious doubt of defendant's liability on this state of facts. It is immaterial for present purposes whether section 329 of the Penal Code or section 14, c. 147, Laws 1885, or both, are still in force, and constitute the law governing this case. The requirements of both statutes are substantially the same, and the sole object of both is to protect the public against the dangerous qualities of poison. It is now well settled, certainly in this state, that where a statute or municipal ordinance imposes upon any person a specific duty for the protection or benefit of others, if he neglects to perform that duty he is liable to those for whose protection or benefit it was imposed for any injuries of the character which the statute or ordinance was designed to prevent, and which were proximately produced by such neglect. . . .

Defendant contends that this is only true where a right of action for the alleged negligent act existed at common law; that no liability existed at common law for selling poison without labelling it, and therefore none exists under this statute, no right of civil action being given by it. Without stopping to consider the correctness of the assumption that selling poison without labelling it might not be actionable negligence at common law, it is sufficient to say that, in our opinion, defendant's contention proceeds upon an entire misapprehension of the nature and gist of a cause of action of this kind. The common law gives a right of action to every one sustaining injuries caused proximately by the negligence of another. The present is a common-law action, the gist of which is defendant's negligence, resulting in the death of plaintiff's intestate. Negligence is the breach of legal duty. It is immaterial whether the duty is one imposed by the rule of common law requiring the exercise of ordinary care not to injure another, or is imposed by a statute designed for the protection of others. In either case the failure to perform the duty constitutes negligence, and renders the party liable for injuries resulting from it. The only difference is that in the one case the measure of legal duty is to be determined upon common-law principles, while in the other the statute fixes it, so that the violation of the statute constitutes conclusive evidence of negligence, or, in other words, negligence per se. The action in the latter case is not a statutory one, nor does the statute give the right of action in any other sense except that it makes an act negligent which otherwise might not be such, or at least only evidence of negligence. All that the statute does is to establish a fixed standard by which the fact of negligence may be determined. The gist of the action is still negligence, or the non-performance of a legal duty to the person injured.

What has been already said suggests the answer to the further contention that if any civil liability exists it is only against the clerk who sold the poison, and who alone is criminally liable. Whether the act constituting the actionable negligence was such on common-law principles, or is made such by statute, the doctrine of agency applies, to wit, that the master is civilly liable for the negligence of his servant committed in the course of his employment, and resulting in injuries to third persons.

Judgment affirmed.

NOTES

1. Defective statutes as a source of duty. Assume that an otherwise valid criminal safety statute is invalid because of a technical defect in the enacting procedure. Could it nevertheless be used to set the standard of care in a negligence action? How would Thayer answer this question? In Clinkscales v. Carver, 136 P.2d 777, 778-779 (Cal. 1943), Traynor, J., held that while the state could not criminally enforce its laws when it erected a stop sign pursuant to a defective statute, it nonetheless "was negligence as a matter of law to disregard the stop sign."

If a through artery has been posted with stop signs by the public authorities in the customary way and to all appearances by regular procedure, any reasonable man should know that the public naturally relies upon their observance. If a driver from a side street enters the ostensibly protected boulevard without stopping, in disregard of the posted safeguards, contrary to what drivers thereon could reasonably have expected him to do, he is guilty of negligence regardless of any irregularity attending the authorization of the signs.

2. *Subsequently enacted statutes.* In Hammond v. International Harvester Co., 691 F.2d 646, 651 (3d Cir. 1982), the defendant manufactured a skid load tractor which, at the option of the purchaser, was not equipped with a roll-over protective structure and side screens (ROPS) that could have prevented the driver from falling out of the operator's seat. On the question of whether the tractor was defectively designed without the ROPS, the court allowed the plaintiff, an employee of the purchaser, to introduce into evidence OSHA regulations, effective only after the manufacture of the vehicle, requiring the use of a removable ROPS for tractors that were used both outdoors and inside farm buildings with low clearances. "We recognize that these OSHA regulations do not directly govern the instant case because the tractor in question was manufactured at least six months prior to the effective date of the regulations. Nevertheless, OSHA's very decision to promulgate these regulations provides strong support for the proposition that a loader tractor —even one which must frequently pass through a low door — does not possess every element necessary to make it safe for use unless it comes equipped with a ROPS." How should a manufacturer design his equipment when he has knowledge of pending regulations? Should the defendant be allowed to introduce evidence that the dangers in removing and reattaching the ROPS exceeded any benefits that it might provide? Could it do so if the regulation had been in effect at the time of the accident?

3. *Who is protected by statute?* As a matter of hornbook law, only those persons who are supposed to receive the protection of the statute are entitled to maintain a suit for its breach. But with modern regulatory schemes, it is sometimes difficult to identify the members of a protected class. Under OSHA, for example,

> Each employer —
> (1) Shall furnish to each of his employees employment and a place of employment which are free from recognized hazards that are causing or are likely to cause death or serious physical harm to his employees;
> (2) Shall comply with Occupational Safety and Health standards promulgated under this chapter. 29 U.S.C. Sec. 654(a)

In Teal v. Du Pont de Nemours & Co., 728 F.2d 789 (6th Cir. 1984), the plaintiff, an employee of an independent contractor, was injured when he fell seventeen feet from a ladder that Du Pont had maintained in violation of a specific OSHA rule that required a clearance of not less than seven inches "from the centerline of the runs, cleats or steps to the nearest permanent object in back of the ladder." 29 C.F.R. §1910.27(c)(4). The defendant's violation was negligence per se, but the defendant argued that since Section 654(1) was restricted to an employer's own employees, that Section 654(a)(2) also did not run in favor of this plaintiff. The court rejected that argument on the ground that the statute as a whole was enacted "to assure so far as possible every working man and woman in the Nation safe and healthful working conditions," (Section 651(b)). It therefore concluded that this provision was enacted "for the special benefit of *all* employees, including the employees of an independent contractor, who perform work at another employer's workplace."

Where statutes have more limited objectives, the scope of the statutory duty has been narrower. In Fitzwater v. Sunset Empire, Inc., 502 P.2d 214, 217 (Or. 1972), the court denied the plaintiff a cause of action for negligence when defendant, although required to do so by municipal ordinance, had not removed ice and snow from the public sidewalk that served as the ingress to and egress from its restaurant:

> At common law the abutting owner had no duty to pedestrians to keep the public sidewalk clear of ice and snow. An ordinance requiring removal of the ice and snow does not impose liability on the abutting owner to third persons injured as a result of his failure to remove the ice and snow. The duty belongs to the municipality and the courts have construed the ordinances as an effort by the city "to require the abutting property owner to aid the city in the performance of its duty," not to create a liability in favor of third persons.. . . The penalty and abatement of the nuisance provisions in the ordinance are additional measures to help the city enforce the ordinance. If the city had intended by the ordinance to give an injured third party a right of action against the abutting owner, it could have so provided in the ordinance.

Why is the defendant's argument that the legislature could have provided for the private cause of action persuasive in *Fitzwater*, but not in *Osborne?*

4. *Actions "for any injuries of the character which the statute or ordinance was designed to prevent."* The dominant issue in *Osborne* has arisen in a wide range of contexts, with mixed results. In Gorris v. Scott, L.R. 9 Ex. 125, 129 (1874). The plaintiff had shipped a number of sheep with the defendant shipowner who failed to pen them in accordance with the requirement of the Contagious Disease (Animals) Act of 1869. The animals were washed overboard in the storm and "were lost by reason of the neglect to comply" with administrative orders issued pursuant to

the statute. Notwithstanding this causal connection between plaintiff's harm and defendant's breach of statutory duty, Kelly, C.B., denied plaintiff's recovery:

> [I]f we could see that it was the object, or among the objects of this Act, that the owners of sheep and cattle coming from a foreign port should be protected by the means described against the danger of their property being washed overboard, or lost by the perils of the sea, the present action would be within the principle.
>
> But, looking at the Act, it is perfectly clear that its provisions were all enacted with a totally different view; there was no purpose, direct or indirect, to protect against such damage; but, as is recited in the preamble, the Act is directed against the possibility of sheep or cattle being exposed to disease on their way to this country.. . . That being so, if by reason of the default in question the plaintiffs' sheep had been overcrowded, or had been caused unnecessary suffering, and so had arrived in this country in a state of disease, I do not say that they might not have maintained this action. But the damage complained of here is something totally apart from the object of the Act of Parliament, and it is in accordance with all the authorities to say that the action is not maintainable.

Could the plaintiff have maintained an action for breach of the contract of carriage?

Gorris was a case with a clear disjunction between the harm to which the statute was directed, and the harm sustained by the plaintiff. A similar result was reached in Di Caprio v. New York Central Ry., 131 N.E. 746 (N.Y. 1921), where the defendant failed to erect a fence required by statute to keep livestock off the tracks. Recovery was denied when the plaintiff's small son wandered on the track and was killed. What result if the boy had been killed while trying to drive cattle off the tracks?

In more recent cases courts have tended to find subsidiary statutory purposes consistent with *Gorris'* view that a statute could have multiple objectives. In de Haen v. Rockwood Sprinkler Co., 179 N.E. 764 (N.Y. 1932), defendant violated a statute requiring work elevators on construction jobs to have gates on the open sides in order to prevent workmen from falling down. A workman left a steam radiator near the open shaft which toppled over, hitting a worker coming up in the elevator. The statutory gate could have prevented the injury. Cardozo, C.J., concluded that if the risk of falling objects had been called to the legislature's attention, it would have included it as one of the hazards to be avoided. "A safeguard has been commanded, but without enumeration of the hazards to be avoided. In the revealing light of experience the hazards to be avoided are disclosed to us as the hazards that ensued."

A greater impatience with the statutory purpose doctrine was expressed by the United States Supreme Court in Kernan v. American Dredging Co., 355 U.S. 426 (1958), where a seaman lost his life when an open-flame kerosene lamp on the deck of a scow ignited inflammable vapors lying above an accumulation of petroleum products that had collected on the surface of a river. A Coast Guard regulation required that such lamps be at a height of not less than eight feet, but the lamp in question was less than three feet above the water. If the lamp had been mounted at the required height, it would not have ignited the vapors. Even though it appeared that the regulation was aimed at the risk of collision and not of fire, the Court, in a five-to-four decision, permitted recovery on the ground that "many of the refined distinctions necessary in common law tort doctrine," including the statutory purpose limitation, did not apply in the special context of the Federal Employers' Liability Act and the Jones Act.

Finally, in Stimpson v. Wellington Service Corp., 246 N.E.2d 801, 805 (Mass. 1969), defendant drove a 137-ton rig over city streets without having obtained the needed statutory permit. The weight of defendant's truck dislocated and broke the pipes in plaintiff's building, flooding the premises. The court found that the statute had a dual purpose. "Undoubtedly the primary purpose of the statute was to protect the ways themselves from injury from overloaded vehicles. But the Cambridge authorities, in considering an application for a permit under the statute, should have weighed as well other possible effects of the proposal, particularly because of the prohibition of the city ordinance against moving over city streets vehicles so loaded as to be likely to injure property. Failure to apply for a permit meant that the appropriate authority did not have the opportunity to appraise the risks and probabilities and to refuse the permit or impose conditions."

5. *Private rights of action under federal statutes.* In recent times, one vital question is whether plaintiffs may maintain tort actions for defendant's breach of a *federal* statute or regulation. Here all the usual difficulties are compounded because the right has to be tested under both federal and state law. At the federal level, the original tendency was to freely imply causes of action, as is done in state courts. Thus, in J. I. Case Co. v. Borak, 377 U.S. 426 (1964), the Supreme Court held that, in light of the "broad remedial purposes" of that statute, a shareholder had an implied cause of action for damages against his corporation for misrepresentations in violation of Section 14(a) of the Securities Exchange Act of 1934, which prohibits the use of false or misleading information in proxy fights for corporate control. Subsequently, however, the Supreme Court has taken a much more restrictive view of the availability of federal relief. Thus in the watershed case of Cort v. Ash, 422 U.S. 66, 78 (1975), the Court held that there was no private action for damages (as opposed to injunctive relief) in favor of a corporate shareholder against the corporate directors for violation of 18 U.S.C. §610, which as a criminal matter prohibits corporations from making "a contribution

or expenditure in connection with any election at which Presidential and Vice Presidential electors . . . are to be voted for." It observed:

> In determining whether a private remedy is implicit in a statute not expressly providing one, several factors are relevant. First, is the plaintiff "one of the class for whose *especial* benefit the statute was enacted," . . . that is, does the statute create a federal right in favor of the plaintiff? Second, is there any indication of legislative intent, explicit or implicit, either to create such a remedy or to deny one?. . . Third, is it consistent with the underlying purposes of the legislative scheme to imply such a remedy for the plaintiff?. . . And finally, is the cause of action one traditionally relegated to state law, in an area basically the concern of the States, so that it would be inappropriate to infer a cause of action based solely on federal law?

Subsequent Supreme Court decisions only confirm the hostile attitude to implied private rights of action. Section 10 of the 1899 Rivers and Harbors Act proscribed the "creation of any obstruction not affirmatively authorized by Congress, to the navigable . . . waters of the United States." In California v. Sierra Club, 451 U.S. 287 (1981), the Supreme Court, reversing the court of appeals below, held that the statute did not authorize a private right of action to persons harmed by the diversion of public waters on the ground that their damages were not special under the Cort v. Ash test. And in City of Milwaukee v. State of Illinois, 451 U.S. 304 (1981), the Court refused to allow a private federal cause of action for nuisance, which it regarded as inconsistent with the comprehensive scheme of control imposed by the federal water pollution acts. Is the decision sound if, at the time of passage, it had been common practice in both state and federal courts freely to imply private rights of action? See Stewart and Sunstein, Public Programs and Private Rights, 95 Harv. L. Rev. 1195 (1982), where the authors insist that the background understanding is important in these cases. Most recently in Virginia Bankshares v. Sandberg, 501 U.S. 1083 (1991), Justice Souter noted that "the recognition of any private right of action for violating a federal statute must ultimately rest on congressional intent to provide a private remedy."

In the event of no federal preemption, express or implied, is the state free to adopt or reject the federal standard as a basis for a private suit? In Lowe v. General Motors, 624 F.2d 1373 (5th Cir. 1980), the court held the plaintiff stated a valid state law cause of action when he alleged that the recall and notice practices of the defendant General Motors did not comply with the National Traffic and Motor Vehicle Safety Act, 15 U.S.C.A. §1402(a) on the ground that the tests of Cort v. Ash were inapplicable to a wrongful death action maintained under Alabama law. "This Court has often held that a violation of a Federal law or regulation can be evidence of negligence, and even evidence of negligence per se."

Martin v. Herzog
126 N.E. 814 (N.Y. 1920)

[The decedent was killed in a collision between the buggy he was driving and defendant's automobile. The accident occurred after dark, and decedent was driving the buggy without any lights, in violation of a statute. The defendant requested a ruling that the absence of a light on the plaintiff's vehicle was "prima facie evidence of contributory negligence." This request was refused, and the jury was instructed that it might consider the absence of lights as some evidence of negligence, but not conclusive evidence of negligence. The plaintiff then requested a charge that "the fact that the plaintiff's intestate was driving without a light is not negligence in itself," and to this the court acceded. The jury found the defendant liable and the decedent free from contributory negligence and the plaintiff had judgment. The appellate division reversed for error in the instructions. Affirmed.]

CARDOZO, J. We think the unexcused omission of the statutory signals is more than some evidence of negligence. It *is* negligence in itself. Lights are intended for the guidance and protection of other travelers on the highway (Highway Law, sec. 329a). By the very terms of the hypothesis, to omit, willfully or heedlessly, the safeguards prescribed by law for the benefit of another that he may be preserved in life or limb, is to fall short of the standard of diligence to which those who live in organized society are under a duty to conform. . . . In the case at hand, we have an instance of the admitted violation of a statute intended for the protection of travelers on the highway, of whom the defendant at the time was one. Yet the jurors were instructed in effect that they were at liberty in their discretion to treat the omission of lights either as innocent or as culpable. They were allowed to "consider the default as lightly or gravely" as they would (Thomas, J., in the court below). They might as well have been told that they could use a like discretion in holding a master at fault for the omission of a safety appliance prescribed by positive law for the protection of a workman. Jurors have no dispensing power by which they may relax the duty that one traveler on the highway owes under the statute to another. It is error to tell them that they have. The omission of these lights was a wrong, and being wholly unexcused was also a negligent wrong. No license should have been conceded to the triers of the facts to find it anything else.

We must be on our guard, however, against confusing the question of negligence with that of the causal connection between the negligence and the injury. A defendant who travels without lights is not to pay damages for his fault unless the absence of lights is the cause of the disaster. A plaintiff who travels without them is not to forfeit the right to damages unless the absence of lights is at least a contributing cause of the disaster. To say that conduct is negligence is not to say that it is always contributory negligence.

. . . A statute designed for the protection of human life is not to be brushed aside as a form of words, its commands reduced to the level of cautions, and the duty to obey attenuated into an option to conform.

NOTES

1. Negligence per se and excuses. In Day v. Pauly, 202 N.W. 363 (Wis. 1925), plaintiff made a left-hand turn at an intersection and collided with a southbound car. The highway commission or state police had placed roadmarkings that indicated it was proper for the plaintiff to "cut the corner" when switching from an eastbound to a northbound highway. The court directed that judgment be entered for defendant on the ground that plaintiff's violation of statute was not excused by the actions of the public officials. The court criticized the administrative officers of the state who had encouraged and directed motorists to operate their vehicles in a manner contrary to the legislatively established standard.

Other efforts to escape the doctrine of negligence per se have proved more successful. In Tedla v. Ellman, 19 N.E.2d 987, 989 (N.Y. 1939), the plaintiff and her brother, a deaf mute, were walking along a divided highway shortly after dark, pushing baby carriages filled with junk that they had collected for sale as part of their regular business. Instead of walking on the far left-hand side of the double highway, as required by statute, so that they would be facing oncoming traffic, they walked on the far right-hand side, so that the traffic going in their direction approached them from behind. Defendant struck them with his car, hurting the plaintiff and killing her brother. The defendant's negligence was clearly established at trial and judgment was entered for plaintiff. The only issue on appeal was "whether, as a matter of law, disregard of the statutory rule that pedestrians shall keep to the left of the center line of a highway constitutes contributory negligence which bars any recovery by the plaintiff." To answer that question, Judge Lehman noted that prior to the enactment of the statute, the common-law custom usually required pedestrians to walk against traffic in order to be alert to dangers from oncoming traffic. The general customary rule, however, also contained a customary exception that required pedestrians to walk with the traffic when the traffic coming from behind was much lighter than the oncoming traffic. The case thus presented a knotty issue of statutory construction: should the court read into the legislation the customary exception when the statute embodied the customary rule? If the statute had defined "specified safeguards against recognized dangers," Judge Lehman would have been prepared to apply the rule in Martin v. Herzog. But since this statute was designed to "codify, supplement or even change common-law rules" themselves designed to prevent accidents, Lehman thought it proper to imply the exception to the statute for the benefit of the plaintiff. The argument appears to turn on legislative intent, as Lehman dismissed the defendant's contentions as follows:

> Disregard of the statutory rule of the road and observance of a rule based on immemorial custom, it is said, is negligence which as matter of law is a proximate cause of the accident, though observance of the statutory rule might, under the circumstances of the particular case, expose a pedestrian to serious danger from which he would be free if he followed the rule that had been established by custom. If that be true, then the Legislature has decreed that pedestrians must observe the general rule of conduct which it has prescribed for their safety even under circumstances where observance would subject them to unusual risk; that pedestrians are to be charged with negligence as a matter of law for acting as prudence dictates. It is unreasonable to ascribe to the Legislature an intention that the statute should have so extraordinary a result, and the courts may not give to a statute an effect not intended by the Legislature.

The one-sentence dissent argued that the plaintiff's action should have been dismissed on the authority of Martin v. Herzog.

The Restatement (Second) of Torts §288A, comment *i*, illustration 6 endorses the court's position in *Tedla*. The Restatement also notes that violations of a statute may be excused by necessity or emergency, or by reason of incapacity, just as is the case with various forms of common-law negligence. With *Tedla* contrast Alley v. Siepman, 214 N.W.2d 7 (S.D. 1974), where the plaintiff, a 15-year-old girl, was struck by defendant's car while jaywalking. The plaintiff contended that it was customary for local citizens to violate the jaywalking statute, but the court did "not regard the showing of a custom or practice of violating the law as a legal excuse not to follow the law." But it did excuse her conduct by recognizing a lower standard of care for infants.

2. Statutory breach and plaintiff's conduct. The court found a novel way to escape the negligence per se doctrine in Johnson v. Garnand, 501 P.2d 32 (Ariz. App. 1972). There the defendant had driven his car a short distance straight ahead although the pavement markings required him to make a left-hand turn. Under the negligence per se doctrine defendant was negligent as a matter of law, yet he won by showing that it was customary for close to 95 percent of the drivers in defendant's position to proceed in violation of the pavement markings. Even though the custom did not excuse defendant's negligence, the court held it admissible on the question of plaintiff's contributory negligence and sustained a jury verdict for defendant because plaintiff had known about such custom.

Brown v. Shyne
151 N.E. 197 (N.Y. 1926)

LEHMAN, J. The plaintiff employed the defendant to give chiropractic treatment to her for a disease or physical condition. The defendant had no license to practice medicine, yet he held himself out as being able to diagnose and treat disease, and under the provisions of the Public Health Law (Cons. Laws, ch. 45) he was guilty of a misdemeanor. The plaintiff became paralyzed after she had received nine treatments by the defendant. She claims, and upon this appeal we must assume, that the paralysis was caused by the treatment she received. She has recovered judgment in the sum of $10,000 for the damages caused by said injury.

At the close of the plaintiff's case the plaintiff was permitted to amend the complaint to allege "that in so treating the plaintiff the defendant was engaged in the practice of medicine contrary to and in violation of the provisions of the Public Health Law of the State of New York in such case made and provided, he at the time of so treating plaintiff not being a duly licensed physician or surgeon of the State of New York." Thereafter the trial judge charged the jury that they might bring in a verdict in favor of the plaintiff if they found that the evidence established that the treatment given to the plaintiff was not in accordance with the standards of skill and care which prevail among those treating disease. He then continued: "This is a little different from the ordinary malpractice case, and I am going to allow you, if you think proper under the evidence in the case, to predicate negligence upon another theory. The public health laws of this State prescribe that no person shall practice medicine unless he is licensed so to do by the Board of Regents of this State and registered pursuant to statute . . . This statute to which I have referred is a general police regulation. Its violation, and it has been violated by the defendant, is some evidence, more or less cogent, of negligence which you may consider for what it is worth, along with all the other evidence in the case. If the defendant attempted to treat the plaintiff and to adjust the vertebrae in her spine when he did not possess the requisite knowledge and skill as prescribed by the statute to know what was proper and necessary to do under the circumstances, or how to do it, even if he did know what to do, you can find him negligent." In so charging the jury that from the violation of the statute the jury might infer negligence which produced injury to the plaintiff, the trial justice in my opinion erred.

The provisions of the Public Health Law prohibiting the practice of medicine without a license granted upon proof of preliminary training and after examination intended to show adequate knowledge, are of course intended for the protection of the general public against injury which unskilled and unlearned practitioners might cause. If violation of the statute by the defendant was the proximate cause of the plaintiff's injury, then the plaintiff may recover upon proof of violation; if violation of the statute has no direct bearing on the injury, proof of the violation becomes irrelevant. For injury caused by neglect of duty imposed by the penal law there is civil remedy; but of course the injury must follow from the neglect.

Proper formulation of general standards of preliminary education and proper examination of the particular applicant should serve to raise the standards of skill and care generally possessed by members of the profession in this State; but the license to practice medicine confers no additional skill upon the practitioner; nor does it confer immunity from physical injury upon a patient if the practitioner fails to exercise care. Here, injury may have been caused by lack of skill or care; it would not have been obviated if the defendant had possessed a license yet failed to exercise the skill and care required of one practicing medicine. True, if the defendant had not practiced medicine in this State, he could not have injured the plaintiff, but the protection which the statute was intended to provide was against risk of injury by the unskilled or careless practitioner, and unless the plaintiff's injury was caused by carelessness or lack of skill, the defendant's failure to obtain a license was not connected with the injury. The plaintiff's cause of action is for negligence or malpractice. The defendant undertook to treat the plaintiff for a physical condition which seemed to require remedy. Under our law such treatment may be given only by a duly qualified practitioner who has obtained a license.

The defendant in offering to treat the plaintiff held himself out as qualified to give treatment. He must meet the professional standards of skill and care prevailing among these who do offer treatment lawfully. If injury follows through failure to meet those standards, the plaintiff may recover. The provisions of the Public Health Law may result in the exclusion from practice of some who are unqualified. Even a skilled and learned practitioner who is not licensed commits an offense against the State; but against such practitioners the statute was not intended to protect, for no protection was needed, and neglect to obtain a license results in no injury to the patient and, therefore, no private wrong. The purpose of the statute is to protect the public against unfounded assumption of skill by one who undertakes to prescribe or treat for disease. In order to show that the plaintiff has been injured by defendant's breach of the statutory duty, proof must be given that defendant in such treatment did not exercise the care and skill which would have been exercised by qualified practitioners within the State, and that such lack of skill and care caused the injury. Failure to obtain a license as required by law gives rise to no remedy if it has caused no injury. No case has been cited where neglect of a statutory duty has given rise to private cause of action where it has not appeared that private injury has been caused by danger against which the statute was intended to afford protection, and which obedience to the statute would have obviated. . . .

It is said that the trial justice did not charge that plaintiff might recover for defendant's failure to obtain a license but only that failure to obtain a license might be considered "some evidence" of defendant's negligence. Argument is made that even if neglect of the statutory duty does not itself create liability, it tends to prove that injury was caused by lack of skill or care. That can be true only if logical inference may be drawn from defendant's failure to obtain or perhaps seek a license that he not only lacks the skill and learning which would enable him to diagnose and treat disease generally, but also that he lacks even the skill and learning necessary for the physical manipulation he gave to this plaintiff. Evidence of defendant's training, learning and skill and the method he used in giving the treatment was produced at the trial and upon such evidence the jury could base a finding either of care or negligence, but the absence of a license does not seem to strengthen inference that might be drawn from such evidence, and a fortiori would not alone be a basis for such inference. Breach or neglect of duty imposed by statute or ordinance may be evidence of negligence only if there is logical connection between the proven neglect of statutory duty and the alleged negligence.

CRANE, J., dissenting. . . . I think this rule all too liberal to the defendant. What he did was prohibited by law. He could not practice medicine without violating the law. The law did not recognize him as a physician. How can the courts treat him as such? Provided his act, in violation of the law, is the direct and proximate cause of injury, in my judgment he is liable, irrespective of negligence. It seems somewhat strange that the courts, one branch of the law, can hold up for such a man the standards of the licensed physician, while the Legislature, another branch of the law, declares that he cannot practice at all as a physician. The courts thus afford the protection which the Legislature denies.

What is the rule which is to guide us in determining whether a violation of a statute or ordinance is evidence of negligence? It is no answer to say that the statute provides a penalty, and, therefore, no other consequences can follow. Such is not the law. We are to determine it, as I read the authorities, from the purpose and object of the law, and also from the fact whether a violation of the law may be the direct and proximate cause of an injury to an individual. . . .

The prohibition against practicing medicine without a license was for the very purpose of protecting the public from just what happened in this case. The violation of this statute has been the direct and proximate cause of the injury. The courts will not determine in face of this statute whether a faith healer, a patent medicine man, a chiropractor, or any other class of practitioner acted according to the standards of his own school, or according to the standards of a duly licensed physician. The law, to insure against ignorance and carelessness, has laid down a rule to be followed, namely, examinations to test qualifications, and a license to practice. If a man, in violation of this statute, takes his chances in trying to cure disease, and his acts result directly in injury, he should not complain if the law, in a suit for damages, says that his violation of the statute is some evidence of his incapacity.

NOTES

1. Medical practice without a license. May the plaintiff argue that she would have escaped injury if the defendant had not treated her at all? May the defendant argue that the plaintiff could recover only if she received treatment inferior to that provided by a licensed physician?

Section 4504 of the New York Civil Practice Law and Rules (1994) provides:

> (d) Proof of negligence; unauthorized practice of medicine. In any action for damages for personal injuries or death against a person not authorized to practice medicine . . . for any act or acts constituting the practice of medicine, when such act or acts were a competent producing proximate or contributing cause of such injuries or death, the fact that such person practiced medicine without being so authorized shall be deemed prima facie evidence of negligence.

Does the statute overrule *Brown?* Does it adopt the position of the dissent?

2. Trespassers on the highway. In Johnson v. Boston & Maine R.R., 143 A. 516, 521-22 (N.H. 1928), plaintiff was hurt in a collision with defendant's train while he was driving an automobile without the operator's license required by statute. The defendant pleaded plaintiff's breach of statute as a defense. In allowing this defense, the court had the following to say, in part:

> The legislature laid down a rule of conduct. It has not said merely that whoever drives without a license shall be punished by the state. In addition to that provision it has enacted another, specifically forbidding the act of driving. . . . It did this to protect lawful travelers.
>
> The argument that lack of license is not causal, and that therefore the violation is immaterial, ignores the terms of the statute, puts the facts upon which the prohibition depends in the place of the things prohibited, and thus reaches a conclusion based upon false premises.
>
> . . . Because an unlicensed driver was in fact competent, or might be so, it has been held that the prohibition might be disregarded, upon the ground that the violation was not causal. This amounts to substituting

the judgment of the court for that of the legislature in fixing the line between legal and illegal conduct. . . .

It may be conceded that in many instances the unlicensed driver is as fit as the licensed. But in order to keep out the unfit the legislature made this positive limitation of right. Its reasonableness is beyond dispute. There is no other practical way to accomplish the desired result. The fit can protect themselves by procuring a license. If they do not, they cannot complain of being classed with the unfit.

The statute involved in the *Johnson* case read as follows: "No person shall operate a motor vehicle upon any way in this state unless licensed." But in 1937 the legislature added to this language the following words: "and if any person shall operate a motor vehicle in violation of this section such violation in any civil action shall be prima facie evidence of his unfitness to drive a motor vehicle." The New Hampshire court, on the basis of this amendment, overruled Johnson v. Boston & Maine R.R. "in its entirety." Today's test is whether the operator is actually unfit to drive. See Fuller v. Sirois, 82 A.2d 82 (N.H. 1951).

Ross v. Hartman
139 F.2d 14 (D.C. Cir. 1943)

EDGERTON, J. This is an appeal by the plaintiff from a judgment for the defendant in a personal injury action.

The facts were stipulated. Appellee's agent violated a traffic ordinance of the District of Columbia[1] by leaving appellee's truck unattended in a public alley, with the ignition unlocked and the key in the switch. He left the truck outside a garage "so that it might be taken inside the garage by the garage attendant for night storage," but he does not appear to have notified anyone that he had left it. Within two hours an unknown person drove the truck away and negligently ran over the appellant.

The trial court duly directed a verdict for the appellee on the authority of Squires v. Brooks, 44 App. D.C. 320. That case was decided in 1916. On facts essentially similar to these, and despite the presence of a similar ordinance, this court held that the defendant's act in leaving the car unlocked was not a "proximate" or legal cause of the plaintiff's injury because the wrongful act of a third person intervened. We cannot reconcile that decision with facts which have become clearer and

---

1. "Locks on Motor Vehicles. Every motor vehicle shall be equipped with a lock suitable to lock the starting lever, throttle, or switch, or gear-shift lever, by which the vehicle is set in motion, and no person shall allow any motor vehicle operated by him to stand or remain unattended on any street or in any public place without first having locked the lever, throttle, or switch by which said motor vehicle may be set in motion." Traffic and Motor Vehicle Regulations for the District of Columbia, Section 58.

principles which have become better established than they were in 1916, and we think it should be overruled.

Everyone knows now that children and thieves frequently cause harm by tampering with unlocked cars. The danger that they will do so on a particular occasion may be slight or great. In the absence of an ordinance, therefore, leaving a car unlocked might not be negligent in some circumstances, although in other circumstances it might be both negligent and a legal or "proximate" cause of a resulting accident.

But the existence of an ordinance changes the situation. If a driver causes an accident by exceeding the speed limit, for example, we do not inquire whether his prohibited conduct was unreasonably dangerous. It is enough that it was prohibited. Violation of an ordinance intended to promote safety is negligence. If by creating the hazard which the ordinance was intended to avoid it brings about the harm which the ordinance was intended to prevent, it is legal cause of the harm. This comes only to saying that in such circumstances the law has no reason to ignore and does not ignore the causal relation which obviously exists in fact. The law has excellent reason to recognize it, since it is the very relation which the makers of the ordinance anticipated. This court has applied these principles to speed limits and other regulations of the manner of driving.

The same principles govern this case. The particular ordinance involved here is one of a series which require, among other things, that motor vehicles be equipped with horns and lamps. Ordinary bicycles are required to have bells and lamps, but they are not required to be locked. The evident purpose of requiring motor vehicles to be locked is not to prevent theft for the sake of owners or the police, but to promote the safety of the public in the streets. An unlocked motor vehicle creates little more risk of theft than an unlocked bicycle, or for that matter an unlocked house, but it creates much more risk that meddling by children, thieves, or others will result in injuries to the public. The ordinance is intended to prevent such consequences. Since it is a safety measure, its violation was negligence. This negligence created the hazard and thereby brought about the harm which the ordinance was intended to prevent. It was therefore a legal or "proximate" cause of the harm. Both negligence and causation are too clear in this case, we think, for submission to a jury.

The fact that the intermeddler's conduct was itself a proximate cause of the harm, and was probably criminal, is immaterial. Janof v. Newsom, 60 App. D.C. 291, 53 F.2d 149, involved a statute which forbade employment agencies to recommend servants without investigating their references. An agency recommended a servant to the plaintiff without investigation, the plaintiff employed the servant, and the servant robbed the plaintiff. This court held the agency responsible for the plaintiff's loss. In that case as in this, the conduct of the defendant or his agent was negligent precisely because it created a risk that a third person would act improperly. In such circumstances the fact that a third person does act improperly is not an intelligible reason for excusing the defendant.

There are practical as well as theoretical reasons for not excusing him. The rule we are adopting tends to make the streets safer by discouraging the hazardous conduct which the ordinance forbids. It puts the burden of the risk, as far as may be, upon those who create it. Appellee's agent created a risk which was both obvious and prohibited. Since appellee was responsible for the risk, it is fairer to hold him responsible for the harm than to deny a remedy to the innocent victim.

Reversed.

NOTES

1. *Keys and thieves: common-law negligence.* The fact situation of Ross v. Hartman is one that appears with surprising frequency in appellate decisions, where defendants have enjoyed a fair degree of success. In Richards v. Stanley, 271 P.2d 23, 26-27 (Cal. 1954), plaintiff was hurt by the negligent driving of a thief who had stolen defendant's car, which had been left with the key in the ignition. The San Francisco Municipal Code contained a proviso that stated: "nor shall this section or any violation thereof be admissible as evidence affecting recovery in any civil action for theft of such motor vehicle, or the insurance thereon, or have any other bearing in any civil action." The penal sanction set forth in the ordinance was that any police officer finding keys left in the ignition lock in violation of this section must remove them and take them to the officer in charge at the nearest police station. The court, through Traynor, J., held that the proviso barred the statutory cause of action. It also held that plaintiff had no action for common-law negligence, observing:

> The problem is not answered by pointing out that there is a foreseeable risk of negligent driving on the part of thieves. There is a foreseeable risk of negligent driving whenever anyone drives himself or lends his car to another. That risk has not been considered so unreasonable, however, that an owner is negligent merely because he drives himself, or lends his car to another, in the absence of knowledge on his part of his own or the other's incompetence. Moreover, by leaving the key in the car the owner does not assure that it will be driven, as he does when he lends it to another. At most he creates a risk that it will be stolen and driven. The risk that it will be negligently driven is thus materially less than in the case in which the owner entrusts his car to another for the very purpose of the latter's use.
>
> In one sense the problem presented involves the duty of the owner of an automobile so to manage it as not to create an unreasonable risk of

harm to others. It bears emphasis, however, that when Mrs. Stanley left the car it was in a position where it could harm no one, and no harm occurred until it had been taken by a thief. Thus a duty to prevent such harm would involve more than just the duty to control the car, it would involve a duty to prevent action of a third person. Ordinarily, however, in the absence of a special relationship between the parties, there is no duty to control the conduct of a third person so as to prevent him from causing harm to another. Moreover, this rule is applicable even in cases in which the third person's conduct is made possible only because the defendant has relinquished control of his property to the third person, at least if the defendant has no reason to believe that the third person is incompetent to manage it. . . .

In the present case Mrs. Stanley did not leave her car in front of a school where she might reasonably expect irresponsible children to tamper with it, see Restatement, Torts §302, illus. 7, nor did she leave it in charge of an intoxicated passenger as did defendant in Morris v. Bolling, 218 S.W.2d 754. By leaving the key in her car she at most increased the risk that it might be stolen. Even if she should have foreseen the theft, she had no reason to believe that the thief would be an incompetent driver. In view of the fact that the risk of negligent driving she created was less than the risk she might intentionally have created without negligence by entrusting her car to another, and in the light of the rule that she owed no duty to protect plaintiff from harm resulting from the activities of third persons, we conclude that her duty to exercise reasonable care in the management of her automobile did not encompass a duty to protect plaintiff from the negligent driving of a thief.

Two judges dissented on the ground that the plaintiff's common-law claim should have been left to the jury. If Justice Traynor's position is rejected, how should the case be decided if the thief non-negligently struck the plaintiff?

2. *Keys and thieves: statutory duty.* There has been a sharp split of authority on the precise question raised in Ross v. Hartman. For a flat-footed denial that breach of an ignition key statute is actionable negligence see Meihost v. Meihost, 139 N.W.2d 116 (Wis. 1966), where the key was left in the glove compartment of an otherwise unlocked car, in violation of a Milwaukee city ordinance. The court said that this was "an anti-theft rather than a safety measure." In agreement with this is Kiste v. Red Cab, Inc., 106 N.E.2d 395 (Ind. App. 1952), a case that arose under the Uniform Traffic Act in Indiana. However, in Ney v. Yellow Cab Co., 117 N.E.2d 74 (Ill. 1954), it was held — also under the Uniform Traffic Act of Illinois (and one should consider the possibility of one rule for "yellow" cabs and another rule for "red" ones) — that the provision was a safety rather than simply a traffic measure and that the case should go to the jury on the issue of defendant's negligence.

3. *Outmoded statutes.* How should the courts treat administrative regulations that are "on the books," but no longer enforced? In Lucy Webb Hayes National Training School v. Perotti, 419 F.2d 704, 712 (D.C. Cir. 1969), at page 219 supra, the decedent killed himself by jumping

through a glass window shortly after he was committed to the defendant institution. The applicable regulations for private hospitals, which were enacted in 1909, prohibited hospitals from keeping "any delirious or maniacal patient" in a room "not properly barred or closed." Plaintiff argued that the negligence per se doctrine announced in Ross v. Hartman, at page 266 supra, should govern. The court disagreed:

> We do not find it necessary to decide whether an exception should be read into the doctrine announced in Ross v. Hartman for cases where a municipal ordinance is old and outmoded. The traffic ordinance in *Ross* was one directed straight to the motoring public, who were expected to know and heed its requirements. In this case, the regulation related to the licensing of private hospitals in the District of Columbia.
>
> The Department of Public Health, which apparently is responsible for the enforcement of the regulation involved, approved the design of Sibley Memorial Hospital, . . . and recommended that the Commissioners of the District of Columbia license its operation, which they did. The situation thus resembles that in Hecht v. McLaughlin [214 F.2d 212 (D.C. Cir. 1954)] where the plaintiff asserted that the defendant store had violated a municipal regulation providing that doors should not swing into passageways. We noted that "there is unequivocal evidence that the Company obtained the approval of public and architectural authorities before installing this door . . . ," and went on to conclude: "This is indicative of care on the Company's part quite inconsistent with the theory that violation of the regulation alone, all else aside, is negligence as [a] matter of law. To apply this doctrine to the facts of this case would be essentially unfair."
>
> The same reasoning applies to this case. Regulations relating to a licensing process are often enacted with the reasonable expectation that the licensing authority will exercise some judgment in applying the general rule to the specific case. To invoke a doctrine of negligence per se in such circumstances robs the regulation of the flexibility that its draftsmen may well have envisioned for it. We conclude that in this case the instruction that violation of the regulation would be negligence per se was erroneous, and requires a new trial. The correct standard, as enunciated in *McLaughlin,* is that the hospital's negligence should be "decided on all relevant evidence, including violation of any safety regulation found to be applicable, and consequently admissible in evidence, but including also facts tending to show due care" on the part of the hospital in the construction and operation of [its facilities].

Vesely v. Sager
486 P.2d 151 (Cal. 1971)

WRIGHT, C.J.: In this case we are called upon to decide whether civil liability may be imposed upon a vendor of alcoholic beverages for providing alcoholic drinks to a customer who, as a result of intoxication, injures a third person. The traditional common law rule would deny recovery on the ground that the furnishing of alcoholic beverages is not the proximate cause of the injuries suffered by the third person. We have determined that this rule is patently unsound and that civil liability results when a vendor furnishes alcoholic beverages to a customer in violation of Business and Professions Code section 25602 and each of the conditions set forth in Evidence Code section 669, subdivision (a), is established.

Since neither issue is presented in the instant case, we do not decide whether a noncommercial furnisher of alcoholic beverages may be subject to civil liability under section 25602 or whether a person who is served alcoholic beverages in violation of the statute may recover for injuries suffered as a result of that violation. . . .

Plaintiff Miles Vesely brought this action to recover for personal injuries and property damage sustained in an automobile accident. The only defendant involved on this appeal is William A. Sager, individually and doing business as the Buckhorn Lodge. Other defendants are James G. O'Connell, the driver of the vehicle which collided with plaintiff's automobile, and Earl Dirks, the owner of the car driven by O'Connell.

The facts which are alleged in the complaint and which we must accept for the purposes of this appeal are as follows: [That Sager owned the Buckhorn Lodge, located near the top of Mount Baldy; that he served extensive amounts of liquor to O'Connell into the wee hours of the morning; that Sager knew that O'Connell would drive Dirks' car down "a very steep, winding, and narrowing mountain road"; and that O'Connell then drove the car down the road, veered to the other side, and struck the plaintiff's car.]

Defendant Sager demurred to the complaint on the ground that a "seller of intoxicating liquors is not liable for injuries resulting from intoxication" of a buyer thereof, . . .

The trial court sustained the demurrer without leave to amend, granted the motion to strike, and dismissed the complaint as to defendant Sager. Plaintiff appeals.

Until fairly recently, it was uniformly held that an action could not be maintained at common law against the vendor of alcoholic beverages for furnishing such beverages to a customer who, as a result of being intoxicated, injured himself or a third person. The rationale for the common law rule was that the consumption and not the sale of liquor was the proximate cause of injuries sustained as a result of intoxication. "The rule was based on the obvious fact that one cannot be intoxicated by reason of liquor furnished him if he does not drink it." (*Nolan v. Morelli* (226 A.2d 383 (Conn. 1967))). The common law rule has been substantially abrogated in many states by statutes which specifically impose civil liability upon a furnisher of intoxicating liquor under specified circumstances. California, however, has not enacted similar legislation. . . .

[Subsequently] various courts in other jurisdictions have reevaluated the common law rule that the vendor of intoxicating liquor cannot be held liable for injuries resulting from intoxication, and in particular the rule that the seller cannot be held liable for furnishing alcoholic beverages to a customer who injures a third person. A substantial number, if not a majority, have decided that the sale of alcoholic beverages may be the proximate cause of such injuries and that liability may be imposed upon the vendor in favor of the injured third person. . . .

To the extent that the common law rule of nonliability is based on concepts of proximate cause, we are persuaded by the reasoning of the cases that have abandoned that rule. The decisions in those jurisdictions which have abandoned the common law rule invoke principles of proximate cause similar to those established in this state by cases dealing with matters other than the furnishing of alcoholic beverages. Under these principles an actor may be liable if his negligence is a substantial factor in causing an injury, and he is not relieved of liability because of the intervening act of a third person if such act was reasonably foreseeable at the time of his negligent conduct. Moreover, "If the likelihood that a third person may act in a particular manner is the hazard or one of the hazards which makes the actor negligent, such an act whether innocent, negligent, intentionally tortious or criminal does not prevent the actor from being liable for harm caused thereby." . . .

The central question in this case, therefore, is not one of proximate cause, but rather one of duty: Did defendant Sager owe a duty of care to plaintiff or to a class of persons of which he is a member?

A duty of care, and the attendant standard of conduct required of a reasonable man, may of course be found in a legislative enactment which does not provide for civil liability. In this state a presumption of negligence arises from the violation of a statute which was enacted to protect a class of persons of which the plaintiff is a member against the type of harm which the plaintiff suffered as a result of the violation of the statute. The Legislature has recently codified this presumption with the adoption of Evidence Code section 669: "The failure of a person to exercise due care is presumed if: (1) He violated a statute, ordinance, or regulation of a public entity; (2) The violation proximately caused death or injury to person or property; (3) The death or injury resulted from an occurrence of the nature which the statute, ordinance, or regulation was designed to prevent; and (4) The person suffering the death or the injury to his person or property was one of the class of persons for whose protection the statute, ordinance, or regulation was adopted." (Subd. (a).)

In the instant case a duty of care is imposed upon defendant Sager by Business and Professions Code section 25602, which provides: "Every person who sells, furnishes, gives, or causes to be sold, furnished, or given away, any alcoholic beverage to any habitual or common drunkard or to any obviously intoxicated person is guilty of a misdemeanor." This provision was enacted as part of the Alcoholic Beverage Control Act of 1935 and was adopted for the purpose of protecting members of the general public from injuries to person and damage to property resulting from the excessive use of intoxicating liquor.

From the facts alleged in the complaint it appears that plaintiff is within the class of persons for whose protection section 25602 was enacted and that the injuries he suffered resulted from an occurrence that the statute was designed to prevent. Accordingly, if these two elements are proved at trial, and if it is established that Sager violated section 25602 and that the violation proximately caused plaintiff's injuries, a presumption will arise that Sager was negligent in furnishing alcoholic beverages to O'Connell.

Defendant Sager maintains, however, that a change in the common law rule governing the liability of a tavern keeper to an injured third person is unwarranted and that if there is to be a change in the rule, it should be made by the Legislature, not by the courts. . . . [The court then concludes, first, that it is entitled to reject judicially "the patently unsound" view that the supply of alcohol is not the proximate cause of the subsequent injuries. The court then held that its decision advanced the public policy objectives of its statutory scheme under 25602. and overruled prior California cases to the contrary.]

MCCOMB, J., PETERS, J., TOBRINER, J., MOSK, J., BURKE, J., and SULLIVAN, J., concurred.

NOTES

1. Dram statute legislation in California. Vesely v. Sager was one of the early cases that allowed a private person to maintain a cause of action when a defendant retail establishment served liquor in breach of the dram statute. Subsequent California decisions moved in the same direction. *Vesely* was extended in Ewing v. Cloverleaf Bowl, 572 P.2d 1155 (Cal. 1978), where a bartender served the decedent, who had wanted to get drunk to celebrate his 21st birthday, ten shots of 151 proof rum. The willful misconduct of the bartender was held to overcome the contributory negligence of his patron. And in Coulter v. Superior Court, 577 P.2d 669 (Cal. 1978), the California Supreme Court held that both the dram shop act and "modern" common law negligence principles allowed an action by an injured party against a non-commercial supplier of alcohol — there an apartment owner and apartment manager — to an obviously intoxicated person when the provider knows that the person to whom the alcohol is provided intends to drive. Under the California cases, what is the liability of the Los Angeles Dodgers if they allow ticketholders to have "tailgate parties" (picnics on the backs of their station wagons) at which liquor is consumed in the parking lot? Whatever the precise scope of dram statute liability, it appears not to have gone down well with California voters. The California dram shop decisions have been overruled by legislation. Cal. Bus. & Prof. Code §25602 (1994):

§25602. SALES TO HABITUAL DRUNKARDS; CIVIL LIABILITY: CONSUMPTION OF ALCOHOLIC BEVERAGES AS PROXIMATE CAUSE OF INJURIES INFLICTED UPON ANOTHER BY AN INTOXICATED PERSON

(a) Every person who sells, furnishes, gives, or causes to be sold, furnished, or given away, any alcoholic beverage to any habitual or common drunkard or to any obviously intoxicated person is guilty of a misdemeanor.

(b) No person who sells, furnishes, gives or causes to be sold, furnished, or given away, any alcoholic beverage pursuant to subdivision (a) of this section shall be civilly liable to any injured person or the estate of such person for injuries inflicted on that person as a result of intoxication by the consumer of such alcoholic beverage.

(c) The Legislature hereby declares that this section shall be interpreted so that the holdings in cases such as Vesely v. Sager, . . . and Coulter v. Superior Court, be abrogated in favor of prior judicial interpretation finding the consumption of alcoholic beverages rather than the serving of alcoholic beverages as the proximate cause of injuries inflicted upon another by an intoxicated person.

Why the explicit case citations in section (c)?

The statute was sustained against constitutional attacks, though with obvious misgivings, in Cory v. Shierloh, 629 P.2d 8 (Cal. 1981). "Each day the devastating effects of the drinking driver rage unabated with all their tragic social and economic consequences. We do not speculate on the influences that might have prompted the Legislature to answer this acute and growing problem by narrowly *restricting* rather than *enlarging* civil liability. In the final analysis the Legislature must answer to an informed, and perhaps ultimately aroused, public opinion for its action. We do not substitute our judgment for its own."

2. *Dram statute liability outside California.* In stark contrast with *Coulter* is Edgar v. Kajet, 375 N.Y.S.2d 548 (N.Y. Sup. Ct. 1975), where the court refused to extend liability under the New York dram shop act to an employer who furnished liquor free of charge to its employees at one of the firm's parties. The court feared that the creation of liability might open up a "virtual pandora's box," and concluded that the decision to impose liability was one best left to the legislature: "For example, how is a host at a social gathering to know when the tolerance of one of his guests has been reached? To what extent should a host refuse to serve drinks to those nearing the point of intoxication? Further, how is a host to supervise his guests' social activities? The implications are almost limitless as to situations that might arise when liquor is dis-

pensed at a social gathering, holiday parties, family celebrations, out-door barbecues and picnics, to cite a few examples. If civil liability were imposed on [defendant] herein, it could be similarly imposed on every host who, in a spirit of friendship, serves liquor."

The Pennsylvania Supreme Court took a more nuanced view on the liability of the social host. In Klein v. Raysinger, 470 A.2d 507 (Pa. 1983), the court expressly parted company with *Coulter* by holding that there was no common liability on the part of a social host who served alcoholic beverages to adults who later injured persons on the highway. In the companion case of Congini by Congini v. Portersville Valve Co., 470 A.2d 515 (Pa. 1983), however, the same court allowed an action against a social host who served liquor to a minor in violation of the local criminal code, which made it a summary criminal offense to serve liquor to anyone "less than 21 years of age." Subsequently both *Klein* and *Congini* were analyzed extensively in Fassett v. Delta Kappa Epsilon, 807 F.2d 1150 (3d Cir. 1986). There the Third Circuit, predicting the direction of Pennsylvania law, held that persons who gave "substantial" assistance to the party who actually served the alcohol could be sued for "accomplice" liability. See Restatement (Second) of Torts §876. The court held that the four roommates who had held the party could all be sued, even though only one had acted as bartender, because the others had either purchased liquor, "worked the door," or invited the fraternity to use the apartment. But in Kapres v. Heller, 640 A.2d 888 (Pa. 1994), the Pennslvania Supreme Court showed the Third Circuit to be a bad prophet when it explicitly disapproved of *Fassett* by holding that since all minors are regarded as "incompetent," that "one minor does not owe a duty to another minor regarding the furnishing or con-sumption of alcohol."

As dram shop actions have increased in frequency and importance, common-law principles have been been modified and restricted by stat-utes that reflect very different political judgments in the various states, so that it is now almost impossible to state the common law in this area. For a summary of some of the recent cases and statutory innovations, see 3 Harper, James and Gray §17.5 n.21.

F. JUDGE AND JURY

The law of negligence extends beyond abstract theory and asks how legal institutions apply these commands to particular cases. In our legal system, the responsibility for deciding questions of fact, especially those of negligence, is divided between judge and jury. One possible division would grant the jury complete sway in deciding individual cases, as if the jury were told: "You are to decide, on the basis of all you have heard and in terms of your sense of fairness, whether the defendant should pay for the damage sustained by the plaintiff in this case." That solution has been rejected, typically for two reasons. First, judges have feared that the jury might abuse its unlimited power by deciding cases contrary to *established* principles of law, especially when motivated by the more obvious forms of passion and prejudice, or perhaps by more subtle forms of class, social, or economic bias. Second, judges believe that unlimited jury discretion repudiates or at least undermines the central principle of distributive justice — that like cases should be decided alike, no matter what substantive principles are selected.

For these two reasons, then, judges have always exerted some control over the decision-making power of juries. One form of control is in the instructions that the judges give to the jury at the close of the case. These instructions embody the relevant principles of law. And much of the substantive law is made when the lawyers for either party challenge those instructions on appeal. Appellate courts set aside jury verdicts reached after erroneous and prejudicial instructions are given precisely because they believe that juries should and do follow the instructions they receive, and that these instructions must therefore reflect the substantive law.

Sometimes the mistakes in instruction can be quite minor. In Louisville & Nashville R.R. v. Gower, 3 S.W. 824, 827 (Tenn. 1887), plaintiff, an employee of the defendant railroad, was hurt while attempting to couple two cars. Snodgrass, J., speaking for the court, said in part:

> The charge was otherwise incorrect and misleading, particularly in defining the care necessary to have been exercised by Plaintiff Gower in order to entitle him to recovery. The Court, after telling the jury that "it was the duty of the plaintiff to exercise such a degree of care in making the coupling as a man of ordinary prudence" would have done, adds: "Just such care as one of you, similarly employed, would have exercised under such circumstances. If he exercised that degree of care, and was nevertheless injured, he is entitled to your verdict. If he failed to exercise that degree of care, he can not recover."
>
> The charge as to the exercise of such care as a man of ordinary prudence would have done was correct, but it was thought not full enough by the judge, who illustrated what he meant by reference to the care which each one of the jurymen would have exercised. His charge, so limited, was erroneous. It does not appear that all or any of the members of the jury were men of ordinary prudence, and yet the judge tells them that what he means by the "exercise of such care as a man of ordinary prudence would have exercised" is that it was the exercise of such care as one of them would have exercised if similarly situated. Under this instruction, if any member of the jury thought he would have done what Gower did in the coupling, he would of course have determined that Gower acted with the care required, and was entitled to recover. This

illustration, used to define what he meant by "the care of a man of ordinary prudence" and thereby becoming its definition, was erroneous. The care he was required to exercise was that of a man of ordinary prudence in that dangerous situation, and not "just such care as one of the jury similarly situated" would have done, be that much or little as each member might be very prudent or very imprudent.

The court then reversed plaintiff's judgment and remanded for a new trial because of this and two other errors in the trial of the case.

The second form of judicial control over the jury is the power of the court to keep certain questions of fact from the jury. In Metropolitan Railway v. Jackson, 3 A.C. 193, 197 (1877), the issue on appeal was, "Was there at the trial any evidence of negligence by the defendant that ought to have been left to a jury?" Chancellor Cairns remarked as follows:

> There was not, at your Lordships' bar, any serious controversy as to the principles applicable to a case of this description. The Judge has a certain duty to discharge, and the jurors have another and a different duty. The Judge has to say whether any facts have been established by evidence from which negligence *may be* reasonably inferred; the jurors have to say whether, from those facts, when submitted to them, negligence *ought to be* inferred. It is, in my opinion, of the greatest importance in the administration of justice that these separate functions should be maintained, and should be maintained distinct. It would be a serious inroad on the province of the jury, if, in a case where there are facts from which negligence may reasonably be inferred, the Judge were to withdraw the case from the jury upon the ground that, in his opinion, negligence ought not to be inferred; and it would, on the other hand, place in the hands of the jurors a power which might be exercised in the most arbitrary manner, if they were at liberty to hold that negligence might be inferred from any state of facts whatever.

As the opinion in Metropolitan Railway v. Jackson suggests, the traditional role of the jury is to find the "facts" to which it then applies the "law." Obviously, the concept of negligence fits uneasily into this sharp dichotomy of *law* and *fact*. Would it be helpful to think of negligence as a "mixed issue of law and fact," as it is frequently called?

The materials that follow have several themes: What is the role of the jury in law and in actual practice in setting the standard of care? What difference does it make whether the court or the jury decides this issue? How does the court limit or control the jury's exercise of discretion? How does the presence of the jury affect the litigation strategy of the lawyers? Is there any way to assure uniformity of jury decisions in similar cases? And is the jury in fact applying a different system of law from the one formally set out and approved in appellate decisions? See generally James, Functions of Judge and Jury in Negligence Cases, 58 Yale L.J. 667 (1949).

Holmes, The Common Law
110-111, 120-124 (1881)

Again, any legal standard must, in theory, be one which would apply to all men, not specially excepted, under the same circumstances. It is not intended that the public force should fall upon an individual accidentally, or at the whim of any body of men. The standard, that is, must be fixed. In practice, no doubt, one man may have to pay and another may escape, according to the different feelings of different juries. But this merely shows that the law does not perfectly accomplish its ends. The theory or intention of the law is not that the feeling of approbation or blame which a particular twelve may entertain should be the criterion. They are supposed to leave their idiosyncrasies on one side, and to represent the feeling of the community. The ideal average prudent man, whose equivalent the jury is taken to be in many cases, and whose culpability or innocence is the supposed test, is a constant, and his conduct under given circumstances is theoretically always the same.

Finally, any legal standard must, in theory, be capable of being known. When a man has to pay damages, he is supposed to have broken the law, and he is further supposed to have known what the law was.

If, now, the ordinary liabilities in tort arise from failure to comply with fixed and uniform standards of external conduct, which every man is presumed and required to know, it is obvious that it ought to be possible, sooner or later, to formulate these standards at least to some extent, and that to do so must at last be the business of the court. It is equally clear that the featureless generality, that the defendant was bound to use such care as a prudent man would do under the circumstances, ought to be continually giving place to the specific one, that he was bound to use this or that precaution under these or those circumstances. The standard which the defendant was bound to come up to was a standard of specific acts or omissions, with reference to the specific circumstances in which he found himself. If in the whole department of unintentional wrongs the courts arrived at no further utterance than the question of negligence, and left every case, without rudder or compass, to the jury, they would simply confess their inability to state a very large part of the law which they required the defendant to know, and would assert, by implication, that nothing could be learned by experience. But neither courts nor legislatures have ever stopped at that point. . . .

The principles of substantive law which have been established by the courts are believed to have been somewhat obscured by having presented themselves oftenest in the form of rulings upon the sufficiency of evidence. When a judge rules that there is no evidence of negligence, he does something more than is embraced in an ordinary ruling that there is no evidence of a fact. He rules that the acts or omissions proved or in question do not constitute a ground of legal liability, and in this way the law is gradually enriching itself from daily life, as it should. Thus, in Crafter v. Metropolitan Railway Co. [L.R. 1 C.P. 300 (1866)], the plaintiff slipped on the defendant's stairs and was severely hurt. The cause of his slipping was that the brass nosing of the stairs had been worn smooth by travel over it, and a builder testified that in his opinion the staircase was unsafe by reason of this circumstance and the absence of a hand-rail. There was nothing to contradict this except that great numbers of persons had passed over the stairs and that no accident had happened there, and the plaintiff had a verdict. The court set the verdict aside, and ordered a non-suit. The ruling was in form that there was no evidence of negligence to go to the jury; but this was obviously equivalent to saying, and did in fact mean, that the railroad company had done all that it was bound to do in maintaining such a staircase as was proved by the plaintiff. A hundred other equally concrete instances will be found in the text-books.

On the other hand, if the court should rule that certain acts or omissions coupled with damage were conclusive evidence of negligence unless explained, it would, in substance and in truth, rule that such acts or omissions were a ground of liability, or prevented a recovery, as the case might be. Thus it is said to be actionable negligence to let a house for a dwelling knowing it to be so infected with small-pox as to be dangerous to health, and concealing the knowledge. To explain the acts or omissions in such a case would be to prove different conduct from that ruled upon, or to show that they were not, juridically speaking, the cause of the damage complained of. The ruling assumes, for the purposes of the ruling, that the facts in evidence are all the facts.

The cases which have raised difficulties needing explanation are those in which the court has ruled that there was prima facie evidence of negligence, or some evidence of negligence to go to the jury.

Many have noticed the confusion of thought implied in speaking of such cases as presenting mixed questions of law and fact. No doubt, as has been said above, the averment that the defendant has been guilty of negligence is a complex one: first, that he has done or omitted certain things; second, that his alleged conduct does not come up to the legal standard. And so long as the controversy is simply on the first half, the whole complex averment is plain matter for the jury without special instructions, just as a question of ownership would be where the only dispute was as to the fact upon which the legal conclusion was founded. But when a controversy arises on the second half, the question whether the court or the jury ought to judge of the defendant's conduct is wholly unaffected by the accident, whether there is or is not also a dispute as to what that conduct was. If there is such a dispute, it is entirely possible to give a series of hypothetical instructions adapted to every state of facts which it is open to the jury to find. If there is no such dispute, the court may still take their opinion as to the standard. The problem is to explain the relative functions of court and jury with regard to the latter.

When a case arises in which the standard of conduct, pure and simple, is submitted to the jury, the explanation is plain. It is that the court, not entertaining any clear views of public policy applicable to the matter, derives the rule to be applied from daily experience, as it has been agreed that the great body of the law of tort has been derived. But the court further feels that it is not itself possessed of sufficient practical experience to lay down the rule intelligently. It conceives that twelve men taken from the practical part of the community can aid its judgment. Therefore it aids its conscience by taking the opinion of the jury.

But supposing a state of facts often repeated in practice, is it to be imagined that the court is to go on leaving the standard to the jury forever? Is it not manifest, on the contrary, that if the jury is, on the whole, as fair a tribunal as it is represented to be, the lesson which can be got from that source will be learned? Either the court will find that the fair teaching of experience is that the conduct complained of usually is or is not blameworthy, and therefore, unless explained, is or is not a ground of liability; or it will find the jury oscillating to and fro, and will see the necessity of making up its mind for itself. There is no reason why any other such question should not be settled, as well as that of liability for stairs with smooth strips of brass upon their edges. The exceptions would mainly be found where the standard was rapidly changing, as, for instance, in some questions of medical treatment.

If this be the proper conclusion in plain cases, further consequences ensue. Facts do not often exactly repeat themselves in practice; but cases with comparatively small variations from each other do. A judge who has long sat at nisi prius ought gradually to acquire a fund of experience which enables him to represent the common sense of the community in ordinary instances far better than an average jury. He should be able to lead and to instruct them in detail, even where he thinks it desirable, on the whole, to take their opinion. Furthermore, the sphere in which he is able to rule without taking their opinion at all should be continually growing.

Baltimore and Ohio R.R. v. Goodman
275 U.S. 66 (1927)

HOLMES, J. This is a suit brought by the widow and administratrix of Nathan Goodman against the petitioner for causing his death by running him down at a grade crossing. The defence is that Goodman's own negligence caused the death. At the trial, the defendant asked the

Court to direct a verdict for it, but the request, and others looking to the same direction, were refused, and the plaintiff got a verdict and a judgment which was affirmed by the Circuit Court of Appeals. 10 F.(2d) 58.

Goodman was driving an automobile truck in an easterly direction and was killed by a train running southwesterly across the road at a rate of not less than sixty miles an hour. The line was straight, but it is said by the respondent that Goodman "had no practical view" beyond a section house two hundred and forty-three feet north of the crossing until he was about twenty feet from the first rail, or, as the respondent argues, twelve feet from danger, and that then the engine was still obscured by the section house. He had been driving at the rate of ten or twelve miles an hour, but had cut down his rate to five or six miles at about forty feet from the crossing. It is thought that there was an emergency in which, so far as appears, Goodman did all that he could.

We do not go into further details as to Goodman's precise situation, beyond mentioning that it was daylight and that he was familiar with the crossing, for it appears to us plain that nothing is suggested by the evidence to relieve Goodman from responsibility for his own death. When a man goes upon a railroad track he knows that he goes to a place where he will be killed if a train comes upon him before he is clear of the track. He knows that he must stop for the train, not the train stop for him. In such circumstances it seems to us that if a driver cannot be sure otherwise whether a train is dangerously near he must stop and get out of his vehicle, although obviously he will not often be required to do more than to stop and look. It seems to us that if he relies upon not hearing the train or any signal and takes no further precaution he does so at his own risk. If at the last moment Goodman found himself in an emergency it was his own fault that he did not reduce his speed earlier or come to a stop. It is true as said in Flannelly v. Delaware & Hudson Co., 225 U.S. 597, that the question of due care very generally is left to the jury. But we are dealing with a standard of conduct, and when the standard is clear it should be laid down once for all by the Courts. See Southern Pacific Co. v. Berkshire, 254 U.S. 415.

Judgment reversed.

Pokora v. Wabash Ry.
292 U.S. 98 (1934)

[The defendant had four tracks at a level crossing — as plaintiff approached them, — a switch track, a through track, and then two more switch tracks. Because of the boxcars on the first track, he could not see the main track. Plaintiff stopped, tried to look, and listened, but he heard no bell or whistle. He did not get out of his truck to obtain a better view as the dictum in Baltimore & Ohio R.R. v. Goodman seemed to require under such circumstances. The trial court directed a verdict for defendant on its finding that plaintiff had been contributorily negligent and this judgment was affirmed below. Reversed and remanded.]

CARDOZO, J. Standards of prudent conduct are declared at times by courts, but they are taken over from the facts of life. To get out of a vehicle and reconnoitre is an uncommon precaution, as everyday experience informs us. Besides being uncommon, it is very likely to be futile, and sometimes even dangerous. If the driver leaves his vehicle when he nears a cut or curve, he will learn nothing by getting out about the perils that lurk beyond. By the time he regains his seat and sets his car in motion, the hidden train may be upon him. . . . Often the added safeguard will be dubious though the track happens to be straight, as it seems that this one was, at all events as far as the station, about five blocks to the north. A train traveling at a speed of thirty miles an hour will cover a quarter of a mile in the space of thirty seconds. It may thus emerge out of obscurity as the driver turns his back to regain the waiting car, and may then descend upon him suddenly when his car is on the track. Instead of helping himself by getting out, he might do better to press forward with all his faculties alert. So a train at a neighboring station, apparently at rest and harmless, may be transformed in a few seconds into an instrument of destruction. At times the course of safety may be different. One can figure to oneself a roadbed so level and unbroken that getting out will be a gain. Even then the balance of advantage depends on many circumstances and can be easily disturbed. Where was Pokora to leave his truck after getting out to reconnoitre? If he was to leave it on the switch, there was the possibility that the box cars would be shunted down upon him before he could regain his seat. The defendant did not show whether there was a locomotive at the forward end, or whether the cars were so few that a locomotive could be seen. If he was to leave his vehicle near the curb, there was even stronger reason to believe that the space to be covered in going back and forth would make his observations worthless. One must remember that while the traveler turns his eye in one direction, a train or a loose engine may be approaching from the other.

Illustrations such as these bear witness to the need for caution in framing standards of behavior that amount to rules of law. The need is the more urgent when there is no background of experience out of which the standards have emerged. They are then, not the natural flowerings of behavior in its customary forms, but rules artificially developed, and imposed from without. Extraordinary situations may not wisely or fairly be subjected to tests or regulations that are fitting for the common-place or normal. In default of the guide of customary conduct, what is suitable for the traveler caught in a mesh where the ordinary safeguards fail him is for the judgment of a jury. The opinion in Goodman's case has been a source of confusion in the federal courts to the extent that it imposes a standard for application by the judge, and has had only wavering support in the courts of the states. We limit it accordingly.

NOTE

Stop, look, and listen. Goodman is one of the most discussed cases in the common-law literature. For a critical response see Note, Aftermath of the Supreme Court's Stop, Look and Listen Rule, 43 Harv. L. Rev. 926 (1930). The note argues that "the actual decision is hardly open to criticism," as "[t]he crossing in question was quite clear, and was only obstructed to one approaching as Goodman did" (Id. at 927 and n.5), although the point was not stressed by Holmes. In any event, the decision had its practical impact. Shortly after the *Goodman* case came down from the Supreme Court, there appeared on every railroad station platform a poster quoting the admonitory sentences from Holmes's opinion, threatening with death all readers who might later cross railroad tracks if they did not "stop, look and listen."

Although many commentators have tended to read *Pokora* as doing away with *Goodman, Goodman* has been cited hundreds of times, often with approval, since it was decided in 1927. The cases in which it has not been applied, moreover, have often involved situations in which it is no longer clear that the railroad has the right of way. In Toschi v. Christian, 149 P.2d 848, 851 (Cal. 1944), plaintiff was hurt when the truck he was driving was struck at a crossing by defendant's train. The crossing was located in the heart of the business district, and the defendant customarily employed flagmen to signal to drivers that the tracks were clear. At the time of this particular accident, defendant's flagman was literally experimenting with mirrors, and without the flagman's guidance, plaintiff drove his truck across the tracks. "As he drove onto the first track . . . light from the mirror, with which the flagman was still playing, was flashed in his eyes, blinding him. He stopped, and immediately his truck was struck. . . ."

The court noted:

> The "stop, look and listen" rule, urged by defendants, will not be applied to factual bases where its application would be unreasonable. In the circumstances of this case, which comprise a six-track railroad yard crossing, switching operations progressing almost constantly, the employment of two flagmen by the railroad, whose duties involve traffic control on the highway and to some extent on the railroad, and a practical necessity for travelers on the highway to rely on the flagmen's signals because ordinarily it would be impossible for such travelers after they had ob-

served railroad traffic approaching to know whether it would cross or stop short of the highway, the "stop, look and listen" rule is not wholly appropriate and cannot operate to establish contributory negligence as a matter of law.

A clear deference to jury determinations in crossing accidents is found in McEvers v. Missouri Pacific R.R. Co., 528 F.2d 220 (7th Cir. 1975). There the plaintiff stopped his truck, loaded with 20 tons of coal, some 30 feet from the tracks and looked both ways. His view was obstructed in part by a shack about 450 feet down the track, and in part by the curvature of the main track. The plaintiff then proceeded at two miles an hour toward the track, not looking again in the direction of the shack for the 10 or 12 seconds it took him to reach the track, even though his view of the tracks was now unobstructed. He continued to proceed at a rate of two miles per hour across the tracks. The plaintiff sustained personal injuries when he was at the last moment unable to move his rig across the track. The jury found for the plaintiff, and the trial judge then gave the defendant a directed verdict. On appeal the jury verdict was reinstated, the court noting that under Illinois law "the usual duty of a highway traveler to stop, look, and listen at a railroad crossing may be qualified, or even excused, by the existence of 'facts such as obstructions to view or distractions that might mislead' the driver." The court then concluded that the plaintiff "offered evidence of obstructions to view or misleading conditions" sufficient to "render plausible his assertion that he looked but did not see the train." Note that in diversity cases, federal courts today must apply state law under Erie R.R. v. Tompkins, 304 U.S. 64 (1938).

Wilkerson v. McCarthy
336 U.S. 53 (1949)

[This was an action against the trustees of the Denver & Rio Grande Western Railroad, brought in a state court in Utah under the Federal Employers' Liability Act (FELA). That act made every interstate railroad liable in damages for injuries to its employees caused under certain conditions by the negligence of the railroad through any of its officers, agents, or employees, "or by reason of any defect or insufficiency, due to its negligence" in any of its premises or equipment. It allowed suit to be brought in either the federal or state courts, at the option of the plaintiff.

In this case plaintiff was taking a shortcut over a pit in the repair shop and slipped from the rather narrow boardwalk into the pit, sustaining injury. This boardwalk had oil and grease spilled on it. The evidence showed that the railroad had taken steps to prevent employees from casually using this boardwalk as a shortcut by chaining off access to it. At any rate, the trial court in Utah directed a verdict for the defendant on the ground that there was no evidence of its negligence to submit to the jury. The Utah Supreme Court affirmed, one judge dissenting. The United States Supreme Court then granted certiorari, the only issue being whether or not there was evidence of the railroad's negligence to submit to the jury. Reversed.

This case is included here because of the extraordinary importance lent such a simple issue and because of the strong undercurrent of feeling exhibited in some of the opinions. Also, it shows how widely the Court was split on the issue of whether or not there was evidence of negligence to submit to a jury. Of course, what is really "on trial" before the Supreme Court is the workman's compensation idea versus negligence as the basis of liability. On the political undercurrents in this case see Alderman, What the New Supreme Court Has Done to the Old Law of Negligence, 18 Law & Contemp. Probs. 110 (1953).]

BLACK, J. [after concluding that there was evidence of negligence to submit to a jury]. There are some who think that recent decisions of this Court which have required submission of negligence questions to a jury make, "for all practical purposes, a railroad an insurer of its employees." . . . This assumption, that railroads are made insurers where the issue of negligence is left to the jury, is inadmissible. It rests on another assumption, this one unarticulated, that juries will invariably decide negligence questions against railroads. . . . Courts should not assume that in determining these questions of negligence juries will fall short of a fair performance of their constitutional function. In rejecting a contention that juries could be expected to determine certain disputed questions on whim, this Court, speaking through Mr. Justice Holmes, said: "But it must be assumed that the constitutional tribunal does its duty and finds facts only because they are proved." Aikens v. Wisconsin, 195 U.S. 194, 206.

In reaching its conclusion as to negligence, a jury is frequently called upon to consider many separate strands of circumstances, and from these circumstances to draw its ultimate conclusion on the issue of negligence. Here there are many arguments that could have been presented to the jury in an effort to persuade it that the railroad's conduct was not negligent, and many counter arguments which might have persuaded the jury that the railroad was negligent. The same thing is true as to whether petitioner was guilty of contributory negligence. Many of such arguments were advanced by the Utah Supreme Court to support its finding that the petitioner was negligent and the railroad was not. But the arguments made by the State Supreme Court are relevant and appropriate only for consideration by the jury, the tribunal selected to pass on the issues. For these reasons, the trial court should have submitted the case to the jury, and it was error for the Utah Supreme Court to affirm its action in taking the case from the jury.

FRANKFURTER, J., concurring. Trial by jury as guaranteed by the Constitution of the United States and by the several States presupposes a jury under proper guidance of a disinterested and competent trial judge. . . . It is an important element of trial by jury which puts upon the judge the exacting duty of determining whether there is solid evidence on which a jury's verdict could be fairly based. When a plaintiff claims that an injury which he has suffered is attributable to a defendant's negligence — want of care in the discharge of a duty which the defendant owed to him — it is the trial judge's function to determine whether the evidence in its entirety would rationally support a verdict for the plaintiff, assuming that the jury took, as it would be entitled to take, a view of the evidence most favorable to the plaintiff. If there were a bright line dividing negligence from non-negligence, there would be no problem. Only an incompetent or a wilful judge would take a case from the jury when the issue should be left to the jury. But since questions of negligence are questions of degree, often very nice differences of degree, judges of competence and conscience have in the past, and will in the future, disagree as to whether proof in a case is sufficient to demand submission to the jury. The fact that a third court thinks there was enough to leave the case to the jury does not indicate that the other two courts were unmindful of the jury's function. The easy but timid way out for a trial judge is to leave all cases tried to a jury for jury determination, but in so doing he fails in his duty to take a case from the jury when the evidence would not warrant a verdict by it. A timid judge, like a biased judge, is intrinsically a lawless judge.

These observations are especially pertinent to suits under the Federal Employers' Liability Act. The difficulties in these cases derive largely from the outmoded concept of "negligence" as a working principle for the adjustments of injuries inevitable under the technological circumstances of modern industry. This cruel and wasteful mode of dealing with industrial injuries has long been displaced in industry generally by the insurance principle that underlies workmen's compensation laws. For reasons that hardly reflect due regard for the interests of railroad employees, "negligence" remains the basis of liability for injuries to them. It is, of course, the duty of courts to enforce the Federal Employers' Liability Act, however outmoded and unjust in operation it may be. But so long as negligence rather than workmen's compensation is the basis of recovery, just so long will suits under the Federal Employers' Liability Act lead to conflicting opinions about "fault" and "proximate cause." The law reports are full of unedifying proof of these conflicting views, and that too by judges who seek conscientiously to perform their duty by neither leaving everything to a jury nor, on the other hand, turning the Federal Employers' Liability Act into a workmen's compensation law.

Considering the volume and complexity of the cases which obviously call for decision by this Court, and considering the time and thought that the proper disposition of such cases demands, I do not think we should take cases merely to review facts already canvassed by two and sometimes three courts even though those facts may have been erroneously appraised. The division in this Court would seem to demonstrate beyond peradventure that nothing is involved in this case except the drawing of allowable inferences from a necessarily unique set of circumstances. For this Court to take a case which turns merely on such an appraisal of evidence, however much hardship in the fallible application of an archaic system of compensation for injuries to railroad employees may touch our private sympathy, is to deny due regard to the considerations which led the Court to ask and Congress to give the power to control the Court's docket. Such power carries with it the responsibility of granting review only in cases that demand adjudication on the basis of importance to the operation of our federal system; importance of the outcome merely to the parties is not enough. It has been our practice to dismiss a writ of certiorari even after it was granted where argument exposed a want of conflict or revealed that the case involved no more than its particular facts. I believe we should adhere to this practice in the present case.

I would, therefore, dismiss the petition as having been improvidently granted. Since, however, that is not to be done, I too have been obliged to recanvass the record and likewise think that there was here enough evidence to go to the jury.

VINSON, C.J., dissenting [his entire opinion follows]. In my view of the record, there is no evidence, nor any inference which reasonably may be drawn from the evidence when viewed in the light most favorable to the petitioner, which could sustain a verdict for him. This leads me to conclude that the trial court properly directed a verdict for the respondents, and I would affirm.

JACKSON, J., dissenting. The trial court, after hearing all the evidence and seeing the witnesses, directed a verdict of no cause of action. The Utah Supreme Court, in a careful opinion, decided two propositions: First, whether this Court still holds that a plaintiff "in order to recover must still show negligence on the part of the employer." It resolved its doubts by relying upon statements of this Court to the effect that it still does adhere to that requirement. Second, whether there is any evidence of negligence. On a careful analysis, it found no evidence whatever of negligence in this case. Following established principles of law, it concluded that it would have been error to let such a case go to the jury, and therefore affirmed the trial court's refusal so to do.

This Court now reverses and, to my mind at least, espouses the doctrine that any time a trial or appellate court weighs evidence or examines facts it is usurping the jury's function. But under that rule every claim of injury would require jury trial, even if the evidence showed no possible basis for a finding of negligence. Determination of whether there could be such a basis is a function of the trial court, even though it involves weighing evidence and examining facts. I think we are under a duty to examine the record impartially if we take such cases and to sustain the lower courts where, as here, a finding of negligence would obviously be without basis in fact.

I am not unaware that even in this opinion the Court continues to pay lip service to the doctrine that liability in these cases is to be based only upon fault. But its standard of fault is such in this case as to indicate that the principle is without much practical meaning.

This record shows that both the wheel pit into which plaintiff fell and the board on which he was trying to cross over the pit were blocked off by safety chains strung between posts. Plaintiff admits he knew the chains were there to keep him from crossing over the pit and to require him to go a few feet farther to walk around it. After the chains were put up, any person undertaking to use the board as a cross walk had to complete involved contortions and gymnastics, particularly when, as was the case with petitioner, a car was on the track 23½. A casual examination of the model filed as an exhibit in this Court shows how difficult was such a passage. Nevertheless, the Court holds that if employees succeeded in disregarding the chains and forced passage frequently enough to be considered "customary," and the railroad took no further action, its failure so to do was negligence. The same rule would no doubt apply if the railroad's precautions had consisted of a barricade, or an armed guard. I think the railroad here could not fairly be found guilty of negligence and that there was no jury question.

If in this class of cases, which forms a growing proportion of its total, this Court really is applying accepted principles of an old body of liability law in which lower courts are generally experienced, I do not see why they are so baffled and confused at what goes on here. On the other hand, if this Court considers a reform of this law appropriate and within the judicial power to promulgate, I do not see why it should constantly deny that it is doing just that.

I think a comparison of the State Supreme Court's opinion, 112 Utah 300, 187 P.2d 188, with the opinion of this Court will fairly raise, in the minds of courts below and of the profession, the question I leave to their perspicacity to answer: In which proposition did the Supreme Court of Utah really err?

NOTES

1. Liability rules under the FELA. The FELA, under which Wilkerson v. McCarthy was litigated, marked the first stage of federal intervention in the tort law. It first went into effect in 1908, but covered only railroad employees engaged in interstate commerce. Substantively, the FELA abrogated the fellow servant doctrine whereby one employee could not sue the employer for the wrongs of a fellow employee. See infra Chapter 4 Section C. The FELA also made it unlawful for the railroad to contract out of its tort liability under the statutory system. In 1939 the statute was revised to extend its reach to all railroad employees. The 1939 revisions also eliminated the defense of assumption of risk in all its forms, and provided that contributory negligence should not bar an employee's action, but rather that "the damages shall be diminished by the jury in proportion to the amount of negligence attributable to such employee."

The FELA, however, is not a workers' compensation statute, under which the decisive test is whether the harm arises out of the employment relationship. To this day, the FELA still requires proof of negligence. As *Wilkerson* reveals, the evidence of negligence can be very thin, and subsequent cases have confirmed that so long as the employer negligence has played "any part, even the slightest" in bringing about the injury, then recovery under the FELA is appropriate. See Rogers v. Missouri Pacific Ry. Co., 352 U.S. 500 (1957). The jury thus occupies the dominant role, so the employer can obtain a directed verdict on the issue of its negligence only in "exceptional" cases. See generally Ackley v. Chicago & North Western Transportation Co., 820 F.2d 263 (8th Cir. 1987).

2. Should tort actions be left to the jury? The disputes over the allocation of power in the ordinary negligence case often skirt the larger issue of whether negligence cases, or indeed all tort actions, should be tried by juries at all. The civil law countries of western Europe do not use juries to assess either liability or damages, and even the English courts rely on juries only in exceptional cases. Ward v. James, [1966] 1 Q.B. 273, 295. "Whenever a man is on trial for serious crime, or when in a civil case a man's honour or integrity is at stake, or when one or other party must be deliberately lying, then the trial by jury has no equal. But in personal injury cases trial by jury has given place of late to trial by judge alone, the reason being simply this, that in these cases trial by a judge alone is more acceptable to the great majority of people."

The arguments for and against the use of juries are numerous and familiar. On the positive side, juries represent the sense of the community that can prove decisive on the reasonableness judgments required under a negligence system. Juries also place a distinct check on the domination of the legal system by government officials and professional people. On the negative side, the jury system is expensive to run and depends heavily on taxing unwilling individuals who are paid a fraction of their market wage for jury duty. Juries may be subject to passion and prejudice, and, even when fair-minded, find themselves unable to cope with the complex technical issues raised by medical malpractice and products liability claims. In order to cope with the expense of juries, it has been suggested that smaller juries, perhaps with 6 instead of 12 jurors, be used. While this proposal may reduce the direct costs of running a jury, it could also reduce the sense of community participation and diversity, and with it the reliability of jury efforts. For evaluations of these proposals see Diamond and Zeisel, "Convincing Empirical Evidence" on the Six-Member Jury, 41 U. Chi. L. Rev. 281 (1974); Klevorick and Rothschild, A Model of the Jury Decision Process, 8 J. Legal Stud. 141 (1979); Lempert, Uncovering "Nondiscernible" Differences: Empirical Research and the Jury-Size Cases, 73 Mich. L. Rev. 643 (1975).

There has been only a limited amount of hard empirical work on jury behavior, for it is generally considered unethical to monitor the deliberations of actual juries and too expensive to impanel mock juries in sufficient numbers to obtain a reliable data base. The Chicago jury study undertaken in the 1960s defended the use of the civil jury on the ground that it tended to reach the same results as judges sitting as triers of facts, and that the judges themselves were generally pleased with the operation of the jury system. See Kalven, The Dignity of the Civil Jury, 50 Va. L. Rev. 1055 (1964). A more recent study that followed on the Chicago study, Sentell, The Georgia Jury and Negligence: The View From the Trenches, 28 Ga. L. Rev. 1 (1993), relied on survey data of trial lawyers, and found a significant (but far from unanimous) sentiment that today many judges are more pro-plaintiff than juries, at least on the issue of liability. On the question of damages, however, judges were generally thought less likely to award "runaway verdicts" than a jury.

The full range of this debate on jury behavior is beyond the scope of this book, but it is instructive perhaps to close with one excerpt that evaluates the operation of a jury on a relatively limited question, choosing damages in ordinary negligence actions. The techniques used are those of modern econometric analysis; they depend upon the awards made in actual jury trials, in this instance those that have taken place in Cook County, Illinois.

> . . . This model predicts the award a defendant would pay as a function of the number of other defendants, the number of plaintiffs and their injuries, the type of legal case, and characteristics of the defendant. Corporations, governments, doctors, and hospitals appear to suffer from a "deep-pocket" image. Compared with individual defendants, our model predicts that corporate defendants pay 34 percent larger awards, after

controlling for plaintiffs' injuries and type of legal case. If the plaintiff is permanently and severely injured, the deep-pocket effect is much stronger — a corporate defendant pays almost 4.5 times as much as an individual, on average. Similarly, government defendants are estimated to pay 50 percent more than individuals (averaged over all plaintiff injuries; there were too few cases of permanently and severely injured plaintiffs suing government defendants to analyze these separately). Finally, medical malpractice awards against doctors are almost 2.5 times as great as awards against other individuals in average case types, and awards against hospitals are 85 percent larger.

Legal standards to the contrary, the type of defendant appears to influence jury awards. Defendants who can be presumed to be wealthy, heavily insured, or able to distribute the costs of awards among their customers or shareholders are forced to pay larger awards. As a result, different types of defendants face unequal incentives to prevent accidents. Relatively poor defendants may invest too little in safety, or relatively rich defendants may invest too much.

There are several plausible explanations for the observed jury behavior. First, jurors may balance the benefit of greater compensation for the plaintiff against the harm to the defendant. While a relatively modest award against an individual defendant might cause him great financial hardship, the same award against a corporation would impose only miniscule losses on each of its stockholders. In addition, it may be impossible for jurors to separate the insult implicit in a tort from the harm to the plaintiff. Thus jurors may require doctors to provide greater compensation to victims of malpractice, not only because doctors are usually heavily insured and are wealthier than other defendants, but also because of the special trust a patient places in his or her doctor.

Hammitt, Carroll, and Relles, Tort Standards and Jury Decisions, 14 J. Legal Stud. 751, 754-756 (1985).

What implications do these data have for the application of the Hand formula? Note that the data presented do not indicate whether the same variation in levels of damage awards is found in bench trials.

G. PROOF OF NEGLIGENCE

1. Problems of Proof

It should be fairly obvious that success in prosecuting or defending negligence actions hinges greatly on what the parties can prove at trial. Of course the parties must investigate, collect, and preserve many types of evidence, no small difficulty given the long delays between the occurrence of an accident and the final determination of a case. Much relevant evidence comes from lay witnesses, and is addressed to questions such as, was the defendant driving the yellow car? Or, was the light green or red when the intersection collision took place? In most litigation, especially the modern medical malpractice and products liability actions, expert evidence will be critical on matters such as the proper standard of care or causation. Such expert testimony is always surrounded with ambiguity. Even though experts may not take contingent fees, they are chosen by the parties, and have therefore some stake in the outcome of the case. In many cases experts are full-time professionals with allegiances to either plaintiffs or defendants. The preparation and cross-examination of expert witnesses is therefore a major element in the success of most modern tort litigation, though the practical and strategic issues are outside the scope of this book.

On the particular question of negligence, Clarence Morris has observed that "the plaintiff has usually exhausted the possibilities of proof once he has shown: (1) what defendant did, (2) how dangerous it was, (3) defendant's opportunity to discern danger, (4) availability of safer alternatives, and (5) defendant's opportunity to know about safer alternatives." Morris, Proof of Negligence, 47 Nw. U. L. Rev. 817, 834 (1953).

In this section, however, we shall not be primarily concerned with these general matters of proof, since they are properly taken up in courses on evidence or trial practice, or as part of clinical education. One question of proof has, however, a long and close association with the law of tort. The doctrine of res ipsa loquitur — literally Latin for the thing speaks for itself — has frequently been invoked when the plaintiff seeks to establish the defendant's negligence by circumstantial evidence. In some cases, the plaintiff seeks to reach and persuade a jury on the strength of the doctrine itself. Other times the plaintiff combines the doctrine with lay and expert testimony. This section traces the development and use of the doctrine, first with ordinary accident cases, and then in medical malpractice cases.

2.   Res Ipsa Loquitur

Byrne v. Boadle
159 Eng. Rep. 299 (Ex. 1863)

[Plaintiff's declaration stated that he was passing along the highway in front of defendant's premises when he was struck and badly hurt by a barrel of flour that was apparently being lowered from a window above which was on the premises of the defendant, a dealer in flour. Several witnesses testified that they saw the barrel fall and hit plaintiff. The defendant claimed "that there was no evidence of negligence for the jury." The trial court, agreeing, nonsuited plaintiff after the jury had assessed the damages at £50 and the trial court gave plaintiff leave to move the Court of Exchequer to enter a verdict for him in that amount.

Having obtained a rule nisi to enter a verdict for plaintiff "on the ground of this direction [of the trial court] in ruling that there was no evidence of negligence on the part of the defendant," defendant's attorney showed cause, arguing that it was consistent with the evidence that the purchaser of the flour or some complete stranger was supervising the lowering of the barrel of flour and that its fall was not attributable in any way to defendant or his servants. Pollock, C.B.: "The presumption is that the defendant's servants were engaged in removing the defendant's flour. If they were not it was competent to the defendant to prove it." Defendant's attorney went on to observe that "Surmise ought not to be substituted for strict proof when it is thought to fix a defendant with serious liability. The plaintiff should establish his case by affirmative evidence. . . . The plaintiff was bound to give affirmative proof of negligence. But there was not a scintilla of evidence, unless the occurrence is of itself evidence of negligence." Pollock, C.B.: "There are certain cases of which it may be said res ipsa loquitur and this seems one of them. In some cases the Court had held that the mere fact of the accident having occurred is evidence of negligence, as, for instance, in the case of railway collisions." Then followed a discussion between defendant's counsel and the judges of the Court of Exchequer over the relevance of certain precedents involving railroads.]

POLLOCK, C.B. We are all of opinion that the rule must be absolute to enter the verdict for the plaintiff. The learned counsel was quite right in saying that there are many accidents from which no presumption of negligence can arise, but I think it would be wrong to lay down as a rule that in no case can presumption of negligence arise from the fact of an accident. Suppose in this case the barrel had rolled out of the warehouse and fallen on the plaintiff, how could he possibly ascertain from what cause it occurred? It is the duty of persons who keep barrels in a warehouse to take care that they do not roll out, and I think that such a case would, beyond all doubt, afford prima facie evidence of negligence. A barrel could not roll out of a warehouse without some negligence, and to say that a plaintiff who is injured by it must call witnesses from the warehouse to prove negligence seems to me preposterous. So in the building or repairing a house, or putting pots on the chimneys, if a person passing along the road is injured by something falling upon him, I think the accident alone would be prima facie evidence of negligence. Or if an article calculated to cause damage is put in a wrong place and does mischief, I think that those whose duty it was to put it in the right place are prima facie responsible, and if there is any state of facts to rebut the presumption of negligence, they must prove them. The present case upon the evidence comes to this, a man is passing in front of the premises of a dealer in flour, and there falls down upon him a barrel of flour. I think it apparent that the barrel was in the custody of the defendant who occupied the premises, and who is responsible for the acts of his servants who had the control of it; and in my opinion the fact of its falling is prima facie evidence of negligence, and the plaintiff who was injured by it is not bound to show that it could not fall without negligence, but if there are any facts inconsistent with negligence it is for the defendant to prove them.

NOTES

1. Res ipsa loquitur and circumstantial evidence. The function of res ipsa loquitur is to aid the plaintiff in proving the elements of a negligence case by circumstantial evidence. In Byrne v. Boadle, was the critical difficulty in establishing negligence in the handling of the barrel, or in showing that the person who dropped the barrel was someone for whom the defendant was responsible? In this connection, what is the relationship between res ipsa loquitur and the law of vicarious liability for employees and independent contractors? See note 1 supra at page 152 and Chapter 5.

One of the standard statements of the doctrine of res ipsa loquitur is that of Chief Justice Erle in Scott v. London & St. Katherine Docks Co., 159 Eng. Rep. 665 (Ex. 1865). "There must be reasonable evidence of negligence; but where the thing is shown to be under the management of the defendant or his servants, and the accident is such as in the ordinary course of things does not happen if those who have the management use proper care, it affords reasonable evidence, in the absence of explanation by the defendants, that the accident arose from want of care."

In Wakelin v. London & S.W. Ry. Co., [1886] 12 A.C. 41, 45-46 (H.L.E.), plaintiff's deceased was killed when he was struck by one of defendant's trains. The view of the track was unobstructed at the time of the accident, and there was no specific evidence of any negligent act or omission by the defendant. The trial judge allowed the case to go to the jury, which returned a verdict for plaintiff; but the decision was overturned by the House of Lords, with Lord Halsbury noting:

> In this case I am unable to see any evidence of how this unfortunate calamity occurred. One may surmise, and it is but surmise and not evidence, that the unfortunate man was knocked down by a passing train while on the level crossing; but assuming in the plaintiff's favour that fact to be established, is there anything to shew that the train ran over the man rather than that the man ran against the train? I understand the admission in the answer to the sixth interrogatory to be simply an admission that the death of the plaintiff's husband was caused by contact with

the train. If there are two moving bodies which come in contact, whether ships, or carriages, or even persons, it is not uncommon to hear the person complaining of the injury describe it as having been caused by his ship, or his carriage, or himself having been run into, or run down, or run upon; but if a man ran across an approaching train so close that he was struck by it, is it more true to say that the engine ran down the man, or that the man ran against the engine? Neither man nor engine were intended to come in contact, but each advanced to such a point that contact was accomplished. . . .

Should the doctrine of res ipsa loquitur as formulated in *Scott* be of any assistance to the plaintiff?

Within the American context, the basic conditions for applying res ipsa loquitur were set out in Wigmore on Evidence §2509 (1st ed. 1905). Thereafter they were stated in canonical form by Prosser as follows:

> (1) The event must be of a kind which ordinarily does not occur in the absence of someone's negligence;
> (2) It must be caused by an agency or instrumentality within the exclusive control of the defendant; and
> (3) It must not have been due to any voluntary action or contribution on the part of the plaintiff. [Prosser and Keeton at 244.]

The Restatement (Second) of Torts for its part takes a somewhat more expansive view of the doctrine.

> §328 D. RES IPSA LOQUITUR
> (1) It may be inferred that harm suffered by the plaintiff is caused by negligence of the defendant when
>> (a) the event is of a kind which ordinarily does not occur in the absence of negligence;
>> (b) other responsible causes, including the conduct of plaintiff and third persons, are sufficiently eliminated by the evidence; and
>> (c) the indicated negligence is within the scope of the defendant's duty to the plaintiff.
> (2) It is the function of the court to determine whether the inference may be reasonably drawn by the jury, or whether it must be necessarily drawn.
> (3) It is the function of the jury to determine whether the inference is to be drawn in any case where different conclusions may be reasonably reached.

2. *Res ipsa loquitur and guest statutes.* In its conventional form, res ipsa governs only negligence cases, and applies with difficulty when the defendant's liability is predicated on grounds other than negligence. In Galbraith v. Busch, 196 N.E. 36 (N.Y. 1935), the plaintiff was a guest in an automobile owned by her daughter and driven by the defendant Busch under the daughter's direction. The plaintiff was injured when the car suddenly swerved from the highway. Yet the road was in good

condition, the weather was clear, and the traffic was light. The trial
judge held that these circumstances were sufficient to raise a presumption of negligence, which shifted the burden of proof to the defendant,
who in turn offered no evidence, itself acknowledged by Judge Lehman
in the court of appeal as a "suspicious form of conduct." Lehman, J.,
then noted that the burden of proof "perhaps, logically and properly"
should be shifted to the defendant if "it owed a duty to the plaintiff to
exercise reasonable care both in the operation and maintenance or
repair of the automobile." Nonetheless he held that in this case the
applicable substantive law precluded the invocation of res ipsa loquitur.

> Here the plaintiff was only a guest in the car. She assumed the risk of
> any defect in the automobile which was not known to the defendants.
> They assumed the duty to exercise reasonable care for her protection in
> the operation of the automobile. They were under no duty to exercise
> care to discover and repair defects not known to them. The evidence,
> though unexplained, cannot possibly lead to an inference that the acci-
> dent was due to lack of care in the operation of the automobile, for the
> probability that it occurred from a break in its mechanism is at least
> equally great. All that the evidence shows is that the accident may have
> occurred from any one of many causes, including, perhaps, negligence
> in operation. If knowledge of the actual cause is confined to the defen-
> dants, then the plaintiff cannot prove any cause of action without calling
> them as witnesses. Nonetheless, the plaintiff fails to make out a prima
> facie case without such proof and cannot place upon the defendants the
> burden of exculpating themselves from the charge of neglect of duty
> until evidence showing prima facie that there is such negligence has been
> presented.

Why did none of the three occupants of the car take the stand?

Galbraith was apparently overruled ("sapped of all practical application to the real world") in Pfaffenbach v. White Plains Express Corp.,
216 N.E.2d 324, 325-326 (N.Y. 1966). There, plaintiff was a passenger
in her friend's automobile who was injured when the car was struck by
the defendant's truck, which had skidded across the midline of the
highway. Defendant gave no explanation of the accident. The court
held that whenever a vehicle comes over to the wrong side of the road
a prima facie case of negligence is made out, subject, of course, to
explanation by the defendant.

In his concurrence in *Pfaffenbach*, Burke, J., observed:

> Proof of "mere skidding" is prima facie evidence of negligence in this
> case where the plaintiff was *not* a passenger in defendant-respondent's
> car. There are obvious distinctions between a plaintiff who is a guest-
> passenger and one who is a stranger. The former not only assumes some
> risk in accepting gratuitous transportation but also is in the advantageous
> position of having the opportunity to observe whether the defendant ex-
> ercised reasonable care in the operation of the vehicle. (Galbraith v.
> Busch) On the other hand, the stranger who is injured by defendant's

vehicle's skidding into the opposite flowing lane of traffic or up onto a sidewalk, under conditions known to the defendant alone, is at a singular disadvantage. . . . In such a case [, moreover,] the plaintiff does not assume the same risk of unknown defects as would the owner of the vehicle or his guests. . . .

3. From the terrace, hotel, etc. In Larson v. St. Francis Hotel, 188 P.2d 513, 515 (Cal. App. 1948), the plaintiff, while walking on the sidewalk next to the hotel, was hit by a chair apparently thrown out of one of the hotel windows as "the result of the effervescence and ebullition of San Franciscans in their exuberance of joy on V-J Day, August 14, 1945." The court refused to apply res ipsa loquitur:

> Applying the rule to the facts of this case, it is obvious that the doctrine does not apply. While, as pointed out by plaintiff, the rule of exclusive control "is not limited to the actual physical control but applies to the right of control of the instrumentality which causes the injury" it is not clear to us how this helps plaintiff's case. A hotel does not have exclusive control, either actual or potential, of its furniture. Guests have, at least, partial control. Moreover, it cannot be said that with the hotel using ordinary care "the accident was such that in the ordinary course of events . . . would not have happened." On the contrary, the mishap would quite as likely be due to the fault of a guest or other person as to that of defendants. The most logical inference from the circumstances shown is that the chair was thrown by some such person from a window. It thus appears that this occurrence is not such as ordinarily does not happen without the negligence of the party charged, but, rather, one in which the accident ordinarily might happen despite the fact that the defendants used reasonable care and were totally free from negligence. To keep guests and visitors from throwing furniture out windows would require a guard to be placed in every room in the hotel, and no one would contend that there is any rule of law requiring a hotel to do that.

In Connolly v. Nicollet Hotel, 95 N.W.2d 657, 669 (Minn. 1959), defendant's hotel was "taken over" by a Junior Chamber of Commerce national convention, and the management had ample notice of drinking, revelry, and hooliganism on the premises. Plaintiff was injured when struck by some unidentified falling object. The court distinguished the *Larson* case by noting that *Larson* involved a surprise celebration, while the events in the instant case were the culmination of many days of riotous celebration. In an opinion that never used the words "res ipsa loquitur," the court reversed the trial judge's decision for defendant, and allowed the plaintiff to get to the jury. "We have said many times that the law does not require every fact and circumstance which make up a case of negligence to be proved by direct and positive evidence or by the testimony of eye-witnesses, and the circumstantial evidence alone may authorize a finding of negligence. Negligence may be inferred from all the facts and surrounding circumstances, and where the evidence of such facts and circumstances is such as to take the case out of the realm of conjecture and into the field of legitimate inference from established facts, a prima facie case is made."

Should the doctrine of vicarious liability be extended to cover wrongs committed by guests on the premises of hotels?

4. Acts of God and res ipsa loquitur. How ought res ipsa loquitur to apply when a ship or plane is lost without a trace? In Walston v. Lambersten, 349 F.2d 660 (9th Cir. 1965), defendant's boat disappeared at sea while crab fishing. The ship was in seaworthy condition when it left port and had been seen by other fishermen "going along just like a duck, easy." Plaintiffs suggested that the ship might have sunk because of a sudden redistribution of its weight after the catch had been taken aboard. The court of appeals affirmed the district court's refusal to apply res ipsa loquitur, noting that "the sea itself contains many hazards, and an inference of liability of the shipowner for the mysterious loss of his vessel should not be lightly drawn." One such hazard mentioned at trial was that of striking "deadheads," such as partially submerged logs.

5. Directed verdicts with res ipsa loquitur. The usual effect of res ipsa loquitur is to allow plaintiff's case to reach the jury. In some instances, however, the evidence has proved strong enough to allow for a directed verdict, as the Restatement view implies.

In Newing v. Cheatham, 540 P.2d 33 (Cal. 1975), plaintiffs' decedent was killed when a plane owned and piloted by defendant's decedent crashed in mountainous terrain about 13 miles east of Tijuana, Mexico. The plaintiff's evidence indicated that the only possible cause of the crash was the negligence of the defendant in running out of fuel while in flight. The defendant had been drinking beer for about an hour on the morning of the crash. When the wreckage of the plane was examined, the smell of alcohol was found on the defendant's breath, as well as on the breath of a second passenger. None was found on the decendent's breath. Eight or nine empty beer cans were also uncovered. Visibility was excellent; the weather was calm; there was no evidence of a mid-air collision; the plane's clock indicated that the crash took place at a time when it could be reasonably expected for the plane's fuel supply to be exhausted; and after the crash the plane's fuel tanks did not contain sufficient fuel to feed the motor.

The evidence also pointed to the defendant's exclusive control over the plane. He owned the plane; he was the only licensed pilot on board the aircraft; he was at the controls when the crash took place; and the applicable federal air regulations imposed upon him ultimate responsibility while the plane was in flight. Finally no evidence suggested that the decedent's voluntary conduct could have contributed to the crash, since the decedent did not know how to fly and at the time of the crash was seated in a rear seat out of reach of the controls. On this record the supreme court upheld the trial court's ruling that the circumstantial evidence in the case was sufficient to take the case from the jury.

A similar effort to obtain a directed verdict was rebuffed in Imig v.

Beck, 503 N.E.2d 324, 329-330 (Ill. 1986). There the plaintiff was injured while driving westward in his parents' van when struck by a car that was being towed eastward on the same road by a wrecker owned by one defendant and driven by the other. The wrecker had remained on the south side of the highway throughout, but the collision took place on the north side of the highway when the towed car unaccountably veered across the midline of the road. The defendants testified that they had checked the rig between the wrecker and the car just before the accident and had found nothing wrong with it, and plaintiff offered no specific evidence of negligence. The jury returned a verdict for the defendant, which was entered by the trial judge. That decision was reversed on appeal by the intermediate court, which ordered a directed verdict entered for the plaintiffs on the issue of liability. The original jury verdict was reinstated by the Illinois Supreme Court, which held that the doctrine of res ipsa loquitur did not allow the plaintiff to prevail.

> Since the doctrine gives rise only to a permissive inference, in most cases a directed verdict for the plaintiff will not be appropriate, even where the defendant presents no explanation or rebuttal, because it must be left to the jury whether to draw the inference of negligence from the circumstances of the occurence. However, as the appellate court majority correctly reasoned, in exceptional cases the plaintiff may be entitled either to a directed verdict or to a judgment notwithstanding the verdict because the unrebutted *prima facie* proof of negligence is so strong that all of the evidence, when viewed in its aspect most favorable to the defendant, so overwhelmingly favors the plaintiff that no contrary jury verdict based on that evidence could ever stand.

The court then held that this high standard was not met in this case.

> The defendants offered evidence to the effect that the wrecker was properly equipped to tow a vehicle, that the wrecker passed the proper safety inspections, that on the night of the accident the towed vehicle was properly attached to the wrecker, that both the towing mechanism and the towed vehicle were checked one mile before the accident, that the wrecker remained in its proper lane of travel, and that the stabilizer bar was welded together.

6. *References.* Carpenter, The Doctrine of Res Ipsa Loquitur, 1 U. Chi. L. Rev. 519 (1934); Prosser, Res Ipsa Loquitur in California, 37 Cal. L. Rev. 183 (1949), reprinted in Prosser, Selected Topics on the Law of Torts 302 (1954).

Colmenares Vivas v. Sun Alliance Insurance Co.
807 F.2d 1102 (1st Cir. 1986)

BOWNES, C.J.: Appellants are plaintiffs in a diversity action to recover damages for injuries they suffered in an accident while riding an escalator. After the parties had presented their evidence, the defendants moved for and were granted a directed verdict. The court held that there was no evidence of negligence and that the doctrine of res ipsa loquitur, which would raise a presumption of negligence, did not apply. We reverse the directed verdict and remand the case to the district court because we hold that res ipsa loquitur does apply.

I

The relevant facts are not in dispute. On February 12, 1984, Jose Domingo Colmenares Vivas and his wife, Dilia Arreaza de Colmenares, arrived at the Luis Munoz Marin International Airport in Puerto Rico. They took an escalator on their way to the Immigration and Customs checkpoint on the second level. Mrs. Colmenares was riding the escalator on the right-hand side, holding the moving handrail, one step ahead of her husband. When the couple was about halfway up the escalator, the handrail stopped moving, but the steps continued the ascent, causing Mrs. Colmenares to lose her balance. Her husband grabbed her from behind with both hands and prevented her from falling, but in doing so, he lost his balance and tumbled down the stairs. Mr. and Mrs. Colmenares filed a direct action against the Sun Alliance Insurance Company (Sun Alliance), who is the liability insurance carrier for the airport's owner and operator, the Puerto Rico Ports Authority (Ports Authority). Sun Alliance brought a third-party contractual action against Westinghouse Electric Corporation (Westinghouse) based on a maintenance contract that required Westinghouse to inspect, maintain, adjust, repair, and replace parts as needed for the escalator and handrails, and to keep the escalator in a safe operating condition . . .

The trial was conducted on January 30 and 31, 1986. Appellants called four witnesses. The Ports Authority's contract and maintenance supervisor testified about his daily weekday inspections of the escalator, about the maintenance contract with Westinghouse, about inspection and maintenance procedures, and about the accident report and subsequent repair and maintenance of the escalator.[1] The Ports Authority's assistant chief of operations testified about the accident report. Appellants' testimony concerned the accident and their injuries.

. . . After hearing the parties' arguments, the court ruled that there was no evidence that the Ports Authority had been negligent, and that the case could not go to the jury based on res ipsa loquitur because at

---

1. A record of a subsequent repair made to the escalator was admitted to impeach the contract and maintenance supervisor's testimony. The record indicated that a sprocket was changed on February 23 in making repairs to the right-hand side handrail. Because appellants presented their case and base this appeal on the applicability of res ipsa loquitur, we do not consider whether evidence of this repair required the court to submit the case to the jury on the issue of negligence.

least one of the requirements for its application — that the injury-causing instrumentality was within the exclusive control of the defendant —
was not met. . .

II. RES IPSA LOQUITUR

Under Puerto Rico law, three requirements must be met for res ipsa
loquitur ("the thing speaks for itself") to apply: "(1) the accident must
be of a kind which ordinarily does not occur in the absence of someone's negligence; (2) it must be caused by an agency or instrumentality
within the exclusive control of the defendant; [and] (3) it must not be
due to any voluntary action on the part of the plaintiff." *Community
Partnership v. Presbyterian Hosp.*, 88 P.R.R. 379, 386 (1963). If all three
requirements are met, the jury may infer that the defendant was negligent even though there is no direct evidence to that effect. *Id.* at 398.

A. THE FIRST REQUIREMENT: INFERENCE OF NEGLIGENCE

The first requirement that must be met for res ipsa loquitur to apply
is that "the accident must be such that in the light of ordinary experience it gives rise to an inference that someone has been negligent." It
is not clear to us whether the district court decided that this requirement was met, although the court did suggest that it was giving the
benefit of the doubt on this question to the appellants. We hold that
this requirement was met because an escalator handrail probably would
not stop suddenly while the escalator continues moving unless someone
had been negligent.[2]
This requirement would not be met if appellants had shown nothing
more than that they had been injured on the escalator, because based
on this fact alone it would not be likely that someone other than the
appellants had been negligent. See *Conway v. Boston Elevated Ry. Co.*,
152 N.E. 94 (Mass. 1926) (negligence element not satisfied when all
that had been shown was that a child's hand had been caught beneath
the escalator handrail belt); *Fuller v. Wurzburg Dry Goods Co.*, 158 N.W.
1026 (Mich. 1916) (negligence may not be inferred from a fall on an
escalator because the plaintiff did not show that the escalator was improperly constructed or that it malfunctioned). Here, it was not disputed that the handrail malfunctioned and stopped suddenly, an event

2. In some jurisdictions, the courts have taken the position that escalator operators
are common carriers owing the highest degree of care to their passengers . . . To our
knowledge, the Puerto Rico courts have not equated escalators to common carriers, and
such a determination is not properly made by this court in the first instance. For the
purposes of this appeal, however, it would not matter if the stricter standard did apply,
because we hold that an inference of negligence has been raised even under the lower
reasonable care standard.

that foreseeably could cause riders to lose their balance and get injured. Thus, the evidence gave rise to an inference that someone probably had been negligent in operating or maintaining the escalator, and the first requirement for the application of res ipsa loquitur was met.

B.   THE SECOND REQUIREMENT: EXCLUSIVE CONTROL

The second requirement for res ipsa loquitur to apply is that the injury-causing instrumentality — in this case, the escalator — must have been within the exclusive control of the defendant. The district court found that this requisite was not met, despite the parties' stipulation that "[t]he escalator in question is property of and is under the control of the Puerto Rico Ports Authority." We agree that this stipulation was not by itself enough to satisfy the res ipsa loquitur requirement. It did not exclude the possibility that someone else also had control over the escalator; indeed, the stipulation said that Westinghouse maintained the escalator. We hold, however, that the Ports Authority effectively had exclusive control over the escalator because the authority in control of a public area had a nondelegable duty to maintain its facilities in a safe condition.

Few courts have required that control literally be "exclusive." . . . The exclusive control requirement, then, should not be so narrowly construed as to take from the jury the ability to infer that a defendant was negligent when the defendant was responsible for the injury-causing instrumentality, even if someone else might also have been responsible. The purpose of the requirement is not to restrict the application of the res ipsa loquitur inference to cases in which there is only one actor who dealt with the instrumentality, but rather "to eliminate the possibility that the accident was caused by a *third party.*" It is not necessary, therefore, for the defendant to have had actual physical control; it is enough that the defendant, and not a third party, was ultimately responsible for the instrumentality. Thus, res ipsa loquitur applies even if the defendant shares responsibility with another, or if the defendant is responsible for the instrumentality even though someone else had physical control over it. It follows that a defendant charged with a nondelegable duty of care to maintain an instrumentality in a safe condition effectively has exclusive control over it for the purposes of applying res ipsa loquitur. Unless the duty is delegable, the res ipsa loquitur inference is not defeated if the defendant had shifted physical control to an agent or contracted with another to carry out its responsibilities.

We hold that the Ports Authority could not delegate its duty to maintain safe escalators. There are no set criteria for determining whether a duty is nondelegable; the critical question is whether the responsibility is so important to the community that it should not be transferred to another. The Ports Authority was charged with such a responsibility. It was created for a public purpose, which included the operation and management of the airport. A concomitant of this authority is the duty to keep the facilities it operates in a reasonably safe condition. The public is entitled to rely on the Ports Authority — not its agents or contractors — to see that this is done. The Ports Authority apparently recognized this responsibility, for its maintenance and contract supervisor conducted daily weekday inspections of the escalators despite the maintenance contract with Westinghouse.

Duties have been seen as nondelegable in several analogous situations. For example, a public authority may not delegate to an independent contractor its responsibility to see that work in a public place is done carefully. Also, a government may not delegate its responsibility to maintain safe roads and similar public places. Finally, an owner has a nondelegable duty to keep business premises safe for invitees. These examples demonstrate a general tort law policy not to allow an entity to shift by contract its responsibility for keeping an area used by the public in a safe condition. It would be contrary to this policy to allow the owner and operator of an airport terminal to delegate its duty to keep its facility safe. We hold, therefore, that the district court erred in ruling that the exclusive control requirement was not met.

C. The Third Requirement: The Plaintiff's Actions

The third requirement that must be met for res ipsa loquitur to apply is that the accident must not have been due to the plaintiff's voluntary actions. The district court found, and we agree, that there was no evidence that Mr. and Mrs. Colmenares caused the accident. Indeed, there is no indication that they did anything other than attempt to ride the escalator in the ordinary manner. Therefore, we hold that all three requirements were met and that the jury should have been allowed to consider whether the Ports Authority was liable based on the permissible inference of negligence raised by the application of res ipsa loquitur. . . .

Torruella, C.J.: I must regretfully dissent . . .

In my view, *solely* because the handrail stopped and Mrs. Colmenares fell, without further evidence as to why or how the handrail malfunctioned, does not give rise to an inference of *negligence* by the Ports Authority. . . .

The malfunctioning of an escalator presents an even stronger argument against the raising of an inference of negligence without additional proof as to the cause of the malfunction. Although a court can take notice that an escalator is a complicated piece of machinery, it has no basis of common knowledge for inferring that its malfunction is the result of the operator's negligence . . .

Appellant presented no evidence from which a jury could infer lack of diligence or foresight by appellees and thus negligence.

NOTES

1. Assessing the probabilities of negligence. Conceptually the most difficult part of the res ipsa loquitur test comes from attaching a precise meaning to the phrase "ordinarily does not occur in the absence of negligence." Linguistically, this phrase has generally been taken to signify either "(1) that the probability of the injury given the exercise of reasonable care is quite small, or (2) that the probability of the injury given reasonable care is smaller than the probability of the injury given negligence, or (3) that the probability of the injury given reasonable care is much smaller than the probability of the injury given negligence." Kaye, Probability Theory Meets Res Ipsa Loquitur, 77 Mich. L. Rev. 1456, 1465 (1979). Yet, as Kaye points out, none of these three commonsense statements captures the ultimate issue, whether the probability that the defendant was negligent, given the occurrence of the injury, is greater than 50 percent. The first expression only notes that the probability of accident is quite small when there is reasonable care, but if the defendant exercises reasonable care an overwhelming proportion of the time, then it still might be more likely than not that reasonable care was exercised in the particular case.

Thus suppose that it is established that a hand grenade has prematurely exploded because it contains a defective fuse, see, e.g., Monigal v. Gearhart Industries, Inc., 788 F.2d 321 (5th Cir. 1986), and assume further that the only question is whether the defective fuse escaped detection because it was negligently inspected before shipment. In dealing with this question, it is useful to consider two examples. First, suppose there is a one-in-a-thousand chance of a defective grenade slipping through a reasonable inspection and a 50 percent chance of a defective grenade slipping through when it does not. If the defendant is careful 99.9 percent of the time, then if one million units are produced, 999,000 of them are properly inspected. Of these we should expect to see 999 instances of failure, none of which are attributable to negligence. By the same token, we should expect to see 500 failures (half of the 1,000 units that remain), and all of these attributable to negligence. To be sure, any negligently prepared unit is much more likely to be defective than a carefully manufactured one (as in Kaye's proposition (2)), for a 50 percent failure rate is 500 times a 0.1 percent failure rate. Yet — and the point is critical — by the same token it is more likely (by odds 999 to 500) that any defective unit comes from the group of carefully inspected grenades than from the group of negligently inspected grenades.

The conclusions here, however, are very sensitive to the choice of numbers. Suppose now that the defendant was careful only 99 percent of the time, and was careless 1 percent of the time. If the probability of a bad grenade slipping through the careful inspection is still 0.1 percent, then 990 defective grenades would be produced when care was exercised (one one-thousandth of 990,000). In addition, however, 5,000 defective units (half of 10,000) would be produced with negligence, making it more likely by over 5 to 1 odds that the grenade came from the badly inspected batch.

These two examples show that the hard question therefore in all cases is to link two numbers: the probability of negligence given the accident, with the increase in the likelihood of an accident given the shift from care to negligence. Kaye's article contains a formal demonstration, invoking the use of Bayes' theorem, of why in general that jump should be made only in the third situation set out above, namely, the probability of injury when defendant takes due care is much smaller than the probability of injury when the defendant is negligent.

On the intricacies of statistical inference, see also Comment, Mathematics, Fuzzy Negligence and the Logic of Res Ipsa Loquitur, 75 Nw. U. L. Rev. 147 (1980).

2. Res ipsa loquitur and the duty to inspect. The question of inspection often turns out to be critical whenever the defendant is not personally charged with the admitted negligence of some third party. In Brown v. Racket Club of Bricktown, 471 A.2d 25 (N.J. 1984), the plaintiffs were injured during a fashion show when the interior wood stairway on which they were standing "abruptly" pulled away from the wall and collapsed. The stairway in question had been attached to the wall by plain nails, a form of construction that was concededly negligent. But this defective construction had been undertaken by the original builder of the clubhouse, who, owing to his "financial difficulties," had sold the clubhouse to the defendant. It was conceded that the defendant was not vicariously liable for the negligence of its predecessor in title, (sound?) and that the defect in question was latent. Nonetheless the court held that there was a sufficient case to go to the jury on the ground that the negligence of a third party in constructing the stairway did not negate the defendant's negligence in failing to discover the defect, since owners are under a general duty to inspect the premises and "to discover their actual condition and any latent defects." Restatement (Second) of Torts §343, comment *b*. The court then held that the plaintiff could reach the jury notwithstanding the testimony of defendant's President that he had made a casual inspection of the stairs and had "failed to notice anything unusal" that would lead him to inspect how the stairs were connected to the wall or to seek an engineering or structural inspection.

3. Exclusive control with multiple defendants. The requirement of "exclusive" control has been the source of extensive litigation. In Winans v. Rockwell International Corp., 705 F.2d 1449, 1454 (5th Cir. 1983), the court refused to apply the doctrine in an airplane crash case against a large number of manufacturers and repairers of the doomed plane because the plaintiffs had not joined in the suit the company that had undertaken the most recent set of repairs. "The problem with applying res ipsa loquitur in this case was not that too many defendants were joined; it was that too few were joined."

Similarly, in Victory Park Apartments, Inc. v. Axelson, 367 N.W.2d 155 (N.D. 1985), the court refused to apply res ipsa on behalf of a landlord whose building was damaged by a fire that started in the defendant's apartment while she was out for the afternoon. The court noted that there was clear evidence that the fire had been started by a cigarette that had negligently been left burning in the defendant's couch earlier in the day. Nevertheless it held that this negligence had not been brought "home" to the defendant because the fire could have been started by either of the defendant's two guests, both of whom had smoked cigarettes in the apartment. Is the defendant under a special duty to inspect for smoldering cigarettes left by others? Could the defendant be held strictly liable under the doctrine of Tuberville v. Stamp, supra at page 17, note 1?

4. Exclusive control and the workers' compensation statutes. In some instances an injured party is prevented from suing his employer in tort because of the exclusive remedy provisions of the workers' compensation statutes, which block the tort remedy. In these cases the question arises whether or not the plaintiff can show that some third-party defendant has "exclusive" control of the dangerous instrumentality to support the use of res ipsa. In Miles v. St. Regis Paper Co., 467 P.2d 307, 310 (Wash. 1970), the decedent, an employee of the "D" Street Rafting Company, was crushed to death by a load of logs that suddenly rolled off the defendant railroad's flatcar while he was releasing one of its binders. There was conflicting evidence as to whether the accident could have been caused by the movement of the train and indeed whether the train had moved at all. The workers' compensation statute precluded a tort remedy against the rafting company, whose employees had directed the unloading operation. Nonetheless the railroad company, which responded to the orders of employees of the rafting company, was found to have "exclusive control" over the movement of the train.

> The question of control poses a close and difficult problem. Appellant makes a strong argument that employees of "D" Street Rafting Company had exclusive control of not only the unloading of the logs involving the use of the crane, but also other operations, including positioning of the cars and movement of the train. There is conflicting testimony, and the hand on the throttle of the switch engine was obviously the hand of

the engineer or the fireman (employees of the railroad). Furthermore, any movement of the train ultimately was the responsibility and within the exclusive control of such employees. It is not denied that movement of the train and positioning of the railroad flatcars loaded with logs occurred in accordance with the unloading plans and desires of employees of "D" Street Rafting Company, communicated by hand signal or otherwise to the foreman of the railroad switching crew and relayed by him to the engine crew. We believe that the ultimate decision to move the train was made by employees of the railroad. Thus, in terms of the requisites for application of res ipsa loquitur in this case, we are convinced that at the time of the accident the train of flatcars loaded with logs was in the "exclusive control" of the railroad.

The dissent argued that the right of control remained with the employees of the "D" Street Rafting Company throughout.

5. *Plaintiff's conduct and conduct of a third party.* In many negligence actions the dangerous instrumentality in question has passed through the hands of a third party, only to cause injury while being used by the plaintiff. In these cases, "the plaintiff's mere possession of a chattel which injures him does not prevent a res ipsa case where it is made clear that he has done nothing abnormal and *has used the thing only for the purpose for which it was intended.*" Prosser, Res Ipsa Loquitur in California, 37 Cal. L. Rev. 183, 201-202 (1949). Much the same standard governs the use of the instrumentality while in the possession of a third party. It follows therefore that the use of res ipsa depends upon meticulously following a dangerous instrumentality through a "chain of custody" that begins with the defendant and ends with the plaintiff.

In Honea v. Coca-Cola Bottling Co., 183 S.W.2d 968 (Tex. 1944), plaintiff, aged 15, was carrying cases of Coca-Cola, each containing 24 bottles arranged in 4 rows of 6 bottles and weighing about 40 pounds. In order to lift the cases, plaintiff grasped two bottles at the ends of the two middle rows and clasped them together rather than using the handles on the case. One of the bottles he grasped exploded, badly cutting his hand. Plaintiff did not allege any specific negligence by the defendant, but instead relied on res ipsa loquitur, which required him to show by a preponderance of the evidence that neither plaintiff nor anyone else had mishandled the bottles from the time they left defendant's possession until the time they reached plaintiff's hands. On the last point the court held that the trial court erred by refusing to allow plaintiff's testimony that all of defendant's employees lifted the bottles in the same manner and that, indeed, they had told him to lift them that way. The court remanded for a new trial on the effect of plaintiff's conduct, noting that custom is evidence, although not conclusive, on the standard of care.

Likewise res ipsa loquitur was held applicable in Benedict v. Eppley Hotel Co., 65 N.W.2d 224, 229 (Neb. 1954). There the plaintiff-appellee was injured when a folding chair collapsed after she had been sitting on it for some 20 or 30 minutes while participating in a bingo game. After the accident it was discovered that the screws and bolts on one side of the chair were missing.

> The applicability of the doctrine of res ipsa loquitur to this case is denied by appellant because it asserts that its chair occupied by appellee at the time of the accident was in her exclusive possession and control from the time she got it from a person who had been using it, moved it up to the table, and sat on it, a period of about 30 minutes. Her acts in reference to the chair were limited to transportation of it from where she first saw it in the hallway connecting the Embassy Room and the ballroom of the Rome Hotel to the table in the latter room where the game was in progress and sitting on it. She occupied the chair as an invitee of appellant. She had no right or duty to examine it for defects. She had a right to assume it was a safe instrumentality for the use she had been invited by appellant to make of it. Appellant had the ownership, possession, and control of the chair under the circumstances of this case and it was obligated to maintain it in a reasonably safe condition for the invited use made of it by the appellee. The fact that the chair when it was being properly used for the purpose for which it was made available gave way permits an inference that it was defective and unsafe and that appellant had not used due care in reference to it.

Ybarra v. Spangard
154 P.2d 687 (Cal. 1944)

GIBSON, C.J. This is an action for damages for personal injuries alleged to have been inflicted on plaintiff by defendants during the course of a surgical operation. The trial court entered judgments of nonsuit as to all defendants and plaintiff appealed.

On October 28, 1939, plaintiff consulted defendant Dr. Tilley, who diagnosed his ailment as appendicitis, and made arrangements for an appendectomy to be performed by defendant Dr. Spangard at a hospital owned and managed by defendant Dr. Swift. Plaintiff entered the hospital, was given a hypodermic injection, slept, and later was awakened by Doctors Tilley and Spangard and wheeled into the operating room by a nurse whom he believed to be defendant Gisler, an employee of Dr. Swift. Defendant Dr. Reser, the anesthetist, also an employee of Dr. Swift, adjusted plaintiff for the operation, pulling his body to the head of the operating table and, according to plaintiff's testimony, laying him back against two hard objects at the top of his shoulders, about an inch below his neck. Dr. Reser then administered the anesthetic and plaintiff lost consciousness. When he awoke early the following morning he was in his hospital room attended by defendant Thompson, the special nurse, and another nurse who was not made a defendant.

Plaintiff testified that prior to the operation he had never had any pain in, or injury to, his right arm or shoulder, but that when he awakened he felt a sharp pain about half way between the neck and the point of the right shoulder. He complained to the nurse, and then to Dr. Tilley, who gave him diathermy treatments while he remained in the hospital. The pain did not cease, but spread down to the lower part of his arm, and after his release from the hospital the condition grew worse. He was unable to rotate or lift his arm, and developed paralysis and atrophy of the muscles around the shoulder. He received further treatments from Dr. Tilley until March, 1940, and then returned to work, wearing his arm in a splint on the advice of Dr. Spangard.

Plaintiff also consulted Dr. Wilfred Sterling Clark, who had X-ray pictures taken which showed an area of diminished sensation below the shoulder and atrophy and wasting away of the muscles around the shoulder. In the opinion of Dr. Clark, plaintiff's condition was due to trauma or injury by pressure or strain, applied between his right shoulder and neck.

Plaintiff was also examined by Dr. Fernando Garduno, who expressed the opinion that plaintiff's injury was a paralysis of traumatic origin, not arising from pathological causes, and not systemic, and that the injury resulted in atrophy, loss of use and restriction of motion of the right arm and shoulder.

Plaintiff's theory is that the foregoing evidence presents a proper case for the application of the doctrine of res ipsa loquitur, and that the inference of negligence arising therefrom makes the granting of a nonsuit improper. Defendants take the position that, assuming that plaintiff's condition was in fact the result of an injury, there is no showing that the act of any particular defendant, nor any particular instrumentality, was the cause thereof. They attack plaintiff's action as an attempt to fix liability "en masse" on various defendants, some of whom were not responsible for the acts of others; and they further point to the failure to show which defendants had control of the instrumentalities that may have been involved. Their main defense may be briefly stated in two propositions: (1) that where there are several defendants, and there is a division of responsibility in the use of an instrumentality causing the injury, and the injury might have resulted from the separate act of either one of two or more persons, the rule of res ipsa loquitur cannot be invoked against any one of them; and (2) that where there are several instrumentalities, and no showing is made as to which caused the injury or as to the particular defendant in control of it, the doctrine cannot apply. We are satisfied, however, that these objections are not well taken in the circumstances of this case.

The doctrine of res ipsa loquitur has three conditions: "(1) the accident must be of a kind which ordinarily does not occur in the absence of someone's negligence; (2) it must be caused by an agency or instrumentality within the exclusive control of the defendant; (3) it must not have been due to any voluntary action or contribution on the part of the plaintiff." (Prosser, Torts, p. 295.) It is applied in a wide variety of situations, including cases of medical or dental treatment and hospital care. . . .

There is, however, some uncertainty as to the extent to which res ipsa loquitur may be invoked in cases of injury from medical treatment. This is in part due to the tendency, in some decisions, to lay undue emphasis on the limitations of the doctrine, and to give too little attention to its basic underlying purpose. The result has been that a simple, understandable rule of circumstantial evidence, with a sound background of common sense and human experience, has occasionally been transformed into a rigid legal formula, which arbitrarily precludes its application in many cases where it is most important that it should be applied. If the doctrine is to continue to serve a useful purpose, we should not forget that "the particular force and justice of the rule, regarded as a presumption throwing upon the party charged the duty of producing evidence, consists in the circumstance that the chief evidence of the true cause, whether culpable or innocent, is practically accessible to him but inaccessible to the injured person." (9 Wigmore, Evidence [3d ed. 1940], §2509, p. 382.)

The present case is of a type which comes within the reason and spirit of the doctrine more fully perhaps than any other. The passenger sitting awake in a railroad car at the time of a collision, the pedestrian walking along the street and struck by a falling object or the debris of an explosion, are surely not more entitled to an explanation than the unconscious patient on the operating table. Viewed from this aspect, it is difficult to see how the doctrine can, with any justification, be so restricted in its statement as to become inapplicable to a patient who submits himself to the care and custody of doctors and nurses, is rendered unconscious, and receives some injury from instrumentalities used in his treatment. Without the aid of the doctrine a patient who received permanent injuries of a serious character, obviously the result of someone's negligence, would be entirely unable to recover unless the doctors and nurses in attendance voluntarily chose to disclose the identity of the negligent person and the facts of establishing liability. If this were the state of the law of negligence, the courts, to avoid gross injustice, would be forced to invoke the principles of absolute liability, irrespective of negligence, in actions by persons suffering injuries during the course of treatment under anesthesia. But we think this juncture has not yet been reached, and the doctrine of res ipsa loquitur is properly applicable to the case before us.

The condition that the injury must not have been due to the plaintiff's voluntary action is of course fully satisfied under the evidence produced herein; and the same is true of the condition that the accident must be one which ordinarily does not occur unless someone was negligent. We have here no problem of negligence in treatment, but of distinct injury to a healthy part of the body not the subject of treatment, nor within the area covered by the operation. The decisions in this state make it clear that such circumstances raise the inference of negligence, and call upon the defendant to explain the unusual result. . . .

The argument of defendants is simply that plaintiff has not shown an injury caused by an instrumentality under a defendant's control, because he has not shown which of the several instrumentalities that he came in contact with while in the hospital caused the injury; and he has not shown that any one defendant or his servants had exclusive control over any particular instrumentality. Defendants assert that some of them were not the employees of other defendants, that some did not stand in any permanent relationship from which liability in tort would follow, and that in view of the nature of the injury, the number of defendants and the different functions performed by each, they could not all be liable for the wrong, if any.

We have no doubt that in a modern hospital a patient is quite likely to come under the care of a number of persons in different types of contractual and other relationships with each other. For example, in the present case it appears that Doctors Smith, Spangard and Tilley were physicians or surgeons commonly placed in the legal category of independent contractors and Dr. Reser, the anesthetist, and defendant Thompson, the special nurse, were employees of Dr. Swift and not of the other doctors. But we do not believe that either the number or relationship of the defendants alone determines whether the doctrine of res ipsa loquitur applies. Every defendant in whose custody the plaintiff was placed for any period was bound to exercise ordinary care to see that no unnecessary harm came to him and each would be liable for failure in this regard. Any defendant who negligently injured him, and any defendant charged with his care who so neglected him as to allow injury to occur, would be liable. The defendant employers would be liable for the neglect of their employees and the doctor in charge of the operation would be liable for the negligence of those who became his temporary servants for the purpose of assisting in the operation.

In this connection, it should be noted that while the assisting physicians and nurses may be employed by the hospital, or engaged by the patient, they normally become the temporary servants or agents of the surgeon in charge while the operation is in progress, and liability may be imposed upon him for their negligent acts under the doctrine of respondeat superior. Thus a surgeon has been held liable for the negligence of an assisting nurse who leaves a sponge or other object inside a patient, and the fact that the duty of seeing that such mistakes do not occur is delegated to others does not absolve the doctor from responsibility for their negligence. . . .

It may appear at the trial that, consistent with the principles outlined above, one or more defendants will be found liable and others absolved, but this should not preclude the application of the rule of res ipsa loquitur. The control, at one time or another, of one or more of the various agencies or instrumentalities which might have harmed the plaintiff was in the hands of every defendant or of his employees or temporary servants. This, we think, places upon them the burden of initial explanation. Plaintiff was rendered unconscious for the purpose of undergoing surgical treatment by the defendants; it is manifestly unreasonable for them to insist that he identify any one of them as the person who did the alleged negligent act.

The other aspect of the case which defendants so strongly emphasize is that plaintiff has not identified the instrumentality any more than he has the particular guilty defendant. Here, again, there is a misconception which, if carried to the extreme for which defendants contend, would unreasonably limit the application of the res ipsa loquitur rule. It should be enough that the plaintiff can show an injury resulting from an external force applied while he lay unconscious in the hospital; this is as clear a case of identification of the instrumentality as the plaintiff may ever be able to make.

[The court then discusses a series of precedents.]

In the face of these examples of liberalization of the tests for res ipsa loquitur, there can be no justification for the rejection of the doctrine in the instant case. As pointed out above, if we accept the contention of defendants herein, there will rarely be any compensation for patients injured while unconscious. A hospital today conducts a highly integrated system of activities, with many persons contributing their efforts. There may be, e.g., preparation for surgery by nurses and interns who are employees of the hospital; administering of an anesthetic by a doctor who may be an employee of the hospital, an employee of the operating surgeon, or an independent contractor; performance of an operation by a surgeon and assistants who may be his employees, employees of the hospital, or independent contractors; and post surgical care by the surgeon, a hospital physician, and nurses. The number of those in whose care the patient is placed is not a good reason for denying him all reasonable opportunity to recover for negligent harm. It is rather a good reason for re-examination of the statement of legal theories which supposedly compel such a shocking result.

We do not at this time undertake to state the extent to which the reasoning of this case may be applied to other situations in which the doctrine of res ipsa loquitur is invoked. We merely hold that where a plaintiff receives unusual injuries while unconscious and in the course of medical treatment, all those defendants who had any control over his body or the instrumentalities which might have caused the injuries may properly be called upon to meet the inference of negligence by giving an explanation of their conduct.

The judgment is reversed.

NOTES

1. Conspiracy of silence. To what extent should res ipsa be used to overcome the "conspiracy of silence" among physicians?

Prosser, Selected Topics on the Law of Torts 346 (1954): "One may suspect that the courts are not reluctant to use res ipsa loquitur as a deliberate instrument of policy to even the balance against the professional conspiracy of silence; but with two exceptions the decisions give no hint of anything more than the obvious inference from the circumstantial evidence alone," citing Ybarra v. Spangard and Dierman v. Providence Hospital, 188 P.2d 12 (Cal. 1947).

Even if most physicians will not testify against fellow physicians when the evidence of liability is overwhelming, is res ipsa loquitur the answer to this problem? Note that in Ybarra v. Spangard defendants at the new trial testified that to their knowledge nothing had gone wrong in the operation. The California Court of Appeals held that the trial judge could still find for the plaintiff on the strength of the circumstantial evidence in the case. Ybarra v. Spangard, 208 P.2d 445 (Cal. App. 1949). For criticism of Ybarra v. Spangard see Seavey, Res Ipsa Loquitur: Tabula in Naufragio, 63 Harv. L. Rev. 643 (1950).

2. Common understanding and res ipsa loquitur. One of the major problems in the use of res ipsa loquitur in medical malpractice cases is whether plaintiff should be allowed to go to the jury without the benefit of expert testimony on his behalf. In general, the courts have held that he may do so when there is "common knowledge" that the harm would not have occurred without defendant's negligence, as, for example, when a hot water bottle was applied that burned plaintiff. However, when medical judgments and procedures are concerned, the common knowledge rule is difficult to apply indeed. Thus in Farber v. Olkon, 254 P.2d 520 (Cal. 1953), the plaintiff, a mental incompetent, suffered broken bones after being subjected to electroshock therapy. The court explicitly distinguished *Ybarra* treating it as a case where "plaintiff while unconscious on an operating table received injuries to a healthy part of his body, not subject to treatment or within the area covered by his operation." It then refused to apply the common knowledge test given the undisputed testimony by defendant's experts "that electroshock therapy is designed to have 'an effect upon the entire body' " in the hope that the convulsion will improve the patient's mental condition. Likewise in Salgo v. Stanford University Board of Trustees, 317 P.2d 170

(Cal. 1957), the court held that progress in medical research might well be thwarted if jurors were allowed to find negligence on the basis of their common knowledge when new procedures were tried. Accordingly, it required expert evidence to establish negligence when paralysis had resulted from a translumbar aortogram, a procedure in which the aorta is injected with fluids in order to find blockages in the circulatory system.

Other cases, however, have upheld a finding of negligence on the basis of common knowledge alone. Thus, in Bardessono v. Michels, 478 P.2d 480, 486 (Cal. 1971), plaintiff received a series of injections of cortisone and local anesthetic for the treatment of tendonitis in his shoulder. All the injections caused plaintiff excruciating pain, and shortly after their completion he developed partial paralysis. The court held that the jury was properly instructed when told that "it could infer negligence from the happening of the accident alone." The court distinguished *Salgo* and said:

> In cases in which the physician or surgeon has injected a substance into the body, the courts have followed the test that if the routine medical procedure is relatively commonplace and simple, rather than special, unusual and complex, the jury may properly rely upon its common knowledge in determining whether the accident is of a kind that would ordinarily not have occurred in the absence of someone's negligence. Whether the case falls into the category of the commonplace or the unusual must necessarily turn upon a conglomerate of medical facts; only if the facts clearly show that the procedure is so unusual and complex that the jury could not rest their understanding of it upon their common knowledge should the court refuse a tendered res ipsa loquitur instruction, based on common knowledge.

If the needle damaged one of the plaintiff's nerves, does that establish negligence, or only causation? In *Bardessono*, defendant testified that she had made the same sort of injection hundreds of times without adverse effects. How should the jury have weighed that evidence?

A sharp contrast in attitude on the use of res ipsa loquitur in medical malpractice cases is found in Greenberg v. Michael Reese Hospital, 396 N.E.2d 1088, 1094 (Ill. App. 1979), aff'd in part and rev'd in part, 415 N.E.2d 390, 397 (Ill. 1980). Plaintiff had been treated with radiation for enlarged tonsils and adenoids during the 1940s and 1950s, when such treatment was routine at Michael Reese Hospital. The treatment was discontinued when it was discovered that it could result in tumorous growths in or near the thyroid gland. The court said:

> Plaintiffs contend that res ipsa loquitur is proper in tonsillar irradiation cases because of the close parallel to radiation burn situations where res ipsa historically attends.
> . . . However, we believe that radiation burns, typically the result of an unintentional or accidental application of excess radiation, are far

different from tumor development, usually a product not of accidental overdosage but an unanticipated long term side effect of planned treatment.

The inferences to be drawn from the two types of cases are different and distinguishable. In the radiation burn cases, the reasoning takes two steps: first, that there is no medical reason to use radiation sufficient to cause extensive burns and, second, that the doctor in fact used excess radiation and therefore was negligent. Here, however, plaintiffs concede that irradiation of tonsils was a widely used therapeutic treatment, specifically chosen by the referring physician in the light of surgical dangers and poliomyelitic implications. The only possible inference which res ipsa loquitur could provide in the case at bar is that tumors, having resulted in some percentage of cases from either organic or external stimulus, are the result of negligent medical judgment. Res ipsa loquitur arises from a clearly negligent act (i.e., application of excessive doses of radiation) which leads to an almost certain outcome (radiation burns). Unlike these radiation burn cases, the original diagnostic decision to use tonsillar irradiation is at best debatably negligent. Whether or not a medical judgment to use an alternative form of therapy is legally negligent is properly contested at trial, and should not be subject to a presumption of negligence arising solely from the bad result.

The Illinois Supreme Court remanded on the res ipsa question, stating only that "we are unable to say that no set of facts can be proved which will entitle plaintiff to recover," without addressing the difference between excess radiation and tumor cases. Can res ipsa loquitur be used on the causal question of whether the radiation caused the tumors?

3. *"Conditional" res ipsa loquitur.* The doctrine of res ipsa loquitur has also been extended in recent years to actions against multiple defendants sued under different substantive theories. In Anderson v. Somberg, 338 A.2d 1, 4-5, 9-10 (N.J. 1975), plaintiff suffered serious injuries when the tip of a surgical forcep (a rongeur) broke off in his spinal canal and remained lodged there despite the efforts of defendant physician to remove it. The plaintiff brought actions against four separate defendants: against the physician, for negligence in the operation; against the hospital, for negligently furnishing a defective instrument; against the medical distributor who supplied the rongeur, on a warranty theory; and against the manufacturer of the rongeur, on a strict products liability theory. The jury returned a verdict in favor of each of the four defendants against the plaintiff; the decision was reversed by the appellate division, which held that the jury was obligated to impose liability on at least one of the named defendants. The New Jersey Supreme Court, by a four-to-three vote, applied res ipsa loquitur to this case of multiple defendants, noting that this "development represents a substantial deviation from earlier conceptions of res ipsa loquitur and has more accurately been called "akin to res ipsa loquitur," or "conditional res ipsa loquitur."

A sharp dissent mentioned the four named defendants and continued:

> There is no other defendant in the case. And yet the record is replete with testimony that other surgeons — perhaps as many as twenty — have used the rongeur during the four years that it has formed part of the surgical equipment of the hospital, and that any one or more of them may perfectly well have been responsible for so injuring the instrument that it came apart while being manipulated in plaintiff's incision or that it may have been weakened to near breaking point by cumulative misuse, entirely by persons not now before the court. In the face of this uncontroverted proof that the surgical instrument had been used upon approximately twenty earlier occasions and possibly by the same number of different surgeons, in the hands of any of whom it may have been fatally misused, how then can it be said that the wrongdoer is surely in court? There is a far greater likelihood that he is no party to this litigation at all and that his identity will never be established.

How effective is the response of the court that the defendants are free before the new trial to take further discovery and join additional defendants to the suit? Might the rongeur have broken without any party's being responsible? What if, for example, a sudden convulsion required the surgeon to quickly twist the instrument?

A more cautious attitude toward the use of res ipsa loquitur in medical malpractice cases is found in Quin v. George Washington University, 407 A.2d 580 (D.C. Ct. App. 1979). In *Quin* the decedent died of massive internal bleeding after having his spleen removed. The question was whether the bleeding was triggered by a weakness in the wall of the splenic vein or was due to improper suturing of the end of the vein during surgery. Since the evidence was divided as to the place of the injury, the court affirmed the refusal of the judge below to give a conditional res ipsa loquitur instruction, that res ipsa loquitur would apply if the source of the bleeding was found to be at the place of the suture. Are special verdicts an adequate protection against the confusion that might be created by a conditional res ipsa loquitur instruction? If so, how might one have been framed in *Quin*?

For the connections between vicarious liability and res ipsa loquitur in the medical setting see Hardy v. Brantley, 471 So. 2d 358 (Miss. 1985), infra at page 459.

4. Statutory modification of res ipsa loquitur in medical malpractice cases. Given the application of res ipsa and the common knowledge rule in recent years, it is not surprising that medical groups have sought to limit their scope. Consider the following Nevada statute (N.R.S. 41A.100 (1993)).

> Liability for personal injury or death shall not be imposed upon any provider of medical care based on alleged negligence in the perfor-

mance of such care unless evidence consisting of expert medical testimony, material from recognized medical tests or treatises or the regulations of the licensed health care facility wherein such alleged negligence occurred is presented to demonstrate the alleged deviation from the accepted standard of care in the specific circumstances of the case and to prove causation of the alleged personal injury or death, except that such evidence consisting of expert medical testimony, text or treatise material or facility regulations is not required and a rebuttable presumption that the personal injury or death was caused by negligence arises where evidence is presented that the personal injury or death occurred in any one or more of the following circumstances:

1. A foreign substance other than medication or a prosthetic device was unintentionally left within the body of a patient following surgery;

2. An explosion or fire originating in a substance used in treatment occurred in the course of treatment;

3. An unintended burn caused by heat, radiation or chemicals was suffered in the course of medical care;

4. An injury was suffered during the course of treatment to a part of the body not directly involved in such treatment or proximate thereto; or

5. A surgical procedure was performed on the wrong patient or the wrong organ, limb or part of a patient's body.

5. *The future of res ipsa loquitur.* By all accounts res ipsa loquitur is a fixed point in the law of negligence, but the question arises, whether the use of the doctrine will be on the increase or the wane given the predictable advances of technology that affect all areas of productive life. On this score the prognosis is mixed. At one level the increase in technology reduces the probability of an adverse outcome. Thus the improvement in technology for administering and monitoring anesthesia has resulted in a decline in the attendant risks of surgery. Yet precisely because the procedures are now more capable of control, in the cases that do arise the use of res ipsa loquitur may be yet more attractive, since it becomes more likely that the accidents that do occur could have been avoided by the exercise of reasonable care. The same logic can be extended to other forms of accidents as well: in earlier times, the crash of a commercial airliner was more likely to be regarded as an act of God, given the low level of instrumentation available to monitor flight and weather conditions. But the advances in technology can now be taken to increase the likelihood that the accidents that do occur could have been avoided by taking precautions. For a defense of the "counterintuitive idea" that the lower the costs of precautions the greater likelihood of using res ipsa loquitur to establish negligence, see Grady, Res Ipsa Loquitur and Compliance Error, 142 U. Pa. L. Rev. 887 (1994).

Chapter Four
Plaintiff's Conduct

A. INTRODUCTION

This chapter examines the ways in which the plaintiff's own conduct can affect his right to recover for the harm he has suffered. The question is of immediate importance once the defendant is allowed to say that the plaintiff's harm was his own fault. As is often the case with legal principles, the force of this commonsense notion resists any easy transformation into workable and clear rules.

In one sense the phrase "it was not my fault" does not raise the issues discussed in this chapter. Thus when the plaintiff is the only person involved in bringing about the accident, the defendant can say quite simply that the plaintiff was the cause of his own harm: since the plaintiff has failed to make out a prima facie case, contributory negligence and assumption of risk need never be raised as independent affirmative defenses. The defendant's objection amounts to a general denial that the defendant had anything to do with the matter, a defense which is as valid in a strict liability system as it is in a negligence system.

The argument that the plaintiff should not recover because his injury was his own fault also arises in contexts where the defendant plainly has had at least something to do with bringing about the plaintiff's harm, as when the defendant negligently runs over the plaintiff who has darted into the street from between two parked cars. Notwithstanding the plaintiff's good prima facie case, the further question now is whether the plaintiff's own involvement in bringing about the injury is sufficient to *disentitle* him in whole or in part from recovering damages.

In this chapter we will examine the two major versions of the "plaintiff's own conduct" defense: contributory negligence and assumption of risk. Contributory negligence is established when the plaintiff has not taken reasonable care, and in consequence of his default has suffered injury. At common law the plaintiff's negligence, if established on the facts, generally acted as a complete bar to recovery, subject to a number of important exceptions looking to the defendant's "last clear chance" to avoid the harm, or to his willfulness in causing it.

The second of our two defenses is assumption of risk. Unlike contributory negligence, it does not ask whether the plaintiff's conduct has inadvertently fallen below an acceptable standard of care and it does not embody in any obvious way an implicit causal component. Instead it asks whether the plaintiff has deliberately and willingly encountered a known risk created by the defendant's negligence, and holds that, if he has, he should not be allowed to recover for the consequent harm. Like the defense of contributory negligence, assumption of risk has a kind of intuitive plausibility, but has generated protracted and often bitter controversy. Its place in tort law has been passionately defended in the name of laissez-faire or individual responsibility. Just as passionately, it has been attacked as inconsistent with modern social norms of responsibility. Some have even argued that, properly understood, assumption of risk has no place at all in a mature system of tort law. See, e.g., James, Assumption of Risk, 61 Yale L.J. 141 (1952).

With the contours of contributory negligence and assumption of risk thus established, we will investigate the recent surge, both by legislation and at common law, toward comparative negligence. That principle requires that the plaintiff's negligence should not necessarily bar his cause of action, but should only reduce the amount of damages recoverable. We will have to examine, therefore, the complexities raised by the new rule, the way that comparative negligence treats the traditional doctrines of both contributory negligence and assumption of risk, and how it meshes with a strict liability system.

B.   CONTRIBUTORY NEGLIGENCE

1.   Basic Doctrine

Butterfield v. Forrester
103 Eng. Rep. 926 (K.B. 1809)

This was an action on the case for obstructing a highway, by means of which obstruction the plaintiff, who was riding along the road, was thrown down with his horse, and injured, &c. At the trial before Bayley,

J., at Derby, it appeared that the defendant, for the purpose of making some repairs to his house, which was close by the road side at one end of the town, had put up a pole across this part of the road, a free passage being left by another branch or street in the same direction. That the plaintiff left a public house not far distant from the place in question at 8 o'clock in the evening in August, when they were just beginning to light candles, but while there was light enough left to discern the obstruction at 100 yards distance: and the witness, who proved this, said that if the plaintiff had not been riding very hard he might have observed and avoided it: the plaintiff however, who was riding violently, did not observe it, but rode against it, and fell with his horse and was much hurt in consequence of the accident; and there was no evidence of his being intoxicated at the time. On this evidence Bayley, J., directed the jury, that if a person riding with reasonable and ordinary care could have seen and avoided the obstruction; and if they were satisfied that the plaintiff was riding along the street extremely hard, and without ordinary care, they should find a verdict for the defendant: which they accordingly did.

Vaughan Serjt. now objected to this direction, on moving for a new trial; and referred to Buller's Ni. Pri. 26, where the rule is laid down, that "if a man lay logs of wood across a highway though a person may with care ride safely by, yet if by means thereof my horse stumble and fling me, I may bring an action."

BAYLEY, J. The plaintiff was proved to be riding as fast as his horse could go, and this was through the streets of Derby. If he had used ordinary care he must have seen the obstruction so that the accident appeared to happen entirely from his own fault.

LORD ELLENBOROUGH, C.J. A party is not to cast himself upon an obstruction which has been made by the fault of another, and avail himself of it, if he do not himself use common and ordinary caution to be in the right. In cases of persons riding upon what is considered to be the wrong side of the road, that would not authorise another purposely to ride up against them. One person being in fault will not dispense with another's using ordinary care for himself. Two things must concur to support this action, an obstruction in the road by the fault of the defendant, and no want of ordinary care to avoid it on the part of the plaintiff.

Per Curiam. Rule refused.

Beems v. Chicago, Rock Island & Peoria R.R. Co.
12 N.W. 222 (Iowa 1882)

BECK, J. . . . . We will now consider the action of the court in overruling the [railroad's] motion for judgment non-obstante. The intestate met his death in making an attempt to uncouple the tender from a car. The special findings of the jury show that when he went between the cars to uncouple them they were moving at an improper and unusual rate of speed. Counsel for defendant insist that this finding establishes the fact of contributory negligence on the part of the intestate. The petition alleges that defendant's employees in charge of the engine were negligent, in failing to obey a direction given them by a signal made by the intestate to check the speed of the cars. The testimony tends to support this allegation. The jury were authorized to find from the testimony that deceased made two attempts to uncouple the cars while they were moving. After the first attempt he came out from between the cars, and signaled directions to check their speed; he immediately went again between the cars to make the second attempt to uncouple them. His signal was not obeyed. He was authorized to believe that the motion of the car would be checked, and he was not required to wait, before acting, to discover whether obedience would be given to his signal. The jury could have found that after the signal had been given, and after he had gone between the cars, if their speed had been checked, he would not have been exposed to danger. His act, therefore, in going between the cars after having made the signal to check their speed, was not necessarily contributory negligence. . . .

The court instructed the jury that if intestate's foot was caught between the rails and he "was thus held and run over, *without any negligence on the part of the other employees of defendant,* such as is charged in the petition, then the plaintiff cannot recover anything." The defendant asked an instruction, which was refused, to the effect that if the intestate's foot was caught between the rails the defendant is not liable, even though the jury should find the negligence charged in the petition. The instruction given is correct. If intestate was run over by reason of defendant's negligence, surely it cannot be claimed that defendant is not liable, because intestate's foot was caught between the rails. It would be a strange doctrine to hold that defendant could back its trains with unusual speed, without obeying signals to move more slowly, and thus negligently run over a brakesman, and would not be liable, for the reason that the unfortunate man was fastened to the spot by his foot being held between the rails. Whatever was the intestate's condition at the time of the accident, whether free to move, or fastened to the place, the defendant is liable if its cars were negligently driven over him.

Schwartz, Tort Law and the Economy in Nineteenth-Century America: A Reinterpretation
90 Yale L.J. 1717, 1759-1762 (1981)

Professor Friedman describes the tort defense of contributory negligence as a "cunning trap" set by courts for nineteenth-century accident victims;[310] Professor Malone argues that nineteenth-century courts frequently were aggressive in withdrawing the contributory negligence issue from the jury in order carefully to monitor industry liability.[311] These assessments are contradicted, however, by the nineteenth–century experience in New Hampshire and California.

Each state's Supreme Court from an early date accepted the traditional rule of contributory negligence as a complete defense. Both Courts were openly ambivalent about the rule, however. . . .

The California Court placed the contributory-negligence burden of proof on the defendant, and regarded a technical misassignment of the burden of proof as reversible error, even when the defendant was the Central Pacific. . . . When allocating decisionmaking between judge and jury, the New Hampshire Court specified that the contributory negligence issue could be taken away from the jury only in "extraordinary" circumstances; the California Court frequently used language almost as strong.

In administering tort appeals, the two states' Courts developed a variety of maxim-like ideas emphasizing the lenient and forgiving quality of the contributory negligence standard. Thus, a plaintiff was not required to exercise "great care" or to behave in a "very timid or cautious" way; contributory negligence was not proven by an "indiscretion" or a mere "error of judgment," let alone by a "misjudgment" in retrospect. If the plaintiff was "startled and alarmed," that was taken into account in evaluating the reasonableness of his conduct. Momentary distraction is a "most common occurrence" on city streets and "falls far short" of contributory negligence. If the plaintiff forgot what he knew about the particular danger, the Court could say that "people are liable to lapses of memory." Attenuating maxims like these were almost totally lacking in the Courts' opinions dealing with the possible negligence of tort defendants, who were frequently held to a standard of the "utmost care." Whatever, then, the symmetry in form of the doctrines of negligence and contributory negligence, they were administered under an emphatic, if implicit, double standard. . . .[333]

310. L. Friedman, A History of American Law (1973), at 411-412. According to Professor Levy, nineteenth-century plaintiffs making "a misstep, however slight, from the ideal standard of conduct," were routinely and unfairly denied recoveries. L. Levy, The Law of the Commonwealth and Chief Justice Shaw (1957) at 319. For acceptance of the doctrine of "slight" contributory negligence, see W. Prosser, Law of Torts 421 (4th ed. 1971).

311. Malone, The Formative Era of Contributory Negligence, at 151, 152, 182.

Professors Levy and Ursin — supposedly writing about California law specifically — claim that "the nineteenth-century [contributory negligence] doctrine could fairly have been called the rule of railroad and industrial immunity." Levy & Ursin, Tort Law in California: At the Crossroads, 67 Calif. L. Rev. 497, 509 (1979).

333. That is, when the conduct of the defendant and the plaintiff combined to expose the plaintiff to a major risk, the Courts subjected the defendant to a stern negligence obligation even while defining the plaintiff's contributory negligence obligation in a mild and permissive way. . . .

[Professor Schwartz then observes that a detailed analysis of the disposition of all contributory negligence cases in California and New Hampshire is consistent with the impression created by judicial language. Contributory negligence is rarely found as a matter of law; jury verdicts for the plaintiff on the issue are both frequent and usually upheld; jury verdicts for defendants are often set aside, typically because of a defect in jury instructions.]

NOTE

The scope and function of contributory negligence. Professor Schwartz continues his attack on the proposition that American tort law gave special protection to industry and corporations in Schwartz, The Character of Early American Tort Law, 36 U.C.L.A. L. Rev. 641 (1989).

Apart from the history, there has been an extensive debate over whether any defense based upon plaintiff's misconduct is needed. Within the framework of the negligence system it has been suggested that this defense may not be necessary. See W. Landes and R. Posner, The Economic Structure of Tort Law 75-76 (1987). Under the Hand formula, the argument proceeds, the defendant can always escape liability by showing that he took cost-justified precautions against accidents. The "no-negligence" defense, therefore, provides the rational defendant with all the protection needed against unwarranted suits. Notwithstanding this argument, the defense is retained because the negligence of the defendant will be hotly contested in some cases in which the negligence of the plaintiff is evident.

Where a strict liability system is in place, however, contributory negligence (or at least some defense based upon plaintiff's misconduct) is much more critical. Since the defendant may be held prima facie responsible even if he took all cost-justified precautions, the defense is necessary to limit liability when the plaintiff is in a better position to prevent the harm; otherwise a plaintiff may run extreme risks to take advantage of the defendant's strict liability. What happens to this analysis when possible errors in the application of the negligence law are taken into account?

One possible variation is to marry strict liability to a contributory negligence defense. See Brown, Toward an Economic Theory of Liability, 2 J. Legal Stud. 323, 351 (1973). Yet such a system is oddly asymmetrical. Consider the case in which two cars crash head-on when neither driver is negligent. Under the system of strict liability with contributory

---

A conventional economic analysis of the contributory negligence problem, see R. Posner, Economic Analysis of Law, 123, 124 (2d ed. 1977), would find this double standard plainly out of order.

negligence, each driver would be required to compensate the other for his loss (why?): the relative extent of the two sets of injuries, itself largely a matter of luck, would simply be reversed by legal action, since now each party would have to shoulder the other's loss. In order to escape this inelegance, it is possible to develop a system of strict liability that is based solely upon causal connections. If the prima facie case was that the defendant struck the plaintiff, then the causal defense is simply that the plaintiff blocked the defendant's right of way, as by entering an intersection when the light was red or by crossing the midline of the highway. There need be no additional proof that the violation of the rule of the road was brought about by the negligence or wrongful intention of the plaintiff. See the excerpt from H. Laurence Ross, Settled Out of Court, supra Chapter 3 at page 207. It is of course odd to speak of "strict liability defenses" to a strict liability prima facie case, since there is no obvious sense in which a person can be liable to himself. Yet once it is recognized that causal principles operate on both the plaintiff's and defendant's sides, the rules of fairness require apportionment between the causal contributions of the two parties such that in the case of the head-on collision mentioned above the crucial determinants would be the mass and the velocity of the two automobiles immediately prior to impact.

For a more complete account of the way in which cases of joint causation should be approached within a thoroughgoing system of strict liability see Epstein, Defenses and Subsequent Pleas in a System of Strict Liability, 3 J. Legal Stud. 165, 174-185 (1974).

Gyerman v. United States Lines Co.
498 P.2d 1043 (Cal. 1972)

[The plaintiff, a longshoreman in the employ of the Associated Banning Company, was injured while unloading fishmeal sacks that had just been brought into the warehouse of the defendant United States Lines. Fishmeal, it seems, is a very difficult cargo to handle because it is packaged in sacks that have a tendency to rip and spill. In order to combat this danger, several common precautions are usually taken: only 18 to 22 sacks of fishmeal are placed on any one pallet and then only three or four layers high; the sacks are "bulkheaded," or tied together, in order to prevent them from falling; and, for maximum stability, they are placed as are bricks in a wall, with no sack directly on top of another. The plaintiff had been assigned to "break down" the sacks into units that were only two pallets high. Before he began work, he noted that the sacks were not properly arranged. There were 30 sacks per pallet; the sacks were not bulkheaded; and they were not arranged in brick-like fashion. He complained to Noel, the United States Lines chief marine clerk, that it was dangerous to proceed with the work in question, but was told that nothing could be done about it.

At no time, however, did the plaintiff speak to his own supervisor, even though the union contract with his employer provided that "Longshoremen shall not be required to work when in good faith they believe that to do so is to immediately endanger health and safety" and established a grievance procedure "to determine whether a condition is safe or unsafe." During the first three days of his work an unusually large number of sacks fell off the forklift, but no harm resulted. On the afternoon of the fourth day, about 12 sacks simultaneously fell off a load that he was moving and one of them, after bumping into the others, came toward him. Although the exact physical sequence of events was never established, the plaintiff did sustain injuries to his back and legs as a result of the incident. The trial judge, sitting without a jury, found that the defendant, United States Lines, was negligent in its failure to stack the fishmeal sacks in a safe way, conduct that was also a violation of the statutory duty to furnish every employee a "safe" place of employment. He found further that the defendant's negligence was a proximate cause of the plaintiff's harm. But he also found that the plaintiff's negligence in failing to stop work in the face of a known danger barred his cause of action. After disposing of two preliminary procedural points, the appellate court then considered the effect of plaintiff's contributory negligence upon his cause of action.]

SULLIVAN, J. . . . .

3.   CONTRIBUTORY NEGLIGENCE. . . .

"Contributory negligence is conduct on the part of the plaintiff which falls below the standard to which he should conform for his own protection, and which is a legally contributing cause co-operating with the negligence of the defendant in bringing about the plaintiff's harm." (Rest. 2d Torts (1965) §463.) The question of contributory negligence is ordinarily one of fact for the determination of the trier of fact.

"A plaintiff is required to exercise only that amount of care which would be exercised by a person of ordinary prudence in the same circumstances." Where a person must work under possibly unsafe or dangerous conditions, the amount of care he must exercise for his own safety may well be less than would otherwise be required by reason of the necessity of his giving attention to his work. The burden of proving that the plaintiff was negligent and that such negligence was a proximate cause of the accident is on the defendant.

In the instant case, absent evidence of the contract governing plaintiff's employment and of the custom and practice affecting stevedoring, we doubt that the record would provide evidentiary support for the finding that plaintiff violated a standard of due care for his own safety. Considered in the light of the realities of his working life, the laborer's duty may become considerably restricted in scope. In some instances he may find himself powerless to abandon the task at hand with impunity whenever he senses a possible danger; in others, he may be uncertain as to which person has supervision of the job or control of the place of employment, and therefore unsure as to whom he should direct his complaint; in still others, having been encouraged to continue working under conditions where danger lurks but has not materialized, he may be baffled in making an on-the-spot decision as to the imminence of harm. All of these factors enter into a determination whether his conduct falls below a standard of due care.

In the case before us the standard of due care required of laborers in general is explicated by evidence of duty imposed by contract and by custom upon the particular type of laborer involved. Custom alone, of course, does not create the standard of proper diligence. "Indeed in most cases reasonable prudence is in fact common prudence but strictly it is never its measure. . . ." (The T. J. Hooper). Nevertheless, although custom does not fix the standard of care, evidence of custom is ordinarily admissible for its bearing upon contributory negligence.

[The court then reviewed the facts of the case and concluded that the evidence supported the finding that the plaintiff failed to use ordinary care for his own protection.]

We must now inquire whether defendant sustained its burden of establishing that plaintiff's failure to report the unsafe condition was a "legally contributing cause . . . in bringing about the plaintiff's harm." (Rest. 2d Torts, §463.) As previously noted, the trial court appears to have determined that plaintiff's failure was a proximate cause of his injuries because if plaintiff had reported the condition it would have been corrected.

On this issue the positions of the parties may be summarized thusly: Plaintiff argues that the burden was on defendant to prove that if plaintiff *had* reported the condition to his own supervisor instead of to defendant's supervisor, the condition would have been corrected or made safer. Defendant asserts that it was not incumbent upon it to prove that the condition complained of was correctable and that in any event there is evidence supporting the trial court's finding.

The burden of proof rests on each party to a civil action as to each fact essential to his claim or defense. A party claiming a person failed to exercise due care has the burden of proof on that issue. The burden of proving all aspects of the affirmative defense of contributory negligence, including causation, rests on the defendant, unless the elements of the defense may be inferred from the plaintiff's evidence. The burden must be met by more than conjecture or speculation. Merely because plaintiff asserts that his own negligence, if any, could not have caused his injury, does not shift to him the burden of proof on the issue. Otherwise denial of any essential element of the defense case would shift the burden of proof on that issue to the plaintiff.

"The plaintiff's negligence is a legally contributing cause of his harm if, but only if, it is a substantial factor in bringing about his harm and there is no rule restricting his responsibility for it." (Rest. 2d Torts, §465(1).) The rules determining this causal connection between the plaintiff's negligence and his harm are the same as those determining the causal relation between the defendant's negligence and the harm resulting to others.

The fundamental question, then, is whether the plaintiff, as "the negligent actor has so produced the harm to himself . . . for which he is sought to be held responsible . . . as to make the law regard his conduct as the cause of the harm. . . ." (Rest. 2d Torts, pp. 425-426.) His "conduct must be a substantial factor operating with the defendant's negligence in bringing about the plaintiff's harm. . . ." (Rest. 2d Torts, §465, com. b); that is, it must have "such an effect in producing the harm as to lead reasonable men to regard it as a cause, using that word in the popular sense, in which there always lurks the idea of responsibility. . . ." (Rest. 2d Torts, §431, com. a.)

We turn now to the facts of the case before us. It is obvious, of course, from what we have said that plaintiff did not create or maintain the dangerous and unsafe conditions of storage. The trial court found upon substantial evidence that defendant negligently maintained and operated its warehouse under those conditions. It was defendant who had control of the cargo and directed its disposition and high stacking throughout the warehouse. Defendant alone created this risk of harm which materialized in the toppling of the stacks.

Nor did the trial court find that plaintiff was negligent in his operation of the forklift or in his "breaking down" the particular stack of fishmeal whose sacks fell from the top of the load and injured him. In short there is no finding that any negligent conduct of plaintiff, operating with defendant's negligence, brought about the shifting and eventual dislodging of the sacks. According to the trial court's findings, plaintiff's negligence consisted solely in *his failure to report* the dangerous condition to his own supervisor. Our task then is to find in the record evidence showing, or from which it can be reasonably inferred, that this omission was a substantial factor in bringing about plaintiff's harm.

Defendant's theory of causation is that if plaintiff had reported the dangerous condition to his Associated Banning supervisor, that firm would have made the condition safer. An examination of the record, however, discloses no evidence establishing this theory. Indeed, although defendant vigorously asserts that the record supports a finding of proximate cause, it points to only one page of the extensive record for such evidence. At this part of the record, defendant's witness Hargett responded on direct examination to a question about what a longshoreman should do upon encountering an unsafe condition. Hargett replied that he would have to get another lot to work on or "have supervision called, . . . and we would have sent men there to take care of the situation, if he was in such a condition he couldn't operate."

In our view this testimony does not show that the stacks would have been made safer. Although it indicates that the problem would have received immediate attention, it provides no clue as to what, if anything, could have been done to break down the stacks of fishmeal more safely than by the use of forklifts. Indeed, other than the vague statement as to sending "men there to take care of the situation" no evidence at all was offered as to specific measures that would be taken. Nor does evidence as to the existence of a grievance procedure, formalized in the ILWU-PMA contract constitute proof that in the particular situation culminating in plaintiff's injury, steps would have been taken to make the situation safer. Finally the trial court's suggestions made in its memorandum of decision that the offending bags could have been removed by using ladders or having other forklift drivers remove them one at a time are not based upon evidence in the record and therefore do not support the finding. Indeed such suggestions only point up the complete lack of defense evidence in the record on this critical issue. The record does not establish that plaintiff's failure to report the dangerous condition was a substantial factor in bringing about the fall of the sacks.

In view of the foregoing we conclude that defendant did not meet its burden of proving that plaintiff's contributory negligence was a proximate cause of his injuries.

[The court then remanded the case for a retrial on the questions of the plaintiff's contributory negligence and its causal connection to the plaintiff's own harm. It noted that though the plaintiff's negligence had been sufficiently established by evidence below, the court was "not satisfied" that in the instant case the two issues were so "separate and distinct" that the issue of proximate cause could not be tried alone "without such confusion or uncertainty as would amount to a denial of a fair trial."]

The issue of defendant's negligence has been properly determined and we see no reason why it should be relitigated. Retrial should be had on the issue of plaintiff's contributory negligence (including the issue of whether such negligence, if any, was the proximate cause of the accident) and, if such issue is resolved favorably to plaintiff, on the issue of damages.

The judgment is reversed and the cause is remanded with directions for a new trial limited to the issues of plaintiff's contributory negligence and of damages. Each party shall bear his or its own costs on appeal.

WRIGHT, C.J., McCOMB, PETERS, TOBRINER, and BURKE, JJ., concurred.

NOTES

1. Contributory negligence and breach of statutory duty. Should the defense of contributory negligence be excluded in *Gyerman* because the improper stacking of the fishmeal sacks violated defendant's statutory duty to provide a safe place to work? In Osborne v. Salvation Army, 107 F.2d 929, 931-932 (2d Cir. 1939), the plaintiff, a resident of the defendant's home for unemployed and destitute men, was ordered by the defendant to clean windows from the outside, but was not furnished any of the safety equipment required under state law. The plaintiff, also obligated by the statute to observe those same safety precautions, fell and hurt himself while attempting to lift the lower section of a window. The court first decided that the plaintiff was an employee within the meaning of the safety statute (sound result? why?), and then addressed the question of whether the plaintiff's cause of action was barred by his own conduct. It observed:

> The better reasoned decisions have held that assumption of risk and contributory negligence, which the trial judge allowed to go to the jury, are not valid defenses in cases where the violation of a statute enacted for the benefit of a class of which the plaintiff is a member is involved. If the plaintiff's injuries arose from the violation, defendant's liability was absolute irrespective of any proof of negligence.
>
> It is the general rule that a plaintiff may not waive a statute enacted for his protection and that he cannot do so because of assumption of risk is clear. To bar recovery in an action brought under the statute because the plaintiff's acts contributed to his injuries would seem to render its enforcement entirely ineffective. There is no practical difference in such cases between the defense of assumption of risk and that of contributory negligence.

In Koenig v. Patrick Construction Corp., 83 N.E.2d 133, 135 (N.Y. 1948), the court offered the following justification for the rule that contributory negligence should not be a defense when the defendant is in breach of safety regulations:

> Workmen such as the present plaintiff, who ply their livelihoods on ladders and scaffolds, are scarcely in a position to protect themselves from accident. They usually have no choice but to work with the equipment at hand, though danger looms large. The legislature recognized this and to guard against the known hazards of the occupation required the employer to safeguard the workers from injury caused by faulty or inadequate equipment. If the employer could avoid this duty by pointing to the concurrent negligence of the injured worker in using the equip-

ment, the beneficial purpose of the statute might well be frustrated and nullified.

Why is it impossible for the workmen to decline employment if they think that the risks it involves are too great? Does the level of compensation offered for their services reflect the risk of their employment? Can one make the argument that individual employees are powerless when they are represented by a union that is able to bargain with the employer on safety issues?

2. *Contributory negligence and cases of custodial care.* What is the level of care to be expected of those individuals who, by virtue of being in custodial care, have demonstrated their inability to act reasonably on their own behalf? The problem is raised with suitable vividness in Padula v. State, 398 N.E.2d 548, 551 (N.Y. 1979). The two plaintiffs, inmates at the Iroquois Narcotic Rehabilitation Center, and several of their friends were able, through the negligence of the center's guards, to gain access to the center's printing room. There they found some ditto fluid, rich in methyl alcohol, which they drank after mixing it "with an orange preparation called Tang." One of the plaintiffs died and another became blind. The question was whether their contributory negligence barred their cause of action. The court of appeals held that it did not, relying heavily upon its earlier decision in Fuller v. Preis, infra at page 506, to the effect that actions done under an irresistible impulse, even without specific proof of a mental disease, do not sever causal connection. It then continued:

> [W]hatever the contributory or comparative negligence rule may ultimately be held to be as to a person under the influence of drugs in a noncustodial situation as to which we express no opinion, we think that in relation to persons in the custody of the State for treatment of a drug problem, contributory (or comparative) negligence should turn not on whether the drug problem or its effects be categorized as a mental disease nor on whether the injured person understood what he was doing, but on whether based upon the entire testimony presented (including objective behavioral evidence, claimant's subjective testimony and the opinions of experts) the trier of fact concludes that the injured person was able to control his actions.

The court was particularly impressed by the clear testimony that "not only Padula and Modaferi [the blind claimant] but six other residents drank the Ditto-Tang concoction notwithstanding that the warning [which spoke of death or blindness] had been read to them." Is any action possible against the supplier of the methyl alcohol? Might the court better hold that contributory negligence is never a defense for persons in custodial institutions?

3. *Contributory negligence and private necessity.* Suppose that the plaintiff runs into the path of a negligently speeding car on the public highway

in order to escape from a gang attack. Should the defense of contributory negligence be available to the defendant, given that the plaintiff blocked his right of way, or is the plaintiff's misconduct excused on account of the emergency? In Raimondo v. Harding, 341 N.Y.S.2d 679 (App. Div. 1973), the court reversed the decision below, noting that a "person faced with an emergency and who acts, without opportunity for deliberation, to avoid an accident may not be charged with contributory negligence if he acts as a reasonably prudent person would act under the same emergency circumstances, even though it appears afterwards that he did not take the safest course or exercise the best judgment." Is the result in *Raimondo* consistent with Vincent v. Lake Erie, supra at page 56?

4. Causation and contributory negligence. On the principal issue in the case, the relationship between contributory negligence and causation, the Restatement (Second) of Torts has the following provision:

§465. CAUSAL RELATION BETWEEN HARM AND PLAINTIFF'S NEGLIGENCE
(1) The plaintiff's negligence is a legally contributing cause of his harm if, but only if, it is a substantial factor in bringing about his harm and there is no rule restricting his responsibility for it.

(2) The rules which determine the causal relation between the plaintiff's negligent conduct and the harm resulting to him are the same as those determining the causal relation between the defendant's negligent conduct and resulting harm to others.

The complications that can arise in the application of these causal rules are perhaps best illustrated by two famous Connecticut cases. In Smithwick v. Hall & Upson Co. 21 A. 924 (Conn. 1890), plaintiff was working on a platform erected in front of defendant's icehouse, about 15 feet above the ground. This platform was fairly narrow and had a railing along it on the west side of the door where the ice was put in; but on the east side of the door it had no railing. Plaintiff was warned by defendant's foreman not to work on the east side because it was dangerous to do so. The foreman did not tell plaintiff why it was dangerous, but he had in mind the fact that he might slip and fall, because there was no railing there. While plaintiff was working on the east end of the platform, the whole front of the icehouse at that point buckled outward and the falling bricks knocked plaintiff off the platform to the ground. Defendant was clearly negligent in maintaining a defective and weakened icehouse, of which defect and danger plaintiff could have had no knowledge. Defendant opposed plaintiff's recovery of the damages he sustained on the ground that he was contributorily negligent for entering an area where he had been warned not to go. But the court, on appeal, dismissed this contention, declaring that while plaintiff, by working at the east end of the platform, may have been negligent with respect to the danger of slipping and falling, his conduct was not negligent with respect to the danger which actually occurred and, hence, could not have been a proximate cause of his injuries but was only a "mere condition" thereof. To anticipate the foreseeability language often used in proximate cause cases, the plaintiff's own harm did not "fall within the risk" of the types of injuries that generated the duty to take care in the first instance. See discussion of Wagon Mound, infra Chapter 6 at page 531.

The companion case is Mahoney v. Beatman, 147 A. 762 (Conn. 1929). Plaintiff was driving a Rolls Royce at about 60 miles per hour, while it was still daylight, on a gravel-shouldered, two-lane concrete turnpike, with a clear view in both directions. Defendant was approaching in a Nash from the other direction. He turned to speak to somebody in the back seat, and permitted the Nash to cross over the middle of the highway into plaintiff's lane. Plaintiff, in order to avoid a head-on collision, pulled the Rolls Royce partly off onto the shoulder, leaving only his left wheels on the pavement. The Nash hit and grazed the Rolls Royce's left-hand front hub cap and spare tire, causing an estimated two hundred dollars' worth of damage. The Rolls Royce proceeded for about 125 feet along the road then suddenly turned across the highway, climbed a small bank, and hit a tree and a stone wall, sustaining about $5,650 in additional damage.

The trial court, sitting without a jury, found that defendant's Nash was on the wrong side of the road, that the speed of the Rolls Royce was "unreasonable but it did not contribute to the collision which was due entirely to the negligence of the defendant," and that the speed of the Rolls Royce did, however, "materially hamper plaintiff's chauffeur in controlling the car after the collision and owing to it he completely lost control of it." Thereupon the trial court awarded "nominal damages" of $200 to the plaintiff. On appeal plaintiff was given judgment for $5,850 for damage to his car. The Supreme Court of Connecticut treated the defendant's negligence as *the* proximate cause of plaintiff's entire damage. Its opinion is a confused attempt at applying the Restatement's "substantial factor" rule of proximate cause.

In *Mahoney* the plaintiff's contributory negligence in driving too fast did not contribute to the collision, which might just as well have happened had he been driving at 45 miles per hour. Yet the speeding did obviously contribute to the balance of the damage to the Rolls Royce, since plaintiff no doubt could have brought the Rolls under control after the collision had it been traveling at a reasonable rate of speed. What result if there had been a comparative negligence statute in Connecticut at that time? See generally Green, *Mahoney v. Beatman:* A Study in Proximate Cause, 39 Yale L.J. 532 (1930), reprinted in Green, Judge and Jury 226 (1930); Epstein, Defenses and Subsequent Pleas in a System of Strict Liability, 3 J. Legal Stud. 165, 181-184 (1974).

5. *Burden of proof on contributory negligence. Gyerman* follows the universal modern rule that the defendant bears the burden of proof on the issues of contributory negligence and its causal relationship to plain-

tiff's harm. Nevertheless, a significant minority of states once required the plaintiff to establish his or her freedom from contributory negligence as a part of the basic cause of action. The rule probably arose out of confusion over the relationship between contributory negligence and proximate causation in an age when the intervening negligence of another actor, including the plaintiff, was sufficient to negative the causal connection between the defendant's negligence and the plaintiff's harm. See the discussion of the last wrongdoer rule infra at page 503, note 2. Since the plaintiff bore the burden of proof on proximate cause, it therefore followed that he had to demonstrate that his own conduct did not sever the causal connection between defendant's conduct and his injury. From that position it was but a small step to say that the plaintiff bore the burden of proof on contributory negligence.

The argument from causal intervention will only work when the negligence of the plaintiff, as in *Gyerman,* follows that of the defendant. It will not work in the reverse case, when the defendant's negligence follows that of the plaintiff.

The minority view is subject to the obvious criticism that if the burden of pleading and proving defendant's basic negligence is on the plaintiff, then by parity of reasoning the burden of pleading and proving contributory negligence should be on the defendant. Placing the burden of proving no contributory negligence on the plaintiff created unfortunate complications in wrongful death actions in which the decedent was unable to testify about the reasonableness of his conduct at the time of death. The difficulties were only compounded where there were no eyewitnesses to the accident. Some courts therefore created a special presumption that the plaintiff had exercised due care to escape this problem. That presumption was then extended to defendants who for some reason were also unable to testify at trial. Today both presumptions have been rendered obsolete by the general rule that each side now has the burden of proving the negligence of its adversary, and the few cases that have discussed the special presumption in death cases have rejected it entirely. See Rice v. Shuman, 519 A.2d 391 (Pa. 1986).

LeRoy Fibre Co. v. Chicago, Milwaukee & St. Paul Ry.
232 U.S. 340 (1914)

[As part of its business of making flax, plaintiff stored about 700 tons of straw in 230 stacks on its land. The stacks were lined up in two rows; about seventy feet from the first row and eighty-five feet from the second ran the defendant's right of way. One day a high wind carried sparks from a passing train to one of the stacks of flax located in the row farther from the tracks. The fire started by the sparks eventually spread so that all of the flax was destroyed. It was correctly found by the jury below, first, that the defendant's servants had negligently operated its locomotive by allowing it to emit large quantities of sparks and live cinders and, second, that this act of negligence was a cause of the plaintiff's harm. The jury, consistent with its instructions, also found the plaintiff guilty of contributory negligence by placing the exposed stacks within one hundred feet of the railroad's right of way. The question was whether there was any question of contributory negligence to leave to the jury at all.]

McKENNA, J. . . . The questions certified present two facts — (1) The negligence of the railroad was the immediate cause of the destruction of the property. (2) The property was placed by its owner near the right of way of the railroad, but on the owner's own land.

The query is made in the first two questions whether the latter fact constituted evidence of negligence of the owner to be submitted to the jury. It will be observed, the use of the land was of itself a proper use — it did not interfere with nor embarrass the rightful operation of the railroad. It is manifest, therefore, the questions certified . . . are but phases of the broader one, whether one is limited in the use of one's property by its proximity to a railroad or, to limit the proposition to the case under review, whether one is subject in its use to the careless as well as to the careful operation of the road. We might not doubt that an immediate answer in the negative should be given if it were not for the hesitation of the Circuit Court of Appeals evinced by its questions, and the decisions of some courts in the affirmative. That one's uses of his property may be subject to the servitude of the wrongful use by another of his property seems an anomaly. It upsets the presumptions of law and takes from him the assumption and the freedom which comes from the assumption, that the other will obey the law, not violate it. It casts upon him the duty of not only using his own property so as not to injure another, but so to use his own property that it may not be injured by the wrongs of another. How far can this subjection be carried? Or, confining the question to railroads, what limits shall be put upon their immunity from the result of their wrongful operation? In the case at bar, the property destroyed is described as inflammable, but there are degrees of that quality; and how wrongful must be the operation? In this case, large quantities of sparks and "live cinders" were emitted from the passing engine. Houses may be said to be inflammable, and may be, as they have been, set on fire by sparks and cinders from defective or carelessly handled locomotives. Are they to be subject as well as stacks of flax straw, to such lawless operation? And is the use of farms also, the cultivation of which the building of the railroad has preceded? Or is that a use which the railroad must have anticipated and to which it hence owes a duty, which it does not owe to other uses? And why? The question is especially pertinent and immediately shows that the rights of one man in the use of his property cannot be limited by the wrongs of another. The doctrine of contributory negligence is entirely out of place. Depart from the simple requirement of the law, that every one must use his property so as not to injure others, and you pass to refinements and confusing considerations. There is no embarrassment in the principle even to the operation of a railroad. Such operation is a legitimate use of property; other property in its vicinity may suffer inconveniences and be subject to risks by it, but a risk from wrongful operation is not one of them.

The legal conception of property is of rights. When you attempt to limit them by wrongs, you venture a solecism. If you declare a right is subject to a wrong you confound the meaning of both. It is difficult to deal with the opposing contention. There are some principles that have axiomatic character. The tangibility of property is in its uses and that the uses by one owner of his property may be limited by the wrongful use of another owner of his, is a contradiction. But let us pass from principle to authority. . . .

HOLMES, J., partially concurring. . . . If a man stacked his flax so near to a railroad that it obviously was likely to be set fire to by a well-managed train, I should say that he could not throw the loss upon the road by the oscillating result of an inquiry by the jury whether the road had used due care. I should say that although of course he had a right to put his flax where he liked upon his own land, the liability of the railroad for a fire was absolutely conditioned upon the stacks being at a reasonably safe distance from the train. . . .

If I am right so far, a very important element in determining the right to recover is whether the plaintiff's flax was so near to the track as to be in danger from even a prudently managed engine. Here certainly, except in a clear case, we should call in the jury. I do not suppose that anyone would call it prudent to stack flax within five feet of the engines or imprudent to do it at a distance of half a mile, and it would not be absurd if the law ultimately should formulate an exact measure, as it has tended to in other instances; but at present I take it that if the question I suggest be material we should let the jury decide whether seventy feet was too near by the criterion that I have proposed. . . .

I do not think we need trouble ourselves with the thought that my view depends upon differences of degree. The whole law does so as soon as it is civilized. Negligence is all degree — that of the defendant here degree of the nicest sort; and between the variations according to distance that I suppose to exist and the simple universality of the rules in the Twelve Tables or the Leges Barbarorum, there lies the culture of two thousand years.

I am authorized to say that the Chief Justice concurs in the opinion that I express.

NOTE

Reciprocal causation. LeRoy Fibre illustrates the close connection between the conceptions of property rights and causation. In the Court's
view, the issue of contributory negligence cannot arise because the
plaintiff (even by stacking his flax close to the tracks) has done nothing
to invade physically the right of way owned by the railroad. The case is
thus similar to Smith v. Kenrick, supra Chapter 2 at page 127, where it
was held that a mine owner was under no duty to erect a barrier to keep
"foreign" water discharged by the defendant from flooding his mine.
Holmes' dissenting opinion stresses less the physical invasion (here by
plaintiff of defendant's property) and more the cheaper precautions
that the plaintiff could take to prevent the fire. His position had in fact
received a fair bit of support in some of the earlier nineteenth-century
cases that dealt with the duties of farmers to minimize their losses from
fires set by passing locomotives. Thus, in Kansas Pacific Ry. v. Brady, 17
Kan. 380, 386 (1877), the defendant railroad set fire to plaintiff's hay,
which was stacked between one and one-half and two miles away from
the tracks. The court first found that there was evidence of defendant's
negligence in the operation of the train, and then turned to the question of contributory negligence:

> If the defendant was negligent at all as against the plaintiffs, it was
> really as much because said hay was stacked in a dangerous place, and
> because dry grass was allowed to intervene all the way from the stack to
> the railway track, as because said fire was permitted to escape. Now as the
> burning of said hay was the result of the acts and omissions of both the
> plaintiffs and the defendant, it would seem that the acts and omissions
> of both parties should have been submitted to the jury. Both parties may
> have been negligent, and the acts and omissions of both should have
> been subject to the scrutiny of the jury. But it is claimed that the plaintiffs
> could not under any circumstances be considered negligent. It is claimed
> that they had a right to stack their hay as they did stack it, in a dangerous
> place, with dry grass all around it, and without taking any precautions for
> its protection. And this is claimed upon the theory that every man has a
> right to use his own property as he pleases without reference to the great
> inconvenience he may thereby impose upon others. Is this theory, or
> rather the plaintiffs' application thereof, correct? . . . Why should any
> person be allowed to invite the destruction of his own property by his
> own negligence, so that he might by recovering for the loss thereof lessen
> the estate of another to that extent? Why should any person be allowed
> to so use his own property that in the natural course of things he would
> most likely injure the estate of another to the extent of the value of such
> property? Or, why should he have it within his power to so use his own
> property as to make it so hazardous for others to use theirs that such
> others must necessarily abandon the use of theirs?

In Svea Insurance Co. v. Vicksburg, S. & P. Ry., 153 F. 773 (W.D. La.
1907), the court noted that fire cases required the jury to take into

account the "reciprocal duties" of both parties. This theme of reciprocity has received its most famous elaboration in Coase, The Problem of Social Cost, 3 J.L. & Econ. 1, 2 (1960).

> The question is commonly thought of as one in which *A* inflicts harm on *B* and what has to be decided is: how should we restrain *A*? But this is wrong. We are dealing with a problem of a reciprocal nature. To avoid the harm to *B* would inflict harm on *A*. The real question that has to be decided is: should *A* be allowed to harm *B* or should *B* be allowed to harm *A*? The problem is to avoid the more serious harm. I instanced . . . the case of a confectioner the noise and vibrations from whose machinery disturbed a doctor in his work. To avoid harming the doctor would inflict harm on the confectioner. The problem posed by this case was essentially whether it was worth while, as a result of restricting the methods of production which could be used by the confectioner, to secure more doctoring at the cost of a reduced supply of confectionery products. Another example is afforded by the problem of straying cattle which destroy crops on neighbouring land. If it is inevitable that some cattle will stray, an increase in the supply of meat can only be obtained at the expense of a decrease in the supply of crops. The nature of the choice is clear: meat or crops. What answer should be given is, of course, not clear unless we know the value of what is obtained as well as the value of what is sacrificed to obtain it. To give another example, Professor George J. Stigler instances the contamination of a stream. If we assume that the harmful effect of the pollution is that it kills the fish, the question to be decided is: is the value of the fish lost greater or less than the value of the product which the contamination of the stream makes possible.

For a general discussion of these fire cases see Grady, Common Law Control of Strategic Behavior: Railroad Sparks and The Farmer, 17 J. Legal Stud. 15 (1988), attacking the rigid property rights logic of McKenna, J., in *LeRoy Fibre*.

Derheim v. N. Fiorito Co.
492 P.2d 1030 (Wash. 1972)

[The plaintiff's car collided with defendant's truck when defendant made a left turn in violation of rules of the road. The plaintiff was not wearing a seat belt at the time of the accident. The defendant sought to introduce expert evidence at trial to establish that the plaintiff's conduct was a form of contributory negligence and should in any event be taken into account to reduce damages under the doctrine of avoidable consequences. The trial judge, however, refused to allow the defendant to amend his answer to raise the seat belt defense, and he also refused to allow the defendant's expert to testify that if the plaintiff had worn his seat belt at the time of the accident, he would not have suffered the injuries for which the suit was brought. After a verdict and judgment for the plaintiff, the case was certified for immediate hearing by the Washington Supreme Court because of its important substantive issue.]

HUNTER, J. . . . We are thus called upon to determine the rule in this state with respect to the so-called "seat belt defense." No subject in the field of automobile accident litigation, with the possible exception of no-fault insurance, has received more attention in recent years than has the seat or lap belt defense. The question being one of first impression in this state, we have reviewed the published material extensively, concluding that while the research and statistical studies indicate a far greater likelihood of serious injuries in the event of nonuse, nevertheless the courts have been inconsistent in their handling of the defense. This inconsistency seems to result from the fact that the defense does not fit conveniently into the familiar time-honored doctrines traditionally used by the courts in deciding tort cases. Thus, the conduct in question (failure to buckle up) occurs *before* defendant's negligence, as opposed to contributory negligence which customarily is thought of in terms of conduct contributing to the accident itself. While more precisely, contributory negligence is conduct contributing, with the negligence of the defendant in bringing about the plaintiff's harm, it is a rare case indeed where the distinction need be made. Furthermore, while states with comparative negligence do not have the problem to the same extent, contributory negligence in many states (such as Washington) is a complete bar to any recovery by a plaintiff — an obvious unjust result to apply in seat belt cases. The same result would be reached if the defense were presented in terms of assumption of risk, that is, that one who ventures upon the highway without buckling up is voluntarily assuming the risk of more serious injuries resulting from a possible accident proximately caused by the negligence of another.

The doctrine of avoidable consequences has been suggested as a possible solution to this conceptual dilemma, but here again, the problem is one of appearing to stretch the doctrine to fit an unusual fact pattern. As a legal theory, avoidable consequences is closely akin to mitigation of damages, and customarily is applied when plaintiff's conduct *after* the occurrence fails to meet the standards of due care. Moreover, courts have traditionally said that a defendant whose negligence proximately causes an injury to plaintiff, "takes the plaintiff as he finds him."

The practical implications of allowing seat belt evidence, has also given the courts pause. For example, most automobiles are now manufactured with shoulder straps in addition to seat belts, and medical evidence could be anticipated in certain cases that particular injuries would not have resulted if both shoulder belts and seat belts had been used. Additionally, many automobiles are now equipped with headrests which are designed to protect one from the so-called whiplash type of injury. But to be effective, its height must be adjusted by the occupant. Should the injured victim of a defendant's negligence be penalized in ascertainment of damages for failure to adjust his headrest? Furthermore, the courts are aware that other protective devices and measures are undergoing testing in governmental and private laboratories, or are on the drawing boards. The concern is, of course, that if the seat belt defense is allowed, would not the same analysis require the use of all safety devices with which one's automobile is equipped. A further problem bothers the courts, and that is the effect of injecting the seat belt issue into the trial of automobile personal injury cases. The courts are concerned about unduly lengthening trials and if each automobile accident trial is to provide an arena for a battle of safety experts, as well as medical experts, time and expense of litigation might well be increased.

These problems, legal and practical, are found in reviewing the most recent cases decided by other jurisdictions confronting the issue.

[The court then reviewed a series of very recent cases in other jurisdictions, some accepting and some rejecting the "seat belt defense," and continued:]

We believe the cases in those jurisdictions rejecting the "seat belt defense" are the better reasoned cases. It seems extremely unfair to mitigate the damages of one who sustains those damages in an accident for which he was in no way responsible, particularly when, as in this jurisdiction, there is no statutory duty to wear seat belts.

Moreover, in the state of Washington the installation of seat belts is required only in cars sold in this state manufactured after 1964. RCW 46.37.510. The problem of unequal treatment of owners and occupants of motor vehicles immediately arises. To charge a person with negligence for failure to wear an available seat belt and thereby require a mitigation of his damages resulting therefrom, would constitute preferential treatment to owners of vehicles who failed to have their cars equipped with seat belts, and passengers who knowingly enter cars not equipped with seat belts who sustained injuries. Under the proposed rule, no mitigation of their damages resulting from their failure to wear seat belts would be required. The resolution of this problem encompasses the legislative judgment of whether all vehicles on the roads or highways should be equipped with seat belts.

In addition, the state of Washington has not adopted the doctrine of comparative negligence. As viewed by the court of Alabama, the admission of evidence on the "seat belt defense" issue is tantamount to adopting the rule of comparative negligence. This poses a question of a change in public policy as to the doctrine of comparative negligence, which issue is not properly before us in this case.

For the reasons heretofore stated, we believe the trial court was correct in refusing admission of evidence on the "seat belt defense."

The judgment of the trial court is affirmed.

NOTES

1. The seat belt defense. Contrast the opinion of the Washington court in *Derheim* with the following observations of the New York Court of Appeals in Spier v. Barker, 323 N.E.2d 164, 167-168, (N.Y. 1974):

> Despite the fact that the "seat belt defense," as it is commonly known, has received extensive examination in other jurisdictions as well as several legal periodicals, it is raised as a matter of first impression in this court. We today hold that nonuse of an available[2] seat belt, and expert testimony in regard thereto, is a factor which the jury may consider, in light of all the other facts received in evidence, in arriving at its determination as to whether the plaintiff has exercised due care, not only to avoid injury to himself, but to mitigate any injury he would likely sustain. However, as the trial court observed in its charge, the plaintiff's nonuse of an available seat belt should be strictly limited to the jury's determination of the plaintiff's damages and should not be considered by the triers of fact in resolving the issue of liability. Moreover, the burden of pleading and proving that nonuse thereof by the plaintiff resulted in increasing the extent of his injuries and damages, rests upon the defendant. That is to say, the issue should not be submitted to the jury unless the defendant can demonstrate, by competent evidence, a causal connection between the plaintiff's nonuse of an available seat belt and the injuries and damages sustained . . . .
>
> Since section 383 of the Vehicle and Traffic Law does not require occupants of a passenger car to make use of available seat belts, we hold that a plaintiff's failure to do so does not constitute negligence per se. Even in jurisdictions in which some form of the seat belt defense has been adopted, the negligence per se approach has been rejected because legislation, which does not require use of the device, "cannot be considered a safety statute in a sense that it is negligence per se for an occupant of an automobile to fail to use available seat belts." (Bentzler v. Braun, 34 Wis. 2d 362, 385.) Likewise, we do not subscribe to the holdings of those cases in which the plaintiff's failure to fasten his seat belt may be determined by the jury to constitute contributory negligence as a matter of common law. In our view, the doctrine of contributory negligence is applicable only if the plaintiff's failure to exercise due care causes, in whole or in part, *the accident,* rather than when it merely exacerbates or enhances the severity of his injuries. That being the case, holding a nonuser contributorily negligent would be improper since it would impose liability upon the plaintiff for all his injuries though use of a seat belt might have prevented none or only a portion of them. Having disapproved of these two variations of the seat belt defense, we address ourselves to the defendants' contention that nonuse of an available seat belt may be con-

2. It has been intimated that reducing recovery solely in cases of nonuse of an available seat belt creates an invidious distinction. However, as one author has asserted, the distinction is not only justified but rational since the effort entailed in using an available seat belt is far less than the expense of arranging to have seat belts installed (see Comment, Self-Protective Safety Device: An Economic Analysis, 40 U. Chi. L. Rev. 421, 439). Furthermore, the distinction will eventually become academic in as much as section 383 of the Vehicle and Traffic Law requires seat belts to be installed for each passenger seat position in all new passenger cars sold or registered in New York after January 1, 1968.

sidered by the jury in assessing the plaintiff's damages where it is shown that the seat belt would have prevented at least a portion of the injuries.

As Prosser has indicated, the plaintiff's duty to mitigate his damages is equivalent to the doctrine of avoidable consequences, which precludes recovery for any damages which could have been eliminated by reasonable conduct on the part of the plaintiff (Prosser, Torts [4th ed.], §65, pp. 442-444). Traditionally both of these concepts have been applied only to postaccident conduct, such as a plaintiff's failure to obtain medical treatment after he has sustained an injury. To do otherwise, it has been argued, would impose a preaccident obligation upon the plaintiff and would deny him the right to assume the due care of others. We concede that the opportunity to mitigate damages prior to the occurrence of an accident does not ordinarily arise, and that the chronological distinction, on which the concept of mitigation damages rest, is justified in most cases. However, in our opinion, the seat belt affords the automobile occupant an unusual and ordinarily unavailable means by which he or she may minimize his or her damages *prior* to the accident. Highway safety has become a national concern; we are told to drive defensively and to "watch out for the other driver." When an automobile occupant may readily protect himself, at least partially, from the consequences of a collision, we think that the burden of buckling an available seat belt may, under the facts of the particular case, be found by the jury to be less than the likelihood of injury when multiplied by its accompanying severity.

Another objection frequently raised is that the jury will be unable to segregate the injuries caused by the initial impact from the injuries caused by the plaintiff's failure to fasten his seat belt. In addition to underestimating the abilities of those trained in the field of accident reconstruction, this argument fails to consider other instances in which the jury is permitted to apportion damages (i.e., as between an original tortfeasor and a physician who negligently treats the original injury).

The difference in position between *Derheim* and *Spier* persists today, with perhaps a majority of the cases favoring *Derheim*'s pronouncement that the failure to use a seat belt cannot be used to establish contributory negligence. See the compilation in 3 Harper, James and Gray, Torts §22.10, n.17.

2. Statutory response to the seat belt defense. The role of the seatbelt defense in tort litigation is today heavily regulated by statute, as about 30 states have adopted different regimes, most of which sharply restricted the availability of defense. For a table see V. Schwartz, Comparative Negligence (2d ed. 1986) (Appendix D, 1993 Supp. 136-137).

Washington and New York have both joined the list of states that have legislated on the issue, and each has followed the path set out in its earlier common-law decisions. Wash. Rev. Code Ann., ch. 46.61.688(6), enacted in 1986, provides categorically that failure to use a seat belt as required by statute "does not constitute negligence, nor may failure to wear a safety belt assembly be admissible as evidence of negligence in any civil action." A similar rule of inadmissibility applies to the failure to use "a separate child passenger restraint" device for children under

5 years old. Wash. Rev. Code Ann. ch. 46.61.687(3). The 1984 New York statute for its part provides that noncompliance with its seat belt law "shall not be admissible as evidence in any civil action in a court of law in regard to the issue of liability but may be introduced into evidence in mitigation of damages provided the party introducing said evidence has pleaded such non-compliance as an affirmative defense." N.Y. Veh. & Traf. Law §1229-c 8 (McKinney 1994). The Illinois statute follows the Washington rule on the nonadmissibility of contributory negligence, but regards any violation of the statute as a "petty offence, subject to a fine not to exceed $25." 625 ILCS 5/12-603.1 (1993). Louisiana shows a similar vacillation. At one point it allowed seat belt evidence in the damage phase of the trial but limited any reduction in awards to two percent. La. Rev. Stat. Ann. §32.295.1 (West 1989). Today seat belt users enjoy a ten percent discount on any fine for a moving violation. LSA-RS 32: 295 (I) (1994 Supp.)

Why should a statute call for a small fine, or a forgiveness on other fines, but preclude the use of its violation as a tort defense? Would it have been preferable for the statute to provide that any failure to comply with the commands of section(a) result in a reduction of tort damages by 25 percent, regardless of the particular circumstances of the accident?

3. *The helmet defense.* Closely allied to the question of whether individual users of automobiles should wear seat belts is the question of whether motorcyclists and their passengers should be required to wear helmets. As with seat belts, the helmet issue has both a legislative and a common-law dimension. In Dare v. Sobule, 674 P.2d 960, 963 (Colo. 1984), the court held that a defendant could not use proof that the decedent was not wearing a helmet to either bar or diminish damages after the legislature repealed its law requiring helmets in 1977 for reasons similar to those articulated in *Derheim*.

> First, a defendant should not diminish the consequences of his negligence by the failure of the injured party to anticipate defendant's negligence in causing the accident itself. Second, a defense premised on an injured party's failure to wear a protective helmet would result in a windfall to tortfeasors who pay only partially for the harm their negligence caused. Third, allowing the defense would lead to a veritable battle of experts as to what injuries would have or have not been avoided had the plaintiff been wearing a helmet.

The rise and fall of helmet statutes has been influenced by federal intervention. In 1966 the federal government tied the distribution of funds for highway construction to states' willingness to pass motorcycle helmet laws. These were introduced in 47 states by 1975, and the number of motorcycle fatalities fell by about half from about 12 per 10,000 riders to about 6 per 10,000 riders. In 1976 Congress repealed its 1966 statute; 27 states then proceeded to repeal or modify their helmet laws, so that by 1978 fatality rates climbed to about 9 per 10,000, where it has remained roughly constant until today. The recent trend has been for states to reinstitute or tighten the helmet laws. The movement has been spurred in part by the effort to reduce medical costs, which in California have totaled between $60 and $100 million in public funds alone. See generally *Bareheaded Motorcyclists Pressed Anew to Cover Up*, N. Y. Times, Jan. 14, 1989, at 16.

2.   Last Clear Chance

Fuller v. Illinois Central R.R.
56 So. 783 (Miss. 1911)

[Decedent, a man of over 70, was riding his one-horse wagon on a north-south dirt road that crossed a straight stretch of railroad track that ran perpendicular to it. The decedent had his head down; he did not stop, look or listen, and did not observe defendant's oncoming train. This train, a light one, came down the tracks one-half an hour late, faster than usual or appropriate at around 40 miles per hour. The decedent was in plain view on the track some 660 feet from the crossing, and the uncontradicted evidence was that the defendant's engineer could have stopped the light train within 200 feet. The record was silent as to what the engineer of the train did or thought when the decedent came into plain view on the tracks, but he did not slow the train down. The only signal he gave was a routine whistle-blast some 20 seconds before the train crashed into the wagon. The decedent was instantly killed. To the defense of contributory negligence, the plaintiff alleged that the defendant's servant had the last clear chance to avoid injury either by braking or promptly sounding a warning whistle. At trial judgment was given for the defendant.]

McLAIN, J. . . . The rule is settled beyond controversy or doubt, first, that all that is required of the railroad company as against a trespasser is the abstention from wanton or willful injury, or that conduct which is characterized as gross negligence; second, although the injured party may be guilty of contributory negligence, yet this is no defense if the injury were willfully, wantonly, or recklessly done or the party inflicting the injury was guilty of such conduct as to characterize it as gross; and, third, that the contributory negligence of the party injured will not defeat the action if it is shown that the defendant might by the exercise of reasonable care and prudence have avoided the consequence of the injured party's negligence. This last principle is known as the doctrine of the "last clear chance." The origin of this doctrine is found in the celebrated case of Davies v. Mann, 10 Mees & W. 545. The plaintiff in that case fettered the front feet of his donkey, and turned him into the public highway to graze. The defendant's wagon, coming down a slight descent at a "smartish" pace, ran against the donkey, and knocked it down, the wheels of the wagon passing over it, and the donkey was killed. In that case Lord Abinger, C.B., says: "The defendant has not denied that the ass was lawfully in the highway, and therefore we must assume it to have been lawfully there. But, even were it otherwise, it would have made no difference, for, as the defendant might by proper care have avoided injuring the animal and did not, he is liable for the consequences of his negligence, though the animal might have been improperly there." While Park, B., says: "Although the ass might have been wrongfully there, still the defendant was bound to go along the road at such a pace as would be likely to prevent mischief. Were this not so, a man might justify the driving over goods left on the public highway or even a man lying asleep there, or probably running against the carriage going on the wrong side of the road." It is impossible to follow this case through its numerous citations in nearly every jurisdiction subject to Anglo-American jurisprudence. For the present it will be sufficient to say that the principle therein announced has met with practically almost universal favor. It has been severely criticized by some textwriters. The groans, ineffably and mournfully sad, of Davies' dying donkey, have resounded around the earth. The last lingering gaze from the soft, mild eyes of this docile animal, like the last parting sunbeams of the softest day in spring, has appealed to and touched the hearts of men. There has girdled the globe a band of sympathy for Davies' immortal "critter." Its ghost, like Banquo's ghost, will not down at the behest of the people who are charged with inflicting injuries, nor can its groanings be silenced by the rantings and excoriations of carping critics. The law as enunciated in that case has come to stay. The principle has been clearly and accurately stated in 2 Quarterly Law Review, p. 207, as follows: "The party who last has a clear opportunity of avoiding the accident, notwithstanding the negligence of his opponent, is considered solely responsible for it". . . .

. . . The facts in the instant case show that for a distance of six hundred and sixty feet west of the crossing where Mr. Fuller was run over and injured the track was perfectly straight.; that there were no obstructions; that there was nothing to prevent those in charge of the train from seeing the perilous position of the plaintiff, and it may be that, if the engineer and fireman were on the lookout, they saw, or by the exercise of reasonable care and diligence might have seen, the perilous position of the plaintiff. No alarm was given. Nothing was done to warn the deceased of the approaching train. He evidently was unconscious of its approach.

The only warning that was given him was too late to be of any benefit whatever, as the train was upon him at the time the two short blasts of the whistle were given. . . . Even if the engineer had not made an effort to stop or check his train, but had contented himself with given the alarm at the point when he did see, or could have seen by the exercise of reasonable care on his part, the catastrophe in all probability could have been averted.

It must be observed that this is not the case of a pedestrian who approaches or who is on the track. In such cases the engineer has the right ordinarily to act upon the assumption that the party will get out of danger., Mr. Fuller was in a wagon, and the engineer could have seen that he was going to cross the track, and could only with difficulty extricate himself from his perilous position. . . .

Reversed and remanded

American Law Institute, Restatement (Second) of Torts
(1966)

§479.   LAST CLEAR CHANCE: HELPLESS PLAINTIFF

A plaintiff who has negligently subjected himself to a risk of harm from the defendant's subsequent negligence may recover for harm caused thereby if, immediately preceding the harm,

(a) the plaintiff is unable to avoid it by the exercise of reasonable vigilance and care, and

(b) the defendant is negligent in failing to utilize with reasonable care and competence his then existing opportunity to avoid the harm, when he

(i) knows of the plaintiff's situation and realizes or has reason to realize the peril involved in it or

(ii) would discover the situation and thus have reason to realize the peril, if he were to exercise the vigilance which it is then his duty to the plaintiff to exercise.

§480.   LAST CLEAR CHANCE: INATTENTIVE PLAINTIFF

A plaintiff who, by the exercise of reasonable vigilance, could discover the danger created by the defendant's negligence in time to avoid the harm to him, can recover if, but only if, the defendant

(a) knows of the plaintiff's situation, and

(b) realizes or has reason to realize that the plaintiff is inattentive and therefore unlikely to discover his peril in time to avoid the harm, and

(c) thereafter is negligent in failing to utilize with reasonable care and competence his then existing opportunity to avoid the harm.

NOTES

1. Scope of the defense. The doctrine of last clear chance enjoyed considerable influence in an earlier era when contributory defense operated as a complete bar to the plaintiff's recovery. In order to make out the defense, however, the plaintiff usually had to show that the defendant was guilty of something more than ordinary negligence, which as the Restatement implied presupposes some knowledge that the plaintiff is in peril, or "negligence so reckless as to betoken indifference to knowledge." Woloszynowski v. New York Central R.R. Co., 172 N.E. 471, 472 (N.Y. 1930). The plaintiff was able to carry that burden in the grisly case of Kumkumian v. City of New York, 111 N.E.2d 865, 868 (N.Y 1953), a wrongful death action in which the City's subway train ran over the decedent who was lying on the track some 1400 feet before the station. The train had come to a stop when its tripping device came in contact three times with something on the tracks. Each time the brakeman inspected the tracks and each time found nothing. Only after the third time did the brakeman and engineer discover the decedent's mangled corpse, "actually steaming" on the track. Froessel, J., held that the trial judge properly left the case to the jury on a theory of last clear chance:

> In the case before us, the brakes were tripped, not once or twice, but thrice. The motorman and conductor, both experienced men, made no investigation and took no corrective action until after the third stop, although there was ample time to have done so. The motorman did not so much as open the door and glance the length of his own car, but, "Without any lapse of time, except the time necessary to perform the operations," he reset the brakes immediately after each of the first two stops, an act which in itself could be found to have been sufficient to apprise him that the emergency system was in good working order.
>
> The evidence in this record would support an inference that decedent was struck successively by the tripcocks of the first, second and third cars, thus actuating the brakes. Moreover, the inference is permissible that the fatal injuries were not incurred until after the second stop and were received under the third and fourth cars of the train. . . .
>
> Surely we cannot say, as a matter of law, under the last clear chance doctrine, that the motorman and conductor were not negligent in *twice* disregarding the emergency equipment, which is not placed in service to be ignored, and were merely chargeable with an error of judgment. At least it became a question of fact as to whether such conduct constitutes "negligence so reckless as to betoken indifference to knowledge" and whether they "ignored the warning" while there was still opportunity to avoid the accident. It matters not that they received the warning through a faultless mechanical instrumentality rather than a human agency, so long as they had "the requisite knowledge upon which a reasonably prudent man would act." The jury was entitled to find that lack of knowledge on the part of defendant's employees as to decedent's position of danger did not come about through mere lack of vigilance in observing the tracks, but rather as the result of their own willful indifference to the

emergency called to their attention by the automatic equipment, to which clear warning they paid no heed. When they did belatedly carry out their plain duty to investigate, they found decedent, and it may be inferred that they would have seen him had they carried out that duty after the second stop — still belatedly, yet in time to have saved his life. We are of the opinion that plaintiff made out at least a prima facie case under the doctrine of last clear chance.

Justice Fuld wrote a brief dissent denying the applicability of last clear chance. "Certainly, neither the motorman nor the conductor knew that any person was in peril in time to have prevented his death, and the evidence is insufficient to support the inference that they *should* have known."

2. *Sequential conduct.* Although the doctrine of last clear chance has generally been regarded as a transitional doctrine (see James, Last Clear Chance — Transitional Doctrine, 47 Yale L.J. 704 (1938)), it has remained a favorite in the law and economics movement. The problem here has been analyzed as one of trying to induce optimal levels of precaution when the actions of the plaintiff and defendant, instead of occurring simultaneously and independently of each other, take place sequentially, when the second party knows, or has reason to know, of the risk already created by the actions of the first. The situation is conveniently illustrated by Davies v. Mann, 152 Eng. Rep. 588 (Ex. 1842), so poignantly retold in *Fuller* where the plaintiff first left his donkey in plain view on the highway, only to have it run over by the defendant's wagon. When the defense of contributory negligence is made absolute, it will reduce the likelihood that the plaintiff will leave his donkey in the road in the first place, and hence the risk of accidents. Yet by the same token the contributory negligence defense reduces the incentive to the defendant to avoid killing the donkey even when that is possible.

The doctrine of last clear chance can be viewed as a rough-and-ready effort to split the difference by placing the loss where it best reduces the likelihood of an accident. When the defendant knows or has reason to know of the danger in question, the duty to take care places the loss on him. When there is no such knowledge or reason to know, the loss is left on the plaintiff. The last clear chance exception to contributory negligence applies only in a small fraction of cases, so the plaintiff can hardly count on it to protect his interests when deciding where to leave his donkey. Yet when the defendant knows or has reason to know the risk, his cost of avoidance is low, so the exception to the contributory negligence rule bites where it is likely to be most effective.

For general discussions of this problem see Shavell, Torts in Which Victim and Injurer Act Sequentially, 26 J.L. & Econ. 589 (1983); Wittman, Optimal Pricing of Sequential Inputs: Last Clear Chance, Mitigation of Damages, and Related Doctrines in the Law, 10 J. Legal Stud. 65 (1981).

C. IMPUTED CONTRIBUTORY NEGLIGENCE

Mills v. Armstrong (The *Bernina*)
13 App. Cas. 1 (H.L.E. 1888)

[Plaintiffs' decedents were employees on the SS *Bushire* when that ship collided with the SS *Bernina,* due to the mutual negligence of those in charge of and operating each ship. The trial court imputed the contributory negligence of those in charge of their ship to the decedents so as to bar their recovery under the traditional law. The court of appeals reversed the decision of the trial judge, and its decision was affirmed in the House of Lords.]

LORD HERSCHELL. . . . The question arises whether, under these circumstances, the appellants are liable. The appellants having, as they admit, been guilty of negligence from which the respondents have suffered loss, a prima facie case of liability is made out against them. How do they defend themselves? They do not allege that those whom the respondents represent were personally guilty of negligence which contributed to the accident. Nor, again, do they allege that there was contributory negligence on the part of any third person standing in such a legal relation towards the deceased men as to cause the acts of that third person, on principles well settled in our law, to be regarded as their acts, as, e.g., the relation of master and servant, or employer and agent acting within the scope of his authority. But they rest their defence solely upon the ground that those who were navigating the vessel in which the deceased men were being carried were guilty of negligence, without which the disaster would not have occurred. In support of the proposition that this establishes a defence they rely upon the case of Thorogood v. Bryan [137 Eng. Rep 452 (1849)] which undoubtedly does support their contention. This case was decided as long ago as 1849, and has been followed in some other cases; but though it was early subjected to adverse criticism, it has never come for revision before a Court of Appeal until the present occasion. That action was one brought under Lord Campbell's Act against the owner of an omnibus by which the deceased man was run over and killed. The omnibus in which he had been carried had set him down in the middle of the road instead of drawing up to the kerb, and before he could get out of the way he was run over by the defendant's omnibus, which was coming along at too rapid a pace to be able to pull up. The learned judge directed the jury that "if they were of opinion that want of care on the part of the driver of Barber's omnibus in not drawing up to the kerb to put the deceased down, or any want of care on the part of the deceased himself, had been conducive to the injury, in either of those cases — notwithstanding the defendant, by her servant, had been guilty of negligence — their verdict must be for the defendant." The jury gave a verdict for the defendant, and the question was then raised, on a rule for a new trial on the ground of misdirection, whether the ruling of the learned judge was right. The Court held that it was.

It is necessary to examine carefully the reasoning by which this conclusion was arrived at. Coltman, J., said: "It appears to me that, having trusted the party by selecting the particular conveyance, the plaintiff has so far identified himself with the owner and her servants, that if any injury results from their negligence, he must be considered a party to it. In other words, the passenger is so far identified with the carriage in which he is travelling, that want of care of the driver will be a defence of the driver of the carriage which directly caused the injury." [The other two judges agreed, for the same reasons.]

With the utmost respect for these eminent judges, I must say that I am unable to comprehend this doctrine of identification upon which they lay so much stress. In what sense is the passenger by a public stagecoach, because he avails himself of the accommodation afforded by it, identified with the driver? The learned judges manifestly do not mean to suggest (though some of the language used would seem to bear that construction) that the passenger is so far identified with the driver that the negligence of the latter would render the former liable to third persons injured by it. I presume that they did not even mean that the identification is so complete as to prevent the passenger from recovering against the driver's master: though if "negligence of the owner's servants is to be considered negligence of the passenger," or if he "must be considered a party" to their negligence, it is not easy to see why it should not be a bar to such an action. In short, as far as I can see, the identification appears to be effective only to the extent of enabling another person whose servants have been guilty of negligence to defend himself by the allegation of contributory negligence on the part of the person injured. But the very question that had to be determined was, whether the contributory negligence of the driver of the vehicle was a defence as against the passenger when suing another wrongdoer. To say that it is a defence because the passenger is identified with the driver, appears to me to beg the question, when it is not suggested that this identification results from any recognised principles of law, or has any other effect than to furnish that defence, the validity of which was the very point in issue. Two persons may no doubt be so bound together by the legal relation in which they stand to each other, that the acts of one may be regarded by the law as the acts of the other. But the relation between the passenger in a public vehicle, and the driver of it, certainly is not such as to fall within any of the recognised categories in which the act of one man is treated in law as the act of another.

I pass now to the other reasons given for the judgment in Thorogood v. Bryan. Maule, J., says: "On the part of the plaintiff it is suggested that a passenger in a public conveyance has no control over the driver. But I think that cannot with propriety be said. He selects the conveyance. He enters into a contract with the owner, whom by his servant, the driver, he employs to drive him. If he is dissatisfied with the mode of conveyance he is not obliged to avail himself of it. . . . But, as regards the present plaintiff, he is not altogether without fault; he chose his own conveyance, and must take the consequences of any default on the part of the driver whom he thought fit to trust."

I confess I cannot concur in this reasoning. I do not think it well founded either in law or in fact. What kind of control has the passenger over the driver which would make it reasonable to hold the former affected by the negligence of the latter? And is it any more reasonable to hold him so affected because he chose the mode of conveyance, that is to say, drove in an omnibus rather than walked, or took the first omnibus that passed him instead of waiting for another? And when it is attempted to apply this reasoning to passengers travelling in steam-ships or on railways, the unreasonableness of such a doctrine is even more glaring.

The only other reason given is contained in the judgment of Cress-well, J., in these words: "If the driver of the omnibus the deceased was in had by his negligence or want of due care and skill contributed to an injury from a collision, his master clearly could maintain no action. And I must confess I see no reason why a passenger who employs the driver to convey him stands in any better position." Surely, with defer-ence, the reason for the difference lies on the very surface. If the master in such a case could maintain no action, it is because there existed between him and the driver the relation of master and servant. It is clear that if his driver's negligence alone had caused the collision, he would have been liable to an action for the injury resulting from it to third parties. The learned judge would, I imagine, in that case have seen a reason why a passenger in the omnibus stood in a better position than the master of the driver. I have now dealt with all the reasons on which the judgment in Thorogood v. Bryan was founded, and I entirely agree with the learned judges in the Court below in thinking them inconclusive and unsatisfactory.

NOTES

1. American response to Thorogood v. Bryan. American courts first adopted both the argument and the results of the English court in Thorogood v. Bryan. As the years passed, however, the rule was sub-jected to constant criticism and, for reasons much like those that per-suaded the House of Lords in Mills v. Armstrong, state after state repudiated it. Today the general rule in virtually all jurisdictions is that the negligence of the driver will not be imputed to the passenger, in the usual collision case, by virtue of the driver-passenger relationship alone.

2. *Joint enterprise and the "both ways test."* While the rule in Mills v. Armstrong is the law today everywhere, it is generally subject to one exception of great importance. When the defendant can establish that the passenger and the driver have entered into some relationship that makes the passenger vicariously liable for the torts of the driver, then the courts may impute the negligence of the driver to the passenger. Although a joint enterprise could conceivably be found from the simple driver-passenger relationship, the courts have tended to construe the requirements of a joint enterprise narrowly, sometimes dwelling on the "community of interest" that such an enterprise presupposes. See Restatement (Second) of Torts §491, comments *b* & *g*.

The hostile attitude toward the joint enterprise rule is well illustrated by Dashiell v. Keauhou-Kona Co., 487 F.2d 957, 959-961 (9th Cir. 1973). There Mr. Dashiell was injured, partly through the negligence of his wife, who was driving a golf cart in which he was a passenger. The defendant, whose negligence was established, sought to take advantage of the joint enterprise defense, but the court by a vote of two to one reversed the judgment given the defendant below, holding the joint enterprise defense inapplicable as a matter of law:

> We find that on the facts of this case, at no time did the relationship of joint enterprise or joint venture exist between Mr. and Mrs. Dashiell within the meaning of imputed negligence. This is not a typical case of a business venture of a character similar to a partnership where two or more parties undertake, for some pecuniary purpose, a contractual obligation resulting in the liability of each for the negligence of the other. . . .
>
> Additionally, applying the concept of imputed contributory negligence to the facts of this case would needlessly frustrate some basic policies of tort law. Mr. Dashiell was found by the jury to be blameless, and since negligence law is based on personal fault, it would be both illogical and inequitable to deny him recovery unless he were under a duty to control the actions of Mrs. Dashiell as she drove the golf cart. The record reflects no basis on which to find any duty of control. The original purpose of defining the joint enterprise relationship was vicarious liability, in order to increase the number of those liable to provide a financially responsible person to injured third parties. That purpose is absent when related to the Dashiells; in fact, application of the imputed contributory negligence rule would have the opposite effect of freeing from liability another party who is at fault even though the person denied recovery is blameless.

The decision in *Dashiell* reflects the modern dissatisfaction with the once fashionable "both ways test," which essentially held that if *A* could be held vicariously liable for the torts of *B*, then the contributory negligence of *B* should be imputed to *A* in order to bar *A*'s recovery. Should Mr. Dashiell be vicariously liable if Mrs. Dashiell had injured the defendant? What result in *The Bernina* under the both ways test?

3. *Imputed negligence in parent-child cases.* In Hartfield v. Roper, 21 Wend. 615, 618-619 (N.Y. 1839), the court held that the action of a 2- or 3-year-old infant was barred by the negligence of his parents in allowing him to wander into a roadway, where he was struck and injured by a sleigh driven by the defendants Roper and Newall. The court ventured the opinion that it was both "folly and gross neglect" for the child's parents to allow him to wander into the road. While conceding that such parental foolishness could not excuse or justify either the voluntary injury or gross neglect of the defendants, the court nonetheless concluded that the plaintiff could not recover:

> The child has a right to the road for the purposes of travel, attended by the proper escort. But at the tender age of two or three years, and even more, the infant cannot personally exercise that degree of discretion, which becomes instinctive at an advanced age, and for which the law must make him responsible, through others, if the doctrine of mutual care between the parties using the road is to be enforced at all in his case. It is perfectly well settled, that, if the party injured by a collision on the highway has drawn the mischief upon himself by his own neglect, he is not entitled to an action, even though he be lawfully in the highway pursuing his travels, which can scarcely be said of a toppling infant, suffered by his guardians to be there, either as a traveller or for the purpose of pursuing his sports. The application may be harsh when made to small children; as they are known to have no personal discretion, common humanity is alive to their protection; but they are not, therefore, exempt from the legal rule, when they bring an action for redress; and there is no other way of enforcing it, except by requiring due care at the hands of those to whom the law and the necessity of the case has delegated the exercise of discretion. An infant is not *sui juris*. He belongs to another, to whom discretion in the care of his person is exclusively confided. That person is keeper and agent for this purpose; and in respect to third persons, his act must be deemed that of the infant; his neglect, the infant's neglect. Suppose a hopeless lunatic suffered to stray by his committee, lying in the road like a log, shall the traveller, whose sleigh unfortunately strikes him, be made amenable in damages? The neglect of the committee to whom his custody is confided shall be imputed to him. It is a mistake to suppose that because the party injured is incapable of personal discretion, he is, therefore, above all law. An infant or lunatic is liable personally for wrongs which he commits against the person and property of others. And when he complains of wrongs to himself, the defendant has a right to insist that he should not have been the heedless instrument of his own injury. He cannot, more than any other, make a profit of his own wrong. *Volenti non fit injuria.* If his proper agent and guardian has suffered him to incur mischief, it is much more fit that he should look for redress to that guardian, than that the latter should negligently allow his ward to be in the way of travellers, and then harass them in courts of justice, recovering heavy verdicts for his own misconduct.

The decision in *Hartfield* was roundly denounced by Prosser as one of those "bleak decisions that have here and there marred the face of our law." Prosser and Keeton, Torts 531, and has been repudiated by either common-law decision or statute in virtually all jurisdictions. New York, for example, overturned the rule by statute in 1935. N. Y. Dom. Rel. Law §73, now N.Y. Gen. Oblig. Law §3-111 (McKinney 1989). More recent cases illustrate the same hostility. See generally Gregory, Vicarious Responsibility and Contributory Negligence, 41 Yale L.J. 831 (1932); 2 Harper, James and Gray, Torts ch. 23.

D. ASSUMPTION OF RISK

Lamson v. American Axe & Tool Co.
58 N.E. 585 (Mass. 1900)

Tort, under the employers' liability act, St. 1887, c. 270, for personal injuries occasioned to the plaintiff while in the defendant's employ. Trial in the Superior Court, before Lawton, J., who directed the jury to return a verdict for the defendant; and the plaintiff alleged exceptions, which appear in the opinion.

HOLMES, C. J. This is an action for personal injuries caused by the fall of a hatchet from a rack in front of which it was the plaintiff's business to work at painting hatchets, and upon which the hatchets were to be placed to dry when painted. The plaintiff had been in the defendant's employment for many years. About a year before the accident new racks had been substituted for those previously in use, and it may be assumed that they were less safe and were not proper, but were dangerous on account of the liability of the hatchets to fall from the pegs upon the plaintiff when the racks were jarred by the motion of machinery near by. The plaintiff complained to the superintendent that the hatchets were more likely to drop off than when the old racks were in use, and that now they might fall upon him, which they could not have done from the old racks. He was answered in substance that he would have to use the racks or leave. The accident which he feared happened, and he brought this suit.

The plaintiff, on his own evidence, appreciated the danger more than any one else. He perfectly understood what was likely to happen. That likelihood did not depend upon the doing of some negligent act by people in another branch of employment, but solely on the permanent conditions of the racks and their surroundings and the plaintiff's continuing to work where he did. He complained, and was notified that he could go if he would not face the chance. He stayed and took the risk. . . . He did so none the less that the fear of losing his place was one of his motives.

Exceptions overruled.

NOTES

1. The fellow servant rule. The decision of the Massachusetts Supreme Judicial Court represents only one manifestation of the assumption of risk defense in the area of its birth, the law of industrial accidents. Nearly 60 years before, Chief Justice Shaw (following the English decision of Priestly v. Fowler, 150 Eng. Rep. 1030 (Ex. 1837)) had endorsed that rule in one of its most demanding forms, the fellow servant rule — also known as the doctrine of common employment. Farwell v. Boston & Worcester R.R. Corp., 45 Mass. 49, 58-59 (1842). In *Farwell* the defendant employed the plaintiff as an engineer. While engaged in his work, the plaintiff lost his right hand when another of the defendant's servants carelessly threw the wrong switch down the line. The employer had not been negligent in the selection and supervision of the "trusty" switchman. The question before the court was whether the railroad could be charged with the negligence of its employee in an action brought by that employee's fellow servant. Shaw conceded that the principle of vicarious liability could be used against the railroad by a *stranger* injured by its servant. But he denied that the principle applied to the plaintiff, who in his view had assumed the risk: "the implied contract of the master does not extend to indemnify the servant against the negligence of anyone but himself." Shaw then contrasted the position of an employee with that of a passenger:

> The liability of passenger carriers is founded on similar considerations. They are held to the strictest responsibility for care, vigilance and skill, on the part of themselves and all persons employed by them, and they are paid accordingly. The rule is founded on the expediency of throwing the risk upon those who can best guard against it. Story on Bailments, §590 et seq.

Shaw then concluded as follows:

> In applying these principles to the present case, it appears that the plaintiff was employed by the defendants as an engineer, at the rate of wages usually paid in that employment, being a higher rate than the plaintiff had before received as a machinist. It was a voluntary undertaking on his part, with a full knowledge of the risks incident to the employment; and the loss was sustained by means of an ordinary casualty, caused by the negligence of another servant of the company. Under these circumstances, the loss must be deemed to be the result of a pure accident,

like those to which all men, in all employments, and at all times, are more or less exposed; and like similar losses from accidental causes, it must rest where it first fell, unless the plaintiff has a remedy against the person actually in default; of which we give no opinion.

The fellow servant rule was, if anything, far more uncompromising than the assumption of risk rule in *Lamson*. In *Farwell*, for example, the risk was assumed by status alone, since the plaintiff was in total ignorance of the dangerous condition that could cause harm. In an unavailing effort to limit the impact of the fellow servant rule, the plaintiff's counsel in *Farwell* sought to limit it to the conditions applicable in Priestly v. Fowler, where the two servants (jointly loading a butcher's wagon) were in face-to-face contact, and not under the immediate supervision of their common employer. But Shaw resisted any compromise of the basic principle, holding that the rule applied to employees who worked in "different departments" of the same business, however defined.

The common employment rule did not long retain the pristine simplicity it possessed in *Farwell*. Of the many exceptions to the rule, perhaps the most important is the "vice-principal" exception, whereby certain duties of the employer discharged by supervisory personnel were regarded as nondelegable: the duty to supply the proper equipment, to furnish a safe work place, and the like. The precise delineation of this exception created large numbers of inconsistent judicial decisions, collected in C. Labatt, Master and Servant §§1433-1553 (2d ed. 1913). Indeed the whole vice-principal exception was in fact repudiated in England, by Lord Cairns, in the celebrated (or infamous) case of Wilson v. Merry, 1 L.R.-S. & D. App. 326 (1868), which reaffirmed *Priestly* in its original rigor.

The compromises with the basic principle did not, however, satisfy the critics of the fellow servant rule. See 1 T. G. Shearman and A. A. Redfield, Negligence vi, vii (5th ed. 1898), in which the authors said:

> A small number of able judges, devoted, from varying motives, to the supposed interests of the wealthy classes, and caring little for any others, boldly invented an exception to the general rule of masters' liability, by which servants were deprived of its protection. Very appropriately, this exception was first announced in South Carolina, then the citadel of human slavery. It was eagerly adopted in Massachusetts, then the centre of the factory system, where some decisions were then made in favor of great corporations, so preposterous that they have been disregarded in every other State, without even the compliment of refutation. It was promptly followed in England, which was then governed exclusively by landlords and capitalists. . . .
>
> As the courts, while asserting unlimited power to create new and bad law, denied their power to correct their own errors, the legislature intervened, and to a large extent the whole defence of "common employment" has been taken away in Great Britain. And now, not a single voice

is raised in Great Britain in justification of the doctrine once enforced by the unanimous opinions of the English courts. The infallible Chief Justice Shaw and Chancellor Cairns have fallen so low, on *this* point at least, that "there are none so poor as to do them reverence. . . ."

That same view has been voiced by twentieth-century writers as well. See L. Friedman, A History of American Law 413, 414 (1973); see also Schwartz, Tort Law and the Economy in Nineteenth-Century America: A Reinterpretation, 90 Yale L.J. 1717, 1768-1775 (1981). For a defense of the rule on the contractual grounds originally advanced by Shaw see Posner, A Theory of Negligence, 1 J. Legal Stud. 29, 67-71 (1972).

2. *Employer liability acts.* In order to understand *Lamson* it should be noted that his action was brought not at common law, but under the Massachusetts Employers' Liability Act. Based on an English statute of the same name (43 Vict. c. 42 (1880)), the act, among other things, introduced a general principle of negligence liability and abolished the fellow servant rule. See generally Epstein, The Historical Origins and Economic Structure of Workers' Compensation Law, 16 Ga. L. Rev. 775 (1982). Rejection of the fellow servant rule did not, however, by itself delineate the substitute rules of employer's liability. Assumption of risk as defined in *Lamson*, like its parallel in England (see, e.g., Thomas v. Quartermaine, 18 Q.B.D. 685 (1887); Smith v. Baker, [1891] A.C. 325), quickly became part of new law pertaining to actions brought under the Employers' Liability Act as well as actions brought at common law.

The newer versions of assumption of risk, however, depended critically upon the continued willingness to work in the face of known risks. In St. Louis Cordage v. Miller, 126 F. 495 (1903), Sanborn, J., urged a classic defense of the doctrine on freedom of contract grounds. Lord Bramwell took a similar stance in Smith v. Baker & Sons, [1891] A.C. 325, 344, where the plaintiff, while engaged in his employment, was injured when a stone that was being lifted over his head fell and hit him. The House of Lords accepted the plaintiff's contention that he did not assume the risk because he did not have specific knowledge that he was about to be struck, but Bramwell, that staunch and unreconstructed defender of laissez-faire, dissented, putting his case in the language of the bargain.

It is a rule of good sense that if a man voluntarily undertakes a risk for a reward which is adequate to induce him, he shall not, if he suffers from the risk, have a compensation for which he did not stipulate. He can, if he chooses, say, "I will undertake the risk for so much, and if hurt, you must give me so much more, or an equivalent for the hurt." But drop the maxim. Treat it as a question of bargain. The plaintiff here thought the pay worth the risk, and did not bargain for a compensation if hurt: in effect, he undertook the work, with its risks, for his wages and no more. He says so. Suppose he had said, "If I am to run this risk, you must give me 6*s.* a day and not 5*s.*," and the master agreed, would he in reason have a claim if he got hurt? Clearly not. What difference is there if the master says, "No I will only give you 5s."? None. I am ashamed to argue it.

How does Bramwell know that the bargain between the parties precluded compensation in the event of injury? How could he, or the majority of the House of Lords, find out whether it did? In one sense, the latent issue in *Smith* was not whether this plaintiff had assumed the risk in question, but whether he would as a matter of law be allowed to assume it. The movement toward limiting or banning the assumption of risk defense in industrial accident cases moved by degrees, and culminated in its abolition by a 1939 amendment to the Federal Employers' Liability Act (45 U.S.C.A. §54). The defense is also eliminated in suits against the employer under the standard workers' compensation statute of the sort introduced in most states shortly after the First World War. But the defense does continue to operate in actions brought against third parties not covered by these statutes. See Dullard v. Berkely Assoc. Co., 606 F.2d 890 (2d Cir. 1979) (general contractors); Gyerman v. United States Lines Co., supra at page 325 (warehouse owners), and most important, product manufacturers and suppliers. See, e.g., Micallef v. Miehle Co., infra at page 786.

At common law, how does assumption of risk differ from contributory negligence? Is it enough to say that assumption of risk is a defense even when the plaintiff's conduct is reasonable, if it is risky? See Bohlen, Voluntary Assumption of Risk, 20 Harv. L. Rev. 14, 17-18 (1906).

3. *Risk premium.* Both Shaw in *Farwell* and Bramwell in *Smith* alluded to the relationship between higher wages and assumption of the risk of injury on the job. These remarks may well be an early effort to ask whether workers engaged in dangerous employments receive a "risk premium" to cover such risk. If that premium is present, then in effect the worker has received a sum of money that "compensates" for the loss in question before it occurs. Measuring the risk premium today is a chancy business at best, and even if some premium exists, there is a further question of whether it is adequate. Some of the most careful empirical work on this question has been done by W. Kip Viscusi, Risk by Choice 43-44 (1983), who reports as follows:

> In my study of workers' subjective risk perceptions, I found that workers who believed that they were exposed to dangerous or unhealthy conditions received over $900 annually (1980 prices) in hazard pay. It is especially noteworthy that an almost identical figure was obtained when I used an objective industry injury risk measure as the risk variable. The similarity of the findings using subjective and objective measures of risk lends strong empirical support to the validity of the risk premium analysis.
>
> Unfortunately, these results do not enable us to conclude that markets work perfectly. Is the premium less or more than would prevail if workers

and employers were fully cognizant of the risks? The size of the premium only implies that compensating differentials are one element of market behavior. A more meaningful index is the wage premium per unit of risk. If it is very likely that a worker will be killed or injured, a $900 risk premium can be seen as a signal that the compensating differential process is deficient. The average blue-collar worker, however, faces an annual occupational death risk of only about 1/10,000 and a less than 1/25 risk of an injury severe enough to cause him to miss a day or more of work. Consequently, the observed premium per unit of risk is quite substantial, with the implicit value of life being on the order of $2 million or more for many workers.

The safety incentives created by market mechanisms are much stronger than those created by OSHA standards; a conservative estimate of the total job risk premiums for the entire private sector is $69 billion, or almost 3,000 times the total annual penalties now levied by OSHA. Whereas OSHA penalties are only 34 cents per worker, market risk premiums per worker are $925 annually. This figure would be even higher if we added in the premiums that are displaced by the workers' compensation system, which provides an additional $11.8 billion in compensation to workers.

Murphy v. Steeplechase Amusement Co.
166 N.E. 173 (N.Y. 1929)

CARDOZO, C.J. The defendant, Steeplechase Amusement Company, maintains an amusement park at Coney Island, New York. One of the supposed attractions is known as "The Flopper." It is a moving belt, running upward on an inclined plane, on which passengers sit or stand. Many of them are unable to keep their feet because of the movement of the belt, and are thrown backward or aside. The belt runs in a groove, with padded walls on either side to a height of four feet, and with padded flooring beyond the walls at the same angle as the belt. An electric motor, driven by current furnished by the Brooklyn Edison Company, supplies the needed power.

Plaintiff, a vigorous young man, visited the park with friends. One of them, a young woman, now his wife, stepped upon the moving belt. Plaintiff followed and stepped behind her. As he did so, he felt what he describes as a sudden jerk, and was thrown to the floor. His wife in front and also friends behind him were thrown at the same time. Something more was here, as every one understood, than the slowly-moving escalator that is common in shops and public places. A fall was foreseen as one of the risks of the adventure. There would have been no point to the whole thing, no adventure about it, if the risk had not been there. The very name above the gate, the Flopper, was warning to the timid. If the name was not enough, there was warning more distinct in the experience of others. We are told by the plaintiff's wife that the members of her party stood looking at the sport before joining in it themselves. Some aboard the belt were able, as she viewed them, to sit down with decorum or even to stand and keep their footing; others jumped or fell. The tumbling bodies and the screams and laughter supplied the merriment and fun. "I took a chance," she said when asked whether she thought that a fall might be expected.

Plaintiff took the chance with her, but, less lucky than his companions, suffered a fracture of a knee cap. He states in his complaint that the belt was dangerous to life and limb in that it stopped and started violently and suddenly and was not properly equipped to prevent injuries to persons who were using it without knowledge of its dangers, and in a bill of particulars he adds that it was operated at a fast and dangerous rate of speed and was not supplied with a proper railing, guard or other device to prevent a fall therefrom. No other negligence is charged.

We see no adequate basis for a finding that the belt was out of order. It was already in motion when the plaintiff put his foot on it. He cannot help himself to a verdict in such circumstances by the addition of the facile comment that it threw him with a jerk. One who steps upon a moving belt and finds his heels above his head is in no position to discriminate with nicety between the successive stages of the shock, between the jerk which is a cause and the jerk, accompanying the fall, as an instantaneous effect. There is evidence for the defendant that power was transmitted smoothly, and could not be transmitted otherwise. If the movement was spasmodic, it was an unexplained and, it seems, an inexplicable departure from the normal workings of the mechanism. An aberration so extraordinary, if it is to lay the basis for a verdict, should rest on something firmer than a mere descriptive epithet, a summary of the sensations of a tense and crowded moment. But the jerk, if it were established, would add little to the case. Whether the movement of the belt was uniform or irregular, the risk at greatest was a fall. This was the very hazard that was invited and foreseen.

Volenti non fit injuria. One who takes part in such a sport accepts the dangers that inhere in it so far as they are obvious and necessary, just as a fencer accepts the risk of a thrust by his antagonist or a spectator at a ball game the chance of contact with the ball. The antics of the clown are not the paces of the cloistered cleric. The rough and boisterous joke, the horseplay of the crowd, evokes its own guffaws, but they are not the pleasures of tranquillity. The plaintiff was not seeking a retreat for meditation. Visitors were tumbling about the belt to the merriment of onlookers when he made his choice to join them. He took the chance of a like fate, with whatever damage to his body might ensue from such a fall. The timorous may stay at home.

A different case would be here if the dangers inherent in the sport were obscure or unobserved, or so serious as to justify the belief that precautions of some kind must have been taken to avert them. Nothing happened to the plaintiff except what common experience tells us may happen at any time as the consequence of a sudden fall. Many a skater or a horseman can rehearse a tale of equal woe. A different case there would also be if the accidents had been so many as to show that the game in its inherent nature was too dangerous to be continued without change. The president of the amusement company says that there had never been such an accident before. A nurse employed at an emergency hospital maintained in connection with the park contradicts him to some extent. She says that on other occasions she had attended patrons of the park who had been injured at the Flopper, how many she could not say. None, however, had been badly injured or had suffered broken bones. Such testimony is not enough to show that the game was a trap for the unwary, too perilous to be endured. According to the defendant's estimate, two hundred and fifty thousand visitors were at the Flopper in a year. Some quota of accidents was to be looked for in so great a mass. One might as well say that a skating rink should be abandoned because skaters sometimes fall.

There is testimony by the plaintiff that he fell upon wood, and not upon a canvas padding. He is strongly contradicted by the photographs and by the witnesses for the defendant, and is without corroboration in the testimony of his companions who were witnesses on his behalf. If his observation was correct, there was a defect in the equipment, and one not obvious or known. The padding should have been kept in repair to break the force of any fall. The case did not go to the jury, however, upon any such theory of the defendant's liability, nor is the defect fairly suggested by the plaintiff's bill of particulars, which limits his complaint. The case went to the jury upon the theory that negligence was dependent upon a sharp and sudden jerk.

The judgment of the Appellate Division and that of the Trial Term [for the plaintiff] should be reversed, and a new trial granted, with costs to abide the event.

POUND, CRANE, LEHMAN, KELLOGG and HUBBS, JJ., concur; O'BRIEN, J., dissents.

NOTES

1. *Assumption of risk and the duty to warn.* Why did Cardozo remand the case instead of giving judgment for the defendant?

One important issue in these amusement park cases is the extent to which assumption of risk can survive the recent expansion of the duty to warn. For an instructive contrast with *Murphy,* consider Russo v. Range, Inc., 395 N.E.2d 10, 13-14 (Ill. App. 1979), where the plaintiff was injured while riding down the "giant slide" that was owned and operated by the defendant. Before he entered the amusement park, he purchased a ticket that on the reverse side read "the person using this ticket so assumes all risk of personal injury." At the top of the slide itself was a warning and instructions for the proper use of the slide. The plaintiff also admitted that he had taken several similar rides at the amusement park before the accident. Nonetheless, the court refused to award the defendant a summary judgment on the question of assumption of risk because there was no written contract that exonerated the defendant from all liability. The court stated:

> Russo alleges that he had no knowledge that the slide would cause his body to fly in the air as he rode it — the event which he says caused his injury. . . .
>
> Clearly, the Range presents a strong argument that Russo knew the risk of injury he was to encounter on the slide and that he assumed it. But that argument is based as much on inferences from the facts as it is predicated on the law. From these same facts the Range relies on it is possible to infer that Russo's ride down the slide was an abnormal occurrence caused by some danger unknown to him and a risk he did not assume. It is the presence of this possibility which precludes summary judgment.

When will a directed verdict on assumption of risk be possible given the rationale in *Russo?* Is there any parallel here between the assumption of risk defense and the treatment of informed consent?

2. *Spectator sports and assumption of risk.* A good deal of litigation turns on the risks taken by spectators who attend athletic events. One key issue in these cases concerns the extent to which the average person has an awareness of the risks associated with the game in progress. In some cases this inquiry is undertaken at a wholesale level, for the knowledge of risks is thought to be so evident that the individual plaintiff is not allowed to show a personal lack of awareness of the danger. Thus, it is generally regarded as common knowledge that spectators at baseball games may be struck by batted balls, but at one time at least it was doubted whether the ordinary person had knowledge of the risk of being struck by an errant puck at a hockey game. See Thurman v. Ice Palace, 97 P.2d 999 (Cal. App. 1939), allowing the question of assumption of risk to go to the jury when the game of hockey was "new" in California. The question of assumption of risk has come up in connection with almost every sport. For basketball see McFetridge v. Harlem Globe Trotters, 365 P.2d 918 (N.M. 1961); for wrestling see Dusckiewicz v. Carter, 52 A.2d 788 (Vt. 1947); for horse shows see Wooldridge v. Summers, 3 W.L.R. 616 (1962 C.A.); for auto racing, Celli v. Sports Club, 105 Cal. Rptr. 904 (Cal. App. 1972); for baseball, Neinstein v. Los Angeles Dodgers, Inc., 229 Cal. Rptr. 612 (Cal. 1986). See generally Harper, James and Gray §21.2 n.15.

3. *Assumption of risk in professional sports.* The extent to which professional athletes assume the risks of injury incident to their trade has also

been litigated in recent cases. In Maddox v. City of New York, 487
N.E.2d 553, 556-557 (N.Y. 1985), the plaintiff was an outfielder for the
New York Yankees whose professional career was effectively ended after
he sustained severe damage to his knee when he slipped in the "wet
and muddy" outfield while chasing after a fly ball. The suit was brought
against the Yankees as his employer, the Mets as lessees of Shea Stadium, and New York City as its owner. The plaintiff knew about the
general condition of the field, and the court held that "[h]is continued
participation in the game in light of that awareness constituted assumption of risk as a matter of law, entitling defendants to a summary judgment." The court reasoned as follows:

> There is no question that the doctrine requires not only knowledge of
> the injury-causing defect but also appreciation of the resultant risk, but
> awareness of the risk is not to be determined in a vacuum. It is, rather,
> to be assessed against the background of the skill and experience of the
> particular plaintiff, and in that assessment a higher degree of awareness
> will be imputed to a professional than to one with less than professional
> experience in the particular sport. In that context plaintiff's effort to
> separate the wetness of the field, which he testified was above the
> grassline, from the mud beneath it in which his foot became lodged must
> be rejected for not only was he aware that there was "some mud" in the
> centerfield area, but also it is a matter of common experience that water
> of sufficient depth to cover grass may result in the earth beneath being
> turned to mud. We do not deal here . . . with a hole in the playing field
> hidden by grass, but with water, indicative of the presence of mud, the
> danger of which plaintiff was sufficiently aware to complain to the
> grounds keepers. It is not necessary to the application of assumption of
> risk that the injured plaintiff have foreseen the exact manner in which
> his or her injury occurred, so long as he or she is aware of the potential
> for injury of the mechanism from which the injury results.

The issue of assumption of risk was, however, left to the jury in Ash-
croft v. Calder Race Course, 492 So. 2d 1309 (Fla. 1986), where the
plaintiff, a jockey, received serious injuries "when his horse veered
across the race course and toward an exit gap." While the court recognized that "express" assumption of risk (i.e., "plaintiff's consent to take
certain chances") was a defense in horse racing, it held, as a matter of
law, that the defense was not applicable here. It therefore reversed the
decision of the trial judge to allow the case to go to the jury. "Riding
on a track with a negligently placed exit gap is not an inherent risk in
the sport of horse racing. We therefore find as a matter of law that
there was no express assumption of risk with respect to the negligent
placement of the exit gap. . . ."

4. *Primary and secondary assumption of risk.* In Meistrich v. Casino Arena
Attractions, Inc. 155 A.2d 90 (N.J. 1959), the plaintiff fell while skating
on defendant's rink. Plaintiff's evidence showed "that defendant departed from the usual procedure in preparing the ice, with the result

that it became too hard and hence too slippery for the patron of average ability using skates sharpened for the usual surface." Weintraub, C.J., speaking for a unanimous court, held that a jury could infer that the defendant's negligence was a proximate cause of the accident. It also held that a "jury could permissibly find he carelessly contributed to his injury when, with that knowledge, he remained on the ice and skated cross-hand with another." He nonetheless ordered a new trial because what it regarded as a faulty instruction below on assumption of risk, namely: "that assumption of risk may be found if plaintiff knew or reasonably should have known of the risk, notwithstanding that a reasonably prudent man would have continued in the face of the risk."

Weintraub, C.J., critically reviewed the history of assumption of risk in industrial accidents, and in the course of its opinion articulated the distinction between primary and secondary assumption of risk as follows:

> We here speak solely of the area in which injury or damage was neither intended nor expressly contracted to be non-actionable. In this area, assumption of risk has two distinct meanings. In one sense (sometimes called its "primary" sense), it is an alternative expression for the proposition that defendant was not negligent, i.e., either owed no duty or did not breach the duty owed. In its other sense (sometimes called "secondary"), assumption of risk is an affirmative defense to an established breach of duty. In its primary sense, it is accurate to say plaintiff assumed the risk whether or not he was "at fault," for the truth thereby expressed in alternate terminology is that defendant was not negligent. But in its secondary sense, i.e., as an affirmative defense to an established breach of defendant's duty, it is incorrect to say plaintiff assumed the risk whether or not he was at fault. . . .
>
> In applying assumption of risk in its secondary sense in areas other than that of master and servant, our cases have consistently recognized the ultimate question to be whether a reasonably prudent man would have moved in the face of a known risk, dealing with the issue as one of law or leaving it to the jury upon the same standard which controls the handling of the issue of contributory negligence. . . .
>
> Hence we think it clear that assumption of risk in its secondary sense is a mere phase of contributory negligence, the total issue being whether a reasonably prudent man in the exercise of due care (a) would have incurred the known risk and (b) if he would, whether such a person in the light of all the circumstances including the appreciated risk would have conducted himself in the manner in which plaintiff acted.
>
> Thus in the area under discussion there are but two basic issues: (1) defendant's negligence, and (2) plaintiff's contributory negligence. In view of the considerations discussed above, it has been urged that assumption of risk in both its primary and secondary senses serves merely to confuse and should be eliminated. James, Assumption of Risk, 61 Yale L.J. 141, 169 (1952).

Is *Murphy* a case of primary or secondary assumption of risk? Unlike the situation in *Lamson* or *Murphy,* the plaintiff in *Meistrich* knew that the defendant was in breach of its obligation to provide a safe skating surface before he fell. Why then is he not under an obligation to leave the ice? If he does, can he get his money back?

5. *Assumption of risk and abandonment of rights.* Many other cases raise the question of how the doctrine of assumption of risk should apply in its secondary sense when the defendant has negligently or unlawfully created a dangerous condition. In Marshall v. Ranne, 511 S.W.2d 255, 260 (Tex. 1974), the defendant's mad boar bit the plaintiff while the plaintiff was walking from his house to his car. The plaintiff knew of the mad condition of the boar and often had complained about it to the defendant. An expert marksman, he also had passed up several good opportunities to shoot the boar, not wanting to do such an "unneighborly thing." At trial the jury found denied plaintiff's recovery, first because he had been contributorily negligent in not shooting the boar when he had the chance, and second because he voluntarily assumed the risk of harm. The supreme court, reversing the decision below, held that contributory negligence was not a defense in a case of strict liability. It then addressed the question of voluntary assumption of risk:

> We hold that there was no proof that plaintiff had a free and voluntary choice, because he did not have a free choice of alternatives. He had, instead, only a choice of evils, both of which were wrongfully imposed upon him by the defendant. He could remain a prisoner inside his own house or he could take the risk of reaching his car before defendant's hog attacked him. Plaintiff could have remained inside his house, but in doing so, he would have surrendered his legal right to proceed over his own property to his car so he could return to his home in Dallas. The latter alternative was forced upon him against his will and was a choice he was not legally required to accept. . . . The dilemma which defendant forced upon plaintiff was that of facing the danger or surrendering his rights with respect to his own real property, and that was not, as a matter of law the voluntary choice to which the law entitled him.
>
> See Restatement (Second) of Torts §496E.

One complication in these cases concerns the appropriate measure of damages, given that the plaintiff may take insufficient care if full tort recovery is allowed. See in connection with this the suggestion in Rose-Ackerman, Dikes, Dams, and Vicious Harms: Entitlement and Efficiency in Tort Law, 18 J. Legal Stud. 25, 26 (1989), where the following rule is proposed: "victims should be paid for the level of preventive activity that would be efficient *plus* the consequential damage that would have resulted if these precautions had been taken. The payment would be made to all victims *whether or not they actually have taken care.* Since the level of damages is independent of their behavior, victims would have an incentive to act efficiently." Should the rule apply even if there is only a one percent chance that a rabid animal will bite its owner's neighbor? Or if the precautions when taken only reduce, but do not eliminate, the chance of being attacked? See also Mansfield, Informed Choice in the Law of Torts, 22 La. L. Rev. 17 (1961).

6. Assumption of risk: the fireman's rule. One context in which the defense of assumption of risk refuses to die, even in New Jersey, involves the so-called fireman's rule, which in fact extends to police officers and other public officials charged with the maintenance of public order. Thus, when a public officer responds to a fire alarm or a request for police assistance brought about by the negligent or indeed criminal conduct of the defendant, recovery is barred for injuries thereby incurred. The fireman's rule is based squarely on the doctrine of assumption of risk: "one who has knowingly and voluntarily confronted a hazard cannot recover for injuries sustained thereby." See Walters v. Sloan, 571 P.2d 609 (Cal. 1979). The public policy reasons behind the principle were well set out by Weintraub, C.J., shortly after his opinion in *Meistrich,* in Krauth v. Geller, 157 A.2d 129, 130-131 (N.J. 1959):

> [I]t is the fireman's business to deal with that very hazard [the fire] and hence, perhaps by analogy to the contractor engaged as an expert to remedy dangerous situations, he cannot complain of negligence in the creation of the very occasion for his engagement. In terms of duty, it may be said there is none owed the fireman to exercise care so as not to require the special services for which he is trained and paid. Probably most fires are attributable to negligence, and in the final analysis the policy decision is that it would be too burdensome to charge all who carelessly cause or fail to prevent fires with the injuries suffered by the expert retained with public funds to deal with those inevitable, although negligently created, occurrences. Hence, for that risk, the fireman should receive appropriate compensation from the public he serves both in pay which reflects the hazard and in workmen's compensation benefits for the consequences of the inherent risks of the calling.

Some limits have been imposed on the scope of the fireman's rule. Thus in Donohue v. San Francisco Housing Authority, 20 Cal. Rptr. 2d 148, 150-51 (Cal. App. 1993), a fireman entered a building maintained by the SFHA during an unannounced fire safety inspection. He sued for injuries incurred when he slipped on the wet, slick steps and his action was not barred by the fireman's rule because "the firefighter's rule does not apply because it does not bar recovery for independent acts of misconduct which were not the cause of the plaintiff's presence on the scene. . . . The negligent conduct at issue was SFHA's failure to install non-slip adhesive treads on the stairs coupled with the improper maintenance practice of hosing down the stairs. Neither of these acts was the reason for plaintiff's presence." What result if the plaintiff slipped on steps lacking proper treads while fighting a fire? Should the fireman's rule protect defendants who are guilty of arson? To all suits brought by workers injured in the course of their employment?

Obstetrics & Gynecologists v. Pepper
693 P.2d 1259 (Nev. 1985)

PER CURIAM. This appeal concerns the enforceability of an arbitration agreement between appellant medical clinic and respondent patient. Following a hearing, the district court denied appellant's motions to stay respondent's action for negligence pending arbitration and to direct arbitration to proceed. On the record before us, we are not persuaded that the district court erred.

Appellant clinic requires its patients to sign the arbitration agreement at issue before receiving treatment. The agreement provides that all disputes between the parties shall be submitted to binding arbitration. The parties expressly waive their right to a trial. According to the standard procedure of the clinic, the receptionist hands the patient the arbitration agreement along with two information sheets, and informs him or her that any questions he or she may have regarding the agreement will be answered. The patient must sign the agreement before receiving treatment; the physician signs later. If the patient refuses to sign the arbitration agreement, the clinic refuses treatment. Ostensibly, even in the absence of an arbitration agreement, the clinic will consent to provide treatment in some emergency situations, but the record does not reflect that this has ever in fact occurred. The agreement does not give the patient any option to revoke within a specified period of time; once the patient signs the agreement he or she cannot regain the right to a trial.

On November 28, 1979, respondent Rhonda Pepper entered appellant medical clinic to obtain a prescription for an oral contraceptive. Respondent's signature appears on the agreement; however, respondent stated in an affidavit that she has no recollection of either signing the agreement or of its being explained to her. On July 20, 1980, respondent suffered a cerebral incident which left her partially paralyzed. Subsequently respondent filed suit against appellant medical clinic, alleging that the cerebral incident had been caused by the clinic's negligence in prescribing the contraceptive, which was contraindicated by her medical history. Appellant moved to stay the lawsuit pending arbitration and to order arbitration to proceed. Each party submitted an affidavit, and a hearing was held. The district court denied both motions, and ordered respondent's counsel to prepare findings of fact and conclusions of law, to be filed after approval by appellant's counsel.

Counsel being unable to reach agreement, no findings of fact and conclusions of law were ever filed.

NRS 38.045 provides that if a party requests a court to compel arbitration pursuant to a written agreement to arbitrate, and the opposing party denies the existence of such an agreement, the court shall summarily determine the issue. Since appellant set up the existence of the agreement to preclude the lawsuit from proceeding, it had the burden of showing that a binding agreement existed. After reviewing the facts, we cannot say that the district court erred in finding that appellant did not sustain that burden.

Initially, we note that the district court did not enter any findings of fact and conclusions of law. The absence of express findings renders it impossible for us to know on what grounds the district court refused to enforce the arbitration agreement. We have previously held, however, that in the absence of express findings, this court will imply findings where the evidence clearly supports the judgment.

The district court could certainly have found that the arbitration agreement was an adhesion contract. An adhesion contract has been defined as a standardized contract form offered to consumers of goods and services essentially on a "take it or leave it" basis, without affording the consumer a realistic opportunity to bargain, and under such conditions that the consumer cannot obtain the desired product or service except by acquiescing to the form of the contract. The distinctive feature of an adhesion contract is that the weaker party has no choice as to its terms. Wheeler v. St. Joseph Hospital, 133 Cal. Rptr. 775, 783 (Cal. App. 1976). The arbitration agreement before us clearly falls into this category. It was prepared by appellant medical clinic and presented to respondent as a condition of treatment. Respondent had no opportunity to modify any of its terms; her choices were to sign the agreement as it stood or to forego treatment at the clinic.

An adhesion contract need not be unenforceable if it falls within the reasonable expectations of the weaker or "adhering" party and is not unduly oppressive. However, courts will not enforce against an adhering party a provision limiting the duties or liabilities of the stronger party absent plain and clear notification of the terms and an understanding consent.

The district court held a hearing to determine whether an enforceable arbitration agreement existed between the parties. The parties were entitled to present oral testimony at the hearing; instead, they chose to rely on the affidavits they had submitted. Consequently, we must look for facts supporting the decision of the district court in the affidavits of respondent and of appellant's receptionist. The affidavits do not compel the conclusion that respondent knowingly consented to the terms of the agreement. Respondent stated that she did not remember receiving any information regarding the terms of the arbitration agreement. Appellant's receptionist stated that the general policy of the clinic was to inform the patient that any questions he or she might have would be answered. The contents of both affidavits are perfectly consistent with the conclusion that the agreement was never explained to respondent. On these facts the district court may well have found that respondent did not give an informed consent to the agreement and that no meeting of the minds occurred.

Consequently, we conclude that appellant has failed to demonstrate that the district court erred. As the moving party, appellant had the burden of persuading the district court that the arbitration agreement which it wished to enforce was a valid contract. We cannot say as a matter of law that appellant sustained that burden. Since appellant's counsel failed to pursue the entry of findings of facts and conclusions of law, we are bound to presume that the district court found that respondent did not give a knowing consent to the arbitration agreement prepared by appellant clinic.

 Accordingly, we affirm the judgment of the district court and remand for further proceedings.

NOTES

1. The role of arbitration agreements. If the plaintiff had admitted signing the release form, would she have been bound to accept arbitration given that the defendant group had offered its services only on a "take-it-or-leave-it basis"? If the applicable state law prevents physicians and hospitals from contracting out of their medical malpractice tort liabilities, may they stipulate by contract for an arbitral forum that might offer them, as health care providers, systematically more favorable results? What if the administrative expenses of arbitration are far lower than the corresponding costs of jury trials? If the fees of Obstetrics and Gynecology were lower than those charged by comparable groups whose contracts did not contain an arbitration clause?

2. Institutional arbitration. With *Pepper* contrast the earlier case of Madden v. Kaiser Foundation Hospitals, 552 P.2d 1178, 1185 (Cal. 1976), upholding an arbitration clause contained in a contract between a state employee and the defendant foundation. The contract was negotiated on behalf of the individual employee by an appropriate state board, and the plaintiff selected her own health maintenance organization from a list of available groups, some of which offered the plaintiff the right to a jury trial. The defendant's plan required arbitration of all medical disputes on a take-it-or-leave-it basis. The plaintiff was held bound by the terms of the clause even though she claimed to be unaware of its inclusion in the agreement.

In the characteristic adhesion contract case, the stronger party drafts the contract, and the weaker has no opportunity, either personally or through an agent, to negotiate concerning its terms. The Kaiser plan, on the other hand, represents the product of negotiation between two parties, Kaiser and the board, possessing parity of bargaining strength. Although plaintiff did not engage in the personal negotiation of the contract's terms, she and other public employees benefitted from representation by a board, composed in part of persons elected by the affected employees, which exerted its bargaining strength to secure medical protection for employees on more favorable terms than any employee could individually obtain.

Should ordinary individuals not represented by third-party group agents be deprived the option of relinquishing their right to a jury trial?

3. Contracting out of medical malpractice liability generally. The arbitration question is but the tip of the iceberg in the larger dispute of whether the general principle of freedom of contract should govern medical malpractice litigation. Professor Robinson puts the case for market freedom forcefully:

> The affirmative case for contract is simple and powerful. In terms of utilitarian efficiency, contractual arrangements allow parties to achieve the most efficient combination of efforts to manage risk in accordance with their respective comparative advantages and their respective risk preferences. The moral argument proceeds along similar lines but emphasizes the fact that contractual allocation promotes individual freedom of choice, constrained only by the need to accommodate the divergent interests of the contracting parties. To justify private ordering one need not suppose that it always yields "good" or "fair" results. It is enough that, in general, private parties are likely to achieve results that are at least as good and fair for themselves as would be achieved by paternalistic intervention.

Robinson, Rethinking the Allocation of Medical Malpractice Risks between Patients and Providers, 49 Law & Contemp. Probs. 172, 189 (1986).

Robinson's article (as well as others by Danzon, Epstein, and Havighurst) provoked the following defense of the tort system from the English scholar P. S. Atiyah, Medical Malpractice and the Contract/Tort Boundary, id. at 296-297:

> The real market enthusiasts appear to envisage a situation in which a competitive market offers a range of benefit and risk packages suitable to the individual desires, risk-averseness, and wallets of various patients. If all the bargaining is in practice to be done collectively (by employers and unions whose interests of course are not always identical with those of employees), however, the reality is that the rules which will govern the physician/patient relationship will not be tailored to the individual patient's needs at all. They will be fixed by third parties, just as much as the tort rules are. There may, it is true, be more choice available in the

market, but this argument takes us back to our starting point about information, risk evaluation, and bargaining power. If the patient does not understand the differences in the packages offered to him, choice by itself means little, and the presumption of efficiency in outcome is rebutted.

A further problem to which little attention seems to have been paid concerns the long-term nature of the physician/patient relationship. If the terms are fixed at the outset of this relationship and continue to bind for years afterwards, it again seems unreal to think of these terms as truly negotiated or agreed-upon terms in relation to incidents occurring years after the terms were initially agreed to — and perhaps forgotten. If, on the other hand, the terms are changed frequently by third party negotiations, with little knowledge by the patient and with his consent perhaps even being presumed, the argument that this is an efficient outcome of market choices looks thin indeed.

A third reason for doubting whether contract, as the law of the market, is an appropriate legal category for health care provision. . . . is the ethical position that people have a *right* to a decent standard of health care, and that they should not be required to pay for this as though it were an "optional extra," like whitewall tires or fancy trim. This ethical stance no doubt stems in part from the general egalitarian principles referred to earlier. It has also derived strength from Bernard Williams's well known suggestion that it is a necessary truth that the proper ground for the distribution of health care is ill health. The reformers criticize this idea on the ground that much health care provided today is not needed at all, and may indeed be medically quite useless. Furthermore, even with medical procedures which may have some therapeutic value, it is still necessary to decide whether the benefit exceeds the cost, and that decision can only be properly made by the patient himself, since the true value of the benefits depends on his own evaluation of them. These criticisms of the extreme ethical position may be well founded, but they do not begin to touch the ethical argument as to medical procedures which *are* genuinely necessary.

See generally, Symposium, Medical Malpractice: Can the Private Sector Find Relief?, 49 Law & Contemp. Probs. 1-348 (1986). See also P. Danzon, Medical Malpractice: Theory, Evidence, and Public Policy 208-217 (1985), for a qualified endorsement of the contract solution, and P. Weiler, Medical Malpractice On Trial 113 (1991), for a "highly dubious [view] of the brave new world of no-liability," which Weiler thinks is the probable outcome of any wholly free contractual regime on issues of malpractice liability. In Weiler's view the need for physician and institutional incentives dominate. "It is unlikely that even a more informed consumer in the health care market or a more aggressive government regulatory agency will provide sufficient incentive to the hospital and its physician committee structure to commit the resources and energies needed to make the institution less hazardous to the health of its patients."

4. Assumption of risk by contract: other contexts. Express contracts limiting tort liability have been used with varying success in other contexts. In

Jefferson County Bank of Lakewood v. Armored Motor Service, 366 P.2d 13 (Colo. 1961), the court upheld an exculpation clause in a contract between a bank and an armored carrier that had limited the carrier's liability to $30,000 "for each sealed shipment entrusted to the defendant's possession by the bank." The court stressed that this private contract had been "negotiated on a basis of equal bargaining power, knowledge of the facts, and with a thorough understanding of the import of the contract provisions. The variable charges made for the armored car service were in proportion to the maximum liability assumed." The court also noted that general disclaimers by public carriers would be against public policy.

Contractual disclaimers have fared less well, however, when they have involved personal injuries to individual consumers. Thus, in Henrioulle v. Marin Ventures, Inc., 573 P.2d 465, 467 (Cal. 1978), the California Supreme Court struck down this exculpation clause in a standard form lease:

> INDEMNIFICATION: Owner shall not be liable for any damage or injury to Tenant, or any other person, or to any property occurring on the premises, or any part thereof, or in the common areas thereof, and Tenant agrees to hold Owner harmless from any claims for damages no matter how caused.

Henrioulle relied on the critical decision in Tunkl v. Regents of University of California, 383 P.2d 441 (Cal. 1963), criticized by Robinson, supra, which had invalidated similarly broad exemption clauses in the standard hospital admission form.

> In *Tunkl*, six criteria are used to identify the kind of agreement in which an exculpatory clause is invalid as contrary to public policy. "[1] It concerns a business of a type generally thought suitable for public regulation. [2] The party seeking exculpation is engaged in performing a service of great importance to the public, which is often a matter of practical necessity for some members of the public. [3] The party holds himself out as willing to perform this service for any member of the public who seeks it, or at least any member coming within certain established standards. [4] As a result of the essential nature of the service, in the economic setting of the transaction, the party invoking exculpation possesses a decisive advantage of bargaining strength against any member of the public who seeks his services. [5] In exercising a superior bargaining power the party confronts the public with a standardized adhesion contract of exculpation, and makes no provision whereby a purchaser may pay additional fees and obtain protection against negligence. [6] Finally, as a result of the transaction, the person or property of the purchaser is placed under the control of the seller, subject to the risk of carelessness by the seller or his agents."

The court then held that this residential agreement met the *Tunkl* agreement. Sound? *Henrioulle* in a sense ratified the statutory law of

California. Two years before the case was handed down, section 1953 of the California Civil Code made it "void as contrary to public policy" to waive or modify "[h]is right to have the landlord exercise a duty of care to prevent personal injury or personal property damage where that duty is imposed by law." Cal. Civ. Code c. 302, §1 (West 1994).

E. COMPARATIVE NEGLIGENCE

1. At Common Law

Beach, Contributory Negligence
12-13 (2d ed. 1892)

The reasons of the rule which denies relief to a plaintiff guilty of contributory negligence have been previously stated. The common law refuses to apportion damages which arise from negligence. This it does upon considerations of public convenience and public policy, and upon this principle, it is said, depends also the rule which makes the contributory negligence of a plaintiff a complete defense. For the same reason, when there is an action in tort, where injury results from the negligence of two or more persons, the sufferer has a full remedy against any one of them, and no contribution can be enforced between the tort feasors. The policy of the law in this respect is founded upon the inability of human tribunals to mete out exact justice. A perfect code would render each man responsible for the unmixed consequences of his own default; but the common law, in view of the impossibility of assigning all effects to their respective causes, refuses to interfere in those cases where negligence is the issue, at the instance of one whose hands are not free from the stain of contributory fault, and where accordingly the impossibility of apportioning the damage between the parties does not exist, the rule is held not to apply.

Li v. Yellow Cab Co. of California
532 P.2d 1226 (Cal. 1975)

[The accident in question resulted from the negligence of both parties. The plaintiff had attempted to cross three lanes of oncoming traffic in order to enter a service station; the defendant's driver was traveling at an excessive speed when he ran a yellow light just before he struck the plaintiff's car. The trial court held that the plaintiff was barred from recovery by her own contributory negligence.]

SULLIVAN, J. In this case we address the grave and recurrent question whether we should judicially declare no longer applicable in California courts the doctrine of contributory negligence, which bars all recovery when the plaintiff's negligent conduct has contributed as a legal cause in any degree to the harm suffered by him, and hold that it must give way to a system of comparative negligence, which assesses liability in direct proportion to fault. As we explain in detail infra, we conclude that we should. In the course of reaching our ultimate decision we conclude that: (1) The doctrine of comparative negligence is preferable to the "all-or-nothing" doctrine of contributory negligence from the point of view of logic, practical experience, and fundamental justice; (2) judicial action in this area is not precluded by the presence of section 1714 of the Civil Code, which has been said to "codify" the "all-or-nothing" rule and to render it immune from attack in the courts except on constitutional grounds; (3) given the possibility of judicial action, certain practical difficulties attendant upon the adoption of comparative negligence should not dissuade us from charting a new course — leaving the resolution of some of these problems to future judicial or legislative action; (4) the doctrine of comparative negligence should be applied in this state in its so-called "pure" form under which the assessment of liability in proportion to fault proceeds in spite of the fact that the plaintiff is equally at fault as or more at fault than the defendant and finally; (5) this new rule should be given a limited retrospective application.

I

[The court then notes the then dominant common-law rule that treats contributory negligence as an absolute defense subject to a limited last clear chance exception.]

It is unnecessary for us to catalogue the enormous amount of critical comment that has been directed over the years against the "all-or-nothing" approach of the doctrine of contributory negligence. The essence of that criticism has been constant and clear: the doctrine is inequitable in its operation because it fails to distribute responsibility in proportion to fault. Against this have been raised several arguments in justification, but none have proved even remotely adequate to the task.[4] The basic

---

4. Dean Prosser, in a 1953 law review article on the subject which still enjoys considerable influence, addressed himself to the commonly advanced justificatory arguments in the following terms: "There has been much speculation as to why the rule thus declared found such ready acceptance in later decisions, both in England and in the United States. The explanations given by the courts themselves never have carried much conviction. Most of the decisions have talked about 'proximate cause,' saying that the plaintiff's negligence is an intervening, insulating cause between the defendant's negligence and the injury. But this cannot be supported unless a meaning is assigned to proximate

objection to the doctrine — grounded in the primal concept that in a system in which liability is based on fault, the extent of fault should govern the extent of liability — remains irresistible to reason and all intelligent notions of fairness.

Furthermore, practical experience with the application by juries of the doctrine of contributory negligence has added its weight to analyses of its inherent shortcomings: "Every trial lawyer is well aware that juries often do in fact allow recovery in cases of contributory negligence, and that the compromise in the jury room does result in some diminution of the damages because of the plaintiff's fault. But the process is at best a haphazard and most unsatisfactory one." (Prosser, Comparative Negligence.) . . . It is manifest that this state of affairs, viewed from the standpoint of the health and vitality of the legal process, can only detract from public confidence in the ability of law and legal institutions to assign liability on a just and consistent basis. . . .

It is in view of these theoretical and practical considerations that to this date 25 states,[6] have abrogated the "all-or-nothing" rule of contributory negligence and have enacted in its place general apportionment *statutes* calculated in one manner or another to assess liability in proportion to fault. In 1973 these states were joined by Florida, which effected the same result by *judicial* decision. (Hoffman v. Jones (Fla. 1973) 280 So. 2d 431.) We are likewise persuaded that logic, practical experience,

---

cause which is found nowhere else. If two automobiles collide and injure a bystander, the negligence of one driver is not held to be a superseding cause which relieves the other of liability; and there is no visible reason for any different conclusion when the action is by one driver against the other. It has been said that the defense has a penal basis, and is intended to punish the plaintiff for his own misconduct; or that the court will not aid one who is himself at fault, and he must come into court with clean hands. But this is no explanation of the many cases, particularly those of the last clear chance, in which a plaintiff clearly at fault is permitted to recover. It has been said that the rule is intended to discourage accidents, by denying recovery to those who fail to use proper care for their own safety; but the assumption that the speeding motorist is or should be, meditating on the possible failure of a lawsuit for his possible injuries lacks all reality, and it is quite as reasonable to say that the rule promotes accidents by encouraging the negligent defendant. Probably the true explanation lies merely in the highly individualistic attitude of the common law of the early nineteenth century. The period of development of contributory negligence was that of the industrial revolution, and there is reason to think that the courts found in this defense, along with the concepts of duty and proximate cause, a convenient instrument of control over the jury, by which the liabilities of rapidly growing industry were curbed and kept within bounds." (Prosser, Comparative Negligence (1953) 41 Cal. L. Rev. 1, 3-4; fns. omitted.)

6. Arkansas, Colorado, Connecticut, Georgia, Hawaii, Idaho, Maine, Massachusetts, Minnesota, Mississippi, Nebraska, Nevada, New Hampshire, New Jersey, North Dakota, Oklahoma, Oregon, Rhode Island, South Dakota, Texas, Utah, Vermont, Washington, Wisconsin, Wyoming. (Schwartz, Comparative Negligence (1974), Appendix A, pp. 367-369.) [Today comparative negligence, either by common law or statute, represents the law of at least 45 states as well as Puerto Rico and the Virgin Islands. — Ed.] In the federal sphere, comparative negligence of the "pure" type (see infra) has been the rule since 1908 in cases arising under the Federal Employers' Liability Act (see 45 U.S.C. §53) and since 1920 in cases arising under the Jones Act (see 46 U.S.C. §688) and the Death on the High Seas Act (see 46 U.S.C. §766).

and fundamental justice counsel against the retention of the doctrine
rendering contributory negligence a complete bar to recovery — and
that it should be replaced in this state by a system under which liability
for damage will be borne by those whose negligence caused it in direct
proportion to their respective fault. . . .[6a]

II

It is urged that any change in the law of contributory negligence must
be made by the Legislature, not by this court. Although the doctrine of
contributory negligence is of judicial origin — its genesis being traditionally attributed to the opinion of Lord Ellenborough in Butterfield
v. Forrester (K.B. 1809) 103 Eng. Rep. 926 — the enactment of section
1714 of the Civil Code in 1872 codified the doctrine as it stood at that
date and, the argument continues, rendered it invulnerable to attack
in the courts except on constitutional grounds.

[The court then exhaustively examined Section 1714 of the California Civil Code, which provides that "Everyone is responsible, not only
for the result of his willful acts, but also for an injury occasioned to
another by his want of ordinary care or skill in the management of his
property or person, except so far as the latter has, willfully or by want
of ordinary care, brought the injury upon himself. The extent of liability in such cases is defined by the Title on Compensatory Relief." The
court concluded that "it was not the intention of the Legislature in
enacting section 1714 of the Civil Code, as well as other sections of that
code declarative of the common law, to insulate the matters therein
expressed from further judicial development; rather it was the intention of the Legislature to announce and formulate existing common
law principles and definitions for purposes of orderly and concise presentation and with a distinct view toward continuing judicial evolution."]

III

We are thus brought to the second group of arguments which have
been advanced by defendants and the amici curiae supporting their
position. Generally speaking, such arguments expose considerations of

---

6a. In employing the generic term "fault" throughout this opinion we follow a usage
common to the literature on the subject of comparative negligence. In all cases, however, we intend the term to import nothing more than "negligence" in the accepted
legal sense. [In the original advance sheets, the court stated a comparative negligence
test that would allocate liability "in direct proportion to the extent of the parties' causal
responsibility." 119 Cal. Rptr. 858 (1975), advance sheets only. Footnote 6a did not
appear. — Ed.]

a practical nature which, it is urged, counsel against the adoption of a rule of comparative negligence in this state even if such adoption is possible by judicial means.

The most serious of these considerations are those attendant upon the administration of a rule of comparative negligence in cases involving multiple parties. One such problem may arise when all responsible parties are not brought before the court: it may be difficult for the jury to evaluate relative negligence in such circumstances, and to compound this difficulty; such an evaluation would not be res judicata in a subsequent suit against the absent wrongdoer. Problems of contribution and indemnity among joint tortfeasors lurk in the background.

A second and related major area of concern involves the administration of the actual process of fact-finding in a comparative negligence system. The assigning of a specific percentage factor to the amount of negligence attributable to a particular party, while in theory a matter of little difficulty, can become a matter of perplexity in the face of hard facts.

The temptation for the jury to resort to a quotient verdict in such circumstances can be great. These inherent difficulties are not, however, insurmountable. Guidelines might be provided the jury which will assist it in keeping focussed upon the true inquiry and the utilization of special verdicts or jury interrogatories can be of invaluable assistance in assuring that the jury has approached its sensitive and often complex task with proper standards and appropriate reverence.

The third area of concern, the status of the doctrines of last clear chance and assumption of risk, involves less the practical problems of administering a particular form of comparative negligence than it does a definition of the theoretical outline of the specific form to be adopted. Although several states which apply comparative negligence concepts retain the last clear chance doctrine, the better reasoned position seems to be that when true comparative negligence is adopted, the need for last clear chance as a palliative of the hardships of the "all-or-nothing" rule disappears and its retention results only in a windfall to the plaintiff in direct contravention of the principle of liability in proportion to fault. As for assumption of risk, we have recognized in this state that this defense overlaps that of contributory negligence to some extent and in fact is made up of at least two distinct defenses. "To simplify greatly, it has been observed . . . that in one kind of situation, to wit, where a plaintiff *unreasonably* undertakes to encounter a specific known risk imposed by a defendant's negligence, plaintiff's conduct, although he may encounter that risk in a prudent manner, is in reality a form of contributory negligence. . . . Other kinds of situations within the doctrine of assumption of risk are those, for example, where plaintiff is held to agree to relieve defendant of an obligation of reasonable conduct toward him. Such a situation would not involve contributory negligence but rather a reduction of defendant's duty of care." We think it clear that the adoption of a system of comparative negligence should entail the merger of the defense of assumption of risk into the general scheme of assessment of liability in proportion to fault in those particular cases in which the form of assumption of risk involved is no more than a variant of contributory negligence.

Finally there is the problem of the treatment of willful misconduct under a system of comparative negligence. In jurisdictions following the "all-or-nothing" rule, contributory negligence is no defense to an action based upon a claim of willful misconduct (see Rest. 2d Torts, §503), and this is the present rule in California.[19] As Dean Prosser has observed, "[this] is in reality a rule of comparative fault which is being applied, and the court is refusing to set up the lesser fault against the greater." (Prosser, Torts, supra, §65, p. 426.) The thought is that the difference between willful and wanton misconduct and ordinary negligence is one of kind rather than degree in that the former involves conduct of an entirely different order,[20] and under this conception it might well be urged that comparative negligence concepts should have no application when one of the parties has been guilty of willful and wanton misconduct. It has been persuasively argued, however, that the loss of deterrent effect that would occur upon application of comparative fault concepts to willful and wanton misconduct as well as ordinary negligence would be slight, and that a comprehensive system of comparative negligence should allow for the apportionment of damages in all cases involving misconduct which falls short of being intentional. The law of punitive damages remains a separate consideration. . . .

The existence of the foregoing areas of difficulty and uncertainty has not diminished our conviction that the time for a revision of the means for dealing with contributory fault in this state is long past due and that it lies within the province of this court to initiate the needed change by our decision in this case. Two of the indicated areas (i.e., multiple parties and willful misconduct) are not involved in the case before us, and we consider it neither necessary nor wise to address ourselves to specific problems of this nature which might be expected to arise. . . .

---

19. BAJI No. 3.52 (1971 re-revision) currently provides: "Contributory negligence of a plaintiff is not a bar to his recovery for an injury caused by the wilful or wanton misconduct of a defendant. [¶] Wilful or wanton misconduct is intentional wrongful conduct, done either with knowledge, express or implied, that serious injury to another will probably result, or with a wanton and reckless disregard of the possible results. An intent to injure is not a necessary element of wilful or wanton misconduct. [¶] To prove such misconduct it is not necessary to establish that defendant himself recognized his conduct as dangerous. It is sufficient if it be established that a reasonable man under the same or similar circumstances would be aware of the dangerous character of such conduct."

20. "Disallowing the contributory negligence defense in this context is different from last clear chance; the defense is denied not because defendant had the last opportunity to avoid the accident but rather because defendant's conduct was so culpable it was different in 'kind' from the plaintiff's. The basis is culpability rather than causation." (Schwartz, supra, §5.1, p. 100; fn. omitted.)

Our decision in this case is to be viewed as a first step in what we deem to be a proper and just direction, not as a compendium containing the answers to all questions that may be expected to arise. Pending future judicial or legislative developments, we are content for the present to assume the position taken by the Florida court in this matter: "We feel the trial judges of this State are capable of applying [a] comparative negligence rule without our setting guidelines in anticipation of expected problems. The problems are more appropriately resolved at the trial level in a practical manner instead of a theoretical solution at the appellate level. The trial judges are granted broad discretion in adopting such procedures as may accomplish the objectives and purposes expressed in this opinion." (280 So. 2d at pp. 439-440.)

It remains to identify the precise form of comparative negligence which we now adopt for application in this state. Although there are many variants, only the two basic forms need be considered here. The first of these, the so-called "pure" form of comparative negligence, apportions liability in direct proportion to fault in all cases. This was the form adopted by the Supreme Court of Florida in Hoffman v. Jones, supra, and it applies by statute in Mississippi, Rhode Island, and Washington. Moreover it is the form favored by most scholars and commentators. The second basic form of comparative negligence, of which there are several variants, applies apportionment based on fault *up to the point* at which the plaintiff's negligence is equal to or greater than that of the defendant — when that point is reached, plaintiff is barred from recovery. Nineteen states have adopted this form or one of its variants by statute. The principal argument advanced in its favor is moral in nature: that it is not morally right to permit one more at fault in an accident to recover from one less at fault. Other arguments assert the probability of increased insurance, administrative, and judicial costs if a "pure" rather than a "50 percent" system is adopted, but this has been seriously questioned.

We have concluded that the "pure" form of comparative negligence is that which should be adopted in this state. In our view the "50 percent" system simply shifts the lottery aspect of the contributory negligence rule to a different ground. As Dean Prosser has noted, under such a system "[i]t is obvious that a slight difference in the proportionate fault may permit a recovery and there has been much justified criticism of a rule under which a plaintiff who is charged with 49 percent of the total negligence recovers 51 percent of his damages, while one who is charged with 50 percent recovers nothing at all."[22] (Prosser, Comparative Negligence, supra, 41 Cal. L. Rev. 1, 25; fns. omitted.) In effect "such a rule distorts the very principle it recognizes, i.e., that

---

22. This problem is compounded when the injurious result is produced by the combined negligence of several parties. For example in a three-car collision a plaintiff whose negligence amounts to one-third or more recovers nothing; in a four-car collision the plaintiff is barred if his negligence is only one-quarter of the total.

persons are responsible for their acts to the extent their fault contributes to an injurious result. The partial rule simply lowers, but does not eliminate, the bar of contributory negligence."

We also consider significant the experience of the State of Wisconsin, which until recently was considered the leading exponent of the "50 percent" system. There that system led to numerous appeals on the narrow but crucial issue whether plaintiff's negligence was equal to defendant's. Numerous reversals have resulted on this point, leading to the development of arcane classifications of negligence according to quality and category. (See cases cited in Vincent v. Pabst Brewing Co., 177 N.W.2d 513, at 513 (dissenting opn.).) This finally led to a frontal attack on the system in the *Vincent* case, cited above, wherein the state supreme court was urged to replace the statutory "50 percent" rule by a judicially declared "pure" comparative negligence rule. The majority of the court rejected this invitation, concluding that the Legislature had occupied the field, but three concurring justices and one dissenter indicated their willingness to accept it if the Legislature failed to act with reasonable dispatch. The dissenting opinion of Chief Justice Hallows, which has been cited above, stands as a persuasive testimonial in favor of the "pure" system. We wholeheartedly embrace its reasoning.

[The court then held its rule should apply in all cases in which the trial had not yet begun. It noted that there was some unfairness in denying the benefits of the comparative negligence rule to other plaintiffs who had sought to raise the issue on appeal while granting them to Nga Li, but justified its result by noting that it provided a good incentive in future cases for parties to "raise issues involving renovation of unsound or outmoded legal doctrines." The judgment was reversed. There were two other opinions in the case. Mosk, J., concurring and dissenting, took exception to that portion of the opinion that held the rule of comparative negligence should apply to all cases in which the trial had not yet begun. Clark, J., (McComb, J., concurring) dissented on the ground that section 1714 of the Civil Code codified the common law rule on contributory negligence, which could only be displaced by other legislation.]

NOTES

1. *Historical origins of the comparative negligence system.* Although comparative negligence has met with widespread favor only in recent years, its possibilities have long been known to lawyers. A form of comparative negligence was enacted in Georgia as early as 1855; a pure comparative negligence system was adopted in Mississippi as early as 1919; and comparative negligence was introduced by legislation in Wisconsin in 1931.

There has also been fleeting judicial acknowledgment of comparative negligence. In Galena & Chicago Union R.R. v. Jacobs, 20 Ill. 478,

496-497 (1858), a 4-year-old boy was run over by an engine. In assessing the effect of the contributory negligence of the boy and his parents, the court concluded that

> . . . in this, as in all like cases, the degrees of negligence must be measured and considered, and wherever it shall appear that the plaintiff's negligence is comparatively slight, and that of the defendant gross, he shall not be deprived of his action.

While *Galena Railroad* removed the defense of contributory negligence in some cases, it did not replace the all-or-nothing rule with proportionate recovery in cases where both parties were at fault. Moreover, it was exceedingly difficult to define "gross" negligence and to set up a satisfactory guide for the jury to determine it in any particular case. In any event, this common-law doctrine was short-lived. See City of Lanark v. Dougherty, 38 N.E. 892 (Ill. 1894), where the court simply stated: "The doctrine of comparative negligence is no longer the law of this court."

From its humble roots comparative negligence has become a veritable giant. As recently as 1968 only five states had adopted some form of comparative negligence by statute. Then the dam broke. Between 1969 and 1973 some 19 more states adopted some form of comparative negligence by legislation so that by the time Hoffman v. Jones and *Li* were decided, the common-law rule had been abandoned in about half the states. Today virtually all states have some form of comparative negligence usually by legislation and occasionally by judicial decision. For a detailed tally see V. Schwartz, Comparative Negligence 1-2 (2d ed. 1986 & 1993 Supp.).

For a comment on *Li*, see Fleming, Foreword: Comparative Negligence At Last — by Judicial Choice, 64 Cal. L. Rev. 239 (1976).

2. *Comparative negligence in admiralty.* The traditional rule for the apportionment of damages in admiralty cases was the rule of "divided damages," whereby an equal division of property damage was required whenever two ships were guilty of negligence, no matter what their relative degrees of fault. The Schooner Catharine v. Dickinson, 58 U.S. 170 (1854). In United States v. Reliable Transfer Co., 421 U.S. 397, 405, 411 (1975), the plaintiff's tanker, the *Mary A. Whalen,* crashed into the rocks after her captain attempted dangerous turning maneuvers that failed in part because the Coast Guard had failed to maintain its breakwater lights. "The District Court found that the vessel's grounding was caused 25% by the failure of the Coast Guard to maintain the breakwater light and 75% by the fault of the *Whalen,*" but owing to the admiralty rules divided damages equally. A unanimous Supreme Court jettisoned the rule of divided damages in favor of the pure form of comparative negligence less than two months before Li v. Yellow Cab. Through Justice Stewart it said:

An equal division of damages is a reasonably satisfactory result only where each vessel's fault is approximately equal and each vessel thus assumes a share of the collision damages in proportion to its share of the blame, or where proportionate degrees of fault cannot be measured and determined on a rational basis. The rule produces palpably unfair results in every other case. For example, where one ship's fault in causing a collision is relatively slight and her damages small, and where the second ship is grossly negligent and suffers extensive damage, the first ship must still make a substantial payment to the second. "This result hardly commends itself to the sense of justice any more appealingly than does the common law doctrine of contributory negligence. . . ." G. Gilmore & C. Black, The Law of Admiralty 528 (2d ed. 1975). . . .

We hold that when two or more parties have contributed by their fault to cause property damage in a maritime collision or stranding, liability for such damage is to be allocated among the parties proportionately to the comparative degree of their fault, and that liability for such damages is to be allocated equally only when the parties are equally at fault or when it is not possible fairly to measure the comparative degree of their fault.

By its decision, the Supreme Court brought the admiralty rules applied in United States courts into conformity with those applied by all other leading maritime nations. See the Maritime Conventions Act, 1 & 2 Geo. V., c. 57, and the comparative negligence rules applicable in personal injury actions under the Jones Act, 46 U.S.C. §688 (1994).

3. *"Impure" comparative negligence by judicial legislation.* In Bradley v. Appalachian Power Co., 256 S.E.2d 879, 885 (W. Va. 1979), the West Virginia Supreme Court adopted comparative negligence by judicial action but declined to follow *Li* in its choice of the pure form. Instead the court took a more restrained approach:

We do not accept the major premise of pure comparative negligence that a party should recover his damages regardless of his fault, so long as his fault is not 100 percent. Without embarking on an extended philosophical discussion of the nature and purpose of our legal system, we do state that in the field of tort law we are not willing to abandon the concept that where a party substantially contributes to his own damages, he should not be permitted to recover for any part of them. We do recognize that the present rule that prohibits recovery to the plaintiff if he is at fault in the slightest degree is manifestly unfair, and in effect rewards the substantially negligent defendant by permitting him to escape any responsibility for his negligence.

Our present judicial rule of contributory negligence is therefore modified to provide that a party is not barred from recovering damages in a tort action so long as his negligence or fault does not equal or exceed the combined negligence or fault of the other parties involved in the accident.

Does the *Bradley* rule encourage the plaintiff to join as many parties to the suit as possible? What should be done if, for example, a landlord and tenant are joined in a suit arising out of a single defendant upon common property?

4. Economic analysis of comparative negligence. The efficiency analysis of comparative negligence has been, on balance, somewhat more tentative than the fairness arguments made in its favor. Once again the issue is how to coordinate the behavior of two parties, each of whom will vary the level of care provided as a function of the level of care provided by the other side. At one level, therefore, the familiar paradox of the Hand formula reasserts itself in this context. Where the parties and the court both possess full information, negligent behavior will not occur. Suppose that the expected loss is $100 and the optimal levels of precautions are $30 by the plaintiff and $40 by the defendant. If comparative negligence were to leave the plaintiff with 20 percent of the expected loss, it might appear that the precaution would not be taken because plaintiff's cost of avoidance ($30) is greater than his residual loss ($20). Nonetheless, this analysis is incomplete because it does not take into account the response of the defendant, who will prefer to spend the $40 on precaution in order to avoid the $80 worth of loss. Yet once that step is taken, the plaintiff will now prefer to take precautions as well, for the $30 spent could avoid a $100 loss that might otherwise occur. See R. Posner, Economic Analysis of Law 171-172 (4th ed. 1992). See also S. Shavell, An Economic Analysis of Accident Law 15-16 (1987); Haddock and Curran, An Economic Theory of Comparative Negligence, 14 J. Legal Stud. 49 (1985); Cooter and Ulen, An Economic Case for Comparative Negligence, 61 N.Y.U. L. Rev. 1067 (1986).

The analysis, however, is somewhat more complicated, because it cannot be assumed that the anticipated loss will remain at $100 regardless of whether the defendant takes precautions. Nor can it be assumed that either side has any information on the relation between the dollar cost of precautions and expected damages when the initial decisions are made. Therefore, these results are subject to wide variation once the possibility of error is introduced, be it by the parties or by the trier of fact, just as was the case when the Hand formula was applied in other contexts. Thus if in the above example the defendant thought he would have to spend $50 in order to avoid a 40 percent chance of a $100 loss, he would not take precautions and thus would be held negligent. But if the plaintiff knew or had reason to believe that the defendant would make this blunder, then his best decision, if fully informed, is not to take care, because the $30 precaution is now more expensive than the $20 in unrecoverable losses. The errors of one party thus invite strategic responses by the other.

In practice, moreover, the efficiency of the comparative negligence rule is affected by a wide range of considerations, which includes (a) the risk that the defendant will be insolvent, (b) the possibility of jury error, (c) the payment of contingent fees and other expenses of suit, (d) the lower standard for contributory negligence, and (e) the internal difficulties of the Hand formula. See generally Schwartz, Contributory and Comparative Negligence: A Reappraisal, 87 Yale L.J. 697

(1978). For an empirical study which suggests that less care is taken in states applying comparative rather than contributory negligence see Flanigan et al., Experience From Early Tort Reforms: Comparative Negligence Since 1974, 56 J. Risk & Insurance 525 (1989).

How would the analysis be altered under the old admiralty rule of even division? Under the 50 percent negligence threshold, as in Wisconsin and West Virginia?

2. By Legislation

As the decision of the California Supreme Court in Li v. Yellow Cab points out, there has been a massive legislative move towards comparative negligence within the past 15 years. A representative sample of the possible forms of comparative negligence legislation is given below. For a full collection of the statutes see V. Schwartz, Comparative Negligence, appendix B (2d ed. 1986 & 1993 Supp.). Note that the statutes in question can, and often do, provide more than the formula for apportioning losses between plaintiff and defendant.

Federal Employers' Liability Act
35 Stat. 66 (1908), 45 U.S.C. §53 (1994)

§53. That in all actions hereafter brought against any such common carrier or railroad under or by virtue of any of the provisions of this Act to recover damages for personal injuries to an employee, or where such injuries have resulted in his death, the fact that the employee may have been guilty of contributory negligence shall not bar a recovery, but the damages shall be diminished by the jury in proportion to the amount of negligence attributable to such employee: *Provided,* that no such employee who may be injured or killed shall be held to have been guilty of contributory negligence in any case where the violation by such common carrier of any statute enacted for the safety of employees contributed to the injury or death of such employee.

New York
N.Y. Civ. Prac. Law §§1411-1412 (McKinney 1994)

§1411. In any action to recover damages for personal injury, injury to property, or wrongful death, the culpable conduct attributable to the claimant or to the decedent, including contributory negligence or assumption of risk, shall not bar recovery, but the amount of damages otherwise recoverable shall be diminished in the proportion which the culpable conduct attributable to the claimant or decedent bears to the culpable conduct which caused the damages.

§1412. Culpable conduct claimed in diminution of damages, in accordance with section fourteen hundred eleven, shall be an affirmative defense to be pleaded and proved by the party asserting the defense.

Pennsylvania
42 Pa. Cons. Stat. Ann. §7102 (Purdon 1994)

(a) General rule. In all actions brought to recover damages for negligence resulting in death or injury to person or property, the fact that the plaintiff may have been guilty of contributory negligence shall not bar a recovery by the plaintiff or his legal representative where such negligence was not greater than the causal negligence of the defendant or defendants against whom recovery is sought, but any damages sustained by the plaintiff shall be diminished in proportion to the amount of negligence attributed to the plaintiff.

(b) Recovery against joint defendant; contribution. Where recovery is allowed against more than one defendant, each defendant shall be liable for that proportion of the total dollar amount awarded as damages in the ratio of the amount of his causal negligence to the amount of causal negligence attributed to all defendants against whom recovery is allowed. The plaintiff may recover the full amount of the allowed recovery from any defendant against whom the plaintiff is not barred from recovery. Any defendant who is so compelled to pay more than his percentage share may seek contribution.

(c) Downhill skiing.

(1) The General Assembly finds that the sport of downhill skiing is practiced by a large number of citizens of this Commonwealth and also attracts to this Commonwealth large numbers of nonresidents significantly contributing to the economy of this Commonwealth. It is recognized that as in some other sports, there are inherent risks in the sport of downhill skiing.

(2) The doctrine of voluntary assumption of risk as it applies to downhill skiing injuries and damages is not modified by subsections (a) and (b).

Wisconsin
Stat. Ann. §895.045 (West 1994)

§895.045. Contributory negligence shall not bar recovery in an action by any person or his legal representative to recover damages for negligence resulting in death or in injury to person or property, if such negligence was not greater than the negligence of the person against whom recovery is sought, but any damages allowed shall be diminished in the proportion to the amount of negligence attributable to the person recovering.*

NOTE

Comparative negligence and the control of juries. It seems quite possible that special verdicts may well have an important role to play in the administration of a comparative negligence system. In the typical accident case brought in a comparative negligence jurisdiction, the final award to the plaintiff is dependent upon both the extent of his damages and the degree of his negligence. A verdict that states only a dollar figure as the plaintiff's award is therefore difficult to interpret, particularly in connection with the possible posttrial motions. An award of $60,000 to a plaintiff who has suffered $150,000 damages could be attacked as inadequate if a finding of contributory negligence totally bars the plaintiff's recovery, since there is no reason for awarding only partial compensation. In a pure comparative negligence jurisdiction, however, the verdict is quite consistent with a finding that the plaintiff was 60 percent negligent. General verdicts make it quite difficult to review the conduct of a jury on posttrial motions or on appeal. Special verdicts promise greater control.

Should special verdicts on the questions of, first, the degree of negligence of each party and, second, on the total amount of damages that would have been recoverable if the plaintiff were not negligent, be required in all cases in which plaintiff's negligence is at issue? Or should the special verdicts be ordered at the request of either party or otherwise left to the discretion of the court? Note that the Idaho statute allows any party to request the court to "direct the jury to find separate special verdicts determining the amount of damages and the percentage of negligence attributable to each party," after which the court makes the appropriate reduction in damages for the successful plaintiff. The Idaho statute only allows recovery when the plaintiff's negligence "was not as great as the negligence or gross negligence of the person against whom recovery is sought." Idaho Code §6-801 (1994). Is there a greater need for the special verdict here or under pure comparative negligence?

---

*The original 1931 Wisconsin comparative negligence statute contained the words "not as great as" instead of the current words "not greater than." — ED.

3. A Common Law Reprise

Knight v. Jewett
834 P.2d 696 (Cal. 1992)

GEORGE, J. In this case, and in the companion case of Ford v. Gouin, 834 P.2d 724 (Cal. 1992), we face the question of the proper application of the "assumption of risk" doctrine in light of this court's adoption of comparative fault principles in Li v. Yellow Cab Co.

[Plaintiff Kendra Knight and defendant Michael Jewett both participated in a game of touch football that took place at the home of the mutual friend. The game was coed, with four or five players on each side, and about ten minutes into it, the plaintiff testified that she told the defendant "not to play so rough" or she would "stop playing." She stated that although he said nothing, he seemed to "acknowledge her statement" and would play less rough "prospectively." The defendant testified that the plaintiff asked him to "be careful," but did not remember her saying that she would stop playing. At any rate, on the next play the plaintiff was injured when struck by the defendant. He testified that he leaped to intercept a pass, touched the ball, and fell on the plaintiff's hand. She and her coparticipant Andrea Starr testified that defendant ran over defendant's hand while chasing Starr who had already caught the ball. The suit was brought to recover damages to her broken little finger, which had to be amputated when successive operations could not restore its use or relieve her pain.

Both sides moved for summary judgment. In support of its motion, which the trial judge granted, the defendant contended that] that "reasonable implied assumption of risk" continues to operate as a complete defense after Li and that plaintiff's action was barred under that doctrine. In this regard, defendant asserted that "[b]y participating in [the touch football game that resulted in her injury], plaintiff . . . impliedly agreed to reduce the duty of care owed to her by defendant . . . to only a duty to avoid reckless or intentionally harmful conduct," and that the undisputed facts established both that he did not intend to injure plaintiff and that the acts of defendant which resulted in plaintiff's injury were not reckless.

[In arguing against the defendant's summary judgment motion, plaintiff made two basic arguments The legal argument was that the doctrine of "reasonable implied assumption of risk" had been eliminated by the adoption of comparative fault principles, and thus . . . the basic premise of defendant's summary judgment motion was untenable. . . .] Furthermore, plaintiff maintained that even were [assumption of risk a recognized defense under comparative fault] there were numerous disputed material facts that precluded the granting of summary judgment in favor of defendant. . . . [T]here was a clear dispute between defendant's and plaintiff's recollection of the specific facts of the play in which plaintiff was injured, and, in particular, of the details of defendant's conduct that caused plaintiff's injury. She claimed that under the facts as described by plaintiff and Starr, defendant's conduct was at least reckless.

[P]laintiff [also] vigorously disputed defendant's claim that, by participating in the game in question, she impliedly had agreed to reduce the duty of care, owed to her by defendant, to only a duty to avoid reckless or intentionally harmful conduct. Plaintiff maintained in her declaration that in view of the casual, social setting, the circumstance that women and men were joint participants in the game, and the rough dirt surface on which the game was played, she anticipated from the outset that it was the kind of "mock" football game in which there would be no forceful pushing or hard hitting or shoving. . . .

. . . Plaintiff maintained that her statement during the game established that a disputed factual issue existed as to whether she voluntarily had chosen to assume the risks of the type of conduct allegedly engaged in by defendant.

II

As every leading tort treatise has explained, the assumption of risk doctrine long has caused confusion both in definition and application, because the phrase "assumption of risk" traditionally has been used in a number of very different factual settings involving analytically distinct legal concepts. . . .

In some settings — for example, most cases involving sports-related injuries — past assumption of risk decisions largely have been concerned with defining the contours of the legal duty that a given class of defendants — for example, owners of baseball stadiums or ice hockey rinks — owed to an injured plaintiff. In other settings, the assumption of risk terminology historically was applied to situations in which it was clear that the defendant had breached a legal duty of care to the plaintiff, and the inquiry focused on whether the plaintiff knowingly and voluntarily had chosen to encounter the specific risk of harm posed by the defendant's breach of duty. . . .

Prior to the adoption of comparative fault principles of liability, there often was no need to distinguish between the different categories of assumption of risk cases, because if a case fell into either category, the plaintiff's recovery was totally barred. With the adoption of comparative fault, however, it became essential to differentiate between the distinct categories of cases that traditionally had been lumped together under the rubric of assumption of risk. This court's seminal compara-

tive fault decision in *Li* explicitly recognized the need for such differentiation, and attempted to explain which category of assumption of risk
cases should be merged into the comparative fault system and which
category should not. Accordingly, in considering the current viability
of the assumption of risk doctrine in California, our analysis necessarily
begins with the *Li* decision.

[The review of *Li* is omitted.]

With respect to the effect of the adoption of comparative negligence
on the assumption of risk doctrine — the issue before us today — the
Li decision stated as follows: "As for assumption of risk, we have recognized in this state that this defense overlaps that of contributory negligence to some extent and in fact is made up of at least two distinct
defenses. 'To simplify greatly, it has been observed . . . that in one
kind of situation, to wit, where a plaintiff unreasonably undertakes to
encounter a specific known risk imposed by a defendant's negligence,
plaintiff's conduct, although he may encounter that risk in a prudent
manner, is in reality a form of contributory negligence. . . . Other
kinds of situations within the doctrine of assumption of risk are those,
for example, where plaintiff is held to agree to relieve defendant of an
obligation of reasonable conduct toward him. Such a situation would
not involve contributory negligence, but rather a reduction of defendant's duty of care.' We think it clear that the adoption of a system
of comparative negligence should entail the merger of the defense of
assumption of risk into the general scheme of assessment of liability
in proportion to fault in those particular cases in which the form of
assumption of risk involved is no more than a variant of contributory
negligence."

[W]e believe it becomes clear that the distinction in assumption of
risk cases to which the *Li* court referred in this passage was not a distinction between instances in which a plaintiff unreasonably encounters a
known risk imposed by a defendant's negligence and instances in which
a plaintiff reasonably encounters such a risk. Rather, the distinction to
which the *Li* court referred was between (1) those instances in which
the assumption of risk doctrine embodies a legal conclusion that there
is "no duty" on the part of the defendant to protect the plaintiff from
a particular risk — the category of assumption of risk that the legal
commentators generally refer to as "primary assumption of risk" — and
(2) those instances in which the defendant does owe a duty of care to
the plaintiff but the plaintiff knowingly encounters a risk of injury
caused by the defendant's breach of that duty — what most commentators have termed "secondary assumption of risk." Properly interpreted,
the relevant passage in *Li* provides that the category of assumption of
risk cases that is not merged into the comparative negligence system
and in which the plaintiff's recovery continues to be completely barred
involves those cases in which the defendant's conduct did not breach a

legal duty of care to the plaintiff, i.e., "primary assumption of risk" cases, whereas cases involving "secondary assumption of risk" properly are merged into the comprehensive comparative fault system adopted in *Li*.

Although the difference between the "primary assumption of risk"/ "secondary assumption of risk" nomenclature and the "reasonable implied assumption of risk"/"unreasonable implied assumption of risk" terminology embraced in many of the recent Court of Appeal decisions may appear at first blush to be only semantic, the significance extends beyond mere rhetoric. First, in "primary assumption of risk" cases — where the defendant owes no duty to protect the plaintiff from a particular risk of harm — a plaintiff who has suffered such harm is not entitled to recover from the defendant, whether the plaintiff's conduct in undertaking the activity was reasonable or unreasonable. Second, in "secondary assumption of risk" cases — involving instances in which the defendant has breached the duty of care owed to the plaintiff — the defendant is not entitled to be entirely relieved of liability for an injury proximately caused by such breach, simply because the plaintiff's conduct in encountering the risk of such an injury was reasonable rather than unreasonable. Third and finally, the question whether the defendant owed a legal duty to protect the plaintiff from a particular risk of harm does not turn on the reasonableness or unreasonableness of the plaintiff's conduct, but rather on the nature of the activity or sport in which the defendant is engaged and the relationship of the defendant and the plaintiff to that activity or sport. For these reasons, use of the "reasonable implied assumption of risk"/"unreasonable implied assumption of risk" terminology, as a means of differentiating between the cases in which a plaintiff is barred from bringing an action and those in which he or she is not barred, is more misleading than helpful.

Our reading of *Li*, insofar as it draws a distinction between assumption of risk cases in which the defendant has not breached any legal duty to the plaintiff and those in which the defendant has breached a legal duty, is supported not only by the language of *Li* itself and the authorities it cites, but also, and perhaps most significantly, by the fundamental principle that led the *Li* court to replace the all-or-nothing contributory negligence defense with a comparative fault scheme. In "primary assumption of risk" cases, it is consistent with comparative fault principles totally to bar a plaintiff from pursuing a cause of action, because when the defendant has not breached a legal duty of care to the plaintiff, the defendant has not committed any conduct which would warrant the imposition of any liability whatsoever, and thus there is no occasion at all for invoking comparative fault principles. By contrast, in the " secondary assumption of risk" context, the defendant has breached a duty of care owed to the plaintiff. When a risk of harm is created or imposed by a defendant's breach of duty, and a plaintiff who chose to encounter the risk is injured, comparative fault principles preclude automatically placing all of the loss on the plaintiff, because the injury in such a case may have been caused by the combined effect of the defendant's and the plaintiff's culpable conduct. To retain assumption of risk as a complete defense in such a case would fly in the face of *Li*'s basic holding that when both parties are partially at fault for an injury, a rule which places all of the loss on one of the parties is inherently inequitable. . . .

The dissenting opinion [of Kennard, J.] suggests, however, that, even when a defendant has breached its duty of care to the plaintiff, a plaintiff who reasonably has chosen to encounter a known risk of harm imposed by such a breach may be totally precluded from recovering any damages, without doing violence to comparative fault principles, on the theory that the plaintiff, by proceeding in the face of a known risk, has "impliedly consented" to any harm. For a number of reasons, we conclude this contention does not withstand analysis.

[George, J., first argues that Kennard's position is inconsistent with the text of *Li*.]

Second, the implied consent rationale rests on a legal fiction that is untenable, at least as applied to conduct that represents a breach of the defendant's duty of care to the plaintiff. It may be accurate to suggest that an individual who voluntarily engages in a potentially dangerous activity or sport "consents to" or "agrees to assume" the risks inherent in the activity or sport itself, such as the risks posed to a snow skier by moguls on a ski slope or the risks posed to a water skier by wind-whipped waves on a lake. But it is thoroughly unrealistic to suggest that, by engaging in a potentially dangerous activity or sport, an individual consents to (or agrees to excuse) a breach of duty by others that increases the risks inevitably posed by the activity or sport itself, even where the participating individual is aware of the possibility that such misconduct may occur.

A familiar example may help demonstrate this point. Although every driver of an automobile is aware that driving is a potentially hazardous activity and that inherent in the act of driving is the risk that he or she will be injured by the negligent driving of another, a person who voluntarily chooses to drive does not thereby "impliedly consent" to being injured by the negligence of another, nor has such a person "impliedly excused" others from performing their duty to use due care for the driver's safety. Instead, the driver reasonably expects that if he or she is injured by another's negligence, i.e., by the breach of the other person's duty to use due care, the driver will be entitled to compensation for his or her injuries. Similarly, although a patient who undergoes elective surgery is aware that inherent in such an operation is the risk of injury in the event the surgeon is negligent, the patient, by voluntarily encountering such risk, does not "impliedly consent" to negligently inflicted injury or "impliedly agree" to excuse the surgeon from a normal duty of care, but rather justifiably expects that the surgeon will be liable in the event of medical malpractice. . . .

[George, J., concludes that Kennard, J., improperly relied on pre-*Li* cases.]

It may be helpful at this point to summarize our general conclusions as to the current state of the doctrine of assumption of risk in light of the adoption of comparative fault principles in *Li*, general conclusions that reflect the view of a majority of the justices of the court (i.e., the three justices who have signed this opinion and Justice Mosk [concurring and dissenting]. In cases involving "primary assumption of risk" — where, by virtue of the nature of the activity and the parties' relationship to the activity, the defendant owes no legal duty to protect the plaintiff from the particular risk of harm that caused the injury — the doctrine continues to operate as a complete bar to the plaintiff's recovery. In cases involving "secondary assumption of risk" — where the defendant does owe a duty of care to the plaintiff, but the plaintiff proceeds to encounter a known risk imposed by the defendant's breach of duty — the doctrine is merged into the comparative fault scheme, and the trier of fact, in apportioning the loss resulting from the injury, may consider the relative responsibility of the parties. . . .

III

[George, J., then concurred with the "overwhelming authority" in coparticipant sports cases that the defendant's only duty was to avoid reckless or intentional harm to the plaintiff, so that the defense of primary assumption of risk was established, wholly without regard to "the plaintiff's subjective knowledge or appreciation of the potential risk."]

In reaching the conclusion that a coparticipant's duty of care should be limited in this fashion, the cases have explained that, in the heat of an active sporting event like baseball or football, a participant's normal energetic conduct often includes accidentally careless behavior. The courts have concluded that vigorous participation in such sporting events likely would be chilled if legal liability were to be imposed on a participant on the basis of his or her ordinary careless conduct. The cases have recognized that, in such a sport, even when a participant's conduct violates a rule of the game and may subject the violator to internal sanctions prescribed by the sport itself, imposition of legal liability for such conduct might well alter fundamentally the nature of the sport by deterring participants from vigorously engaging in activity that falls close to, but on the permissible side of, a prescribed rule.

[The court then brushed aside plaintiff's suggestion that genuine disputes over material facts precluded summary judgment, noting that the conduct alleged by the plaintiff "is not even closely comparable to the kind of conduct — so reckless as to be totally outside the range of the ordinary activity involved in the sport — that is a prerequisite to the imposition of legal liability upon a participant in such a sport."]

Lucas, C.J., and Arabian, J., concur.

[Mosk, J., concurring and dissenting, took the position that the summary judgment was proper in this case given that "the liability of sports participants should be limited to those cases in which their misconduct falls outside the range of the ordinary activity involved in the sport." He also urged that the defense of assumption of risk be eliminated "entirely" because of the massive confusion that has surrounded its use, and that comparable fault principles be applied across the board.]

Panelli, J, concurring and dissenting. I concur in the majority opinion solely with respect to the result reached. . . . I dissent, however, from the reasoning of the majority opinion. Instead, I reach a like result by adopting and applying the "consent-based" analysis set forth in the dissenting opinion by Justice Kennard. [Panelli, J., then concluded that the evidence showed that "plaintiff knew and appreciated that physical injury resulting from contact, such as being knocked to the ground, was possible when playing touch football. Defendant was not required to prove more, such as that plaintiff knew or appreciated that a 'serious injury' or her particular injury could result from the expected physical contact."]

Baxter, J., concurs.

Kennard, J., dissenting. . . . The defense of assumption of risk, whether the risk is assumed expressly or by implication, is based on consent. Thus, in both the express and implied forms, the defense is a specific application of the maxim that one "who consents to an act is not wronged by it." (Civ. Code, §3515.) This consent, we have explained, "will negative liability."

The elements of implied assumption of risk deserve some explanation. To establish the defense, a defendant must prove that the plaintiff voluntarily accepted a risk with knowledge and appreciation of that risk. The normal risks inherent in everyday life, such as the chance that one who uses a public highway will be injured by the negligence of another motorist, are not subject to the defense, however, because they are general rather than specific risks. . . .

[Kennard, J., then urged adoption of a rule whereby the assumption of *specific* risks must be voluntary and based on "actual knowledge of the specific danger involved."]

The defense of implied assumption of risk [recognizes] that a person generally should be required to accept responsibility for the normal consequence of a freely chosen course of conduct. . . . In those cases in which a plaintiff's decision to encounter a specific known risk was not the result of carelessness (that is, when the plaintiff's conduct is not merely a form of contributory negligence), nothing in this court's adoption in *Li* of a system of comparative fault suggests that implied assumption of risk must or should be eliminated as a complete defense to an action for negligence. I would hold, therefore, that the defense continues to exist in such situations unaffected by this court's adoption in *Li* of a comparative fault system.

NOTES

1. Comparative negligence: old questions, new context. In theory, comparative negligence only changes the consequences of the plaintiff's negligence, without altering the principles that determine negligence in the first place. In fact, many of the collateral rules that grew up under the older regime of the absolute defense have been reevaluated under the new legal order. Last clear chance is one such rule, and assumption of risk in *Knight* is yet another. A sampler of some other relevant developments includes:

(a) Strict liability causes of action. In Albrecht v. Groat, 588 P.2d 229 (Wash. 1978), the Washington Supreme Court held that comparative negligence principles did not apply to strict liability actions brought against a common carrier. In its view, Wash. Rev. Code §4.22.010 "is meant to apply only where the contributory negligence of plaintiff might otherwise bar recovery." Since such was not the case with respect to common carriers, it concluded that the statute should not be applied to reduce the plaintiff's right of action.

In Seay v. Chrysler Corp., 609 P.2d 1382 (Wash. 1980), the Washington Supreme Court extended *Albrecht* to products liability actions, basing its decision on the language of the Washington statute, thereby going against the dominant judicial trend on the point. The Massachusetts Supreme Judicial Court for its part did not allow comparative negligence to be used as a defense in a breach of warranty suit. Correia v. Firestone Tire & Rubber Co., 446 N.E.2d 1033 (Mass. 1983). For a more exhaustive treatment see Daly v. General Motors, infra at page 851.

(b) Willful misconduct. There has been broad disagreement over the proper treatment of the willful and wanton misconduct of both plaintiffs and defendants under the comparative negligence theory. In Sorenson v. Allred, 169 Cal. Rptr. 441 (Cal. App. 1980), the court took its cue from *Li* and ruled that the plaintiff's recovery was diminished by her own negligence, even though the defendant's misconduct was willful and wanton. The court noted that the elimination of such "buzz" words as willful misconduct, last clear chance, and assumption of risk could only "streamline" the trial of most cases. It rejected the contrary argument based upon the principles of deterrence, thinking it "altogether apparent that people in general and motorists in particular, do not act with any deliberative thought as to consequences which are not immediately apparent," noting in this connection the widespread failure to use seat belts.

The opposite conclusion has been reached in other jurisdictions. Thus in Burke v. 12 Rothschild's Liquor Mart, 593 N.E.2d 522, 532 (Ill. 1992), the court wrote: "Because of the qualitative difference between simple negligence and willful and wanton conduct, and because willful and wanton conduct carries a degree of opprobrium not found in merely negligent behavior, we hold that a plaintiff's negligence cannot be compared with a defendant's willful and wanton conduct." The court then left open the question of "whether a plaintiff's willful and wanton conduct can be compared with the willful and wanton conduct of the defendant." Likewise, in Davies v. Butler, 602 P.2d 605 (Nev. 1979), the Nevada Supreme Court broke with *Li,* stating that "in the absence of a clear legislative directive, we decline to abrogate the long-standing rule that mere negligence on the part of a plaintiff will not constitute a defense to the wanton or willful misconduct of a defendant."

(c) Intentional torts. Munoz v. Olin, 142 Cal. Rptr. 667, 674 (Cal. App. 1977), a wrongful death action, was brought against a policeman who shot the decedent, who was suspected of arson. In the opinion of the court, comparative negligence principles were "wholly misplaced":

> If Munoz's actions gave rise to the reasonable cause to arrest and to believe it was necessary to employ deadly force to effect that arrest then there was no liability, and if his actions did not there was full liability and there would be no room for the operation of the concept of comparative fault. The doctrine of comparative negligence was adopted as a substitute for the all or nothing rule of contributory negligence previously followed in this state, it was not a substitute for the defense of privilege to commit an intentional tort. The jury's verdict which found Munoz 35% responsible is fatally inconsistent with a finding of liability in the defendant.

The opposite view was taken in Blazovic v. Andrich, 590 A.2d 222, 231 (N.J. 1991), a case arising out of a barroom brawl, where the court deviated from the majority view and stated

> We reject the concept that intentional conduct is "different in kind" from both negligence and wanton and willful conduct, and consequently cannot be compared with them. Instead, we view intentional wrongdoing as "different in degree" from either negligence or wanton and willful conduct. To act intentionally involves knowingly or purposefully engaging in conduct "substantially certain to result in injury to another." In contrast, wanton and willful conduct poses a highly unreasonable risk of harm likely to result in injury. Neither that difference nor the divergence between intentional conduct and negligence precludes comparison by a jury. The different levels of culpability inherent in each type of conduct will merely be reflected in the jury's apportionment of fault. By viewing

the various types of tortious conduct in that way, we adhere most closely
to the guiding principle of comparative fault — to distribute the loss in
proportion to the respective faults of the parties causing that loss.

The upshot was that plaintiff's recovery against the owner of a bar was
reduced to reflect the intentional wrongs of its patrons who had previously settled with the plaintiff.

(d) Violation of safety act. Hardy v. Monsanto Enviro-Chem Systems,
Inc., 323 N.W.2d 270, 273, 274 (Mich. 1982), illustrates how the shift
from contributory to comparative negligence can lead a court to alter
its view of underlying substantive issues. Prior to the advent of comparative negligence, Michigan refused to treat the plaintiff's violation of a
safety act as a form of contributory negligence. Funk v. General Motors,
220 N.W.2d 641 (Mich. 1974). But it reversed field on the point after
the advent of its comparative negligence regime:

> Since the defense of comparative negligence serves not to undermine
> but to enhance safety in the workplace, we are of the view that compara-
> tive negligence is available in those cases where [prior decisions like *Koe-
> nig*, supra at page 330] formerly prohibited the application of the
> contributory negligence defense. . . .
>
> [A]t some point a worker must be charged with *some* responsibility for
> his own safety-related behavior. If a worker continues to work under ex-
> tremely unsafe conditions when a reasonable worker under all the facts
> and circumstances would "take a walk," the trier of fact might appropri-
> ately reduce the plaintiff's recovery under comparative negligence. Com-
> parative negligence enhances the goal of safety in the workplace under
> these conditions since it gives the worker some financial incentive to act
> in a reasonable and prudent fashion.

With *Hardy* contrast Roy Crook and Sons, Inc. v. Allen, 778 F.2d 1037
(5th Cir. 1985), where the court refused to reduce the recovery in a
wrongful death case under the FELA and the Jones Act by the wrongful
conduct of the decedent when the defendant was in violation of a safety
statute passed for his protection. The decision rested on the explicit
language of the FELA which contained both a comparative negligence
provision and an exception for safety statutes, supra at 384.

(e) Avoidable consequences. In Ostrowski v. Azzara, 545 A.2d 148
(N.J. 1988), the defendant physician argued that the plaintiff could not
recover for her major circulatory complications sustained after a routine operation to repair an irritated toe because these complications
could have been avoided if she had quit smoking and watched her
weight as she had been advised by her doctors to do. The New Jersey
court held that the comparative principles applied to the plaintiff's
failure to mitigate damages. "[I]t would be the bitterest irony if the rule
of comparative negligence, designed to ameliorate the harshness of
contributory negligence, should serve to shut out any recovery to one

who would otherwise have recovered under the law of contributory negligence. Put the other way, absent a comparative negligence act, it
would have never been thought that 'avoidable consequences' or 'mitigation of damages' attributable to post-accident conduct of any claimant would have included a shutout of apportionable damages
proximately caused by another's negligence." What result if 30 percent
of the harm was caused solely by the defendant while the other 70
percent was caused by the defendant but could have been mitigated by
the plaintiff?

(f) Seat belt defense. In Amend v. Bell, 570 P.2d 138 (Wash. 1977),
the Washington Supreme Court held that its decision in Derheim v.
Fiorito, supra at page 338, rejecting the seat belt defense, remained
good law even under the state's pure comparative negligence rule. In
the absence of a statutory requirement, the court did not want to en-
mesh itself in "a veritable battle of experts" over the nature and effects
of the seat belt defense. That result was codified by statute, supra at
page 342.

The integration of the seat belt defense with comparative negligence
was also addressed in Iowa Code Ann. §321.449, which allowed for a
reduction "by an amount not to exceed five percent of the damages
awarded after any reductions for comparative fault."

(g) Imputed negligence. Schmidt v. Martin, 510 P.2d 1244 (Kan.
1973), was a wrongful death action brought by parents against the
driver of the other car. The court refused to impute the negligence of
the decedent's uncle in driving a car while babysitting for the decedent.
"If the doctrine of imputed negligence ever had any validity in parent-
custodian situations, it should not be applied today in a world of working mothers and the universal use of babysitters. In many cases arising
today the custodian of a child is simply not subject to such a right of
control by the parent as to justify imputed liability on the basis of an
agency relationship." Schmidt was decided when contributory negligence was still an absolute bar in Kansas, and before the passage of its
statute (see page 439 infra), making defendants liable solely for their
own share of the harm. Ironically, therefore, the outcome sought by
the defendant in Schmidt has been achieved today in a more general
way. If Schmidt arose today the plaintiffs would have to successfully sue
both the driver of the other car and the decedent's uncle to obtain full
recovery.

2. Insurance complications. One of the collateral complications of the
comparative negligence rule concerns the amount of damages that can
be recovered when, as so often happens in routine collision cases, each
party is a tortfeasor as well as an accident victim. When contributory
negligence was an absolute bar it was difficult, if not impossible, for
both parties to obtain judgment, since if both were at fault typically
neither could recover. Accident cases therefore resulted in a single

judgment against one defendant that was then discharged by the insurance carrier up to the limits of its policy. Today, comparative negligence makes it possible for each party to recover from the other. Thus, assume that *A* has $100,000 in damages and was 25 percent responsible for her loss, while *B* has $200,000 in damages and was 75 percent responsible for his loss. If *A* alone were injured, she should recover $75,000 in damages from *B*. Likewise, if *B* alone were injured, he should be able to recover $50,000 in damages from *A*. The question that faced the California Supreme Court in Jess v. Herrmann, 604 P.2d 208 (Cal. 1979), was whether, as the statute seemed to require, the two damage awards should be set off against each other, so that the insurer of *B* pays *A* $25,000, or whether, in the alternative, *A*'s insurer should pay *B* $50,000 *and* *B*'s insurer should pay *A* $75,000.

The California Supreme Court held that the statutory set-off was available only when the parties in question were not covered by insurance. In its view, the function of insurance could not in fact be well served if the application of the mandatory set-off rule were allowed to produce "the anomalous situation in which a liability insurer's responsibility under its policy depends as much on the extent of injury suffered by its own insured as on the amount of damages sustained by the person its insured has negligently injured." The dissent argued that the court misconstrued the applicable statutory language; that it did not sufficiently appreciate the types of procedure that could be used to protect the interests of the various insurers, if not sued in their own names; and that it did not explain the way in which the rule was to operate in situations in which either or both parties had limited insurance coverage.

Florida, another of the early comparative negligence states, has reached a similar result. See Stuyvesant Insurance Co. v. Bournazian, 342 So. 2d 471 (Fla. 1977). See generally Fleming, Report to the Joint Committee of the California Legislature on Tort Liability on the Problems Associated with *American Motorcycle Association v. Superior Court*, 30 Hastings L.J. 1464 (1979).

Is the decision in question a victory or a defeat for the insurance industry? Is it relevant in this regard that the typical automobile insurance policy runs for six months or a year?

Chapter Five
Multiple Defendants: Joint, Several, and Vicarious Liability

A. INTRODUCTION

One of the most salient features of modern tort law is the rise of lawsuits in which the plaintiff simultaneously seeks recovery from a large number of multiple defendants. The rise of multiple party litigation is a direct consequence of the expansion of tort liability into different areas. We have already seen that actions for medical injuries can be brought simultaneously against the many physicians who provided professional services, against the hospital and its staff, and against the many different suppliers of the equipment and medicines that are used for medical treatment. Similar expansions of liability make it possible to sue not only the other driver in an automobile intersection case, but the manufacturer or dealer of the automobile, and the public and private parties responsible for designing the overall traffic system. And the modern growth of toxic torts often allows the injured party to sue any of the literally hundreds of persons who might have contributed some small fraction of the waste whose release is said to cause damage.

This proliferation of novel theories of liability makes it imperative that the tort law develop principles to govern the complexities of multiple party litigation. This chapter groups together a broad range of issues raised by multiple party litigation. The first section deals with the question of joint and several liability among various codefendants. At the outset a bit of clarification is needed, for while the terms "joint-and-several" are often run together as if a single word, they in fact represent distinct concepts. "Joint liability" implies that each of several defendants is responsible for the entire loss which (almost by definition) they all caused in part. "Several liability" holds each defendant responsible only for his proportionate share of the loss. If the plaintiff sues two defendants, a jointly liable defendant can be held for the full loss, while the severally liable defendant can only be held liable for half. The issues quickly become quite fearsome, and are broken down into two parts: the first deals with the rights of the plaintiff against each of the multiple defendants, and second deals with the rights of the defendants among each other. At this juncture it is assumed that each defendant is causally responsible for the plaintiff's loss. Chapter 6 will examine the factual and legal issues that lie behind those causal judgments.

In the second section we turn from joint and several liability to a discussion of the principles used to determine the liability for employers for the wrongs of their servants and their independent contractors. Here the liability of one person — the employer — is said to be "vicarious" in that it bears responsibility solely for what another party — the employee — has done. Vicarious liability cases do *not* involve two independent causal agents, each partially responsible for the harm. As with joint causation, the problem has two distinct parts. The first concerns the ability of the plaintiff to sue both employer and employee, and the second concerns the adjustment of rights between the two defendants. As with the causation issue, matters can become quite complex when single individuals have two or more employers, and more complicated still when multiple individuals with different employers are all involved in the same incident, as typically happens today in environmental litigation. Good luck!

B.   JOINT AND SEVERAL LIABILITY

1.   Toward the Plaintiff

Kingston v. Chicago & N.W. Ry.
211 N.W. 913 (Wis. 1927)

OWEN, J. . . . We therefore have this situation: The northeast fire was set by sparks emitted from defendant's locomotive. This fire, according to the finding of the jury, constituted a proximate cause of the destruction of plaintiff's property. This finding we find to be well supported by the evidence. We have the northwest fire, of unknown origin. This fire, according to the finding of the jury, also constituted a proximate cause of the destruction of the plaintiff's proper. This finding we also find to be well supported by the evidence. We have a union of these two fires 940 feet north of plaintiff's property, from which point the united fire bore down upon and destroyed the property. We therefore have two separate, independent, and distinct agencies, each of which constituted the proximate cause of plaintiff's damage, and either of which, in the absence of the other, would have accomplished such result.

It is settled in the law of negligence that any one of two or more joint tortfeasors, or one of two or more wrongdoers whose concurring acts of negligence result in injury, are each individually responsible for the entire damage resulting from their joint or concurrent acts of negligence. This rule also obtains "where two causes, each attributable to the negligence of a responsible person, concur in producing an injury to another, either of which causes would produce it regardless of the other,. . . because, whether the concurrence be intentional, actual, or constructive, each wrongdoer, in effect, adopts the conduct of his co-actor, and for the further reason that it is impossible to apportion the damage or to say that either perpetrated any distinct injury that can be separated from the whole. The whole loss must necessarily be considered and treated as an entirety." Cook v. M., St. P. & S.S.M.R. Co., 98 Wis. 624 (74 N.W. 561), at p. 642. That case presented a situation very similar to this. One fire, originating by sparks emitted from a locomotive, united with another fire of unknown origin and consumed plaintiff's property. There was nothing to indicate that the fire of unknown origin was not set by some human agency. The evidence in the case merely failed to identify the agency. In that case it was held that the railroad company which set one fire was not responsible for the damage committed by the united fires because the origin of the other fire was not identified . . .

Emphasis is placed upon the fact, especially in the opinion, that one fire had "no responsible origin." At other times in the opinion the fact is emphasized that it had no "known responsible origin." The plain inference from the entire opinion is that if both fires had been of responsible origin, or of known responsible origin, each wrongdoer would have been liable for the entire damage. The conclusion of the court exempting the railroad company from liability seems to be based upon the single fact that one fire had no responsible origin or no known responsible origin. It is difficult to determine just what weight was accorded to the fact that the origin of the fire was unknown. If the conclusion of the court was founded upon the assumption that the fire of unknown origin had no responsible origin, the conclusion announced may be sound and in harmony with well settled principles of negligence.

From our present consideration of the subject we are not disposed to criticise the doctrine which exempts from liability a wrongdoer who sets a fire which unites with a fire originating from natural causes, such as lightning, not attributable to any human agency, resulting in damage. It is also conceivable that a fire so set might unite with a fire of so much greater proportions, such as a raging forest fire, as to be enveloped or swallowed up by the greater holocaust, and its identity destroyed, so that the greater fire could be said to be an intervening or superseding cause. But we have no such situation here. These fires were of comparatively equal rank. If there was any difference in their magnitude or threatening aspect, the record indicates that the northeast fire was the larger fire and was really regarded as the menacing agency. At any rate there is no intimation or suggestion that the northeast fire was enveloped and swallowed up by the northwest fire. We will err on the side of the defendant if we regard the two fires as of equal rank.

According to well settled principles of negligence, it is undoubted that if the proof disclosed the origin of the northwest fire, even though its origin be attributed to a third person, the railroad company, as the originator of the northeast fire, would be liable for the entire damage. There is no reason to believe that the northwest fire originated from any other than human agency. It was a small fire. It had traveled over a limited area. It had been in existence but for a day. For a time it was thought to have been extinguished. It was not in the nature of a raging forest fire. The record discloses nothing of natural phenomena which could have given rise to the fire. It is morally certain that it was set by some human agency.

Now the question is whether the railroad company, which is found to have been responsible for the origin of the northeast fire, escapes liability because the origin of the northwest fire is not identified, although there is no reason to believe that it had any other than human origin. An affirmative answer to that question would certainly make a wrongdoer a favorite of the law at the expense of an innocent sufferer. The injustice of such a doctrine sufficiently impeaches the logic upon which it is founded. Where one who has suffered damage by fire proves the origin of a fire and the course of that fire up to the point of the destruction of his property, one has certainly established liability on the part of the originator of the fire. Granting that the union of that fire with another of natural origin, or with another of much greater proportions, is available as a defense, the burden is on the defendant to show that by reason of such union with a fire of such character the fire set by him was not the proximate cause of the damage. No principle of justice requires that the plaintiff be placed under the burden of specifically identifying the origin of both fires in order to recover the damages for which either or both fires are responsible. . . .

While under some circumstances a wrongdoer is not responsible for damage which would have occurred in the absence of his wrongful act, even though such wrongful act was a proximate cause of the accident, that doctrine does not obtain "where two causes, each attributable to the negligence of a responsible person, concur in producing an injury to another, either of which causes would produce it regardless of the other." This is because "it is impossible to apportion the damage or to say that either perpetrated any distinct injury that can be separated from the whole," and to permit each of two wrongdoers to plead the wrong of the other as a defense to his own wrongdoing would permit both wrongdoers to escape and penalize the innocent party who has been damaged by their wrongful acts.

The fact that the northeast fire was set by the railroad company, which fire was a proximate cause of plaintiff's damage, is sufficient to affirm the judgment. This conclusion renders it unnecessary to consider other grounds of liability stressed in respondent's brief.

By the Court. — Judgment affirmed.

NOTES

1. Fires: human and natural. Kingston addresses two situations: one in which both fires are set by human causes, and a second where only one such fire is set. Is it wise to adopt a rule of joint and several liability where both fires are set by human origin and a rule of no liability when only one set fire is so set? Why not a rule of several liability that holds the named defendant responsible for one-half the damage regardless of how the other fire was set?

What weight should be attached when the two fires arrive at different times? In particular ought there to be a substantial difference in the outcome of the following two cases? Case 1: Fire *A* of natural origin burns plaintiff's premises. Minutes later fire *B*, set by defendant, reaches plaintiff's property. Fire *B* could have destroyed plaintiff's property if fire *A* had not destroyed it first. Case 2: Same sequence of events, only fire *A* is of human origin and *B* is of natural origin. Should the twice-blessed plaintiff be better off in the second case than he is in the first? Case 3: Same as above, only both fires are of human origin.

2. Apportionment of damages. The typical case of joint and several liability arises when it is conceded that each of two or more defendants plays some causal role in bringing about the injury. On this question, the Restatement has proved to be exceptionally influential. Its key provision provides:

§433A: APPORTIONMENT OF HARM TO CAUSES
(1) Damages for harm are to be apportioned among two or more causes where
    (a) there are distinct harms, or
    (b) there is a reasonable basis for determining the contribution of each cause to a single harm.
(2) Damages for any other harm cannot be apportioned among two or more causes.

Comment . . .

d. Divisible harm. . . . [W]here the cattle of two or more owners trespass upon the plaintiff's land and destroy his crop, the aggregate harm is a lost crop, but it may nevertheless be apportioned among the owners of the cattle, on the basis of the number owned by each, and the reasonable assumption that the respective harm done is proportionate to that number. . . .

Such an apportionment is commonly made in cases of private nuisance, where the pollution of a stream, or flood, or smoke or dust or noise, from different sources, has interfered with the plaintiff's use or enjoyment of his land. Thus where two or more factories independently pollute a stream the interference with the plaintiff's use of the water may be treated as divisible in terms of degree, and may be apportioned among the owners of the factories, on the basis of evidence of the respective quantities of pollution discharged into the stream.

The cases that illustrate the problems raised by this provision are legion. In Smith v. J. C. Penney Co., Inc., 525 P.2d 1299, 1305-1306 (Or. 1974), the plaintiff was wearing a coat purchased from J. C. Penney made of flammable material supplied, as the jury found, by defendant Bunker-Ramo. The coat was set ablaze by a fire started through the negligence of the defendant service station employees. Bunker-Ramo contended that since "there is no way to segregate the damages as between the various defendants," plaintiff should not recover from any of them. The court, however, thought otherwise:

> There was evidence in this case that as a practical matter plaintiff's injuries were indivisible; that is, the jury could not make any reasonable determination that certain injuries were caused by the gasoline fire and other injuries were caused by the coat.
>
> An employee of the Enco Service Station had gasoline sprayed on his trousers and was engulfed in the same fire as plaintiff, yet suffered only minor burns to his legs. The jury could infer from this that plaintiff would not have incurred severe burns to her lower extremities if she had not been wearing the coat. There was evidence that burning material dripped from the coat, although there was no direct evidence that such dripping material landed on plaintiff's legs or feet. There was evidence that the burning coat radiated such heat that the jury could find it burned plaintiff's lower extremities. There also was testimony that the fierce burning of the coat and the emission of gases in the process would have impeded a wearer from rapidly escaping a fire.
>
> Most important is that there is evidence that the greatest injury to plaintiff arises out of the totality of her condition. There is testimony that she is physically and psychologically permanently disabled and unable to lead a normal life. This cannot be attributed to a burn on her foot, her head, or her body but only to her entire condition.

Should the gasoline station be held liable for the full extent of the damage, given that its employee suffered only minor burns from the same fire?

In Maddux v. Donaldson, 108 N.W.2d 33, 35 (Mich. 1961), *X*'s auto skidded and crashed into the auto in which plaintiffs were riding, whereupon an oncoming auto driven by *Y* also hit plaintiff's helpless car, adding to their damages. As Smith, J., pointed out, the question whether successive acts of negligence may be treated as a joint tort in the absence of concert of action among the defendants has become crucially important, with much authority pro and con. "There is authority, in this situation," he observed, "that plaintiff must separate the injuries, ascribing some to one tort-feasor and the balance to the other, much as a housewife separates the colored and the white goods before laundering." With three justices dissenting vigorously, the court concluded that the plaintiffs could treat this situation as a joint tort and hold *X* and *Y* jointly and severally liable for all the damages, even though that might mean "that a tort-feasor [might] pay more than his theoretical share of the damages accruing out of a confused situation which his wrong has helped to create."

3. Apportionment under CERCLA. The Restatement apportionment rules have exerted a great influence on the courts who have struggled to fill in the gaps in CERCLA (Comprehensive Environmental Response, Compensation and Liability Act) (aka Superfund) that imposes strict and joint liability on various defendants. One difficult question that arises under CERCLA is whether to apportion when apportionment is possible. In the leading case of United States v. Chem-Dyne Corp. 572 F. Supp. 802 (S.D. Ohio 1983), the court applied the Restatement approach when it refused to grant a summary judgment calling for apportionment among codefendants with respect to a dumpsite that "contains a variety of waste from 289 generators or transporters, consisting of about 608,000 pounds of material," much of it from unascertained sources, which made it impossible to determine in advance whether apportionment was possible. A more flexible rule, allowing for apportionment in some cases of apparently indivisible harms was followed in Allied Corp. v. Acme Solvents Reclaiming, Inc., 691 F. Supp. 1100 (N.D. Ill. 1988).

Apportionment under the Restatement rule led to a hot dispute in Matter of Bell Petroleum Services, Inc., 3 F.3d 889, 903-904 (5th Cir. 1993), where three successive operators — Leigh, Bell, Sequa — ran chrome-plating operations on an industrial site from 1967 to 1977. The United States sued all three parties for chromium contamination of the ground water. The United States settled with Bell for $1,000,000 and with Leigh for $100,000, and then sought to hold Sequa responsible for $1,866,000 for past damages, and to keep it jointly and severally liable (with other defendants) for all future costs needed to maintain the groundwater system. Sequa challenged the suit on the ground that the costs attributable to the chromium contamination could be apportioned among the defendants, and, after being rebuffed in the District

Court, was successful in the Fifth Circuit. Jolly, J., first relied explicitly on the illustrations from comment *d* to hold that a reasonable ground for apportionment existed, and remanded the case to the District Court.

> Even though it is not possible to determine with absolute certainty the exact amount of chromium each defendant introduced into the ground-water, there is sufficient evidence from which a reasonable and rational approximation of each defendant's individual contribution to the contamination can be made.. . . In response to the EPA's motion for summary judgment [against apportionment], Sequa introduced evidence regarding chrome flake purchases during each operator's tenure. It also introduced evidence with respect to the value of the chrome-plating done by each, as well as summaries of sales. Given the number of years that had passed since the activities were conducted, the records of these activities were not complete. However, there was testimony from various witnesses regarding the rinsing and wastewater disposal practices of each defendant, and the amount of chrome-plating activity conducted by each.
>
> During [the hearing on joint responsibility], Sequa introduced expert testimony regarding a volumetric approach to apportionment. The first expert, Henderson, calculated the total amount of chromium that had been introduced into the environment by Leigh, Bell, and Sequa, collectively and individually. The second expert, Mooney, calculated the amount of chromium that would have been introduced into the environment by each operator on the basis of electrical usage records.
>
> In addition to rejecting apportionment because of competing theories, the district court also rejected volume as a basis for apportionment, because there was no method of dividing the liability among the defendants which would rise to any level of fairness above mere speculation. It stated that each of the proposed apportionment methods involved significant assumption factors, because records had been lost, and because the theories differed significantly.
>
> The existence of competing theories of apportionment is an insufficient reason to reject all of those theories. It is true, as the district court noted, that the records of chrome-plating activity were incomplete. However, under the facts and circumstances of this case, and in the light of the other evidence that is available, that factor may be taken into account in apportioning Sequa's share of the liability. Finally, the fact that Sequa's experts relied on certain assumptions in forming their opinions is not fatal to Sequa's ability to prove that there is a reasonable basis for apportionment. Expert opinions frequently include assumptions. If those assumptions are well-founded and reasonable, and not inconsistent with the facts as established by other competent evidence, they may be sufficiently reliable to support a conclusion that a reasonable basis for apportionment exists.

The dissenting opinion of Parker, J., argued that "while Sequa met its *legal* burden of establishing that the type of harm involved is capable of apportionment, it failed to meet its factual burden relative to apportionment."

4. Theoretical allocation of damages between joint tortfeasors. The ever-expanding notions of causation and responsibility have continued to increase the pressure on the rules of contribution and indemnity. Thus, when both defendants are present and able to pay the loss, how should it be allocated between them? One proposal that has attracted considerable attention is that by Rizzo and Arnold, Causal Apportionment in the Law of Torts: An Economic Theory, 80 Colum. L. Rev. 1399 (1980). In order to get some sense of the problem assume that there are two actions, one by defendant *A* and the other by defendant *B*. The probability of harm given *A*'s act alone could be set at 20 percent; the probability of harm given *B*'s act alone could be set at 40 percent. Both acts occur and the harm follows. How should the loss be apportioned between the two defendants? Rizzo and Arnold propose that it be allocated in accordance with their "probabilistic marginal product." More simply stated, each party bears a fraction of the loss whose numerator is equal to the probability that his act alone would cause harm and whose denominator is the possibility that either act taken independently would cause harm. In the example given above, *A*'s portion of the harm is 0.2/(0.2 + 0.4), or one-third, while *B*'s portion of the harm is 0.4/(0.2 + 0.4), or two-thirds.

The use of this formula presupposes, of course, that there is some reasonably precise way to measure the independent probability of the actions of both *A* and *B*, which might be difficult if they are not recurrent events for which probability estimates are easily available. The formula has also been criticized on the ground that it does not provide any obvious answer for the common case in which the probability of harm, given the wrongful conduct of *A* or *B,* with either acting alone, is zero. See Kruskal, Terms of Reference: Singular Confusion about Multiple Causation, 15 J. Legal Stud. 427 (1986). For other ins and outs of the debate see Kaye and Aicken, A Comment on Causal Apportionment, 13 J. Legal Stud. 191 (1984), and Rizzo and Arnold, Causal Apportionment: Reply to the Critics, 15 J. Legal Stud. 219 (1986). What is wrong with a simple solution that says in all joint causation cases the liability is divided by the number of codefendants? See infra at page 430, note 5.

Summers v. Tice
199 P.2d 1 (Cal. 1948)

CARTER, J. Each of the two defendants appeals from a judgment against them in an action for personal injuries. Pursuant to stipulation the appeals have been consolidated.

Plaintiff's action was against both defendants for an injury to his right eye and face as the result of being struck by bird shot discharged from a shotgun. The case was tried by the court without a jury and the court found that on November 20, 1945, plaintiff and the two defendants were hunting quail on the open range. Each of the defendants was armed with a 12 gauge shotgun loaded with shells containing 7-½ size shot. Prior to going hunting plaintiff discussed the hunting procedure with defendants, indicating that they were to exercise care when shooting and to "keep in line." In the course of hunting plaintiff proceeded up a hill, thus placing the hunters at the points of a triangle. The view of defendants with reference to plaintiff was unobstructed and they knew his location. Defendant Tice flushed a quail which rose in flight to a 10-foot elevation and flew between plaintiff and defendants. Both defendants shot at the quail, shooting in plaintiff's direction. At that time defendants were 75 yards from plaintiff. One shot struck plaintiff in his eye and another in his upper lip. Finally it was found by the court that as the direct result of the shooting by defendants the shots struck plaintiff as above mentioned and that defendants were negligent in so shooting and plaintiff was not contributorily negligent.

[The court upheld the findings below on defendants' negligence and plaintiff's lack of contributory negligence and assumption of risk.]

The problem presented in this case is whether the judgment against both defendants may stand. It is argued by defendants that they are not joint tort feasors, and thus jointly and severally liable, as they were not acting in concert, and that there is not sufficient evidence to show which defendant was guilty of the negligence which caused the injuries — the shooting by Tice or that by Simonson. Tice argues that there is evidence to show that the shot which struck plaintiff came from Simonson's gun because of admissions allegedly made by him to third persons and no evidence that they came from his gun. Further in connection with the latter contention, the court failed to find on plaintiff's allegation in his complaint that he did not know which one was at fault — did not find which defendant was guilty of the negligence which caused the injuries to plaintiff.

Considering the last argument first, we believe it is clear that the court sufficiently found on the issue that defendants were jointly liable and that thus the negligence of both was the cause of the injury or to that legal effect. It found that both defendants were negligent and "That as a direct and proximate result of the shots fired by *defendants, and each of them,* a birdshot pellet was caused to and did lodge in plaintiff's right eye and that another birdshot pellet was caused to and did lodge in plaintiff's upper lip." In so doing the court evidently did not give credence to the admissions of Simonson to third persons that he fired the shots, which it was justified in doing. It thus determined that the negligence of both defendants was the legal cause of injury — or that both were responsible. Implicit in such finding is the assumption that the court was unable to ascertain whether the shots were from the gun of one defendant or the other or one shot from each of them. The one shot that entered plaintiff's eye was the major factor in assessing damages and that shot could not have come from the gun of both defendants. It was from one or the other only.

It has been held that where a group of persons are on a hunting party, or otherwise engaged in the use of firearms, and two of them are negligent in firing in the direction of a third person who is injured thereby, both of those so firing are liable for the injury suffered by the third person, although the negligence of only one of them could have caused the injury. (Moore v. Foster, 182 Miss. 15; Oliver v. Miles, 144 Miss. 852.) These cases speak of the action of defendants as being in concert as the ground of decision, yet it would seem they are straining that concept and the more reasonable basis appears in Oliver v. Miles, supra. There two persons were hunting together. Both shot at some partridges and in so doing shot across the highway injuring plaintiff who was travelling on it. The court stated they were acting in concert and thus both were liable. The court then stated: "We think that . . . each is liable for the resulting injury to the boy, although no one can say definitely who actually shot him. *To hold otherwise would be to exonerate both from liability, although each was negligent, and the injury resulted from such negligence.*" [Emphasis added.]

When we consider the relative position of the parties and the results that would flow if plaintiff was required to pin the injury on one of the defendants only, a requirement that the burden of proof on that subject be shifted to defendants becomes manifest. They are both wrong-doers — both negligent toward plaintiff. They brought about a situation where the negligence of one of them injured the plaintiff, hence it should rest with them each to absolve himself if he can. The injured party has been placed by defendants in the unfair position of pointing to which defendant caused the harm. If one can escape, the other may also and plaintiff is remediless. Ordinarily defendants are in a far better position to offer evidence to determine which one caused the injury. . . .

Cases are cited for the proposition that where two or more tort feasors acting independently of each other cause an injury to plaintiff, they are not joint tort feasors and plaintiff must establish the portion of the damage caused by each, even though it is impossible to prove the portion of the injury caused by each. In view of the foregoing discussion it is apparent that defendants in cases like the present one may be treated as liable on the same basis as joint tort feasors, and hence the last-cited cases are distinguishable inasmuch as they involve independent tort feasors.

In addition to that, however, it should be pointed out that the same reasons of policy and justice shift the burden to each of defendants to absolve himself if he can — relieving the wronged person of the duty of apportioning the injury to a particular defendant, apply here where we are concerned with whether plaintiff is required to supply evidence for the apportionment of damages. If defendants are independent tort feasors and thus each liable for the damage caused by him alone, and, at least, where the matter of apportionment is incapable of proof, the innocent wronged party should not be deprived of his right to redress. The wrongdoers should be left to work out between themselves any apportionment. Some of the cited cases refer to the difficulty of apportioning the burden of damages between the independent tort feasors, and say that where factually a correct division cannot be made, the trier of fact may make it the best it can, which would be more or less a guess, stressing the factor that the wrongdoers are not in a position to complain of uncertainty.

It is urged that plaintiff now has changed the theory of his case in claiming a concert of action; that he did not plead or prove such concert. From what has been said it is clear that there has been no change in theory. The joint liability, as well as the lack of knowledge as to which defendant was liable, was pleaded and the proof developed the case under either theory. We have seen that for the reasons of policy discussed herein, the case is based upon the legal proposition that, under the circumstances here presented, each defendant is liable for the whole damage whether they are deemed to be acting in concert or independently.

The judgment is affirmed.

NOTE

Alternative liability. Prior to *Summers,* courts were more reluctant to indulge in the fancy footwork needed to apportion harm. In Adams v. Hall, 2 Vt. 9, 11 (1829), the plaintiff's sheep were killed by two dogs, one owned by one defendant and the second by the other. Once the evidence showed that the two dogs did not have a common owner, the court refused to allow the plaintiff recovery against either. "Hall was under no obligation to keep the other defendant's dog from killing sheep; nor *vice versa.* Then, shall each become liable for the injury done by the other's dog, merely because the dogs, without the knowledge or consent of the owners did the mischief in company? We think not." Hutchinson, J., then analogized the case to one where two servants of different owners combined to destroy property without the knowledge and consent of their masters, and concluded that there too neither master would be liable.

Summers marks a departure from the prior common-law rule and presents a situation where either *A or B* is causally responsible for the plaintiff's harm, and thus differs from *Kingston,* where *both A and B* are causally responsible. Is a regime of joint and several liability equally appropriate for both situations? A regime of several liability only? On the court's reasoning in *Summers,* what result if there were ten persons in the hunting party? One hundred? How would the decision look to you if both defendants were covered by liability insurance issued by the same carrier?

The result in Summers v. Tice has been adopted in the Restatement (Second) of Torts §433B(3). For one dramatic application see Hall v. E. I. du Pont de Nemours & Co., 345 F. Supp. 353 (E.D.N.Y. 1972), where 13 infant plaintiffs, all injured in separate blasting cap accidents, sued each of six corporate defendants. The defendants argued that the plaintiffs should not be allowed to shift the burden of proof on causation because the caps could have been made by parties not named as defendants in the suit, including foreign manufacturers and domestic companies that had gone out of business. The court held, however, that if the plaintiffs could establish that it was more likely than not that one of the named defendants manufactured the particular cap that caused each injury, then the burden was on each defendant to show that its cap was not involved in that particular incident. Even with the identification of each cap established, there are further issues to be resolved in blasting cap cases. See Pittsburg Reduction Co. v. Horton, at page 499, note 3.

Sindell v. Abbott Laboratories
607 P.2d 924 (Cal. 1980)

MOSK, J. This case involves a complex problem both timely and significant: may a plaintiff, injured as the result of a drug administered to her mother during pregnancy, who knows the type of drug involved but cannot identify the manufacturer of the precise product, hold liable for her injuries a maker of a drug produced from an identical formula?

Plaintiff Judith Sindell brought an action against eleven drug companies and Does 1 through 100, on behalf of herself and other women similarly situated. The complaint alleges as follows:

Between 1941 and 1971, defendants were engaged in the business of manufacturing, promoting, and marketing diethylstilbesterol (DES), a drug which is a synthetic compound of the female hormone estrogen. The drug was administered to plaintiff's mother and the mothers of the class she represents, [1] for the purpose of preventing miscarriage. In

1. The plaintiff class alleged consists of "girls and women who are residents of California and who have been exposed to DES before birth and who may or may not know the fact or the dangers" to which they were exposed. Defendants are also sued as representatives of a class of drug manufacturers which sold DES after 1941.

1947, the Food and Drug Administration authorized the marketing of DES as a miscarriage preventative, but only on an experimental basis, with a requirement that the drug contain a warning label to that effect.

DES may cause cancerous vaginal and cervical growths in the daughters exposed to it before birth, because their mothers took the drug during pregnancy. The form of cancer from which these daughters suffer is known as adenocarcinoma, and it manifests itself after a minimum latent period of 10 or 12 years. It is a fast-spreading and deadly disease, and radical surgery is required to prevent it from spreading. DES also causes adenosis, precancerous vaginal and cervical growths which may spread to other areas of the body. The treatment for adenosis is cauterization, surgery, or cryosurgery. Women who suffer from this condition must be monitored by biopsy or colposcopic examination twice a year, a painful and expensive procedure. Thousands of women whose mothers received DES during pregnancy are unaware of the effects of the drug.

In 1971, the Food and Drug Administration ordered defendants to cease marketing and promoting DES for the purpose of preventing miscarriages, and to warn physicians and the public that the drug should not be used by pregnant women because of the danger to their unborn children.*

During the period defendants marketed DES, they knew or should have known that it was a carcinogenic substance, that there was a grave danger after varying periods of latency it would cause cancerous and precancerous growths in the daughters of the mothers who took it, and that it was ineffective to prevent miscarriage. Nevertheless, defendants continued to advertise and market the drug as a miscarriage preventative. They failed to test DES for efficacy and safety; the tests performed by others, upon which they relied, indicated that it was not safe or effective. In violation of the authorization of the Food and Drug administration, defendants marketed DES on an unlimited basis rather than as an experimental drug, and they failed to warn of its potential danger.[2]

Because of defendants' advertised assurances that DES was safe and effective to prevent miscarriage, plaintiff was exposed to the drug prior to her birth. She became aware of the danger from such exposure within one year of the time she filed her complaint. As a result of the DES ingested by her mother, plaintiff developed a malignant bladder tumor which was removed by surgery. She suffers from adenosis and must constantly be monitored by biopsy or colposcopy to insure early warning of further malignancy.

*It should also be noted that DES continues to be used today for purposes other than the prevention of miscarriage in pregnancy. — ED.

2. It is alleged also that defendants failed to determine if there was any means to avoid or treat the effects of DES upon the daughters of women exposed to it during pregnancy, and failed to monitor the carcinogenic effects of the drug.

The first cause of action alleges that defendants were jointly and individually negligent in that they manufactured, marketed and promoted DES as a safe and efficacious drug to prevent miscarriage, without adequate testing or warning, and without monitoring or reporting its effects.

A separate cause of action alleges that defendants are jointly liable regardless of which particular brand of DES was ingested by plaintiff's mother because defendants collaborated in marketing, promoting and testing the drug, relied upon each other's tests, and adhered to an industry-wide safety standard. DES was produced from a common and mutually agreed upon formula as a fungible drug interchangeable with other brands of the same product; defendants knew or should have known that it was customary for doctors to prescribe the drug by its generic rather than its brand name and that pharmacists filled prescriptions from whatever brand of the drug happened to be in stock.

Other causes of action are based upon theories of strict liability, violation of express and implied warranties, false and fraudulent representations, misbranding of drugs in violation of federal law, conspiracy and "lack of consent."

Each cause of action alleges that defendants are jointly liable because they acted in concert, on the basis of express and implied agreements, and in reliance upon and ratification and exploitation of each other's testing and marketing methods.

Plaintiff seeks compensatory damages of $1 million and punitive damages of $10 million for herself. For the members of her class, she prays for equitable relief in the form of an order that defendants warn physicians and others of the danger of DES and the necessity of performing certain tests to determine the presence of disease caused by the drug, and that they establish free clinics in California to perform such tests.

Defendants demurred to the complaint. While the complaint did not expressly allege that plaintiff could not identify the manufacturer of the precise drug ingested by her mother, she stated in her points and authorities in opposition to the demurrers filed by some of the defendants that she was unable to make the identification, and the trial court sustained the demurrers of these defendants without leave to amend on the ground that plaintiff did not and stated she could not identify which defendant had manufactured the drug responsible for her injuries. Thereupon, the court dismissed the action. This appeal involves only five of ten defendants named in the complaint. . . .[4]

---

4. Abbott Laboratories, Eli Lilly and Company, E.R. Squibb and Sons, The Upjohn Company, and Rexall Drug Company are respondents. The action was dismissed or the appeal abandoned on various grounds as to other defendants named in the complaint; e.g., one defendant demonstrated it had not manufactured DES during the period plaintiff's mother took the drug.

This case is but one of a number filed throughout the country seeking to hold drug manufacturers liable for injuries allegedly resulting from DES prescribed to the plaintiff's mothers since 1947. According to a note in the Fordham Law Review, estimates of the number of women who took the drug during pregnancy range from 1-½ million to 3 million. Hundreds, perhaps thousands, of the daughters of these women suffer from adenocarcinoma, and the incidence of vaginal adenosis among them is 30 to 90 percent. (Comment, DES and a Proposed Theory of Enterprise Liability (1978) 46 Fordham L. Rev. 963, 964-967 [hereafter Fordham Comment].) Most of the cases are still pending. . . .

We begin with the proposition that, as a general rule, the imposition of liability depends upon a showing by the plaintiff that his or her injuries were caused by the act of the defendant or by an instrumentality under the defendant's control.

There are, however, exceptions to this rule. Plaintiff's complaint suggests several bases upon which defendants may be held liable for her injuries even though she cannot demonstrate the name of the manufacturer which produced the DES actually taken by her mother. The first of these theories, classically illustrated by Summers v. Tice [supra at page 407], places the burden of proof of causation upon tortious defendants in certain circumstances. The second basis of liability emerging from the complaint is that defendants acted in concert to cause injury to plaintiff. There is a third and novel approach to the problem, sometimes called the theory of "enterprise liability," but which we prefer to designate by the more accurate term of "industry-wide" liability, which might obviate the necessity for identifying the manufacturer of the injury-causing drug. We shall conclude that these doctrines, as previously interpreted, may not be applied to hold defendants liable under the allegations of this complaint. However, we shall propose and adopt a fourth basis for permitting the action to be tried, grounded upon an extension of the *Summers* doctrine.

Plaintiff places primary reliance upon cases which hold that if a party cannot identify which of two or more defendants caused an injury, the burden of proof may shift to the defendants to show that they were not responsible for the harm. This principle is sometimes referred to as the "alternative liability" theory. . . .

The rule developed in *Summers* has been embodied in the Restatement of Torts. (Rest. 2d Torts, §433B, subsec. (3).[11]) Indeed, the *Summers* facts are used as an illustration (p. 447).

___

11. §433B, subsection (3) of the Restatement provides: "Where the conduct of two or more actors is tortious, and it is proved that harm has been caused to the plaintiff by only one of them, but there is uncertainty as to which one has caused it, the burden is upon each such actor to prove that he has not caused the harm." The reason underlying the rule is "the injustice of permitting proved wrongdoers, who among them have in-

[The court then noted that the loss of evidence on identification was the fault of neither the plaintiff nor the defendant, being largely attributable to the passage of time and the destruction of records.]

Thus we conclude that the fact defendants do not have greater access to information which might establish the identity of the manufacturer of the DES which injured plaintiff does not per se prevent application of the *Summers* rule.

Nevertheless, plaintiff may not prevail in her claim that the *Summers* rationale should be employed to fix the whole liability for her injuries upon defendants, at least as those principles have previously been applied. There is an important difference between the situation involved in *Summers* and the present case. There, all the parties who were or could have been responsible for the harm to the plaintiff were joined as defendants. Here, by contrast, there are approximately 200 drug companies which made DES, any of which might have manufactured the injury-producing drug.

Defendants maintain that, while in *Summers* there was a 50 percent chance that one of the two defendants was responsible for the plaintiff's injuries, here since any one of 200 companies which manufactured DES might have made the product which harmed plaintiff, there is no rational basis upon which to infer that any defendant in this action caused plaintiff's injuries, nor even a reasonable possibility that they were responsible.

These arguments are persuasive if we measure the chance that any one of the defendants supplied the injury-causing drug by the number of possible tortfeasors. In such a context, the possibility that any of the five defendants supplied the DES to plaintiff's mother is so remote that it would be unfair to require each defendant to exonerate itself. There may be a substantial likelihood that none of the five defendants joined in the action made the DES which caused the injury, and that the offending producer not named would escape liability altogether. While we propose, infra, an adaptation of the rule in *Summers* which will substantially overcome these difficulties, defendants appear to be correct that the rule, as previously applied, cannot relieve plaintiff of the burden of proving the identity of the manufacturer which made the drug causing her injuries.

II

The second principle upon which plaintiff relies is the so-called "concert of action" theory.. . . [The court rejected this theory on the

---

flicted an injury upon the entirely innocent plaintiff, to escape liability merely because the nature of their conduct and the resulting harm has made it difficult or impossible to prove which of them has caused the harm." (Rest. 2d Torts, §433B, com. *f*, p. 446.)

ground that there was no evidence that "they assisted and encouraged one another to inadequately test DES and to provide inadequate warnings."]

III

A third theory upon which plaintiff relies is the concept of industry-wide liability, or according to the terminology of the parties, "enterprise liability." This theory was suggested in Hall v. E. I. Du Pont de Nemours & Co., Inc. [supra at page 411]. . . .

Under the theory of industry-wide liability . . . each manufacturer could be liable for all injuries caused by DES by virtue of adherence to an industry-wide standard of safety. . . .

The [Fordham] Comment proposes seven requirements for a cause of action based upon industry-wide liability,[24] and suggests that if a plaintiff proves these elements, the burden of proof of causation should be shifted to the defendants, who may exonerate themselves only by showing that their product could not have caused the injury.

We decline to apply this theory in the present case. At least 200 manufacturers produced DES; *Hall,* which involved 6 manufacturers representing the entire blasting cap industry in the United States, cautioned against application of the doctrine espoused therein to a large number of producers. Moreover, in *Hall,* the conclusion that the defendants jointly controlled the risk was based upon allegations that they had delegated some functions relating to safety to a trade association. There are no such allegations here, and we have concluded above that plaintiff has failed to allege liability on a concert of action theory.

Equally important, the drug industry is closely regulated by the Food and Drug Administration, which actively controls the testing and manufacture of drugs and the method by which they are marketed, including the contents of warning labels. To a considerable degree, therefore, the standards followed by drug manufacturers are suggested or com-

---

24. The suggested requirements are as follows:

1. There existed an insufficient, industry-wide standard of safety as to the manufacture of the product.

2. Plaintiff is not at fault for the absence of evidence identifying the causative agent but, rather, this absence of proof is due to defendant's conduct.

3. A generically similar defective product was manufactured by all the defendants.

4. Plaintiff's injury was caused by this defect.

5. Defendants owed a duty to the class of which plaintiff was a member.

6. There is clear and convincing evidence that plaintiff's injury was caused by a product made by one of the defendants. For example, the joined defendants accounted for a high percentage of such defective products on the market at the time of plaintiff's injury.

7. All defendants were tortfeasors.

pelled by the government. Adherence to those standards cannot, of course, absolve a manufacturer of liability to which it would otherwise be subject. But since the government plays such a pervasive role in formulating the criteria for the testing and marketing of drugs, it would be unfair to impose upon a manufacturer liability for injuries resulting from the use of a drug which it did not supply simply because it followed the standards of the industry.

IV

If we were confined to the theories of *Summers* and *Hall,* we would be constrained to hold that the judgment must be sustained. Should we require that plaintiff identify the manufacturer which supplied the DES used by her mother or that all DES manufacturers be joined in the action, she would effectively be precluded from any recovery. As defendants candidly admit, there is little likelihood that all the manufacturers who made DES at the time in question are still in business or that they are subject to the jurisdiction of the California courts. There are, however, forceful arguments in favor of holding that plaintiff has a cause of action.

In our contemporary complex industrialized society, advances in science and technology create fungible goods which may harm consumers and which cannot be traced to any specific producer. The response of the courts can be either to adhere rigidly to prior doctrine, denying recovery to those injured by such products, or to fashion remedies to meet these changing needs. . . .

The most persuasive reason for finding plaintiff states a cause of action is that advanced in *Summers:* as between an innocent plaintiff and negligent defendants, the latter should bear the cost of the injury. Here, as in *Summers,* plaintiff is not at fault in failing to provide evidence of causation, and although the absence of such evidence is not attributable to the defendants either, their conduct in marketing a drug the effects of which are delayed for many years played a significant role in creating the unavailability of proof.

From a broader policy standpoint, defendants are better able to bear the cost of injury resulting from the manufacture of a defective product. . . .

Where, as here, all defendants produced a drug from an identical formula and the manufacturer of the DES which caused plaintiff's injuries cannot be identified through no fault of plaintiff, a modification of the rule of *Summers* is warranted. As we have seen, an undiluted *Summers* rationale is inappropriate to shift the burden of proof of causation to defendants because if we measure the chance that any particular manufacturer supplied the injury-causing product by the number of producers of DES, there is a possibility that none of the five defendants in this case produced the offending substance and that the responsible manufacturer, not named in the action, will escape liability.[28]

But we approach the issue of causation from a different perspective: we hold it to be reasonable in the present context to measure the likelihood that any of the defendants supplied the product which allegedly injured plaintiff by the percentage which the DES sold by each of them for the purpose of preventing miscarriage bears to the entire production of the drug sold by all for that purpose. Plaintiff asserts in her briefs that Eli Lilly and Company and 5 or 6 other companies produced 90 percent of the DES marketed. If at trial this is established to be the fact, then there is a corresponding likelihood that this comparative handful of producers manufactured the DES which caused plaintiff's injuries, and only a 10 percent likelihood that the offending producer would escape liability.

If plaintiff joins in the action the manufacturers of a substantial share of the DES which her mother might have taken, the injustice of shifting the burden of proof to defendants to demonstrate that they could not have made the substance which injured plaintiff is significantly diminished. While 75 to 80 percent of the market is suggested as the requirement by the Fordham Comment (at p. 996), we hold only that a substantial percentage is required.

The presence in the action of a substantial share of the appropriate market also provides a ready means to apportion damages among the defendants. Each defendant will be held liable for the proportion of the judgment represented by its share of that market unless it demonstrates that it could not have made the product which caused plaintiff's injuries. In the present case, as we have seen, one DES manufacturer was dismissed from the action upon filing a declaration that it had not manufactured DES until after plaintiff was born. Once plaintiff has met her burden of joining the required defendants, they in turn may cross-complaint against other DES manufacturers, not joined in the action, which they can allege might have supplied the injury-causing product.

Under this approach, each manufacturer's liability would approximate its responsibility for the injuries caused by its own products. Some minor discrepancy in the correlation between market share and liability is inevitable; therefore, a defendant may be held liable for a somewhat

---

28. The Fordham Comment explains the connection between percentage of market share and liability as follows: "[I]f X Manufacturer sold one-fifth of all the DES prescribed for pregnancy and identification could be made in all cases, X would be the sole defendant in approximately one-fifth of all cases and liable for all the damages in those cases. Under alternative liability, X would be joined in all cases in which identification could not be made, but liable for only one-fifth of the total damages in these cases. X would pay the same amount either way. Although the correlation is not, in practice, perfect [footnote omitted], it is close enough so that defendants' objections on the ground of fairness lose their value."

different percentage of the damage than its share of the appropriate market would justify. It is probably impossible, with the passage of time, to determine market share with mathematical exactitude. But just as a jury cannot be expected to determine the precise relationship between fault and liability in applying the doctrine of comparative fault or partial indemnity, the difficulty of apportioning damages among the defendant producers in exact relation to their market share does not seriously militate against the rule we adopt. As we said in *Summers* with regard to the liability of independent tortfeasors, where a correct division of liability cannot be made "the trier of fact may make it the best it can."

We are not unmindful of the practical problems involved in defining the market and determining market share,[29] but these are largely matters of proof which properly cannot be determined at the pleading stage of these proceedings. Defendants urge that it would be both unfair and contrary to public policy to hold them liable for plaintiff's injuries in the absence of proof that one of them supplied the drug responsible for the damage. Most of their arguments, however, are based upon the assumption that one manufacturer would be held responsible for the products of another or for those of all other manufacturers if plaintiff ultimately prevails. But under the rule we adopt, each manufacturer's liability for an injury would be approximately equivalent to the damages caused by the DES it manufactured.[30]

The judgments are reversed.

BIRD, C.J., and NEWMAN and WHITE,* JJ., concur.

RICHARDSON, J., dissenting. . . . Recovery is permitted from a handful of defendants *each* of whom *individually* may account for a comparatively small share of the relevant market, so long as the *aggregate* business of those who have been sued is deemed "substantial." In other words, a particular defendant may be held proportionately liable *even though mathematically it is much more likely than not that it played no role whatever in causing plaintiffs' injuries.* Plaintiffs have strikingly capsulated their reasoning by insisting ". . . that while one manufacturer's product may not have injured a particular plaintiff, we can assume that it

---

29. Defendants assert that there are no figures available to determine market share, that DES was provided for a number of uses other than to prevent miscarriage and it would be difficult to ascertain what proportion of the drug was used as a miscarriage preventative, and that the establishment of a time frame and area for market share would pose problems.

30. The dissent concludes by implying the problem will disappear if the Legislature appropriates funds "for the education, identification, and screening of persons exposed to DES." While such a measure may arguably be helpful in the abstract, it does not address the issue involved here: damages for injuries which have been or will be suffered. Nor, as a principle, do we see any justification for shifting the financial burden for such damages from drug manufacturers to the taxpayers of California.

*Assigned by the Chairman of the Judicial Council.

injured a different plaintiff and all we are talking about is a mere matching of plaintiffs and defendants." (Counsel's letter (Oct. 16, 1979) p. 3.) In adopting the foregoing rationale the majority rejects over 100 years of tort law which required that before tort liability was imposed a "matching" of defendant's conduct and plaintiff's injury was absolutely essential. Furthermore, in bestowing on plaintiffs this new largess the majority sprinkles the rain of liability upon all the joined defendants alike — those who may be tortfeasors and those who may have had nothing at all to do with plaintiffs' injury — and an added bonus is conferred. Plaintiffs are free to pick and choose their targets. . . .

Additionally, it is readily apparent that "market share" liability will fall unevenly and disproportionately upon those manufacturers who are amenable to suit in California. On the assumption that no other state will adopt so radical a departure from traditional tort principles, it may be concluded that under the majority's reasoning those defendants who are brought to trial in this state will bear effective joint responsibility for 100 percent of plaintiffs' injuries despite the fact that their "substantial" aggregate market share may be considerably less. This undeniable fact forces the majority to concede that, "a defendant may be held liable for a somewhat different percentage of the damage than its share of the appropriate market would justify." . . . With due deference, I suggest that the complete unfairness of such a result in a case involving only five of two hundred manufacturers is readily manifest. . . .

[The dissent then castigated the court for adopting the "deep pocket" mentality.]

CLARK and MANUEL, JJ., concur.

Rehearing denied. CLARK, RICHARDSON and MANUEL, JJ., dissenting.

NOTES

1. *Market share in DES cases.* The plaintiff's victory in *Sindell* goes only to the first issue in this long and complicated litigation. On remand, what is to be done in order to establish the market share analysis, given the administrative problems to which the court referred in footnote 29? In determining the appropriate market share for each defendant, it is important to note that DES has been in the public domain from the time of its synthesis by a British research team in 1938. DES was manufactured by many regional and local producers as well as by the large national drug manufacturers — perhaps 300 in total. The drug also has many different uses, and is produced in many different tablet sizes, so it is difficult to make any inference back from gross sales (if such numbers are known) to percentage of the market in DES for the prevention

of pregnancy miscarriage. In addition, the plaintiffs were born in different years, when the markets were differently constituted. They were
also born in different places. It is estimated, for example, that one-half
of the women involved were born not in California, but elsewhere in
the United States. Does it make sense to construct a national market for
DES? To permit defendants to introduce evidence of local variation?

Sindell itself was settled in September 1983, before any of these factual issues were raised in discovery. Before settlement was reached the
trial judge had granted the defendant's motion to reject the plaintiff as
a proper class representative because her chief complaint was bladder
cancer, which is normally not associated with DES. The plaintiff received $20,000 for her individual claim. Extensive litigation of individ-
ual claims has of course proceeded apace.

2. *DES: joint and several, or proportionate liability?* One major theoretical question in *Sindell* is whether the absence of any hard evidence on
the question of causal identification makes it impossible for the plaintiff
to proceed against a class of defendants, one of whom must have supplied the DES pills that caused her injury. Here if all the suppliers could
be joined as defendants in the case, then the case for liability is simply
that each defendant is required to pay exactly that amount that it would
have to pay if perfect identification were possible in each individual
case. Matters become somewhat more difficult when some of the suppliers cannot be joined as defendants or are otherwise insolvent, for the
question then arises: who shall pick up that loss, the codefendants or
the individual plaintiffs? If the principle of joint and several liability as
announced in *Summers* applies, then any single defendant should in
principle be responsible for the full measure of the losses, no matter
how small its share of the market. The California Supreme Court
stepped back from that implication in Murphy v. E.R. Squibb & Sons,
710 P.2d 247, 255 (Cal. 1985), by holding that the "substantial share"
requirement of *Sindell* was not met when the plaintiff brought her suit
against only one manufacturer, Squibb. "Since Squibb had only a 10
percent share of the DES market, there is a only a 10 percent chance
that it produced the drug causing plaintiff's injuries, and a 90 percent
chance that another manufacturer was the producer."

Subsequently in Brown v. Superior Court (Abbott Laboratories), 751
P.2d 470, 486-487 (Cal. 1988), the California Supreme Court, again
speaking through Judge Mosk, backpedaled from its *Sindell* opinion. It
first held that each defendant was only responsible for its proportionate
share of the loss.

> It is apparent that the imposition of joint liability on defendants in a
> market share action would be inconsistent with this rationale. Any defen-
> dant could be held responsible for the entire judgment even though its
> market share may have been comparatively insignificant. Liability would
> in the first instance be measured not by the likelihood of responsibility
> for the plaintiff's injuries but by the financial ability of a defendant to

undertake payment of the entire judgment or a large portion of it. A defendant that paid a larger percentage of the judgment than warranted by its market share would have the burden of seeking indemnity from other defendants, and it would bear the loss if producers of DES that might have been held liable in the action were not amenable to suit, or if a codefendant was bankrupt. In short, the imposition of joint liability among defendant manufacturers in a market share action would frustrate *Sindell's* goal of achieving a balance between the interests of DES plaintiffs and manufacturers of the drug.

On a second point Mosk, J., also narrowed the scope of the *Sindell* doctrine by holding "that a plaintiff who proceeds on a market share theory may not prosecute a cause of action for fraud or breach of warranty" because she would not be able to "show not only the fact that common representations were made by defendants but also the state of mind or knowledge of the defendant making them. . . ."

Both *Sindell* and *Brown* were examined a year later in New York in Hymowitz v. Eli Lilly & Co., 539 N.E.2d 1069, 1078 (N.Y. 1989). The New York court first joined with *Sindell* in rejecting the concert of action theory — which would have allowed full recovery against any supplier regardless of its market share — a theory with which the court had flirted with in Bichler v. Lilly & Co., 436 N.E.2d 182 (N.Y. 1982). Then elaborating on *Brown,* the New York court adopted a system of proportionate liability based upon the sales of each pharmaceutical company in the "national market" for DES used in pregnancy.

> [B]ecause liability here is based on the overall risk produced, and not causation in a single case, there should be no exculpation of a defendant who, although a member of the market producing DES for pregnancy use, appears not to have caused a particular plaintiff's injury. It is merely a windfall for a producer to escape liability solely because it manufactured a more identifiable pill, or sold only to certain drugstores. These fortuities in no way diminish the culpability of a defendant for marketing the product, which is the basis of liability here.
>
> Finally, we hold that the liability of DES producers is several only, and should not be inflated when all participants in the market are not before the court in a particular case. We understand that, as a practical matter, this will prevent some plaintiffs from recovering 100% of their damages. However, we eschewed exculpation to prevent the fortuitous avoidance of liability, and thus, equitably, we decline to unleash the same forces to increase a defendant's liability beyond its fair share of responsibility.

It is important to understand *Hymowitz's* logic for excluding exculpation evidence in individual cases. While that evidence allows a defendant to escape liability in a given case, it will not reduce its overall burden, for its share of liability for the remaining cases in the pool should increase in an amount that exactly offsets its saving in the individual case. Thus if there are four defendants with equal 25 percent shares in the market, and one can establish that it was not responsible in five of the one hundred cases, then once the pool is readjusted, it will be responsible for 25/95ths of the remaining judgments. So if each case is worth $100,000, its liability will still be $2.5 million whether it pays $25,000 for each of 100 cases, or pays 25/95ths of $100,000 for each of 95 cases. Since the gains and losses net out, even the defendants profit in the long run if *none* can exonerate itself in the individual case, for the total administrative costs are reduced and the total amount paid to resolve all claims does not increase.

3. Setting market shares. Under *Sindell* liability is not prorated in accordance with the number of firms, but with the market shares of each. In McCormack v. Abbott Laboratories, 617 F. Supp. 1521, 1527 (D. Mass. 1985), Judge Garrity explained how to compute the shares of individual defendants in a system of proportionate liability. He first held that any defendant that could establish its market share could be held for no greater sum, and that the remainder should be divided among the remaining defendants in equal proportion. "Assume hypothetically, five prima facie defendants, of whom one shows an actual share of 12%. The four remaining defendants will each be potentially liable for 22%. Suppose, instead, that one shows an actual share of 12% and a second of 13% — the three remaining defendants will then each be potentially liable for 25%." This system of allocation does not allow any plaintiff to recover from any defendant the share attributable to absent third parties. "Assume hypothetically, five prima facie defendants who show that their actual shares are, respectively, 5%, 10%, 15%, 20% and 25%. Plaintiff could recover a maximum of 75% of her damages."

4. Market share: beyond DES. In recent years the courts have proved unwilling to extend *Sindell* beyond DES to other substances that have been implicated in mass torts. Thus in Starling v. Seaboard Coast Line R. Co., 533 F. Supp. 183, 191 (S.D. Ga. 1982), the court stressed the nonfungible nature of asbestos products, which broke any "correspondence between the total volume of asbestos produced and the injury caused."

> The injuries caused by asbestos exposure are not restricted to asbestos products — other products, such as cigarettes, may have caused or contributed to the injury. Additionally, products containing asbestos are not uniformly harmful — many products contain different degrees of asbestos. Thus "the total risk created by any manufacturer would be a function of both its share of the market and the relative harmfulness of its products"; but a company's market share could not be adjusted for the latter relation.

Is this an argument against market share or all tort liability?

In Shackil v. Lederle Laboratories, 561 A.2d 511, 523 (N.J. 1989), the New Jersey Supreme Court also refused to extend the market share doctrine to diphtheria-pertussis-tetanus (DPT) vaccine, whose pertussis component caused in the infant plaintiff a seizure disorder resulting in serious, permanent brain damage. The court first noted that all DPT vaccines were not prepared in the same way and did not necessarily hold out the same level of risk, making it difficult to extend the market share doctrine from the DES cases. But its basic concerns went beyond the technical aspects of the market share doctrine. The court first noted that the very high levels of death and disability from pertussis, numbering in the thousands per year, had been reduced by the pertussis vaccine by well over 99 percent between 1943 and 1976. Nonetheless, it noted that today the vaccine is produced by only two firms. "The market's fragility has been reflected in the exorbitant increase in the price of the DPT vaccine from eleven cents per dose in 1984 to $11.40 a dose in 1986 (eight dollars of which goes to insurance costs)." In its view the National Childhood Vaccine Compensation Injury Act of 1986 (42 U.S.C. 300aa-1-34), for which Congress allocated up to $80,000,000 in 1989, offered a better "no-fault" solution to the compensation problem without posing a threat to the underlying market. The court noted that it might not be "inhospitable" to the market share doctrine in an "appropriate case." But as regards DPT it concluded that "the imposition of market-share liability in this case would cut against the societal goals of maintaining an adequate supply of life-saving vaccines and of developing safer alternatives to current methods of vaccinations." The dissent criticized the court on the ground that it "rejected the market-share theory by addressing the 'unavoidably unsafe' issue." See infra Chapter 9.

Sindell has spawned an enormous amount of academic literature. See, e.g., Kaye, The Limits of the Preponderance of the Evidence Standard: Justifiably Naked Statistical Evidence and Multiple Causation, [1982] Am. B. Found. Res. J. 487; Robinson, Multiple Causation in Tort Law: Reflections on the DES Cases, 68 Va. L. Rev. 713 (1982): Note, Market Share Liability: An Answer to the DES Causation Problem, 94 Harv. L. Rev. 668 (1981); Epstein, Two Fallacies in the Law of Joint Torts, 73 Geo. L.J. 1377, 1378 (1985).

2. Between Codefendants

American Motorcycle Association v. Superior Court
578 P.2d 899 (Cal. 1978)

[In this action the California Supreme Court was called upon to address an issue left open in Li v. Yellow Cab, supra at page 373, namely, the proper apportionment of liability in suits against multiple defendants. At the outset, the court stated its conclusions on the issues of law before it:

(1) That the doctrine subjecting multiple defendants to "joint and several liability" to a single plaintiff was neither abolished nor limited by the decision in *Li*.

(2) That a doctrine of partial equitable indemnity should be adopted at common law to permit apportionment of loss among codefendants on pure comparative principles.

(3) That the California contribution statutes do not "preclude" the development of a common-law doctrine of comparative indemnity, and

(4) That under this system of equitable contribution, any defendant may maintain an action against any other party, whether or not joined in the original suit, but that the trial judge may postpone trial of the indemnity action in order "to avoid unduly complicating the plaintiff's suit."]

TOBRINER, J. . . . In light of these determinations, we conclude that a writ of mandate should issue, directing the trial court to permit petitioner-defendant to file a cross-complaint for partial indemnity against previously unjoined alleged concurrent tortfeasors.

1. THE FACTS

[The plaintiff, Glen Gregos, was injured in a novice motorcycle race that he claimed was negligently organized and run by two defendants, the American Motorcycle Association (AMA) and the Viking Motorcycle Club (Viking). Thereafter the AMA sought leave of the court to file a cross-complaint against Gregos' parents, alleging their negligence and improper supervision of their minor son. It also asked declaratory relief that its portion of the judgment be reduced by the amount of the "allocable negligence" of the parents. The plaintiff then obtained a writ of mandate from the intermediate court, and the case was then brought to the supreme court because of the obvious importance of the issues it raised.]

2. THE ADOPTION OF COMPARATIVE NEGLIGENCE IN *LI* DOES NOT WARRANT THE ABOLITION OF JOINT AND SEVERAL LIABILITY OF CONCURRENT TORTFEASORS . . .

In the instant case AMA argues that the *Li* decision, by repudiating the all-or-nothing contributory negligence rule and replacing it by a rule which simply diminishes an injured party's recovery on the basis of his comparative fault, in effect undermined the fundamental rationale of the entire joint and several liability doctrine as applied to concurrent tortfeasors. . . .

AMA argues that after *Li* (1) there *is* a basis for dividing damages, namely on a comparative negligence basis, and (2) a plaintiff is no longer necessarily "innocent," for *Li* permits a negligent plaintiff to recover damages. AMA maintains that in light of these two factors it is logically inconsistent to retain joint and several liability of concurrent tortfeasors after *Li*. As we explain, for a number of reasons we cannot accept AMA's argument.

First, the simple feasibility of apportioning fault on a comparative negligence basis does not render an indivisible injury "divisible" for purposes of the joint and several liability rule. As we have already explained, a concurrent tortfeasor is liable for the whole of an indivisible injury whenever his negligence is a proximate cause of that injury. In many instances, the negligence of each of several concurrent tortfeasors may be sufficient, in itself, to cause the entire injury; in other instances, it is simply impossible to determine whether or not a particular concurrent tortfeasor's negligence, acting alone, would have caused the same injury. Under such circumstances, a defendant has no equitable claim vis à vis an injured plaintiff to be relieved of liability for damage which he has proximately caused simply because some other tortfeasor's negligence may also have caused the same harm. In other words, the mere fact that it may be possible to assign some percentage figure to the relative culpability of one negligent defendant as compared to another does not in any way suggest that each defendant's negligence is not a proximate cause of the entire indivisible injury.

Second, abandonment of the joint and several liability rule is not warranted by AMA's claim that, after *Li*, a plaintiff is no longer "innocent." Initially, of course, it is by no means invariably true that after *Li* injured plaintiffs will be guilty of negligence. In many instances a plaintiff will be completely free of all responsibility for the accident, and yet, under the proposed abolition of joint and several liability, such a completely faultless plaintiff, rather than a wrongdoing defendant, would be forced to bear a portion of the loss if any one of the concurrent tortfeasors should prove financially unable to satisfy his proportioned share of the damages.

Moreover, even when a plaintiff is partially at fault for his own injury, a plaintiff's culpability is not equivalent to that of a defendant. In this setting, a plaintiff's negligence relates only to a failure to use due care for his own protection, while a defendant's negligence relates to a lack of due care for the safety of others. Although we recognized in *Li* that a plaintiff's self-directed negligence would justify reducing his recovery in proportion to his degree of fault for the accident,[2] the fact remains that insofar as the plaintiff's conduct creates only a risk of self-injury, such conduct, unlike that of a negligent defendant, is not tortious.

Finally, from a realistic standpoint, we think that AMA's suggested abandonment of the joint and several liability rule would work a serious and unwarranted deleterious effect on the practical ability of negligently injured persons to receive adequate compensation for their injuries. One of the principal by-products of the joint and several liability rule is that it frequently permits an injured person to obtain full recovery for his injuries even when one or more of the responsible parties do not have the financial resources to cover their liability. In such a case the rule recognizes that fairness dictates that the "wronged party should not be deprived of his right to redress," but that "[t]he wrongdoers should be left to work out between themselves any apportionment." (Summers v. Tice (1948) 33 Cal. 2d 80, 88, 199 P.2d 1, 5.) The *Li* decision does not detract in the slightest from this pragmatic policy determination.

[The court then noted that the overwhelming weight of judicial and academic opinion supports its conclusion.]

3. UPON REEXAMINATION OF THE COMMON LAW EQUITABLE INDEMNITY DOCTRINE IN LIGHT OF THE PRINCIPLES UNDERLYING *LI*, WE CONCLUDE THAT THE DOCTRINE SHOULD BE MODIFIED TO PERMIT PARTIAL INDEMNITY AMONG CONCURRENT TORTFEASORS ON A COMPARATIVE FAULT BASIS . . .

In California, as in most other American jurisdictions, the allocation of damages among multiple tortfeasors has historically been analyzed in terms of two, ostensibly mutually exclusive, doctrines: contribution and

2. A question has arisen as to whether our *Li* opinion, in mandating that a plaintiff's recovery be diminished in proportion to the plaintiff's negligence, intended that the plaintiff's conduct be compared with each individual tortfeasor's negligence, with the cumulative negligence of all named defendants or with all other negligent conduct that contributed to the injury. The California BAJI Committee, which specifically addressed this issue after *Li*, concluded that "the contributory negligence of the plaintiff must be proportioned to the combined negligence of plaintiff and of all the tortfeasors, whether or not joined as parties . . . whose negligence proximately caused or contributed to plaintiff's injury."

We agree with this conclusion, which finds support in decisions from other comparative negligence jurisdictions. In determining to what degree the injury was due to the fault of the plaintiff, it is logically essential that the plaintiff's negligence be weighed against the combined total of all other causative negligence; moreover, inasmuch as a plaintiff's actual damages do not vary by virtue of the particular defendants who happen to be before the court, we do not think that the damages which a plaintiff may recover against defendants who are joint and severally liable should fluctuate in such a manner.

indemnification. In traditional terms, the apportionment of loss between multiple tortfeasors has been thought to present a question of contribution; indemnity, by contrast, has traditionally been viewed as concerned solely with whether a loss should be entirely shifted from one tortfeasor to another, rather than whether the loss should be shared between the two. As we shall explain, however, the dichotomy between the two concepts is more formalistic than substantive, and the common goal of both doctrines, the equitable distribution of loss among multiple tortfeasors, suggests a need for a reexamination of the relationship of these twin concepts.

Early California decisions, relying on the ancient law that "the law will not aid a wrongdoer," embraced the then ascendant common law rule denying a tortfeasor any right to contribution whatsoever. In 1957, the California Legislature enacted a bill to ameliorate the harsh effects of that "no contribution" rule; this legislation did not, however, sweep aside the old rule altogether, but instead made rather modest inroads into the contemporary doctrine, restricting a tortfeasor's statutory right of contribution to a narrow set of circumstances. We discuss the effect of the 1957 contribution legislation in more detail below; at this point it is sufficient to note that the passage of the 1957 legislation had the effect of foreclosing any evolution of the California common law contribution doctrine beyond its pre-1957 "no contribution" state. Over the past two decades, common law developments with respect to the allocation of loss between joint tortfeasors in this state have all been channeled instead through the equitable indemnity doctrine.

Although early common law decisions established the broad rule that a tortfeasor was never entitled to contribution, it was not long before situations arose in which the obvious injustice of requiring one tortfeasor to bear an entire loss while another more culpable tortfeasor escaped with impunity led common law courts to develop an equitable exception to the no contribution rule. . . .

[T]he equitable indemnity doctrine originated in the common sense proposition that when two individuals are responsible for a loss, but one of the two is more culpable than the other, it is only fair that the more culpable party should bear a greater share of the loss. Of course, at the time the doctrine developed, common law precepts precluded any attempt to ascertain comparative fault; as a consequence, equitable indemnity, like the contributory negligence doctrine, developed as an all-or-nothing proposition.

Because of the all-or-nothing nature of the equitable indemnity rule, courts were, from the beginning, understandably reluctant to shift the entire loss to a party who was simply slightly more culpable than another. As a consequence, throughout the long history of the equitable indemnity doctrine courts have struggled to find some linguistic formulation that would provide an appropriate test for determining when the relative culpability of the parties is sufficiently disparate to warrant placing the entire loss on one party and completely absolving the other.

A review of the numerous California cases in this area reveals that the struggle has largely been a futile one. . . .

Indeed, some courts, as well as some prominent commentators,[4] after reviewing the welter of inconsistent standards utilized in the equitable indemnity realm, have candidly eschewed any pretense of an objectively definable equitable indemnity test. . . .

If the fundamental problem with the equitable indemnity doctrine as it has developed in this state were simply a matter of an unduly vague or imprecise linguistic standard, the remedy would be simply to attempt to devise a more definite verbal formulation. In our view, however, the principal difficulty with the current equitable indemnity doctrine rests not simply on a question of terminology, but lies instead in the all-or-nothing nature of the doctrine itself.

[The court then relied on Dole v. Dow Chemical (page 436 infra) and its companion case of Kelly v. Long Island Lighting Company, 286 N.E.2d 241 (N.Y. 1972).]

In order to attain such a system in which liability for an indivisible injury caused by concurrent tortfeasors will be borne by each individual tortfeasor "in direct proportion to [his] respective fault," we conclude that the current equitable indemnity rule should be modified to permit a concurrent tortfeasor to obtain partial indemnity from other concurrent tortfeasors on a comparative fault basis. In reaching this conclusion, we point out that in recent years a great number of courts, particularly in jurisdictions which follow the comparative negligence rule, have for similar reasons adopted, as a matter of common law, comparable rules providing for comparative contribution or comparative indemnity.

---

4. Dean Prosser was at a loss in attempting to state the applicable standard: "Out of all this, it is extremely difficult to state any general rule or principle as to when indemnity will be allowed and when it will not. It has been said that it is permitted only where the indemnitor has owed a duty of his own to the indemnitee; that it is based on a 'great difference' in the gravity of the fault of the two tortfeasors; or that it rests upon a disproportion or difference in character of the duties owed by the two to the injured plaintiff. Probably none of these is the complete answer, and, as is so often the case in the law of torts, no one explanation can be found which will cover all the cases. Indemnity is a shifting of responsibility from the shoulders of one person to another; and the duty to indemnify will be recognized in cases where community opinion would consider that in justice the responsibility should rest upon one rather than the other. This may be because of the relation of the parties to one another, and the consequent duty owed; or it may be because of a significant difference in the kind or quality of their conduct." (Prosser, Law of Torts, supra, §52, p. 313.)

4. CALIFORNIA'S CONTRIBUTION STATUTES DO NOT
    PRECLUDE THIS COURT FROM ADOPTING COMPARATIVE
    PARTIAL INDEMNITY AS A MODIFICATION OF THE
    COMMON LAW EQUITABLE INDEMNITY DOCTRINE

None of the parties to the instant proceeding, and none of the numerous amici who have filed briefs, seriously takes issue with our conclusion
that a rule of comparative partial indemnity is more consistent with
the principles underlying *Li* than the prior "all-or-nothing" indemnity
doctrine. The principal argument raised in opposition to[5] the recogni-

5. Sections 875 to 879 provide:

  Section 875:

  (a) Where a money judgment has been rendered jointly against two or more
  defendants in a tort action there shall be a right of contribution among them as
  hereinafter provided.

  (b) Such right of contribution shall be administered in accordance with the
  principles of equity.

  (c) Such right of contribution may be enforced only after one tortfeasor has,
  by payment, discharged the joint judgment or has paid more than his pro rata
  share thereof. It shall be limited to the excess so paid over the pro rata share of
  the person so paying and in no event shall any tortfeasor be compelled to make
  contribution beyond his own pro rata share of the entire judgment.

  (d) There shall be no right of contribution in favor of any tortfeasor who has
  intentionally injured the injured person.

  (e) A liability insurer who by payment has discharged the liability of a tortfeasor judgment debtor shall be subrogated to his right of contribution.

  (f) This title shall not impair any right of indemnity under existing law, and
  where one tortfeasor judgment debtor is entitled to indemnity from another
  there shall be no right of contribution between them.

  (g) This title shall not impair the right of a plaintiff to satisfy a judgment in
  full as against any tortfeasor judgment debtor.

  Section 876:

  (a) The pro rata share of each tortfeasor judgment debtor shall be determined
  by dividing the entire judgment equally among all of them.

  (b) Where one or more persons are held liable solely for the tort of one of
  them or of another, as in the case of the liability of a master for the tort of his
  servant, they shall contribute a single pro rata share, as to which there may be
  indemnity between them.

  Section 877:

  Where a release, dismissal with or without prejudice, or a covenant not to sue
  or not to enforce judgment is given in good faith before verdict or judgment to
  one or more of a number of tortfeasors claimed to be liable for the same tort —

  (a) It shall not discharge any other such tortfeasor from liability unless its
  terms so provide, but it shall reduce the claims against the others in the amount
  stipulated by the release, the dismissal or the covenant, or in the amount of the
  consideration paid for it whichever is the greater; and

  (b) It shall discharge the tortfeasor to whom it is given from all liability for any
  contribution to any other tortfeasors.

  [Section 877.5 sets out a detailed procedure for cases in which the plaintiff has
  entered into "sliding scale" agreements with one or more defendants whereby
  any defendant's liability is "dependent upon the amount of recovery which the
  plaintiff is able to recover from the nonagreeing defendant or defendants." The
  parties must give notice of the agreement to the court and disclosure of its existence (but not its terms) must be made to the jury whenever a defendant party

tion of a common law comparative indemnity rule is the claim that California's existing contribution statutes, section 875 et seq. of the Code of Civil Procedure, preclude such a judicial development. As we explain, we reject the contention on a number of grounds.

First, as we have already noted, the New York Court of Appeals adopted a similar partial indemnity rule in Dole v. Dow Chemical Co., supra, despite the existence of a closely comparable statutory contribution scheme.[6] . . . The *Dole* court, viewing the statute as simply a partial legislative modification of the harsh common law "no contribution" rule, found nothing in the New York statutory scheme to indicate that the Legislature had intended to preclude judicial extension of the statutory apportionment concept through the adoption of a common law partial indemnification doctrine.

[The court then argued that the case for comparative negligence among codefendants is even stronger under the California statute because of the express preservation of indemnity actions in section 875(f). It also argued that the legislature, although it could not foresee in 1957 the advent of the *Li* decision, "had no intention of completely withdrawing the allocation of loss issue from judicial review." The court then addressed the question of settlements.]

[Section 877's policy of encouraging settlements] can, and should, be preserved as an integral part of the partial indemnity doctrine that we adopt today. Thus, while we recognize that section 877, by its terms, releases a settling tortfeasor only from liability for contribution and not partial indemnity, we conclude from a realistic perspective the legislative policy underlying the provision dictates that a tortfeasor who has entered into a "good faith settlement" with the plaintiff must also be discharged from any claim for partial or comparative indemnity that may be pressed by a concurrent tortfeasor. As the Court of Appeal noted recently in Stambaugh v. Superior Court, 132 Cal. Rptr. 843, 846 (Cal. App. 1976) "Few things would be better calculated to frustrate

becomes a witness for the plaintiff in the case, except where such disclosure creates undue confusion or prejudice or otherwise misleads the jury.

Section 878 governs the entrance of judgments by one joint tortfeasor against another. Section 879 is a general severance provision that provides in standard form that if one section is declared invalid the other provisions of the section remain in force.]

6. At the time of the *Dole* decision, the New York contribution statute provided: "Where a money judgment has been recovered jointly against defendants in an action for a personal injury or for property damage, each defendant who has paid more than his pro rata share shall be entitled to contribution from the other defendants with respect to the excess paid over and above his pro rata share; provided, however that no defendant shall be compelled to pay to any other such defendant an amount greater than his own pro rata share of the entire judgment. Recovery may be had in a separate action or a judgment in the original action against a defendant who has appeared may be entered on motion made on notice in the original action." (N.Y.C.P.L.R., former §1401, repealed N.Y.L. 1974, ch. 742, §1.)

[section 877's] policy, and to discourage settlement of disputed tort claims, than knowledge that such a settlement lacked finality and would lead to further litigation with one's joint tortfeasors, and perhaps further liability." This observation is as applicable in a partial indemnity framework as in the contribution context. Moreover, to preserve the incentive to settle which section 877 provides to injured plaintiffs, we conclude that a plaintiff's recovery from nonsettling tortfeasors should be diminished only by the amount that the plaintiff has actually recovered in a good faith settlement, rather than by an amount measured by the settling tortfeasor's proportionate responsibility for the injury.

Accordingly, . . . we hold that under the common law of this state a concurrent tortfeasor may seek partial indemnity from another concurrent tortfeasor on a comparative fault basis. . . .

Let a peremptory writ of mandate issue directing the trial court (1) to vacate its order denying AMA leave to file its proposed cross-complaint, and (2) to proceed in accordance with the views expressed in this opinion. Each party shall bear its own costs.

CLARK, J., dissenting. . . . The majority reject the *Li* principle in two ways. First, they reject it by adopting joint and several liability holding that each defendant — including the marginally negligent one — will be responsible for the loss attributable to his codefendant's negligence. To illustrate, if we assume that the plaintiff is found 30 percent at fault, the first defendant 60 percent, and a second defendant 10 percent, the plaintiff under the majority's decision is entitled to a judgment for 70 percent of the loss against each defendant, and the defendant found only 10 percent at fault may have to pay 70 percent of the loss if his codefendant is unable to respond in damages.

The second way in which the majority reject *Li*'s irresistible principle is by its settlement rules. Under the majority opinion, a good faith settlement releases the settling tortfeasor from further liability, and the "plaintiff's recovery from nonsettling tortfeasors should be diminished only by the amount that the plaintiff has actually recovered in a good faith settlement, rather than by an amount measured by the settling tortfeasor's proportionate responsibility for the injury."[1] The settlement rules announced today may turn *Li*'s principle upside down — the extent of dollar liability may end up in inverse relation to fault.

Whereas the joint and several liability rules violate the *Li* principle when one or more defendants are absent or unable to respond in damages, the settlement rules will ordinarily preclude effecting the majori-

---

1. Although one of the most important matters determined by today's decision, the issue of pro rata reduction or dollar amount reduction was barely mentioned and the relative merits of the two systems were not briefed or argued by the parties or by any of the numerous amici. The overwhelming weight of authority — contrary to the majority — is for pro rata reduction rather than settlement amount reduction.

ty's principle in cases when all defendants are involved in the litigation and are solvent. To return to my 30-60-10 illustration and further assuming both defendants are solvent, the plaintiff is ordinarily eager to settle quickly to avoid the long delay incident to trial. Further, he will be willing to settle with either defendant because under the majority's suggested rules, he may then pursue the remaining defendant for the balance of the recoverable loss (70 percent) irrespective whether the remaining defendant was 10 percent at fault or 60 percent at fault. The defendants' settlement postures will differ substantially. Realizing the plaintiff is eager for quick recovery and is capable of pursuing the codefendant, the defendant 60 percent liable for the loss will be prompted to offer a sum substantially below his share of fault, probably paying 20 to 40 percent of the loss. The defendant only 10 percent at fault will be opposed to such settlement, wishing to limit his liability. To compete with his codefendant in settlement offers he will be required to offer substantially in excess of his 10 percent share of the loss, again frustrating the *Li* principle that the extent of liability should be governed by the extent of fault. Should he fail to settle, the 10 percent at fault defendant runs the risk that his codefendant will settle early for perhaps half of his own liability, while the lesser negligent person must eventually pay the remainder, not only frustrating the *Li* principle but turning it upside down. In any event, it is extremely unlikely he can settle for his 10 percent share. . . .

Adherence to the *Li* principle that the extent of liability is governed by the extent of fault requires that only a limited form of joint and several liability be retained in cases where the plaintiff is negligent. The issue of joint and several liability presents the problem whether the plaintiff or the solvent defendants should bear the portion of the loss attributable to unknown defendants or defendants who will not respond in damages due to lack of funds.

Consistent with the *Li* principle — the extent of liability is governed by the extent of fault — the loss attributable to the inability of one defendant to respond in damages should be apportioned between the negligent plaintiff and the solvent negligent defendant in relation to their fault. Returning to my 30-60-10 illustration, if the 60 percent at fault defendant is unable to respond, the 30 percent at fault plaintiff should be permitted to recover 25 percent of the entire loss from the 10 percent at fault solvent defendant based on the 3 to 1 ratio of fault between them. (The solvent defendant would have added to his 10 percent liability one-fourth of the 60 percent or 15 percent to reach the 25 percent figure.) To the extent that anything is recovered from the 60 percent at fault defendant, the money should be apportioned on the basis of the 3 to 1 ratio. The system is based on simple mechanical calculations from the jury findings.

Placing the entire loss attributable to the insolvent defendant solely on the negligent plaintiff or solely on the solvent negligent defendant is not only contrary to the *Li* principle, but also undermines the entire system of comparative fault. If the portion attributable to the insolvent defendant is placed upon the negligent plaintiff, the solvent defendant will attempt to reduce his liability by magnifying the fault of the insolvent defendant. Should the insolvent's portion be placed solely upon the solvent defendant — as done by the majority's application of joint and several liability — the plaintiff will have an incentive to magnify the fault of the insolvent defendant. . . .

Similarly, settlement rules should also reflect the *Li* principle. When a defendant settles, he should be deemed to have settled his share of the total liability and the pleadings and releases should so reflect. The nonsettling defendant should be liable only for the portion of the loss attributable to him — deducting from the total loss the amount attributable to the plaintiff's negligence and the amount attributable to the settling defendant's negligence. This rule adopted by Wisconsin would force a plaintiff to demand settlements reasonably commensurate to the fault of the settling defendant because he will no longer be able to settle quickly and cheaply, then holding the remaining defendants for part of his codefendant's share of the loss. Granted, the nonsettling defendant will have an incentive to magnify the fault of the settling defendant, but it is not unfair to place the burden of defending the settling defendant upon the plaintiff for three reasons: He is the one who chose to settle, the settlement has eliminated any right of contribution or partial indemnity of the nonsettling defendant, and the plaintiff in obtaining his settlement may secure the cooperation of the settling defendant for the later trial. . . .

I do not suggest return to the old contributory negligence system. The true criticism of that system remains valid: one party should not be required to bear a loss which by definition two have caused. However, in departing from the old system of contributory negligence numerous approaches are open, but the Legislature rather than this court is the proper institution in a democratic society to choose the course. To accommodate the true criticism, for example, it might be proper to take the position that a negligent plaintiff forfeits part — but not all — of his recovery in a percentage fixed by the Legislature. A fixed percentage approach would eliminate the impossible task of comparing apples and oranges placed upon the trier of fact by *Li* and would provide the consistency, certainty and predictability which foster compromise and settlement. Although the percentage would be arbitrary, the allocation of loss as demonstrated above is necessarily arbitrary under the present system.

NOTES

1. Contribution at common law. The general common-law rules sharply limited the circumstances in which one tortfeasor could recover from another. In Union Stock Yds. Co. v. Chicago, Burlington & Quincy R. Co., 196 U.S. 217 (1905), the plaintiff terminal company was not allowed contribution against the defendant railroad since both were guilty of "like negligence" in failing to discover the missing nut on the brake staff that caused the accident. Day, J., contrasted the case with Gray v. Boston Light Co., 114 Mass. 149, 154 (1873), where recovery was allowed when the defendant light company attached heavy wire to the plaintiff-landowner's chimney, which then toppled onto a traveler on the street below. The Massachusetts court held that the no-contribution rule "does not apply when one does the act or creates the nuisance, and the other does not join therein, but is exposed to liability and suffers damage. . . . In such cases the parties are not in pari delicto as to each other, though as to third persons either may be held liable." In *Union Stock Yards* should the action for contribution be allowed if the cost of inspection was low to the railroad and high to the stockyard? How do the two above cases come out under a rule that allows the passive party to obtain contribution or indemnity against the active one? Under a rule that allows the party secondarily responsible an action against the party primarily responsible?

2. Release of joint tortfeasors. One of the recurrent questions in cases involving two or more defendants concerns the effect that a release given by the plaintiff to one defendant has on the cause of action that he or she might have maintained against the others. In cases of joint tortfeasors who have acted in concert, the traditional common-law rule was that the release of one, regardless of the amount of consideration received in exchange, destroys the cause of action against the others, unless there has been an express reservation of rights. The "logic" behind that result was that the joint tortfeasors were but one person in law who owed a single indivisible obligation to the plaintiff. The effect of the rule has been to give a "free ride" to the other defendants in the frequent cases in which the attorneys did not appreciate the legal consequences of the release. This traditional common-law rule was not only applied to cases in which there were true joint tortfeasors, acting in concert, but to any case of multiple defendants as well, as, for example, when an injured party sues both the automobile driver who struck him and the treating physician. The recent trend of cases has been to reject the automatic release rule, at least with respect to independent tortfeasors. The new presumption is that the cause of action against the physician for medical malpractice is not released by any settlement with another tortfeasor in the absence of a clear manifestation of intent to the contrary. See, e.g., Krenz v. Medical Protective Co. of Fort Wayne, 204 N.W.2d 663 (Wis. 1973); Cal. Civ. Proc. Code §§875-879, supra at page 430, note 5. Is there any reason why the same rule should not apply to joint tortfeasors who originally acted in concert?

3. *Dole v. Dow: joint tortfeasors and workers' compensation.* The first important modern case to repudiate the general "no contribution" rule, and its elaborate exceptions, between joint tortfeasors was Dole v. Dow Chemical Co., 282 N.E.2d 288, 292 (N.Y. 1972). Defendant Dow Chemical supplied the George Urban Milling Company with a poison, methyl bromide, used in the control of insects and pests. Urban fumigated its storage bin with the methyl bromide, but did not allow sufficient time for it to dissipate before allowing its employee, Dole, to enter the bin, where he subsequently died. The plaintiff sued Dow for not giving the decedent a direct warning about the dangerous properties of the methyl bromide. Dow denied its own negligence, and brought a suit against Urban, claiming that Urban itself was negligent in failing to comply with Dow's detailed instructions for using methyl bromide. The court first held that Dow's "active negligence" barred its contribution suit, even if Urban's negligence was active as well. (Sound under *Union Stock Yards?*) It then sidestepped the New York contribution statute by holding that it only applied where the plaintiff had joined both defendants in the original action. It then showed its obvious impatience with the traditional rules and concluded that "where a third party is found to have been responsible for a part, but not all, of the negligence for which a defendant is cast in damages, the responsibility for that party is recoverable by the prime defendant against the third party. To reach that end there must necessarily be an apportionment of responsibility in negligence between those parties."

Dole thus routinely permits a flank attack by a plaintiff against an employer who is protected against direct suit for damages by the exclusive remedy provisions of the workers' compensation statutes. In this sense, the institutional importance of the no contribution rule is far greater than it was at common law, for there the plaintiff could in fact procure a partial direct recovery against multiple defendants. Do both *Dole* and *American Motorcycle* pay sufficient attention to their respective statutory schemes? In particular, when will the contribution provisions of section 875 et seq. apply in California? For more on exclusive remedies, see Chapter 13, Section D.

4. *A defense of the common-law regime?* American Motorcycle may not represent the last word on contribution and apportionment. A spirited defense of the common-law rules of barring contribution and limiting equitable indemnity may be advanced on several grounds. First, the bar

on contribution and indemnity may have superior incentive effects no matter what rule of liability is adopted. Thus the total amount of compensation is limited by the amount of damages sustained. Assuming that most individuals are risk-averse — i.e., fear uncertainty — then the all-or-nothing common-law contribution rule induces a greater level of accident avoidance for any given level of damages. Equitable indemnity is then reserved for cases where one defendant clearly has the superior capacity to avoid the risk in question. Second, the administrative costs of a pure apportionment regime are apt to be substantial, since many lawsuits are necessary to adjust completely the rights and duties of all interested parties. Moreover, as Clark, J., pointed out in dissent, the settlement may result in the more responsible defendant paying less of the total loss, which in turn weakens the incentive effect of the contribution rule. Is there any reason to adopt the complicated ad hoc rules for apportionment laid down by the California Supreme Court instead of the statutory pro rata rules for contribution rendered a dead letter in *American Motorcycle?* For a detailed account of the efficiency point see Landes and Posner, Joint and Multiple Tort Feasors: An Economic Analysis, 9 J. Legal Stud. 517 (1980).

5. *Contribution: strict liability and negligence.* The decision in *American Motorcycle* only addressed the problem of apportionment when the substantive theories of liability were all based upon negligence theories. What happens, however, when a given plaintiff sues two defendants, one on a negligence theory and the other on a strict liability theory? In Safeway Stores, Inc. v. Nest-Kart, 579 P.2d 441, 446 (Cal. 1978), the plaintiff was injured when a supermarket cart collapsed. Two actions were commenced — one in negligence against Safeway, the supermarket owner, and the other in strict liability against Nest-Kart, the cart manufacturer. The jury found that Safeway was 80 percent responsible and Nest-Kart 20 percent responsible.

Safeway's motion to apportion losses evenly between the defendants was granted, and Nest-Kart's appeal followed. Safeway's argument on appeal was that no principles of apportionment could operate with negligence and strict liability theories. This was rejected by the court:

> Indeed, if further confirmation of the feasibility of applying a comparative fault system in this context is needed, the proceedings in the instant case clearly furnish such proof. Here the jury, after considering evidence which demonstrated both that the shopping cart was defective and that Safeway had not utilized due care in maintaining its cart in safe working condition, apparently had no difficulty in finding both the manufacturer and Safeway liable for the accident, and apportioning the lion's share (80 percent) of the fault for the accident to Safeway, rather than to the manufacturer. We see no reason to assume that a similar common sense determination of proportional fault or proportional responsibility will be beyond the ken of other juries in similar cases.

Finally, we note that a contrary conclusion, which confined the operation of the comparative indemnity doctrine to cases involving solely negligent defendants, would lead to bizarre, and indeed irrational, consequences. Thus, if we were to hold that the comparative indemnity doctrine could only be invoked by a negligent defendant but not a strictly liable defendant, a manufacturer who was actually negligent in producing a product would frequently be placed in a better position than a manufacturer who was free from negligence but who happened to produce a defective product, for the negligent manufacturer would be permitted to shift the bulk of liability to more negligent cotortfeasors, while the strictly liable defendant would be denied the benefit of such apportionment.

How does the *Safeway* decision bear on the question of whether contributory negligence should be allowed as a defense in products liability cases? See Daly v. General Motors, reprinted infra at page 851.

6. *Insolvent defendants in joint tortfeasor cases.* Yet a further complication arises when one or more of multiple defendants are insolvent. *American Motorcycle* seems to hold that the remaining defendants bear all of the risk of an insolvent codefendant, but the California Supreme Court appears to have changed course on this question in Evangelatos v. Superior Ct., 753 P.2d 585, 590 (Cal. 1988):

Subsequent cases established that under the principles articulated in *American Motorcycle*, . . . a defendant may pursue a comparative equitable indemnity claim against other tortfeasors either (1) by filing a cross-complaint in the original tort action or (2) by filing a separate indemnity action after paying more than its proportionate share of the damages through the satisfaction of a judgment or through a payment in settlement. . . . In addition, more recent decisions also make clear that if one or more tortfeasors prove to be insolvent and are not able to bear their fair share of the loss, the shortfall created by such insolvency should be apportioned equitably among the remaining culpable parties — both defendants and plaintiffs.

To revert to Justice Clark's 30/60/10 hypothetical, if the 60 percent defendant is insolvent, *American Motorcycle* placed 70 percent of the loss on the 10 percent defendant. *Evangelatos* splits that 60 percent loss between plaintiff and defendant in accordance with their responsibility so that the plaintiff can recover only 25 percent from the solvent defendant, representing his own 10 percent responsibility plus one quarter (10 divided by 40) of the remaining 60 percent of the loss, or 15 percent.

7. *Several liability for multiple defendants?* With *American Motorcycle* compare Brown v. Keill, 580 P.2d 867, 873-874 (Kan. 1978), where the court found that the Kansas comparative negligence statute (K.S.A. 60-258a) (allowing recovery if plaintiff's negligence "was less than" defendant's causal negligence) did in fact abrogate the traditional rule that held

concurrent tortfeasors jointly and severally liable for the plaintiff's harm. The key provision for these purposes is subsection (d), which provides:

> Where the comparative negligence of the parties in any action is an issue and recovery is allowed against more than one party, each such party shall be liable for that portion of the total dollar amount awarded as damages to any claimant in the proportion that the amount of his causal negligence bears to the amount of the causal negligence attributed to all parties against whom such recovery is allowed.

The court first held that the plain language of the statute compelled the result. It then argued that a limitation of losses for defendants was not inconsistent with sound social policy:

> The perceived purpose in adopting K.S.A. 60-258a is fairly clear. The legislature intended to equate recovery and duty to pay to degree of fault. Of necessity, this involved a change of both the doctrine of contributory negligence and of joint and several liability. There is nothing inherently fair about a defendant who is 10% at fault paying 100% of the loss, and there is no social policy that should compel defendants to pay more than their fair share of the loss. Plaintiffs now take the parties as they find them. If one of the parties at fault happens to be a spouse or a governmental agency and if by reason of some competing social policy the plaintiff cannot receive payment for his injuries from the spouse or agency, there is no compelling social policy which requires the codefendant to pay more than his fair share of the loss. The same is true if one of the defendants is wealthy and the other is not. Previously, when the plaintiff had to be totally without negligence to recover and the defendants had to be merely negligent to incur an obligation to pay, an argument could be made which justified putting the burden of seeking contribution on the defendants. Such an argument is no longer compelling because of the purpose and intent behind the adoption of the comparative negligence statute.

Does the reasoning of the Kansas court require the retention of joint and several liability when the plaintiff is wholly without fault?

8. *Statutory modifications of joint and several liability.* Most statutes take the opposite position on joint and several liability and hold each defendant responsible for the whole. See, e.g., Minn. Stat. Ann. §604.02 (1978). More recently, the question of joint and several liability has been a hot item for legislative reform as many states have decided to modify the common-law rules. One chief concern has been with the marginal defendant whose tiny fraction of loss has required it to bear the full damages attributable to more culpable, but wholly or largely insolvent, defendants. One possible response to this problem is to adopt the outright abolition of the rule, as was done by statutes in Colorado, Utah, and Wyoming. See Colo. Rev. Stat. §13-21-111.5; Utah Code Ann. §78-27-38; Wyo. Stat. §1-1-109. Yet another response is to limit

the plight of marginal defendants noted in Clark's *American Motorcycle* dissent. Thus the 1989 amendments to the Minnesota statute provide that for cases of pesticide control, water pollution control, waste management, and various others forms of environmental risks, "a person whose fault is 15 percent or less is liable for a percentage of the whole award no greater than four times the percentage . . ." Minn. Stat. Ann. §604.02.1 (1989). Another approach, taken by New Hampshire in N.H. Rev. Stat. Ann. §507:7-e, allows a judgment for the full amount of damages to be entered against a defendant found 50 or more percent at fault, but allows only for several liability against a defendant found less than 50 percent at fault.

California modified its own joint and several liability rule by popular referendum designed to counteract what the referendum identified as "the deep pocket rule." The proponents of the referendum claimed that the new innovations in tort law had threatened local governments and private businesses with substantial losses and had forced local governments to curtail essential local services. Its substantive portion reads as follows:

§1431.2 SEVERAL LIABILITY FOR NONECONOMIC DAMAGES.
(a) In any action for personal injury, property damage, or wrongful death, based upon principles of comparative fault, the liability of each defendant for noneconomic damages shall be several only and shall not be joint. Each defendant shall be liable only for the amount of noneconomic damages allocated to that defendant in direct proportion to that defendant's percentage of fault, and a separate judgment shall be rendered against that defendant for that amount.

Illinois (735 ILCS 5/2-1117) adopts a complex amalgam of the above schemes, whereby joint and several liability apply across all defendants "for plaintiff's past and future medical and medically related expenses." But for pain and suffering joint and several liability is imposed only on those defendants found more than 25 percent responsible than plaintiff's injury, with several liability for less responsible defendants. Is an ordinary tort action under negligence or strict liability principles "based upon the principles of comparative fault"? Does this section apply in those cases in which the plaintiff is free of any contributory negligence? What are the arguments for and against abolishing the rule of joint and several liability for local and state governments but not for private parties?

What rules should govern contribution between joint tortfeasors where plaintiffs must cross the 50 percent threshold to make recovery? One possibility is to insist that the plaintiff in an indemnity action be less responsible than the party from whom the indemnity is sought. That possibility was rejected in Bielski v. Schulze, 114 N.W.2d 105 (Wis. 1962), when the Wisconsin court rejected the broad contention that there was a necessary link between comparative negligence and apportionment between joint tortfeasors, allowing contribution even though the party from whom it was exacted was less than half responsible for the loss to the injured party.

Matter of Oil Spill by the Amoco Cadiz
954 F.2d 1279 (7th Cir. 1992).

Before BAUER, Chief Judge, EASTERBROOK, Circuit Judge, and FAIR-CHILD, Senior Circuit Judge.

PER CURIAM.

On the morning of March 16, 1978, the supertanker AMOCO CADIZ broke apart in a severe storm, spewing most of its load of 220,000 tons of Iranian crude into the seas off Brittany. The wreck resulted in one of the largest oil spills in history, damaging approximately 180 miles of coastline in one of the most important tourist and fishing regions in France. The clean up took more than six months and involved equipment and resources from all over the country. The disaster has had lasting effects on the environment, the economy, and the people of Brittany, and has resulted in numerous lawsuits. Thirteen years later, the matter is before us. In this consolidated appeal, we are asked to resolve a myriad of issues involving jurisdiction, liability, and damages. Before we begin, a brief history of the litigation and its cast of characters is in order.

[For these purposes, it is sufficient to note that Amoco and its various subsidiaries entered into a contract to purchase the Amoco Cadiz from Astilleros Espanoles, S.A., "the shipbuilder who constructed the fleet in which Columbus voyaged to the New World."]

The contract required that the ship be built according to the American Bureau of Shipping's ("ABS") Rules for Building and Classing Steel Vessels. The ABS is a not-for-profit maritime classification society headquartered in New York that promulgates rules and sets standards for shipbuilding, design, and seaworthiness. The ABS's technical staff in London reviewed Astilleros's proposed plan for the AMOCO CADIZ to ensure that it complied with the ABS's Rules. The ABS examined the "general arrangement" plans — plans featuring the layout and list of components used in the various parts of the ship — as well as drawings related to the detailed design of the ship. (By "detailed design," we mean items as small as nuts and bolts.) The ABS stamped the plans and drawings with its Maltese cross emblem to signify its approval. The Amoco-Astilleros contract incorporated the general arrangement plans and required Astilleros to submit them to Amoco for acceptance prior to construction. Astilleros did so, but did not pass along to Amoco its detailed design drawings, calculations, or fabrication drawings showing the mechanical details of the steering mechanism's component parts. Amoco reviewed the design of the steering gear system and approved it on October 19, 1971. Amoco later made two modifications to the system: it designed a low fluid level alarm for the replenishment gravity tank and increased the size of the rudder. It chose not to include an optional hand charging pump. Astilleros's representatives came to Chicago for a two-day meeting in June 1972 to firm up technical details. . . .

II

In the aftermath of the environmental disaster, various parties brought lawsuits. The Republic of France ("France") sued Amoco to recover for pollution damages and clean up costs. Similar actions were brought by the French administrative departments of Côtes du Nord and Finistere ("the Côtes du Nord parties"), numerous municipalities called "communes," and various French individuals, businesses, and associations, including hoteliers and fisherman who lost business as a result of the oil spill ("the French claimants"). The Côtes du Nord parties and the French claimants charged Astilleros with negligence in designing and constructing the tanker. The lawsuits were filed in Illinois and New York. Astilleros appeared and moved to dismiss the claims against it for lack of personal and subject matter jurisdiction and for *forum non conveniens*. Both the Côtes du Nord parties and Amoco sued Bugsier, the owner of the tug PACIFIC, claiming that it was negligent in attempting to tow the AMOCO CADIZ. The Bugsier suits were stayed pending arbitration in London. Bugsier filed a limitation action in the lawsuits in which the Côtes du Nord parties were claimants.

[Huge portions of the opinion are omitted, dealing with issues of jurisdiction, liability, and damages. The following section addresses the question of contribution between joint tortfeasors.]

VII

D

The American Bureau of Shipping (ABS) certified that the AMOCO CADIZ was properly designed and constructed. Every year the ABS recertified the AMOCO CADIZ as seaworthy. Amoco believes that the ABS accordingly bears some of the responsibility for the loss; so do the Côtes du Nord parties, which sued the ABS and settled their claims against it. After settling with the Côtes du Nord parties, the ABS paid the French State for a release in advance of litigation. The district court deducted from the judgment against Amoco the amounts the plaintiffs have received from the ABS.

Amoco is dissatisfied with this approach and wants either contribution from the ABS or a reduction in the plaintiffs' claims by the amount of the ABS's responsibility. It cannot have the former in this action, for the ABS is not a party. Amoco's suit seeking contribution from the ABS remains on the district court's docket. (We express no opinion on the question whether Amoco ultimately will be entitled to contribution.) Far better, from Amoco's perspective, would be a decision that it is not liable at all for that portion of the loss reflecting the ABS's share of the fault. A reduction in the allowable claims would eliminate Amoco's risk that it will lose the litigation against the ABS (or be unable to collect any judgment it receives); it also would reduce the headaches Amoco will confront as it tries to enforce its judgment for indemnity from Astilleros. Such a reduction is appropriate, Amoco submits, because the plaintiffs settled their claims against the ABS on terms satisfactory to themselves. Amoco asks: if the ABS bears 20% of the fault and the plaintiffs settled for 10 centimes on the franc for that share of the damages, why should they be able to collect the other 90 from Amoco? According to Amoco, maritime law enforces a general comparative fault approach under which each party is responsible only for its own share. It relies on Leger v. Drilling Well Control, Inc., 592 F.2d 1246 (5th Cir. 1979).

All parties cast the question as one of American maritime law without explaining why. Contribution and comparative fault usually go with the substantive law. [The court then mused that French law might in principle apply.] Nonetheless, because none of the parties has argued that French law applies, and no one has furnished us with the tools to decide the question under French law, we shall fashion some federal admiralty law — while making it explicit that all questions of choice of law are open for decision when the question is properly argued.

There are four potential rules:

No contribution: All defendants are jointly and severally liable for the full damages. A plaintiff may decide to collect any part of an award from any of the defendants. No one may obtain contribution from another person.

Contribution: All defendants are jointly and severally liable for the full damages. The prevailing plaintiff may decide to collect any part of the award from any of the defendants. A party called on to pay more of the award than its share of fault implies may obtain contribution from a party called on to pay less than its share.

Contribution plus settlement bar: The same as the contribution rule, except that one party may obtain contribution only from another that proceeds to judgment. By settling, a party escapes any liability for contribution. (Variant: By settling in good faith, that is, for a bona fide estimate of liability at trial, a party escapes any liability for contribution.)

Claim reduction: Defendants are jointly and severally liable, unless one or more settles. By accepting a settlement from any party, the plaintiff forgoes the ability to collect from the remaining defendants any damages attributable to the settling party's share of fault. The remaining defendants are not entitled to contribution from the settling party — because after claim reduction there is no "excess" payment for which contribution would be appropriate. This is sometimes called the "comparative fault" rule.

. . . [N]o contribution is the common law rule in federal cases and remains the norm unless a statute calls for different treatment. [The Court then reviewed various statutory schemes, and noted that a contribution rule had been adopted generally in admiralty cases.]

. . . Many states have adopted the settlement-bar rule by statute. Uniform Contribution Among Tortfeasors Act s. 4(b) (1955 rev.).

Amoco asks us to adopt the fourth approach, claim reduction. No case in the Supreme Court has done so for any subject. For that matter, the Court has never used a settlement-bar rule. [The court then noted that the Fifth Circuit in *Leger* had adopted a claim reduction rule for admiralty cases, and at one time that rule was thought to be "gaining ground."]

What has caused the approach of *Leger* to lose the ground it once held? The answer is Edmonds v. Compagnie Generale Transatlantique, 443 U.S. 256 (1979). . . . Edmonds, a longshoreman injured in an accident aboard a vessel, sued the shipowner. A jury determined that the stevedore contractor (Edmonds' employer) was 70% at fault, that the vessel was 20% at fault, and that Edmonds bore the remaining 10% of the responsibility. The Supreme Court held that the shipowner must pay 90% of the damages — all save the portion attributable to the plaintiff. This looks like a simple application of joint and several liability for an indivisible injury until you recognize that the reason Edmonds had not sued his employer was the existence of a workers' compensation system that not only forbids suits by longshoremen against their employers but also bars shipowners from collecting from stevedores. This law induced the court of appeals to analogize the stevedore to a settling defendant and adopt a system of comparative fault, reducing the longshoreman's claim against the vessel to the portion of the loss attributable to the vessel's fault. The Supreme Court reversed this decision and reiterated the rule of joint and several liability.

Although *Edmonds* is based in part on an interpretation of the Longshore and Harbor Workers' Compensation Act and does not involve a formal settlement with a responsible party, . . . the Court also exercised some of its common law power in admiralty cases and considered whether claim reduction would be wise. It concluded that claim reduction is unwise, for two reasons: it complicates litigation, and it reduces injured persons' recoveries. The Court acknowledged the inequity of requiring a person 20% at fault to pay 90% of the damages but observed that such disproportion has been tolerated since the creation of the rule of joint and several liability. Attempts to redress this inequity create problems of their own, including failure to compensate the victim if one of the responsible parties cannot (or, as in *Edmonds,* need not) pay. "Contribution remedies the unjust enrichment of the concurrent tortfeasor [not called on to pay] . . . and while it may sometimes limit the ultimate loss of the tortfeasor chosen by the plaintiff, it does not justify allocating more of the loss to the innocent employee, who was not unjustly enriched." 443 U.S. at 272 n. 30. . . .

Perhaps a court should struggle against the implications of *Edmonds,* . . . if claim reduction were strongly preferable for reasons of efficiency or economy. . . . But the intervening decade has not made the arguments lopsided. Contribution and associated issues have been the subject of extended academic inquiry in the last decade. See, e.g., Landes & Posner, The Economic Structure of Tort Law 201-15 (1987); Shavell, Economic Analysis of Accident Law 164-67 (1987); Easterbrook, Landes & Posner, Contribution Among Antitrust Defendants: A Legal and Economic Analysis, 23 J.L. & Econ. 331 (1980); Kornhauser & Revesz, Sharing Damages Among Multiple Tortfeasors, 98 Yale L.J. 831 (1989); Polinsky & Shavell, Contribution and Claim Reduction Among Antitrust Defendants: An Economic Analysis, 33 Stan. L. Rev. 447 (1981). These assessments are in concord on the following conclusions about the different rules in any system where liability is based on fault (we disregard the complications introduced by strict liability):

No contribution: This approach promotes settlements, not only because by settling a party buys peace but also because, by concentrating full liability on those who hold out through trial and judgment, it creates a distinct possibility that those who settle first will pay a lower share of the total damages. This effect magnifies the plaintiff's total recoveries, for every dollar from a settling defendant is recovered with certainty even if the plaintiff would have failed at trial, and if the plaintiff succeeds at trial it always obtains full compensation. The magnification effect ensures adequate deterrence as well as full compensation; indeed it may over-compensate and thus over-deter. No contribution is also the cheapest for the courts, as there is no collateral litigation.

Contribution: Instead of the rush to settle under the no-contribution rule there is competition not to settle — for a settling defendant pays cash with certainty but does not buy peace, and may be called on to pay a full share if the plaintiff wins at trial, while a party going to trial may be able to obtain contribution from another defendant. Plaintiffs receive the actuarially correct amount of damages (the magnification effect discussed above disappears). Costs of administering the legal system rise, for courts must apportion damages. The costs of doing this may be steep, if the parties cannot agree on who should be responsible.

Contribution plus settlement bar: This removes the disincentive to settlement (now the settling defendant buys peace) but is otherwise similar to contribution. Administrative costs are higher than under no contribution, for even though it will not generally be necessary to decide on degrees of fault, it may be essential to inquire into the bona fides of a settlement, which extinguishes other defendants' right of contribution. Determining bona fides may require a mini-trial of the merits, to see whether the settling party indeed made a payment reasonably related to the strength of the plaintiff's claim.

Claim reduction: The effect on settlement is uncertain — defendants would love to settle (for they can buy peace, just as under no contribution), but settlement is costly for the plaintiffs, who get cash but relinquish not only their claim against the settling party but also a share of the claims against other parties. Bargaining should lead to actuarially fair settlements (if all defendants are solvent, an important qualification), and thus claim reduction has no ex ante effect on total compensation and deterrence — hence the attraction noted in *Donovan* [v. Robbins, 752 F.2d 1170 (7th Cir. 1985)]. Claim reduction may require substantial ancillary litigation to fix the amount of the carve-out. Further complications arise if the plaintiff settled with one party because of doubts about solvency, perhaps for the limit of insurance. Would claims against other defendants be reduced by the settling party's fault or only by the extent the settling party could have chipped into the pot after trial?

It should be clear from this recitation that none of the four approaches is without its problems, and that claim reduction in particular is no panacea. It creates a substantial possibility of extended collateral litigation. Take this case as an example. Thirteen years have passed since the grounding, almost two of them spent in trials on liability and damages. The record still does not permit a confident assessment of the ABS's proportionate fault (if any). A trial between the plaintiffs and Amoco over ABS's fault would be a curious adventure. ABS itself, the party with the best knowledge of its activities, would be on the sidelines (for it has settled); Amoco would try to magnify the ABS's contributions (to reduce its own liability) and the plaintiffs to belittle the ABS's role. Such a contest would make more sense if the ABS were brought back in, but as its own liability is fixed it would have no incentive to litigate (and such post-settlement litigation would remove the principal incentive to settle — the prospect of saving the costs of litigation). And the ABS is not necessarily the end. Amoco might point a finger at Bugsier, the owner of the tug PACIFIC. (Note that the French State never sued the ABS; it was brought into the picture only by the Côtes du Nord parties.) We are confident that the case would at last come to an end, but maybe not in this century. At all events, why should the judicial system invest so heavily in adjusting accounts among wrongdoers? Neither justification for the tort system — compensation of victims and the creation of incentives to take care — would be served by this collateral litigation. Conducting such cases would detract from the time courts have available to handle new claims by deserving persons.

"Whittling away at a case is more attractive if its core principle is wrong than if it is right, for why strain to curtail the application of sound rules?" Travis v. Gary Community Mental Health Center, Inc., 921 F.2d 108, 109 (7th Cir. 1990). Amoco does not persuade us that the core principle of *Edmonds* is wrong, given the difficulties with each of the alternatives. We therefore disagree with . . . *Leger*, and we decline to adopt a carve-out rule. Whether to [allow] Amoco contribution from the ABS, or [to adopt] the settlement-bar rule, is a question for another day. Only the claim reduction alternative would have required the district court to determine in this proceeding the degree of fault, if any, attributable to the ABS, and we approve the district court's decision not to adopt that alternative.

NOTES

1. Settlement of multiple-party actions. As both Clark's dissent in *American Motorcycle* and *Amoco Cadiz* indicate, many strategic complications intrude in the settlement of suits against multiple defendants. The exact nature of the legal incentives depends in part upon the effect of the earlier settlements upon the liability of the remaining defendants. Thus section 877 of the California statute allows contribution by a settling defendant against other defendants, but only for an amount in excess of its pro rata share. In contrast, N.Y. Gen. Oblig. Law §15-108 (1974), passed by the New York legislature in response to *Dole,* fully protects any defendant who settles with the plaintiff from action for indemnity or contribution brought by a codefendant. In addition, the New York statute further provides that the plaintiff cannot recover from the remaining defendants any damages that on comparative principles are properly attributable to the settling defendant. For its part, the Restatement (Second) of Torts §885 notes that the release of one joint tortfeasor "diminishes the claim, at least to the amount of the payment made" but does not specify by what formula. In *Amoco Cadiz,* should contribution be allowed or should the settlement-bar rule be followed?

The entire question has generated fearsome complications and deep divisions of opinion over the merits of the various approaches. Much of the discussion has focused on the choice between a rule that disallows contribution between codefendants, but reduces the plaintiff's recovery from the nonsettling tortfeasor by the amount recovered from the settling tortfeasor (the so-called pro tanto approach followed by the district court in *Amoco Cadiz*) or whether to follow the claim-reduction method, sometimes called the "apportioned set-off rule."

To see the difference in the simplest setting, assume that two defendants are equally responsible for the $100 loss of the plaintiff. Under the pro tanto rule, if the plaintiff settles with one defendant for $20, then the plaintiff's verdict against the second defendant will be entered for $80. Under the apportioned set-off rule the $20 settlement cuts out 50 percent of the claim against the remaining defendant whose liability is now at most $50. The upshot is that under apportionment the plaintiff can never recoup from the second defendant the $30 forgone in the first settlement. By the same token the second defendant has no need for any recourse against the settling defendant since the two claims are treated independently. Similarly where the first settlement for some reason gives an excess award of $70, the apportionment rule still lets the plaintiff recover $50 from the nonsettling defendant. Independence is thus preserved both ways and not solely for the advantage of the defendant. See Austin v. Raymark Industries, 841 F.2d 1184 (1st Cir. 1988).

2. *Incentive effects of settlement rules.* For an exhaustive analysis of the incentive effects of the various rules among separate defendants, see Kornhauser and Revesz, Settlements Under Joint and Several Liability, 68 N.Y.U. L. Rev. 427 (1993). There the authors develop the thesis that the pro tanto method invites different settlement strategies where the risks that each defendant faces are *independent,* such that the success against one defendant "does not depend upon whether the plaintiff prevails against, loses to, or settles with the other defendant," or perfectly *correlated,* such that success or failure against one defendant implies the same result against the other.

Consider first the "independent" situation in which administrative costs are treated as zero, and both defendants are fully solvent. Suppose the plaintiff with $100 in damages has two independent 50 percent recoveries, one against each of two defendants. In total, her expected recovery from litigation is $75. She will recover the full $100 if both defendants are found liable, or if either is, that is, in 75 percent of the cases. But she will recover nothing in the 25 percent of cases where neither is found liable. Here settlement is not possible. Note that each defendant expects to pay nothing in half the cases. In 25 percent of the cases, each defendant will be liable alone, and in 25 percent of the cases, each defendant will have half the total liability of $100. Taking these two possibilities together, the expected liability for each defendant is $(0.25)($100) + (0.25)($50) = 37.50. So if plaintiff offers to take $37.50 from each defendant (the maximum either would pay), then at most one defendant would accept that offer. Yet once the first defendant takes the offer, it is no longer in the interest of the second defendant to follow suit, for it faces liability only for the 50 percent of the time that it loses, in which event it can set off the $37.50 the plaintiff has recovered from the other defendant. In the end therefore its expected liability from continuing with litigation after the other defendant has settled is $(0.50)(\$100 - \$37.50) = \$31.25$, so it will not settle for more than that amount. It follows therefore that the plaintiff's total anticipated recovery, given its initial settlement is reduced to $37.50 + $31.25 = $68.75, which is lower than its expected $75 recovery from suing both defendants. So the settlement cannot work. Indeed Revesz and Kornhauser show that no pair of offers to both defendants can leave all three parties better off from settlement that from suit. Neither defendant will pay more than $37.50 to avoid suit, and if the plaintiff takes less, then for each dollar below that figure she gains only $0.50 in additional value against the nonsettling defendant. Litigation remains her superior choice.

Where the probabilities of success or failure are correlated, then settlement is possible, for now the plaintiff's success from litigation is reduced to only $50, since in half the cases she will lose against both parties. Under these circumstances an offer of (say) $10 to one defendant will be accepted, since it will leave both parties better off: the plaintiff has an anticipated recovery of $10 + (0.50)($90) for $55, while the settling defendant reduces its exposure from $25 to $10. Indeed settlement with both parties is possible, for if plaintiff offers to take $25 from one defendant, that offer will be accepted, and thereafter the second defendant is better off taking any offer up to $37.50 given that its residual liability is equal to $(0.50)(\$75)$. In essence when the claims are correlated, the plaintiff gives up nothing by settling with one plaintiff, whereas she must give up something when the claims against the two defendants are independent. Settlement is easier when claims correlate than when they are independent.

These illustrations are all influenced by their restrictive assumptions. In most cases, litigation costs could be positive (which would tend to drive parties to settlement), and there could be genuine uncertainties as to the extent of damages or the solvency of codefendants. In addition, most cases will involve intermediate states in which there is rough independence on some issues (say liability) and rough correlation on other issues (say damages). The mindboggling complications that follow are, to say the least, not easily summarized. Note that none of these strategic complications arise under the apportioned set-off rule because there the separation of the basic claim into two parts means that each claim is independent of the other, so that the settlement or litigation of one claim does not alter the exposure of the other defendant.

3. *Mary Carter agreements.* In Booth v. Mary Carter Paint Co, 202 So. 2d 385 (Fla. App. 1967), the court approved an agreement whereby a "settling" defendant remained in a case with his codefendants even after signing a secret agreement with the plaintiff which allowed him to

reduce his share of the total damage award as the amounts of damages levied against his codefendants increased. These "Mary Carter" agreements came under constant attack and in Ward v. Ochoa, 284 So. 2d 385 (Fla. 1973), the court held that these agreements had to be disclosed to the other side during discovery and to the jury at the request of other codefendants. The disclosure remedy did not prevent the settling defendant from participating in all phases of litigation, including the use of preemptory challenges and cross-examination. In order to obviate the confusion of roles that could thereby develop, a unanimous court prospectively held that all such agreements were void and against public policy in Dosdourian v. Carsten, 624 So. 2d 241, 245, 246 (Fla. 1993). Grimes, J., wrote:

> The main argument in favor of Mary Carter agreements is that they promote settlement. However, while it is true that a Mary Carter agreement accomplishes a settlement with one of the defendants, the intent of the agreement is to proceed with the trial against the other. Some agreements even give the settling defendant veto authority over a prospective settlement with the other defendant. Therefore, the existence of Mary Carter agreements may result in an increased number of trials, and they certainly increase the likelihood of post trial attacks on verdicts alleged to have been unfairly obtained as a result of such agreements. Of course, if the existence of the agreement is known, it is possible that the other defendant may feel compelled to also reach a settlement. However, in that event the remaining defendant may have been unfairly coerced into settling for more than his fair share of liability. . . .
>
> We are convinced that the only effective way to eliminate the sinister influence of Mary Carter agreements is to outlaw their use. We include within our prohibition any agreement which requires the settling defendant to remain in the litigation, regardless of whether there is a specified financial incentive to do so.

See generally Entman, Mary Carter Agreements: An Assessment of Attempted Solutions, 38 U. Fla. L. Rev. 521 (1986).

C. VICARIOUS LIABILITY

Ira S. Bushey & Sons, Inc. v. United States
398 F.2d 167 (2d Cir. 1968)

FRIENDLY, J. While the United States Coast Guard vessel *Tamaroa* was being overhauled in a floating drydock located in Brooklyn's Gowanus Canal, a seaman [named Lane] returning from shore leave late at night, in the condition for which seamen are famed, turned some wheels on the drydock wall. He thus opened valves that controlled the flooding of the tanks on one side of the drydock. Soon the ship listed, slid off the blocks and fell against the wall. Parts of the drydock sank, and the ship partially did — fortunately without loss of life or personal injury. The drydock owner [Bushey] sought and was granted compensation by the District Court for the Eastern District of New York in an amount to be determined, 276 F. Supp. 518; the United States appeals. . . .

The Government attacks imposition of liability on the ground that Lane's acts were not within the scope of his employment. It relies heavily on §228(1) of the Restatement of Agency 2d which says that "conduct of a servant is within the scope of employment if, but only if: . . . (c) it is actuated, at least in part by a purpose to serve the master." Courts have gone to considerable lengths to find such a purpose, as witness a well-known opinion in which Judge Learned Hand concluded that a drunken boatswain who routed the plaintiff out of his bunk with a blow, saying "Get up, you big son of a bitch, and turn to," and then continued to fight, might have thought he was acting in the interest of the ship. Nelson v. American-West African Line, 86 F.2d 730 (2d Cir. 1936). It would be going too far to find such a purpose here; while Lane's return to the *Tamaroa* was to serve his employer, no one has suggested how he could have thought turning the wheels to be, even if — which is by no means clear — he was unaware of the consequences.

In light of the highly artificial way in which the motive test has been applied, the district judge believed himself obliged to test the doctrine's continuing vitality by referring to the larger purposes respondeat superior is supposed to serve. He concluded that the old formulation failed this test. We do not find his analysis so compelling, however, as to constitute a sufficient basis in itself for discarding the old doctrine. It is not at all clear, as the court below suggested, that expansion of liability in the manner here suggested will lead to a more efficient allocation of resources. As the most astute exponent of this theory has emphasized, a more efficient allocation can only be expected if there is some reason to believe that imposing a particular cost on the enterprise will lead it to consider whether steps should be taken to prevent a recurrence of the accident. Calabresi, The Decision for Accidents: An Approach to Non-Fault Allocation of Costs, 78 Harv. L. Rev. 713, 725-34 (1965). And the suggestion that imposition of liability here will lead to more intensive screening of employees rests on highly questionable premises, see Comment, Assessment of Punitive Damages Against an Entrepreneur for the Malicious Torts of His Employees, 70 Yale L.J. 1296, 1301-1304 (1961).[5] The unsatisfactory quality of the allocation of resource rationale is especially striking on the facts of this case. It could well be that

5. We are not here speaking of cases in which the enterprise has negligently hired an employee whose undesirable propensities are known or should have been. See Koehler v. Presque-Isle Transp. Co., 141 F.2d 490 (2d Cir.), cert. denied, 322 U.S. 764 (1943).

application of the traditional rule might induce drydock owners, prodded by their insurance companies, to install locks on their valves to avoid similar incidents in the future, while placing the burden on shipowners is much less likely to lead to accident prevention.[7] It is true, of course, that in many cases the plaintiff will not be in a position to insure, and so expansion of liability will, at the very least, serve respondeat superior's loss spreading function. See Smith, Frolic and Detour, 23 Colum. L. Rev. 444, 456 (1923). But the fact that the defendant is better able to afford damages is not alone sufficient to justify legal responsibility, see Blum & Kalven, Public Law Perspectives on a Private Law Problem (1965), and this overarching principle must be taken into account in deciding whether to expand the reach of respondeat superior.

A policy analysis thus is not sufficient to justify this proposed expansion of vicarious liability. This is not surprising since respondeat superior, even within its traditional limits, rests not so much on policy grounds consistent with the governing principles of tort law as in a deeply rooted sentiment that a business enterprise cannot justly disclaim responsibility for accidents which may fairly be said to be characteristic of its activities. It is in this light that the inadequacy of the motive test becomes apparent. Whatever may have been the case in the past, a doctrine that would create such drastically different consequences for the actions of the drunken boatswain in *Nelson* and those of the drunken seaman here reflects a wholly unrealistic attitude toward the risks characteristically attendant upon the operation of a ship. We concur in the statement of Mr. Justice Rutledge in a case involving violence injuring a fellow-worker, in this instance in the context of workmen's compensation:

"Men do not discard their personal qualities when they go to work. Into the job they carry their intelligence, skill, habits of care and rectitude. Just as inevitably they take along also their tendencies to carelessness and camaraderie, as well as emotional make-up. In bringing men together, work brings these qualities together, causes frictions between them, creates occasions for lapses into carelessness, and for fun-making and emotional flare-up. . . . These expressions of human nature are incidents inseparable from working together. They involve risks of injury and these risks are inherent in the working environment." Hartford Accident & Indemnity Co. v. Cardillo, 112 F.2d 11, 15 (1940). . . . Further supporting our decision is the persuasive opinion of Justice Traynor in Carr v. Wm. C. Crowell Co., 171 P.2d 5 (Cal. 1946) [employer liable for violent acts of servant against employee of a sub-

---

7. Although it is theoretically possible that shipowners would demand that drydock owners take appropriate action, see Coase, The Problem of Social Cost, 3 J.L. & Econ. 1 (1960), this would seem unlikely to occur in real life. [Why? — Ed.]

contractor working on the same construction job], followed in Fields v. Sanders, 180 P.2d 684 (Cal. 1947) [employer liable for violent acts of driver against another driver in traffic dispute].

Put another way, Lane's conduct was not so "unforeseeable" as to make it unfair to charge the Government with responsibility. . . . Here it was foreseeable that crew members crossing the drydock might do damage, negligently or even intentionally, such as pushing a Bushey employee or kicking property into the water. Moreover, the proclivity of seamen to find solace for solitude by copious resort to the bottle while ashore has been noted in opinions too numerous to warrant citation. Once all this is granted, it is immaterial that Lane's precise action was not to be foreseen. . . . Consequently, we can no longer accept our past decisions that have refused to move beyond the *Nelson* rule, Brailas v. Shepard S.S. Co., 152 F.2d 849 (2d Cir. 1945), Kable v. United States, 169 F.2d 90, 92 (2d Cir. 1948), since they do not accord with modern understanding as to when it is fair for an enterprise to disclaim the actions of its employees.

One can readily think of cases that fall on the other side of the line. If Lane had set fire to the bar where he had been imbibing or had caused an accident on the street while returning to the drydock, the Government would not be liable; the activities of the "enterprise" do not reach into areas where the servant does not create risks different from those attendant on the activities of the community in general. We agree with the district judge that if the seaman "upon returning to the drydock, recognized the Bushey security guard as his wife's lover and shot him," 276 F. Supp. at 530, vicarious liability would not follow; the incident would have related to the seaman's domestic life, not to his seafaring activity, and it would have been the most unlikely happenstance that the confrontation with the paramour occurred on a drydock rather than at the traditional spot. Here Lane had come within the closed-off area where his ship lay, to occupy a berth to which the Government insisted he have access, cf. Restatement, Agency 2d, §267, and while his act is not readily explicable, at least it was not shown to be due entirely to facets of his personal life. The risk that seamen going and coming from the *Tamaroa* might cause damage to the drydock is enough to make it fair that the enterprise bear the loss. It is not a fatal objection that the rule we lay down lacks sharp contours in the end, as Judge Andrews said in a related context, "it is all a question [of expediency,] . . . of fair judgment, always keeping in mind the fact that we endeavor to make a rule in each case that will be practical and in keeping with the general understanding of mankind." Palsgraf v. Long Island R.R. Co., 162 N.E. 99, 104 (N.Y. 1928) (dissenting opinion). . . .

[Affirmed.]

NOTES

1. Respondeat superior: history. Vicarious liability refers generally to the liability that one person has for the acts of another. Historically, the term has religious origins, in the responsibility that the vicar has for the faithful. Today the religious origins of the phrase are largely forgotten but the principle of vicarious liability, or as it is sometimes termed, respondeat superior (let the superior answer) enjoys an unquestioned acceptance in all common-law jurisdictions. Its universal adoption makes the undercurrent of academic dissatisfaction with the rule somewhat surprising, stemming in large measure from an inability to identify and defend its precise rationale. Thus Holmes, in his famous articles on Agency, 4 Harv. L. Rev. 345 (1891), 5 Harv. L. Rev. 1 (1891), treated the doctrine of respondeat superior as an anomaly that "must be explained by some cause not manifest to common sense alone." His doubt stemmed from his nineteenth-century view that individual conduct alone was the basis of individual responsibility. In this vein, he wrote: "I assume that common-sense is opposed to making one man pay for another man's wrong, unless he has actually brought the wrong to pass. . . . I therefore assume that common-sense is opposed to the fundamental theory of agency. . . ." The sentiment was echoed in another early article, Y. B. Smith, Frolic and Detour, 23 Colum. L. Rev. 444, 454 (1923): "If one turns to the opinions of judges or books upon the subject seeking a justification, disappointment is almost inevitable. True it is that many reasons have been given, but none of them are satisfying. Perhaps this may account for the fact that most legal scholars who have written about the doctrine have disapproved of it; or, it may be that the cause is deeper than this."

For a sustained attack on vicarious liability as a doctrine that "has attained its luxuriant growth through carelessness and false analogy" see T. Baty, Vicarious Liability (1916). What made the doctrine of respondeat superior even more remarkable to many of the earlier commentators was that it was a bastion of strict liability that withstood the late-nineteenth-century conquest of tort law by negligence principles. Thus, while typically respondeat superior could apply only if the servant negligently discharged his duties, the defendant employer did not have to be similarly negligent in selecting or supervising the employee. To the contrary, an unbroken line of cases has held an employer responsible for the employee's negligence even when the employer had expressly, indeed emphatically, forbidden the very conduct that constituted employee negligence. See Limpus v. London General Omnibus Co., 158 Eng. Rep. 993 (Ex. 1862). Notwithstanding some early hesitation, it became established, after 1700 or so, that vicarious liability turned on the tort arising out of the servant's employment, not on the negligence of the employer in selection or supervision, and certainly not on the narrow theory that the employer had authorized, whether expressly or impliedly, the commission of the very tort for which he was vicariously charged. 1 Bl. Comm. 429, Hern v. Nichols, 91 Eng. Rep. 256 (Ex. 1708).

Much effort has been made to justify the stringent rules of respondeat superior within the traditional negligence framework. One justification for vicarious liability that was advanced as early as the nineteenth century was that of the deep pocket. In River Wear Commissioners v. Adamson, 2 A.C. 743 (H.L.(E.) 1876), Lord Blackburn was explicit: "In the great majority of cases the servant actually guilty of the negligence is poor, and unable to make good the damage, especially if it is considerable, and the master is at least comparatively rich, and consequently it is generally better to fix the master with liability; but there is also concurrent liability in the servant, who is not discharged from liability because his master also is liable." A similar conclusion is reached in Smith, Frolic, and Detour, 23 Colum. L. Rev. 444, 455-456 (1923). There Young B. Smith, following Baty's work on vicarious liability, listed the nine traditional rationales for vicarious liability: control; profit; revenge; carefulness and choice; identification; evidence; indulgence; danger; and satisfaction. Having concluded that none of these could account for the doctrine, he offered his own explanation: "A reason which occurs to the writer is that which has been offered in justification of workmen's compensation statutes. In substance it is the belief that it is socially more expedient to spread or distribute among a large group of the community the losses which experience has taught are inevitable in the carrying on of industry, than to cast the loss upon a few." Why isn't loss-spreading more cheaply accomplished through first-party insurance?

2. *Efficiency arguments.* More recently, the effort has been made to defend vicarious liability on more general efficiency grounds by placing greater stress on loss prevention. See Sykes, The Economics of Vicarious Liability, 93 Yale L.J. 1231 (1984). Sykes explicitly compares two possible legal regimes. In the first, that of pure personal liability, the injured third party has recourse only against the employee, who in turn can seek an indemnity against the employer. In the second system of vicarious liability, the employer is directly liable, with possible rights of indemnity against the erring employee. As between the employer and the employee, Sykes observes that the employer is usually the superior risk bearer because of the greater access to insurance markets, especially when the employer is a public corporation whose shareholders are able to diversify their own private holdings by investing in many different firms. The direct action against the employer tends to place the loss initially on the superior risk bearer. Vicarious liability also reduces the risk that the insolvency of a particular employee will impose

an uncompensated risk on a third party and the doctrine reduces the need to have an extensive network of voluntary contracts between employee and employer to make the employer the ultimate risk bearer when the employee is, in fact, solvent.

3. Frolic and detour. Once the case for vicarious liability has been accepted, it is still necessary to determine its extent. Employees do not always act as employees when they are supposed to be on the job. It becomes necessary to determine therefore which acts are within the scope of employment and which fall outside of it. Thus difficulties frequently arise when the employee deviates from the route set by his employer for personal reasons. Here the general position today is, roughly, that the employer is liable for small deviations, but not for large ones. See, for example, Riley v. Standard Oil Co., 132 N.E. 97 (N.Y. 1921), where the court recognized that "[n]o hard and fast rule on the subject either in space or time can be applied," and then held that driving four blocks out of the way on a personal errand did not take the employee out of his master's employment.

One way to analyze the desirability of this rule is to ask whether it will tend to increase the number of overall accidents. The outcome is, however, unclear. On the one hand, imposing vicarious liability creates a strong incentive for the employer to monitor the behavior of the employee. If the deviation is effectively curtailed, then one possibility is that the employee will choose to engage in the same mission outside of work, thus having to travel a greater distance and probably having a higher accident rate. Alternatively, the errand may become so burdensome that the employee will not undertake it at all. In the first case, using an expansive vicarious liability rule will tend to increase the number of accidents. In the second case, the expansive rule will reduce the accident level. It is, however, often unclear which result will hold, or whether the employee is more likely to abandon a particular private errand if the deviation is large or small. It is therefore not surprising that no hard and fast rule can be developed to cover these cases. See generally Sykes, The Boundaries of Vicarious Liability: An Economic Analysis of the Scope of Employment Rule and Related Legal Doctrines, 101 Harv. L. Rev. 563 (1988).

4. Intentional torts. One of the most troublesome areas of vicarious liability concerns intentional harms committed by employees. In Lancaster v. Norfolk & Western Railway, 773 F.2d 807, 819-820 (7th Cir. 1985), the plaintiff was driven into "a descent of madness" from which the medical experts on both sides agreed he would never recover. The source of his condition was a series of abusive and indecent acts (including "goosing") by his supervisory personnel, Lachrone, Tynan, and Funderburk. In affirming a judgment for the plaintiff against the railroad, Posner, J., noted that theories of "direct negligence" offered an alternative route for recovery against the employer when the torts of the employee fall outside the scope of employment.

The issue of respondeat superior is more difficult with regard to Funderburk, whose "goosing" of Lancaster was not related to Funderburk's supervisory duties; it was the pure expression of perversion, infantilism, bad taste, or some combination of these things. The usual view, as we saw earlier, is that when the motive for the employee's intentional tort is personal — which is to say unrelated to his employer's objectives and therefore not in furtherance of those objectives — the employer is not liable under a theory of respondeat superior. But the case also went to the jury on the alternative theory to respondeat superior that the railroad was negligent in failing to prevent its employees from committing a series of intentional torts against Lancaster ("direct negligence"), and, as shown earlier, liability for direct negligence does not require proof that the employee was acting in furtherance of his employer's objectives. It does require, of course, proof of the railroad's negligence. Lancaster had to show that the railroad should have known that its supervisors were misbehaving, more concretely, that the railroad had information about their propensities, and failed to act on the information.

Posner, J., then held that in this connection "the railroad" was sufficiently identified with its "master mechanics," who in the ordinary execution of their duties would have gotten "wind" of the situation and been able to do something to counteract it.

5. *Vicarious liability and sexual harassment.* The recent upsurge of cases on sexual harassment posed the question whether the employer can be held responsible in tort for the misconduct of individual employees. In Meritor Savings Bank v. Vinson, 477 U.S. 57 (1986), the Supreme Court first held that sexual harassment was a form of sex discrimination under Title VII of the Civil Rights Act of 1964. The Court then refused to issue any definitive rule on the question of the bank's liability for the wrongful acts of its employee. It did reject two extreme positions, however. The first, accepted by the court of appeals below, had held the employer "automatically" liable for the wrongs of the supervisory employee, whether or not it had notice of those wrongs. The second, championed by the bank, argued that liability could not be found unless the employee first pursued available remedies against the employer under the applicable grievance provisions. It then concluded enigmatically: "As to employer liability, we conclude that the Court of Appeals was wrong to entirely disregard agency principles and impose absolute liability on employers for the acts of their supervisors, regardless of the circumstances of a particular case." Should sexual harassment be regarded as a "frolic and detour" of the employee? Is the proper rule here to impose liability only when the employer has reasonable cause to detect and prevent the illegal behavior, as in *Lancaster?*

6. *The "borrowed servant."* When a given person works for two employers, which should be held vicariously liable? The problem arises is the construction industry, where, for example, a general contractor who needs to have specialized work done with cranes, hires a crane and operator from a crane company. The control and supervision over the

operator is usually divided between the two firms. The crane company retains the general power to hire and fire and to impose safety regulations, work rules, and the like; the construction company designates the operator's particular tasks on the job. Which of the two firms must respond in damages for the wrongful acts of the servant? Cardozo gave this answer: "The rule now is that as long as the employee is furthering the business of his general employer by the service rendered to another, there will be no inference of a new relation unless command has been surrendered, and no inference of its surrender from the mere fact of its division." Charles v. Barrett, 135 N.E. 199 (N.Y. 1922). What is wrong with a rule that makes the two employers jointly and severally liable, leaving them free to work out the arrangements between themselves by way of contribution and indemnity? See Mersey Docks & Harbour Board v. Coggins & Griffith (Liverpool) Ltd., [1947] A.C. 1, where the general employer's action for indemnity was denied, with the court unwilling to find a shift in employer without the express or implied consent of the employee. See generally Note, Borrowed Servants and the Theory of Enterprise Liability, 76 Yale L.J. 807, 820 (1967).

7. *Employer's indemnification.* The rule of respondeat superior governs only the relationship between the employer and the injured third party. It does not speak to the division of burden between the employer and the servant after the third party has been paid. Since the employer is only vicariously responsible, there has been much sentiment to allow him, as the passive and innocent party, to recoup his losses against the individual employee whose active negligence caused the original accident and, therefore, the employer's loss. At present that right of indemnification has been nearly universally adopted in all American courts. See, e.g., Fireman's Fund American Ins. Co. v. Turner, 488 P.2d 429 (Or. 1971); and in England see Lister v. Romford Ice & Cold Storage, [1957] A.C. 555.

While the doctrine of indemnification is secure in the judicial setting, there has been extensive academic criticism of it. See, e.g., James, Indemnity, Subrogation, and Contribution and the Efficient Distribution of Accident Losses, 21 NACCA L.J. 360 (1958); Williams, Vicarious Liability and the Master's Indemnity, 20 Mod. L. Rev. 220, 437 (1957). But see Jolowicz, The Right to Indemnity Between Master and Servant [1958] Cambridge L.J. 21, a defense of Lister v. Romford Ice.

8. *Beyond vicarious liability: owner-consent statutes.* Even when the immediate tortfeasor is not the employee of the defendant, principles of vicarious liability may still be an important source of liability, as with the owner-consent statutes on the books in many jurisdictions. These statutes enable the victim of a tort to sue not only the driver of a vehicle but also its owner. For example, section 388 of the New York Vehicle and Traffic Law provides:

Every owner of a vehicle used or operated in this state shall be liable and responsible for death or injuries to person or property resulting from negligence in the use or operation of such vehicle, in the business of such owner, or otherwise, by any person using or operating the same with the permission, express or implied of such owner.

As drafted, the statute goes far beyond the ordinary common-law principles of vicarious liability, for liability attaches even if the driver is not engaged in the business of the owner. To be sure, since the statute applies in ordinary agency cases, it simplifies litigation without changing results within that limited class. The dominant sense of these provisions, however, is that the automobile itself forms an effective unit around which to build protection for innocent traffic victims, since an owner is likely to allow persons without liability insurance to use the car.

Hardy v. Brantley
471 So. 2d 358 (Miss. 1985)

ROBERTSON, J., for the Court:

I

Evidence in this medical malpractice action reflects that practically no one ever dies of a perforated duodenal ulcer, but Brad Ewing did. The testimony also suggests that detection of a perforated ulcer is a relatively straight forward diagnosis provided the proper tests are run, but an emergency room physician misdiagnosed Brad Ewing's condition following which Brad died.

Because of outmoded rules we have finally dispatched in Hall v. Hilbun, 466 So. 2d 856 (Miss. 1985), Brad Ewing's personal representative was denied a fair opportunity to prove a claim of malpractice against the emergency physician and the hospital. We reverse and remand for a new trial under the *Hall* principles. Beyond that we clarify our law regarding the liability of a hospital for the malpractice of its emergency physician and provide that under certain circumstances the hospital may incur vicarious liability under the theory of respondeat superior. . . .

[The statement of facts, most favorable to the plaintiff, revealed that the decedent came to the emergency room of Hinds General Hospital with severe stomach pains. Once there he was treated by the defendant Brantley, who had mistreated the decedent's duodenal ulcer by failing to order or perform the necessary urine, stool, and blood tests and

X rays. Dr. Brantley then allowed the decedent to go home after his condition had stabilized with the use of Tylenol and Valium. The next day the decedent's condition worsened and he was brought back to the emergency room, where he died. The autopsy revealed that the decedent had died from an untreated duodenal ulcer from which he had suffered for a period of between 48 and 72 hours before his death. Those portions of the opinion reversing the trial court's decision to exclude the testimony of the plaintiff's key medical witness are omitted.]

II

B

The record reflects that Dr. Terry K. Brantley is one of three physicians organized as The Hinds Emergency Group (HEG). At all relevant times, Dr. Brantley served as an emergency physician at Hinds General in accordance with a rather elaborate contract between Hinds General and HEG.

> The contract provides that HEG shall have the complete and sole responsibility for furnishing professional services in the Emergency Department of . . . [Hinds General] so as to provide twenty-four hour coverage.

HEG was obligated to provide an emergency physician to render emergency care to each patient presenting himself at the emergency room, except patients known to have their own private physician.

Fees for services rendered by HEG were to be determined by HEG subject to review by Hinds General's administrator. The Hinds General accounting department was charged administratively with all billings and collections on behalf of HEG, for which services HEG paid to Hinds General 20 per cent of all such billings.

HEG agreed that during the term of the agreement none of its physicians would maintain an office for the private practice of medicine other than in the Emergency Department of the hospital and

> that they [HEG physicians] will confine their practice to emergency coverage at this Hospital . . . ,

except as otherwise expressly authorized by Hinds General's administrator.

Significantly, the contract then provided:

> 10. *Disclaimer.* In this performance of the work, duties and obligations devolving upon him under this agreement, it is mutually understood and

agreed that The Hinds Emergency Group is at all times acting and performing as an independent contractor providing to the Hospital the services of Emergency Physicians who are practicing their profession in medicine and surgery and specializing in Emergency care. The Hospital shall neither have nor exercise any control or direction over the methods by which the Hinds Emergency Group or its contract physicians shall perform their professional work and functions; *the sole interest and responsibility of the Hospital is to ensure that the Emergency Department and service covered by this agreement shall be performed and rendered in a competent, efficient, and satisfactory manner.* The standards of medical practice and professional duties of the partners and the contract physicians of the Hinds Emergency Group shall be determined by the medical staff of the Hospital. All applicable provisions of law and other rules and regulations of any and all governmental authorities relating to licensing and regulations of Physicians and Hospital and to the operation of the department shall be fully complied with by all parties hereto; in addition, the parties shall also operate and conduct the department in accordance with the standards and recommendations of the Joint Commission on Accreditation of Hospitals, the bylaws of the Hospital, and the bylaws, rules and regulations of the medical staff as may be in effect from time to time. Nothing in this agreement shall be in any way construed to constitute The Hinds Emergency Group or the Emergency Physicians as agents or employees of the Hospital, nor shall anything contained herein be construed to constitute the Hospital as agent for The Hinds Emergency Group or the Emergency Physicians except as specifically provided for in respect to billing and collection matters set forth in Paragraph 2 above.

11. *Liability Insurance.* The Hinds Emergency Group shall at its own expense or at the expense of its Emergency Physicians, cause each of its Emergency Physicians to carry professional liability insurance to cover himself, with a minimum of $100,000.00 for each person and $300,000.00 for each incident.

12. *Indemnity.* The Hinds Emergency Group shall defend, indemnify and hold Hospital, its Board of Trustees, employees and agents harmless from and against any and all claims, demands, liabilities, damages and expenses for injury to persons or damage to property caused or asserted to have been caused by the negligent or intentional acts of The Hinds Emergency Group or its employees, agents or partners. [Emphasis supplied.]

There is no evidence in the record that Brad or Larry Ewing had any knowledge of this agreement or its terms. . . .

[The court, having completed its examination of the expert witness question, then continued.]

IV

With respect to the Defendant Hinds General we must go further. It will be recalled that at the conclusion of Plaintiff's proof the trial judge directed a verdict in favor of Hinds General as well as Dr. Brantley. We are told that this ruling was correct, among other reasons, because Dr.

Brantley was an independent contractor and the hospital can have no liability for his defaults, if any.

We regard the question whether a hospital operating an emergency [room] may be held liable vicariously or under the theory of respondeat superior for the conduct of emergency room physicians retained by the hospital as one of first impression in this state. Porter v. Pandey, 423 So. 2d 126 (Miss. 1982), addresses a related topic but fails to consider the respondeat superior theory.

In its brief Hinds General makes much of its contractual arrangement with Dr. Brantley and the members of the Hinds Emergency Group, the details of which are recited in Section II(B) above. The hospital and the emergency room physicians (or any other health care providers for that matter), of course, are free to make as between themselves whatever agreement they may desire. To be specific, the hospital and the emergency physicians are certainly free to agree, if they wish, that the physician shall have full control of patient care, even to the point of agreeing to indemnify the hospital for liability vicariously incurred. Our concern, however, regards the rights and duties of the hospital vis-à-vis the patient, not the emergency room physician.

In this context, we sense a core of logic in cases from other states that appear to hold the hospital vicariously liable for the negligence or malpractice of staff physicians, no matter what the contract between them may say.[5] The seminal case is Brown v. Lasociet Francise de Bienfaisance Mutuelle, 71 P. 156 (CAl. 1903), which based its findings of agency upon two facts: (1) the patient seeks treatment from the hospital as opposed to a particular doctor, and (2) the hospital paid the doctor a salary. In Kober v. Stewart, 417 P.2d 476 (Mont. 1966), the Montana court followed this lead, and in spite of a contractual arrangement very similar to the one here, found a hospital to be vicariously liable for the acts of X-Ray technicians provided by an X-Ray clinic because (1) no one requested the services of the particular radiologist, (2) the three radiologists rotated their periods of service at the hospital, (3) a hospital employee asked the radiologist to read the X-Rays, (4) the radiologist was on call, (5) it was the hospital's standard procedure to call its own radiologist, (6) the hospital owned and operated the equipment and sent one bill including the doctor's fee, and (7) the clinic received a percentage of gross receipts. . . .

[The court then reviewed several relevant cases and concluded.]

Having in mind the considerations and premises set forth in the above authorities, we have concluded that the better rule to be followed in this state henceforth is this: Where a hospital holds itself out to the

---

5. There is no evidence in this record that either Brad Ewing or any members of his family had any knowledge of the contents of the agreement [between] Hinds General and HEG.

public as providing a given service, in this instance, emergency services, and where the hospital enters into a contractual arrangement with one or more physicians to direct and provide the service, and where the patient engages the services of the hospital without regard to the identity of a particular physician and where as a matter of fact the patient is relying upon the hospital to deliver the desired health care and treatment, the doctrine of respondeat superior applies and the hospital is vicariously liable for damages proximately resulting from the neglect, if any, of such physicians. By way of contrast and distinction, where a patient engages the services of a particular physician who then admits the patient to a hospital where the physician is on staff, the hospital is not vicariously liable for the neglect of defaults of the physician.[6]. . .

DAN M. LEE, J., concurring in part and dissenting in part: I concur in Parts I-III of the majority opinion. I must dissent, however, to Part IV of the majority opinion. Porter v. Pandey, 423 So. 2d 126 (Miss. 1982), was decided only three years ago. I am unconvinced that that decision was wrong and see no reason to overrule it. The majority's decision to impose liability on a hospital for the negligent actions of a physician independent contractor is certain to have a negative impact in terms of health care costs and availability. Because I would leave the business of running hospitals to physicians and hospital administrators I would adhere to the rule that the negligence of an independent contracting physician is not imputable to the hospital. I would affirm the trial court's decision to grant a directed verdict as to Hinds General.

NOTES

1. *Independent physicians.* Porter v. Pandey, 423 So. 126 (Miss. 1982), discussed in *Hardy*

> [O]ur statutes provide that a license to practice medicine may be issued only to a duly qualified *person* and there is no statutory authority which permits a hospital to diagnose and order treatment for a patient. [Plaintiff] is urging this Court to impose a duty on a hospital to supervise the attending physician of a patient, and in effect, to second guess the attending physician's diagnosis and treatment. If we were to impose that duty on hospitals, hospitals would then be required to engage in the practice of medicine contrary to our statute. This we decline to do.

Hardy continues to gain ground today. In Gilbert v. Frank, 599 N.E.2d 143, 148 (Ill. App. 1992), the court declined to hold the hospital vicariously liable on the ground that the "split second decisions" re-

6. We are aware of the emerging trend in other states to adopt a theory of corporate negligence in the adjudication of patient claims against hospitals. . . .

quired in emergency rooms "demands recognition of the independent relationship between a hospital and an emergency room physician and militates strongly against extension of a hospital's vicarious liability to physicians who are not actual agents or employees of the hospital." But in Gilbert v. Sycamore Municipal Hospital, 622 N.E.2d 788, 794 (Ill. 1993), the Illinois Supreme Court reversed the appellate court, explicitly followed *Hardy*, and answered its own question in the negative: "Can a hospital always escape liability for the rendering of negligent health care because the person rendering the care was an independent contractor, regardless of how the hospital holds itself out to the public, regardless of how the treating physician held himself or herself out to the public with the knowledge of the hospital, and regardless of the perception created in the mind of the public?"

2. *Who is an independent contractor?* Both inside and outside the medical context, it is often important to classify given persons. The working distinction between the independent contractor and the employee was stated in Sanford v. Goodridge, 13 N.W.2d 40, 43 (Iowa 1944) as follows:

> The principles governing the determination of the question as to whether a contract is independent upon the part of the contractor or one of employment is easy of statement but sometimes difficult of application. An independent contractor is one who, by virtue of his contract, possesses independence in the manner and method of performing the work he has contracted to perform for the other party to the contract. This other party to the contract must relinquish the right of control ordinarily enjoyed by an employer of labor and reserve only control as to the results of the contract before the independent-contractor relationship is created. Whether the party for whom the work was to be performed had the right to dictate and control the manner, means, and details of performing the service is the test to be applied. If he did have such rights, then, under the doctrine of respondeat superior, he is liable for the workman's tort. If he did not have such rights, then the workman did not have a master who could be required to respond in damages to the person injured by the workman.

The court then held that a route driver for the defendant newspaper, who injured the plaintiff in a traffic accident, was not an independent contractor, given that the employer retained effective control over his day-to-day operations. The court adopted this view of the relationship notwithstanding the language in the contract that described the route operator as an independent contractor. "It will not do for an employer to make a contract which in many clauses loudly proclaims the independence of his contracting workman and in other clauses circumvents this granted freedom by retaining in himself all the control that employers ordinarily possess over their employees." What result if the servant delivered papers for many different newspaper companies from the same vehicle?

3. Vicarious liability for independent contractors. While the employer is normally responsible for all torts of employees that arise out of and in the scope of employment, the general rule for independent contractors exempts the employer from liability. A landowner is not normally responsible in tort for the intersection collision caused by a roofer on his way from the home office to the job site. But the rule is subject to an important exception when the independent contractor does work on the premises of the employer. "When the injury is a direct result of the work contracted for, it is generally held that if the owner of a lot employs a contractor to make an excavation on it which removes the lateral support of a building of an adjoining owner the doctrine of respondeat superior is applicable, and the liability of the owner of the lot is to be determined as though he actually made the excavation himself." Law v. Phillips, 68 S.E.2d 452, 459 (W. Va. 1952). The same principle applies to damage from blasting or the cutting of electrical conduits, water pipes, or gasoline lines located below the ground. See, e.g., Brown v. Wisconsin National Gas Co., 208 N.W.2d 769 (Wis. 1973).

The Restatement of Torts states the applicable principle as follows:

§427. NEGLIGENCE AS TO DANGER INHERENT IN THE WORK
One who employs an independent contractor to do work involving a special danger to others which the employer knows or has reason to know to be inherent in or normal to the work, or which he contemplates or has reason to contemplate when making the contract, is subject to liability for physical harm caused to such others by the contractor's failure to take reasonable precautions against such danger.

This principle was applied in Western Stock Center v. Sevit, Inc., 578 P.2d 1045, 1050 (Colo. 1978). There, a tenant brought an action against the landlord for property damage and lost profits when his demised premises were burned by a fire set by an independent contractor hired by the defendant landlord. The landlord had contracted for the removal of "various ammonia pipes, valves and fittings" from his building for salvage purposes, and the fire was set by an electrical torch used by the contractor. In allowing the jury to pass on the question of whether use of the electric cutting torch was inherently dangerous under the circumstances, the court relied on section 427 and observed as follows:

It is important not to confuse the "inherently dangerous" exception with the "ultrahazardous activity" rule applied in real property trespass cases. In Colorado, blasting with dynamite and impounding water have been held to be ultrahazardous activities. Landowners who carry on these ultrahazardous activities on their land are strictly liable for all damages proximately caused to others by the activities. Thus, liability is imposed on the landowner regardless of whether he was negligent in conducting the activity. In contrast, under the "inherently dangerous activity" rule, an employer is only liable for damages if the independent contractor is negligent in performing the work. As with the doctrine of respondeat superior, the "inherently dangerous" exception is not a strict liability concept.

Chapter Six

Causation

A. INTRODUCTION

The questions of joint causation that were discussed in the last chapter might be said to put the cart before the horse, for the "jointness" questions only become important after the causation questions have been resolved. These issues of causation, moreover, form an indispensable element of every tort case, regardless of its underlying theory of liability. Once the plaintiff has established that the defendant has engaged in some wrongful conduct, it becomes necessary to link that conduct to the harm suffered by the plaintiff. In practice that question of linkage generally raises two distinct issues, which shall be considered in turn in this chapter: cause in fact and proximate cause.

Under the rubric of "cause in fact" we address generally the empirical questions of causal connection that have to be resolved in any tort suit. In the ordinary highway case, for example, the defendant will triumph on the cause-in-fact question if he can show that the plaintiff had the injury prior to the collision. The defendant did not cause (in fact) any harm which occurred before his wrongful conduct; nor is the defendant responsible for any harm that was caused by some independent event. The same type of cause-in-fact analysis carries over to far more complicated causal connections, including those involving the covert operation of drugs and chemicals that may be responsible for some disease or disability suffered by the plaintiff. In the modern setting, moreover, issues of cause in fact are no longer limited to situations in which the plaintiff searches for a discrete cause of a known and certain harm. Especially thorny issues arise when the plaintiff claims that the defendant's conduct has caused not an injury itself, but has only created an increased risk or hazard of an injury that is itself compensable.

The second inquiry into causation addresses the distinct issue of "proximate" or "legal" causation. Here the issues are not factual but conceptual: when are harms attributable to the defendant whose own actions are combined with those of other persons and natural events? This issue of proximate cause arises only after it is first established that some harmful consequence suffered by the plaintiff was caused in fact by the defendant, at least in the loose sense of "but for" causation: "but for the negligence, or other wrongful conduct of the defendant, the plaintiff would not have been injured." Often the chain of events and actions that links the plaintiff's injury to the defendant's conduct is long and tortuous. The issue of proximate causation asks whether the defendant's conduct could be regarded as a "substantial factor" in bringing about plaintiff's harm, and that inquiry often is translated into one that asks whether any of the human actions or natural events that occur after defendant's conduct but before the plaintiff's harm severs the causal connection between them.

Analytically, the problem of proximate cause in turn can be addressed in two distinct ways. One possibility is to ask whether the chain of events that in fact occurred was sufficiently "foreseeable," "natural," or "probable" at the outset for the defendant to be held liable for the ultimate harm that ensued, assuming that causation in fact can be established. That judgment is made from the standpoint of the defendant at the time the tortious act was committed. The second approach starts with the injury and works back toward the wrongful action of the defendant, seeking to determine whether any act of a third party or the plaintiff, or any natural event, severed the causal connection between the harm and the defendant's wrongful conduct. Here the question is only whether, when all the evidence is in, it is permissible to say that the defendant "did it," that is, brought about the plaintiff's harm. The interaction between the "foresight" and "directness" perspectives, as they are respectively called, is the subject of Section C of this chapter. Here the materials are organized in historical sequence to trace the evolution and permutation of the basic doctrine from its nineteenth-century origins to its more contemporary applications.

As a rough generalization, the cause-in-fact issues appear to have gained importance relative to the proximate-cause issues in the past generation. Why might this be so?

B.   CAUSE IN FACT

New York Central R.R. v. Grimstad
264 F. 334 (2d Cir. 1920)

Action of Elfrieda Grimstad, administratrix of the estate of Angell Grimstad, deceased, against the New York Central Railroad Company. Judgment for plaintiff, and defendant brings error. Reversed.

WARD, C.J. This is an action under the Federal Employers' Liability Act (Comp. St. Sec. 8657-8665) to recover damages for the death of Angell Grimstad, captain of the covered barge *Grayton*, owned by the defendant railroad company. The charge of negligence is failure to equip the barge with proper life-preservers and other necessary and proper appliances, for want of which the decedent, having fallen into the water, was drowned.

The barge was lying on the port side of the steamer *Santa Clara*, on the north side of Pier 2, Erie Basin, Brooklyn, loaded with sugar in transit from Havana to St. John, N.B. The tug *Mary M*, entering the slip between Piers 1 and 2, bumped against the barge. The decedent's wife, feeling the shock, came out from the cabin, looked on one side of the barge, and saw nothing, and then went across the deck to the other side of the barge, and discovered her husband in the water about 10 feet from the barge holding up his hands out of the water. He did not know how to swim. She immediately ran back into the cabin for a small line, and when she returned with it he had disappeared.

It is admitted that the decedent at the time was engaged in interstate commerce. The court left it to the jury to say whether the defendant was negligent in not equipping the barge with life-preservers and whether, if there had been a life-preserver on board, Grimstad would have been saved from drowning.

The jury found as a fact that the defendant was negligent in not equipping the barge with life-preservers. Life-preservers and life belts are intended to be put on the body of a person before getting into the water, and would have been of no use at all to the decedent. On the other hand, life buoys are intended to be thrown to a person when in the water, and we will treat the charge in the complaint as covering life buoys.

Obviously the proximate cause of the decedent's death was his falling into the water, and in the absence of any testimony whatever on the point, we will assume that this happened without negligence on his part or on the part of the defendant. On the second question, whether a life buoy would have saved the decedent from drowning, we think the jury were left to pure conjecture and speculation. A jury might well conclude that a light near an open hatch or rail on the side of a vessel's deck would have prevented a person's falling into the hatch or into the water, in the dark. But there is nothing whatever to show that the decedent was not drowned because he did not know how to swim, nor anything to show that, if there had been a life buoy on board, the decedent's wife would have got it in time, that is, sooner than she got the small line, or, if she had, that she would have thrown it so that her husband could have seized it, or, if she did, that he would have seized it, or that, if he did, it would have prevented him from drowning.

The court erred in denying the defendant's motion to dismiss the complaint at the end of the case.

Judgment reversed.

NOTES

1. *The life you save.* . . . In Ford v. Trident Fisheries, 122 N.E. 389, 390 (Mass. 1919), the decedent fell overboard from his shipping vessel and drowned. The negligence alleged by the plaintiff was that the rescue boat was "lashed to the deck instead of being suspended from davits" from which it could be easily lowered. The court held that even if the defendant was negligent, "there is nothing to show they in any way contributed to Ford's death. He disappeared when he fell from the trawler, and it does not appear that if the boat had been suspended from davits and a different method of propelling it had been used he could have been rescued."

What is the precedential value of *Grimstad*? In Kirincich v. Standard Dredging Co., 112 F.2d 163, 164 (3d Cir. 1940), where "the deceased fell off a dredge close to shore and was carried away by the falling tide while shipmates tried to save him with inadequate life-saving equipment, such inadequacy of equipment being the negligence alleged." The trial judge had dismissed plaintiff's cause of action. That judgment was reversed and the case remanded for trial. Clark, C.J., speaking for the court, observed in part:

> . . . In the light, then, of this logic and these examples, would Kirincich have drowned even if a larger and more buoyant object than the inch heaving line had been thrown within two feet of him? If he could swim, even badly, there would be no doubt. Assuming he could not, we think he might (the appropriate grammatical mood) have saved himself through the help of something which he could more easily grasp. We can take judicial notice of the instinct of self-preservation that at first compensates for lack of skill. A drowning man comes to the surface and clutches at what he finds there — hence the significance of size and buoyancy in life saving apparatus. In other words, we prefer the doctrine of Judge Learned Hand in the case of Zinnel v. United States Shipping Board Emergency Fleet Corp., 2 Cir., 10 F.2d 47, 49: "Thereof course remains the question whether they might have also said that the fault

caused the loss. About that we agree no certain conclusion was possible. Nobody could, in the nature of things, be sure that the intestate would have seized the rope, or, if he had not, that it would have stopped his body. But we are not dealing with a criminal case, nor are we justified, where certainty is impossible, in insisting upon it. . . . we think it a question about which reasonable men might at least differ whether the intestate would not have been saved, had it been there," to that of his colleague, Judge Hough, dissenting in that case, and concurring in the earlier case of New York Central R. Co. v. Grimstad, 2 Cir., 264 F. 334, 335.

The modern cases are explicit in conferring upon the jury broad powers of decision in cases of rescue at sea. In Reyes v. Vantage Steamship Co., 609 F.2d 140, 144 (5th Cir. 1980), the decedent, while drunk, jumped off his boat and tried to swim to a mooring buoy some several hundred feet away. Immediately after striking the water he was seen by members of the crew who were aware that he was in mortal danger. The decedent struggled against a strong current only to drown, his energy spent, some 20 feet from the buoy. Since the ship was under a duty of maritime rescue, the only question was the causal connection between its failure and the decedent's drowning. Coast Guard regulations required a ship to have a rocket-powered line-throwing appliance capable of throwing at least 1,500 feet of line. The district court first denied relief. On appeal the court initially entered a judgment for the plaintiff, but on rehearing reversed and remanded for a finding on causation. "The District Court on remand must be prepared to determine whether there was time for a crew member to go to the hypothetical storage location, obtain the hypothetical line-throwing appliance, move it to the appropriate firing location, and fire the appliance — all before Reyes went limp in the water." The court noted that it was also necessary to take into account "some possibility that a line or lines fired over or near Reyes might have harmed him or perhaps impeded his labored swimming," as well as the likelihood that the line would have reached Reyes and whether he "would have obeyed an order" to take it. The court then refused to place "the difficult burden of proving causation on the widow of the deceased seaman." On remand the district court entered a judgment for the plaintiff, finding that defendant's negligence was 15 percent of the cause of death.

2. *Switching the burden of proof on causation.* In Haft v. Lone Palm Hotel, 478 P.2d 465, 474-475 (Cal. 1970), the plaintiffs brought wrongful death actions when a father and son drowned in the pool operated at the defendant's Palm Springs motel. The applicable statute provided that "lifeguard service shall be provided or signs shall be erected clearly indicating that such service is not provided." The defendant neither provided the lifeguard service nor posted the signs; and there was no evidence as to how the deaths actually took place. The court, through

Tobriner, J., first observed that "to hold that a pool owner, who has failed to satisfy either of the section's alternative requirements, may limit his liability to that resulting from his "lesser" failure to erect a sign, would of course effectively read out of the section the primary requirement of providing lifeguard service." (Sound?) He then addressed the burden of proof on causation as follows:

> The troublesome problems concerning the causation issue in the instant case of course arise out of the total lack of direct evidence as to the precise manner in which the drownings occurred. Although the paucity of evidence on causation is normally one of the burdens that must be shouldered by a plaintiff in proving his case, the evidentiary void in the instant action results primarily from defendants' failure to provide a lifeguard to observe occurrences within the pool area. The main purpose of the lifeguard requirement is undoubtedly to aid those in danger, but an attentive guard does serve the subsidiary function of witnessing those accidents that do occur. The absence of such a lifeguard in the instant case thus not only stripped decedents of a significant degree of protection to which they were entitled, but also deprived the present plaintiffs of a means of definitively establishing the facts leading to the drownings.
>
> Clearly, the failure to provide a lifeguard greatly enhanced the chances of the occurrence of the instant drownings. In proving (1) that defendants were negligent in this respect, and (2) that the available facts, at the very least, strongly suggest that a competent lifeguard, exercising reasonable care, would have prevented the deaths, plaintiffs have gone as far as they possibly can under the circumstances in proving the requisite causal link between defendants' negligence and the accidents. To require plaintiffs to establish "proximate causation" to a greater certainty than they have in the instant case, would permit defendants to gain the advantage of the lack of proof inherent in the lifeguardless situation which they have created. Under these circumstances the burden of proof on the issue of causation should be shifted to defendants to absolve themselves if they can.

Stimpson v. Wellington Service Corp.
246 N.E.2d 801 (Mass. 1969)

[The defendants drove their 137-ton rig over a public way in violation of statutory weight limitations. The plaintiff complained of damages when pipes in his basement became uncoupled. The jury found for plaintiff, and one of the questions on appeal was whether plaintiff could connect the flooding in his basement with defendants' violation of the statute.]

WHITTEMORE, J. . . . The verdicts were supported by proof of negligence and not founded in speculation and conjecture.

Apart from the excluded expert testimony it was a reasonable conclusion from the evidence that the great pressure in the street had caused a lowering of the connecting pipe in that part of its forty foot length that underlay the rig. An expert was not essential to demonstrate that the effect of downward movement on that part of the rigid pipe that was in the street would be an upward thrust of its other end inside the foundation wall on which it rested. It was also a reasonable layman's conclusion that all rigid pipes on the basement side of the coupling would as a result be under stress and that a fracture at some point in the system was likely.

That the fracture occurred a number of hours after the time when the stress was created in the system did not make the cause conjectural. A delay between the distortion and the break was entirely consistent with initial slight adjustment in the position of the relatively rigid pipes which created tension throughout all of them, and the eventual release of the tension by a break occurring at the weakest point in the system.

In this the jurors were concerned with the operation of established physical principles and circumstances to which they could apply their knowledge and experience. The plaintiffs were not bound to exclude the operation of other possible causes. It is sufficient if the cause shown is made to appear the probable cause of the accident. Restatement 2d:Torts, §433, comment f.

It follows that the expert testimony, although not required to take the case to the jury, was not founded on conjecture and was admissible. . . .

NOTES

1. *Slip-and-fall cases.* Another group of cases that raises many difficult questions of cause in fact are the so-called slip-and-fall cases. For our purposes, it suffices to note two variations on the theme. In Reynolds v. Texas & Pacific Ry. Co., 37 La. Ann. 694, 698 (1885), plaintiff, a 250-pound woman, after hurrying out of a lighted waiting room, fell down the unlighted steps leading to the train platform. The defendant argued that "she might well have made the mis-step and fallen even had it been broad daylight," but the court affirmed judgment for plaintiff, noting:

> We concede that this is possible, and recognize the distinction between post hoc and propter hoc. But where the negligence of the defendant greatly multiplies the chances of accident to the plaintiff, and is of a character naturally leading to its occurrence, the mere possibility that it might have happened without the negligence is not sufficient to break the chain of cause and effect between the negligence and the injury. Courts, in such matters, consider the natural and ordinary course of events, and do not indulge in fanciful suppositions. The whole tendency of the evidence connects the accident with the negligence.

Compare McInturff v. Chicago Title and Trust, 243 N.E.2d 657, 662 (Ill. App. 1968), where decedent fell down a stairway in defendant's building and was found dead at the bottom. There were no eyewitnesses to the accident, but plaintiff's evidence did establish that the stairs were worn down in violation of a city ordinance and that there was no railing on the right-hand side of the stairwell. The jury's decision in favor of plaintiff was overturned on appeal:

> The fragmentary evidence on the issue of the defendant's negligence did not establish any relationship between the alleged negligence and the proximate cause of decedent's fall and injury. There was no direct evidence relative to what took place prior to and at the time of decedent's injury. There was no proof that the condition of the stairway, or the alleged failure to comply with the handrail ordinances, caused the injury or damage suffered by the plaintiff. The burden was on the plaintiff to establish by a preponderance of the evidence the causal relation between the alleged negligence and the injury sustained by the decedent. Absent proof of a causal relationship between the condition of the stairs and the decedent's death, the plaintiff was not entitled to recover. Damages cannot be assessed on mere surmise or conjecture as to what probably happened to cause his injury and death.

   2. *Cause in fact in products liability cases.* In Engberg v. Ford Motor Co., 205 N.W.2d 104, 106 (S.D. 1973), plaintiff's husband was killed when he drove his station wagon, which he had purchased two weeks previously from the defendant, off the highway into a ditch. No other cars were involved in the accident and the parties were unable to establish the precise sequence of events leading up to the decedent's death. Plaintiff's cause of action was based upon the theory that defendant's car was defectively manufactured in that its seat belt was of insufficient strength to withstand the impact of a crash. Plaintiff introduced evidence that the decedent's seat belt was found "buckled but broken" after the fatal crash, and that there was no blood inside the car. Her expert witnesses further testified that

> the seat belt severed in this case because the boot and belt were rubbing on the frame of the seat causing them to give way under the pressure of less than expectable force. He also stated that in his opinion, the design of the assembly and the installation of the belt was improper to prevent the rubbing that caused the severance. He further testified, over the defendant's objection, that the absence of internal damage to the vehicle indicated that the fatal injury occurred outside of the car and that had the seat belt remained intact and the decedent remained inside the car, the amount of injury would have been minor.
>   [The defendant's expert witness in turn testified that] the boot and seat belt could not in any way come into contact with the frame of the seat. He also testified that based upon the type and location of the cut, it was his opinion that the seat belt had been severed by the metal capsule that ties together the wires of the seat and that the capsule had been moved from where it was originally installed by the manufacturer.

There was additional evidence in the case that the decedent did not properly adjust his seat belt before the crash and that there was ample room for him to slip out under the belt when the crash took place.

The court held that the case was properly left for the jury because defendant could not show that plaintiff's version of the case was "contradicted by its undisputed physical facts," and it further rejected the defendant's contention that it was pure "speculation" to conclude that the decedent would have survived if the seat belt had remained intact. What additional facts need to be established in order for the defendant to be entitled to a directed verdict? For the plaintiff to be entitled to a directed verdict?

"Proximate cause is a rule of physics and not a criterion of negligence." Collier v. Citizens Coach Co., 330 S.W.2d 74, 76 (Ark. 1959). Is that true or false in light of the cases thus far considered? Reconsider the answer in both normative and positive terms at the end of this chapter.

Richardson v. Richardson-Merrell
649 F. Supp. 799 (D.D.C. 1986)

JACKSON, D.J.: This products liability case is presently before the Court on defendant's motion for judgment n.o.v. or a new trial following a jury verdict for plaintiffs of $1.16 million after a lengthy trial. It is one of a number of cases filed across the country in which the plaintiffs allege that a child's congenital limb deformities were caused by Bendectin, an anti-nauseant medication manufactured by defendant to be taken orally by the mother during pregnancy to alleviate "morning sickness."

This trial was a virtual reprise of Oxendine v. Merrell Dow Pharmaceuticals, Inc., 506 A.2d 1100 (D.C. 1986), the only other such case known to the Court to have been tried to conclusion in a plaintiff's verdict which has survived all post-trial proceedings to date. The trial judge in Oxendine set aside the verdict and judgment with only a brief statement of reasons, but the District of Columbia Court of Appeals reversed, in an opinion which, although accurately summarizing the testimony, did not address the significance of certain evidence bearing upon the current state of scientific knowledge. In consequence, it judicially reopened an esoteric twenty-year-old controversy which is by now essentially settled within the scientific community.

This Court, having heard substantially the same evidence as the trial judge in Oxendine, is of the same opinion as to its efficacy. No reasonable jury could find on the basis thereof that this infant plaintiff's birth defects were more likely than not to have been caused by her intrauterine exposure to Bendectin; alternatively, even if such a finding were reasonable, it is nevertheless so clearly contrary to the weight of the evidence that the case must be retried. For the reasons hereinafter set forth, therefore, defendant's motion will be granted, and judgment notwithstanding the verdict will be entered for defendant, with a new trial granted in the alternative.

I

Carita Richardson, the fourth child of Etheleen and Samuel Richardson, was born in the District of Columbia on February 16, 1976. Her siblings were normal at birth. At her birth Carita had a deformed left arm, with an underdeveloped humerus fused to the radius at the elbow, terminating in a hand with only two digits. Her right arm was normal. The right and left femurs were likewise underdeveloped, and, while her lower left leg was normal, she had no lower right leg at all. An appendage resembling a foot (later amputated) was attached directly to her right hip.

Etheleen Richardson (then aged 38) conceived Carita approximately May 28, 1975. She developed "morning sickness," i.e., the nausea which occasionally occurs in early pregnancy (onset at about 21-28 days *post* conception) and began taking Bendectin, on her doctor's prescription, on or about June 28, 1975, two tablets at night and one in the morning, for at least the duration of the period of organogenesis, when Carita's limbs were forming *in utero* (from about the 24th through the 56th days *post* conception).

In 1975 Bendectin contained 10 mg. each of dicyclomine hydrochloride, doxylamine succinate, and pyridoxine hydrochloride — an anticholergenic, antihistamine, and Vitamin B-6, respectively — the latter two ingredients included for their ostensible anti-nausea and antiemetic properties.

Bendectin (also known as "Debendox" in the British Commonwealth, and "Lenotan" in West Germany) had been marketed by Merrell-Dow Pharmaceuticals, Inc., or its predecessors, Wm. S. Merrell Co. and Richardson-Merrell, Inc. (hereinafter "Merrell"), as an anti-nauseant since 1956. In the United States it has always been available only by prescription; in some other countries it was sold over-the-counter.

Expert witnesses for both sides generally agreed that congenital birth defects are present in approximately two to four per cent of all live births; that limb reduction defects, specifically, occur at a rate of approximately three per thousand; that genetic or chromosomal abnormalities account for from 10 to about 15 per cent of all birth defects, and maternal illnesses, e.g. diabetes, or viral or bacterial infections, will explain perhaps three to five per cent more; and that there is a large category — a majority — to which no cause can be ascribed with certainty. They are also agreed that "environmental" factors can and do cause some of the remainder, including substances ingested by the mother. Plaintiffs assert that Carita Richardson's afflictions were caused by the Bendectin her mother took in the summer of 1975. Defendant denies it, but, being without evidence to implicate another of the known causes of birth defects, places Carita in the "unknown" category for which science has yet to find an explanation.[3]

Unable to prove directly how Bendectin actually (or could have) affected Carita while in her mother's womb, plaintiffs here proceeded (as did the plaintiff in *Oxendine*) with circumstantial evidence.[4] Through the testimony of experts in several disciplines — pharmacology, embryology, veterinary medicine, and the like — they established the similarity of the chemical structure of doxylamine to that of other antihistamines known to be teratogenic in animals. Witnesses described the effects of Bendectin components in solution in *in vitro* experiments upon frog nerve fibers and the mesenchyme cells of mouse limb buds, postulating that other effects might occur in the human intra-uterine environment, when Bendectin is infused *via* the mother, which could inhibit the development of fetal organs. And they criticized the animal experiments conducted by Merrell in 1963 and 1966, suggesting that Merrell's raw data had been misassessed, and the number of tests and dosage levels had been insufficient to dispel doubts about Bendectin's safety. Moreover, when such observations as Merrell had made were properly interpreted, they said, the studies did indicate Bendectin's teratogenic potential in animals which raised suspicions of a similar effect in humans.

Defendant's case consisted, in part, of discipline-by-discipline retorts to plaintiffs' witnesses, supplemented by the testimony of several clinicians with extensive experience in prescribing Bendectin for pregnant women or in treating malformed children, all of whom were certain no connection existed between the medication and the malformations. At least equally well-qualified defense experts asserted that a structural chemical resemblance does not import similar chemical activity; that *in vitro* studies on animal tissues have never been scientifically validated as

3. There is no evidence to suggest that Bendectin is a selective teratogen (other than the fact that the vast majority of Bendectin-exposed infants are normal); that Etheleen or Carita Richardson had a peculiar suseptibility to it or any of its components; or that the composition of the drug distributed in the District of Columbia differed from that distributed elsewhere.

4. There is, of course, no direct evidence of Bendectin's actual physiological effects upon the human fetus. No such experiments have been, or could lawfully or ethically be, conducted.

Plaintiffs were not permitted to introduce into evidence, nor were their experts allowed to rely upon, so-called "drug experience reports" or "adverse reaction reports," i.e., anecdotal case reports of birth defects observed in the offspring of mothers whose histories included Bendectin usage. The Court made a disputed preliminary finding that such reports are neither exceptions to the hearsay rule nor data reasonably relied upon by experts in the field of making determinations of causality.

predictors of physiological effects upon living human beings, and, indeed, are generally regarded as useless for the purpose; and that Merrell's animal tests had been, in fact, both properly conducted and properly interpreted, reflecting precisely the conclusions Merrell had drawn from them. Moreover, they declared, animal studies, too, are of limited usefulness in assessing a drug's teratogenic potential in humans; of some 600 known animal teratogens, only a small fraction of them have been shown to have such an effect upon human embryos. All defense witnesses, as might be expected, were of the opinion that Bendectin is not a human teratogen.

Plaintiffs' principal witness on causation was, as in *Oxendine,* Dr. Alan K. Done, a pediatrician, and until three years ago, a professor of pediatrics, pharmacology, and toxicology at Wayne State University in Detroit.[6] Based upon his knowledge of Bendectin's chemical structure, the *in vitro* studies, the animal teratology studies conducted by Merrell (and others), and the "human data" he had reviewed, i.e., epidemiological studies which he found defective, inconclusive, or both, Dr. Done stated that, in his opinion, to a "reasonable degree of medical certainty," Bendectin was not only "capable" of causing birth defects in humans, but that it had, in fact, caused those limb defects with which Carita Richardson had been born.

II

It was Dr. Done's testimony in principal part upon which the D.C. Court of Appeals relied in holding the *Oxendine* case to have been a " 'classic battle of the experts . . . in which the jury must decide the victor,' " *Oxendine,* 506 A.2d at 1110, *quoting Ferebee v. Chevron Chemical Co.,* 736 F.2d 1529, 1535 (D.C. Cir.), and reinstating the jury verdict for plaintiff.

[The court then summarized the testimony of defendant's Dr. Seltser, who had published extensively on Bendectin. Dr. Seltser stated that studies conducted throughout the world on Bendectin had "uniformly reported no statistically significant correlation to have been found between pre-natal exposure to Bendectin and the limb reduction defects it was suspected of causing." The court then noted that an expert panel convened by the Food and Drug Administration (FDA) in 1980 had reached the same conclusion after an exhaustive review of the subject at which 30 experts, including Dr. Done, had testified. The FDA "announced its agreement with its findings, a position it has not changed in the meantime nor been given reason to do so."]

6. Since May 1983, Dr. Done has been a proprietor (or an investor in) and for a time the chief executive officer, of an enterprise known as the Association of Consulting Toxicologists which provides "medicolegal and forensic investigation" services.

III

It is unnecessary to revive debate upon the wisdom of that rule of law which, for purposes of awarding damages in personal injury cases, allows unschooled triers-of-fact, whether judges or juries, to resolve those "complex and refractory causal issues . . . at the frontier of current medical and epidemiological inquiry," *Ferebee,* 736 F.2d at 1534, for it is obvious that Bendectin's teratogenicity *vel non* is no longer such an issue. The ominous hypothesis of two decades ago, namely, that Bendectin might be another Thalidomide, has been reduced to the status of a perdurable superstition by the worldwide epidemiological investigations it provoked, surviving mainly by the *post hoc ergo propter hoc* logic which beckons whenever deformed babies are born to women who have taken any suspect substance.

Though Dr. Done might disagree, there is now nearly universal scientific consensus that Bendectin has not been shown to be a teratogen, and, the issue being a scientific one, reasonable jurors could not reject that consensus without indulging in precisely the same speculation and conjecture which the multiple investigations undertook, but failed, to confirm. That Dr. Done remains an unbeliever and was willing to testify to his disbelief "with reasonable medical certainty" does not mandate that this case be left as the jury decided it. Without a genuine basis "in or out of the record," even his expert "theoretical speculations" are insufficient to sustain the plaintiffs' burden of proving, by a preponderance of the evidence, that Bendectin not only causes congenital defects generally, but that, in particular, it caused those limb reduction defects with which Carita Richardson was most unfortunately born.

For the foregoing reasons, therefore, it is this 19th day of December, 1986,

ORDERED, that defendant's motions for judgment n.o.v. and for a new trial in the alternative, are granted.

NOTES

1. Bendectin: expert evidence and epidemiology. The decision in *Richardson* was affirmed in Richardson by Richardson v. Richardson-Merrell, Inc., 857 F.2d 823 (D.C. Cir. 1988), and today represents the dominant view that Bendectin should not be regarded as a cause of certain birth defects. See also Lynch v. Merrell-National Laboratories Division of Richardson Merrell, Inc. 646 F. Supp. 856 (D. Mass. 1986), aff'd 830 F.2d 1190 (1st Cir. 1987). The major exception to the general rule is Oxendine v. Merrell Dow Pharmaceuticals, 506 A.2d 1100, 1110 (D.C. App. 1986), where a $750,000 jury award to the plaintiff was first overturned by the trial judge and then reinstated by the Court of Appeals:

> Where the [trial] court erred was in failing to consider the same expert's testimony that all of the studies, *taken in combination,* did support such a finding, as he carefully and repeatedly explained.
>
> In ruling on a motion for judgment n.o.v., the court must view the evidence as a whole, not in fragments. Like the pieces of a mosaic, the individual studies showed little or nothing when viewed separately from one another, but they combined to produce a whole that was greater than the sum of its parts: a foundation for Dr. Done's opinion that Bendectin caused appellant's birth defects. The evidence also established that Dr. Done's methodology was generally accepted in the field of teratology, and his qualifications as an expert have not been challenged. Because he fully explained to the jury that his opinion was based on *all* of the studies, we cannot say that no reasonable juror could reach a verdict in favor of appellant. Hence we must reverse the order granting a judgment n.o.v.

Notwithstanding its vindication by the FDA and its general success in tort litigation, Richardson-Merrell has pulled Bendectin from the market because of its fear of continued law suits. "(W)hile Bendectin usage declined from 1 million new therapy starts in 1979 to zero in 1984, there has been no change in the incidence of birth defects." *Lynch,* 830 F.2d at 1194.

The battle of experts reached the United States Supreme Court in Daubert v. Merrell Dow Pharmaceuticals, Inc., 113 S. Ct. 2786 (1993), after the defendant obtained summary judgment at trial on the causation issue after the plaintiff had assembled a team of eight recognized experts who were prepared to testify that Bendectin could indeed cause birth defects, largely by reinterpreting the data contained in peer review studies that had denied the causal association between Bendectin and birth defects. The Supreme Court rejected the traditional test of Frye v. United States, 293 F. 1013, 1014 (1923), which allowed as admissible only that expert testimony "generally accepted" as reliable by the scientific community. It then remanded the case for further consideration, noting that both lower courts erroneously "focused almost exclusively on 'general acceptance,' as gauged by publication and the decision of other courts," not taking into account sufficiently other measures of reliability and relevance, including the tightness of "fit" between the evidence presented and the charge to be proved. On remand, Kozinski, J., upheld summary judgment on the revised standard, noting that none of plaintiff's experts "are proposing to testify about matters growing naturally and directly out of research they have conducted independent of the litigation," and far from publishing their results in peer-reviewed journals, "the only places their theories and studies have been published is in the pages of the federal and state reports." See Daubert v. Merrell Dow Pharmaceuticals, Inc., — F.3d — (9th Cir. 1995).

2. *The Agent Orange litigation.* Proving causation in fact was also the

central issue in the Agent Orange suits brought mainly by servicemen and their offspring who claimed that Agent Orange (or more specifically dioxin, a deadly byproduct of its production) caused a large class of serious illnesses and birth defects. The individual suits were consolidated before Weinstein, J., where they were prosecuted as a class action, with individual plaintiffs having the right to opt out of the class. The main class was settled for $180,000,000, with the moneys placed in a trust fund for distribution to the victims. In a subsequent action, Weinstein, J., dismissed the suits of those plaintiffs who had opted out of the class because the evidence (including animal and epidemiological studies) did not support proof of causal connection.

> There is no evidence that plaintiffs were exposed to the far higher concentrations involved in both the animal and industrial studies. The animal studies are not helpful in the instant case because they involve different biological species. They are of so little probative value and are so potentially misleading as to be inadmissible.

See In re "Agent Orange" Product Liability Litigation, 611 F. Supp. 1223, 1241 (E.D.N.Y. 1985). Why should the settlement have provided for any award given the summary judgment that followed? Does the issue have to do with the risk that any summary judgment award could be overturned on appeal? Note that the $180,000,000 was placed in a fund for distribution to various veterans for their illnesses and their children's birth defects. The distribution of those moneys was itself held up when one veteran's group claimed that the proposed plan of distribution was improperly based on degrees of disability and not on levels of exposure to Agent Orange. See In re "Agent Orange" Product Liability Litigation, 804 F.2d 19 (2d Cir. 1986). On Agent Orange generally see P. Schuck, Agent Orange on Trial: Mass Toxic Disasters in the Courts (1986).

The Agent Orange cases illustrate the three levels of causation that must be established in toxic torts, which are summarized by Professor Abraham in Individual Action and Collective Responsibility: The Dilemma of Mass Tort Reform, 73 Va. L. Rev. 845, 860, 867-868 (1987), as follows:

> To meet traditional burdens of proof in a regime that emphasizes individual responsibility, the plaintiff must show what I shall call *substance, source,* and *exposure* causation. That is, he must prove that the substance for which the defendant is responsible can cause his injury or disease, that the defendant and not someone else was the source of the substance, and that he was in fact exposed to the substance in a way that has caused his disease. In many cases, proof of some of these elements is simple; in some cases, proof of one automatically proves another. For example,

when a particular disease is caused almost exclusively by a particular substance, the occurrence of the disease is the substance's "signature." Proof
that the plaintiff has the disease, therefore, is also proof of both exposure
and substance causation. In many cases, however, meeting the traditional
burden of proof as to each of these elements is no minor accomplishment.

Abraham then expressed his doubt that the traditional tort models
could work in cases like Agent Orange where no signature disease is
found.

> In sum, the justification for imposing collective responsibility in a large
> variety of nonsignature disease cases is not easy to find. Often no collec-
> tive action of even the attenuated sort that might warrant a finding of
> collective responsibility in other mass tort situations can be identified;
> the use of collective responsibility as a surrogate for individual responsi-
> bility does not necessarily have the incentive effects that might otherwise
> justify its imposition; and in any case, the data necessary to support the
> probabilistic measures of causation that could serve as surrogates for
> causal responsibility will rarely be available. The entire effort usually re-
> quires more than the legal or scientific state of the art is capable of pro-
> viding.

Herskovits v. Group Health Cooperative
664 P.2d 474 (Wash. 1983)

DORE, J.: This appeal raises the issue of whether an estate can maintain an action for professional negligence as a result of failure to timely
diagnose lung cancer, where the estate can show probable reduction in
statistical chance for survival but cannot show and/or prove that with
timely diagnosis and treatment, decedent probably would have lived to
normal life expectancy.

Both counsel advised that for the purpose of this appeal we are to
assume that the respondent Group Health Cooperative of Puget Sound
and its personnel negligently failed to diagnose Herskovits' cancer on
his first visit to the hospital and *proximately* caused a 14 percent reduction in his chances of survival. It is undisputed that Herskovits had less
than a 50 percent chance of survival at all times herein.

The main issue we will address in this opinion is whether a patient,
with less than a 50 percent chance of survival, has a cause of action
against the hospital and its employees if they are negligent in diagnos-
ing a lung cancer which reduces his chances of survival by 14 percent.

The personal representative of Leslie Herskovits' estate initiated this
survivorship action against Group Health Cooperative of Puget Sound
(Group Health), alleging failure to make an early diagnosis of her husband's lung cancer. Group Health moved for summary judgment for

dismissal on the basis that Herskovits *probably* would have died from lung cancer even if the diagnosis had been made earlier, which the trial court granted.

I

. . . At hearing on the motion for summary judgment, plaintiff was unable to produce expert testimony that the delay in diagnosis "probably" or "more likely than not" caused her husband's death. . .

Dr. Ostrow [plaintiff's expert] testified that if the tumor was a "stage 1" tumor in December 1974, Herskovits' chance of a 5-year survival would have been 39 percent. In June 1975, his chances of survival were 25 percent assuming the tumor had progressed to "stage 2." Thus, the delay in diagnosis may have reduced the chance of a 5-year survival by 14 percent. . .

Plaintiff contends that medical testimony of a reduction of chance of survival from 39 percent to 25 percent is sufficient evidence to allow the proximate cause issue to go to the jury. Defendant Group Health argues conversely that Washington law does not permit such testimony on the issue of medical causation and requires that medical testimony must be at least sufficiently definite to establish that the act complained of "probably" or "more likely than not" caused the subsequent disability. It is Group Health's contention that plaintiff must prove that Herskovits "probably" would have survived had the defendant not been allegedly negligent; that is, the plaintiff must prove there was at least a 51 percent chance of survival. . .

II

This court has held that a person who negligently renders aid and consequently increases the risk of harm to those he is trying to assist is liable for any physical damages he causes. Brown v. MacPherson's, Inc., 86 Wash. 2d 293, 299, 545 P.2d 13 (1975). In *Brown,* the court cited Restatement (Second) of Torts §323 (1965), which reads:

> One who undertakes . . . to render services to another which he should recognize as necessary for the protection of the other's person or things, is subject to liability to the other for physical harm resulting from his failure to exercise reasonable care to perform his undertaking, if
> (a) his failure to exercise such care increases the risk of such harm, . . .

This court heretofore has not faced the issue of whether, under section 323(a), proof that the defendant's conduct increased the risk of death by decreasing the chances of survival is sufficient to take the issue of proximate cause to the jury. Some courts in other jurisdictions have allowed the proximate cause issue to go to the jury on this type of proof. See Hamil v. Bashline, 481 Pa. 256, 392 A.2d 1280 (1978). These courts emphasized the fact that defendants' conduct deprived the decedents of a "significant" chance to survive or recover, rather than requiring proof that with absolute certainty the defendants' conduct caused the physical injury. The underlying reason is that it is not for the wrongdoer, who put the possibility of recovery beyond realization, to say afterward that the result was inevitable.

Other jurisdictions have rejected this approach, generally holding that unless the plaintiff is able to show that it was *more likely than not* that the harm was caused by the defendant's negligence, proof of a decreased chance of survival is not enough to take the proximate cause question to the jury. Cooper v. Sisters of Charity, Inc., 27 Ohio St. 2d 242, 272 N.E.2d 97 (1971). These courts have concluded that the defendant should not be liable where the decedent more than likely would have died anyway.

The ultimate question raised here is whether the relationship between the increased risk of harm and Herskovits' death is sufficient to hold Group Health responsible. Is a 36 percent (from 39 percent to 25 percent) reduction in the decedent's chance for survival sufficient evidence of causation to allow the jury to consider the possibility that the physician's failure to timely diagnose the illness was the proximate cause of his death? We answer in the affirmative. To decide otherwise would be a blanket release from liability for doctors and hospitals any time there was less than a 50 percent chance of survival, regardless of how flagrant the negligence.

III

We are persuaded by the reasoning of the Pennsylvania Supreme Court in Hamil v. Bashline, *supra*. While *Hamil* involved an original survival chance of greater than 50 percent, we find the rationale used by the *Hamil* court to apply equally to cases such as the present one, where the original survival chance is less than 50 percent.

[In *Hamil* the decedent's wife took him to an emergency room, where he was negligently treated for a heart attack and died. The plaintiff's expert testified that with proper treatment the decedent would have had a 75-percent chance of survival. The court allowed the case to go to the jury.]

CONCLUSION

Both counsel have agreed for the purpose of arguing this summary judgment that the defendants were negligent in failing to make a diagnosis of cancer on Herskovits' initial visit in December 1974, and that such negligence was the proximate cause of reducing his chances of survival by 14 percent. It is undisputed that Herskovits had less than a 50 percent chance of survival at that time. Based on this agreement and Dr. Ostrow's deposition and affidavit, a prima facie case is shown. We reject Group Health's argument that plaintiffs *must show* that Herskovits "probably" would have had a 51 percent chance of survival if the hospital had not been negligent. We hold that medical testimony of a reduction of chance of survival from 39 percent to 25 percent is sufficient evidence to allow the proximate cause issue to go to the jury.

Causing reduction of the opportunity to recover (loss of chance) by one's negligence, however, does not necessitate a total recovery against the negligent party for all damages caused by the victim's death. Damages should be awarded to the injured party or his family based only on damages caused directly by premature death, such as lost earnings and additional medical expenses, etc.

We reverse the trial court and reinstate the cause of action.

ROSELLINI, J., concurs.

PEARSON, J. (concurring) — I agree with the majority that the trial court erred in granting defendant's motion for summary judgment. I cannot, however, agree with the majority's reasoning in reaching this decision.

[Pearson, J., then conducted an exhaustive review of the cases and explicitly adopted the position in King, Causation, Valuation, and Chance in Personal Injury Torts Involving Preexisting Conditions and Future Consequences, 90 Yale L.J. 1353 (1981).]

King's basic thesis is explained in the following passage, which is particularly pertinent to the case before us.

> Causation has for the most part been treated as an all-or-nothing proposition. Either a loss was caused by the defendant or it was not. . . . A plaintiff ordinarily should be required to prove by the applicable standard of proof that the defendant caused the loss in question. *What* caused a loss, however, should be a separate question from what the *nature and extent* of the loss are. This distinction seems to have eluded the courts, with the result that lost chances in many respects are compensated either as certainties or not at all.

To illustrate, consider the case in which a doctor negligently fails to diagnose a patient's cancerous condition until it has become inoperable. Assume further that even with a timely diagnosis the patient would have had only a 30% chance of recovering from the disease and surviv-

ing over the long term. There are two ways of handling such a case.
Under the traditional approach, this loss of a not-better-than-even
chance of recovering from the cancer would not be compensable because it did not appear more likely [than] not that the patient would
have survived with proper care. Recoverable damages, if any, would
depend on the extent to which it appeared that cancer killed the patient sooner than it would have with timely diagnosis and treatment,
and on the extent to which the delay in diagnosis aggravated the patient's condition, such as by causing additional pain. A more rational
approach, however, would allow recovery for the loss of the chance of
cure even though the chance was not better than even. The probability
of long-term survival would be reflected in the amount of damages
awarded for the loss of the chance. While the plaintiff here could not
prove by a preponderance of the evidence that he was denied a cure by
the defendant's negligence, he could show by a preponderance that he
was deprived of a 30% chance of a cure. [90 Yale L.J. at 1363-1364.]

Under the all-or-nothing approach typified by Cooper v. Sisters of
Charity, Inc., a plaintiff who establishes that but for the defendant's
negligence the decedent had a 51-percent chance of survival may maintain an action for that death. The defendant will be liable for all damages arising from the death, even though there was a 49-percent chance
it would have occurred despite his negligence. On the other hand, a
plaintiff who establishes that but for the defendant's negligence the
decedent had a 49-percent chance of survival recovers nothing.

[The dissent of Brachtenberg, J., is omitted.]

DOLLIVER, J. (dissenting) . . . I favor the opposing view and believe
the reasoning in Cooper v. Sisters of Charity, Inc., also cited by the
majority, is more persuasive. In discussing the rule to be adopted the
Ohio Supreme Court stated:

> A rule, which would permit a plaintiff to establish a jury question on
> the issue of proximate cause upon a showing of a "substantial possibility"
> of survival, in our judgment, suffers the same infirmity as a rule which
> would permit proof of a "chance of recovery" to be sufficient. While the
> substantial possibility concept appears to connote a weightier burden
> than the chance of recovery idea, both derogate well-established and val-
> uable proximate cause considerations. Traditional proximate cause stan-
> dards require that the trier of the facts, at a minimum, must be provided
> with evidence that a result was more likely than not to have been caused
> by an act, in the absence of any intervening cause.
>
> Lesser standards of proof are understandably attractive in malpractice
> cases where physical well being, and life itself, are the subject of litiga-
> tion. The strong intuitive sense of humanity tends to emotionally direct
> us toward a conclusion that in an action for wrongful death an injured
> person should be compensated for the loss of any chance for survival,
> regardless of its remoteness. However, we have trepidations that such a
> rule would be so loose that it would produce more injustice than justice.
> Even though there exists authority for a rule allowing recovery based

upon proof of causation by evidence not meeting the standard of probability, we are not persuaded by their logic. . . .

We consider the better rule to be that in order to comport with the
standard of proof of proximate cause, plaintiff in a malpractice case must
prove that defendant's negligence, *in probability*, proximately caused the
death.

(Citations omitted.) *Cooper*, at 251-252.

NOTES

1. Judicial response in the lost chance doctrine. The judicial response to
the lost chance doctrine is sharply split. At present it appears that a
clear majority (16) of those states which have considered the doctrine
have accepted it, while a smaller group (6) has adhered to the traditional rejection of the doctrine, with still fewer states (4) undecided.
For a tally see Fennell v. Southern Maryland Hosp., 580 A.2d 206, 209
nn. 1-3 (Md. 1990). Since that time, litigation on the subject has proceeded apace, with the "lost opportunity doctrine gaining ground." In
Safidi v. Seiler, 574 A.2d 398 (N.J. 1990), the doctrine was used to require the jury to apportion the risk of death of a premature baby "in
cases in which the defendant's negligence combines with a *preexistent*
condition to cause an injury." And in Delaney v. Cade, 873 P.2d 175
(Kan. 1994), the court adopted the lost chance doctrine to apportion
losses between a prior automobile accident and subsequent medical
malpractice, so long as there was a "substantial loss of the chance." But
the court refused plaintiff's invitation to "permit the jury to determine
the loss of chance of survival or better recovery no matter how small
such chance may be."

The lost chance doctrine was rejected, however, in *Fennell* out of a
concern for how the doctrine fit into the large system of damage compensation.

> If loss of chance damages are to be recognized, amendments to the
> wrongful death statute should also be considered. As a class, medical
> malpractice plaintiffs benefit from the fact that they are entitled to re-
> cover 100% of their damages from a defendant whose negligence caused
> only 51% of their loss because it is more probable than not that the
> defendant's negligence caused the loss. Reciprocally, a defendant whose
> negligence caused less than 50% of a plaintiff's loss pays nothing because
> it is [more] probable that the negligence did not cause the loss. If a
> plaintiff whose decedent had a 49% chance of survival, which was lost
> through negligent treatment, is permitted to recover 49% of the value of
> the decedent's life, then a plaintiff whose decedent had a 51% chance of
> survival, which was lost through negligent treatment, perhaps ought to
> have recovery limited to 51% of the value of the life lost. The latter result
> would require a change in our current wrongful death statute.

Fennell's concern can be recast as a question that asks about the optimal level of deterrence supplied by the tort system. Here the difficulty is that the errors in individual cases under the lost chance doctrine will not "cancel out" in the long run, so that defendants may be systematically overtaxed for harms that they did *not* cause. Suppose there are 100 cases. Defendant has a 25 percent chance of causing the death in 50 of them and a 75 percent chance of causing the death in the other 50. On balance the defendant has caused half the deaths $[(0.25 \times 50) + (0.75 \times 50) = 50]$. Yet under the *Herskovits* rule the defendant will be charged for 62.5 deaths $[(0.25 \times 50) + (1 \times 50) = 62.5]$, which leads to overdeterrence. The *Fennell* rule on this view tends to yield better results because the defendants are undercharged when the chance of loss is less than 50 percent but overcharged when it is more. The two errors seem to balance each other out, at least if the losses are evenly distributed about a mean of 50 percent probability. In that case it can be shown formally that the all-or-nothing rule reduces the level of error below what it would be with a proportionate share rule. See Kaye, The Limits of the Preponderance of the Evidence Standard: Justifiably Naked Statistical Evidence and Multiple Causation, 1982 Am. B. Found. Res. J. 713.

Kaye's conclusion will not hold, however, when defendant undertakes a large number of similar actions, each of which is less than 50 percent likely to cause harm. The refusal to allow any plaintiff to recover now results in systematic underdeterrence, for a defendant who is, say, 40 percent responsible for loss in each of 100 cases pays nothing at all. See S. Shavell, Economic Analysis of Accident Law 117 (1987), which criticizes the 50 percent threshold on the ground that it "will result in injurers' never being liable for the losses they cause; it may thus provide grossly inadequate incentives to reduce risk."

2. Compensation for future tortious risk only. The use of probabilistic tests to award tort damages can be extended from cases of existing injury to cases to make the simple creation of tortious risk as compensable, without actual injury. Suppose a release of radioactive materials yields a 10 percent increase in the expected number of cancers in a community over the next 30 years. The 50 percent cutoff denies recovery in all cases, and thus leads to underdeterrence so the defendant would not be required to internalize any of the known (statistical) losses that it generated. Yet if it were required to pay for all 110 cancer cases, then it would be being charged for losses that it did not cause and thus would be induced to take precautions that were not cost-justified under the circumstances.

One possible escape is to make the additional "tortious risk" compensable, even without actual injury. Professor Robinson advances this position in Probabilistic Causation and Compensation for Tortious Risk, 14 J. Legal Stud. 779, 782-783 (1985):

It should be emphasized at the outset that, in this context at least, the issue of liability for risk creation does not entail changing the standards for defining what activities (risks) are tortious. Instead it redefines compensable "injury" to make "tortious" risk a basis of liability — adjusting compensation according to a probabilistic measure of anticipated loss. We might analogize such a tort action to a contract action for anticipatory breach. Although there are, of course, differences in the contract and tort enforcement rationales, the case for "anticipatory" enforcement is similar in some ways. In both cases the practical impetus for such an action arises from the need to have prompt enforcement in order to permit the victim to make adjustments to ameliorate the threatened injury. In the tort context there is an even stronger transactional efficiency argument for early evaluation of (arguably) tortious risks, since the evidence relevant to such an evaluation is likely to decay faster than it does in the typical contract case. The point is of special concern in those tort cases where immediate risks may not manifest themselves as actual injury for periods of a decade or more.

How does one handle the proliferation of law suits that result if all plaintiffs can sue today for losses that might not occur tomorrow? How should the estimates of increased risk be made?

3. *Uncertain future harms from present torts.* The questions of probabilistic causation raised in *Herskovits* have arisen in other contexts as well. In Jackson v. Johns-Manville Sales Corp., 781 F.2d 394, 413, 414 (5th Cir. 1986), the plaintiff had already contracted asbestosis and was now suing to recover for the 50 percent chance that he would contract cancer as well. The defendant insisted that the plaintiff could not recover for that loss at present "since the development of cancer represents a future injury based on a presently existing cause of action." The plaintiff for his part insisted that the action *had* to be allowed because a suit for future cancer would have been barred by the procedural rule that prevents a "splitting of a cause of action," in this instance between asbestosis and cancer. The court first concluded that the plaintiff's cause of action was not confined to asbestosis as such but allowed recovery "for probable future consequences."

> Of course, a plaintiff who sues with nothing more than hand calluses may have a significantly lower likelihood of developing cancer than does a plaintiff who exhibits asbestosis. That would be a question for the jury, to be decided by listening to and evaluating conflicting medical testimony. This plaintiff, however, has asbestosis; and evidence adduced at trial indicates that he has a greater than fifty percent chance of getting cancer. Recovery for that possibility is permissible under Mississippi law.

The court also allowed the plaintiff to recover for the fear of future cancer.

> Jackson's fear is plainly a present injury. It is a fear which he experiences every day and every night. It is a fear which is exacerbated each

time he learns that another victim of asbestos has died of lung cancer. It is fear which, regardless of whether Jackson actually gets cancer, will haunt him for the rest of his life. Jackson's claim is not merely that he *might* get cancer, or that there is a remote possibility that he will. Jackson has established that there is a greater than fifty percent chance that he *will* get cancer. Who can gainsay that this knowledge causes him anguish, or that this anguish is reasonable? Certainly not this court and, in our view, not the Mississippi Supreme Court.

The dissent urged that the entire matter be remitted for consideration by the Mississippi Supreme Court in light of the importance of the issues involved. How should the prospects of future cancer be evaluated if the plaintiff's life expectancy was already drastically reduced by the asbestosis? Should the damages be apportioned if the plantiff also fears another attack of abestososis?

4. *Enhanced risk of injury and medical monitoring.* In Mauro v. Raymark Industries, 561 A.2d 257, 263 (N.J. 1989), the court refused to allow plaintiff to recover for the increased chance of contracting asbestos where the probability of getting the disease was less than 50 percent, given that suit could always be brought when the asbestos-related injury first manifested itself. The court held, however, that the inability to maintain an action for enhanced risk did not bar suit to cover the costs of medical monitoring, even if the likelihood of ultimate injury were below 50 percent. The claim for medical monitoring covers the cost of periodic medical examinations that are themselves made necessary because of the risk of future injury. The court rejected any necessary connection between the enhanced risk claim and the medical monitoring claim, quoting from its earlier decision in Ayers v. Jackson Township, 525 A.2d 287, 312-313 (N.J. 1987):

> Although we rejected the enhanced-risk claim in *Ayers . . .* we upheld the right of plaintiffs with an unquantified enhanced risk of disease due to exposure to toxic chemicals to recover for medical-surveillance expenses:
>
>> Accordingly, we hold that the cost of medical surveillance is a compensable item of damages where the proofs demonstrate, through reliable expert testimony predicated upon the significance and extent of exposure to chemicals, the toxicity of the chemicals, the seriousness of the diseases for which individuals are at risk, the relative increase in the chance of onset of disease in those exposed, and the value of early diagnosis, that such surveillance to monitor the effect of exposure to toxic chemicals is reasonable and necessary. In our view, this holding is thoroughly consistent with our rejection of plaintiffs' claim for damages based on their enhanced risk of injury. That claim seeks damages for the impairment of plaintiffs' health, without proof of its likelihood, extent, or monetary value. In contrast, the medical surveillance claim seeks reimbursement for the specific dollar costs of periodic examinations that are medically necessary notwithstanding the fact that the extent of plaintiffs' impaired health is unquantified.

Nor is there any question concerning the right of a plaintiff who has sustained physical injury because of exposure to toxic chemicals to recover damages for emotional distress based on a reasonable concern that he or she has an enhanced risk of further disease.

How do the ordinary rules of mitigation of damages apply to cases of medical monitoring? How should the costs of this item of recovery be apportioned if the plaintiff requires medical monitoring and treatment for conditions that are unrelated to the risk of an asbestos-based injury?

C. PROXIMATE CAUSE (HEREIN OF DUTY)

1. Physical Injury

Bacon, Maxims

Reg. I. In jure non remota causa sed proxima spectatur. It were infinite for the law to judge the causes, and their impulsions one of another; therefore it contenteth it selfe with the immediate cause, and judgeth of acts by that, without looking to any further degree.

Street, Foundations of Legal Liability
Vol. I, p. 110 (1906)

The terms "proximate" and "remote" are thus respectively applied to recoverable and non-recoverable damages. . . . It is unfortunate that no definite principle can be laid down by which to determine this question. It is always to be determined on the facts of each case upon mixed considerations of logic, common sense, justice, policy and precedent. . . . The best use that can be made of the authorities on proximate cause is merely to furnish illustrations of situations which judicious men upon careful consideration have adjudged to be on one side of the line or the other.

Ryan v. New York Central R. Co.
35 N.Y. 210 (1866)

On the 15th July 1854, in the city of Syracuse, the defendants, by the careless management, or through the insufficient condition, of one of their engines, set fire to their woodshed, and a large quantity of wood therein. The plaintiff's house, situated at a distance of one hundred and thirty feet from the shed, soon took fire from the heat and sparks, and was entirely consumed, notwithstanding diligent efforts were made to save it. A number of other houses were also burned by the spreading of the fire.

These facts having been proved on the part of the plaintiff, the defendants' counsel moved for a nonsuit, which was granted, and an exception taken. And the judgment having been affirmed at general term, the plaintiff appealed to this court.

HUNT, J. [after stating the facts]. The question may be thus stated: A house in a populous city takes fire, through the negligence of the owner or his servant; the flames extend to and destroy an adjacent building: Is the owner of the first building liable to the second owner for the damage sustained by such burning?

It is a general principle, that every person is liable for the consequences of his own acts; he is thus liable in damages for the proximate results of his own acts, but not for remote damages. It is not easy, at all times, to determine what are proximate and what are remote damages. . . .

[After discussing cases of direct ignition of plaintiff's property by defendants' negligence, the court continued:] Thus far the law is settled, and the principle is apparent. If, however, the fire communicates from the house of A. to that of B., and that is destroyed, is the negligent party liable for his loss? And if it spreads thence to the house of C., and thence to the house of D., and thence consecutively through the other houses, until it reaches and consumes the house of Z., is the party liable to pay the damages sustained by these twenty-four sufferers? The counsel for the plaintiff does not distinctly claim this, and I think it would not be seriously insisted, that the sufferers could recover in such case. Where, then, is the principle upon which A. recovers and Z. fails?

It has been suggested, that an important element exists in the difference between an intentional firing and a negligent firing merely; that when a party designedly fires his own house or his own fallow-land, not intending, however, to do any injury to his neighbor, but a damage actually results, that he may be liable for more extended damages than where the fire originated in accident or negligence. It is true, that the most of the cases where the liability was held to exist, were cases of an intentional firing. The case, however, of Vaughan v. Menlove (3 Bing. N.C. 468) was that of a spontaneous combustion of a hay-rick; the rick was burned, the owner's buildings were destroyed, and thence the fire spread to the plaintiff's cottage, which was also consumed; the defendant was held liable.

Without deciding upon the importance of this distinction, I prefer to place my opinion upon the ground, that, in the one case, to wit, the destruction of the building upon which the sparks were thrown by the negligent act of the party sought to be charged, the result was to have been anticipated, the moment the fire was communicated to the building; that its destruction was the ordinary and natural result of its being fired. In the second, third or twenty-fourth case, as supposed, the destruction of the building was not a natural and expected result of the first firing. That a building upon which sparks and cinders fall should be destroyed or seriously injured, must be expected, but that the fire should spread and other buildings be consumed, is not a necessary or a usual result. That it is possible, and that it is not unfrequent, cannot be denied. The result, however, depends, not upon any necessity of a further communication of the fire, but upon a concurrence of accidental circumstances, such as the degree of the heat, the state of the atmosphere, the condition and materials of the adjoining structures and the direction of the wind. These are accidental and varying circumstances; the party has no control over them, and is not responsible for their effects.

My opinion, therefore, is, that this action cannot be sustained, for the reason that the damages incurred are not the immediate but the remote result of the negligence of the defendants. The immediate result was the destruction of their own wood and sheds beyond that, it was remote. . . .

To sustain such a claim as the present, and to follow the same to its legitimate consequences, would subject to a liability against which no prudence could guard, and to meet which no private fo .une would be adequate. Nearly all fires are caused by negligence, in its extended sense. In a country where wood, coal, gas and oils are universally used, where men are crowded into cities and villages, where servants are employed, and where children find their home in all houses, it is impossible, that the most vigilant prudence should guard against the occurrence of accidental or negligent fires. A man may insure his own house, or his own furniture, but he cannot insure his neighbor's building or furniture, for the reason that he has no interest in them. To hold that the owner must not only meet his own loss by fire, but that he must guaranty the security of his neighbors on both sides, and to an unlimited extent, would be to create a liability which would be the destruction of all civilized society. No community could long exist, under the operation of such a principle. In a commercial country, each man, to some extent, runs the hazard of his neighbor's conduct, and each, by insurance against such hazards, is enabled to obtain a reasonable security against loss. To neglect such precaution, and to call upon his neighbor, on whose premises a fire originated, to indemnify him instead, would be to award a punishment quite beyond the offence committed. It is to be considered, also, that if the negligent party is liable to the owner of a remote building thus consumed, he would also be liable to the insurance companies who should pay losses to such remote owners. The principle of subrogation would entitle the companies to the benefit of every claim held by the party to whom a loss should be paid.

. . . The remoteness of the damage, in my judgment, forms the true rule on which the question should be decided, and which prohibits a recovery by the plaintiff in this case. Judgment should be affirmed.

NOTES

1. *Fire!* The reception given to the *Ryan* rule has not always been favorable. Speaking of *Ryan* and the similar case of Kerr v. Pennsylvania R.R., 62 Pa. 353 (1870), the United States Supreme Court, in Milwaukee & St. P. Ry. v. Kellogg, 94 U.S. 469 (1876), said: "Those cases have been the subject of much criticism since they were decided; and it may, perhaps, be doubted whether they have always been quite understood. If they were intended to assert the doctrine that when a building has been set on fire through the negligence of a party, and a second building has been fired from the first, it is a conclusion of law that the owner of the second has no recourse to the negligent wrong-doer, they have not been accepted as authority for such a doctrine, even in the States where the decisions were made." See generally Schwartz, Tort Law and the Economy in Nineteenth-Century America: A Reinterpretation, 90 Yale L.J. 1717, 1746-1747 (1981). See also note to *Leroy Fibre*, supra at 337.

2. *"Ordinary and natural result of defendant's negligence."* *Ryan* is noted for the narrow construction that it gives to the phrase "ordinary and natural result" (of the defendant's negligence). The proper construction of this phrase arises not only with intervening natural events, but also with intervening human conduct. Yet in this context the phrase has been given a somewhat broader interpretation even in the early nineteenth-century cases. Thus, in *City of Lincoln*, 15 P.D. 15, 18 (1889), the plaintiff's vessel, the *Albatross,* was totally disabled in a collision with the *City of Lincoln* that was wholly the fault of the latter. The *Albatross* lost its compass, log, log glass, and charts, and the captain was unsuccessful in his efforts to bring the ship to port. The court first noted that the "only inquiry in all these cases is whether the damage complained of is the natural and reasonable result of the defendant's act," a test which it found was satisfied if the damage was "such a consequence as in the ordinary course of things would flow from the act." Lindley, L.J. then continued:

> We have then to consider what is the meaning of "the ordinary course of things." Sir Walter Phillimore has asked us to exclude from it all human conduct. I can do nothing of the kind. I take it that reasonable human conduct is part of the ordinary course of things. So far as I can see my way to any definite proposition I should say that the ordinary course of things does not exclude all human conduct, but includes at least the reasonable conduct of those who have sustained the damage,

and who are seeking to save further loss. That principle was acted on in Jones v. Boyce, which I have always regarded as sound law. Let us see, then, what occurred in the present case, and what was the real cause of the loss of this vessel. It was the fact that the captain was, by the collision, deprived of the means of ascertaining his position and of properly navigating his ship. He was deprived of his compass, his log-line, and his charts. His ship was not utterly unmanageable but she was in a very bad state, and the necessary consequence of all this was that this captain lost his vessel without any negligence on his part. Under these circumstances the case falls within the rule I have laid down as to the term "ordinary course of things." Therefore, I am of opinion that the owners of the *City of Lincoln* must pay for the loss of the *Albatross*.

3. Plaintiff's response to emergencies. The problem of intervening actions can also arise in cases in which a sudden emergency requires immediate action by the plaintiff. Thus, in Jones v. Boyce, 171 Eng. Rep. 540, 541 (K.B. 1816), cited in *The City of Lincoln,* plaintiff jumped from defendant's coach after it had gotten out of control, and in so doing broke his leg. It was established both that defendant was negligent and that plaintiff would not have been hurt if he had remained in his place. In instructing the jury, Lord Ellenborough stated:

> To enable the plaintiff to sustain the action, it is not necessary that he should have been thrown off the coach; it is sufficient if he was placed by the misconduct of the defendant in such a situation as obliged him to adopt the alternative of a dangerous leap, or to remain at certain peril; if that position was occasioned by the default of the defendant, the action may be supported. On the other hand, if the plaintiff's act resulted from a rash apprehension of danger, which did not exist, and the injury which he sustained is to be attributed to rashness and imprudence, he is not entitled to recover.

The jury found for the plaintiff.

The same result was reached on this side of the Atlantic in Tuttle v. Atlantic City R.R., 49 A. 450, 451 (N.J. 1901). There one of defendant's trains jumped the tracks while being moved around a freight yard in "a flying drill" and headed toward the plaintiff. "Acting under the impulse of fear," she ran for safety and hurt her knee. If she had stayed put, she would not have been struck. The court affirmed the judgment of the jury, noting that it would be truly "extraordinary" for the plaintiff not to try to escape. "The true rule governing cases of this character may be stated as follows: That if a defendant, by negligence, puts the plaintiff under a reasonable apprehension of personal physical injury, and plaintiff, in a reasonable effort to escape, sustains physical injury, a right of action arises to recover for the physical injury and the mental disorder naturally incident to its occurrence."

Occasionally courts have used a foresight limitation to bar recovery in cases such as these. Thus, in Mauney v. Gulf Refining Co., 9 So. 2d

780, 782 (Miss. 1942), the plaintiff, carrying her 2-year-old child in her arms, tripped over a chair in her husband's cafe while trying to flee after being warned by neighbors that defendant's delivery truck was on fire and likely to explode. The court denied recovery on the ground that if the plaintiff "didn't see a chair in her own place of business, it would impose an inadmissible burden upon the defendants to say that they should have foreseen from across the street and through the walls of a building on another corner what appellant didn't see right at her feet. . . ." What degree of precision is required in working a foreseeability test? Is there any difficulty in holding the defendant liable under a directness standard?

Berry v. The Borough of Sugar Notch
43 A. 240 (Pa. 1899)

. . . Trespass for personal injuries. Before Woodward, P.J. . . .

Verdict and judgment for plaintiff for $3,162.50. Defendant appealed. . . .

FELL, J. The plaintiff was a motorman in the employ of the Wilkes-Barre and Wyoming Valley Traction Company on its line running from Wilkes-Barre to the borough of Sugar Notch. The ordinance by virtue of which the company was permitted to lay its track and operate its cars in the borough of Sugar Notch contained a provision that the speed of the cars while on the streets of the borough should not exceed eight miles an hour. On the line of the road, and within the borough limits, there was a large chestnut tree, as to the condition of which there was some dispute at the trial. The question of the negligence of the borough in permitting it to remain must, however, be considered as set at rest by the verdict. On the day of the accident the plaintiff was running his car on the borough street in a violent wind-storm, and as he passed under the tree it was blown down, crushing the roof of the car and causing the plaintiff's injury. There is some conflict of testimony as to the speed at which the car was running, but it seems to be fairly well established that it was considerably in excess of the rate permitted by the borough ordinance.

We do not think that the fact that the plaintiff was running his car at a higher rate of speed than eight miles an hour affects his right to recover. It may be that in doing so he violated the ordinance by virtue of which the company was permitted to operate its cars in the streets of the borough, but he certainly was not for that reason without rights upon the streets. Nor can it be said that the speed was the cause of the accident, or contributed to it. It might have been otherwise if the tree had fallen before the car reached it; for in that case a high rate of speed might have rendered it impossible for the plaintiff to avoid a collision which he either foresaw or should have foreseen. Even in that case the ground for denying him the right to recover would be that he had been guilty of contributory negligence, and not that he had violated a borough ordinance. The testimony however shows that the tree fell upon the car as it passed beneath. With this phase of the case in view, it was urged on behalf of the appellant that the speed was the immediate cause of the plaintiff's injury, inasmuch as it was the particular speed at which he was running which brought the car to the place of the accident at the moment when the tree blew down. This argument, while we cannot deny its ingenuity, strikes us, to say the least, as being somewhat sophistical. That his speed brought him to the place of the accident at the moment of the accident was the merest chance, and a thing which no foresight could have predicted. The same thing might as readily have happened to a car running slowly, or it might have been that a high speed alone would have carried him beyond the tree to a place of safety. It was also argued by the appellant's counsel that, even if the speed was not the sole efficient cause of the accident, it at least contributed to its severity, and materially increased the damage. It may be that it did. But what basis could a jury have for finding such to be the case and, should they so find, what guide could be given them for differentiating between the injury done this man and the injury which would have been done a man in a similar accident on a car running at a speed of eight miles an hour or less?

The judgment is affirmed.

NOTES

1. Coincidence and causation. Berry involved a case where plaintiff's breach of a safety statute was not causally connected with his injuries because it did not increase the risk or hazard of his being struck. Is it relevant that the increased speed reduced the time that the plaintiff was exposed to potential injury? Increased the possibility of damage in the event of a collision with a fallen log?

The problem of coincidence has also arisen in a somewhat different form in Central of Georgia Ry. Co. v. Price, 32 S.E. 77, 77-78 (Ga. 1898), where the plaintiff was not dropped off at her station through the negligence of the railroad, and spent the night at a hotel to which she had been escorted by the railroad's conductor. At the hotel, she was given a furnished room outfitted with a kerosene lamp, which exploded and set fire to the mosquito netting covering the bed. In her efforts to put out the fire, the plaintiff severely burnt her hands. The court first rejected her argument that the railroad should be liable because the hotel proprietor was its agent. It then held that the plaintiff's harm was too remote from the railroad's negligence:

The negligence of the company consisted in passing the station where the passenger desired to alight, without giving her an opportunity to get off. Taking her version of the manner in which she was injured, the injury was occasioned by the negligence of the proprietor of the hotel or his servants in giving her a defective lamp. The negligence of the company in passing her station was therefore not the natural and proximate cause of her injury. There was the interposition of a separate, independent agency, — the negligence of the proprietor of the hotel, over whom, as we have shown, the railway company neither had nor exercised any control. The injuries to the plaintiff were not the natural and proximate consequences of carrying her beyond her station, but were unusual, and could not have been foreseen or provided against by the highest practicable care. The plaintiff was not entitled to recover for such injuries, and the court erred in overruling the motion for new trial.

The risks to which the plaintiff was exposed were quite different in Hines v. Garrett, 108 S.E. 690, 695 (Va. 1921), where a railroad conductor negligently carried the 19-year-old plaintiff almost a mile past her stop at night, thus forcing her to walk back this distance through an unsettled area. During her walk back she was raped once by a soldier and once by a hobo, both unidentified. Allowing her to recover against the railroad, the court said, in part: "We do not wish to be understood as questioning the general proposition that no responsibility for a wrong attaches whenever an independent act of a third person intervenes between the negligence complained of and the injury. But . . . this proposition does not apply where the very negligence alleged consists of exposing the injured party to the act causing the injury. It is perfectly well settled and will not be seriously denied that whenever a carrier has reason to anticipate the danger of an assault upon one of its passengers, it rests under the duty of protecting such passenger against the same."

2. *Independent and dependent causation.* Still another variation on the causal theme arises when each of two successive acts is sufficient to harm plaintiff, but where the plaintiff is exposed to the second cause only because of the prior negligence of the first. In these situations, the second act is said to be "dependent" on the first, so that the second defendant is normally responsible for the additional damages, if any brought about by his action. In Dillon v. Twin State G. & E. Co., 163 A. 111, 115 (N.H. 1932), plaintiff's decedent, a boy of 14, lost his balance while trespassing on the superstructure of a bridge and then grabbed defendant's high-voltage wires as he fell. The current killed him and the shock apparently threw his body back onto the girder. The defendant power company was not found responsible or negligent in any way for the boy's fall given his trespass, but it was found negligent and responsible for the boy's exposure to the uncovered charged wires. The defendant's motion for a directed verdict on the issue of liability was denied, and that decision was affirmed on appeal. Allen, J., wrote:

The circumstances of the decedent's death give rise to an unusual issue of its cause. In leaning over from the girder and losing his balance he was entitled to no protection from the defendant to keep from falling. Its only liability was in exposing him to the danger of the charged wires. If but for the current in the wires he would have fallen down on the floor of the bridge or into the river, he would without doubt have been either killed or seriously injured. Although he died from electrocution, yet, if by reason of his preceding loss of balance he was bound to fall except for the intervention of the current, he either did not have long to live or was to be maimed. In such an outcome of his loss of balance, the defendant deprived him not of a life of normal expectancy, but of one too short to be given pecuniary allowance, in one alternative, and not of normal but of limited, earning capacity, in the other.

If it were found that he would have thus fallen with death probably resulting, the defendant would not be liable, unless for conscious suffering found to have been sustained from the shock. In that situation his life or earning capacity had no value. To constitute actionable negligence there must be damage, and damage is limited to those elements the statute prescribes.

If it should be found that but for the current he would have fallen with serious injury, then the loss of life or earning capacity resulting from the electrocution would be measured by its value in such injured condition. Evidence that he would be crippled would be taken into account in the same manner as though he had already been crippled.

His probable future but for the current thus bears on liability as well as damages. Whether the shock from the current threw him back on the girder or whether he would have recovered his balance, with or without the aid of the wire he took hold of if it had not been charged, are issues of fact, as to which the evidence as it stands may lead to different conclusions.

3. *An apparent condition of safety.* Problems of causal intervention also arise when dangerous objects are passed from hand to hand. In Pittsburg Reduction Co. v. Horton, 113 S.W. 647, 648-649 (Ark. 1908), the defendant discarded a dynamite cap on its unenclosed plant premises near a public school. The cap was picked up by Charlie Copple, age 10, who placed it in a tin box with other caps, and played with it on several occasions in his house. His mother, who later testified that she did not know what they were, would pick the caps up when Charlie was done playing. About a week after he found the cap, Charlie traded it to Jack Horton, age 13, for some writing paper. Horton thought that "the cap was the shell of a .22 cartridge that had been shot." He was picking the dirt out of the cap with a match when the cap exploded, so injuring his hand that it had to be amputated. Charlie's father, a miner, denied knowing that the cap was in the house until after the accident. Horton brought suit against the defendant company and its foreman, but his claim was denied.

In the present case the facts are practically undisputed. Charlie Copple's father was an employee of a company engaged in a similar business to that of appellant company. Naturally, his avocation and the proximity of his residence to the mines made both himself and his wife familiar with the nature of explosives. True, Mrs. Copple says that she did not know what the shells contained, but she did know that they were shells for some kind of explosives, that her son brought them home, and that he played with them. She admits that when he would leave them on the floor she would pick them up and lay them away for him. This continued for a week, and then, with her knowledge, he carried them to school. Her course of conduct broke the causal connection between the original negligent act of appellant and the subsequent injury of the plaintiff. It established a new agency, and the possession of Charlie Copple of the caps or shells was thereafter referable to the permission of his parents, and not to the original taking. Charlie Copple's parents having permitted him to retain possession of the caps, his further acts in regard to them must be attributable to their permission, and were wholly independent of the original negligence of appellants. This is but an application of the well established general rule that, to charge a person with liability for damages, the negligence alleged must be found to have been the proximate cause of the injury to the plaintiff.

Horton and similar cases were analyzed in great detail in Beale, The Proximate Consequences of An Act, 33 Harv. L. Rev. 633, 650, 651, 656 (1920), where the following two generalizations were offered:

> If the defendant's active force has come to rest, but in a dangerous position, creating a new or increasing an existing risk of loss, and the foreseen danger comes to pass, operating harmfully on the condition created by defendant and causing the risked loss, we say that the injury thereby created is a proximate consequence of the defendant's act. . . .
>
> On the other hand, where defendant's active force has come to rest in a position of apparent safety, the court will follow it no longer; if some new force later combines with this condition to create harm, the result is remote from the defendant's act.

With reference to cases like *Horton* Beale concluded that "if the explosive gets into the hands of an adult the defendant's force has ceased to be an active danger; if the explosive thereafter gets into the hands of a child, defendant is not the proximate cause of anything this child may do with it." Should the result be the same even if the adult did not know that the cap was dangerous? The result in *Horton* has also been defended in Grady, Proximate Cause and the Law of Negligence, 69 Iowa L. Rev. 363, 420 (1984): "In situations when the last wrongdoer would feel especially disposed to remain at a low level of precaution because of an expectation that the original wrongdoer would be held liable for a lion's share of the expected harm that would result from their joint omissions, the direct-consequences doctrine cuts off the liability of the original wrongdoer and makes the last wrongdoer solely responsible for the damage. This was the result in the *Horton* case." Why not allow the first wrongdoer an action of indemnity against the intermediate wrongdoer instead of cutting off all relief? What likelihood is there that Horton will sue the Copples?

Brower v. New York Central & H.R.R.
103 A. 166 (N.J. 1918)

SWAYZE, J.: This is a case of a grade-crossing collision. We are clear that the questions of negligence and contributory negligence were for the jury. If there were nothing else, the testimony of the plaintiff as to signals of the flagman would carry the case to the jury. The only question that has caused us difficulty is that of the extent of the defendant's liability. The complaint avers that the horse was killed, the wagon and harness, and the cider and barrels with which the wagon was loaded, were destroyed. What happened was that as a result of the collision, aside from the death of the horse and the destruction of the wagon, the contents of the wagon, consisting of empty barrels and a keg of cider, were scattered and probably stolen by people at the scene of the accident. The driver, who was alone in charge for the plaintiff, was so stunned that one of the railroad detectives found him immediately after the collision in a fit. There were two railroad detectives on the freight train to protect the property it was carrying against thieves, but they did nothing to protect the plaintiff's property. The controversy on the question of damages is as to the right of the plaintiff to recover the value of the barrels, cider and blanket. An objection was based solely on the ground that the complaint alleged that they were destroyed; counsel said "there is no use proving value unless they were destroyed." We think that if they were taken by thieves, they were destroyed as far as was important to the case; at least the averment was sufficient to justify the evidence and the charge, since the case was fully tried. It is now argued that the defendant's negligence was not in any event the proximate cause of the loss of this property since the act of the thieves intervened. The rule of law which exempts the one guilty of the original negligence from damage due to an intervening cause is well settled. The difficulty lies in the application. Like the question of proximate cause, this is ordinarily a jury question. . . .

We think these authorities justified the trial judge in his rulings as to the recovery of the value of the barrels, cider and blanket. The negligence which caused the collision resulted immediately in such a condition of the driver of the wagon that he was no longer able to protect his employer's property; the natural and probable result of his enforced abandonment of it in the street of a large city was its disappearance and the wrongdoer cannot escape making reparation for the loss caused by depriving the plaintiff of the protection which the presence of the driver in his right senses would have afforded. "The act of a third person," said the Supreme Judicial Court of Massachusetts, "intervening and contributing a condition necessary to the injurious effect of the original negligence, will not excuse the first wrongdoer, if such act ought to have been foreseen." Lane v. Atlantic Works, 111 Mass. 136. A railroad company which found it necessary or desirable to have its freight train guarded by two detectives against thieves is surely chargeable with knowledge that portable property left without a guard was likely to be made off with. Again, strictly speaking, the act of the thieves did not intervene between defendant's negligence and the plaintiff's loss; the two causes were to all practical intent simultaneous and concurrent; it is rather a case of a joint tort than an intervening cause. Lord Cairns dwelt on the importance of the different acts having occurred or been done continuously. Sneesby v. Lancashire and Yorkshire Railway Co., L.R., 1 Q.B.D. 42, 44. An illustration will perhaps clarify the case. Suppose a fruit vendor at his stand along the street is rendered unconscious by the negligence of the defendant, who disappears, and boys in the street appropriate the unfortunate vendor's stock in trade; could the defendant escape liability for their value? We can hardly imagine a court answering in the affirmative. Yet the case is but little more extreme than the jury might have found the present case. . . .

GARRISON, J., dissenting. The collision afforded an opportunity for theft of which a thief took advantage, but I cannot agree that the collision was therefore the proximate cause of loss of the stolen articles. Proximate cause imports unbroken continuity between cause and effect, which, both in law and in logic, is broken by the active intervention of an independent criminal actor. This established rule of law is defeated if proximate cause be confounded with mere opportunity for crime. A maladjusted switch may be the proximate cause of the death of a passenger who was killed by the derailment of the train, or by the fire or collision that ensued, but it is not the proximate cause of the death of a passenger who was murdered by a bandit who boarded the train because of the opportunity afforded by its derailment. This clear distinction is not met by saying that criminal intervention should be foreseen, for this implies that crime is to be presumed and the law is directly otherwise.

NOTES

1. Deliberate intervention by third parties. The position taken in the *Brower* dissent was endorsed in Watson v. Kentucky & Indiana Bridge & Ry. Co., 126 S.W. 146, 151 (Ky. 1910), where a tank car containing gasoline derailed through defendant's negligence. As the gas leaked out, a man named Duerr threw a match on it, starting a large fire. The defendant introduced evidence that Duerr had just been discharged by the defendant, had intended to commit arson, and had been indicted for the crime. The plaintiff produced evidence that suggested that Duerr was lighting a cigar when he carelessly threw the match on the gasoline. The court held that the jury should decide whether Duerr had acted maliciously or negligently, but that if his actions were malicious, then the defendant was entitled to a directed verdict on proximate cause grounds.

> If, however, the act of Duerr in lighting the match and throwing it into the vapor or gas arising from the gasoline was malicious, and done for the purpose of causing the explosion, we do not think appellees would be responsible, for while the appellee Bridge & Railroad Company's negligence may have been the efficient cause of the presence of the gas in the street, and it should have understood enough of the consequences thereof to have foreseen that an explosion was likely to result from the inadvertent or negligent lighting of a match by some person who was ignorant of the presence of the gas or of the effect of lighting or throwing a match in it, it could not have foreseen or deemed it probable that one would maliciously or wantonly do such an act for the evil purpose of producing the explosion. Therefore, if the act of Duerr was malicious, we quite agree with the trial court that it was one which the appellees could not reasonably have anticipated or guarded against, and in such case the act of Duerr, and not the primary negligence of the appellee Bridge & Railroad Company, in any of the particulars charged, was the efficient or proximate cause of appellant's injuries. The mere fact that the concurrent cause or intervening act was unforeseen will not relieve the defendant guilty of the primary negligence from liability, but if the intervening agency is something so unexpected or extraordinary as that he could not or ought not to have anticipated it, he will not be liable and certainly he is not bound to anticipate the criminal acts of others by which damage is inflicted, and hence is not liable therefor.

2. *Alternative tests of proximate causation.* Cases like *Brower* and *Watson* call into question the proper test of causation. Under the earliest tests of proximate causation, the defendant was held liable only when he was the "last wrongdoer" whose conduct contributed to the loss. Here the last wrongdoer need not be the same as the last actor, for a subsequent actor may undertake acts that are either blameless or even praiseworthy. The efforts of the captain to save his ship in *The City of Lincoln* would not sever causal connection, and so too the effort of the plaintiff to escape a moving train in *Tuttle*. Likewise, the actions of infants and incompetents would not break the chain of causation, especially to the extent that a negligence system does not regard these actions as tortious. Nevertheless the test is highly restrictive, for it blocks causal recovery not only when the deliberate wrong of a third party intervenes but also when the negligence of a third party intervenes as well. Although this "last wrongdoer" test had some early champions (see T. Beven, Negligence in Law 45 (3d ed. 1908)), it was implicitly, but necessarily, rejected in both *Watson* and *Brower*.

Even after the last wrongdoer test was jettisoned, many causal theorists continued to believe that deliberate and malicious acts should in general negative causal connection. Thus Hart and Honore offer this general test of causation: "The general principle of the traditional doctrine is that *the free, deliberate and informed act or omission of a human being, intended to exploit the situation created by the defendant, negatives any causal connection.*" Causation in the Law 136 (2d ed. 1985) (italics in original). There is a commonsense defense of this position that rests on the observation that the original actor did not constrain the conduct of the malicious intervenor, but only facilitated his mischief. Yet it was just the creation of additional opportunities for harm that allowed the plaintiff to recover against the railroad in Hines v. Garratt (supra at page 498) or indeed in *Brower* itself.

3. *The Restatement approach.* The question of deliberate third party intervention, with the context of the Restatement's "substantial factor" test, is taken up in two critical provisions of the Restatement (Second).

§448. INTENTIONALLY TORTIOUS OR CRIMINAL ACTS DONE UNDER OPPORTUNITY AFFORDED BY ACTOR'S NEGLIGENCE
The act of a third person in committing an intentional tort or crime is a superseding cause of harm to another resulting therefrom, although the actor's negligent conduct created a situation which afforded an opportunity to the third person to commit such a tort or crime, unless the actor at the time of his negligent conduct realized or should have realized the likelihood that such a situation might be created, and that a third person might avail himself of the opportunity to commit such a tort or crime.

§449. TORTIOUS OR CRIMINAL ACTS THE PROBABILITY OF WHICH MAKES ACTOR'S CONDUCT NEGLIGENT
If the likelihood that a third person may act in a particular manner is the hazard or one of the hazards which makes the actor negligent, such an act whether innocent, negligent, intentionally tortious, or criminal does not prevent the actor from being liable for harm caused thereby.

The case for the Restatement position is that the defendant should be liable precisely because the third party *did* exploit the dangerous condition created by the defendant. Thus the situation in *Watson,* for example, would be quite different if Duerr had independently laid plans to set off an explosion near the railroad's cars, a most unlikely supposition on the facts of the case. In addition it is clear, both in *Brower* and *Watson,* that there are distinct limits to causal responsibility, wholly without reference to foreseeability, even if the malicious acts of a third party do not sever causal connection. Thus, in *Brower* the consequences of defendant's action cease once the railroad gathers up the barrels and places them under a competent guard. In *Watson* the liability ends once the spilled gasoline is collected and removed to a position of safety.

The post-Restatement cases generally take the view that the foreseeable deliberate intervention of a third party rarely severs causal connection. In Landeros v. Flood, 551 P.2d 389 (Cal. 1976), the court held that if a physician negligently failed to identify a "battered child," he could be held for the damages resulting from the child's return to his offending parent because, although the subsequent beatings were deliberate, malicious, and criminal, they were also tragically foreseeable.

Similarly, in Bigbee v. Pacific Telephone & Telegraph Co., 565 P.2d 947 (Cal. 1983), the plaintiff was trapped in a telephone booth located in a parking lot 15 feet from a major thoroughfare. The plaintiff saw an oncoming car careening out of control. He was then struck by Leona Roberts, a drunk driver, when he was unable to wrestle the door open in time to escape. After holding that the phone company could be found negligent both in its placement and its maintenance of the booth, Bird, C.J., brushed aside the defendant's proximate cause argument, noting that it "is of no consequence that the harm to the plaintiff came about through the negligent or reckless acts of Roberts," citing Restatement (Second) Torts §449.

One last variation is Atherton v. Devine, 602 P.2d 634, 636-637 (Okla. 1979). There the plaintiff was injured in a road accident attributable to the negligence of the defendant. The ambulance that took the plaintiff to the hospital was in turn involved in another collision, aggravating the original injuries. The Oklahoma Supreme Court, reversing the decision below, held that the first collision was a "substantial factor" in causing the subsequent injury:

> It has long been the rule in Oklahoma that an original wrongdoer, negligently causing injury to another is liable for the negligence of a physician who treats the injured person where the negligent treatment results in the aggravation of injuries, so long as the injured person exercises good faith in the choice of his physician. . . .
>
> As a matter of principle, there would seem to be no material distinction between medical treatment required because of the tortious act, and transportation required to reach an institution where medical treatment is available. The use of an ambulance, like the use of a surgeon's scalpel, is necessitated by the tortfeasor's wrong, and either may be used negligently.

4. Plaintiff's suicide as an intervening cause. These different approaches are tested by those situations where the plaintiff's decedent, having been hurt by the wrongful conduct of the defendant, commits suicide while suffering from nervous shock or mental depression brought about by the accident.

The early cases, reflecting the common law's awe of suicide, saw it as an intervening cause. In Scheffer v. Railroad Co., 105 U.S. 249 (1881), a wrongful death action, plaintiff alleged that defendant's negligent conduct had so hurt decedent's brain and nervous system that he consequently became insane, suffered delusions, and committed suicide. Defendant demurred; the Supreme Court affirmed a judgment sustaining the demurrer, denying that either Scheffer's insanity or his suicide was the natural and probable consequence of the negligence of defendant's officers.

More recent cases, however, show greater willingness to allow the question to go to the jury. In Fuller v. Preis, 322 N.E.2d 263, 266, 269 (N.Y. 1974), the decedent, a medical doctor, walked away from an automobile accident in the belief that he was uninjured. About seven months after the accident he executed his will and two days later took his life. In the period between the accident and his death, the decedent experienced recurrent seizures that required him to abandon his medical practice. In addition, his wife, partially paralyzed by polio, suffered "nervous exhaustion" and his mother became ill with cancer. The New York Court of Appeals, speaking through Breitel, C.J., held that it was a question for the jury whether the cause of the decedent's death was the automobile accident or the illnesses of his wife and mother. On the question of causation it noted:

> The only authentic issue is whether the suicide was an "irresistible impulse" caused by traumatic organic brain damage. The issue is limited on this appeal because of the theory of the case based on the traditional but not entirely satisfactory concept of the "irresistible impulse." Medical and legal lore have developed an incisive critique of that concept but its evolution or clarification must await another day and another case. It has been cogently argued that it ought to be sufficient to accept mental illness, traumatic in origin, as a substantial cause of particular behavior, including suicide. . . .
>
> A suicide is a strange act and no rationalistic approach can fit the act into neat categories of rationality or irrationality. When the suicide is preceded by a history of trauma, brain damage, epileptic seizures, aberrational conduct, depression and despair, it is at the very least a fair issue of fact whether the suicide was the rational act of a sound mind or the irrational act or irresistible impulse of a deranged mind evidenced by a physically damaged brain.

More recently in Stafford v. Neurological Medicine, Inc., 811 F.2d 470 (8th Cir. 1987), the defendant medical group sent a diagnosis to the plaintiff that falsely stated she had an incurable brain tumor. Shortly thereafter the plaintiff killed herself. The trial judge had held that the plaintiff's suicide barred the cause of action, but on appeal the court held that there was a jury case on whether she had an "irresistible impulse" caused by the faulty diagnosis. Given the dispute between plaintiff's and defendant's experts, the case was left to the jury.

Wagner v. International Ry.
133 N.E. 437 (N.Y. 1921)

CARDOZO, J. [after a brief statement of preliminary facts about the electric railway's trestle:] Plaintiff and his cousin Herbert boarded a car at a station near the bottom of one of the trestles. Other passengers, entering at the same time, filled the platform, and blocked admission to the aisle. The platform was provided with doors, but the conductor did not close them. Moving at from six to eight miles an hour, the car, without slackening, turned the curve. There was a violent lurch, and Herbert Wagner was thrown out, near the point where the trestle changes to a bridge. The cry was raised, "Man overboard." The car went on across the bridge, and stopped near the foot of the incline. Night and darkness had come on. Plaintiff walked along the trestle, a distance of four hundred and forty-five feet, until he arrived at the bridge, where he thought to find his cousin's body. He says that he was asked to go there by the conductor. He says, too, that the conductor followed with a lantern. Both these statements the conductor denies. Several other persons, instead of ascending the trestle, went beneath it, and discovered under the bridge the body they were seeking. As they stood there, the plaintiff's body struck the ground beside them. Reaching the bridge, he had found upon a beam his cousin's hat, but nothing else. About him, there was darkness. He missed his footing, and fell.

The trial judge held that negligence toward Herbert Wagner would not charge the defendant with liability for injuries suffered by the plaintiff unless two other facts were found: First, that the plaintiff had been invited by the conductor to go upon the bridge; and second, that the conductor had followed with a light. Thus limited, the jury found in favor of the defendant. Whether the limitation may be upheld, is the question to be answered.

Danger invites rescue. The cry of distress is the summons to relief. The law does not ignore these reactions of the mind in tracing conduct to its consequences. It recognizes them as normal. It places their effects within the range of the natural and probable. The wrong that imperils life is a wrong to the imperiled victim; it is a wrong also to his rescuer. The state that leaves an opening in a bridge is liable to the child that falls into the stream, but liable also to the parent who plunges to its aid. . . . The railroad company whose train approaches without signal is a wrongdoer toward the traveler surprised between the rails, but a wrongdoer also to the bystander who drags him from the path (Eckert v. L.I.R.R. Co., 43 N.Y. 502). . . . The rule is the same in other jurisdictions. . . . The risk of rescue, if only it be not wanton, is born of the occasion. The emergency begets the man. The wrongdoer may not have foreseen the coming of a deliverer. He is accountable as if he had . . .

The defendant says that we must stop, in following the chain of causes, when action ceases to be "instinctive." By this, is meant, it seems, that rescue is at the peril of the rescuer, unless spontaneous and immediate. If there has been time to deliberate, if impulse has given way to judgment, one cause, it is said, has spent its force, and another has intervened. In this case, the plaintiff walked more than four hundred feet in going to Herbert's aid. He had time to reflect and weigh; impulse had been followed by choice; and choice, in the defendant's view, intercepts and breaks the sequence. We find no warrant for thus shortening the chain of jural causes. We may assume, though we are not required to decide, that peril and rescue must be in substance one transaction; that the sight of the one must have aroused the impulse to the other; in short, that there must be unbroken continuity between the commission of the wrong and the effort to avert its consequences. If all this be assumed, the defendant is not aided. Continuity in such circumstances is not broken by the exercise of volition . . . So sweeping an exception, if recognized, would leave little of the rule. "The human mind," as we have said (People v. Majone, 91 N.Y. 211, 212), "acts with celerity which it is sometimes impossible to measure." The law does not discriminate between the rescuer oblivious of peril and the one who counts the cost. It is enough that the act, whether impulsive or deliberate, is the child of the occasion.

The defendant finds another obstacle, however, in the futility of the plaintiff's sacrifice. [The court then discussed whether or not plaintiff was contributorily negligent and concluded that under the emergency conditions he was not.]

Whether Herbert Wagner's fall was due to the defendant's negligence, and whether plaintiff in going to the rescue, as he did, was foolhardy or reasonable in the light of the emergency confronting him, were questions for the jury.

NOTE

Danger invites rescue? Is the decision in *Wagner* a fair extension of *The City of Lincoln* or of *Tuttle?* Should the plaintiff's recovery be barred if the conductor had mounted adequate rescue efforts without the plaintiff's assistance? In Talbert v. Talbert, 199 N.Y.S.2d 212 (N.Y. Sup. Ct. 1960), plaintiff was harmed while rescuing his father, the defendant, who had locked himself in a garage and turned on the motor of his car in an effort to take his own life. The court, influenced by the decisions in Eckert v. Long Island R.R. at page 191 supra and in *Wagner,* held that plaintiff stated a cause of action. The court followed the rule set out by Professor Bohlen in his Studies in the Law of Torts, p. 569 n.33:

> The rescuer's right of action, therefore must rest upon the view that one who imperils another, at a place where there may be bystanders, must take into account the chance that some bystander will yield to the meritorious impulse to save life or even property from destruction, and attempt a rescue. If this is so, the right of action depends not upon the wrongfulness of the defendant's conduct in its tendency to imperil the person whose rescue is attempted, but upon its tendency to cause the

rescuer to take the risk involved in the attempted rescue. And it would seem that a person who carelessly exposes himself to danger or who attempts to take his life in a place where others may be expected to be, does commit a wrongful act towards them in that it exposes them to a recognizable risk of injury.

In re Polemis & Furness, Withy & Co.
[1921] 3 K.B. 560

BANKES, L.J. By a time charterparty dated February 21, 1917, the respondents chartered their vessel to the appellants. Clause 21 of the charterparty was in these terms. [The clause stated the contingencies under which the charterer was not liable to the ship as follows:

"The act of God, the King's enemies, loss or damage from fire on board in hulk or craft, or on shore, arrest and/or restraint of princes, rulers, and people, collision, an act, neglect, or default whatsoever of pilot, master, or crew in the management or navigation of the ship, and all and every of the dangers and accidents of the seas, canals, and rivers, and of navigation of whatever nature or kind always mutually excepted." The court then held that the clause would not shield the respondents for liability for the consequences of their negligence.]

The vessel was employed by the charterers to carry a cargo to Casablanca in Morocco. The cargo included a quantity of benzine or petrol in cases. While discharging at Casablanca a heavy plank fell into the hold in which the petrol was stowed, and caused an explosion, which set fire to the vessel and completely destroyed her. The owners claimed the value of the vessel from the charterers, alleging that the loss of the vessel was due to the negligence of the charterers' servants. The charterers contended that they were protected by the exception of fire contained in clause 21 of the charterparty, and they also contended that the damages claimed were too remote. The claim was referred to arbitration, and the arbitrators stated a special case for the opinion of the Court. Their findings of fact are as follows.

(*a*) That the ship was lost by fire.

(*b*) That the fire arose from a spark igniting petrol vapour in the hold.

(*c*) That the spark was caused by the falling board coming into contact with some substance in the hold.

(*d*) That the fall of the board was caused by the negligence of the Arabs (other than the winchman) engaged in the work of discharging.

(*e*) That the said Arabs were employed by the charterers or their agents the Cie. Transatlantique on behalf of the charterers, and that the said Arabs were the servants of the charterers.

(*f*) That the causing of the spark could not reasonably have been anticipated from the falling of the board, though some damage to the ship might reasonably have been anticipated.

(*g*) There was no evidence before us that the Arabs chosen were known or likely to be negligent.

Then they state the damages, £196,165 1*s*. 11*d*. These findings are no doubt intended to raise the question whether the view taken, or said to have been taken, by Pollock, C.B., in Rigby v. Hewitt, (5 Ex. 243) and Greenland v. Chaplin (5 Ex. 248), or the view taken by Channell, B., and Blackburn, J., in Smith v. London & South Western Ry. Co. (3 L. R. 6 C.P. 21), is the correct one. . . .

Assuming the Chief Baron to have been correctly reported in the Exchequer Reports, the difference between the two views is this: According to the one view, the consequences which may reasonably be expected to result from a particular act are material only in reference to the question whether the act is or is not a negligent act; according to the other view, those consequences are the test whether the damages resulting from the act, assuming it to be negligent, are or are not too remote to be recoverable. [Bankes, L.J., then quoted from H.M.S. London, [1914] P. 72, in part, as follows:] ". . . In Smith v. London and South Western Ry. Co., Channell, B., said: 'Where there is no direct evidence of negligence, the question what a reasonable man might foresee is of importance in considering the question whether there is evidence for the jury of negligence or not . . . but when it has been once determined that there is evidence of negligence, the person guilty of it is equally liable for its consequences, whether he could have foreseen them or not.' And Blackburn, J., in the same case said: 'What the defendants might reasonably anticipate is only material with reference to the question, whether the defendants were negligent or not, and cannot alter their liability if they were guilty of negligence' " . . .

In the present case the arbitrators have found as a fact that the falling of the plank was due to the negligence of the defendants' servants. The fire appears to me to have been directly caused by the falling of the plank. Under these circumstances I consider that it is immaterial that the causing of the spark by the falling of the plank could not have been reasonably anticipated. The appellants' junior counsel sought to draw a distinction between the anticipation of the extent of damage resulting from a negligent act, and the anticipation of the type of damage resulting from such an act. He admitted that it could not lie in the mouth of a person whose negligent act had caused damage to say that he could not reasonably have foreseen the extent of the damage, but he contended that the negligent person was entitled to rely upon the fact that he could not reasonably have anticipated the type of damage which resulted from his negligent act. I do not think that the distinction can be admitted. Given the breach of duty which constitutes the negligence, and given the damage as a direct result of that negligence, the anticipations of the person whose negligent act has produced the damage appear to me to be irrelevant. I consider that the damages claimed are not too remote.

WARRINGTON, L.J. [referring to a discussion by Beven on Negligence, observed:] . . . The result may be summarised as follows: The presence or absence of reasonable anticipation of damage determines the legal quality of the act as negligent or innocent. If it be thus determined to be negligent, then the question whether particular damages are recoverable depends only on the answer to the question whether they are the direct consequence of the act. Sufficient authority for the proposition is afforded by Smith v. London and South Western Ry. Co., in the Exchequer Chamber, and particularly by the judgments of Channell, B., and Blackburn, J. . . . In the present case it is clear that the act causing the plank to fall was in law a negligent act, because some damage to the ship might reasonably be anticipated. If this is so then the appellants are liable for the actual loss, that being on the findings of the arbitrators the direct result of the falling board. . . .

SCRUTTON, L.J. . . . The second defence is that the damage is too remote from the negligence, as it could not be reasonably foreseen as a consequence. On this head we were referred to a number of well known cases in which vague language, which I cannot think to be really helpful, has been used in an attempt to define the point at which damage becomes too remote from, or not sufficiently directly caused by, the breach of duty, which is the original cause of action, to be recoverable. For instance, I cannot think it useful to say the damage must be the natural and probable result. This suggests that there are results which are natural but not probable, and other results which are probable but not natural. I am not sure what either adjective means in this connection; if they mean the same thing, two need not be used; if they mean different things, the difference between them should be defined. And as to many cases of fact in which the distinction has been drawn, it is difficult to see why one case should be decided one way and one another. . . . To determine whether an act is negligent, it is relevant to determine whether any reasonable person would foresee that the act would cause damage; if he would not, the act is not negligent. But if the act would or might probably cause damage, the fact that the damage it in fact causes is not the exact kind of damage one would expect is immaterial, so long as the damage is in fact directly traceable to the negligent act, and not due to the operation of independent causes having no connection with the negligent act, except that they could not avoid its results. Once the act is negligent, the fact that its exact operation was not foreseen is immaterial. . . . In the present case it was negligent in discharging cargo to knock down the planks of the temporary staging, for they might easily cause some damage either to workmen, or cargo, or the ship. The fact that they did directly produce an unexpected result, a spark in an atmosphere of petrol vapour which caused a fire, does not relieve the person who was negligent from the damage which his negligent act so directly caused.

NOTE

Culpability versus compensation. Should culpability be judged by one standard and compensation by another? Professor Seavey has said, "Prima facie at least, the reasons for creating liability should limit it." Seavey, Mr. Justice Cardozo and the Law of Torts, 39 Colum. L. Rev. 29; 52 Harv. L. Rev. 372; 48 Yale L.J. 390 (1939). How does Seavey's argument apply when a theory of strict liability is adopted?

Whatever its merits the *Polemis* rule has long been followed in most American jurisdictions. Perhaps the leading American statement of the rule is that of Mitchell, J., in Christianson v. Chicago, St. P., M. and O. Ry., 69 N.W. 640, 641 (Minn. 1896):

> What a man may reasonably anticipate is important, and may be deci-
> sive, in determining whether an act is negligent, but is not at all decisive
> in determining whether that act is the proximate cause of an injury which
> ensues. If a person had no reasonable ground to anticipate that a particu-
> lar act would or might result in any injury to anybody, then, of course,
> the act would not be negligent at all but, if the act itself is negligent, then
> the person guilty of it is equally liable for all its natural and proximate
> consequences, whether he could have foreseen them or not. . . . Conse-
> quences which follow in unbroken sequence, without an intervening ef-
> ficient cause, from the original negligent act, are natural and proximate
> and for such consequences the original wrongdoer is responsible, even
> though he could not have foreseen the particular results which did
> follow.

Does the foresight test require a court to take into account more than the actual sequence of events to determine causal connection? Is there any reason why this should be done? Is the same sort of inquiry required under a directness test?

Palsgraf v. Long Island R.R.
162 N.E. 99 (N.Y. 1928)

Appeal from a judgment of the Appellate Division of the Supreme Court in the second judicial department, entered December 16, 1927, affirming a judgment in favor of plaintiff entered upon a verdict.

[The following excerpts are from the majority opinion of Seeger, J., in the Appellate Division, 222 App. Div. 166 (1927):]

The defendant contends that the accident was not caused by the negligence of the defendant.

The sole question of defendant's negligence submitted to the jury was whether the defendant's employees were "careless and negligent in the way they handled this particular passenger after he came upon the platform and while he was boarding the train." This question of negligence was submitted to the jury by a fair and impartial charge and the verdict was supported by the evidence. The jury might well find that the act of the passenger in undertaking to board a moving train was negligent, and that the acts of the defendant's employees in assisting him while engaged in that negligent act were also negligent. Instead of aiding or assisting the passenger engaged in such an act, they might better have discouraged and warned him not to board the moving train. It is quite probable that without their assistance the passenger might have succeeded in boarding the train and no accident would have happened, or without the assistance of these employees the passenger might have desisted in his efforts to board the train. In any event, the acts of defendant's employees, which the jury found to be negligent, caused the bundle to be thrown under the train and to explode. It is no answer or defense to these negligent acts to say that the defendant's employees were not chargeable with notice that the passenger's bundle contained an explosive. . . .

It must be remembered that the plaintiff was a passenger of the defendant and entitled to have the defendant exercise the highest degree of care required of common carriers.

[The dissenting opinion of Lazansky, P.J., in the appellate division reads as follows:]

The facts may have warranted the jury in finding the defendant's agents were negligent in assisting a passenger in boarding a moving train in view of the fact that a door of the train should have been closed before the train started, which would have prevented the passenger making the attempt. There was also warrant for a finding by the jury that as a result of the negligence of the defendant a package was thrown between the platform and train, exploded, causing injury to plaintiff, who was on the station platform. In my opinion, the negligence of defendant was not a proximate cause of the injuries to plaintiff. Between the negligence of defendant and the injuries, there intervened the negligence of the passenger carrying the package containing an explosive. This was an independent, and not a concurring act of negligence. The explosion was not reasonably probable as a result of defendant's act of negligence. The negligence of defendant was not a likely or natural cause of the explosion, since the latter was such an unusual occurrence. Defendant's negligence was a cause of plaintiff's injury, but too remote.

[The appellate division split three to two on this case. The court of appeals split four to three on the appeal.]

CARDOZO, C.J. Plaintiff was standing on a platform of defendant's railroad after buying a ticket to go to Rockaway Beach. A train stopped at the station, bound for another place. Two men ran forward to catch it. One of the men reached the platform of the car without mishap, though the train was already moving. The other man, carrying a package, jumped aboard the car, but seemed unsteady as if about to fall. A guard on the car, who had held the door open, reached forward to help him in, and another guard on the platform pushed him from behind. In this act, the package was dislodged, and fell upon the rails. It was a package of small size, about fifteen inches long, and was covered by a newspaper. In fact it contained fireworks, but there was nothing in its appearance to give notice of its contents. The fireworks when they fell exploded. The shock of the explosion threw down some scales at the other end of the platform, many feet away. The scales struck the plaintiff, causing injuries for which she sues.

The conduct of the defendant's guard, if a wrong in its relation to the holder of the package, was not a wrong in its relation to the plaintiff, standing far away. Relatively to her it was not negligence at all. Nothing in the situation gave notice that the falling package had in it the potency of peril to persons thus removed. Negligence is not actionable unless it involves the invasion of a legally protected interest, the violation of a right. "Proof of negligence in the air, so to speak, will not do." (Pollock, Torts, p. 455 [11th ed.]). The plaintiff as she stood upon the platform of the station might claim to be protected against intentional invasion of her bodily security. Such invasion is not charged. She might claim to be protected against unintentional invasion by conduct involving in the thought of reasonable men an unreasonable hazard that such invasion would ensue. These, from the point of view of the law, were the bounds of her immunity, with perhaps some rare exceptions, survivals for the most part of ancient forms of liability, where conduct is held to be at the peril of the actor (Sullivan v. Dunham, 161 N.Y. 290). If no hazard was apparent to the eye of ordinary vigilance, an act innocent and harmless, at least to outward seeming, with reference to her, did not take to itself the quality of a tort because it happened to be a wrong, though apparently not one involving the risk of bodily insecurity, with reference to someone else. "In every instance, before negligence can be predicated of a given act, back of the act must be sought and found a duty to the individual complaining, the observance of which would have averted or avoided the injury" (McSherry, C.J., in W. Va. Central R. Co. v. State, 96 Md. 652, 666). "The ideas of negligence and duty are strictly correlative" (Bowen, L.J., in Thomas v. Quartermaine, 18 Q.B.D. 685, 694). The plaintiff sues in her own right for a wrong personal to her, and not as the vicarious beneficiary of a breach of duty to another.

A different conclusion will involve us, and swiftly too, in a maze of contradictions. A guard stumbles over a package which has been left upon a platform. It seems to be a bundle of newspapers. It turns out to be a can of dynamite. To the eye of ordinary vigilance, the bundle is abandoned waste, which may be kicked or trod on with impunity. Is a passenger at the other end of the platform protected by the law against the unsuspected hazard concealed beneath the waste? If not, is the result to be any different, so far as the distant passenger is concerned, when the guard stumbles over a valise which a truckman or a porter has left upon the walk? The passenger far away, if the victim of a wrong at all, has a cause of action, not derivative, but original and primary. His claim to be protected against invasion of his bodily security is neither greater nor less because the act resulting in the invasion is a wrong to another far removed. In this case, the rights that are said to have been violated, the interests said to have been invaded, are not even of the same order. The man was not injured in his person nor even put in danger. The purpose of the act, as well as its effect, was to make his person safe. If there was a wrong to him at all, which may very well be doubted, it was a wrong to a property interest only, the safety of his package. Out of this wrong to property, which threatened injury to nothing else, there has passed, we are told, to the plaintiff by derivation or succession a right of action for the invasion of an interest of another order, the right to bodily security. The diversity of interests emphasizes the futility of the effort to build the plaintiff's right upon the basis of a wrong to some one else. The gain is one of emphasis, for a like result would follow if the interests were the same. Even then, the orbit of the danger as disclosed to the eye of reasonable vigilance would be the orbit of the duty. One who jostles one's neighbor in a crowd does not invade the rights of others standing at the outer fringe when the unintended contact casts a bomb upon the ground. The wrongdoer as to them is the man who carries the bomb, not the one who explodes it without suspicion of the danger. Life will have to be made over, and human nature transformed, before prevision so extravagant can be accepted as the norm of conduct, the customary standard to which behavior must conform.

The argument for the plaintiff is built upon the shifting meanings of such words as "wrong" and "wrongful," and shares their instability. What the plaintiff must show is "a wrong" to herself, i.e. a violation of her own right, and not merely a wrong to someone else, nor conduct "wrongful" because unsocial, but not "a wrong" to any one. We are told that one who drives at reckless speed through a crowded city street is guilty of a negligent act and, therefore, of a wrongful one irrespective of the consequences. Negligent the act is, and wrongful in the sense that it is unsocial, but wrongful and unsocial in relation to other travelers, only because the eye of vigilance perceives the risk of damage. If the same act were to be committed on a speedway or a race course, it would lose its wrongful quality. The risk reasonably to be perceived defines the duty to be obeyed, and risk imports relation; it is risk to

another or to others within the range of apprehension (Seavey, Negligence, Subjective or Objective, 41 H.L. Rv. 6). This does not mean, of
course, that one who launches a destructive force is always relieved of
liability if the force, though known to be destructive, pursues an unexpected path. "It was not necessary that the defendant should have had
notice of the particular method in which an accident would occur, if
the possibility of an accident was clear to the ordinarily prudent eye"
(Munsey v. Webb, 231 U.S. 150, 156). Some acts, such as shooting, are
so imminently dangerous to any one who may come within reach of the
missile, however unexpectedly, as to impose a duty of prevision not far
from that of an insurer. Even today, and much oftener in earlier stages
of the law, one acts sometimes at one's peril (Jeremiah Smith, Tort and
Absolute Liability, 30 H.L. Rv. 328; Street, Foundations of Legal Liability, vol. 1, pp. 77, 78). Under this head, it may be, fall certain cases of
what is known as transferred intent, an act willfully dangerous to *A*
resulting by misadventure in injury to *B* (Talmage v. Smith, 101 Mich.
370, 374). These cases aside, wrong is defined in terms of the natural
or probable, at least when unintentional (Parrot v. Wells-Fargo Co.
[The Nitro-Glycerine Case], [82 U.S.] 15 Wall. [524 (1872).]) The
range of reasonable apprehension is at times a question for the court,
and at times, if varying inferences are possible, a question for the jury.
Here, by concession, there was nothing in the situation to suggest to
the most cautious mind that the parcel wrapped in newspaper would
spread wreckage through the station. If the guard had thrown it down
knowingly and willfully, he would not have threatened the plaintiff's
safety, so far as appearances could warn him. His conduct would not
have involved, even then, an unreasonable probability of invasion of
her bodily security. Liability can be no greater where the act is inadvertent.

Negligence, like risk, is thus a term of relation. Negligence in the
abstract, apart from things related, is surely not a tort, if indeed it is
understandable at all. Negligence is not a tort unless it results in the
commission of a wrong, and the commission of a wrong imports the
violation of a right, in this case, we are told, the right to be protected
against interference with one's bodily security. But bodily security is
protected, not against all forms of interference or aggression, but only
against some. One who seeks redress at law does not make out a cause
of action by showing without more that there has been damage to his
person. If the harm was not willful, he must show that the act as to him
had possibilities of danger so many and apparent as to entitle him to
be protected against the doing of it though the harm was unintended.
Affront to personality is still the keynote of the wrong. Confirmation of
this view will be found in the history and development of the action on
the case. Negligence as a basis of civil liability was unknown to mediae-
val law. For damage to the person, the sole remedy was trespass, and

trespass did not lie in the absence of aggression, and that direct and personal. Liability for other damage, as where a servant without orders from the master does or omits something to the damage of another, is a plant of later growth. When it emerged out of the legal soil, it was thought of as a variant of trespass, an offshoot of the parent stock. This appears in the form of action, which was known as trespass on the case. . . . The victim does not sue derivatively, or by right of subrogation, to vindicate an interest invaded in the person of another. Thus to view his cause of action is to ignore the fundamental difference between tort and crime. He sues for breach of a duty owing to himself.

The law of causation, remote or proximate, is thus foreign to the case before us. The question of liability is always anterior to the question of the measure of the consequences that go with liability. If there is no tort to be redressed, there is no occasion to consider what damage might be recovered if there were a finding of a tort. We may assume, without deciding, that negligence, not at large or in the abstract, but in relation to the plaintiff, would entail liability for any and all consequences, however novel or extraordinary. There is room for argument that a distinction is to be drawn according to the diversity of interests invaded by the act, as where conduct negligent in that it threatens an insignificant invasion of an interest in property results in an unforeseeable invasion of an interest of another order, as e.g., one of bodily security. Perhaps other distinctions may be necessary. We do not go into the question now. The consequences to be followed must first be rooted in a wrong.

The judgment of the Appellate Division and that of the Trial Term should be reversed, and the complaint dismissed, with costs in all courts.

ANDREWS, J., dissenting. Assisting a passenger to board a train, the defendant's servant negligently knocked a package from his arms. It fell between the platform and the cars. Of its contents the servant knew and could know nothing. A violent explosion followed. The concussion broke some scales standing a considerable distance away. In falling they injured the plaintiff, an intending passenger.

Upon these facts may she recover the damages she has suffered in an action brought against the master? The result we shall reach depends upon our theory as to the nature of negligence. Is it a relative concept — the breach of some duty owing to a particular person or to particular persons? Or where there is an act which unreasonably threatens the safety of others, is the doer liable for all its proximate consequences, even where they result in injury to one who would generally be thought to be outside the radius of danger? This is not a mere dispute as to words. We might not believe that to the average mind the dropping of the bundle would seem to involve the probability of harm to the plaintiff standing many feet away whatever might be the case as to the owner or to one so near as to be likely to be struck by its fall. If, however, we adopt the second hypothesis we have to inquire only as to the relation between cause and effect. We deal in terms of proximate cause, not of negligence.

Negligence may be defined roughly as an act or omission which unreasonably does or may affect the rights of others, or which unreasonably fails to protect oneself from the dangers resulting from such acts. Here I confine myself to the first branch of the definition. Nor do I comment on the word "unreasonable." For present purposes it sufficiently describes that average of conduct that society requires of its members. . . .

But we are told that "there is no negligence unless there is in the particular case a legal duty to take care, and this duty must be one which is owed to the plaintiff himself and not merely to others." (Salmond, Torts, 24 [6th ed.].) This, I think too narrow a conception. Where there is the unreasonable act, and some right that may be affected there is negligence whether damage does or does not result. That is immaterial. Should we drive down Broadway at a reckless speed, we are negligent whether we strike an approaching car or miss it by an inch. The act itself is wrongful. It is a wrong not only to those who happen to be within the radius of danger but to all who might have been there — a wrong to the public at large. Such is the language of the street. Such is the language of the courts when speaking of contributory negligence. Such again and again their language in speaking of the duty of some defendant and discussing proximate cause in cases where such a discussion is wholly irrelevant on any other theory. As was said by Mr. Justice Holmes many years ago, "the measure of the defendant's duty in determining whether a wrong has been committed is one thing, the measure of liability when a wrong has been committed is another." (Spade v. Lynn & Boston R.R. Co., 172 Mass. 488.) Due care is a duty imposed on each one of us to protect society from unnecessary danger, not to protect A, B or C alone.

It may well be that there is no such thing as negligence in the abstract. "Proof of negligence in the air, so to speak, will not do." In an empty world negligence would not exist. It does involve a relationship between man and his fellows. But not merely a relationship between man and those whom he might reasonably expect his act would injure. Rather, a relationship between him and those whom he does in fact injure. If his act has a tendency to harm some one, it harms him a mile away as surely as it does those on the scene. We now permit children to recover for the negligent killing of the father. It was never prevented on the theory that no duty was owing to them. A husband may be compensated for the loss of his wife's services. To say that the wrongdoer was negligent as to the husband as well as to the wife is merely an attempt to fit facts to theory. An insurance company paying a fire loss recovers its payment of the negligent incendiary. We speak of subrogation — of suing in the right of the insured. Behind the cloud of words is the fact they hide, that the act, wrongful as to the insured, has also injured the company. Even if it be true that the fault of father, wife or insured will prevent recovery, it is because we consider the original negligence not the proximate cause of the injury. (Pollock, Torts, 463 [12th ed.].)

In the well-known Polemis Case, Scrutton, L.J., said that the dropping of a plank was negligent for it might injure "workman or cargo or ship." Because of either possibility the owner of the vessel was to be made good for his loss. The act being wrongful the doer was liable for its proximate results. Criticized and explained as this statement may have been, I think it states the law as it should be and as it is. (Smith v. London & South Western Ry. Co., 6 C.P. 14 [1870].)

The proposition is this. Every one owes to the world at large the duty of refraining from those acts that may unreasonably threaten the safety of others. Such an act occurs. Not only is he wronged to whom harm might reasonably be expected to result, but he also who is in fact injured, even if he be outside what would generally be thought the danger zone. There needs be duty due the one complaining but this is not a duty to a particular individual because as to him harm might be expected. Harm to some one being the natural result of the act, not only that one alone, but all those in fact injured may complain. We have never, I think, held otherwise. Indeed in the Di Caprio case [231 N.Y. 94] we said that a breach of a general ordinance defining the degree of care to be exercised in one's calling is evidence of negligence as to every one. We did not limit this statement to those who might be expected to be exposed to danger. Unreasonable risk being taken, its consequences are not confined to those who might probably be hurt.

If this be so, we do not have a plaintiff suing by "derivation or succession." Her action is original and primary. Her claim is for a breach of duty to herself — not that she is subrogated to any right of action of the owner of the parcel or of a passenger standing at the scene of the explosion.

The right to recover damages rests on additional considerations. The plaintiff's rights must be injured, and this injury must be caused by the negligence. We build a dam, but are negligent as to its foundations. Breaking, it injures property down stream. We are not liable if all this happened because of some reason other than the insecure foundation. But when injuries do result from our unlawful act we are liable for the consequences. It does not matter that they are unusual, unexpected, unforeseen and unforeseeable. But there is one limitation. The damages must be so connected with the negligence that the latter may be said to be the proximate cause of the former.

These two words have never been given an inclusive definition. What is a cause in a legal sense, still more what is a proximate cause, depend in each case upon many considerations, as does the existence of negligence itself. Any philosophical doctrine of causation does not help us. A boy throws a stone into a pond. The ripples spread. The water level rises. The history of that pond is altered to all eternity. It will be altered by other causes also. Yet it will be forever the resultant of all causes combined. Each one will have an influence. How great only omniscience can say. You may speak of a chain, or if you please, a net. An analogy is of little aid. Each cause brings about future events. Without each the future would not be the same. Each is proximate in the sense it is essential. But that is not what we mean by the word. Nor on the other hand do we mean sole cause. There is no such thing.

Should analogy be thought helpful, however, I prefer that of a stream. The spring, starting on its journey, is joined by tributary after tributary. The river, reaching the ocean, comes from a hundred sources. No man may say whence any drop of water is derived. Yet for a time distinction may be possible. Into the clear creek, brown swamp water flows from the left. Later, from the right comes water stained by its clay bed. The three may remain for a space, sharply divided. But at last, inevitably no trace of separation remains. They are so commingled that all distinction is lost.

As we have said, we cannot trace the effect of an act to the end, if end there is. Again, however, we may trace it part of the way. A murder at Serajevo may be the necessary antecedent to an assassination in London twenty years hence. An overturned lantern may burn all Chicago. We may follow the fire from the shed to the last building. We rightly say the fire started by the lantern caused its destruction.

A cause, but not the proximate cause. What we do mean by the word "proximate" is, that because of convenience, of public policy, of a rough sense of justice, the law arbitrarily declines to trace a series of events beyond a certain point. This is not logic. It is practical politics. Take our rule as to fires. Sparks from my burning haystack set on fire my house and my neighbor's. I may recover from a negligent railroad. He may not. Yet the wrongful act as directly harmed the one as the other. We may regret that the line was drawn just where it was, but drawn somewhere it had to be. We said the act of the railroad was not the proximate cause of our neighbor's fire. Cause it surely was. The words we used were simply indicative of our notions of public policy. Other courts think differently. But somewhere they reach the point where they cannot say the stream comes from any one source. . . .

It is all a question of expediency. There are no fixed rules to govern our judgment. There are simply matters of which we may take account. We have in a somewhat different connection spoken of "the stream of events." We have asked whether that stream was deflected — whether it was forced into new and unexpected channels. This is rather rhetoric than law. There is in truth little to guide us other than common sense.

There are some hints that may help us. The proximate cause, involved as it may be with many other causes, must be, at the least, something without which the event would not happen. The court must ask itself whether there was a natural and continuous sequence between cause and effect. Was the one a substantial factor in producing the other? Was there a direct connection between them, without too many intervening causes? Is the effect of cause on result not too attenuated? Is the cause likely, in the usual judgment of mankind, to produce the result? Or by the exercise of prudent foresight could the result be foreseen? Is the result too remote from the cause, and here we consider remoteness in time and space. . . . Clearly we must so consider, for the greater the distance either in time or space, the more surely do other causes intervene to affect the result. When a lantern is overturned the firing of a shed is a fairly direct consequence. Many things contribute to the spread of the conflagration — the force of the wind, the direction and width of streets, the character of intervening structures, other factors. We draw an uncertain and wavering line, but draw it we must as best we can.

Once again, it is all a question of fair judgment, always keeping in mind the fact that we endeavor to make a rule in each case that will be practical and in keeping with the general understanding of mankind. . . .

This last suggestion is the factor which must determine the case before us. The act upon which defendant's liability rests is knocking an apparently harmless package onto the platform. The act was negligent. For its proximate consequences the defendant is liable. If its contents were broken, to the owner; if it fell upon and crushed a passenger's foot, then to him. If it exploded and injured one in the immediate vicinity, to him also . . . Mrs. Palsgraf was standing some distance away. How far cannot be told from the record — apparently twenty-five or thirty feet. Perhaps less. Except for the explosion, she would not have been injured. We are told by the appellant in his brief "it cannot be denied that the explosion was the direct cause of the plaintiff's injuries." So it was a substantial factor in producing the result — there was here a natural and continuous sequence — direct connection. The only intervening cause was that instead of blowing her to the ground the concussion smashed the weighing machine which in turn fell upon her. There was no remoteness in time, little in space. And surely, given such an explosion as here it needed no great foresight to predict that the natural result would be to injure one on the platform at no greater distance from its scene than was the plaintiff. Just how no one might be able to predict. Whether by flying fragments, by broken glass, by wreckage of machines or structures no one could say. But injury in some form was most probable.

Under these circumstances I cannot say as a matter of law that the plaintiff's injuries were not the proximate result of the negligence. That is all we have before us. The court refused to so charge. No request was made to submit the matter to the jury as a question of fact, even would that have been proper upon the record before us.

The judgment appealed from should be affirmed, with costs.

NOTES

1. The secret history of Palsgraf v. Long Island R.R. *Palsgraf* has inspired extensive detective work to uncover its facts. Judge Noonan, Persons and Masks of the Law ch. 4 (1976) notes, among other things, that the "plaintiff was a Brooklyn janitress and ex-housewife, 43 years of age" who earned $416 per year. She was accompanied on the trip by her two daughters. Noonan suggests that the "scales must have been toppled *not by the explosion* of the fireworks but by the crowd running in panic on the platform" and that although the plaintiff "had been hit by the scales on the arm, hip and thigh" the chief source of her complaint was "a stammer and stutter" that appeared about one week after the accident, and which may have been intensified by the litigation itself.

Not to be outdone, Judge Posner disputes Noonan's explanation of the source of injury. In Cardozo: A Study in Reputation 38-39 (1990), he relies on a front page New York Times report of the accident, "Bomb Blast Injures 13 in Station Crowd," (August 25, 1924, p.1) that stated the explosion was not only loud enough to cause a stampede but violent enough to cause extensive damage to the train station, and to send several of the 13 people it injured to the hospital with minor injuries. Posner then identifies a number of errors in Cardozo's account of the facts which render it "both elliptical and slanted."

> The plaintiff is described as standing on the platform rather than as waiting for a train; the effect is to downplay the carrier-passenger relationship (created by the purchase of the ticket) that entitled Mrs. Palsgraf under traditional legal principles to the highest degree of care. The bundle is described as small even though the witnesses had described it as large. There is no hint of the magnitude of the explosion, a reticence that makes the collapse of the scale seem freakish. The scale is described as being "at the other end of the platform, many feet away," but this characterization has no basis in the record, which discloses neither the location of the scale nor its distance from the explosion.

Evidence from Palsgraf's daughter suggests that she stood only ten feet from the explosion, which injured her directly. What difference, if any, do these factual errors make to the legal relationship between proximate cause and the duty of care? If Palsgraf was not "standing far away," should she recover as a "foreseeable plaintiff"? Should a total stranger injured by the blast be able to recover from the railroad if its conductors had innocently set off the bomb?

Palsgraf may also have influenced the development of tort theory even before it reached the Court of Appeal. In Palsgraf Revisited, 52 Mich. L. Rev. 1, 4-5 (1953), reprinted in Selected Topics on the Law of Torts 191, 195-196 (1954), Dean Prosser reports some scuttlebutt that is interesting if true — "one of those accidents which shape the course of the law." Professor Bohlen, Reporter for the Restatement of the Law of Torts, got hold of the *Palsgraf* case after it was decided by the Appellate Division and used the case in preparation of a draft to be discussed before the Advisory Council. Chief Judge Cardozo was a member of the council, but he could not participate in the discussion since the case might come before his court — as it did. But he listened to a lively debate that resulted in the adoption of Section 281 of the Restatement of Torts, which reads as follows:

> The actor is liable for an invasion of an interest of another, if:
>   (a) the interest invaded is protected against unintentional invasion, and
>   (b) the conduct of the actor is negligent with respect to such interest or any other similar interest of the other which is protected against unintentional invasion, and
>   (c) the actor's conduct is a legal cause of the invasion . . .
> [The Restatement Comment on clause (b), above, reads:]
> c. *Risk to class of which plaintiff is member.* If the actor's conduct creates a recognizable risk of harm only to a particular class of persons, the fact that it causes harm to a person of a different class, to whom the actor could not reasonably have anticipated injury, does not render the actor liable to the persons so injured.

In any event, Cardozo was convinced by the majority of the council, and when the *Palsgraf* case did come before his court, his opinion reflected what he had heard the learned professors and other judges say, as well as his own thoughts.

2. *Duty and foresight.* The *Palsgraf* decision calls into question the relationship between the duty of care and the tests used to determine the remoteness of damage. In many cases when the defendant does not have notice of the dangerous conditions created by a third party it may be said that there is no negligence at all. In the famous Nitroglycerine Case, 82 U.S. 524 (1872), an unmarked package containing nitroglycerine was delivered to defendant's place of business, located

in its landlord's building. When the defendant's servants tried to open the package, it exploded, killing them and damaging the building. The Supreme Court noted that different outcomes were required for the servants' wrongful death action and the landlord's property damage claim. For property damage the landlord could recover without proof of negligence, basing its case on a covenant in its lease with the defendant. For the death actions the lease was, however, inapplicable, and the cause of action failed for want of proof of negligence, given that the parcel gave no notice of its dangerous contents. For the suggestion that *Palsgraf* should be understood on those "notice" grounds only, see the opinion of Judge Friendly in Petition of Kinsman, 338 F.2d 708 (2d Cir. 1964), from which excerpts are reprinted at page 541, note 5 infra. For an extended discussion of the duty of care in connection with affirmative duties see Chapter 7.

3. Harm within the risk. One of the many ways to look at *Palsgraf* switches attention from the duty owed to the plaintiff to the nature of the risk by asking whether the harm suffered by the plaintiff fell within the class of risks against which the defendant had a duty to guard. See L. Green, Rationale of Proximate Cause 40-41 (1927). This approach has given rise to several notable examples. In the first, put by Professor Seavey, the defendant leaves a ten-pound can of nitroglycerin on a table from which it is knocked off by a child; it hurts the child's foot but, miraculously, does not explode. If defendant had left a can of water of similar size on the table, he could not be held negligent: since the risk that materialized was unrelated to the explosive power of the nitroglycerin, the plaintiff could not recover. See Seavey, Mr. Justice Cardozo and the Law of Torts, 39 Colum. L. Rev. 20; 52 Harv. L. Rev. 372; 48 Yale L.J. 390 (1939); compare Restatement of Torts §281, illus. 2.

The second case, put by Professor Keeton, is central to his important work Legal Cause in the Law of Torts (1963). The defendant "negligently" places unlabeled rat poison on a shelf full of food. The shelf happens to be near a stove that gives off heat, and the heat causes the poison to explode, injuring the plaintiff. Keeton argues that this plaintiff should be denied recovery. How does the foresight theory allow him to reach that result? Is it proper to say that the negligent *aspect* of the defendant's conduct is the cause of the plaintiff's harm in either of these cases? See Larrimore v. American National Ins. Co., 184 Okla. 614, 89 P.2d 340 (1939). Williams, The Risk Principle, 77 Law Q. Rev. 179, 185-190 (1961).

4. The "substantial factor" test. For all Cardozo's eloquence, some of the most memorable phrases in *Palsgraf* come from Andrews's dissenting opinion. In particular, his question, whether the defendant's conduct was a "substantial factor" in producing the harm, was adopted as the test of legal, or proximate, cause under the Restatement (Second) of Torts.

§431. WHAT CONSTITUTES LEGAL CAUSE

The actor's negligent conduct is a legal cause of harm to another if

    (a) his conduct is a substantial factor in bringing about the harm, and

    (b) there is no rule of law relieving the actor from liability because of the manner in which his negligence has resulted in the harm.

Comment:

a. Distinction between substantial cause and cause in the philosophical sense. In order to be a legal cause of another's harm, it is not enough that the harm would have occurred had the actor not be negligent. Except as stated in §432 (2) [dealing with joint causation], this is necessary, but it is not itself sufficient. The negligence must also be a substantial factor in bringing about the plaintiff's harm. The word "substantial" is used to denote the fact that the defendant's conduct has such an effect in producing the harm as to lead reasonable men to regard it as a cause, using that word in the popular sense, in which there always lurks the idea of responsibility, rather than in the so-called "philosophic sense," which includes everyone of the great number of events without which any happening would not have occurred. Each of these events is a cause in the so-called "philosophical sense," yet the effect of many of them is so insignificant that no ordinary mind would think of them as causes.

5. *Jury instructions on proximate causation.* One recurrent question in the law of proximate cause is how to instruct juries on the substantial factor test championed by the Restatement (Second). That issue came to a head in Mitchell v. Gonzales, 819 P.2d 872, 877-878 (Cal. 1991). There 12-year-old Damechie Mitchell drowned while vacationing with the defendants and their 14-year-old son Luis. Damechie did not know how to swim, but with the Gonzales's permission went out on a raft with Luis and his sister Yoshi. Damechie drowned when the boys engaged in horseplay on the raft while Luis's father slept on the beach. The decedent's parents charged Luis with negligence for his conduct on the raft, and his parents with negligent supervision. The jury found that the defendants were negligent, but that their negligence was not the proximate cause of the death. At trial the judge gave the defendants' requested instruction (BAJI 3.75), a "but for" test of cause in fact which provides: "A proximate cause of injury is a cause which in natural and continuous sequence produces the injury, and without which the injury would not have occurred." The test gets its name from the "without which" clause, and also adopts the precise language of the *Andrews* dissent. The rival "substantial factor" instruction (BAJI No. 3.76) requested by the plaintiff reads: "A legal cause of injury is a cause which is a substantial factor in bringing about injury."

By a divided vote, the court held that the but for instruction was always prejudicial to the plaintiffs. The court first noted its dislike for the term "proximate cause," which it regarded with Prosser as little more than an unfortunate "legacy of Sir Francis Bacon." It then commented on the proximate cause definition as follows:

The misunderstanding engendered by the term "proximate cause" has been documented. In a scholarly study of 14 jury instructions, BAJI No. 3.75 produced proportionally the most misunderstanding among laypersons. (Charrow, Making Legal Language Understandable: A Psycholinguistic Study of Jury Instructions (1979) 79 Colum. L. Rev. 1306, 1353.) The study noted two significant problems with BAJI No. 3.75. First, because the phrase "natural and continuous sequence" precedes "the verb it is intended to modify, the construction leaves the listener with the impression that the cause itself is in a natural and continuous sequence. Inasmuch as a single 'cause' cannot be in a continuous sequence, the listener is befuddled." Second, in one experiment, "the term 'proximate cause' was misunderstood by 23% of the subjects. . . . They interpreted it as 'approximate cause,' 'estimated cause,' or some fabrication." . . .

In contrast, the "substantial factor" test, incorporated in BAJI No. 3.76 and developed by the Restatement Second of Torts, section 431 has been comparatively free of criticism and has even received praise. "As an instruction submitting the question of causation in fact to the jury in intelligible form, it appears impossible to improve on the Restatement's 'substantial factor [test.]' " (Prosser, Proximate Cause in California, 38 Cal. L. Rev. 369, 421.) It is "sufficiently intelligible to any layman to furnish an adequate guide to the jury, and it is neither possible nor desirable to reduce it to lower terms." (Id., at p. 379.)

Moreover, the "substantial factor" test subsumes the "but for" test. "If the conduct which is claimed to have caused the injury had nothing at all to do with the injuries, it could not be said that the conduct was a factor, let alone a substantial factor, in the production of the injuries." [Prosser, supra]

Not only does the substantial factor instruction assist in the resolution of the problem of independent causes, as noted above, but "[i]t aids in the disposition . . . of two other types of situations which have proved troublesome. One is that where a similar, but not identical result would have followed without the defendant's act; the other where one defendant has made a clearly proved but quite insignificant contribution to the result, as where he throws a lighted match into a forest fire. But in the great majority of cases, *it produces the same legal conclusion as the but-for test.* Except in the classes of cases indicated, no case has been found where the defendant's act could be called a substantial factor when the event would have occurred without it; nor will cases very often arise where it would not be such a factor when it was so indispensable a cause that without it the result would not have followed." (Prosser & Keeton on Torts, supra, §41, at pp. 267-268, italics added.) Thus, "[t]he substantial factor language in BAJI No. 3.76 makes it the preferable instruction over BAJI No. 3.75."

The court then concluded that the No. 3.75 instruction was prejudicial error in the case before it because its misunderstanding of proximate cause "overemphasized the condition temporally closest to the death," Damechie's inability to swim, and downplayed the extent to which the negligent supervision of Mr. and Mrs. Gonzales contributed to the loss. Kennard, J., dissented on the ground that the court should not displace an instruction that had been in standard use for around 50 years without developing a "better instruction" capable of providing

"meaningful guidance" on the proximate cause issue. In his view, "proximate cause includes two elements: an element of physical or logical
causation, known as cause in fact, and a more normative or evaluative
element, which the term 'proximate' imperfectly conveys." In his view,
No. 3.76 does not supply "meaningful guidance" on that critical normative question. Which set of instructions would be appropriate in
Palsgraf? The following case?

Marshall v. Nugent
222 F.2d 604 (1st Cir. 1955)

[Much abbreviated, the substantial facts of the case are as follows: A
truck owned by the defendant oil company cut the corner as it headed
north around a sharp curve on an icy New Hampshire highway, forcing
off the road a southbound car driven by the plaintiff's son-in-law, Harriman. Prince, the driver of the truck, offered to help pull Harriman's
car back onto the highway and suggested that the plaintiff go around
the curve to the south in order to warn oncoming cars of the unexpected danger. As the plaintiff was getting into position on the west side
of the highway, the defendant, Nugent, who was driving northbound,
suddenly saw his way blocked by the oil truck on one side of the road
and Prince and Harriman on the other. In an effort to avoid a collision
with them, he pulled the car over to the left, where it went into a skid,
hit a plank guard fence on the western side of the highway, and glanced
off it into the plaintiff, severely hurting him.

The jury returned a verdict for Nugent (sound?) and another for
Marshall against the oil company. The second contention of the oil
company on appeal was that the wrongful conduct of its driver was not
the proximate cause of the plaintiff's injury.]

MAGRUDER, C.J. . . . Coming then to contention (2) above mentioned, this has to do with the doctrine of proximate causation, a doctrine which appellant's arguments tend to make out to be more
complex and esoteric than it really is. To say that the situation created
by the defendant's culpable acts constituted "merely a condition," not
a cause of plaintiff's harm, is to indulge in mere verbiage, which does
not solve the question at issue, but is simply a way of stating the conclusions, arrived at from other considerations, that the casual relation between the defendant's act and the plaintiff's injury is not strong
enough to warrant holding the defendant legally responsible for the
injury.

The adjective "proximate," as commonly used in this connection, is
perhaps misleading, since to establish liability it is not necessarily true
that the defendant's culpable act must be shown to have been the next
or immediate cause of the plaintiff's injury. In many familiar instances,

the defendant's act may be more remote in the chain of events and the plaintiff's injury may more immediately have been caused by an intervening force of nature, or an intervening act of a third person whether culpable or not, or even an act by the plaintiff bringing himself in contact with the dangerous situation resulting from the defendant's negligence. Therefore, perhaps, the phrase "legal cause," as used in Am. L. Inst., Rest. of Torts §431, is preferable to "proximate cause"; but the courts continue generally to use "proximate cause," and it is pretty well understood what is meant.

Back of the requirement that the defendant's culpable act must have been a proximate cause of the plaintiff's harm is no doubt the widespread conviction that it would be disproportionately burdensome to hold a culpable actor potentially liable for all the injurious consequences that may flow from his act, i.e., that would not have been inflicted "but for" the occurrence of the act. This is especially so where the injurious consequence was the result of negligence merely. And so, speaking in general terms, the effort of the courts has been, in the development of this doctrine of proximate causation, to confine the liability of a negligent actor to those harmful consequences which result from the operation of the risk, or of a risk, the foreseeability of which rendered the defendant's conduct negligent.

Of course, putting the inquiry in these terms does not furnish a formula which automatically decides each of an infinite variety of cases. Flexibility is still preserved by the further need of defining the risk, or risks, either narrowly, or more broadly, as seems appropriate and just in the special type of case.

Regarding motor vehicle accidents in particular, one should contemplate a variety of risks which are created by negligent driving. There may be injuries resulting from a direct collision between the carelessly driven car and another vehicle. But such direct collision may be avoided, yet the plaintiff may fall and injure himself in frantically racing out of the way of the errant car. Or the plaintiff may be knocked down and injured by a human stampede as the car rushes toward a crowded safety zone. Or the plaintiff may faint from intense excitement stimulated by the near collision, and in falling sustain a fractured skull. Or the plaintiff may suffer a miscarriage or other physical illness as a result of intense nervous shock incident to a hair-raising escape. This bundle of risks could be enlarged indefinitely with a little imagination. In a traffic mix-up due to negligence, before the disturbed waters have become placid and normal again, the unfolding of events between the culpable act and the plaintiff's eventual injury may be bizarre indeed; yet the defendant may be liable for the result. In such a situation, it would be impossible for a person in the defendant's position to predict in advance just how his negligent act would work out to another's injury. Yet this in itself is no bar to recovery.

When an issue of proximate cause arises in a borderline case, as not infrequently happens, we leave it to the jury with appropriate instructions. We do this because it is deemed wise to obtain the judgment of the jury, reflecting as it does the earthy viewpoint of the common man — the prevalent sense of the community — as to whether the causal relation between the negligent act and the plaintiff's harm which in fact was a consequence of the tortious act is sufficiently close to make it just and expedient to hold the defendant answerable in damages. That is what the courts have in mind when they say the question of proximate causation is one of fact for the jury. . . .

Exercising [our] judgment on the facts in the case at bar, we have to conclude that the district court committed no error in refusing to direct a verdict for the defendant Socony on the issue of proximate cause. . . .

Plaintiff Marshall was a passenger in the oncoming Chevrolet car, and thus was one of the persons whose bodily safety was primarily endangered by the negligence of Prince, as might have been found by the jury, in "cutting the corner" with the Socony truck in the circumstances above related. In that view, Prince's negligence constituted an irretrievable breach of duty to the plaintiff. Though this particular act of negligence was over and done with when the truck pulled up alongside of the stalled Chevrolet without having actually collided with it, still the consequences of such past negligence were in the bosom of time, as yet unrevealed.

If the Chevrolet had been pulled back onto the highway, and Harriman and Marshall, having got in it again, had resumed their journey and had had a collision with another car five miles down the road, in which Marshall suffered bodily injuries, it could truly be said that such subsequent injury to Marshall was a consequence in fact of the earlier delay caused by the defendant's negligence, in the sense that but for such delay the Chevrolet car would not have been at the fatal intersection at the moment the other car ran into it. But on such assumed state of facts, the courts would no doubt conclude, "as a matter of law," that Prince's earlier negligence in cutting the corner was not the "proximate cause" of this later injury received by the plaintiff. That would be because the extra risks to which such negligence by Prince had subjected the passengers in the Chevrolet car were obviously entirely over; the situation had been stabilized and become normal, and, so far as one could foresee, whatever subsequent risks the Chevrolet might have to encounter in its resumed journey were simply the inseparable risks, no more and no less, that were incident to the Chevrolet's being out on the highway at all. But in the case at bar, the circumstances under which Marshall received the personal injuries complained of presented no such clear-cut situation.

As we have indicated, the extra risks created by Prince's negligence were not all over at the moment the primary risk of collision between the truck and the Chevrolet was successfully surmounted. Many cases have held a defendant, whose negligence caused a traffic tie-up, legally liable for subsequent property damage or personal injuries more immediately caused by an oncoming motorist. This would particularly be so where, as in the present case, the negligent traffic tie-up and delay occurred in a dangerous blind spot, and where the occupants of the stalled Chevrolet, having got out onto the highway to assist in the operation of getting the Chevrolet going again, were necessarily subject to risks of injury from cars in the stream of northbound traffic coming over the crest of the hill. It is true, the Chevrolet car was not owned by the plaintiff Marshall, and no doubt, without violating any legal duty to Harriman, Marshall could have crawled up onto the snowbank at the side of the road out of harm's way and awaited there, passive and inert, until his journey was resumed. But the plaintiff, who as a passenger in this Chevrolet car had already been subjected to a collision risk by the negligent operation of the Socony truck, could reasonably be expected to get out onto the highway and lend a hand to his host in getting the Chevrolet started again, especially as Marshall himself had an interest in facilitating the resumption of the journey in order to keep his business appointment in North Stratford. Marshall was therefore certainly not an "officious intermeddler," and whether or not he was barred by contributory negligence in what he did was a question for the jury, as we have already held. The injury Marshall received by being struck by the Nugent car was not remote, either in time or place, from the negligent conduct of defendant Socony's servant, and it occurred while the traffic mix-up occasioned by defendant's negligence was still persisting, not after the traffic flow had become normal again. In the circumstances presented we conclude that the district court committed no error in leaving the issue of proximate cause to the jury for determination.

NOTE

Bizarre causal chains. Marshall v. Nugent is only one of many cases where courts have had to trace through bizarre causal chains from the defendant's act to the plaintiff's harm in order to establish liability. In Brown v. Travelers Indemnity Co., 28 N.W.2d 306 (Wis. 1947), the defendant, plaintiff's husband, negligently struck a cow on the highway, knocking it into a ditch and dazing it. Plaintiff, who was in the car, got out and went to a nearby farmhouse to report the incident. When she returned shortly thereafter, the cow, somewhat recovered but apparently still dazed, started out of the ditch and away from the scene of the accident, knocking down the plaintiff and hurting her severely. The

court, two justices dissenting, affirmed a judgment for the plaintiff, noting that "the mere fact that the injured cow unexpectedly regained
consciousness and in an attempt to escape from the place injured the
plaintiff is not a superseding cause of the harm which resulted from
the collision."

See also In re Guardian Casualty Co., 2 N.Y.S.2d 232, 234 (N.Y. App.
Div. 1938). There a taxicab, operated by Monarch Transportation Co.,
and insured by Consolidated Indemnity and Insurance Co., collided
with the car of one Haas, insured by Guardian Casualty Co., under
circumstances indicating mutual negligence. The cab was thrust across
the sidewalk, hit a stone building, and actually embedded itself into the
stonework. The decedent, who ran a laundry in the building, stood
watching as the cab was being removed half an hour later, and was
killed when struck by a stone that fell when the taxicab, without negligence, was being removed. In a suit against the insolvent insurers, the
court held that the death of the decedent was not too remote a consequence of the initial negligence of the two defendant drivers.

> The present defendants, whose wrongful acts caused a vehicle to be
> projected across a sidewalk and against a building, with such force as to
> loosen parts of the structure, must have foreseen the necessity of removal
> of the vehicle from the sidewalk. They might reasonably have anticipated
> that parts of the structure which were dislodged by the blow would fall
> into the highway. That a passing pedestrian might be injured when such
> an event took place in a city street, was also foreseeable. It would seem
> plain that although the injury to the pedestrian did not occur for some
> minutes after the application of the original force, because of the circum-
> stances that the dislodged stones were temporarily held in place by the
> vehicle, this would not alter the case, when there is nothing to show the
> application of a new force causing the stone to fall.

Overseas Tankship (U.K.) Ltd. v. Morts Dock & Engineering Co., Ltd. (The Wagon Mound (No. 1))
[1961] A.C. 388 (P.C. Aust.)

[The appellants, defendants in the original cause of action, had carelessly discharged oil from their ship while it was berthed in Sydney harbor. After their ship set sail, the oil was carried by the wind and tide to
the respondent's wharf, which was used for repair work on other ships
in the harbor. Plaintiff's supervisor was concerned about the spread of
the oil and he ordered his workmen to do no welding or burning in
the area until further orders. He then made some inquiries, which,
coupled with his own knowledge, satisfied him that the oil was not
flammable. He accordingly instructed his men to resume their welding
operations, and directed them as well to take care that no flammable
material should fall off the wharf into the oil.

About two and one-half days later, the respondent's wharf was destroyed when the oil caught fire. "The outbreak of fire was due, as the trial judge found, to the fact that there was floating in the oil underneath the wharf a piece of debris on which lay some smouldering cotton waste or rag which had been set on fire by molten metal falling from the wharf: that the cotton waste or rag burst into flames: that the flames from the cotton waste set the floating oil afire either directly or by first setting fire to a wooden pile coated with oil, and that after the floating oil became ignited; the flames spread rapidly over the surface of the oil and quickly developed into a conflagration which severely damaged the wharf." "The trial judge also made the all-important finding, which must be set out in his own words: 'The *raison d'etre* of furnace oil is, of course, that it shall burn, but I find the defendant did not know and could not reasonably be expected to have known that it was capable of being set afire when spread on water.' " The trial judge also found that the oil had caused, apart from the conflagration, some slight damage when it mucked up the respondent's wharf.]

VISCOUNT SIMONDS . . . There can be no doubt that the decision of the Court of Appeal in *Polemis* plainly asserts that, if the defendant is guilty of negligence, he is responsible for all the consequences whether reasonably foreseeable or not. The generality of the proposition is perhaps qualified by the fact that each of the Lords Justices refers to the outbreak of fire as the direct result of the negligent act. There is thus introduced the conception that the negligent actor is not responsible for consequences which are not "direct," whatever that may mean. It has to be asked, then, why this conclusion should have been reached. The answer appears to be that it was reached upon a consideration of certain authorities, comparatively few in number, that were cited to the court. Of these, three are generally regarded as having influenced the decision. The earliest in point of date was Smith v. London & South Western Railway Co. ((1870) L.R. 6 C.P. 14). In that case it was said that "when it has been once determined that there is evidence of negligence, the person guilty of it is equally liable for its consequences, whether he could have foreseen them or not" (see per Channell, B., ibid., 21). Similar observations were made by other members of the court. Three things may be noted about this case: the first, that for the sweeping proposition laid down no authority was cited: the second, that the point to which the court directed its mind was not unforeseeable damage of a different kind from that which was foreseen, but more extensive damage of the same kind: and the third, that so little was the mind of the court directed to the problem which has now to be solved that no one of the seven judges who took part in the decision thought it necessary to qualify in any way the consequences for which the defendant was to be held responsible. It would perhaps not be improper to say that the law of negligence as an independent tort was then of recent growth and that its implications had not been fully examined.

[The Privy Council then considered the H.M.S. London [1914] P. 72 and Weld Blundell v. Stephens [1970] A.C. 956, and concluded with a famous passage from the latter case by Lord Sumner:] "What a defendant ought to have anticipated as a reasonable man is material when the question is whether or not he was guilty of negligence, that is, of want of due care according to the circumstances. This, however, goes to culpability, not to compensation."

[After discussion of some other English precedents, the opinion continues:] The impression that may well be left on the reader of the scores of cases in which liability for negligence has been discussed is that the courts were feeling their way to a coherent body of doctrine and were at times in grave danger of being led astray by scholastic theories of causation and their ugly and barely intelligible jargon. . . .

Enough has been said to show that the authority of *Polemis* has been severely shaken though lip service has from time to time been paid to it. In their Lordships' opinion it should no longer be regarded as good law. It is not probable that many cases will for that reason have a different result, though it is hoped that the law will be thereby simplified, and that in some cases, at least, palpable injustice will be avoided. For it does not seem consonant with current ideas of justice or morality that for an act of negligence, however slight or venial, which results in some trivial foreseeable damage the actor should be liable for all consequences however unforeseeable and however grave, so long as they can be said to be "direct." It is a principle of civil liability, subject only to qualifications which have no present relevance, that a man must be considered to be responsible for the probable consequences of his act. To demand more of him is too harsh a rule, to demand less is to ignore that civilized order requires the observance of a minimum standard of behaviour.

This concept applied to the slowly developing law of negligence has led to a great variety of expressions which can, as it appears to their Lordships, be harmonized with little difficulty with the single exception of the so-called rule in *Polemis*. For, if it is asked why a man should be responsible for the natural or necessary or probable consequences of his act (or any other similar description of them) the answer is that it is not because they are natural or necessary or probable, but because, since they have this quality, it is judged by the standard of the reasonable man that he ought to have foreseen them. Thus it is that over and over again it has happened that in different judgments in the same case, and sometimes in a single judgment, liability for a consequence has been imposed on the ground that it was reasonably foreseeable or, alternatively, on the ground that it was natural or necessary or probable. The two grounds have been treated as coterminous, and so they largely are. But, where they are not, the question arises to which the wrong answer was given in *Polemis*. For, if some limitation must be imposed upon the consequences for which the negligent actor is to be held responsible — and all are agreed that some limitation there must be — why should that test (reasonable foreseeability) be rejected which, since he is judged by what the reasonable man ought to foresee, corresponds with the common conscience of mankind, and a test (the "direct" consequence) be substituted which leads to nowhere but the never-ending and insoluble problems of causation. "The lawyer," said Sir Frederick Pollock, "cannot afford to adventure himself with philosophers in the logical and metaphysical controversies that beset the idea of cause." Yet this is just what he has most unfortunately done and must continue to do if the rule in *Polemis* is to prevail. A conspicuous example occurs when the actor seeks to escape liability on the ground that the "chain of causation" is broken by a nova causa or novus actus interveniens. . . .

In the same connection may be mentioned the conclusion to which the Full Court finally came in the present case. Applying the rule in *Polemis* and holding therefore that the unforeseeability of the damage by fire afforded no defence, they went on to consider the remaining question. Was it a "direct" consequence? Upon this Manning, J., said: "Notwithstanding that, if regard is had separately to each individual occurrence in the chain of events that led to this fire, each occurrence was improbable and, in one sense, improbability was heaped upon improbability, I cannot escape from the conclusion that if the ordinary man in the street had been asked, as a matter of common sense, without any detailed analysis of the circumstances, to state the cause of the fire at Morts Dock, he would unhesitatingly have assigned such cause to spillage of oil by the appellant's employees." Perhaps he would, and probably he would have added: "I never should have thought it possible." But with great respect to the Full Court this is surely irrelevant, or, if it is relevant, only serves to show that the *Polemis* rule works in a very strange way. After the event even a fool is wise. But it is not the hindsight of a fool; it is the foresight of the reasonable man which alone can determine responsibility. The *Polemis* rule by substituting "direct" for "reasonably foreseeable" consequence leads to a conclusion equally illogical and unjust.

At an early stage in this judgment their Lordships intimated that they would deal with the proposition which can best be stated by reference to the well-known dictum of Lord Sumner: "This however goes to culpability not to compensation." It is with the greatest respect to that very learned judge and to those who have echoed his words, that their Lordships find themselves bound to state their view that this proposition is fundamentally false.

It is, no doubt, proper when considering tortious liability for negligence to analyse its elements and to say that the plaintiff must prove a duty owed to him by the defendant, a breach of that duty by the defendant, and consequent damage. But there can be no liability until the damage has been done. It is not the act but the consequences on which tortious liability is founded. Just as (as it has been said) there is no such thing as negligence in the air, so there is no such thing as liability in the air. Suppose an action brought by A. for damage caused by the carelessness (a neutral word) of B., for example, a fire caused by the careless spillage of oil. It may, of course, become relevant to know what duty B. owed to A., but the only liability that is in question is the liability for damage by fire. It is vain to isolate the liability from its context and to say that B. is or is not liable, and then to ask for what damage he is liable. For his liability is in respect of that damage and no other. If, as admittedly it is, B.'s liability (culpability) depends on the reasonable foreseeability of the consequent damage, how is that to be determined except by the foreseeability of the damage which in fact happened — the damage in suit? And if that damage is unforeseeable so as to displace liability at large, how can the liability be restored so as to make compensation payable?

But, it is said, a different position arises if B.'s careless act has been shown to be negligent and has caused some foreseeable damage to A. Their Lordships have already observed that to hold B. liable for consequences however unforeseeable of a careless act, if, but only if, he is at the same time liable for some other damage however trivial, appears to be neither logical nor just. This becomes more clear if it is supposed that similar unforeseeable damage is suffered by A. and C. but other foreseeable damage, for which B. is liable, by A. only. A system of law which would hold B. liable to A. but not to C. for the similar damage suffered by each of them could not easily be defended. Fortunately, the attempt is not necessary. For the same fallacy is at the root of the proposition. It is irrelevant to the question whether B. is liable for unforeseeable damage or that he is liable for foreseeable damage, as irrelevant as would the fact that he had trespassed on Whiteacre be to the question whether he has trespassed on Blackacre. Again, suppose a claim by A. for damage by fire by the careless act of B. Of what relevance is it to that claim that he has another claim arising out of the same careless act? It would surely not prejudice his claim if that other claim failed: it cannot assist it if it succeeds. Each of them rests on its own bottom, and will fail if it can be established that the damage could not reasonably be foreseen. We have come back to the plain common sense stated by Lord Russell of Killowen in Bourhill v. Young ([1943] A.C. 92, 101). As Denning, L.J., said in King v. Phillips ((1953) 1 Q.B. 429, 441): "There can be no doubt since Bourhill v. Young that the test of *liability for shock* is foreseeability of *injury by shock*." Their Lordships substitute the word "fire" for "shock" and endorse this statement of the law. . . .

[Appeal allowed.]

NOTES

1. The passing of causation. One of the major arguments for the foresight test is that it allows the courts to dispense with the technical and nearly insoluble conundrums of causation. Even if the argument is sound (is it?), the foresight test raises unique problems of its own. Chief among them is how the events that led to the plaintiff's harm ought to be described and evaluated. Professor Morris discusses this point in his Torts 174-177 (1953):

> Once misconduct causes damage, a specific accident has happened in a particular way and has resulted in a discrete harm. When, after the event, the question is asked, "Was the particular accident and the resulting damages foreseeable?", the cases fall into the three classes:
>
> (1) In some cases damages resulting from misconduct are so typical that judge and jurors cannot possibly be convinced that they were unforeseeable. If Mr. Builder negligently drops a brick on Mr. Pedestrian who is passing an urban site of a house under construction, even though the dent in Pedestrian's skull is microscopically unique in pattern, Builder could not sensibly maintain that the injury was unforeseeable.
>
> (2) In some cases freakishness of the facts refuses to be downed and any description that minimizes it is viewed as misdescription. For example, in a recent Louisiana case [Lynch v. Fisher, 41 So. 2d 692 (La. App. 1949)] a trucker negligently left his truck on the highway at night without setting out flares. A car crashed into the truck and caught fire. A passerby came to the rescue of the car occupants — a man and wife. After the rescuer got them out of the car he returned to the car to get a floor mat to pillow the injured wife's head. A pistol lay on the mat rescuer wanted to use. He picked it up and handed it to the husband. The accident had unbeknownst to the rescuer, temporarily deranged the husband, and he shot rescuer in the leg. Such a consequence of negligently failing to guard a truck with flares is so unarguably unforeseeable that no judge or juror would be likely to hold otherwise. (Incidentally the Louisiana court held the trucker liable to the rescuer on the ground that foreseeability is not a requisite of liability.)
>
> (3) Between these extremes are cases in which consequences are neither typical nor wildly freakish. In these cases unusual details are arguably — but only arguably significant. If they are held significant, then the consequences are unforeseeable; if they are held unimportant then the consequences are foreseeable.

Into which class does *Polemis* fall? The *Wagon Mound?* Need the defendant only foresee "in a general way" the consequences of his act, and not the "precise details of its occurrence"?

2. A foreseeable kind of damage. The application of the foresight test has troubled English courts since *Wagon Mound* (*No. 1*) in yet another context: how does one determine whether the harm suffered by plaintiff was foreseeable? Consider Doughty v. Turner Manufacturing Co., Ltd., [1964] 1 Q.B. 518, where the Court of Appeal sought to apply the rule of *Wagon Mound* (*No. 1*). There one of defendant's employees knocked an asbestos cement cover into a vat of extremely hot solution of sodium cyanide — eight times as hot as boiling water. This was negligent, since the falling cover might have splashed some of the molten substance on someone standing nearby. Actually nobody was hurt by the splash; but after a short time the asbestos cement cover caused an explosion in the vat that hurled the molten substance into the air, some of it hurting the plaintiff, who stood fairly nearby. There was absolutely no reason for anyone to suspect that this cover, when immersed, would explode. Because there had been some negligence, the trial court allowed recovery; but the court of appeal reversed because the damage was the consequence of a risk or hazard with respect to which defendant had not been negligent. Does *Doughty* present any problems of causal intervention?

Contrast Hughes v. Lord Advocate, [1963] A.C. 837. There defendant's servants were working on an underground cable to which they had access through an open manhole nine feet deep. The manhole was covered by a shelter-tent. When defendant's servants left the work area, they lighted four paraffin warning lamps, left a ladder near the manhole, and pulled a tarpaulin over the entrance to the tent. Plaintiff, aged eight, and his uncle, aged ten, came by and started to play with the equipment with a view toward descending into the manhole. Plaintiff tripped over one of the paraffin lamps, which then fell into the hole. An explosion ensued when, as best could be determined, "paraffin escaped from the tank, formed vapour and was ignited by the flame." The respondents argued that the explosion was unforeseeable, even if some harm from burning by the lamp was foreseeable, but the House of Lords rejected the argument, holding that the damage was not of a different type from that which was foreseeable, given that paraffin lamps were a "known source of danger." Is the distinction between burning and explosion "too fine to warrant acceptance"? If that is so, why is the distinction between splashing and exploding acceptable? Does *Hughes* present the troublesome questions of causal intervention referred to in *Wagon Mound* (*No. 1*)? In this connection note that defendant, on appeal, did not press the argument that plaintiff's trespass barred his recovery.

3. Foresight v. directness. The debate over the proper standard for remoteness of damage is carried on in these opinions at a very abstract level, so it is often difficult to determine exactly what is at stake in the two positions. Indeed, an instructive way to approach the discussion of proximate cause is to ask whether *Wagon Mound* (*No. 1*) can be reconciled with *In re Polemis* even under the "direct consequences" test. To do so, it is important to examine the precise sequence of events between defendant's wrongful conduct and plaintiff's harm. In *Polemis* no human act intervened between the dropping of the plank and the burning of the ship; the only causal complication was the presence of fumes in the hold of the ship. In *Wagon Mound (No. 1)*, however, the causal chain contained at least two human acts between the spillage of the oil from defendant's ship and the destruction of plaintiff's wharf: first, the consultations by plaintiff's dock supervisor, and second, the ignition of the fire by the oxyacetylene torches used by plaintiff's servants. If the conduct of plaintiff's servants supports some affirmative defense, either of assumption of risk or contributory negligence, then it is possible both to keep the directness test of *Polemis* and to defend the result in *Wagon Mound*. Note too that if either of these defenses is feasible, the plaintiff must proceed gingerly on the foresight question, for if defendant's servants could have foreseen the harm, then so too could the plaintiff's.

The importance of plaintiff's conduct is illustrated by the subsequent decision of the Privy Counsel in Overseas Tankship (U.K.) Ltd. v. The Miller Steamship Co., [1967] 1 A.C. 617, 642-643, better known as *Wagon Mound (No. 2)*. The facts in that case were the same as in *Wagon Mound (No. 1)* except that the plaintiff in *Wagon Mound (No. 2)* was the owner of a ship that was destroyed in the same fire involved in *Wagon Mound (No. 1)*. Plaintiff shipowner was not, of course, bound by the prior decision; nor was it troubled by possible charges of contributory negligence or assumption of risk. As against the plaintiff, the conduct of the servants of Morts Dock (plaintiff in *Wagon Mound (No. 1)*) was of possible importance only on the issue of causation, where in the modern view it could not, as intervening negligence, be decisive. See supra at page 503. Plaintiff therefore introduced evidence to show that some risk of harm by fire was reasonably foreseeable to defendant's engineer. Lord Reid, speaking for the Privy Council, distinguished *Wagon Mound (No. 1)* and affirmed a judgment for plaintiff. He then discussed Bolton v. Stone, at page 150 supra, concluding:

> The House of Lords held that the risk was so small that in the circumstances a reasonable man would have been justified in disregarding it and taking no steps to eliminate it.
> But it does not follow that, no matter what the circumstances may be, it is justifiable to neglect a risk of such a small magnitude. A reasonable man would only neglect such a risk if he had some valid reason for doing so, e.g., that it would involve considerable expense to eliminate the risk. He would weigh the risk against the difficulty of eliminating it. If the activity which caused the injury to Miss Stone had been an unlawful activity, there can be little doubt but that Bolton v. Stone would have been decided differently. In their Lordships' judgment Bolton v. Stone did not alter the general principle that a person must be regarded as negligent if he does not take steps to eliminate a risk which he knows or ought to know is a real risk and not a mere possibility which would never influence

the mind of a reasonable man. What that decision did was to recognise and give effect to the qualification that it is justifiable not to take steps to eliminate a real risk if it is small and if the circumstances are such that a reasonable man, careful of the safety of his neighbour, would think it right to neglect it.

In the present case there was no justification whatever for discharging the oil into Sydney Harbour. Not only was it an offence to do so, but it involved considerable loss financially. If the ship's engineer had thought about the matter, there could have been no question of balancing the advantages and disadvantages. From every point of view it was both his duty and his interest to stop the discharge immediately.

Lord Reid then concluded: "The findings show that he [the ship's engineer] ought to have known that it is possible to ignite this kind of oil on water, and that the ship's engineer probably ought to have known that this had in fact happened before. The most that can be said to justify inaction is that he would have known that this could only happen in very exceptional circumstances. But that does not mean that a reasonable man would dismiss such a risk from his mind and do nothing when it was so easy to prevent it." Does this amount to a repudiation of Bolton v. Stone? An adoption of the Hand formula for negligence? On the two *Wagon Mound* cases see 82 Law Q. Rev. 444 (1966).

4. *The thin skull rule, or "You take your victim as you find him."* One rule of tort law left unshaken by *Wagon Mound (No. 1)* provides that the defendant takes his victim as he finds him. In Smith v. Brain Leech & Co. Ltd., [1962] 2 Q.B. 405, plaintiff's deceased was burned on his lip by splashing molten metal because defendant negligently failed to provide an adequate guard. Because of prior exposures of another kind in the past, deceased had (according to the court) developed a tendency toward cancer. In any event, the burned lip did develop into cancer, from which he died. The court acknowledged that death by cancer was unforeseeable; but even after *Wagon Mound (No. 1)* the court allowed recovery, expressing certainty that the Privy Council had no intention of changing the "take plaintiff as he is" principle and equating this case with the classic instance of the thin-skulled person.

On the thin skull rule and its relationship to the problems of causal intervention see Seavey, Mr. Justice Cardozo and the Law of Torts, 39 Colum. L. Rev. 20, 32-33; 52 Harv. L. Rev. 372, 384-385; 48 Yale L.J. 390, 402-403 (1939):

> The second group of cases involves only the question of damages. It is assumed in these cases that the defendant is a tortfeasor with respect to the plaintiff and the question is as to the extent of the harm for which he is liable. The type case is that where one negligently strikes another causing him immediate serious harm, as a result of which he is taken to a hospital and subsequently suffers further harm or dies because of intervening negligence or extraneous events, such as the burning of the hospital. With reference to this type of situation, the problem may be as

to liability for the harm immediately ensuing upon the negligent act or for the harm which subsequently develops. As to the first, it accords with our general sense of justice that the tortfeasor should be liable irrespective of the unexpectedness of such harm. Thus where the defendant has negligently struck a person whose skull is so fragile that it is broken by the comparatively slight blow, all courts are agreed that the defendant is liable for the wholly unexpected breaking. This is true not only with reference to physical harm but also other forms of harm. If a person were negligently to incapacitate another who has a yearly earning capacity of a hundred thousand dollars, there is liability for the resulting loss though so great a loss could not have been anticipated. It may be that this is a possible explanation for the reaction of the King's Bench in its famous but doubtful decision of the Polemis case, in which the defendant whose workman negligently dropped a plank into the hold of a ship filled with gasoline vapor was made liable for the destruction of the ship resulting from the ensuing explosion. In this, as in other cases, the courts are agreed that the negligent person takes his victims as they are.

The causal complications of the thin skull rule are graphically illustrated by Steinhauser v. Hertz, 421 F.2d 1169, 1172 (2d Cir. 1970). There plaintiff, a 14-year-old child, was a passenger in her parents' car when it was tortiously struck by the driver of defendant's car. The car itself was badly damaged, but none of the passengers, including plaintiff, suffered any physical injuries. Shortly after the accident plaintiff began to behave in a strange manner; she became "highly agitated," "glassy-eyed," and "nervous." Her condition worsened; she was institutionally treated for schizophrenia and even after her release required further medical treatment, with reinstitutionalization a likely prospect. The question in this case was whether plaintiff could recover from defendant the costs associated with her psychological condition. In an effort to show that the collision was not responsible for plaintiff's psychological condition, defendant introduced evidence at trial about plaintiff's medical history, which included a mild concussion suffered two years before the road accident. Plaintiff's attorney argued that the accident was a "precipitating cause of a quiescent disease." The judge instructed the jury that recovery was permissible only if plaintiff were normal before the accident, but not if "this plaintiff had this disease all along." Proximate cause was in the words of the trial judge "a big word" for what ordinary people call cause. The jury, which asked the judge how it should decide the case if it regarded the accident as the "precipitating factor," was reread the previous instructions on causation. The jury returned a verdict for defendant; the decision was reversed on appeal, Friendly, J., writing as follows:

> It is plain enough that plaintiffs were deprived of a fair opportunity to have the jury consider the case on the basis of the medical evidence they had adduced. The testimony was that before the accident Cynthia was *neither* a "perfectly normal child" *nor* a schizophrenic, but a child with

some degree of pathology which was activated into schizophrenia by an emotional trauma although it otherwise might not have blossomed. Whatever the medical soundness of this theory may or may not be, and there does not seem in fact to have been any dispute about it, see Guttmacher and Weihofen, Psychiatry and the Law 43-55 (1952), plaintiffs were entitled to have it fairly weighed by the jury. They could not properly be pinioned on the dilemma of having either to admit that Cynthia was already suffering from active schizophrenia or to assert that she was wholly without psychotic tendencies. The jury's question showed how well they had perceived the true issue. When they were told in effect that plaintiffs could recover only if, contrary to ordinary experience, the accident alone produced the schizophrenia, the result was predestined.

5. American response to Polemis *and* Wagon Mound (No. 1). The difficult facts of Petition of Kinsman Transit Company, 338 F.2d 708, 723-725 (2d Cir. 1964), afforded Judge Friendly the opportunity to comment on the English debate over proximate cause. There a January thaw on the Buffalo River released large cakes of ice which, because of high water, banged into and loosened a negligently tied and improperly tended ship so that it started downstream, careening into another ship and knocking it loose. Both ships then drifted on and crashed into a drawbridge maintained by the City of Buffalo at a point before the river flows into Lake Erie. The two ships and the drawbridge made an effective dam against which floating ice accumulated, causing flooding for miles. This action was brought against the owner of the first ship and the city. The above events all occurred at night, when no traffic was expected on the river.

The crew tending the drawbridge was, or so the court held, under a statutory duty to raise the drawbridge not only for ships passing by in the course of navigation but also for drifting vessels. If the crew had displayed the required alertness by raising the bridge in time, all of the harm in issue could have been avoided. By a two-to-one vote the court held both defendants jointly responsible for plaintiff's damages, which were apportioned between them. Judge Friendly made these observations about *Wagon Mound (No. 1)*:

> The effect of unforeseeability of damage upon liability for negligence has recently been considered by the Judicial Committee of the Privy Council, Overseas Tankship (U.K.) Ltd. v. Morts Dock & Engineering Co. (The Wagon Mound). The Committee there disapproved the proposition, thought to be supported by Re Polemis and Furness, Withy & Co. Ltd., "that unforeseeability is irrelevant if damage is 'direct.' " We have no difficulty with the result of The Wagon Mound, in view of the finding that the appellant had no reason to believe that the floating furnace oil would burn, see also the extended discussion in Miller S.S. Co. v. Overseas Tankship (U.K.) Ltd., The Wagon Mound No. 2. On that view the decision simply applies the principle which excludes liability where the injury sprang from a hazard different from that which was improperly risked. Although some language in the judgment goes beyond this, we

would find it difficult to understand why one who had failed to use the care required to protect others in the light of expectable forces should be exonerated when the very risks that rendered his conduct negligent produced other and more serious consequences to such persons than were fairly foreseeable when he fell short of what the law demanded. Foreseeability of danger is necessary to render conduct negligent where as here the damage was caused by just those forces whose existence required the exercise of greater care than was taken — the current, the ice, and the physical mass of the Shiras, the incurring of consequences other and greater than foreseen does not make the conduct less culpable or provide a reasoned basis for insulation. See Hart and Honoré, Causation in the Law 234-248 (1959). The oft-encountered argument that failure to limit liability to foreseeable consequences may subject the defendant to a loss wholly out of proportion to his fault seems scarcely consistent with the universally accepted rule that the defendant takes the plaintiff as he finds him and will be responsible for the full extent of the injury even though a latent susceptibility of the plaintiff renders this far more serious than could reasonably have been anticipated. See Prosser, Torts 260.

The weight of authority in this country rejects the limitation of damages to consequences foreseeable at the time of the negligent conduct when the consequences are "direct," and the damage, although other and greater than expectable, is of the same general sort that was risked. . . . Other American courts, purporting to apply a test of foreseeability to damages, extend that concept to such unforeseen lengths as to raise serious doubt whether the concept is meaningful; indeed, we wonder whether the British courts are not finding it necessary to limit the language of The Wagon Mound as we have indicated.

We see no reason why an actor engaging in conduct which entails a large risk of small damage and a small risk of other and greater damage, of the same general sort, from the same forces, and to the same class of persons, should be relieved of responsibility for the latter simply because the chance of its occurrence, if viewed alone, may not have been large enough to require the exercise of care. By hypothesis, the risk of the lesser harm was sufficient to render his disregard of it actionable; the existence of a less likely additional risk that the very forces against whose action he was required to guard would produce other and greater damage than could have been reasonably anticipated should inculpate him further rather than limit his liability.

2.   Emotional Distress

Thus far the question of proximate causation has been addressed largely with physical injuries. But other forms of consequences can flow from wrongful acts as well, chiefly mental shock or emotional distress, for which claims are increasingly common today. As with physical injury claims one line of defense simply denies the connection between the distress and the defendant's conduct. But a second line of defense is that even if the harm in question is caused by defendant's conduct, that cause is not the proximate cause of the injury in question. Over the last century there has been an expansion of liability in emotional distress cases, but the area is still filled with extensive limitations on recovery which leaves the entire area filled with fine distinctions and artificial rules.

Mitchell v. Rochester Railway Co.
45 N.E. 354 (N.Y. 1896)

MARTIN, J. The facts in this case are few, and may be briefly stated. On the 1st day of April, 1891, the plaintiff was standing upon a cross walk on Main Street, in the city of Rochester, awaiting an opportunity to board one of the defendant's cars which had stopped upon the street at that place. While standing there, and just as she was about to step upon the car, a horse car of the defendant came down the street. As the team attached to the car drew near, it turned to the right, and came close to the plaintiff, so that she stood between the horses' heads when they were stopped. She testified that from fright and excitement caused by the approach and proximity of the team she became unconscious, and also that the result was a miscarriage, and consequent illness. Medical testimony was given to the effect that the mental shock which she then received was sufficient to produce that result. Assuming that the evidence tended to show that the defendant's servant was negligent in the management of the car and horses, and that the plaintiff was free from contributory negligence, the single question presented is whether the plaintiff is entitled to recover for the defendant's negligence which occasioned her fright and alarm, and resulted in the injuries already mentioned. While the authorities are not harmonious upon this question, we think the most reliable and better-considered cases, as well as public policy, fully justify us in holding that the plaintiff cannot recover for injuries occasioned by fright, as there is no immediate personal injury. If it be admitted that no recovery can be had for fright occasioned by the negligence of another, it is somewhat difficult to understand how a defendant would be liable for its consequences. Assuming that fright cannot form the basis of an action, it is obvious that no recovery can be had for injuries resulting therefrom. That the result may be nervous disease, blindness, insanity, or even a miscarriage, in no way changes the principle. These results merely show the degree of fright or the extent of the damages. The right of action must still depend upon the question whether a recovery may be had for fright. If it can, then an action may be maintained, however slight the injury. If not, then there can be no recovery, no matter how grave or serious the consequences. Therefore, the logical result of the respondent's concession would seem to be, not only that no recovery can be had for mere fright, but also that none can be had for injuries which are the direct consequences of it. If the right of recovery in this class of cases should be once established, it would naturally result in a flood of litigation in cases where the injury complained of may be easily feigned without detection, and where the damages must rest upon mere conjecture or speculation. The difficulty which often exists in cases of alleged physical injury, in determining whether they exist, and if so, whether they were caused by the negligent act of the defendant, would not only be greatly increased, but a wide field would be opened for fictitious or speculative claims. To establish such a doctrine would be contrary to principles of public policy.

Moreover, it cannot be properly said that the plaintiff's miscarriage was the proximate result of the defendant's negligence. Proximate damages are such as are the ordinary and natural results of the negligence charged, and those that are usual and may, therefore, be expected. It is quite obvious that the plaintiff's injuries do not fall within the rule as to proximate damages. The injuries to the plaintiff were plainly the result of an accidental or unusual combination of circumstances, which could not have been reasonably anticipated, and over which the defendant had no control, and, hence, her damages were too remote to justify a recovery in this action. These considerations lead to the conclusion that no recovery can be had for injuries sustained by fright occasioned by the negligence of another, where there is no immediate personal injury. [Reversed and dismissed.]

NOTES

1. Coping with the physical injury rule. The early opposition to allowing recovery for negligently inflicted emotional distress thus rested on two distinct grounds. The first was that the damages were too "remote" and the second was the fear that a large number of false and ungrounded suits would be brought if the basic action were allowed. Yet, as long as the requirement of actual impact remained, the courts were quick to convert any impact, however slight, into the basis of plaintiff's cause of action for emotional distress. In effect, courts treated the emotional distress as parasitic damages upon the most nominal of invasions. In Comstock v. Wilson, 177 N.E. 431 (N.Y. 1931), recovery was allowed for a slight jolt in a very minor automobile collision. In Porter v. Delaware, L. & W. Ry., 63 A. 860 (N.J. 1906), the plaintiff recovered when "something" slight hit her neck and she got dust in her eyes. In Kenney v. Wong Len, 128 A. 343 (N.H. 1925), the requisite impact was found when the hair of a mouse in a spoonful of stew touched the roof of the plaintiff's mouth. And finally, in Christy Bros. Circus v. Turnage, 144 S.E. 680 (Ga. App. 1928), the hapless plaintiff recovered when one of defendant's horses "evacuated his bowels" in plaintiff's lap, "in full view of many people . . . all of whom laughed at the occurrence."

2. *Within the zone of danger.* While some courts were probing the limits of the impact rule, other courts were reexamining its foundations. The counterattack started in England, where both the remoteness of damage and floodgates arguments were rejected in Dulieu v. White & Sons, [1901] 2 K.B. 669, 677, 681. There the plaintiff gave premature birth to her child after nearly being run over by the defendant's team of horses while working behind the counter in her husband's public house. After an exhaustive review of the prior case law, Kennedy, J., rejected *Mitchell* and allowed the plaintiff's action. On the question of remoteness of damage, he wrote:

> Why is the accompaniment of physical injury essential? For my own part, I should not like to assume it to be scientifically true that a nervous shock which causes serious bodily illness is not actually accompanied by physical injury, although it may be impossible, or at least difficult, to detect the injury at the time in the living subject. I should not be surprised if the surgeon or the physiologist told us that nervous shock is or may be in itself an injurious affection of the physical organism. Let it be assumed, however, that the physical injury follows the shock, but that the jury are satisfied upon proper and sufficient medical evidence that it follows the shock as its direct and natural effect, is there any legal reason for saying that the damage is less proximate in the legal sense than damage which arises contemporaneously? "As well might it be said" (I am quoting from the judgment of Palles, C.B.) "that a death caused by poison is not to be attributed to the person who administered it because the mortal effect is not produced contemporaneously with its administration." Remoteness as a legal ground for the exclusion of damage in an action of tort means, not severance in point of time, but the absence of direct and natural causal sequence — the inability to trace in regard to the damage the "propter hoc" in a necessary or natural descent from the wrongful act. As a matter of experience, I should say that the injury to health which forms the main ground of damages in actions of negligence, either in cases of railway accidents or in running-down cases, frequently is proved, not as a concomitant of the occurrence, but as one of the sequelae. . . .

Thereafter Kennedy, J., rejected any concern about spurious claims, saying:

> I should be sorry to adopt a rule which would bar all such claims on grounds of policy alone, and in order to prevent the possible success of unrighteous or groundless actions. Such a course involves the denial of redress in meritorious cases, and it necessarily implies a certain degree of distrust, which I do not share, in the capacity of legal tribunals to get at the truth in this class of claim. My experience gives me no reason to suppose that a jury would really have more difficulty in weighing the medical evidence as to the effects of nervous shock through fright, than in weighing the like evidence as to the effects of nervous shock through a railway collision or a carriage accident, where, as often happens, no

palpable injury, or very slight palpable injury, has been occasioned at the time.

Accordingly, Kennedy J., allowed the action even where the harm does not arise from actual impact subject to one critical limitation: the plaintiff was not "entitled to maintain this action if the nervous shock was produced, not by the fear of bodily injury to herself, but by horror or vexation arising from the sight of mischief being threatened or done either to some other person, or to her own or her husband's property, by the intrusion of the defendant's van and horses."

3. *Empirical complications.* Is the concern with fraud or error in nervous shock cases understated in *Dulieu?* In 1944 a doctor-lawyer made an exhaustive survey of actions brought for physical injuries resulting from negligently inflicted fright and concluded: "On the basis of all available factors, we thought at least 7/10 or 21/30 of the 301 cases examined should have been decided in defendant's favor. In practice, defendants were able to obtain jury verdicts in 7 cases only, to get directed verdicts in 25, and on appeal to prevail in but 19 additional cases. Thus, defendant prevailed in only 51 cases or 5/30 of the total series. In all, plaintiff won or still might win, 25/30 of the 301 cases. . . . Law, in a commendable desire to be forward looking, outran scientific standards. Taking all cases decided between 1850 and 1944, the net balance of justice would have been greater had all courts denied damages for injury imputed to psychic stimuli alone." Smith, Relation of Emotions to Injury and Disease: Legal Liability for Psychic Stimuli, 30 Va. L. Rev. 193, 284-285 (1944), and defended again in Smith, Problems of Proof in Psychic Injury Cases, 14 Syracuse L. Rev. 586 (1963).

Dillon v. Legg
441 P.2d 912 (Cal. 1968)

[While driving his automobile, defendant struck and killed Erin Lee Dillon, a child, as she was crossing a public street. Out of her death arose a law suit with three separate claims. The first was brought by the decedent's mother and minor sister, Cheryl, for wrongful death. The second was brought by the mother for nervous shock and serious mental and physical pain suffered in consequence of defendant's negligence. The third was brought by the minor sister, Cheryl, also for emotional and physical suffering. The evidence established that the mother was in "close proximity" to Erin Lee at the time of the collision, but that defendant's car never threatened the mother's safety since she was outside the "zone of danger." The trial court dismissed the mother's action for emotional distress on the authority of Amaya v. Home Ice, Fuel & Supply Co., 379 P.2d 513 (Cal. 1963), because the complaint did not allege that she suffered her fright and distress out of fear for her own safety. However, Cheryl's action for emotional distress was not dismissed, because the evidence raised the possibility that she was in the zone of danger or feared for her own safety. The mother appealed from the judgment dismissing her action for negligent infliction of emotional distress.

Noting that the mother's claim was supported by considerations of "natural justice," the court concluded that her claim, so founded, should not be "frustrated" because of judicial fears that such claims would invite fraudulent claims or "would involve the courts in the hopeless task of defining the extent of the tortfeasor's liability." It then continued with a critical analysis of the *Amaya* case.]

TOBRINER, J.* . . . [W]e can hardly justify relief to the sister for trauma which she suffered upon apprehension of the child's death and yet deny it to the mother merely because of a happenstance that the sister was some few yards closer to the accident. The instant case exposes the hopeless artificiality of the zone-of-danger rule. In the second place, to rest upon the zone-of-danger rule when we have rejected the impact rule becomes even less defensible. We have, indeed, held that impact is not necessary for recovery. The zone-of-danger concept must, then, inevitably collapse because the only reason for the requirement of presence in that zone lies in the fact that one within it will fear the danger of *impact*. At the threshold, then, we point to the incongruity of the rules upon which any rejection of plaintiff's recovery must rest.

We further note, at the outset, that defendant has interposed the defense that the contributory negligence of the mother, the sister, and the child contributed to the accident. If any such defense is sustained and defendant found not liable for the death of the child because of the contributory negligence of the mother, sister or child, we do not believe that the mother or sister should recover for the emotional trauma which they allegedly suffered. In the absence of the primary liability of the tort-feasor for the death of the child, we see no ground for an independent and secondary liability for claims for injuries by third parties. The basis for such claims must be adjudicated liability and fault of defendant; that liability and fault must be the foundation for the tort-feasor's duty of due care to third parties who, as a consequence of such negligence, sustain emotional trauma.

We turn then to an analysis of the concept of duty, which, as we have stated, has furnished the ground for the rejection of such claims as the instant one. Normally the simple facts of plaintiff's complaint would establish a cause of action: the complaint alleges that defendant drove his car (1) negligently, as a (2) proximate result of which plaintiff suffered (3) physical injury. Proof of these facts to a jury leads to recovery in dam-

---

*Tobriner, J., while on the California Court of Appeals, wrote the opinion in *Amaya*, later reversed by the California Supreme Court, allowing the plaintiff to recover for nervous shock even though he was beyond the zone of danger. 23 Cal. Rptr. 131 (1962) — ED.

ages; indeed, such a showing represents a classic example of the type of accident with which the law of negligence has been designed to deal.

The assertion that liability must nevertheless be denied because defendant bears no "duty" to plaintiff "begs the essential question — whether the plaintiff's interests are entitled to legal protection against the defendant's conduct. . . . It [duty] is a shorthand statement of a conclusion, rather than an aid to analysis in itself. . . . But it should be recognized that 'duty' is not sacrosanct in itself, but only an expression of the sum total of those considerations of policy which lead the law to say that the particular plaintiff is entitled to protection." (Prosser, Law of Torts, [(3rd ed. 1964)] at pp. 332-333.)

The history of the concept of duty in itself discloses that it is not an old and deep-rooted doctrine but a legal device of the latter half of the nineteenth century designed to curtail the feared propensities of juries toward liberal awards. "It must not be forgotten that 'duty' got into our law for the very purpose of combatting what was then feared to be a dangerous delusion (perhaps especially prevalent among juries imbued with popular notions of fairness untempered by paramount judicial policy), viz. that the law might countenance legal redress for all foreseeable harm." (Fleming, An Introduction to the Law of Torts (1967) p. 47.)

[The court then returned to its initial concern, whether the concept of duty should be invoked to protect against an "onslaught of fraudulent and indefinable claims."]

1. *This court in the past has rejected the argument that we must deny recovery upon a legitimate claim because other fraudulent ones may be urged. . . .*

Indubitably juries and trial courts, constantly called upon to distinguish the frivolous from the substantial and the fraudulent from the meritorious, reach some erroneous results. But such fallibility, inherent in the judicial process, offers no reason for substituting for the case-by-case resolution of causes an artificial and indefensible barrier. Courts not only compromise their basic responsibility to decide the merits of each individually but destroy the public's confidence in them by using the broad broom of "administrative convenience" to sweep away a class of claims a number of which are admittedly meritorious. The mere assertion that fraud is possible, "a possibility [that] exists to some degree in all cases" does not prove a present necessity to abandon the neutral principles of foreseeability, proximate cause and consequential injury that generally govern tort law.

Indeed, we doubt that the problem of the fraudulent claim is substantially more pronounced in the case of a mother claiming physical injury resulting from seeing her child killed than in other areas of tort law in which the right to recover damages is well established in California. For example, a plaintiff claiming that fear for his own safety resulted in physical injury makes out a well recognized case for recovery.

Moreover, damages are allowed for "mental suffering," a type of injury, on the whole, less amenable to objective proof than the physical injury involved here; the mental injury can be in aggravation of, or "parasitic to," an established tort. In fact, fear for another, even in the absence of resulting physical injury, can be part of these parasitic damages. And emotional distress, if inflicted intentionally, constitutes an independent tort. The danger of plaintiffs' fraudulent collection of damages for nonexistent injury is at least as great in these examples as in the instant case.

In sum, the application of tort law can never be a matter of mathematical precision. In terms of characterizing conduct as tortious and matching a money award to the injury suffered as well as in fixing the extent of injury, the process cannot be perfect. Undoubtedly, ever since the ancient case of the tavern-keeper's wife who successfully avoided the hatchet cast by an irate customer (I. de S. et ux v. W. de S., Y.B. 22 Edw. iii, f. 99, pl. 60 (1348)), defendants have argued that plaintiffs' claims of injury from emotional trauma might well be fraudulent. Yet we cannot let the difficulties of adjudication frustrate the principle that there be a remedy for every substantial wrong.

> 2. *The alleged inability to fix definitions for recovery on the different facts of future cases does not justify the denial of recovery on the specific facts of the instant case; in any event, proper guidelines can indicate the extent of liability for such future cases. . . .*

Since the chief element in determining whether defendant owes a duty or an obligation to plaintiff is the foreseeability of the risk, that factor will be of prime concern in every case. Because it is inherently intertwined with foreseeability such duty or obligation must necessarily be adjudicated only upon a case-by-case basis. We cannot now predetermine defendant's obligation in every situation by a fixed category; no immutable rule can establish the extent of that obligation for every circumstance of the future. We can, however, define guidelines which will aid in the resolution of such an issue as the instant one.

We note, first, that we deal here with a case in which plaintiff suffered a shock which resulted in physical injury and we confine our ruling to that case. In determining, in such a case, whether defendant should reasonably foresee the injury to plaintiff, or, in other terminology, whether defendant owes plaintiff a duty of due care, the courts will take into account such factors as the following: (1) Whether plaintiff was located near the scene of the accident as contrasted with one who was a distance away from it. (2) Whether the shock resulted from a direct emotional impact upon plaintiff from the sensory and contemporaneous observance of the accident, as contrasted with learning of the accident from others after its occurrence. (3) Whether plaintiff and the victim were closely related, as contrasted with an absence of any relationship or the presence of only a distant relationship.

The evaluation of these factors will indicate the degree of the defendant's foreseeability: obviously defendant is more likely to foresee that a mother who observes an accident affecting her child will suffer harm than to foretell that a stranger witness will do so. Similarly, the degree of foreseeability of the third person's injury is far greater in the case of his contemporaneous observance of the accident than that in which he subsequently learns of it. The defendant is more likely to foresee that shock to the nearby, witnessing mother will cause physical harm than to anticipate that someone distant from the accident will suffer more than a temporary emotional reaction. All these elements, of course, shade into each other; the fixing of obligation, intimately tied into the facts, depends upon each case.

In light of these factors the court will determine whether the accident and harm was *reasonably* foreseeable. Such reasonable foreseeability does not turn on whether the particular defendant as an individual would have in actuality foreseen the exact accident and loss; it contemplates that courts, on a case-to-case basis, analyzing all the circumstances, will decide what the ordinary man under such circumstances should reasonably have foreseen. The courts thus mark out the areas of liability, excluding the remote and unexpected.

In the instant case, the presence of all the above factors indicates that plaintiff has alleged a sufficient prima facie case. Surely the negligent driver who causes the death of a young child may reasonably expect that the mother will not be far distant and will upon witnessing the accident suffer emotional trauma. As Dean Prosser has stated: "when a child is endangered, it is not beyond contemplation that its mother will be somewhere in the vicinity, and will suffer serious shock." . . .

The fear of an inability to fix boundaries has not impelled the courts of England to deny recovery for emotional trauma caused by witnessing the death or injury of another due to defendant's negligence. We set forth the holdings of some English cases merely to demonstrate that courts can formulate and apply such limitations of liability.

[The court then reviewed the English cases which are favorable to recovery in nervous shock cases.]

Thus we see no good reason why the general rules of tort law, including the concepts of negligence, proximate cause, and foreseeability, long applied to all other types of injury, should not govern the case now before us. . . .

In short, the history of the cases does not show the development of a logical rule but rather a series of changes and abandonments. Upon the argument in each situation that the courts draw a Maginot Line to withstand an onslaught of false claims, the cases have assumed a variety of postures. At first they insisted that there be no recovery for emotional trauma at all. Retreating from this position, they gave relief for such trauma only if physical impact occurred. They then abandoned the requirement for physical impact but insisted that the victim fear for her own safety, holding that a mother could recover for fear for her children's safety if she simultaneously entertained a personal fear for herself. They stated that the mother need only be in the "zone of danger." The final anomaly would be the instant case in which the sister, who observed the accident, would be granted recovery because she was in the "zone of danger," but the *mother,* not far distant, would be barred from recovery.

The successive abandonment of these positions exposes the weakness of artificial abstractions which bar recovery contrary to the general rules. As the commentators have suggested, the problem should be solved by the application of the principles of tort, not by the creation of exceptions to them. Legal history shows that artificial islands of exceptions, created from the fear that the legal process will not work, usually do not withstand the waves of reality and, in time, descend into oblivion. . . .

Yet for some artificial reason this delimitation of liability is alleged to be unworkable in the most egregious case of them all: the mother's emotional trauma at the witnessed death of her child. If we stop at this point, however, we must necessarily question and reject not merely recovery here, but the viability of the judicial process for ascertaining liability for tortious conduct itself. To the extent that it is inconsistent with our ruling here, we therefore overrule Amaya v. Home Ice, Fuel & Supply Co.

To deny recovery would be to chain this state to an outmoded rule of the 19th century which can claim no current credence. No good reason compels our captivity to an indefensible orthodoxy.

The judgment is reversed.

TRAYNOR, C.J. I dissent for the reasons set forth in Amaya v. Home Ice, Fuel & Supply Co. In my opinion that case was correctly decided and should not be overruled.

BURKE, J. [dissenting, questioned the guidelines set forth in the majority opinion]. . . . What if the plaintiff was honestly *mistaken* in believing the third person to be in danger or to be seriously injured? What if the third person had assumed the risk involved? How "close" must the relationship be between the plaintiff and the third person? I.e., what if the third person was the plaintiff's beloved niece or nephew, grandparent, fiancé, or lifelong friend, more dear to the plaintiff than her immediate family? Next, how "near" must the plaintiff have been to the scene of the accident, and how "soon" must shock have been felt? Indeed, what is the magic in the plaintiff's being actually present? Is the shock any less real if the mother does not know of the accident until her injured child is brought into her home? On the other hand, is it any less real if the mother is physically present at the scene but is nevertheless unaware of the danger or injury to her child until after the accident has occurred? No answers to these questions are to be found in today's majority opinion. Our trial courts, however, will not so easily escape the burden of distinguishing between litigants on the basis of such artificial and unpredictable distinctions.

NOTES

1. Foreseeability in emotional distress cases. In Tobin v. Grossman, 249 N.E.2d 419, 422-423, 424-425 (N.Y. 1969), the plaintiff suffered "physical injuries caused by shock and fear" when her 2-year-old son was seriously injured in an automobile accident. The plaintiff did not see the accident, but heard the screech of brakes and arrived on the scene, only a few feet away, moments later. In denying the cause of action, Breitel, J., took direct issue with Dillon v. Legg's heavy reliance on foreseeability, and predicted that if actions of this sort were allowed, they could not in principle or practice be confined to close family members who witnessed the accident.

> On foreseeability, it is hardly cogent to assert that the negligent actor if he could foresee injury to the child that he should not also foresee at the same time harm to the mother who, especially in the case of children of tender years, is likely to be present or about. But foreseeability, once recognized, is not so easily limited. Relatives, other than the mother, such as fathers or grandparents, or even other caretakers, equally sensitive and as easily harmed, may be just as foreseeably affected. Hence, foreseeability would, in short order, extend logically to caretakers other than the mother, and ultimately to affected bystanders. . . .
>
> The final and most difficult factor is any reasonable circumscription, within tolerable limits required by public policy, of a rule creating liability. Every parent who loses a child or whose child of any age suffers an injury is likely to sustain grievous psychological trauma, with the added risk of consequential physical harm. Any rule based solely on eyewitnessing the accident could stand only until the first case comes along in which the parent is in the immediate vicinity but did not see the accident. Moreover, the instant advice that one's child has been killed or injured, by telephone, word of mouth, or by whatever means, even if delayed, will have in most cases the same impact. The sight of gore and exposed bones is not necessary to provide special impact on a parent. Again, the logical difficulty of excluding the grandparent, the relatives, or others in loco parentis, and even the conscientious and sensitive caretaker, from a right to recover, if in fact the accident had the grave consequences claimed, raises subtle and elusive hazards in devising a sound rule in this field.

Judge Breitel underestimated the resolve of the California courts on the two requirements of close relationship and direct observation. On the first issue, Elden v. Sheldon, 758 P.2d 582 (Cal. 1988), the court denied claims for the negligent infliction of emotional distress (and loss of consortium) to an unmarried cohabitant involved in an automobile accident, who not only witnessed her death but was injured himself. The court in *Elden* construed the third prong of the *Dillon* test — that the plaintiff be "closely related" to the victim — to allow actions brought by married persons for injuries to a spouse and by one sibling for injury to another. It held, however, that *Dillon*'s general foreseeability language did not allow damage actions when the victim was a "close friend" and held that unmarried cohabitants stood in no better position, given the "state's interest in promoting marriage."

On the second issue, the court refused to bend in Thing v. La Chusa, 771 P.2d 814, 815 (Cal. 1989), when it denied recovery for emotional distress to a mother who had not witnessed the automobile accident that injured her child. Eagleson, J., rejected *Dillon*'s assertion that "foreseeability" was the touchstone of duty, on the ground that the concept was "amorphous." Instead he opted for a "bright line" rule. "In so doing we balance the impact of arbitrary lines which deny recovery to some victims whose injury is very real against that of imposing liability out of proportion to culpability for negligent acts. We also weigh in the balance the importance to the administration of justice of clear guidelines under which litigants and trial courts may resolve disputes." Accordingly, the court concluded that

> the societal benefits of certainty in the law, as well as traditional concepts of tort law, dictate limitation of bystander recovery of damages for emotional distress. In the absence of physical injury or impact to the plaintiff himself, damages for emotional distress should be recoverable only if the plaintiff: (1) is closely related to the injury victim; (2) is present at the scene of the injury-producing event at the time it occurs and is then aware that it is causing injury to the victim, and (3) as a result suffers emotional distress beyond that which would be anticipated in a disinterested witness.

2. Direct victims. *Dillon* was concerned only with the potential liabilities to strangers who suffered emotional distress in consequence of defendant's wrong. Recovery for emotional distress often arises out of a network of consensual arrangements, and in this context, the California courts have sometimes allowed recovery for plaintiffs who did not witness physical harm to certain close relations. In Molien v. Kaiser Foundation Hospitals, 616 P.2d 813, 817 (Cal. 1980), the defendant's employee, Dr. Kilbridge, negligently provided the plaintiff's wife with an erroneous report that she had contracted an infectious type of syphilis. She in turn had to undergo unnecessary medical treatment and became "upset and suspicious that her husband had engaged in extramarital sexual activities." Their marriage broke up from the ensuing tension and hostility, and husband's suit for emotional distress was allowed, notwithstanding the limitations in *Dillon* on the ground that the plaintiff was a "direct victim" of the defendant's action. Mosk, J., used the general foreseeability analysis of *Dillon* to permit recovery even though the plaintiff was not in any zone of danger.

> In the case at bar the risk of harm to plaintiff was reasonably foreseeable to defendants. It is easily predictable that an erroneous diagnosis of syphilis and its probable source would produce marital discord and resultant emotional distress to a married patient's spouse; Dr. Kilbridge's advice to Mrs. Molien to have her husband examined for the disease confirms that plaintiff was a foreseeable victim of the negligent diagnosis. Because the disease is normally transmitted only by sexual relations, it is rational to anticipate that both husband and wife would experience anxiety, suspicion, and hostility when confronted with what they had every reason to believe was reliable medical evidence of a particularly noxious infidelity.

Molien for its part has generated an entire jurisprudence on the question of who counts as a "direct victim" who can recover for emotional distress without being exposed to direct physical harm or witnessing physical injury to close personal relations. The California court has eschewed the general foreseeability analysis, and focused on the question of whether the defendant has assumed some direct duty to the plaintiff. Thus in Huggins v. Longs Drug Stores California, Inc., 862 P.2d 148, 152-153 (Cal. 1993), the court refused to allow the plaintiffs to recover when the defendant pharmacy filled prescriptions for five times the dosage ordered by the physician, resulting in medical harm to the child. Baxter, J., first noted that the parents could not recover as bystanders under *Dillon* and then denied recovery on the ground that there was no direct or special relationship between the defendant and the plaintiff parents:

> Since *Molien* was decided, we have made clear that despite its broad references to foreseeability, the opinion should be read as basing the defendant doctor's direct-victim liability only upon his assumption of a direct duty toward the husband. That duty did not arise simply because the doctor's misdiagnosis "necessarily involved him directly . . . but because the doctor directed his patient, the wife to advise the plaintiff of the diagnosis.
>
> That limitation on direct victim liability under *Molien* was confirmed in Ochoa v. Superior Court, 703 P.2d 1 (Cal. 1985), where plaintiffs alleged emotional distress from observing the defendant juvenile authorities' wrongful refusal to provide or allow direly needed medical care for the plaintiffs' son, who subsequently died from the consequent neglect. Though upholding plaintiffs' claim for recovery as bystanders, we rejected their claim as direct victims under *Molien*. . . .
>
> More recently we have allowed recovery for parental emotional distress

from professional mistreatment of a child by health care providers who were concurrently treating the parents as patients. In Marlene F. v. Affiliated Psychiatric Medical Clinic, 770 P.2d 278 (Cal. 1989), the defendant psychotherapist was treating both the plaintiff mothers and their sons for intrafamily difficulties. We held that because the plaintiffs were themselves patients, they could recover damages for emotional distress caused by the defendant's sexual abuse of the sons. Similarly, in Burgess v. Superior Court, 831 P.2d 1197 (Cal. 1992), we held that a mother could recover damages for emotional distress as the direct victim of medical malpractice that inflicted permanent brain damage injury upon her child through deprivation of oxygen during childbirth. Again, liability was based on the defendant's physician-patient relationship with, and consequent duty of care toward, the mother as well as the child.

When the plaintiff is not the defendant's patient, however, "courts have not extended the *Molien* direct-victim cause of action to emotional distress which is derived solely from a reaction to another's injury." . . .

That principle was applied in Schwarz v. Regents of University of California, 276 Cal. Rptr. 470, 483 (Cal. App. 1990), where a father was denied recovery for emotional distress as the alleged direct victim of a psychotherapist whom the father had retained to treat his son and who facilitated and concealed the mother's removal of the son to London, England. . . . "[T]he simple existence of a contract between a parent and a medical caregiver to provide medical treatment for a child is not in itself sufficient to impose on the caregiver a duty of care owed to the patient."

Direct-victim claims have not been confined to suits against physicians. In Christensen v. Superior Court (Pasadena Crematorium of Altadena, RPI), 820 P.2d 181, 191, 202 (Cal. 1991), the defendant crematorium was charged with treating the remains of the plaintiff's deceased in a disrespectful and undignified manner, with selling its body parts without the consent of family members, with failing to place the decedent's remains in a separate container, and with selling gold and other remains from his body. Baxter, J., treated the entire family, not only the contracting party, as direct victims under *Molien*.

> One of several children of the decedent may arrange for the services on behalf of all siblings, as well as surviving spouse or parent of the decedent. If so, the crematory or mortuary assumes a duty to all of these family members. There is no reason to assume that the person who makes the arrangements is any more susceptible to emotion if the services are not competently performed than are the other family members. Indeed, in light of the emotional impact of the death of a close family member of the bereaved, it may be the relative least affected who is chosen by the family to represent them in arranging for funeral and related services.

Baxter, J., also refused to allow the plaintiffs a claim for the intentional infliction of emotional distress by extreme and outrageous conduct. "It is not enough that the conduct be intentional and outrageous. It must be conduct directed at the plaintiff, or occur in the presence of a plaintiff of whom the defendant is aware."

3. Dillon's *reception outside California*. Dillon and its progeny have been subject to intensive examination in other states. *Dillon* was rejected in favor of *Amaya's* zone-of-danger approach of in Rickey v. Chicago Transit Authority, 457 N.E.2d 1 (Ill. 1983). On the other hand, *Dillon* has received a broad construction in a few states. See, e.g., Dziokonski v. Babineau, 380 N.E.2d 1295, 1302 (Mass. 1978), where it was held that "allegations concerning a parent who sustains substantial physical harm as a result of severe mental distress over some peril or harm to his minor child caused by the defendant's negligence state a claim for which relief might be granted, where the parent either witnesses the accident or soon comes on the scene while the child is still there."

Still other courts have respected the bright-line limitations in *Dillon*, even after accepting its basic principle. For example, Hawaii adopted the *Dillon* rule in Rodrigues v. State, 472 P.2d 509 (Haw. 1970). Yet in Kelley v. Kokua Sales and Supply, Ltd., 532 P.2d 673 (Haw. 1975), a divided court denied recovery in the case of a decedent, a California resident, who died of a heart attack shortly after being informed by telephone that his daughter and grandchild had been killed in a road accident. The court, unquestionably motivated by the fear of unlimited liability, invoked the language of "duty of care" and "foresight of consequences" to justify its denial of recovery.

More recently in Dunphy v. Gregor, 642 A.2d 372 (N.J. 1994), the New Jersey Supreme Court split the difference. It followed a narrow reading of *Dillon*, and required a plaintiff to have observed the death or injury of another person, but it repudiated *Elden*, by allowing an unmarried cohabitant to maintain the action. "The State's interest in marriage would not be harmed if unmarried cohabitants are permitted to prove on a case-by-case basis that they enjoy a steadfast relationship that is equivalent to a legal marriage and thus equally deserves legal protection."

See generally Nolan and Ursin, Negligent Infliction of Emotional Distress: Coherence Emerging From Chaos, 33 Hastings L.J. 583 (1982); Diamond, *Dillon v. Legg* Revisited: Toward a Unified Theory of Compensating Bystanders and Relatives for Intangible Injuries, 35 Hastings L. J. 477 (1984), which was relied on by the majority in *Thing*.

4. *The "at risk" plaintiff: of drugs and toxic torts*. Nervous shock cases do not arise only with traumatic accidents or imminent threats thereof to the plaintiff or to some third party. In the medical area, damages have been sought by daughters without physical injuries at the date of suit, as "at risk" plaintiffs who have a chance of between one in a thousand and one in ten thousand of getting adenocarcinoma, a very seri-

ous form of cancer. In Payton v. Abbott Labs, 437 N.E.2d 171, 193 (Mass. 1982), the court rejected the plaintiffs' efforts and held that the plaintiff must prove that

> a plaintiff's physical harm must either cause or be caused by the emotional distress alleged, and that the physical harm must be manifested by objective symptomatology and substantiated by expert medical testimony. Finally, the emotional distress for which compensation is sought must be reasonably foreseeable: unless a plaintiff proves that the defendant knew or should have known of special factors affecting that plaintiff's response to the circumstances of the case, the plaintiff can recover only for that degree of emotional distress which a reasonable person, normally constituted, would have experienced under those circumstances. Whether the emotional distress which a plaintiff is alleged to have experienced is reasonable, is to be determined by the finder of fact.

A parallel question of emotional distress in toxic tort contexts arose in Potter v. Firestone Tire & Rubber Co., 863 P.2d 795, 810, 811 (Cal. 1993), where the defendant's local employees, in conscious violation of federal and state statutes, and internal company policy, dumped certain toxic wastes into an unauthorized dump site in order to economize on costs. Firestone's toxins (unique to its manufacturing processes) made their way into the plaintiffs' wells, and the knowledge of the contamination created emotional distress for which they claimed relief, even though none of them suffered from cancerous or precancerous conditions. Plaintiffs urged that they should be allowed to recover if they could show that exposure to defendant's toxins led to some "significant increase in the risk of cancer." Defendants insisted that recovery should be allowed only where there was some sign of physical injury from the ingested toxic substances.

Baxter, J., rejected both extremes. As to the defendant's proposed test, he concluded that "the physical injury requirement is a hopelessly imprecise screening device — it would allow recovery for fear of cancer whenever such distress accompanies or results in any physical injury, no matter how trivial, yet would disallow recovery in all cases where the fear is both serious and genuine but no physical injury has yet manifested itself." He concluded that the plaintiffs' test "provides no protection against unreasonable claims based on wholly speculative fears. For example, a plaintiff's risk of contracting cancer might be significantly increased by 100 or more percent due to a particular toxic exposure, yet the actual risk of the feared cancer might itself be insignificant and no more than a mere possibility." He therefore hewed to a middle path and required, as in *Payton,* that the plaintiff "pleads and proves that the fear stems from a knowledge, corroborated by reliable medical and scientific opinion, that it is more likely than not that the feared cancer will develop in the future due to the toxic exposure." The court thought that only this limitation would confine liability to manageable limits, control insurance costs, and make it possible to have funds available for the serious cases of cancer that do arise.

In the instant case, the court did, however, allow recovery (including recovery for medical monitoring costs) on the strength of the "increased risk" test because the defendant's systematic violation of statutory and internal policies constituted "fraud, malice and oppression" under California law, which dispensed with the need for meeting the higher standard. It also rejected defendant's contention that no recovery should be allowed since the plaintiffs were smokers whose toxic intake from smoking contained toxic chemicals (e.g., benzene) in concentrations 2,500 times of that found in the wastes, saying that defendant "had failed to establish a causal link between plaintiffs' smoking and the harm they suffered, i.e. their fear of a significant increased risk of cancer." Should medical monitoring expenses be allowed if the cigarettes pose the far greater risk of cancer?

Chapter Seven
Affirmative Duties

A. INTRODUCTION

In the previous chapters we have examined the law of tort largely (but not exclusively) in connection with the harms that the defendant has inflicted upon the plaintiff by misfeasance, or such positive acts as hitting or beating or creating traps and other dangerous conditions. In this chapter the focus shifts to those cases in which the defendant is said to be liable for a nonfeasance, or failure to act, because he is under an affirmative duty to aid, assist, or protect the plaintiff from harms that the defendant did not cause or bring about. As will become evident, the line between misfeasance and nonfeasance is not always clear. The discussion of the duties that landowners owe to trespassers, for example, involves both an examination of the types of acts that cause harm and the failure to take steps to protect trespassers from dangerous conditions or equipment on the landowner's premises.

In accordance with this general plan, the first part of this chapter examines a hardy problem of enduring philosophical interest: when are individuals liable for failing to rescue strangers in imminent peril of life or limb? Prominent in this area are the so-called good Samaritan cases, where the defendant was in no sense responsible for creating the dangerous condition or situation that brought forth the need to rescue in the first place. Thereafter the discussion is extended to the less controversial settings when the defendant has created the dangerous situation requiring rescue by conduct which itself may be either tortious or nontortious.

The second set of issues concerns the duties that landowners and occupiers owe to persons who enter their premises. These entries may be unlawful, as with trespassers, or lawful as with persons who have received permission from the landowner. Despite these fluctuations in judicial attitude, it is still generally accepted that the trespasser takes, at the very least, the risk of purely accidental injuries, even if entitled to recover for deliberate and perhaps recklessly inflicted injuries. On the other hand, the landowner clearly owes some duty of care to persons lawfully on the premises, and the critical issues are at what level and to which persons. The traditional common-law cases distinguished between social guests (called "licensees") and business visitors (called "invitees"), and imposed a lower duty to the former — to warn of latent defects — than it did for the latter — to take reasonable care to keep the premies safe. Many states today reject this distinction and impose a uniform duty of reasonable care for the benefit of licensees and invitees alike.

The third set of issues arises in cases where the defendant makes a gratuitous undertaking to provide some benefit or assistance to the plaintiff. These cases are, in a sense, contractual in that they rest upon defendant's promise, express or implied, to the plaintiff. But the defendant's undertakings have not been bargained for by the plaintiff, and historically these cases have been treated as part of the tort law.

The fourth set of issues arises in cases where the defendant *does* owe a duty to prevent harms to the person or property of the plaintiff because the defendant stands in some sort of "special relationship" either to the plaintiff, or, alternatively, to the person who threatens harm or injury to the plaintiff. The first subclass of special relationship cases concerns, for example, the duties a landlord owes to his tenant, a hotel to its guests, a club to its members, or a university to its students. In these cases the defendant may be called upon to guard against various contingencies from the simple loss or destruction of property entrusted to its care, to the defective conditions of premises under its control, or today to the criminal act of a third party. The second subclass of special relationship cases includes situations in which prisons and hospitals have charge of persons who, once they are released, commit acts of violence against third parties. Until recently, contemporary tort law has been to expand the class of affirmative duties that large (and not-so-large) social institutions — schools, hotels, hospitals, landlords, common carriers — owe their customers and clients, but there is today some clear evidence of stabilization or contraction.

B. THE DUTY TO RESCUE

Buch v. Amory Manufacturing Co.
44 A. 809 (N.H. 1897)

[The plaintiff, aged 8 years, trespassed in defendant's mill, where weaving machinery was in operation. An overseer observed him there and told him to leave. Plaintiff did not go because he did not understand English and the overseer did not put him out, although it was apparent that the running machinery presented an obvious hazard to a child of plaintiff's age. Plaintiff had his hand crushed in a machine that his brother, aged 13, an employee, was trying to teach him to run. The trial court denied a motion for a directed verdict. Defendant appealed. Verdict for plaintiff set aside and judgment for defendant.]

CARPENTER, C.J. Assuming, then, that the plaintiff was incapable either of appreciating the danger or of exercising the care necessary to avoid it, is he, upon the facts stated, entitled to recover? He was a trespasser in a place dangerous to children of his age. In the conduct of their business and management of their machinery the defendants were without fault. The only negligence charged upon, or attributed to, them is that, inasmuch as they could not make the plaintiff understand a command to leave the premises, and ought to have known that they could not, they did not forcibly eject him. Actionable negligence is the neglect of a legal duty. The defendants are not liable unless they owed to the plaintiff a legal duty which they neglected to perform. With purely moral obligations the law does not deal. For example, the priest and Levite who passed by on the other side were not, it is supposed, liable at law for the continued suffering of the man who fell among thieves, which they might and morally ought to have prevented or relieved. Suppose *A,* standing close by a railroad, sees a two-year-old babe on the track and a car approaching. He can easily rescue the child with entire safety to himself, and the instincts of humanity require him to do so. If he does not, he may, perhaps, justly be styled a ruthless savage and a moral monster; but he is not liable in damages for the child's injury, or indictable under the statute for its death. . . .

What duties do the owners owe to a trespasser upon their premises? They may eject him, using such force and such only as is necessary for the purpose. They are bound to abstain from any other or further intentional or negligent acts of personal violence, — bound to inflict upon him by means of their own active intervention no injury which by due care they can avoid. They are not bound to warn him against hidden or secret dangers arising from the condition of the premises, or to protect him against any injury that may arise from his own acts or those of other persons. In short, if they do nothing, let him entirely alone, in no manner interfere with him, he can have no cause of action against them for any injury that he may receive. On the contrary, he is liable to them for any damage that he by his unlawful meddling may cause them or their property. What greater or other legal obligation was cast on these defendants by the circumstance that the plaintiff was (as is assumed) an irresponsible infant?

If landowners are not bound to warn an adult trespasser of hidden dangers, — dangers which he by ordinary care cannot discover and, therefore, cannot avoid, — on what ground can it be claimed that they must warn an infant of open and visible dangers which he is unable to appreciate? No legal distinction is perceived between the duties of the owners in one case and the other. The situation of the adult in front of secret dangers which by no degree of care he can discover, and that of the infant incapable of comprehending danger, is in a legal aspect exactly the same. There is no apparent reason for holding that any greater or other duty rests upon the owners in one case than in the other.

There is a wide difference — a broad gulf — both in reason and in law, between causing and preventing an injury; between doing by negligence or otherwise a wrong to one's neighbor, and preventing him from injuring himself; between protecting him against injury by another and guarding him from injury that may accrue to him from the condition of the premises which he has unlawfully invaded. The duty to do no wrong is a legal duty. The duty to protect against wrong is, generally speaking and excepting certain intimate relations in the nature of a trust, a moral obligation only, not recognized or enforced by law. Is a spectator liable if he sees an intelligent man or an unintelligent infant running into danger and does not warn or forcibly restrain him? What difference does it make whether the danger is on another's land, or upon his own, in case the man or infant is not there by his express or implied invitation? If A sees an eight-year-old boy beginning to climb into his garden over a wall stuck with spikes and does not warn him or drive him off, is he liable in damages if the boy meets with injury from the spikes? I see my neighbor's two-year-old babe in dangerous proximity to the machinery of his windmill in his yard, and easily might, but do not, rescue him. I am not liable in damages to the child for his injuries, nor, if the child is killed, punishable for manslaughter by the common law or under the statute (P.S., c. 278, S. 8), because the child and I are strangers, and I am under no legal duty to protect him. Now suppose I see the same child trespassing in my own yard and meddling in like manner with the dangerous machinery of my own windmill. What additional obligation is cast upon me by reason of the child's trespass? The mere fact that the child is unable to take care of himself does not impose on me the legal duty of protecting him in the one case more than in the other. Upon what principle of law can an infant by coming unlawfully upon my premises impose upon me the legal duty of a guardian? None has been suggested, and we know of none.

An infant, no matter of how tender years, is liable in law for his trespasses. . . . If, then, the defendants' machinery was injured by the plaintiff's act in putting his hand in the gearing, he is liable to them for the damages in an action of trespass and to nominal damages for the wrongful entry. It would be no answer to such an action that the defendants might by force have prevented the trespass. It is impossible to hold that while the plaintiff is liable to the defendants in trespass, they are liable to him in case for neglecting to prevent the act which caused the injury both to him and them. Cases of enticement, allurement, or invitation of infants to their injury, or setting traps for them, and cases relating to the sufficiency of public ways, or to the exposure upon them of machinery attractive and dangerous to children, have no application here.

Danger from machinery in motion in the ordinary course of business cannot be distinguished from that arising from a well, pit, open scuttle, or other stationary object. The movement of the works is a part of the regular and normal condition of the premises. . . . The law no more compels the owners to shut down their gates and stop their business for the protection of a trespasser than it requires them to maintain a railing about an open scuttle or to fence in their machinery for the same purpose.

NOTE

The no duty synthesis. While *Buch* is by far the most famous of the no-duty case, it does not stand alone in the common law. In Mangan v. Atterton L.R. 1 Ex. 239, 240 (1866), the defendant whitesmith left exposed on a public street (as he customarily did) "a machine for crushing oil-cake, unfenced and without superintendence." The machine was operated by a handle on one side and had exposed crushing rollers on the other side. The handle could have been, but was not secured by wires. The 4-year-old plaintiff came along the street under the care of his 7-year-old brother in the company of friends, and stuck his hand in the cogs at his brother's direction while his brother turned the wheel, crushing the plaintiff's hand. The trial judge directed the jury to find that if it thought that "the machine was dangerous, and one that should not have been left unguarded in the way of ignorant people, and especially children, without, at all events, the handle being removed or fastened up and the cogs thrown out of gear," then they could award damages to the plaintiff. On appeal the £10 verdict for the plaintiff was reversed. Martin, B., held that the defendant's act was not the proximate cause of the harm "because the accident was directly caused by the act of the boy himself." Bramwell, B., concurred, saying: "The defendant is no more liable than if he had exposed goods coloured with poisonous paint, and the child had sucked them. It may seem a harsh way of putting it, but suppose this machine had been of a very delicate construction, and had been injured by the child's fingers, would not the child, in spite of his tender years, have been liable to an action as a tortfeasor? That shews that it is impossible to hold the defendant liable."

The same hostility toward tort liability is found in the more modern decision of Yania v. Bigan, 155 A.2d 343, 345, 346 (Pa. 1959). There the decedent and defendant were operators of nearby strip mines. One day Yania was visiting Bigan's land to discuss business. Located on the land was a worked-out strip-mine in which about 8 to 10 feet of water stood in a cut some 16 or 18 feet deep. Yania jumped into the cut and drowned, and the complaint in the wrongful death action that ensued charged Bigan "with three-fold negligence: (1) by urging, enticing, taunting and inveigling Yania to jump into the water; (2) by failing to warn Yania of a dangerous condition on the land; i.e., the cut wherein lay 8 to 10 feet of water; (3) by failing to go to Yania's rescue after he jumped into the water."

Jones, J., then dismissed all three parts of the claim. The first count failed because the

> complaint does not allege that Yania slipped or that he was pushed or that Bigan made any *physical* impact on his person. On the contrary, the only inference deducible from the facts alleged in the complaint is that Bigan, by the employment of cajolery and inveiglement, caused such a *mental* impact on Yania that the latter was deprived of his volition and freedom of choice and placed under a compulsion to jump into the water. Had Yania been a child of tender years or a person mentally deficient then it is conceivable that taunting and enticement could constitute actionable negligence if it resulted in harm. However to contend that such conduct directed to an adult in full possession of all his mental faculties constitutes actionable negligence is not only without precedent but completely without merit.

On the second count, Jones, J., held that Yania knew of the dangers since he himself was a strip-mine operator and was well aware of the obvious dangers of jumping into the water. Jones, J., then addressed the third claim as follows:

> Lastly, it is urged that Bigan failed to take the necessary steps to rescue Yania from the water. The mere fact that Bigan saw Yania in a position of peril in the water imposed upon him no legal, although a moral, obligation or duty to go to his rescue unless Bigan was legally responsible in whole or in part, for placing Yania in the perilous position. The language of this Court in Brown v. French, 104 Pa. 604, 607, 608 is apt. "If it appeared that the deceased, by his own carelessness, contributed in any degree to the accident which caused the loss of his life, the defendant ought not to have been held to answer for the consequences resulting

from that accident. . . . He voluntarily placed himself in the way of danger, and his death was the result of his own act . . . That his undertaking was an exceedingly reckless and dangerous one, the event proves, but there was no one to blame for it but himself. He had the right to try the experiment, obviously dangerous as it was, but then also upon him rested the consequences of that experiment, and upon no one else he may have been, and probably was, ignorant of the risk which he was taking upon himself, or knowing it, and trusting to his own skill he may have regarded it as easily superable. But in either case, the result of his ignorance, or of his mistake, must rest with himself — and cannot be charged to the defendants.

Ames, Law and Morals
22 Harv. L. Rev. 97, 110-113 (1908)

The law is utilitarian. It exists for the realization of the reasonable needs of the community. If the interest of an individual runs counter to this chief object of the law, it must be sacrificed. That is why, in the cases just considered and others that will occur to you, the innocent suffer and the wicked go unpunished. . . .

It remains to consider whether the law should ever go so far as to give compensation or to inflict punishment for damage which would not have happened but for the wilful inaction of another. I exclude cases in which, by reason of some relation between the parties like that of father and child, nurse and invalid, master and servant and others, there is a recognized legal duty to act. In the case supposed the only relation between the parties is that both are human beings. As I am walking over a bridge a man falls into the water. He cannot swim and calls for help. I am strong and a good swimmer, or, if you please, there is a rope on the bridge, and I might easily throw him an end and pull him ashore. I neither jump in nor throw him the rope, but see him drown. Or, again, I see a child on the railroad track too young to appreciate the danger of the approaching train. I might easily save the child, but do nothing, and the child, though it lives, loses both legs. Am I guilty of a crime, and must I make compensation to the widow and children of the man drowned and to the wounded child? Macaulay, in commenting upon his Indian Criminal Code, puts the case of a surgeon refusing to go from Calcutta to Meerut to perform an operation, although it should be absolutely certain that this surgeon was the only person in India who could perform it, and that, if it were not performed, the person who required it would die.

We may suppose again that the situation of imminent danger of death was created by the act, but the innocent act, of the person who refuses to prevent the death. The man, for example, whose eye was penetrated by the glancing shot of the careful pheasant hunter, stunned by the shot, fell face downward into a shallow pool by which he was standing. The hunter might easily save him, but lets him drown.

In the first three illustrations, however revolting the conduct of the man who declined to interfere, he was in no way responsible for the perilous situation, he did not increase the peril, he took away nothing from the person in jeopardy, he simply failed to confer a benefit upon a stranger. As the law stands today there would be no legal liability, either civilly or criminally, in any of these cases. The law does not compel active benevolence between man and man. It is left to one's conscience whether he shall be the good Samaritan or not.

But ought the law to remain in this condition? Of course any statutory duty to be benevolent would have to be exceptional. The practical difficulty in such legislation would be in drawing the line. But that difficulty has continually to be faced in the law. We should all be better satisfied if the man who refuses to throw a rope to a drowning man or to save a helpless child on the railroad track could be punished and be made to compensate the widow of the man drowned and the wounded child. We should not think it advisable to penalize the surgeon who refused to make the journey. These illustrations suggest a possible working rule. One who fails to interfere to save another from impending death or great bodily harm, when he might do so with little or no inconvenience to himself, and the death or great bodily harm follows as a consequence of his inaction, shall be punished criminally and shall make compensation to the party injured or to his widow and children in case of death. The case of the drowning of the man shot by the hunter differs from the others in that the hunter, although he acted innocently, did bring about the dangerous situation. Here, too, the lawyer who should try to charge the hunter would lead a forlorn hope. But it seems to me that he could make out a strong case against the hunter on common law grounds. By the early law, as we have seen, he would have been liable simply because he shot the other. In modern times the courts have admitted as an affirmative defense the fact that he was not negligent. May not the same courts refuse to allow a defense, if the defendant did not use reasonable means to prevent a calamity after creating the threatening situation? Be that as it may, it is hard to see why such a rule should not be declared by statute, if not by the courts.

Epstein, A Theory of Strict Liability
2 J. Legal Stud. 151, 198-200 (1973)

Under Ames' good Samaritan rule, a defendant in cases of affirmative acts would be required to take only those steps that can be done "with little or no inconvenience." But if the distinction between causing harm and not preventing harm is to be disregarded, why should the difference in standards between the two cases survive the reform of the law? The only explanation is that the two situations are regarded at bottom as raising totally different issues, even for those who insist upon the immateriality of this distinction. Even those who argue, as Ames does, that the law is utilitarian must in the end find some special place for the claims of egoism which are an inseparable byproduct of the belief that individual autonomy — individual liberty — is a good in itself not explainable in terms of its purported social worth. It is one thing to *allow* people to act as they please in the belief that the "invisible hand" will provide the happy congruence of the individual and the social good. Such a theory, however, at bottom must regard individual autonomy as but a means to some social end. It takes a great deal more to assert that men are *entitled* to act as they choose (within the limits of strict liability) even though it is certain that there will be cases where individual welfare will be in conflict with the social good. Only then is it clear that even freedom has its costs: costs revealed in the acceptance of the good Samaritan doctrine.

But are the alternatives more attractive? Once one decides that as a matter of statutory or common law duty, an individual is required under some circumstances to act at his own cost for the exclusive benefit of another, then it is very hard to set out in a principled manner the limits of social interference with individual liberty. Suppose one claims, as Ames does, that his proposed rule applies only in the "obvious" cases where everyone (or almost everyone) would admit that the duty was appropriate: to the case of the man upon the bridge who refuses to throw a rope to a stranger drowning in the waters below. Even if the rule starts out with such modest ambitions, it is difficult to confine it to those limits. Take a simple case first. *X* as a representative of a private charity asks you for $10 in order to save the life of some starving child in a country ravaged by war. There are other donors available but the number of needy children exceeds that number. The money means "nothing" to you. Are you under a legal obligation to give the $10? Or to lend it interest-free? Does $10 amount to a substantial cost or inconvenience within the meaning of Ames' rule? It is true that the relationship between the gift to charity and the survival of an unidentified child is not so apparent as is the relationship between the man upon the bridge and the swimmer caught in the swirling seas. But lest the physical imagery govern, it is clear that someone will die as a consequence of your inaction in both cases. Is there a duty to give, or is the contribution a matter of charity?

Consider yet another example where services, not cash, are in issue. Ames insists that his rule would not require the only surgeon in India capable of saving the life of a person with a given affliction to travel across the subcontinent to perform an operation, presumably because the inconvenience and cost would be substantial. But how would he treat the case if some third person were willing to pay him for all of his efforts? If the payment is sufficient to induce the surgeon to act, then there is no need for the good Samaritan doctrine at all. But if it is not, then it is again necessary to compare the costs of the physician with the benefits to his prospective patient. It is hard to know whether Ames would require the forced exchange under these circumstances. But it is at least arguable that under his theory forced exchanges should be required, since the payment might reduce the surgeon's net inconvenience to the point where it was trivial.

Once forced exchanges, regardless of the levels of payment, are accepted, it will no longer be possible to delineate the sphere of activities in which contracts (or charity) will be required in order to procure desired benefits and the sphere of activity in which those benefits can be procured as of right. Where tests of "reasonableness" — stated with such confidence, and applied with such difficulty — dominate the law of tort, it becomes impossible to tell where liberty ends and obligation begins; where contract ends, and tort begins. In each case, it will be possible for some judge or jury to decide that there was something else which the defendant should have done, and he will decide that on the strength of some cost-benefit formula that is difficult indeed to apply. These remarks are conclusive, I think, against the adoption of Ames' rule by judicial innovation, and they bear heavily on the desirability of the abandonment of the good Samaritan rule by legislation as well. It is not surprising that the law has, in the midst of all the clamor for reform, remained unmoved in the end, given the inability to form alternatives to the current position.

Bender, A Lawyer's Primer on Feminist Theory and Tort
38 J. Leg. Ed. 34-35 (1988)

How would this drowning-stranger hypothetical look from a new legal perspective informed by a feminist ethic based upon notions of caring, responsibility, interconnectedness, and cooperation? If we put abstract reasoning and autonomy aside momentarily, we can see what else matters. In defining duty, what matters is that someone, a human being, a part of us, is drowning and will die without some affirmative action. This seems more urgent, more imperative, more important than any possible infringement of individual autonomy by the imposition of an affirmative duty. If we think about the stranger as a human being for a moment, we may realize that much more is involved than balancing one person's interest in having his life saved and another's interest in not having affirmative duties imposed upon him in the absence of a special relationship, although even then the balance seems to me to weigh in favor of imposing a duty or standard of care that requires action. The drowning stranger is not the only person affected by the lack of care. He is not detached from everyone else. He no doubt has people who care about him — parents, spouse, children, friends, colleagues; groups he participates in — religious, social, athletic, artistic, political, educational, work-related; he may even have people who depend upon him for emotional or financial support. He is interconnected with others. If the stranger drowns, many will be harmed. It is not an isolated event with one person's interests balanced against another's. When our legal system trains us to understand the drowning-stranger story as a limited event between two people, both of whom have interests at least equally worth protecting, and when the social ramifications we credit most are the impositions on personal liberty of action, we take a human situation and translate it into a cold, dehumanized algebraic equation. We forget that we are talking about human death or grave physical harms and their reverberating consequences when we equate the consequences with such things as one person's momentary freedom not to act. People are decontextualized for the analysis, yet no one really lives an acontextual life. What gives us the authority to take contextual, actual problems and encode them in a language of numbers, letters, and symbols that represents no reality in any actual person's life?

. . . . Why should our autonomy or freedom not to rescue weigh more heavily in law than a stranger's harms and the consequent harms to people with whom she is interconnected?

NOTES

1. An affirmative duty to rescue. What are the possible grounds on which to construct an argument for or against a generalized duty to rescue strangers? In particular, is it possible to argue, as is urged by Judge Posner, Epstein's Tort Theory: A Critique, 8 J. Legal Stud. 457, 460 (1979), that a duty to rescue might be justified on quasi-consensual grounds:

> Suppose that if all the members of society could somehow be assembled they would agree unanimously that, as a reasonable measure of mutual protection, anyone who can warn or rescue someone in distress at negligible cost to himself (in time, danger, or whatever) should be required to do so. These mutual promises of assistance would create a contract that Epstein would presumably enforce since he considers the right to make binding contracts a fundamental one. However, there are technical obstacles — in this case insurmountable ones — to the formation of an actual contract among so many people. Transaction costs are prohibitive. If, moved by these circumstances, a court were to impose tort liability on a bystander who failed to assist a person in distress, such liability would be a means of carrying out the original desires of the parties just as if it were an express contract that was being enforced.

The point of this example is that tort duties can sometimes (perhaps, as we shall see, generally) be viewed as devices for vindicating the principles that underlie freedom of contract. It may be argued, however, that the contract analogy is inapplicable because the bystander would not be compensated for coming to the rescue of the person in distress. But this argument overlooks the fact that the consideration for the rescue is not payment when the rescue is effected but a commitment to reciprocate should the roles of the parties some day be reversed. Liability would create a mutual protective arrangement under which everyone was obliged to attempt a rescue when circumstances dictated and, in exchange, was entitled to the assistance of anyone who might be able to help him should he ever find himself in a position of peril.

If the duty to rescue were recognized, what would be the elements of a successful cause of action? In particular, how would one identify the proper defendant? Handle the case of multiple defendants? Define and prove cause in fact and proximate cause? Handle the issue of contributory negligence? See, on these problems, Epstein, Causation and Corrective Justice, A Reply to Two Critics, 8 J. Legal Stud. 477, 490-492 (1979). And for the affirmative case for the duty of rescue see Weinrib, The Case for a Duty to Rescue, 90 Yale L.J. 247 (1980), and Heyman, Foundations of the Duty to Rescue, 47 Vand. L. Rev. 673, 747-748 (1994), which advocates a duty to rescue that "would require a citizen in an emergency situation to take action reasonably necessary to prevent either a crime of violence or a substantial risk of death or serious bodily harm to another, unless that action would involve a substantial risk of death or serious bodily harm to the rescuer or others."

2. Restitution and rescue. As a common-law matter, is it better to approach the rescue problem with restitution instead of tort doctrines? Whereas the tort solution requires a large judgment against the able defendant who does not rescue, the restitution solution provides a much smaller payment to the enterprising person who does rescue. The restitution scheme reduces the number of cases in which the legal rule will be invoked, and it eliminates the vexing problems of multiple causation that arise whenever many persons are in a position to undertake a rescue (or to call the police) and none in fact does. Yet how are the levels of compensation to be fixed? Is it sound policy to pay rescuers out of public funds? See the thoughtful article by Dawson, Rewards for the Rescue of Human Life, in The Good Samaritan and the Law (Ratcliffe ed. 1966), in which a very cautious attitude is taken toward the creation of the restitution remedies. Yet restitution remedies have been favored relative to tort ones for professional rescuers who might be discouraged by the threat of tort suits from making the heavy investments necessary to carry out rescues at sea. See Landes and Posner, Salvors, Finders, Good Samaritans, and Other Rescuers: An Economic Study of Law and Altruism, 7 J. Legal Stud. 83, 119-127 (1978).

3. Legislation and the good Samaritan. The problem of the good Samaritan has provoked a number of legislative responses, some of which are designed to induce efforts to rescue by insulating the rescuer against liability for ordinary negligence, and others by imposing affirmative duties to rescue, subject to the payment of fines. In both cases the rescuer remains liable for willful misconduct. For example, Kansas Statute §§865-2891 (a) & (d) provide:

> (a) Any health care provider who in good faith renders emergency care or assistance at the scene of an emergency or accident including treatment of a minor without first obtaining the consent of the parent or guardian of such minor shall not be liable for any civil damages for acts or omissions other than damages occasioned by gross negligence or by willful and wanton acts or omissions by such persons in rendering emergency care.
>
> (d) Any provision herein contained notwithstanding, the ordinary standards of care and rules of negligence shall apply in those cases wherein emergency care and assistance is rendered in any physician's or dentist's office, clinic, emergency room or hospital with or without compensation.

Vermont Statute, title 12, §519 provides:

> (a) A person who knows that another is exposed to grave physical harm shall, to the extent that the same can be rendered without danger or peril to himself or without interference with important duties owed to others, give reasonable assistance to the exposed person unless that assistance or care is being provided by others.
>
> (b) A person who provides reasonable assistance in compliance with subsection (a) of this section shall not be liable in civil damages unless his acts constitute gross negligence or unless he will receive or expects to receive remuneration. Nothing contained in this subsection shall alter existing law with respect to tort liability of a practitioner of the healing arts for acts committed in the ordinary course of his practice.
>
> (c) A person who willfully violates subsection (a) of this section shall be fined not more than $100.00.

Does the Vermont statute adopt a straight negligence approach in rescue cases? Does it authorize the creation of a private cause of action? See, on the statute, Franklin, Vermont Requires Rescue: A Comment, 25 Stan. L. Rev. 51 (1972).

Montgomery v. National Convoy & Trucking Co.
195 S.E. 247 (S.C. 1937)

[Defendants' trucks had stalled on an icy highway without their fault, blocking the road completely. About fifteen minutes later plaintiff's car came over a hill and started down toward the trucks before plaintiff or plaintiff's driver could see them. The trucks were then about 50 feet away, not being previously visible because of the hill. In view of the icy condition of the road, plaintiff's car could not be stopped. "The agents of the [defendants] operating the trucks knew, or had every reason to know, that once a car had passed the crest of the hill and started down the decline, . . . it would be impossible to stop such automobile or motor vehicle due to the icy condition of the highway, regardless of the rate of speed at which such automobile may be traveling." Defendants' drivers had ample time to place a warning signal at the top of the hill where it could have been observed by the plaintiff's chauffeur who, well aware of the dangerous condition of the road, could have stopped before the collision that injured plaintiff. The defendants' motion for a directed verdict was refused, and the jury awarded plaintiff the full amount demanded, $3,000. The defendants appealed.]

BAKER, J. One may be negligent by acts of omission as well as of commission, and liability therefor will attach if the act of omission of a duty owed another, under the circumstances, is the direct, proximate and efficient cause of the injury. It is only where the evidence is susceptible of but one reasonable inference that the Court may declare what that inference is and take the case from the consideration of the jury. . . .

One of the acts of negligence alleged in the complaint is the failure of the appellants to warn approaching vehicles of the conditions existing, and this necessarily means that the warning should be given at a point where it would be effective. That appellants recognized that they owed a duty to others using the highway cannot be questioned, since they at some time put out flares and left the lights on their trucks. But if appellants owed a duty to others using the highway, and this cannot be disputed, the performance of such duty was not met by merely having lights at the point where the trucks blocked the highway, but it was incumbent on the appellants to take such precautions as would reasonably be calculated to prevent injury.

For the moment let us repeat some of the facts. There is a curve in the highway at the crest of a long hill. A short distance to the south of the curve and crest of the hill two trucks are stalled and block the entire road. It is a much-traveled highway. Respondent's chauffeur testified that due to the curve in the road and the hill, the lights of an automobile approaching from the north would not focus on the trucks until the automobile was within a little over fifty feet from the trucks. Once a car passed the crest of the hill and commenced to descend on the south side, it could not be stopped due to the ice on the highway — the slippery condition thereof, which was known or should have been known to appellants. No flagman nor warning of any description was placed at the crest of the hill to warn approaching cars. That a warning at the crest of the hill would have been effective and prevented the injury is fully demonstrated from other evidence had upon the trial. The danger of the situation was so self-evident that a jury could have concluded that the omission to warn approaching travelers from the north at a point where the warning would be effective, amounted not only to negligence, but to willfulness. However, the jury in this case have vindicated their intelligence and freedom from passion when they found only inadvertence.

NOTES

1. Misfeasance and nonfeasance. The distinction between misfeasance and nonfeasance is relatively clear in those cases in which it matters most: when the defendant has not rescued the plaintiff from some peril that the defendant has not created. The distinction between misfeasance and nonfeasance is both less critical and more difficult to draw when the defendant has created the dangerous condition in question but has failed to neutralize the danger so created. That situation arose in *Montgomery,* where the defendants, without fault, blocked the highway when their trucks stalled on an icy highway. A similar situation arose in Newton v. Ellis, 119 Eng. Rep. 424 (K.B. 1855). The defendant, while under contract with the local board of health, dug a hole in a public highway that he left unlighted at night. Shortly thereafter the plaintiff, while driving along, fell into the hole. The three judges who heard the case denied that the action was one for nonfeasance. Coleridge, J., remarked: "This is not a case of not doing: the defendant does something, omitting to secure protection for the public. He is not sued for not putting up a light, but for the complex act." Erle, J., agreed, saying: "Here the cause of action is the making the hole, compounded with the not putting up a light. When these two are blended, the result is no more than if two positive acts were committed, such as digging the hole and throwing out the dirt: the two would make up one act." Compare the account of negligence given by Baron Alderson in Blyth v. Birmingham Water Works, supra at page 189.

Suppose that *A,* while driving, hits *B* because *A* has failed to brake in time to stop. Can *A* argue that this is a simple case of nonfeasance for which he is not responsible? Why not?

2. The duty to rescue under strict liability. In cases like *Montgomery* the duty to rescue only arose because the defendants could not be held liable under a negligence system for originally blocking the highway, which occurred without his fault. The analysis of that case would be, however, quite different if a rule of strict liability applied to highway accidents. On that view, the defendant could not rely on the inevitable accident defense when its trucks first stalled. Nonetheless it could escape or reduce its liability by showing that the plaintiff proceeded too rapidly in light of the poor road conditions. Given the potentially extensive liability that defendant would face under strict liability, it would have a strong incentive to post warnings at the top of the road, both to reduce the charges of having its own property damaged in the collision and to bolster its assumption of risk or contributory negligence defenses against any potential plaintiffs who saw, or could have seen, the warnings. The broader strict liability theory therefore narrows the need for any fresh tortious duty to take affirmative care, given the prior dangerous situation. What analysis should apply if a bystander is in a position to warn oncoming cars of the peril, but chooses to continue on his way?

There are other situations in which a strict liability rule could well prevent some of the problems of the duty to rescue. In Louisville & Nashville R. Co. v. Scruggs, 49 So. 399 (Ala. 1909), defendant's freight train was stopped at a certain place when a fire engine drove up to extinguish a fire in plaintiff's house, just across the tracks. Defendant's employees refused to move the train except on the dispatcher's orders and, by the time they came, plaintiff's house was destroyed. The Alabama Supreme Court denied recovery, since the defendant's use of its land was "merely passive," adding that "The law imposes no duty on one man to aid another in the preservation of the latter's property, but only the duty not to injure another's property in the use of his own." The court did concede that had the fire department already placed the hose across the track to plaintiff's house, then if defendant's engineer deliberately or negligently ran over the hose, defendant would have been liable to the plaintiff for resulting damage to his home. One judge dissented, thinking the attitude of defendant's employees showed "an indifference to the situation and emergency that was little short of shocking." Should it make a difference if the local rules of the road give fire engines the right of way over all other traffic? If so, how might the plaintiff state his cause of action?

Scruggs provoked the following response in Hale, Prima Facie Torts, Combination, and Non-Feasance, 46 Colum. L. Rev. 196, 214 (1946):

> Perhaps judicial reluctance to recognize affirmative duties is based on one or both of two inarticulate assumptions. One of these is that a rugged, independent individual needs no help from others, save such as they may be disposed to render him out of kindness, or such as he can induce them to render by the ordinary process of bargaining, without having the government step in to make them help. All he is supposed to ask of the government is that it interfere to prevent others from doing him positive harm. The other assumption is that when a government *requires* a person to act, it is necessarily interfering more seriously with his liberty than when it places limits on his freedom to act — to make a man serve another is to make him a slave, while to forbid him to commit affirmative wrongs is to leave him still essentially a freeman. Neither of these assump-

tions is universally true. Neither was true in [*Scruggs*]. No matter how rugged the owner of the burning building, his property depended for its preservation on the affirmative acts of the railroad employees — acts which they were evidently not disposed to render out of kindness, and which he was in no position to induce them to perform by bargaining. Nor would a legal duty to move the train have subjected either the employees or the railroad company itself to anything having the slightest resemblance to slavery.

3. The duty to rescue those whom you have harmed. A somewhat different variation on the same theme arises when the defendant has already harmed the plaintiff in ways for which there is no independent tortious liability. That result could arise either because the defendant himself was not negligent in his primary conduct or because the contributory negligence of the plaintiff (as is no longer generally the case) is a complete bar to liability. The situation today is governed by the Restatement (Second) of Torts, which provides as follows:

§322. DUTY TO AID ANOTHER HARMED BY ACTOR'S CONDUCT
If the actor knows or has reason to know that by his conduct, whether tortious or innocent, he has caused such bodily harm to another as to make him helpless and in danger of further harm, the actor is under a duty to exercise reasonable care to prevent such further harm.

On the application of section 322, see Summers v. Dominguez, 84 P.2d 237 (Cal. App. 1938). There the plaintiff was struck by the defendant's truck while walking on the side of a public highway. The defendant, who had had a couple of drinks, stopped his truck and called out to the victim, but hearing no response continued on his way. He was tracked down by some efficient detective work after someone found the plaintiff in bad shape the next day. The defense rested its case on the ground that the plaintiff's walking on the public highway was per se negligence. In upholding the plaintiff's cause of action for the failure to aid, the court relied upon the comment to section 322: "The liability which this Section recognizes is not imposed as a penalty for the actor's original misconduct, but for a breach of a separate duty to aid and protect the other after his helpless condition caused by the actor's misconduct is or should be known."

The disposition of highway accident cases today is often governed by statutes such as California Vehicle Code §20003, which provides as follows:

§20003. DUTY TO GIVE INFORMATION AND RENDER AID
(a) The driver of any vehicle involved in an accident resulting in injury to or death of any person shall also give his name, address and the registration number of the vehicle he is driving, and the name of the owner to the person struck or the driver or occupants of any vehicle collided with or shall give such information to any traffic or police officer at the

scene of the accident and shall render to any person injured in the accident reasonable assistance, including the carrying or the making arrangements for the carrying of such person to a physician, surgeon or hospital for medical or surgical treatment if it is apparent that such treatment is necessary or if such carrying is requested by the injured person.

Might such a duty be imposed by statute on any licensed driver? On a bystander? If so, should compensation be provided? Payable by whom?

4. *Aid to the helpless: once begun, then undone.* In Black v. New York, N.H. & H. R.R., 79 N.E. 797, 798 (Mass. 1907), plaintiff boarded defendant's suburban train, apparently very intoxicated, but not raucous — just helpless. When he reached his stop the conductor and the brakeman took him out of the car and carried him halfway up a flight of stairs, where they left him. The plaintiff balanced himself for a short while and then fell backward, "turned a complete somersault and struck on the back of his head," and was badly hurt. In deciding that there was a jury case, the court said in part:

> They [defendant's servants] were under no obligation to remove him from the car, or to provide for his safety after he left the car. But they voluntarily undertook to help him from the car, and they were bound to use ordinary care in what they did that might affect his safety. Not only in the act of removal, but in the place where they left him, it was their duty to have reasonable regard for his safety in view of his manifest condition. The jury might have found that they were negligent in leaving him on the steps where a fall would be likely to do him much harm.

Compare Zelenko v. Gimbel Bros., 287 N.Y.S. 134, 135 (N.Y. Sup. Ct. 1935), where the court said:

> But there are many ways that a defendant's duty to act may arise. Plaintiff's intestate was taken ill in defendant's store. We will assume that the defendant owed her no duty at all; that defendant could have let her be and die. But if a defendant undertakes a task, even if under no duty to undertake it, the defendant must not omit to do what an ordinary man would do in performing the task.
>
> Here the defendant undertook to render medical aid to the plaintiff's intestate. Plaintiff says that defendant kept his intestate for six hours in an infirmary without any medical care. If defendant had left plaintiff's intestate alone, beyond doubt some bystander, who would be influenced more by charity than by legalistic duty, would have summoned an ambulance. Defendant segregated this plaintiff's intestate where such aid could not be given and then left her alone.
>
> The plaintiff is wrong in thinking that the duty of a common carrier of passengers is the same as the duty of this defendant. The common carrier assumes its duty by its contract of carriage. This defendant assumed its duty by meddling in matters with which legalistically it had no concern. The plaintiff is right in arguing that when the duty arose, the same type of neglect is actionable in both cases.

See Restatement (Second) of Torts §324:

§324. DUTY OF ONE WHO TAKES CHARGE OF ANOTHER WHO IS HELPLESS
One who, being under no duty to do so, takes charge of another who is helpless adequately to aid or protect himself is subject to liability to the other for any bodily harm caused to him by
    (a) the failure of the actor to exercise reasonable care to secure the safety of the other while within the actor's charge, or
    (b) the actor's discontinuing his aid or protection, if by so doing he leaves the other in a worse position than when the actor took charge of him.

Does it make sense to have a rule that allows one person to glory in the suffering of another while penalizing his neighbor for honest if inept efforts to aid? Compare the following two cases: In the first, *A*, coming upon the scene of an accident, picks up *B*, who is helpless, and starts to drive him to a hospital. En route she drives negligently and has a collision, and *B*'s injuries are aggravated. In the second, *A*, coming upon the scene of an accident, picks up *B*, who is helpless, and starts to drive him to a hospital. A moment later *A* changes her mind and returns *B* to the scene of the accident. Assume that prompt medical care would have greatly reduced the harm to *B* and that this was obvious to *A*.

5. *Cracks in the good Samaritan doctrine.* In Soldano v. O'Daniels, 190 Cal. Rptr. 310 (Cal. App. 1983), the decedent was in imminent danger of being shot at Happy Jack's Saloon when another patron ran across the street to the defendant's restaurant and asked the defendant's bartender to allow him to use the phone or to make an emergency call to the police on his behalf. The bartender refused to honor the request and the killing took place as feared. The court rebuffed the defendant's argument that there was no duty to aid or assist the plaintiff. It first agreed with Prosser that the common-law rule denying the duty to rescue violates "common decency" and is "revolting to any moral sense." It then held that the defendant, while not required to rescue, did have "to permit the patron from Happy Jack's to place a call to the police or to place the call himself" Restatement (Second) of Torts §327 renders any person who "knows or has reason to know that a third person is giving or is ready to give another aid necessary to prevent physical harm to [an endangered person]" tortiously liable if he "negligently prevents or disables the third person from giving such aid."

6. *Constitutional dimensions of the duty to rescue.* In DeShaney v. Winnebago County Department of Social Services, 489 U.S 189, 196 (1989), the plaintiff, a child left permanently retarded after being repeatedly and savagely beaten by his father, brought an action for damages under the due process clause of the Fourteenth Amendment against the

county social services department for its failure to protect him from child abuse. The injuries arose even though department personnel had visited the boy and his father over a period of two years and had seen clear signs of child abuse. The gist of the complaint was that the failure to intercede "deprived" the plaintiff of his constitutional liberty. The Court rejected the cause of action, holding that the due process clause generally confers "no affirmative right to government aid, even where such aid may be necessary to secure life, liberty, or property interests of which the government itself may not deprive the individual. . . . If the Due Process clause does not require the State to provide its citizens with particular protective services, it follows that the State cannot be held liable under the Clause for injuries that could have been averted had it chosen to provide them." Should the cause of action have been allowed as a matter of state tort law? Does it make a difference that the department had assumed some supervision over the case?

The limits of *DeShaney* were explored at length in K.H. Through Murphy v. Morgan, 914 F.2d 846, 859 (7th Cir. 1990). There K.H. had been subjected to massive child abuse by her natural parents at a very young age and had been taken into custody by the state, which then placed her in a long series of foster-care situations, some of which resulted in further abuse of her. In a section 1983 action against the guardianship administrator (Morgan), Posner, J., held in line with the tort law: "Once the state assumes custody of a person, it owes him a rudimentary duty of safekeeping no matter how perilous his circumstances when he was free." Posner then found a clear breach of duty when a child in state custody is "handed over by state officers to a foster parent or other custodian, private or public, *whom the state knows or suspects to be a child abuser.*" Yet owing to the financial difficulties and professional uncertainties in these placement situations, Posner rejected the plaintiff's assertion that she had a specific right not to be "shuttled . . . among" foster homes and remanded the case to determine whether she could recover under his proposed standard after taking into account both financial restraints and the limits of professional judgment on matters of child care.

C. DUTIES OF OWNERS AND OCCUPIERS

Robert Addie & Sons (Collieries), Ltd. v. Dumbreck
[1929] A.C. 358

[The defendant colliers operated a haulage system in their own fields near a public road in order to remove coal ashes from the pithead where mining operations were going on. The haulage system employed an endless wire cable; at one end of the system, near the mouth of the mine, there was an eight-horsepower engine that was used intermittently to operate the system. At the other end, which was not visible to anyone working the electrical motor, was a large, heavy horizontal wheel around which the cable passed at a rate of two to two and one-half miles per hour when the system was in use. The wheel in question was protected only by four boards that were placed upon its top; there was a space of eight or nine inches between these boards and the bed of ashes beneath the wheel. The court below found that the wheel was dangerous and attractive to children.

The field in which the haulage system was located was surrounded by a hedge that contained a number of gaps, making it inadequate to keep little children away from the wheel. In fact, many people used the field as a shortcut and many children played there. Though the defendant's servants from time to time warned children to stay out of the field and admonished adults not to cross, they knew their warnings had little or no effect. The defendant's servants did maintain a watch over the field, but to protect the defendant's property, not the persons who trespassed on it. There were two gates to the field, at one of which was posted a notice that read "Trespassers will be prosecuted."

The plaintiff's son was a 4-year-old boy who had been warned by the plaintiff not to go into the field and not to play with the wheel. The exact circumstances of his death were not determined, but it appeared that he had either been "sitting on the cover of the wheel or in a position in front of and in close proximity to the pulley and rope, being caught and drawn into the mechanism when it was set in motion by the defendant's servants."

The court below had awarded the plaintiff judgment on the ground that the accident was due to the fault of the defendant in not taking suitable precautions to avoid accidents to persons using the fields before activating the haulage system.

The defendant appealed.]

HAILSHAM, L.C. . . . The first and in my opinion the only question which arises for determination is the capacity in which the deceased child was in the field and at the wheel on the occasion of the accident. There are three categories in which persons visiting premises belonging to another person may fall; they may go

1. By the invitation, express or implied, of the occupier;
2. With the leave and license of the occupier, and
3. As trespassers.

It was suggested in argument that there was a fourth category of persons who were not on the premises with the leave or license of the occupier, but who were not pure trespassers. I cannot find any foundation for this suggestion either in English or Scotch law, and I do not think that the category exists.

The duty which rests upon the occupier of premises towards the persons who come on such premises differs according to the category into which the visitor falls. The highest duty exists towards those persons who fall into the first category, and who are present by the invitation of the occupier. Towards such persons the occupier has the duty of taking reasonable care that the premises are safe.

In the case of persons who are not there by invitation, but who are there by leave and licence, express or implied, the duty is much less stringent — the occupier has no duty to ensure that the premises are safe, but he is bound not to create a trap or allow a concealed danger to exist upon the said premises, which is not apparent to the visitor, but which is known — or ought to be known — to the occupier.

Towards the trespasser the occupier has no duty to take reasonable care for his protection or even to protect him from concealed danger. The trespasser comes on to the premises at his own risk. An occupier is in such a case liable only where the injury is due to some wilful act involving something more than the absence of reasonable care. There must be some act done with the deliberate intention of doing harm to the trespasser, or at least some act done with reckless disregard of the presence of the trespasser. . . .

The only question, therefore, that remains for decision in this case is whether, upon the findings of fact of the Court of Session (which are not open to review), the respondent's son may properly be regarded as having been at the wheel at the time of the accident with the leave and license of the appellants. If this had been proved, I should have been prepared to hold that the wheel, which was at times stationary and which was started without any warning, and which was, in the words of the Court of Session, "dangerous and attractive to children and insufficiently protected at the time of the accident," amounted to a trap, and that the respondent would therefore have been entitled to recover. But in my opinion, the findings of fact effectually negative that view. It is found that the appellants warned children out of the field and reproved adults who came there, and all that can be said is that these warnings were frequently neglected and that there was a gap in the hedge through which it was easy to pass on to the field. I cannot regard the fact that the appellants did not effectively fence the field or the fact that their warnings were frequently disregarded as sufficient to justify an inference that they permitted the children to be on the field, and, in the absence of such a permission, it is clear that the respondent's child was merely a trespasser. The sympathy which one cannot help feeling for the unhappy father must not be allowed to alter one's view of the law, and I have no doubt that in law the respondent's son was a mere trespasser, and that as such the appellants owed him no duty to protect him from injury. On these grounds I am of opinion that this appeal succeeds and must be allowed with costs, and I move your Lordships accordingly.

VISCOUNT DUNEDIN . . . What I particularly wish to emphasize is that there are the three different classes — invitees, licensees, trespassers. I think, in the Scottish cases at least, there has been a little laxity in distinguishing between invitees and licensees. The best test of who is an invitee is, I think, given by Lord Kinnear in *Devlin*'s case. He must be on the land for some purpose in which he and the proprietor have a joint interest. A licensee is a person whom the proprietor has not in any way invited — he has no interest in his being there — but he has either expressly permitted him to use his lands or knowledge of his presence more or less habitual having been brought home to him, he has then either accorded permission or shown no practical anxiety to stop his further frequenting the lands. The trespasser is he who goes on the land without invitation of any sort and whose presence is either unknown to the proprietor or, if known, is practically objected to.

Now the line that separates each of these three classes is an absolutely rigid line. There is no half-way house, no no-man's land between adjacent territories. When I say rigid, I mean rigid in law. When you come to the facts it may well be that there is great difficulty — such difficulty as may give rise to difference of judicial opinion — in deciding into which category a particular case falls, but a judge must decide and, having decided, then the law of that category will rule and there must be no looking to the law of the adjoining category. I cannot help thinking that the use of epithets, "bare licensees," "pure trespassers" and so on, has much to answer for in obscuring what I think is a vital proposition that, in deciding cases of the class we are considering, the first duty of the tribunal is to fix once and for all into which of the three classes the person in question falls. . . .

Something has been said about fencing. There is no duty on a proprietor to fence his land against the world under sanction that, if he does not, those who come over it become licensees. Of course, a proprietor may do nothing at all to prevent people coming over his lands and they may come so often that permission will be held to be implied, or he may do something, but that something so half-heartedly as to be equivalent to doing nothing. For instance, a mere putting up of a notice "No Trespassers Allowed" or "Strictly Private," followed, when people often come, by no further steps, would, I think, leave it open for a judge or jury to hold implied permission. But when a proprietor protests and goes on protesting, turning away people when he meets them, as he did here, and giving no countenance in anything that he does to their presence there, then I think no Court has a right to say that permission must be implied. As I have said, circumstances vary infinitely and you cannot ab ante furnish a test which will fit every case; but it is permission that must be proved, not tolerance, though tolerance in some circumstances may be so pronounced as to lead to a conclusion that it was really tantamount to permission. I, therefore, find that the child who met with an accident in this case was a trespasser.

[Appeal allowed.]

NOTES

1. *Liability to trespassers.* In Excelsior Wire Rope Co., Ltd. v. Callan, [1930] A.C. 404, decided the year after *Addie,* the House of Lords upheld a judgment on behalf of two infant plaintiffs whose hands had been crushed when caught between the wire rope and the pulley used to operate the defendant's haulage system. There were obvious similarities to *Addie.* The House of Lords, treating the plaintiffs as trespassers, nonetheless distinguished *Addie* and held that the defendant's servants had acted in reckless disregard of the plaintiffs' welfare. The haulage system was located in an open field next to a playground run by the local town corporation for the benefit of its children. The field was constantly "swarming" with children, who left the playground to play games such as hide and seek on and about the defendant's machinery. The defendant's servants knew that the children constantly played upon the machinery, and the House of Lords found them in reckless disregard of their duty, even though they first cleared the area of children, when "they started the machinery without being clear that the wire was free from children." How is *Callan* distinguishable from *Addie?* In this connection note that Lord Buckmaster concluded his judgment by saying that the defendants were in breach of their duty because it was "well known" to them "that when this machine was going to start it was extremely likely that children would be there and, with the wire in motion, would be exposed to grave danger."

The "willful and wanton" exception to the general rule was seized upon by the Federal Court of Appeals in Gould v. DeBeve, 330 F.2d 826 (D.C. Cir. 1964). There the plaintiff, a $2\frac{1}{2}$-year-old infant, and his mother were staying temporarily with a mrs. Dodd, under an arrangement whereby Mrs. DeBeve reimbursed Mrs. Dodd for half the rent owed to the landlord. The landlord did not know of this arrangement, and it was, in addition, contrary to an express provision of Mrs. Dodd's lease that restricted occupation of her apartment to herself and to members of her immediate family. The day of the accident was extremely hot. The two women had left a bedroom window open even though its screen was warped and cracked, indeed defective in almost every conceivable way. The plaintiff, while playing by the open window, knocked out the loose screen and fell to the ground, sustaining injuries. The court expressed an obvious distaste for a rule that treats alike all trespassers, from guileless infants to persistent poachers. But it did not upset the determination below that the plaintiff was indeed a trespasser in the apartment. Instead it upheld the jury verdict for the plaintiff by noting it was proper to find the defendants guilty of "wilful and wanton misconduct" in ignoring their statutory obligation to replace the defective screen after they had received urgent requests from Mrs. Dodd to do so. Although the statute only provided that the screens "be so maintained as to prevent effectively the entrance of flies and mosquitoes into the building," the court found that the defendant's statutory obligation "certainly comprehends, in the Washington summer when windows must be raised, screens which keep flies out and young children in."

2. *Trespassers on land adjacent to the public way.* Suppose the plaintiff misses a turn and stops on private land that is not distinguishable in any way from the public road. If the land is dangerous (perhaps because of the removal of some previous structure, or as a result of some recent excavation), should the trespass bar the plaintiff's cause of action? The general view has allowed plaintiff to recover under limited circumstances. In Hardcastle v. South Yorkshire Ry. & River Dun Co., 157 Eng. Rep. 761, 764 (Ex. 1859), Pollock, C.B., said: "We think that the proper and true test of legal liability is, whether the excavation be substantially adjoining the way, and it would be very dangerous if it were otherwise — if in every case it was to be left as a fact to the jury, whether the excavation were sufficiently near to the highway to be dangerous." The American cases have tended to follow the same line, although there may be greater latitude in imposing liability for hazards that are not abutting the public way. See Sinclair Tex. Pipe Line Co. v. Patterson, 54 P.2d 204 (Okla. 1936). The rule in question has also been applied to private roads that have not been marked off with sufficient clearness. See, e.g., Aluminum Co. of America v. Walden, 322 S.W.2d 696 (Ark. 1959).

3. *Attractive nuisance: origins.* The rigors of the common-law rules regarding trespassers have also been eased by the widespread adoption of the attractive nuisance doctrine that allows infant trespassers to recover when lured onto defendant's premises by some attractive condition created and maintained by the defendant, such as railway turntables, explosives, electrical conduits, smoldering fires, and rickety structures. Exposure to liability under the doctrine is, however, not unlimited, for the case law has not extended it to cover "rivers, creeks, ponds, wagons, axes, plows, woodpiles, haystacks," and the like. Franich v. Great Northern Ry. Co., 260 F.2d 599 (9th Cir. 1958).

Some of the earlier common-law cases, such as *Buch* supra refused to impose duties on landowners toward infant trespassers, who sought in effect to profit from their own wrong. In addition, the attractive nuisance doctrine was frequently rejected on grounds that, once recognized, the duties it envisioned could not be confined or limited. This argument was made forcefully by Mitchell, J., in Twist v. Winona & St. P. Ry., 39 N.W. 402, 404 (Minn. 1888):

> To the irrepressible spirit of curiosity and intermeddling of the average boy there is no limit to the objects which can be made attractive play-things. In the exercise of his youthful ingenuity, he can make a plaything out of almost anything, and then so use it as to expose himself to danger. If all this is to be charged to natural childish instincts, and the owners of property are to be required to anticipate and guard against it, the result would be that it would be unsafe for a man to own property, and the duty of the protection of children would be charged upon every member of the community except the parents or the children themselves.

See also Smith, Liability of Landowners to Children Entering Without Permission, 11 Harv. L. Rev. 349 (1898).

Nonetheless the attractive nuisance doctrine owes its start to Railroad Company v. Stout, 84 U.S. 657, 661 (1873), where the Court allowed the plaintiff, a 6-year-old child, to recover for injuries sustained when his foot was caught between the fixed rail of the roadbed and the turning rail of a turntable while playing with friends. The Court wrote that "if from the evidence given it might justly be inferred by the jury that the defendant, in the construction, location, management, or condition of its machine had omitted that care and attention to prevent the occurrence of accidents which prudent and careful men ordinarily bestow, the jury was at liberty to find for the plaintiff." What result under *Mangan* supra at page 563?

4. Restatement reformulation of the attractive nuisance doctrine. Section 339 of the Restatement (Second) of Torts has had enormous influence on the law of attractive nuisance. As stated, the purpose of this section is to reconcile "the public interest in the possessor's free use of his own land for his own purposes" (comment *n*) with the general law of negligence.

§339. ARTIFICIAL CONDITIONS HIGHLY DANGEROUS TO TRESPASSING
        CHILDREN

A possessor of land is subject to liability for physical harm to children trespassing thereon caused by an artificial condition upon the land if

(a) the place where the condition exists is one upon which the possessor knows or has reason to know that children are likely to trespass, and

(b) the condition is one of which the possessor knows or has reason to know and which he realizes or should realize will involve an unreasonable risk of death or serious bodily harm to such children, and

(c) the children because of their youth do not discover the condition or realize the risk involved in intermeddling with it or in coming within the area made dangerous by it, and

> (d) the utility to the possessor of maintaining the condition and the burden of eliminating the danger are slight as compared with the risk to children involved, and
>
> (e) the possessor fails to exercise reasonable care to eliminate the danger or otherwise to protect the children.

Though on its face the rule looks to be very broad, its application is hedged in with substantial limitations that mark a retreat from the broad position staked out in *Stout*. First, as stated, the rule only applies to "artificial conditions on the land." While the Restatement itself takes no position on whether section 339 should apply to natural conditions, most cases hold it does not. Thus, in Loney v. McPhillips, 521 P.2d 340 (Or. 1974), the court held that, in part to encourage private landowners to make their land available to the public for recreational purposes, section 339 did not apply when a 13-year-old boy drowned while trespassing in an ocean cove owned by the defendant. Is the result consistent with the general law of negligence? For a criticism of the position see Prosser, Trespassing Children, 47 Cal. L. Rev. 427 (1959).

Second, the section only applies when the owner "knows or has reason to know that children are likely to trespass." This phrase is used in opposition to the phrase "should know" and was adopted to make it clear that the possessor is under no duty to investigate the land to determine whether trespassing children are present.

Third, the assumption of risk language in clause (c) has been used to bar a number of claims. See, e.g., Holland v. Baltimore & Ohio R.R., 431 A.2d 597 (D.C. 1981), where a defendant obtained a judgment notwithstanding the verdict against a 9-year-old plaintiff who was injured while jumping trains, on the ground that the dangers were obvious even to one his age.

Recent cases show a similar reluctance to impose liability on landowners for the injuries sustained by children. In Merrill v. Central Maine Power Co., 628 A.2d 1062 (Me. 1993), the court relied on section 339 when it refused to allow a 9-year-old plaintiff to recover on an attractive nuisance theory when he climbed over a fence surrounding defendant's electrical power substation and badly burned himself while trying to cook an eel against a live wire. And in Corson v. Kosinski, 3 F.3d 1146 (7th Cir. 1993), the plaintiff fell from the roof of defendant's apartment house while playing with other children. Defendant's summary judgment was affirmed when it was established that the children had never played on the roof prior to the day of injury, so that the defendant had no reason to expect the children to play there, even if they had made frequent forays into the yard and often gathered on the front porch.

5. *Licensees versus invitees.* The classical common law devoted considerable ingenuity to refining the difference between a licensee and an

invitee with reference to the purpose of the visit. But there are a host of marginal cases identified in Licensor-Licensee, 25 Conn. B.J. 123, 131 (1951):

> When a customer goes into a store to buy something and actually makes the purchase, the problem is easy. But how about the person who is merely "shopping" or who accompanies a friend who makes a purchase or children who accompany their parents or one who drops into a hotel or store to go to the toilet or use the telephone, or to mail a letter? And what of a worker looking for a job which he may or may not get? Then there is the problem of public officials of one kind or another who enter another's premises, not with his permission, but because they have legal authority to do so in the discharge of their duties.

One way to meet these difficulties is to focus not on the nature of the visit but on the nature of the premises. Those who run business premises, or premises to which the public generally is invited, are subject to the rules for invitees; those who maintain private or residential premises are not. The nature of the premises, not the business, generally controls. See Prosser, Business Visitors and Invitees, 26 Minn. L. Rev. 573 (1942), taking up this position, which has been adopted in the Restatement (Second) of Torts:

> §332. INVITEE DEFINED
> (1) An invitee is either a public invitee or a business visitor.
> (2) A public invitee is a person who is invited to enter or remain on land as a member of the public for a purpose for which the land is held open to the public.
> (3) A business visitor is a person who is invited to enter or remain on land for a purpose directly or indirectly connected with business dealings with the possessor of the land.

Yet even under this view some hard cases remain. In Lemon v. Busey, 461 P.2d 145 (Kan. 1969), a 5-year-old child was brought to the defendant church by her grandmother, a part-time church employee. The arrangement was "for the convenience of her grandmother and parents" and the church at no time supervised the child. While her grandmother was busy at work, the child wandered off and fell to her death from a roof that she had probably reached through an unlocked elevator door or fire escape. The court held that she was a licensee and denied liability.

With *Lemon* contrast Post v. Lunney, 261 So. 2d 146 (Fla. 1972). There the plaintiff had paid five dollars to go on a tour of defendant Marjorie Merriweather Post's home, where she "tripped on a piece of transparent vinyl which had been placed over a valuable oriental rug, and fractured her hip." The trial judge called the plaintiff a licensee because the visit was not, as the older conception of invitee required, to their mutual economic advantage, given that the five dollars paid by the plaintiff did not go to the defendant. The Florida Supreme Court rejected that contention and treated the plaintiff as a public invitee. Should it make any difference whether the vinyl was placed over the oriental rug solely in preparation for the tour?

In Hopkins v. Fox & Lazo Realtors, 625 A.2d 1110, 1119 (N.J. 1993), the plaintiff, who had accompanied her son and daughter-in-law in an open house tour organized by the defendant broker, slipped and fell while coming down the steps. Without explicitly abrogating the common-law categories, the court returned to first principles in analyzing the broker's duty. Accordingly, it treated the broker as though it were the possessor of the premises, who along with the homeowner had to inspect the premises for dangerous conditions. "That inspection would impose on the broker the duty to warn of any such discoverable physical features or conditions of the property that pose a hazard or danger to such visitors."

6. Duties to firefighters, police officers, and other public officials. The question of classification has also proved difficult for public officials who enter private property to discharge public duties without obtaining the landowner's consent. Given the difficulty of classifying public officials as either licensees or invitees, some writers have suggested that they be treated as a class of entrants sui generis. See, e.g., Bohlen, The Duty of a Landowner Towards Those Entering His Premises of Their Own Right, 69 U. Pa. L. Rev. 142, 237, 340 (1921). Today when public officials arrive under ordinary circumstances — to collect garbage or to make routine inspections — the tendency is to treat them as business visitors. Thus in treating a police officer delivering a summons as an implied invitee, the court in Mounsey v. Ellard, 297 N.E.2d 43, 47 (Mass. 1973) observed:

> It seems logical to contend that if the trashman and mailman can rely on the appearance of safety of an intended mode of approach which they necessarily use in the performance of their official duties, the police officer should be afforded the same right. At the very least, [our cases] have established the occupier's and landowner's obligation to keep the access routes to his house in reasonably safe condition for those who are required to use them in the performance of their official duties. The mere fact that a policeman rather than a mailman delivered the criminal summons should not affect the standard of care owed by the occupier or owner. Thus, we could rest our decision in the instant case on the narrow ground that the plaintiff was an implied invitee to whom the defendants owed a duty to keep the route of access to their premises in reasonably safe condition.

The court then went on to reject the common-law classification of invitees and licensees, following the lead of the next case.

Rowland v. Christian
443 P.2d 561 (Cal. 1968)

[On November 30, 1963, the plaintiff, James Rowland, entered the apartment of Nancy Christian at Christian's invitation. While using the bathroom fixtures, the porcelain handle on one of the water faucets broke, severing the nerves and tendons of his right hand. The defendant knew of the crack in the faucet and two weeks before the incident had asked her landlord to repair it, but she gave the plaintiff no warning of its dangerous condition. The defendant's affidavits did not show that the defect was "obvious or even nonconcealed" or that the plaintiff knew or had reason to know of the defect. The defendant moved for a summary judgment, alleging first that the plaintiff was a social guest and, second, that the twin defenses of assumption of risk and contributory negligence barred the action. The trial court granted the motion. Reversed.]

PETERS, J. . . . Section 1714 of the Civil Code provides: "Every one is responsible, not only for the result of his willful acts, but also for an injury occasioned to another by his want of ordinary care or skill in the management of his property or person, except so far as the latter has, willfully or by want of ordinary care, brought the injury upon himself. . . ." This code section, which has been unchanged in our law since 1872, states a civil law and not a common law principle.

Nevertheless, some common law judges and commentators have urged that the principle embodied in this code section serves as the foundation of our negligence law. Thus in a concurring opinion, Brett, M.R., in Heaven v. Pender (1883) 11 Q.B.D. 503, 509, states: "whenever one person is by circumstances placed in such a position with regard to another that every one of ordinary sense who did think would at once recognise that if he did not use ordinary care and skill in his own conduct with regard to those circumstances he would cause danger of injury to the person or property of the other, a duty arises to use ordinary care and skill to avoid such danger."

Although it is true that some exceptions have been made to the general principle that a person is liable for injuries caused by his failure to exercise reasonable care in the circumstances, it is clear that in the absence of statutory provision declaring an exception to the fundamental principle enunciated by section 1714 of the Civil Code, no such exception should be made unless clearly supported by public policy.

A departure from this fundamental principle involves the balancing of a number of considerations; the major ones are the foreseeability of harm to the plaintiff, the degree of certainty that the plaintiff suffered injury, the closeness of the connection between the defendant's conduct and the injury suffered, the moral blame attached to the defendant's conduct, the policy of preventing future harm, the extent of the burden to the defendant and consequences to the community of imposing a duty to exercise care with resulting liability for breach, and the availability, cost, and prevalence of insurance for the risk involved.

One of the areas where this court and other courts have departed from the fundamental concept that a man is liable for injuries caused by his carelessness is with regard to the liability of a possessor of land for injuries to persons who have entered upon that land. It has been suggested that the special rules regarding liability of the possessor of land are due to historical considerations stemming from the high place which land has traditionally held in English and American thought, the dominance and prestige of the landowning class in England during the formative period of the rules governing the possessor's liability, and the heritage of feudalism.

The departure from the fundamental rule of liability for negligence has been accomplished by classifying the plaintiff either as a trespasser, licensee, or invitee and then adopting special rules as to the duty owed by the possessor to each of the classifications. Generally speaking a trespasser is a person who enters or remains upon land of another without a privilege to do so; a licensee is a person like a social guest who is not an invitee and who is privileged to enter or remain upon land by virtue of the possessor's consent, and an invitee is a business visitor who is invited or permitted to enter or remain on the land for a purpose directly or indirectly connected with business dealings between them.

Although the invitor owes the invitee a duty to exercise ordinary care to avoid injuring him, . . . the general rule is that a trespasser and licensee or social guest are obliged to take the premises as they find them insofar as any alleged defective condition thereon may exist, and that the possessor of the land owes them only the duty of refraining from wanton or willful injury. The ordinary justification for the general rule severely restricting the occupier's liability to social guests is based on the theory that the guest should not expect special precautions to be made on his account and that if the host does not inspect and maintain his property the guest should not expect this to be done on his account.

An increasing regard for human safety has led to a retreat from this position, and an exception to the general rule limiting liability has been made as to active operations where an obligation to exercise reasonable care for the protection of the licensee has been imposed on the occupier of land. . . . In an apparent attempt to avoid the general rule limiting liability, courts have broadly defined active operations, sometimes giving the term a strained construction in cases involving dangers known to the occupier.

Thus in Hansen v. Richey, 46 Cal. Rptr. 909, an action for wrongful death of a drowned youth, the court held that liability could be predicated not upon the maintenance of a dangerous swimming pool but upon negligence "in the active conduct of a party for a large number of youthful guests in the light of knowledge of the dangerous pool." . . .

Another exception to the general rule limiting liability has been recognized for cases where the occupier is aware of the dangerous condition, the condition amounts to a concealed trap, and the guest is unaware of the trap. In none of these cases, however, did the court impose liability on the basis of a concealed trap; in some liability was found on another theory, and in others the court concluded that there was no trap. A trap has been defined as a "concealed" danger, a danger with a deceptive appearance of safety. It has also been defined as something akin to a spring gun or steel trap. . . . [I]t is pointed out that the lack of definiteness in the application of the term "trap" to any other situation makes its use argumentative and unsatisfactory.

The cases dealing with the active negligence and the trap exceptions are indicative of the subtleties and confusion which have resulted from application of the common law principles governing the liability of the possessor of land. Similar confusion and complexity exist as to the definitions of trespasser, licensee, and invitee.

In refusing to adopt the rules relating to the liability of a possessor of land for the law of admiralty, the United States Supreme Court stated: "The distinctions which the common law draws between licensee and invitee were inherited from a culture deeply rooted to the land, a culture which traced many of its standards to a heritage of feudalism. In an effort to do justice in an industrialized urban society, with its complex economic and individual relationships, modern common-law courts have found it necessary to formulate increasingly subtle verbal refinements, to create subclassifications among traditional common-law categories, and to delineate fine gradations in the standards of care which the landowner owes to each. Yet even within a single jurisdiction, the classifications and subclassifications bred by the common law have produced confusion and conflict. As new distinctions have been spawned, older ones have become obscured. Through this semantic morass the common law has moved, unevenly and with hesitation, towards 'imposing on owners and occupiers a single duty of reasonable care in all circumstances.' " (Footnotes omitted.) (Kermarec v. Compagnie Generale, 358 U.S. 625, 630-631.)

The courts of this state have also recognized the failings of the common law rules relating to the liability of the owner and occupier of land. In refusing to apply the law of invitees, licensees, and trespassers to determine the liability of an independent contractor hired by the occupier, we pointed out that application of those rules was difficult and often arbitrary. . . .

There is another fundamental objection to the approach to the question of the possessor's liability on the basis of the common law distinctions based upon the status of the injured party as a trespasser, licensee, or invitee. Complexity can be borne and confusion remedied where the underlying principles governing liability are based upon proper considerations. Whatever may have been the historical justifications for the common law distinctions, it is clear that those distinctions are not justified in the light of our modern society and that the complexity and confusion which has arisen is not due to difficulty in applying the original common law rules — they are all too easy to apply in their original formulation — but is due to the attempts to apply just rules in our modern society within the ancient terminology.

Without attempting to labor all of the rules relating to the possessor's liability, it is apparent that the classifications of trespasser, licensee, and invitee, the immunities from liability predicated upon those classifications, and the exceptions to those immunities, often do not reflect the major factors which should determine whether immunity should be conferred upon the possessor of land. Some of those factors, including the closeness of the connection between the injury and the defendant's conduct, the moral blame attached to the defendant's conduct, the policy of preventing future harm, and the prevalence and availability of insurance, bear little, if any, relationship to the classifications of trespasser, licensee, and invitee and the existing rules conferring immunity.

Although in general there may be a relationship between the remaining factors and the classifications of trespasser, licensee, and invitee, there are many cases in which no such relationship may exist. Thus, although the foreseeability of harm to an invitee would ordinarily seem greater than the foreseeability of harm to a trespasser, in a particular case the opposite may be true. The same may be said of the issue of certainty of injury. The burden to the defendant and consequences to the community of imposing a duty to exercise care with resulting liability for breach may often be greater with respect to trespassers than with respect to invitees, but it by no means follows that this is true in every case. In many situations, the burden will be the same, i.e., the conduct necessary upon the defendant's part to meet the burden of exercising due care as to invitees will also meet his burden with respect to licensees and trespassers. The last of the major factors, the cost of insurance, will, of course, vary depending upon the rules of liability adopted, but there is no persuasive evidence that applying ordinary principles of negligence law to the land occupier's liability will materially reduce the prevalence of insurance due to increased cost or even substantially increase the cost.

Considerations such as these have led some courts in particular situations to reject the rigid common law classifications and to approach the issue of the duty of the occupier on the basis of ordinary principles of negligence. (E.g., Gould v. DeBeve, 330 F.2d 826, 829-830 (1964)). And the common law distinctions after thorough study have been repudiated by the jurisdiction of their birth. (Occupiers' Liability Act, 1957, 5 and 6 Eliz. 2, ch. 31.)

A man's life or limb does not become less worthy of protection by the law nor a loss less worthy of compensation under the law because he has come upon the land of another without permission or with permission but without a business purpose. Reasonable people do not ordinarily vary their conduct depending upon such matters, and to focus upon the status of the injured party as a trespasser, licensee, or invitee in order to determine the question whether the landowner has a duty of care, is contrary to our modern social mores and humanitarian values. The common law rules obscure rather than illuminate the proper considerations which should govern determination of the question of duty.

. . . We decline to follow and perpetuate such rigid classifications. The proper test to be applied to the liability of the possessor of land in accordance with section 1714 of the Civil Code is whether in the management of his property he has acted as a reasonable man in view of the probability of injury to others, and, although the plaintiff's status as a trespasser, licensee, or invitee may in the light of the facts giving rise to such status have some bearing on the question of liability, the status is not determinative.

Once the ancient concepts as to the liability of the occupier of land are stripped away, the status of the plaintiff relegated to its proper place in determining such liability, and ordinary principles of negligence applied, the result in the instant case presents no substantial difficulties. As we have seen, when we view the matters presented on the motion for summary judgment as we must, we must assume defendant Miss Christian was aware that the faucet handle was defective and dangerous, that the defect was not obvious, and that plaintiff was about to come in contact with the defective condition, and under the undisputed facts she neither remedied the condition nor warned plaintiff of it. Where the occupier of land is aware of a concealed condition involving in the absence of precautions an unreasonable risk of harm to those coming in contact with it and is aware that a person on the premises is about to come in contact with it, the trier of fact can reasonably conclude that a failure to warn or to repair the condition constitutes negligence. Whether or not a guest has a right to expect that his host will remedy dangerous conditions on his account, he should reasonably be entitled to rely upon a warning of the dangerous condition so that he, like the host, will be in a position to take special precautions when he comes in contact with it.

It may be noted that by carving further exceptions out of the traditional rules relating to the liability to licensees or social guests, other jurisdictions reach the same result, that by continuing to adhere to the strained construction of active negligence or possibly, by applying the trap doctrine the result would be reached on the basis of some California precedents, and that the result might even be reached by a continued expansion of the definition of the term "invitee" to include all persons invited upon the land who may thereby be led to believe that the host will exercise for their protection the ordinary care of a reasonable man. However, to approach the problem in these manners would only add to the confusion, complexity, and fictions which have resulted from the common law distinctions.

The judgment is reversed.

TRAYNOR, C.J., and TOBRINER, MOSK and SULLIVAN, JJ., concur.

BURKE, J., dissenting. I dissent. In determining the liability of the occupier or owner of land for injuries, the distinctions between trespassers, licensees and invitees have been developed and applied by the courts over a period of many years. They supply a reasonable and workable approach to the problems involved, and one which provides the degree of stability and predictability so highly prized in the law. The unfortunate alternative, it appears to me, is the route taken by the majority in their opinion in this case that such issues are to be decided on a case by case basis under the application of the basic law of negligence, bereft of the guiding principles and precedent which the law has heretofore attached by a virtue of the relationship of the parties to one another.

Liability for negligence turns upon whether a duty of care is owed, and if so, the extent thereof. Who can doubt that the corner grocery, the large department store, or the financial institution owes a greater duty of care to one whom it has invited to enter its premises as a prospective customer of its wares or services than it owes to a trespasser seeking to enter after the close of business hours and for a nonbusiness or even an antagonistic purpose? I do not think it unreasonable or unfair that a social guest (classified by the law as a licensee, as was plaintiff here) should be obliged to take the premises in the same condition as his host finds them or permits them to be. Surely a homeowner should not be obliged to hover over his guests with warnings of possible dangers to be found in the condition of the home (e.g., waxed floors, slipping rugs, toys in unexpected places, etc., etc.). Yet today's decision appears to open the door to potentially unlimited liability despite the purpose and circumstances motivating the plaintiff in entering the premises of another, and despite the caveat of the majority that the status of the parties may "have some bearing on the question of liability . . . ," whatever the future may show that language to mean.

In my view, it is not a proper function of this court to overturn the learning, wisdom and experience of the past in this field. Sweeping modifications of tort liability law fall more suitably within the domain of the Legislature, before which all affected interests can be heard and which can enact statutes providing uniform standards and guidelines for the future.

I would affirm the judgment for defendant.

McComb J., concurs.

NOTES

1. Response to Rowland v. Christian. Is it necessary to abolish the distinction between licensees and invitees in order to deny the defendant's motion for summary judgment? Note that prior to Rowland v. Christian, California had not accepted the view adopted in section 342 of the Restatement (Second) of Torts that the possessor of real property was under a duty to warn a licensee of concealed dangerous conditions. See, e.g., Fisher v. General Petroleum Corp., 267 P.2d 841 (Cal. App. 1954); Hansen v. Richey, 46 Cal. Rptr. 909 (Cal. App. 1965). On remand in *Rowland,* will the plaintiff be able to prevail if the defendant can show that the defect was patent? Will the defendant be able to escape liability if the defect was concealed?

The responses of other jurisdictions that have considered Rowland v. Christian have not been uniform. A majority of the courts that have reconsidered the question after *Rowland* have decided to adhere to the traditional distinctions. See, e.g., DiGildo v. Caponi, 247 N.E.2d 732 (Ohio 1969); Astleford v. Milner Enterprises Inc., 233 So. 2d 524 (Miss. 1970). Yet approximately 15 states have followed *Rowland* across the board. See, e.g., Pickard v. City and County of Honolulu, 452 P.2d 445 (Haw. 1969); Mile High Fence Co. v. Radovich, 489 P.2d 308 (Colo. 1971); Basso v. Miller, 352 N.E.2d 868 (N.Y. 1976).

In New Hampshire the adoption of the *Rowland* position took place in two stages. In Sargent v. Ross, 308 A.2d 528, 531 (N.H. 1973), the court abolished the distinction between licensees and invitees, holding that a landlord owes a general duty of care to all persons on his premises. Under previous law, the landlord was liable in tort for injuries "resulting from defective and dangerous conditions in the premises if the injury [was] attributable to (1) a hidden danger in the premises of which the landlord but not the tenant is aware, (2) premises leased for public use, (3) premises retained under the landlord's control, such as common stairways, or (4) premises negligently repaired by the landlord." The New Hampshire Supreme Court then completed the process of adopting *Rowland* in Ouellette v. Blanchard, 364 A.2d 631 (N.H. 1976), noting it was "not disposed to limit our holding to abolishment of two-thirds of the trichotomy and to retain the category of trespassers as a legal area of immunity." But it did qualify its result by saying that "a landowner cannot be expected to maintain his premises in a safe condition for a wandering tramp or a person who enters against the known wishes of the landowner."

2. Duties to trespassers after Rowland v. Christian. Still other states have followed *Rowland* insofar as it eliminates the distinction between licensees and invitees. See, e.g., Jones v. Hansen, 867 P.2d 303 (Kan. 1994). And other states have followed by statute. Thus Illinois law now provides that "The distinction under the common law between invitees and licensees as to the duty owed by an owner or occupier of any premises to such entrants is abolished. The duty owed to such entrants is that of reasonable care under the circumstances regarding the state of the premises or acts done or omitted on them. (Ill. Rev. Stat. 1994, ch. 80, ¶302.)

As is evident from these developments, *Rowland* has met with greater resistance on its extension of the ordinary duty of care to trespassers. The English case of British Rys. Bd. v. Herrington, [1972] A.C. 877 held that the trespasser was entitled to "humane treatment" but not the ordinary duty of care. Likewise, the Minnesota Supreme Court, in Peterson v. Balach, 199 N.W.2d 639, 642 (Minn. 1972), observed:

> [T]he considerations governing a landowner's or occupant's liability to trespassers may be fundamentally different from his duty to those whom he has expressly or by implication invited onto his property. Burglars are trespassers; vandals are trespassers. We have criminal statutes governing trespassers. Minn. St. 609.605. Sweeping away all distinction between trespassers and social guests and business invitees is a drastic step to take because there may be, and often is, good reason to distinguish between a trespasser and a social guest. There is little or no reason to distinguish between a social guest and a business invitee.
>
> Our course of action emulates the changes made in England by the Occupiers' Liability Act, 1957 (5 & 6 Eliz. II, c. 31). That act abolished the distinction between invitees, licensees and so-called contractual visitors but made no change in the law as to the liability of an occupant of land to trespassers.

The Massachusetts Supreme Judicial Court, however, cast its lot with *Rowland* in Pridgen v. Boston Housing Authority, 308 N.E.2d 467, 476-477 (Mass. 1974). The plaintiff, an 11-year-old boy, lifted an escape hatch in the ceiling of an elevator and climbed into the elevator shaft. He slipped off the elevator roof and became trapped. His mother, having learned of her son's predicament, asked one of the defendant's servants to turn off "the lights" to keep her son from being injured, but he failed to shut down the power to the elevators in time to prevent the boy's legs from being crushed by the moving elevator. The court, much troubled by the influence of the good Samaritan doctrine on common law, observed:

> In the context of the relationship between an owner or occupier (owner) of the property and a trapped, imperiled and helpless trespasser

thereon, we reject any rule which would exempt the owner from liability if he knowingly refrains from taking reasonable action which he is in a position to take and which would prevent injury or further injury to the trespasser. It should not be, it cannot be, and surely it is not now the law of this Commonwealth that the owner in such a situation is rewarded with immunity from liability as long as he ignores the plight of the trapped trespasser and takes no affirmative action to help him. Thus, in the case before us it is unthinkable to have a rule which would hold the authority liable if one of its employees, acting in the course of his employment, pushed the "go" button on the elevator although he knew Joseph Pridgen was trapped in the elevator shaft, but would not hold it liable if, being reasonably able to do so, the employee knowingly failed or refused to turn off the switch to the electrical power for the same elevator.

This is not a case of an intruder who is cut during the act of pushing his fist through the glass in a door which the owner has no duty to open for him; rather, we are dealing with one who is injured after his original trespass is effectively frustrated by virtual physical entrapment in a position of peril. We hold that as to the latter trespasser the owner owes a duty to exercise reasonable care to prevent injury or further injury to him, including, if necessary, the duty to take reasonable affirmative action. We reject any notion that this is a duty which can never be violated by nonfeasance. The owner in such a situation is required to act if, in the same circumstances, an ordinary and reasonably prudent person would have acted, and, in doing so, he must exercise the degree and standard of care which would have been exercised by an ordinary and reasonably prudent person in those circumstances.

It then concluded that the "common duty of reasonable care" owed to an invitee or licensee "is owed by an owner to a trespasser who has become helplessly trapped on the premises to the owner's knowledge." Is the result here consistent with the statutory treatment of the good Samaritan problem, at page 561 supra, which in general requires proof of willful misconduct, recklessness, or gross negligence to hold a rescuer liable? How ought this case to be decided under Addie v. Dumbreck or under Excelsior Wire Rope Ltd. v. Callan? Under section 339 of the Restatement? Indeed, does section 339 survive under Rowland v. Christian?

3. Obvious conditions. Restatement (Second) of Torts, section 343 provides:

> A possessor of land is subject to liability for physical harm caused to his invitees by a condition on the land if, but only if, he
> (a) knows or by the exercise of reasonable care would discover the condition, and should realize that it involves an unreasonable risk of harm to such invitees, and
> (b) should expect that they will not discover or realize the danger, or will fail to protect themselves against it, and
> (c) fails to exercise reasonable care to protect them against the danger.

Restatement (Second) of Torts, section 343A provides:

> (1) A possessor of land is not liable to his invitees for physical harm caused to them by any activity or condition on the land whose danger is known or obvious to them, unless the possessor should anticipate the harm despite such knowledge or obviousness.

These provisions were applied in Ward v. K-Mart Corp., 554 N.E.2d 223, 230-231 (Ill. 1990). There the plaintiff was injured when he walked into a concrete post located on defendant's premises about 19 inches from the rear wall of the K-Mart store. On entering the store, plaintiff had noticed the post, but he had forgotten about it momentarily while leaving the store carrying a large bathroom mirror which obscured his view. Plaintiff then walked into the post, sustaining injuries to his face and partial loss of vision. A jury verdict for the plaintiff for $68,000 was overruled by the trial court, but was reinstated by the Illinois Supreme Court. Ryan, J., first noted that Illinois had by statute abolished the distinction between licensees and invitees and that the landowner owed to both a duty "of reasonable care under the circumstances regarding the state of the premises or acts done or omitted on them. Ill. Rev. Stat. ch. 80, §302 (1994). Ryan, J., then refused to hold that the defendant had automatically discharged its duty of care for dangerous conditions that are open and obvious.

> A rule more consistent with an owner's or occupier's general duty of reasonable care, however, recognizes that the "obviousness" of a condition or the fact that the injured party may have been in some sense "aware" of it may not always serve as adequate warning of the condition and of the consequences of encountering it. . . .
>
> The manifest trend of the courts in this country is away from the traditional rule absolving, ipso facto, owners and occupiers of land from liability for injuries resulting from known or obvious conditions, and toward the standard expressed in section 343A(1) of the Restatement (Second) of Torts (1965). . . .

Ryan, J., then reinstated the judgment for the plaintiff on the strength of these provisions, saying:

> [I]n the case at bar it was reasonably foreseeable that a customer would collide with the post while exiting defendant's store carrying merchandise which could obscure view of the post. Defendant invited customers to use that door through which plaintiff entered and exited, and many customers did use it. Defendant had reason to anticipate that customers shopping in the store would, even in the exercise of reasonable care, momentarily forget the presence of the posts which they may have previously encountered by entering through the customer entrance door. It was also reasonably foreseeable that a customer carrying a large item which he had purchased in the store might be distracted and fail to see

the post upon exiting through the door. It should be remembered that the post was located immediately outside the entrance to the Home Center section of defendant's store. Defendant had every reason to expect that customers would carry large, bulky items through that door, particularly where, as here, the large overhead door was closed. The burden on the defendant of protecting against this danger would be slight. A simple warning or a relocation of the post may have sufficed. It is also relevant that there were no windows or transparent panels on the customer entrance doors to permit viewing of the posts from the interior of the store.

4. *Strict liability for owners and occupiers. Rowland* adopted a general negligence standard of landowners toward all entrants on their property. More recently, it has been suggested that landlords (but not necessarily apartment dwellers themselves) be subjected to the strict liability rules applied to product sellers. That position was endorsed by the California Supreme Court in Becker v. IRM Corporation, 698 P.2d 116, 122-23 (Cal. 1985). There the plaintiff slipped and fell against an untempered shower door and severely lacerated his arm. It was undisputed that the defect was latent and that the risk of injury would have been substantially reduced if the door had been made of tempered glass. The plaintiff settled his suit against the door assembler and the builder, and then proceeded on a strict liability action against the defendant landlord, who had purchased the building from a prior owner. Justice Broussard first noted that lower courts — heavily influenced by the rise of strict products liability and the implied warranties of habitability for residential leases, not waivable by contract — had created pockets of strict liability for landlords. Justice Broussard then continued as follows:

> We are satisfied that the rationale of the foregoing cases, establishing the duties of a landlord and the doctrine of strict liability in tort, requires us to conclude that a landlord engaged in the business of leasing dwellings is strictly liable in tort for injuries resulting from a latent defect in the premises when the defect existed at the time the premises were let to the tenant. . . .
>
> The tenant renting the dwelling is compelled to rely upon the implied assurance of safety made by the landlord. It is also apparent that the landlord by adjustment of price at the time he acquires the property, by rentals or by insurance is in a better position to bear the costs of injuries due to defects in the premises than the tenants.
>
> In these circumstances, strict liability in tort for latent defects existing at the time of renting must be applied to insure that the landlord who markets the product bears the costs of injuries resulting from the defects "rather than the injured persons who are powerless to protect themselves."

The dissent of Lucas, J., protested the result:

> Any landlord, even one renting the family home for a year, will now be insurer for defects in any wire, screw, latch, cabinet door, pipe or other

article on and in his premises at the time they are let despite the fact that he neither installed the item nor had any knowledge or reason to know of the defect. I believe, in conformance with the almost unanimous judgment of other jurisdictions considering this issue, that such imposition of liability is inappropriate.

Note that the court in *Becker* left open in footnotes two questions: first, whether the doctrine of strict liability applies to patent defects, and second, whether "the landlord is strictly liable for defects in the property which develop after the property is leased." How should these be answered?

See generally Smith v. Arbaugh's Restaurant Inc., 469 F.2d 97 (D.C. Cir. 1973), where Leventhal, J., was uneasy about the ability of private homeowners to bear the additional insurance costs imposed by strict liability. See also Ursin, Strict Liability for Defective Business Premises — One Step Beyond *Rowland* and *Greenman*, 22 U.C.L.A. L. Rev. 820 (1975).

The California Court of Appeals refused to extend the strict liability rule in *Becker* to commercial lessors in Muro v. Superior Court, 229 Cal. Rptr. 383 (Cal. App. 1986), noting that there was no shortage of commercial real estate, and that commercial landlords were subject neither to the implied warranty of habitability nor to extensive direct government regulation.

5. *Duties to strangers after Rowland v. Christian. Rowland* has also had an important impact upon the rules governing the liability of owners and occupiers to persons who have not entered their land. In this context one critical distinction is that between natural and artificial conditions upon the land. Artificial conditions raise no special problems because the normal "act" requirement of both negligence and strict liability theories is satisfied. Natural conditions are more problematic because now the "act" requirement is not (at least not obviously) satisfied. The stranger cannot rely upon affirmative duties born of the informal consensual arrangements of the invitee and licensee. In consequence, the duty issue becomes a stumbling block in the path of the stranger's recovery. In Pontardawe Rural District Council v. Moore-Gwyn, [1929] 1 Ch. 656, a large boulder tumbled down the side of a mountain, crashing into the plaintiff's house. The court denied the plaintiff recovery because the fall of the rocks was attributable only to weathering and not to the defendant's mining operations. The ownership of the dangerous instrumentality did not per se ground a cause of action, nor did it matter if the defendant had the better opportunity to observe changes in the rock formations.

In Noble v. Harrison, [1926] 2 K.B. 332, the plaintiff was struck when a tree branch overhanging a public way fell upon his motor coach. The court denied the plaintiff recovery under a nuisance theory, and held that Rylands v. Fletcher was confined in its application to things noxious in themselves and that it made no difference "whether the tree was planted or self-sown." The court did not explicitly address the question of liability in negligence, but did note that "neither the defendant nor his servants knew that the bough was dangerous, but that the fracture was due to a latent defect not discoverable by any reasonably careful inspection."

The American case law has generally followed the English rules, with decisions in 13 states, allowing negligence actions for harm caused by falling trees but not by other natural conditions. See, e.g., Taylor v. Olsen, 578 P.2d 779 (Or. 1978). See also Noel, Nuisances from Land in its Natural Condition, 56 Harv. L. Rev. 772, 796-797 (1943), where the author observed: "Where a planted tree has become dangerous to persons on the highway or on adjoining land, and causes harm, the fault lies not in the planting of the tree but in permitting it to remain after it has become unsafe."

The most radical departure from the common-law rule is found in Sprecher v. Adamson Co., 636 P.2d 1121, 1125, 1126 (Cal. 1981), where the court was prepared to impose an affirmative duty on one Malibu landowner to prevent a mudslide after heavy rains that would damage the home of his downhill neighbor. Bird, C.J., showed her obvious hostility to the misfeasance-nonfeasance distinction at common law and placed heavy reliance upon Rowland v. Christian. "In rejecting the common law rule of non-liability for natural conditions, the courts have recognized the inherent injustice involved in a rule which states that 'a landowner may escape all liability for serious damage to his neighbors [or those using a public highway], merely by allowing nature to take its course.' . . . Whatever the rule may once have been, it is now clear that a duty to exercise due care can arise out of possession alone." Richardson, J., concurring, found it "exceedingly difficult to imagine what respondents *reasonably* could have done to prevent or reduce the damage caused by the natural condition here present." Id. at 1136.

6. Statutory rules on occupier's liability. The entire area of occupier's liability is one that has received increased legislative attention in recent years. In one development, "premises guest statutes" have protected landowners from suits by either "a guest without payment or . . . a trespasser" when the landowner or occupier has not acted either intentionally or in the "wilful and wanton disregard of the rights of others." See Delaware Premises Guest Stat., Del. Code Ann. Tit. 25, §1501, sustained against constitutional challenge in Bailey v. Pennington, 406 A.2d 44 (Del. 1979).

Statutes now found in most jurisdictions provide extensive protection to landowners, in sharp contrast with the judicial philosophy of *Rowland*. See, for example, New Jersey Landowner's Liability Act, N.J. Rev. Stat. Ann. §2A:42A-2 et seq. (West 1987 & 1994 Supp.), which provides:

a. An owner, lessee or occupant of premises, whether or not posted . . . , and whether or not improved or maintained in a natural condition, or used as part of a commercial enterprise, owes no duty to keep the premises safe for entry or use by others for sport and recreational activities, or to give warning of any hazardous condition of the land or in connection with the use of any structure or by reason of any activity on such premises to persons entering for such purposes . . .

b. An owner, lessee or occupant of premises who gives permission to another to enter upon such premises for a sport or recreational activity or purpose does not thereby (1) extend any assurance that the premises are safe for such purpose, or (2) constitute the person to whom permission is granted an invitee to whom a duty of care is owed, or (3) assume responsibility for or incur liability for any injury to person or property caused by any act of persons to whom the permission is granted.

Sport and recreational activities were given a broad and comprehensive statutory definition, and the statute contained a presumption that it was to "be liberally construed to serve as an inducement to the owners, lessees and occupants of property, that might otherwise be reluctant to do so for fear of liability, to permit persons to come onto their property for sport and recreational activities." Id. §2A:42A-5.1 This statute did not, however, protect a landowner against suit by a good Samaritan who drowned while trying to rescue two 15-year-old boys who had fallen through thin ice on the defendant's reservoir on the first day of the skating season, as the court held that the rescuer was not engaged in recreational activities. Harrison v. Middlesex Water Co., 403 A.2d 910, 914 (N.J. 1979).

California has a virtually identical statute, Civil Code section 846, first passed in 1963, which has been held to provide "an exception from the general rule that a private landowner owes a duty of reasonable care to any person coming on the land," such that "the landowner's duty to the nonpaying, uninvited recreational user is, in essence, that owed a trespasser under the common law as it existed prior to Rowland v. Christian." Ornelas v. Randolph, 847 P.2d 560, 562 (Cal. 1993). In *Ornelas* the court read the "recreational use" language broadly and concluded "that entering and using defendant's property to play on his farm equipment invokes the immunity provisions of section 846. As noted, a 'recreational' injury may result as readily from playing on a manmade object as on a natural edifice. Therefore, for our purposes here, clambering about on farm equipment is no different in kind from scaling a cliff or climbing a tree."

See generally Barrett, Good Sports and Bad Lands: The Application of Washington's Recreational Use Statute Limiting Landowner Liability, 53 Wash. L. Rev. 1 (1977).

D. GRATUITOUS UNDERTAKINGS

Coggs v. Bernard
92 Eng. Rep. 107 (K.B. 1703)

[Assumpsit. The defendant had moved casks of brandy owned by the plaintiff from one place to another. Through the defendant's negligence, some of the casks were split open and great quantities of brandy were lost. The defendant moved for an arrest of the judgment in plaintiff's favor because it had not been alleged that he was a common porter or that he had received any reward or consideration. Notwithstanding, the plaintiff had judgment.]

GOULD, J. I think this is a good declaration. The objection that has been made is, because there is not any consideration laid. But I think it is good either way, and that any man, that undertakes to carry goods, is liable to an action, be he a common carrier, or whatever he is, if through his neglect they are lost, or come to any damage: and if a praemium be laid to be given, then it is without question so. The reason of the action is, the particular trust reposed in the defendant, to which he has concurred by his assumption, and in the executing which he has miscarried by his neglect. But if a man undertakes to build a house, without any thing to be had for his pains, an action will not lie for nonperformance, because it is nudum pactum. . . .

HOLT, C.J. . . . But secondly it is objected, that there is no consideration to ground this promise upon, and therefore the undertaking is but nudum pactum. But to this I answer, that the owner's trusting him with the goods is a sufficient consideration to oblige him to a careful management. Indeed if the agreement had been executory, to carry these brandies from the one place to the other such a day, the defendant had not been bound to carry them. But this is a different case, for assumpsit does not only signify a future agreement, but in such a case as this, it signifies an actual entry upon the thing, and taking the trust upon himself. And if a man will do that, and miscarries in the performance of his trust, an action will lie against him for that, though no body could have compelled him to do the thing.

NOTES

1. Contract without consideration. Coggs v. Bernard, discussed at page 172, note 2 supra, on the issue of degrees of negligence, bears as well on the question of whether gratuitous promises can be a source of affirmative duties. The crux of the matter here is consideration. Is the court right that consideration can be "found" in this essentially gratuitous transaction, given that the general formula requires a benefit to the promisor or a detriment to the promisee? Note too that civil law treats these cases as contract cases without invoking the idea of consideration. Thus the Roman learning on bailments, extensively relied upon by Lord Holt in Coggs v. Bernard, allows the plaintiff to recover on contractual grounds for the improper performance of the duty, even though the promisor can withdraw if he changes his mind before performance was due. The doctrine of consideration, which in its heyday was the exclusive test for enforceable contractual promises at the common law, functions in the civil law mainly as the test for enforceability for fully executory agreements, not as the test of whether there was a contract at all.

The interaction between tort and contract is illustrated again by another famous early case. In Thorne v. Deas, 4 Johns. Cas. 84 (N.Y. Sup. Ct. 1809), the plaintiff was captain of a ship and, as he was about to leave on a voyage, he suggested to his co-owner, the defendant, that they insure the ship before he left. Defendant told plaintiff to go ahead and sail — that he would insure the ship on plaintiff's departure. Relying on defendant's promise, plaintiff sailed. Defendant failed to insure the ship, which was subsequently wrecked. On his return home, plaintiff sued defendant for his loss. The court denied recovery, Chief Justice Kent noting that this was "an action on the case, for a *non-feasance*" and that it could not lie because of "the want of a consideration for the promise." Kent observed, however, that the plaintiff's case was good under Roman contract law. The contract of mandate — a gratuitous promise to undertake something to the benefit of the promisee or a third party — gave rise to a good prima facie case even with the absence of consideration.

Since the contract option was foreclosed by the English consideration rules, the plaintiff was required to frame his action in tort. Kent's position was that the law could not first deny recovery for breach of a promise unsupported by consideration and then turn around and allow recovery on the same facts by calling it a tort. Plaintiff could recover, however, Kent continued, if he could show that defendant had engaged in misfeasance — had actually started to perform and had done so negligently. Would the actions of the defendant have been tortious without reference to the former promise? If not, why does the ineffective promise make them actionable?

2. Section 90 of the Restatement (Second) of Contracts:

§90. PROMISE REASONABLY INDUCING ACTION OR FORBEARANCE
(1) A promise which the promisor should reasonably expect to induce action or forbearance on the part of the promisee or a third person and which does induce such action or forbearance is binding if injustice can be avoided only by enforcement of the promise. The remedy granted for breach may be limited as justice requires.

Is this section of assistance to the plaintiff in Coggs v. Bernard or Thorne v. Deas? Does it depend on the interpretation given to the concept of reliance?

On section 90 and this area in general see Seavey, Reliance upon Gratuitous Promises or Other Conduct, 64 Harv. L. Rev. 913, 926-927 (1951), who observed: "The colloquial explanation for the rule of the section is that it creates 'promissory estoppel.' Estoppel is basically a tort doctrine and the rationale of the section is that justice requires the defendant to pay for the harm caused by foreseeable reliance upon the performance of his promise. The wrong is not primarily in depriving the plaintiff of the promised reward but in causing the plaintiff to change position to his detriment. . . . In a case like Thorne v. Deas, however, the continuing representation becomes fraudulent when the promisor decides not to perform and does not inform the plaintiff, knowing that he still relies upon performance."

Erie R.R. v. Stewart
40 F.2d 855 (6th Cir. 1930)

HICKENLOOPER, C.J. Stewart, plaintiff below, was a passenger in an automobile truck, sitting on the front seat to the right of the driver, a fellow employee of the East Ohio Gas Company. He recovered a judgment in the District Court for injuries received when the truck was struck by one of the defendant's trains at the 123d Street crossing in the city of Cleveland. Defendant maintained a watchman at this crossing, which was admittedly heavily traveled, but the watchman was either within the shanty or just outside of it as the train approached, and he gave no warning until too late to avoid the accident. . . .

The second contention of appellant presents the question whether the court erred in charging the jury that the absence of the watchman, where one had been maintained by the defendant company at a highway crossing over a long period of time to the knowledge of the plaintiff, would constitute negligence as a matter of law. In the present case it is conceded that the employment of the watchman by the defendant was voluntary upon its part, there being no statute or ordinance requiring the same, and that plaintiff had knowledge of this practice and relied upon the absence of the watchman as an assurance of safety and implied invitation to cross. We are not now concerned with the extent of the duty owing to one who had no notice of the prior practice, nor, in this aspect of the case, with the question of contributory negligence and the extent to which the plaintiff was relieved from the obligation of vigilance by the absence of the watchman. The question is simply whether there was any positive duty owing to the plaintiff in respect to the maintenance of such watchman, and whether a breach of such duty is so conclusively shown as to justify a peremptory charge of negligence. The question whether such negligence was the proximate cause of the injury was properly submitted to the jury.

Where the employment of a watchman or other precaution is required by statute, existence of an absolute duty to the plaintiff is conclusively shown, and failure to observe the statutory requirement is negligence per se. . . . Conversely, where there is no duty prescribed by statute or ordinance, it is usually a question for the jury whether the circumstances made the employment of a watchman necessary in the exercise of due care. Where the voluntary employment of a watchman was unknown to the traveler upon the highway, the mere absence of such watchman could probably not be considered as negligence toward him as a matter of law, for in such case there is neither an established duty positively owing to such traveler as a member of the general public, nor had he been led into reliance upon the custom. The question would remain simply whether the circumstances demanded such employment. But where the practice is known to the traveler upon the highway, and such traveler has been educated into reliance upon it, some positive duty must rest upon the railway with reference thereto. The elements of invitation and assurance of safety exist in this connection no less than in connection with contributory negligence. The company has established for itself a standard of due care while operating its trains across the highway, and, having led the traveler into reliance upon such standard, it should not be permitted thereafter to say that no duty required, arose from or attached to these precautions.

This duty has been recognized as not only actual and positive, but as absolute, in the sense that the practice may not be discontinued without exercising reasonable care to give warning of such discontinuance, although the company may thereafter do all that would otherwise be reasonably necessary. American Law Institute, Restatement of the Law of Torts, Tentative Draft No. 4, Comment f to §183. Conceding for the purposes of this opinion that, in cases where a watchman is voluntarily employed by the railway in an abundance of precaution, the duty is not absolute, in the same sense as where it is imposed by statute, still, if there be some duty, it cannot be less than that the company must use reasonable care to see that reliance by members of the educated public upon its representation of safety is not converted into a trap. Responsibility for injury will arise if the service be negligently performed or abandoned without other notice of that fact. . . .

So, in the present case, the evidence conclusively establishes the voluntary employment of a watchman, knowledge of this fact and reliance upon it by the plaintiff, a duty, therefore, that the company, through the watchman, will exercise reasonable care in warning such travelers as plaintiff, the presence of the watchman thereabouts, and no explanation of the failure to warn. Therefore, even though the duty be considered as qualified, rather than absolute, a prima facie case was established by plaintiff, requiring the defendant to go forward with evidence to rebut the presumption of negligence thus raised, or else suffer a verdict against it on this point. . . . No such evidence was introduced by defendant. No other inference than that of negligence could therefore be drawn from the evidence. If, perhaps, the rule was stated more broadly than this in the charge, the error, if any, was harmless as applied to the present case. . . .

[Affirmed.]

TUTTLE, J. I concur in the result reached by the opinion of the majority of the court. I cannot, however, concur in the views, expressed in that opinion, which would make the actionable negligence of the defendant dependent upon the knowledge of the plaintiff, previous to his injury, of the custom of the defendant in maintaining a watchman at the crossing where such injury occurred. It is settled law that a railroad company operating trains at high speed across a public highway owes to travelers properly using such highway the duty to exercise reasonable care to give such warning of approaching trains as may be reasonably required by the particular circumstances. It is equally well settled that the standard of duty thus owed to the public, at least where not otherwise prescribed by statutory law, consists of that care and prudence which an ordinarily prudent person would exercise under the same circumstances. I am satisfied that where, as here, a railroad company has established a custom, known to the general public, of maintaining a watchman at a public crossing with instructions to warn the traveling public of the approach of trains, such railroad company, in the exercise of that reasonable care which it owes to the public, should expect, and is bound to expect, that any member of the traveling public approaching such crossing along the public highway is likely to have knowledge of and to rely upon the giving of such warning. Such knowledge, with the consequent reliance, may be acquired by a traveler at any time, perhaps only a moment before going upon the crossing, and this also the railroad company is bound to anticipate. Having, in effect, given notice to the public traveling this highway that it would warn them of trains at this crossing, I think that it was bound to assume (at least in the absence of knowledge to the contrary) that every member of such public would receive, and rely on, such notice. Under such circumstances such a railroad company, in my opinion, owes to every traveler so approaching this crossing a duty to give such a warning, if reasonably possible, and a reasonably prudent railroad company would not fail, without sufficient cause, to perform that duty. It follows that the unexplained failure, as in the present case, of the defendant to give this customary warning to the plaintiff, a traveler on the highway approaching this crossing, indicates, as a matter of law, actionable negligence for which it is liable. While undoubtedly lack of reliance by plaintiff upon the custom of the defendant has an important bearing and effect upon the question whether the plaintiff was guilty of contributory negligence, it seems to me clear that the knowledge or lack of knowledge of the plaintiff, unknown to the defendant, concerning such customs cannot affect the nature or extent of the duty owed to the plaintiff by the defendant or the performance of such duty. As therefore the conclusions expressed in the opinion of a majority of the court are, to the extent which I have thus indicated, not in accord with my own views in this connection, I have felt it my duty to briefly state such views in this separate concurring opinion.

Marsalis v. LaSalle
94 So. 2d 120 (La. App. 1957)

McBRIDE, J. Plaintiffs bring this suit for damages against Shelby P. LaSalle, the defendant, as a result of Mrs. Marsalis' having been bitten or scratched by a Siamese cat on January 12, 1953, in a store in Jefferson Parish, of which the defendant is proprietor, the occurrence having taken place while Mrs. Marsalis, who was accompanied by her husband, was shopping. The cat is the pet of defendant's minor son. Mrs. Marsalis is asserting her claim for personal injuries and her husband is seeking reimbursement of the cost of the medical treatment of his wife. From a judgment in favor of plaintiffs, defendant appeals.

While the testimony on the point is in conflict, we believe that it preponderates to the effect that after Mrs. Marsalis sustained her injury, Marsalis requested defendant to keep the cat under observation for fourteen days until it could be determined whether the animal was rabid and what medical precautions Mrs. Marsalis should take against being infected by rabies. We quote Marsalis' words:

"Then I asked Mr. LaSalle to lock the cat up for 14 days, and we had a little discussion about the time element relative to keeping a cat up that had bitten someone to note its condition after that period of time, and I asked him to be sure and lock it up, because I didn't want my wife to take rabies treatment because there were numerous cats in the neighborhood that were reported rabid in the Jefferson Herald and Times, and a number of the papers, and there was quite an incident — . . .

"I asked him to keep the cat up, to lock it up, and he said he would. . . ."

The defendant denies there had been any such conversation regarding the restraining of the cat for the purpose of observation, and his testimony is that neither Mr. nor Mrs. Marsalis considered the injury dangerous. He quoted Mrs. Marsalis as having said:

"Oh, it is nothing; don't worry about it."

We do not doubt that the defendant and his wife, she having been present in the store when the incident occurred, well knew of the serious consequences that could arise from the bite of an animal, nor do we doubt that they agreed to be cooperative in the matter by observing the state of health of the cat during the period of incubation of rabies. At one point we find Mrs. LaSalle let slip this significant statement:

"Well, I think my husband notified me not to let it out and I have got that much sense to know that if a cat ever scratches anybody —"

According to her statement the cat stayed:

". . . indoors where we always kept it on the opposite side of the grocery, it's a basement house, and part of the basement is the store and the opposite side is our domicile and that's where he was. He was supposed to be at all times."

At any rate, on the evening of the fourth or fifth day after the episode in the grocery store the cat escaped and the only explanation given is by Mrs. LaSalle, who testified that this occurred as she and some friends were making their exit via the basement door. The cat was gone for about a month, and in the meantime its whereabouts was not known. Upon returning home the animal gave no evidence whatever of being infected.

Two days after she had sustained the injuries, Mrs. Marsalis sought advice from her friend and neighbor, Dr. Homer Kirgis, whose specialty is in the medical field of neurosurgery. He thought Mrs. Marsalis should first determine whether the cat had been inoculated and then consult her family physician. When it was learned a few days later that the animal had strayed from defendant's premises, Dr. Kirgis urged Mrs. Marsalis to see her family doctor and admonished her to contact the Pasteur Treatment Ward of the Charity Hospital in New Orleans. However, Dr. Kirgis subsequently undertook to administer the Pasteur treatment himself at his home, the first injection being made about January 23, 1953. This treatment consists of a number of injections of a prophylactic vaccine for rabies and we are informed that some persons are extremely allergic to the serum. Mrs. Marsalis was evidently in this category as she suffered a noxious reaction to the serum which brought about some ill effects. . . .

It is uncontroverted that there is no liability in defendant merely because the cat bit or scratched Mrs. Marsalis. Never before had the animal exhibited any vicious traits or tendencies and it had been, as the court found, a gentle and well-behaved pet and defendant was guilty of no negligence in allowing it to frequent his premises.

[The court then referred to a number of cases standing for the proposition "that one who voluntarily undertakes to care for, or to afford relief or assistance to, an ill, injured, or helpless person is under a legal obligation to use reasonable care and prudence in what he does."]

Our belief is that the above-discussed rule with respect to the duties of one who voluntarily undertakes to care for or to afford relief or assistance to an injured or distressed person is broad enough to have full application to the instant case. Perhaps the defendant, LaSalle, initially owed no duty whatever to Mrs. Marsalis, but when he once agreed to restrain and keep the cat under observation, he was bound to use reasonable care and prudence in doing so and to assume and exercise reasonable care and common humanity. It may be that Mrs. Marsalis had open to her some other course by which she could have had the cat incarcerated and examined in order to determine if it was rabid, but she unquestionably and in good faith relied upon defendant to carry out the agreement which he voluntarily made, thus foregoing such other possible available protection. It was of extreme importance to know if the cat had rabies so she could regulate her course of conduct with reference to the injury. We do not doubt for one moment that both defendant and his wife were fully cognizant that such injuries could be quite serious and exceedingly dangerous in the event the offending animal was infected with rabies. In fact we feel sure of our ground in saying this because of the statement of Mrs. LaSalle: "I have got that much sense to know that if a cat ever scratches anybody —."

LaSalle's liability would then depend on whether he used reasonable care with reference to keeping the cat, for as it developed later the Pasteur treatment was entirely unnecessary and the escape of the cat was the direct and proximate cause of the necessity for the injections and the ill effects which Mrs. Marsalis suffered as a result thereof.

Neither defendant nor his wife took any especial steps or means to prevent the cat from straying from their premises. The cat, which was three years old, had always been kept in the basement and was allowed access to the yard from time to time. No change whatever in the animal's usual routine was undertaken and we must hold that defendant failed to use ordinary or reasonable care to see to it that the animal was kept secure, and, hence, defendant is liable unto plaintiffs for whatever damages they sustained as a result of such lack of care. [The court then discussed some of the medical testimony and proceeded as follows]:

However, Dr. Kirgis' testimony is sufficient to show that Mrs. Marsalis reacted unfavorably during the course of the injections, and it appears that she suffered headaches, fever, disorientation and nausea, and, of course, she is entitled to recover damages from the defendant, not only because she was compelled to submit to the fourteen injections, but also because of the effects of her reaction. The trial judge set her recovery at $3,000, but we believe that this award is excessive in view of the failure of Mrs. Marsalis to prove that her hospital stays and the attention rendered her by Dr. Mattingly were a result of the administration of the Pasteur injections.

NOTE

Reliance in action. Do the results in *Stewart* and *Marsalis* square with a reliance theory? The Restatement (Second) of Torts provides:

§323. NEGLIGENT PERFORMANCE OF UNDERTAKING TO RENDER SERVICES
One who undertakes, gratuitously or for consideration, to render services to another which he should recognize as necessary for the protection of the other's person or things, is subject to liability to the other for physical harm resulting from his failure to exercise reasonable care to perform his undertaking, if
(a) his failure to exercise such care increases the risk of such harm, or
(b) the harm is suffered because of the other's reliance upon the undertaking.

The principle contained in this provision is invoked with great frequency today in suits against the government for breach of its various regulatory duties. In this connection, the leading case is still Indian Towing v. United States, 350 U.S. 61, 64-65 (1955). There, the U.S. Coast Guard was in charge of the operation of a lighthouse whose light was negligently allowed to go out, whereupon the plaintiff's barge ran aground. The plaintiff's action was brought under the Federal Tort Claims Act, which imposes upon the government the duties of a private party acting under like circumstances. Frankfurter, J., allowed the cause of action, noting "it is hornbook tort law that one who undertakes to warn the public of danger and thereby induces reliance must peform his good Samaritan task in a careful manner."

Moch Co. v. Rensselaer Water Co.
159 N.E. 896 (N.Y. 1928)

CARDOZO, C.J. The defendant, a water works company under the laws of this State, made a contract with the city of Rensselaer for the supply of water during a term of years. Water was to be furnished to the city for sewer flushing and street sprinkling; for service to schools and public buildings; and for service at fire hydrants, the latter service at the rate of $42.50 a year for each hydrant. Water was to be furnished to private takers within the city at their homes and factories and other industries at reasonable rates, not exceeding a stated schedule. While this contract was in force, a building caught fire. The flames, spreading to the plaintiff's warehouse near by, destroyed it and its contents. The defendant according to the complaint was promptly notified of the fire, "but omitted and neglected after such notice, to supply or furnish sufficient or adequate quantity of water, with adequate pressure to stay, suppress or extinguish the fire before it reached the warehouse of the plaintiff, although the pressure and supply which the defendant was equipped to supply and furnish, and had agreed by said contract to supply and furnish, was adequate and sufficient to prevent the spread of the fire to and the destruction of the plaintiff's warehouse and its contents." By reason of the failure of the defendant to "fulfill the provisions of the contract between it and the city of Rensselaer," the plaintiff is said to have suffered damage, for which judgment is demanded. A motion, in the nature of a demurrer, to dismiss the complaint, was denied at Special Term. The Appellate Division reversed by a divided court.

Liability in the plaintiff's argument is placed on one or other of three grounds. The complaint, we are told, is to be viewed as stating: (1) A cause of action for breach of contract within Lawrence v. Fox (20 N.Y. 268); (2) a cause of action for a common-law tort, within MacPherson v. Buick Motor Company (217 N.Y. 382); or (3) a cause of action for the breach of a statutory duty. These several grounds of liability will be considered in succession.

(1) We think the action is not maintainable as one for breach of contract.

No legal duty rests upon a city to supply its inhabitants with protection against fire. That being so, a member of the public may not maintain an action under Lawrence v. Fox against one contracting with the city to furnish water at the hydrants, unless an intention appears that the promisor is to be answerable to individual members of the public as well as to the city for any loss ensuing from the failure to fulfill the promise. No such intention is discernible here. On the contrary, the contract here is significantly divided into two branches: One a promise to the city for the benefit of the city in its corporate capacity, in which branch is included the service at the hydrants; and the other a promise to the city for the benefit of private takers, in which branch is included the service at their homes and factories. In a broad sense it is true that every city contract, not improvident or wasteful, is for the benefit of the public. More than this, however, must be shown to give a right of action to a member of the public not formally a party. The benefit, as it is sometimes said, must be one that is not merely incident and secondary. It must be primary and immediate in such a sense and to such a degree as to bespeak the assumption of a duty to make reparation directly to the individual members of the public if the benefit is lost. The field of obligation would be expanded beyond reasonable limits if less than this were demanded as a condition of liability. A promisor undertakes to supply fuel for heating a public building. He is not liable for breach of contract to a visitor who finds the building without fuel, and thus contracts a cold. . . .

[Cardozo then notes that the overwhelming authority treats the benefit to the public under these contracts as incidental and secondary.]

An intention to assume an obligation of indefinite extension to every member of the public is seen to be the more improbable when we recall the crushing burden that the obligation would impose. . . . If the plaintiff is to prevail, one who negligently omits to supply sufficient pressure to extinguish a fire started by another assumes an obligation to pay the ensuing damage, though the whole city is laid low. A promisor will not be deemed to have had in mind the assumption of a risk so overwhelming for any trivial reward. . . .

(2) We think the action is not maintainable as one for a common-law tort.

"It is ancient learning that one who assumes to act, even though gratuitously, may thereby become subject to the duty of acting carefully, if he acts at all" (Glanzer v. Shepard, 233 N.Y. 236, 239). The plaintiff would bring its case within the orbit of that principle. The hand once set to a task may not always be withdrawn with impunity though liability would fail if it had never been applied at all. A time-honored formula often phrases the distinction as one between misfeasance and nonfeasance. Incomplete the formula is, and so at times misleading. Given a relation involving in its existence a duty of care irrespective of a contract, a tort may result as well from acts of omission as of commission in the fulfillment of the duty thus recognized by law. What we need to know is not so much the conduct to be avoided when the relation and its attendant duty are established as existing. What we need to know is the conduct that engenders the relation. It is here that the formula, however incomplete, has its value and significance. If conduct has gone forward to such a stage that inaction would commonly result, not negatively merely in withholding a benefit, but positively or actively in working an injury, there exists a relation out of which arises a duty to go forward (Bohlen, Studies in the Law of Torts, p. 87). So the surgeon who operates without pay is liable though his negligence is in the omission to sterilize his instruments; the engineer, though his fault is in the failure to shut off steam; the maker of automobiles, at the suit of some one other than the buyer, though his negligence is merely in inadequate inspection (MacPherson v. Buick Motor Co., 217 N.Y. 382). The query always is whether the putative wrongdoer has advanced to such a point as to have launched a force or instrument of harm, or has stopped where inaction is at most a refusal to become an instrument for good.

The plaintiff would have us hold that the defendant, when once it entered upon the performance of its contract with the city, was brought into such a relation with every one who might potentially be benefited through the supply of water at the hydrants as to give to negligent performance, without reasonable notice of a refusal to continue, the quality of a tort. There is a suggestion of this thought in Guardian Trust Co. v. Fisher (200 U.S. 57), but the dictum was rejected in a later case decided by the same court (German Alliance Ins. Co. v. Home Water

Supply Co., 226 U.S. 220) when an opportunity was at hand to turn it into law. We are satisfied that liability would be unduly and indeed indefinitely extended by this enlargement of the zone of duty. The dealer in coal who is to supply fuel for a shop must then answer to the customers if fuel is lacking. The manufacturer of goods, who enters upon the performance of his contract, must answer, in that view, not only to the buyer, but to those to his knowledge are looking to the buyer for their own sources of supply. Everyone making a promise having the quality of a contract will be under a duty to the promisee by virtue of the promise, but under another duty, apart from contract, to an indefinite number of potential beneficiaries when performance has begun. The assumption of one relation will mean the involuntary assumption of a series of new relations, inescapably hooked together. Again we may say in the words of the Supreme Court of the United States: "The law does not spread its protection so far" (Robins Dry Dock & Repair Co. v. Flint, [275 U.S. 303]; cf. Byrd v. English, 117 Ga. 191). We do not need to determine now what remedy, if any, there might be if the defendant had withheld the water or reduced the pressure with a malicious intent to do injury to the plaintiff or another. We put aside also the problem that would arise if there had been reckless and wanton indifference to consequences measured and foreseen. Difficulties would be present even then, but they need not now perplex us. What we are dealing with at this time is a mere negligent omission, unaccompanied by malice or other aggravating elements. The failure in such circumstances to furnish an adequate supply of water is at most the denial of a benefit. It is not the commission of a wrong.

(3) We think the action is not maintainable as one for the breach of a statutory duty.

The defendant, a public service corporation, is subject to the provisions of the Transportation Corporations Act. The duty imposed upon it by that act is in substance to furnish water, upon demand by the inhabitants, at reasonable rates, through suitable connections at office, factory or dwelling, and to furnish water at like rates through hydrants or in public buildings upon demand by the city, all according to its capacity. We find nothing in these requirements to enlarge the zone of liability where an inhabitant of the city suffers indirect or incidental damage through deficient pressure at the hydrants. The breach of duty in any case is to the one to whom service is denied at the time and at the place where services to such one is due. The denial, though wrongful, is unavailing without more to give a cause of action to another. We may find a helpful analogy in the law of common carriers. A railroad company is under a duty to supply reasonable facilities for carriage at reasonable rates. It is liable, generally speaking, for breach of a duty imposed by law if it refuses to accept merchandise tendered by a shipper. The fact that its duty is of this character does not make it liable to some one else who may be counting upon the prompt delivery of the merchandise to save him from loss in going forward with his work. If the defendant may not be held for a tort at common law, we find no adequate reason for a holding that it may be held under the statute.

The judgment should be affirmed with costs.

NOTES

1. The privity limitation and the waterworks cases. Moch represents an uneasy mixture between gratuitous and commercial transactions. On the one hand the contract provided for reimbursement to the water company for the services provided. Yet on the other hand, the plaintiff was not a party to the agreement in question, even if a taxpayer of the local community that funded the contract. Cardozo's opinion addresses both sides of the dilemma, first by negating liability on contractual grounds by refusing to recognize the plaintiff as a third-party beneficiary, and then by refusing to impose upon the defendant a duty to act carefully assuming that it has acted gratuitously. The decision itself has met with a divided press. The case was criticized in Seavey, Reliance upon Gratuitous Promises or Other Conduct, 64 Harv. L. Rev. 913, 920-921 (1951):

> Closely allied to this group are those which may be described as "waterworks" cases. These are cases in which a waterworks company, having undertaken to keep a specific pressure in hydrants, has failed to maintain the pressure, as a result of which the plaintiff's house is destroyed when it would have been saved had the pressure been sufficient. By and large, recovery has been denied. This result may perhaps be justified on the ground that it is advisable to protect water companies from the extensive liability which might arise from the destruction of a large part of the city because of the lack of water pressure. To the contrary, however, the modern tendency is to impose strict liability upon those in control of a situation which, if things go wrong, may result in a holocaust. Further, it is difficult to differentiate this type of case from that where a person has negligently broken a water main and is held responsible for harm caused by the consequent lack of pressure. The earlier cases, however, were decided at a time when nonfeasance and lack of privity were sufficient to prevent liability and the subsequent cases have followed these precedents. Even Cardozo, in what is perhaps his most unsatisfactory opinion in the field of torts, rested his decision, in part, upon the nonfeasance of the waterworks company.

Moch also has its strong defenders. Professor Gregory, Gratuitous Undertakings and the Duty of Care, 1 DePaul L. Rev. 30, 59-60 (1951), first takes Cardozo to task for "soar[ing] off into the ethereal sphere of cryptic verbalism in a most unsatisfactory manner," but then defends his result as follows:

The real reason for the decision in the *Moch* case seems to be that fire insurance companies, and not water companies, are the appropriate social institutions for bearing losses by fire under these circumstances. Practically all property owners today carry fire insurance. They pay plenty for the protection they get and the insurance companies are professional risk-bearers, well able to shoulder the losses which occur. Indeed, losses by fire should be left finally on them unless there is some good reason for allowing them to shift the burden elsewhere. . . .

Certainly Cardozo realized that a decision for the Moch Company was tantamount to a decision for Moch's fire insurance underwriter against the water company. Any right acknowledged to Moch would be equitably assigned by subrogation to its fire insurance carrier — and would quickly be asserted. But what could the water company do about administering this risk? It always received $42.50 per hydrant per annum, regardless of the nature of the property holdings near any particular hydrant or of the changes which took place in the neighborhoods. That left it virtually nothing to fund against the contingency of loss which might be indirectly occasioned through an inadvertent failure of the water pressure. . . .

Cardozo thought the sum of $42.50 insufficient to warrant the conclusion that a negligent water company should be made to relieve a fire insurance company from bearing the ultimate risk of loss by fire. . . .

Should the plaintiff in *Moch* be able to recover on the strength of Restatement (Second) of Torts §324A?

§324A. LIABILITY TO THIRD PERSON FOR NEGLIGENT PERFORMANCE
    OF UNDERTAKING

One who undertakes, gratuitously or for consideration, to render services to another which he should recognize as necessary for the protection of a third person or his things, is subject to liability to the third person for physical harm resulting from his failure to exercise reasonable care to protect his undertaking, if

(a) his failure to exercise reasonable care increases the risk of such harm, or

(b) he has undertaken to perform a duty owed by the other to the third person, or

(c) the harm is suffered because of reliance of the other or the third person upon the undertaking.

2. *Judicial developments since* Moch. Strauss v. Belle Realty Co., 482 N.E.2d 34, 38 (N.Y. 1985), arose out of the great New York power failure of 1977, for which the defendant, Consolidated Edison, had already been found grossly negligent. The power failure cut off the pumps used to circulate water upstairs in defendant Belle Realty's building. The plaintiff, a 77-year-old tenant in Belle's building, was injured when he fell in the dark on some defective basement stairs in search of water. Both the plaintiff and Belle were customers of Con Ed, but only Belle had a direct contractual relation with the utility. The court refused to extend the utility's liability in negligence to the plaintiff tenant:

[W]e deal here with a system-wide power failure occasioned by what has already been determined to be the utility's gross negligence. If liability could be found here, then in logic and fairness the same result must follow in many similar situations. For example, a tenant's guests and invitees, as well as persons making deliveries or repairing equipment in the building, are equally persons who must use the common areas, and for whom they are maintained. Customers of a store and occupants of an office building stand in much the same position with respect to Con Edison as tenants of an apartment building. In all cases the numbers are to a certain extent limited and defined, and while identities may change, so do those of apartment dwellers. While limiting recovery to customers in this instance can hardly be said to confer immunity from negligence on Con Edison, permitting recovery to those in plaintiff's circumstances would, in our view, violate the court's responsibility to define an orbit of duty that places controllable limits on liability. . . .

In sum, Con Edison is not answerable to the tenant of an apartment building injured in a common area as a result of Con Edison's negligent failure to provide electric service as required by its agreement with the building owner.

Nonetheless, a number of important jurisdictions have deviated from *Moch.* See, e.g., Doyle v. South Pittsburgh Water Co., 199 A.2d 875, 878 (Pa. 1964), where Musmanno, J., held that the case fell "squarely within the rule that where a party to a contract assumes a duty to the other party to the contract, and it is foreseeable that a breach of that duty will cause injury to some third person not a party to the contract, the contracting party owes a duty to all those falling within the foreseeable orbit of the risk of harm." Other cases have relied more heavily on a pure theory of negligence. See, e.g., Harris v. Board of Water & Sewer Commissioners of Mobile, 320 So. 2d 624, 629 (Ala. 1975), which held that "given the fact that the hydrant was installed, the failure to use reasonable care in its maintenance, including the supplying of water thereto, is a sufficient breach of duty to provide a party with a cause of action under the theory of simple negligence."

Intermediate positions are also possible. Thus in Weinberg v. Dinger, 524 A.2d 366, 378 (N.J. 1987), the court decided to partially abandon its former uneasy adherence to the *Moch* rule. The court first showed its concern with the high insurance costs that water companies might have to bear, and then wrote as follows:

We believe that the imposition on a water company of liability for subrogation claims of carriers who pay fire losses caused by the company's negligent failure to maintain adequate water pressure would inevitably result in higher water rates paid by the class of consumers that paid for the fire insurance. The result of imposing subrogation-claim liability on water companies in such cases would be to shift the risk from the fire-insurance company to the water company, and, ultimately, to the consumer in the form of increased water rates. Thus, the consumer would pay twice — first for property insurance premiums, and then in the form of higher water rates to fund the cost of the water company's liability insurance. We find this result contrary to public policy.

Accordingly, we abrogate the water company's immunity for losses caused by the negligent failure to maintain adequate water pressure for fire fighting only to the extent of claims that are uninsured or underinsured. To the extent that such claims are insured and thereby assigned to the insurance carrier as required by statute, *N.J.S.A.* 17:36-5:20, we hold that the carrier's subrogation claims are unenforceable against the water company.

Note that the contract at issue in *Weinberg* provided as follows:

> 8. The Company will use due diligence at all times to provide continuous service of the character or quality proposed to be supplied; but in case the service shall be interrupted or irregular or defective or fail, the Company shall be liable and obligated only to use reasonably diligent efforts in light of the circumstances then existing to restore or correct its characteristics. . . .
> 10. The standard terms and conditions contained in this tariff are a part of every contract for service entered into by the Company and govern all classes of service where applicable.

What result if homeowner fire insurance contracts are redrafted to provide that no coverage shall exist when the fire in question could have been avoided by the due care of the water company?

3. Privity and leases. The scope of the privity limitation has also been at issue when the guest of a tenant has sought to sue the tenant's landlord for breach of a covenant of repair that in terms benefited the tenant alone. In Cullings v. Goetz, 176 N.E. 397, 397-398 (N.Y. 1931), Cardozo, J., denied the guest's action against the landlord. After noting the division of opinion on the question, he continued:

> Generally, however, in this country as in England, a covenant to repair does not impose upon the lessor a liability in tort at the suit of the lessee or of others lawfully on the land in the right of the lessee. . . . The tenant and no one else may keep visitors away till the danger is abated, or adapt the warning to the need. The landlord has at most a privilege to enter for the doing of the work, and at times not even that if the occupant protests.

Cardozo's opinion was overruled in New York in Putnam v. Stout, 345 N.E.2d 319, 325-326 (N.Y. 1976), a case in which the plaintiff suffered "serious injuries when her left shoe became caught in a hole causing her to fall on her back in the driveway adjoining a supermarket and parking lot" leased by a supermarket chain from a private landowner. In place of *Cullings* the court in *Putnam* decided to adopt the Restatement rule:

A lessor of land is subject to liability for physical harm caused to his lessee and others upon the land with the consent of the lessee or his sublessee by a condition of disrepair existing before or arising after the lessee has taken possession if

(a) the lessor, as such, has contracted by a covenant in the lease or otherwise to keep the land in repair, and

(b) the disrepair creates an unreasonable risk to persons upon the land which the performance of the lessor's agreement would have prevented, and

(c) the lessor fails to exercise reasonable care to perform his contract. (Restatement, Torts 2d, §357.)

We overrule Cullings v. Goetz and adopt the Restatement formulation as the law rule to be applied. The Restatement rule rests on a combination of factors which, we think, more accurately and realistically place an increased burden on a lessor who contracts to keep the land in repair: First, the lessor has agreed, for a consideration, to keep the premises in repair; secondly, the likelihood that the landlord's promise to make repairs will induce the tenant to forego repair efforts which he otherwise might have made; thirdly, the lessor retains a reversionary interest in the land and by his contract may be regarded as retaining and assuming the responsibility of keeping his premises in safe condition; finally, various social policy factors must be considered: (a) tenants may often be financially unable to make repairs; (b) their possession is for a limited term and thus the incentive to make repairs is significantly less than that of a landlord; and (c) in return for his pecuniary benefit from the relationship, the landlord could properly be expected to assume certain obligations with respect to the safety of the others. We hold, therefore, that a landlord may be liable for injuries to persons coming onto his land with the consent of his lessee solely on the basis of his contract or covenant to keep the premises in repair.

4. Insurance carriers, safety regulations, and workers' compensation: one more fond look at the duty of care. Under the general law, an insurance company that conducts inspections of an employer's workplace could be held liable in negligence to a worker who is injured by some condition that could have been discovered and corrected by reasonable care. Just that result was reached in Nelson v. Union Wire Rope Corp., 199 N.E.2d 769 (Ill. 1964), which thus worked an end run around the exclusive remedy provisions of the workers' compensation statutes banning tort actions against the employer. The result in *Nelson* was altered by statute in 1969, which provided:

No common law or statutory right to recover damages from the employer, his insurer, his broker, any service organization retained by the employer, his insurer or his broker to provide safety service, advice or recommendations for the employer or the agents or employees of any of them for injury or death sustained by any employee while engaged in the line of his duty as such employee, other than the compensation herein provided, is available to any employee who is covered by the provisions of this Act. . . . [Ill. Rev. Stat. 1969, ch. 48, par. 138.5(a).]

In Reid v. Employers Mutual Liability Insurance Co., 319 N.E.2d 769, 772 (Ill. 1974), the court explained the reason for the statute as follows:

> It is also apparent that the actions of defendant of which plaintiff complains in this case were directly related to its function as a compensation carrier. It is undoubtedly true that the safety inspections conducted by defendant inured to its financial benefit by reducing accidents and thereby reducing its exposure on its workmen's compensation policy. However, it is also obvious that the employees were beneficiaries of such safety inspections and accident-prevention programs. If compensation carriers were held subject to liability for making the type of safety inspections occurring here, it is quite likely that the insurers would choose to escape liability by not making any safety inspections on the premises of its insureds. It is difficult to believe that the legislature would have intended such a result.

The pattern developed in Illinois — judicial recognition of a cause of action followed by its legislative nullification — has been followed in other jurisdictions. See generally A. Larson, The Law of Workmen's Compensation §72.90 (1989). Yet here some states have created constitutional obstacles against the tort immunity of the compensation carrier. See, e.g., Johnson v. American Mutual Liability Ins. Co., 394 So. 2d 1 (Ala. 1980), holding that the legislature could not immunize an insurance carrier from tort liability for a negligent inspection.

Legislation aside, what might an insurance company do in order to protect itself from the possibility of suit if it conducts safety inspections for its own benefit? In Stacy v. Aetna Casualty & Surety Co., 484 F.2d 289, 293 (5th Cir. 1973), the insurance company rested its successful defense in part upon the following clause in its contract with the plaintiff's employer:

> The company and any rating authority having jurisdiction by law shall each be permitted but not obligated to inspect at any reasonable time the work places, operations, machinery and equipment covered by this policy. Neither the right to make inspections nor the making thereof, nor any report thereon shall constitute an undertaking on behalf of or for the benefit of the insured or others, to determine or warrant that such work places, operations, machinery or equipment are safe.

Should the plaintiff be able to argue that since he is not a party to the provisions of the agreement, he should not be bound by any of its terms?

The question of privity arises again both in connection with defective products (see Chapter 9) and negligent misrepresentation (see Chapter 16).

E. SPECIAL RELATIONSHIPS

American Law Institute, Restatement (Second) of Torts
(1965)

§315. GENERAL PRINCIPLE

There is no duty so to control the conduct of a third person as to prevent him from causing physical harm to another unless

(a) a special relation exists between the actor and the third person which imposes a duty upon the actor to control the third person's conduct, or

(b) a special relation exists between the actor and the other which gives the other a right to protection.

NOTE

On the borderland of nonfeasance. In Weirum v. RKO General Inc, 539 P.2d 36, 40, 41 (Cal. 1975), the defendant's disk jockey, the Real Don Steele, staged a novel promotional contest. He would drive around town announcing that he "had bread to spread" and give his location on the air. The first contestant to reach that location and answer some simple quiz questions correctly would win small prizes. Two teenage drivers got into an 80-miles-per-hour drag race in an effort to reach Steele at his new location, and forced decedent's car off the highway, where it overturned, killing him. The California Court of Appeals, over a dissent, reversed plaintiff's judgment against the radio station, saying that the station "had no control, or right to control, over the conduct of the drivers of other cars on the highway." 119 Cal. Rptr. 468 (1975). The California Supreme Court reinstated the plaintiff's judgment in a unanimous decision, insisting that liability here did not open up a Pandora's box:.

> We are not persuaded that the imposition of a duty here will lead to unwarranted extensions of liability. Defendant is fearful that entrepreneurs will henceforth be burdened with an avalanche of obligations: an athletic department will owe a duty to an ardent sports fan injured while hastening to purchase one of a limited number of tickets; a department store will be liable to injuries incurred in response to a "while-they-last" sale. This argument, however, suffers from a myopic view of the facts presented here. The giveaway contest was no commonplace invitation to an attraction available on a limited basis. It was a competitive scramble in which the thrill of the chase to be the one and only victor was intensified by the live broadcasts which accompanied the pursuit. In the assertedly analogous situations described by defendant, any haste involved in the purchase of the commodity is an incidental and unavoidable result

of the scarcity of the commodity itself. In such situations there is no attempt, as here, to generate a competitive pursuit on public streets, accelerated by repeated importuning by radio to be the very first to arrive at a particular destination. Manifestly the "spectacular" bears little resemblance to daily commercial activities.

The court then rebuffed an effort to use section 315 to limit liability:

> The rule stated in Restatement section 315 is merely a refinement of the general principle . . . that one is not obligated to act as a "good samaritan." This doctrine is rooted in the common law distinction between action and inaction, or misfeasance and nonfeasance. Misfeasance exists when the defendant is responsible for making the plaintiff's position worse, i.e., defendant has created a risk. Conversely, nonfeasance is found when the defendant has failed to aid plaintiff through beneficial intervention. As section 315 illustrates, liability for nonfeasance is largely limited to those circumstances in which some special relationship can be established. If, on the other hand, the act complained of is one of misfeasance, the question of duty is governed by the standards of ordinary care discussed above.
>
> Here, there can be little doubt that we review an act of misfeasance to which section 315 is inapplicable. Liability is not predicated upon defendant's failure to intervene for the benefit of decedent but rather upon its creation of an unreasonable risk of harm to him. Defendant's reliance upon cases which involve the failure to prevent harm to another is therefore misplaced . . .

Kline v. 1500 Massachusetts Avenue Apartment Corp.
439 F.2d 477 (D.C. Cir. 1970)

WILKEY, J. The appellee apartment corporation states that there is "only one issue presented for review . . . whether a duty should be placed on a landlord to take steps to protect tenants from foreseeable criminal acts committed by third parties." The District Court as a matter of law held that there is no such duty. We find that there is, and that in the circumstances here the applicable standard of care was breached. We therefore reverse and remand to the District Court for the determination of damages for the appellant.

I

The appellant, Sarah B. Kline, sustained serious injuries when she was criminally assaulted and robbed at approximately 10:15 in the evening by an intruder in the common hallway of an apartment house at 1500 Massachusetts Avenue. This facility, into which the appellant Kline moved in October 1959, is a large apartment building with approximately 585 individual apartment units. It has a main entrance on Massachusetts Avenue, with side entrances on both 15th and 16th Streets. At the time the appellant first signed a lease a doorman was on duty at the main entrance twenty-four hours a day, and at least one employee at all times manned a desk in the lobby from which all persons using the elevators could be observed. The 15th Street door adjoined the entrance to a parking garage used by both the tenants and the public. Two garage attendants were stationed at this dual entranceway; the duties of each being arranged so that one of them always was in position to observe those entering either the apartment building or the garage. The 16th Street entrance was unattended during the day but was locked after 9:00 P.M.

By mid-1966, however, the main entrance had no doorman, the desk in the lobby was left unattended much of the time, the 15th Street entrance was generally unguarded due to a decrease in garage personnel, and the 16th Street entrance was often left unlocked all night. The entrances were allowed to be thus unguarded in the face of an increasing number of assaults, larcenies, and robberies being perpetrated against the tenants in and from the common hallways of the apartment building. These facts were undisputed. . . . The landlord had notice of these crimes and had in fact been urged by appellant Kline herself prior to the events leading to the instant appeal to take steps to secure the building.

Shortly after 10:00 P.M. on November 17, 1966, Miss Kline was assaulted and robbed just outside her apartment on the first floor above the street level of this 585 unit apartment building. This occurred only two months after Leona Sullivan, another female tenant, had been similarly attacked in the same commonway.

II

At the outset we note that of the crimes of violence, robbery, and assault which had been occurring with mounting frequency on the premises at 1500 Massachusetts Avenue, the assaults on Miss Kline and Miss Sullivan took place in the hallways of the building, which were under the exclusive control of the appellee landlord. Even in those crimes of robbery or assault committed in individual apartments, the intruders of necessity had to gain entrance through the common entry and passageways. These premises fronted on three heavily traveled streets, and had multiple entrances. The risk to be guarded against therefore was the risk of unauthorized entrance into the apartment house by intruders bent upon some crime of violence or theft.

While the apartment lessees themselves could take some steps to guard against this risk by installing extra heavy locks and other security devices on the doors and windows of their respective apartments, yet this risk in the greater part could only be guarded against by the landlord. No individual tenant had it within his power to take measures to guard the garage entranceways, to provide scrutiny at the main entrance of the building, to patrol the common hallways and elevators, to set up any kind of a security alarm system in the building, to provide additional locking devices on the main doors, to provide a system of announcement for authorized visitors only, to close the garage doors at appropriate hours, and to see that the entrance was manned at all times.

The risk of criminal assault and robbery on a tenant in the common hallways of the building was thus entirely predictable; that same risk had been occurring with increasing frequency over a period of several months immediately prior to the incident giving rise to this case; it was a risk whose prevention or minimization was almost entirely within the power of the landlord; and the risk materialized in the assault and robbery of appellant on November 17, 1966.

III

In this jurisdiction, certain duties have been assigned to the landlord because of his *control* of common hallways, lobbies, stairwells, etc., used by all tenants in multiple dwelling units. This Court in Levine v. Katz, 407 F.2d 303, 304 (D.C. Cir. 1968), pointed out that:

> It has long been well settled in this jurisdiction that, where a landlord leases separate portions of property and reserves under his own control the halls, stairs, or other parts of the property for use in common by all tenants, he has a duty to all those on the premises of legal right to use ordinary care and diligence to maintain the retained parts in a reasonably safe condition.

While Levine v. Katz dealt with a physical defect in the building leading to plaintiff's injury, the rationale as applied to predictable criminal acts by third parties is the same. The duty is the landlord's because by his control of the areas of common use and common danger he is the only party who has the *power* to make the necessary repairs or to provide the necessary protection.

As a general rule, a private person does not have a duty to protect another from a criminal attack by a third person. We recognize that this rule has sometimes in the past been applied in landlord-tenant law, even by this court. Among the reasons for the application of this rule to landlords are: judicial reluctance to tamper with the traditional common law concept of the landlord-tenant relationship; the notion that the act of a third person in committing an intentional tort or crime is a superseding cause of the harm to another resulting therefrom; the oftentimes difficult problem of determining foreseeability of criminal acts; the vagueness of the standard which the landlord must meet; the economic consequences of the imposition of the duty; and conflict with the public policy allocating the duty of protecting citizens from criminal acts to the government rather than the private sector.

But the rationale of this very broad general rule falters when it is applied to the conditions of modern day urban apartment living, particularly in the circumstances of this case. The rationale of the general rule exonerating a third party from any duty to protect another from a criminal attack has no applicability to the landlord-tenant relationship in multiple dwelling houses. The landlord is no insurer of his tenants' safety, but he certainly is no bystander. And where, as here, the landlord has notice of repeated criminal assaults and robberies, has notice that these crimes occurred in the portion of the premises exclusively within his control, has every reason to expect like crimes to happen again, and has the exclusive power to take preventive action, it does not seem unfair to place upon the landlord a duty to take those steps which are within his power to minimize the predictable risk to his tenants. . . .

[The court then relied upon Javins v. First National Realty Corporation, 428 F.2d 1071 (D.C. Cir. 1970), which imposed an implied warranty of habitability for residential leases in multiple dwellings.]

In the case at bar we place the duty of taking protective measures guarding the entire premises and the areas peculiarly under the landlord's control against the perpetration of criminal acts upon the landlord, the party to the lease contract who has the effective capacity to perform these necessary acts.

[The court then noted that innkeepers were held liable to their guests for assaults and molestations by third parties, "be they innkeeper's employees, fellow guests or intruders."] Other relationships in which similar duties have been imposed include landowner-invitee, businessman-patron, employer-employee, school district-pupil, hospital-patient, and carrier-passenger. In all, the theory of liability is essentially the same: that since the ability of one of the parties to provide for his own protection has been limited in some way by his submission to the control of the other, a duty should be imposed upon the one possessing control (and thus the power to act) to take reasonable precautions to protect the other one from assaults by third parties which, at least, could reasonably have been anticipated. However, there is no liability normally imposed upon the one having the power to act if the violence is sudden and unexpected provided that the source of the violence is not an employee of the one in control.

We are aware of various cases in other jurisdictions following a different line of reasoning, conceiving of the landlord and tenant relationship along more traditional common law lines, and on varying fact situations reaching a different result from that we reach here. Typical of these is a much cited (although only a 4-3) decision of the Supreme Court of New Jersey, Goldberg v. Housing Authority of Newark [186 A.2d 291(N.J. 1962)], relied on by appellee landlord here. There the court said:

> Everyone can foresee the commission of crime virtually anywhere and at any time. If foreseeability itself gave rise to a duty to provide "police" protection for others, every residential curtilage, every shop, every store, every manufacturing plant would have to be patrolled by the private arm of the owner. And since hijacking and attack upon occupants of motor vehicles are also foreseeable, it would be the duty of every motorist to provide armed protection for his passengers and the property of others. Of course, none of this is at all palatable.

This language seems to indicate that the court was using the word *foreseeable* interchangeably with the word *possible*. In that context, the statement is quite correct. It would be folly to impose liability for mere possibilities. But we must reach the question of liability for attacks which are foreseeable in the sense that they are *probable* and *predictable*. . . . As between tenant and landlord, the landlord is the only one in the position to take the necessary acts of protection required. He is not an insurer, but he is obligated to minimize the risk to his tenants. Not only as between landlord and tenant is the landlord best equipped to guard against the predictable risk of intruders, but even as between landlord and the police power of government, the landlord is in the best position to take the necessary protective measures. Municipal police cannot patrol the entryways and the hallways, the garages and the basements of private multiple unit apartment dwellings. They are neither equipped, manned, nor empowered to do so. In the area of the predictable risk which materialized in this case, only the landlord could have taken measures which might have prevented the injuries suffered by appellant.

We note that in the fight against crime the police are not expected to do it all; every segment of society has obligations to aid in law enforcement and to minimize the opportunities for crime. . . .

IV

We now turn to the standard of care which should be applied in judging if the landlord has fulfilled his duty of protection to the tenant. Although in many cases the language speaks as if the standard of care itself varies, in the last analysis the standard of care is the same — reasonable care in all the circumstances. . . .

We therefore hold in this case that the applicable standard of care in providing protection for the tenant is that standard which this landlord himself was employing in October 1959 when the appellant became a resident on the premises at 1500 Massachusetts Avenue. The tenant was led to expect that she could rely upon this degree of protection. While we do not say that the precise measures for security which were then in vogue should have been kept up (e.g., the number of people at the main entrances might have been reduced if a tenant-controlled inter-com-automatic latch system had been installed in the common entryways), we do hold that the same relative degree of security should have been maintained. [The court then held that liability was "clear" on the face of the record and remanded the case to the district court on the issue of damages only.]

Having said this, it would be well to state what is *not* said by this decision. We do not hold that the landlord is by any means an insurer of the safety of his tenants. His duty is to take those measures of protection which are within his power and capacity to take, and which can reasonably be expected to mitigate the risk of intruders assaulting and robbing tenants. The landlord is not expected to provide protection commonly owed by a municipal police department; but as illustrated in this case, he is obligated to protect those parts of his premises which are not usually subject to periodic patrol and inspection by the municipal police. We do not say that every multiple unit apartment house in the District of Columbia should have those same measures of protection which 1500 Massachusetts Avenue enjoyed in 1959, nor do we say that 1500 Massachusetts Avenue should have precisely those same measures in effect at the present time. Alternative and more up-to-date methods may be equally or even more effective.

Granted, the discharge of this duty of protection by landlords will cause, in many instances, the expenditure of large sums for additional equipment and services, and granted, the cost will be ultimately passed on to the tenant in the form of increased rents. This prospect, in itself, however, is no deterrent to our acknowledging and giving force to the duty, since without protection the tenant already pays in losses from theft, physical assault and increased insurance premiums.

The landlord is entirely justified in passing on the cost of increased protective measures to his tenants, but the rationale of compelling the landlord to do it in the first place is that he is the only one who is in a position to take the necessary protective measures for overall protection of the premises, which he owns in whole and rents in part to individual tenants.

Reversed and remanded to the District Court for the determination of damages.

MacKinnon, J., dissenting. [The dissent first argued that liability was not established on the record, so that the case should, even on the court's view of the substantive law, be retried de novo. In particular, the dissent noted that the evidence on the number and frequency of previous criminal attacks was insufficient, as only one of the 20 incidents involved both an assault and robbery. It also argued that the notice to the landlord was only of theft, and that there was no evidence in the record that the landlord knew of the previous assault upon Leona Sullivan. It continued:]

The evidence introduced by the plaintiff is also deficient in my opinion in not proving that the alleged negligence was the proximate cause of the assault or that it contributed to it in any way. Plaintiff's evidence did not negate that it was a tenant, guest or person properly on the property who committed the offense, and while the panel opinion throughout asserts that an "intruder" committed the offense, there is no proof of that fact. So plaintiff's evidence failed to prove a nexus between the alleged deficiencies of the appellee and the cause of any damage to appellant. . . .

As for the claim that appellant was led to believe she would get the same standard of protection in 1966 that was furnished in 1959, there is obviously nothing to this point. She was not led to expect that. She personally observed the changes which occurred in this respect. They were obvious to her each day of her life. And since her original lease had terminated and her tenancy in 1966 was on a month to month basis, whatever contract existed was created at the beginning of the month and since there was no evidence of any alteration in the security precautions during the current month, there is no basis for any damage claim based on contract. . . .

In my opinion the decision in Goldberg v. Housing Authority of Newark, 186 A.2d 291 (N.J. 1962), answers all appellant's arguments. It is just too much, absent a contractual agreement, to require or expect a combination office-apartment building such as is involved here to provide police patrol protection or its equivalent in the block-long, well-lighted passageways. Yet nothing short of that will meet the second guessing standard of protection the panel opinion practically directs. If tenants expect such protection, they can move to apartments where it is available and presumably pay a higher rental, but it is a mistake in my judgment to hold an office-apartment building to such a requirement when the tenant knew for years that such protection was not being afforded.

NOTES

1. Contract or special relationship? If the defendant landlord could have taken effective steps to prevent crimes in common areas at a lower cost than its tenants, then why didn't it assume that liability in its standard residential lease? In dealing with the contract alternative, should the court in *Kline* take into account the question of administrative costs? Contributory negligence? Does some defect in the bargaining process prevent the correct allocative result from being obtained by contract?

Whatever the answer to the last question, it is clear that the *Kline* approach has met with widespread approval insofar as it reverses the older common-law rule that imposed no duty on a landlord to shield tenants from the criminal attacks of strangers. Thus in Johnston v. Harris, 198 N.W.2d 409 (Mich. 1972), the court found that a landlord could be held responsible for the assault and robbery of his tenant when the assailant lurked in the poorly lighted and unlocked vestibule of the defendant's four-unit apartment house. The dissent argued that it was a mistake to require the defendant to assume the public function of police protection when the city itself had been unable to stem the increase in crime.

The duty of care was extended to the tenant's invitees in Sampson v. Saginaw Professional Building, Inc., 224 N.W.2d 843 (Mich. 1975). There, by a vote of four to three, the Michigan Supreme Court allowed an employee of a tenant in the defendant's building to recover damages when she was robbed and stabbed by an out-patient of a state mental clinic that was another tenant in the building. Noting the exclusive control that the defendant retained over the building's common areas, the court held that it "is his duty to insure that these areas are kept in good repair and reasonably safe for the use of his tenants and invitees." With the duty thus established, the court said the question of whether the defendant had taken reasonable care was for the jury, whose verdict it found justified under the circumstances. Even though there had been no incident during the nine years that the mental clinic had been tenant in the building, the other tenants had "voiced concern and uneasiness" about the manner in which the mental patients behaved while in the building. Should the state mental clinic be held liable for the incident? What result if the injury is inflicted by a disgruntled employee just fired by another tenant?

2. The procession of liability.

a. Colleges and universities. In Peterson v. San Francisco Community College District, 685 P.2d 1193, 1197 (Cal. 1984), the California Supreme Court held that a community college district had a duty to protect a college student against a foreseeable criminal assault that took place in broad daylight on campus — here, on a stairway in a parking lot — on the strength of the special relationship between institution and student. "There is no question that if the defendant district here were a private landowner operating a parking lot on its premises it would owe plaintiff a duty to exercise due care for her protection." The court ruled that the plaintiff was entitled to reach the jury on two allegations of negligence: first, on whether the defendant had properly trimmed the hedge and foliage that concealed the perpetrator before he committed the crime and, second, on whether it had a duty to warn the plaintiff about the hazards in question, given that it had not corrected them. How might such a warning be given? Be updated?

b. Common carriers. In Lopez v. Southern California Rapid Transit District, 710 P.2d 907, 910-911 (Cal. 1985), the court rejected the argument that the duty would impose a "colossal financial burden" on the transit district given the far-flung operations of its system.

> Finding such a duty to exist is not the functional equivalent of finding a duty to provide an armed security guard on every bus. There are a number of actions a carrier might take short of placing an armed guard on each bus which, in a given case, might be sufficient to meet the duty imposed [by statute to exercise "utmost care"]. For instance, where the disorderly conduct of certain passengers threatens the safety of others, the bus driver (subject, of course, to reasonable concern for his own safety), might warn the unruly passengers to quiet down or get off the bus; alert the police and summon their assistance; or, if necessary, eject the unruly passengers (Civ. Code, §2188). Carriers could provide radio communication between the bus driver and local police or bus headquarters to enable the driver to call for assistance when needed, and buses could be equipped with alarm lights (Veh. Code, §25275.5) to alert nearby police or carrier personnel of criminal activity taking place on board the bus. Bus drivers, especially those on routes with a history of criminal activity, could be trained to recognize and deal with potentially volatile situations.

c. Condominiums. In Frances T. v. Village Green Owners Association, 723 P.2d 573 (Cal. 1986), the plaintiff was "molested, raped and robbed" by an unidentified assailant who entered her condominium unit at night after the condominium board refused to allow plaintiff to install lights by her own unit for her own self-protection. The court first held that the liability imposed on landlords in *Kline* should be extended to condominium boards and to their individual members who function as the de facto landlord of the premises. Mosk, J., dissented on the ground that any parallels between a condominium board and an ordinary landlord were wholly flawed and that there was no special relationship between a condominium association and its unit member.

Note that some California lawyers have described the decision as "crazy" because of the obstacles it placed in the way of "quality people" who might otherwise volunteer for service on these boards. Legislation limiting the liability of officers and directors of nonprofit institutions has been passed in several states, and has been introduced in California. See Bishop, *Coast Case Raises Risk of Directors*, N.Y. TIMES, Oct. 26, 1986, Business section, at 1.

d. Shopping malls. In Ann M. v. Pacific Plaza Shopping Center, 863 P.2d 207, 210, 215-216 (Cal. 1993), the court refused to allow the plaintiff, who had been raped inside her place of employment in the defendant's shopping mall, to maintain a suit against her employer's landlord. The plaintiff's employer had signed a lease that gave defendant exclusive control over all common areas. Plaintiff was raped around 8:00 a.m. by a customer who entered the store from the mall when she was alone in her shop. There was some evidence that the tenants in the shopping mall had complained of lack of security and the presence of transients, but the merchants association had considered the possible options and "decided not to hire [walking] security patrols, because the cost would be prohibitive. . . . According to the lease, if the shopping center had provided the requested patrols, the tenants would have borne the cost in the form of increased rent." So alternative arrangements were made for another security company to drive by three or four times a day.

In its earlier decision of Isaacs v. Huntington Memorial Hospital, 695 P.2d 653 (Cal. 1985), the court held that the plaintiff could show the increased risk of criminal activities from "the totality of circumstances," even if there were no "similar acts" of the sort that harmed the plaintiff. In *Ann M.* the court consciously retreated from *Isaacs*, Panelli, J., saying:

> While there may be circumstances where the hiring of security guards will be required to satisfy a landowner's duty of care, such action will rarely, if ever, be found to be a "minimal burden." The monetary costs of security guards is not insignificant. Moreover, the obligation to provide patrols adequate to deter criminal conduct is not well defined. "No one really knows why people commit crime, hence no one really knows what is 'adequate' deterrence in any given situation. Finally, the social costs of imposing a duty on landowners to hire private police forces are also not insignificant. For these reasons, we conclude that a high degree of foreseeability is required in order to find that the scope of a landlord's duty of care includes the hiring of security guards. We further conclude that the requisite degree of foreseeability rarely, if ever, can be proven in the absence of prior similar incidents of violent crime on the landlord's premises. To hold otherwise would be to impose an unfair burden upon landlords and, in effect, would force landlords to become the insurers of public safety, contrary to well established policy in this state.

Isaacs, however, continues to gain support outside California. See, e.g., Seibert v. Vic Regnier Builders, Inc., 856 P.2d 1332 (Kan. 1993), applying the rule for the benefit of a plaintiff robbed in the defendant's parking lot.

3. *Contributory negligence.* What role does an injured plaintiff have in *Kline* situations? In Wassell v. Adams, 865 F.2d 849, 855 (7th Cir. 1989), the plaintiff was raped and sodomized when, hearing a knock, she opened the door to her hotel room in the middle of the night under the mistaken belief that it was her fiancé at the door. The plaintiff argued that the defendants, operators of the motel, had failed to warn her of the risks of staying in a motel in a high-crime area. The jury assessed the plaintiff's damages at $850,000, but found her 97 percent

negligent, leaving an award of $25,500, roughly the expenses of her therapy for posttraumatic stress. Posner, J., upheld the award:

> [I]t is absurd to think that hoteliers are required to give so *obvious* a warning any more than they must warn guests not to stick their fingers into the electrical outlets. Everyone, or at least the average person, knows better than to open his or her door to a stranger in the middle of the night. The problem was not that Susan thought that she *should* open her bedroom door in the middle of the night to anyone who knocked, but that she wasn't thinking clearly. A warning would not have availed against a temporary, sleep-induced lapse.

Tarasoff v. Regents of University of California
551 P.2d 334 (Cal. 1976)

TOBRINER, J. On October 27, 1969, Prosenjit Poddar killed Tatiana Tarasoff. Plaintiffs, Tatiana's parents, allege that two months earlier Poddar confided his intention to kill Tatiana to Dr. Lawrence Moore, a psychologist employed by the Cowell Memorial Hospital at the University of California at Berkeley. They allege that on Moore's request, the campus police briefly detained Poddar, but released him when he appeared rational. They further claim that Dr. Harvey Powelson, Moore's superior, then directed that no further action be taken to detain Poddar. [Elsewhere in the opinion it was noted: "Poddar had persuaded Tatiana's brother to share an apartment with him near Tatiana's residence; shortly after her return from Brazil, Poddar went to her residence and killed her."] No one warned plaintiffs of Tatiana's peril.

Concluding that these facts set forth causes of action against neither therapists and policemen involved, nor against the Regents of the University of California as their employer, the superior court sustained defendants' demurrers to plaintiffs' second amended complaints without leave to amend. This appeal ensued. . . .

Plaintiffs' complaints predicate liability on two grounds: defendants' failure to warn plaintiffs of the impending danger and their failure to bring about Poddar's confinement pursuant to the Lanterman-Petris-Short Act (Welf. & Inst. Code, §5000ff.). Defendants, in turn, assert that they owed no duty of reasonable care to Tatiana and that they are immune from suit under the California Tort Claims Act of 1963 (Gov. Code, §810ff.). . . .

2. PLAINTIFFS CAN STATE A CAUSE OF ACTION AGAINST
    DEFENDANT THERAPISTS FOR NEGLIGENT FAILURE TO PROTECT
    TATIANA

The second cause of action can be amended to allege that Tatiana's death proximately resulted from defendant's negligent failure to warn

Tatiana or others likely to apprise her of her danger. Plaintiffs contend that as amended, such allegations of negligence and proximate causation, with resulting damages, establish a cause of action. Defendants, however, contend that in the circumstances of the present case they owed no duty of care to Tatiana or her parents and that, in the absence of such duty, they were free to act in careless disregard of Tatiana's life and safety.

In analyzing this issue, we bear in mind that legal duties are not discoverable facts of nature, but merely conclusory expressions that, in cases of a particular type, liability should be imposed for damage done. As stated in Dillon v. Legg, 441 P.2d 912, 916 (Cal. 1968): "The assertion that liability must . . . be denied because defendant bears no 'duty' to plaintiff 'begs the essential question — whether the plaintiff's interests are entitled to legal protection against the defendant's conduct. . . . [Duty] is not sacrosanct in itself, but only an expression of the sum total of those considerations of policy which lead the law to say that the particular plaintiff is entitled to protection.' (Prosser, Law of Torts [3d ed. 1964] at pp. 332-333.)"

In the landmark case of Rowland v. Christian, 443 P.2d 561 (Cal. 1968), Justice Peters recognized that liability should be imposed "for an injury occasioned to another by his want of ordinary care or skill" as expressed in section 1714 of the Civil Code. Thus, Justice Peters, quoting from Heaven v. Pender (1883) 11 Q.B.D. 503, 509, stated: " 'whenever one person is by circumstances placed in such a position with regard to another . . . that if he did not use ordinary care and skill in his own conduct . . . he would cause danger of injury to the person or property of the other, a duty arises to use ordinary care and skill to avoid such danger.' "

We depart from "this fundamental principle" only upon the "balancing of a number of considerations"; major ones "are the foreseeability of harm to the plaintiff, the degree of certainty that the plaintiff suffered injury, the closeness of the connection between the defendant's conduct and the injury suffered, the moral blame attached to the defendant's conduct, the policy of preventing future harm, the extent of the burden to the defendant and consequences to the community of imposing a duty to exercise care with resulting liability for breach, and the availability, cost and prevalence of insurance for the risk involved."

The most important of these considerations in establishing duty is foreseeability. As a general principle, a "defendant owes a duty of care to all persons who are foreseeably endangered by his conduct, with respect to all risks which make the conduct unreasonably dangerous." As we shall explain, however, when the avoidance of foreseeable harm requires a defendant to control the conduct of another person, or to warn of such conduct, the common law has traditionally imposed liability only if the defendant bears some special relationship to the dangerous person or to the potential victim. Since the relationship between a therapist and his patient satisfies this requirement, we need not here decide whether foreseeability alone is sufficient to create a duty to exercise reasonable care to protect a potential victim of another's conduct.

Although, as we have stated above, under the common law, as a general rule, one person owed no duty to control the conduct of another the courts have carved out an exception to this rule[5] in cases in which the defendant stands in some special relationship to either the person whose conduct needs to be controlled or in a relationship to the foreseeable victim of that conduct (see Rest. 2d Torts, §§315-320). Applying this exception to the present case, we note that a relationship of defendant therapists to either Tatiana or Poddar will suffice to establish a duty of care; as explained in section 315 of the Restatement Second of Torts, a duty of care may arise from either "(a) a special relation . . . between the actor and the third person which imposes a duty upon the actor to control the third person's conduct, or (b) a special relation . . . between the actor and the other which gives to the other a right of protection."

Although plaintiff's pleadings assert no special relation between Tatiana and defendant therapists, they establish as between Poddar and defendant therapists the special relation that arises between a patient and his doctor or psychotherapist. Such a relationship may support affirmative duties for the benefit of third persons. Thus, for example, a hospital must exercise reasonable care to control the behavior of a patient which may endanger other persons.[7] A doctor must also warn a patient if the patient's condition or medication renders certain conduct, such as driving a car, dangerous to others.

Although the California decisions that recognize this duty have involved cases in which the defendant stood in a special relationship *both*

---

5. This rule derives from the common law's distinction between misfeasance and nonfeasance, and its reluctance to impose liability for the latter. (See Harper & Kime, The Duty to Control the Conduct of Another (1934) 43 Yale L.J. 886, 887.) Morally questionable, the rule owes its survival to "the difficulties of setting any standards of unselfish service to fellow men, and of making any workable rule to cover possible situations where fifty people might fail to rescue. . . ." (Prosser, Torts (4th ed. 1971) §56, p. 341.) Because of these practical difficulties, the courts have increased the number of instances in which affirmative duties are imposed not by direct rejection of the common law rule, but by expanding the list of special relationships which will justify departure from that rule. (See Prosser, supra, §56, at pp. 343-350.)

7. When a "hospital has notice or knowledge of facts from which it might reasonably be concluded that a patient would be likely to harm himself *or others* unless preclusive measures were taken, then the hospital must use reasonable care in the circumstances to prevent such harm." (Vistica v. Presbyterian Hospital, 432 P.2d 193, 196 (Cal. 1967).) (Emphasis added.) A mental hospital may be liable if it negligently permits the escape or release of a dangerous patient. Greenberg v. Barbour (E.D. Pa. 1971) 322 F. Supp. 745, upheld a cause of action against a hospital staff doctor whose negligent failure to admit a mental patient resulted in that patient assaulting the plaintiff.

to the victim and to the person whose conduct created the danger,[9] we do not think that the duty should logically be constricted to such situations. Decisions of other jurisdictions hold that the single relationship of a doctor to his patient is sufficient to support the duty to exercise reasonable care to protect others against dangers emanating from the patient's illness. The courts hold that a doctor is liable to persons infected by his patient if he negligently fails to diagnose a contagious disease (Hofmann v. Blackmon 241 So. 2d 752 (Fla. App. 1970)), or, having diagnosed the illness, fails to warn members of the patient's family.

Since it involved a dangerous mental patient, the decision in Merchants Nat. Bank & Trust Co. of Fargo v. United States 272 F. Supp. 409 (D.N.D. 1967) comes closer to the issue. The Veterans Administration arranged for the patient to work on a local farm, but did not inform the farmer of the man's background. The farmer consequently permitted the patient to come and go freely during nonworking hours; the patient borrowed a car, drove to his wife's residence and killed her. Notwithstanding the lack of any "special relationship" between the Veterans Administration and the wife, the court found the Veterans Administration liable for the wrongful death of the wife. . . .

Defendants contend, however, that imposition of a duty to exercise reasonable care to protect third persons is unworkable because therapists cannot accurately predict whether or not a patient will resort to violence. In support of this argument amicus representing the American Psychiatric Association and other professional societies cites numerous articles which indicate that therapists, in the present state of the art, are unable reliably to predict violent acts; their forecasts, amicus claims, tend consistently to overpredict violence, and indeed are more often wrong than right. Since predictions of violence are often erroneous, amicus concludes, the courts should not render rulings that predicate the liability of therapists upon the validity of such predictions. . . .

We recognize the difficulty that a therapist encounters in attempting to forecast whether a patient presents a serious danger of violence. Obviously we do not require that the therapist, in making that determination, render a perfect performance; the therapist need only exercise "that reasonable degree of skill, knowledge, and care ordinarily possessed and exercised by members of [that professional specialty] under similar circumstances." Within the broad range of reasonable practice

---

9. Ellis v. D'Angelo, 253 P.2d 675 (Cal. App. 1953), upheld a cause of action against parents who failed to warn a babysitter of the violent proclivities of their child; Johnson v. State of California, 447 P.2d 352 (Cal. 1968), upheld a suit against the state for failure to warn foster parents of the dangerous tendencies of their ward; Morgan v. City of Yuba, 41 Cal. Rptr. 508 (Cal. App. 1964), sustained a cause of action against a sheriff who had promised to warn decedent before releasing a dangerous prisoner, but failed to do so.

and treatment in which professional opinion and judgment may differ, the therapist is free to exercise his or her own best judgment without liability; proof, aided by hindsight, that he or she judged wrongly is insufficient to establish negligence.

In the instant case, however, the pleadings do not raise any question as to failure of defendant therapists to predict that Poddar presented a serious danger of violence. On the contrary, the present complaints allege that defendant therapists did in fact predict that Poddar would kill, but were negligent in failing to warn. . . .

[The court then held that its recent decision in People v. Burnick, 535 P.2d 352 (Cal. 1975), which held that proof beyond a reasonable doubt was required in order to commit a person as a mentally disordered sex offender, did not preclude the creation of a duty to warn in the instant case.]

The risk that unnecessary warnings may be given is a reasonable price to pay for the lives of possible victims that may be saved. We would hesitate to hold that the therapist who is aware that his patient expects to attempt to assassinate the President of the United States would not be obligated to warn the authorities because the therapist cannot predict with accuracy that his patient will commit the crime. . . .

We recognize the public interest in supporting effective treatment of mental illness and in protecting the rights of patients to privacy (see In re Liftschutz, 467 P.2d 557), and the consequent public importance of safeguarding the confidential character of psychotherapeutic communication. Against this interest, however, we must weigh the public interest in safety from violent assault. The Legislature has undertaken the difficult task of balancing the countervailing concerns. In Evidence Code section 1014, it established a broad rule of privilege to protect confidential communications between patient and psychotherapist. In Evidence Code section 1024, the Legislature created a specific and limited exception to the psychotherapist-patient privilege: "There is no privilege . . . if the psychotherapist has reasonable cause to believe that the patient is in such mental or emotional condition as to be dangerous to himself or to the person or property of another and that disclosure of the communication is necessary to prevent the threatened danger."

We realize that the open and confidential character of psychotherapeutic dialogue encourages patients to express threats of violence, few of which are ever executed. Certainly a therapist should not be encouraged routinely to reveal such threats; such disclosures could seriously disrupt the patient's relationship with his therapist and with the persons threatened. To the contrary, the therapist's obligations to his patient require that he not disclose a confidence unless such disclosure is necessary to avert danger to others, and even then that he do so discreetly, and in a fashion that would preserve the privacy of his patient to the fullest extent compatible with the prevention of the threatened danger. (See Fleming & Maximov, The Patient or His Victim: The Therapist's Dilemma (1974) 62 Cal. L. Rev. 1025, 1065-1066.)

The revelation of a communication under the above circumstances is not a breach of trust or a violation of professional ethics as stated in the Principles of Medical Ethics of the American Medical Association (1957) section 9: "A physician may not reveal the confidence entrusted to him in the course of medical attendance . . . *unless he is required to do so by law or unless it becomes necessary in order to protect the welfare of the individual or of the community.*" (Emphasis added.) We conclude that the public policy favoring protection of the confidential character of patient-psychotherapist communications must yield to the extent to which disclosure is essential to avert danger to others. The protective privilege ends where the public peril begins.

Our current crowded and computerized society compels the interdependence of its members. In this risk-infested society we can hardly tolerate the further exposure to danger that would result from a concealed knowledge of the therapist that his patient was lethal. If the exercise of reasonable care to protect the threatened victim requires the therapist to warn the endangered party or those who can reasonably be expected to notify him, we see no sufficient societal interest that would protect and justify concealment. The containment of such risks lies in the public interest. For the foregoing reasons, we find that plaintiffs' complaints can be amended to state a cause of action against defendants Moore, Powelson, Gold, and Yandell and against the Regents as their employer, for breach of a duty to exercise reasonable care to protect Tatiana.

[The court then held that defendant therapists were not immune from liability for their failure to warn under the discretionary function exception to the California Tort Claims Act. It further held that both defendant therapists and defendant police officers were immune from liability for failure to confine Poddar. Finally, the court concluded that the police defendants "do not have any such special relationship to either Tatiana or to Poddar sufficient to impose upon such defendants a duty to warning respecting Poddar's violent intentions."]

WRIGHT, C.J., and SULLIVAN and RICHARDSON, JJ., concur.

MOSK, J., concurring and dissenting. I concur in the result in this instance only because the complaints allege that defendant therapists did in fact predict that Poddar would kill and were therefore negligent in failing to warn of that danger. Thus the issue here is very narrow: we are not concerned with whether the therapists, pursuant to the standards of their profession, "should have" predicted potential violence; they allegedly did so in actuality. Under these limited circumstances I agree that a cause of action can be stated. . . .

CLARK, J., dissenting. Until today's majority opinion, both legal and medical authorities have agreed that confidentiality is essential to effectively treat the mentally ill, and that imposing a duty on doctors to disclose patient threats to potential victims would greatly impair treatment. Further, recognizing that effective treatment and society's safety are necessarily intertwined, the Legislature has already decided effective and confidential treatment is preferred over imposition of a duty to warn.

The issue whether effective treatment for the mentally ill should be sacrificed to a system of warnings is, in my opinion, properly one for the Legislature, and we are bound by its judgment. Moreover, even in the absence of clear legislative direction, we must reach the same conclusion because imposing the majority's new duty is certain to result in a net increase in violence.

McComb, J., concurred.

NOTES

1. Tarasoff's *California aftermath.* Under the rationale of the court is the case easier, or more difficult, because the defendants were medical professionals instead of ordinary individuals? Does it make a difference whether we focus upon the competence of psychiatrists to detect dangerous persons or upon the need for confidentiality in patient-psychiatrist relationships? If so, on which should we focus?

The precise limits of the *Tarasoff* decision have been the subject of much litigation in recent years. In Beauchene v. Synanon Foundation, 151 Cal. Rptr. 796 (Cal. App. 1979), the California Court of Appeals held that a *private* rehabilitation center owed no duty of care to members of the public at large when it accepted individuals referred to it by the state prison system as a condition of their parole. The court held that the absence of a duty of care was fatal to both the plaintiff's claims, to wit, that the assailant had been improperly admitted into the program and that he or she had been improperly supervised once admitted. Should the same result apply when a private institution treats defendants without a criminal conviction?

In the subsequent California Supreme Court case of Thompson v. County of Alameda, 614 P.2d 728, 736 (Cal. 1980), a juvenile with a long and sorrowful personal history of violence and sexual abuse was released into custody of his mother, even though the county knew that the youth had "indicated that he would, if released, take the life of a young child residing in the neighborhood." Although no particular person was identified, the juvenile in fact murdered the plaintiff's son in his mother's garage within 24 hours of his release. The plaintiffs argued that warnings should have been issued to (a) the police, (b) the parents in the neighborhood, and/or (c) the juvenile's mother. The contention was rejected by the court:

Unlike members of the general public, in *Tarasoff* . . . the potential victims were specifically known and designated individuals. The warnings which we therein required were directed at making those individuals aware of the danger to which they were uniquely exposed. The threatened targets were precise. In such cases, it is fair to conclude that warnings given discreetly and to a limited number of persons would have a greater effect because they would alert those particular targeted individuals of the possibility of a specific threat pointed at them. In contrast, the warnings sought by plaintiffs would of necessity have to be made to a broad segment of the population and would be only general in nature. In addition to the likelihood that such generalized warnings when frequently repeated would do little as a practical matter to stimulate increased safety measures, as we develop below, such extensive warnings would be difficult to give.

Tobriner, J., dissented on the ground that warnings should have been given to the mother, who "might" have taken additional steps to control the conduct of her son.

The issue of the therapist's care in California is today governed by California Civil Code §43.92 (1994), which provides:

(a) There shall be no monetary liability on the part of, and no cause of action shall arise against, any person who is a psychotherapist . . . in failing to warn of and protect from a patient's threatened violent behavior or failing to predict and warn of and protect from a patient's violent behavior except where the patient has communicated to the psychotherapist a serious threat of physical violence against a reasonably identifiable victim or victims.

(b) If there is a duty to warn and protect under the limited circumstances specified above, the duty shall be discharged by the psychotherapist making reasonable efforts to communicate the threat to the victims or victim and to a law enforcement agency.

2. Beyond California. Notwithstanding the California statute, the influence of *Tarasoff* has extended beyond California, where other courts have been willing to give the decision a more expansive reading than it has received in California. More specifically, some courts have rejected the proposition that the therapist's sole duty is to warn identifiable third parties of the risk of injury, and have insisted that other precautions, including confinement if necessary, may be required to prevent injuries to the public at large. See, e.g., Hamman v. County of Maricopa, 775 P.2d 1122 (Ariz. 1989), allowing an action for negligent misrepresentation even when the assailant did not make any explicit threats against the plaintiff.

The duties on defendants are especially high where they take steps that facilitate attacks by persons within their care on innocent plaintiffs. One particularly chilling example is Lundgren v. Fultz, 354 N.W.2d 25, 29 (Minn. 1984). In that case, Fultz, a graduate student in theoretical physics at the University of Minnesota, was under the care of Dr. David

Cline of the university's Department of Psychiatry. Fultz was by all accounts severely disturbed and had an obvious fixation with guns. "Fultz told one doctor that his guns meant more to him than his penis, and Dr. Cline thought his 'defensive pattern of interest' characteristic of introspective males who have great concern about their masculinity." Diagnosed as a paranoid schizophrenic, Fultz was treated and then discharged in January 1969. Thereafter he purchased several guns, one of which he brandished during a campus demonstration. His guns were confiscated by the police department, and Fultz was again treated by Dr. Cline, first on an in-patient and then on an out-patient basis. When treatment was finished, Fultz asked the police for the return of his guns, which they refused to do without assurances from Cline that Fultz was "cured," which Cline provided them in writing. Three weeks later "Fultz entered a restaurant near the University and shot and killed Ruth Lundgren in an unprovoked and random attack. Fultz eventually committed suicide while serving a prison sentence for murder." The summary judgment entered for the defendant was reversed by the state supreme court, which on the strength of the evidence reasoned as follows:

> A jury could conclude that the psychiatrist's letter caused the police to return these guns and, thus, materially increased the danger that Fultz posed. A jury could also conclude that Fultz presented a danger to the public when armed with the handguns that figured so largely in his psychosis and that someone in Dr. Cline's position should have foreseen that harm to a member of the public might result.
>
> In holding that this plaintiff has stated a cause of action, we recognize that, in other cases, policy considerations have made courts reluctant to extend the psychiatrist's duty to control the conduct of the patient too far. In Cairl v. State, 323 N.W.2d 20 (Minn. 1982), for example, this court refused to impose a duty to warn potential victims of a patient's dangerous propensities unless the patient has made specific threats against identifiable persons. 323 N.W.2d at 25-26. The court was concerned that if such a duty were imposed, the resulting "cacophony" of warnings would add greatly to the stigma of mental illness while contributing little to public protection. Id. In Leverett v. State, 399 N.E.2d 106, 110 (Ohio App. 1978), the Ohio Court of Appeals declined to impose a duty to readmit a patient. The court felt that this obligation would force psychiatrists to rely, at their peril, on lay persons' opinions of the danger posed by a patient.
>
> The policy considerations underlying the denial of a psychiatrist's duty in those cases are not present here. This case has its own special facts, including, as it does, the use of a handgun. In this case, a jury could find that Dr. Cline assisted his patient in gaining access to deadly handguns and that the patient later used one of those guns in a random homicide. There is a limit to the protection given the discretion in a professional relationship. That limit is exceeded where a psychiatrist places the gun in a potential assassin's hand under the guise of fostering trust between patient and psychiatrist. We do not believe that the imposition of a duty in those circumstances would contribute to the stigma of mental illness or impair a psychiatrist's professional discretion.

Could the police department be found negligent for turning over the guns after receiving Dr. Cline's letter? Should it have gotten a second opinion before so acting?

When the special circumstances found in *Lundgren* have not been present, plaintiffs have had a more difficult time securing recovery. In Higgins v. Salt Lake County, 855 P.2d 231 (Utah 1993), the 10-year-old plaintiff Shaundra was stabbed three times by Carolyn Trujillo, a paranoid schizophrenic who had been treated on and off at the defendant's mental hospital. Trujillo harbored grudges against the plaintiff "because she believed Shaundra had struck her six year old daughter," and "because [Shaundra] refused to give her cigarettes and was 'a slut.' " After Trujillo had been convicted of a second degree felony and confined for being mentally ill, plaintiff sued the hospital claiming that it both "owed a general duty to any third party foreseeably at risk from their negligence in treating and supervising Trujillo, and second, that a special relationship existed between defendants and Trujillo. . . ." The court rejected the first claim on the ground that the duty was too onerous given the imperfect nature of psychiatric prediction and the need to preserve confidential relations between patients and their psychiatrists. The court then held that the second duty would arise only if the plaintiff were identifiable as a likely victim of the assailant, and remanded the case for further hearings to determine whether "proper examination and diagnosis would have disclosed that Trujillo was brooding over Shaundra and had targeted her for an attack. . . ."

Summary judgment for the defendant was, however, affirmed in Bucher v. Oregon, 853 P.2d 798, 804-805 (Or. 1993), where a felon, with no previous record of violence, escaped from a remote forest worksite, and stole a gun from his mother's house, which he used to kill one plaintiff and injure a second. "While it is generally foreseeable that criminals may escape and engage in criminal activity while at large, that level of foreseeability does not make the criminal's acts the legal responsibility of everyone who may have contributed in some way to the criminal opportunity." The court further held that in the absence of knowledge of the "specific danger presented by the prisoner to the plaintiffs," the defendant discharged its duty when it "promptly advised the appropriate police agencies of the escape."

Chapter Eight
Traditional Strict Liability

A. INTRODUCTION

One major theme of this casebook concerns the recurrent tension and interaction between the theory of negligence and that of strict liability. In this chapter we will pursue yet another aspect of that theme by looking in detail at those areas of the tort law that resisted incorporation into a general negligence system at a time when its influence was at its peak. The particular historical bastions of strict liability grouped together in this chapter involve liability for conversion, for animals, for so-called ultrahazardous activities, and for nuisance. Three of these areas of tort liability are quite ancient, and were, it will be recalled, treated by Judge Blackburn as instances of the "true rule" (of bringing, keeping, and collecting) that he announced in Rylands v. Fletcher. The last head of liability — ultrahazardous activities — has developed in the United States in large measure from the effort to rationalize and generalize from Rylands v. Fletcher. *Rylands*, then, provides the most convenient point of departure for determining how these rules relate to each other and to *Rylands* itself. In order to place the subject matter in perspective, it is helpful at this point to reread the opinions in Rylands v. Fletcher, supra at page 120.

B.   CONVERSION

Moore v. The Regents of the University of California
249 Cal. Rptr. 494 (Cal. App. 1988)

ROTHMAN, Associate Justice.

I.   BACKGROUND

In 1976, plaintiff and appellant sought medical treatment at the Medical Center of the University of California, Los Angeles (UCLA), for a condition known as hairy-cell leukemia. He was seen by Dr. David W. Golde, who confirmed the diagnosis. As a necessary part of the treatment for this disease, plaintiff's spleen was removed at UCLA in October of 1976.

Without plaintiff's knowledge or consent, Dr. Golde and Shirley G. Quan, a UCLA employee, determined that plaintiff's cells were unique. Through the science of genetic engineering, these defendants developed a cell-line from plaintiff's cells which is capable of producing pharmaceutical products of enormous therapeutic and commercial value. The Regents, Golde and Quan patented the cell-line along with methods of producing many products therefrom. In addition, these defendants entered into a series of commercial agreements for rights to the cell-line and its products with Sandoz Pharmaceuticals Corporation (Sandoz) and Genetics Institute, Inc. (Genetics). The market potential of products from plaintiff's cell-line was predicted to be approximately three billion dollars by 1990. Hundreds of thousands of dollars have already been paid under these agreements to the developers. Without informing plaintiff, and in pursuit of their research efforts, Golde and UCLA continued to monitor him and take tissue samples from him for almost seven years following the removal of his spleen. . . .

IV.   DISCUSSION: SUFFICIENCY OF THE CONVERSION CAUSE OF ACTION

A.   THE ELEMENTS OF CONVERSION

. . . Conversion is "a distinct act of dominion wrongfully exerted over another's personal property in denial of or inconsistent with his title or rights therein, . . . without the owner's consent and without lawful justification." It is " 'an act of wilful interference with a chattel, done without lawful justification, by which any person entitled thereto is deprived of use and possession.' "

For conversion, a plaintiff need only allege: "(1) plaintiffs' ownership or right to possession of the property at the time of the conversion; (2) defendants' conversion by a wrongful act or disposition of plaintiffs' property rights; and (3) damages."

Conversion is a strict liability tort. "The foundation for the action of conversion rests neither in the knowledge nor the intent of the defendant. It rests upon the unwarranted interference by defendant with the dominion over the property of the plaintiff from which injury to the latter results. Therefore, neither good nor bad faith, neither care nor negligence, neither knowledge nor ignorance, are of the gist of the action. The plaintiff's right of redress no longer depends upon his showing, in any way, that the defendant did the act in question from wrongful motives, or generally speaking, even intentionally; and hence the want of such motives, or of intention, is no defense. Nor, indeed, is negligence any necessary part of the case. Here, then, is a class of cases in which the tort consists in the breach of what may be called an absolute duty; the act itself (in some cases it must have caused damage) is unlawful and redressible as a tort."

In a leading case on the subject, Poggi v. Scott, 139 P. 815 (Cal. 1915), the defendant bought a building in which plaintiff had been a subtenant, using a basement space to store numerous barrels of a "sound wine, seven years old." The defendant, unaware that the barrels contained wine, thought they were junk and sold them. He was held liable in spite of his lack of knowledge or intent. "The foundation for the action of conversion rests neither in the knowledge nor the intent of the defendant. It rests upon the unwarranted interference by defendant with the dominion over the property of the plaintiff from which injury to the latter results."

B.   TISSUE OF A LIVING PERSON AS A FORM OF TANGIBLE PERSONAL PROPERTY

The complaint alleges that plaintiff's tissues, including his spleen, blood, and the cell-line derived from his cells "are his tangible personal property." This is the crux of plaintiff's case for conversion. . . .

[The court then concludes that the broad definition of property rights, which "refers not to a particular material object but to the right and interest or domination rightfully obtained over such object, with the unrestricted right to its use, enjoyment and disposition" is sufficient to cover body parts and fluids.]

Defendants' position that plaintiff cannot own his tissue, but that they can, is fraught with irony. Apparently, defendants see nothing abnormal in their exclusive control of plaintiff's excised spleen, nor in their patenting of a living organism derived therefrom. We cannot reconcile defendant's assertion of what appears to be their property interest in removed tissue and the resulting cell-line with their contention that the source of the material has no rights therein.

Defendants also claim that plaintiff cannot have an interest in the cell-line derived from his tissues since he is only the source of the thing studied. "Thus, the cells involved have no inherent value until a cell line is derived and created to produce useful products. Plaintiff tries to obscure this unassailable fact by creating the impression his cells *themselves* have miraculous curative powers. . . ." (Emphasis in original.)

Defendants contend that plaintiff has no property right in the knowledge gained or the new things made in the course of the study of his cells. This is an inaccurate characterization of this case. Plaintiff's complaint does not allege a conversion of ideas gained from study of his cells, but conversion of the cells, and their progeny, themselves. Plaintiff was not simply the object of study to increase knowledge. His spleen and cells were taken by defendants to their laboratory, where they extracted his genetic material, placed it in a growth medium, and, by cell division, created an "immortal" cell-line — one that could forever produce products of enormous commercial value to defendants. . . .

The fact that defendants' skill and efforts modified the tissue and enhanced its value does not negate the existence of a conversion. Any questions as to defendants' alteration of plaintiff's tissue go to what damages, if any, he might be entitled if successful at trial.

[The court then rejects the argument that the plaintiff's spleen could not be converted because it has no value.]

[The court then rejected the argument that recognizing the tort of conversion would inhibit medical research.]

C.　Issue of Abandonment of Tissue in Surgery

Defendants argue that even if plaintiff's spleen is personal property, its surgical removal was an abandonment by him of a diseased organ. They assert that he cannot, therefore, bring an action for conversion.

The essential element of abandonment is the intent to abandon. The owner of the property abandoned must be " 'entirely indifferent as to what may become of it or as to who may thereafter possess it.' "

"It may be said that abandonment is made up of two elements, act and intent, and the intent must be gathered from all the facts and circumstances of the case."

[The court holds it is a question of fact whether the bodily tissue was abandoned.] Nothing in the complaint indicates that plaintiff had an intent to abandon his spleen, and we do not find that, as a matter of law, anyone who consents to surgery abandons all removed tissue to the first person to claim it. Certainly, in the example of an unconscious patient, the concept of abandonment becomes ridiculous.

D. ISSUE OF THE SCOPE OF CONSENT TO TISSUE REMOVAL

Defendants next contend that there was no conversion since the plaintiff consented to the removal of the spleen and other tissues.

[The court held that no consent was given for commercial exploitation.]

GEORGE, Associate Justice. I dissent.

[The dissent argued that the plaintiff had not established that his body parts and fluids were personal property for the purposes of the law of conversion because they did not come within the standard definitions of goods and chattels. It also argued that there had been an abandonment of any property right. It then argued that any damage award should be negligible because the cell-line "evolved into something of great value only through the unusual scientific expertise of defendants, like unformed clay or stone transformed by the hands of a master sculptor into a valuable work of art." It then concluded that allowing the cause of action could unduly inhibit medical research.]

Moore v. Regents of the University of California
793 P.2d 479 (Cal. 1990)

PANELLI, Justice. We granted review in this case to determine whether plaintiff has stated a cause of action against his physician and other defendants for using his cells in potentially lucrative medical research without his permission. Plaintiff alleges that his physician failed to disclose preexisting research and economic interests in the cells before obtaining consent to the medical procedures by which they were extracted. The superior court sustained all defendants' demurrers to the third amended complaint, and the Court of Appeal reversed. We hold that the complaint states a cause of action for breach of the physician's disclosure obligations, but not for conversion.

[The court first restated the facts and reviewed the literature on informed consent, and concluded.]

Accordingly, we hold that a physician who is seeking a patient's consent for a medical procedure must, in order to satisfy his fiduciary duty and to obtain the patient's informed consent, disclose personal interests unrelated to the patient's health, whether research or economic, that may affect his medical judgment.

B. CONVERSION

Moore also attempts to characterize the invasion of his rights as a conversion — a tort that protects against interference with possessory and ownership interests in personal property. He theorizes that he continued to own his cells following their removal from his body, at least for the purpose of directing their use, and that he never consented to their use in potentially lucrative medical research. Thus, to complete Moore's argument, defendants' unauthorized use of his cells constitutes a conversion. As a result of the alleged conversion, Moore claims a proprietary interest in each of the products that any of the defendants might ever create from his cells or the patented cell line.

No court, however, has ever in a reported decision imposed conversion liability for the use of human cells in medical research. While that fact does not end our inquiry, it raises a flag of caution. In effect, what Moore is asking us to do is to impose a tort duty on scientists to investigate the consensual pedigree of each human cell sample used in research. To impose such a duty, which would affect medical research of importance to all of society, implicates policy concerns far removed from the traditional, two-party ownership disputes in which the law of conversion arose. Invoking a tort theory originally used to determine whether the loser or the finder of a horse had the better title, Moore claims ownership of the results of socially important medical research, including the genetic code for chemicals that regulate the functions of every human being's immune system.

. . . [W]e first consider whether the tort of conversion clearly gives Moore a cause of action under existing law. We do not believe it does. Because of the novelty of Moore's claim to own the biological materials at issue, to apply the theory of conversion in this context would frankly have to be recognized as an extension of the theory. Therefore, we consider next whether it is advisable to extend the tort to this context.

1.   MOORE'S CLAIM UNDER EXISTING LAW

"To establish a conversion, plaintiff must establish an actual interference with his ownership or right of possession. . . . Where plaintiff neither has title to the property alleged to have been converted, nor possession thereof, he cannot maintain an action for conversion."[19]

Since Moore clearly did not expect to retain possession of his cells following their removal, to sue for their conversion he must have retained an ownership interest in them.[20] But there are several reasons to

---

19. While it ordinarily suffices to allege ownership generally, it is well established that a complaint's contentions or conclusions of law do not bind us. Moore's novel allegation that he "owns" the biological materials involved in this case is both a contention and a conclusion of law.

20. In his complaint, Moore does not seek possession of his cells or claim the right to possess them. This is consistent with Health and Safety Code section 7054.4, which provides that "human tissues . . . following conclusion of scientific use shall be disposed of by interment, incineration, or any other method determined by the state department [of health services] to protect the public health and safety."

doubt that he did retain any such interest. First, no reported judicial decision supports Moore's claim, either directly or by close analogy. Second, California statutory law drastically limits any continuing interest of a patient in excised cells. Third, the subject matters of the Regents' patent — the patented cell line and the products derived from it — cannot be Moore's property.

Neither the Court of Appeal's opinion, the parties' briefs, nor our research discloses a case holding that a person retains a sufficient interest in excised cells to support a cause of action for conversion. We do not find this surprising, since the laws governing such things as human tissues, transplantable organs, blood, fetuses, pituitary glands, corneal tissue, and dead bodies deal with human biological materials as objects sui generis, regulating their disposition to achieve policy goals rather than abandoning them to the general law of personal property. It is these specialized statutes, not the law of conversion, to which courts ordinarily should and do look for guidance on the disposition of human biological materials. . . .

2. SHOULD CONVERSION LIABILITY BE EXTENDED?

There are three reasons why it is inappropriate to impose liability for conversion based upon the allegations of Moore's complaint. First, a fair balancing of the relevant policy considerations counsels against extending the tort. Second, problems in this area are better suited to legislative resolution. Third, the tort of conversion is not necessary to protect patients' rights. For these reasons, we conclude that the use of excised human cells in medical research does not amount to a conversion.

Of the relevant policy considerations, two are of overriding importance. The first is protection of a competent patient's right to make autonomous medical decisions. That right, as already discussed, is grounded in well-recognized and long-standing principles of fiduciary duty and informed consent. This policy weighs in favor of providing a remedy to patients when physicians act with undisclosed motives that may affect their professional judgment. The second important policy consideration is that we not threaten with disabling civil liability innocent parties who are engaged in socially useful activities, such as researchers who have no reason to believe that their use of a particular cell sample is, or may be, against a donor's wishes.

To reach an appropriate balance of these policy considerations is extremely important. . . .

We need not, however, make an arbitrary choice between liability and nonliability. Instead, an examination of the relevant policy considerations suggests an appropriate balance: Liability based upon existing disclosure obligations, rather than an unprecedented extension of the conversion theory, protects patients' rights of privacy and autonomy without unnecessarily hindering research.

To be sure, the threat of liability for conversion might help to enforce patients' rights indirectly. This is because physicians might be able to avoid liability by obtaining patients' consent, in the broadest possible terms, to any conceivable subsequent research use of excised cells. Unfortunately, to extend the conversion theory would utterly sacrifice the other goal of protecting innocent parties. Since conversion is a strict liability tort, it would impose liability on all those into whose hands the cells come, whether or not the particular defendant participated in, or knew of, the inadequate disclosures that violated the patient's right to make an informed decision. In contrast to the conversion theory, the fiduciary-duty and informed-consent theories protect the patient directly, without punishing innocent parties or creating disincentives to the conduct of socially beneficial research.

To expand liability by extending conversion law into this area would have a broad impact. [The court then concludes that the creation of tort liability will dull the incentives for medical innovation.] If the use of cells in research is a conversion, then with every cell sample a researcher purchases a ticket in a litigation lottery. Because liability for conversion is predicated on a continuing ownership interest, "companies are unlikely to invest heavily in developing, manufacturing, or marketing a product when uncertainty about clear title exists."

If the scientific users of human cells are to be held liable for failing to investigate the consensual pedigree of their raw materials, we believe the Legislature should make that decision.

Finally, there is no pressing need to impose a judicially created rule of strict liability, since enforcement of physicians' disclosure obligations will protect patients against the very type of harm with which Moore was threatened. So long as a physician discloses research and economic interests that may affect his judgment, the patient is protected from conflicts of interest. Aware of any conflicts, the patient can make an informed decision to consent to treatment, or to withhold consent and look elsewhere for medical assistance. As already discussed, enforcement of physicians' disclosure obligations protects patients directly, without hindering the socially useful activities of innocent researchers.

For these reasons, we hold that the allegations of Moore's third amended complaint state a cause of action for breach of fiduciary duty or lack of informed consent, but not conversion.

Lucas, C.J., and Eagleson and Kennard, JJ., concur.

[The concurring opinion Arabian, Justice is omitted.]

Broussard, Justice, concurring and dissenting. . . .

II

. . . I dissent from the majority's conclusion that the facts alleged in this case do not state a cause of action for conversion.

If this were a typical case in which a patient consented to the use of his removed organ for general research purposes and the patient's doctor had no prior knowledge of the scientific or commercial value of the patient's organ or cells, I would agree that the patient could not maintain a conversion action. In that common scenario, the patient has abandoned any interest in the removed organ and is not entitled to demand compensation if it should later be discovered that the organ or cells have some unanticipated value. I cannot agree, however, with the majority that a patient may never maintain a conversion action for the unauthorized use of his excised organ or cells, even against a party who knew of the value of the organ or cells before they were removed and breached a duty to disclose that value to the patient. Because plaintiff alleges that defendants wrongfully interfered with his right to determine, prior to the removal of his body parts, how those parts would be used after removal, I conclude that the complaint states a cause of action under traditional, common law conversion principles. . . .

MOSK, Justice, dissenting.

[Mosk, J., first argues that an acceptance of legislative dominance does not require judicial passivity on the application of traditional common-law principles of conversion to "the recent explosive growth in the commercialization of biotechnology." He then argues that the current legislative schemes do not preclude the sale of human organs removed for medical reasons. He then turns to a comparison of conversion with the informed consent action. After noting the difficulties of proving causation in informed consent cases, he continues:]

The second reason why the nondisclosure cause of action is inadequate for the task that the majority assign to it is that it fails to solve half the problem before us: it gives the patient only the right to refuse consent, i.e., the right to prohibit the commercialization of his tissue; it does not give him the right to grant consent to that commercialization on the condition that he share in its proceeds. . . .

Reversing the words of the old song, the nondisclosure cause of action thus accentuates the negative and eliminates the positive: the patient can say no, but he cannot say yes and expect to share in the proceeds of his contribution. Yet . . . there are sound reasons of ethics and equity to recognize the patient's right to participate in such benefits. The nondisclosure cause of action does not protect that right; to that extent, it is therefore not an adequate substitute for the conversion remedy, which does protect the right.

Third, the nondisclosure cause of action fails to reach a major class of potential defendants: all those who are outside the strict physician-patient relationship with the plaintiff. . . .

To the extent that a plaintiff such as Moore is unable to plead or prove a satisfactory theory of secondary liability, the nondisclosure cause of action will thus be inadequate to reach a number of parties to the commercial exploitation of his tissue. Such parties include, for example, any physician-researcher who is not personally treating the patient, any other researcher who is not a physician, any employer of the foregoing (or even of the treating physician), and any person or corporation thereafter participating in the commercial exploitation of the tissue. Yet some or all of those parties may well have participated more in, and profited more from, such exploitation than the particular physician with whom the plaintiff happened to have a formal doctor-patient relationship at the time.

NOTES

1. The reach of conversion. As *Moore* notes conversion was viewed traditionally as a strict liability action, and the early law developing its scope was heavily entangled with the early development of the forms of action, where the chief difficulty was in setting the boundaries between conversion and trespass to chattels. Trespass to chattels required the plaintiff to show that the defendant carried off goods which were then in the plaintiff's possession. The Latin name for the wrong was de bonis asportatis — the asportation of chattels. The tort was regarded as an offense to possession alone, so the plaintiff could maintain the action even if some third party had a title paramount to either plaintiff's or defendant's. In contrast, conversion could be brought by any party who claimed either ownership rights in the thing or some right to its immediate possession.

The differences in basic theory led quickly to refinements in the decided cases as courts struggled to identify the situations in which only one action or the other was proper. Thus conversion alone was held to lie for *A* against *C* where *C* had taken the property from *B*, who had previously taken it from *A*. Trespass was inappropriate because the possession at the time of *C*'s wrong rested in *B*. See J. B. Ames, Lectures in Legal History 60-61 (1913). Conversion, however, was proper because the plaintiff as owner had the immediate right to possession. See Gordon v. Harper, 101 Eng. Rep. 828 (K.B. 1796). For the complications created when chattels were bailed, mortgaged, leased, or subject to contract of sale see The Winkfield, [1902] P. 42. See generally 1 Harper, James and Gray, Torts §§2.16-2.25.

On the other hand, only trespass would lie when the defendant had taken possession of the plaintiff's goods without claiming ownership of them. See, e.g., Fouldes v. Willoughby, 151 Eng. Rep. 1153 (Ex. 1841), where the plaintiff passenger brought an action in conversion against a defendant ferryman who removed plaintiff's horses from his ferry before setting sail. In dismissing the action, Lord Abinger, C.B., said that "a simple asportation of a chattel, without any intention of making any further use of it, although it may be a sufficient foundation for an action of trespass, is not sufficient to establish a conversion." The defendant in *Fouldes* offered to justify his conduct by saying that he removed the animals in order to induce the plaintiff, who was misbehaving, to leave the ferry. Should the success of the defense depend upon the choice of the original action? On trespass and conversion see generally F. Pollock and R. Wright, Possession in the Common Law (1888); 1 Harper, James and Gray, Torts §§2.14-2.15. On the earlier history of the various writs see F. W. Maitland, The Forms of Action At Common Law, Lectures V and VI (1936).

2. *Trespass and conversion: the measure of damage.* Notwithstanding the different theories for trespass and conversion, many wrongs fall within the scope of both. From the early 1600s it was settled that the plaintiff could elect the more advantageous action when both were available. The choice in many cases rested upon the type of relief the plaintiff wanted to secure. Originally conversion proceeded on a theory of the "forced sale," under which the defendant, as the owner of the plaintiff's property, was now made to buy it at the full market price — even if the defendant was willing to return it. Today that rule has been relaxed in most jurisdictions, so that the innocent converter may generally return the property taken, at least if it has not suffered substantial damage, conditional upon payment for the loss of interim use or for repairs.

Historically, the rule was otherwise with trespass for chattels, for here the damages in question were limited to the reduction in value of the chattel. The defendant was therefore able to force the plaintiff to take the chattel back, so that the full price was awarded only in cases of complete destruction.

3. *Reference.* Comment, Ownership of Human Tissue: Life After *Moore v. Regents of the University of California,* 75 U. Va. L. Rev. 1363 (1989).

C. ANIMALS

Baker v. Snell
[1908] 2 K.B. 825

COZENS-HARDY, M.R. This is an appeal from a decision of the Divisional Court directing a new trial of an action commenced in the county court by a young woman who had been bitten by a dog owned by her master and known by that master to be ferocious and given to bite.

[The statement of facts is taken from the opinion of Channell, J., in the Divisional Court, [1908] 2 K.B. 353-354: "The action is for damages for injury caused by the bite of a dog belonging to the defendant. The plaintiff was a maidservant in his employment. He had had the dog for some time, and there was evidence on which the jury might have found that the dog was accustomed to bite mankind and that the defendant knew it. Indeed, the dog had bitten the plaintiff herself before. It appeared that the defendant was in the habit of entrusting the dog to his potman with directions to take it out for a run early in the morning and then bring it back and chain it up before the maidservants were down. One morning he took it into the kitchen where the plaintiff and the defendant's other servants were at breakfast, and, presumably by way of a foolish practical joke, said, 'I will bet the dog will not bite any one,' and then, 'Go it, Bob,' whereupon the dog bit the plaintiff."]

The learned county court judge nonsuited the plaintiff on the ground that the conduct of the barman who had the dog in charge amounted to an assault by him. In the Divisional Court both the learned judges thought that there had not been a satisfactory trial and that the action must go down for a new trial. Channell, J., based his decision on the ground stated in the following passage: "The potman was the defendant's servant, and was entrusted by him with the custody of the dog. Instead of performing his duty of keeping the dog securely, he incited it to fly at the plaintiff. The question whether the defendant is liable for that depends upon whether the man's wrongful act was done in the course of his employment, or whether it was done for purposes of his own. If it could be shewn that the man did it maliciously to gratify some grudge against the plaintiff, his master would not be liable. But there was no evidence of that. In my view the potman's act amounted to nothing more than a foolish and wanton act done in neglect of his duty to keep the dog safe; and if that is the right view, the defendant would be responsible. But the question is one of fact which ought to have been left to the jury." I entirely adopt that view, and that, no doubt, is in itself a sufficient reason for affirming the decision of the Court below, but as a matter of wider interest has been raised, and as it has been dealt with by both Channell and Sutton, JJ., I think it right to state, shortly, my view on the point. If a man keeps an animal whose nature is ferocious, or an animal of a class not generally ferocious, but which is known to the owner to be dangerous, is the owner of that animal liable only if he neglects his duty of keeping it safe or is negligent in the discharge of that duty, or is he bound to keep it secure at his peril? In my opinion the latter is the correct proposition of law, and I think that it is not open to the Court to decide the other way. In 1846, in May v. Burdett [9 Q.B. 101], the law was laid down by the Court of

Queen's Bench in the case of a monkey. The action was brought by a man and his wife to recover damages for a bite to the female plaintiff, and the declaration stated that the defendant wrongfully kept a monkey, well knowing that it was of a mischievous and ferocious nature and used and accustomed to attack and bite mankind, and that it was dangerous to allow it to be at large, and that the monkey, whilst the defendant kept the same as aforesaid, did attack, bite, and injure the female plaintiff. The case was elaborately argued. Lord Denman, C.J., delivering the judgment of the Court, said "A great many cases and precedents were cited upon the argument: and the conclusion to be drawn from them appears to us to be that the declaration is good upon the face of it; and that whoever keeps an animal accustomed to attack and bite mankind, with knowledge that it is so accustomed, is prima facie liable in an action on the case at the suit of any person attacked and injured by the animal, without any averment of negligence or default in the securing or taking care of it. The gist of the action is the keeping the animal after knowledge of its mischievous propensities." And again, at the end of his judgment, after referring to a passage in Hale's Pleas of the Crown, vol. 1, p. 430b, he says: "It was said, indeed, further, on the part of the defendant, that, the monkey being an animal ferae naturae, he would not be answerable for injuries committed by it, if it escaped and went at large without any default on the part of the defendant, during the time it had so escaped and was at large, because at that time it would not be in his keeping nor under his control: but we cannot allow any weight to this objection: for, in the first place, there is no statement in the declaration that the monkey had escaped, and it is expressly averred that the injury occurred whilst the defendant kept it: we are besides of opinion, as already stated, that the defendant, if he would keep it, was bound to keep it secure at all events." . . . The matter came up again, not directly, but in a shape which led to some observations by the Court, in Nichols v. Marsland. [In the course of his judgment, Bramwell, B., observed in a discussion concerned with the limits of the rule in Rylands v. Fletcher: "I am by no means sure that, if a man kept a tiger, and lightning broke his chain and he got loose and did mischief, the man who kept him would not be liable."]

. . . If it be true, as I think it is, that it is a wrongful act for a person to keep an animal which he knows to be dangerous, that is an authority, not merely of the Court of Exchequer, but also of the Court of Appeal, that the person so keeping it is liable for the consequences of his wrongful act, even though the immediate cause of damage is the act of a third party. The case of Filburn v. People's Palace and Aquarium Co. [25 Q.B.D. 258 (1890)] is also a strong authority for the same proposition. In that case the action was brought to recover damages for injuries sustained by the plaintiff by his being attacked by an elephant which was the property of the defendants and was being exhibited by them.

The defendants did not know the elephant to be dangerous, but they were nevertheless held liable because the elephant was of a class of animals which were dangerous by nature. Lord Esher said in his judgment in that case that the law recognized two distinct classes of animals, animals which were dangerous by nature and animals which were generally not dangerous; but where animals of the latter class were dangerous to the owner's knowledge, he put them into the same class as animals which were dangerous by nature. Then, after referring to certain descriptions of animals which were not dangerous, he continued: "Unless an animal is brought within one of these two descriptions — that is, unless it is shewn to be either harmless by its very nature, or to belong to a class that has become so by what may be called cultivation — it falls within the class of animals as to which the rule is, that a man who keeps one must take the responsibility of keeping it safe. It cannot possibly be said that an elephant comes within the class of animals known to be harmless by nature, or within that shewn by experience to be harmless in this country, and consequently it falls within the class of animals that a man keeps at his peril, and which he must prevent from doing injury under any circumstances, unless the person to whom the injury is done brings it on himself." On these authorities, and in accordance with what in my judgment is settled law, I think that the matter ought to go down for a new trial, not merely on the ground stated by Channell, J., though I agree that is sufficient, but also on the ground as to which he expressed some doubt, but on which Sutton, J., appears to have based his decision.

FARWELL, L.J. I agree. I take the same view as Channell, J., did as regards the potman's authority, but I do not agree with him in thinking that the liability of the keeper of a savage animal does not extend to damage directly brought about by the intervening voluntary act of a third party. Sutton, J., also did not agree with him, because he bases his judgment upon May v. Burdett. The cases, in my opinion, establish that the law recognizes two classes of animals — animals ferae naturae and animals mansuetae naturae. Any animal of the latter class when known to its owner to be dangerous falls within the former class, and any one who keeps an animal of that nature does a wrongful act and is liable for the consequences under whatever circumstances arising, except where the plaintiff by his own conduct has brought the injury upon himself.

NOTES

1. Personal injuries caused by animals. Liability for animals may be divided roughly into two general parts: damage to persons and damage to real property. As regards the former, the liability rules tend to be strict, at least for animals that are held to be dangerous by nature. For those animals that are tame by nature, the rules are a bit more complex. Normally, negligence must be proved to hold the owner responsible for the animal, but a strict liability rule applies for domestic animals which, as individuals, have shown dangerous propensities, even if they have not bitten. The common statement that every dog is entitled to one free bite is not an accurate reflection of the general law; a demonstrated tendency to bite is enough. Restatement (Second) Torts §509 comment *g*. What is wrong with a unified prima facie case that states simply "your dog bit me"?

2. *Remoteness of damage.* It is generally accepted that the owner of the animal is responsible for the damage it does to the plaintiff's real property and to animals peacefully grazing there, see, e.g., Lee v. Riley, 144 Eng. Rep. 629 (C.B. 1865). Yet problems may arise in setting the limits of liability. In Williams v. Goodwin, 116 Cal. Rptr. 200, 208 (Cal. App. 1974), the plaintiff was working in his garden when, without provocation, he was attacked by the defendant's trespassing bull. The defendant's motion for nonsuit was granted by the trial judge, but recovery was allowed on appeal.

> The sequence of events from entry upon the land to attack upon plaintiff, without interposition of any independent operative agency, compels the conclusion that plaintiff's injuries were the direct consequence of the trespass. Moreover, to conclude under these circumstances that an attack such as occurred with resulting injury was not reasonably to be expected would require a departure from logic. The manifest danger that inheres in exposure of the person to the immediate presence of an uncontrolled bull is strongly suggested by human experience and common sense. Thus, it is of no significance that defendant's bull did not pause to forage plaintiff's crop either before the attack, after the attack, or at all, or that plaintiff's injuries were not sustained in the course of an effort to expel the animal or to protect his property.

See also Restatement (Second) of Torts §504, which provides that the strict liability of the "possessor" of trespassing livestock does "not extend to harm (a) not reasonably to be expected from the intrusion, (b) done by animals straying onto abutting land while driven on the highway, or (c) brought about by the unexpectable operation of a force of nature, action of another animal or intentional, reckless or negligent conduct of a third person."

Since liability is restricted to the "possessors" of livestock, "one who has transferred the possession of his livestock to a bailee is not liable under the rule stated in this Section. The bailee by taking possession becomes solely liable." §504 comment *e*. Why not a rule that holds the owner liable to the stranger, with an action over against the bailee for breach of contractual duty, if any? In addition, comment *g* declares: "In determining whether particular harm to the land or to chattels on it or to the person of the possessor or of members of his household is of a kind that might reasonably be expected to follow from the trespass, account must be taken of the natural propensities of the particular kind of animal. Thus any trespassing bull may be expected to attack and gore any other animal, or any person who gets in his way."

3. Affirmative defenses. The strict liability principle is at its greatest strength when animals attack or injure strangers. But the rule has been relaxed in a variety of controlled settings. In City and County of Denver v. Kennedy, 476 P.2d 762 (Colo. App. 1970), the Colorado Court of Appeals held that its state's general rule of strict liability (Collins v. Otto, 369 P.2d 564 (Colo. 1962)) did not apply to animals kept in public zoos. Although it agreed in general that the keeping or harboring of an animal is "in defiance of the safety and desires of the surrounding society," it nonetheless concluded that it would be improper to apply that rule to a zoo, which is maintained and operated "in response to the public's obvious desires," and "unrealistic" to hold that the operation of the zoo "exposes the public to an inordinate risk" of harm. It therefore decided that the case should be decided under negligence principles. In a subsequent appeal of the same case, Kennedy v. City and County of Denver, 506 P.2d 764 (Colo. 1972), the court held that the plaintiff made out a jury case in negligence by showing that the defendant's zebra pit was constructed so that a person could easily reach over the barriers and come in direct physical contact with the animals.

A similar result has been held for animals in national parks. In Rubenstein v. United States, 338 F. Supp. 654 (N.D. Cal. 1972), aff'd 488 F.2d 1071 (9th Cir. 1973), the plaintiff, while sleeping in his tent in Yellowstone Park, was attacked and mauled by a bear. Before the incident took place, however, the plaintiff had received written warnings from the park authorities about the dangers of camping out in the park. The decision in the case was reached on the ground that the defendants were not guilty of actionable negligence, having discharged their duty to warn. The same result is required under a theory of strict liability, since the written warnings are sufficient to compel the finding that the plaintiff assumed the risk of injury.

4. Distress damage feasant. Distress damage feasant refers to "the taking of chattels, whether animate or inanimate, that are doing damage to or (perhaps) encumbering land, or depasturing chattels, and the retaining of them by way of security until compensation is paid." G. Williams, Liability for Animals 7 (1939). This self-help remedy was critical in most disputes between farmers arising from trespassing cattle, and it offers a partial explanation for the dominance of the strict liability rule for trespassing animals. Thus in Marshall v. Welwood, 38 N.J.L. 339, 341 (1876) — which, like Losee v. Buchanan, rejected Rylands v. Fletcher in a suit against the owner of an exploding boiler — Beasley, C.J., argued that "the right to plead that the escape had occurred by inevitable accident would have seriously impaired, if it did not entirely frustrate, the process of distress damage feasant. Custom has had much to do in giving shape to the law, and what is highly convenient readily runs into usage, and is accepted as a rule. It would but rarely occur that cattle would escape from a vigilant owner. . . ."

Note also that in England, when it was proposed to subject the law of cattle trespass to the general principles of negligence, Report of the Committee on the Law of Civil Liability for Damage Done by Animals, CMD 8746, ¶3 (1953), it was rejected in large measure because of the protests of the farmers themselves. As the report stated, "This class of liability is of interest only to farmers and landowners and the general public are not affected thereby."

5. *"Fencing in" and "fencing out."* In Garcia v. Sumrall, 121 P.2d 640, 644 (Ariz. 1942), the court said:

> Under the common law it was presumed to be the duty of the owners of animals to keep the same properly enclosed and under control, and if they failed to do so and the animals trespassed upon the property of another, fenced or unfenced, the owners of the animals were liable for damages. This rule, however, has been greatly modified in America, and particularly in what is commonly referred to as the grazing states. The situation in these states may be briefly stated as follows:
>
> A very large percentage of the land therein is owned by the United States government, only an extremely small portion being under private ownership. Much of this land is valuable only for the pasturage of meat animals. The federal government for many years recognized the custom existing of allowing such animals to run at large upon the land and acquiesced therein, but forbade its enclosure by fences. The result was that if the old common law rule of trespass was applied, it would have been practically impossible to use these federal lands for grazing, for the animals running at large thereon, due to their natural instincts, would be practically certain to trespass upon any privately owned lands lying adjacent to the open range. For this reason many, if not most, of the western states adopted statutes similar to ours above referred to. The obvious purpose and effect of these statutes was to change the common law rule and to make the owner of private premises fence his land to keep animals out, rather than to compel the owner of the animals to fence the land upon which they were grazing in order to keep them in. But notwithstanding this, it was practically universally held in the states having such laws that they did not have the effect of permitting those grazing animals upon the public domain to commit acts of willful trespass by deliberately and intentionally causing their animals to trespass upon private property.

One recurrent issue is whether a defendant who simply lets his animals roam the open fields with the knowledge that they might enter another's land has committed a willful trespass? In *Garcia*, the court noted a division of authority on the question and opted for a higher standard, taking the view adopted in Colorado and Wyoming that requires the plaintiff to show "some overt and unlawful act on the part of the defendant which tends to increase the natural propensity of cattle to wander and to direct them upon the premises of another." Some decisions, however, hold the cattleowner on a open range will be liable for an intentional tort when he places cattle on his own land in a manner and location that makes it substantially certain that they will stray. *Lazarus v. Phelps*, 152 U.S. 81 (1894).

6. Fencing out: historical, economic, and social complications. "Fencing out" statutes mark a departure from the usual principles of property law insofar as they require a plaintiff to take affirmative action to protect the exclusive use of land. These fencing laws occupied center stage throughout much of the nineteenth century, when they were the subject of an intense and bitter political rivalry. This early history has been well documented in R. Ellickson, Order without Law: How Neighbors Settle Disputes chs. 2 & 3 (1991); and in Vogel, The Coase Theorem and California Animal Trespass Law, 16 J. Legal Stud. 149 (1987). Fencing has always been an expensive proposition, especially since fences had to withstand the incessant pounding of large herds of thirst-crazed animals. In the nineteenth century the cost of a fence could easily exceed the value of the fenced land, and today it runs around $1 per linear foot. Ellickson, at 65.

With the high cost of fencing, it is not surprising that state legislatures vacillated on who must build them. In California, for example, an "open range" statute (whereby the landowner was under a duty to fence out with a "lawful fence") was adopted for the entire state in 1850. By 1915, the increased pressure from expanding agricultural interests led to "closed range" statutes (whereby the ranchers were under a duty to control their cattle) for most of the state, except for the state's six sparsely populated northern counties. Today this divided regime generally holds, although Shasta County, in the north, is now governed by a complex system that allows the local Board of Supervisors to designate certain county lands as either open or closed range. See Ellickson, at 42-48.

The choice between open and closed range not only has dramatic economic consequences for both ranchers and farmers, but also influences the pattern of negotiations over the use of land. As Vogel points out, supra at 176, moving from open-range rules (favoring the rancher) to the closed-range rules (favoring the farmer) reduces the costs of negotiating a change in the patterns of land use. Under an open-range system, a single landowner cannot in practice buy off some ranchers and hope to preserve his land for agricultural uses. Those ranchers not bound by the agreement could still let their cattle roam at will. Yet when the rights to exclude belong to the farmer, a voluntary agreement can allow some ranchers limited grazing rights without opening the land up to all ranchers. Placing exclusive rights in the farmer thus facilitates consensual reassignments of rights as the open-range rules do not.

These titanic struggles over fencing laws do not occur when all participants are by degrees both ranchers and farmers, as is now the case in

Shasta County. Now a general norm of reciprocity applies. Ellickson has reported, for example, that in ordinary low-level interactions between ranchers in Shasta County, virtually none of the local citizens and officials knew the details of the substantive law. Rather, as Ellickson notes, their conduct was routinely guided by a general, informal norm "that a rancher should keep his animals from eating a neighbor's grass, regardless of whether a range is open or closed." Given reciprocity, the costs of care for another's animals are not normally compensated in cash by the true owner, for in the long run the accounts tend to balance out over separate transactions. What does Ellickson's account say of the relative influence of law and custom in solving concrete disputes?

D.   ULTRAHAZARDOUS OR ABNORMALLY DANGEROUS ACTIVITIES

Spano v. Perini Corp.
250 N.E.2d 31 (N.Y. 1969)

FULD, C.J. The principal question posed on this appeal is whether a person who has sustained property damage caused by blasting on nearby property can maintain an action for damages without a showing that the blaster was negligent. Since 1893, when this court decided the case of Booth v. Rome, W. & O.T.R.R. Co. (140 N.Y. 267), it has been the law of this State that proof of negligence was required unless the blast was accompanied by an actual physical invasion of the damaged property — for example, by rocks or other material being cast upon the premises. We are now asked to reconsider that rule.

The plaintiff Spano is the owner of a garage in Brooklyn which was wrecked by a blast occurring on November 27, 1962. There was then in that garage, for repairs, an automobile owned by the plaintiff Davis which he also claims was damaged by the blasting. Each of the plaintiffs brought suit against the two defendants who, as joint venturers, were engaged in constructing a tunnel in the vicinity pursuant to a contract with the City of New York. The two cases were tried together, without a jury, in the Civil Court of the City of New York, New York County, and judgments were rendered in favor of the plaintiffs. The judgments were reversed by the Appellate Term and the Appellate Division affirmed that order, granting leave to appeal to this court.

It is undisputed that, on the day in question (November 27, 1962), the defendants had set off a total of 194 sticks of dynamite at a construction site which was only 125 feet away from the damaged premises. Although both plaintiffs alleged negligence in their complaints, no attempt was made to show that the defendants had failed to exercise reasonable care or to take necessary precautions when they were blasting. Instead, they chose to rely, upon the trial, solely on the principle of absolute liability either on a tort theory or on the basis of their being third-party beneficiaries of the defendants' contract with the city. At the close of the plaintiff Spano's case, when defendants' attorney moved to dismiss the action on the ground, among others, that no negligence had been proved, the trial judge expressed the view that the defendants could be held liable even though they were not shown to have been careless. The case then proceeded, with evidence being introduced solely on the question of damages and proximate cause. Following the trial, the court awarded damages of some $4,400 to Spano and of $329 to Davis.

On appeal, a divided Appellate Term reversed that judgment, declaring that it deemed itself concluded by the established rule in this State requiring proof of negligence. Justice Markowitz, who dissented, urged that the *Booth* case should no longer be considered controlling precedent.

The Appellate Division affirmed; it called attention to a decision in the Third Department (Thomas v. Hendrickson Bros., 30 A.D.2d 730, 731), in which the court observed that "[i]f *Booth* is to be overruled, 'the announcement thereof should come from the authoritative source and not in the form of interpretation or prediction by an intermediate appellate court.' "

In our view, the time has come for this court to make that "announcement" and declare that one who engages in blasting must assume responsibility, and be liable without fault, for any injury he causes to neighboring property.

The concept of absolute liability in blasting cases is hardly a novel one. The overwhelming majority of American jurisdictions have adopted such a rule. Indeed, this court itself, several years ago, noted that a change in our law would "conform to the more widely (indeed almost universally) approved doctrine that a blaster is absolutely liable for any damages he causes, with or without trespass." (Schlansky v. Augustus V. Riegel, Inc., 9 N.Y.2d 493, 496.)

We need not rely solely, however, upon out-of-state decisions in order to attain our result. Not only has the rationale of the *Booth* case been overwhelmingly rejected elsewhere but it appears to be fundamentally inconsistent with earlier cases in our own court which had held, long before *Booth* was decided, that a party was absolutely liable for damages to neighboring property caused by explosions. (See, e.g., Hay v. Cohoes Co., 2 N.Y. 159; Heeg v. Licht, 80 N.Y. 579.) In the *Hay* case, for example, the defendant was engaged in blasting an excavation for a canal and the force of the blasts caused large quantities of earth and stones to be thrown against the plaintiff's house, knocking down his stoop and part of his chimney. The court held the defendant *absolutely* liable for the damage caused, stating (2 N.Y., at pp. 160-161):

"It is an elementary principle in reference to private rights, that every individual is entitled to the undisturbed possession and lawful enjoyment of his own property. The mode of enjoyment is necessarily limited by the rights of others — otherwise it might be made destructive of their rights altogether. Hence the maxim sic utere tuo, &c. The defendants had the right to dig the canal. The plaintiff had the right to the undisturbed possession of his property. If these rights conflict, the former must yield to the latter, as the more important of the two, since, upon grounds of public policy, it is better that one man should surrender a particular use of his land, than that another should be deprived of the beneficial use of his property altogether, which might be the consequence if the privilege of the former should be wholly unrestricted. The case before us illustrates this principle. For if the defendants in excavating their canal, in itself a lawful use of their land, could, in the manner mentioned by the witnesses, demolish the stoop of the plaintiff with impunity, they might, for the same purpose, on the exercise of reasonable care, demolish his house, and thus deprive him of all use of his property."

Although the court in *Booth* drew a distinction between a situation — such as was presented in the *Hay* case — where there was "a physical invasion" of, or trespass on, the plaintiff's property and one in which the damage was caused by "setting the air in motion, or in some other unexplained way," it is clear that the court, in the earlier cases, was not concerned with the particular manner by which the damage was caused but by the simple fact that any explosion in a built-up area was likely to cause damage. Thus, in Heeg v. Licht the court held that there should be absolute liability where the damage was caused by the accidental explosion of stored gunpowder, even in the absence of a physical trespass (p. 581):

"The defendant had erected a building and stored materials therein, which from their character were liable to and actually did explode, causing injury to the plaintiff. The fact that the explosion took place tends to establish that the magazine was dangerous and liable to cause damage to the property of persons residing in the vicinity. . . . The fact that the magazine was liable to such a contingency, which could not be guarded against or averted by the greatest degree of care and vigilance, evinces its dangerous character. . . . In such a case, the rule which exonerates a party engaged in a lawful business, when free from negligence, has no application."

Such reasoning should, we venture, have led to the conclusion that the *intentional* setting off of explosives — that is, blasting — in an area in which it was likely to cause harm to neighboring property similarly results in absolute liability. However, the court in the *Booth* case rejected such an extension of the rule for the reason that "[t]o exclude the defendant from blasting to adapt its lot to the contemplated uses, at the instance of the plaintiff, would not be a compromise between conflicting rights, but an extinguishment of the right of the one for the benefit of the other" (140 N.Y., at p. 281). The court expanded on this by stating, "This sacrifice, we think, the law does not exact. Public policy is promoted by the building up of towns and cities and the improvement of property. Any unnecessary restraint on freedom of action of a property owner hinders this."

This rationale cannot withstand analysis. The plaintiff in *Booth* was not seeking, as the court implied, to "exclude the defendant from blasting" and thus prevent desirable improvements to the latter's property. Rather, he was merely seeking compensation for the damage which was inflicted upon his own property as a result of that blasting. The question, in other words, was not *whether* it was lawful or proper to engage in blasting but *who* should bear the cost of any resulting damage — the person who engaged in the dangerous activity or the innocent neighbor injured thereby. Viewed in such a light, it clearly appears that *Booth* was wrongly decided and should be forthrightly overruled.

In more recent cases, our court has already gone far toward mitigating the harsh effect of the rule laid down in the *Booth* case. Thus, we have held that negligence can properly be inferred from the mere fact that a blast has caused extensive damage, even where the plaintiff is unable to show "the method of blasting or the strength of the charges or the character of the soil or rock." (Schlansky v. Augustus V. Riegel, Inc., 9 N.Y.2d 493, 497.) But, even under this liberal interpretation of *Booth,* it would still remain possible for a defendant who engages in blasting operations — which he realizes are likely to cause injury — to avoid liability by showing that he exercised reasonable care. Since blasting involves a substantial risk of harm no matter the degree of care exercised, we perceive no reason for ever permitting a person who engages in such an activity to impose this risk upon nearby persons or property without assuming responsibility therefor.

Indeed, the defendants devote but brief argument in defense of the *Booth* rule. The principal thrust of their argument is directed not to the requisite standard of care to be used but, rather, to the sufficiency of the plaintiffs' pleadings and the proof adduced on the issue of causation. [The court then disposed of both these points in plaintiff's favor.]

The order appealed from should be reversed, with costs, and the matter remitted to the Appellate Division for further proceedings in accordance with this opinion.

NOTES

1. Influence of the forms of action. The rule in Booth v. Rome, discussed in *Spano,* rested in part on the distinction between trespass and case. The argument was that the plaintiff could characterize the physical entry of rocks or other materials upon his land as a direct invasion by the defendant such that the rules of trespass, including those that specified liability without fault, applied. When the damage was caused only by vibration or concussion, however, the injury was "indirect" and the applicable rules were those of trespass on the case, including their negligence requirement. This argument could be attacked on narrow grounds by noting that even when rocks and debris are thrown onto the plaintiff's land, trespass should not lie because defendant's direct and immediate act was the pushing of the plunger and not the throwing of the rocks. The more powerful line of attack, however, is a variation of the Holmes argument in The Common Law, at page 140 supra that contends that the substantive ground for relief should not turn on the procedural requirements of the forms of action. See Whitman Hotel Corp. v. Elliot & Watrous Engineering Co., 79 A.2d 591 (Conn. 1951). Note how history has afforded Holmes only partial vindication of his views. With blasting cases, the theory of liability is uniform regardless of the mode of causation, but that uniform theory turns out to be one of strict liability and not of negligence.

2. Survival of the forms of action. In Laird v. Nelms, 406 U.S. 797, 800 (1972), the plaintiffs sued for damage to their property caused by the sonic booms of military planes flying overhead. In a split decision the Supreme Court recognized that the general rule of strict liability was applicable in blasting cases, but nonetheless held for the government, because in its view the plaintiff's cause of action did not fall within the provision of the Federal Torts Claims Act (28 U.S.C. §1346(b)). That act makes the United States liable for injuries to personal property "caused by the negligent or wrongful act or omission of any employee of the government while acting within the scope of his office or employment, under circumstances where the United States, if a private person, would be liable to the claimant in accordance with the law of the place where the act or omission occurred." Even though plaintiff's cause of action was valid under state law, the Court decided that the plaintiffs' case failed under the statute because they could not establish "the negligent or wrongful act" of the defendant. The plaintiffs conceded that there was no negligence, and the Court thought they could only recover for wrongfulness if they could establish a trespass at common law. Thus, the cause of action failed because "the presently prevailing view as to the theory of liability for blasting damage is frankly conceded to be strict liability for undertaking an ultrahazardous activity rather than any attenuated notion of common law trespass."

What result if the government plane invades the plaintiff's airspace, where the only real damage is that caused by vibration, not the intrusion? See United States v. Causby, 328 U.S. 256 (1946). On the general question of airplane noise see Baxter and Altree, Legal Aspects of Airport Noise, 15 J.L. & Econ. 1 (1972).

Madsen v. East Jordan Irrigation Co.
125 P.2d 794 (Utah 1942)

PRATT, J. This is an appeal from a decree of the lower court sustaining a general demurrer to appellant's amended complaint and entering judgment for the respondent.

The facts, as alleged in the amended complaint, are as follows: Appellant owns the Madsen Mink Farm in Sandy, Utah, using said farm to breed and raise mink for sale. The farm is located 100 yards north of respondent's irrigation canal and, on May 5, 1941, respondent, in repairing its canal, blasted with explosives, causing vibrations and noises which frightened the mother mink and caused 108 of them to kill 230 of their "kittens" (offspring). The appellant further alleges that, by nature, habit and disposition all mink, when with and attending their young, are highly excitable and, when disturbed, will become terrified and kill their young. Appellant places a value of $25 each on said "kittens" and seeks to recover $5,750 as damages. . . .

Respondent, in his brief, contends that, because the injury in the present case was consequential rather than immediate, the amended complaint does not state facts sufficient to constitute a cause of action in trespass. He further contends that the amended complaint did not state facts sufficient to constitute a cause of action in case.

It is conceded that the rule of absolute liability prevails when one uses explosives and the blasting of said explosives results in hurling of rock, earth or debris which causes injury to another. . . . The weight of authority sustains the position that there is no distinction in liability for damage in nonconcussion and concussion cases. . . .

The minority rule, led by New York [prior to *Spano*], holds that negligence must be alleged in concussion cases. . . . Had the concussion in the instant case killed the kittens directly, without the intervention of the mother minks, the majority rule of liability in concussion cases would have been applicable, but the case at bar presents the additional element of the mother minks' independent acts, thereby raising a question of proximate causation. Query: Did the mother minks' intervention break the chain of causation and therefore require an allegation of negligence?

Many years ago (1896) a Maine court held that the intervening act of an animal broke the chain of causation to such extent that blasting could not be considered the proximate cause of injury and negligence on the part of the blaster had to be proved. Wadsworth v. Marshall, 88 Me. 263, 34 A. 30. In the *Wadsworth* case, the plaintiff was riding along a public highway near which defendant was operating a quarry. He exploded a blast which frightened plaintiff's horse and she (plaintiff) was injured. There was a Maine statute requiring persons engaged in blasting to give reasonable notice of their intention to blast to all persons in the vicinity of the blast. The trial court excluded testimony as to the viciousness and nervousness of plaintiff's horse, proceeding upon the ground that defendant violated the statute by failing to give the required notice and therefore he was liable regardless of the character of the horse or any negligence of the plaintiff. The appellate court reversed the lower court's decision, holding that it would be a harsh construction of the statute to hold that the negligence of the quarry-man in not giving notice subjected him to liability for damages largely, if not wholly, resulting from the negligence of the traveler in riding an unsuitable horse. The court ruled that "the established doctrine of contributory negligence, as a defense, applies to this class of actions."

While the above ruling interjects an element — contributory negligence — which is absent in the present case, it impresses one with the thought that he who fires explosives is not liable for every occurrence following the explosion which has a semblance of connection to it. Jake's horse might become so excited that he would run next door and kick a few ribs out of Cy's jersey cow, but is such a thing to be anticipated from an explosion? Whether the cases are concussion or nonconcussion, the results chargeable to the nonnegligent user of explosives are those things ordinarily resulting from an explosion. Shock, air vibrations, thrown missiles are all illustrative of the anticipated result of explosives; they are physical as distinguished from mental in character. The famous *Squib* case does not mitigate what has been said in the preceding lines. That was a case where the mental reaction was to be anticipated as an instinctive matter of self-preservation. In the instant case, the killing of their kittens was not an act of self-preservation on the part of the mother mink but a peculiarity of disposition which was not within the realm of matters to be anticipated. Had a squib been thrown and suddenly picked up by a dog, in fun, and carried near another, it is ventured that we would not have had a famous *Squib* case, as such a result would not have been within the realm of anticipation.

We are of the opinion that the lower court properly sustained the demurrer.

American Law Institute, Restatement (Second) of Torts
(1977)

§519.   GENERAL PRINCIPLE

(1) One who carries on an abnormally dangerous activity is subject to liability for harm to the person, land or chattels of another resulting from the activity, although he has exercised the utmost care to prevent the harm.

(2) This strict liability is limited to the kind of harm, the possibility of which makes the activity abnormally dangerous.

Comment: . . .

c. The word "care" includes care in preparation, care in operation and skill both in operation and preparation.

Comment on Subsection (2):

e. Extent of protection. The rule of strict liability stated in Subsection (1) applies only to harm that is within the scope of the abnormal risk that is the basis of the liability. One who carries on an abnormally dangerous activity is not under strict liability for every possible harm that may result from carrying it on. For example, the thing that makes the storage of dynamite in a city abnormally dangerous is the risk of harm to those in the vicinity if it should explode. If an explosion occurs and does harm to persons, land or chattels in the vicinity, the rule stated in Subsection (1) applies. If, however, there is no explosion and for some unexpected reason a part of the wall of the magazine in which the dynamite is stored falls upon a pedestrian on the highway upon which the magazine abuts, the rule stated in Subsection (1) has no application. In this case the liability, if any, will be dependent upon proof of negligence in the construction or maintenance of the wall. So also, the transportation of dynamite or other high explosives by truck through the streets of a city is abnormally dangerous for the same reason as that which makes the storage of the explosives abnormally dangerous. If the dynamite explodes in the course of the transportation, a private person transporting it is subject to liability under the rule stated in Subsection (1), although he has exercised the utmost care. On the other hand, if the vehicle containing the explosives runs over a pedestrian, he cannot recover unless the vehicle was driven negligently.

Illustration:

1. *A,* with reasonable care, carries on blasting operations in a closely settled rural district. *A* has no reason to know of the presence of *B*'s mink ranch nearby. The noise of the blasting frightens the mink and

the fright causes them to kill their young. *A* is not subject to strict liability to *B* for the loss of the mink.

§520.   Abnormally Dangerous Activities

In determining whether an activity is abnormally dangerous, the following factors are to be considered:

(a) existence of a high degree of risk of some harm to the person, land or chattels of others;

(b) likelihood that the harm that results from it will be great;

(c) inability to eliminate the risk by the exercise of reasonable care;

(d) extent to which the activity is not a matter of common usage;

(e) inappropriateness of the activity to the place where it is carried on and;

(f) extent to which its value to the community is outweighed by its dangerous attributes.

Comment: . . .

b. Distinguished from negligence. The rule stated in §519 is applicable to an activity that is carried on with all reasonable care, and that is of such utility that the risk which is involved in it cannot be regarded as so great or so unreasonable as to make it negligence merely to carry on the activity at all. (See §282). If the utility of the activity does not justify the risk it creates, it may be negligence merely to carry it on, and the rule stated in this Section is not then necessary to subject the defendant to liability for harm resulting from it.

c. Relation to nuisance. If the abnormally dangerous activity involves a risk of harm to others that substantially impairs the use and enjoyment of neighboring lands or interferes with rights common to all members of the public the impairment or interference may be actionable on the basis of a public or a private nuisance. (See §822, and Comment *a* under that Section). The rule of strict liability stated in §519 frequently is applied by many courts in these cases under the name of "absolute nuisance," even when the harm that results is physical harm to person, land or chattels.

d. Purpose of activity. In the great majority of the cases that involve abnormally dangerous activities the activity is carried on by the actor for purposes in which he has a financial interest, such as a business conducted for profit. This, however, is not necessary for the existence of such an activity. The rule here stated is equally applicable when there is no pecuniary benefit to the actor. Thus a private owner of an abnormally dangerous body of water who keeps it only for his own use and pleasure as a swimming pool is subject to the same liability as one who operates a reservoir of water for profit.

e. Not limited to the defendant's land. In most of the cases to which the rule of strict liability is applicable the abnormally dangerous activity is conducted on land in the possession of the defendant. This, again, is not necessary to the existence of such an activity. It may be carried on in a public highway or other public place or upon the land of another. . . .

Comment on Clause (c):

h. Risk not eliminated by reasonable care. Another important factor to be taken into account in determining whether the activity is abnormally dangerous is the impossibility of eliminating the risk by the exercise of reasonable care. Most ordinary activities can be made entirely safe by the taking of all reasonable precautions; and when safety cannot be attained by the exercise of due care there is reason to regard the danger as an abnormal one. . . .

Comment on Clause (d):

i. Common usage. An activity is a matter of common usage if it is customarily carried on by the great mass of mankind or by many people in the community. It does not cease to be so because it is carried on for a purpose peculiar to the individual who engages in it. Certain activities, notwithstanding their recognizable danger, are so generally carried on as to be regarded as customary. Thus automobiles have come into such general use that their operation is a matter of common usage. This, notwithstanding the residue of unavoidable risk of serious harm that may result even from their careful operation, is sufficient to prevent their use from being regarded as an abnormally dangerous activity. On the other hand, the operation of a tank or any other motor vehicle of such size and weight as to be unusually difficult to control safely, or to be likely to damage the ground over which it is driven, is not yet a usual activity for many people, and therefore the operation of such a vehicle may be abnormally dangerous.

Although blasting is recognized as a proper means of excavation for building purposes or of clearing woodland for cultivation, it is not carried on by any large percentage of the population, and therefore it is not a matter of common usage. Likewise the manufacture, storage, transportation and use of high explosives, although necessary to the construction of many public and private works, are carried on by only a comparatively small number of persons and therefore are not matters of common usage. So likewise, the very nature of oil lands and the essential interest of the public in the production of oil require that oil wells be drilled, but the dangers incident to the operation are characteristic of oil lands and not of lands in general, and relatively few persons are engaged in the activity. . . .

Comment on Clause (f):

k. Value to the community. Even though the activity involves a serious risk of harm that cannot be eliminated with reasonable care and it is not a matter of common usage, its value to the community may be such that the danger will not be regarded as an abnormal one. . . .

Comment:

l. Function of court. Whether the activity is an abnormally dangerous one is to be determined by the court, upon consideration of all the factors listed in this Section, and the weight given to each that it merits upon the facts in evidence. In this it differs from questions of negligence. Whether the conduct of the defendant has been that of a reasonable man of ordinary prudence or in the alternative has been negligent is ordinarily an issue to be left to the jury. . . . The imposition of strict liability, on the other hand, involves a characterization of the defendant's activity or enterprise itself, and a decision as to whether he is free to conduct it at all without becoming subject to liability for the harm that ensues even though he has used all reasonable care. This calls for a decision of the court; and it is no part of the province of the jury to decide whether an industrial enterprise upon which the community's prosperity might depend is located in the wrong place or whether such an activity as blasting is to be permitted without liability in the center of a large city.

§522.   Contributing Actions of Third Persons, Animals and Forces of Nature

One carrying on an ultrahazardous activity is liable for harm under the rule stated in §519, although the harm is caused by the unexpectable

   (a) innocent, negligent or reckless conduct of a third person, or
   (b) action of an animal, or
   (c) operation of a force of nature.

§523.   Assumption of Risk

The plaintiff's assumption of the risk of harm from an abnormally dangerous activity bars his recovery for the harm.

§524.   Contributory Negligence

(1) Except as stated in Subsection (2), the contributory negligence of the plaintiff is not a defense to the strict liability of one who carries on an abnormally dangerous activity.

(2) The plaintiff's contributory negligence in knowingly and unreasonably subjecting himself to the risk of harm from the activity is a defense to the strict liability.

§524A.   PLAINTIFF'S ABNORMALLY SENSITIVE ACTIVITY

There is no strict liability for harm caused by an abnormally dangerous activity if the harm would not have resulted but for the abnormally sensitive character of the plaintiff's activity.

NOTES

1. Definition of abnormally dangerous activities. Sections 519 and 520 of the Restatement (Second) of Torts are modifications of the provisions of the first Restatement that in 1934 endorsed a principle of strict liability for all "ultrahazardous activities." The two Restatements have many points of similarity, notwithstanding the rejection by the Restatement (Second) of the term *ultra*hazardous as inelegant, if not ungrammatical. Both versions of the Restatement followed the common law in deciding that certain *classes* of activities, such as drilling for oil, see Green v. General Petroleum Corp., 270 P. 952 (Cal. 1928), or fumigation, see Luthringer v. Moore, 190 P.2d 1 (Cal. 1948), are covered by the provisions. Why is a categorical approach adopted here when negligence liability is usually determined on a case-by-case basis? How successful are the authors of the Restatement (Second) in defining the area of "abnormally dangerous activities"? In particular, why doesn't the general Hand formula for negligence not apply to all abnormally dangerous activities? Does comment *k* endorse or reject the rule in Rylands v. Fletcher? Note that comment *c* to the 1934 Restatement on "ultrahazardous subject matter" concluded: *"Caveat:* The Institute expresses no opinion as to whether the construction and use of a large tank or artificial reservoir in which a large body of water or other fluid is collected is or is not an ultrahazardous activity."

The Restatement's insistence that the social value of an activity be taken into account in determining whether it is abnormally dangerous was ably criticized in Koos v. Roth, 652 P.2d 1255, 1261, 1262 (Or. 1982), where Linde, J., in upholding a strict liability action for fire damage, observed:

> There are at least two reasons not to judge civil liability for unintended harm by a court's views of the utility or value of the harmful activity. One reason lies in the nature of the judgment. Utility and value often are subjective and controversial. They will be judged differently by those who profit from an activity and those who are endangered by it, and between

one locality and another. The use of explosives to remove old buildings for a new highway or shopping center may be described as slum clearance or as the destruction of historic landmarks and neighborhoods. On a smaller scale, it may celebrate a traditional holiday which some may value more highly than either buildings or roads. Highly toxic materials may be necessary to the production of agricultural pesticides, or of drugs, or of chemical or bacteriological weapons, or of industrial products of all sorts; does liability for injury from their storage or movement depend on the utility of these products? Judges, like others, may differ about such values; they can hardly be described as conclusions of law. . . .

The second reason why the value of a hazardous activity does not preclude strict liability for its consequences is that the conclusion does not follow from the premise. In the prior cases, the court did not question the economic value of blasting, cropdusting, or storing natural gas. In an action for damages, the question is not whether the activity threatens such harm that it should not be continued. The question is who shall pay for harm that has been done. The loss has occurred. It is a cost of the activity whoever bears it. To say that when the activity has great economic value the cost should be borne by others is no more or less logical than to say that when the costs of an activity are borne by others it gains in value. This, in effect, is postulated in the argument that the industry which relies on field burning is highly valuable but could not survive the cost difference of insurance against strict liability instead of negligence.

2. Common usage. What is the function of the common usage requirement set out in section 520(d)? If it is taken seriously, how can blasting, fumigating, or the manufacturing of explosives not be matters of common usage?

One notable effort to make sense out of the common usage requirement in the Restatement is found in Fletcher, Fairness and Utility in Tort Theory, 85 Harv. L. Rev. 537, 541-542, 547-548 (1972).

I shall propose a specific standard of risk that makes sense of the Restatement's emphasis on uncommon, extra-hazardous risks, but which shows that the Restatement's theory is part of a larger rationale of liability that cuts across negligence, intentional torts, and numerous pockets of strict liability. The general principle expressed in all of these situations governed by diverse doctrinal standards is that a victim has a right to recover for injuries caused by a risk greater in degree and different in order from those created by the victim and imposed on the defendant — in short, for injuries resulting from nonreciprocal risks. Cases of liability are those in which the defendant generates a disproportionate, excessive risk of harm, relative to the victim's risk-creating activity. For example, a pilot or an airplane owner subjects those beneath the path of flight to nonreciprocal risks of harm. Conversely, cases of nonliability are those of reciprocal risks, namely those in which the victim and the defendant subject each other to roughly the same degree of risk. For example, two airplanes flying the same vicinity subject each other to reciprocal risks of a mid-air collision. Of course, there are significant problems in determining when risks are nonreciprocal, and we shall turn to these difficulties later. For now, it is sufficient to note that the paradigm of reciprocity represents (1) a bifurcation of the questions of who is entitled to compensation and who ought to pay, (2) a commitment to resolving both of those issues by looking only to the activity of the victim and the risk-creator, and (3) a specific criterion for determining who is entitled to recover for loss, namely all those injured by nonreciprocal risks. . . .

The rationale of nonreciprocal risk-taking accounts as well for pockets of strict liability outside the coverage of the Restatement's sections on extra-hazardous activities. For example, an individual is strictly liable for damage done by a wild animal in his charge, but not for damage committed by his domesticated pet. Most people have pets, children, or friends whose presence creates some risk to neighbors and their property. These are risks that offset each other; they are, as a class, reciprocal risks. Yet bringing an unruly horse into the city goes beyond the accepted and shared level of risks in having pets, children, and friends in one's household. If the defendant creates a risk that exceeds those to which he is reciprocally subject, it seems fair to hold him liable for the results of his aberrant indulgence. Similarly, according to the latest version of the Restatement, airplane owners and pilots are strictly liable for ground damage, but not for mid-air collisions. Risk of ground damage is nonreciprocal; homeowners do not create risks to airplanes flying overhead. The risks of mid-air collisions, on the other hand, are generated reciprocally by all who fly the air lanes. Accordingly, the threshold of liability for damage resulting from mid-air collisions is higher than mere involvement in the activity of flying. To be liable for collision damage to another flyer, the pilot must fly negligently or the owner must maintain the plane negligently; they must generate abnormal risks of collision to the other planes aflight.

Fletcher's norm of reciprocity works well with repeat low-level interferences that might be characterized as reciprocal, see infra at page 689, note 6, but it works less well with personal injuries where the harms can be very substantial. Often, as with dangerous animals, both actions are allowed instead of neither. How should it be decided which approach, two actions or none, is superior?

3. *Aviation as abnormally dangerous activity.* Should aviation be regarded as an abnormally dangerous activity? In the 1934 Restatement, aviation was so regarded on the ground that "one of the risks of aviation is that the plane being flown at a high altitude and over a large area may encounter dangerous weather conditions which would be altogether abnormal on the surface of the earth." This explanation is very difficult to accept today, especially given that more lives have been lost per passenger mile in automobile accidents — governed by negligence principles under the Restatement — than in airplane accidents. The strict liability principles contained in sections 519 and 520 do not reach the airplane any more than they reach the automobile. Thus in Boyd v. White, 276 P.2d 92 (Cal. App. 1954), the court denied recovery, concluding "the operation of an airplane in the year 1954 is not such a dangerous activity that it can be placed in this category." Similarly in Wood v. United Air Lines, Inc., 223 N.Y.S.2d 692 (Sup. Ct. Trial Term 1961), arising out of a mid-air collision, which resulted in damage to

plaintiff's apartment, sought summary judgment on the ground that defendant committed "trespass as a matter of law." But the court rejected the argument on the ground that trespass was an intentional tort, so that at the very least an intention to invade defendant's land had to be established. "In the instant case it would seem to be apparent that there was no intent to crash. Neither is there any indication that the collision which led to the crash occurred during the course of attempting to make a landing. No evidentiary facts are adduced on the instant motion to show that the plane was in any wise under the pilot's control when, as alleged in the amended complaint, it 'plunged down' onto the street . . ." In line with these cases, the tenth tentative draft of the Restatement proposed that ground damage caused by airplanes be actionable only if caused by an intentional trespass or the negligence of the defendant, except where the aircraft is "abnormally dangerous" or is operated in "an abnormally dangerous manner." But that provision was rejected in favor of the strict liability rule now contained in section 520A:

§520A. GROUND DAMAGE FROM AIRCRAFT
If physical harm to land or to persons or chattels on the ground is caused by the ascent, descent or flight of aircraft, or by the dropping or falling of an object from the aircraft,
    (a) the operator of the aircraft is subject to liability for the harm, even though he has exercised the utmost care to prevent it, and
    (b) the owner of the aircraft is subject to similar liability if he has authorized or permitted the operation.

Is section 520A consistent with the general liability provisions of section 520? And does it represent an adequate causal account of aviation accidents? See Schwartz, The Vitality of Negligence and the Ethics of Strict Liability, 15 Ga. L. Rev. 963, 1000 (1981), in which the author observed that "airplane flying being an activity which is normally very safe, an ordinary-language inquiry into causation would almost certainly concern itself with identifying the specific non-normal feature that could explain why the particular crash occurred."

4. Ultrahazardous activities: causal complications. In Yukon Equipment v. Fireman's Fund Insurance Company, 585 P.2d 1206, 1211 (Alaska 1978), the defendants were sued for damage caused by the explosion of their storage magazine, which was located in a suburb of Anchorage. The damage was caused when four young thieves set off the explosives in order to conceal evidence of their theft. The court first noted that the storage of explosives was governed by the principles of strict liability set forth in the leading case of Exner v. Sherman Power Construction Co., 54 F.2d 510 (2d Cir. 1931), and that its application was not defeated by virtue of the fact that the petitioners had located their plant in a remote part of town nearly one mile from the nearest public highway.

The petitioners also argued that the conduct of the four thieves should be treated as a superseding cause that negatived tortious liability, but this argument was rejected because "incendiary destruction of premises by thieves to cover evidence of theft is not so uncommon an occurrence that it can be regarded as highly extraordinary." Is this decision consistent with *Madsen*?

Indiana Harbor Belt R.R. Co. v. American Cyanamid Co.
916 F.2d 1174 (7th Cir. 1990)

POSNER, C.J. American Cyanamid Company, the defendant in this diversity tort suit governed by Illinois law, is a major manufacturer of chemicals, including acrylonitrile, a chemical used in large quantities in making acrylic fibers, plastics, dyes, pharmaceutical chemicals, and other intermediate and final goods. On January 2, 1979, at its manufacturing plant in Louisiana, Cyanamid loaded 20,000 gallons of liquid acrylonitrile into a railroad tank car that it had leased from the North American Car Corporation. The next day, a train of the Missouri Pacific Railroad picked up the car at Cyanamid's siding. The car's ultimate destination was a Cyanamid plant in New Jersey served by Conrail rather than by Missouri Pacific. The Missouri Pacific train carried the car north to the Blue Island railroad yard of Indiana Harbor Belt Railroad, the plaintiff in this case, a small switching line that has a contract with Conrail to switch cars from other lines to Conrail, in this case for travel east. The Blue Island yard is in the Village of Riverdale, which is just south of Chicago and part of the Chicago metropolitan area.

The car arrived in the Blue Island yard on the morning of January 9, 1979. Several hours after it arrived, employees of the switching line noticed fluid gushing from the bottom outlet of the car. The lid on the outlet was broken. After two hours, the line's supervisor of equipment was able to stop the leak by closing a shut-off valve controlled from the top of the car. No one was sure at the time just how much of the contents of the car had leaked, but it was feared that all 20,000 gallons had, and since acrylonitrile is flammable at a temperature of 30 degrees Fahrenheit or above, highly toxic, and possibly carcinogenic, the local authorities ordered the homes near the yard evacuated. The evacuation lasted only a few hours, until the car was moved to a remote part of the yard and it was discovered that only about a quarter of the acrylonitrile had leaked. Concerned nevertheless that there had been some contamination of soil and water, the Illinois Department of Environmental Protection ordered the switching line to take decontamination measures that cost the line $981,022.75, which it sought to recover by this suit.

One count of the two-count complaint charges Cyanamid with having maintained the leased tank car negligently. The other count asserts that the transportation of acrylonitrile in bulk through the Chicago metropolitan area is an abnormally dangerous activity, for the consequences of which the shipper (Cyanamid) is strictly liable to the switching line, which bore the financial brunt of those consequences because of the decontamination measures that it was forced to take. After the district judge denied Cyanamid's motion to dismiss the strict liability count, the switching line moved for summary judgment on that count — and won. . . .

The parties agree that the question whether placing acrylonitrile in a rail shipment that will pass through a metropolitan area subjects the shipper to strict liability is, as recommended in Restatement (Second) of Torts §520, comment l (1977), a question of law, so that we owe no particular deference to the conclusion of the district court . . .

The roots of section 520 are in nineteenth-century cases. The most famous one is Rylands v. Fletcher, [casebook at page 120] but a more illuminating one in the present context is Guille v. Swan, 19 Johns. (N.Y.) 381 (1822) supra at page 110. A man took off in a hot-air balloon and landed, without intending to, in a vegetable garden in New York City. A crowd that had been anxiously watching his involuntary descent trampled the vegetables in their endeavor to rescue him when he landed. The owner of the garden sued the balloonist for the resulting damage, and won. Yet the balloonist had not been careless. In the then state of ballooning it was impossible to make a pinpoint landing.

Guille is a paradigmatic case for strict liability. (a) The risk (probability) of harm was great, and (b) the harm that would ensue if the risk materialized could be, although luckily was not, great (the balloonist could have crashed into the crowd rather than into the vegetables). The confluence of these two factors established the urgency of seeking to prevent such accidents. (c) Yet such accidents could not be prevented by the exercise of due care; the technology of care in ballooning was insufficiently developed. (d) The activity was not a matter of common usage, so there was no presumption that it was a highly valuable activity despite its unavoidable riskiness. (e) The activity was inappropriate to the place in which it took place — densely populated New York City. The risk of serious harm to others (other than the balloonist himself, that is) could have been reduced by shifting the activity to the sparsely inhabited areas that surrounded the city in those days. (f) Reinforcing (d), the value to the community of the activity of recreational ballooning did not appear to be great enough to offset its unavoidable risks.

These are, of course, the six factors in section 520. They are related to each other in that each is a different facet of a common quest for a proper legal regime to govern accidents that negligence liability cannot adequately control. The interrelations might be more perspicuous if the six factors were reordered. One might for example start with (c), inability to eliminate the risk of accident by the exercise of due care. The baseline common law regime of tort liability is negligence. When it is a workable regime, because the hazards of an activity can be avoided by being careful (which is to say, nonnegligent), there is no need to switch to strict liability. Sometimes, however, a particular type of accident cannot be prevented by taking care but can be avoided, or its consequences minimized, by shifting the activity in which the accident occurs to another locale, where the risk or harm of an accident will be less ((e)), or by reducing the scale of the activity in order to minimize the number of accidents caused by it ((f)). Shavell, Strict Liability versus Negligence, 9 J. Legal Stud. 1 (1980). By making the actor strictly liable — by denying him in other words an excuse based on his inability to avoid accidents by being more careful — we give him an incentive, missing in a negligence regime, to experiment with methods of preventing accidents that involve not greater exertions of care, assumed to be futile, but instead relocating, changing, or reducing (perhaps to the vanishing point) the activity giving rise to the accident. The greater the risk of an accident ((a)) and the costs of an accident if one occurs ((b)), the more we want the actor to consider the possibility of making accident-reducing activity changes; the stronger, therefore, is the case for strict liability. Finally, if an activity is extremely common ((d)), like driving an automobile, it is unlikely either that its hazards are perceived as great or that there is no technology of care available to minimize them; so the case for strict liability is weakened.

The largest class of cases in which strict liability has been imposed under the standard codified in the Second Restatement of Torts involves the use of dynamite and other explosives for demolition in residential or urban areas. Restatement, supra, §519, comment d. Explosives are dangerous even when handled carefully, and we therefore want blasters to choose the location of the activity with care and also to explore the feasibility of using safer substitutes (such as a wrecking ball), as well as to be careful in the blasting itself. Blasting is not a commonplace activity like driving a car, or so superior to substitute methods of demolition that the imposition of liability is unlikely to have any effect except to raise the activity's costs.

Against this background we turn to the particulars of acrylonitrile. Acrylonitrile is one of a large number of chemicals that are hazardous in the sense of being flammable, toxic, or both; acrylonitrile is both, as are many others. [Judge Posner then summarizes a list of 125 such substances, some more and some less dangerous than acrylonitrile.] Every shipper of any of these materials would therefore be strictly liable for the consequences of a spill or other accident that occurred while the material was being shipped through a metropolitan area. The plaintiff's lawyer further acknowledged the irrelevance, on her view of the case, of the fact that Cyanamid had leased and filled the car that spilled the acrylonitrile; all she thought important is that Cyanamid introduced the product into the stream of commerce that happened to pass through the Chicago metropolitan area. Her concession may have been incautious. One might want to distinguish between the shipper who merely places his goods on his loading dock to be picked up by the carrier and the shipper who, as in this case, participates actively in the transportation. But the concession is illustrative of the potential scope of the district court's decision.

No cases recognize so sweeping a liability. Several reject it, though none has facts much like those of the present case. [A discussion of some cases not following the Restatement rule is omitted.]

Siegler v. Kuhlman, 502 P.2d 1181 (Wash. 1972), also imposed strict liability on a transporter of hazardous materials, but the circumstances were again rather special. A gasoline truck blew up, obliterating the plaintiff's decedent and her car. The court emphasized that the explosion had destroyed the evidence necessary to establish whether the accident had been due to negligence; so, unless liability was strict, there would be no liability — and this as the very consequence of the defendant's hazardous activity. . . .

So we can get little help from precedent, and might as well apply section 520 to the acrylonitrile problem from the ground up. To begin with, we have been given no reason, whether the reason in *Siegler* or any other, for believing that a negligence regime is not perfectly adequate to remedy and deter, at reasonable cost, the accidental spillage of acrylonitrile from rail cars. Acrylonitrile could explode and destroy evidence, but of course did not here, making imposition of strict liability on the theory of the *Siegler* decision premature. More important, although acrylonitrile is flammable even at relatively low temperatures, and toxic, it is not so corrosive or otherwise destructive that it will eat through or otherwise damage or weaken a tank car's valves although they are maintained with due (which essentially means, with average) care. No one suggests, therefore, that the leak in this case was caused by the inherent properties of acrylonitrile. It was caused by carelessness — whether that of the North American Car Corporation in failing to maintain or inspect the car properly, or that of Cyanamid in failing to maintain or inspect it, or that of the Missouri Pacific when it had custody of the car, or that of the switching line itself in failing to notice the ruptured lid, or some combination of these possible failures of care. Accidents that are due to a lack of care can be prevented by taking care; and when a lack of care can (unlike *Siegler*) be shown in court, such accidents are adequately deterred by the threat of liability for negligence.

It is true that the district court purported to find as a fact that there is an inevitable risk of derailment or other calamity in transporting "large quantities of anything." This is not a finding of fact, but a truism: anything can happen. The question is, how likely is this type of accident if the actor uses due care? For all that appears from the record of the case or any other sources of information that we have found, if a tank car is carefully maintained the danger of a spill of acrylonitrile is negligible. If this is right, there is no compelling reason to move to a regime of strict liability, especially one that might embrace all other hazardous materials shipped by rail as well. This also means, however, that the amici curiae who have filed briefs in support of Cyanamid cry wolf in predicting "devastating" effects on the chemical industry if the district court's decision is affirmed. If the vast majority of chemical spills by railroads are preventable by due care, the imposition of strict liability should cause only a slight, not as they argue a substantial, rise in liability insurance rates, because the incremental liability should be slight. The amici have momentarily lost sight of the fact that the feasibility of avoiding accidents simply by being careful is an argument against strict liability. . . .

The district judge and the plaintiff's lawyer make much of the fact that the spill occurred in a densely inhabited metropolitan area. Only 4,000 gallons spilled; what if all 20,000 had done so? Isn't the risk that this might happen even if everybody were careful sufficient to warrant giving the shipper an incentive to explore alternative routes? Strict liability would supply that incentive. But this argument overlooks the fact that, like other transportation networks, the railroad network is a hub-and-spoke system. And the hubs are in metropolitan areas. Chicago is one of the nation's largest railroad hubs. In 1983, the latest year for which we have figures, Chicago's railroad yards handled the third highest volume of hazardous-material shipments in the nation. East St. Louis, which is also in Illinois, handled the second highest volume. With most hazardous chemicals (by volume of shipments) being at least as hazardous as acrylonitrile, it is unlikely — and certainly not demonstrated by the plaintiff — that they can be rerouted around all the metropolitan areas in the country, except at prohibitive cost. Even if it were feasible to reroute them one would hardly expect shippers, as distinct from carriers, to be the firms best situated to do the rerouting. Granted, the usual view is that common carriers are not subject to strict liability for the carriage of materials that make the transportation of them abnormally dangerous, because a common carrier cannot refuse service to a shipper of a lawful commodity. Restatement, supra, §521. Two courts, however, have rejected the common carrier exception. If it were rejected in Illinois, this would weaken still further the case for imposing strict liability on shippers whose goods pass through the densely inhabited portions of the state.

The difference between shipper and carrier points to a deep flaw in the plaintiff's case. Unlike *Guille,* and unlike *Siegler,* and unlike the storage cases, beginning with *Rylands* itself, here it is not the actors — that is, the transporters of acrylonitrile and other chemicals — but the manufacturers, who are sought to be held strictly liable. A shipper can in the bill of lading designate the route of his shipment if he likes, 49 U.S.C. §11710(a)(1), but is it realistic to suppose that shippers will become students of railroading in order to lay out the safest route by which to ship their goods? Anyway, rerouting is no panacea. Often it will increase the length of the journey, or compel the use of poorer track, or both. When this happens, the probability of an accident is increased, even if the consequences of an accident if one occurs are reduced; so the expected accident cost, being the product of the probability of an accident and the harm if the accident occurs, may rise. It is easy to see how the accident in this case might have been prevented at reasonable cost by greater care on the part of those who handled the tank car of acrylonitrile. It is difficult to see how it might have been prevented at reasonable cost by a change in the activity of transporting the chemical. This is therefore not an apt case for strict liability. . . .

In emphasizing the flammability and toxicity of acrylonitrile rather than the hazards of transporting it, as in failing to distinguish between the active and the passive shipper, the plaintiff overlooks the fact that ultrahazardousness or abnormal dangerousness is, in the contemplation of the law at least, a property not of substances, but of activities: not of acrylonitrile, but of the transportation of acrylonitrile by rail through populated areas. Natural gas is both flammable and poisonous, but the operation of a natural gas well is not an ultrahazardous activity. Whatever the situation under products liability law (section 402A of the Restatement), the manufacturer of a product is not considered to be engaged in an abnormally dangerous activity merely because the product becomes dangerous when it is handled or used in some way after it leaves his premises, even if the danger is foreseeable. The plaintiff does not suggest that Cyanamid should switch to making some less hazardous chemical that would substitute for acrylonitrile in the textiles and other goods in which acrylonitrile is used. Were this a feasible method of accident avoidance, there would be an argument for making manufacturers strictly liable for accidents that occur during the shipment of their products (how strong an argument we need not decide). Apparently it is not a feasible method.

The relevant activity is transportation, not manufacturing and shipping. This essential distinction the plaintiff ignores. But even if the plaintiff is treated as a transporter and not merely a shipper, it has not shown that the transportation of acrylonitrile in bulk by rail through populated areas is so hazardous an activity, even when due care is exercised, that the law should seek to create — perhaps quixotically — incentives to relocate the activity to nonpopulated areas, or to reduce the scale of the activity, or to switch to transporting acrylonitrile by road rather than by rail, perhaps to set the stage for a replay of Siegler v. Kuhlman. It is no more realistic to propose to reroute the shipment of all hazardous materials around Chicago than it is to propose the relocation of homes adjacent to the Blue Island switching yard to more distant suburbs. It may be less realistic. Brutal though it may seem to say it, the inappropriate use to which land is being put in the Blue Island yard and neighborhood may be, not the transportation of hazardous chemicals, but residential living. The analogy is to building your home between the runways at O'Hare.

The briefs hew closely to the Restatement, whose approach to the issue of strict liability is mainly allocative rather than distributive. By this we mean that the emphasis is on picking a liability regime (negligence or strict liability) that will control the particular class of accidents in question most effectively, rather than on finding the deepest pocket and placing liability there. At argument, however, the plaintiff's lawyer invoked distributive considerations by pointing out that Cyanamid is a huge firm and the Indiana Harbor Belt Railroad a fifty-mile-long switching line that almost went broke in the winter of 1979, when the accident occurred. Well, so what? A corporation is not a living person but a set of contracts the terms of which determine who will bear the brunt of liability. Tracing the incidence of a cost is a complex undertaking which the plaintiff sensibly has made no effort to assume, since its legal relevance would be dubious. We add only that however small the plaintiff may be, it has mighty parents: it is a jointly owned subsidiary of Conrail and the Soo line.

The case for strict liability has not been made. Not in this suit in any event. We need not speculate on the possibility of imposing strict liability on shippers of more hazardous materials, such as . . . bombs . . . any more than we need differentiate (given how the plaintiff has shaped its case) between active and passive shippers. We noted earlier that acrylonitrile is far from being the most hazardous among hazardous materials shipped by rail in highest volume. Or among materials shipped, period. . . .

The judgment is reversed (with no award of costs in this court) and the case remanded for further proceedings, consistent with this opinion, on the plaintiff's claim for negligence.

Reversed and remanded, with directions.

NOTES

1. The strict liability alternative. In Siegler v. Kuhlman, 502 P.2d 1181, 1184-1185 (Wash. 1973), the court defended the use of the strict liability regime of Rylands v. Fletcher for gasoline transported on public highways as follows:

> In many respects, hauling gasoline as freight is no more unusual, but more dangerous, than collecting water. When gasoline is carried as cargo — as distinguished from fuel for the carrier vehicle — it takes on uniquely hazardous characteristics, as does water impounded in large quantities. Dangerous in itself, gasoline develops even greater potential for harm when carried as freight — extraordinary dangers deriving from sheer quantity, bulk and weight, which enormously multiply its hazardous properties. And the very hazards inhering from the size of the load, its bulk or quantity and its movement along the highways presents another reason for application of the Fletcher v. Rylands rule not present in the impounding of large quantities of water — the likely destruction of cogent evidence from which negligence or want of it may be proved or disproved. It is quite probable that the most important ingredients of proof will be lost in a gasoline explosion and fire. Gasoline is always dangerous whether kept in large or small quantities because of its volatility, inflammability and explosiveness. But when several thousand gallons of it are allowed to spill across a public highway — that is, if, while in transit as freight, it is not kept impounded — the hazards to third persons are so great as to be almost beyond calculation. As a consequence of its escape from impoundment and subsequent explosion and ignition, the evidence in a very high percentage of instances will be destroyed, and the reasons for and causes contributing to its escape will quite likely be lost in the searing flames and explosions.

Do the different properties of acrylonitrile justify a different response? Note that in *Indiana Harbor Belt R.R.* the action was brought against the shipper but not the carrier. How does the Restatement rule apply to transporters? Posner's opinion represents one of the first explicit efforts to incorporate into the case law the activity-level/care-level distinction of Professor Shavell (see supra at page 199) by showing how difficult it would be for either the shipper or carrier to reroute the shipment of acrylonitrile. Posner's strategy has been critiqued in Gilles, Rule-Based Negligence and the Regulation of Activity Levels, 21 J. Legal Stud. 319, 337 (1992) as follows:

> On the record before the court, Posner's conclusion seems perfectly sound. But surely his ability to arrive at that conclusion undercuts the premise on which he undertook the inquiry in the first place. To conclude that spills of acrylonitrile probably could not "have been prevented at reasonable cost by a change in the activity of transporting the chemical" is, in substance, to determine that, as a rule, it is not negligent to transport acrylonitrile by rail rather than by other means or by rail through metropolitan areas rather than rerouting to avoid them. That is a rule-based determination of the very same activity-level negligence claims that Posner assumed the negligence standard could not handle.

E. NUISANCE

1. Private Nuisance

Morgan v. High Penn Oil Co.
77 S.E.2d 682 (N.C. 1953)

Appeal by defendants from Rudisill, J., and a jury, at January Term, 1953, of Guilford.

Civil action to recover temporary damages for a private nuisance, and to abate such nuisance by injunction.

The salient facts appear in the numbered paragraphs which immediately follow. . . .

2. The land of the plaintiffs is a composite tract, which they acquired by two separate purchases antedating 3 August, 1945. It contains a dwelling-house, a restaurant, and accommodations for thirty-two habitable trailers. The dwelling-house existed at the time of the purchases of the plaintiffs, and has been occupied by them as their home since 3 August, 1945. The plaintiffs constructed the restaurant and the trailer accommodations immediately after they established their residence on the premises, and have been renting these improvements since their completion to third persons. They have been supplementing their income from these sources by taking lodgers in their dwelling. . . .

5. The High Penn Oil Company operated the oil refinery at virtually all times between 10 October, 1950, and the date of the rendition of the judgment in this action. . . .

9. The oil refinery is approximately 1,000 feet from the dwelling of the plaintiffs.

10. These structures are situated within a radius of one mile of the oil refinery: a church; at least twenty-nine private dwellings; four tourist and trailer camps; a grocery store; two restaurants; a nursery appropriated to the propagation of young trees, shrubs, and plants; three motor vehicle service stations; two motor vehicle repair shops; a railroad track; the terminus of a gasoline pipe line; numerous large storage tanks capable of storing sixty million gallons of gasoline; and the headquarters of at least four motor truck companies engaged in the transportation of petroleum products and other property for hire. Railway tank cars and motor tank trucks are filled with gasoline at the storage tanks for conveyance to various places at virtually all hours of the day and night. . . .

16. The evidence of the plaintiffs tended to show that for some hours on two or three different days during each week of its operation by the High Penn Oil Company, the oil refinery emitted nauseating gases and odors in great quantities; that the nauseating gases and odors invaded

the nine acres owned by the plaintiffs and the other lands located within "a mile and three-quarters or two miles" of the oil refinery in such amounts and in such densities as to render persons of ordinary sensitiveness uncomfortable and sick; that the operation of the oil refinery thus substantially impaired the use and enjoyment of the nine acres by the plaintiffs and their renters; and that the defendants failed to put an end to the atmospheric pollution arising out of the operation of the oil refinery after notice and demand from the plaintiffs to abate it. The evidence of the plaintiffs tended to show, moreover, that the oil refinery was the only agency discharging gases or odors in annoying quantities into the air in the Friendship section. . . .

18. [The jury found that the defendant's oil refinery was a nuisance and awarded the plaintiff $2,500 in damages; and the trial judge then enjoined the defendant "from continuing the nuisance alleged in the complaint." The defendant excepted and appealed.]

ERVIN, J. . . . The High Penn Oil Company contends that the evidence is not sufficient to establish either an actionable or an abatable private nuisance. This contention rests on a twofold argument somewhat alternative in character. The High Penn Oil Company asserts primarily that private nuisances are classified as nuisances per se or at law, and nuisances per accidens or in fact; that when one carries on an oil refinery upon premises in his rightful occupation, he conducts a lawful enterprise, and for that reason does not maintain a nuisance per se or at law; that in such case the oil refinery can constitute a nuisance per accidens or in fact to the owner of neighboring land if, and only if, it is constructed or operated in a negligent manner; that there was no testimony at the trial tending to show that the oil refinery was constructed or operated in a negligent manner; and that consequently the evidence does not suffice to establish the existence of either an actionable or an abatable private nuisance. The High Penn Oil Company insists secondarily that the plaintiffs in a civil action can recover only on the case presented by their complaint; that the complaint in the instant action states a cause of action based solely on negligence; that there was no testimony at the trial indicating that the oil refinery was constructed or operated in a negligent manner; and that consequently the evidence is not sufficient to warrant the relief sought and obtained by the plaintiffs, even though it may be ample to establish a nuisance. . . .

The High Penn Oil Company asserts with complete correctness that private nuisances may be classified as nuisances per se or at law, and nuisances per accidens or in fact. A nuisance per se or at law is an act, occupation, or structure which is a nuisance at all times and under any circumstances, regardless of location or surroundings. Nuisances per accidens or in fact are those which become nuisances by reason of their location, or by reason of the manner in which they are constructed, maintained, or operated. The High Penn Oil Company also asserts with complete correctness that an oil refinery is a lawful enterprise and for that reason cannot be a nuisance per se or at law. The High Penn Oil Company falls into error, however, when it takes the position that an oil refinery cannot become a nuisance per accidens or in fact unless it is constructed or operated in a negligent manner.

Negligence and nuisance are distinct fields of tort liability. While the same act or omission may constitute negligence and also give rise to a private nuisance per accidens or in fact, and thus the two torts may coexist and be practically inseparable, a private nuisance per accidens or in fact may be created or maintained without negligence. Most private nuisances per accidens or in fact are intentionally created or maintained, and are redressed by the courts without allegation or proof of negligence. . . .

The law of private nuisance rests on the concept embodied in the ancient legal maxim Sic utere tuo ut alienum non laedas, meaning, in essence, that every person should so use his own property as not to injure that of another. As a consequence, a private nuisance exists in a legal sense when one makes an improper use of his own property and in that way injures the land or some incorporeal right of one's neighbor.

Much confusion exists in respect to the legal basis of liability in the law of private nuisance because of the deplorable tendency of the courts to call everything a nuisance, and let it go at that. The confusion on this score vanishes in large part, however, when proper heed is paid to the sound propositions that private nuisance is a field of tort liability rather than a single type of tortious conduct; that the feature which gives unity to this field of tort liability is the interest invaded, namely, the interest in the use and enjoyment of land; that any substantial non-trespassory invasion of another's interest in the private use and enjoyment of land by any type of liability forming conduct is a private nuisance; that the invasion which subjects a person to liability for private nuisance may be either intentional or unintentional; that a person is subject to liability for an intentional invasion when his conduct is unreasonable under the circumstances of the particular case; and that a person is subject to liability for an unintentional invasion when his conduct is negligent, reckless or ultrahazardous. . . .

An invasion of another's interest in the use and enjoyment of land is intentional in the law of private nuisance when the person whose conduct is in question as a basis for liability acts for the purpose of causing it, or knows that it is resulting from his conduct, or knows that it is substantially certain to result from his conduct. Restatement of the Law of Torts, section 825. A person who intentionally creates or maintains a private nuisance is liable for the resulting injury to others regardless of the degree of care or skill exercised by him to avoid such injury. . . .

One of America's greatest jurists, the late Benjamin N. Cardozo, made this illuminating observation on this aspect of the law: "Nuisance as a concept of the law has more meanings than one. The primary meaning does not involve the element of negligence as one of its essential factors. One acts sometimes at one's peril. In such circumstances, the duty to desist is absolute whenever conduct, if persisted in, brings damage to another. Illustrations are abundant. One who emits noxious fumes or gases day by day in the running of his factory may be liable to his neighbor though he has taken all available precautions. He is not to do such things at all, whether he is negligent or careful." McFarlane v. City of Niagara Falls, 247 N.Y. 340, 160 N.E. 391.

When the evidence is interpreted in the light most favorable to the plaintiffs, it suffices to support a finding that in operating the oil refinery the High Penn Oil Company intentionally and unreasonably caused noxious gases and odors to escape onto the nine acres of the plaintiffs to such a degree as to impair in a substantial manner the plaintiffs' use and enjoyment of their land. This being so, the evidence is ample to establish the existence of an actionable private nuisance, entitling the plaintiffs to recover temporary damages from the High Penn Oil Company. When the evidence is taken in the light most favorable to the plaintiffs, it also suffices to warrant the additional inferences that the High Penn Oil Company intends to operate the oil refinery in the future in the same manner as in the past; that if it is permitted to carry this intent into effect, the High Penn Oil Company will hereafter cast noxious gases and odors onto the nine acres of the plaintiffs with such recurring frequency and in such annoying density as to inflict irreparable injury upon the plaintiffs in the use and enjoyment of their home and their other adjacent properties; and that the issuance of an appropriate injunction is necessary to protect the plaintiffs against the threatened irreparable injury. This being true, the evidence is ample to establish the existence of an abatable private nuisance, entitling the plaintiffs to such mandatory or prohibitory injunctive relief as may be required to prevent the High Penn Oil Company from continuing the nuisance.

The contention of the High Penn Oil Company that the complaint states a cause of action based solely on negligence is untenable. To be sure, the plaintiffs assert that the defendants were "negligent and careless" in specified particulars in constructing and operating the oil refinery. When the complaint is construed as a whole, however, it alleges facts which show a private nuisance resulting from an intentional and unreasonable invasion of the plaintiffs' interest in the use and enjoyment of their land.

For the reasons given, the evidence is sufficient to withstand the motion of the High Penn Oil Company for a compulsory nonsuit.

NOTES

1. Definition of nuisance. Compare the definition of a nuisance given in Morgan v. High Penn with that provided by the California Civil Code:

> §3479. NUISANCE DEFINED
> Anything which is injurious to health, or is indecent or offensive to the senses, or an obstruction to the free use of property, so as to interfere with the comfortable enjoyment of life or property, or unlawfully obstructs the free passage or use, in the customary manner, of any navigable lake, or river, bay, stream, canal, or basin, or any public park, square, street, or highway, is a nuisance.

Does the statute or the common-law rule require that the nuisance in question be created by some act of the defendant? In Puritan Holding Co. v. Holloschitz, 372 N.Y.S.2d 500 (N.Y. Sup. Ct. 1975), the court held the defendant liable in nuisance when she abandoned and left in disrepair a building she owned in an urban renewal area in which property values had shown a marked increase. The court noted that she had acted in violation of the local administrative ordinance that required vacant buildings to be guarded or sealed. It further stated that her conduct might not constitute a nuisance in an area that had already deteriorated, and allowed plaintiff damages measured by the loss in market value attributable to the defendant's nuisance.

The act requirement was also tested in Merriam v. McConnell, 175 N.E.2d 293 (Ill. App. 1961), where the court held that the bugs infesting the plaintiff's trees did not constitute a nuisance because the defendant had not placed them there. See also Robinson v. Whitelaw, 364 P.2d 1085 (Utah 1961), which denied an action for damage caused by sand and dirt deposited on plaintiff's property after the defendant cut the sagebrush and natural growth off his land to make way for future cultivation that he never undertook. The court noted that the "defendant would have difficulty in stopping the wind or replacing the sagebrush. . . ." What result if the land were cleared in order to vex the plaintiff?

2. Trespass or nuisance. The line between trespassory and nontrespassory invasions, referred to in *Morgan* has often proved important to draw, often for reasons that have little to do with plaintiff's basic right of action. Thus, in Martin v. Reynolds Metals Co., 342 P.2d 790 (Or. 1959), the defendants had released quantities of fluoride gas that became airborne and settled on adjacent land, rendering it unfit for cattle grazing and watering. The defendants claimed that the plaintiff's cause of action sounded in nuisance, for which the applicable statute of limitations was only two years. The court, however, agreed with the plaintiff's contention that the defendant's conduct amounted to an actionable trespass, to which a six-year statute of limitation applied.

The court noted, too, that the question of trespass or nuisance could be important on substantive issues as well, pointing out that the defense of "coming to the nuisance," at page 700 infra, is, almost by definition, inapplicable to a trespass case. If trespass involves the direct and immediate application of force against the person or property of another, can the court's position in *Martin* be defended? See Merrill, Trespass, Nuisance, and the Costs of Determining Property Rights, 14 J. Legal Stud. 13 (1985).

3. *Fear of invasion as a nuisance.* How indispensable is the nontrespassory invasion to the right of action? In Adkins v. Thomas Solvent Co., 487 N.W.2d 715, 726, 728 (Mich. 1992), toxic leaks from the defendant's operations leaked into the groundwater system. Some 22 of the original plaintiffs sought recovery not for physical damage but for the depreciation in property values attributable to unfavorable publicity and the *unfounded* belief that such contamination would take place. The expert evidence from both parties established that plaintiffs' "properties were not and would never be subject to ground water contamination emanating from the defendants' property." Boyle, J., first reviewed the historical evolution of nuisance law and noted that the historical evolution of the law of nuisance involved a relaxation of the requirement that the defendant enter the plaintiff's land, but did not eliminate the need for nontrespassory invasive conduct lacking in this case, and it held that "negative publicity resulting in unfounded fear about dangers in the vicinity of the property does not constitute a significant interference with the use and enjoyment of land." It also observed:

> In short we do not agree with the dissent's suggestion that wholly unfounded fears of third parties regarding the conduct of a lawful business satisfy the requirement for a legally cognizable harm injury as long as property values decline. Indeed we would think it only "odd" (Levin, J., dissenting) but anachronistic that a claim of nuisance in fact could be based on unfounded fears regarding persons with AIDS moving into a neighborhood, the establishment of otherwise lawful group homes for the disabled, or unrelated persons living together, merely because the fears experienced by third parties would cause a decline in property values.

The dissent of Levin, J., took a narrower view of the scope of liability:

> We would hold that a homeowner may maintain a nuisance action to recover damages for a decline in the market value of his home that reflects interference with the use and enjoyment of his home by a condition tortiously created or maintained by the defendant on neighboring property, and that the homeowner may do so without demonstrating interference with use or enjoyment that might result in further, separately compensable injuries to persons or property.

How should the court decide the case if a buyer backed out of a purchase on the strength of the unfounded rumors? If it were unclear that the threatened pollution might reach the plaintiff's property? How should regulators respond to the risks?

4. *Reasonableness in the law of nuisance.* Most accounts of the nuisance law provide that the defendant's invasive conduct is actionable only if it constitutes an "unreasonable" interference with the plaintiff's use and enjoyment of his or her own property. One view is that this reasonableness language imports general negligence principles into the law of nuisance, so that the ultimate question is whether the expected benefits of the challenged activities exceed their expected costs. Thus section 826 of the Restatement (Second) provides:

> §826. UNREASONABLENESS OF INTENTIONAL INVASION
> An intentional invasion of another's interest in the use and enjoyment of land is unreasonable if
>   (a) the gravity of the harm outweighs the utility of the actor's conduct, or
>   (b) the harm caused by the conduct is serious and the financial burden of compensating for this and similar harm to others would not make the continuation of the conduct not feasible.

This view appears to have been adopted in Copart Industries, Inc. v. Consolidated Edison, 362 N.E.2d 968, 971 (N.Y. 1977). There the plaintiff, an operator of a new car storage and preparation business, alleged that the emissions from the smokestacks of a nearby Con Ed plant damaged the finishes on his and his customers' cars, forcing him out of business. The Court of Appeals affirmed the judgment for the defendant below, noting the limited basis of liability in nuisance cases:

> Despite early private nuisance cases, which apparently assumed that the defendant was strictly liable, today it is recognized that one is subject to liability for a private nuisance if his conduct is a legal cause of the invasion of the interest in the private use and enjoyment of land and such invasion is (1) intentional and unreasonable, (2) negligent or reckless, or (3) actionable under the rules governing liability for abnormally dangerous conditions or activities.

A more hostile reception to negligence principles in nuisance cases is found in Jost v. Dairyland Power Cooperative, 172 N.W.2d 647, 650-652 (Wis. 1969), where discharges of sulfur dioxide resulted in substantial damages to the plaintiff's land. There the court adopted a strict liability rule for damages that the jury had found "substantial":

> Plaintiffs' attorney from the outset made it clear that liability was predicated on the *fact* that sulphur dioxide gases were emitted into the atmosphere, despite complaints over a period of several years. There was no attempt to hinge plaintiffs' case on the theory that the defendant was not

exercising due care. Under the plaintiffs' theory, which we deem to be a correct one, it is irrelevant that defendant was conforming to industry standards of due care if its conduct created a nuisance.

The court relied here on the explication of substantial injury contained in section 827 of the Second Restatement:

> [W]here the invasion involves physical damage to tangible property, the gravity of the harm is ordinarily regarded as great even though the extent of the harm is relatively small. But where the invasion involves only personal discomfort and annoyance, the gravity of the harm is generally regarded as slight unless the invasion is substantial and continuing. . . .
>
> In any event it is apparent that a continued invasion of a plaintiff's interests by nonnegligent conduct, when the actor knows of the nature of the injury inflicted, is an intentional tort, and the fact the hurt is administered nonnegligently is not a defense for liability.

Does *Jost* tie reasonableness solely to the *level* of the defendant's invasive activities, so that once a given threshold is reached the case is actionable under a strict liability theory?

5. *Absolute property rights.* The rhetoric of absolute property rights, which is so dominant in the law of trespass, takes on much more muted tones in the law of nuisance where the hard-edges of property boundaries yield if only because the number and frequency of low-level invasions makes it quite undesirable to give universal redress for all nuisance-like events. For an elaboration of concern see Epstein, Nuisance Law: Corrective Justice and its Utilitarian Constraints, 8 J. Legal Stud. 49, 74-79, 82-90 (1979), where the following considerations are used to justify the relaxation of the otherwise absolute common-law right to be wholly free from physical interference with the possession or use of property:

1. High administrative costs for claim resolution;
2. High transaction costs for voluntary reassignment of rights;
3. Low value to the interested parties of the ownership rights whose rearrangement is mandated by the public rule;
4. Presence of implicit in-kind compensation from all to all that precludes any systematic redistribution of wealth among the interested parties.

6. *Live and let live.* One discrete application of the above concerns is found in the "live and let live" rule whose rationale is put in modern language by Bramwell, B., in Bamford v. Turnley, 122 Eng. Rep. 27, 32-33 (Ex. 1862):

> The instances put during the argument, of burning weeds, emptying cess-pools, making noises during repairs, and other instances which be

nuisances if done wantonly or maliciously, nevertheless may be lawfully done. It cannot be said that such acts are not nuisances, because, by the hypothesis they are; and it cannot be doubted that, if a person maliciously and without cause made close to a dwelling-house the same offensive smells as may be made in emptying a cesspool, an action would lie. Nor can these cases be got rid of as extreme cases, because such cases properly test a principle. Nor can it be said that the jury settle such questions by finding there is no nuisance, though there is. . . .

There must be, then, some principle on which such cases must be excepted. It seems to me that that principle may be deduced from the character of these cases, and is this, viz., that those acts necessary for the common and ordinary use and occupation of land and houses may be done, if conveniently done, without submitting those who do them to an action. . . . There is an obvious necessity for such a principle as I have mentioned. It is as much for the advantage of one owner as of another for the very nuisance the one complains of, as the result of the ordinary use of his neighbour's land, he himself will create in the ordinary use of his own, and the reciprocal nuisances are of a comparatively trifling character. The convenience of such a rule may be indicated by calling it a rule of give and take, live and let live. . . .

The public consists of all the individuals of it, and a thing is only for the public benefit when it is productive of good to those individuals on the balance of loss and gain to all. So that if all the loss and all the gain were borne and received by one individual, he on the whole would be the gainer. But whenever this is the case, — whenever a thing is for the public benefit, properly understood, — the loss to the individuals of the public who lose will bear compensation out of the gains of those who gain. It is for the public benefit there should be railways, but it would not be unless the gain of having the railway was sufficient to compensate the loss occasioned by the use of the land required for its site; and accordingly no one thinks it would be right to take an individual's land without compensation to make a railway.

Bramwell's endorsement of the "live and let live" principle shows the connection between the requirement of just compensation and the principle of reciprocity. Since all interferences are "reciprocal" in character, no party may easily claim that he has been made worse off or that his neighbor alone has profited, for virtually *all* parties are left better off under the regime of "live and let live" for minimal harms. Because that system eliminates litigation over relatively small inconveniences, it reduces the administrative costs necessary to police the unhappy interactions between neighbors. As stated, moreover, the rule contains its own limitations. When it is clear that the damage in question is substantial, it becomes more likely, first, that the inconvenience to the two parties will no longer be of equal magnitude and, second, that the administrative costs of dispute resolution will shrink in comparison to the amount in controversy.

For the classic discussion of the impact of transaction costs on market transactions see Coase, The Problem of Social Cost, 3 J.L. & Econ. 1 (1960). For the connection between Bramwell's general views and the modern tests of social welfare see Coleman, Efficiency, Utility and Wealth Maximization, 8 Hofstra L. Rev. 509 (1980). For the connection between nuisance law and eminent domain see R. Epstein, Takings: Private Property and the Power of Eminent Domain 199-202, 229-238 (1985).

7. *Locality rule.* The principle of reciprocity also helps explain another feature of nuisance law that has no parallel in the law of trespass, the so-called locality rule. Its underpinnings are well illustrated by a passage from the opinion of Earl, J., in Campbell v. Seaman, 63 N.Y. 568, 576-577 (1876), a case in which the fumes from the defendant's brick factory destroyed the trees and vegetation upon the plaintiff's land.

> It is a general rule that every person may exercise exclusive dominion over his own property, and subject it to such uses as will best subserve his private interests. Generally, no other person can say how he shall use or what he shall do with his property. But this general right of property has its exceptions and qualifications. Sic utere tuo ut alienum non laedas is an old maxim which has a broad application. It does not mean that one must never use his own so as to do any injury to his neighbor or his property. Such a rule could not be enforced in civilized society. Persons living in organized communities must suffer some damage, annoyance and inconvenience from each other. For these they are compensated by all the advantages of civilized society. If one lives in the city he must expect to suffer the dirt, smoke, noisome odors, noise and confusion incident to city life. . . .
>
> But every person is bound to make a reasonable use of his property so as to occasion no unnecessary damage or annoyance to his neighbor. If he make an unreasonable, unwarrantable or unlawful use of it, so as to produce material annoyance, inconvenience, discomfort or hurt to his neighbor, he will be guilty of a nuisance to his neighbor. And the law will hold him responsible for the consequent damage. As to what is a reasonable use of one's own property cannot be defined by any certain general rules, but must depend upon the circumstances of each case. A use of property in one locality and under some circumstances may be lawful and reasonable, which, under other circumstances, would be unlawful, unreasonable and a nuisance. To constitute a nuisance, the use must be such as to produce a tangible and appreciable injury to neighboring property, or such as to render its enjoyment specially uncomfortable or inconvenient.
>
> Within the rules thus referred to, that defendant's brick burning was a nuisance to plaintiffs cannot be doubted.

As the outcome in *Campbell* indicates, the locality rule does not afford a defendant absolute immunity from suit. "A dweller in towns cannot expect to have as pure air, as free from smoke, smell and noise as if he lived in the country . . . and yet an excess of smoke, smell, and noise may give a cause of action, but in each of such cases it becomes a question of degree. . . ." Colls v. Home & Colonial Stores, [1904] A.C. 179, 185.

Fontainebleau Hotel Corp. v. Forty-Five Twenty-Five, Inc.
114 So. 2d 357 (Fla. App. 1959)

PER CURIAM. This is an interlocutory appeal from an order temporarily enjoining the appellants from continuing with the construction of a fourteen-story addition to the Fontainebleau Hotel, owned and operated by the appellants. Appellee, plaintiff below, owns the Eden Roc Hotel, which was constructed in 1955, about a year after the Fontainebleau, and adjoins the Fontainebleau on the north. Both are luxury hotels, facing the Atlantic Ocean. The proposed addition to the Fontainebleau is being constructed twenty feet from its north property line, 130 feet from the mean high water mark of the Atlantic Ocean, and 76 feet 8 inches from the ocean bulkhead line. The 14-story tower will extend 160 feet above grade in height and is 416 feet long from east to west. During the winter months, from around two o'clock in the afternoon for the remainder of the day, the shadow of the addition will extend over the cabana, swimming pool, and sunbathing areas of the Eden Roc, which are located in the southern portion of its property.

In this action, plaintiff-appellee sought to enjoin the defendants-appellants from proceeding with the construction of the addition to the Fontainebleau (it appears to have been roughly eight stories high at the time suit was filed), alleging that the construction would interfere with the light and air on the beach in front of the Eden Roc and cast a shadow of such size as to render the beach wholly unfitted for the use and enjoyment of its guests, to the irreparable injury of the plaintiff; further, that the construction of such addition on the north side of defendant's property, rather than the south side, was actuated by malice and ill will on the part of the defendants' president toward the plaintiff's president; and that the construction was in violation of a building ordinance requiring a 100-foot setback from the ocean. It was also alleged that the construction would interfere with the easements of light and air enjoyed by plaintiff and its predecessors in title for more than twenty years and "impliedly granted by virtue of the acts of the plaintiff's predecessors in title, as well as under the common law and the express recognition of such rights by virtue of Chapter 9837, Laws of Florida 1923. . . ." Some attempt was also made to allege an easement by implication in favor of the plaintiff's property, as the dominant, and against the defendants' property, as the servient, tenement.

The defendants' answer denied the material allegations of the complaint, pleaded laches and estoppel by judgment.

The chancellor heard considerable testimony on the issues made by the complaint and the answer and, as noted, entered a temporary injunction restraining the defendants from continuing with the construction of the addition. His reason for so doing was stated by him, in a memorandum opinion, as follows:

"In granting the temporary injunction in this case the Court wishes to make several things very clear. The ruling is not based on any alleged presumptive title nor prescriptive right of the plaintiff to light and air nor is it based on any deed restrictions nor recorded plats in the title of the plaintiff nor of the defendant nor of any plat of record. It is not based on any zoning ordinance nor on any provision of the building code of the City of Miami Beach nor on the decision of any court, nisi prius or appellate. It is based solely on the proposition that no one has a right to use his property to the injury of another. In this case it is clear from the evidence that the proposed use by the Fontainebleau will materially damage the Eden Roc. There is evidence indicating that the construction of the proposed annex by the Fontainebleau is malicious or deliberate for the purpose of injuring the Eden Roc, but it is scarcely sufficient, standing alone, to afford a basis for equitable relief."

This is indeed a novel application of the maxim sic utere tuo ut alienum non laedas. This maxim does not mean that one must never use his own property in such a way as to do any injury to his neighbor. It means only that one must use his property so as not to injure the lawful *rights* of another. In Reaver v. Martin Theatres, Fla. 1951, 52 So. 2d 682, 683, 25 A.L.R.2d 1451, under this maxim, it was stated that "it is well settled that a property owner may put his own property to any reasonable and lawful use, so long as he does not thereby deprive the adjoining landowner of any right of enjoyment of his property *which is recognized and protected by law, and so long as his use is not such a one as the law will pronounce a nuisance.*" [Emphasis supplied.]

No American decision has been cited, and independent research has revealed none, in which it has been held that — in the absence of some contractual or statutory obligation — a landowner has a legal right to the free flow of light and air across the adjoining land of his neighbor. Even at common law, the landowner had no legal right, in the absence of an easement or uninterrupted use and enjoyment for a period of 20 years, to unobstructed light and air from the adjoining land. And the English doctrine of "ancient lights" has been unanimously repudiated in this country. 1 Am. Jur., Adjoining Landowners, §49, p. 533.

There being, then, no legal right to the free flow of light and air from the adjoining land, it is universally held that where a structure serves a useful and beneficial purpose, it does not give rise to a cause of action, either for damages or for an injunction under the maxim sic utere tuo ut alienum non laedas, even though it causes injury to another by cutting off the light and air and interfering with the view that would otherwise be available over adjoining land in its natural state, regardless of the fact that the structure may have been erected partly for spite.

We see no reason for departing from this universal rule. If, as contended on behalf of plaintiff, public policy demands that a landowner in the Miami Beach area refrain from constructing buildings on his premises that will cast a shadow on the adjoining premises, an amendment of its comprehensive planning and zoning ordinance, applicable to the public as a whole, is the means by which such purpose should be achieved. (No opinion is expressed here as to the validity of such an ordinance, if one should be enacted pursuant to the requirements of law. But to change the universal rule — and the custom followed in this state since its inception — that adjoining landowners have an equal right under the law to build to the line of their respective tracts and to such a height as is desired by them (in the absence, of course, of building restrictions or regulations) amounts, in our opinion, to judicial legislation. As stated in Musumeci v. Leonardo [77 R.I. 255, 75 A.2d 177], "So use your own as not to injure another's property is, indeed, a sound and salutary principle for the promotion of justice, but it may not and should not be applied so as gratuitously to confer upon an adjacent property owner incorporeal rights incidental to his ownership of land which the law does not sanction."

[Reversed.]

NOTES

1. *Cast a giant shadow: an easement of light.* As the court in *Fontainebleau* noted, American courts traditionally rejected a common-law easement for the light and air that pass over a neighbor's property on the ground that such a rule would inhibit the growth of both towns and industry. Height restrictions have, however, often been imposed by legislation and these have uniformly been sustained against challenges under the takings clause of the Constitution. On the vexed relationship between the law of nuisance and the law of eminent domain see generally Michelman, Property, Utility, and Fairness: Comments on the Ethical Formulations of "Just Compensation" Law, 80 Harv. L. Rev. 1165 (1967); see also Miller v. Schoene, 276 U.S. 272 (1928).

A very different approach to the easement of light was taken in Prah v. Maretti, 321 N.W.2d 182, 189-190, 191 (Wis. 1982). There the plaintiff and the defendant owned adjoining plots in a subdivision, with the defendant's land located to the south of the plaintiff's. The defendant wished to construct a house on his plot that conformed to all applicable subdivision and zoning restrictions. The plaintiff sought to enjoin the proposed construction until the defendant relocated it on the site, claiming that the defendant's proposed house would impair the efficiency of the plaintiff's solar heating system by blocking off the sunlight during part of the year.

The trial court granted the defendant's motion for summary judgment, but the Wisconsin Supreme Court reversed, and explicitly repudiated *Fontainebleau,* holding that summary judgment was precluded on the ground that an "unreasonable obstruction of access to sunlight might be a private nuisance." The court noted that easements of light could be acquired by prescription under the English doctrine of "ancient lights" and everywhere by express grant. It then addressed the traditional reluctance to respect solar easements:

> First, society has increasingly regulated the use of land by the landowner for the general welfare.
> Second, access to sunlight has taken on a new significance in recent years. In this case the plaintiff seeks to protect access to sunlight, not for aesthetic reasons or as a source of illumination but as a source of energy. Access to sunlight as an energy source is of significance both to the landowner who invests in solar collectors and to a society which has an interest in developing alternative sources of energy.
> Third, the policy of favoring unhindered private development in an expanding economy is no longer in harmony with the realities of our society. The need for easy and rapid development is not as great today as it once was, while our perception of the value of sunlight as a source of energy has increased significantly.
> Courts should not implement obsolete policies that have lost their vigor over the course of the years. The law of private nuisance is better suited to resolve landowners' disputes about property development in the 1980's than is a rigid rule which does not recognize a landowner's interest in access to sunlight.
> [The court then concluded that summary judgment was inappropriate because:] The application of the reasonable use standard in nuisance cases normally requires a full exposition of all underlying facts and circumstances. Too little is known in this case of such matters as the extent of the harm to the plaintiff, the suitability of solar heat in that neighborhood, the availability of remedies to the plaintiff, and the costs to the defendant of avoiding the harm.

A lengthy dissent argued many points including, first, that there was no "invasion" by the defendant, second, that solar energy had not proved itself in the marketplace, and, third, that the elaborate legislative scheme in place should not be displaced by a parallel judicial innovation.

In Tenn v. 889 Associates, Ltd., 500 A.2d 366, 371 (N.H. 1985), the court sought to steer a middle course between *Fontainebleau* and *Prah*. The court first rejected the hard-line proposition that the doctrine of ancient lights could never limit a neighbor's right to build, and held that "there is no reason in principle why the law of nuisance should not be applied to claims for the protection of a property owner's interests in light and air." Nonetheless, on the facts of the case it refused to enjoin defendant's plans to construct a six-story office building at the property line just south of the plaintiff's own six-story building.

> The sites were in the downtown commercial area of Manchester, where buildings commonly buttress and block the sides of adjacent structures. Moreover, the defendant proposed to do no more than the plaintiff's own predecessor had done, by building right to the lot line and to a

height of six stories. If, as the plaintiff claimed, this would require expenditures for additional artificial lighting and ventilation systems, she failed to present any evidence that the costs would exceed what was customarily necessary for such buildings.

On the question of private nuisances and solar easements see generally Williams, Solar Access and Property Rights: A Maverick Analysis, 11 Conn. L. Rev. 430, 443 (1979); Goble, Solar Access and Property Rights: Reply to a "Maverick" Analysis, 12 Conn. L. Rev. 270 (1980).

2. *Spite fences.* It has often been held that "a fence erected maliciously, and with no other purpose than to shut out the light and air from a neighbor's window, is a nuisance." Flaherty v. Moran, 45 N.W. 381 (Mich. 1890). This proposition tracks the logic of the live and let live rule insofar as it rests on the belief that all individuals are better off if each is denied the right to construct fences solely out of malice. Yet those courts that regard spite fences as actionable nuisances are quick to qualify their conclusions. Thus, in Kuzniak v. Kozminski, 65 N.W. 275 (Mich. 1895), the defendant moved his coal and wood shed close to the plaintiff's property line, where it blocked the light and air to plaintiff's windows. The shed was moved in part out of malice, but nonetheless the court refused to extend the spite fence doctrine because the shed itself served some "useful purpose." What about spite fences with useful functions? How might *Prah* be distinguished from the spite fence cases?

3. *Noninvasive nuisances: of ugly things and beautiful views.* Is it a nuisance if the defendant paints his house the most horrendous shade of pink, thereby driving down the value of the neighboring houses? Is there ever a form of aesthetic blight so inconsistent with the character of a neighborhood that it should be treated by the courts as a nuisance? In Mathewson v. Primeau, 395 P.2d 183 (Wash. 1964), the court, while willing to enjoin the raising of hogs on the defendant's land because their odors reached the plaintiff's property, nonetheless refused to require the defendant to remove the collection of junk from his land, holding the law of nuisance was not concerned with aesthetics. Is that result better defended by arguing that if there is no physical invasion there is no nuisance, or by arguing that while there may be aesthetic nuisances in some cases, it is impossible to specify by common-law adjudication the appropriate standards to govern them?

Rodgers v. Elliott
15 N.E. 768 (Mass. 1888)

[The facts of the case, somewhat abbreviated, are as follows: The defendant operated a large church bell in a small Massachusetts town, which he rang regularly each day. The plaintiff was recovering from a serious case of sunstroke in a house located not far from the church. One Saturday the plaintiff suffered severe convulsions attributed by his physician to the noise generated by the bell. After the Saturday episode the physician informed the defendant of the condition of his patient and indicated that further convulsions would ensue if the defendant rang the bell the next day. After he received this warning, the defendant said he would ring his bell as usual the next day because he had no love for the plaintiff. He added that he would ring it even if his mother were ill. The next day the defendant rang his bell and the plaintiff suffered further damage, for which he brought this action.]

KNOWLTON, J. The defendant was the custodian and authorized manager of property of the Roman Catholic Church used for religious worship. The acts for which the plaintiff seeks to hold him responsible were done in the use of this property, and the sole question before us is whether or not that use was unlawful. The plaintiff's case rests upon the proposition that the ringing of the bell was a nuisance. The consideration of this proposition involves an inquiry into what the defendant could properly do in the use of the real estate which he had in charge, and what was the standard by which his rights were to be measured.

It appears that the church was built upon a public street in a thickly settled part of the town, and if the ringing of the bell on Sundays had materially affected the health or comfort of all in the vicinity, whether residing or passing there, this use of the property would have been a public nuisance, for which there would have been a remedy by indictment. Individuals suffering from it in their persons or their property could have recovered damages for a private nuisance. Wesson v. Washburn Iron Co., 13 Allen 95.

In an action of this kind, a fundamental question is, by what standard, as against the interests of a neighbor, is one's right to use his real estate to be measured. In densely populated communities the use of property in many ways which are legitimate and proper necessarily affects in greater or less degree the property or persons of others in the vicinity. In such cases the inquiry always is, when rights are called in question, what is reasonable under the circumstances. If a use of property is objectionable solely on account of the noise which it makes, it is a nuisance, if at all, by reason of its effect upon the health or comfort of those who are within hearing. The right to make a noise for a proper purpose must be measured in reference to the degree of annoyance which others may reasonably be required to submit to. In connection with the importance of the business from which it proceeds, that must be determined by the effect of noise upon people generally, and not upon those, on the one hand, who are peculiarly susceptible to it, or those, on the other, who by long experience have learned to endure it without inconvenience; not upon those whose strong nerves and robust

health enable them to endure the greatest disturbances without suffering, nor upon those whose mental or physical condition makes them
painfully sensitive to everything about them.

That this must be the rule in regard to public nuisances is obvious. It
is the rule as well, and for reasons nearly if not quite as satisfactory, in
relation to private nuisances. Upon a question whether one can lawfully
ring his factory bell, or run his noisy machinery, or whether the noise
will be a private nuisance to the occupant of a house near by, it is
necessary to ascertain the natural and probable effect of the sound
upon ordinary persons in that house, — not how it will affect a particular person, who happens to be there to-day, or who may chance to come
to-morrow. St. Helen's Smelting Co. v. Tipping, 11 H.L. Cas. 642.

In the case of Westcott v. Middleton, 16 Stew. (N.J.) 478, it appeared
that the defendant carried on the business of an undertaker, and the
windows of the plaintiff's house looked out upon his yard, where boxes
which had been used to preserve the bodies of the dead were frequently
washed, and where other objects were visible and other work was going
on, which affected the tender sensibilities of the plaintiff, and caused
him great discomfort. Vice-Chancellor Bird, in dismissing the bill for
an injunction against carrying on the business there, said: "The inquiry
inevitably arises, if a decision is rendered in Mr. Westcott's favor because he is so morally or mentally constituted that the particular business complained of is an offence or a nuisance to him, or destructive
to his comfort or his enjoyment of his home, how many other cases will
arise and claim the benefit of the same principle, however different the
facts may be, or whatever may be the mental condition of the party
complaining. . . . A wide range has indeed been given to courts of
equity in dealing with these matters; but I can find no case where the
court has extended aid unless the act complained of was, as I have
above said, of a nature to affect all reasonable persons, similarly situated, alike."

If one's right to use his property were to depend upon the effect of
the use upon a person of peculiar temperament or disposition, or upon
one suffering from an uncommon disease, the standard for measuring
it would be so uncertain and fluctuating as to paralyze industrial enterprises. The owner of a factory containing noisy machinery, with dwelling-houses all about it, might find his business lawful as to all but one
of the tenants of the houses, and as to that one, who dwelt no nearer
than the others, it might be a nuisance. The character of his business
might change from legal to illegal, or illegal to legal, with every change
of tenants of an adjacent estate or with an arrival or departure of a
guest or boarder at a house near by or even with the wakefulness or the
tranquil repose of an invalid neighbor on a particular night. Legal
rights to the use of property cannot be left to such uncertainty. When
an act is of such a nature as to extend its influence to those in the

vicinity, and its legal quality depends upon the effect of that influence, it is as important that the rightfulness of it should be tried by the experience of ordinary people, as it is, in determining a question as to negligence, that the test should be the common care of persons of ordinary prudence, without regard to the peculiarities of him whose conduct is on trial.

In the case at bar it is not contended that the ringing of the bell for church services in the manner shown by the evidence materially affected the health or comfort of ordinary people in the vicinity, but the plaintiff's claim rests upon the injury done him on account of his peculiar condition. However his request should have been treated by the defendant upon considerations of humanity, we think he could not put himself in a place of exposure to noise, and demand as of legal right that the bell should not be used.

The plaintiff, in his brief, concedes that there was no evidence of express malice on the part of the defendant, but contends that malice was implied in his acts. In the absence of evidence that he acted wantonly, or with express malice, this implication could not come from his exercise of his legal rights. How far and under what circumstances malice may be material in cases of this kind, it is unnecessary to consider.

Judgment on the verdict.

NOTES

1. Extrasensitive plaintiffs under the law of nuisance. Is there any way to reconcile the result in Rodgers v. Elliott with the general rule applicable in trespass and negligence cases, that the defendant takes his victim as he finds him? If it had been found in Rodgers v. Elliott that an ordinary person would have suffered substantial discomfort but no physical injuries from the ringing of the bells, could the plaintiff have recovered for the full extent of his injuries? Could the defendant claim a prescriptive easement, based on long use, against the public at large?

The Restatement (Second) of Torts follows the rule in *Rodgers* by stating in section 821F: "There is liability for a nuisance only to those to whom it causes significant harm, of a kind that would be suffered by a normal person in the community or by property in normal condition and used for a normal purpose."

2. The extrasensitive use of plaintiff's property. The extrasensitivity issue in nuisance cases arises not only in connection with personal injuries, but also with property damage. In Belmar Drive-In Theater v. Illinois State Toll Highway Comm., 216 N.E.2d 788 (Ill. 1966), the defendants operated a toll-road service center that was adjoined to the plaintiff's outdoor movie theater. The charge in the complaint was that the "brilliant artificial lights" used in the service area "dispelled" the darkness, making it impossible for the plaintiff to exhibit his outdoor movies, reducing the value of the plaintiff's theater. The court denied the plaintiff's cause of action, relying on the extrasensitivity test. How should *Belmar* be decided if the plaintiff must show the defendant's "invasion" of his premises? What if the defendant could have constructed its tollway service center so as not to cast light on the plaintiff's theater? Does it make a difference that the defendant was a governmental agency?

Belmar was expressly distinguished in Page County Appliance Center v. Honeywell, 347 N.W.2d 171, 175, 176 (Iowa 1984). There the defendant Honeywell installed a computer in a local travel agency as part of defendant ITT's plan to lease computers to retail travel outlets nationwide. The computer leaked extensive amounts of radiation, which interfered with the pictures on display television sets in plaintiff's nearby appliance store. Honeywell's efforts to fix the computers were to no avail because the "interference-causing radiation was a design and not a service problem." The jury awarded the plaintiff $221,000 in damages ($71,000 compensatory, $150,000 exemplary) and the judge required Honeywell to make full indemnity to ITT. The judgment was affirmed on appeal.

> In the case before us, ITT asserts the Appliance Center's display televisions constituted a hypersensitive use of its premises as a matter of law, and equates this situation to cases involving light thrown on outdoor theater screens in which light-throwing defendants have carried the day. *See Belmar . . .*
>
> We cannot equate the rare outdoor theater screen with the ubiquitous television that exists, in various numbers in almost every home. Clearly, the presence of televisions on any premises is not such an abnormal condition that we can say, as a matter of law, that the owner has engaged in a *peculiarly* sensitive use of the property.

On the question of extrasensitivity see generally Ellickson, Alternatives to Zoning: Covenants, Nuisance Rules, and Fines as Land Use Controls, 40 U. Chi. L. Rev. 681, 751-757 (1973).

Ensign v. Walls
34 N.W.2d 549 (Mich. 1948)

CARR, J. Defendant herein has for some years past carried on at 13949 Dacosta Street, in the City of Detroit, the business of raising, breeding and boarding St. Bernard dogs. Plaintiffs are property owners and residents in the immediate neighborhood. Claiming that the business conducted by defendant constituted a nuisance as to them and their property, plaintiffs brought suit for injunctive relief. The bill of complaint alleged that obnoxious odors came from defendant's premises at all times, that the continual barking of the dogs interfered with and disturbed plaintiffs in the use and enjoyment of their respective properties, that the premises were infested with rats and flies, and that on occasions dogs escaped from defendant's premises and roamed about the neighborhood. Defendant in her answer denied that her business was conducted in such a manner as to constitute a nuisance, and claimed further that she had carried on the business at the premises in question since 1926, that she had invested a considerable sum of money in the purchase of the property and in the subsequent erection of buildings thereon, and that under the circumstances plaintiffs were not entitled to the relief sought. . . .

[The court then concluded that the evidence supported the finding that the defendant's business constituted a nuisance to the plaintiffs and that the defendant had not acquired by prescriptive use the right to continue the nuisance.]

The record discloses that the plaintiffs, or the majority of them at least, have moved into the neighborhood in recent years. In view of this situation it is claimed by defendant that, inasmuch as she was carrying on her business of raising, breeding and boarding dogs on her premises at the time plaintiffs established their residences in the neighborhood, they cannot now be heard to complain. Such circumstance may properly be taken into account in a proceeding of this nature in determining whether the relief sought ought, in equity and good conscience, to be granted. Doubtless under such circumstances courts of equity are more reluctant to restrain the continued operation of a lawful business than in instances where it is sought to begin in a residential district a business of such character that it will constitute a nuisance. The Supreme Court of Pennsylvania in Wier's Appeal, 74 Pa. 230, declared the commonly accepted rule as follows:

"There is a very marked distinction to be observed in reason and equity between the case of a business long established in a particular locality, which has become a nuisance from the growth of population and the erection of dwellings in proximity to it, and that of a new erection threatened in such a vicinity. Carrying on an offensive trade for any number of years in a place remote from buildings and public roads, does not entitle the owner to continue it in the same place after houses have been built and roads laid out in the neighborhood, to the occupants of which and travellers upon which it is a nuisance. As the city extends, such nuisances should be removed to the vacant grounds beyond the immediate neighborhood of the residences of the citizens. This, public policy, as well as the health and comfort of the population of the city, demand. It certainly ought to be a much clearer case, however, to justify a court of equity in stretching forth the strong arm of injunction to compel a man to remove an establishment in which he has invested his capital and been carrying on business for a long period of time, from that of one who comes into a neighborhood proposing to establish such a business for the first time, and who is met at the threshold of his enterprise by a remonstrance and notice that if he persists in his purpose, application will be made to a court of equity to prevent him." . . .

In Campbell v. Seaman, 63 N.Y. 568, 20 Am. Rep. 567, the court enjoined the operation of a brick manufacturing plant on the ground that it was a nuisance. The plant was established a number of years previously, before neighboring residences were constructed. In rejecting the claim that equitable relief should be denied because of such circumstance, it was said:

"One cannot erect a nuisance upon his land adjoining vacant lands owned by another and thus measurably control the uses to which his neighbor's land may in the future be subjected. He may make a reasonable and lawful use of his land and thus cause his neighbor some inconvenience, and probably some damage which the law would regard as damnum absque injuria. But he cannot place upon his land anything which the law would pronounce a nuisance, and thus compel his neighbor to leave his land vacant, or to use it in such way only as the neighboring nuisance will allow." . . .

Defendant cites and relies on prior decisions of this court in each of which consideration was given to the circumstance that the parties seeking relief had established residences near the business the operation of which was sought to be enjoined. That such a circumstance may properly be considered in any case of this character in determining whether equitable relief should be granted is scarcely open to question. However it is not necessarily controlling. Looking to all the facts and circumstances involved, the question invariably presented is whether the discretion of the court should be exercised in favor of the parties seeking relief. In the case at bar the trial court came to the conclusion that the nuisance found by him to exist ought to be abated, and that such action was necessary in order to protect the plaintiffs in their rights and in the use and enjoyment of their homes. It may be assumed that new residences will be built in the community in the future, as they have been in the past, and that in consequence the community will become more and more thickly populated. This means of course that the injurious results of the carrying on of defendant's business, if the nuisance is not abated, will be greater in the future than it has been in the past. Such was obviously the view of the trial judge, and we cannot say that he abused his discretion in granting relief. On the contrary we think his conclusions were fully justified by the record.

Defendant also argues that the further carrying on of the business should not have been enjoined but rather that the court should have regulated its future operation in such manner as to "eliminate claimed objections." No specific suggestions are offered, however, as to the manner in which the result suggested can be accomplished. In view of the nature of the business it seems apparent, if defendant is permitted to continue it on her premises, the same conditions will necessarily attend its carrying on as the trial judge found existed at the time of the hearing before him. The record does not indicate that any suggestion was made during the course of the trial that the offensive features of the business could be avoided by any reasonable means. Rather, defendant insisted that plaintiffs' rights were not invaded by her acts, that no nuisance existed, and that plaintiffs were not entitled to the relief sought.

The decree of the Circuit Court is affirmed. Plaintiffs may have costs.

NOTES

1. Coming to the nuisance. The decision in Ensign v. Walls adopts the general view that it is no defense to show that the plaintiff came to the nuisance. The argument in support of the majority position finds its basis in the plaintiff's right to the exclusive use and control of his own land and holds that the defendant is not entitled to acquire by her unilateral conduct an easement to cause damage to the plaintiff's property. The case, briefly put, is that an acceptance of the coming to the nuisance defense allows the "theft" of an incorporeal interest in real property.

The minority view on the coming to the nuisance question usually rests its case on some version of assumption of risk. Thus in Bove v. Donner-Hanna Coke Corp., 258 N.Y.S. 229, 234 (N.Y. 1932), the plaintiff sought to enjoin the operation of defendant's coke oven, which was located on the opposite side of the street. The region was industrialized when the plaintiff moved into it, but a hickory grove was located on the site of the defendant's coke oven. The court rejected the plaintiff's request for an injunction with these words:

> With all the dirt, smoke and gas which necessarily come from factory chimneys, trains and boats, and with full knowledge that this region was especially adapted for industrial rather than residential purposes, and that factories would increase in the future, plaintiff selected this locality as the site of her future home. She voluntarily moved into this district, fully aware of the fact that the atmosphere would constantly be contaminated by dirt, gas and foul odors and that she could not hope to find in this locality the pure air of a strictly residential zone. She evidently saw certain advantages in living in this congested center. This is not the case of an industry, with its attendant noise and dirt, invading a quiet, residential district. It is just the opposite. Here a residence is built in an area naturally adapted for industrial purposes and already dedicated to that use. Plaintiff can hardly be heard to complain at this late date that her peace and comfort have been disturbed by a situation which existed, to

some extent at least, at the very time she bought her property, and which condition she must have known would grow worse rather than better as the years went by.

The opinion concluded with a marked deference to local zoning authorities, with the court holding that it was "not for the court to step in and override such decision, and condemn as a nuisance a business which is being conducted in an approved and expert manner, at the very spot where the council said it might be located."

Note the equivocation of the Restatement (Second) of Torts on the question. Section 840C provides that assumption of risk should be a defense in nuisance actions "to the same extent as in other tort actions." Thereafter section 840D on coming to the nuisance provides: "The fact that the plaintiff has acquired or improved his land after a nuisance interfering with it has come into existence is not in itself sufficient to bar his action, but is a factor to be considered in determining whether the nuisance is actionable."

The approach taken in *Bove* has been followed in the California Code of Civil Procedure, section 731a:

> Whenever any city, city and county, or county shall have established zones or districts under the authority of law wherein certain manufacturing or commercial airport uses are expressly permitted, except in an action to abate a public nuisance brought in the name of the people of the State of California, no person or persons, firm or corporation shall be enjoined or restrained by the injunctive process from the reasonable and necessary operation of any such industrial or commercial zone or airport of any use expressly permitted therein, nor shall such use be deemed a nuisance without evidence of the employment of unnecessary and injurious methods of operation.

How do *Bove* and section 731 compare with Bramwell's views in Powell v. Fall, supra at page 136, and Bamford v. Turnley, supra at page 689, note 6? Should an action be allowed for persons who live outside the designated zones?

The question of statutory authorization has come up in other contexts as well. In Varjabedian v. City of Madera, 572 P.2d 43 (Cal. 1977), the defendant operated a municipal sewage dump pursuant to general statutory authorization. The defendant argued that the complaint for damages had to be dismissed because section 3482 of the California Civil Code provides that "Nothing which is done or maintained under the express authority of a statute can be deemed a nuisance." The court rejected that argument on the ground that nothing in the statute "expressly sanctions the production of any particular level of odors." What result if the creation of a sewage system necessarily entails some minimum level of offensive odors? Should recovery under the statute be limited to negligence causes of action?

The California Supreme Court also upheld the plaintiff's claim for damages based upon a constitutional theory of "inverse condemnation," on the ground that it was peculiarly damaged by the defendant's activities. See the discussion of public nuisances infra at page 717. Note that the ability to maintain a constitutional claim may not permit the recovery of any additional element of damages, but it might, as was noted in *Varjabedian*, allow the plaintiff to recover pre-judgment interest or some expenses of litigation.

2. *Economic analysis and the coming to the nuisance rule.* There has also been a spirited attack on the coming to the nuisance rule in the law and economics literature. See Baxter and Altree, Legal Aspects of Airport Noise, 15 J.L. & Econ. 1 (1972), where the authors argue that the optimum use of land will be achieved with the following liability rule: "of two incompatible land uses the one which had but did not take the opportunity to avoid creating costs of incompatibility should bear the costs." From this premise it follows in general that the first party to invest in a given area should be protected and, to use the authors' phrase, "the unavoidable reciprocal costs" that arise when a second party makes an incompatible use of his own land should be borne by the second party. The temporal element is given a dominance under this formulation that under the traditional nuisance law was reserved for the spatial element.

The purpose of the Baxter-Altree rule is to discourage any wasteful investment that the second user might otherwise make if he knew he could collect full damages or enjoin the prior use. But it does not indicate what restrictions, if any, should be placed on the *initial* decision by the first user. If their proposal is followed, then it appears that the plaintiff is left remediless in the standard coming to the nuisance case. One possible escape from that conclusion is to allow the plaintiff a remedy at the time the defendant begins his potentially noxious use equal to the diminution in market value of the property in question. This approach minimizes the incentive for a plaintiff to develop property prematurely in order to protect its future use.

The situation here is very much bound up with the debate over the reciprocal nature of causation, on which see the excerpt from Coase, The Problem of Social Cost, at page 338 supra. Note that many of the cases considered by Coase involve coming to the nuisance situations, often complicated by assertions that the plaintiff is making an extrasensitive use of property. See Cooke v. Forbes, L.R. 5 Eq. 166 (1867) (sulfur fumes from defendant's property interfered with plaintiff's "delicate" manufacturing process); Sturges v. Bridgman, 11 Ch. D. 852 (1879) (doctor's examining room next to pharmacist's mortar and pestle); Webb v. Bird, 10 C.B. (N.S.) 268, 142 Eng. Rep. 455 (1861) (plaintiff's windmill subjected to blockage of wind by defendant); Bryant v. Lefever, 4 C.P.D. 172 (1879) (defendant's chimney blocked escape of fumes from plaintiff's premises).

The entire question of coming to the nuisance has been much debated in the academic literature. See Calabresi and Hirschoff, Toward a Test for Strict Liability in Torts, 81 Yale L.J. 1055, 1080-1082 (1972); Ellickson, Alternatives to Zoning, 40 U. Chi. L. Rev. 681, 758-761 (1973); Epstein, Defenses and Subsequent Pleas in a System of Strict Liability, 3 J. Legal Stud. 165, 197-201 (1974); Michelman, Property, Utility and Fairness, 80 Harv. L. Rev. 1165, 1235-1245 (1967).

Boomer v. Atlantic Cement Co.
257 N.E.2d 870 (N.Y. 1970)

BERGAN, J. Defendant operates a large cement plant near Albany. These are actions for injunction and damages by neighboring land owners alleging injury to property from dirt, smoke and vibration emanating from the plant. A nuisance has been found after trial, temporary damages have been allowed; but an injunction has been denied.

The public concern with air pollution arising from many sources in industry and in transportation is currently accorded ever wider recognition accompanied by a growing sense of responsibility in State and Federal Governments to control it. Cement plants are obvious sources of air pollution in the neighborhoods where they operate.

But there is now before the court private litigation in which individual property owners have sought specific relief from a single plant operation. The threshold question raised by the division of view on this appeal is whether the court should resolve the litigation between the parties now before it as equitably as seems possible; or whether, seeking promotion of the general public welfare, it should channel private litigation into broad public objectives.

A court performs its essential function when it decides the rights of parties before it. Its decision of private controversies may sometimes greatly affect public issues. Large questions of law are often resolved by the manner in which private litigation is decided. But this is normally an incident to the court's main function to settle controversy. It is a rare exercise of judicial power to use a decision in private litigation as a purposeful mechanism to achieve direct public objectives greatly beyond the rights and interests before the court.

Effective control of air pollution is a problem presently far from solution even with the full public and financial powers of government. In large measure adequate technical procedures are yet to be developed and some that appear possible may be economically impracticable.

It seems apparent that the amelioration of air pollution will depend on technical research in great depth on a carefully balanced consideration of the economic impact of close regulation; and of the actual effect on public health. It is likely to require massive public expenditure and to demand more than any local community can accomplish and to depend on regional and interstate controls.

A court should not try to do this on its own as a by-product of private litigation and it seems manifest that the judicial establishment is neither equipped in the limited nature of any judgment it can pronounce nor prepared to lay down and implement an effective policy for the elimination of air pollution. This is an area beyond the circumference of one private lawsuit. It is a direct responsibility for government and should not thus be undertaken as an incident to solving a dispute between property owners and a single cement plant — one of many — in the Hudson River valley.

The cement making operations of defendant have been found by the court at Special Term to have damaged the nearby properties of plaintiffs in these two actions. That court, as it has been noted, accordingly found defendant maintained a nuisance and this has been affirmed at the Appellate Division. The total damage to plaintiffs' properties is, however, relatively small in comparison with the value of defendant's operation and with the consequences of the injunction which plaintiffs seek.

The ground for the denial of injunction, notwithstanding the finding both that there is a nuisance and that plaintiffs have been damaged substantially, is the large disparity in economic consequences of the nuisance and of the injunction. This theory cannot, however, be sustained without overruling a doctrine which has been consistently reaffirmed in several leading cases in this court and which has never been disavowed here, namely that where a nuisance has been found and where there has been any substantial damage shown by the party complaining an injunction will be granted.

The rule in New York has been that such a nuisance will be enjoined although marked disparity be shown in economic consequence between the effect of the injunction and the effect of the nuisance.

The problem of disparity in economic consequence was sharply in focus in Whalen v. Union Bag & Paper Co. (208 N.Y. 1). A pulp mill entailing an investment of more than a million dollars polluted a stream in which plaintiff, who owned a farm, was "a lower riparian owner." The economic loss to plaintiff from this pollution was small. This court, reversing the Appellate Division, reinstated the injunction granted by the Special Term against the argument of the mill owner that in view of "the slight advantage to plaintiff and the great loss that will be inflicted on defendant" an injunction should not be granted. "Such a balancing of injuries cannot be justified by the circumstances of this case," Judge Werner noted. He continued: "Although the damage to the plaintiff may be slight as compared with the defendant's expense of abating the condition, that is not a good reason for refusing an injunction."

Thus the unconditional injunction granted at Special Term was reinstated. The rule laid down in that case, then, is that whenever the damage resulting from a nuisance is found not "unsubstantial," viz., $100 a year, injunction would follow. This states a rule that had been followed in this court with marked consistency .

There are cases where injunction has been denied. McCann v. Chasm Power Co. (211 N.Y. 301) is one of them. There, however, the damage shown by plaintiffs was not only unsubstantial, it was non-existent. Plaintiffs owned a rocky bank of the stream in which defendant had raised the level of the water. This had no economic or other adverse consequence to plaintiffs, and thus injunctive relief was denied. Similar is the basis for denial of injunction in Forstmann v. Joray Holding Co. (244 N.Y. 22) where no benefit to plaintiffs could be seen from the injunction sought. Thus if, within Whalen v. Union Bag & Paper Co. which authoritatively states the rule in New York, the damage to plaintiffs in these present cases from defendant's cement plant is "not unsubstantial," an injunction should follow.

Although the court at Special Term and the Appellate Division held that injunction should be denied, it was found that plaintiffs had been damaged in various specific amounts up to the time of the trial and damages to the respective plaintiffs were awarded for those amounts. The effect of this was, injunction having been denied, plaintiffs could maintain successive actions at law for damages thereafter as further damage was incurred.

The court at Special Term also found the amount of permanent damage attributable to each plaintiff, for the guidance of the parties in the event both sides stipulated to the payment and acceptance of such permanent damage as a settlement of all the controversies among the parties. The total of permanent damages to all plaintiffs thus found was $185,000. This basis of adjustment has not resulted in any stipulation by the parties.

This result at Special Term and at the Appellate Division is a departure from a rule that has become settled but to follow the rule literally in these cases would be to close down the plant at once. This court is fully agreed to avoid that immediately drastic remedy; the difference in view is how best to avoid it.

One alternative is to grant the injunction but postpone its effect to a specified future date to give opportunity for technical advances to permit defendant to eliminate the nuisance; another is to grant the injunction conditioned on the payment of permanent damages to plaintiffs which would compensate them for the total economic loss to their property present and future caused by defendant's operations. For reasons which will be developed the court chooses the latter alternative.

If the injunction were to be granted unless within a short period — e.g., 18 months — the nuisance be abated by improved methods, there would be no assurance that any significant technical improvement would occur.

The parties could settle this private litigation at any time if defendant paid enough money and the imminent threat of closing the plant would build up the pressure on defendant. If there were no improved techniques found, there would inevitably be applications to the court at Special Term for extensions of time to perform on showing of good faith efforts to find such techniques.

Moreover, techniques to eliminate dust and other annoying by-products of cement making are unlikely to be developed by any research the defendant can undertake within any short period, but will depend on the total resources of the cement industry nationwide and throughout the world. The problem is universal wherever cement is made.

For obvious reasons the rate of the research is beyond control of defendant. If at the end of 18 months the whole industry has not found a technical solution a court would be hard put to close down this one cement plant if due regard be given to equitable principles.

On the other hand, to grant the injunction unless defendant pays plaintiffs such permanent damages as may be fixed by the court seems to do justice between the contending parties. All of the attributions of economic loss to the properties on which plaintiffs' complaints are based will have been redressed.

The nuisance complained of by these plaintiffs may have other public or private consequences, but these particular parties are the only ones who have sought remedies and the judgment proposed will fully redress them. The limitation of relief granted is a limitation only within the four corners of these actions and does not foreclose public health or the public agencies from seeking proper relief in a proper court.

It seems reasonable to think that the risk of being required to pay permanent damages to injured property owners by cement plant owners would itself be a reasonable effective spur to research for improved techniques to minimize nuisance.

The power of the court to condition on equitable grounds the continuance of an injunction on the payment of permanent damages seems undoubted.

The damage base here suggested is consistent with the general rule in those nuisance cases where damages are allowed. "Where a nuisance is of such a permanent and unabatable character that a single recovery can be had, including the whole damage past and future resulting therefrom, there can be but one recovery" (66 C.J.S., Nuisances, §140, p. 947). It has been said that permanent damages are allowed where the loss recoverable would obviously be small as compared with the cost of removal of the nuisance.

Thus it seems fair to both sides to grant permanent damages to plaintiffs which will terminate this private litigation. The theory of damage is the "servitude on land" of plaintiffs imposed by defendant's nuisance. (See United States v. Causby, 328 U.S. 256, 261, 262, 267, where the term "servitude" addressed to the land was used by Justice Douglas relating to the effect of airplane noise on property near an airport.)

The judgment, by allowance of permanent damages imposing a servitude on land, which is the basis of the actions, would preclude future recovery by plaintiffs or their grantees.

This should be placed beyond debate by a provision of the judgment that the payment by defendant and the acceptance by plaintiffs of permanent damages found by the court shall be in compensation for a servitude on the land.

Although the Trial Term has found permanent damages as a possible basis of settlement of the litigation, on remission the court should be entirely free to re-examine this subject. It may again find the permanent damage already found or make new findings.

The orders should be reversed, without costs, and the cases remitted to Supreme Court, Albany County to grant an injunction which shall be vacated upon payment by defendant of such amounts of permanent damage to the respective plaintiffs as shall for this purpose be determined by the court.

JASEN, J., dissenting. I agree with the majority that a reversal is required here, but I do not subscribe to the newly enunciated doctrine of assessment of permanent damages, in lieu of an injunction, where substantial property rights have been impaired by the creation of a nuisance.

It has long been the rule in this State, as the majority acknowledges, that a nuisance which results in substantial continuing damage to neighbors must be enjoined. To now change the rule to permit the cement company to continue polluting the air indefinitely upon the payment of permanent damages is, in my opinion, compounding the magnitude of a very serious problem in our State and Nation today.

In recognition of this problem, the Legislature of this State has enacted the Air Pollution Control Act (Public Health Law, §§1264-1299m) declaring that it is the State policy to require the use of all available and reasonable methods to prevent and control air pollution (Public Health Law, §1265).

The harmful nature and widespread occurrence of air pollution have been extensively documented. Congressional hearings have revealed that air pollution causes substantial property damage, as well as being a contributing factor to a rising incidence of lung cancer, emphysema, bronchitis and asthma.

The specific problem faced here is known as particulate contamination because of the fine dust particles emanating from defendant's cement plant. The particular type of nuisance is not new, having appeared in many cases for at least the past 60 years. It is interesting to

note that cement production has recently been identified as a significant source of particulate contamination in the Hudson Valley. This
type of pollution, wherein very small particles escape and stay in the
atmosphere, has been denominated as the type of air pollution which
produces the greatest hazard to human health. We have thus a nuisance
which not only is damaging to the plaintiffs, but also is decidedly harmful to the general public.

I see grave dangers in overruling our long-established rule of granting an injunction where a nuisance results in substantial continuing
damage. In permitting the injunction to become inoperative upon the
payment of permanent damages, the majority is, in effect, licensing a
continuing wrong. It is the same as saying to the cement company, you
may continue to do harm to your neighbors so long as you pay a fee for
it. Furthermore, once such permanent damages are assessed and paid,
the incentive to alleviate the wrong would be eliminated, thereby continuing air pollution of an area without abatement.

It is true that some courts have sanctioned the remedy here proposed
by the majority in a number of cases, but none of the authorities relied
upon by the majority are analogous to the situation before us. In those
cases, the courts, in denying an injunction and awarding money damages, grounded their decision on a showing that the use to which the
property was intended to be put was primarily for the public benefit.
Here, on the other hand, it is clearly established that the cement company is creating a continuing air pollution nuisance primarily for its
own private interest with no public benefit.

This kind of inverse condemnation may not be invoked by a private
person or corporation for private gain or advantage. Inverse condemnation should only be permitted when the public is primarily served in
the taking or impairment of property. The promotion of the interests
of the polluting cement company has, in my opinion, no public use or
benefit.

Nor is it constitutionally permissible to impose servitude on land,
without consent of the owner, by payment of permanent damages
where the continuing impairment of the land is for a private use. This
is made clear by the State Constitution (art. I, §7, subd. [a]) which
provides that "[p]rivate property shall not be taken for *public use* without just compensation" (emphasis added). It is, of course, significant
that the section makes no mention of taking for a *private* use.

In sum, then, by constitutional mandate as well as by judicial pronouncement, the permanent impairment of private property for private purposes is not authorized in the absence of clearly demonstrated
public benefit and use.

I would enjoin the defendant cement company from continuing the
discharge of dust particles upon its neighbors' properties unless, within
18 months, the cement company abated this nuisance.

NOTES

1. Permanent and temporary damages. Injunctions aside, damages are one possible remedy for a plaintiff in a nuisance action. In such situations the court frequently must decide whether to award the plaintiff periodic damages or a single lump-sum payment in full satisfaction for his loss. As might be expected, there are advantages and disadvantages to both rules. Temporary damages allow the court to make an accurate assessment of actual harm without having to guess about the course of future events. But they place great administrative burdens on the system, and they burden the plaintiff with the inconvenience of having to bring multiple actions for the redress of one continuing wrong. Permanent damages raise the converse problems, for they place great emphasis on the original valuation. Yet they can often avoid a multiplicity of subsequent actions. Nonetheless, the dispute may well continue, especially if the defendant increases the level of interference with the plaintiff's land beyond what was expected. How does one measure damages in such a case? Determine the point at which the statute of limitations starts to run? Given the difficulties in choosing between permanent and temporary damages, does it make sense to allow the plaintiff to elect which remedy he desires?

2. Mitigation of damages. With either permanent or temporary damages, the plaintiff's mitigation of the loss must be taken into account. Thus in Belkus v. City of Brockton, 184 N.W. 812 (Mass. 1933), the plaintiff's land had been flooded at various times in the six years prior to suit. The court allowed the plaintiff to recover for the costs of raising the level of his basement in order to prevent its being flooded from a culvert improperly maintained by the defendant municipality. Should the costs of repair be allowed after a single flooding? In Stratford Theater, Inc. v. Town of Stratford, 101 A.2d 279 (Conn. 1953), the plaintiff's theater had been "frequently" flooded from a broken sewer line. The plaintiff was allowed to recover the expense, not of altering his own property, but of repairing the defendant's broken line. If the plaintiff had not chosen to make the repairs, could it recover for the value of the nuisance not averted, even if greater than the cost of repairs?

The opposite position on mitigation has been forcefully asserted in an oft-quoted but little-followed passage:

> A person injured by a nuisance, is not precluded from a recovery by the fact that he might, by small exertion and a small expenditure, have prevented the injury, the rule being, that as it was the defendant's duty to abstain from the creation of the nuisance, and having created it adjoining owners are not bound to guard against the consequences ensuing therefrom, when in order to do so they are required to expend time or money. . . . A party is not bound to expend a dollar, or to do any act to secure for himself the exercise or enjoyment of a legal right of which he

is deprived by reason of the wrongful acts of another. [H. Wood, The Law of Nuisances §§844, 435 (3rd ed. 1893).]

3. Permanent injunctions. Wood's position represents the strongest manifestation of the autonomy principle in connection with damage suits for harm already caused. The same principle can be applied as well to grant injunctive relief as a matter of course for individuals who have been substantially inconvenienced by the defendant's nuisance. In practice, as both *Ensign* and *Boomer* suggest, courts do not follow an inflexible rule that always grants an immediate injunction as a matter of course. Nonetheless they are typically quite cautious in denying injunctive relief for a number of reasons, each of which is relevant but none wholly dispositive. In some cases an injunction is awarded because there are serious risks that the defendant will be insolvent. In other cases the injunction has the desirable effect of providing protection to other, innocent third parties who have not joined in the original suit, perhaps because their losses, while not trivial, are below the cost of suit. See Menell, A Note on Private Versus Social Incentives to Sue in a Costly Legal System, 12 J. Legal Stud. 41 (1983). In addition, the injunction reduces the need for the court (which may still, however, be needed to assess interim damages) to determine exactly the subjective valuation that the plaintiff attaches to privacy and seclusion.

These factors have for the most part inclined courts to treat injunctions as a presumptive if not an absolute remedy. But even before *Boomer,* some cases have balked at granting injunctive relief. Thus, in the early case of Madison v. Tennessee Copper Co., 83 S.W. 658, 666, 667 (Tenn. 1904), the plaintiffs were all owners of "thin mountain lands, of little agricultural value." The defendants for their part operated two large copper smelting plants that the plaintiffs sought to shut down. The court refused this last request, noting:

> Shall the complainants be granted, in the way of damages, the full measure of relief to which their injuries entitle them, or shall we go further, and grant their request to blot out two great mining and manufacturing enterprises, destroy half of the taxable values of a county, and drive more than 10,000 people from their homes? We think there can be no doubt as to what the true answer to this question should be.
>
> In order to protect by injunction several small tracts of land, aggregating in value less than $1,000, we are asked to destroy other property worth nearly $2,000,000, and wreck two great mining and manufacturing enterprises, that are engaged in work of very great importance, not only to their owners, but to the state, and to the whole country as well, to depopulate a large town, and deprive thousands of working people of their homes and livelihood, and scatter them broadcast. The result would be practically a confiscation of the property of the defendants for the benefit of the complainants — an appropriation without compensation. The defendants cannot reduce their ores in a manner different from that they are now employing, and there is no more remote place to which

they can remove. The decree asked for would deprive them of all of their rights.

Madison offers a graphic illustration of the risks of strategic bargaining behavior by aggrieved plaintiffs when there is an enormous disparity in value. More specifically, if the injunction were granted, the parties would have both have incentives to renegotiate the deal. Since the defendant's property was worth $2,000,000 and the plaintiff's property was worth but $1,000, any bargain to dissolve the injunction and paid the plaintiff a sum in excess of $1,000 but less than $2,000,000 would leave both sides better off. The size of the bargaining range ($1,999,000) is so enormous that the plaintiffs could hold out for a very large portion of the gain when the defendants resume their activities.

Injunctive relief thus poses two major risks: first, that parties will waste enormous resources in bargaining over the surplus and, second, that they will not be able to reach any agreement at all given the tendency to bluff and bluster. (The parallel to the private necessity cases in chapter one should be reviewed.) The damage remedy makes this outcome unlikely because the plaintiff is at most entitled to $1,000, which the defendant would happily pay to continue business as before. Note, however, that the social desirability of injunctive relief diminishes as the size and subjective nature of the plaintiff's interest becomes larger and the size of the defendant's interest shrinks. Now estimation of the plaintiff's interest is more difficult to make, so damages are a less reliable remedy. In addition, the smaller bargaining range makes it more likely that the parties can reach agreement to remove the injunction. It is possible therefore to conceive of situations in which the damage rule dominates the injunctive rule, and vice versa. Accordingly, there is no hard and fast rule as to when injunctive relief should yield to damages, even though the polar cases are tolerably easy to identify. On the proper mix between injunctions and damages see Ellickson, Alternatives to Zoning: Covenants, Nuisance Rules, and Fines as Land Use Controls, 40 U. Chi. L. Rev. 681, 738-748 (1973); Polinsky, Resolving Nuisance Disputes: The Simple Economics of Injunctive and Damage Remedies, 32 Stan. L. Rev. 1075 (1980). For the English law, which generally favors the injunction, see Ogus and Richardson, Economics and the Environment: A Study of Private Nuisance, 36 Cambridge L.J. 284 (1977).

4. *Injunctions for threatened harms.* Injunctive relief is ordinarily allowed against ongoing or even imminent harms. But suppose the defendant's activities only increase the risk of some future actionable harm? Here the general tendency is to deny the immediate injunction, in part because injunctive relief is still available in the future should the harm become imminent, and in part because damages remain as a backstop for and a deterrent to consummated harms.

Suppose the plaintiff seeks to enjoin the operation of a prison, a pest house, a reform school, or housing for people with AIDS or the homeless. Quite often he fails because he cannot establish that the mere operation of the facility is in itself a nuisance. See, e.g., Nicholson v. Connecticut Half-Way House, 218 A.2d 383 (Conn. 1966), where the plaintiffs, residents of a middle-class neighborhood, were unsuccessful in their efforts to enjoin the operation of a half-way house for parolees from state prisons. The court noted that the defendant's plans called for strict control upon the number of persons living in the house, for the exclusion of sex offenders, drug addicts, and alcoholics, and for extensive supervision of the parolees. The court did not deny that the presence of the defendant's facility introduced fear and unhappiness into the neighborhood or that it lowered the values of the surrounding property; nor did it rule out the possibility that some relief should be in order if it could be established that the actual operation of the facility interfered with the peace and comfort of the neighborhood.

If some resident of the half-way house in *Nicholson* committed a crime in the neighborhood, should the operators of the home be held strictly responsible? What if the residents of the house made loud noises at night, or generally littered the public streets? Is a funeral home a nuisance if it depresses the neighbors? If it has black drapes?

5. *Discretion to issue injunctions.* Although courts have the undeniable power to issue injunctions in nuisance cases, they may at their discretion refuse to enjoin an activity or, in the alternative, issue them only if certain conditions are satisfied. In Pendoley v. Ferreira, 187 N.E.2d 142 (Mass. 1963), the court delayed the enforcement of an injunction against the continued operation of defendants' piggery in order to permit the defendants to engage in "an orderly, rather than a hurried, liquidation of their pigs," and allow them "opportunity to find new premises."

Judicial discretion on injunctive relief does not extend only to the all-or-nothing choice of injunction or no injunction. It is possible to permit the defendant to continue in business, but only on condition that certain specific measures are taken to eliminate the objectionable features of that enterprise. Thus, in Quinn v. American Spiral Spring & Manufacturing Co., 141 A. 855 (Pa. 1928), the defendant was allowed to continue operation of its factory, but only on condition that it re-arrange its heavy machinery in order to reduce the inconvenience to the plaintiff. And in Hansen v. Independent School Dist. No. 1, 98 P.2d 959 (Idaho 1939), the defendant school board was allowed to continue to schedule night baseball games on the school's athletic fields, but only on condition that it control the illumination of its lights, terminate the games at a reasonable hour, and limit the parking in the neighborhood. Similar flexibility was shown in Pritchett v. Board of Commissioners, 85 N.E. 32 (Ind. App. 1908), where the court tailored the plaintiff's injunction to allow the defendant to continue operating its prison on condition that it shutter and close all windows of the prison that overlooked the plaintiff's house to spare the plaintiff from hearing profanity and "wild, boisterous and indecent noises" from inside the prison. On this general question of "balancing the equities" see Developments in the Law — Injunctions, 78 Harv. L. Rev. 994 (1965); Note, An Economic Analysis of Land Use Conflicts, 21 Stan. L. Rev. 293 (1969).

6. *Purchased injunctions.* Thus far we have considered three possible solutions to the nuisance problem: damages, injunctions (permanent or temporary), and, of course, no remedy at all. A fourth solution, often missed by courts and commentators alike, is what might be best termed a "purchased injunction." The plaintiff may enjoin the defendant, but only if he is prepared to compensate the defendant for the loss incurred. For the original recognition of this approach see Calabresi and Malamed, Property Rules, Liability Rules, and Inalienability: One View of the Cathedral, 85 Harv. L. Rev. 1089, 1115-1123 (1972). One notable case that illustrates the use of purchased injunctions is Spur Industries, Inc. v. Del E. Webb Development Co., 494 P.2d 700, 707-708 (Ariz. 1972). There the defendants operated a cattle feedlot on the outskirts of Phoenix. The plaintiff development corporation purchased land near the plaintiff's lot that it then developed into a tract of private homes. At first the plaintiff developed land that was not in the immediate vicinity of the defendant's feedlot; but later it built homes close to the lot. The odors and flies from the feedlot made it impossible for the new residents to enjoy the outdoor amenities promised by the plaintiff, and also made it impossible for the plaintiff to market the unsold homes near the defendant's feedlot. The court held that the defendant's activities constituted an actionable nuisance and enjoined its operation. The court noted, however, that it would have applied the coming to the nuisance defense if the plaintiff had not sold some of the units to individual purchasers. It then continued:

> There was no indication in the instant case at the time Spur and its predecessors located in western Maricopa County that a new city would spring up, fullblown, alongside the feeding operation and that the developer of that city would ask the court to order Spur to move because of the new city. Spur is required to move not because of any wrongdoing on the part of Spur, but because of a proper and legitimate regard of the courts for the rights and interests of the public.
>
> Del Webb, on the other hand, is entitled to the relief prayed for (a permanent injunction), not because Webb is blameless, but because of the damage to the people who have been encouraged to purchase homes in Sun City. It does not equitably or legally follow, however, that Webb, being entitled to the injunction, is then free of any liability to Spur if Webb has in fact been the cause of the damage Spur has sustained. It does not seem harsh to require a developer, who has taken advantage of the lesser land values in a rural area as well as the availability of large

tracts of land on which to build and develop a new town or city in the area, to indemnify those who are forced to leave as a result.

Having brought people to the nuisance to the foreseeable detriment of Spur, Webb must indemnify Spur for a reasonable amount of the cost of moving or shutting down. It should be noted that this relief to Spur is limited to a case wherein a developer has, with foreseeability, brought into a previously agricultural or industrial area the population which makes necessary the granting of an injunction against a lawful business and for which the business has no adequate relief.

Do the purchasers of the individual units take title subject to the defenses available against the plaintiff, their predecessor in title?

2. Public Nuisance

Anonymous
Y.B. Mich. 27 Hen. 8, f. 27, pl. 10 (1535)

One brought a Writ sur son cas [on his case] against another. He alleged that, whereas the plaintiff had used to have a way from his house to a close over the King's highway for carriage and re-carriage, etc., the defendant had stopped the King's highway, so that the plaintiff could not go to his aforesaid close, to his tort and damage.

BALDWIN, C.J. It seems to me that this action does not lie to the plaintiff for the stopping of the highway; for the King has the punishment of that, and he has his plaint in the Leet and there he has his redress, because it is a common nuisance to all the King's lieges, and so there is no reason for a private particular person to have an accion sur son cas; for if one person shall have an action for this, by the same reason every person shall have an action, and so he will be punished a hundred times on the same case.

FITZHERBERT, J., to the contrary. I agree well that each nuisance done in the King's highway is punishable in the Leet and not by an action, unless it be where one man has suffered greater hurt or inconvenience than the generality have; but he who has suffered such greater displeasure or hurt can have an action to recover the damage which he has by reason of this special hurt. So if one makes a ditch across the highway, and I come riding along the way in the night and I and my horse are thrown into the ditch so that I have great damage and displeasure thereby, I shall have an action here against him who made this ditch across the highway, because I have suffered more damage than any other person. So here the plaintiff had more convenience by this highway than any other person had, and so when he is stopped he suffers more damage because he has no way to go to his close. Wherefore it seems to me that he shall have this action pour ce special matiere [for his special harm]: but if he had not suffered greater damage than all others suffered, then he would not have the action. Quod Nota. [Which was noted.]

NOTE

Public nuisances. The common-law distinction between public and private nuisances made in 1535 holds true in general outline today. Restatement (Second) of Torts §§821B-821E. General damages from public nuisances are controlled only by direct public action, usually administrative regulation or criminal prosecution. The private action is maintainable only for "special," "peculiar," or "disproportionate" harm to the individual plaintiff. The reasons for this division lie less in matters of justice than in matters of administration. As general damages are of low level and are widely diffused across an extended population, private actions for admitted grievances are simply too costly to maintain. The enforcement function is therefore centralized to preserve the deterrent and control functions of the tort law, even though direct compensation to aggrieved parties is necessarily abandoned. When, however, the harms are "special," private actions may again be maintained, as in all ordinary tort situations, for now the administrative burdens are more easily negotiable. See generally Epstein, Nuisance Law: Corrective Justice and Its Utilitarian Constraints, 8 J. Legal Stud. 49, 98-102 (1979). What is the relationship between the live and let live doctrine and the law of public nuisances?

Within this framework, how should one draw the distinction between general and special damages? Although general formulas are hard to state, it is clear that private actions have always been appropriate in at least two classes of cases: total loss of access to private land and personal injuries. At the other extreme, no private action may be brought for delays in traffic, even if they lead to disruption of important business or personal plans. The difficult intermediate cases involve partial loss of access. In Smith v. City of Boston, 61 Mass. 254, 255-256 (1851), Boston closed down a street to make way for a new railroad line and the plaintiff, in consequence, lost access to the closed street, even though he retained access to other nearby streets. Shaw, C.J., denied the action on the ground that "[t]he damage complained of in this case, though it may be greater in degree, in consequence of the proximity of the petitioner's estates, does not differ in kind from that of any other members of the community who would have had occasion more or less frequently to pass over the discontinued highway." Does Shaw's reasoning apply to a gas station that receives 90 percent of its business from the street that was closed? Note that partial loss of access, even for isolated plaintiffs, generally remains uncompensable, either as a private nuisance or under special statutory schemes that incorporate the distinction between general and special damages. See, e.g., Malone v. Commonwealth, 389 N.E.2d 975 (Mass. 1979), where a statutory claim for special damages was denied when the plaintiff's gift shop was deprived of its direct access to a state highway so that the store could only be reached by a connector road. Can the loss of partial access ever form the basis of a constitutional claim for the taking of private property without just compensation?

Union Oil Co. v. Oppen
501 F.2d 558 (9th Cir. 1974)

[The appellees, plaintiffs below, were commercial fishermen who sued the Union Oil Company in negligence for the economic losses they suffered when the oil pollution in the Santa Barbara Channel killed the fish upon which their commercial livelihood depended. The district court denied the Union Oil Company a partial summary judgment and refused to strike from the plaintiffs' cause of action the demand for compensation for "ecological damage," which included their lost commercial profits.]

SNEED, J. Defendants support their motion for partial summary judgment by pointing to the widely recognized principle that no cause of action lies against a defendant whose negligence prevents the plaintiff from obtaining a prospective pecuniary advantage. As the defendants see it, any diminution of the sea life in the Santa Barbara Channel caused by the occurrence, which, it must be remembered, is attributable to the defendants' negligence by reason of the parties' Stipulation, consists of no more than the loss of an economic advantage which is not a "legally cognizable injury" and thus not "legally compensable."

Their argument has strength. It rests upon the proposition that a contrary rule, which would allow compensation for all losses of economic advantages caused by defendant's negligence, would subject the defendant to claims based upon remote and speculative injuries which he could not foresee in any practical sense of the term. Accordingly, in some cases it has been stated as the general rule that the negligent defendant owes no duty to plaintiffs seeking compensation for such injuries. In other of the cases, the courts have invoked the doctrine of proximate cause to reach the same result; and in yet a third class of cases the "remoteness" of the economic loss is relied upon directly to deny recovery. The consequence of these cases is that a defendant is normally relieved of the burden to defend against such claims, and the courts of a class of cases the resolution of which is particularly difficult.

The general rule has been applied in a wide variety of situations. Thus, the negligent destruction of a bridge connecting the mainland with an island, which caused a loss of business to the plaintiff who was a merchant on the island, has been held not to be actionable. Rickards v. Sun Oil Company, 41 A.2d 267, 23 N.J. Misc. 89 (1945). A plaintiff engaged in commercial printing has been held unable to recover against a negligent contractor who, while engaged in excavation pursuant to a contract with a third party, cut the power line upon which the plaintiff's presses depended. Byrd v. English, 117 Ga. 191, 43 S.E. 419 (1903). . . . A defendant who negligently injures a third person entitled to life-care medical services by the plaintiff is liable to the third person but not to the plaintiff. Fifield Manor v. Finston, 54 Cal. 2d 632, 7 Cal. Rptr. 377, 354 P.2d 1073 (1960) (subrogation also denied because third party's claim not assignable). The operators of a dry dock are not liable in admiralty to charterers of a ship, placed by its owners in the dry dock, for negligent injury to the ship's propeller where the injury deprived the charterer of the use of the ship. Robins Dry Dock & Repair Company v. Flint, 275 U.S. 303 (1927). Mr. Justice Holmes, in writing this opinion, observed that ". . . a tort to the person or property of one man does not make the tort-feasor liable to another merely because the injured person was under a contract with that other, unknown to the doer of the wrong." 275 U.S. at 309.

[The court then reviewed the California cases on products liability and thereafter concluded that the defendant owed the plaintiffs a duty of care to avoid damaging the aquatic life in the Santa Barbara Channel and, thereby, the plaintiff's business.]

[T]he question must be asked whether the defendants could reasonably have foreseen that negligently conducted drilling operations might diminish aquatic life and thus injure the business of commercial fishermen. We believe the answer is yes. The dangers of pollution were and are known even by school children. The defendants understood the risks of their business and should reasonably have foreseen the scope of its responsibilities. To assert that the defendants were unable to foresee that negligent conduct resulting in a substantial oil spill could diminish aquatic life and thus injure the plaintiffs is to suppose a degree of general ignorance of the effects of oil pollution not in accord with good sense.

An examination of the other factors . . . only strengthens our conclusion that the defendants in this case owed a duty to the plaintiffs. Thus, the fact that the injury flows directly from the action of escaping oil on the life in the sea, . . . the public's deep disapproval of injuries to the environment and the strong policy of preventing such injuries, all point to existence of a required duty.

The same conclusion is reached when the issue before us is approached from the standpoint of economics. Recently a number of scholars have suggested that liability for losses occasioned by torts should be apportioned in a manner that will best contribute to the achievement of an optimum allocation of resources. See e.g., Calabresi, The Cost of Accidents, 69-73 (1970) (hereinafter Calabresi); Coase, The Problem of Social Cost, 3 J. Law & Econ. 1 (1960). This optimum, in theory, would be that which would be achieved by a perfect market system. In determining whether the cost of an accident should be borne by the injured party or be shifted, in whole or in part, this approach requires the court to fix the identity of the party who can avoid the costs most cheaply. Once fixed, this determination then controls liability.

It turns out, however, that fixing the identity of the best or cheapest cost-avoider is more difficult than might be imagined. In order to facilitate this determination, Calabresi suggests several helpful guidelines. The first of these would require a rough calculation designed to exclude as potential cost-avoiders those groups/activities which could avoid accident costs only at an extremely high expense. Calabresi at 140-143. While not easy to apply in any concrete sense, this guideline does suggest that the imposition of oil spill costs directly upon such groups as the consumers of staple groceries is not a sensible solution. Under this guideline, potential liability becomes resolved into a choice between, on an ultimate level, the consumers of fish and those of products derived from the defendants' total operations.

To refine this choice, Calabresi goes on to provide additional guidelines which, in this instance, have proven none too helpful. For example, he suggests an evaluation of the administrative costs which each party would be forced to bear in order to avoid the accident costs. Calabresi at 143-144. He also states that an attempt should be made to avoid an allocation which will impose some costs on those groups or activities which neither consume fish nor utilize those products of the defendants derived from their operations in the Santa Barbara Channel. Calabresi at 144-150. On the record before us, we have no way of evaluating the relative administrative costs involved. However, we do recognize that it is probable that by imposing liability on the defendants some portion of the accident costs in this case may be borne by those who neither eat fish nor use the petroleum products derived from the defendants' operations in Santa Barbara.

Calabresi's final guideline, however, unmistakably points to the defendants as the best cost-avoider. Under this guideline, the loss should be allocated to that party who can best correct any error in allocation, if such there be, by acquiring the activity to which the party has been made liable. Calabresi at 150-152. The capacity "to buy out" the plaintiffs if the burden is too great is, in essence, the real focus of Calabresi's approach. On this basis there is no contest — the defendants' capacity is superior.

NOTES

1. Protection of wild animals: the common pool. Why is the plaintiff in *Oppen* barred from bringing an ordinary tort action for nuisance? One possible explanation is that no one owned the fish when they were killed. "The plaintiffs who do not own the fish cannot complain if the Union Oil company captures them. As they cannot complain of capture, they cannot complain of destruction after capture. As they cannot complain of destruction after capture, they cannot complain of destruction before capture." Epstein, Nuisance Law: Corrective Justice and Its Utilitarian Constraints, 8 J. Legal Stud. 49, 52 (1979). This position overlooks, however, the problem of the common pool — i.e., that resources not subject to private ownership will be destroyed or consumed too rapidly. Since the fish are unowned, any individual actor motivated by self-interest will not need to take into account the social losses that accrue from the damage done to the pool of fish through capture and destruction. See generally Sweeney, Tollison, and Willett, Market Failure, the Common-Pool Problem, and Ocean Resource Exploitation, 17 J.L. & Econ. 179 (1974). *Oppen* may be interpreted as providing the tort action to a nonowner to prevent the premature destruction of valuable resources.

Overconsumption or destruction of common-pool resources are generally thought to furnish the most powerful justifications for state regulation. But it is less clear that the response should take the form of a private action for commercial fishermen, given the need to protect common pool resources from both pollution and chronic overfishing. Still another difficulty with the private action involves determining which individuals have standing to bring suit for their economic losses. Pruitt v. Allied Chemical Corp., 523 F. Supp. 975 (E.D. Va. 1981), arose out of the spillage of kepone into the James River and the Chesapeake Bay. The district court allowed the suits of the commercial fishermen and the marina, boat, tackle, and bait shop owners. It denied the actions of the various seafood wholesalers, retailers, and distributors who purchased and marketed the seafood of the commercial fishermen on the ground that the harm suffered was "insufficiently direct." It also refused to allow actions by employees of the various groups named. Does the directness test serve to distinguish the various interests? What if the loss of a large fish wholesaler was larger in dollar amount than that of a small commercial fisherman? How can a double counting of losses be prevented?

Note here the close affinity between the physical damage cases and the cases of pure economic loss treated in Chapter 17.

2. Public regulation and the protection of the common pool: CERCLA. As with public nuisances generally, the weakness of the private remedial system has led to extensive direct regulation of activities that pose dangers to the environment. Since 1980, CERCLA (Comprehensive Environmental Response, Compensation, and Liability Act of 1980 — Pub. L. No. 96-510, 94 Stat. 2767, 2781-2785 (1980)) — often known as the Superfund — has provided for an extensive scheme of regulation that, inter alia, require parties to provide the government with notice, first, of any discharge of pollutants into the environment, and second, of the storage or collection of any dangerous substance in a "facility," broadly defined under the statute. The statute also imposes taxes on the sale of certain designated chemicals and the shipment of waste products to disposal sites. And it gives specific authorization for the cleanup of major dumpsites. These may be undertaken by the Environmental Protection Agency (EPA) alone or in cooperation with state agencies and cover the costs of clean up of any pollution spills.

The basic rules of liability under CERCLA have two notable features. First, whatever the ambiguities in the original drafting, it is now settled that all persons in the chain of distribution are jointly, severally, and strictly liable for the cleanup costs. State of New York v. Shore Realty Corp., 759 F.2d 1032, 1039-1042 (2d Cir. 1985) (holding that states can enjoin dumpsite operations as public nuisances under state law, even if they cannot obtain injunctive relief under CERCLA). CERCLA imposes strict *retroactive* liability on defendants for wastes that were lawfully deposited in the dumpsites prior to the passage of the statute. Similarly the class of potentially responsible parties (PRPs) under the statute has been broadly construed to include not only generators and transporters of hazardous wastes material but also former owners of the dumpsite, for however short a period, even if they have done no dumping themselves. CERCLA covers passive leakages as well as discharges or dumping from cities, and plaintiffs under CERCLA are not subject to "the onerous burden of pinpointing at what precise point a leakage might have begun." Nurd v. William E. Hooper & Sons Co., 966 F.2d 837 (4th Cir. 1992).

CERCLA also presents difficult issues of causation and remedy. In United States v. Alcan Corporation, 964 F.2d 252 (3d Cir. 1992), Alcan released into the Susquehanna River a treated waste emulsion that contained minute quantities of copper, chromium, lead, and zinc, all of which are hazardous substances under CERCLA. The amounts in question were far below those which could be released under applicable environmental regulations, and were "indeed, orders of magnitude below ambient or naturally occurring background levels." Greenberg, J., nonetheless held that there was no minimum level of release necessary to trigger private liability for clean-up costs under the statute. Once a release was established, the government, as plaintiff under CERCLA, "need not establish a direct causal connection between the defendant's hazardous substances and the release or the plaintiff's incurrence of response costs." The court then went on to hold that the common-law provisions on joint and several liability governed the case, and remanded for further determination as to whether Alcan's releases were sufficiently "divisible" from pollution caused by other sources so that it could be held accountable only for its distinct harm. What is the best response where low-level emissions from multiple parties require a government-organized clean up? See generally Harris and Milan, Avoiding Joint and Several Liability Under CERCLA, 23 Env. L. Rptr. 1726 (1992).

3. *The general theory of environmental law.* The CERCLA represents only one limited effort to cope with the endless variety of environmental problems. Air pollution, for example, is an area in which private remedies work fitfully, if at all, since we no longer have nuisance cases with, at most, a small number of parties on either side. The remedial structure of the private law of nuisance breaks down when the nuisances are created by large numbers of individuals, most of whom happen to be the victims of the very nuisances they have created. The contrast with the single defendant, so critical in *Boomer,* must be repeatedly stressed. Yet with large number situations, administratively it seems impossible (class actions not to the contrary) to tolerate a mass of damages actions brought by everybody against everybody, or, in the extreme case, to allow a single individual to enjoin all use of the automobile. We are thus again drawn to direct public controls over such things as automobile emissions.

Choosing the right form of pollution regulation is formidable, to say the least; and here it is only possible to mention the various strategies that might be adopted. One system is a tax that requires each polluter to bear the economic costs of the pollution while allowing the basic activities to continue even though they cause inconvenience or discomfort to others. Taxes are a form of strict liability on the defendant without direct compensation to the plaintiff, who might prove less willing to undertake clean-up actions that could prove uneconomical without the prospect of tort recovery. Taxes also create their own set of political and administrative problems. How does one determine the level of the tax? When to change it? What to do with the proceeds? Whether to treat rich and poor alike?

Another approach is the public analogue to the private injunction, thus prohibiting the offending activity altogether, as, for example, banning the use of high-sulfur fuel in home furnaces in urban areas. How will it be possible to decide whether the costs of prohibition are justified by the benefits conferred upon society? Taxes allow private parties to help make those choices for us; what scheme must be used for public prohibition?

A less crude, but more complex variation contemplates direct controls short of prohibition. Thus, a particular activity may be allowed to continue, but only if done in conformity with certain conditions established by the state. A firm may be allowed to burn coal, but only on condition that it install scrubbers in its chimneys. With these last two alternatives, how does one decide what conditions should attach to what uses? Is it possible to frame regulations that take into account the alternatives to pollution open to each firm? Do taxes or injunctions possess more of the desirable features of a market system? See generally Polinsky, Controlling Externalities and Protecting Entitlements: Property Right, Liability Rule, and Tax-Subsidy Approaches, 8 J. Legal Stud. 1 (1979).

Chapter Nine
Products Liability

A. INTRODUCTION

In this chapter we will turn our attention to products liability law, an area that has become so important that it is today virtually a field of law in itself. As befits its complexity, products liability law has a rich and dense history which can be roughly divided into four periods beginning shortly after the onset of the Industrial Revolution in the first half of the nineteenth century and extending to the present day.

The first period ran roughly from the middle of the nineteenth century to the early twentieth century. During this period, the major question was whether any suits against product manufacturers or distributors of products should be allowed at all. The dominant question was whether the "privity" limitation prevented the injured party — whether consumer, user, or bystander — from bringing a suit against the "remote" seller of the product in question. The early case of Winterbottom v. Wright, 152 Eng. Rep. 402 (Ex. 1842), held that an injured consumer or user had an action only against the immediate vendor of the product, while a bystander could sue only the party then in possession of the product immediately before the injury occurred. The remainder of the nineteenth century witnessed a steady, but limited, erosion of this basic principle as exceptions were created, roughly speaking, for products that held hidden dangers which manifested themselves in ordinary use.

At the beginning of the second period, the privity limitation was overthrown in its entirety in MacPherson v. Buick Motor Co., 111 N.E. 1050

(N.Y. 1916), which imposed a general liability for negligence on a remote seller, that is, one who has no direct contractual relationship with the injured party. The third stage of liability law was inaugurated with the famous concurring opinion of Justice Traynor in Escola v. Coca-Cola Bottling Co., 150 P.2d 436 (Cal. 1944), which urged that strict liability, and not negligence, principles should govern the manufacturer's liability. Traynor's view began to receive widespread judicial acceptance in the early 1960s and quickly became the dominant view when in 1965 the American Law Institute incorporated a general principle of strict liability into section 402A of the Restatement (Second) of Torts. The three dominant themes in the Restatement debates focused on the role of manufacturers: their market power, their capacity to obtain insurance, and their ability to internalize the costs of accidents associated with their products. Taken together, these three pointed to "absolute liability. The presuppositions themselves do not incorporate any conceptual limit to manufacturer's liability." Priest, The Invention of Enterprise Liability: A Critical History of the Intellectual Foundations of Modern Tort Law, 14 J. Legal Stud. 461, 527 (1985). On the early development of strict liability through the second Restatement see also R. Epstein, Modern Products Liability Law (1980); Prosser, The Assault Upon the Citadel (Strict Liability to the Consumer), 69 Yale L.J. 1099 (1960).

The fourth and present stage of products liability law began with a series of important (what are now widely known as) defective design and duty to warn cases, decided in the decade after the 1965 Restatement. These cases, which ironically enough have expanded liability within the traditional framework of negligence law, form the centerpiece of modern products liability law.

Today products liability law is big business, and it is useful to give some basic information about its overall scope before turning to discrete legal issues. The first and most obvious fact about the system is that the volume of litigation has soared in the 30 years since the Second Restatement. The total number of product liability actions in federal court has increased from 2,393 in 1975 (the date corresponding to the first crisis in the products liability insurance market) to 13,408 in 1989. A huge fraction of this increase has come in asbestos cases, which by 1991 represented over 60 percent of the products liability cases in federal courts, although suits against pharmaceutical companies continue to occupy a substantial portion of the docket. See W. Viscusi, Reforming Products Liability Law 18-19 (1991). The volume of litigation in other product-related areas have varied within a far smaller range over that same period; airline cases, for example, have gone from 301 suits to 185, and motor vehicle cases have increased from 438 to 662. The level of damages has about doubled between 1980 and 1988, in large part in response to rising medical costs during this period of time. Only in the last few years has there been a decline in suits. Thus from July 1989 through June 1990, the total number of new civil suits filed in federal courts was 177,545, of which 19,428 were products related. From July 1990 through June 1991, 170,342 new suits were filed in federal courts, of which 13,188 were products liability cases. Of the more than 32,000 product liability suits filed in those two years, some 7,150 were for asbestos injuries. See Annual Report of the Director of the Administrative Office of the United States Court 138, 143 (1991).

Even a small number of suits can bring about dramatic results. It is estimated that about $100,000 in the cost of each new private plane covers potential liability insurance, where about 90 percent of the crashes result in product liability actions. The production of private planes accordingly dropped from 17,000 per year in 1979 to little more than 1,000 by 1987, and today most new planes are sold in kit form to be assembled by the purchaser. Only in 1994 did Congress respond to this problem by passing a statute of repose to protect manufacturers of old claims against suit. See infra at page 770. Similarly, as much as 25 percent of the cost of the ordinary ladder can be traced to costs associated with product liability actions. Ironically, however, the rapid increase in the overall level of product litigation has been matched by a long and steady decline in accident levels. From 1930 to 1985, workplace accidents has declined from fifteen to five per one hundred thousand, while home accident and vehicular accident rates have fallen dramatically as well. There seems to be little, if any, correlation between the decline in accident rates and the expansion in tort liability, for the decline in rates has been steady and consistent both before and after the initial expansion of products liability law, between 1968 and 1975.

See generally Priest, Products Liability Law and the Accident Rate, in Liability: Perspectives and Policy (R. Litan and C. Winston eds., 1988); W. Kip Viscusi, Reforming Products Liability Law chs. 1 & 2 (1991); Paul Rubin, Tort Reform by Contract 67 (1993); National Safety Council, Accident Facts (1989). For a very different view of this issue see Croley and Hanson, What Liability Crisis? An Alternative Explanation for Recent Events in Product Liability, 8 Yale J. on Reg. 1 (1991), arguing that the recent developments in products liability have properly forced manufacturers to bear the full pecuniary and nonpecuniary costs of marketing defective products. For a critique of Croley and Hanson see Priest, Can Absolute Manufacturer Liability be Defended?, 9 Yale J. on Reg. 237 (1992).

The concerns with the expansion of products liability law have not been confined to academic circles. Clearly some move has been afoot in the cases as well. Professors James Henderson and Theodore Eisenberg's recent major study of product liability litigation concludes that with the independent efforts at legislative reforms from the early to mid-1980s "products liability had turned an important corner. The judges whom the state legislatures sought to rein in had already begun a trend of doctrinal change favoring defendants. This trend is evident in an increasing percentage of published opinions, both routine and groundbreaking, favoring defendants. At the trial court level, at a time when plaintiffs' likelihood of success in products cases is said by many to be increasing, it has been moving in quite the opposite direction." Henderson and Eisenberg, The Quiet Revolution in Products Liability: An Empirical Study of Legal Change, 37 U.C.L.A. L. Rev. 479, 481 (1990). Their conclusion has been challenged by Professor Gary Schwartz: "As far as appellate doctrine is concerned, their use of the term 'revolution' is perhaps unfortunate; what they primarily describe is not the overruling of precedents but rather the rejection by the judiciary of further expansions of products liability doctrine. They can call this a 'revolution' because it stands in such contrast to the growth of doctrine that had occurred between 1960 and the early 1980s." Schwartz, The Beginning and the Possible End of the Rise of Modern American Tort Law, 26 Ga. L. Rev. 601, 604 (1992).

Owing to the vastness of modern products liability law, virtually every issue of tort liability — the basis of liability, causation, proof, defenses, damages — that has been examined in the ordinary tort case reasserts itself in the context of modern products liability litigation and can easily fill a casebook of its own. See, e.g., J. Henderson and A. Twerski, Products Liability: Problems and Process (2d ed. 1992). The materials presented here are designed to give a sense of both the historical origins and the current controversies of products liability law. Of necessity they cover only a tiny fraction of a rich and complex field.

B.   EXPOSITION

Winterbottom v. Wright
152 Eng. Rep. 402 (Ex. 1842)

[The defendant contracted with the Postmaster-General to supply mail coaches to carry the mail and to see that the coaches would "be kept in a fit, proper, safe, and secure state and condition for said purpose," and under this contract he assumed "the sole and exclusive duty, charge, care, and burden of the repairs, state, and condition" thereof. Atkinson, knowing of the contract, himself contracted with the Postmaster-General to supply horses and drivers for the coaches. The plaintiff was one of the drivers so provided. While the plaintiff was driving the coach serviced by defendant, he was hurt when a latent defect caused the coach to break down, throwing plaintiff to the ground and injuring him. The defendant demurred to the defendant's action.

Perhaps a brief observation is in order at this point. It has frequently been said that the plaintiff sued on the contract between the defendant and Postmaster-General, to which he was not a party. But there is ample evidence that he was suing in tort, and looked to the contract only as a source for the defendant's duty of care. See the argument of counsel in the original report, as well as the concluding two sentences of Lord Abinger's opinion below.]

ABINGER, C.B. I am clearly of opinion that the defendant is entitled to our judgment. We ought not to permit a doubt to rest upon this subject, for our doing so might be the means of letting in upon us an infinity of actions. This is an action of the first impression, and it has been brought in spite of the precautions which were taken, in the judgment of this Court in the case of Levy v. Langridge [150 Eng. Rep. 863 (Ex. 1836), a case of fraudulent representation by the seller to the purchaser], to obviate any notion that such an action could be maintained. We ought not to attempt to extend the principle of that decision, which, although it has been cited in support of this action, wholly fails as an authority in its favour; for there the gun was bought for the use of the son, the plaintiff in that action, who could not make the bargain himself, but was really and substantially the party contracting. Here the action is brought simply because the defendant was a contractor with a third person; and it is contended that thereupon he became liable to everybody who might use the carriage. If there had been any ground for such an action, there certainly would have been some precedent of it; but with the exception of actions against innkeepers, and some few other persons, no case of a similar nature has occurred in practice. That is a strong circumstance, and is of itself a great authority against its maintenance. It is however contended, that this contract being made on the behalf of the public by the Postmaster-General, no action could be maintained against him, and therefore the plaintiff must have a remedy against the defendant. But that is by no means a necessary consequence — he may be remediless altogether. There is no privity of contract between these parties; and if the plaintiff can sue, every passenger, or even any person passing along the road, who was injured by the upsetting of the coach, might bring a similar action. Unless we confine the operation of such contracts as this to the parties who entered into them, the most absurd and outrageous consequences, to which I can see no limit, would ensue. Where a party becomes responsible to the public, by undertaking a public duty, he is liable, though the injury may have arisen from the negligence of his servant or agent. So, in cases of public nuisances, whether the act was done by the party as a servant, or in any other capacity, you are liable to an action at the suit of any person who suffers. Those, however, are cases where the real ground of the liability is the public duty, or the commission of the public nuisance. There is also a class of cases in which the law permits a contract to be turned into a tort; but unless there has been some public duty undertaken, or public nuisance committed, they are all cases in which an action might have been maintained upon the contract. Thus, a carrier may be sued either in assumpsit or case; but there is no instance in which a party, who was not privy to the contract entered into with him, can maintain any such action. The plaintiff in this case could not have brought an action on the contract; if he could have done so, what would have been his situation, supposing the Postmaster-General had released the defendant? That would, at all events, have defeated his claim altogether. By permitting this action, we should be working this injustice, that after the defendant had done everything to the satisfaction of his employer, and after all matters between them had been adjusted, and all accounts settled on the footing of their contract, we should subject them to be ripped open by this action of tort being brought against him.

NOTE

The American reception of Winterbottom v. Wright. During the nineteenth century, Winterbottom v. Wright was a leading case not only in England but also in the United States. Several nineteenth-century cases, however, carved out exceptions to its categorical prohibition. The overall position in the United States at about the turn of the century is best summarized in Huset v. J. I. Case Threshing Machine Co., 120 F. 865, 867-871 (8th Cir. 1903). There Judge Sanborn gave this rationale for the general rule and its major exceptions:

> [T]he natural and probable effect of the negligence of the contractor or manufacturer will generally be limited to the party for whom the article is constructed, or to whom it is first sold, and, perhaps more than all this, for the reason that a wise and conservative public policy has impressed the courts with the view that there must be a fixed and definite limitation to the liability of manufacturers and vendors for negligence in the construction and sale of complicated machines and structures which are to be operated or used by the intelligent and the ignorant, the skillful and the incompetent, the watchful and the careless, parties that cannot be known to the manufacturers or vendors, and who use the articles all over the country hundreds of miles distant from the place of their manufacture or original sale, a general rule has been adopted and has become established by repeated decisions of the courts of England and of this country that in these cases the liability of the contractor or manufacturer for negligence in the construction or sale of the articles which he makes or vends is limited to the persons to whom he is liable under his contracts of construction or sale. The limits of the liability for negligence and for breaches of contract in cases of this character are held to be identical. The general rule is that a contractor, manufacturer, or vendor is not liable to third parties who have no contractual relations with him for

negligence in the construction, manufacture, or sale of the articles he handles. Winterbottom v. Wright, ...

But while this general rule is both established and settled, there are, as is usually the case, exceptions to it as well defined and settled as the rule itself. There are three exceptions to this rule.

The first is that an act of negligence of a manufacturer or vendor which is imminently dangerous to the life or health of mankind, and which is committed in the preparation or sale of an article intended to preserve, destroy, or affect human life, is actionable by third parties who suffer from the negligence. . . .

The second exception is that an owner's act of negligence which causes injury to one who is invited by him to use his defective appliance upon the owner's premises may form the basis of an action against the owner. . . .

The third exception to the rule is that one who sells or delivers an article which he knows to be imminently dangerous to life or limb to another without notice of its qualities is liable to any person who suffers an injury therefrom which might have been reasonably anticipated, whether there were any contractual relations between the parties or not.

The court then held that the complaint alleged a cause of action under the third exception: the defendant's threshing machine was said to be constructed so that the cylinder covering upon which its operator had to walk could not support his weight, that defect was latent in that it could not be discovered by ordinary inspection, and that it was known by the defendant. The court then remanded the case for trial, noting that it was "perhaps improbable" that the defendant had knowledge of the imminently dangerous character of the machine at the time of delivery.

MacPherson v. Buick Motor Co.
111 N.E. 1050 (N.Y. 1916)

Appeal, by permission, from a judgment of the Appellate Division of the Supreme Court in the third judicial department, entered January 8, 1914, affirming a judgment in favor of plaintiff entered upon a verdict.

CARDOZO, J. The defendant is a manufacturer of automobiles. It sold an automobile to a retail dealer. The retail dealer resold to the plaintiff. While the plaintiff was in the car, it suddenly collapsed. He was thrown out and injured. One of the wheels was made of defective wood, and its spokes crumbled into fragments. The wheel was not made by the defendant; it was bought from another manufacturer. There is evidence, however, that its defects could have been discovered by reasonable inspection, and that inspection was omitted. There is no claim that the defendant knew of the defect and willfully concealed it. The case, in other words, is not brought within the rule of Kuelling v. Lean Mfg. Co. (183 N.Y. 78). The charge is one, not of fraud, but of negligence.

The question to be determined is whether the defendant owed a duty of care and vigilance to any one but the immediate purchaser.

The foundations of this branch of the law, at least in this state, were laid in Thomas v. Winchester (6 N.Y. 397). A poison was falsely labeled. The sale was made to a druggist, who in turn sold to a customer. The customer recovered damages from the seller who affixed the label. "The defendant's negligence," it was said, "put human life in imminent danger." A poison falsely labeled is likely to injure anyone who gets it. Because the danger is to be foreseen, there is a duty to avoid the injury. Cases were cited by way of illustration in which manufacturers were not subject to any duty irrespective of contracts. The distinction was said to be that their conduct, though negligent, was not likely to result in injury to any one except the purchaser. We are not required to say whether the chance of injury was always as remote as the distinction assumes. Some of the illustrations might be rejected to-day. The *principle* of the distinction is for present purposes the important thing.

Thomas v. Winchester became quickly a landmark of the law. In the application of its principle there may at times have been uncertainty or even error. There has never in this state been doubt or disavowal of the principle itself. The chief cases are well known, yet to recall some of them will be helpful. Loop v. Litchfield (42 N.Y. 351) is the earliest. It was the case of a defect in a small balance wheel used on a circular saw. The manufacturer pointed out the defect to the buyer, who wished a cheap article and was ready to assume the risk. The risk can hardly have been an imminent one, for the wheel lasted five years before it broke. In the meanwhile the buyer had made a lease of the machinery. It was held that the manufacturer was not answerable to the lessee. Loop v. Litchfield was followed in Losee v. Clute (51 N.Y. 494), the case of the explosion of a steam boiler. That decision has been criticised (Thompson on Negligence, 233 Shearman & Redfield on Negligence [6th ed.], §117) but it must be confined to its special facts. It was put upon the ground that the risk of injury was too remote. The buyer in that case had not only accepted the boiler, but had tested it. The manufacturer knew that his own test was not the final one. The finality of the test has a bearing on the measure of diligence owing to persons other than the purchaser (Beven, Negligence [3d ed.], pp. 50, 51, 54; Wharton, Negligence [2d ed.], §134).

These early cases suggest a narrow construction of the rule. Later cases, however, evince a more liberal spirit. First in importance is Devlin v. Smith (89 N.Y. 470). The defendant, a contractor, built a scaffold for a painter. The painter's servants were injured. The contractor was held liable. He knew that the scaffold, if improperly constructed, was a most dangerous trap. He knew that it was to be used by the workmen. He was building it for that very purpose. Building it for their use, he owed them a duty, irrespective of his contract with their master, to build it with care.

From Devlin v. Smith we pass over intermediate cases and turn to the latest case in this court in which Thomas v. Winchester was followed. That case is Statler v. Ray Mfg. Co. (195 N.Y. 478, 480). The defendant manufactured a large coffee urn. It was installed in a restaurant. When heated, the urn exploded and injured the plaintiff. We held that the manufacturer was liable. We said that the urn "was of such a character inherently that, when applied to the purposes for which it was designed, it was liable to become a source of great danger to many people if not carefully and properly constructed."

It may be that Devlin v. Smith and Statler v. Ray Mfg. Co. have extended the rule of Thomas v. Winchester. If so, this court is committed to the extension. The defendant argues that things imminently dangerous to life are poisons, explosives, deadly weapons — things whose normal function it is to injure or destroy. But whatever the rule in Thomas v. Winchester may once have been, it has no longer that restricted meaning. A scaffold (Devlin v. Smith, supra) is not inherently a destructive instrument. It becomes destructive only if imperfectly constructed. A large coffee urn . . . may have within itself, if negligently made, the potency of danger, yet no one thinks of it as an implement whose normal function is destruction. What is true of the coffee urn is equally true of bottles of aerated water (Torgeson v. Schultz, 192 N.Y. 156). We have mentioned only cases in this court. But the rule has received a like extension in our courts of intermediate appeal. In Burke v. Ireland (26 App. Div. 487), in an opinion by Cullen, J., it was applied to a builder who constructed a defective building; in Kahner v. Otis Elevator Co. (96 App. Div. 169) to the manufacturer of an elevator; in Davis v. Pelham Hod Elevating Co. (65 Hun. 573 affirmed in this court without opinion, 146 N.Y. 363) to a contractor who furnished a defective rope with knowledge of the purpose for which the rope was to be used. We are not required at this time either to approve or to disapprove the application of the rule that was made in these cases. It is enough that they help to characterize the trend of judicial thought.

[Cardozo, J., then reviewed the parallel English decisions.]

We hold, then, that the principle of Thomas v. Winchester is not limited to poisons, explosives, and things of like nature, to things which in their normal operation are implements of destruction. If the nature of a thing is such that it is reasonably certain to place life and limb in peril when negligently made, it is then a thing of danger. Its nature gives warning of the consequences to be expected. If to the element of danger there is added knowledge that the thing will be used by persons other than the purchaser, and used without new tests, then, irrespective of contract, the manufacturer of this thing of danger is under a duty to make it carefully. That is as far as we are required to go for the decision of this case. There must be knowledge of a danger, not merely possible, but probable. It is *possible* to use almost anything in a way that will make it dangerous if defective. That is not enough to charge the manufacturer with a duty independent of his contract. Whether a given thing is dangerous may be sometimes a question for the court and sometimes a question for the jury. There must also be knowledge that in the usual course of events the danger will be shared by others than the buyer. Such knowledge may often be inferred from the nature of the transaction. But it is possible that even knowledge of the danger and of the use will not always be enough. The proximity or remoteness of the relation is a factor to be considered. We are dealing now with the liability of the manufacturer of the finished product, who puts it on the market to be used without inspection by his customers. If he is negligent, where danger is to be foreseen, a liability will follow. We are not required at this time to say that it is legitimate to go back of the manufacturer of the finished product and hold the manufacturers of the component parts. To make their negligence a cause of imminent danger, an independent cause must often intervene; the manufacturer of the finished product must also fail in *his* duty of inspection. It may be that in those circumstances the negligence of the earlier members of the series is too remote to constitute, as to the ultimate user, an actionable wrong. . . . We leave that question open. We shall have to deal with it when it arises. The difficulty which it suggests is not present in this case. There is here no break in the chain of cause and effect. In such circumstances, the presence of a known danger, attendant upon a known use, makes vigilance a duty. We have put aside the notion that the duty to safeguard life and limb, when the consequences of negligence may be foreseen, grows out of contract and nothing else. We have put the source of the obligation where it ought to be. We have put its source in the law.

From this survey of the decisions, there thus emerges a definition of the duty of a manufacturer which enables us to measure this defendant's liability. Beyond all question, the nature of an automobile gives warning of probable danger if its construction is defective. This automobile was designed to go fifty miles an hour. Unless its wheels were sound and strong, injury was almost certain. It was as much a thing of danger as a defective engine for a railroad. The defendant knew the danger. It knew also that the car would be used by persons other than the buyer. This was apparent from its size; there were seats for three persons. It was apparent also from the fact that the buyer was a dealer in cars, who bought to resell. The maker of this car supplied it for the use of purchasers from the dealer just as plainly as the contractor in Devlin v. Smith supplied the scaffold for use by the servants of the owner. The dealer was indeed the one person of whom it might be said with some approach to certainty that by him the car would not be used. Yet the defendant would have us say that he was the one person whom it was under a legal duty to protect. The law does not lead us to so inconsequent a conclusion. Precedents drawn from the days of travel by stage coach do not fit the conditions of travel today. The principle that the danger must be imminent does not change, but the things subject to the principle do change. They are whatever the needs of life in a developing civilization require them to be.

In reaching this conclusion, we do not ignore the decisions to the contrary in other jurisdictions. It was held in Cadillac M.C. Co. v. Johnson (221 Fed. Rep. 801) that an automobile is not within the rule of Thomas v. Winchester. There was, however, a vigorous dissent. Opposed to that decision is one of the Court of Appeals of Kentucky (Olds Motor Works v. Shaffer, 145 Ky. 616). The earlier cases are summarized by Judge Sanborn in Huset v. J. I. Case Threshing Machine Co. (120 Fed. Rep. 865). Some of them, at first sight inconsistent with our conclusion, may be reconciled upon the ground that the negligence was too remote, and that another cause had intervened. But even when they cannot be reconciled, the difference is rather in the application of the principle than in the principle itself. Judge Sanborn says, for example, that the contractor who builds a bridge, or the manufacturer who builds a car, cannot ordinarily foresee injury to other persons than the owner as the probable result. We take a different view. We think that injury to others is to be foreseen not merely as a possible, but as an almost inevitable result. (See the trenchant criticism in Bohlen, supra, at p. 351.) Indeed, Judge Sanborn concedes that his view is not to be reconciled with our decision in Devlin v. Smith (supra). The doctrine of that decision has now become the settled law of this state, and we have no desire to depart from it.

In England the limits of the rule are still unsettled. Winterbottom v. Wright is often cited. The defendant undertook to provide a mail coach to carry the mail bags. The coach broke down from latent defects in its construction. The defendant, however, was not the manufacturer. The court held that he was not liable for injuries to a passenger. The case was decided on a demurrer to the declaration. Lord Esher points out in Heaven v. Pender (11 Q.B.D. 503) that the form of the declaration was subject to criticism. It did not fairly suggest the existence of a duty aside from the special contract which was the plaintiff's main reliance. At all events, in Heaven v. Pender (supra) the defendant, a dock owner, who put up a staging outside a ship, was held liable to the servants of the ship owner. In Elliot v. Hall (15 Q.B.D. 315) the defendant sent out a defective truck laden with goods which he had sold. The buyer's servants unloaded it, and were injured because of the defects. It was held that the defendant was under a duty "not to be guilty of negligence with regard to the state and condition of the truck." [Then, after a brief discussion of some English cases obliquely touching on the issue involved, Cardozo, J., proceeded as follows:] From these cases a consistent principle is with difficulty extracted. The English courts, however, agree with ours in holding that one who invites another to make use of an appliance is bound to the exercise of reasonable care. That at bottom is the underlying principle of Devlin v. Smith. The contractor who builds the scaffold invites the owner's workmen to use it. The manufacturer who sells the automobile to the retail dealer invites the dealer's customers to use it. The invitation is addressed in the one case to determinate persons and in the other to an indeterminate class, but in each case it is equally plain, and in each its consequences must be the same.

There is nothing anomalous in a rule which imposes upon A, who has contracted with B, a duty to C and D and others according as he knows or does not know that the subject-matter of the contract is intended for their use. We may find an analogy in the law which measures the liability of landlords. If A leases to B a tumbledown house he is not liable, in the absence of fraud, to B's guests who enter it and are injured. This is because B is then under the duty to repair it, the lessor has the right to suppose that he will fulfill that duty, and, if he omits to do so, his guests must look to him. But if A leases a building to be used by the lessee at once as a place of public entertainment, the rule is different. There injury to persons other than the lessee is to be foreseen, and foresight of the consequences involves the creation of a duty.

In this view of the defendant's liability there is nothing inconsistent with the theory of liability on which the case was tried. It is true that the court told the jury that "an automobile is not an inherently dangerous vehicle." The meaning, however, is made plain by the context. The meaning is that danger is not to be expected when the vehicle is well constructed. The court left it to the jury to say whether the defendant ought to have foreseen that the car, if negligently constructed, would become "imminently dangerous." Subtle distinctions are drawn by the defendant between things inherently dangerous and things imminently dangerous, but the case does not turn upon these verbal niceties. If danger was to be expected as reasonably certain, there was a duty of vigilance, and this whether you call the danger inherent or imminent. In varying forms that thought was put before the jury. We do not say that the court would not have been justified in ruling as a matter of law that the car was a dangerous thing. If there was any error, it was none of which the defendant can complain.

We think the defendant was not absolved from a duty of inspection because it bought the wheels from a reputable manufacturer. It was not merely a dealer in automobiles. It was a manufacturer of automobiles. It was responsible for the finished product. It was not at liberty to put the finished product on the market without subjecting the component parts to ordinary and simple tests. Under the charge of the trial judge nothing more was required of it. The obligation to inspect must vary with the nature of the thing to be inspected. The more probable the danger, the greater the need of caution. There is little analogy between this case and Carlson v. Phoenix Bridge Co. (132 N.Y. 273), where the defendant bought a tool for a servant's use. The making of tools was not the business in which the master was engaged. Reliance on the skill of the manufacturer was proper and almost inevitable. But that is not the defendant's situation. Both by its relation to the work and by the nature of its business, it is charged with a stricter duty.

Other rulings complained of have been considered, but no error has been found in them.

The judgment should be affirmed with costs.

BARTLETT, C.J., dissenting. . . . [In Thomas v. Winchester] Chief Judge Ruggles, who delivered the opinion of the court, distinguished between an act of negligence imminently dangerous to the lives of others and one that is not so, saying: "If A. build a wagon and sell it to B., who sells it to C. and C. hires it to D., who in consequence of the gross negligence of A. in building the wagon is overturned and injured, D. cannot recover damages against A., the builder. A.'s obligation to build the wagon faithfully, arises solely out of his contract with B. The public have nothing to do with it. . . . So, for the same reason, if a horse be defectively shod by a smith, and a person hiring the horse from the owner is thrown and injured in consequence of the smith's negligence in shoeing the smith is not liable for the injury." . . .

I do not see how we can uphold the judgment in the present case without overruling what has been so often said by this court and other courts of like authority in reference to the absence of any liability for negligence on the part of the original vendor of an ordinary carriage to any one except his immediate vendee. The absence of such liability was the very point actually decided in the English case of Winterbottom v. Wright, and the illustration quoted from the opinion of Chief Judge Ruggles in Thomas v. Winchester assumes that the law on the subject was so plain that the statement would be accepted almost as a matter of course. In the case at bar the defective wheel on an automobile moving only eight miles an hour was not any more dangerous to the occupants of the car than a similarly defective wheel would be to the occupants of a carriage drawn by a horse at the same speed; and yet unless the courts have been all wrong on this question up to the present time there would be no liability to strangers to the original sale in the case of the horse-drawn carriage.

NOTES

1. A landmark case. MacPherson v. Buick is a great landmark in the history of our law. Before it came down, the opinion of Sanford, J., in Huset v. J. I. Case stated the law in virtually all jurisdictions, including

New York. After MacPherson v. Buick, one jurisdiction after another abandoned the privity rule in cases involving physical injuries caused by defective products. One early response to *MacPherson* was Johnson v. Cadillac Motor Car Co., which on rehearing reversed its earlier decision, 221 F. 801 (2d Cir. 1915), on the strength of Judge Cardozo's opinion. "We cannot believe that the liability of a manufacturer of automobiles has any analogy to the liability of a manufacturer of 'tables, chairs, pictures or mirrors hung on walls.' The analogy is rather that of a manufacturer of unwholesome food or of a poisonous drug. It is every bit as dangerous to put upon the market an automobile with rotten spokes as it is to send out to the trade rotten foodstuffs." Johnson v. Cadillac Motor Car Co., 261 F. 878 (2d Cir. 1919). Other cases also extended the scope of *MacPherson*. Thus in Smith v. Peerless Glass Co., 181 N.E. 576 (N.Y. 1932), the court allowed a direct action for negligence to be brought against the manufacturer of a component part, such as the wheelmaker in *MacPherson*. Today every jurisdiction in the United States follows the *MacPherson* rule. In 1966 Mississippi became the last state to fall into line, in State Stove Mfg. Co. v. Hodges, 189 So. 2d 113 (Miss. 1966), when that court in a single step both rejected the privity doctrine *and* embraced a theory of strict liability for defective products. For a provocative discussion of the early evolution of products liability law see E. Levi, An Introduction to Legal Reasoning 7-19 (1949).

2. *The fate of Winterbottom v. Wright in English law.* In Donoghue v. Stevenson, [1932] A.C. 562, 580, 599 (Scot.), the plaintiff sued the defendant for the physical harm that allegedly resulted when she drank the remains of a decomposed snail left in an opaque bottle of ginger beer marketed by the defendant. While the House of Lords went out of its way to avoid overruling Winterbottom v. Wright, it took exception to its view of privity. Lord Atkin adopted both "broad" and "narrow" grounds for his decision. Referring first to the "general public sentiment of moral wrongdoing from which the offenders must pay," Lord Atkin first stated his famous "neighbour rule":

> The rule that you are to love your neighbour becomes in law, you must not injure your neighbour; and the lawyer's question, Who is my neighbour? receives a restricted reply. You must take reasonable care to avoid acts or omissions which you can reasonably foresee would be likely to injure your neighbour. Who, then, in law, is my neighbour? The answer seems to be — persons who are so closely and directly affected by my act that I ought reasonably to have them in contemplation as being so affected when I am directing my mind to the acts or omissions which are called in question.

Of equal importance in the development of English law is Atkin's narrow rule:

> [A] manufacturer of products which he sells in such a form as to show
> that he intends them to reach the ultimate consumer in the form in
> which they left him, with no reasonable possibility of intermediate exami-
> nation, and with the knowledge that the absence of reasonable care in
> the preparation or putting up of the products is likely to result in injury
> to the consumer's life or property, owes a duty to the consumer to take
> that reasonable care.

Note that this last rule is capable of the same sort of expansion as the
principle of MacPherson v. Buick. To manufacturers we can analogize
architects, retailers, or repairmen; to sales we can analogize contracts
of hire or gifts of free samples. Users can be treated like consumers.
One early instance of the growth of the English law is Grant v. Austra-
lian Knitting Mills, [1936] A.C. 562 (P.C. 1935) (Aust.), where the Privy
Council allowed the plaintiff's action for personal injury when the defendant sold packaged ready-to-wear underpants without having first
removed the salts used to shrink the fabric during manufacture. The
salts combined with the perspiration in the plaintiff's skin to create
sulfuric acid, which in turn burned the plaintiff. Should it be a defense
in the action if a friend made the plaintiff a present of the underpants?
Any defense if the plaintiff's skin was extrasensitive?

Escola v. Coca-Cola Bottling Co. of Fresno
150 P.2d 436 (Cal. 1944)

[The plaintiff was a waitress. As part of her job, she was placing into
the restaurant's refrigerator bottles of Coca-Cola that had been delivered to the restaurant at least 36 hours earlier. As she put the fourth
bottle into the refrigerator, it exploded in her hand, causing severe
injuries. The plaintiff alleged that the defendant had been negligent in
selling "bottles containing said beverage which on account of excessive
pressure of gas or by reason of some defect in the bottle was dangerous
. . . and likely to explode."

The jury entered a verdict for the plaintiff that was affirmed on appeal. Gibson, J., wrote as follows: "The bottle was admittedly charged
with gas under pressure, and the charging of the bottle was within the
exclusive control of the defendant. As it is a matter of common knowledge that an overcharge would not ordinarily result without negligence, it follows under the doctrine of res ipsa loquitur that if the bottle
was in fact excessively charged an inference of defendant's negligence
would arise."]

TRAYNOR, J. I concur in the judgment, but I believe the manufacturer's negligence should no longer be singled out as the basis of a plaintiff's right to recover in cases like the present one. In my opinion it
should now be recognized that a manufacturer incurs an absolute liabil-

ity when an article that he has placed on the market, knowing that it is to be used without inspection, proves to have a defect that causes injury to human beings. MacPherson v. Buick Motor Co. established the principle, recognized by this court, that irrespective of privity of contract, the manufacturer is responsible for an injury caused by such an article to any person who comes in lawful contact with it. In these cases the source of the manufacturer's liability was his negligence in the manufacturing process or in the inspection of component parts supplied by others. Even if there is no negligence, however, public policy demands that responsibility be fixed wherever it will most effectively reduce the hazards to life and health inherent in defective products that reach the market. It is evident that the manufacturer can anticipate some hazards and guard against the recurrence of others, as the public cannot. Those who suffer injury from defective products are unprepared to meet its consequences. The cost of an injury and the loss of time or health may be an overwhelming misfortune to the person injured, and a needless one, for the risk of injury can be insured by the manufacturer and distributed among the public as a cost of doing business. It is to the public interest to discourage the marketing of products having defects that are a menace to the public. If such products nevertheless find their way into the market it is to the public interest to place the responsibility for whatever injury they may cause upon the manufacturer, who, even if he is not negligent in the manufacture of the product, is responsible for its reaching the market. However intermittently such injuries may occur and however haphazardly they may strike, the risk of their occurrence is a constant risk and a general one. Against such a risk there should be general and constant protection and the manufacturer is best situated to afford such protection.

The injury from a defective product does not become a matter of indifference because the defect arises from causes other than the negligence of the manufacturer, such as negligence of a submanufacturer of a component part whose defects could not be revealed by inspection, or unknown causes that even by the device of res ipsa loquitur cannot be classified as negligence of the manufacturer. The inference of negligence may be dispelled by an affirmative showing of proper care. If the evidence against the fact inferred is "clear, positive, uncontradicted, and of such a nature that it cannot rationally be disbelieved, the court must instruct the jury that the nonexistence of the fact has been established as a matter of law." An injured person, however, is not ordinarily in a position to refute such evidence or identify the cause of the defect, for he can hardly be familiar with the manufacturing process as the manufacturer himself is. In leaving it to the jury to decide whether the inference has been dispelled, regardless of the evidence against it, the negligence rule approaches the rule of strict liability. It is needlessly circuitous to make negligence the basis of recovery and impose what is in reality liability without negligence. If public policy demands that a manufacturer of goods be responsible for their quality regardless of negligence there is no reason not to fix that responsibility openly.

In the case of foodstuffs, the public policy of the state is formulated in a criminal statute. . . . Statutes of this kind result in a strict liability of the manufacturer in tort to the member of the public injured.

The statute may well be applicable to a bottle whose defects cause it to explode. In any event it is significant that the statute imposes criminal liability without fault, reflecting the public policy of protecting the public from dangerous products placed on the market, irrespective of negligence in their manufacture. While the Legislature imposes criminal liability only with regard to food products and their containers, there are many other sources of danger. It is to the public interest to prevent injury to the public from any defective goods by the imposition of civil liability generally.

The retailer, even though not equipped to test a product, is under an absolute liability to his customer, for the implied warranties of fitness for proposed use and merchantable quality include a warranty of safety of the product. This warranty is not necessarily a contractual one; see 1 Williston on Sales, 2d ed., §§197-201, for public policy requires that the buyer be insured at the seller's expense against injury. The courts recognize, however, that the retailer cannot bear the burden of this warranty, and allow him to recoup any losses by means of the warranty of safety attending the wholesaler's or manufacturer's sale to him. . . . Such a procedure, however, is needlessly circuitous and engenders wasteful litigation. Much would be gained if the injured person could base his action directly on the manufacturer's warranty.

The liability of the manufacturer to an immediate buyer injured by a defective product follows without proof of negligence from the implied warranty of safety attending the sale. Ordinarily, however, the immediate buyer is a dealer who does not intend to use the product himself, and if the warranty of safety is to serve the purpose of protecting health and safety it must give rights to others than the dealer. In the words of Judge Cardozo in the *MacPherson* case: "The dealer was indeed the one person of whom it might be said with some approach to certainty that by him the car would not be used. Yet, the defendant would have us say that he was the one person whom it was under a legal duty to protect. The law does not lead us to so inconsequent a solution." While the defendant's negligence in the *MacPherson* case made it unnecessary for the court to base liability on warranty, Judge Cardozo's reasoning recognized the injured person as the real party in interest and effectively disposed on the theory that the liability of the manufacturer incurred by his warranty should apply only to the immediate purchaser. It thus paves the way for a standard of liability that would make the manufacturer guarantee the safety of his product even when there is no negligence.

This court and many others have extended protection according to such a standard to consumers of food products, taking the view that the right of a consumer injured by unwholesome food does not depend "upon the intricacies of the law of sales" and that the warranty of the manufacturer to the consumer in absence of privity of contract rests on public policy. Dangers to life and health inhere in other consumers' goods that are defective and there is no reason to differentiate them from the dangers of defective food products.

In the food products cases the courts have resorted to various fictions to rationalize the extension of the manufacturer's warranty to the consumer: that a warranty runs with the chattel; that the cause of action of the dealer is assigned to the consumer; that the consumer is a third party beneficiary of the manufacturer's contract with the dealer. They have also held the manufacturer liable on a mere fiction of negligence: "Practically he must know it [the product] is fit, or bear the consequences if it proves destructive." Such fictions are not necessary to fix the manufacturer's liability under a warranty if the warranty is severed from the contract of sale between the dealer and the consumer and based on the law of torts as a strict liability. Warranties are not necessarily rights arising under a contract. An action on a warranty "was, in its origin, a pure action of tort," and only late in the historical development of warranties was an action in assumpsit allowed. (Ames, The History of Assumpsit, 2 Harv. L. Rev. 1, 8; 4 Williston on Contracts (1936) §970.) "And it is still generally possible where a distinction of procedure is observed between actions of tort and of contract to frame the declaration for breach of warranty in tort." (Williston, loc. cit.; see Prosser, Warranty on Merchantable Quality, 27 Minn. L. Rev. 117, 118.) On the basis of the tort character of an action on a warranty, recovery has been allowed for wrongful death as it could not be in an action for breach of contract. . . .

As handicrafts have been replaced by mass production with its great markets and transportation facilities, the close relationship between the producer and consumer of a product has been altered. Manufacturing processes, frequently valuable secrets, are ordinarily either inaccessible to or beyond the ken of the general public. The consumer no longer has means or skill enough to investigate for himself the soundness of a product, even when it is not contained in a sealed package, and his erstwhile vigilance has been lulled by the steady efforts of manufacturers to build up confidence by advertising and marketing devices such as trademarks. (See Thomas v. Winchester, 6 N.Y. 697; Baxter v. Ford Motor Co., 168 Wash. 546.) Consumers no longer approach products warily but accept them on faith, relying on the reputation of the manufacturer or the trademark. Manufacturers have sought to justify that faith by increasingly high standards of inspection and a readiness to make good on defective products by way of replacements and refunds. (See Bogert and Fink, Business Practices Regarding Warranties in the Sale of Goods, 25 Ill. L. Rev. 400.) The manufacturer's obligation to the consumer must keep pace with the changing relationship between them; it cannot be escaped because the marketing of a product has become so complicated as to require one or more intermediaries. Certainly there is greater reason to impose liability on the manufacturer than on the retailer who is but a conduit of a product that he is not himself able to test.

The manufacturer's liability should, of course, be defined in terms of the safety of the product in normal and proper use, and should not extend to injuries that cannot be traced to the product as it reached the market.

NOTE

Command decision. Traynor's concurrence in Escola v. Coca-Cola offers a rich variety of justifications for strict liability for manufactured products, each of which raises its own complications.

a. Loss minimization. One rationale is that the manufacturer is in the best position to minimize the losses that arise out of the general use of its product. If that is the correct rationale, however, should we also require strict liability for defective premises of commercial enterprises, or for that matter, strict liability for automobile accidents, at least when business enterprises are defendants? Recall Hammontree v. Jenner, at page 157 supra. On this rationale, what adjustments should be made if the plaintiff or a third party is in a better position to take the desired precautions? Is it consistent with the loss minimization rationale to allow the manufacturer to contract out of liability with the consumer? Does a negligence rule fail to create all the necessary incentives for the manufacturer to take appropriate cost-justified precautions?

For an early criticism of strict liability in products cases see Plant, Strict Liability of Manufacturers for Injuries Caused by Defects in Products — An Opposing View, 24 Tenn. L. Rev. 938, 945 (1957), where it is noted that "[t]he element which is most disturbing to manufacturers is not the potential judgment of legal liability but the injury which is done to the reputation of the product and its producers."

b. Loss spreading. A second defense of the strict liability rule in *Escola* rests upon the ability of the defendant to spread and to cushion the "overwhelming misfortune" to the injured person or his family. This risk-spreading rationale for strict liability has not escaped judicial challenge. In Wights v. Staff Jennings, Inc., 405 P.2d 624, 628 (Or. 1965), the court observed:

> The rationale of risk spreading and compensating the victim has no special relevancy to cases involving injuries resulting from the use of defective goods. The reasoning would seem to apply not only in cases involving personal injuries arising from the *sale* of defective goods, but equally to any case where an injury results from the risk creating conduct of the seller in any stage of the production and distribution of goods. Thus a manufacturer would be strictly liable even in the absence of fault for any injury to a person struck by one of the manufacturer's trucks being used in transporting his goods to market. It seems to us that the enterprise liability rationale employed in the *Escola* case proves too much and that if adopted would compel us to apply the principle of strict liability in all future cases where the loss could be distributed.

c. Elimination of proof complications. A third strand in Traynor's case for strict liability in Escola v. Coca-Cola rests on its circumvention of res ipsa loquitur. Note that this rationale found voice in strict liability actions brought under the Rylands v. Fletcher line of cases. See Chapter 2, supra at 120. In all contexts, the effect of the strict liability rule is to switch the residual risk of unavoidable accidents from the defendant to the plaintiff. In connection with exploding pop bottles, that risk is generally quite small given the stringent quality control and inspection devices that are part of the manufacturing process. How does the doctrine of res ipsa loquitur apply when misconduct by the plaintiff or a third party is also in issue? Should it make any difference that the plaintiff in *Escola* could not produce the pieces of the broken bottle for inspection and examination?

d. The foodstuffs analogy. A fourth defense of the general strict liability doctrine rests on the analogy between adulterated foodstuffs and product defects generally. In this regard, the law after *MacPherson* and before *Escola* generally drew a distinction between foodstuffs that were and were not sold in sealed containers. For goods sold in sealed containers, the general rule exempted the retailer from liability but allowed a direct suit against the manufacturer, albeit on a negligence theory. See, e.g., Richenbacher v. California Packing Corp., 145 N.E. 281 (Mass. 1924), sustaining the use of res ipsa loquitur when the plaintiff's mouth was cut by some heavy gray glass found in a container of spinach. In contrast, when goods were not so packaged, the general rule imposed a negligence liability, if at all, on the retailer but not on the ultimate supplier of the food. Is *Richenbacher* an easier case for res ipsa loquitur than *Escola*? Why?

e. Corrective justice. One last argument for strict liability in products cases — one not pressed by Traynor — is the same argument made on behalf of strict liability in ordinary trespass cases, or even under the rule in Rylands v. Fletcher: that is, to establish the causal connection between the plaintiff and the defendant's act (here, the defective bottling under pressure that caused harm) and then to ask whether, prima facie, the loss should be placed upon the party who created that condition or the party who suffered from it. In this context, however, it is important to note one structural difference between the two types of cases. With abnormally dangerous activities, the defendant is virtually always in possession of the dangerous instrumentality just before it causes the accident and thus is in a powerful position to prevent harm. Accordingly, in this context, the class of defenses based upon plaintiff's conduct remains quite small (see supra Chapter 2 at 131, note 7 and Chapter 8 at 669). With products liability the defendant is *never* in possession of the dangerous product when it causes injury. Given this fact, the older privity limitation becomes more defensible on the ground that it makes liability track possession, save in those few cases in which a party out of possession is in a better position to avoid the loss. See Epstein, The Historical Origins and Economic Structure of Workers' Compensation Law, 16 Ga. L. Rev. 775, 806-808 (1982), where privity for workplace injuries is defended on the ground that employer's liability is both cheaper and more efficient than manufacturer's liability.

On *Escola* see generally Owen, Rethinking the Policies of Strict Products Liability, 33 Vand. L. Rev. 681 (1980), which argues that the various loss-shifting and loss-spreading rationales are defective because they "suffer incurably from being one-directional — they argue only that payment should be made," but do not identify those cases that the defendant ought to win.

McCabe v. Liggett Drug Co.
112 N.E.2d 254 (Mass. 1953)

Contract or Tort. Writ in the Superior Court dated July 22, 1949.

A count in tort was waived by the plaintiff. The action was tried on a count in contract before Meagher, J.

WILLIAMS, J. This is an action of contract to recover compensation for personal injuries resulting from the use of a metal coffee maker purchased from the defendant. The declaration is in one count and alleges breaches of implied warranties of fitness and merchantability. After a verdict for the plaintiff, the judge, on motion of the defendant and subject to the plaintiff's exception, entered a verdict for the defendant under leave reserved.

[Huwe, acting as agent for the plaintiff, had purchased a metal coffee maker, called "Lucifer Lifetime," which he had seen on display at the defendant's store. It was delivered to the plaintiff in a sealed cardboard container. Thereafter the plaintiff assembled and used the coffee maker in the proper manner. The first several times she used it she noticed that the water was slow in going up into the upper bowl. The next time she used it, again in a normal and proper manner, she noticed that the water was not going up into the bowl at all. The entire coffeemaker then exploded, causing the plaintiff to be burned.]

The defendant was notified of the occurrence by letter from the plaintiff's attorney dated June 16, 1949. Therein it was stated that the plaintiff was injured on June 9, 1949, "when the top part of a coffee maker apparently having the trademark 'Lucifer Lifetime' exploded and flew off while being used by her in her home according to the instructions in the circular which accompanied the purchase thereof made at your store on or about May 20, 1949," and that damages were claimed "because the appliance was not fit for the purposes for which it was sold and purchased."

The transaction appears to have been a sale by description. Huwe described the article which he wished to purchase to be one of the metal coffee makers which he had previously seen on sale. The clerk knew to what merchandise he referred and delivered to him a coffee maker of the designated type. The sale carried an implied warranty by the seller that the appliance was a coffee maker of merchantable quality. G. L. (Ter. Ed.) c.106, §17 (2). Merchantable quality means that goods are reasonably suitable for the ordinary uses for which goods of that description are sold. Whether this coffee maker was of such quality depended on its capability, when properly used, to make coffee. This presented a question of fact for the jury. The evidence consisted of the coffee maker and the testimony of the plaintiff concerning the so called explosion. The jury could find that she assembled the parts of the appliance, measured the coffee and water, and applied heat to the water in the lower bowl in accordance with instructions and in the manner that an ordinary person would be expected to proceed in using the appliance to make coffee. The evidence, we think, was sufficient to warrant them in finding why the coffee maker blew up when so used.

[The court then reviewed plaintiff's expert testimony that the "notches" in the coffee maker's filtration system were "inadequate to provide for the release of the pressure which developed from the boiling water," especially if they became clogged by the "congealing" of the coffee grounds.]

. . . Where it is a matter of common knowledge and experience that a process will uniformly or generally produce a certain result a jury of ordinary men may infer the cause from proof of the effect. Here it may be presumed the jury knew that the operation of the coffee maker depended on the pressure of steam on the water in the lower bowl and that the only means provided for relieving this pressure was the tube by which the water would escape into the upper bowl.

The fact that the apparatus violently burst apart in the manner described showed that the accumulating pressure was not being released and in the absence of explanation was itself evidence of a defective condition. The jury could find that the explosion was caused by the failure of the water to rise into the upper bowl and from an examination of the notches in the filter that this failure was due to an inadequate outlet and the clogging effect of coffee grounds which would collect around the notches.

If the coffee maker was so imperfect in design that it could not be used without the likelihood of an explosion it could be found that the appliance was not reasonably fit for making coffee and therefore not merchantable. The plaintiff was not deprived of her right to rely upon the implied warranty either by a failure to inspect or by an inspection before use, as it could have been found that the defect in design would not be obvious to an ordinary person on inspection.

The judge was not justified in entering the verdict for the defendant on the ground that, as contended by the defendant, the notice required by G. L. (Ter. Ed.) c.106, §38, was insufficient, in not stating the exact date of the purchase or the name of the purchaser. Information as to the exact date of the sale was here of little if of any importance to the seller. The defendant had been selling these coffee makers over a period of a week. Presumably all were constructed alike. No claim was made that there was a defect in the particular appliance which was not common to all. The notice indicated a date of purchase within the period when they were being sold and was sufficient to enable the defendant to examine into any fault in their common design. The name of the person who actually made the purchase did not enter into the transaction with the defendant and the failure to state it did not invalidate the notice.

[Reversed with judgment for the plaintiff on the jury verdict].

NOTES

1. Implied warranties: privity complications. McCabe is illustrative of the litigation under the older sales acts (i.e., before the introduction of the Uniform Commercial Code) for injuries caused by defective products. The case itself was brought by the injured purchaser against the retailer, where the privity limitation could not operate to defeat the plaintiff's cause of action. In Chysky v. Drake Brothers Co., 139 N.E. 576, 578 (N.Y. 1923), the plaintiff, a waitress, was given a piece of the defendant's cake for lunch; she bit on a concealed nail that had been baked into the cake and suffered injuries to her mouth. Section 96 of the New York Personal Property Code then provided that "there is no implied warranty or condition as to the quality or fitness for any particular purpose of goods supplied under a contract to sell or a sale, except as follows: 1. Where the buyer, expressly or by implication, makes known to the seller the particular purpose for which the goods are required, and it appears that the buyer relies on the seller's skill or judgment (whether he be the grower or manufacturer or not), there is an implied warranty that the goods shall be reasonably fit for such purpose." The court of appeals held that the plaintiff's cause of action failed under this section, stating that "[t]he general rule is that a manufacturer or seller of food, or other articles of personal property, is not liable to third persons, under an implied warranty, who have no contractual relations with him. The reason for this rule is that privity of contract does not exist between the seller and such third persons, and unless there be privity of contract, there can be no implied warranty."

Chysky v. Drake was gutted, if not expressly overturned, 38 years later in Greenberg v. Lorenz, 173 N.E.2d 773 (N.Y. 1961). There the plaintiff was injured when she ate some canned salmon that contained sharp metal slivers. The salmon had been sold by the defendant retail food dealer to her father. The court below dismissed the plaintiff's complaint on the authority of Chysky v. Drake, because the plaintiff had not purchased the salmon. The Court of Appeals took the injustice of Chysky v. Drake as a given and then rejected it. Assuming it was not fatal to the plaintiff's case that she did not purchase the can of salmon, can she still be denied recovery on the grounds that neither she nor her father relied upon the skill and judgment of the seller, here a retailer and not a manufacturer? As between the retailer and the plaintiff, who was in the better position to discover the metal bits in the salmon can?

2. UCC Section 2-318. The problem raised in both Chysky v. Drake and Greenberg v. Lorenz is no longer governed by section 96 of the New York statute. Today, the operative section is section 2-318 of the Uniform Commercial Code, which offers three possible approaches to the scope of the warranty.

§2-318. THIRD PARTY BENEFICIARIES OF WARRANTIES EXPRESS OR IMPLIED . . .

Alternative A

A seller's warranty whether express or implied extends to any natural person who is in the family or household of his buyer or who is a guest in his home if it is reasonable to expect that such person may use, consume or be affected by the goods and who is injured in person by breach of the warranty. A seller may not exclude or limit the operation of this section.

Alternative B

A seller's warranty whether express or implied extends to any natural person who may reasonably be expected to use, consume or be affected by the goods and who is injured in person by breach of the warranty. A seller may not exclude or limit the operation of this section.

Alternative C

[handwritten: ∃ c can recover for property but can exclude econ. loss ∃ corporations]

A seller's warranty whether express or implied extends to any person who may reasonably be expected to use, consume or be affected by the goods and who is injured by breach of the warranty. A seller may not exclude or limit the operation of this section with respect to injury to the person of an individual to whom the warranty extends.

[handwritten: ⟶ someone else's property unless limited]

[handwritten margin: now from ...fing; β √]

New York originally adopted alternative A. In 1975, however, it adopted alternative B (N.Y. U.C.C. Law §2-318 (Consol. 1994)). Under any of these variations, should the seller be held under a theory of implied warranty when he deals in prepackaged goods that he has no opportunity to inspect? Does the UCC improve the law by eliminating the requirement that the buyer rely upon the skill and judgment of the seller? If *X* steals a roll from *Y,* who had purchased it from *Z,* should *X* be able to recover from *Z* under the variations of section 2-318 when injured by a piece of sharp metal baked into the roll? Why should the parties be unable to contract out of this provision?

[handwritten margin: can't limit personal injury — can limit property damage]

3. Defective products and the theory of the implied warranty: Henningsen v. Bloomfield Motors, Inc., 161 A.2d 69 (N.J. 1960). Henningsen purchased a new Plymouth automobile, manufactured by the defendant Chrysler Corporation, from defendant Bloomfield Motors, Inc. Henningsen then gave the car to his wife, in circumstances indicating to the dealer his intention to make a gift. The contract of sale between Mr. Henningsen and the two defendants contained language that expressly disclaimed all warranties by the dealer or manufacturer, except one that limited the liability of the defendants *to the original purchaser* to the replacement of defective parts within 90 days or 4,000 miles, whichever occurred first. Shortly after the car was purchased, the plaintiff, Mrs. Henningsen, was driving along a clear road when the steering mechanism suddenly went awry. The car went out of control and veered off the road and into a wall, injuring her. She sued on theories of negligence and warranty, the court dismissing the negligence claim. The jury found for the plaintiff against both defendants on the warranty claim and the defendants appealed. In his very lengthy opinion, Judge Francis examined the expansion of the law of warranties within the framework of the law of sales. He noted how the courts had been prepared to extend the implied warranty of merchantability to individuals who were not party to the original sales agreement, a development he found absolutely necessary since manufacturers insulated themselves from sales act liability to consumers by a complex web of contracts. He then demonstrated the limited protection made available to the plaintiff under this express warranty, noting that its terms were a "sad commentary" on the marketing practices of automobile manufacturers. Although he thought it technically possible to infer the ordinary warranty of merchantability even in the teeth of the disclaimer clause,

Judge Francis did not resort to these interpretative techniques, but instead struck down the disclaimer clause on the ground that it "was not fairly obtained." He held therefore that the benefit of the implied warranty ran in favor of the plaintiff: "[U]nder modern marketing conditions, when a manufacturer puts a new automobile in the stream of trade and promotes its purchase by the public, an implied warranty that it is reasonably suitable for use as such accompanies it into the hands of the ultimate purchaser. Absence of agency between the manufacturer and the dealer who makes the ultimate sale is immaterial." He then held that modern economic conditions required the same implied warranty to run in favor of Mrs. Henningsen as well. "In our judgment, the principles of those cases and the supporting texts are just as proximately applicable to her situation. We are convinced that the cause of justice in this area of the law can be served only by recognizing that she is such a person who, in the reasonable contemplation of the parties to the warranty, might be expected to become a user of the automobile. Accordingly, her lack of privity does not stand in the way of prosecution of the injury suit against the defendant Chrysler."

In 1966, Prosser wrote of *Henningsen:* "In the field of products liability, the date of the fall of the citadel of privity can be fixed with some certainty. It was May 9, 1960, when the Supreme Court of New Jersey announced the decision in Henningsen v. Bloomfield Motors Inc." Prosser, The Fall of the Citadel (Strict Liability to the Consumer), 50 Minn. L. Rev. 791 (1966). In recent years, however, its importance appears to have waned somewhat, not because courts reject its outcome, but ironically because its implied warranty theory left products liability actions too closely tied to the law of sales.

   4. *Strict liability in torts: The* Greenman *reformulation.* In Greenman v. Yuba Power Products, Inc., 377 P.2d 897, 900-901 (Cal. 1962), the plaintiff's wife gave him a product manufactured by the defendant, a Shopsmith, a combination power tool that could be used as a saw, a drill, and a wood lathe. The plaintiff then read the manufacturer's brochure, which contained the following statements: "(1) WHEN SHOPSMITH IS IN HORIZONTAL POSITION — Rugged construction of frame provides rigid support from end to end. Heavy centerless-ground steel tubing insures perfect alignment of components. (2) SHOPSMITH maintains its accuracy because every component has positive locks that hold adjustments through rough or precision work." In the course of working the lathe, a piece of wood "suddenly flew out of the machine and struck him on the forehead, inflicting serious injury." There was substantial evidence that the plaintiff's injuries were caused by the defective construction of the Shopsmith, whose set screws were of insufficient strength to hold the wood in place while the lathe was being operated. (What concept of defect is involved?) The plaintiff recovered

damages from the manufacturer for negligence and breach of both express and implied warranties.

One of defendant's contentions on appeal was that the plaintiff's cause of action was barred because he failed to give notice of his injury within a "reasonable time" as required by §1769 of the California Civil Code. Justice Traynor, speaking for the entire court, avoided the effect of the warranty provisions by making clear his preference for the tort theory of strict liability:

> Manufacturer is strictly liable in tort when an article he places on the market, knowing that it is to be used without inspection for defects, proves to have a defect that causes injury to a human being. Recognized first in the case of unwholesome food products, such liability has now been extended to a variety of other products that create as great or greater hazards if defective.
>
> Although in these cases strict liability has usually been based on the theory of an express or implied warranty running from the manufacturer to the plaintiff, the abandonment of the requirement of a contract between them, the recognition that the liability is not assumed by agreement but imposed by law, and the refusal to permit the manufacturer to define the scope of its own responsibility for defective products make clear that the liability is not one governed by the law of contract warranties but by the law of strict liability in tort. Accordingly, rules defining and governing warranties that were developed to meet the needs of commercial transactions cannot properly be invoked to govern the manufacturer's liability to those injured by their defective products unless those rules also serve the purposes for which such liability is imposed.
>
> We need not recanvass the reasons for imposing strict liability on the manufacturer. The purpose of such liability is to insure that the costs of injuries resulting from defective products are borne by the manufacturers that put such products on the market rather than by the injured persons who are powerless to protect themselves. Sales warranties serve this purpose fitfully at best. In the present case, for example, plaintiff was able to plead and prove an express warranty only because he read and relied on the representations of the Shopsmith's ruggedness contained in the manufacturer's brochure. Implicit in the machine's presence on the market, however, was a representation that it would safely do the jobs for which it was built. Under these circumstances, it should not be controlling whether plaintiff selected the machine because of the statements in the brochure, or because of the machine's own appearance of excellence that belied the defect lurking beneath the surface, or because he merely assumed that it would safely do the jobs it was built to do. It should not be controlling whether the details of the sales from manufacturer to retailer and from retailer to plaintiff's wife were such that one or more of the implied warranties of the sales act arose. (Civ. Code, §1735.) "The remedies of injured consumers ought not to be made to depend upon the intricacies of the law of sales." To establish the manufacturer's liability it was sufficient that plaintiff proved that he was injured while using the Shopsmith in a way it was intended to be used as a result of a defect in design and manufacture of which plaintiff was not aware that made the Shopsmith unsafe for its intended use.

5. Strict liability, common carriers, and government regulation. The last of the important pre-Restatement cases was Goldberg v. Kollsman Instruments Corp., 191 N.E.2d 81, 83-84, 85 (N.Y. 1963). There the plaintiff's daughter was killed in a plane crash. She brought a suit in negligence against the carrier, American Airlines, and two strict liability actions, one against Lockheed, the airplane manufacturer, and the second against Kollsman, as the manufacturer of a defective altimeter, charging both "with breaching their respective implied warranties of merchantability and fitness." By a four-to-three vote, the Court of Appeals applied *Greenman's* strict liability rationale to Lockheed but refused to extend it to Kollsman: "Adequate protection is provided for the passengers by casting in liability the airplane manufacturer which put into the market the completed aircraft."

The dissent by Burke, J., took a far more skeptical view of any direct action against either Lockheed or Kollsman:

> If it were a case where a defendant sold a food or other household product to a member of a family, the warranty incident thereto would extend to all for whose consumption or use the product was obviously purchased. The conclusion reached by the majority might be correct even if the defective product were sold to an employer for the use of his employees. This, however, is none of those cases. The conditions present in those cases are entirely different. There the manufacturer knew that the article he made was not to be inspected thereafter. Here the Federal regulations provide for rigorous inspection and certification for the Federal Aviation Agency. There the risk of loss was a trap for the unwary. Here all are aware of the hazards attending air travel and accident and special insurance is readily available at moderate rates. Plaintiff is purchaser of a service from an airline seeking to assert a warranty cause of action against Lockheed, the assembler of an airplane, and Kollsman, the manufacturer of an allegedly defective component part thereof. In such a situation we see no satisfactory basis on which to uphold against Lockheed a cause of action not grounded in negligence, while disallowing it against the manufacturer of an alleged defective part.
>
> First, we do not find a cause of action stated under the implied warranty provisions of section 96 of the Personal Property Law. Plaintiff purchased no goods; she entered into a contract of carriage with American Airlines. By a long line of cases in this court, the most recent being Kilberg v. Northeast Airlines (9 N.Y.2d 34), it is settled that the measure of American Airlines' duty towards plaintiff was an undertaking of reasonably safe carriage. This duty is, of course, discharged by the use of due care. Crucial is the fact that this duty would be unaffected if American assembled its own planes, even if they contained a latent defect. Why, then, should plaintiff's rights be any greater simply because American chose to contract this work out instead of doing it itself?

Burke, J., then observed that American Airlines was the "proper enterprise" on which to fasten liability given that it "deals directly with the public" and "assumes the responsibility of selecting and using those goods itself as a capital asset in the conduct of a service enterprise such as common carriage."

> Whatever conclusions may flow from the fact that the accident was caused by a defective altimeter should be merged in whatever responsibility the law may place on the airline with which plaintiff did business. To extend warranty law to allow plaintiff to select a defendant from a multiplicity of enterprises in a case such as this would not comport with the rationale of enterprise liability and would only have the effect of destroying whatever rights that exist among the potential defendants by virtue of agreement among themselves. If, on the other hand, plaintiff's maximum rights lie against the carrier, the rules of warranty can perform their real function of adjusting the rights of the parties to the agreements through which the airline acquired the chattel that caused the accident.

Does Burke's position amount to a defense of the privity limitation in all common carrier cases?

C.   THE RESTATEMENT

1.   The Fundamental Text

American Law Institute, Restatement (Second) of Torts

(1966)

[handwritten annotation: does not seem to cover bystanders, but the courts allow injured bystanders to sue the original manufacturer]

§402A.   SPECIAL LIABILITY OF SELLER OF PRODUCT FOR PHYSICAL HARM TO USER OR CONSUMER

(1) One who sells any product in a defective condition unreasonably dangerous to the user or consumer or to his property is subject to liability for physical harm thereby caused to the ultimate user or consumer, or to his property, if

   (a) the seller is engaged in the business of selling such a product, and

   (b) it is expected to and does reach the user or consumer without substantial change in the condition in which it is sold.

(2) The rule stated in Subsection (1) applies although

   (a) the seller has exercised all possible care in the preparation and sale of his product, and

   (b) the user or consumer has not bought the product from or entered into any contractual relation with the seller.

Caveat:

The Institute expresses no opinion as to whether the rules stated in this Section may not apply

(1) to harm to persons other than users or consumers

(2) to the seller of a product expected to be processed or otherwise substantially changed before it reaches the user or consumer or

(3) to the seller of a component part of a product to be assembled.

Comments: . . .

f. Business of selling. The rule stated in this Section applies to any person engaged in the business of selling products for use or consumption. It therefore applies to any manufacturer of such a product, to any wholesale or retail dealer or distributor, and to the operator of a restaurant. It is not necessary that the seller be engaged solely in the business of selling such products. Thus the rule applies to the owner of a motion picture theatre who sells popcorn or ice cream, either for consumption on the premises or in packages to be taken home.

The rule does not, however, apply to the occasional seller of food or other such products who is not engaged in that activity as a part of his business. Thus it does not apply to the housewife who, on one occasion, sells to her neighbor a jar of jam or a pound of sugar. Nor does it apply to the owner of an automobile who, on one occasion, sells it to his neighbor, or even sells it to a dealer in used cars, and this even though he is fully aware that the dealer plans to resell it. The basis for the rule is the ancient one of the special responsibility for the safety of the public undertaken by one who enters into the business of supplying human beings with products which may endanger the safety of their persons and property, and the forced reliance upon that undertaking on the part of those who purchase such goods. This basis is lacking in the case of the ordinary individual who makes the isolated sale, and he is not liable to a third person, or even to his buyer, in the absence of his negligence. . . .

g. Defective condition. The rule stated in this Section applies only where the product is, at the time it leaves the seller's hands, in a condition not contemplated by the ultimate consumer, which will be unreasonably dangerous to him. The seller is not liable when he delivers the product in a safe condition, and subsequent mishandling or other causes make it harmful by the time it is consumed. The burden of proof that the product was in a defective condition at the time that it left the hands of the particular seller is upon the injured plaintiff and unless evidence can be produced which will support the conclusion that it was then defective, the burden is not sustained.

Safe condition at the time of delivery by the seller will, however, include proper packaging, necessary sterilization, and other precautions required to permit the product to remain safe for a normal length of time when handled in a normal manner.

h. A product is not in defective condition when it is safe for normal handling and consumption. If the injury results from abnormal handling, as where a bottled beverage is knocked against a radiator to remove the cap, or from abnormal preparation for use, as where too much salt is added to food, or from abnormal consumption, as where a child eats too much candy and is made ill, the seller is not liable. . . .

The defective condition may arise not only from harmful ingredients, not characteristic of the product itself either as to presence or quantity, but also from foreign objects contained in the product, from decay or deterioration before sale, or from the way in which the product is prepared or packed. No reason is apparent for distinguishing between the product itself and the container in which it is supplied; and the two are purchased by the user or consumer as an integrated whole. Where the container is itself dangerous, the product is sold in a defective condition. Thus a carbonated beverage in a bottle which is so weak, or cracked, or jagged at the edges, or bottled under such excessive pressure that it may explode or otherwise cause harm to the person who handles it, is in a defective and dangerous condition. The container cannot logically be separated from the contents. . . .

i. Unreasonably dangerous. The rule stated in this Section applies only where the defective condition of the product makes it unreasonably dangerous to the user or consumer. Many products cannot possibly be made entirely safe for all consumption, and any food or drug necessarily involves some risk of harm, if only from over-consumption. Ordinary sugar is a deadly poison to diabetics, and castor oil found use under Mussolini as an instrument of torture. That is not what is meant by "unreasonably dangerous" in this Section. The article sold must be dangerous to an extent beyond that which would be contemplated by the ordinary consumer who purchases it, with the ordinary knowledge common to the community as to its characteristics. Good whiskey is not unreasonably dangerous merely because it will make some people drunk, and is especially dangerous to alcoholics; but bad whiskey, containing a dangerous amount of fusel oil, is unreasonably dangerous. Good tobacco is not unreasonably dangerous merely because the effects of smoking may be harmful; but tobacco containing something like marijuana may be unreasonably dangerous. Good butter is not unreasonably dangerous merely because, if such be the case, it deposits cholesterol in the arteries and leads to heart attacks; but bad butter, contaminated with poisonous fish oil, is unreasonably dangerous.

j. Directions or warning. In order to prevent the product from being unreasonably dangerous, the seller may be required to give directions or warning, on the container, as to its use. The seller may reasonably assume that those with common allergies, as for example to eggs or strawberries, will be aware of them, and he is not required to warn against them. Where, however, the product contains an ingredient to which a substantial number of the population are allergic, and the ingredient is one whose danger is not generally known, or if known is one which the consumer would reasonably not expect to find in the product, the seller is required to give warning against it, if he has knowledge, or by the application of reasonable, developed human skill and foresight should have knowledge, of the presence of the ingredient and the danger. Likewise in the case of poisonous drugs, or those unduly dangerous for other reasons, warning as to use may be required. But a seller is not required to warn with respect to products, or ingredients in them, which are only dangerous or potentially so, when consumed in excessive quantity, or over a long period of time, when the danger, or potentiality of danger, is generally known and recognized. Again the dangers of alcoholic beverages are an example, as are also those of foods containing such substances as saturated fats, which may over a period of time have a deleterious effect upon the human heart. Where warning is given, the seller may reasonably assume that it will be read and heeded; and a product bearing such a warning, which is safe for use if it is followed, is not in defective condition, nor is it unreasonably dangerous.

   k. Unavoidably unsafe products. There are some products which, in the present state of human knowledge, are quite incapable of being made safe for their intended and ordinary use. These are especially common in the field of drugs. An outstanding example is the vaccine for the Pasteur treatment of rabies, which not uncommonly leads to very serious and damaging consequences when it is injected. Since the disease itself invariably leads to a dreadful death, both the marketing and the use of the vaccine are fully justified, notwithstanding the unavoidable high degree of risk which they involve. Such a product, properly prepared, and accompanied by proper directions and warning, is not defective, nor is it *unreasonably* dangerous. The same is true of many other drugs, vaccines, and the like, many of which for this very reason cannot legally be sold except to physicians, or under the prescription of a physician. It is also true in particular of many new or experimental drugs as to which, because of lack of time and opportunity for sufficient medical experience, there can be no assurance of safety, or perhaps even of purity of ingredients, but such experience as there is justifies the marketing and use of the drug notwithstanding a medically recognizable risk. The seller of such products, again with the qualification that they are properly prepared and marketed, and proper warning is given, where the situation calls for it, is not to be held to strict liability for unfortunate consequences attending their use, merely because he has undertaken to supply the public with an apparently useful and desirable product, attended with a known but apparently reasonable risk.

   m. "Warranty". . . . . The rule stated in this Section does not require any reliance on the part of the consumer upon the reputation, skill, or judgment of the seller who is to be held liable, nor any representation or undertaking on the part of that seller. The seller is strictly liable although, as is frequently the case, the consumer does not even know who he is at the time of consumption. The rule stated in this Section is not governed by the provisions of the Uniform Sales Act, or those of the Uniform Commercial Code, as to warranties; and it is not affected by limitations on the scope and content of warranties, or by limitation to "buyer" and "seller" in those statutes. Nor is the consumer required to give notice to the seller of his injury within a reasonable time after it occurs, as is provided by the Uniform Act. . . .

n. *Contributory negligence.* Since the liability with which this Section deals is not based upon negligence of the seller, but is strict liability, the rule applied to strict liability cases (see §524) applies. Contributory negligence of the plaintiff is not a defense when such negligence consists merely in a failure to discover the defect in the product, or to guard against the possibility of its existence. On the other hand the form of contributory negligence which consists in voluntarily and unreasonably proceeding to encounter a known danger, and commonly passes under the name of assumption of risk, is a defense under this Section as in other cases of strict liability. If the user or consumer discovers the defect and is aware of the danger, and nevertheless proceeds unreasonably to make use of the product and is injured by it, he is barred from recovery.

NOTES

1. Restatement of Torts section 402A. Section 402A and its comments have for 30 years formed the basic text of modern products liability in the tort law. At its inception section 402A sought to capture the ever-more-popular shift from negligence to strict liability that was occurring while the American Law Institute was debating its scope. Thus, this section appears as a "special" addition to chapter 14 of the Restatement concerned with "Liability of Persons Supplying Chattels For the Use of Others." Even before its final publication, however, it had become clear that its strict liability rule reached far beyond the contaminated foodstuffs cases so conspicuous in earlier tort litigation. In order to deal with the unique issues raised, for example, by pharmaceuticals, the drafters of the Restatement sought to resolve many hard questions only in the comments to the basic text, comments which, over time, have become as important as the basic provision itself. Whatever its "special" origin, the strict liability rule of section 402A now dominates the law, so that it heavily influences the law in the few states that have not officially embraced its position. For accounts of the Restatement adoption see R. Epstein, Modern Products Liability Law ch. 6 (1980); Priest, The Invention of Enterprise Liability: A Critical History of the Intellectual Foundations of Modern Tort Law, 14 J. Legal Stud. 461, 505-519 (1985).

2. Bystander's recovery. Today the case law has outstripped the Second

Restatement by allowing injured bystanders to sue the original manufacturer. The Restatement's hesitation in the bystander case rested in
part upon the uncertainty in the 1965 case law and in part upon the
confusion about the basic theory applicable to products liability cases.
Thus, any version of implied warranty or the misrepresentation theories
makes it difficult to hold the defendant accountable to the injured bystander. The bystander is not lured into using the product by the defendant's representations and is not an immediate or ultimate beneficiary
of any warranty from any seller or manufacturer. The bystander's case
for strict liability in tort is far stronger: as with abnormally dangerous
activities, the bystander is best able to claim to have been hurt by a
process that was in no sense his making. And it is he who can best resist
charges that he misused the product or used it with full knowledge of
its dangerous characteristics.

Whatever the precise reasons, the liability of the manufacturer or
seller to the bystander is everywhere allowed under the case law. See,
e.g., Elmore v. American Motors Corp., 451 P.2d 84 (Cal. 1969); Cod-
ling v. Paglia, 298 N.E.2d 622 (N.Y. 1973). For commentators' reactions
on the bystander question see generally Kalven, Tort Law — Tort
Watch, 34 A.T.L.J. 1, 44-59 (1972); Noel, Defective Products: Extension
of Strict Liability to Bystanders, 38 Tenn. L. Rev. 1 (1970). In practice,
however, bystander cases turn out to be relatively infrequent since the
vast bulk of suits are brought by injured consumers or users of the
product in question.

The American Law Institute, Restatement of the Law of Products Liability
(Tentative Draft #1 1994)

§1.   COMMERCIAL SELLER'S LIABILITY FOR HARM CAUSED BY DEFECTIVE PRODUCTS

(a) One engaged in the business of selling products who sells a defective product is subject to liability for harm to persons or property
caused by the product defect.

(b) A product is defective only if, at the time of sale, it contains
a manufacturing defect, is defective in design or is defective due to
inadequate instructions or warnings.

§2.   CATEGORIES OF PRODUCT DEFECTS

For purposes of determining liability under Section 1:

(a) A product contains a manufacturing defect when the product
departs from its intended design even though all possible care was
exercised in the preparation and marketing of the product;

(b) A product is defective in design when the foreseeable risks of harm posed by the product could have been reduced by the adoption of a reasonable alternative design by the seller or a predecessor in the commercial chain of distribution and the omission of the alternative design renders the product not reasonably safe;

(c) A product is defective because of inadequate instructions or warnings when the foreseeable risks of harm posed by the product could have been reduced by the provision of reasonable instructions or warnings by the seller or a predecessor in the commercial chain of distribution and the omission of the instructions or warnings renders the product not reasonably safe.

NOTE

Into the next generation. The current drafts of the new products liability Restatement reflect a growing dissatisfaction with the treatment of the subject under current §402A. The original caveats on such issues as bystander liability have disappeared, for example, and all the rules on construction, design, and warning defects are brought within a single comprehensive section, which then imposes an absolute duty to sell products that conform to the manufacturer's own intended design, but a more limited obligation to make those designs, warnings, and instructions "reasonably safe." Many of the old rules, however, still carry over, such as that which excludes "casual sellers" from the operation of this provision. See Section 1, comment *c.* Subsequent provisions of the Restatement draft examine each class of defects, and contain additional provisions to deal with prescription drugs, issues of causation, and affirmative defenses. These provisions will be set out in connection with the specific topics they examine. For an early discussion of the revisions of the Second Restatement see Henderson and Twerski, A Proposed Revision of Section 402A of the Restatement (Second) of Torts, 77 Cornell L. Rev. 1512 (1992), whose views take on special significance since they are the joint reporters for the ALI revision.

2.   Tort or Contract?: The Scope of Section 402A

Casa Clara Condominium Association v. Charley Toppino & Sons
620 So. 2d 1244 (Fla. 1993)

McDONALD, JUSTICE. . . . The issue is whether a homeowner can recover for purely economic losses from a concrete supplier under a negligence theory. We agree with the district court that such a recovery cannot be had and approve the decisions under review and disapprove the conflicting decisions.

Charley Toppino & Sons, Inc., a dissolved corporation, supplied concrete for numerous construction projects in Monroe County. Apparently, some of the concrete supplied by Toppino contained a high content of salt that caused the reinforcing steel inserted in the concrete to rust, which, in turn, caused the concrete to crack and break off. The petitioners own condominium units and single-family homes built with, and now allegedly damaged by, Toppino's concrete. In separate actions the homeowners sued numerous defendants and included claims against Toppino for breach of common law implied warranty, products liability, negligence, and violation of the building code. The circuit court dismissed all counts against Toppino in each case. On appeal the district court applied the economic loss rule and held that, because no person was injured and no other property damaged, the homeowners had no cause of action against Toppino in tort. The district court also held that Toppino, a supplier, had no duty to comply with the building code.

Plaintiffs find a tort remedy attractive because it often permits the recovery of greater damages than an action on a contract and may avoid the conditions of a contract. The distinction between "tort recovery for physical injuries and warranty recovery for economic loss" rests

> on an understanding of the nature of the responsibility a manufacturer must undertake in distributing his products. He can appropriately be held liable for physical injuries caused by defects by requiring his goods to match a standard of safety defined in terms of conditions that create unreasonable risks of harm. *He cannot be held for the level of performance of his products in the consumer's business unless he agrees that the product was designed to meet the consumer's demands.*

Seely v. White Motor Co., 403 P.2d 145, 151 (Cal. 1965) (emphasis supplied). An individual consumer, on the other hand,

> should not be charged at the will of the manufacturer with bearing the risk of physical injury when he buys a product on the market. He can, however, be fairly charged with the risk that the product will not match his economic expectations unless the manufacturer agrees that it will.

Id. *Seely* sets out the economic loss rule, which prohibits tort recovery when a product damages itself, causing economic loss, but does not cause personal injury or damage to any property other than itself. E.g., East River Steamship Corp. v. Transamerica Delaval, Inc. 476 U.S. 858 (1986); Florida Power & Light Co. v. Westinghouse Elec. Corp., 510 So. 2d 899 (Fla. 1987); Danforth v. Acorn Structures, Inc., 608 A.2d 1194 (Del. 1992). The rule is "the fundamental boundary between contract law, which is designed to enforce the expectancy interests of the parties, and tort law, which imposes a duty of reasonable care and thereby encourages citizens to avoid causing physical harm to others." Sidney R. Barrett, Jr., Recovery of Economic Loss in Tort for Construction Defects: A Critical Analysis, 40 S.C. L. Rev. 891, 894 (1989).

Economic loss has been defined as "damages for inadequate value, costs of repair and replacement of the defective product, or consequent loss of profits — without any claim of personal injury or damage to other property." Note, Economic Loss in Products Liability Jurisprudence, 66 Colum. L. Rev. 917, 918 (1966). It includes "the diminution in the value of the product because it is inferior in quality and does not work for the general purposes for which it was manufactured and sold." Comment, Manufacturers' Liability to Remote Purchasers for "Economic Loss" Damages — Tort or Contract?, 114 U. Pa. L. Rev. 539, 541 (1966). In other words, economic losses are "disappointed economic expectations," which are protected by contract law, rather than tort law. This is the basic difference between contract law, which protects expectations, and tort law, which is determined by the duty owed to an injured party. For recovery in tort "there must be a showing of harm above and beyond disappointed expectations. A buyer's desire to enjoy the benefit of his bargain is not an interest that tort law traditionally protects." Redarowicz v. Ohlendorf, 441 N.E.2d 324, 327 (Ill. 1982).

The homeowners are seeking purely economic damages — no one has sustained any physical injuries and no property, other than the structures built with Toppino's concrete, has sustained any damage. They argue that holding them to contract remedies is unfair and that homeowners in general should be excepted from the operation of the economic loss rule. We disagree.

In tort a manufacturer or producer of goods "is liable whether or not it is negligent because 'public policy demands that responsibility be fixed wherever it will most effectively reduce the hazards to life and health inherent in defective products that reach the market.'" East River, 476 U.S. at 866 (quoting Escola v. Coca Cola Bottling Co., (Traynor, J., concurring)). Thus, the "basic function of tort law is to shift the burden of loss from the injured plaintiff to one who is at fault . . . or to one who is better able to bear the loss and prevent its occurrence." Barrett, supra at 935. The purpose of a duty in tort is to protect society's interest in being free from harm, Spring Motors Distributors, Inc. v. Ford Motor Co., 489 A.2d 660 (N.J. 1985), and the cost of protecting society from harm is borne by society in general. Contractual duties, on the other hand, come from society's interest in the performance of promises. Id. When only economic harm is involved, the question becomes "whether the consuming public as a whole should bear the cost of economic losses sustained by those who failed to bargain for adequate contract remedies." Barrett, supra at 933.

We are urged to make an exception to the economic loss doctrine for homeowners. Buying a house is the largest investment many consumers ever make, see Conklin v. Hurley, 428 So. 2d 654 (Fla. 1983), and homeowners are an appealing, sympathetic class. If a house causes economic disappointment by not meeting a purchaser's expectations, the resulting failure to receive the benefit of the bargain is a core concern of contract, not tort, law. East River, 476 U.S. at 870. There are protections for homebuyers, however, such as statutory warranties, the general warranty of habitability, and the duty of sellers to disclose defects, as well as the ability of purchasers to inspect houses for defects. Coupled with homebuyers' power to bargain over price, these protections must be viewed as sufficient when compared with the mischief that could be caused by allowing tort recovery for purely economic losses. Therefore, we again "hold contract principles more appropriate than tort principles for recovering economic loss without an accompanying physical injury or property damage." Florida Power & Light, 510 So. 2d at 902. If we held otherwise, "contract law would drown in a sea of tort." East River, 476 U.S. at 866. We refuse to hold that homeowners are not subject to the economic loss rule.

The homeowners also argue that Toppino's concrete damaged "other" property because the individual components and items of building material, not the homes themselves, are the products they purchased. We disagree. The character of a loss determines the appropriate remedies, and, to determine the character of a loss, one must look to the product purchased by the plaintiff, not the product sold by the defendant. Generally, house buyers have little or no interest in how or where the individual components of a house are obtained. They are content to let the builder produce the finished product, i.e., a house. These homeowners bought finished products — dwellings — not the individual components of those dwellings. They bargained for the finished products, not their various components. The concrete became an integral part of the finished product and, thus, did not injure "other" property.

We also disagree with the homeowners that the mere possibility that the exploding concrete will cause physical injury is sufficient reason to abrogate the economic loss rule. This argument goes completely against the principle that injury must occur before a negligence action exists. Because an injury has not occurred, its extent and the identity of injured persons is completely speculative. Thus, the degree of risk is indeterminate, with no guarantee that damages will be reasonably related to the risk of injury, and with no possibility for the producer of a product to structure its business behavior to cover that risk. Agreeing with the homeowners' argument would make it difficult "to maintain a realistic limitation on damages." East River, 476 U.S. at 871.

Therefore, we approve the district court's opinions and hold that the economic loss rule applies to the purchase of houses. The cases in conflict, Adobe, Drexel, and Latite, incorrectly refused to apply the economic loss rule to what should have been contract actions, and we disapprove them. We also agree with the district court that the homeowners cannot recover against Toppino under a building code.

It is so ordered.

OVERTON, GRIMES and HARDING, JJ., concur.

BARKETT, CHIEF JUSTICE, concurring in part, dissenting in part.

If the allegations of the homeowners in this case are true, their homes are literally crumbling around them because the concrete supplied by Toppino was negligently manufactured. The homeowners assert that the concrete is now cracking and breaking apart and poses a danger of serious injury. The courts, including this one, have said "too bad."

I find that answer unacceptable in light of the principle underlying Florida's access to courts provision: that absent compelling, countervailing public policies, wrongs must have remedies. Art. I, §21, Fla. Const. I understand and accept that sometimes the remedies provided cannot be in the full measure that pure justice unfettered by pragmatism can provide. Thus, some applications of the economic loss doctrine may have acceptable viability. But surely it stretches reason to apply the doctrine in this context to deny these homeowners any remedy.

Their claim for breach of implied warranty has been denied (they lack privity with Toppino); their claim that Toppino violated the Florida Building Codes Act has been denied (Toppino, as a material supplier, is not governed by the Standard Building Code); and now their claim in tort has been denied because, notwithstanding their alleged ability to prove that their houses are falling down around them, they have not suffered any damage to their property on the basis that homes are "products."

A key premise underlying the economic loss rule is that parties in a business context have the ability to allocate economic risks and remedies as part of their contractual negotiations. That premise does not exist here. Moreover, I cannot subscribe to the majority's view that the defective concrete has not damaged "other property" in the form of the houses' individual components. . . .

KOGAN, J., concurs.

SHAW, JUSTICE, concurring and dissenting.

While I basically agree that, under a negligence theory, purely economic loss cannot be recovered by parties to a contract when the loss is to the property that is the subject of the contract, I find the logic of the restriction inapplicable in this instance. The rationale of the economic loss rule is that parties who have bargained for the distribution of risk of loss should not be permitted to circumvent their bargain after loss occurs to the property that was the subject of the bargain. . . .

While I agree with the majority opinion that parties who have freely bargained and entered a contract relative to a particular subject matter should be bound by the terms of that contract including the distribution of loss, I feel that the theory is stretched when it is used to deny a cause of action to an innocent third party who the defendant knew or should have known would be injured by the tortious conduct. Toppino knew that the concrete that was the subject matter of the bargain between Toppino and the general contractor would be incorporated into homes that would be bought and occupied by innocent third parties.

When the concrete proved to be contaminated, damages were not limited to simply the loss of concrete; innocent third parties suffered various degrees of damage to structures using the concrete. In my mind, the economic loss theory was never intended to defeat a tort cause of action that would otherwise lie for damages caused to a third party by a defective product.

BARKETT, C.J., and KOGAN, J., concur.

NOTES

1. *Tort or contract: the minority view and intermediate views.* The interaction between contract and tort has long been a vexatious element of the American tort law. Today, the position in *Casa Clara* represents the majority position in the United States, and has been adopted by the United States Supreme Court in admiralty cases as well. East River Steamship Co v. Transmerica Delaval, Inc., 476 U.S. 858 (1986). For a recent tally on the cases see Jones, Product Defects Causing Commercial Loss: The Ascendency of Contract over Tort, 44 U. Miami L. Rev. 731, 799 (1990).

Nonetheless there remains powerful, if minority, support for the proposition that section 402A overrides warranty disclaimers even for pure economic loss. Thus Peters, J., dissenting in *Seely*, 403 P.2d 145, 153-154, put the case in its strongest light:

> Given the rationale of Greenman v. Yuba Power Products, Inc., it cannot properly be held that plaintiff may not recover the value of his truck and his lost profits on the basis of strict liability. The nature of the damage sustained by the plaintiff is immaterial, so long as it proximately flowed from the defect. What *is* important is not the nature of the damage but the relative roles played by the parties to the purchase contract and the nature of their transaction. . . .
>
> Of course, the application of the strict liability theory to property damage (including "economic loss") will limit the applicability of several sections of the recently enacted Commercial Code dealing with implied warranties (see, e.g., Com. Code, §§2607, 2719). But this result, even if unfortunate, follows from the rationale of *Greenman*, which limited the effect of a statute requiring the purchaser to give defendant notice of a

breach of warranty within a reasonable time (former Civ. Code, §1769). In the present case, it is not necessary to "extend" *Greenman* in order to reach the proper result. All that is required is that we apply its reasoning to a factual situation which cannot be distinguished analytically from that case.

In *Greenman* we allowed recovery for "personal injury" damages. It is well established that such an award may include compensation for past loss of time and earnings due to the injury, for loss of future earning capacity, and for increased living expenses caused by the injury. There is no logical distinction between these losses and the losses suffered by plaintiff here. All involve economic loss, and all proximately arise out of the purchase of a defective product. I find it hard to understand how one might, for example, award a traveling salesman lost earnings if a defect in his car causes his *leg* to break in an accident but deny that salesman his lost earnings if the defect instead disables only his *car* before any accident occurs. The losses are exactly the same; the chains of causation are slightly different, but both are "proximate." Yet the majority would allow recovery under strict liability in the first situation but not in the second. This, I submit, is arbitrary.

An intermediate position, that applies section 402A only to "sudden" damage to the thing sold, was defended in Pennsylvania Glass Sand Corp. v. Caterpillar Tractor Co., 652 F.2d 1165, 1172-1173, 1174 (3d Cir. 1981), where the court first concluded that "the principles of warranty law remain the appropriate vehicle to redress a purchaser's disappointed expectations" as to its level of performance, but that warranty was "ill-suited to correct problems of hazardous problems that cause physical injury." The court then concluded that it was proper under Pennsylvania law to "classify damage to a defective product resulting from an unreasonably dangerous condition as physical injury compensable under §402A." It held that the tort law was applicable because the damage was "the result of a fire — a sudden and highly dangerous occurrence" and because "the alleged defect — a faulty design that failed to contain the fire and led to greatly enhanced damage — constitutes a safety hazard that posed a serious risk of harm to people and property." It also noted that economic interests were not at stake since the loader had worked well and the plaintiff was not trying to protect its expectation interest in the form of the benefit of the bargain.

2. *Physical and economic harm.* The line between physical and economic harm, announced in *Seely* and adopted in *Casa Clara* was tested in Adams-Arapahoe School, District No. 28-J v. GAF Corp., 959 F.2d 868, 872 (10th Cir. 1992). There plaintiff sought to recover the cost of removing from its public schools the vinyl-asbestos-tile (VAT) manufactured by defendant. The asbestos contained in these tiles was tightly bound to them, and did not contaminate the air. The court refused to treat this as a products liability action, here for negligence, on the ground that there was no cognizable physical injury.

The School District's claim of injury in the mere presence of VAT appears to be little more than an invitation to recognize some fictional property damage as a vehicle upon which to carry an economic loss action into the province of tort law. While the presence of asbestos in VAT may well impose increased renovation costs, any additional expense is best characterized as economic loss — consequential damages resulting from the failure of VAT to meet the School District's economic expectations in terms of performance. These additional costs do not present the type of accidental physical injury against which the doctrine of negligence, as described in *Seely* and its progeny, is designed to protect.

The court then stressed that the mere risk of future harm is not sufficient grounds on which to predicate the tort claim. In contrast where the actual release of contaminants has taken place, the ensuing harm is regarded as physical, even if prompt removal prevents physical injuries to any particular person.

3. Express warranties in physical injury cases. In most express warranty cases, it is the defendant who seeks to invoke contract principles to limit the scope of liability. In some instances, however, the plaintiff seeks to sue on express warranty theories when the defendant has made a specific undertaking without incorporating into the contract any limitation on consequential damages. Thus, in Hauter v. Zogarts, 534 P.2d 377 (Cal. 1975), the defendant sold a "Golfing Gizmo" that consisted of a golf ball attached to a cotton and elastic cord. The gizmo was supposed to allow the user to improve his swing without running the risk of physical injury. The defendant's literature urged the user to "drive the ball with full power" and further stated: "COMPLETELY SAFE BALL WILL NOT HIT PLAYER." Plaintiff, a 13-year-old boy struck the ball at an inopportune angle and was hit as the ball came back. The court upheld his cause of action for breach of express warranty and misrepresentation, rejecting the defendant's arguments that the statements made were simple "puffing" and that the device — designed for learners — was warranted as safe only for experienced or skilled golf players.

For plaintiff's express warranty claim, the critical statute is section 2-313 of the Uniform Commercial Code, which provides as follows:

> (1) Express warranties by the seller are created as follows:
> (a) Any affirmation of fact or promise made by the seller to the buyer which relates to the goods and becomes part of the basis of the bargain creates an express warranty that the goods shall conform to the affirmation or promise.
> (b) Any description of the goods which is made part of the basis of the bargaining creates an express warranty that the goods shall conform to the description. . . .

At issue in *Hauter* was the proper interpretation of the "basis of the bargain" language, which, as Tobriner, J., noted, was subject to two possible interpretations. The more modest view holds that the language "merely shifts the burden of proving non-reliance to the seller." The more radical view holds that the language "eliminates the concept of reliance altogether." Tobriner, J., decided not to choose between these two positions because the plaintiff was entitled to recover under either test, given that plaintiff "read and relied upon defendants' representation." Which view is preferable?

4. *Tort or warranty: the statute of limitations.* Under the UCC, claims for breach of warranty are barred by the statute of limitations, which under UCC §2-725 runs four years from the date of sale. In contrast, the tort statute of limitations runs at the earliest from the date of the injury, and in most jurisdictions only from the date at which the plaintiff has discovered, or through the exercise of reasonable diligence could have discovered, the injury in question. At one time some cases held that the UCC statute of limitations applied even to physical injury cases. See Mendel v. Pittsburgh Plate Glass Co., 253 N.E.2d 207 (N.Y. 1969). *Mendel* was in short order overruled by Victorson v. Bock Laundry Machine Co., 335 N.E.2d 275, 279 (N.Y. 1975). There the plaintiff sued for personal injuries allegedly caused by a defective laundry centrifuge extractor manufactured by the defendant. The extractor was sold in 1948 and the injury occurred in 1969. A unanimous court held that the applicable statute of limitations was that for personal injury or property damage, and that it ran only from the time the injury occurred, expressly adopting the argument of the *Mendel* dissent that "it is all but unthinkable that a person should be time-barred from prosecuting a cause of action before he ever had one." In the course of its opinion, the court observed:

> One argument of policy is pressed on us by appellants in these cases. Is it fair or reasonable, they ask, to hold a manufacturer liable for a defect in production many years after the product has left the manufacturer's plant? The predicament of the manufacturer is not then significantly different whether its liability in tort be grounded in theories of negligence or of strict products liability. One can observe that while passage of time may work a deterioration of the manufacturer's capability to defend, by similar token it can be expected to complicate the plaintiff's problem of proving, as he must, that the alleged defect existed at the time the product left the manufacturer's plant. In any event this consideration, of varying weight from case to case, cannot be accorded such significance as to dictate the outcome.

The concern with long-lived products that cause damage long after their initial sale has led many states to adopt so-called statutes of repose. The Pennsylvania version of the statute, for example, provides, with minor exceptions, that any action "brought against any person lawfully performing or furnishing the design, planning, supervision or observation of construction, or construction of any improvement to real property must be commenced within twelve years after the completion of such improvement to recover damages . . ." 42 Pa. Cons. Stat. §5536 (1994). In McConnaughey v. Building Components, Inc., 637 A.2d 1331, 1334 (Pa. 1994), trusses manufactured and supplied by defendant for the construction of plaintiff's barn in 1979 collapsed in 1986, killing 37 dairy cows. Defendant sought refuge under the statute. Papadakos, J., first noted;

> We find that the clear and unambiguous language of the statute of repose establishes that a manufacturer who does nothing other than supply a defective product which is later incorporated into an improvement to real property by others is not within the purview of the statute. . . . The Pennsylvania statute of repose was not intended to apply to manufacturers and suppliers of products, but only to the kinds of economic actors who perform acts of "individual expertise" akin to those commonly thought to be performed by builders.

It then remanded the case to determine "what involvement, if any, [defendant] had in the installation of the finished roof trusses, or the supervision thereof." Is there any reason why a statute of repose, if used at all, should not be applied to suppliers of standardized component parts that others incorporate into real estate? Any reason why it should not apply to personal property, such as the extractor in *Victorson?* Should a statute of repose extend to personal injuries sustained by the plaintiff?

At the federal level, Congress has passed the General Aviation Revitalization Act of 1994, Pub. L. No. 103-298, 49 U.S.C. §40101, which is designed to breathe life into a dormant general aviation industry. The key provision of the Act is an 18-year statute of repose for the benefit of "general aviation," defined roughly to cover planes with a capacity for fewer than 20 passengers that are not used for regularly scheduled commercial flights. The 18-year period generally runs from the date the plane is first put into service and covers the aircraft, any component system or subassembly, or aircraft part originally installed in the aircraft, with new limitations periods running for subsequently installed equipment. The limitations period protects only plane designs for which the Federal Aviation Administration has issued an airworthiness certificate. The protection so afforded extends only to the manufacturer "in its capacity as a manufacturer," so that subsequent services and maintenance, for example, are not covered. In addition, the statute's protection does not apply in cases where (1) the manufacturer knowingly misrepresented or deliberately concealed relevant information to the FAA on a design feature or component that was "causally related" to the claimant's harm, (2) the injured person is "being made a passenger for purposes of receiving treatment for a medical or other emergency," (3) the injured party is not on board the aircraft carrier, and (4) the action is for breach of an express warranty.

5. *Limitations on damages in express warranties.* In Collins v. Uniroyal, Inc., 315 A.2d 16 (N.J. 1974), the defendant tire company sold its Royal Master Tire under a guarantee against "blowouts, cuts, bruises, and similar injury rendering the tire unserviceable," covering the tires as long as they were not "punctured or abused." The guarantee went on to exclude, in italics, all liability for "consequential damage," obligating the tire company only to repair or replace the tire. The decedent was killed in an unexplained tire blowout and the plaintiff was unable to recover under a tort theory because of the inability to identify any defect in the tire. The court then allowed the plaintiff an action for full damages on the warranty provision, holding the defendant to the warranty provided in the first clause of the guarantee but denying it the benefit of the limitation of liability contained in the italicized clause.

The court relied in part upon UCC §2-719, which provides: "Consequential damages may be limited or excluded unless the limitation or exclusion is unconscionable. Limitation of consequential damages for injury to the person in the case of consumer goods is prima facie unconscionable, but limitation of damages where the loss is commercial is not." What is the force of the words "prima facie unconscionable"? Why is it not sufficient to override the presumption on the facts of this case to show that the defendant was under no obligation at all to provide a comprehensive guarantee for its product? How should the case be treated if the warranty excluded consequential damages for harm caused by defective tires? For criticism of *Collins* and of the general unconscionability doctrine see Epstein, Unconscionability: A Critical Reappraisal, 18 J.L. & Econ. 293 (1975). On the general subject of unconscionability see the critical account of Leff, Unconscionability and the Code — The Emperor's New Clause, 115 U. Pa. L. Rev. 485 (1967), and the qualified defense of Ellinghaus, In Defense of Unconscionability, 78 Yale L.J. 757 (1969).

3.   Proper Defendants under Section 402A

Murphy v. E.R. Squibb & Sons, Inc.
710 P.2d 247 (Cal. 1985)

MOSK, J. — We consider issues relating to the liability of a manufacturer and a pharmacy for the production and sale of an allegedly defective drug, stilbestrol (DES). We will decide whether a pharmacy at which the drug was purchased may be held strictly liable for alleged defects in the product (as distinguished from ordinary negligence). . . .

Plaintiff filed an action for personal injuries allegedly resulting from DES taken by her mother in 1951 and 1952 during pregnancy for the purpose of reducing the risk of miscarriage. The complaint sought damages on the theory of strict liability, alleging that the drug was defectively designed, with the result that plaintiff developed clear cell adenocarcinoma at the age of 23. As defendants, plaintiff joined Exclusive Prescription Pharmacy Corporation (Exclusive) where plaintiff's mother purchased the DES, and E.R. Squibb & Sons, Inc. (Squibb). The first cause of action alleged that Squibb was the manufacturer of the DES used by plaintiff's mother. . . .

Before jury selection began, the court granted Exclusive's motion for judgment on the pleadings, holding that a pharmacy may not be held strictly liable for dispensing a prescription drug. The court determined that Exclusive rendered a professional service in supplying the DES, that the consumer of the drug was the doctor who prescribed it rather than plaintiff's mother, and that as a matter of policy the doctrine of strict liability should not be extended to a pharmacy. . . .

THE ACTION AGAINST EXCLUSIVE

In the seminal case of Greenman v. Yuba Power Products, Inc., Justice Traynor, writing for the court, held a manufacturer strictly liable in tort for injuries caused by a defective product which it knew would be used without inspection for defects. In Vandermark v. Ford Motor Co., 391 P.2d 168 (Cal. 1964), the strict liability doctrine was extended to retailers of defective products.

Plaintiff asserts that a pharmacy which sells prescription drugs is in the same position as a retailer of any other consumer product, and that the reasons advanced in *Greenman* and *Vandermark* for imposing strict liability necessarily apply to a pharmacy. Exclusive counters that a pharmacist who dispenses a prescription drug is primarily furnishing a service rather than selling a product, and that the rationale underlying imposition of strict liability does not justify application of the doctrine to him. . . .

There are no cases in California deciding whether a retail pharmacy is strictly liable for injuries caused by an inherent defect in a drug. In Florida, North Carolina and New York a pharmacy is held not to be strictly liable for defects in a prescription drug. These cases rely on section 402A of the Restatement Second of Torts, which declares that unavoidably unsafe products such as drugs are not defective if they are accompanied by an appropriate warning (*id.*, com. k), and that a seller is only required to warn of defects of which he knew or should have known (id., com. j).

It is critical to the issue posed to determine if the dominant role of a pharmacist in supplying a prescription drug should be characterized as the performance of a service or the sale of a product. Both parties accept as a general rule that "those who sell their services for the guidance of others . . . are not liable in the absence of negligence or intentional misconduct." . . .

Magrine v. Krasnica, 227 A.2d 539, 543 (N.J. Super. 1967), held that a dentist was not strictly liable for injuries caused by a needle which broke during the course of treatment due to a latent defect. The court characterized the difference between a sale and a service as follows: "[T]he *essence* of the transaction between the retail seller and the consumer relates to the *article sold*. The seller is *in the business* of supplying the product to the consumer. It is that, and that alone, for which he is paid. A dentist or physician offers, and is paid for, his professional services and skill. That is the *essence* of the relationship between him and his patient." . . .

As might be anticipated, the parties differ sharply as to whether the main function of a pharmacist is to provide a service or to sell a product. Plaintiff asserts that the duties of a pharmacist in filling a prescription do not differ from those of any other retailer: he reads the prescription, fills the container with the proper type and dosage of the medication required, types up a label, attaches it to the container, and exchanges the medication for payment by the customer. In essence, argues plaintiff, a pharmacist is the functional equivalent of "an experienced clerk at a hardware store." . . .

It seems clear to us that the pharmacist is engaged in a hybrid enterprise, combining the performance of services and the sale of prescription drugs. It is pure hyperbole to suggest, as does plaintiff, that the role of the pharmacist is similar to that of a clerk in an ordinary retail store. With a few exceptions, only a licensed pharmacist may dispense prescription drugs, and as indicated above there are stringent educational and professional requirements for obtaining and retaining a license. A pharmacist must not only use skill and care in accurately filling and labelling a prescribed drug, but he must be aware of problems regarding the medication, and on occasion he provides doctors as well as patients with advice regarding such problems. In counseling patients, he imparts the same kind of information as would a medical doctor about the effects of the drugs prescribed. A key factor is that the pharmacist who fills a prescription is in a different position from the ordinary retailer because he cannot offer a prescription for sale except by order of the doctor. In this respect, he is providing a service to the doctor and acting as an extension of the doctor in the same sense as a technician who takes an X-ray or analyzes a blood sample on a doctor's order.

Nevertheless, it cannot be disputed that a sale in fact occurs. There is an obvious distinction between the doctor who provides a patient with a prescription for a defective drug, a dentist who uses a faulty drill or a hospital that uses a defective needle during surgery and a pharmacist who fills a prescription. The pharmacist is in the business of selling prescription drugs, and his role begins and ends with the sale. His services are rendered only in connection with the sale, and a patient who goes to a pharmacy to have a prescription filled generally is seeking to purchase the drug rather than to obtain the advice of the pharmacist.

By contrast, the doctor, dentist and hospital in the cases cited above are not in the business of selling the drug or device; they use the product in the course of treatment as one element in their efforts to effect a cure, and furnishing the services does not depend on sale of a product.

Ordinarily, in deciding whether the sale or service aspect of an enterprise predominates, we would confine our consideration to the type of factors discussed above. In the case of a pharmacy, however, we must broaden our inquiry. The Legislature has provided in section 4046 that the practice of pharmacy is not only a profession (subd. (a)), but also a "dynamic patient-oriented *health service* that applies a scientific body of knowledge to improve and promote patient health by means of appropriate drug use and drug related therapy" (subd. (b)). (Italics added.)

[The court then compares the provisions of this section with section 1606 of the Health and Safety Code, which explicitly treats the sale of blood as a service in order to avoid the use of strict liability rules.]

There is no definitive legislative history of subdivision (b), and we are not certain, therefore, of the Legislature's motivation in shielding pharmacies from strict liability. The Legislature may have determined that it is not in the public interest to subject them to strict liability, because (like the need to assure an adequate supply of blood plasma) the wide availability of a full range of prescription drugs at economical cost outweighs the advantage to the individual consumer of being able to recover for injuries on a strict liability basis rather than to be limited to claims arising from negligence.

If pharmacies were held strictly liable for the drugs they dispense, some of them, to avoid liability, might restrict availability by refusing to dispense drugs which pose even a potentially remote risk of harm, although such medications may be essential to the health or even the survival of patients. Furthermore, in order to assure that a pharmacy receives the maximum protection in the event of suit for defects in a drug, the pharmacist may select the more expensive product made by an established manufacturer when he has a choice of several brands of the same drug. As the Board's amicus brief warns, "Why choose a new company's inexpensive product, which has received excellent reviews in the literature for its quality, over the more expensive product of an established multinational corporation which will certainly have assets available for purpose of indemnification 10, 20, or 30 years down the line?"

The Legislature might have decided also that, since the doctor who ordered the drug provided by the pharmacy cannot be held strictly liable for its defects and in some circumstances the manufacturer who created the defect can also escape liability, it would be unfair and burdensome to expose the pharmacy alone to strict liability since it may provide the drug only on a doctor's prescription, which the pharmacist must strictly follow. Plaintiff emphasizes that some pharmacies are owned by large chain store operations which are as capable as large drug manufacturers to respond in damages. But most pharmacies are not in this category. According to the Board, approximately 3,385 pharmacy permits are held in California by independent operators of 3 or fewer pharmacies, many of which are single drugstores owned by the operating pharmacist. Only 1,165 permits are held by operators of 4 or more pharmacies, and 642 permits are held by hospital pharmacies.

Finally, plaintiff contends that even if the pharmacist is personally exempt from strict liability because he provides a service, the "merchandising organization which employs him . . . should not be so exempted." Plaintiff cites no authority in support of this claim, and we perceive no basis in law or rationale for accepting it. The fact that a pharmacy may be owned by an enterprise which also deals in ordinary merchandise does not justify the conclusion that it should be held strictly liable when it performs a service. Moreover, the policy justifying the grant of immunity from strict liability to the practice of pharmacy would only be effectuated if the pharmacy operation itself is exempted.

For the reasons stated above, we conclude that the trial court was correct in granting judgment on the pleadings to Exclusive. . . .

BIRD, C.J. — I dissent from the affirmance of the judgment in favor of defendant Exclusive Prescription Pharmacy Corporation (Exclusive). Under principles of products liability which are firmly established in this state, a retail druggist is strictly liable in tort for the sale of a defective prescription drug. Today's majority reach the opposite conclusion by retreating from sound principles which, in less turbulent times, were viewed as beyond serious challenge.

Specifically, the majority take a narrow and cramped view of the policies served by strict liability. Several of the most important policies, first articulated in the pioneering opinions of Chief Justice Roger Traynor, are not even mentioned. The majority's failure to address these policies has unfortunate consequences which go beyond their incorrect conclusion regarding liability. . . .

While *Greenman* presented only the question of a manufacturer's liability for a defective product, the policies underlying the strict liability doctrine apply to others in the marketing chain by which the product reaches the consumer. This was made clear a year later in Vandermark v. Ford Motor Co., 391 P.2d 168, 171-72 (Cal. 1968). Chief Justice Traynor's opinion, again expressing the unanimous view of this court, held that a retailer is strictly liable in tort for defects in products it sells.

> Retailers like manufacturers are engaged in the business of distributing goods to the public. They are an integral part of the overall producing and marketing enterprise that should bear the cost of injuries resulting from defective products. In some cases the retailer may be the only member of that enterprise reasonably available to the injured plaintiff. In other cases the retailer himself may play a substantial part in insuring that the product is safe or may be in a position to exert pressure on the manufacturer to that end; the retailer's strict liability thus serves as an added incentive to safety. Strict liability on the manufacturer and retailer alike affords maximum protection to the injured plaintiff and works no injustice to the defendants, for they can adjust the costs of such protection between them in the course of their continuing business relationship. . . .

Accepting the majority's characterization of the retail druggist's business as "a hybrid enterprise, combining the performance of services and the sale of prescription drugs," it is nonetheless abundantly clear that the sale aspect predominates.

The majority's own statistics bear this out. Only 22 percent of patients who purchase prescription drugs are counseled by the retail druggist, who spends an average of only one and one-half hours a day performing this service. Thus, in the vast majority of prescription drug sales transactions, the customer receives only a product and no services from the retail druggist.

KAUS, J., and BROUSSARD, J., concurred.

KAUS, J. — I respectfully dissent.

. . . Unless we are to repudiate the principle set forth by Chief Justice Traynor in Vandermark v. Ford Motor Co., applying strict liability doctrine to retailers of goods generally, if a manufacturer who markets a defective prescription drug may be held strictly liable for resulting injuries, I see no proper basis for exempting a retail pharmacist — certainly a link in the product's marketing chain — from similar liability.[1] It is surely no more difficult for such a pharmacist to obtain contractual or equitable indemnity from the manufacturer, or to insure against such loss in his own right, than it is for the typical "mom-and-pop" grocery or hardware store to take such steps. While . . . doctors and

---

1. I emphasize that the retailer's liability should simply be coextensive with that of the drug manufacturer. If — for reasons not fully explored in existing California cases — it is determined that, in a particular context, a drug manufacturer should not be held strictly liable for harm caused by a prescription drug, the retailer too should escape strict liability. But when the manufacturer may properly be held strictly liable — as would clearly be the case, for example, if it marketed an impure batch of a prescription drug — the retailer of the defective drug should also be strictly liable.

dentists have not been held strictly liable for injuries caused by defective products which they incidentally use in performing their service on patients, I know of no authority which suggests that *the retailer* who sells a doctor or dentist a defective surgical needle or defective orthodontic wire should escape strict liability for a resulting injury to the patient simply because the defective product has been used in the course of a professional service.

NOTES

1. Sales and services. As noted in *Murphy,* section 402A does not apply to persons who provide "services," but is limited to "sellers" under comment *f.* By analogy, liability under the section has been extended to the builders of mass-produced homes, Schipper v. Levitt & Sons, Inc., 207 A.2d 314 (N.J. 1965); to wholesalers and distributors, Barth v. B.F. Goodrich Tire Co., 71 Cal. Rptr. 306 (Cal. App. 1968); and to lessors and bailors of personal property, Cintrone v. Hertz Leasing & Rental Service Co., 212 A.2d 769 (N.J. 1965), and Price v. Shell Oil Co., 466 P.2d 722 (Cal. 1970).

Other cases have also grappled with the identification of product sellers under section 402A. Shaffer v. Victoria Station, Inc., 588 P.2d 233 (Wash. 1978), applied section 402A to injuries caused by a broken wine glass at a restaurant dinner, brushing aside the "gloomy view" that products liability actions would often be brought against "busboys and waiters" and restaurants generally for all manner of ills. Kosters v. The Seven-Up Company, 595 F.2d 347 (6th Cir. 1979), held that under section 402A a franchisor, responsible for "floating" its products into the stream of commerce, was a seller of bottles sold by its distributors, because it "exercised control over the 'type, style, size and design' of the carton in which its product was to be marketed." But Johnson v. William C. Ellis & Sons Iron Works, Inc., 604 F.2d 950 (5th Cir. 1979), held that section 402A did not reach "a repairer, installer or other provider of services . . . for failing to correct or warn of pre-existing defects in the products on which they have contracted to work," at least with respect to conditions that they did not create or exacerbate and that were not within the contracted work.

The proposed Third Restatement does not address all these wrinkles but in its main lines it follows the lead of the Second. The product sellers include "commercial lessors of property for consumer use," and apply "to housing, although sales of real property historically have not been within the ambit of product sales." §1, comment *b.* Third Restatement, §2, comment *k* acknowledges that nonmanufacturing sellers "are often not in a good position to feasibly adopt safer product designs or better instructions or warnings." But it reiterates that nonmanufacturing sellers are nonetheless subject to the same standards applicable to manufacturers: "As long as the plaintiff establishes that the product was defective when it left the hands of a given seller in the distributive chain, liability will attach to that seller." §2, comment *b*. "Thus liability is imposed on a wholesale or retail seller who neither knew nor should have known of the relevant risks, nor was in a position to have taken action to avoid them, so long as a precedecessor in title could have acted reasonably to avoid the risk." §2, comment *k*. Should there be *any* liability where the retailer has no control over the manufacture, design, or warnings associated with a given product? What if the retailer remains in business after the manufacturer has become insolvent?

2. *Used and reconditioned products.* The scope of section 402A has also been raised in connection with the sale of used or reconditioned products. In many circumstances the sellers of these products did not purchase them from the original manufacturer, but obtained them in the open market at the request of a particular client. In Tillman v. Vance Equipment Co., 596 P.2d 1299, 1303-1304 (Or. 1979), the plaintiff was injured by a 24-year-old used crane that his employer had purchased from the defendant, a used equipment dealer, on an "as is" basis. The court refused to extend the strict liability principles of section 402A to this defendant:

> We conclude that holding every dealer in used goods responsible regardless of fault for injuries caused by defects in his goods would not only affect the prices of used goods; it would work a significant change in the very nature of used goods markets. Those markets, generally speaking, operate on the apparent understanding that the seller, even though he is in the business of selling such goods, makes no particular representation about their quality simply by offering them for sale. If a buyer wants some assurance of quality, he typically either bargains for it in the specific transaction or seeks out a dealer who routinely offers it (by, for example, providing a guarantee, limiting his stock of goods to those of a particular quality, advertising that his used goods are specially selected, or in some other fashion). The flexibility of this kind of market appears to serve legitimate interests of buyers as well as sellers.
>
> We are of the opinion that the sale of a used product, without more, may not be found to generate the kind of expectations of safety that the courts have held are justifiably created by the introduction of a new product into the stream of commerce.
>
> As to the risk-reduction aspect of strict products liability, the position of the used-goods dealer is normally entirely outside the original chain of distribution of the product. As a consequence, we conclude, any risk reduction which would be accomplished by imposing strict liability on the dealer in used goods would not be significant enough to justify our taking that step. The dealer in used goods generally has no direct relationship with either manufacturers or distributors. Thus, there is no ready channel of communication by which the dealer and the manufacturer can exchange information about possible dangerous defects in particular product lines or about actual and potential liability claims.

In Crandell v. Larkin, 334 N.W.2d 31 (S.D. 1983), the court agreed with the decision in *Tillman* as it applied to mere sellers of used products, but held that the traditional principles of strict liability did apply to sellers who rebuild or recondition those products. Should the rule apply to defects in the original design? See Michalko v. Cooke Color & Chem. Corp., 451 A.2d 179, 183 (N.J. 1982), where, in accordance with its strict liability principles, the court held:

> [W]hen it is feasible for the rebuilder of machinery or the manu-facturer of component parts to incorporate a safety device and it fails to do so, the rebuilt machine or component part will be deemed to be a defective product when delivered by the manufacturer to its owner. Further, the fact that the product was built according to the plans and specifications of the owner does not constitute a defense to a claim based on strict liability for the manufacture of a defective product when the injuries are suffered by an innocent foreseeable user of the product.

3. Successor liability. One question, much litigated in recent years, has been whether a corporation that has acquired either the assets or the shares of a product seller can be sued for its predecessor's torts after the liquidation of the original corporation. The leading case in support of successor liability is still Ray v. Alad Corporation, 560 P.2d 3, 9 (Cal. 1977), where the new defendant corporation simply took over the busi-ness of the prior corporation and exploited its good will without any change in its operation or its control. The court rested its case for suc-cessor liability on three separate grounds:

> (1) the virtual destruction of the plaintiff's remedies against the original manufacturer caused by the successor's acquisition of the business, (2) the successor's ability to assume the original manufacturer's risk-spread-ing role, and (3) the fairness of requiring the successor to assume a re-sponsibility for defective products that was a burden necessarily attached to the original manufacturer's good will being enjoyed by the successor in the continued operation of the business.

Ray was not followed in Leannais v. Cincinnati, Inc., 565 F.2d 437, 439 (7th Cir. 1977), where the management of the selling corporation had nothing to do with the operation of the new business after the sale. The court held that the transaction did not fall within any of the four exceptions to Wisconsin's general rule of no successor liability:

> (1) when the purchasing corporation expressly or impliedly agreed to assume the selling corporation's liability; (2) when the transaction amounts to a consolidation or merger of the purchaser and seller corpo-rations; (3) when the purchaser corporation is merely a continuation of the seller corporation; or (4) when the transaction is entered into fraudulently to escape liability for such obligations.

Leannais was adopted by the Wisconsin Supreme Court in Tift v. Forage King Industries, Inc., 322 N.W.2d 14 (Wis. 1982), a case that fell under the third exception to the *Leannais* rule. Does *Ray* also fall into exception three?

In Nissen Corp. v. Miller, 594 A.2d 564, 568 (Md. 1991), the Maryland Supreme Court also refused to extend successor liability beyond the four exceptions outlined in *Leannais*. There Nissen Corporation had purchased in January 1981, "the trade name, patents, and inventory and other assets of American Tredex," a treadmill manufacturer, and contractually assumed some of Tredex's fixed contractual liabilities. But "the contract expressly excluded assumption of liability for injuries arising from any product previously sold by American Tredex." American Tredex also agreed to maintain its corporate existence for a five-year period after the sale. The market price paid for the assets, in cash and in notes, reflected its full fair market value. In October 1986, the plaintiff was injured on a treadmill purchased from American Tredex, which had liquidated earlier that year. It sought to maintain an action against Nissen Corporation for its injuries, urging adoption of an additional exception to the general rule of no successor liability whenever there is a "continuity of enterprise" between the prior corporation and its successor, Nissen, even though continuity of ownership is lacking. Plaintiff argued that Nissen had to accept both the benefits and the burdens of any assets purchase, while the defendant argued that the current rules were appropriate because they "have functioned well to balance the rights of creditors and successor corporations by preserving traditional principles of corporate law and promoting the free alienability of business assets while maintaining adequate protection for the interests of consumers and creditors from fraudulent and unjust corporate transactions." The court agreed with the defendant, saying: "It seems patently unfair to require such a party to bear the cost of unassumed and uncontemplated products liability claims primarily because it is still in business and is perceived as a 'deep pocket.' " And it further queried the wisdom of allowing suits against successor corporations that were themselves small businesses.

The rule in *Nissen Corp.* also has an efficiency justification. If the law expressly required a successor corporation to assume indefinitely the tort obligations of its seller, any deals in which the contingent tort liabilities exceed the value of the assets to be sold will not be consummated. In that event, only two alternatives could remain: first, the selling corporation could either liquidate its business, leaving all its potential tort claimants in the lurch, or it could continue to operate the business, but probably less efficiently than its would-be purchaser. Ironically, allowing the buyer not to assume tort liabilities could *increase* the level of tort protection, since the purchase agreement obligated the seller to remain in business for five years after the sale. Should the nonassumption clause be held invalid if such a condition is not found in the purchase agreement?

D. PRODUCT DEFECTS

1. Construction Defects

Pouncey v. Ford Motor Co.
464 F.2d 957 (5th Cir. 1972)

MORGAN, J. C. L. Pouncey, the appellee, was injured while putting antifreeze in his 1966 Ford automobile. While he was accelerating the engine with the hood open, a blade broke off the radiator fan, cut through the water hose, and struck him in the face causing permanent facial disfigurement. Pouncey had purchased the car secondhand approximately six months before the accident from Clement Motor Company of Greenville, Alabama. The car had been driven approximately 62,000 miles at the time of the accident.

Pouncey brought this action below against Ford Motor Company, the appellant, seeking damages for the injury on a products liability theory. The case was tried to a jury which returned a verdict in favor of Pouncey in the amount of $15,000.00. Ford now appeals from the denial by the district court of motions for a directed verdict, and for a judgment notwithstanding the verdict, or in the alternative for a new trial. The main thrust of Ford's appeal is that the evidence was insufficient to support the jury's verdict. Ford also assigns as error certain portions of the court's charge and certain evidentiary rulings. We conclude that all of these contentions are without merit and affirm the judgment of the district court.

As is frequently the case in products liability litigation, the trial produced a conflict in expert testimony. The main thrust of Pouncey's case was that the fan blade failure occurred because of a fatigue fracture in the metal fan blade. It was Pouncey's theory that the premature fatigue failure was caused by an excessive number of inclusions in the metal of the blade. An inclusion is a non-metallic impurity in the steel which weakens the metal.

To substantiate this theory, Pouncey called Dr. C. H. T. Wilkins, a metallurgical engineer, as an expert witness. Dr. Wilkins testified that he cut and mounted a specimen of metal from the failed blade. He also cut and mounted specimens from a blade which had not failed and from another Ford fan blade which had failed. On microscopic examination of this mount, Dr. Wilkins found a "surprising number of inclusions" which he did not expect to find in this type steel. These inclusions, he testified, were an identifiable defect in the metal which served as "stress concentrating areas" and "lowered the endurance limit of the fan."

Dr. Wilkins also testified concerning certain bends and deformations in the blade. He conceded that there appeared to be some bends in the blades but he expressed the opinion that the blade which actually failed was not bent. In his opinion, the bends in the blades were not the cause of the fatigue failure.

Not surprisingly, Ford's expert witnesses took a different view of the facts. Ford first called Dr. Robert Hochman, another metallurgical engineer. Dr. Hochman testified that he received and examined the metal specimen that had been mounted by Dr. Wilkins. It was his opinion that the specimen had been mounted in such a way that acid seeped into the cracks between the specimens of metal, causing an exaggerated appearance of large inclusions. Dr. Hochman remounted and polished the specimens and took photomicrographs of them. These photomicrographs showed an acceptable inclusion level, testified Dr. Hochman, which conformed with standards established by the Society of Automotive Engineers.

Dr. Hochman attributed the fracture to a different source. He testified that one arm of the blade was bent and that this would have a major effect in throwing the fan out of balance. He also noted that the ends of the blades were bent and cracked and that this condition would also tend to imbalance the fan. An out-of-balance condition, Dr. Hochman testified, could cause the blade to vibrate and set up a high stress pattern which would result in the acceleration of metal fatigue. Dr. Hochman also noted a small notch in the fracture surface which could have been attributed to impact damage.

Ford also called two other expert witnesses, both of whom were Ford employees. Mr. Phillip Burch, a Ford design engineer, testified as to the testing procedures utilized by Ford on newly designed radiator fans. Mr. Robert Riding, another Ford engineer, testified concerning alleged bends in the fan blades. He stated in his opinion that the fan failed because of an unbalanced condition in the fan which may have been caused by a front end collision or by rough handling.

[The court then reviewed the expert testimony and concluded that the testimony of the plaintiff's expert went far beyond mere speculation in pinpointing the cause of the fracture. He stated unequivocally that " 'enormous' inclusions not normally found in spring steel were an 'identifiable defect' in the metal which caused premature fatigue failure."]

Ford also contends that the evidence was insufficient to support an inference of negligence either on the part of Ford or Ford's supplier, Fram Corporation. Ford contends that the testimony is undisputed that even under the best quality control program there is always the possibility that isolated pockets of inclusions could be found in metal and that there is no practical means of discovering the particular fans which might have these impurities. Ford argues that the absence of any proof by Pouncey of inadequate quality control procedures on the part of Ford or its supplier bars submission of the issue of Ford's negligence to the jury. Again we disagree.

In this diversity action, federal law, of course, defines the test for sufficiency of evidence to create a jury question. But the law of Alabama governs the substantive measure of care owed by the manufacturer of a product to the ultimate consumer. Under Alabama law, it is settled that a manufacturer's liability for a defective product is predicated upon negligence in the manufacture or design of the product. However, the Alabama courts have freely permitted juries to infer manufacturer negligence from circumstantial evidence where there is in the record direct evidence of an actual defect in the product. . . .

In the case at bar, there was direct evidence that Ford's supplier manufactured the blades with "dirty" spring steel. There is also testimony by Pouncey's expert that Ford and its supplier could reasonably expect a premature fatigue failure from steel with that level of inclusions. Finally, Ford itself offered no evidence as to the quality control procedures actually employed with regard to the radiator fans produced in 1966.[3] The court below committed no error in permitting the jury to infer from this evidence negligence on the part of Ford in placing on the market a defective radiator fan which could reasonably have been expected to produce injury or damage.

[Affirmed].

NOTES

1. Proof of construction defect. As *Pouncey* indicates, the typical construction defect case requires an enormous amount of expert evidence to identify the product's defect and its causal connection to the plaintiff's harm. As a matter of law, the plaintiff in a products liability case is "required to prove that her injury resulted from a condition of the product which was unreasonably dangerous and which existed at the time the product left the manufacturer's control." Moore v. Jewel Tea Co., 253 N.E.2d 636 (Ill. App. 1969). The defect in question need not "manifest" itself at once. Recovery is not barred simply because the plaintiff or a third party has stored or used a product before the injury

---

3. The testimony of Ford design engineer Phillip Burch dealt almost exclusively with the testing of newly designed fans. Burch could offer virtually no information on the tests *actually* conducted on the 1966 production fans.

occurred. See, e.g., Dunham v. Vaughan & Bushnell Mfg. Co., 247 N.E.2d 401 (Ill. 1969), where the plaintiff was allowed to recover even though he used the defendant's hammer for eleven months before it chipped and injured him.

2. *Res ipsa loquitur in products liability cases.* Today, the plaintiff in construction defect cases can reach the jury even without identifying the particular product defect. As Breitel, C.J., wrote in Halloran v. Virginia Chemicals, 361 N.E.2d 991, 993 (N.Y. 1977), "it is now established that, if the plaintiff has proven that the product has not performed as intended and excluded all causes of the accident not attributable to defendant, the fact finder may, even if the particular defect has not been proven, infer that the accident could only have occurred due to some defect in the product or its packaging."

One recent application of this principle is Welge v. Planters Lifesavers Co., 17 F.3d 209, 211, 212 (7th Cir. 1994). There plaintiff "forty-something but young in spirit," "loved to sprinkle peanuts on his ice cream sundaes." He cut his hand badly when a 24-ounce peanut jar collapsed under the weight of his hand as he closed it. One defendant manufactured the jar, a second packed it with peanuts, and the third sold it to Karen Godfrey, with whom plaintiff boarded. The pieces of the jar were recovered after the accident and revealed no evidence of product defect, but the plaintiff introduced uncontradicted evidence that the only alteration to the jar had been the removal of a coupon with an X-acto knife, that he had opened and closed it once without incident, that it had been sitting on top of a refrigerator for a week, and that he had closed the jar in the ordinary fashion. Posner, J., reversed defendant's summary judgment at trial and remanded for trial:

> [T]he defendants point out, it is always *possible* that the jar was damaged while it was sitting unattended on the refrigerator, in which event they are not responsible. Only if it had been securely under lock and key when not being used could the plaintiff and Karen Godfrey be *certain* that nothing happened to damage it after she brought it home. That is true — there are no metaphysical certainties — but it leads nowhere. Elves may have played nine-pins with the jar of peanuts while Welge and Godfrey were sleeping; but elves could remove a jar of peanuts from a locked cupboard. The plaintiff in a products liability case is not required to exclude every possibility, however fantastic or remote, that the defect which led to the accident was caused by someone other than one of the defendants. . . .
>
> The strict-liability element in modern products liability law comes precisely from the fact that a seller subject to that law is liable for defects in his product even if those defects were introduced without the slightest fault of his own for failing to discover them, at some anterior stage of production.

Under this view, what happens if the defect was introduced after the goods had been shipped from Planters to K-Mart?

These questions of proof often give rise to cases closer to the line, especially for long-lived products or those that receive intensive and protracted use. In Jagman v. Simons Abrasive Co., 211 N.W.2d 810 (Wis. 1973), the plaintiff was injured when struck in the face by a grinding wheel that broke into pieces while he was operating it. The plaintiff established that the wheel was of the defendant's manufacture. He further testified that he had used the wheel in the proper manner, that he had not placed undue stress on it, that he had no evidence to believe that any other person had used the wheel while he was away from his job, and that the wheel had several hours of life left at the time the accident took place. The wheel itself was destroyed after it broke. The trial court refused to allow the case to go to the jury, ruling that there was insufficient evidence on the question of "defect." The state supreme court reversed, relying in part on *Dunham*. It noted that the case was "exceedingly close," but allowed the plaintiff to reach the jury on a modified version of res ipsa loquitur, given that the plaintiff's evidence tended to exclude the possibility of any responsible cause of the injury apart from an original product defect. Does the plaintiff's evidence negate the possibility that the wheel was damaged in shipment or in installation?

A more hostile approach toward circumstantial proof of product defect was taken in State Farm Fire & Casualty v. Chrysler Corp., 523 N.E.2d 489, 496 (Ohio 1988). There the plaintiffs' car and home were destroyed by a fire that originated under the dashboard in plaintiffs' car. Prior to the fire, the plaintiffs had had repeated problems with the car's electrical wiring, which the dealer had tried unsuccessfully several times to repair. The plaintiffs' expert attempted to show that the "location, origin and nature" of the fire supported the conclusion that it was attributable to faulty wiring done by Chrysler. The trial judge granted defendant's motion for a directed verdict and its decision was upheld on appeal. "Yet, even when construed in favor of plaintiffs, this evidence does not permit reasonable minds to conclude that the source of the fire was a manufacturing defect in the electrical wiring present *when the automobile left the hands of the manufacturer.* . . . It is equally likely that the defect arose as the result of negligent repair when [the dealer] removed the dashboard of the [plaintiffs'] vehicle." Should the burden of proof be on the dealer and the manufacturer jointly to absolve themselves if they can?

Should res ipsa loquitur, developed in the law of negligence, ever be relevant to a construction defect case brought under section 402A? In this connection recall that three conditions for the doctrine were: (1) an accident that did not ordinarily happen in the absence of negligence; (2) exclusive control in the defendant; and (3) no plaintiff's contribution. In one sense, section 402A permits a powerful application of the doctrine because the negligence of the defendant is immaterial to the theory of relief. The proposed third Restatement §3 follows the case law and allows plaintiffs to recover in construction defect cases without specifying the particular defect responsible for the harm, so long as other causes of harm can be excluded. On the myriad problems of proof of defect in products cases see Rheingold, Proof of Defect in Product Liability Cases, 38 Tenn. L. Rev. 325 (1971).

2. Design Defects

Micallef v. Miehle Co.
348 N.E.2d 571 (1976)

COOKE, J. The time has come to depart from the patent danger rule enunciated in Campo v. Scofield, 95 N.E.2d 802 [N.Y. 1951].

This action was initiated to recover damages for personal injuries, allegedly resulting from negligent design and breach of an implied warranty. Paul Micallef, plaintiff, was employed by Lincoln Graphic Arts at its Farmingdale plant as a printing-press operator. For eight months he had been assigned to operate a photo-offset press, model RU 1, manufactured and sold by defendant Miehle-Goss Dexter, Inc., to his employer. The machine was 150 feet long, 15 feet high and 5 feet wide and was capable of printing at least 20,000 sheets an hour. Then, while working on January 22, 1969, plaintiff discovered that a foreign object had made its way onto the plate of the unit. Such a substance, known to the trade as a "hickie," causes a blemish or imperfection on the printed pages. Plaintiff informed his superior of the problem and told him he was going to "chase the hickie," whereupon the foreman warned him to be careful. "Chasing a hickie" consisted of applying, very lightly, a piece of plastic about eight inches wide to the printing plate, which is wrapped around a circular plate cylinder which spins at high speed. The revolving action of the plate against the plastic removes the "hickie." Unsuccessful in his first removal attempt, plaintiff started anew but this time the plastic was drawn into the nip point between the plate cylinder and an ink-form roller along with his hand. The machine had no safety guards to prevent such occurrence. Plaintiff testified that while his hand was trapped he reached for a shut-off button but couldn't contact it because of its location.

Plaintiff was aware of the danger of getting caught in the press in "chasing hickies." However, it was the custom and usage in the industry to "chase hickies on the run," because once the machine was stopped, it required at least three hours to resume printing and, in such event, the financial advantage of the high speed machine would be lessened. Although it was possible to have "chased the hickie" from another side of the machine, such approach would have caused plaintiff to be in a leaning position and would have increased the chances of scratching the plate. Through its representatives and engineers, defendant had observed the machine in operation and was cognizant of the manner in which "hickies were chased" by Lincoln's employees.

Samuel Aidlin, a professional engineer, had inspected the machine subsequent to the mishap. In his opinion, based upon the custom in the printing industry, it would have been good custom and practice to have placed guards near the rollers where plaintiff's hand entered the machine, the danger of human contact being well known. Moreover, he testified that at least three different types of guards were available, two for over 30 years, that they would not have impeded the practice of "chasing hickies," and that these guards would have protected an employee from exposure to the risk. Based upon the foregoing, both causes of action, negligence and breach of warranty, were submitted to the jury.

Although defendant was found negligent, recovery on that ground was barred by a finding that plaintiff had been contributorily negligent. . . .

We are confronted here with the question as to the continued validity of the patent-danger doctrine of Campo v. Scofield, . . .

Directing our attention to the cause of action for negligence in design, defendant asserts, citing Campo v. Scofield (supra), that the action must be dismissed because the danger created by the absence of safeguards on the machine was open and obvious and, therefore, as the manufacturer it was under no duty to protect plaintiff from such a patent defect. *Campo* set forth the following principles: "The cases establish that the manufacturer of a machine or any other article, dangerous because of the way in which it functions, and patently so, owes to those who use it a duty merely to make it free from latent defects and concealed dangers. Accordingly, if a remote user sues a manufacturer of an article for injuries suffered, he must allege and prove the existence of a latent defect or a danger not known to plaintiff or other users." It was then declared: "If a manufacturer does everything necessary to make the machine function properly for the purpose for which it is designed, if the machine is without any latent defect, and if its functioning creates no danger or peril that is not known to the user, then the manufacturer has satisfied the law's demands. We have not yet reached the state where a manufacturer is under the duty of making a machine accident proof or foolproof. Just as the manufacturer is under no obligation, in order to guard against injury resulting from deterioration, to furnish a machine that will not wear out, so he is under no duty to guard against injury from a patent peril or from a source manifestly dangerous."*

The requirement that a latent defect be proved, before there could be a recovery against a manufacturer in a negligence action, has retained its vitality. The underlying rationale of the court's decision in *Campo* apparently is founded on the notion that it should be the task of the Legislature, not the judiciary, to compel manufacturers to install possible safety devices. *Campo* has been the subject of sustained attack. The major thrust of criticism stems from the belief that, in our highly complex and technological society, we fall victim to the manufacturer who holds himself out as an expert in his field. It is argued that the *Campo* doctrine is "a vestigial carryover from pre-*MacPherson* days when deceit was needed for recovery." (2 Harper and James, Torts §28.5.)

More specifically, it is contended that the application of *Campo* amounts to an assumption of risk defense as a matter of law "with the added disadvantage that the defendant was relieved of the burden of proving that plaintiff had subjectively appreciated a known risk." (Rheingold, Expanding Liability of the Product Supplier: A Primer, 2 Hofstra L. Rev. 521, 541.) *Campo* is viewed as inconsistent because, on the one hand, it places a duty on the manufacturer to develop a reasonably safe product yet eliminates this duty, thereby granting him immunity from answering in damages, if the dangerous character of the product can be readily seen, irrespective of whether the injured user or consumer actually perceived the danger. As Professors Harper and James succinctly assert: "The bottom does not logically drop out of a negligence case against the maker when it is shown that the purchaser knew of the dangerous condition. Thus if the product is a carrot-topping machine with exposed moving parts, or an electric clothes wringer dangerous to the limbs of the operator, and if it would be feasible for the maker of the product to install a guard or safety release, it should be a question for the jury whether reasonable care demanded such a precaution, though its absence is obvious. Surely reasonable men might

---

*The passage in *Campo* continued:

"To illustrate, the manufacturer who makes, properly and free of defects, an axe or a buzz saw or an airplane with an exposed propeller, is not to be held liable if one using the axe or the buzz saw is cut by it, or if some one working around the airplane comes in contact with the propeller. In such cases, the manufacturer has the right to expect that such persons will do everything necessary to avoid such contact, for the very nature of the article gives notice and warning of the consequences to be expected, of the injuries to be suffered. In other words, the manufacturer is under no duty to render a machine or other article 'more' safe as long as the danger to be avoided is obvious and patent to all.

"To impose upon a manufacturer the duty of producing an accident-proof product may be a desirable aim, but no such obligation has been or, in our view, may be imposed by judicial decision. Suffice it to note that, in cases dealing with a manufacturer's liability for injuries to remote users, the stress has always been upon the duty of guarding against *hidden* defects and of giving notice of *concealed* dangers." [ED.]

find here a great danger, even to one who knew the condition and since it was so readily avoidable they might find the maker negligent." (2 Harper and James, Torts §28.5.)

Other jurisdictions have taken a more liberal position. For example, in Palmer v. Massey-Ferguson, 476 P.2d 713 (Wash. App. 1970), the plaintiff brought an action against the manufacturer of a hay baler for injuries sustained while adjusting a drawbar. In response to the defendant's allegations that the patent peril precluded liability, the court said: "The manufacturer of the obviously defective product ought not to escape because the product was obviously a bad one. The law, we think, ought to discourage misdesign rather than encouraging it in its obvious form." Another case, Bexiga v. Havir Mfg. Co., 290 A.2d 281, 286 (N.J. 1972), forcefully stated: "The asserted negligence of plaintiff — placing his hand under the ram while at the same time depressing the foot pedal — was the very eventuality the safety devices were designed to guard against. It would be anomalous to hold that defendant has a duty to install safety devices; but a breach of that duty results in no liability for the very injury the duty was meant to protect against." We find the reasoning of these cases persuasive. *Campo* suffers from its rigidity in precluding recovery whenever it is demonstrated that the defect was patent. Its unwavering view produces harsh results in view of the difficulties in our mechanized way of life to fully perceive the scope of danger, which may ultimately be found by a court to be apparent in manufactured goods as a matter of law. . . . Apace with advanced technology, a relaxation of the *Campo* stringency is advisable. A casting of increased responsibility upon the manufacturer, who stands in a superior position to recognize and cure defects, for improper conduct in the placement of finished products into the channels of commerce furthers the public interest. To this end, we hold that a manufacturer is obligated to exercise that degree of care in his plan or design so as to avoid any unreasonable risk of harm to anyone who is likely to be exposed to the danger when the product is used in the manner for which the product was intended as well as an unintended yet reasonably foreseeable use.

What constitutes "reasonable care" will, of course, vary with the surrounding circumstances and will involve "a balancing of the likelihood of harm, and the gravity of harm if it happens, against the burden of the precaution which would be effective to avoid the harm." Under this approach, "the plaintiff endeavors to show the jury such facts as that competitors used the safety device which was missing here, or that a 'cotter pin costing a penny' could have prevented the accident. The defendant points to such matters as cost, function, and competition as narrowing the design choices. He stresses 'trade-offs.' If the product would be unworkable when the alleged missing feature was added, or would be so expensive as to be priced out of the market, that would be relevant defensive matter." (Rheingold, Expanding Liability of the Product Supplier: A Primer, 2 Hofstra L. Rev. 521, 537.) In this case, there was no evidence submitted at trial to show the cost of guards that could have been attached in relation to the entire cost of the machine.

Also relevant, but by no means exclusive, in determining whether a manufacturer exercised reasonable skill and knowledge concerning the design of the product is whether he kept abreast of recent scientific developments and the extent to which any tests were conducted to ascertain the dangers of the product. This does not compel a manufacturer to clothe himself in the garb of an insurer in his dealings nor to supply merchandise which is accident proof. It does require, however, that legal responsibility, if any, for injury caused by machinery which has possible dangers incident to its use should be shouldered by the one in the best position to have eliminated those dangers.

We next examine the duty owing from a plaintiff or, in other words, the conduct on a plaintiff's part which will bar recovery from a manufacturer. As now enunciated, the patent-danger doctrine should not, in and of itself, prevent a plaintiff from establishing his case. That does not mean, however, that the obviousness of the danger as a factor in the ultimate injury is thereby eliminated, for it must be remembered that in actions for negligent design, the ordinary rules of negligence apply. Rather, the openness and obviousness of the danger should be available to the defendant on the issue of whether plaintiff exercised that degree of reasonable care as was required under the circumstances. . . .

The order of the Appellate Division should be reversed and a new trial granted, with costs to abide the event. BREITEL, C.J., and JASEN, GABRIELLI, JONES, WACHTLER and FUCHSBERG, JJ., concur.

Order reversed, etc.

NOTES

1. Two conceptions of design defect cases. Most of the major themes in design defect litigation are raised by the contrast between *Campo* and *Micallef. Campo* was the leading design defect case before the second Restatement, and *Micallef* represents the modern view. In dispute are two intertwined issues. The first is whether the open and obvious nature of an asserted defect is sufficient to negate all liability or whether it only dispenses with the need for a warning. The second is whether any design requirements should be imposed by legislation or whether these changes can be imposed by judges and juries in common-law adjudication. Once the open and obvious defect test is rejected, the only alternative for it has been various forms of a cost/benefit standard, usually, but not always, under a negligence rubric. The cases in this section indicate the level of vacillation as to the relative weight to be accorded to these two conceptions of product defect. Which is simpler to use? Which will create the better incentives for manufacturers, intermediates, and product users?

2. *Product modification.* A substantial amount of litigation has focused on the question of whether a product alteration made after a manufacturer has shipped goods constitutes a superseding cause sufficient to relieve it of tort liability for design defects. An early case in which subsequent alterations precluded plaintiff's recovery against the manufacturer is Young v. Aeroil Products Co., 248 F.2d 185 (9th Cir. 1957). There the decedent had been crushed to death when the portable elevator he had been operating toppled. The decedent's employer had previously added additional equipment to the elevator, causing its imbalance. Even though the defendant had sold the elevator with the express warranty that it was balanced, the court held that the warranty was unavailing because "[t]he thing being used was not the thing sold."

More recent cases have expanded the scope of the manufacturer's liability for products that have been subsequently modified. In Soler v. Castmaster, Div. of H.P.M. Corp., 484 A.2d 1225, 1231 (N.J. 1984), the defendant manufacturer sold a die casting machine that was manually operated and that was not equipped with any automatic safety gate or interlock device. Subsequently, the plaintiff's employer modified the machine in two ways: it added a trip wire to the machine to make it cycle automatically without operator activation, and at the same time it also added a safety gate. The plaintiff's hand was caught in the machine while he was trying to remove a cast from the molding. The court first concluded that a jury could find the original machine design defective under the risk-utility analysis, and then allowed the jury to decide whether the changes made by the plaintiff's employer insulated the defendant from liability. "The critical question then is whether the original defect in the design of the machine — the absence of a safety gate with interlock — constitutes a proximate cause of the accident, notwithstanding the subsequent substantial alteration." The court further observed that "in applying strict liability 'in torts for design defects, manufacturers cannot escape liability on the grounds of misuse or abnormal use if the actual use proximate to the injury was objectively foreseeable.' Foreseeable misuse or abnormal use can be extended by analogy to foreseeable substantial change of the product from its original design."

In the companion case of Brown v. United States Stove Co., 484 A.2d 1234, 1244 (N.J. 1984), the New Jersey court held that an employer's product modification did exonerate the original manufacturer as a matter of law. The plaintiff was seriously burned while standing near an unvented, freestanding space heater manufactured by the defendant for home use. Some 15 years before the accident, the plaintiff's employer had removed its thermocouple valve and gas safety shut off from its pilot light tube, increasing the flow through the heater 100-fold. The plaintiff's expert testified that these space heaters were often abused when, as here, they were moved between construction sites. He therefore suggested that either the unit should have been redesigned to bear the higher rate of gas flow, or, alternatively, that the defendant could have used "noncommercial left-handed threading and inverted flange connectors, which were available in the 1950's and 1960's" to make the heaters more tamper resistant. A defendant's employee testified that the right-handed threading was used for "serviceability and market convenience." On appeal the court first held that the product alterations were objectively foreseeable, but then awarded defendant judgment on the ground that its original defect, if any, was too remote a cause of the plaintiff's harm. "No evidence was proffered to indicate that with a proper design the removal of the heater's safety features probably could not have been accomplished or even rendered so substantially difficult as to be unlikely. Rather the record discloses that the heater was deliberately altered for the specific purpose of operating it beyond its safe capacity, and, further, it was wilfully, persistently and intensively misused in this fashion for an extraordinarily long period of time, perhaps for as long as fifteen years."

Volkswagen of America, Inc. v. Young
321 A.2d 737 (Md. 1974)

[The decedent in this case had stopped his 1968 Volkswagen Beetle at a red light when he was hit from behind by a 1967 Ford, negligently driven by one William Benson. As a result, decedent's car was pushed forward. The seat bracketing pieces and seat adjustment mechanisms broke away from the body of the car. In the ensuing "second collision" the decedent was hurled into the rear of the car and sustained injuries on impact to his head and torso that resulted in his death. The plaintiff sued Volkswagen in Federal District Court; her complaint alleged that the Beetle was "defectively designed, manufactured, and marketed with defects which rendered it structurally hazardous, not merchantable, and not fit for the purpose intended" in that its entire seat assembly was "unreasonably vulnerable to separation from the floor upon collision." After the complaint was filed, the defendant moved in district court to have a question certified for decision by the Maryland Court of Appeals pursuant to Maryland's Certification of Questions of Law Act. The question certified by the district court was as follows:

"Whether or not, under Maryland law, the definition of the 'intended use' of a motor vehicle includes the vehicle's involvement in a collision; and thus in turn, whether a cause of action is stated against the manufacturer or importer of said vehicle in breach of warranty or negligence or absolute liability or misrepresentation by allegations that the design and manufacture of the vehicle unreasonably increased the risk of injury to occupants following a collision not caused by any defect of the vehicle."

The Maryland court answered the question in the affirmative, holding that the "intended use" of an automobile was not only to provide transportation but also reasonably safe transportation, and that the plaintiff's complaint stated a cause of action in negligence under Maryland law.]

ELDRIDGE, J. . . . This is the first case to reach this Court concerning the extent of an automobile manufacturer's liability for a design defect resulting in enhanced injuries in a motor vehicle accident, where the defect did not cause the initial impact or movement of the injured person. Such cases are often called "second collision" cases or "automobile crashworthiness" cases. They differ from other products liability cases involving defective automobiles by the combination of two factors. First, the alleged defect is in the design of the automobile rather than a negligent deviation during the construction or assembly process from the manner in which the vehicle was supposed to be made. The latter is usually called a "construction defect." Second, the defect is not the cause of the initial impact. Typically, the actions of the driver of the car in which the plaintiff is riding, or the actions of the driver of another vehicle, or the actions of some third person, cause an initial disruption or impact which in turn results in the plaintiff's colliding with the interior (or occasionally the exterior) of the car. The plaintiff's collision with the car is the so-called "second collision." The issue of whether the automobile manufacturer has a duty to take reasonable steps to design its vehicles so as to minimize the injuries caused by "second collisions" has engendered much controversy and comment throughout the nation.

The principal case holding that an automobile manufacturer has no duty to design its cars so as to minimize the injuries suffered in automobile accident is Evans v. General Motors Corporation, 359 F.2d 822 (7th Cir. 1966), cert. denied 385 U.S. 836 (1966). The plaintiff [the decedent] in *Evans* was killed when his 1961 Chevrolet station wagon was struck broadside by another car. He claimed that General Motors was negligent in designing the frame of his car, inasmuch as an "X" type frame rather than a box or perimeter type frame was used, contrary to the construction of some other cars. The claim was that an "X" type frame without side rails would not adequately protect occupants during a side impact collision, and that the defendant manufacturer had created an unreasonable risk of serious injury. The trial court, applying Indiana law, dismissed the complaint for failure to state a claim on which relief could be granted, and the dismissal was affirmed by the

United States Court of Appeals for the Seventh Circuit. The Court of Appeals held that the critical question was the nature of the manufacturer's duty. It went on to conclude that a manufacturer has a duty only to design a car reasonably fit for its intended purpose, and that "[t]he intended purpose of an automobile does not include its participation in collisions with other objects, despite the manufacturer's ability to foresee the possibility that such collisions may occur. As defendant argues, the defendant also knows that its automobiles may be driven into bodies of water, but it is not suggested that defendant has a duty to equip them with pontoons." (359 F.2d at 825.)

The Court of Appeals for the Seventh Circuit also stated as grounds for its decision that a "manufacturer is not under a duty to make his automobile accident-proof or fool-proof" (id. at 824) and that requiring "manufacturers to construct automobiles in which it would be safe to collide . . . [is] a legislative function. . . ." (Ibid.) . . .

The seminal case on the other side of the issue is Larsen v. General Motors Corporation, 391 F.2d 495 (8th Cir. 1968). The plaintiff in *Larsen* suffered severe bodily injuries while driving a 1963 Corvair which collided head-on with another car. The impact caused the steering mechanism to thrust forward into the plaintiff's head. The suit against General Motors charged negligence in the design of the steering assembly and the placement of the component parts of the steering assembly into the structure of the car. It was alleged that General Motors was also negligent in not warning the user of this latent condition. The specific defect relied upon by the plaintiff was that the solid steering shaft was so designed as to extend "without interruption from a point 2.7 inches in front of the leading surface of the front tires to a position directly in front of the driver," exposing him "to an unreasonable risk of injury from the rearward displacement of that shaft in the event of a left-of-center head-on collision. So positioned it receives the initial impact of forces generated by a left-of-center head-on collision. The unabsorbed forces of the collision in this area are transmitted directly toward the driver's head, the shaft acting as a spear aimed at a vital part of the driver's anatomy." 391 F.2d 497, n.2. The plaintiff also pointed out that other cars were designed so as to protect against such rearward displacement, in that the steering column did not protrude beyond the forward surface of the front tires. The lower court in *Larsen* granted General Motors' motion for summary judgment on the theory that the manufacturer had no duty to design a vehicle which would protect the plaintiff from injury in a collision. On appeal, the United States Court of Appeals for the Eighth Circuit reversed, holding that the plaintiff had made out a sufficient case for consideration by the jury.

[The court in *Larsen* gave a broad interpretation to "intended use," stating:] "Automobiles are made for use on the roads and highways in transporting persons and cargo to and from various points. This intended use cannot be carried out without encountering in varying degrees the statistically proved hazard of injury-producing impacts of various types. The manufacturer should not be heard to say that it does not intend its product to be involved in any accident when it can easily foresee and when it knows that the probability over the life of its product is high, that it will be involved in some type of injury-producing accident."

And later the court emphasized (id. at 502):

"The sole function of an automobile is not just to provide a means of transportation, it is to provide a means of safe transportation or as safe as is reasonably possible under the present state of the art."

The Court of Appeals concluded that an automobile manufacturer "is under a duty to use reasonable care in the design of its vehicle to avoid subjecting the user to an unreasonable risk of injury in the event of a collision." (Ibid.)

The *Larsen* court then emphasized the limitations of its holding that it was not making automobile manufacturers "insurers," that it was merely applying common law principles of negligence that the standard for manufacturers was "reasonable care" and that an automobile did not have to be absolutely crash-proof but only designed to provide "a reasonably safe vehicle in which to travel." 391 F.2d at 503.* . . .

In our view, Larsen v. General Motors Corporation, supra, and the cases following it, are more in accord with traditional negligence principles than Evans v. General Motors Corporation, supra. . . .

That the design defect does not cause the initial collision should make no difference if it is a cause of the ultimate injury. Where the injuries to an occupant of a motor vehicle resulted from both the negligence of a driver as well as a negligent condition created by some other entity, this Court has held that both negligent actors may be liable. . . .

In sum, "traditional rules of negligence" lead to the conclusion that an automobile manufacturer is liable for a defect in design which the manufacturer could have reasonably foreseen would cause or enhance injuries on impact, which is not patent or obvious to the user, and which in fact leads to or enhances the injuries in an automobile collision.

The arguments advanced by Volkswagen in the instant case for creating an exception to the application of traditional negligence principles in "second collision" cases are not persuasive. They are essentially the same reasons set forth by the United States Court of Appeals for the Seventh Circuit in *Evans* and the other cases following *Evans*. Volkswa-

*The defendant in *Larsen* received a unanimous verdict after a three-week trial, having introduced scientific evidence that the plaintiff had not been hit by the steering column. For a discussion of the expert evidence introduced at trial, see Bowman, Defense of an Auto Design Negligence Case, 10 For the Defense, No. 5, May, 1969. — ED.

gen's principal arguments are: (1) that the intended purpose of an automobile is transportation and does not include its participation in collisions; (2) that "a manufacturer is not required to produce accident-proof or injury-proof cars"; (3) that manufacturers are not insurers; and (4) that "[d]esign requirements are a legislative, not a judicial function. . . ."

While the intended purpose of an automobile may not be to participate in collisions, the intended purpose includes providing a reasonable measure of safety when, inevitably, collisions do occur. For many years automobiles have been equipped with safety glass, bumpers, windshield wipers, etc. More recently, and largely as a result of governmental action, automobiles are equipped with additional safety devices such as seat belts, shoulder harnesses, padded dashboards, padded visors, non-protruding knobs, etc. Frequent collisions are foreseeable, and the intended purpose of all of these parts of the vehicle is to afford reasonable safety when those collisions occur.

The arguments that there is no duty to design "accident-proof" or "injury-proof" vehicles, and that automobile manufacturers are not insurers, are "straw men." No case has ever held that an automobile manufacturer must design an "accident-proof" or "injury-proof" vehicle or that the manufacturer is an insurer. Concerning two of the examples most often used by the advocates of non-liability for design defects, no one has suggested that an automobile must be designed to withstand a high speed head-on collision with a truck or to float if it leaves the road and goes into a body of water. . . .

The standard to be applied is the traditional one of reasonableness.

The contention that the design of automobiles involves a legislative function and not a judicial function, similarly furnishes no sound reason for exempting automobile "second collision" cases from the normal principles of tort liability. Legislative or administrative requirements that persons or businesses conduct their operations in a particular manner, and adhere to specified standards, have never been viewed as supplanting tort liability. On the contrary, such statutory or regulatory requirements are deemed to furnish standards by which courts or juries determine, along with other circumstances, whether or not conduct is negligent. Failure to adhere to those standards is evidence of negligence for the court or jury to consider. Moreover, the most significant legislation dealing with motor vehicle safety standards makes it clear that Congress did not view the question of safe motor vehicle design as solely a legislative problem. The National Traffic and Motor Vehicle Safety Act of 1966 specifically provided that "Compliance with any Federal motor vehicle safety standard issued under this subchapter does not exempt any person from any liability under common law." 15 U.S.C. 1397 (c). The committee reports and debates specify that the purpose of this provision was to insure that "state common law standards of care" and the principles of "product liability at common law" would continue to be viable, and that the legislative safety standards were not "to affect the rights of parties under common law. . . ." S. Rep. No. 1301, Committee on Commerce, 89 Cong., 2d Sess. 1966, p. 12. . . .

In addition, there can be no recovery if the danger inherent in the particular design was obvious or patent to the user of the vehicle. . . .

With respect to the contention that the complaint sets forth a cause of action under the "strict liability" theory of Restatement 2d, Torts, §402A, this Court has not endorsed the theory of that section. Bona v. Graefe, 285 A.2d 607 (Md. 1972). Regardless of whether the theory of §402A of the Restatement should be accepted in other contexts, we are convinced that it has no proper application to liability for *design* defects in motor vehicles. The thrust of §402A is that a seller of "any product in a defective condition" is liable to a user for harm caused by that defective condition even though "the seller has exercised all possible care in the preparation and sale of his product." This principle obviously changes the standard of care with regard to a *construction defect*. But as to a defect in *design*, it has no special meaning. Since the existence of a defective design depends upon the reasonableness of the manufacturer's action, and depends upon the degree of care which he has exercised, it is wholly illogical to speak of a defective *design* even though the manufacturer has "exercised all possible care" in the preparation of his product. While a few cases applying *Larsen* principles have used language of "strict liability" with respect to design defects, it has been recognized that this results in "no practical difference" from the application of negligence principles. Consequently, the tort liability under Maryland law of a manufacturer or supplier of a motor vehicle, for a defective design which enhances injuries in a collision, depends upon traditional principles of negligence.

NOTES

1. Open and obvious again. While *Young* embraces a general negligence analysis, other cases have nonetheless found it appropriate to award directed verdicts to defendants in design defect cases largely because of the obviousness of the defect involved. In Dreisonstok v. Volkswagenwerk, A.G., 489 F.2d 1066 (4th Cir. 1974), the court, reversing the verdict for plaintiff below, held as a matter of law that a Volkswagen van is not defective simply because it does not provide as much protection against a head-on collision as the ordinary passenger car, which has the motor in front of the passenger compartment. (The design allowed the van to carry large amounts of cargo in a relatively small and maneuverable vehicle.) In Height v. Kawasaki Heavy Industries, 461

A.2d 757 (N.J. Super. 1983), common knowledge was held to preclude a suit against the manufacturer and distributor of a motorcycle whose fuel sprayed out of a gas tank after a collision, especially when the tank design contained a "pressure-relief mechanism" that substantially reduced the risk of a tank explosion. No warning was required because the plaintiff already had adequate knowledge of the need to avoid serious crashes. In Delvaux v. Ford Motor Co., 764 F.2d 469 (7th Cir. 1985), the court held that Wisconsin law precluded any suit on either design or warning grounds against a manufacturer of a convertible car sold without rollbar protection. The risks were clearly "apparent" to all consumers and the only workable modifications would eliminate the main advantage of the design, its open top.

2. *Determining standards for design defects.* As *Young* indicates, design defect liability grew up under the aegis of negligence. While it is possible to use strict liability for the protection of strangers against the defendant's use of force, it is far harder to apply that same standard when the defendant is required to protect the plaintiff against the use (or misuse) of force by the plaintiff or some third party. A motorcycle gasoline tank may be made "totally" safe against impact, but its weight and unwieldiness make it wholly unsuited for highway use. Once absolute protection is rejected as unworkable, the reasonableness standards have to take over.

Setting the standard then becomes the critical task. In some instances standards are set by legislation. See The National Traffic and Motor Vehicle Safety Act, 15 U.S.C.A. §§1381-1431, wherein, for example, regulation No. 216 ("Roofcrush Resistance — Passenger Cars") provides that a force equal to one and one-half times a car's weight or 5,000 pounds, whichever is less, should not move the roof more than five inches when applied to either of its front corners. 49 C.F.R. §571.216 (1994). Yet once it is held that compliance with a statute does not necessarily allow a defendant to escape liability in a design defect case, then courts must resort to various types of cost-benefit tests to determine the applicable standard. Can it be done? For a skeptical response see Henderson, Judicial Review of Manufacturer's Conscious Design Choices: The Limits of Adjudication, 73 Colum. L. Rev. 1531 (1973). In it, Professor Henderson stresses the "polycentric nature" of design decisions, which requires a design engineer to find the proper balance of "such factors as market price, functional utility, and aesthetics, as well, as safety." Henderson urges these are matters that cannot be adequately reexamined in litigation because "courts are not institutionally suited to establishing safety standards." On the general question of liability for design defects see also Nader and Page, Automobile Design and Judicial Process, 55 Cal. L. Rev. 645 (1967).

3. *Enhancement of injury.* As *Young* indicates, the plaintiff in a crashworthiness case typically does not seek to hold the defendant responsi-

ble for the injuries associated with the original impact, but only for those harms that were "enhanced or aggravated" by the defective design. One issue of great importance, therefore, is the burden of proof on the question of enhancement. One position is that no prima facie case is established unless the plaintiff shows that "it is more probable than not that the alleged defect aggravated or enhanced the injuries resulting from the initial collision." See Caiazzo v. Volkswagenwerk, A.G., 647 F.2d 241 (2d Cir. 1981). The alternative position was taken in Mitchell v. Volkswagenwerk, A.G., 669 F.2d 1199, 1204-1205 (8th Cir. 1982), where the court rejected *Caiazzo* as follows:

> The primary difficulty we have with this analysis is that it forces not only the parties but the jury as well to try a hypothetical case. Liability and damage questions are difficult enough within orthodox principles of tort law without extending consideration to a case of a hypothetical victim. More realistically, the parties and juries should direct their attentions to what actually happened rather than what might have happened.
>
> By placing the burden of proof on a plaintiff to prove that the designer was the sole cause of not only an enhanced indivisible injury, but, in addition, that he would not otherwise have received injuries absent a defect, the injured victim is relegated to an almost hopeless state of never being able to succeed against a defective designer. The public interest is little served. We write to reaffirm that *Larsen* was not intended to create a rule which requires the plaintiff to assume an impossible burden of proving a negative fact. A rule of law which requires a plaintiff to prove what portion of indivisible harm was caused by each party and what might have happened in lieu of what did happen requires obvious speculation and proof of the impossible. This approach converts the common law rules governing principles of legal causation into a morass of confusion and uncertainty.

Can any rule on the burden of proof avoid the need to try a "hypothetical case" in a design defect situation? See generally Comment, Apportionment of Damages in the "Second Collision" Case, 63 Va. L. Rev. 475 (1977).

The proposed Restatement Third, section 6, comment *a* takes the same view by holding the seller liable for "all the harm suffered by the plaintiff from both the defect and other causes," when responsibility for the injuries could not be apportioned.

4. *Crashworthiness cases: acceptance, disquiet, and reform?* The crashworthiness doctrine announced in *Larsen* and applied in *Young* is today accepted in every state of the Union. But some courts have expressed misgivings about its potential scope. In Dawson v. Chrysler Corp., 630 F.2d 950, 962-963 (3d Cir. 1980), the plaintiff, a police officer, was hurrying to answer a burglar alarm when his Dodge Monaco patrol car slipped off a rain-soaked highway into an "unyielding" steel pole some 15 inches in diameter. The pole ripped through the side of the car, crushed the plaintiff, and left him a quadriplegic. The plaintiff urged

that the car was defective because it did not have a rigid frame with "a full continuous steel frame extending through the door panels," which would have kept the pole from penetrating the passenger space. The defendant's expert testified that the plaintiff's proposed changes would add between 200 and 250 pounds of weight to the car and cost some $300. He also noted that "deformation" of a car in a crash is in general desirable because it absorbs the impact that would otherwise be transmitted to the occupant. Adams, J., affirmed the plaintiff's jury verdict under New Jersey law but noted his obvious misgivings:

> The result of such arrangement is that while the jury found Chrysler liable for not producing a rigid enough vehicular frame, a factfinder in another case might well hold the manufacturer liable for producing a frame that is too rigid. Yet, as pointed out at trial, in certain types of accidents — head-on collisions — it is desirable to have a car designed to collapse upon impact because the deformation would absorb much of the shock of the collision, and divert the force of deceleration away from the vehicle's passengers. In effect, this permits individual juries applying varying laws in different jurisdictions to set nationwide automobile safety standards and to impose on automobile manufacturers conflicting requirements. It would be difficult for members of the industry to alter their design and production behavior in response to jury verdicts in such cases, because their response might well be at variance with what some other jury decides is a defective design. Under these circumstances, the law imposes on the industry the responsibility of insuring vast numbers of persons involved in automobile accidents. . . .
>
> Although it is important that society devise a proper system for compensating those injured in automobile collisions, it is not at all clear that the present arrangement of permitting individual juries, under varying standards of liability, to impose this obligation on manufacturers is fair or efficient. Inasmuch as it was the Congress that designed this system, and because Congress is the body best suited to evaluate and, if appropriate, to change that system, we decline today to do anything in this regard except to bring the problem to the attention of the legislative branch.

The level of cynicism mounted in Blankenship v. General Motors Corp., 406 S.E.2d 781, 783, 784 (W.Va. 1991), where Neely, J., was induced to join the end of the crashworthiness parade for reasons that have little to do with the intrinsic merits of the doctrine.

> . . . [B]oth the defendant and amicus argue that allowing crashworthiness lawsuits invites juries to second-guess the safety standards promulgated by the National Highway Traffic Safety Administration. Thus, under the common theories of crashworthiness, defendant and amicus argue, different juries will reach different conclusions about the "reasonableness" of safety features, leaving manufacturers in the unenviable position of being unable to predict what juries will deem a "defective product [that] causes personal injury." Furthermore, defendant and amicus argue, juries may find designs approved by federal regulators "defective," giving the whole regulatory effect a certain *Alice in Wonderland* quality.

In all of these regards, the manufacturers and amicus have strong arguments. Nonetheless, West Virginia is a small rural state with .66 percent of the population of the United States. Although some members of this court have reservations about the wisdom of many aspects of the tort law, as a court we are utterly powerless to make the *overall* tort system for cases arising in interstate commerce more rational: Nothing that we do will have any impact whatsoever on the set of economic trade-offs that occur in the *national* economy. And, ironically, trying unilaterally to make the American tort system more rational through being uniquely responsible in West Virginia will only punish our residents severely without, in any regard, improving the system for anyone else. . . .

The defendant before us, General Motors, is the largest producer of automobiles in the world. In light of the fact that all of our sister states have adopted a cause of action for lack of crashworthiness, General Motors is *already* collecting a product liability premium every time it sells a car anywhere in the world, including West Virginia. West Virginians, then, are already paying the product liability premium when they buy a General Motors car, so this Court would be both foolish and irresponsible if we held that while West Virginia must pay the premiums, West Virginians can't collect the insurance after they're injured.

Barker v. Lull Engineering Co.
573 P.2d 443 (Cal. 1978)

TOBRINER, C.J. In August 1970, plaintiff Ray Barker was injured at a construction site at the University of California at Santa Cruz while operating a high-lift loader manufactured by defendant Lull Engineering Co. and leased to plaintiff's employer by defendant George M. Philpott Co., Inc. Claiming that his injuries were proximately caused, inter alia, by the alleged defective design of the loader, Barker instituted the present tort action seeking to recover damages for his injuries. The jury returned a verdict in favor of defendants, and plaintiff appeals from the judgment entered upon that verdict, contending primarily that in view of this court's decision in Cronin v. J. B. E. Olson Corp. 501 P.2d 1153 (Cal. 1972), the trial court erred in instructing the jury "that strict liability for a defect in design of a product is based on a finding that the product was unreasonably dangerous for its intended use. . . ."

As we explain, we agree with plaintiff's objection to the challenged instruction and conclude that the judgment must be reversed. . . .

As we explain in more detail below, we have concluded from this review that a product is defective in design either (1) if the product has failed to perform as safely as an ordinary consumer would expect when used in an intended or reasonably foreseeable manner, or (2) if, in light of the relevant factors discussed below, the benefits of the challenged design do not outweigh the risk of danger inherent in such design. In addition, we explain how the burden of proof with respect to the latter "risk-benefit" standard should be allocated.

This dual standard for design defect assures an injured plaintiff protection from products that either fall below ordinary consumer expectations as to safety, or that, on balance, are not as safely designed as they should be. At the same time, the standard permits a manufacturer who has marketed a product which satisfies ordinary consumer expectations to demonstrate the relative complexity of design decisions and the tradeoffs that are frequently required in the adoption of alternative designs. Finally, this test reflects our continued adherence to the principle that, in a product liability action, the trier of fact must focus on the *product,* not on the *manufacturer's conduct,* and that the plaintiff need not prove that the manufacturer acted unreasonably or negligently in order to prevail in such an action. . . .

1.   THE FACTS OF THE PRESENT CASE

Plaintiff Barker sustained serious injuries as a result of an accident which occurred while he was operating a Lull High-Lift Loader at a construction site. The loader, manufactured in 1967, is a piece of heavy construction equipment designed to lift loads of up to 5,000 pounds to a maximum height of 32 feet. The loader is 23 feet long, 8 feet wide and weighs 17,050 pounds; it sits on four large rubber tires which are about the height of a person's chest, and is equipped with four-wheel drive, an automatic transmission with no park position and a hand brake. Loads are lifted by forks similar to the forks of a forklift.

The loader is designed so that the load can be kept level even when the loader is being operated on sloping terrain. The leveling of the load is controlled by a lever located near the steering column, and positioned between the operator's legs. The lever is equipped with a manual lock that can be engaged to prevent accidental slipping of the load level during lifting.

The loader was not equipped with seat belts or a roll bar. A wire and pipe cage over the driver's seat afforded the driver some protection from falling objects. The cab of the loader was located at least nine feet behind the lifting forks.

On the day of the accident the regular operator of the loader, Bill Dalton, did not report for work, and plaintiff, who had received only limited instruction on the operation of the loader from Dalton and who had operated the loader on only a few occasions, was assigned to run the loader in Dalton's place. The accident occurred while plaintiff was attempting to lift a load of lumber to a height of approximately 18 to 20 feet and to place the load on the second story of a building under construction. The lift was a particularly difficult one because the terrain on which the loader rested sloped sharply in several directions.

Witnesses testified that plaintiff approached the structure with the loader, leveled the forks to compensate for the sloping ground and lifted the load to a height variously estimated between 10 and 18 feet. During the course of the lift plaintiff felt some vibration, and, when it appeared to several coworkers that the load was beginning to tip, the workers shouted to plaintiff to jump from the loader. Plaintiff heeded these warnings and leaped from the loader, but while scrambling away he was struck by a piece of falling lumber and suffered serious injury.

Although the above facts were generally not in dispute, the parties differed markedly in identifying the responsible causes for the accident. Plaintiff contended, inter alia, that the accident was attributable to one or more design defects of the loader. Defendant, in turn, denied that the loader was defective in any respect, and claimed that the accident resulted either from plaintiff's lack of skill or from his misuse of its product.

[The plaintiff claimed that the loader was defective in several respects: first, that it was not equipped with seat belts or a roll-bar; second, that it was not equipped with "outriggers" that might have given it greater lateral stability; third, that it was not equipped with an automatic locking device on its leveling mechanism; and, fourth, that it was not equipped with a separate park gear. In response to this assignment of defects, the defendant argued as follows: first, seat belts or roll-bars were themselves dangerous because they prevented any quick escape from the loader; second, that the outriggers were not needed if the loader was operated on level terrain as was intended, that none of the defendant's competitors had such outriggers, and that a regular crane should have been called in if work on uneven terrain was required; third, that the leveling device used was the most convenient and safe for the operator; and, fourth, that none of the transmissions manufactured for loaders incorporated a park position. The defendant also argued that the plaintiff's inexperience and panic were the sole source of his injury.

The jury returned a verdict for the defendant by a vote of ten to two.]

2. THE TRIAL COURT ERRED IN INSTRUCTING THE JURORS THAT "STRICT LIABILITY FOR A DEFECT IN DESIGN . . . IS BASED ON A FINDING THAT THE PRODUCT WAS UNREASONABLY DANGEROUS FOR ITS INTENDED USE."

Plaintiff principally contends that the trial court committed prejudicial error in instructing the jury "that strict liability for a defect in design of a product is based on a finding that the product was unreasonably dangerous for its intended use. . . ."[4] Plaintiff maintains that

4. The challenged instruction reads in full: "I instruct you that strict liability for the defect in design of a product is based on a finding that the product was unreasonably dangerous for its intended use, and in turn the unreasonableness of the danger must necessarily be derived from the state of the art at the time of the design. The manufac-

this instruction conflicts directly with this court's decision in *Cronin*, decided subsequently to the instant trial, and mandates a reversal of the judgment. Defendants argue, in response, that our *Cronin* decision should not be applied to product liability actions which involve "design defects" as distinguished from "manufacturing defects.". . .

Plaintiff contends that the clear import of . . . *Cronin* is that the "unreasonably dangerous" terminology of the Restatement should not be utilized in defining defect in product liability actions, and that the trial court consequently erred in submitting an instruction which defined a design defect by reference to the "unreasonably dangerous" standard.

In attempting to escape the apparent force of *Cronin*'s explicit language, defendants observe that the flawed hasp which rendered the truck defective in *Cronin* represented a manufacturing defect rather than a design defect, and they argue that *Cronin*'s disapproval of the Restatement's "unreasonably dangerous" standard should be limited to the manufacturing defect context. Defendants point out that one of the bases for our rejection of the "unreasonably dangerous" criterion in *Cronin* was our concern that such language, when used in conjunction with the "defective product" terminology, was susceptible to an interpretation which would place a *dual burden* on an injured plaintiff to prove, first, that a product was defective and, second, that it was additionally unreasonably dangerous. . . . Defendants contend that the "dual burden" problem is present only in a manufacturing defect context and not in a design defect case.

In elaborating this contention, defendants explain that in a manufacturing defect case, a jury may find a product defective because it deviates from the manufacturer's intended result, but may still decline to impose liability under the Restatement test on the ground that such defect did not render the product unreasonably dangerous. In a design defect case, by contrast, defendants assert that a defect is *defined* by reference to the "unreasonably dangerous" standard and, since the two are equivalent, no danger of a dual burden exists. In essence, defendants argue that under the instruction which the trial court gave in the instant case, plaintiff was not required to prove both that the loader was defective and that such defect made the loader unreasonably dangerous, but only that the loader was defectively designed by virtue of its unreasonable dangerousness.

Although defendants may be correct, at least theoretically, in as-

---

turer or lessor are not insurers of their products. However, an industry cannot set its own standards."

Plaintiff's challenge is limited to the portion of the instruction which provides that "strict liability for the defect in design of a product is based on a finding that the product was unreasonably dangerous for its intended use," and accordingly we express no opinion as to the propriety of the remaining portions of the instruction.

serting that the so-called "dual burden" problem is averted when the "unreasonably dangerous" terminology is used in a design defect case simply as a definition of "defective condition" or "defect," defendants overlook the fact that our objection to the "unreasonably dangerous" terminology in *Cronin* went beyond the "dual burden" issue, and was based, more fundamentally, on a substantive determination that the Restatement's "unreasonably dangerous" formulation represented an undue restriction on the application of strict liability principles.

As we noted in *Cronin*, the Restatement draftsmen adopted the "unreasonably dangerous" language primarily as a means of confining the application of strict tort liability to an article which is "dangerous to an extent beyond that which would be contemplated by the ordinary consumer who purchases it, with the ordinary knowledge common to the community as to its characteristics." (Rest. 2d Torts, §402A, com. *i*.) In *Cronin*, however, we flatly rejected the suggestion that recovery in a products liability action should be permitted *only* if a product is more dangerous than contemplated by the average consumer, refusing to permit the low esteem in which the public might hold a dangerous product to diminish the manufacturer's responsibility for injuries caused by that product. As we pointedly noted in *Cronin*, even if the "ordinary consumer" may have contemplated that Shopsmith lathes posed a risk of loosening their grip and letting a piece of wood strike the operator, "another Greenman" should not be denied recovery. . . .

Thus, our rejection of the use of the "unreasonably dangerous" terminology in *Cronin* rested in part on a concern that a jury might interpret such an instruction, as the Restatement draftsman had indeed intended, as shielding a defendant from liability so long as the product did not fall below the ordinary consumer's expectations as to the product's safety.[7] . . . [T]he dangers posed by such a misconception by the jury extend to cases involving design defects as well as to actions involving manufacturing defects: indeed, the danger of confusion is perhaps more pronounced in design cases in which the manufacturer could frequently argue that its product satisfied ordinary consumer expectations since it was identical to other items of the same product line with which the consumer may well have been familiar.

Accordingly, contrary to defendants' contention, the reasoning of *Cronin* does not dictate that that decision be confined to the manufac-

---

7. This is not to say that the expectations of the ordinary consumer are irrelevant to the determination of whether a product is defective, for as we point out below we believe that ordinary consumer expectations are frequently of direct significance to the defectiveness issue. The flaw in the Restatement's analysis, in our view, is that it treats such consumer expectations as a "ceiling" on a manufacturer's responsibility under strict liability principles, rather than as a "floor." As we shall explain, past California decisions establish that *at a minimum* a product must meet ordinary consumer expectations as to safety to avoid being found defective.

turing defect context. . . . Consequently, we conclude that the design defect instruction given in the instant case was erroneous.

3.   A Trial Court May Properly Formulate Instructions to
     Elucidate the "Defect" Concept in Varying
     Circumstances. In Particular, in Design Defect Cases, a
     Court May Properly Instruct a Jury that a Product is
     Defective in Design if (1) the Plaintiff Proves that the
     Product Failed to Perform as Safely as an Ordinary
     Consumer Would Expect When Used in an Intended or
     Reasonably Foreseeable Manner, or (2) the Plaintiff
     Proves that the Product's Design Proximately Caused
     Injury and the Defendant Fails to Prove, in Light of
     the Relevant Factors, that on Balance the Benefits of
     the Challenged Design Outweigh the Risk of Danger
     Inherent in Such Design. . . .

As this court has recognized on numerous occasions, the term defect as utilized in the strict liability context is neither self-defining nor susceptible to a single definition applicable in all contexts.[8] . . . [T]he concept of defect raises considerably more difficulties in the design defect context than it does in the manufacturing or production defect context.

In general, a manufacturing or production defect is readily identifiable because a defective product is one that differs from the manufacturer's intended result or from other ostensibly identical units of the same product line. For example, when a product comes off the assembly line in a substandard condition it has incurred a manufacturing defect. . . . A design defect, by contrast, cannot be identified simply by comparing the injury-producing product with the manufacturer's plans or with other units of the same product line, since by definition the plans and all such units will reflect the same design. Rather than applying any sort of deviation-from-the-norm test in determining whether a product is defective in design for strict liability purposes, our cases have employed two alternative criteria in ascertaining, in Justice Traynor's words, whether there is something "wrong, if not in the manufacturer's manner of production, at least in his product." (Traynor,

---

8. One commentator has observed that, in addition to the deficiencies in the "unreasonably dangerous" terminology noted in *Cronin*, the Restatement's language is potentially misleading because "[i]t may suggest an idea like ultrahazardous, or abnormally dangerous, and thus give rise to the impression that the plaintiff must prove that the product was unusually or extremely dangerous." (Wade, On the Nature of Strict Tort Liability for Products 44 Miss. L.J. 825, 832 (1973).) We agree with this criticism and believe it constitutes a further reason for refraining from utilizing the "unreasonably dangerous" terminology in defining a defective product.

The Ways and Meanings of Defective Products and Strict Liability, 32 Tenn. L. Rev. 363, 366.)

First, our cases establish that a product may be found defective in design if the plaintiff demonstrates that the product failed to perform as safely as an ordinary consumer would expect when used in an intended or reasonably foreseeable manner. This initial standard, somewhat analogous to the Uniform Commercial Code's warranty of fitness and merchantability (Cal. U. Com. Code, §2314), reflects the warranty heritage upon which California product liability doctrine in part rests. As we noted in *Greenman,* "implicit in [a product's] presence on the market . . . [is] a representation that it [will] safely do the jobs for which it was built." When a product fails to satisfy such ordinary consumer expectations as to safety in its intended or reasonably foreseeable operation, a manufacturer is strictly liable for resulting injuries. . . .

As Professor Wade has pointed out, however, the expectations of the ordinary consumer cannot be viewed as the exclusive yardstick for evaluating design defectiveness because "[i]n many situations . . . the consumer would not know what to expect, because he would have no idea how safe the product could be made." . . . Numerous California decisions have implicitly recognized this fact and have made clear, through varying linguistic formulations, that a product may be found defective in design, even if it satisfies ordinary consumer expectations, if through hindsight the jury determines that the product's design embodies "excessive preventable danger," or, in other words, if the jury finds that the risk of danger inherent in the challenged design outweighs the benefits of such design. . . .

A review of past cases indicates that in evaluating the adequacy of a product's design pursuant to this latter standard, a jury may consider, among other relevant factors, the gravity of the danger posed by the challenged design, the likelihood that such danger would occur, the mechanical feasibility of a safer alternative design, the financial cost of an improved design, and the adverse consequences to the product and to the consumer that would result from an alternative design. . . .

Although our cases have thus recognized a variety of considerations that may be relevant to the determination of the adequacy of a product's design, past authorities have generally not devoted much attention to the appropriate allocation of the burden of proof with respect to these matters. . . . The allocation of such burden is particularly significant in this context inasmuch as this court's product liability decisions, from *Greenman* to *Cronin,* have repeatedly emphasized that one of the principal purposes behind the strict product liability doctrine is to relieve an injured plaintiff of many of the onerous evidentiary burdens inherent in a negligence cause of action. Because most of the evidentiary matters which may be relevant to the determination of the adequacy of a product's design under the "risk-benefit" standard —

e.g., the feasibility and cost of alternative designs — are similar to issues typically presented in a negligent design case and involve technical matters peculiarly within the knowledge of the manufacturer, we conclude that once the plaintiff makes a prima facie showing that the injury was proximately caused by the product's design, the burden should appropriately shift to the defendant to prove, in light of the relevant factors, that the product is not defective. Moreover, inasmuch as this conclusion flows from our determination that the fundamental public policies embraced in *Greenman* dictate that a manufacturer who seeks to escape liability for an injury proximately caused by its product's design on a risk-benefit theory should bear the burden of persuading the trier of fact that its product should not be judged defective, the defendant's burden is one affecting the burden of proof, rather than simply the burden of producing evidence. . . .

Because the jury may have interpreted the erroneous instruction given in the instant case as requiring plaintiff to prove that the high-lift loader was ultrahazardous or more dangerous than the average consumer contemplated, and because the instruction additionally misinformed the jury that the defectiveness of the product must be evaluated in light of the product's "intended use" rather than its "reasonably foreseeable use" . . . , we cannot find that the error was harmless on the facts of this case. In light of this conclusion, we need not address plaintiff's additional claims of error, for such issues may not arise on retrial.

The judgment in favor of defendants is reversed.

NOTES

1. What is a design defect? The *Barker* formulation is but one of many different standards for determining design defects propounded in recent years. In Azzarello v. Black Bros. Co., Inc., 391 A.2d 1020, 1027 (Pa. 1978), the plaintiff's hand was injured when caught between two rubber rollers in a coating machine manufactured by the defendant. On the critical question of product defect the court noted that the need to control "giant corporate structures" made it appropriate to follow the lead of the California court in *Cronin* and *Barker* and to reject "the unreasonably dangerous" limitation on product defect. It then held that although the supplier was not "an insurer of all injuries caused by the product," it nonetheless was cast "in the role of a guarantor of his product's safety." The court explained its position as follows:

> For the term guarantor to have any meaning in this context the supplier must at least provide a product which is designed to make it safe for the intended use. Under this standard, in this type case, the jury may find a defect where the product left the supplier's control lacking any element necessary to make it safe for its intended use or possessing any feature

that renders it unsafe for the intended use. It is clear that the term "un-reasonably dangerous" has no place in the instructions to a jury as to the question of "defect" in this type of case. We therefore agree with the court en banc that the use of the term "unreasonably dangerous" in the charge was misleading and that the appellee was entitled to a new trial.

If a manufacturer makes economy and deluxe models of a chain saw, both intended for the same general uses, is the economy model necessarily defective under the *Azzarello* formulation? Presumptively defective? See Linegar v. Armour of America, infra at page 816. Is the *Azzarello* formulation of product defect narrower than that in *Barker*, owing to its repeated reference to intended, as distinguished from foreseeable, use?

A very different approach to the question of design defect was taken in Wilson v. Piper Aircraft Corp., 577 P.2d 1322, 1327-1328 (Or. 1978). There the plaintiffs brought wrongful death actions as the representatives of two passengers who died in the crash of a Piper Cherokee airplane manufactured by the defendants. The plaintiffs' theory was that the plane was defective in design both because of the engine's susceptibility to icing and because of certain design weaknesses in the rear compartment.

In support of their theory that the airplane was dangerously defective because of its susceptibility to icing, plaintiffs alleged the following design defects: (1) the aircraft was not equipped with an injection-type fuel system; (2) the carburetor was not designed and equipped so that it would provide a proper fuel-air mixture under icing conditions; (3) the aircraft was not supplied with an adequate carburetor-heating system; and (4) the aircraft was not equipped with a carburetor heat gauge.

The defendant in turn urged that the product was not defective because its design had been approved by the Federal Aviation Administration (FAA) and had received an FAA certificate of airworthiness. The court first noted that by the statute's own terms, the FAA standard was "minimum" only, and did not provide the defendant with an automatic safe harbor from liability. It then continued, however, to impose stringent requirements on the plaintiff in a design defect case:

> Plaintiffs' allegations amount to a contention that an airplane furnished with a standard aircraft engine is defective because an engine of a different type, or with a different carburetor system, would be safer in one particular. It is not proper to submit such allegations to the jury unless the court is satisfied that there is evidence from which the jury could find the suggested alternatives are not only technically feasible but also practicable in terms of cost and the over-all design and operation of the product. It is part of the required proof that a design feature is a "defect" to present such evidence. In at least some instances in the present case, that requirement has not been met. . . .

There is not, however, any evidence about what effect the substitution of a fuel injected engine in this airplane design would have had upon the airplane's cost, economy of operation, maintenance requirements, over-all performance, or safety in respects other than susceptibility to icing. Plaintiffs' own expert witnesses testified that a carbureted engine of the type used in this airplane was, except for its susceptibility to icing, a highly satisfactory, dependable engine. There was also undisputed evidence that 80 to 90 per cent of all small airplanes comparable to this one are manufactured with carbureted engines rather than with fuel injected engines. There was no explanation of why this is the case.

We also think it is significant that both in 1966, when this airplane was manufactured, and at the present time the FAA safety standards disclose that the agency was aware of the carburetor icing problems and provided for them in its regulations and yet determined that the use of carbureted engines was not unduly dangerous. Although we have held that compliance with the FAA safety standards does not preclude the possibility of liability for a design defect, we nevertheless believe that in a field as closely regulated as aircraft design and manufacture, it is proper to take into consideration, in determining whether plaintiffs have produced sufficient evidence of defect to go to the jury, the fact that the regulatory agency has approved the very design of which they complain after considering the dangers involved.

Linde, J., in his concurrence, placed even greater stress on the FAA standards, noting that although originally it is "defendant's burden to show that a governmental agency has undertaken the responsibility of making substantially the same judgment that the court would otherwise be called on to make — it should then be plaintiff's burden to show that the responsible agency has not in fact made that judgment with respect to the particular 'defect' at issue." Should compliance with the FAA standards be absolute? What about motor vehicle standards?

Note that on rehearing the court in *Wilson* concluded that *Barker* was "not persuasive." In particular it rejected *Barker*'s shifting of the burden of proof, and following the position taken by the overwhelming number of courts today, it held that the plaintiff bears the burden of proof of showing a reasonable alternative design.

2. *State of the art: time of sale or time of trial?* In setting the appropriate standard for product safety, many judicial decisions look to the state of the art in the product supplier's trade or business. The state of the art is generally understood to refer to something more stringent than the "common practice" in the industry, and to embrace the scientific and technical possibilities for product design and improvement. As technology advances, therefore, the question of *when* the state of the art should be measured becomes of crucial importance. At one time some courts supported a test that measured the state of the art at the time of trial and not when the product was marketed, on the ground that a strict liability test charged a defendant with knowledge and technical advances that became available only after the product was sold. See, e.g.,

Keeton, Products Liability — Inadequacy of Information, 48 Tex. L. Rev. 398 (1970). The dominant view today, however, runs in the opposite direction. In Bruce v. Martin Marietta Corp., 544 F.2d 442 (10th Cir. 1976), the court measured the state of the art at the time the defendant's airplane seats entered the stream of commerce, 1952, not at the time of the crash, October 1970. The record also showed that the seats did meet all FAA standards as well as the applicable state of the art for 1952. The court rejected plaintiff's effort to apply more modern standards as to both negligence and strict liability under section 402A. In the court's view the crucial test was the "expectations of the ordinary consumer," who "would not expect a Model T to have safety features which are incorporated in automobiles today."

See *The T. J. Hooper,* supra at page 214. For a defense of the common-practice standard see R. Epstein, Modern Products Liability Law (1980); for an analysis of *Barker* see Schwartz, Forward: Understanding Products Liability, 67 Cal. L. Rev. 435 (1979).

3. Consumer expectations. The consumer expectations test also has considerable influence in foodstuff cases. The traditional law held that the defendant was strictly liable for any "foreign object" that was found within the food, be it a sliver of tin or some waste impurities from animals. But by the same token, the earlier cases refused to hold manufacturers liable under any theory for substances "natural" to the product served. Thus the leading case of Mix v. Ingersoll Candy Co., 59 P.2d 144 (Cal. 1936), held that "[b]ones which are natural to the type of meat served cannot legitimately be called a foreign substance, and a consumer who eats meat dishes ought to anticipate and be on his guard against the presence of such bones." *Mix* was in turn challenged in Mexicali Rose v. The Superior Court (Clark), 822 P.2d 1292 (Cal. 1992), where the plaintiff swallowed a bone in a chicken enchilada. Lucas, C.J., adopted a compromise position holding manufacturers strictly liable for foreign contaminants, but imposing only negligence liability for natural contaminants. Plaintiff urged that with advancing technology, the reasonable expectations of consumers was that food would be free of all contaminants, natural or foreign. Lucas, C.J., agreed, but only in part:

> [W]e agree with plaintiff that a "reasonable expectation" test is applicable in this context and, in part at least, is consistent with the development of tort law in our jurisdiction. Accordingly, we adopt that test as our own. As we further explain, although we conclude that under a reasonable expectation test plaintiff may not state a cause of action under the theories of strict liability or breach of the implied warranties of merchantability or fitness, we conclude that under the same test, he may state a cause of action in negligence based on defendants' asserted failure to exercise due care in the preparation of the chicken enchilada.
>
> [W]e believe it is a question for the trier of fact to determine whether

the presence of the injury-producing substance was caused by the failure of the defendants to exercise reasonable care in the preparation of the food, and whether the breach of the duty to exercise such care caused the consumer's injury. In so concluding, we emphasize that restaurateurs have available all the traditional defenses to a negligence cause of action, including comparative negligence. . . .

A vigorous dissent by Mosk, J., argued for a uniform rule of strict liability:

> A natural object may cause as much harm *and be as unanticipated* as a foreign object in food, so that it is simply illogical to distinguish between the two solely on the basis of their provenance.
> A nutshell in a scoop of ice cream, a bit of crystalized corn in a serving of corn flakes or a chunk of bone in a hamburger is as harmful and unanticipated from the injured consumer's point of view as a bit of rock, glass or wire in the same food products. For social policy reasons we have long held the restaurateur strictly liable for injuries caused by unwholesome food, and there is no reason to abandon this social policy when the object in food that causes the injury is "natural."

4. Subsequent improvements. The substantive dispute in *Bruce* has its evidentiary side as well: can evidence of subsequent design changes be introduced to show the defectiveness of defendant's basic design? In Ault v. International Harvester Co., 528 P.2d 1148, 1151-1152 (Cal. 1974), the California Supreme Court allowed the evidence, saying:

> The contemporary corporate mass producer of goods, the normal products liability defendant, manufactures tens of thousands of units of goods; it is manifestly unrealistic to suggest that such a producer will forego making improvements in its product, and risk innumerable additional lawsuits and the attendant adverse effect upon its public image, simply because evidence of adoption of such improvement may be admitted in an action founded on strict liability for recovery on an injury that preceded the improvement.

Since that time a well-nigh uniform line of decisions have refused to admit the evidence. Federal Rule of Evidence 407 now provides:

> When, after an event, measures are taken which, if taken previously, would have made the event less likely to occur, evidence of the subsequent measures is not admissible to prove negligence or culpable conduct in connection with the event. This rule does not require the exclusion of evidence of subsequent measures when offered for another purpose, such as proving ownership, control, or feasibility of precautionary measures, if controverted, or impeachment.

In Cann v. Ford Motor Co., 658 F.2d 54, 60 (2d Cir. 1981), Meskill, J., relied on Rule 407 to exclude evidence of Ford's redesigned transmission, even under a strict liability theory:

Rule 407 is prompted by the fear that people will be less likely to take subsequent remedial measures if evidence of their repairs or improvements may be used against them in lawsuits arising out of prior accidents. Appellants point out that a negligence action places in issue whether the defendant's conduct was reasonable while a strict liability action involves whether the product was defective; they note that the jury focuses on the *defendant* in a negligence action, but solely upon the *product* in a strict liability action. However, the defendant must pay the judgment in both situations, regardless of where the jury's attention focused when they found against him. Since the policy underlying Rule 407 not to discourage persons from taking remedial measures is relevant to *defendants* sued under either theory, we do not see the significance of the distinction. A potential defendant must be equally concerned regardless of the theoretical rubric under which this highly prejudicial, and extremely damaging, evidence is admitted.

5. *The risk-utility test.* The second prong of the *Barker* opinion announces a risk-utility test for product defects in design cases. In O'Brien v. Muskin Corp., 463 A.2d 298, 302-303, 305-306 (N.J. 1983), Muskin sold a pool that Arthur Henry assembled for use in his back yard. The pool was 20 feet by 24 feet with 4-foot walls. The pool's bottom was made of an embossed vinyl that, when filled with water, left the pool about $3\frac{1}{2}$ feet deep. The plaintiff, then 23-years-old, dove into the pool from either a platform near the pool or from the eight-foot high roof of the Henrys' garage. "As his outstretched hands hit the vinyl-lined pool bottom, they slid apart, and O'Brien struck his head on the bottom of the pool, thereby sustaining injuries." The plaintiff's expert claimed that the pool design was dangerous because

wet vinyl was more than twice as slippery as rubber latex, which is used to line in-ground pools. The trial court, however, sustained an objection to the expert's opinion about alternative kinds of pool bottoms, specifically whether rubber latex was a feasible liner for above-ground pools. The expert admitted that he knew of no above-ground pool lined with a material other than vinyl, but plaintiff contended that vinyl should not be used in above-ground pools, even though no alternative material was available. A second expert testified that the slippery vinyl bottom and lack of adequate warnings rendered the pool unfit and unsafe for its foreseeable uses.

At the close of trial the court took the design case from the jury but on appeal the court allowed the design defect count to go to the jury. In its opinion the court explicitly adopted the risk-utility formula first set out in Wade, On the Nature of Strict Tort Liability for Products, 44 Miss. L.J. 825 (1973). By that formula the relevant factors include:

(1) The usefulness and desirability of the product — its utility to the user and to the public as a whole.

(2) The safety aspects of the product — the likelihood that it will cause injury, and the probable seriousness of the injury.

(3) The availability of a substitute product which would meet the same need and not be as unsafe.

(4) The manufacturer's ability to eliminate the unsafe character of the product without impairing its usefulness or making it too expensive to maintain its utility.

(5) The user's ability to avoid danger by the exercise of care in the use of the product.

(6) The user's anticipated awareness of the dangers inherent in the product and their avoidability, because of general public knowledge of the obvious condition of the product, or of the existence of suitable warnings or instructions.

(7) The feasibility, on the part of the manufacturer, of spreading the loss by setting the price of the product or carrying liability insurance.

The court thereafter observed that although "state-of-the-art evidence may be dispositive on the facts of a particular case, it does not constitute an absolute defense apart from risk-utility analysis. The ultimate burden of proving a defect is on the plaintiff, but the burden is on the defendant to prove that compliance with state-of-the-art, in conjunction with other relevant evidence, justifies placing a product on the market." It then held that for the plaintiff to reach the jury under a risk-utility test, "it was not necessary for plaintiff to prove the existence of alternative, safer designs."

The narrow result in *Muskin* was altered by statute, which provided, among other things, that "the manufacturer or seller should not be liable if: (1) At the time the product left the control of the manufacturer, there was not a practical and technically feasible alternative design that would have prevented the harm without substantially impairing the reasonably anticipated or intended function of the product." N.J. Stat. Ann. §2A:58C-3 (West 1993). The proposed third Restatement takes much the same line by requiring that "plaintiff show a reasonable alternative design . . . even though the plaintiff alleges that the category of product sold by the defendant is sufficiently dangerous that it should not have been marketed at all." Accordingly it explicitly disapproved of the *Muskin* decision, and comment *c*, illustration 4, because "the vinyl pool liner that [the manufacturer] utilized was the best and safest liner available and that no alternative, less slippery liner was feasible."

Thereafter the proposed Restatement, section 2, comment *d* seeks to cover all bases in setting out the standards for design defect cases.

A broad range of factors may legitimately be considered in determining whether an alternative design is reasonable and whether its omission renders the product not reasonably safe. These include, without limitation, the magnitude of foreseeable risks of harm, the nature and strength of consumer expectations, the effects on costs of product, the effects of alternative design on product function, the relative advantages and disadvantages of proposed safety features, product longevity, maintenance and repair, esthetics, and marketability. On the other hand, it is inappropriate to take into account whether the imposition of liability would have a negative effect on corporate earnings, or would reduce employment in a given industry. . . .

When evaluating the reasonableness of a design alternative, the overall safety of the entire product must be considered. It is not sufficient that the alternative design would have reduced or prevented the harm suffered by the plaintiff if it would also introduce into the product other dangers of equal or greater magnitude.

6. Guns: risk-utility and the marketing of dangerous, but nondefective, products. One recurrent question is whether the basic risk-utility analysis may be extended to defect-free products whose very presence in the marketplace may be said to create risks in excess of the product's social utility. In recent years, plaintiffs have advanced such theories against the manufacturers of products such as guns and convertible cars. For the most part the courts have not been sympathetic to these claims. Thus, in Martin v. Harrington & Richardson, 743 F.2d 1200 (7th Cir. 1984), the plaintiff brought suit against the defendant gun manufacturer, asserting that its "liability stems solely from 'the manufacture of an inherently dangerous, nondefective instrument.' " In its effort to escape the defect language of the Restatement (Second) of Torts §402A, the plaintiff resorted to a theory of "abnormally dangerous activities," as set out in §§519 and 520 of the Restatement. See Chapter 8 at page 666. The court rejected the claim on the ground that these two sections apply only to dangerous *activities* and not to dangerous *products*. It also stressed that any such novel changes in Illinois could likewise "require that manufacturers of guns, knives, drugs, alcohol, tobacco and other dangerous products act as insurers against all damages produced by their products." This theory was also rejected in Perkins v. F. I. E. Corp., 762 F.2d 1250 (5th Cir. 1985), which feared the risks of allowing the jury to legislate under so broad a mandate.

A notable exception to the hostility toward liability for generic products is Kelley v. R. G. Industries, 497 A.2d 1143 (Md. 1985), which allowed a victim of an armed robbery an action against the manufacturers of "Saturday Night Specials," which it found useful for criminals but no one else. The proposed Restatement Third, section 2, comment *c* does not take a definitive position on generic product defects, but opts at most for a narrow extension of liability. In its view, given a narrow definition of product type — e.g. "limited to toy guns with the capacity to injure" — a court "might well conclude that liability should attach without proof of a reasonable alternative design."

In the area of prescription drugs plaintiffs have occasionally succeeded with similar claims. In Tobin v. Astra Pharmaceutical Products, Inc., 993 F.2d 528 (6th Cir. 1993), the drug ritodrine was given to the plaintiff, a 19-year-old pregnant woman, causing her heart to fail and forcing her to undergo a heart transplant. Guy, J., held that with evidence of causation established, the defendants could not rely on FDA approval to exempt the drug from further review, and that plaintiff's expert witnesses had placed "sufficient evidence before the jury to conclude that the prudent manufacturer knowing all the risks would not market ritodrine."

The proposed Third Restatement, section 4(b)(4), follows *Tobin* when it provides for a narrow class of design defect prescription drug cases :

> (4) The foreseeable risks of harm posed by the drug or medical device were sufficiently great in relation to its therapeutic benefits as to deter a reasonable medical provider, possessing knowledge of such foreseeable risks, and therapeutic benefits, from prescribing the drug or medical device to any class of patients.

Linegar v. Armour of America
909 F.2d 1150 (8th Cir. 1990)

Before ARNOLD and BOWMAN, Circuit Judges, and HEANEY, Senior Circuit Judge.

BOWMAN, Circuit Judge. This action was brought as a products liability case and heard under the District Court's diversity jurisdiction. Armour of America, Inc. (Armour) appeals a judgment based on a jury verdict in favor of the widow and children of Jimmy Linegar, a Missouri State Highway Patrol trooper who was killed in the line of duty. The jury found that the bullet-resistant vest manufactured by Armour and worn by Linegar at the time of the murder was defectively designed, and it awarded his family $1.5 million in damages. We reverse.

[The decedent was killed during a routine traffic stop by one David Tate, later convicted of capital murder.] None of the shots that hit the contour-style, concealable protective vest Linegar was wearing — there were five such shots — penetrated the vest or caused injury. The wounds Linegar suffered all were caused by shots that struck parts of his body not protected by the vest.

The Missouri State Highway Patrol issued the vest to Linegar when he joined the Patrol in 1981. The vest was one of a lot of various sizes of the same style vest the Patrol purchased in 1979 directly from Armour. The contour style was one of several different styles then on the market. It provided more protection to the sides of the body than the style featuring rectangular panels in front and back, but not as much protection as a wrap-around style. The front and back panels of the contour vest, held together with Velcro closures under the arms, did not meet at the sides of the wearer's body, leaving an area along the sides of the body under the arms exposed when the vest was worn. This feature of the vest was obvious to the Patrol when it selected this vest as standard issue for its troopers and could only have been obvious to any trooper who chose to wear it. The bullet that proved fatal to Linegar entered between his seventh and eighth ribs, approximately three-and-one-fourth inches down from his armpit, and pierced his heart. . . .

To recover under a theory of strict liability in tort for defective design, Missouri law requires that a party prove the following elements: (1) [the] defendant sold the product in the course of its business; (2) the product was then in a defective condition unreasonably dangerous when put to a reasonably anticipated use; (3) the product was used in a manner reasonably anticipated; (4) [the] plaintiff was damaged as a direct result of such defective condition as existed when the product was sold. The jury instructions in this case tracked the applicable law.

While there is some dispute between the parties over various of the elements, we predicate our reversal on the dearth of plaintiff's evidence of element (2). We conclude that, as a matter of law, the contour vest Trooper Linegar was wearing when he was murdered was not defective and unreasonably dangerous. . . .

The Missouri cases leave the meaning of the phrase "unreasonably dangerous" largely a matter of common sense, to the court's or the jury's. . . . The conditions under which a bullet-resistant vest will be called upon to perform its intended function most assuredly will be dangerous, indeed life-threatening, and Armour surely knew that. It defies logic, however, to suggest that Armour reasonably should have anticipated that anyone would wear its vest for protection of areas of the body that the vest obviously did not cover.

Courts applying Missouri law also have applied what has become known as the "consumer expectation" test for unreasonable dangerousness: "The article sold must be dangerous to an extent beyond that which would be contemplated by the ordinary consumer who purchases it, with the ordinary knowledge common to the community as to its characteristics." Restatement (Second) of Torts §402A comment i (1965); . . .

The consumer expectation test focuses attention on the vest's wearer rather than on its manufacturer. The inherent limitations in the amount of coverage offered by Armour's contour vest were obvious to this Court, observing a demonstration from the bench during oral argument, as they would be to anyone with ordinary knowledge, most especially the vest's wearer. A person wearing the vest would no more expect to be shielded from a shot taken under the arm than he would expect the vest to deflect bullets aimed at his head or neck or lower abdomen or any other area not covered by the vest.

Plaintiff insists that the user's expectations should not be considered by us, since doing so would effectively afford Armour the benefit of the "open and obvious" defense, inappropriate, they say, in a defective design strict products liability action. We disagree. Although not conclusive, "[t]he obviousness of a defect or danger is material to the issue whether a product is 'unreasonably dangerous.' " McGowne v. Challenge-Cook Bros., 672 F.2d 652, 663 (8th Cir. 1982). Here, the vest's purported dangerous defect — its lack of closure at the sides — could not have been more open and obvious. An otherwise completely effective protective vest cannot be regarded as dangerous, much less unreasonably so, simply because it leaves some parts of the body obviously exposed.[6] . . .

We have no difficulty in concluding as a matter of law that the product at issue here was neither defective nor unreasonably dangerous. Trooper Linegar's protective vest performed precisely as expected and stopped all of the bullets that hit it. No part of the vest nor any malfunction of the vest caused Linegar's injuries. The vest was designed to prevent the penetration of bullets where there was coverage, and it did so; the amount of coverage was the buyer's choice. The Missouri Highway Patrol could have chosen to buy, and Armour could have sold the Patrol, a vest with more coverage; no one contests that. But it is not the place of courts or juries to set specifications as to the parts of the body a bullet-resistant garment must cover. A manufacturer is not obliged to market only one version of a product, that being the very safest design possible. If that were so, automobile manufacturers could not offer consumers sports cars, convertibles, jeeps, or compact cars. All boaters would have to buy full life vests instead of choosing a ski belt or even a flotation cushion. Personal safety devices, in particular, require personal choices, and it is beyond the province of courts and juries to act as legislators and preordain those choices.

In this case, there obviously were trade-offs to be made. A contour vest like the one here in question permits the wearer more flexibility and mobility and allows better heat dissipation and sweat evaporation, and thus is more likely to be worn than a more confining vest. It is less expensive than styles of vests providing more complete coverage. If manufacturers like Armour are threatened with economically devastating litigation if they market any vest style except that offering maximum coverage, they may decide, since one can always argue that more coverage is possible, to get out of the business altogether. Or they may continue to market the vest style that, according to the latest lawsuit, affords the "best" coverage. Officers who find the "safest" style confining or uncomfortable will either wear it at risk to their mobility or opt not to wear it at all. . . . Law enforcement agencies trying to work within the confines of a budget may be forced to purchase fewer vests

---

6. The wrap-around vest style advocated by appellees as preferable still must have an armhole that will be open some distance below the armpit to allow freedom of movement. See, e.g., Transcript Vol. II at 334 (testimony of Missouri Highway Patrol Trooper Don Phillips that his wrap-around-style vest left a four-inch opening beneath his armpit).

or none at all. How "safe" are those possibilities? "The core concern in strict tort liability law is safety." We are firmly convinced that to allow this verdict to stand would run counter to the law's purpose of promoting the development of safe and useful products, and would have an especially pernicious effect on the development and marketing of equipment designed to make the always-dangerous work of law enforcement officers a little safer.

The death of Jimmy Linegar by the hand of a depraved killer was a tragic event. We keenly feel the loss that this young trooper's family has suffered, and our sympathies go out to them. But we cannot allow recovery from a blameless defendant on the basis of sympathy for the plaintiffs. To hold Armour liable for Linegar's death would cast it in the role of insurer for anyone shot while wearing an Armour vest, regardless of whether any shots penetrated the vest. That a manufacturer may be cast in such a role has been soundly rejected by courts applying Missouri law.

[Reversed.]

NOTES

1. *Obvious design defects: round 3. Linegar* illustrates the continued holding that the consumer expectation test and the open and obvious defect test have on the evaluation of product liability cases. In light of the decision, does it make sense for courts to continue to examine the utility of a product once the defect is found to be obvious? Or should they act on the assumption that users and consumers can make those judgments, without specific demonstrations in each case? The proposed Restatement Third, section 2, comment *e* follows the now dominant position: "The mere fact that a risk presented by a product design is open and obvious, and that the product thus satisfies expectations, does not prevent a finding that the design is defective." It also approves of both *Micallef*, see section 2, illustration 3, and *Linegar*, section 2, illustration 8. Consistent?

2. *The government contractor defense.* Imposing broad-based design defect liability raises special complications when the product in question has been procured for government use. Oftentimes the issue arises in its most pressing form in connection with military conditions, for which the government has issued precise design specifications, thereby precluding the level of individual choice preserved in *Linegar*. In Boyle v. United Technologies Corp. 487 U.S. 500, 512 (1988), the decedent was killed when he was unable to exit from a helicopter escape hatch that he claimed was negligently designed. The Supreme Court, per Scalia, J., refused to allow the plaintiff to try the case under state law, noting that there was a substantial federal interest involved because "the impo-

sition of tort liability will directly affect the terms of Government contracts," by inducing the contractor to decline work or to increase its prices. Scalia, J., then held:

> Liability for design defects in military equipment cannot be imposed pursuant to state law, when (1) the United States approved reasonably precise specifications; (2) the equipment conformed to those specifications; and (3) the supplier warned the United States about the dangers in the use of the equipment that were known to the supplier but not to the United States. . . . The third condition is necessary because, in its absence, the displacement of state tort law would create some incentive for the manufacturer to withhold knowledge of risks, since conveying that knowledge might disrupt the contract but withholding it would produce no liability.

In Scalia's view the government contractor defense is needed to protect the discretion of the United States' military procurement policy, for the government's costs would be increased when contractors passed back the costs of their tort liability, if they accepted the work at all. Justice Brennan dissented on the ground that the Court's government contractors defense might be satisfied by "perhaps no more than a rubberstamp from a federal procurement officer who might or might not have noticed or cared about the defects, or even had the expertise to discover them." Should the government contractors defense apply when the United States purchases stock items? On the scope of the discretionary function exception to government tort liability see Chapter 11, infra at page 955.

3.   The Duty to Warn

MacDonald v. Ortho Pharmaceutical Corp.
475 N.E.2d 65 (Mass. 1985)

Before HENNESSEY, C.J., and LIACOS, ABRAMS, NOLAN and O'CONNOR, JJ.

ABRAMS, JUSTICE. This products liability action raises the question of the extent of a drug manufacturer's duty to warn consumers of dangers inherent in the use of oral contraceptives. The plaintiffs brought suit against the defendant, Ortho Pharmaceutical Corporation (Ortho), for injuries allegedly caused by Ortho's birth control pills, and obtained a jury verdict in their favor. The defendant moved for a judgment notwithstanding the verdict. The judge concluded that the defendant did not owe a duty to warn the plaintiffs, and entered judgment for Ortho. The plaintiffs appealed. We transferred the case to this court on our own motion and reinstate the jury verdict.

We summarize the facts. In September, 1973, the plaintiff Carole D. MacDonald (MacDonald), who was twenty-six years old at the time, obtained from her gynecologist a prescription for Ortho-Novum contraceptive pills, manufactured by Ortho. As required by the then effective regulations promulgated by the United States Food and Drug Administration (FDA), the pill dispenser she received was labeled with a warning that "oral contraceptives are powerful and effective drugs which can cause side effects in some users and should not be used at all by some women," and that "[t]he most serious known side effect is abnormal blood clotting which can be fatal." The warning also referred MacDonald to a booklet which she obtained from her gynecologist, and which was distributed by Ortho pursuant to FDA requirements. The booklet contained detailed information about the contraceptive pill, including the increased risk to pill users that vital organs such as the brain may be damaged[4] by abnormal blood clotting. The word "stroke" did not appear on the dispenser warning or in the booklet.

MacDonald's prescription for Ortho-Novum pills was renewed at subsequent annual visits to her gynecologist. The prescription was filled annually. On July 24, 1976, after approximately three years of using the pills, MacDonald suffered an occlusion of a cerebral artery by a blood clot, an injury commonly referred to as a stroke.[5] The injury caused the death of approximately twenty per cent of MacDonald's brain tissue, and left her permanently disabled. She and her husband initiated an action in the Superior Court against Ortho, seeking recovery for her personal injuries and his consequential damages and loss of consortium.

4. Applicable FDA regulations required that the booklet contain "information in lay language, concerning effectiveness, contraindications, warnings, precautions, and adverse reactions," including a warning "regarding the serious side effects with special attention to thromboembolic disorders and stating the estimated morbidity and mortality in users vs. nonusers." 21 C.F.R. §§130.45(e) & (e)(3). Ortho's booklet contained the following information:

About blood clots

Blood clots occasionally form in the blood vessels of the legs and the pelvis of apparently healthy people and may threaten life if the clots break loose and then lodge in the lung or if they form in other vital organs, such as the brain. It has been estimated that about one woman in 2,000 on the pill each year suffers a blood clotting disorder severe enough to require hospitalization. The estimated death rate from abnormal blood clotting in healthy women under 35 not taking the pill is 1 in 500,000 whereas for the same group taking the pill it is 1 in 66,000. For healthy women over 35 not taking the pill, the rate is 1 in 200,000 compared to 1 in 25,000 for pill users. Blood clots are about three times more likely to develop in women over the age of 34. For these reasons it is important that women who have had blood clots in the legs, lungs, or brain not use oral contraceptives. Anyone using the pill who has severe leg or chest pains, coughs up blood, has difficulty breathing, sudden severe headache or vomiting, dizziness or fainting, disturbances of vision or speech, weakness or numbness of an arm or leg, should call her doctor immediately and stop taking the pill.

5. MacDonald's hospital records refer to her injury as a "cerebral vascular accident," terminology likewise descriptive of brain damage attributable to blood clotting.

MacDonald testified that, during the time she used the pills, she was unaware that the risk of abnormal blood clotting encompassed the risk of stroke, and that she would not have used the pills had she been warned that stroke is an associated risk.[6] The case was submitted to a jury on the plaintiffs' theories that Ortho was negligent in failing to warn adequately of the dangers associated with the pills and that Ortho breached its warranty of merchantability. These two theories were treated, in effect, as a single claim of failure to warn. The jury returned a special verdict, finding no negligence or breach of warranty in the manufacture of the pills. The jury also found that Ortho adequately advised the gynecologist of the risks inherent in the pills;[7] the jury found, however, that Ortho was negligent and in breach of warranty because it failed to give MacDonald sufficient warning of such dangers. The jury further found that MacDonald's injury was caused by Ortho's pills, that the inadequacy of the warnings to MacDonald was the proximate cause of her injury, and that Ortho was liable to MacDonald and her husband.

After the jury verdict, the judge granted Ortho's motion for judgment notwithstanding the verdict, concluding that, because oral contraceptives are prescription drugs, a manufacturer's duty to warn the consumer is satisfied if the manufacturer gives adequate warnings to the prescribing physician, and that the manufacturer has no duty to warn the consumer directly.

The narrow issue, on appeal, is whether, as the plaintiffs contend, a manufacturer of birth control pills owes a direct duty to the consumer to warn her of the dangers inherent in the use of the pill. We conclude that such a duty exists under the law of this Commonwealth.

1.   EXTENT OF DUTY TO WARN. . . .

[The court first noted that the general rule was that the defendant must warn all "persons who it is foreseeable will come in contact with, and

---

6. Subsequent to the events in this case, the FDA regulation was amended by 43 Fed. Reg. 4221 (1978), which replaced the regulation requirement of a specified warning on the pill dispenser, with a requirement that the dispenser contain a warning "of the serious side effects of oral contraceptives, such as thrombophlebitis, pulmonary embolism, myocardial infarction, retinal artery thrombosis, *stroke,* benign hepatic adenomas, induction of fetal abnormalities, and gallbladder disease" (emphasis added). See 21 C.F.R. §310.501(a)(2)(iv) (1984).

7. MacDonald stated at trial that her gynecologist had informed her only that oral contraceptives might cause bloating, and had not advised her of the increased risk of stroke associated with consumption of birth control pills. The physician was not joined as a defendant in this action, and no questions relating to any potential liability on his part are before us.

MacDonald further testified at trial that she had read both the warning on the Dialpak tablet dispenser as well as the booklet which she received from her gynecologist.

consequently be endangered by, that product." It then recognized a "narrow" exception, as set out in Restatement (Second) of Torts §388, comment *n*, when warnings have been given to a responsible intermediary "so that the manufacturer has no duty directly to warn the consumer."[9] It continued:]

The rule in jurisdictions that have addressed the question of the extent of a manufacturer's duty to warn in cases involving prescription drugs is that the prescribing physician acts as a "learned intermediary" between the manufacturer and the patient, and "the duty of the ethical drug manufacturer is to warn the doctor, rather than the patient, [although] the manufacturer is directly liable to the patient for a breach of such duty." McEwen v. Ortho Pharmaceutical Corp., 528 P.2d 522 (Or. 1974). Oral contraceptives, however, bear peculiar characteristics which warrant the imposition of a common law duty on the manufacturer to warn users directly of associated risks. Whereas a patient's involvement in decision-making concerning use of a prescription drug necessary to treat a malady is typically minimal or nonexistent, the healthy, young consumer of oral contraceptives is usually actively involved in the decision to use "the pill," as opposed to other available birth control products, and the prescribing physician is relegated to a relatively passive role.[10]

Furthermore, the physician prescribing "the pill," as a matter of course, examines the patient once before prescribing an oral contraceptive and only annually thereafter. At her annual checkup, the patient receives a renewal prescription for a full year's supply of the pill. Thus, the patient may only seldom have the opportunity to explore her questions and concerns about the medication with the prescribing physician. Even if the physician, on those occasions, were scrupulously to remind the patient of the risks attendant on continuation of the oral contraceptive, "the patient cannot be expected to remember all of the details for a protracted period of time." 35 Fed. Reg. 9002 (1970).

Last, the birth control pill is specifically subject to extensive Federal regulation. The FDA has promulgated regulations designed to ensure that the choice of "the pill" as a contraceptive method is informed by comprehensible warnings of potential side effects. . . . [See note 4 supra.] These regulations, and subsequent amendments, have their basis in the FDA commissioner's finding, after hearings, that "[b]ecause oral

---

9. Ortho points out that a number of courts have reached this result in oral contraceptive cases. See, e.g., Brochu v. Ortho Pharmaceutical Corp., 642 F.2d 652, 656 (1st Cir. 1981) (applying New Hampshire law); Lindsay v. Ortho Pharmaceutical Corp., 637 F.2d 87, 91 (2d Cir. 1980) (applying New York law). . . .

10. According to the American Medical Association, "the medical profession regards the pill, in most cases, as a convenience rather than a traditional medication." Statement of American Medical Association, published in Science News, March 14, 1970, quoted in Comment, Liability of Birth Control Pill Manufacturers, 23 Hastings L.J. 1526, 1532 (1972). . . .

contraceptives are ordinarily taken electively by healthy women who have available to them alternative methods of treatment, and because of the relatively high incidence of serious illnesses associated with their use, . . . users of these drugs should, without exception, be furnished with written information telling them of the drug's benefits and risks." 43 Fed. Reg. 4215 (1978). The FDA also found that the facts necessary to informed decisions by women as to use of oral contraceptives are "too complex to expect the patient to remember everything told her by the physician," and that, in the absence of direct written warnings, many potential users of "the pill" do not receive the needed information "in an organized, comprehensive, understandable, and handy-for-future-reference form." 35 Fed. Reg. 9002 (1970).

The oral contraceptive thus stands apart from other prescription drugs in light of the heightened participation of patients in decisions relating to use of "the pill"; the substantial risks affiliated with the product's use; the feasibility of direct warnings by the manufacturer to the user; the limited participation of the physician (annual prescriptions); and the possibility that oral communications between physicians and consumers may be insufficient or too scanty standing alone fully to apprise consumers of the product's dangers at the time the initial selection of a contraceptive method is made as well as at subsequent points when alternative methods may be considered. We conclude that the manufacturer of oral contraceptives is not justified in relying on warnings to the medical profession to satisfy its common law duty to warn, and that the manufacturer's obligation encompasses a duty to warn the ultimate user. Thus, the manufacturer's duty is to provide to the consumer written warnings conveying reasonable notice of the nature, gravity, and likelihood of known or knowable side effects, and advising the consumer to seek fuller explanation from the prescribing physician or other doctor of any such information of concern to the consumer.[13]

2.   ADEQUACY OF THE WARNING

Because we reject the judge's conclusion that Ortho had no duty to warn MacDonald, we turn to Ortho's separate argument, not reached by the judge, that the evidence was insufficient to warrant the jury's finding that Ortho's warnings to MacDonald were inadequate. Ortho contends initially that its warnings complied with FDA labeling requirements, and that those requirements preempt or define the bounds of

---

13. This opinion does not diminish the prescribing physician's duty to "disclose in a reasonable manner all significant medical information that the physician possesses or reasonably should possess that is material to an intelligent decision by the patient whether to take 'the pill.' " Harnish v. Children's Hosp. Medical Center, 439 N.E.2d 240 (Mass. 1982).

the common law duty to warn. We disagree. The regulatory history of the FDA requirements belies any objective to cloak them with preemptive effect. In response to concerns raised by drug manufacturers that warnings required and drafted by the FDA might be deemed inadequate by juries, the FDA commissioner specifically noted that the boundaries of civil tort liability for failure to warn are controlled by applicable State law. 43 Fed. Reg. 4214 (1978). Although the common law duty we today recognize is to a large degree coextensive with the regulatory duties imposed by the FDA, we are persuaded that, in instances where a trier of fact could reasonably conclude that a manufacturer's compliance with FDA labeling requirements or guidelines did not adequately apprise oral contraceptive users of inherent risks, the manufacturer should not be shielded from liability by such compliance. Thus, compliance with FDA requirements, though admissible to demonstrate lack of negligence, is not conclusive on this issue, just as violation of FDA requirements is evidence, but not conclusive evidence, of negligence. We therefore concur with the plaintiffs' argument that even if the conclusion that Ortho complied with FDA requirements were inescapable, an issue we need not decide, the jury nonetheless could have found that the lack of a reference to "stroke" breached Ortho's common law duty to warn.

The common law duty to warn, like the analogous FDA "lay language" requirement, necessitates a warning "comprehensible to the average user and . . . convey[ing] a fair indication of the nature and extent of the danger to the mind of a reasonably prudent person."

Whether a particular warning measures up to this standard is almost always an issue to be resolved by a jury; few questions are "more appropriately left to a common sense lay judgment than that of whether a written warning gets its message across to an average person." Ferebee v. Chevron Chem. Co., 552 F. Supp. 1293, 1304 (D.D.C. 1982). A court may, as a matter of law, determine "whether the defendant has conformed to that standard, in any case in which the jury may not reasonably come to a different conclusion," Restatement (Second) of Torts §328B(d) and Comment *g* (1965), but judicial intrusion into jury decision-making in negligence cases is exceedingly rare. Further, we must view the evidence in the light most favorable to the plaintiffs. The test is whether "anywhere in the evidence, from whatever source derived, any combination of circumstances could be found from which a reasonable inference could be drawn in favor of the plaintiff."

Ortho argues that reasonable minds could not differ as to whether MacDonald was adequately informed of the risk of the injury she sustained by Ortho's warning that the oral contraceptives could cause "abnormal blood clotting which can be fatal" and further warning of the incremental likelihood of hospitalization or death due to blood clotting in "vital organs, such as the brain." We disagree. "The fact finder may find a warning to be unreasonable, hence inadequate, in its factual content, its expression of the facts, or the method or form in which it is conveyed. . . . The adequacy of such warnings is measured not only by what is stated, but also by the manner in which it is stated. A reasonable warning not only conveys a fair indication of the nature of the dangers involved, but also warns with the degree of intensity demanded by the nature of the risk. A warning may be found to be unreasonable in that it was unduly delayed, reluctant in tone or lacking in a sense of urgency." Seljey v. G.D. Searle Co., 423 N.E.2d 831 (Ohio 1981). We cannot say that this jury's decision that the warning was inadequate is so unreasonable as to require the opposite conclusion as a matter of law. The jury may well have concluded, in light of their common experience and MacDonald's testimony, that the absence of a reference to "stroke" in the warning unduly minimized the warning's impact or failed to make the nature of the risk reasonably comprehensible to the average consumer. Similarly, the jury may have concluded that there are fates worse than death, such as the permanent disablement suffered by MacDonald, and that the mention of the risk of death did not, therefore, suffice to apprise an average consumer of the material risks of oral contraceptive use.

We reverse the judgment, which the judge ordered notwithstanding the verdict, and remand the case to the Superior Court for the entry of judgment for the plaintiffs.

So ordered.

O'CONNOR, JUSTICE (dissenting). . . . I would hold that, as a matter of law, by adequately informing physicians of the risks associated with its product and by complying with applicable FDA regulations, a contraceptive pill manufacturer fulfils the duty to warn that it owes consumers. Therefore, because the jury found that Ortho adequately warned Carole MacDonald's physician of the risks associated with its contraceptive pills and because the MacDonalds presented no evidence that Ortho failed to comply with FDA regulations, I would affirm the judgment for Ortho. . . . In cases involving manufacturers of contraceptive pills, every court but one has adhered to the "prescription drug" rule.

I believe that the "prescription drug" rule, combined with the *Harnish* rule most fairly and efficiently allocates among drug manufacturers, physicians, and drug users, the risks and responsibilities involved with the use of prescription drugs. Furthermore, I believe that those rules best ensure that a prescription drug user will receive in the most effective manner the information that she needs to make an informed decision as to whether to use the drug. The rules place on drug manufacturers the duty to gather, compile, and provide to doctors data regarding the use of their drugs, tasks for which the manufacturers are best suited, and the rules place on doctors the burden of conveying those data to their patients in a useful and understandable manner, a task for which doctors are best suited. Doctors, unlike printed warnings, can tailor to the needs and abilities of an individual patient the information that that patient needs in order to make an informed decision whether to use a particular drug. Manufacturers are not in position to give adequate advice directly to those consumers whose medical histories and physical conditions, perhaps unknown to the consumers, make them peculiarly susceptible to risk. Prescription drugs — including oral contraceptives — differ from other products because their dangers vary widely depending on characteristics of individual consumers. Exposing a prescription drug manufacturer to liability based on a jury's determination that, despite adequately informing physicians of the drug's risks and complying with FDA regulations, the manufacturer failed reasonably to warn a particular plaintiff-consumer of individualized risks is not essential to reasonable consumer protection and places an unfair burden on prescription drug manufacturers.

NOTES

1. *Pharmacists' duty to warn.* In McKee v. American Home Products Corp., 782 P.2d 1045, 1051 (Wash. 1989), the court refused to subject a pharmacist to the duties to warn normally imposed on prescribing physicians.

> In deciding whether to use a prescription drug, the patient relies primarily on the expertise and judgment of the physician. Proper weighing of the risks and benefits of a proposed drug treatment and determining what facts to tell the patient about the drug requires an individualized medical judgment based on knowledge of the patient and his or her medical condition. The physician is not required to disclose all risks associated with a drug, only those that are material. It is apparent that a pharmacist would not be qualified to make such a judgment as to materiality. Moreover, circumstances may exist justifying nondisclosure of even material risks. Requiring the pharmacist to warn of potential risks associated with a drug would interject the pharmacist into the physician-patient relationship and interfere with ongoing treatment. We believe that duty, and any liability arising therefrom, is best left with the physician.

The court also held that a pharmacist could be held liable for prescribing drugs that to his personal knowledge were contraindicated for this particular patient — say because of alcoholism — or for dispensing drugs without a label indicating the maximum safe dosage, given the standard practice to the contrary. *McKee* is followed in the proposed Restatement Third, section 4 (c), which restricts the liability of retail sellers of drugs and medical devices to cases of manufacturing defects (why?) or for failing "to excercise reasonable care in preparing, packaging, labelling, instructing, or warning about the drug or medical device." Is *McKee* consistent with either *MacDonald* or *Murphy,* supra at page 771?

2. *Mass vaccination cases.* Warnings issues have proved critically important in the area of mass immunization programs. Of particular importance are the decisions in Davis v. Wyeth Laboratories, Inc., 399 F.2d 121, 129-131 (9th Cir. 1968), and Reyes v. Wyeth Laboratories, Inc., 498 F.2d 1264 (5th Cir. 1974), both involving liability for the Sabin live virus polio vaccine. In *Davis,* the plaintiff was vaccinated as part of a mass immunization program that was administered by the local pharmacist, there being no physician available to do the job. The program for immunization was promoted by one of the defendant's representatives, whose expenses were reimbursed by the local medical organization. At no point did the defendant inform the plaintiff of the one-in-a-million chance that even when properly prepared and administered the vaccine could cause polio. The court first noted that although the product is inherently dangerous, it could not be regarded as unreasonably dangerous, precluding a finding that liability could follow from contraction of the disease alone. It then held, however, in reliance upon section 402A and comments *j* and *k,* that the plaintiff established a good case by alleging the defendant's failure to warn of inherent defects. It then addressed the defendant's arguments that, even if the duty to warn is generally imposed in products cases, it should not be recognized in the instant case.

> There will, of course, be cases where the personal risk, although existent and known, is so trifling in comparison with the advantage to be gained as to be de minimis. Appellee so characterizes this case. It would approach the problem from a purely statistical point of view: less than one out of a million is just not unreasonable. This approach we reject. When, in a particular case, the risk qualitatively (e.g., of death or major disability) as well as quantitatively, on balance with the end sought to be achieved, is such as to call for a true choice judgment, medical or personal, the warning must be given.
>
> Appellee contends that even under such a test no true choice situation is presented here. It asserts that "common sense and knowledge of the mainstreams of human conduct would unavoidably bring one to the conclusion" that appellant would have chosen to take the risk. It says, "Simply stated that proposition is this: A man has less than one in a million chance of contracting the dreaded disease of polio if he takes the vaccine. If he does not take the vaccine his chances of contracting polio are abundantly increased."
>
> We do not so read the record. The Surgeon General's report of September, 1962, as we have quoted it, predicted that for the 1962 season only .9 persons over 20 years of age out of a million would contract polio from natural sources. While appellant was the father of two young children, he resided in an area that not only was not epidemic but whose immediate past history of incidence was extremely low. We have no way of knowing the extent to which either factor would affect the critical statistics. Thus appellant's risk of contracting the disease without immu-

nization was about as great (or small) as his risk of contracting it from the vaccine. Under these circumstances we cannot agree with appellee that the choice to take the vaccine was clear. . . .

Ordinarily in the case of prescription drugs warning to the prescribing physician is sufficient. . . .

Here, however, although the drug was denominated a prescription drug it was not dispensed as such. It was dispensed to all comers at mass clinics without an individualized balancing by a physician of the risks involved. In such cases (as in the case of over-the-counter sales of nonprescription drugs) warning by the manufacturer to its immediate purchaser will not suffice. The decision (that on balance and in the public interest the personal risk to the individual was worth taking) may well have been that of the medical society and not that of appellee. But just as the responsibility for choice is not one that the manufacturer can assume for all comers, neither is it one that he can allow his immediate purchaser to assume. In such cases, then, it is the responsibility of the manufacturer to see that warnings reach the consumer, either by giving warning itself or by obligating the purchaser to give warning. Here appellee knew that warnings were not reaching the consumer. Appellee had taken an active part in setting up the mass immunization clinic program for the society and well knew that the program did not make any such provision, either in advertising prior to the clinics or at the clinics themselves. On the contrary, it attempted to assure all members of the community that they should take the vaccine.

We conclude that appellee did not meet its duty to warn.

This duty does not impose an unreasonable burden on the manufacturer. When drugs are sold over the counter to all comers warnings normally can be given by proper labeling. Such method of giving warning was not available here, since the vaccine came in bottles never seen by the consumer. But other means of communication such as advertisements, posters, releases to be read and signed by recipients of the vaccine, or oral warnings were clearly available and could easily have been undertaken or prescribed by appellee.

Thereafter, in *Reyes,* the court held that the jury was entitled to decide whether the vaccine was the physical cause of the injury and whether the plaintiff would have changed his behavior if an adequate warning had been provided. "In the absence of evidence rebutting the presumption, a jury finding that the defendant's product was the producing cause of the plaintiff's injury would be sufficient to hold him liable."

Reyes and *Davis* were first-generation cases in which no warnings had been provided. The subsequent round of litigation has focused on the adequacy of the warnings. Givens v. Lederle, 556 F.2d 1341, 1343 (5th Cir. 1977), was another case in which the plaintiff claimed to have contracted polio from the Sabin vaccine — this time when she was present at the inoculation of her infant daughter. Here, however, the defendant Lederle issued a warning to the physician which stated in full:

> Paralytic disease following the ingestion of live polio virus vaccines has been reported in individuals receiving the vaccine, and in some in-

stances, in persons who were in close contact with subjects who had been given live oral polio virus vaccine. Fortunately, such occurrences are rare, and it could not be definitely established that any such case was due to the vaccine strain and was not coincidental with infection due to naturally occurring poliomyelitis, or other enteroviruses.

The package insert also noted that the risk, if any, was one in three million. The physician who in fact inoculated the plaintiff's daughter gave the plaintiff no warning of the risk. At trial, the plaintiff's physician testified that he did not warn the plaintiff of the risk because he thought that the insert was too "nebulous" to require further action on his part. On appeal, the court held that this testimony, together with evidence showing that such infections had occurred, was sufficient to sustain the jury's verdict that the warning was inadequate, especially because the warning itself denied any definite connection between the vaccine and the disease. Dr. Sabin testified for the defendant that his vaccine could not possibly cause polio.

Shortly after the polio cases, the government warnings in the swine flu vaccination program of 1976 produced serious side effects for which the United States (standing in the shoes of the manufacturers) was held liable for its incomplete warnings, often for people who suffered from Guillain-Barre syndrome — a partial paralysis of the legs that in about 5 percent of the cases can result in death. See Unthank v. United States, 732 F.2d 1517 (10th Cir. 1984), where the court noted that "in cases arising out of the Swine Flu Act underlying state laws must be liberally construed in favor of claimants," and further that "it would defy logic and reason to suggest that an adequate warning was provided by the mere mention in the consent form's text that there was a 'possibility of severe or potentially fatal reaction.' " See generally Franklin and Mais, Tort Law and Mass Immunization Programs, 65 Cal. L. Rev. 754 (1977).

3. Reforming mass torts. The number of large damage awards arising out of these cases has driven up costs of vaccines substantially. See Shackil v. Lederle, supra at page 423, note 4. See also Manning, Changing Rules of Tort Law and the Market for Childhood Vaccines, 37 J.L. & Econ. 247, 248 (1994), whose econometric analysis notes that the price of DPT vaccine between 1975 and 1990 increased by over 2,000 percent, of which over 96 percent went to litigation costs. Numbers like these have given rise to much scholarly criticism of the law. See Huber, Safety and the Second Best: The Hazards of Public Risk Management in the Courts, 85 Colum. L. Rev. 277 (1985):

> Which brings us to the whooping cough vaccine, one for which especially precise risk figures are available. In recent decades the vaccine has been used to immunize almost every child in the United States. According to a report by two scientists at the Centers for Disease Control, use of the vaccine prevents an estimated 322,000 cases of whooping

cough per year. An estimated 457 persons per year would die of the disease without the vaccination program; use of the vaccine reduces annual mortality to 44, for a net annual savings of 413 lives. Tragically, however, about 1 in every 310,000 recipients experiences serious, long term brain damage. Without the vaccine there would be 29 such cases per year; vaccine raises that figure to 54 cases, an increase of 25 cases per year. The aggregate figures could scarcely be less ambiguous; receiving the vaccine increases the risk of one particular form of injury a little, but drastically reduces the risk of another.

Huber notes that notwithstanding FDA approval and encouragement of the vaccine program, Wyeth has ceased to produce it solely because of the risk of tort liability, notwithstanding its net social benefits.

One possible reform of the situation would allow the parties by contract to limit the damages payable in the event of an adverse effect. The case for this position is set out in Rubin, Tort Reform by Contract 62-63 (1993):

> For products that reduce risk, the large damage payments associated with payments for nonpecuniary losses can actually lead to consumers facing increased risk. . . .
>
> Consider a hypothetical case of a vaccine that reduces the risk of a fatal illness and entails pecuniary losses of $10,000 and nonpecuniary losses of death valued at $5 million. . . . Risk of injury without the vaccine is .0015, and risk when using the product is .0010 (a one-third reduction in risk). The average and marginal costs of producing the vaccine taking optimal care is $10.
>
> Under a regime of no liability (but with optimal precautions), the competitive price of the vaccine is $10. Under strict liability for monetary damages only, price is $10 + .001 ($10,000) = $10 + $10 = $20, reflecting the .0010 probability of having to pay out $10,000, if the product fails. The value to consumers of the prevention offered by the vaccine is the reduction in monetary losses (estimated as .0005 × $10,000 = $5) plus the amount consumers would have paid for the marginal .0005 reduction in the probability of death (.0005 × $5,000,000 = $2,500), a total of $2,505. If consumer perceptions of relative risks are anywhere close to the truth, consumers will correctly choose to use the vaccine because its benefits of $2,505 greatly exceed its costs of $20.
>
> Now add damage payments for hedonic losses. Price increases by $5,000, reflecting the .0010 chance of making a liability payment of $5 million, for a total price of $5,020. But consumer willingness to pay for the prevention offered by the vaccine is only $2,505. It seems unlikely that consumers would wish to pay anything close to the extra $2,515 for a lottery that awards $5 million in the event of death (the extreme reduction in marginal utility of wealth). Rather, informed consumers would choose not to use the vaccine and instead would live with the greater risk associated with no production at all.

Note that the source of the problem is that the liability payments calculated under a system of strict liability treat the vaccine as though it caused *all* the losses that resulted instead of eliminating one-third of them. The liability system thus registers the manufacture of the drug as the source of a social problem and not as its mitigation.

The questions of liability have, it should be noted, influenced the mode of distribution of drugs that are known to have dangerous side effects. Rubin notes, for example, that the drug clozapine — a powerful treatment for schizophrenia with a .0002 chance of causing death — sells for about $9,000 per year, in part to offset the extensive monitoring costs incurred in the United States, but not, so it appears, in Europe, where the risks of liability are far smaller. See Milt Freudenheim, *Business and Health: Method of Pricing Drug Is Assailed,* N. Y. TIMES, August 28, 1990, at D2, col. 1.

In response to the evident crisis, Congress passed the National Childhood Vaccine Act of 1986, which provides for a complex system of no-fault compensation of up to $250,000 for persons who suffer particular side effects from certain vaccine programs within specified time limits, for example, for the recipient of a measles vaccine who suffers an anaphylactic shock within 24 hours after inoculation. The statute also provides that persons who have met the conditions for no-fault recovery may nonetheless choose to reject the payment and sue for tort damages.

One unanticipated gap in the scheme was revealed in Schafer v. American Cyanamid, 20 F.3d 1, 3 (1st Cir. 1994), where an injured child accepted $750,000 from the vaccine manufacturer under the statute, but her parents withdrew from the scheme and were allowed to bring a tort action for loss of companionship and consortium. Breyer, C.J., acknowledged that the action allowed could well frustrate the cost-reducing program of the Act, but held that he had to allow the action because the statutory bar "applies only to a person who has sustained injury or death," after he or she has "received the vaccine . . . or contracted polio from another person who received an oral polio vaccine."

4. When must a warning be given? The adequacy of warnings has also been litigated in cases involving all manner of household products. A threshold question in these cases is whether the circumstances of a case call for any duty to warn at all. In Ayers v. Johnson & Johnson, 818 P.2d 1337, 1341 (Wash. 1991), David Ayers, then aged 15 months, had taken an unmarked bottle of Johnson's baby oil out of the purse of his 13-year-old-sister. Just as he began to drink the oil, his mother yelled at him, causing him to gasp and inhale the oil in his lungs. Once there the baby oil coated his air sacs and quickly led to oxygen deprivation that resulted in serious injuries: his leg motions became spastic; he had limited control over his head movements; and he suffered retardation, seizures, and lost any ability to speak.

It was agreed on all sides that once David inhaled the baby oil, no medical attention could have prevented these injuries. Plaintiff contended that a warning on the bottle was required to alert users of this risk so that they would take more strenuous efforts to keep baby oil out of the reach of infants in the first place. The plaintiff's mother testified that she read warnings, and kept dangerous products out of the reach of her young children, and instructed her teenage daughters to do the same. Both mother and daughters testified that they thought baby oil could cause diarrhea or stomach upset, but they had no knowledge of its dangerous propensities. Johnson and Johnson argued that it was rank speculation to claim that the additional knowledge would have led to different conduct, since all members of the Ayers family knew that the baby oil was only for external use, and was dangerous if taken internally. The jury found for the plaintiff, and its verdict was sustained on appeal:

> On the basis of this evidence, the jury was entitled to infer that if the Ayerses had known of the dangers of aspiration, they would have treated the baby oil with greater care; that they would have treated it with the caution they used in relation to items they recognized as highly dangerous, like cleaning products; and that had they done so, the accident would have never occurred. We conclude that the evidence of causation presented to the jury was sufficient to sustain the jury's verdict.

Should Johnson and Johnson change the warnings on its bottles? On its package inserts? If a warning should be included, what should it say?

Must a liquor manufacturer warn of the dangers of alcoholic beverages? In Garrison v. Heublein, Inc., 673 F.2d 189 (7th Cir. 1982), the court rejected the plaintiff's claim for "physical and mental injuries as a result of consuming the defendant's product [Smirnoff vodka] over a twenty year period," noting that the risks involved were common knowledge for which the defendant had no duty to warn. The common-knowledge defense, however, was held insufficient to allow the defendant to obtain a summary judgment in Hon v. Stroh Brewery Co., 835 F.2d 510, 511 (3d Cir. 1987), where the plaintiff's husband had died of pancreatitis that the plaintiff alleged had resulted mainly from his consuming about 8 to 12 cans of the defendant's beer each week over a period of several years. The court accepted the plaintiff's claim that a warning was required because it was not common knowledge that "*either* excessive *or* prolonged, even though moderate, use of alcohol may result in diseases of many kinds, including pancreatic disease." The defendant's case, based on comment *j*, was rejected in part because the jury could find that Stroh's advertising campaign linked the consumption of these quantities of beer to the "good life." It wrote that "comment *j* does not say that whenever alcohol is consumed over a long period of time the dangers are necessarily generally known. Rather it says that *when* the danger is generally known, no warning is required." Note that recent federal regulations, 54 Fed. Reg. 7160 (1989), now require the following warning label to be attached conspicuously to containers of alcoholic beverages sold:

> Government warning: [1] According to the Surgeon General, women should not drink alcoholic beverages during pregnancy because of the risk of birth defects. [2] Consumption of alcoholic beverages impairs your ability to drive a car or operate machinery, and may cause health problems.

Is this warning adequate at common law?

5. *Information costs and the duty to warn.* The early products liability cases tended to opt for stringent product warnings. In Jackson v. Coast Paint & Lacquer Co., 499 F.2d 809 (9th Cir. 1974), where the plaintiff-employee's claim that a manufacturer-seller of paint had failed to warn of the dangers of using paints in closed locations was allowed to reach the jury. The warnings supplied said:

> Keep away from heat, sparks, and open flame. USE WITH ADEQUATE VENTILATION. Avoid prolonged contact with skin and breath of spray mist. Close container after each use. KEEP OUT OF REACH OF CHILDREN.

The plaintiff claimed that he thought the warning applied only to the "danger of breath toxic vapors" and did not extend to the risk of fire or explosion. The court allowed the case to reach the jury, which had to answer the question whether "the danger, or potentiality of danger, is *generally* known and recognized" under the standards of comment *n*. The court in *Jackson* also rejected the proposition that the warning to the employer was sufficient under the learned intermediary doctrine, given his lack of any special technical and scientific information.

A sharp change in attitude is found in Cotton v. Buckeye Gas Products Co., 840 F.2d 935, 937-938 (D.C. Cir. 1988). There the plaintiff was injured when gas canisters supplied to his employer by the defendant burst into flames. The canisters contained warnings that the gas was "flammable" and should not be stored in "living areas," and the plaintiff's superiors had instructed him that the valves should be closed when the canisters were moved or changed. The plaintiff had disregarded that instruction. He sued the manufacturer, claiming its warning was inadequate because

> it failed (1) to warn about the explosive properties of propane; (2) to instruct users to shut the valves on used cylinders; (3) to advise users not to use or store the cylinders in enclosed, unventilated areas; and (4) to warn that gas might escape from used cylinders believed to be empty.
>
> Failure-to-warn cases have the curious property that, when the episode is examined in hindsight, it appears as though addition of warnings

keyed to a particular accident would be virtually cost free. What could be simpler than for the manufacturer to add the few simple items noted above? The primary cost is, in fact, the increase in time and effort required for the user to grasp the message. The inclusion of each extra item dilutes the punch of every other item. Given short attention spans, items crowd each other out; they get lost in fine print. Here, in fact, Buckeye responded to the information-cost problem with a dual approach; a brief message on the cannisters themselves and a more detailed one in the NLPGA [National Liquid Propane Gas Association] pamphlet delivered to [the employer] (and posted at the Leesburg Pike construction site where Cotton was employed).

Plaintiff's analysis completely disregards the problem of information costs. He asserts that "it would have been neither difficult nor costly for Buckeye to have purchased or created for attachment to its propane cylinders a clearer, more explicit label, such as the alternatives introduced at trial, warning of propane's danger and how to avoid them." But he offers no reason to suppose that an alternative package of warnings was preferable. He discounts altogether the warnings in the pamphlet, without even considering what the canister warning would have looked like if Buckeye had supplemented it not only with the special items he is personally interested in — in hindsight — but also with all other equally valuable items.

A similar impatience with claims for detailed warnings was found in Todd v. Societe Bic, 9 F.3d 1217 (7th Cir. 1993), where a 4-year-old child set fire to a house with a Bic Lighter, killing an 18-month-old baby. The lighter carried with it a warning directed to parents — KEEP OUT OF REACH OF CHILDREN — and Easterbrook, J., held the defendant was entitled to summary judgment on the warning claim, asking whether "consumers who disdain a bold and (if followed) effective warning will be influenced by smaller and more subtle points?" More concretely, if the parents had not been persuaded to remove the lighter from harm's way by the warning, how could they prove causation when the very child who started the fatal fire had also started a similar fire with a cigarette lighter a week before?

6. *Warnings or design.* The impatience with warnings received a very different spin in Latin, Good Warnings, Bad Products, and Cognitive Limitations, 41 U.C.L.A. L. Rev. 1193 (1994). Latin there rejects the "Rational Risk Calculator Model" of human behavior, often championed by economists, in favor of the rival "Mistake and Momentary Inattention" model, which draws more heavily on the psychological and sociological literature to support the view that even cautious actors are subject to momentary lapses in judgment or attention. From that second perspective, which Latin strongly supports, the clear implication is that even "good" warnings should not be respected when cheap design alternatives are available to protect the users of products from the disastrous consequences of not heeding a warning. The object of Latin's attack is an echo of *Campo* found in Restatement §402A, comment *j*,

"Where warning is given, the seller may reasonably assume that it will be read and heeded." If the Mistake and Momentary Inattention Model is correct, then the correct solution, Latin argues, is to require design changes no matter how strong or "good" the warnings are.

One case criticized by Latin is Skyhook Corp. v. Jasper, 560 P.2d 934 (N.M. 1977) (overruled in Klopp v. Wackenhut Corp., 824 P.2d 293 (N.M. 1992)). There the defendant warned that its crane should never be brought within ten feet of a high-voltage line. Recovery was denied in a wrongful death action stemming from an electrocution when the crane operators moved the crane into the danger zone. Oman, C.J., relied not only on the presumption of comment *j*, but also on the additional facts that the crane had been used without incident for five years, and that both crane operators had been personally told of the risks of letting the crane go near these wires. Is the case for a design change more powerful for an obvious condition (as in *Campo* or *Micallef*) or for a concealed defect for which a comprehensive warning has been issued?

As a variation on the warning question, what should be done with Q-Tips or other cotton swabs? The standard warnings on these products instruct people never to insert them into the ear, even though this is the dominant use, and they are marketed as such. Is the correct remedy to redesign the Q-Tip, strengthen the warning, take the product off the market, or leave things as they are? And as a final variation, should warnings be required in languages other than English? For a negative answer to that question see Ramirez v. Plough, Inc., 863 P.2d 167 (Cal. 1993), holding that the issue was too complicated to be resolved by litigation.

Brown v. Superior Court (Abbott Laboratories)
751 P.2d 470 (Cal. 1988)

MOSK, J.: In current litigation several significant issues have arisen relating to the liability of manufacturers of prescription drugs for injuries caused by their products. Our first and broadest inquiry is whether such a manufacturer may be held strictly liable for a product that is defective in design.

[The discussion of the *Sindell* issues, omitted throughout, is found in Chapter 5, supra at page 411, note 2.]

A number of plaintiffs filed actions in the San Francisco Superior Court against numerous drug manufacturers which allegedly produced DES, a substance plaintiffs claimed was used by their mothers to prevent miscarriage. They alleged that the drug was defective and they were injured *in utero* when their mothers ingested it. . .

The trial court . . . determined that defendants could not be held strictly liable for the alleged defect in DES but only for their failure to warn of known or knowable side effects of the drug.

[The general overview of the history of strict liability in tort from *Escola* to *Barker* is omitted.]

B.   STRICT LIABILITY AND PRESCRIPTION DRUGS

[The court then sets out comment *k* of Restatement §402A and continues.]

Comment *k* has been analyzed and criticized by numerous commentators. While there is some disagreement as to its scope and meaning, there is a general consensus that, although it purports to explain the strict liability doctrine, in fact the principle it states is based on negligence. That is, comment *k* would impose liability on a drug manufacturer only if it failed to warn of a defect of which it either knew or should have known. This concept focuses not on a deficiency in the product — the hallmark of strict liability — but on the fault of the producer in failing to warn of dangers inherent in the use of its product that were either known or knowable — an idea which "rings of negligence," in the words of Cronin [v. J.B.E. Olson Corp.], 501 P.2d 1153 (1972).

Comment *k* has been adopted in the overwhelming majority of jurisdictions that have considered the matter. In California, several decisions of the Courts of Appeal have embraced the comment *k* exemption, but this court has never spoken to the issue.

We are aware of only one decision that has applied the doctrine of strict liability to prescription drugs. (Brochu v. Ortho Pharmaceutical Corp., 642 F.2d 652, 654-657 (1st Cir. 1981).) Most cases have embraced the rule of comment *k* without detailed analysis of its language. A few, notably Kearl v. Lederle Laboratories, 218 Cal. Rptr. 453 (Cal. App. 1985), have conditioned application of the exemption stated therein on a finding that the drug involved is in fact "unavoidably dangerous," reasoning that the comment was intended to exempt only such drugs from strict liability. And in Collins v. Eli Lilly Co., 342 N.W.2d 37, 52 (Wis. 1984), it was held that comment *k* was applicable only if the drug in question was placed on the market without adequate testing because of exigent circumstances.

We appear, then, to have three distinct choices: (1) to hold that the manufacturer of a prescription drug is strictly liable for a defect in its product because it was defectively designed, as that term is defined in *Barker,* or because of a failure to warn of its dangerous propensities even though such dangers were neither known nor scientifically knowable at the time of distribution; (2) to determine that liability attaches only if a manufacturer fails to warn of dangerous propensities of which it was or should have been aware, in conformity with comment *k;* or (3) to decide, like *Kearl,* that strict liability for design defects should apply to prescription drugs unless the particular drug which caused the injury is found to be "unavoidably dangerous."

We shall conclude that (1) a drug manufacturer's liability for a defectively designed drug should not be measured by the standards of strict liability; (2) because of the public interest in the development, availability, and reasonable price of drugs, the appropriate test for determining responsibility is the test stated in comment *k;* and (3) for these same reasons of policy, we disapprove the holding of *Kearl* that only those prescription drugs found to be "unavoidably dangerous" should be measured by the comment *k* standard and that strict liability should apply to drugs that do not meet that description.

1. DESIGN DEFECT

[The court first refuses to apply either "the consumer expectation" or the "safer alternative design" tests of *Barker* to consumer drugs.]

But there is an important distinction between prescription drugs and other products such as construction machinery, the producers of which were held strictly liable. In the latter cases, the product is used to make work easier or to provide pleasure, while in the former it may be necessary to alleviate pain and suffering or to sustain life. Moreover, unlike other important medical products (wheelchairs, for example), harm to some users from prescription drugs is unavoidable. Because of these distinctions, the broader public interest in the availability of drugs at an affordable price must be considered in deciding the appropriate standard of liability for injuries resulting from their use.

Perhaps a drug might be made safer if it was withheld from the market until scientific skill and knowledge advanced to the point at which additional dangerous side effects would be revealed. But in most cases such a delay in marketing new drugs — added to the delay required to obtain approval for release of the product from the Food and Drug Administration — would not serve the public welfare. Public policy favors the development and marketing of beneficial new drugs, even though some risks, perhaps serious ones, might accompany their introduction, because drugs can save lives and reduce pain and suffering.

If drug manufacturers were subject to strict liability, they might be reluctant to undertake research programs to develop some pharmaceuticals that would prove beneficial or to distribute others that are available to be marketed, because of the fear of large adverse monetary judgments. Further, the additional expense of insuring against such liability — assuming insurance would be available — and of research programs to reveal possible dangers not detectable by available scientific methods could place the cost of medication beyond the reach of those who need it most.

. . . The possibility that the cost of insurance and of defending against lawsuits will diminish the availability and increase the price of pharmaceuticals is far from theoretical. Defendants cite a host of examples of products which have greatly increased in price or have been withdrawn or withheld from the market because of the fear that their producers would be held liable for large judgments.

For example, according to defendant E.R. Squibb & Sons, Inc., Benedectin, the only antinauseant drug available for pregnant women, was withdrawn from sale in 1983 because the cost of insurance almost equalled the entire income from sale of the drug. Before it was withdrawn, the price of Benedictin increased by over 300 percent. (132 Chemical Week (June 12, 1983) p. 14.)

Drug manufacturers refused to supply a newly discovered vaccine for influenza on the ground that mass innoculation would subject them to enormous liability. The government therefore assumed the risk of lawsuits resulting from injuries caused by the vaccine. One producer of diphtheria-tetanus-pertussis vaccine withdrew from the market, giving as its reason "extreme liability exposure, cost of litigation and the difficulty of continuing to obtain adequate insurance." (Hearing Before Subcom. on Health and the Environment of House Com. on Energy and Commerce on Vaccine Injury Compensation, 98th Cong., 2d Sess. (Sept. 10, 1984) p. 295.) There are only two manufacturers of the vaccine remaining in the market, and the cost of each dose rose a hundredfold from 11 cents in 1982 to $11.40 in 1986, $8 of which was for an insurance reserve. The price increase roughly paralleled an increase in the number of lawsuits from one in 1978 to 219 in 1985. (232 Science (June 13, 1986) p. 1339.) Finally, a manufacturer was unable to market a new drug for the treatment of vision problems because it could not obtain adequate liability insurance at a reasonable cost. (N.Y. Times (Oct. 14, 1986) p. 10.)

There is no doubt that, from the public's standpoint, these are unfortunate consequences. And they occurred even though almost all jurisdictions follow the negligence standard of comment *k*. It is not unreasonable to conclude in these circumstances that the imposition of a harsher test for liability would not further the public interest in the development and availability of these important products.

We decline to hold, therefore, that a drug manufacturer's liability for injuries caused by the defective design of a prescription drug should be measured by the standard set forth in *Barker*.

2. FAILURE TO WARN

For these same reasons of policy, we reject plaintiff's assertion that a drug manufacturer should be held strictly liable for failure to warn of risks inherent in a drug even though it neither knew nor could have known by the application of scientific knowledge available at the time of distribution that the drug could produce the undesirable side effects suffered by the plaintiff.

Numerous cases have recognized that a product may be defective because of the absence of a warning that was necessary to allow its safe use. While some decisions apply strict liability principles to such a defect by holding that it is irrelevant whether the manufacturer knew of the danger or should have known of it, most jurisdictions hold to the contrary. That is, liability is conditioned on the actual or constructive knowledge of the risk by the manufacturer as of the time the product was sold or distributed. This rule is consistent with comment *j* to section 402A, which confines the duty to warn to a situation in which the seller "has knowledge, or by the application of reasonable, developed human skill and foresight should have knowledge of . . . the danger."

It has been said that to "hold the manufacturer liable for failure to warn of a danger of which it would be impossible to know based on the present state of human knowledge would make the manufacturer the virtual insurer of the product. . . ." (*Woodill v. Parke Davis & Co.*, 402 N.E.2d 194, 199 (Ill. 1980)). The likelihood of the producer's liability would increase with significant advances in scientific knowledge, discouraging the development of new and improved drugs to combat disease. Thus, we disagree with plaintiff's assertion that defendants should be held liable for failing to warn the physician who prescribed DES to plaintiff's mother of alleged defects in the drug that were neither known by defendants nor scientifically knowable at the time the drug was distributed.

3.   THE KEARL TEST

. . . Under *Kearl* the judge should determine, after hearing the evidence, "(1) whether, when distributed, the product was intended to confer an exceptionally important benefit that made its availability highly desirable; (2) whether the then-existing risk posed by the product was both 'substantial' and 'unavoidable'; and (3) whether the interest in availability (again measured as of the time of distribution) outweighs the interest in promoting enhanced accountability through strict liability design defect review." If these questions are answered in the affirmative the liability of the manufacturer is tested by the standards of comment *k*; otherwise, strict liability is the applicable test.

The Court of Appeal in the present case refused to adopt this approach on the ground that it required the trial judge to decide questions of fact which were ordinarily left to the jury, and that it presented the specter of inconsistent verdicts in various trial courts: in one case the question of liability for injuries caused by a specific drug would be tested by a negligence standard, while in another, involving the same drug, the judge might conclude the strict liability was the appropriate test.

[The court then rejected the *Kearl* test for just these reasons. It then concluded:]

Kearl gives the manufacturer a chance to avoid strict liability. But the eligibility of each drug for favorable treatment must be tested at a trial, with its attendant litigation costs, and the drug must survive two risk/benefit challenges, first by the judge and then by the jury. In order to vindicate the public's interest in the availability and affordability of prescription drugs, a manufacturer must have a greater assurance that his products will not be measured by a strict liability standard than is provided by the test stated in *Kearl.* Therefore, we disapprove the portion of *Kearl* which holds that comment *k* should not be applied to a prescription drug unless the trial court first determines that the drug is "unavoidably dangerous."

In conclusion, and in accord with almost all our sister states that have considered the issue, we hold that a manufacturer is not strictly liable for injuries caused by a prescription drug so long as the drug was properly prepared and accompanied by warnings of its dangerous propensities that were either known or reasonably scientifically knowable at the time of distribution.

NOTES

1. Reception of Brown. The decision in *Brown* has met with some resistance in other courts, which have treated it as inconsistent with the broader scope of liability under Barker v. Lull. Thus in Hill v. Searle Laboratories, 884 F.2d 1064, 1069 (8th Cir. 1989), the court reasoned that

> the premise generally relied on by those courts [which refuse to apply strict liability to design defect drug claims] — that the public interest in the development of prescription drug products requires the user to bear all the costs of injury unless the drug product was negligently manufactured or designed or unaccompanied by proper warnings — is unconvincing. In our view, this policy has no greater relevance to prescription drug products than to other products having life-saving characteristics.

Hill's logic was accepted in Shanks v. Upjohn Co., 835 P.2d 1189, 1197-1198 (Alaska 1992), where the decedent shot himself after taking his first dose of Xanax, a central nervous system depressor manufactured by the defendant. Moore, J., held that the plaintiff was entitled to a new trial after the original jury found no liability when instructed only on a negligence theory. In addition to following *Hill,* the court explicitly adopted a generalized risk/utility analysis and a "reasonable physician's expectations" test. It then proceeded to reject comment *k* for three reasons.

> First, we believe that comment *k* has contributed to the confusion which permeates this area of law and blurs the distinctions between negligence and strict liability principles, a distinction we believe warrants preservation.
>
> Secondly, courts are unable to agree as to the comment's scope. Some courts have interpreted comment *k* to exempt all prescription drugs from strict liability. . . . Other courts, without confronting the issue squarely, discuss comment *k* as if it applies to all prescription drugs. Still other courts interpret comment *k* to provide the exception only to those prescription drugs determined on a case-by-case basis to be "unavoidably dangerous." By declining to adopt comment *k*, we hope to avoid contributing to this confusion.
>
> Finally, we believe that the risk/benefit prong of the *Barker* test offers the manufacturers of those products intended to be protected by comment *k* an opportunity to avoid strict liability claims based on a design defect theory.

2. Unavoidably dangerous products.

a. Hepatitis. *Brown*'s rejection of a strict liability principle has not always been followed, at least in the context in which the defect was known, but unavoidable. In Brody v. Overlook Hospital, 296 A.2d 668 (N.J. 1972), the plaintiff died from hepatitis caused by a blood transfusion. At the time the transfusion was made, it was known that blood could be contaminated with the hepatitis virus, but no test could detect it. The trial court held that the "imposition of strict tort liability may well spur the hospital to take a more active role in influencing the bank's collection processes, i.e. more careful screening of donors." The court also thought that strict liability would advance the goal of loss-spreading "among all parties, i.e. donors, blood banks, perhaps its patients. This 'allocative effect' will be felt if hospitals allocate their hepatitis costs as a charge on each unit of blood actually used: physicians will automatically more carefully weigh the risks of surgery and transfusions."

In *Brody* the plaintiff's victory was short-lived, as the decision was reversed by the intermediate court in Brody v. Overlook Hospital, 317 A.2d 393 (N.J. App. Div. 1974), where the court noted, first, that "in December 1966 (when the blood was transfused) there was no known scientific or medical test for determining whether blood drawn from a donor contained serum hepatitis virus," and then used comment *k* to reject the strict liability theory. It also rejected the "loss spreading" or "allocative effect," concluding that this theory "has some weight but not nearly enough when laid beside other more basic considerations. It plays only the part of a makeweight argument." The New Jersey Su-

preme Court affirmed the judgment of the appellate division in a brief
per curiam opinion, 332 A.2d 596 (N.J. 1975).

More than 40 states have enacted legislation adopting the negligence
standard in hepatitis cases, including Illinois, 745 ILCS 40/1-3 (1994).
The Illinois statute first noted that whole blood, plasma, and other body
parts are of great importance to the "health and welfare" of the people
of the state and that a strict liability rule "inhibits the exercise of sound
medical judgment and restricts the availability of important scientific
knowledge, skills and materials." It then provided that any firm engaged in the supply of blood was required only to "warrant" the recipient of the blood or related product that "he has exercised due care
and followed professional standards of care in providing the service
according to the current state of the medical arts," and has complied
with applicable labeling provisions. The Idaho variation adopts a general negligence standard but imposes a strict liability rule on any "paid
blood, organ or tissue donor or a blood, organ or tissue bank operated
for profit." Idaho Code §39-3702 (1994). Is there any reason to suppose
that the commercial provision of blood results in a systematic reduction
in the quality of the blood furnished?

When *Brody* was decided there was no known and reliable test for the
detection of the hepatitis virus in blood. Since that time, tests have been
developed that allow such detection. Is there any way in which this
technological breakthrough could be related to the particular rule of
liability? Does the widespread availability of the test count as an argument in favor of the system of negligence or a system of strict liability?

For early responses to the hepatitis question see Franklin, Tort Liability for Hepatitis: An Analysis and a Proposal, 24 Stan. L. Rev. 439, 474-
475 (1972). See generally Kessel, Transfused Blood, Serum Hepatitis,
and The Coase Theorem, 17 J.L. & Econ. 265 (1974).

b. Asbestos. The single most controversial application of comment *k*
is in the numerous suits for asbestos-related diseases. Asbestos itself fits
within the category of unavoidably dangerous products because it is
both highly useful as an insulation product and because it undeniably
causes many fatal conditions — chief among them asbestosis, mesothe-
lioma, and bronchiogenic carcinoma. The watershed case is Borel v.
Fiberboard Paper Products Corp., 493 F.2d 1076 (5th Cir. 1973), which
affirmed a jury verdict against asbestos manufacturers on behalf of an
insulation worker who had extensive contact with asbestos for more
than 30 years. Wisdom, J., in an exhaustive opinion, held that there was
sufficient evidence of the dangers of asbestos in the medical literature
to impose upon manufacturers — here held to the standard of "experts" in the field — a duty to warn all workers coming in contact with
the product so that they could make an informed choice of whether to
expose themselves to asbestos.

Before *Borel* no plaintiff had ever recovered from an asbestos manufacturer. The decision unleashed a veritable avalanche of suits against asbestos suppliers. By most reckonings they constituted the single largest body of cases in the federal system and by their sheer numbers have overwhelmed the operation of the system: as of March 1991 over 31,000 asbestos cases were pending in federal court alone. For one judge's exasperated evaluation of the system see Cimino v. Raymark Industries, 751 F. Supp. 649 (E.D. Tex. 1990), lamenting the procedural obstacles that result in bankrupt defendants and uncompensated plaintiffs.

Borel does not represent the last word in asbestos litigation. In Beshada v. Johns-Manville Products Corp., 447 A.2d 539 (N.J. 1982), the defendants tried to show that "the danger of which they failed to warn was undiscovered at the time the product was marketed and that it was undiscoverable given the state of scientific knowledge at that time." Noting that there was extensive factual disagreement as to the nature of the defendants' knowledge, the court rejected this "state of the art" defense because it was directed to the issue of the reasonableness of the defendants' behavior when "a major concern of strict liability — ignored by the defendants — is that the distributor of a defective product should compensate its victims for the misfortune that it inflicted upon them."

The court then concluded that a strict liability rule could spread risks efficiently, given that the defendants advanced "no argument as to why risk spreading works better for unknown risks than for unknowable risks." It also stated that its decision advanced the goal of accident avoidance: "By imposing on manufacturers the costs of failure to discover hazards, we create an incentive for them to invest more actively in safety research." Finally, it noted that by eliminating the state-of-the-art defense it eliminated the complicated and expensive scientific determinations of what the state of the art was.

Beshada has not fared well in the courts. New Jersey refused to extend it to prescription drugs in Feldman v. Lederle Laboratories, 479 A.2d 374 (N.J. 1984). And the strict liability approach to warnings was repudiated in Anderson v. Owens-Corning Fiberglas Corp., 810 P.2d 549, 558-559 (Cal. 1991), where Panelli, J., applied *Brown* to asbestos and concluded that the defendant owed no duty to warn of unknown hazards.

> How can one warn of something that is unknowable? If every product that has no warning were defective per se and for that reason subject to strict liability, the mere fact of injury by an unlabelled product would automatically permit recovery. That is not, and has never been, the purpose and goal of the failure-to-warn theory of strict liability. Further, if a warning automatically precluded liability in every case, a manufacturer

or distributor could easily escape liability with overly broad, and thus practically useless, warnings. . . .

We recognize that an important goal of strict liability is to spread the risks and costs of injury to those most able to bear them. However, it was never the intention of the drafters of the doctrine to make the manufacturer or distributor the insurer of the safety of their products. It was never their intention to impose *absolute* liability.

Mosk, J., both concurring and dissenting, took issue with the scope of the majority's opinion. He insisted that his earlier decision in *Brown* should receive a narrower interpretation:

> Here plaintiff alleged, among other claims, that defendants marketed their products "with specific prior knowledge" of the high risks of injury and death from their use. If plaintiff can establish at the new trial that defendants had *actual knowledge,* then state of the art evidence — or what everyone else was doing at the time — would be irrelevant and the trial court could properly exclude it. Actual knowledge may often be difficult to prove, but it is not impossible with adequately probing discovery. Defendants, of course, can produce evidence that they had no such prior actual knowledge.
>
> On the other hand, if plaintiff is only able to show, by medical and scientific data or other means, that defendants *should have known* of the risks inherent in their products, then contrary medical and scientific data and state of the art evidence would be admissible if offered by defendants. 810 P.2d at 563.

If state-of-the-art evidence is admissible on the knowability of the risk, should a negligence rule be used to assess the adequacy of the warning for a known risk? If a manufacturer does not warn of risks of which it has "specific prior knowledge," should it be subject to punitive damages?

c. DES. In Enright by Enright v. Eli Lilly & Co., 570 N.E.2d 198 (N.Y. 1991), the court refused to extend the strict liability to warn to the grandchild of the woman who had first taken DES, on the ground that neither negligence nor strict liability principles justified the imposition of liability for a "pre-conception tort." Wachtler, C.J., first noted the difficulties in proving causation across two or more generations, and limited recovery to persons injured in utero.

> More important, however, is recognition that public policy favors the availability of prescription drugs even though most carry some risks (see *Brown*). That is not to say that drug manufacturers should enjoy immunity from liability stemming from their failure to conduct adequate research and testing prior to the marketing of their products. They do not enjoy such immunity, as evidenced by our recognition of liability in favor of those who have been injured by ingestion or in utero exposure to DES. But we are aware of the dangers of overdeterrence — the possibility that research will be discouraged or beneficial drugs withheld from the mar-

ket. These dangers are magnified in this context, where we are asked to recognize a legal duty toward generations not yet conceived.

d. AIDS. The unavoidably dangerous drug limitation has also held firm in AIDS cases. In Doe v. Miles Laboratories, 927 F.2d 187 (4th Cir. 1991), plaintiff contracted AIDS in September 1983 when given a blood clotting agent, Koyne, which was prepared by concentrating blood plasma donations from about 13,000 individual plasma donors. The Koyne was administered because plaintiff had sustained severe vaginal bleeding after birth. The court upheld a comment *k* defense when it was shown that the Koyne was administered when it was not certain that AIDS was a blood-borne virus, when no test existed to identify the HIV virus, and when the clotting formula was medically essential. The court also held that "we cannot expect [drug companies] to have implemented a blood donor screening program when they did not know that the HIV virus was transmissible through blood or blood products." For criticism of the negligence standard in AIDS cases see Eckert, supra Chapter 3, note 4 at 245.

The approach in these cases has been adopted in the proposed Third Restatement, section 2, comment *i:*

> Unforeseeable risks arising from foreseeable product uses by definition cannot be warned against. Thus, in connection with a claim of inadequate design, instruction, or warning, plaintiff should bear the burden of establishing that the risk in question was known or should have been known to the relevant manufacturing community. The harms that result from unforeseeable risks — for example, in the human body's reaction to a new drug, medical device, or chemical — are not a basis of liability. Of course a seller bears a responsibility to perform reasonable testing prior to marketing a product and to discover risks and risk avoidance measures that such testing should reveal.

King v. E.I. Dupont De Nemours & Co.
996 F.2d 1346 (1st Cir. 1993)

Before BREYER, CHIEF JUDGE, FRIEDMAN, SENIOR CIRCUIT JUDGE, and STAHL, CIRCUIT JUDGE.

FRIEDMAN, SENIOR CIRCUIT JUDGE.

The issue in this case, on appeal from the United States District Court for the District of Maine, 806 F. Supp. 1030 (D.Me. 1992), is whether the Federal Insecticide, Fungicide, and Rodenticide Act (FIFRA), 7 U.S.C. §§136-136y (1988), preempts state tort law claims based upon the alleged failure of the manufacturers of herbicides to provide adequate warning language on the products' labels, which the Environmental Protection Agency (EPA) approved in accordance with FIFRA's requirements. The district court held that FIFRA preempts those state law claims. We affirm.

I

The plaintiffs, King and Higgins (and their wives) filed this diversity tort damage suit against four manufacturers of chemical herbicides. Their second amended complaint alleged that, as part of their duties as employees of the State of Maine, King and Higgins were engaged in the "seasonal spraying of chemical herbicides"; that "[d]uring the chemical spraying operations [they] performed," King and Higgins "were exposed to significant amounts" of specified "chemical products" manufactured by the defendants; and that, "as the direct result of their exposure to the herbicides," King and Higgins have suffered various ailments.

. . . At oral argument, the plaintiffs admitted that the sole basis of their complaint was the defendants' failure to provide adequate warnings.

The parties stipulated that the labels on all the herbicides involved had been submitted to and approved by the EPA, as FIFRA required.

The district court granted the defendants' motion for summary judgment, holding that FIFRA preempted the plaintiffs' claims. The court, following the preemption standards the Supreme Court applied in Cipollone v. Liggett Group, Inc., — U.S. —, 112 S. Ct. 2608, 2617 (1992), held:

> Because the language of FIFRA mandates the preemption of the establishment or enforcement or any common law duty that would impose a labeling requirement inconsistent with those established by the Act, or the EPA's regulations, Plaintiffs' common law failure to warn claims are preempted as a matter of law.

II

A. FIFRA provides a detailed scheme for regulating the content of an herbicide's label. All herbicides sold in the United States must be registered for use by the EPA. The EPA has promulgated comprehensive labeling requirements governing the scope, content, wording and format of herbicide labeling. The manufacturer itself designs and formulates the content of the label, and must file with the EPA a statement which includes "the name of the pesticide," "a complete copy of the labeling of the pesticide, a statement of all claims to be made for it and any directions for its use," and "a full description of the tests made and

the results thereof upon which the claims are based." 7 U.S.C.
§136a(c)(1)(B)-(D).

Section 136v provides in pertinent part:

> (a) In general. A State may regulate the sale or use of any federally regis-
> tered pesticide or device in the State, but only if and to the extent the
> regulation does not permit any sale or use prohibited by this subchapter.
> (b) Uniformity. Such State shall not impose or continue in effect any
> requirements for labeling or packaging in addition to or different from
> those required under this subchapter. Id. §136v.

B. *Cipollone* recently summarized the standards governing preemption analysis:

> The purpose of Congress is the ultimate touchstone of preemption
> analysis. Congress' intent may be explicitly stated in the statute's lan-
> guage or implicitly contained in its structure and purpose. In the absence
> of an express congressional command, state law is pre-empted if that law
> actually conflicts with federal law, or if federal law so thoroughly occupies
> a legislative field as to make reasonable the inference that Congress left
> no room for the States to supplement it.

Cipollone involved similar preemption provisions of the federal statutes governing cigarette labelling and advertising. The suit concerned
a woman who died of lung cancer after smoking for many years. It was a
state tort law diversity suit against the cigarette manufacturers, charging
them with responsibility for her death because, among other things,
"they failed to warn consumers about the hazards of smoking." The
defendants contended that the Federal Cigarette Labelling and Advertising Act (1965 Act) (codified as amended at 15 U.S.C. §§1331-1340
(1988)), and its successor, the Public Health Cigarette Smoking Act
of 1969 (1969 Act), (codified as amended at 15 U.S.C. §§1331-1340),
preempted the claims. Those Acts required health warnings on cigarette packaging, but barred the requirement of such warnings in cigarette advertising.

Section 5 of the 1965 Act, captioned "Preemption," provided in relevant part:

> (b) No statement relating to smoking and health shall be required in
> the advertising of any cigarettes the packages of which are labeled in
> conformity with the provisions of this Act. Federal Cigarette Labelling
> and Advertising Act.

The Court held that this provision "only pre-empted state and federal
rulemaking bodies from mandating particular cautionary statements
and did not pre-empt state law damages actions."

This provision was changed by the 1969 Act to read:

(b) No requirement or prohibition based on smoking and health shall be imposed under State law with respect to the advertising or promotion of any cigarettes the packages of which are labeled in conformity with the provisions of this Act.

The Court held that this provision preempted the plaintiff's state law tort claims based on the defendants' failure to warn of the hazards of cigarette smoking. The Court stated that "[t]he phrase '[n]o requirement or prohibition' sweeps broadly and suggests no distinction between positive enactments and common law; to the contrary, those words easily encompass obligations that take the form of common law rules." It, therefore, "reject[ed] petitioner's argument that the phrase 'requirement or prohibition' limits the 1969 Act's pre-emptive scope to positive enactments by legislatures and agencies." Id. The Court held that "insofar as claims under either failure to warn theory require a showing that respondents' post-1969 advertising or promotions should have included additional, or more clearly stated, warnings, those claims are pre-empted. The Act does not, however, pre-empt petitioner's claims that rely solely on respondents' testing or research practices or other actions unrelated to advertising or promotion." . . .

The Supreme Court itself has indicated that *Cipollone* applies to FIFRA preemption determinations. . . . [T]he Court vacated two courts of appeals judgments that FIFRA impliedly preempted state law failure-to-warn claims and remanded for those courts to reconsider their decisions in light of *Cipollone*.

C. We hold that, in light of *Cipollone*, FIFRA preempts the plaintiffs' state law tort claims based on the defendants' alleged failure to provide adequate warnings about the health hazards of the herbicides they manufactured and sold.

The warnings on the labels of the herbicides King and Higgins used in spraying were approved by the EPA, as FIFRA required. If the plaintiffs could recover on their state law claims that, despite this labeling, the defendants had failed to provide adequate warning, those additional warnings necessarily would be "in addition to or different from those required under this subchapter." 7 U.S.C. §136v(b). The question, therefore, is whether state law liability based upon such defective warning would constitute the "impos[ition]" by the state of "any requirements for labeling or packaging" under section 136v(b). Id.

Cipollone held that the words in the 1969 cigarette statute "'[n]o requirement or prohibition' . . . easily encompass[ed] obligations that take the form of common law rules." The FIFRA language prohibiting the states from "impos[ing] or continu[ing] in effect any requirements," 7 U.S.C. §136v(b), is virtually indistinguishable from the state-imposed "requirement" language that *Cipollone* held preempted the state common law tort claims based on inadequate warning. FIFRA's language, too, preempts the state law lack-of-warning claims involved in this case. . . .

The legislative history of the 1972 amendments to FIFRA, which added section 136v to the statute, supports our conclusion. . . .

Our conclusion accords with the decisions of the three courts of appeals that, since *Cipollone,* have decided the question. . . .

D. The plaintiffs rely on Ferebee v. Chevron Chemical Co., 736 F.2d 1529 (D.C. Cir. 1984). There, the plaintiff became ill and died as a result of his exposure to an herbicide he sprayed. In affirming a jury verdict for the plaintiff, the court held that FIFRA did not preempt the plaintiff's state law tort claims based upon the inadequacy of the warning labels on the herbicide. The court reasoned that "Chevron can comply with both federal and state law by continuing to use the EPA-approved label and by simultaneously paying damages to successful tort plaintiffs such as Mr. Ferebee." Id. at 1541.

In deciding *Ferebee,* the District of Columbia Circuit did not have the benefit of the Supreme Court's subsequent analysis and ruling in *Cipollone.* It is impossible to predict whether, in light of *Cipollone* and the other courts of appeals' decisions discussed above, the District of Columbia Circuit would continue to follow *Ferebee.* In any event, for the reasons set forth in this opinion, we do not find *Ferebee* persuasive.

Affirmed.

NOTE

Preemption in design cases. The question of federal preemption arises not only in warning but also in design cases. The most common dispute is whether a state tort law action is preempted when a particular federal statute or administrative rule gives advance approval to a particular design choice. In Wood v. General Motors Corp., 865 F.2d 395 (1st Cir. 1988), a pre-*Cipollone* case, the court dismissed the plaintiff's claim that the defendant's car was defective because it had not been equipped with a passive restraint system, namely an air bag. The court held that the action was impliedly preempted by the National Traffic and Motor Vehicle Safety Act of 1966, which allowed the Secretary of Transportation to issue safety regulations for active and passive restraint systems. The Secretary's rules, with which GM complied, gave the manufacturer three options: "(1) a passive system for frontal and angular collisions; (2) passive protection from head-on collisions, supplemented by seat-belts and a belt warning system; or (3) lap and shoulder belts, plus a belt warning system." GM had adopted the third alternative. The court held that the comprehensive nature of these regulations precluded any action based on common-law principles alone. "Allowing a common law action holding manufacturers liable for failing to install air bags in motor vehicles would be tantamount to establishing a conflicting safety standard that necessarily encroaches upon the goal of uniformity specifically set forth by Congress in this area." Could *Wood*'s approach be carried over to *Dawson*, supra at page 800?

Unlike *Cipollone*, *Wood* was an implied preemption case that rested on the necessary inconsistency between the federal scheme of regulation and the private right of action. After *Cipollone*, cases of this sort became harder to raise. For example, a preemption claim was rejected in Cleveland v. Piper Aircraft Corp., 985 F.2d 1438, 1446 (10th Cir. 1993), where the jury found that "Piper negligently designed the aircraft without adequate forward vision from the rear seat and negligently failed to provide a rear shoulder harness." Defendant relied on *Wood* to preempt the jury's finding under the Federal Aviation Act, which also explicitly preserves common-law actions. The court rejected defendant's argument that the government's regulations "occupied the field" and thus impliedly preempted state law. In particular, the court noted that the regulations in *Cleveland* did not sanction explicit design choices for the manufacturer. "On the other hand, [t]he requirements cited by Piper do not specify how a manufacturer must ensure visibility. Further, as Piper states, there were no requirements in place on rear seat shoulder harnesses when the FAA certified its approval of the Piper Super Cub."

Shortly thereafter in Myrick v. Freuhauf Corp., 13 F.3d 1516, 1521 (11th Cir. 1994), the court refused to apply an implied preemption analysis under the same National Traffic Safety Act applicable in *Wood*, holding that "the Safety Act does not expressly pre-empt common law liability for a safety defect that is addressed by a safety standard established under the Safety Act." The court held that *Cipollone* effectively eliminated the implied preemption doctrine.

E. PLAINTIFF'S CONDUCT

Daly v. General Motors Corp.
575 P.2d 1162 (Cal. 1978)

RICHARDSON, J. The most important of several problems which we consider is whether the principles of comparative negligence expressed by us in Li v. Yellow Cab Co., apply to actions founded on strict products liability. We will conclude that they do. . . .

[The decedent was driving his Opel southbound on the Harbor Freeway at a speed of between 50 and 70 miles per hour when it struck the metal divider. The car spun around and the decedent was forcibly thrown from the car, sustaining fatal head injuries. The plaintiffs alleged that the door lock was of defective design because of its exposed push button, which, it was claimed, was forced open during the original collision.]

Over plaintiffs' objections, defendants were permitted to introduce evidence indicating that: (1) the Opel was equipped with a seat belt-shoulder harness system, and a door lock, either of which if used, it was contended, would have prevented Daly's ejection from the vehicle; (2) Daly used neither the harness system nor the lock; (3) the 1970 Opel owner's manual contained warnings that seat belts should be worn and doors locked when the car was in motion for "accident security"; and (4) Daly was intoxicated at the time of collision, which evidence the jury was advised was admitted for the limited purpose of determining whether decedent had used the vehicle's safety equipment. After relatively brief deliberations the jury returned a verdict favoring all defendants, and plaintiffs appeal from the ensuing adverse judgment.

STRICT PRODUCTS LIABILITY AND COMPARATIVE FAULT. . . .

Those counseling against the recognition of comparative fault principles in strict products liability cases vigorously stress, perhaps equally, not only the conceptual, but also the semantic difficulties incident to such a course. The task of merging the two concepts is said to be impossible, that "apples and oranges" cannot be compared, that "oil and water" do not mix, and that strict liability, which is not founded on negligence or fault, is inhospitable to comparative principles. The syllogism runs, contributory negligence was only a defense to negligence, comparative negligence only affects contributory negligence, therefore comparative negligence cannot be a defense to strict liability. . . . While fully recognizing the theoretical and semantic distinctions between the twin principles of strict products liability and traditional negligence, we think they can be blended or accommodated.

The inherent difficulty in the "apples and oranges" argument is its insistence on fixed and precise definitional treatment of legal concepts. In the evolving areas of both products liability and tort defenses, however, there has developed much conceptual overlapping and interweaving in order to attain substantial justice. The concept of strict liability itself, as we have noted, arose from dissatisfaction with the wooden formalisms of traditional tort and contract principles in order to protect the consumer of manufactured goods. Similarly, increasing social awareness of its harsh "all or nothing" consequences led us in *Li* to moderate the impact of traditional contributory negligence in order to accomplish a fairer and more balanced result. We acknowledged an intermixing of defenses of contributory negligence and assumption of risk and formally effected a type of merger. . . .

Furthermore, the "apples and oranges" argument may be conceptually suspect. It has been suggested that the term "contributory negligence," one of the vital building blocks upon which much of the argument is based, may indeed itself be a misnomer since it lacks the first element of the classical negligence formula, namely, a duty of care owing to another . . .

We pause at this point to observe that where, as here, a consumer or user sues the manufacturer or designer alone, technically, neither fault nor conduct is really compared functionally. The conduct of one party in combination with the product of another, or perhaps the placing of a defective article in the stream of projected and anticipated use, may produce the ultimate injury. In such a case, as in the situation before us, we think the term "equitable apportionment or allocation of loss" may be more descriptive than "comparative fault."

Given all of the foregoing, we are, in the wake of *Li*, disinclined to resolve the important issue before us by the simple expedient of matching linguistic labels which have evolved either for convenience or by custom. Rather, we consider it more useful to examine the foundational reasons underlying the creation of strict products liability in California to ascertain whether the purposes of the doctrine would be defeated or diluted by adoption of comparative principles. We imposed strict liability against the manufacturer and in favor of the user or consumer in order to relieve injured consumers "from *problems of proof* inherent in pursuing negligence . . . and warranty . . . remedies. . . ." As we have noted, we sought to place the burden of loss on manufacturers rather than ". . . injured persons *who are powerless to protect themselves* . . ." (["*protection of otherwise defenseless victims* of manufacturing defects and the spreading throughout society of the cost of compensating them";] italics added.)

The foregoing goals, we think, will not be frustrated by the adoption of comparative principles. Plaintiffs will continue to be relieved of proving that the manufacturer or distributor was negligent in the production, design, or dissemination of the article in question. Defendant's liability for injuries caused by a defective product remains strict. The principle of protecting the defenseless is likewise preserved, for plaintiff's recovery will be reduced *only* to the extent that his own lack of reasonable care contributed to his injury. The cost of compensating the victim of a defective product, albeit proportionately reduced, remains on defendant manufacturer, and will, through him, be "spread among society." However, we do not permit plaintiff's own conduct relative to the product to escape unexamined, and as to that share of plaintiff's damages which flows from his own fault we discern no reason of policy why it should, following *Li*, be borne by others. Such a result would directly contravene the principle announced in *Li*, that loss should be assessed equitably in proportion to fault.

We conclude, accordingly, that the expressed purposes which persuaded us in the first instance to adopt strict liability in California would not be thwarted were we to apply comparative principles. What would be forfeit is a degree of semantic symmetry. However, in this evolving area of tort law in which new remedies are judicially created, and old defenses judicially merged, impelled by strong considerations of equity and fairness we seek a larger synthesis. If a more just result follows from the expansion of comparative principles, we have no hesitancy in seeking it, mindful always that the fundamental and underlying purpose of *Li* was to promote the equitable allocation of loss among all parties legally responsible in proportion to their fault.

A second objection to the application of comparative principles in strict products liability cases is that a manufacturer's incentive to produce safe products will thereby be reduced or removed. While we fully recognize this concern we think, for several reasons, that the problem is more shadow than substance. First, of course, the manufacturer cannot avoid its continuing liability for a defective product even when the plaintiff's own conduct has contributed to his injury. The manufacturer's liability, and therefore its incentive to avoid and correct product defects, remains; its exposure will be lessened only to the extent that the trier finds that the victim's conduct contributed to his injury. Second, as a practical matter a manufacturer, in a particular case, cannot assume that the user of a defective product upon whom an injury is visited will be blameworthy. Doubtless, many users are free of fault, and a defect is at least as likely as not to be exposed by an entirely innocent plaintiff who will obtain full recovery. In such cases the manufacturer's incentive toward safety both in design and production is wholly unaffected. Finally, we must observe that under the present law, which recognizes assumption of risk as a complete defense to products liability, the curious and cynical message is that it profits the manufacturer to make his product so defective that in the event of injury he can argue that the user had to be aware of its patent defects. To that extent the incentives are inverted. We conclude, accordingly, that no substantial or significant impairment of the safety incentives of defendants will occur by the adoption of comparative principles.

In passing, we note one important and felicitous result if we apply comparative principles to strict products liability. This arises from the fact that under present law when plaintiff sues in negligence his own contributory negligence, however denominated, may diminish but cannot wholly defeat his recovery. When he sues in strict products liability, however, his "assumption of risk" *completely bars* his recovery. Under *Li*, as we have noted, "assumption of risk" is merged into comparative principles. . . . The consequence is that after *Li* in a negligence action, plaintiff's conduct which amounts to "negligent" assumption of risk no longer defeats plaintiff's recovery. Identical conduct, however, in a strict liability case acts as a complete bar under rules heretofore applicable. Thus, strict products liability, which was developed to free injured consumers from the constraints imposed by traditional negligence and warranty theories, places a consumer plaintiff in a worse position than would be the case were his claim founded on simple negligence. This, in turn, rewards adroit pleading and selection of theories. The application of comparative principles to strict liability obviates this bizarre anomaly by treating alike the defenses to both negligence and strict products liability actions. In each instance the defense, if established, will reduce but not bar plaintiff's claim.

A third objection to the merger of strict liability and comparative fault focuses on the claim that, as a practical matter, triers of fact, particularly jurors, cannot assess, measure, or compare plaintiff's negligence with defendant's strict liability. We are unpersuaded by the argument and are convinced that jurors are able to undertake a fair apportionment of liability. . . . [The court then noted that comparative principles had functioned smoothly in the unseaworthiness cases tried in admiralty, even though unseaworthiness is a strict liability concept.]

We find equally unpersuasive a final objection that the merger of the two principles somehow will abolish or adversely affect the liability of such intermediate entities in the chain of distribution as retailers (Vandermark v. Ford Motor Co. . . . and bailors (Price v. Shell Oil Co.) . . . We foresee no such consequence. Regardless of the identity of a particular defendant or of his position in the commercial chain the basis for his liability remains that he has marketed or distributed a defective product. If, as we believe, jurors are capable of assessing fully and fairly the legal responsibility of a manufacturer on a strict liability basis, no reason appears why they cannot do likewise with respect to subsequent distributors and vendors of the product.

We note that the majority of our sister states which have addressed the problem, either by statute or judicial decree, have extended comparative principles to strict products liability.

Our research discloses that of the more than 30 states which have adopted some form of comparative negligence, three (including California) have done so judicially. . . . [The court then noted that its position enjoys considerable academic support, and that the proposed Uniform Comparative Fault Act embraces a comparative fault principle in strict liability actions.]

Having examined the principal objections and finding them not insurmountable, and persuaded by logic, justice, and fundamental fairness, we conclude that a system of comparative fault should be and it is hereby extended to actions founded on strict products liability. In such cases the separate defense of "assumption of risk," to the extent that it is a form of contributory negligence, is abolished. While, as we have suggested, on the particular facts before us, the term "equitable apportionment of loss" is more accurately descriptive of the process, nonetheless, the term "comparative fault" has gained such wide acceptance by courts and in the literature that we adopt its use herein.

. . . We reiterate that our reason for extending a full system of comparative fault to strict products liability is because it is fair to do so. The law consistently seeks to elevate justice and equity above the exact contours of a mathematical equation. We are convinced that in merging the two principles what may be lost in symmetry is more than gained in fundamental fairness.

RETROACTIVITY

. . . We conclude that, for reasons of public policy and the reasonable expectations of the parties to this action and litigants generally, the principles herein expressed shall apply to all cases in which trial has not begun before the date this opinion becomes final in this court. . . .

JEFFERSON, J. concurring and dissenting. . . . What the majority envisions as a fair apportionment of liability to be undertaken by the jury will constitute nothing more than an *unfair reduction* in the plaintiff's total damages suffered, resulting from a jury process that necessarily is predicated on speculation, conjecture and guesswork. . . .

BIRD, C.J., concurs.

MOSK, J., dissenting. I dissent.

This will be remembered as the dark day when this court, which heroically took the lead in originating the doctrine of products liability (Greenman v. Yuba Power Products, Inc.) and steadfastly resisted efforts to inject concepts of negligence into the newly designed tort (Cronin v. J. B. E. Olson Corp.), inexplicably turned 180 degrees and beat a hasty retreat almost back to square one. The pure concept of products liability so pridefully fashioned and nurtured by this court for the past decade and a half is reduced to a shambles.

The majority inject a foreign object — the tort of negligence — into the tort of products liability by the simple expedient of calling negligence something else: on some pages their opinion speaks of "comparative fault," on others reference is to "comparative principles," and elsewhere the term "equitable apportionment" is employed, although this is clearly not a proceeding in equity. But a rose is a rose and negligence is negligence; thus the majority find that despite semantic camouflage they must rely on Li v. Yellow Cab Co., even though *Li* is purely and simply a negligence case which merely rejects contributory negligence and substitutes therefor comparative negligence.

. . . [I]n *Cronin* we stressed that "the very purpose of our pioneering efforts in this field was to relieve the plaintiff from problems of proof inherent in pursuing negligence." And in Luque v. McLean, 501 P.2d

1163 (Cal. 1972), this court unanimously declared that "contributory negligence does not bar recovery in a strict liability action." . . .

The bench and bar have abided by this elementary rule. They have learned to avoid injecting negligence — whether of the defendant or the plaintiff — into a products liability case. And they have understood the reason behind the distinction between negligence of any party and products liability. It was expressed over three decades ago by Justice Traynor in his concurring opinion in Escola v. Coca-Cola Bottling Co. [supra at page 741]. . . .

Transferring the liability, or part of the liability, from the party responsible for putting the article in the stream of commerce to the consumer is precisely what the majority propose to do. They do this by employing a euphemism: the victim's recovery is to be "proportionately reduced." The result, however delicately described, is to dilute the defect of the article by elevating the conduct of the wounded consumer to an issue of equal significance. We can be as certain as tomorrow's daylight that every defendant charged with marketing a defective product will hereafter assert that the injured plaintiff did something, anything, that conceivably could be deemed contributorily negligent: he drove the vehicle with a defective steering mechanism 56 miles an hour instead of 54; or he should have discovered a latent defect hidden in the machinery; or perhaps he should not have succumbed to the salesman's persuasion and purchased the defective object in the first instance. I need no crystal ball to foresee that the pleading of affirmative defenses alleging contributory negligence — or the currently approved substitute terminology — will now become boilerplate. . . .

The defective product is comparable to a time bomb ready to explode; it maims its victims indiscriminately, the righteous and the evil, the careful and the careless. Thus when a faulty design or otherwise defective product is involved, the litigation should not be diverted to consideration of the negligence of the plaintiff. The liability issues are simple: was the product or its design faulty, did the defendant inject the defective product into the stream of commerce, and did the defect cause the injury? The conduct of the ultimate consumer-victim who used the product in the contemplated or foreseeable manner is wholly irrelevant to those issues.

The majority devote considerable effort to rationalizing what has been described as a mixture of apples and oranges. Their point might be persuasive if there were some authority recognizing a defense of contributory products liability, for which they are now substituting comparative products liability. However, all our research to discover such apples and oranges has been fruitless. The conclusion is inescapable that the majority, in avoiding approval of comparative negligence in name as a defense to products liability, are thereby originating a new defense that can only be described as comparative products liability.

We may now anticipate similar defenses in the vast number of other tort actions. Can comparative libel, comparative slander of title, comparative wrongful litigation, comparative nuisance, comparative fraud, be far behind? By whatever name, negligence, heretofore just one subtopic in the elaborate spectrum of torts — which require six volumes and appendices of the Restatement Second of Torts to cover — now seems destined to envelop the entire tort field. . . .

The majority note one "felicitous result" of adopting comparative negligence to products liability: the merger of assumption of risk — which they term a "bizarre anomaly" — into their innovative defense. I find that result neither felicitous nor tenable. In Barker v. Lull Engineering Co., we defined a defective product as one which failed to perform safely when used in an intended or foreseeable manner. If a consumer elects to use a product patently defective when other alternatives are available, or to use a product in a manner clearly not intended or foreseeable, he assumes the risks inherent in his improper utilization and should not be heard to complain about the condition of the object. One who employs a power saw to trim his fingernails — and thereafter finds the number of his fingers reduced — should not prevail to any extent whatever against the manufacturer even if the saw had a defective blade. I would retain assumption of risk as a total defense to products liability, as it always has been.

The majority deny their opinion diminishes the therapeutic effect of products liability upon producers of defective products. It seems self-evident that procedures which evaluate the injured consumer's conduct in each instance, and thus eliminate or reduce the award against the producer or distributor of a defective product, are not designed as an effective incentive to maximum responsibility to consumers. The converse is more accurate: the motivation to avoid polluting the stream of commerce with defective products increases in direct relation to the size of potential damage awards. . . .

I would affirm the judgment.

Rehearing denied. BIRD, C.J., and MOSK, J., dissenting.

NOTES

1. *Contributory negligence in products cases.* Is there any reason why contributory negligence should not be a defense in products liability cases if it is allowed in other types of actions? In particular, what should happen if a bystander sues the driver on an ordinary negligence theory and the car manufacturer on a products liability theory?

While a majority of states today follow the rule in *Daly,* some cases have refused to allow any defense of contributory negligence. For example, in Melia v. Ford Motor Co., 534 F.2d 795 (8th Cir. 1976), the decedent was killed in an intersection collision when she was thrown through the unlocked door on the driver's side of the car. The court first held that it was a jury question whether the design of the door assembly was defective. It then refused to admit evidence on any of the three assignments of contributory negligence raised by the defendant: (1) entering the intersection through a red light, (2) driving with the door unlocked, (3) not using the seat belt. The court stated that "application of the Nebraska comparative negligence statute would, under the language of the statute, be extremely confusing and inappropriate in a strict liability case," and added that it would apply the statute only when the plaintiff's negligence was "slight" in comparison with the defendant's. Note that in state court the plaintiff's contributory negligence had barred her cause of action against the other driver. Melia v. Svoboda, 214 N.W.2d 476 (Neb. 1974).

The proposed Restatement Third of Torts, section 7 and comment *d* sides with the majority on this question to provide that whatever rules apportion damages between plaintiffs and defendants in other cases should carry over to product liability actions. In its view, "all forms of plaintiff's failure to conform to applicable standards of care should be presented to the trier of fact for the purpose of apportionment of liability between the plaintiff and the product seller." It thus took issue with the second Restatement's comment *n* and such cases as Star Furniture Co. v. Pulaski Furniture Co., 297 S.E.2d 854, 863 (W. Va. 1982): "We therefore hold that comparative negligence is available as an affirmative defense in a cause of action founded on strict liability so long as the complained of conduct is not a failure to discover a defect or to guard against it." Proposed comment *d* does suggest, however, that in these latter cases "a trier of fact may decide to allocate little or no responsibility to the plaintiff."

2. Assumption of risk in products cases. As Mosk, J., indicates in his *Daly* dissent, assumption of risk offers a second line of defense in product liability cases. In practice this defense is closely allied with the open and obvious defect question, supra at page 786. Recall that *Micallef* adopted the dominant position by collapsing this form of assumption of risk into contributory negligence when it held that "the openness and obviousness of the danger should be available to the defendant on the issue of whether plaintiff exercised that degree of reasonable care as was required under the circumstances."

In practice the products liability cases have generally given the defense of assumption of risk the same narrow construction that it receives in other areas. In Messick v. General Motors, 460 F.2d 485 (5th Cir. 1972), plaintiff continued to drive his new car, manufactured by defendant, after experiencing trouble with the steering mechanism and the suspension system and after he had repeatedly had mechanics attempt to fix the trouble. In a single-car accident, the car went off the road because of these defects. The court affirmed the judgment below over defendant's demand for a directed verdict. Plaintiff's continued use of the car was not "both voluntary and unreasonable" given that he needed to use the car to earn his living and drove approximately 1,000 miles each week. Why not require the plaintiff to obtain alternative transportation and allow him to charge the defendant for its cost?

In Runnings v. Ford Motor Co., 461 F.2d 1145 (9th Cir. 1972), plaintiff was seriously scalded by steam and boiling water when he attempted to remove the radiator cap on the Econoline van made by defendant. On this model the engine and the radiator were placed inside the cab under a removable hood between the driver's and passenger's seats. The cap could be removed from the inside or by reaching in from the outside. After pouring cold water on the engine to cool it, plaintiff began slowly to remove the cap while inside the cab. The cap suddenly exploded, blowing straight up and shooting steam up against the top of the cab. On contact with the ceiling of the cab, the steam condensed, and boiling water fell on plaintiff, causing his injuries. Plaintiff was aware of how an ordinary radiator cap operated and of the risk of steam and hot water escaping. The court held he could not be said to have assumed the risk in this instance, since it was not shown that he was aware of the specific hazard involved — that the steam would turn to scalding water upon contact with the ceiling. See Twerski, Old Wine in a New Flask — Restructuring Assumption of Risk in the Products Liability Area, 60 Iowa L. Rev. 1 (1974).

3. Plaintiff's misuse of defendant's product. Quite possibly, the most important development in the law of products liability is the radical transformation in judicial attitudes towards plaintiff's misuse of defendant's product, an issue that arises in almost all work-related products liability suits and in many consumer cases as well. Whereas Traynor's opinion in *Escola* contemplated plaintiff's recovery only when plaintiff made "normal and proper use" of the defendant's product, the more recent cases frequently take the line that a plaintiff who makes a "foreseeable misuse" of a product is entitled to the same protection as those who do not, thereby removing from products liability defenses not only plaintiff's failure to discover latent defects in the defendant's products but also active negligence or, arguably, willful misuse of the product.

This approach to the misuse defense is well illustrated by LeBouef v. Goodyear Tire & Rubber Co., 623 F.2d 985, 989 (5th Cir. 1980). The decedent purchased "a new, 1976 Mercury Cougar equipped with a 460 cubic-inch, 425 horsepower engine, and with Goodyear HER78-15 Custom Polysteel Radial Tires." The car was capable of going 100 miles per hour, but the tires had been tested for safety by Goodyear only for speeds of 85 mph. Ford's only warning was "a statement in the Cougar owner's manual that '[c]ontinuous driving over 90 mph requires using high-speed-capability tires'; the manual did not state whether the tires in question were or were not of high-speed-caliber." The decedent was killed when the car veered off the road while being driven at speeds of 100 to 105 mph. Blood tests showed the decedent had been intoxicated. The trial court, sitting without a jury, found that the tire had not been defectively constructed. It nonetheless allowed recovery because of the insufficient warnings about the risk of tread separation at high speeds. It also found that "while Leleux's [the decedent's] excessive speed was a contributory cause of the accident, his intoxication was not." It also rejected the contributory negligence and assumption of risk defenses. On appeal, the decision was affirmed, and the court had this to say about the misuse defense:

> Certainly the operation of the Cougar in excess of 100 miles per hour was not "normal" in the sense of being a routine or intended use. "Normal use," however, is a term of art in the parlance of Louisiana products liability law, delineating the scope of a manufacturer's duty and consequent liability; it encompasses all *reasonably foreseeable* uses of a product. . . . The sports car involved here was marketed with an intended and recognized appeal to youthful drivers. The 425 horsepower engine with which Ford had equipped it provided a capability of speeds over 100 miles per hour, and the car's allure, no doubt exploited in its marketing, lay in no small measure in this power and potential speed. It was not simply foreseeable, but was to be readily expected, that the Cougar would, on occasion, be driven in excess of the 85 miles per hour proven maximum safe operating speed of its Goodyear tires. Consequently, Ford cannot, on the basis of abnormal use, escape its duty either to provide an adequate warning of the specific danger of tread separation at such high speeds or to ameliorate the danger in some other way.

The foreseeable misuse standard has been criticized as creating a "moral hazard" problem by increasing the probability that accident will occur. In addition, foreseeable misuse creates an implicit transfer of wealth from careful to careless drivers, a point perceived long ago in Huset v. J. I. Case, supra at page 732. The transfer arises because the manufacturer cannot differentiate in price charged between a retiree and a travelling salesman, or between the careful driver who has never had a ticket and the teenaged hot-rodder. See Epstein, Products Liability as an Insurance Market, 14 J. Legal Stud. 645 (1985), noting that first-party insurance routinely makes risk classifications that cannot be made when tort insurance is tied to the sale of a product. Should the law expand the role of the misuse defense in a comparative negligence regime?

4. *Contractual defenses to product liability actions.* In many settings express assumption of risk by contract is a complete defense to a tort action. One question is whether product sellers should be able, directly or through intermediaries, to contract out their liability with potential product users. The contract regime could redefine product defect, cap

damages, or eliminate liability altogether. That approach has been uniformly rejected by the courts and it receives a very chilly reception in the proposed Third Restatement of Torts, section 8 which categorically states: "Disclaimers and limitations of remedies by product sellers, waivers by product purchasers, and other similar contractual exculpations, oral or written, do not bar or reduce otherwise valid products liability claims for harm to persons." The explanation for this sweeping prohibition is found in comment *a:* "It is presumed that the plaintiff lacked sufficient information, bargaining power or bargaining position necessary to execute a fair contractual limitation of rights to recover." The rule does not apply to cases of purely economic loss. How would the rest of this chapter have to be written if the contractual waivers were freely accepted in all cases of physical injury or property damages?

Chapter Ten
Damages

Sullivan v. Old Colony Street Ry.
83 N.E. 1091, 1092 (Mass. 1908)

Rugg, C.J. The rule of damages is a practical instrumentality for the administration of justice. The principle on which it is founded is compensation. Its object is to afford the equivalent in money for the actual loss caused by the wrong of another. Recurrence to this fundamental conception tests the soundness of claims for the inclusion of new elements of damage.

Zibbell v. Southern Pacific Co.
116 P. 513, 520 (Cal. 1911)

Henshaw, J. No rational being would change places with the injured man for an amount of gold that would fill the room of the court, yet no lawyer would contend that such is the legal measure of damages.

A. INTRODUCTION

Proof of damages is an essential element of the plaintiff's case in most civil litigation. When liability is clear, both sides will judge their success by the size of the verdict, so that a high damage award may count as a major victory for the plaintiff and a low one as a major defeat. In this day of potential million-dollar verdicts, virtually every major case has the damage element as one of its key components, and it is quite commonplace for both sides to have medical and economic experts testify on three critical elements: pain and suffering, medical expenses, and lost earnings attributable to the accident. For each of these three heads of damages, a jury must take into account both past and future losses. Though substantial concrete evidence may be available for past losses, for future losses only estimates are available, estimates that in cases of permanent injury verge on guesswork.

In working through the complicated rules of damages, it is important not to lose sight of their essential function within the tort system. Within a system of corrective justice, the object of the tort rules is, as Rugg, C.J., suggests, to place the plaintiff in the position that he would have enjoyed if the tort had never been committed. Though money may never be an adequate substitute for irreparable injury, it is better than nothing at all. Damages are also crucial to the deterrence function of tort law because they function as the set of "prices" the defendant must pay for engaging in certain kinds of activities. Damage awards that are too low may induce overinvestment in socially costly activities, by excusing potential defendants from bearing part of the costs they create. Yet damage awards that are too high could induce potential defendants *not* to engage in activities that promise great benefits, either to the individual plaintiff (as in medical situations) or to society at large. To be sure, too much can be made of the deterrent and control function of damages, since a whole host of other sanctions — injunctions, licenses, inspections, and fines — serve to curb harmful behavior. But even with these in place, the tort remedy remains a critical element in our system of social control.

There are a number of other important issues closely associated with the law of damages. In the typical tort action today the plaintiff's lawyer receives compensation in the form of a contingency fee taken out of the plaintiff's damage recovery if the suit is successful. To what extent should damage awards be adjusted to reflect the fees paid third parties? There is also the recurring question of whether the plaintiff, after the tort is completed, is under a duty to mitigate the damages sustained. Next, there is the question of whether the plaintiff's successful award should be reduced by payments received from a so-called collateral source, such as a first-party health plan. Finally, there is the question of the special rules governing the loss of consortium, wrongful death, and — with great importance and constitutional overtones — punitive damages.

B. RECOVERABLE ELEMENTS OF DAMAGES

1. Pain and Suffering

McDougald v. Garber
536 N.E.2d 372 (N.Y. 1989)

WACHTLER, CHIEF JUDGE. This appeal raises fundamental questions about the nature and role of nonpecuniary damages in personal injury litigation. By nonpecuniary damages, we mean those damages awarded to compensate an injured person for the physical and emotional consequences of the injury, such as pain and suffering and the loss of the ability to engage in certain activities. Pecuniary damages, on the other hand, compensate the victim for the economic consequences of the injury, such as medical expenses, lost earnings and the cost of custodial care.

The specific questions raised here deal with assessment of nonpecuniary damages and are (1) whether some degree of cognitive awareness is a prerequisite to recovery for loss of enjoyment of life and (2) whether a jury should be instructed to consider and award damages for loss of enjoyment of life separately from damages for pain and suffering. We answer the first question in the affirmative and the second question in the negative.

I

On September 7, 1978, plaintiff Emma McDougald, then 31 years old, underwent a Caesarean section and tubal ligation at New York Infirmary. Defendant Garber performed the surgery; defendants Armengol and Kulkarni provided anesthesia. During the surgery, Mrs. McDougald suffered oxygen deprivation which resulted in severe brain damage and left her in a permanent comatose condition. This action was brought by Mrs. McDougald and her husband, suing derivatively, alleging that the injuries were caused by the defendants' acts of malpractice.

A jury found all defendants liable and awarded Emma McDougald a total of $9,650,102 in damages, including $1,000,000 for conscious pain and suffering and a separate award of $3,500,000 for loss of the pleasures and pursuits of life. The balance of the damages awarded to her were for pecuniary damages — lost earnings and the cost of custodial and nursing care. Her husband was awarded $1,500,000 on his derivative claim for the loss of his wife's services. On defendants' posttrial motions, the Trial Judge reduced the total award to Emma McDougald to $4,796,728 by striking the entire award for future nursing care

($2,353,374) and by reducing the separate awards for conscious pain and suffering and loss of the pleasures and pursuits of life to a single award of $2,000,000. Her husband's award was left intact. On cross appeals, the Appellate Division affirmed and later granted defendants leave to appeal to this court.

II

We note at the outset that the defendants' liability for Emma McDougald's injuries is unchallenged here.

Also unchallenged are the awards in the amount of $770,978 for loss of earnings and $2,025,750 for future custodial care — that is, the pecuniary damage awards that survived defendants' posttrial motions.

What remains in dispute, primarily, is the award to Emma McDougald for nonpecuniary damages. At trial, defendants sought to show that Mrs. McDougald's injuries were so severe that she was incapable of either experiencing pain or appreciating her condition. Plaintiffs, on the other hand, introduced proof that Mrs. McDougald responded to certain stimuli to a sufficient extent to indicate that she was aware of her circumstances. Thus, the extent of Mrs. McDougald's cognitive abilities, if any, was sharply disputed.

The parties and the trial court agreed that Mrs. McDougald could not recover for pain and suffering unless she were conscious of the pain. Defendants maintained that such consciousness was also required to support an award for loss of enjoyment of life. The court, however, accepted plaintiffs' view that loss of enjoyment of life was compensable without regard to whether the plaintiff was aware of the loss. Accordingly, because the level of Mrs. McDougald's cognitive abilities was in dispute, the court instructed the jury to consider loss of enjoyment of life as an element of nonpecuniary damages separate from pain and suffering. . . .

We conclude that the court erred, both in instructing the jury that Mrs. McDougald's awareness was irrelevant to their consideration of damages for loss of enjoyment of life and in directing the jury to consider that aspect of damages separately from pain and suffering.

III

We begin with the familiar proposition that an award of damages to a person injured by the negligence of another is to compensate the victim, not to punish the wrongdoer. The goal is to restore the injured party, to the extent possible, to the position that would have been occupied had the wrong not occurred. To be sure, placing the burden of compensation on the negligent party also serves as a deterrent, but purely punitive damages — that is, those which have no compensatory purpose — are prohibited unless the harmful conduct is intentional, malicious, outrageous, or otherwise aggravated beyond mere negligence.

Damages for nonpecuniary losses are, of course, among those that can be awarded as compensation to the victim. This aspect of damages, however, stands on less certain ground than does an award for pecuniary damages. An economic loss can be compensated in kind by an economic gain; but recovery for noneconomic losses such as pain and suffering and loss of enjoyment of life rests on "the legal fiction that money damages can compensate for a victim's injury." We accept this fiction, knowing that although money will neither ease the pain nor restore the victim's abilities, this device is as close as the law can come in its effort to right the wrong. We have no hope of evaluating what has been lost, but a monetary award may provide a measure of solace for the condition created.

Our willingness to indulge this fiction comes to an end, however, when it ceases to serve the compensatory goals of tort recovery. When that limit is met, further indulgence can only result in assessing damages that are punitive. The question posed by this case, then, is whether an award of damages for loss of enjoyment of life to a person whose injuries preclude any awareness of the loss serves a compensatory purpose. We conclude that it does not.

Simply put, an award of money damages in such circumstances has no meaning or utility to the injured person. An award for the loss of enjoyment of life "cannot provide [such a victim] with any consolation or ease any burden resting on him . . . He cannot spend it upon necessities or pleasures. He cannot experience the pleasure of giving it away." (*Flannery v. United States*, 4th Cir., 718 F.2d 108, 111.)

We recognize that, as the trial court noted, requiring some cognitive awareness as a prerequisite to recovery for loss of enjoyment of life will result in some cases "in the paradoxical situation that the greater the degree of brain injury inflicted by a negligent defendant, the smaller the award the plaintiff can recover in general damages." The force of this argument, however — the temptation to achieve a balance between injury and damages — has nothing to do with meaningful compensation for the victim. Instead, the temptation is rooted in a desire to punish the defendant in proportion to the harm inflicted. However relevant such retributive symmetry may be in the criminal law, it has no place in the law of civil damages, at least in the absence of culpability beyond mere negligence.

Accordingly, we conclude that cognitive awareness is a prerequisite to recovery for loss of enjoyment of life. We do not go so far, however, as to require the fact finder to sort out varying degrees of cognition and determine at what level a particular deprivation can be fully appreciated. With respect to pain and suffering, the trial court charged simply that there must be "some level of awareness" in order for plaintiff to recover. We think that this is an appropriate standard for all aspects of nonpecuniary loss. No doubt the standard ignores analytically relevant levels of cognition, but we resist the desire for analytical purity in favor of simplicity. A more complex instruction might give the appearance of greater precision but, given the limits of our understanding of the human mind, it would in reality lead only to greater speculation.

We turn next to the question whether loss of enjoyment of life should be considered a category of damages separate from pain and suffering.

IV

There is no dispute here that the fact finder may, in assessing nonpecuniary damages, consider the effect of the injuries on the plaintiff's capacity to lead a normal life. [The court then reviewed movement, within and outside New York, to treat loss of enjoyment as a separate category, in part to facilitate the appellate review of damage awards.]

We do not dispute that distinctions can be found or created between the concepts of pain and suffering and loss of enjoyment of life. If the term "suffering" is limited to the emotional response to the sensation of pain, then the emotional response caused by the limitation of life's activities may be considered qualitatively different. But suffering need not be so limited — it can easily encompass the frustration and anguish caused by the inability to participate in activities that once brought pleasure. Traditionally, by treating loss of enjoyment of life as a permissible factor in assessing pain and suffering, courts have given the term this broad meaning.

If we are to depart from this traditional approach and approve a separate award for loss of enjoyment of life, it must be on the basis that such an approach will yield a more accurate evaluation of the compensation due to the plaintiff. We have no doubt that, in general, the total award for nonpecuniary damages would increase if we adopted the rule. That separate awards are advocated by plaintiffs and resisted by defendants is sufficient evidence that larger awards are at stake here. But a larger award does not by itself indicate that the goal of compensation has been better served.

The advocates of separate awards contend that because pain and suffering and loss of enjoyment of life can be distinguished, they must be treated separately if the plaintiff is to be compensated fully for each distinct injury suffered. We disagree. Such an analytical approach may have its place when the subject is pecuniary damages, which can be calculated with some precision. But the estimation of nonpecuniary damages is not amenable to such analytical precision and may, in fact, suffer from its application. Translating human suffering into dollars and cents involves no mathematical formula; it rests, as we have said, on a legal fiction. The figure that emerges is unavoidably distorted by the translation. Application of this murky process to the component parts of nonpecuniary injuries (however analytically distinguishable they may be) cannot make it more accurate. If anything, the distortion will be amplified by repetition.

Thus, we are not persuaded that any salutary purpose would be served by having the jury make separate awards for pain and suffering and loss of enjoyment of life. We are confident, furthermore, that the trial advocate's art is a sufficient guarantee that none of the plaintiff's losses will be ignored by the jury.

The errors in the instructions given to the jury require a new trial on the issue of nonpecuniary damages to be awarded to plaintiff Emma McDougald. . . .

TITONE, JUDGE (dissenting).

The majority's holding represents a compromise position that neither comports with the fundamental principles of tort compensation nor furnishes a satisfactory, logically consistent framework for compensating nonpecuniary loss. Because I conclude that loss of enjoyment of life is an objective damage item, conceptually distinct from conscious pain and suffering, I can find no fault with the trial court's instruction authorizing separate awards and permitting an award for "loss of enjoyment of life" even in the absence of any awareness of that loss on the part of the injured plaintiff. Accordingly, I dissent. . . .

Unquestionably, recovery of a damage item such as "pain and suffering" requires a showing of some degree of cognitive capacity. Such a requirement exists for the simple reason that pain and suffering are wholly subjective concepts and cannot exist separate and apart from the human consciousness that experiences them. In contrast, the destruction of an individual's capacity to enjoy life as a result of a crippling injury is an objective fact that does not differ in principle from the permanent loss of an eye or limb. As in the case of a lost limb, an essential characteristic of a healthy human life has been wrongfully taken, and, consequently, the injured party is entitled to a monetary award as a substitute, if, as the majority asserts, the goal of tort compensation is "to restore the injured party, to the extent possible, to the position that would have been occupied had the wrong not occurred." . . .

Moreover, the compensatory nature of a monetary award for loss of enjoyment of life is not altered or rendered punitive by the fact that the unaware injured plaintiff cannot experience the pleasure of having it. The fundamental distinction between punitive and compensatory damages is that the former exceed the amount necessary to replace what the plaintiff lost. . . .

SIMONS, KAYE, HANCOCK and BELLACOSA, JJ., concur with WACHTLER, C.J.

TITONE, J., dissents and votes to affirm in a separate opinion in which ALEXANDER, J., concurs.

NOTES

1. Recovery for pain and suffering. In *McDougald* both the majority and dissent agreed that recovery for pain and suffering is appropriate in tort actions. In the usual case, the elements of pain and suffering include worry, anguish, and grief, all notoriously difficult to quantify. The common rule has therefore been subject to a fair bit of academic criticism, the most famous attack being that of Professor Jaffe in his Damages for Personal Injury: The Impact of Insurance, 18 Law & Contemp. Probs. 219, 224-225 (1953):

> But why we may ask *should* the plaintiff be compensated in money for an experience which involves no financial loss? It cannot be on the principle of returning what is his own. Essentially that principle rests on an economic foundation: on maintaining the integrity of the economic arrangements which provide the normally expectable basis for livelihood in our society. Pain is a harm, an "injury," but neither past pain nor its compensation has any consistent economic significance. The past experience is not a loss except in so far as it produced present deterioration. It will be said, however, that these arguments betray a limited, a Philistine view of the law's concern, one that the law has happily transcended. This objection mistakes the argument. Of course the law is concerned, and properly so, with other than economic interests. The criminal law and the tort law *in so far as punitive* (that is to say in so far as the conduct of the plaintiff warrants punishment) is much concerned with the protection of non-economic interests; and to punishment may be added judicial remedies of a preventive character such as the injunction against nuisances, invasions of privacy, etc., and legislative devices such as zoning.
>
> I am aware, however, that though the premise may elude detection, some deep intuition may claim to validate this process of evaluating the imponderable. One who has suffered a violation of his bodily integrity may feel a sense of continuing outrage. This is particularly true where there has been disfigurement or loss of a member (even though not giving rise to economic loss). Because our society sets a high value on money; it uses money or price as a means of recognizing the worth of non-economic as well as economic goods. If, insists the plaintiff, society really values my personality, my bodily integrity, it will signify its sincerity by paying me a sum of money. Damages thus may somewhat reestablish the plaintiff's self-confidence, wipe out his sense of outrage. Furthermore, though money is not an equivalent it may be a consolation, a solatium. These arguments, however, are most valid for disfigurements or loss of member giving rise to a continuing sense of injury. (And in such

cases there may be potential economic injury which cannot be established.) It is doubtful that past pain figures strongly as present outrage. And even granting these arguments there must be set over against them arbitrary indeterminateness of the evaluation. Insurance aside, it is doubtful justice seriously to embarrass a defendant, though negligent, by real economic loss in order to do honor to plaintiff's experience of pain. And insurance present, it is doubtful that the pooled social fund of savings should be charged with sums of indeterminate amount when compensation performs no specific economic function. This consideration becomes the stronger as year after year the amounts set aside for the security account become a larger proportion of the national income.

It is not supposed, however, that even were the reasons of the best — and mine I am sure will fail to satisfy many — the courts will forthwith deny the right of the plaintiff to have these intangibles valued. But putting aside for the moment their bearing on legislation, I would suggest that they are not irrelevant to the judicial creation of new remedies and new items of damage nor to the judicial administration of present items of damage.

Even if it is impossible to make an exact evaluation of the value of pain and suffering, does it follow that it should be assigned a zero value under the tort law, regardless of whether insurance is involved? Is the zero figure equal to the amount that the plaintiff would pay to be rid of the pain? That the defendant would pay in order to remain free of it? Should it make any difference if, as has been suggested, most people when asked in surveys say they are against compensation for pain and suffering?

2. *The "per diem" rule.* Pain and suffering, while an accepted head of damages, has no market value, and thus is enormously difficult to measure. One ingenious suggestion about how to argue pain and suffering to the jury was first advanced by Melvin Belli in a speech to the Mississippi Bar Association on June 2, 1951, later published as M. Belli, The Use of Demonstrative Evidence in Achieving the More Adequate Award, 33-35 (1952).

> This is the key: You must break up the 30-year life expectancy into *finite* detailed periods of time. You must take these small periods of time, seconds and minutes, and determine in dollars and cents what each period is worth. You must start with the seconds and minutes rather than at the other end of thirty years. You cannot stand in front of a jury and say, "Here is a man horribly injured, permanently disabled, who will suffer excruciating pain for the rest of his life, he is entitled to a verdict of $225,000."
>
> You must start at the beginning and show that pain is a continuous thing, second by second, minute by minute, hour by hour, year after year for thirty years. You must interpret one second, one minute, one hour, one year of pain and suffering into dollars and cents and then multiply to your absolute figure to show how you have achieved your result of an award approaching adequacy at $225,000. If you throw a novel figure at a jury or an appellate court of $225,000, without breaking it down, you

are going to frighten both your trier of facts and your reviewer of facts. . . .

When you break down pain and suffering into seconds and minutes and look at it as objectively as this, then you begin to make a jury realize what permanent pain and suffering is and that $60,000 at five dollars a day isn't an adequate award.

As might be expected, the propriety of Belli's argument has been much debated in the appellate opinions. The first leading decision prohibiting the use of the per diem argument was Botta v. Brunner, 138 A.2d 713 (N.J. 1958). Today, however, a majority of the jurisdictions that have considered the matter allow the per diem argument to be made to the jury, subject to a cautionary instruction that the per diem approach is argument, not evidence. See, e.g., Vanskike v. ACF Industries, Inc., 665 F.2d 188 (8th Cir. 1981).

3. *Scheduled damages.* Whatever techniques are used at trial, pain and suffering damages account for much of the enormous variation in the level of awards made to individuals whose conditions are rated as having roughly the same level of severity. The situation is set out in Bovbjerg, Sloan and Blumstein, Valuing Life and Limb in Tort: Scheduling "Pain and Suffering," 83 Nw. U.L. Rev. 908, 923-924 (1989):

> Within an individual severity level, the highest valuation can be scores of times larger than the lowest. Awards for the most serious permanent injuries . . . range in value from a low of $147,000 to a high of $18,100,000. Even considering only the spread between the top and bottom quartiles, the range is great. All the awards in the top 25% of [permanent significant injury cases, such as deafness, loss of limb, loss of eye, or loss of one kidney or lung], for example, are at least six times larger than any of the bottom 25%; the ranges are even larger for lower severity cases. Very large awards are also disproportionately present; the distributions skew to the high end of values, as mean values always far exceed medians. Much of this variation may legitimately reflect claimants' precise individual circumstances, as the tort system intends. [These figures do] not, for instance, control for the age of the claimant, a factor that strongly influences duration of permanent injury. Nor does it control for pre-injury earnings, or the amount of medical care received. Including many other factors in a multiple regression analysis in addition to severity as valuation predictors helps explain some of the differences in awards within individual severity categories. It is not possible to fully and objectively adjust for other circumstances that plausibly influence a jury's valuation, such as the subjective nature of how an injury occurred. No amount of adjusting, however, is likely to fully account for the extreme values. For example, a range of $147,000 to $18,100,000 for awards in compensation for quadriplegia and other injuries requiring lifelong care . . . is inexplicably wide by any standard.

What if compromise verdicts are involved?

In order to control for this abuse, the authors suggest that courts "scheduled" amounts of damages for pain and suffering and other forms of noneconomic loss. One possibility is to establish a matrix that classifies injuries by severity and age. Still another gives a jury the range of awards based on past experience in similar cases to serve as nonbinding benchmarks for recovery. The third approach uses a set of floors and ceilings by which to constrain awards.

Scheduled damages in workers' compensation systems typically make no independent allowance for pain and suffering damages. The same result generally holds for no-fault automobile insurance plans used in many states to supplement the tort system. Elimination of damages for pain and suffering is often found in various first-party insurance schemes, including Social Security Disability Income as well as Medicare and Medicaid. These omissions have been treated as evidence that under an optimal system of compensation injured parties are not in general willing to pay before an accident for recovery for pain and suffering after it occurs. See Danzon, Tort Reform and the Role of Government in Private Insurance Markets, 13 J. Legal Stud. 517 (1984).

4. Fair compensation. There are important theoretical reasons why fully informed persons in a voluntary market might wish to limit the total amount of damages (and hence damages for pain and suffering) that are recoverable after an occurrence of any accident. The basic theoretical insight is developed in Friedman, What Is 'Fair Compensation' For Death or Injury?, 2 Int'l Rev. of Law and Econ. 81, 82 (1982):

> [The basic way of putting the point] is to say that bodily injury makes the victim worse off in two ways. It lowers his effective income by reducing his earning power and imposing costs (a seeing eye dog, hospital bills, etc.). In addition it lowers the value to him of any given income by eliminating the ways in which he can spend it. Death is the extreme case; not only does it lower the victim's income to zero, it simultaneously reduces to zero the benefit he can get by spending any form of income — including damage payments.
>
> One thing this argument suggests is that 'full compensation' — a level of payment for damages which restores the victim to the level of welfare he had before the injury — is in a sense inefficient.

As Friedman explains, the inefficiency arises because, if given a choice, the injured party would rather have received money prior to an accident that he could have spent on other consumer items in his uninjured state. Accordingly, Friedman suggests that the law should permit any person to *sell* insurance on his life, that is, to receive payments for today in exchange for selling to other persons the right to collect damages in the event of death at some future time. The sale of the insurance provides the seller with income at the time when its value is greatest. Simultaneously, placing the tort claim in the hands of the buyer preserves the deterrent effect of the tort law on the injurer.

Friedman's argument also helps explain the procedures that courts do in fact use to determine compensation. The typical major injury case involves the specification of an award that is designed to make some allowance for pain and suffering, medical care, and lost earnings. But there is no pretense that the plaintiff is left with as rich and full a life after injury as was enjoyed before it. While Friedman's argument precludes the possibility of damage awards that render the plaintiff indifferent as regards the pre- versus the post-injury state, it is consistent with the award of very large tort damages in personal injury cases. It is likely therefore that, if permitted, the sales of future tort actions is likely to be restricted to wrongful death cases. On Friedman's approach, what is the correct outcome in *McDougald*?

5. *Increased risk of injury.* The proper treatment of probabilistic events in assessing future pain and suffering divided the court in DePass v. United States, 721 F.2d 203, 210 (7th Cir. 1983). There the plaintiff suffered a traumatic amputation of his left leg below the knee. In addition to the usual elements of pain and suffering, plaintiff's expert witness testified, largely on the strength of an extensive National Institute of Health study done on World War II veterans, that there was "a statistical connection between traumatic limb amputations and future cardiovascular problems and decreased life expectancy." The expert estimated the reduction in life expectancy at 11 years. The government did nothing to counter that evidence, but the trial judge refused to award damages on the ground that it was too speculative. That decision was affirmed by a divided court of appeals per Flaum, J., on the ground that the study used was "inconclusive" and that "Illinois law is not settled as to whether increased risk of future injury is compensable."

The spirited dissent by Posner, J., argued that refusal to award damages for this type of loss was clearly erroneous.

> The district judge's rejection of such evidence, if widely followed, would lead to systematically undercompensating the victims of serious accidents and thus to systematically underdeterring such accidents. Accidents that require the amputation of a limb, particularly a leg, are apparently even more catastrophic than one had thought. They do not just cause a lifetime of disfigurement and reduced mobility; they create a high risk of premature death from heart disease. The goal of awarding damages in tort law is to put the tort victim as nearly as possible in the position he would have occupied if the tort had not been committed. This goal cannot be attained or even approached if judges shut their eyes to consequences that scientists have found are likely to follow from particular types of accident, merely because the scientists' evidence is statistical. But unless I have mistaken the true grounds of the district judge's decision in this case that is what he did.

2.   Economic Losses

O'Shea v. Riverway Towing Co.
677 F.2d 1194 (7th Cir. 1982)

POSNER, J. This is a tort case under the federal admiralty jurisdiction. We are called upon to decide questions of contributory negligence and damage assessment, in particular the question — one of first impression in this circuit — whether, and if so how, to account for inflation in computing lost future wages.

On the day of the accident, Margaret O'Shea was coming off duty as a cook on a towboat plying the Mississippi River. A harbor boat operated by the defendant, Riverway Towing Company, carried Mrs. O'Shea to shore and while getting off the boat she fell and sustained the injury complained of. The district judge found Riverway negligent and Mrs. O'Shea free from contributory negligence, and assessed damages in excess of $150,000. Riverway appeals only from the finding that there was no contributory negligence and from the part of the damage award that was intended to compensate Mrs. O'Shea for her lost future wages. [The court then held that the plaintiff was free of contributory negligence.]

The more substantial issues in this appeal relate to the computation of lost wages. Mrs. O'Shea's job as a cook paid her $40 a day, and since the custom was to work 30 days consecutively and then have the next 30 days off, this comes to $7200 a year although, as we shall see, she never had earned that much in a single year. She testified that when the accident occurred she had been about to get another cook's job on a Mississippi towboat that would have paid her $60 a day ($10,800 a year). She also testified that she had been intending to work as a boat's cook until she was 70 — longer if she was able. An economist who testified on Mrs. O'Shea's behalf used the foregoing testimony as the basis for estimating the wages that she lost because of the accident. He first subtracted federal income tax from yearly wage estimates based on alternative assumptions about her wage rate (that it would be either $40 or $60 a day); assumed that this wage would have grown by between six and eight percent a year; assumed that she would have worked either to age 65 or to age 70; and then discounted the resulting lost-wage estimates to present value, using a discount rate of 8.5 percent a year. These calculations, being based on alternative assumptions concerning starting wage rate, annual wage increases, and length of employment, yielded a range of values rather than a single value. The bottom of the range was $50,000. This is the present value, computed at an 8.5 percent discount rate, of Mrs. O'Shea's lost future wages on the assumption that her starting wage was $40 a day and that it would have grown by six percent a year until she retired at the age of 65. The top of the range was $114,000, which is the present value (again discounted at 8.5 percent) of her lost future wages assuming she would have worked till she was 70 at a wage that would have started at $60 a day and increased by eight percent a year. The judge awarded a figure — $86,033 — near the midpoint of this range. . . .

There is no doubt that the accident disabled Mrs. O'Shea from working as a cook on a boat. The break in her leg was very serious: it reduced the stability of the leg and caused her to fall frequently. It is impossible to see how she could have continued working as a cook, a job performed mostly while standing up, and especially on a boat, with its unsteady motion. But Riverway argues that Mrs. O'Shea (who has not worked at all since the accident, which occurred two years before the trial) could have gotten some sort of job and that the wages in that job should be deducted from the admittedly higher wages that she could have earned as a cook on a boat.

The question is not whether Mrs. O'Shea is totally disabled in the sense, relevant to social security disability cases but not tort cases, that there is no job in the American economy for which she is medically fit. It is whether she can by reasonable diligence find gainful employment, given the physical condition in which the accident left her. Here is a middle-aged woman, very overweight, badly scarred on one arm and one leg, unsteady on her feet, in constant and serious pain from the accident, with no education beyond high school and no work skills other than cooking, a job that happens to require standing for long periods which she is incapable of doing. It seems unlikely that someone in this condition could find gainful work at the minimum wage. True, the probability is not zero; and a better procedure, therefore, might have been to subtract from Mrs. O'Shea's lost future wages as a boat's cook the wages in some other job, discounted (i.e., multiplied) by the probability — very low — that she would in fact be able to get another job. But the district judge cannot be criticized for having failed to use a procedure not suggested by either party. The question put to him was the dichotomous one, would she or would she not get another job if she made reasonable efforts to do so? This required him to decide whether there was a more than 50 percent probability that she would. We cannot say that the negative answer he gave to that question was clearly erroneous.

Riverway argues next that it was wrong for the judge to award damages on the basis of a wage not validated, as it were, by at least a year's employment at that wage. Mrs. O'Shea had never worked full time, had never in fact earned more than $3600 in a full year, and in the year preceding the accident had earned only $900. But previous wages do not put a cap on an award of lost future wages. If a man who had never worked in his life graduated from law school, began working at a law firm at an annual salary of $35,000, and was killed the second day on the job, his lack of a past wage history would be irrelevant to computing his lost future wages. The present case is similar if less dramatic. Mrs. O'Shea did not work at all until 1974, when her husband died. She then lived on her inheritance and worked at a variety of part-time jobs till January 1979, when she started working as a cook on the towboat. According to her testimony, which the trial judge believed, she was then working full time. It is immaterial that this was her first full-time job and that the accident occurred before she had held it for a full year. Her job history was typical of women who return to the labor force after their children are grown or, as in Mrs. O'Shea's case, after their husband dies, and these women are, like any tort victims, entitled to damages based on what they would have earned in the future rather than on what they may or may not have earned in the past. . . .

We come at last to the most important issue in the case, which is the proper treatment of inflation in calculating lost future wages. Mrs. O'Shea's economist based the six to eight percent range which he used to estimate future increases in the wages of a boat's cook on the general pattern of wage increases in service occupations over the past 25 years. During the second half of this period the rate of inflation has been substantial and has accounted for much of the increase in nominal wages in this period; and to use that increase to project future wage increases is therefore to assume that inflation will continue, and continue to push up wages. Riverway argues that it is improper as a matter of law to take inflation into account in projecting lost future wages. Yet Riverway itself wants to take inflation into account — one-sidedly, to reduce the amount of the damages computed. For Riverway does not object to the economist's choice of an 8.5 percent discount rate for reducing Mrs. O'Shea's lost future wages to present value, although the rate includes an allowance — a very large allowance — for inflation.

To explain, the object of discounting lost future wages to present value is to give the plaintiff an amount of money which, invested safely, will grow to a sum equal to those wages. So if we thought that but for the accident Mrs. O'Shea would have earned $7200 in 1990, and we were computing in 1980 (when this case was tried) her damages based on those lost earnings, we would need to determine the sum of money that, invested safely for a period of 10 years, would grow to $7200. Suppose that in 1980 the rate of interest on ultra-safe (i.e., federal government) bonds or notes maturing in 10 years was 12 percent. Then we would consult a table of present values to see what sum of money invested at 12 percent for 10 years would at the end of that time have grown to $7200. The answer is $2318. But a moment's reflection will show that to give Mrs. O'Shea $2318 to compensate her for lost wages in 1990 would grossly undercompensate her. People demand 12 percent to lend money risklessly for 10 years because they expect their principal to have much less purchasing power when they get it back at the end of the time. In other words, when long-term interest rates are high, they are high in order to compensate lenders for the fact that they will be repaid in cheaper dollars. In periods when no inflation is anticipated, the risk-free interest rate is between one and three percent. See references in Doca v. Marina Mercante Nicaraguense, S.A., 634 F.2d 30, 39 n.2 (2d Cir. 1980). Additional percentage points above that level reflect inflation anticipated over the life of the loan. But if there is inflation it will affect wages as well as prices. Therefore to give Mrs. O'Shea $2318 today because that is the present value of $7200 10 years hence, computed as a discount rate — 12 percent — that consists mainly of an allowance for anticipated inflation, is in fact to give her less than she would have been earning then if she was earning $7200 on the date of the accident, even if the only wage increases she would have received would have been those necessary to keep pace with inflation.

There are (at least) two ways to deal with inflation in computing the present value of lost future wages. One is to take it out of both the wages and the discount rate — to say to Mrs. O'Shea, "we are going to calculate your probable wage in 1990 on the assumption, unrealistic as it is, that there will be zero inflation between now and then and, to be consistent, we are going to discount the amount thus calculated by the interest rate that would be charged under the same assumption of zero inflation." Thus, if we thought Mrs. O'Shea's real (i.e., inflation-free) wage rate would not rise in the future, we would fix her lost earnings in 1990 as $7200 and, to be consistent, we would discount that to present (1980) value using an estimate of the real interest rate. At two percent, this procedure would yield a present value of $5906. Of course, she would not invest this money at a mere two percent. She would invest it at the much higher prevailing interest rate. But that would not give her a windfall; it would just enable her to replace her lost 1990 earnings with an amount equal to what she would in fact have earned in that year if inflation continues, as most people expect it to do. (If people did not expect continued inflation, long-term interest rates would be much lower; those rates impound investors' inflationary expectations.)

An alternative approach, which yields the same result, is to use a (higher) discount rate based on the current risk-free 10-year interest rate, but apply that rate to an estimate of lost future wages that includes expected inflation. Contrary to Riverway's argument, this projection would not require gazing into a crystal ball. The expected rate of inflation can, as just suggested, be read off from the current long-term interest rate. If that rate is 12 percent, and if as suggested earlier the real or inflation-free interest rate is only one to three percent, this implies that the market is anticipating 9-11 percent inflation over the next 10 years, for a long-term interest rate is simply the sum of the real interest rate and the anticipated rate of inflation during the term.

Either approach to dealing with inflation is acceptable (they are, in fact, equivalent) and we by no means rule out others; but it is illogical and indefensible to build inflation into the discount rate yet ignore it in calculating the lost future wages that are to be discounted. That results in systematic undercompensation, just as building inflation into the estimate of future lost earnings and then discounting using the real rate of interest would systematically overcompensate. . . .

Applying our analysis to the present case, we cannot pronounce the approach taken by the plaintiff's economist unreasonable. He chose a discount rate — 8.5 percent — well above the real rate of interest, and therefore containing an allowance for inflation. Consistency required him to inflate Mrs. O'Shea's starting wage as a boat's cook in calculating her lost future wages, and he did so at a rate of six to eight percent a year. If this rate had been intended as a forecast of purely inflationary wage changes, his approach would be open to question, especially at the upper end of his range. For if the estimated rate of inflation were eight percent, the use of a discount rate of 8.5 percent would imply that the real rate of interest was only .5 percent, which is lower than most economists believe it to be for any substantial period of time. But wages do not rise just because of inflation. Mrs. O'Shea could expect her real wages as a boat's cook to rise as she became more experienced and as average real wage rates throughout the economy rose, as they usually do over a decade or more. It would not be outlandish to assume that even if there were no inflation, Mrs. O'Shea's wages would have risen by three percent a year. If we subtract that from the economist's six to eight percent range, the inflation allowance built into his estimated future wage increases is only three to five percent; and when we subtract these figures from 8.5 percent we see that his implicit estimate of the real rate of interest was very high (3.5-5.5 percent). This means he was conservative, because the higher the discount rate used the lower the damages calculated.

If conservative in one sense, the economist was most liberal in another. He made no allowance for the fact that Mrs. O'Shea, whose health history quite apart from the accident is not outstanding, might very well not have survived — let alone survived and been working as a boat's cook or in an equivalent job — until the age of 70. The damage award is a sum certain, but the lost future wages to which that award is equated by means of the discount rate are mere probabilities. If the probability of her being employed as a boat's cook full time in 1990 was only 75 percent, for example, then her estimated wages in that year should have been multiplied by .75 to determine the value of the expectation that she lost as a result of the accident; and so with each of the other future years. Cf. Conte v. Flota Mercante del Estado, 277 F.2d 664, 670 (2d Cir. 1960). The economist did not do this, and by failing to do this he overstated the loss due to the accident.

But Riverway does not make an issue of this aspect of the economist's analysis. Nor of another: the economist selected the 8.5 percent figure for the discount rate because that was the current interest rate on Triple A 10-year state and municipal bonds, but it would not make sense in Mrs. O'Shea's federal income tax bracket to invest in tax-free bonds. If he wanted to use nominal rather than real interest rates and wage increases (as we said was proper), the economist should have used a higher discount rate and a higher expected rate of inflation. But as these adjustments would have been largely or entirely offsetting, the failure to make them was not a critical error.

[The court then affirmed the award below because its own analysis convinced it of the reasonableness of its result. It stated, however, that it thought that the calculation of lost earnings "can and should be an analytical rather than an intuitive undertaking," and "for the future" asked "the district judges in this circuit to indicate the steps by which they arrive at damage awards for lost future earnings."]

Judgment affirmed.

NOTES

1. *Discounting to present value.* As Judge Posner's opinion in *O'Shea* makes clear, discounting to present value is an essential task in determining the proper awards for any future item of recovery, whether lost earnings, or, by extension, medical expenses. The requirement for discounting future income streams can be justified by a single proposition: a dollar today is worth more than a dollar next year. The reason for the difference should be apparent to everyone: if a person is in possession of the dollar at the present time he will be able at the end of the year to enjoy both the dollar and the interest earned on it. If he gets the dollar at the end of the year, the interest on it will benefit the person (say, the bank) who has had the use of the dollar in the intermediate period. The question of the value of that one year's use of the dollar is, questions of uncertainty apart, a function of the going rate of interest for the use of money. As interest rates increase, the demand for immediate cash, relative to future payments, increases as well. Accordingly, the discount rate will be steeper. Indeed, the present value of $1.00 is the function of the current rate of interest and the elapsed time until payment is made. It is determined by the formula

$$PV\,\$1.00 = \frac{\$1.00}{(1+i)^n}$$

where $PV\$1.00$ equals the present value of \$1.00, n the number of years until payment is made, and i the uniform rate of interest applicable during the period.

The value of \$1.00 payable at some future time can be calculated by the analogous formula:

$$FV\$1.00 = \$1.00(1+i)^n$$

Inspection of the formula should reveal that the percentage discount for a future payment depends not only on the interest rate, but also on the length of time before payment is due. The longer a creditor must wait for payment, the greater the discount.

2. *Inflation.* Discounting becomes more difficult with inflation. As a general economic proposition, inflation means that it will take more dollars tomorrow to purchase any market basket of goods than it does today. A lender, then, in order to preserve his real economic position over time, will have to receive a payment above and beyond the "real rate" of interest — i.e., the level of interest appropriate when the inflation rate is zero. Most economic studies have indicated that the real rate of interest is somewhere between 1.5 and 3 percent, with 2 percent being perhaps the most commonly cited figure. See, e.g., Gibson, Interest Rates and Inflationary Expectations: New Evidence, 62 Am. Econ. Rev. 854 (1972). As Newman, J., observed in Doca v. Marina Mercante Nicaraguense, S.A., 634 F.2d 30 (2d Cir. 1980), "it is entirely feasible to take inflation into account without making any prediction as to the specific level of future inflation rates. All that is needed is a prediction that in the future inflation rates will bear approximately the same relationship to long-term interest rates that they have in the past."

Neither *O'Shea* nor *Doca* demands that the district courts always use the 2 percent discount rate, with Newman, J., noting that "[l]itigants are free to account for inflation in other ways, or to offer evidence of a rate more appropriate than 2 percent." If inflation is constant across all cases, why should the discount rate vary from case to case? Indeed the case has sometimes been made that the best economic estimations are made if inflation and discounting are ignored altogether. In Kaczkowski v. Bolubasz, 421 A.2d 1027 (Pa. 1980), the Pennsylvania Supreme Court held that "future inflation shall be presumed equal to future interest rates with these factors offsetting. Thus, the courts of this Commonwealth are instructed to abandon the practice of discounting lost future earnings."

That result was in turn supported in Carter and Palmer, Real Rates, Expected Rates, and Damage Awards, 20 J. Legal Stud. 439, 461 (1991), who concluded "that there is, on average, no need to try to estimate nominal or real interest rates, inflation rates, or the aggregate growth of labor productivity in legal cases involving a loss of earning capacity over time. These terms all cancel out in the equation for calculating the present value of the stream of losses." The authors did not control for tax effects of damages, nor take into account the possibility that productivity increases will be smaller as workers approach conventional retirement ages.

Who should bear the burden of proof in those jurisdictions that still treat discounting on a case-by-case basis? In Aldridge v. Baltimore & Ohio Railroad, 789 F.2d 1061, 1067 (4th Cir. 1986), the court held that

> the party who would benefit from the application of a particular economic formula has the burden of producing competent evidence to prove it. Contra DiSabatino v. National Railroad Passenger Corp., 724 F.2d 394, 395 (3d Cir. 1984) (burden of producing evidence of present value of future lost wages rests on plaintiff). If a defendant wishes the fact-finder to reduce the gross amount of future lost wages to present value, he can present evidence probative of an appropriate interest rate and method of discount. The plaintiff, in turn, may offer evidence tending to prove that the award should be increased because inflation will diminish its current value. In that case, the plaintiff must show what kind of and how much inflation. We think this is a sensible approach. In most cases, the factors are simple, and it should be a light burden for the defendant to prove a proper discount rate or for the plaintiff to prove the probable effects of inflation.

3. *Prejudgment interest.* At common law the general rule was that interest for a successful tort plaintiff ran only from the time of judgment, i.e., that moment when the unliquidated amount of the damages imposed by the tort law was fixed by litigation. One obvious objection to this rule is that it allows the defendant, by delay, to reduce the amount paid to the plaintiff, and thereby to frustrate the common-law objective of full compensation to the plaintiff. Consistent with this objection is In re Air Crash Disaster Near Chicago, 644 F.2d 633 (7th Cir. 1981), where the court held that prejudgment interest was recoverable under Illinois law under the general language of the Illinois wrongful death statute, today 740 ILCS 180/2 calling for "fair and just compensation" for pecuniary losses in death cases.

4. *Expected life calculations.* As Posner, J., pointed out, it is important to be careful of general propositions that a plaintiff of a certain age has, say, 20 years of productive work left before retirement. While that may well be the case, any award for future earnings should take into account the possibility of the plaintiff's death or disability before retirement in order not to systematically overstate lost earnings. The proper procedure here is to ask (1) the expected (discounted) earnings of each future year, and (2) the probability that the plaintiff will actually be in the work force in that year. While the probability that the plaintiff would have worked the next year may be close to 100 percent, the same cannot be said of employment 10 or 20 years later. In cases like *O'Shea*

the point is important, since there is a substantial possibility that a woman in her fifties with both weight and health problems will not be able to work, at least at current capacity, until 70 years of age. Nonetheless, as the Supreme Court has observed in Jones & Laughlin Steel Corp. v. Pfeifer, 462 U.S. 523, 533-534 (1983), there is a common perception that these calculations are not made in practice. "Given the complexity of trying to make an exact calculation, litigants frequently follow the relatively simple course of assuming that the worker would have continued to work up to a specific date certain." In calculating the likelihood of future death or disability, should a court confine its attention only to general insurance mortality and disability tables, or should it take into account the individual condition of each particular plaintiff?

5. *Taxation of tort damage awards.* Under the Internal Revenue Code damage awards received in compensation for personal injuries are not taxable, even when they are a substitute for lost income. See I.R.C. §104(a) (1994). One recurrent question is whether damage awards should be reduced to take into account their tax-free status. An early negative answer to that question was offered by Friendly, J., in McWeeney v. New York, N.H. & H.R.R., 282 F.2d 34, 36 (2d Cir. 1960), who argued that any reference to the Internal Revenue Code could only make personal injury litigation more speculative and prolonged than it already is: "Is the jury in each case to speculate, or hear testimony, on the procreative proclivities and potentialities of the plaintiff and his spouse?"

More recent cases have tended to take the opposite position and to take taxes into account and to instruct the jury of that fact. In Norfolk & Western Ry. Co.. v. Liepelt, 444 U.S. 490, 494 (1980), Justice Stevens allowed these damages with instructions into evidence in FELA cases saying:

> Admittedly there are many variables that may affect the amount of a wage earner's future income-tax liability. The law may change, his family may increase or decrease in size, his spouse's earnings may affect his tax bracket, and extra income or unforeseen deductions may become available. But future employment itself, future health, future personal expenditures, future interest rates, and future inflation are also matters of estimate and prediction. Any one of these issues might provide the basis for protracted expert testimony and debate. But the practical wisdom of the trial bar and the trial bench has developed effective methods of presenting the essential elements of an expert calculation in a form that is understandable by juries that are increasingly familiar with the complexities of modern life. We therefore reject the notion that the introduction of evidence describing a decedent's estimated after-tax earnings is too speculative or complex for a jury.

Justice Blackmun's dissent supported the older practice of ignoring taxes in torts cases:

In my view, by mandating adjustment of the award by way of reduction for federal income taxes that would have been paid by the decedent on his earnings, the Court appropriates for the tortfeasor a benefit intended to be conferred on the victim or his survivors. And in requiring that the jury be instructed that a wrongful-death award is not subject to federal income tax, the Court opens the door for a variety of admonitions to the jury not to "misbehave," and unnecessarily interjects what is now to be federal law into the administration of a trial in a state court.

Liepelt was applied in a state law context in Ruff v. Weintraub, 519 A.2d 1384, 1387 (N.J. 1987), where the court declined to " 'give simplicity paramount significance in fashioning the law of damages. Such an approach might aid the judiciary but hardly justice.' Estimating future tax liability is no more speculative or complicated than many of the other factors a jury considers in setting damages for future losses."

The administrative complexities of taking taxes into account provoked, however, a different response in New York, where by statute it is now provided that in medical malpractice cases, evidence of the taxation of lost earnings "shall be admissible for consideration by the court, outside the presence of the jury." The rule further provides that the jury should be instructed that any adjustments for taxes shall be made "if warranted" by the court, which has the power to reduce the award to take into account "the amount of federal, state and local personal income taxes which the court finds, with reasonable certainty, that the plaintiff would have been obligated by law to pay." N.Y. Civ. Prac. L. & R. §4546. What is wrong with an alternative proposal that reduces all damage awards for lost income by a fixed figure, say, 20 percent? Note that the loss in precision is offset by the consistency in results and the reduction in administrative costs.

See generally Morris and Nordstrom, Personal Injury Recoveries and the Federal Income Tax Law, 56 A.B.A. J. (1960).

6. *Imputed income: additions to market losses.* Imputed income from nonmarket activities is another element that must be taken into account in computing damages. The benefits are said to be "imputed" because there is no explicit market transaction that gives direct evidence of their worth. In the law of damages, the most important aspect of imputed income lies in the value of lost services for persons not engaged in ordinary market activities. Thus, serious personal injuries to a housewife may disable her from performing services of great value to herself and her family, and may well require that she go to the marketplace in order to obtain replacement services. See, e.g., Cummings v. Rachner, 257 N.W.2d 808 (Minn. 1977), where the court affirmed an award of $225,000 to the next of kin in a wrongful death action. The 37-year-old decedent was a housewife, "a truly remarkable and exceptional woman." She had been married for 19 years and had had full charge of a household with seven children, including one with learning disabili-

ties. She was active in church and civic affairs and still found time to complete two years of college education before her death. Is the proper measure of damages what she could have earned in the marketplace, less the taxes paid thereon? For a development of this theme see Komesar, Toward a General Theory of Personal Injury Loss, 3 J. Legal Stud. 457 (1974).

Questions of imputed income can also arise with ordinary personal pleasures. In Hogan v. Santa Fe Trail Transportation Co., 85 P.2d 28, 34 (Kan. 1938), the plaintiff, a woman of 63, was an accomplished violinist. After being injured through the defendant's negligence in an automobile collision, she could no longer bend her little finger to play the violin. The plaintiff testified that playing the violin "was my life work. It is just part of me. Every place I go, if I don't have my violin why, I wonder where it is. I have played it all my life. I play solos — solos by myself, with a piano accompaniment." The court held that damages could not be recovered on the ground that they were too speculative. The dissent in the case took quite the opposite view, noting:

> It should be noted on the outset the enjoyment in the instant case was not an imaginary enjoyment. It was a fixed and definite enjoyment which existed at the time of the injury. Nor did it constitute an incidental or merely occasional enjoyment. It was an enjoyment which grew out of and was a part of the regular and ordinary pursuits of the plaintiff's life. It was truly exactly as she stated: "It was my life work. It was just part of me." It constituted the loss of the greatest enjoyment of her life. To say that the loss of such an enjoyment and the comfort to a human being resulting from such enjoyment is compensable in no amount does not appeal to my sense of justice. Neither am I willing to say, that merely by reason of the fact juries and courts are unable to accurately measure such a loss, we will give the injured party nothing to compensate for the loss. Nor is that the law as I understand it to be.

Today the dissent represents the dominant legal position. See, e.g., Mariner v. Marsden, 610 P.2d 6 (Wyo. 1980), allowing compensation for the loss of enjoyment of life.

Firestone v. Crown Center Redevelopment Corp.
693 S.W.2d 99 (Mo. 1985)

Higgins, Judge.

Plaintiff obtained a jury verdict of $15,000,000 damages for injuries suffered when suspended balconies in the Hyatt Regency Kansas City Hotel fell on July 17, 1981. The trial court entered an order granting defendants a new trial unless plaintiff filed a remittitur of $2,250,000 "because the verdict is against the weight of the evidence." Plaintiff filed the required remittitur and the court entered judgment for plaintiff for $12,750,000. Defendants appealed and, in addition to asserting trial errors, claimed the damage award as reduced by remittitur was still excessive. They requested reversal and remand for new trial or alternatively that the verdict be reduced by further remittitur to $7,500,000. Plaintiff responded to the alleged trial errors and under Rule 78.10 requested restoration of the $2,250,000 remittitur required of plaintiff by the trial court as a condition to denial of a new trial to defendants. The Court of Appeals, Western District, affirmed the judgment and transferred the case to this Court where it is determined the same as on original appeal.

This Court affirms the jury's verdict in all respects and remands the cause with directions to set aside the order of remittitur, reinstate the verdict and enter judgment for plaintiff for the verdict sum of $15,000,000.

This Court further determines that this case demonstrates that the doctrine of remittitur should be abolished in Missouri.

[The court then rejected a variety of procedural and substantive challenges that the defendant raised to the verdict below. It then continued:]

This is the first appeal to this Court involving remittitur since promulgation of Rule 78.10, effective Jan. 1, 1981. The rule provides:

> Consenting to a remittitur as a condition to the denial of a new trial does not preclude the consenting party from asserting on appeal that the amount of the verdict was proper or that the amount of the remittitur is excessive. A party consenting to a remittitur may not initiate the appeal on the ground but may raise the same on the other party's appeal.

The amount of damages in a case of this nature is for the jury in the first instance; and in this case the jury awarded plaintiff $15,000,000 which the trial court remitted to $12,750,000 as a condition to denial of a new trial to defendants.

Under the doctrine of remittitur in Missouri, such an order of remittitur by the trial court constitutes a ruling upon the weight of the evidence, *Morris v. Israel Brothers, Inc.*, 510 S.W.2d 437, 447 (Mo. 1974). If there is an abuse of discretion in failing to order a remittitur or in the amount of remittitur ordered the judgment is reviewable by the appellate court.

This Court has often recognized that there is no precise formula for determining whether a verdict is excessive; each case has been considered on its own facts. Although consideration is properly given to the nature and extent of the injuries and the diminished earning capacity, economic conditions, plaintiff's age, and a comparison of the compensation awarded and permitted in cases of comparable injuries, "[t]he ultimate test is what fairly and reasonably compensates plaintiff for the injuries sustained."

Sally Firestone was 34 years old at the time of the skywalk collapse. She was employed at IBM repairing computing systems and received an annual salary of $33,000 including fringe benefits. Outside of work she was very active socially and had a wide range of interests. This was changed drastically by the Hyatt skywalk collapse.

After the accident, Sally was brought to the emergency room of Kansas University Medical Center. She had lost 80 percent of her blood and required massive blood transfusions. The events which followed included: Sally was attached to a mechanical breathing device. She was treated for scalp lacerations. Catheters were inserted, including one to measure the pressure in the pulmonary artery and cardiac functions. This involved the catheter being brought through a vein in the arm up to her heart and into the pulmonary artery. X-rays revealed severe fracture and dislocation of the spine at the level of the fourth, fifth and sixth cervical vertebra — her spinal cord was severed. Sally was classified as a C-5 quadriplegic; she has no movement below the shoulder level with the exception of some use of her biceps enabling her to lift her arms but leaving her without control to lower them. Sally was placed in traction via tongs attached to her skull. An intercranial pressure monitoring device was installed by drilling a hole into the skull. Both of Sally's legs were broken. She developed respiratory distress syndrome requiring a tracheotomy and attachment to a respirator. Her airway passage frequently clogged with phlegm causing her extreme difficulty in breathing. Complications developed and multiple transfusions were necessary. She underwent grueling neurological testing to determine the extent of damage and an operation to stabilize her neck. Following surgery she suffered a gastric hemorrhage, bladder infections and pneumonia.

A total of 3 months was spent in Kansas University Medical Center; $2\frac{1}{2}$ months were in intensive care. Most of this time she was unable to speak due to tubes through her nose and throat. She also had to take anti-seizure drugs which caused hallucinations.

After Sally left Kansas University Medical Center, she spent 4 months at the Craig Institute, a rehabilitation center for brain and spinal cord injuries. There she learned how to operate an electric wheelchair. She had an operation to insert a suprapubic catheter which she is unable to reinsert by herself when necessary. She learned her bowel movements would have to be initiated by suppositories or digital stimulation. Numerous medical complications that arise for quadriplegics were explained to her — among these are respiratory and circulatory problems resulting in lightheadedness, nausea and vomiting.

Sally requires "round-the-clock" attendance, continuing therapy, and expensive specialized equipment. Her psychologist testified she will continue to need professional help in dealing with the emotional aspect of her injury and disability. Both the treating neurosurgeon and a doctor that works primarily with quadriplegics testified that her injuries were the worst they had ever seen.

[The court then accepted the $7,076,711 awarded for the plaintiff's economic loss.]

The jury is vested with a broad discretion in fixing fair and reasonable compensation to an injured party, *Graeff,* 576 S.W.2d at 309, and the foregoing evidence of plaintiff's injuries substantiates the jury's award to her in this case. Such a record does not authorize a trial court in the exercise of reasonable discretion to order any portion of it remitted, and the jury's verdict must be restored.

VII

As indicated at the outset, this case lends emphasis to the problems and conflicting philosophies associated with the remittitur practice and demonstrates a basis for its abolishment. The doctrine is not a provision of statute or rule in Missouri. It has been impressed by practice on the new trial consideration where its application constitutes an invasion of the jury's function by the trial judge. Such applications have been frought with confusion and inconsistency. Its application in the appellate courts has been questioned since its inception in Missouri as an invasion of a party's right to trial by jury and an assumption of a power to weigh the evidence, a function reserved to the trier(s) of fact. This Court has voiced recent concern for reconsideration of the doctrine.

What may have begun with a worthy purpose of bringing uniformity to verdicts and judgments for unliquidated damages has been eroded by added considerations and irreconcilable case by case evaluations.

Abolishment of the remittitur practice in Missouri does no violence to the power and discretion of trial courts to control jury verdicts. . . .

Rule 78.02 continues the authority and discretion of the trial court to grant one new trial on the ground the verdict is against the weight of the evidence. This power and discretion should no longer be adulterated by a remittitur practice which permits the trial court to find error in its trial and excuse the error upon remittitur of a commanded portion of the jury's verdict, only to see the case appealed despite the remittitur, including a charge of error in the amount of remittitur ordered.

The Court concludes that remittitur shall no longer be employed in Missouri.

Accordingly, the verdict of the jury is affirmed and the cause is remanded with directions to set aside the order of remittitur, reinstate the verdict and enter judgment for plaintiff for the verdict sum of $15,000,000; and the doctrine of remittitur is abolished in Missouri.

NOTES

1. Medical expenses. The second major head of economic losses covers medical expenses, both past and future. In dealing with these costs it is first necessary to identify what expenses count as medical expenses. These typically include doctor's and hospital bills as well as the cost of nurses and attendants for persons who have serious permanent disabilities. In addition, in some cases expenses may be recovered for such items as the addition of ramps and handrails in the plaintiff's house, Isgett v. Seaboard Coast Line Railroad Co., 332 F. Supp. 1127 (D. S.C. 1971), or for trips necessary for health reasons.

In principle, the plaintiff is entitled only to the "reasonable cost" of medical expenses, although the price actually paid for services is ordinarily evidence of the reasonableness of the charges in question. As in cases like *Firestone*, special difficulties arise in connection with future medical expenses, which may be extremely difficult to estimate given the uncertainty in the plaintiff's expected life and the changes in medical technology, changes that may either increase or decrease the cost of relevant medical services. In addition, future medical expenses, like lost earnings, must be discounted to their present economic value. See generally 4 Harper, James and Gray, Torts §25.9.

2. Excessive damages. As *Firestone* indicates, courts have long exercised some control over the damage awards that are made in personal injury cases. The question of whether the jury has properly discharged its function can arise in cases in which the award is challenged either as excessive or inadequate. The most common challenges are made for excessive verdicts. In these cases the general rule today is that the jury verdict will be respected "unless the verdict is so plainly and outrageously excessive as to suggest at first blush passion, prejudice, or corruption on the part of the jury." Gorman v. Sacramento County, 268 P.2d 1083, 1088 (Cal. App. 1928). In Addair v. Majestic Petroleum Co., Inc., 232 S.E.2d 821 (W. Va. 1977), the court held that jury awards should stand unless shown to be "monstrous and enormous," quoting Beardmore v. Carrington, 95 Eng. Rep. 790, 793 (K.B. 1764). Under federal practice, "it is the duty of the district judge to set aside an excessive verdict even when such a verdict is supported by substantial evidence 'if he is of the opinion that the verdict is against the clear weight of the evidence, or is based on evidence which is false, or will result in a miscarriage of justice.' " Johnson v. Parrish, 827 F.2d 988, 991 (4th Cir. 1987).

As in *Firestone*, most courts have sustained very large verdicts when the plaintiffs have suffered gruesome injuries. See, e.g., Wry v. Dial, 503 P.2d 979 (Ariz. App. 1973), affirming a $3,500,000 award for a brilliant scientist terribly maimed in a road accident; Murphy v. Colorado Aviation, Inc., 588 P.2d 877 (Colo. App. 1978), affirming a $2,500,000 wrongful death award to the widow of Audie Murphy; and Rodrigues v. McDonnell Douglas Corp., 151 Cal. Rptr. 399 (Cal. App. 1978), affirming a $4,240,000 judgment in favor of a 22-year-old male, recently married, of good habits and disposition, who was paralyzed from the chest down, unable to walk and without control of his bladder, bowel, or sexual functions, with bleeding ulcers, subject to the constant threat of infection, and in constant pain and suffering.

When a verdict is challenged as inadequate some new complications are introduced. First, the verdict might not reflect specific items of loss that have been proved by the plaintiff, such as those for past lost earnings or medical expenses, where there is no real dispute as to the amounts of money involved. In addition, the jury may return an inadequate verdict to "compromise" on the plaintiff's claim, a result that is less likely to happen under a regime of comparative negligence than under the older rules when contributory negligence was a total bar. When compromise verdicts are entered, should they automatically be reversed on the ground that they are necessarily inconsistent with the law? Or should they be accepted as a reflection of genuine disagreement over the underlying liability of the defendant? See generally F. James, G. Hazard, and J. Leubsdorf, Civil Procedure 399 (4th ed. 1992), attacking as "doctrinaire" the view that "it is an abuse of discretion to deny a new trial whenever the verdict is demonstrably inadequate."

3. Remittitur and additur. There is an important debate over the choice of remedy to be awarded once a verdict is held to be excessive or inadequate. As noted in *Firestone,* the remedy of a new trial should in principle be available. But given the costs and delays of a new trial, many states have procedures that allow the prior jury verdict to stand if the plaintiff will accept some lesser amount. Analogous rules can be adopted with respect to additur: the defendant can avoid the cost of a new trial by consenting to a larger verdict equal, perhaps, to the smallest verdict the court would sustain against a charge of inadequacy. The matter of remittitur and additur in federal court raises important constitutional issues, given the Seventh Amendment guarantee of the right to a jury trial. The present practice of allowing remittiturs is probably too well ingrained to be overthrown as an improper judicial invasion of the function of the jury, but in Dimick v. Shiedt, 293 U.S. 474 (1935), the Supreme Court held that using additur in federal court was an unconstitutional invasion of the jury's prerogative. Is it a greater violation of a jury's control over damages for a court to make a larger award than the jury thought reasonable, than to make a smaller one?

4. *Structured settlements.* One way in which the pressure of large verdicts manifests itself is in the increased use of structured settlements. These settlements pay plaintiff's damages in periodic installments rather than in a single lump sum. The structured settlement reduces the need for the parties to make a joint estimate of future levels of inflation, since future payments can be geared to inflation if and when it occurs. Structured settlements are often favored in big cases to reduce the uncertainty in projecting both lost earnings and future medical expenses, either of which can be sizable sums. Their use in smaller cases is, however, sharply limited because of the administrative costs they impose.

Structured settlements may be used by mutual agreement of the parties, even if the common-law rule provides only for lump-sum damages. The more controversial question is whether they may be demanded by one side over the opposition of the other. This matter is the subject of a large variety of recent legislation.

Structured settlements have, for example, been introduced as a response to the medical malpractice crisis at the state level. For example, a 1985 Illinois law (735 ILCS 5/2-1735 et seq.), applicable to medical malpractice actions only, allows either plaintiff or defendant by pretrial motion to elect a structured settlement whenever a good faith estimate places future economic damages over $250,000. The statute then requires the court to award lump-sum damages for present award of economic damages and noneconomic damages. Periodic payments are then made for future economic loss. Any payment for attorney's fees to the plaintiff's lawyer has to take the form of a lump sum, calculated with reference to both the past and future damage awards, and deducted proportionately from both parts of the award. These damage provisions were sustained against various constitutional challenges in Bernier v. Burris, 497 N.E.2d 763 (Ill. 1986). A similar provision is found in California Civil Procedure Code section 667.7 (West 1987), where, when future damages awarded against any "health care provider" exceed $50,000, either party may request that it be paid in whole or in part in periodic payments and not a lump sum. The section was upheld against constitutional challenge in American Bank & Trust Co. v. Community Hospital, 683 P.2d 670 (Cal. 1984).

California has also authorized structured settlements in some suits against public entities. Thus Cal. Gov. Code section 984 (West 1989) provides that non-insured public entities are entitled to impose structured settlements when damage awards exceed $650,00 as of January 1, 1994, $725,000 as of January 1, 1996, with 5 percent annual increases thereafter. The statute calls for 50 percent of the total judgment to be paid immediately, with the remainder to be paid in installments over a period of up to ten years or the expected life of the tort claimant, whichever is less, with interest on the unpaid balance set "at the same rate as one-year treasury bills" as of January 1st of each year. The statute also gives the court jurisdiction to modify the original structured settlement if circumstances require it, and to increase the amounts owing from the public entity in the event of the insolvency of a joint tortfeasor.

More generally, structured settlements may take two forms, and it is important to distinguish between them because they have different incentive effects on a plaintiff's rehabilitative efforts. Thus, if the settlement calls for so much per year as long as the plaintiff needs medical treatment, plaintiffs may unduly prolong treatment in order to continue receiving the payments. On the other hand, if the future payments are for a definite sum and in no sense contingent on the health or conduct of the plaintiff, as is the case with the above statutes, then the payments operate just like a fixed lump-sum payment, without this incentive effect.

Periodic payments contingent upon plaintiff's condition are, however, common in the workers' compensation area, in which the treatment of the injured employee is heavily monitored, typically by the insurance carrier of the compensation employer. The chief advantage of this system is that it avoids the need for making a precise determination of damages at the time of trial when future projections are risky at best. For a defense of the lump-sum common-law system of payments see Rea, Lump-Sum Versus Periodic Damage Awards, 10 J. Legal Stud. 131 (1981).

5. *Caps on damages.* The dramatic increase in the level of damages awarded successful plaintiffs in tort actions has brought forth major legislative responses in many states, especially in connection with medical malpractice. These reforms have met with a mixed fate when subjected to constitutional challenge. A hostile view of the statutory reforms was, for example, taken in Kansas Malpractice Victims v. Bell, 757 P.2d 251, 259-260 (Kan. 1988), where the court struck down a statute that limited the plaintiff's recovery to $1,000,000 and the recovery for noneconomic loss to $250,000 and required the plaintiff to accept an annuity payment for future economic losses. The court held that there was no quid pro quo similar to that found in the workers' compensation cases, and observed that the 5 percent decrease in the payments that any physician must pay to the state fund ("designed to provide additional insurance coverage above the primary coverage limits to all health care providers") was not a sufficient quid pro quo. "Should a doctor decide to pass these savings on to his hundreds of patients each person's savings would be minuscule. In return, the terri-

bly injured patient is denied all remedy for those injuries and losses which exceed the caps."

In contrast, in Fein v. Permanente Medical Group, 695 P.2d 665, 683 (Cal. 1985), the California Supreme Court upheld section 3333.2 of the California Civil Code, which limited recovery for pain and suffering to $250,000, by adopting the deferential "rational basis" standard of review as appropriate to this challenge. It first noted that the statute placed no restrictions on recovery for economic losses, and then it observed that many scholars (including Jaffe, supra at page 870) have attacked the award for pain and suffering in tort cases as matter of first principle. The court then continued:

> Nor can we agree with amicus' contention that the $250,000 limit is unconstitutional because the Legislature could have realized its hoped-for cost savings by mandating a fixed-percentage reduction of all non-economic damage awards. The choice between reasonable alternative methods of achieving a given objective is generally for the Legislature, and there are a number of reasons why the Legislature may have made the choice it did. One of the problems identified in the legislative hearing was the unpredictability of the size of large noneconomic damage awards, resulting from the inherent difficulties in valuing such damages and the great disparity in the price tag which different juries placed on such losses. The Legislature could reasonably have determined that an across-the-board limit would provide a more stable base on which to calculate insurance rates. Furthermore, as one amicus suggests, the Legislature may have felt that the fixed $250,000 limit would promote settlements by eliminating "the unknown possibility of phenomenal awards for pain and suffering that can make litigation worth the gamble." Finally, the Legislature simply may have felt that it was fairer to malpractice plaintiffs in general to reduce only the very large noneconomic damage awards, rather than to diminish the more modest recoveries for pain and suffering and the like in the great bulk of cases. Each of these grounds provides a sufficient rationale for the $250,000 limit.

In General Electric Co. v. Niemet, 866 P.2d 1361, 1364-1365 (Colo. 1994), the court was faced with the challenge of applying its cap on damages to multiple tortfeasors. Colo. Rev. Stat. §13-21-102.5(3)(a) (1993) limits the total amount of noneconomic damages to $250,000, unless the court finds justification by clear and convincing evidence, in which case damages can be awarded up to $500,000. Likewise Colo. Rev. Stat. §13-21-111.5(1) (1993) provides that each defendant should not be held liable for any sum greater than "the degree or percentage of the negligence of fault attributable to such defendant." In case brought against two defendants, the trial judge found that General Electric was 35 percent responsible for plaintiff's injuries and held General Electric responsible therefore for $350,000 of noneconomic damages, given special circumstances. General Electric contended that the

$1,000,000 in total noneconomic losses should first be reduced to $500,000, of which its share was only $175,000. The court rejected that contention. Vollack, J., first noted that one purpose of the statute "was to protect individual defendants from excessive noneconomic damage verdicts, not to deprive injured plaintiffs from recovering compensation for their damages." He then added:

> The goal of the General Assembly in enacting the legislation was to improve the predictability of risks faced by insurance companies. If an insurance company can predict risks with reasonable accuracy, then it can also predict its losses and profits. The concern of an insurance company is the risk associated with insuring each individual insured, not with denying an injured person damages that may be paid by another insurance company or person. Even if an insurance company insured two defendants in one lawsuit, its risk is still predictable. The statutory cap of $250,000, or in some cases up to $500,000, provides a predictable limit for insurance companies, beyond which they cannot be liable for an individual defendant.

McGinley v. United States
329 F. Supp. 62 (E.D. Pa. 1971)

[The plaintiff was a stevedore injured in an accident for which the United States admitted liability. The portion of the opinion reprinted deals with the plaintiff's duty to mitigate damages.]

WOOD, J. . . . This case presents several issues of damages which require discussion. The first is whether we should reduce the amount of plaintiff's recovery because of his failure to undergo further surgery in an attempt to alleviate the pain in his low back. We conclude that his recovery should not be so reduced.

It is, of course, settled law that if injuries may be cured or alleviated by a simple and safe surgical operation, then refusal to submit thereto should be considered in mitigation of damages. This is not true, however, where the operation is a serious one, or one attended by grave risk of death or failure. A plaintiff has a duty to submit to reasonable medical treatment and the test of reasonableness is to be determined by the triers of fact.

The record in this instant case clearly demonstrates that plaintiff has continuously submitted to reasonable medical treatment since he first sustained his injuries. He has already undergone two operations, one for the removal of a herniated cervical disc and the other an exploratory operation on his spine. Moreover he has never refused to submit to further surgery. His physician, Dr. Langfitt, while testifying that another exploratory operation to locate and remove a possible herniated disc might alleviate plaintiff's condition, also testified that he had never, prior to trial, advised plaintiff to have another operation. Consequently this is not a case where a plaintiff has refused to follow the advice of his physician.

The evidence also indicates that the proposed operation is of highly questionable value. In the first instance, such an operation would have only a 60 to 70% chance of being successful. Moreover, it would relieve his disc problem only at the L/5 level of the spine, and the likelihood exists that further surgery would be necessary in a few years to relieve disc problems at other levels of his spine. It is also not inconceivable that further surgery at this time could worsen plaintiff's condition. Finally, an operation such as the one described would obviously be successful only in the event that plaintiff does, in fact, have a herniated disc. If, however, he is suffering from arachnoiditis, as appears likely, such an operation would not relieve his condition. Under these circumstances we do not find it unreasonable for plaintiff to decline to undergo further surgery.

Defendants have also attempted to show that plaintiff, although permanently disabled from his former occupation as head stevedore foreman, can mitigate his damages by obtaining other employment. It has been demonstrated that plaintiff, because of his condition and employment background, is unsuitable for indoor employment. Defendants maintain, however, that he could obtain employment as a checker on the waterfront.

The law requires of an injured party a reasonable effort to mitigate his damages. This includes a duty to seek reasonable alternative employment. We believe that the course which defendants would have plaintiff follow oversteps the bounds of reasonableness.

We have found no case which holds that a disabled plaintiff has a duty not only to obtain alternative employment which he is capable of performing, but also to prepare himself educationally for a job which he is not capable of performing at the time of his injury. Nor do we feel that such a rule is appropriate, especially in a case such as this where the plaintiff has been out of school for approximately thirty years and the amount of time that it would take him to complete the necessary schooling would be extensive. Accordingly, we conclude that plaintiff has no duty to obtain employment as a checker.

NOTES

1. Mitigation of damages. Compare Walker v. International Paper Co., 92 So. 2d 445, 447 (Miss. 1957), a workers' compensation case, in which it was held that the plaintiff, who had suffered a back injury, had not unreasonably refused to undergo surgery to reduce his disability. The plaintiff, an unskilled laborer with a fifth-grade education, expressed eloquently the reactions of generations of reluctant plaintiffs: "He agreed that the physicians know better about it than he, but said it 'ain't their back.' "

See also Adee v. Evanson, 281 N.W.2d 177 (Minn. 1979), where the court observed that the "plaintiff may not insist on chiropractic care instead of surgery, and thereby aggravate damages, unless the jury could find that a reasonable person would do so."

2. *Avoidable consequences and religious liberty.* Some of the most wrenching cases of mitigation of damages arise at the intersection of religious beliefs and medical treatment. In Munn v. Algee, 924 F.2d 568, 575 (5th Cir. 1991), the decedent, a Jehovah's Witness, was seriously injured in a car collision for which defendants were responsible. When brought to the hospital with multiple fractures, Mrs. Munn refused to have a blood transfusion even though her doctors told her it was necessary to save her life, because receiving blood violated her religious principles. The court held that the doctrine of avoidable consequences — which requires a plaintiff to take reasonable postaccident steps to mitigate loss — justified the jury's refusal to award her damages for wrongful death. It therefore upheld a verdict that allowed plaintiff only $10,000 in damages for the eight hours of pain and suffering before her death. The plaintiff had argued that applying the mitigation of damages rule violated her First Amendment right to the free exercise of her religion by forcing her to choose between her religious beliefs and her tort recovery. That conclusion was rebuffed by the court:

> If the jury finds the religion plausible, it will more likely deem the conduct reasonable; on the other hand, if the particular faith strikes the jury as strange or bizarre, the jury will probably conclude that the plaintiff's failure to mitigate was unreasonable. Because the plaintiff's religion is the only basis upon which otherwise unreasonable conduct can be deemed reasonable, the jury undoubtedly assesses the plaintiff's religion in reaching its conclusion. A strong case can be made that the first amendment forbids such an assessment.
>
> However, simply because the case-by-case approach might involve impermissible assessment of a religion's reasonableness does not mean that Munn is entitled to a new trial. Munn himself interjected religion into the case, seeking to explain his wife's conduct. Had he been prohibited from doing so, the jury undoubtedly would have deemed her decision unreasonable. In short, the jury's assessment of Elaine Munn's religion did not harm Munn's case. Consequently, we find the court's application of the case-by-case approach to be, at most, harmless error.

Suppose that the damages for the wrongful death action would have been $1,000,000, but that if the plaintiff had accepted the transfusion and had lived, her damages would have been $2,000,000. Should the doctrine of mitigation of damages preclude the recovery of the smaller sum? Should additional damages be given because the decedent is required to violate her religious beliefs to survive? Does the doctrine that "a tortfeasor takes his victim as he finds him" apply only to physical characteristics or does it extend to religious belief structures as well?

C. CONTINGENCY FEES, FEE-SHIFTING DEVICES, AND SALES OF TORT CLAIMS

Bringing and defending a modern tort claim is everywhere a costly venture. The underlying rules of tort liability are often very complex, the facts of a given case highly uncertain, and the potential damages at stake enormous. Expert witnesses are usually needed to establish critical elements on liability, and are routinely relied on in the damage phase of a trial. This combination of high stakes and high uncertainty means that legal cases will be both expensive to bring and expensive to defend. In the context of the tort system, therefore, it is important to make some quick survey of the standard fee arrangements for tort litigation. Three rules require special attention. First, the plaintiff's lawyer in a damage suit is universally retained on a contingent fee arrangement, while the defendant's lawyer is commonly hired (whether by a firm or an insurance company) on an hourly wage. Second, under the American system each side typically bears its own costs in litigation whether it wins or loses the case. Third, although contingent fee contracts are routinely allowed, an injured party is typically prohibited from making an outright sale of a tort claim to any third party, either before or after it has matured.

1. Contingency Fees

Under the contingent fee system, the plaintiff's attorney agrees to receive compensation for services rendered only out of the funds that the plaintiff receives from the defendant, either by settlement or judgment. In the event that the action is lost, therefore, the plaintiff's attorney receives nothing for time and effort expended. This system is not in general use in any other legal system; indeed, in England, for example, it is specifically prohibited as an "unethical practice." There have been some recent signs of change in England, for at this writing a preliminary study by the Lord Chancellor indicated a willingness to explore the introduction of contingency fees for England, Scotland, and Wales, Lord Chancellor's Department, Contingency Fees Cm 571 (1989), but as of 1994 no law was passed. Today contingency fees are prohbited by the Solicitors Act section 31, which provides, "A solicitor who is retained or employed to prosecute any action, suit or other contentious proceeding shall not enter into agreement or arrangement to receive a contingency fee in respect of that action, suit or other contentious proceeding."

The proponents of the contingent fee system argue that it enables individuals to press forward with claims that would otherwise remain unprosecuted for want of funds. They claim, moreover, that feared abuses are not likely to occur, since lawyers have a strong incentive to choose those cases with the greatest chance of success: they receive no compensation for their services and expenses from suits that fail. The opponents of the system argue, though with less theoretical justification, that it stirs up needless litigation. The dispute over contingent fees has been particularly intense with medical malpractice cases (where the contingency for the lawyer may range anywhere from 25 to 50 percent), and proposals are frequently made to limit the size of the fees the plaintiff's attorney can recover in the event that the case is successful. The New Jersey rules, for example, allow 50 percent of the first $1,500, 40 percent of the next $2,000, $33\frac{1}{3}$ percent of the next $46,500, 20 percent of the next $50,000, and only 10 percent of amounts in excess of $100,000. (Rule 1: 21-7 N.J. Supreme Ct.) The power of the court or legislature to regulate these fees has been sustained against challenges that they improperly restrict the access of injured parties to legal services. Thus, Canon 13 of the New York Bar Association provides: "A contract for a contingent fee, where sanctioned by law, should be reasonable under all the circumstances of the case, including the risk and uncertainty of the compensation, but should always be subject to the supervision of a court, as to its reasonableness." See, Accepting the Canon, Gair v. Peck, 160 N.E.2d 43 (N.Y. 1959).

See also In re Florida Bar, 349 So. 2d 630 (Fla. 1977), where the court noted its disagreement with the New Jersey approach and concluded that "due to the absence of competent evidence demonstrating any significant abuse of the contingent fee arrangements within the State, we reject the proposed amendment [to the state code of professional responsibility,] which would impose a maximum contingent fee schedule and thereby impinge upon the constitutional guarantee of freedom of contract." The court did, however, approve rules requiring disclosure of any division of fees with referring lawyers and the preparation of a closing statement summarizing the distribution of funds received in the case.

One important issue concerning the contingent fee is its relative efficacy versus alternative fee arrangements, most notably the hourly fee arrangement and the fixed fee arrangements. The relative superiority of the contingent fee for the ordinary tort damage action depends critically on its ability to minimize the structural conflict of interests between the lawyer and the client. A description of the nature of these conflicts and their possible resolution is forcefully set out by Judge Easterbrook in Kirchoff v. Flynn, 786 F.2d 320, 324-325 (7th Cir. 1986):

> The market for legal services uses three principal plans of compensation: the hourly fee, the fixed fee, and the contingent fee. The contingent fee serves in part as a financing device, allowing people to hire lawyers without paying them in advance (or at all, if they lose). It also serves as a monitoring device. In any agency relation, the agent may pursue his own goals at the expense of the principal's. A fixed fee creates the incentive to shirk; a lawyer paid a lump sum, win or lose, may no longer work hard enough to present his client's case. Fixed fees therefore are used only in cases where the client can monitor the results and the lawyer's work (did the lawyer secure the divorce or not?) or where the client (or the client's general counsel) is sufficiently sophisticated to assess what the lawyer has accomplished.
>
> An hourly fee creates an incentive to run up hours, to do too much work in relation to the stakes of the case. An hourly fee may be appropriate where it is hard to define output (in litigation, for example, the outcome turns on the merits and not simply the lawyer's skill and dedication), so the hourly method measures and prices the inputs, the attorney's hours. . . .
>
> The contingent fee uses private incentives rather than careful monitoring to align the interests of lawyer and client. The lawyer gains only to the extent his client gains. This interest-alignment device is not perfect. When the lawyer gains 40 cents to the client's dollar, the lawyer tends to expend too little effort; unless concern for his reputation dominates, he would not put in an extra $600 worth of time to obtain an extra $1,000 for his client, because he would receive only $400 for his effort. But imperfect alignment of interests is better than a conflict of interests, which hourly fees may create. The unscrupulous lawyer paid by the hour may be willing to settle for a lower recovery coupled with a payment for more hours. Contingent fees eliminate this incentive and also ensure a reasonable proportion between the recovery and the fees assessed to defendants. Except in grudge litigation, no client, however wealthy, pays a lawyer more than a dollar to pursue a dollar's worth of recovery.

Note that contingent fee arrangements also contain other provisions to reduce the conflict of interest between client and lawyer. Thus, it is generally regarded as a violation of the standards of professional ethics for a lawyer to reject a settlement offer or to settle an outstanding case without first obtaining the approval of the client. See ABA Model Rules of Professional Conduct, Rule 1.2(a). In addition, the standard contract typically allows the client to discharge the attorney from the case if the client is dissatisfied with the handling of the case. Moreover, concerns for professional reputation, and the prospect of future business, often keep plaintiff's lawyer hard at work.

Standing alone, these provisions would seem to place all the cards in the hand of the client; but this balance is redressed in several ways. First, when a client does discharge a lawyer without cause, the court may allow that lawyer a contingent fee based upon the value of work previously done when the claim is finally resolved. The client, moreover, is usually reluctant to undertake that course of action since it is difficult to hire a second lawyer who has to come up to speed in ongoing litigation shaped by another attorney. In addition, the standard contract also allows the lawyer to withdraw from the case if he thinks that it is unwise to pursue the matter further, which might happen if discovery reveals evidence adverse to the client's case. Yet even here withdrawal is normally allowed only with approval of the court, which, although usually granted, may occasionally be denied. For accounts of the contractual features of contingent fee arrangements see Miller, Some Agency Problems in Settlement, 16 J. Legal Stud. 189 (1987). For models of the contingent fee arrangement see Schwartz and Mitchell, An Economic Analysis of the Contingent Fee in Personal Injury Litigation, 22 Stan. L. Rev. 1125 (1970), and the exhaustive study in Clermont and Currivan, Improving on the Contingent Fee, 63 Cornell L. Rev. 529 (1978).

Notwithstanding these safeguards, a more skeptical view of the contingent fee believes that it allows lawyers to reap enormous awards in settling easy cases for large awards. A study by L. Brickman, J. O'Connell and M. Horowitz, Rethinking Contingency Fees: A Proposal to Align the Contingency Fee System with its Policy Roots and Ethical Mandates (1994), claims that the de facto compensation for plaintiff's attorneys reaches $25,000 per hour in cases that carry little risk and that require little skill. The Brickman proposal seeks to counter this risk by allowing defendants a guaranteed opportunity to make settlement offers within 60 days of suit. If accepted, plaintiffs' compensation could be based on an hourly rate of return, or on some modest percentage of the total recovery, say, ten percent. If the offer is refused, however, it then becomes the benchmark against which a contingent fee is calculated in any subsequent settlement. For example, if the settlement offer is for $90,000, and the final settlement is for $100,000, the contingent fee is based on the marginal improvement of $10,000 instead of the full $100,000 in recovery. One possible advantage of this system is that it encourages defendants to make a good first offer, knowing that a low offer, if rejected, could well result down the road in a higher contingent fee to the lawyer and hence less for the plaintiff, who thus will demand even more money to settle. To the plaintiff's bar the proposal represents "something on the fringe." But it has attracted the public support of many prominent conservative scholars who in general favor freedom of contract, and has provoked opposition from plaintiff's lawyers who find themselves defending their contractual prerogatives. See Peter Passell, *Windfall Fees In Injury Cases Under Assault*, N.Y. TIMES, Feb. 11, 1994, at A1.

Whatever the merits of the contingent fee in ordinary tort actions, it is not ideally suited to all situations. There is, for example, no obvious way to value a lawyer's services when injunctive relief is obtained. Since no lawyer wants one-third of the injunction, an hourly fee system is typically required. More important for ordinary tort damage actions is the inescapable conclusion that contingent fee arrangements will not work for compensating the *defendant's* lawyer in a tort action. Until recently, the defendant's lawyer was normally reimbursed on a straight hourly basis for services rendered, even though the hourly fee does not give defense lawyers the same incentives for success as the contingent fee provides for the plaintiff's lawyer. The defense lawyer who obtains, for example, a summary judgment in a difficult case receives relatively little in compensation, while the defense lawyer who loses a large verdict after a protracted trial receives far higher compensation.

Hourly fee arrangements, however, are still common. When these are used in tort defense work, the pull of repeat business tends to keep the relationship in line, as the unexpected successes in some cases offset the unwanted failures in others. But typically there is far greater monitoring of the work of defense lawyers by their clients than of plaintiffs' lawyers by theirs. It is not uncommon for the bills presented to be revised after the fact to take into account exceptional failures or exceptional successes.

In principle, of course, there is, and ought to be, no legal prohibition against the use of contingent fee arrangements on the defendant's side, and there is mounting evidence (in the oral tradition) that some large corporations have experimented with their use. This effort to use contingent fees on the defendant's side has been frequently frustrated by the inability to find a suitable baseline against which to measure the recovery. For the plaintiff the standard baseline is $0.00. In certain extraordinary cases, the parties may stipulate to some higher baseline, if (say) the plaintiff has already received a positive settlement offer before contacting a lawyer. But, on the defendant's side, the contingent fee must be calculated to give the lawyer some fraction of the savings realized from some anticipated verdict or settlement. If the defendant and the lawyer both knew that the proper value of the claim was $1,000,000, then the lawyer's fee could equal one-third of any judgment or settlement below that level. (Thus, the million-dollar case that settles for $400,000 would net the lawyer a fee of $200,000, or 1/3 of $600,000 saved.)

In practice that baseline usually cannot be determined in a precise manner. The ad damnum clause in the complaint is apt to be inflated, and it is often difficult to put any estimated value on a case even after its merits have been investigated. When the defendant is insured, the reserve value that the insurer places on a claim for regulatory purposes might serve as the baseline. But that figure itself is at best an equal mixture of hunch and experience that may have to be revised frequently over the life of the law suit. Its use therefore provides only limited guidance for the determination of the fee when a case is disposed of only for an amount lower than its estimated reservation price, and leads to genuine quandaries when the amount paid exceeds the reservation price.

Notwithstanding these difficulties, as of late more and more firms have been experimenting with other kinds of fee arrangements, both for tort and other litigation. One variation of the contingent fee system is a contract in which the defendant *pays* the lawyer a sum of money up front, in exchange for the lawyer assuming a fraction of the legal liability of the case. The legal fee then becomes the difference between the amount that the lawyer receives from the client (plus interest) and the amount that it loses on the case, either through labor or settlement. But unlike the contingent fee arrangement, the lawyer could *lose* if its share of the total judgment exceeds the amount it was paid up front. It is of course possible to mix and match arrangements, so that the law firm receives some hourly compensation and some lump-sum payment as well. But once the firm is on the hook for its own dollars, the tendency to pad cases with tiers of associates and paralegals is said to disappear, as if by magic.

2.   Fee Shifting

The second dominant feature of the American legal system is its rules for the allocation of costs and attorney's fees. Although the losing side must often compensate the winning side for its "costs," this term has been defined quite narrowly so that usually it includes only such incidental expenses as court filing fees. The largest item of expense in any litigation, however, is attorney's fees; under the American rule these are borne by the respective parties, win or lose. In ordinary tort litigation, attorney's fees are rarely awarded, and only when the prevailing party can clearly demonstrate that the other side advanced a claim or defense that was frivolous or malicious. Cases of malicious prosecution are very difficult to bring. "Suits for malicious prosecution cannot be maintained in Illinois unless the plaintiff alleges and proves that the plaintiff in the original tort action acted maliciously and without probable cause; that the prior cause terminated in the plaintiff's favor; and that some special injury not necessarily resulting in any and all suits prosecuted to recover for like causes of action was suffered." See Berlin v. Nathan, 381 N.E.2d 1367, 1371 (Ill. App. 1978), denying a malicious prosecution claim to a physician who had prevailed in an earlier malpractice claim.

Save in extraordinary circumstances, then, each party bears its own costs in the ordinary tort damage claim in the American system. As is the case with the contingent fee, the American practice on this point stands virtually alone among the advanced industrialized nations. Both the English and the Continental systems use fee shifting, which entitles the winning party to recover its "reasonable" attorney's fees (usually as determined by a taxing master) from the losing party as a matter of course.

The central focus of research on fee-shifting arrangements is its effects on the willingness of the parties to settle or litigate a claim. The standard accounts of this problem treat the litigant as a rational party that seeks to maximize its expected gain through litigation. The basic proposition is that the plaintiff will choose to litigate only when the return from litigation is greater than the expected cost of litigation. Similarly, the defendant will normally choose to litigate (instead of settle) only when the additional expenditures on litigation promise a greater reduction in the amount ultimately paid by settlement or verdict.

On this model, both sides face strong pressures to settle cases short of ultimate verdict. Settlement reduces the total costs of litigation for both sides, and therefore leaves a larger pie for the two sides in the case to share. Settlement also reduces the inherent uncertainty associated with the prosecution of any claim or defense, a clear gain to risk-averse parties.

Within this framework the choice of fee-shifting rules is critical because it influences the willingness to litigate or settle. The relative merits of that choice are clearly revealed in several examples set out in Shavell, Suit, Settlement and Trial: A Theoretical Analysis under Alternative Methods for the Allocation of Legal Costs, 11 J. Legal Stud. 35, 58-60 (1982):

> . . . under the American system, the plaintiff will bring suit if and only if his expected judgment would be at least as large as his legal costs. To illustrate, consider
>
> Example 1: The plaintiff's legal costs from a trial would be $1,000, and he believes that if he prevails he would obtain a judgment for $10,000. Thus, if he thinks the likelihood of prevailing is, say, 75 percent, he will bring suit, for then his expected judgment from a trial would be $7,500 (i.e., 75 percent × $10,000), which would exceed his legal costs of $1,000. However, if he believes the chance of success is only, say, 5 percent, he will not bring suit, since his expected judgment would be $500, which would be less than his legal costs.
>
> Similarly, under the British system, the plaintiff will bring suit if and only if his expected judgment would be at least as large as his expected legal costs — that is, the total legal costs discounted by his probability of losing at trial. Consider now
>
> Example 2: The plaintiff's legal costs and beliefs concerning a judgment are as in the previous example, and the defendant's legal costs from a trial would be $1,500. Consequently, if the plaintiff thinks the probability of prevailing is 75 percent, his expected judgment of $7,500

would exceed his expected legal costs of $625 (i.e., 25 percent × $2,500), so that he would bring suit. But if he thinks the probability is 5 percent, his expected judgment of $500 would be below his expected legal costs of $2,375 (i.e., 95 percent × $2,500), so that he would not bring suit.

Comparing the two systems, it is apparent that *the frequency of suit will be greater under the British system when the plaintiff believes the likelihood of prevailing is sufficiently high — above a "critical" level — and the frequency will be greater under the American system when the likelihood is below the critical level.* This is so because when the plaintiff is relatively optimistic about prevailing, his expected legal costs will be relatively low under the British system — he will be thinking about the possibility of not having to pay any such costs — whereas under the American system he must bear his own costs with certainty. Thus he will be likely to find suit a more attractive prospect under the British system. But when the plaintiff is not optimistic, converse reasoning explains why he would be expected to sue more often under the American system.

The analysis of course becomes even more complicated when either or both sides to the litigation is risk-averse, and thus have an added impulse to settle that a risk-neutral party does not have. Where, therefore, there is a risk-averse plaintiff (the ordinary tort claimant, a large fraction of whose wealth is tied up in an individual claim) and a (relatively) risk-neutral defendant (an insurance company with a large portfolio of cases), the plaintiff will ordinarily be prepared to accept a somewhat lower price than a risk-neutral analysis suggests. Similarly, litigation will be somewhat less frequent since plaintiffs will generally be more reluctant to bring suit given the need for a higher degree of uncertainty for success. Id. at 61-62. The contingent fee arrangement reduces the plaintiff's reluctance to sue, for part of the risk is now borne by the lawyer, who is likely to be more risk-neutral because he has a large portfolio of claims and a greater knowledge and experience of litigation.

The question of fee shifting has been exhaustively studied in a wide range of contexts and under a wide range of alternative assumptions, since many statutes provide for "one-way" fee shifting in favor of the successful plaintiff. For an exhaustive analysis of fee shifting in its private and public contexts see Symposium, Attorney Fee-Shifting, 47 Law & Contemp. Probs. 1-346 (1984), with articles by, among others, Leubsdorf, Rowe, Braeutigam, Owen and Panzar, Fein, and Percival and Miller.

The choice of fee structures and fee-shifting rules may also have an unanticipated effect on the development of the substantive law, for risky claims are more likely to be brought under the American System forbidding cost shifting, because the risks of failure are born in part by the successful defendants. It follows that risky claims will be initiated more often in the United States. Once these claims are established, their riskiness is reduced, and they are more likely to be imitated in England and other common-law jurisdictions that follow a winner-take-all rule. See Prichard, A Systemic Approach to Comparative Law: The Effect of Cost, Fee and Financing Rules on the Development of the Substantive Law, 17 J. Legal Stud. 451 (1988).

3.   Sales of Tort Claims

The present system of tort law allows only the tort victim to press a tort claim. In some sense the contingent fee is an exception to this rule because it functions as a partial sale of a tort claim after the accident has occurred. Two questions then arise: why should total sales be prohibited when these partial sales are allowed, and why should the only eligible purchaser be a contingent fee lawyer? Removing these two restrictions would in effect create an open market for the sale of matured tort claims, unregulated by the current statutes that make maintenance, champerty, and barratry all criminal offenses. The argument in favor of removing that restriction is found in Shukaitis, A Market in Personal Injury Tort Claims, 16 J. Legal Stud. 329, 329-330, 339-340 (1987):

> Allowing victims to sell their claims to third parties, that is, allowing a market in personal injury tort claims, would have significant advantages for tort victims. Compared with litigation, tort victims would be able to receive immediate and certain compensation by selling their claims to purchasers in the market. Compared with settlement, tort victims would receive compensation at a market price closer to what they would expect from a court judgment. Thus compensation by the tort system would be made less dependent on the tort victim's ability to withstand delay and uncertainty. Victims who now do not pursue their claims because of ignorance of their rights or a lack of resources might receive compensation. Some of the incentive problems of hiring an attorney on either a contingent fee or an hourly arrangement would be lessened. And, by increasing the costs of tortfeasors, a market would increase deterrence against harm-causing activities.

Shukaitis then compares the sale of a tort claim with standard fee arrangements.

> There is one important market impediment for the outright sale of tort claims, however. The amount of recovery in a personal injury suit may depend not only on the efforts of the attorney but also on the efforts of the tort victim. After a tort victim sold his interest in a claim, he would have little incentive to appear sympathetic and deserving before a jury. To the extent the tort victim's lack of incentive reduces the expected recovery, the development of a market in claims could be inhibited. Either a purchaser would have to reduce the amount offered for a claim, or he would have to find a way to motivate the tort victim.

There are several ways in which the tort claim purchaser could structure the purchase so as to minimize this incentive problem. For instance, purchasers could require tort victims to cooperate as a condition of purchase; such cooperation clauses are routinely found in standard insurance contracts, which raise the mirror problem with the defense of claims. Purchasers might also pay the purchase price in installments, with payments contingent on cooperation. Finally, purchasers might condition part of the purchase price on the amount of recovery. A purchaser thus might purchase only 90 percent of the claim, leaving the tort victim with 10 percent at risk as an incentive to cooperate in pursuing the claim.

If sales are allowed of matured tort claims, is there any reason to prohibit the sale of unmatured tort claims? That proposal was first raised in Friedman, supra at page 873, and has been urged in a more comprehensive form in Cooter, Towards a Market in Unmatured Tort Claims, 75 Va. L. Rev. 383, 387 (1989). Cooter has defended his proposal as follows:

> A market for UTCs [unmatured tort claims] can be defended solely because it gives people more options. UTCs are no exception to the proposition that both parties benefit in a voluntary exchange. Perhaps less obviously, the market for UTCs may also be defended as a superior vehicle for achieving tort law's two proclaimed goals — deterrence and insurance. If a market in UTCs were established . . . potential victims would substitute cheaper first party insurance for the tort system's current third party insurance scheme. Additionally, competitive pricing of UTCs would result in appropriate deterrence of potential tortfeasors. Because the price of UTCs should vary according to the likelihood and severity of potential torts, the potential tortfeasor faced with purchasing the UTC or risking litigation should take the optimal amount of precaution.

As Cooter points out, there is a certain irony in his proposal because it may reintroduce through the back door many of the standard doctrines of nineteenth-century tort law. Thus, if an employer buys a UTC from its employee, the final position is virtually indistinguishable from the ordinary doctrine of assumption of risk. If a prospective patient can sell his rights to pain and suffering to the employer, who in turn sells them to a health care provider as part of a package for the comprehensive provision of medical care, then pain and suffering damages are effectively eliminated for malpractice actions. Should the legal system allow sales to be made by persons who have no other forms of insurance for personal injury or disability?

Finally, what happens to the position of the potential defendants in a world where injured parties can sell either matured or unmatured claims? The arguments of both Shukaitis and Cooter presuppose that the present rules of tort liability do impose optimal incentives on potential tortfeasors. If that judgment is incorrect, as many believe it to be with both medical malpractice and products liability cases, will the sale of claims only exacerbate the defects of the present system? In this connection is there a difference between the Shukaitis approach, which contemplates sales to professional plaintiffs of matured claims, and the Cooter approach, which contemplates the routine sale of claims to potential defendants?

D.   COLLATERAL BENEFITS

Harding v. Town of Townshend
43 Vt. 536 (1871)

This was an action on the case for damages sustained by the plaintiff by reason of an insufficiency of a highway of the defendant. Trial September term, 1869, Barrett, J., presiding.

Upon the trial, the contest was wholly with reference to the amount of damages the plaintiff was entitled to recover.

The plaintiff was a witness, and on cross-examination the defendant asked him if he had not received money from an accident insurance company on account of the injuries for which he claimed to recover, to which the plaintiff objected, but the court overruled the objection and permitted the inquiry to be put and answered, to which the plaintiff excepted. The plaintiff answered that he had received $130, and that the expenses of the insurance were $7. At the request of the defendant, the court charged the jury that the $123, the net proceeds of the insurance, should be deducted from the damages sustained by the plaintiff, to which the plaintiff excepted.

This ruling was made upon an understanding that in case it should be reversed, the sum of $123 should be added to the verdict and final judgment rendered for the amount in the supreme court. Verdict for the plaintiff for $1,913.31.

PECK, J. There is no technical ground which necessarily leads to the conclusion that the money received by the plaintiff of the accident insurance company should operate as a defense, or enure to the benefit of the defendant. The insurer and the defendant are not joint tortfeasors or joint debtors so as to make a payment or satisfaction by the former operate to the benefit of the latter. Nor is there any legal privity between the defendant and the insurer so as to give the former a right to avail itself of a payment by the latter. The policy of insurance is collateral to the remedy against the defendant, and was procured solely by the plaintiff and at his expense, and to the procurement of which the defendant was in no way contributory. It is in the nature of a wager between the plaintiff and a third person, the insurer, to which the defendant was in no measure privy, either by relation of the parties or by contract or otherwise. It cannot be said that the plaintiff took out the policy in the interest or behalf of the defendant; nor is there any legal principle which seems to require that it be ultimately appropriated to the defendant's use and benefit.

But it is urged, on the part of the defense, that the plaintiff is entitled to but one satisfaction for the injury he has sustained. If we assume this to be a correct proposition, the question arises whether the defendant stands in a condition to make this objection. This depends on the question who, as between the insurer and the defendant, ought to pay the damage — which of the two ought primarily to make compensation to the plaintiff and ultimately to bear the loss? If the insurer ought ultimately to bear the loss, the defendant is entitled in this action to have the benefit of that payment; but if the defendant should ultimately bear the loss, then the payment by the insurer and the collection of the entire damage of the defendant only creates an equity between the plaintiff and the insurer, to be ultimately adjusted between them, in which the defendant has no interest, and with which he has no concern. The statute imposes upon the towns severally the duty of keeping their highways in good and sufficient repair, and makes each town liable for any special damage happening to any person by reason of the insufficiency or want of repair of any highway in such town. The defendant is found liable in consequence of the breach of this duty. The defendant town, therefore, in respect to the injury the plaintiff has sustained, is the wrong-doer; and whether such by some positive, affirmative act, or by culpable negligence, does not vary the principle applicable to the case. In such case, as between the insurer and the wrong-doer, in reason and justice the burden of making compensation to the injured party ought to be ultimately borne by the party thus in fault. The party whose wrongful act or culpable negligence caused the injury ought to make compensation and bear the loss. Therefore, if there is any such connection between these two remedies as to have the enforcement of one operate in defense or mitigation of the other, it is the insurer, and not the town, that should be entitled to this benefit. It would seem to be a perversion of justice to subrogate the wrong-doer, who has caused the loss, to the rights of the injured party as to his remedy against the insurer. But it is not uncommon that the insurer, who has paid the loss, is put in place of the insured and subrogated to his rights in respect to his remedies against others for the injury. Randal v. Cockran, 1 Vesey, sen., 98, is an instance of the application of this principle in equity.

In principle the question involved in this case has been settled in analogous cases. In Mason v. Sainsbury, 3 Doug., 61, it was held that in an action against the Hundred under stat. Geo. I., to recover for the destruction of the plaintiff's house by a mob, the fact that the plaintiff had received the amount of his loss from the insurer would not avail the defendant in defense. In that case it appeared that the action was prosecuted for the benefit of the insurer; but it establishes the principle that the right of the insurer is paramount to that of the wrong-doer, *or one in place of the wrong-doer.* So in Clark v. The Inhabitants of the Hundred of Blythiny, 2 B. & C., 254, (9 E. Com. L., 77,) it was decided that the owner of certain stacks of hay and corn which were maliciously set on fire, who had received the amount of his loss from an insurance office, could nevertheless recover the amount in an action against the Hundred under the stat. Geo. I. In the case at bar, the town is certainly no less to be regarded as in fault for the insufficiency of its highways, than the Hundred for crimes committed by individuals within its limits. In Yates v. Whyte, and others, 33 E. Com. L. R., 349, (4 Bing. New Cases, 272,) in an action for damage to plaintiff's ship by collision with defendant's ship, it was held defendant was not entitled to deduct from the amount of damages a sum paid to plaintiff by insurers in respect to such damage. The same decision was made in a similar case of collision of vessels, The Propeller Monticello v. Gilbert Mollison, in Admiralty, 17 How., 152. In that case there had been an abandonment to the insurers and an acceptance of the abandonment by the insurers, who had paid the insurance prior to the filing of the libel; and Grier, J., says that the doctrine, that in such case the fact that the injured party has received satisfaction from insurers cannot avail the defendant, is well settled at common law, and received in courts of admiralty. We are referred by defendant's counsel to Bird v. Randall, 3 Burr., 1345, in support of the proposition that the defendant can avail himself of such payment. But in that case the plaintiff, having sued and collected of the servant the full stipulated penalty as damages for permanently abandoning his service, it was held that the plaintiff could not afterwards recover of the defendant for procuring or enticing the servant thus to abandon his master's service. In that case the servant and defendant were both wrong-doers, and in principle stood in the relation of joint tortfeasors, and hence the one who did the act that caused the injury having made full satisfaction therefor, the other could not be held liable for the same injury for having aided in procuring the servant to do the wrongful act. . . .

Judgment of the county court reversed, and judgment for the plaintiff for the amount of the verdict, and the $123 to be added thereto.

NOTES

1. Varieties of collateral benefits. The proper treatment of collateral source payments is an issue not only with insurance payments made directly to the plaintiff but with other types of payments as well. In

Motts v. Michigan Cab. Co., 264 N.W. 855 (Mich. 1936), the court refused to reduce the plaintiff's award by the amount of the salary paid
by the plaintiff's employer pursuant to their employment contract.
Kentucky courts have taken a similar position both for payments from
the Welfare Fund of the United Mine Workers, see Conley v. Foster,
335 S.W.2d 904 (Ky. 1960), and with the plaintiff's sick or vacation pay,
see Davidson v. Vogler, 507 S.W.2d 160 (Ky. 1974).

Is there any reason to adopt a different rule for collateral services
given to the plaintiff? In Coyne v. Campbell, 183 N.E.2d 891, 894 (N.Y.
1962), the New York Court of Appeals treated that difference as decisive when the plaintiff, himself a physician, received free medical care
from his professional colleagues, including his uncle. The strong dissent by Fuld, J., asked, "what difference should it make, either to the
plaintiff or to the defendant, whether an injured plaintiff has his medical bills taken care of by an insurer or by a wealthy uncle or by a fellow
doctor? Certainly, neither the uncle, who acted out of affection, nor
the doctor, impelled by so-called professional courtesy, intended to
benefit the tort-feasor."

2. *Government benefits and the collateral source rule.* The collateral source
rule gives rise to special complications when the government is both a
tortfeasor liable under the Federal Torts Claims Act and the supplier
of various first-party benefits under, for example, both Social Security
and veterans benefits programs. In this context the government's position typically is that the monies paid out under other government programs are not monies from collateral sources, and hence should be
used to reduce the government's tort obligation. That position has received mixed success in the courts. In Steckler v. United States, 549
F.2d 1372, 1379 (10th Cir. 1977), the government sought to set off both
veterans benefits and Social Security from the tort award. The court
accepted the government's position that it was necessary to deduct
veterans benefits in order to prevent the plaintiff from recovering "double payment" for the same injury from the same source. The court refused, however, to allow the government a total setoff for Social
Security. "The part contributed by the worker and the employers has
the aspects of social insurance and as such is collateral to monies contributed by the government." The part of Social Security attributable
to general government contributions, however, was not collateral, and
hence should be used as a setoff against tort damages, like veterans
benefits. *Steckler* then placed the burden on the plaintiff to determine
how much of the Social Security payment counted as a nondeductible
collateral source.

Steckler was modified in Berg v. United States, 806 F.2d 978, 985 (10th
Cir. 1986). "We are now convinced that it is in fact impossible to distinguish accurately which part of a fund that has been produced by millions of contributors is attributable to the government and which part

is attributable to a particular injured party. Therefore we require that the plaintiff bear the burden of showing only that he or she contributed to a special fund that is separate and distinct from general government revenues." The court then held that Medicare benefits, funded under Social Security, so qualified as collateral sources.

That approach was followed in Molzof v. United States, 6 F.3d 461, 465, 466 (7th Cir. 1993), where Cudahy, J., following Wisconsin law, refused to allow the government to set off benefits it paid out through its Veterans Administration program against damages awarded against it under the Federal Torts Claims Act. In meeting the argument that the government should not have to pay twice for the same injuries, he wrote: "Just because both recoveries come from the *defendant,* however, does not necessarily mean that they are coming from the same *source.* . . . Thus, in order to determine whether the collateral source rule is applicable, courts have looked to the nature of the payment and the reason the payment is being made rather than simply looking at whether the defendant is paying twice." He then concluded that the collateral source rule applied against the government because the money for the claim came "from a specially funded source distinct from the unsegregated revenues of the Federal treasury." That same rule was applied to a private defendant in Karsten v. Kaiser Foundation Health Plan, Inc., 808 F. Supp. 1253, 1256-57 (1992), where services received by the plaintiff as a member of defendant's health plan were not set off against a malpractice award recovered from that defendant on the ground that payments from the defendant "as insurer" were different from payments from the defendant "as tortfeasor." "It is axiomatic that the plaintiff is entitled to receive the benefit of her bargain under the insurance contract, irrespective of the fact that the carrier servicing that contract may also be the tortfeasor." What if the contract provided explicitly for the set off from tort awards?

3. *Statutory modification of the collateral source rule.* In recent years the tort crisis has brought forth a wide range of statutory modifications to the common-law collateral source rule. One reason why legislatures have adopted this approach is that the collateral source rule, whether right or wrong, has a clear enough structure to allow for modification. In some instances, the statutes are perfectly general and apply to all tort actions; see, e.g., Conn. Gen. Stat. §§52-225a-225d (1992 & Supp. 1994), which provides that collateral payments must be deducted from tort awards in personal injury and death cases, except in those cases in which the collateral source has the right of subrogation, which allows it to recoup its own moneys paid to the tort plaintiff. In other cases the statutes are more directed to actions brought against certain classes of defendants, see California Government Code §985 et seq (West Supp. 1989), which creates a complex set of rules whenever damage actions are successful against public entities. These rules provide that publicly

funded collateral sources, including MediCal and Aid to Families with Dependent Children, should be reimbursed from a tort recovery for any payments to tort claimants "on such terms as may be just." The statute also provides for private collateral sources, such as health maintenance organizations or private disability insurance: "the court may, after considering the totality of all circumstances and on terms as may be just, determine what portion of the collateral source benefits will be reimbursed from the judgment to the provider of the collateral source payment, used to reduce the verdict or accrue to the benefit of the plaintiff." A subsequent amendment modifies §52-225c, so that insurers cannot recover from settlements as they can from judgments. Ct. ALS 297 §24 (1993). Given the high rate of settlement is this provision a de facto restoration of the common-law rule?

Still other collateral source statutes are directed only to specific causes of action, most notably medical malpractice. According to the California Civil Code:

> §3333.1. NEGLIGENCE OF HEALTH CARE PROVIDER; EVIDENCE OF
> BENEFITS AND PREMIUMS PAID; SUBROGATION
> (a) In the event the defendant so elects, in an action for personal injury against a health care provider based upon professional negligence, he may introduce evidence of any amount payable as a benefit to the plaintiff as a result of the personal injury pursuant to the United States Social Security Act, any state or federal income disability or worker's compensation act, any health, sickness or income-disability insurance, accident insurance that provides health benefits or income-disability coverage, and any contract or agreement of any group, organization, partnership, or corporation to provide, pay for, or reimburse the cost of medical, hospital, dental, or other health care services. Where the defendant elects to introduce such evidence, the plaintiff may introduce evidence of any amount which the plaintiff has paid or contributed to secure his right to any insurance benefits concerning which the defendant has introduced evidence.

A New York statute, N.Y. Civ. Prac. L. & R. §4545(a) (1994), allows recovery to be reduced for any present or future payment, subject to reasonable estimation. The amount recoverable is then increased by an amount equal to (1) the cost of keeping the benefit in place during the previous two years plus (2) the projected contractual cost of keeping the benefits in place in the future. The purpose of the New York statute is to place the plaintiff in the same position that he would have been in if he had not procured any collateral coverage at all. A simple reduction of tort damages by the amount of the collateral source would have left the injured party worse off, by the amount of past and future premiums, than he would have been if he had not purchased insurance at all.

4. Subrogation and reimbursement. As noted above a second way to avoid the difficulty of double payments is to have to allow the parties that have paid the collateral benefit to recover them from the award.

Systems of this sort can come in two varieties. The first, subrogation, gives the collateral source the power to participate in, or even control, the tort litigation, and to recover its expenses from the tort claimant. The second, reimbursement, leaves the injured party in full control over the litigation, and allows the insurer to recover its expenses only from the proceeds of recovery.

One question common to both systems concerns the proper order of recovery when the amount paid by the tortfeasor is insufficient to cover both damages for pain and suffering and for lost medical expenses, where the subrogee has a right to the second but not to the first. The normal default rule appears to be that the injured party must be compensated in full for pain and suffering damages before the subrogee is entitled to reimbursement for medical expenses. One critical question is whether these rules can be altered by a contract providing that the right of subrogation or reimbursement "comes first" even if the injury party has not made a full recovery. A clause of that sort was invalidated on both contractual and "equitable" grounds in Powell v. Blue Cross and Blue Shield, 581 So. 2d 772, 777 (Ala. 1990), where the court said:

> Our review of the origins and development of the law of subrogation persuades us that a prerequisite to the right of subrogation is the full compensation of the insured. In effect, an attempt to contract away this prerequisite to the right of subrogation would defeat the right itself. This is not compatible with the principle of fairness that underlies all equitable doctrines. Therefore, we hold that the insurer has no right to subrogation unless and until the insured is made whole for his loss.
>
> For the purposes of subrogation, the test for when the insured has been made whole is whether the injured plaintiff has been completely compensated for *all* of his loss. Likewise, *all* sources of reimbursement must be considered in determining the extent to which the plaintiff has been compensated. It is when the plaintiff's recovery from all sources excess the sum total of the plaintiff's damages that the right to subrogation arises.

The rules on subrogation have influenced the pattern of litigation and settlement of the underlying tort claims. In order to determine the amount of medical expenses awarded by a jury, special verdicts are often used to divide medical claims, to which subrogation is applied, from other claims for which it is not. In Westendorf by Westendorf v. Stasson, 330 N.W.2d 699, 702 (Minn. 1983), a settlement of the underlying tort dispute contained a clause that said that all "payments to be made hereunder are solely attributable to the pain and suffering and permanent injury" of the plaintiff and the loss of consortium to her spouse. Simonett, J., refused to honor that clause:

> When, however, plaintiffs' claim is settled without a verdict, the application of the reimbursement provision is more problematic. In such a case, any allocation is left to the bargaining of the parties to the tort action, and it is not surprising if the parties give little solicitude to the

reimbursement rights of the health care provider. The enrollee, even though entitled to recover medical expenses from a third party, may elect not to do so here. . . . Because the parties to the settlement agreement have characterized their settlement as excluding any damages for medical expenses, it does not follow, however, that this characterization is binding on the HMO provider. The effect of the HMO's reimbursement clause should not depend on a settlement bargain to which it was not privy. The settlement should not be determinative of how the proceeds are allocated.

If the settlement excludes compensation for medical expenses, can the health care provider also have a direct action against the tort defendant? For the position that such actions are excluded by the prohibition on assignment of tort claims (and splitting of causes of action) see Allstate Insurance Co. v. Druke, 576 P.2d 489 (Ariz. 1978).

5. *Collateral uses of collateral benefits.* Should the defendant be permitted to introduce evidence of collateral benefits to establish the plaintiff's motive to malinger or otherwise extend the period of apparent disability? In Eichel v. New York Central Railroad Co., 375 U.S. 253, 255 (1963), the United States Supreme Court adopted an ironclad rule against the practice. "In our view the likelihood of misuse by the jury clearly outweighs the value of this evidence. Insofar as the evidence bears on the issue of malingering, there will generally be other evidence having more probative value and involving less likelihood of prejudice than the receipt of a disability pension."

State courts have usually disagreed with the Supreme Court's strict prohibition, preferring to give discretion, albeit in varying degrees, to the trial judge. In Hrnjak v. Graymar, Inc., 484 P.2d 599 (Cal. 1971), the court parted company with *Eichel* and left it in the discretion of the trial judge whether to allow evidence of collateral benefits on the question of malingering. It further held that "the evidence must have substantial probative value as proof that the plaintiff is a malingerer," as gathered from the full trial record. On the facts, it then reversed the trial judge for an abuse of discretion for admitting evidence of collateral benefits, noting that it "taxes credulity" to think that a plaintiff would malinger for about $700 per year, the money left to him after his medical expenses were deducted from his insurance proceeds.

E.   WRONGFUL DEATH AND LOSS OF CONSORTIUM

The close connection between the actions for wrongful death and loss of consortium justifies their unified treatment. Both types of suit vindicate the "relational" interest of the plaintiff to the person injured or killed. This relational interest rests on the evident social fact that individuals owe obligations of duty and support to other persons: husband and wife to each other; parent to child; and servant to employer. The protection of relational interests introduces an added note of complexity into the law, for now the legal system must coordinate the actions of the injured party with those who claim through that party.

The chief common-law protection of relational interests was found in the action quod servitium amiserit ("because the service has been lost") given only to a man whenever the defendant injured his wife, child, or servant, thereby preventing them from rendering him valuable services. 3 Bl. Comm.; 142 Kendrick v. McCrary, 11 Ga. 603 (1852). The statement of the general rule left unsettled two key questions about the reach of the action. First, could an action for loss of services be brought by a wife or a child? Second, could the action for loss of services be allowed for wrongful death? The history of these two developments did not proceed in an orderly fashion. To organize the discussion, we will first consider the history of actions for wrongful death and related causes. Thereafter we will turn to those for loss of consortium.

1. Wrongful Death

a. History

The orderly development of wrongful death cases at common law was prevented by Lord Ellenborough in his famous, if ill-considered, opinion in Baker v. Bolton, 170 Eng. Rep. 1033 (K.B. 1808). That case decided that a husband suffered no damage when his wife was not merely injured, but killed, by the wrongful conduct of the defendant. The plaintiff in Baker v. Bolton was thus allowed to recover damages for the loss of his wife's services and consortium for the month between injury and death, but was denied damages for services and consortium lost after her death. The precedents were at best scattered and inconclusive. See Holdsworth, Origin of the Rule in Baker v. Bolton, 32 Law Q. Rev. 431 (1916). Nevertheless, Lord Ellenborough treated the matter as though it had long been settled on the highest authority: "In a civil court," he said, "the death of a human being could not be complained of as an injury; and in this case the damages as to the plaintiff's wife must stop with the period of her existence." There was thus no action for wrongful death at common law.

The situation stood unchanged in England until the passage of Lord Campbell's Act of 1846 (Fatal Accidents Act, 9 & 10 Vict. c. 93 (1846)). The statutory preamble treated Baker v. Bolton as decisive authority against allowing the action at the common law. Its operative provision then provided that "whenever the death of a person is caused by the wrongful act, neglect or default of another, such as would (if death had not ensued) have entitled the injured person to sue and recover damages in respect thereof, then the person who would have been liable if death had not ensued shall be liable to an action for damages, although the death shall have been caused under circumstances as amount to a felony." The last clause was inserted to make it clear that the plaintiff in the wrongful death action did not have to first prosecute the defendant for any possible felony. The statute then designated the class of dependents (since expanded by the Fatal Accidents Act, 1959 §1 (1)) entitled to the action: husband, wife, parent, child, grandparent, or grandchild of the deceased. How might the plaintiffs entitled to bring suit for wrongful death be specified at common law?

Under Lord Campbell's statute, dependents are subject to any defenses that could have been raised against the decedent had he lived, including his contributory negligence and assumption of risk. The English statute is quite unspecific on the question of damages, providing only that, however assessed, they should be divided among the class of eligible beneficiaries in proportions seen fit by the jury. But in subsequent judicial opinions, the English court adopted a rule that required damages to be apportioned "in reference to a reasonable expectation of pecuniary benefit as of right, or otherwise, from the continuance of the life." Franklin v. South Eastern Ry. Co., 157 Eng. Rep. 448 (Ex. 1858).

After the passage of the statute some plaintiffs tried to recover at common law those elements of damages not listed in the wrongful death statutes. The most famous cases of this sort were Osborn v. Gillett, L.R. 8 Ex. 88 (1873), where the plaintiff was denied recovery for burial expenses, then not provided for under the statute, and Admiralty Commissioners v. S.S. Amerika, [1917] A.C. 38, where the plaintiffs sought to recover the amount of ex gratiae pensions they had paid out to the relatives of the crew lost when the defendant ship sank an admiralty submarine. In both cases the plaintiffs were rebuffed on the strength of Baker v. Bolton. While that decision might well never have survived in the absence of legislative reform, the passage of the death statute effectively foreclosed any common law development in England long after its errors were openly acknowledged. The courts declined to tread where Parliament had intervened, partly out of deference to Parliament and partly out of fear of the complications that a dual scheme for wrongful death actions could create.

The history of wrongful death in the United States also exhibits complex interaction between common law and legislation. In the early colonial period, particularly in Massachusetts, local tribunals probably made awards for wrongful death that were not sanctioned by statute or at common law. Even after the decision in Baker v. Bolton, it appeared that some courts at least were prepared to develop wrongful death actions on their own, Plummer v. Webb, 19 Fed. Cas. 894 (No. 11234) (1825); Ford v. Monroe, 20 Wend. 210 (N.Y. Sup. Ct. 1838), although the rarity of such actions suggests that they were not well established.

Until 1848 Baker v. Bolton was not even cited in an American court. In that year, however, the Massachusetts Supreme Judicial Court, in Carey v. Berkshire R.R., 55 Mass. 475 (1848), relied on Baker v. Bolton to deny the plaintiff a common-law action for wrongful death. The case could have been distinguished from Baker v. Bolton on the ground that the plaintiff in *Carey* was the wife, who had no action at common law for the loss of services or consortium even if her husband had been injured instead of killed. That explanation, however, could not have accounted for the result in the companion case to *Carey*, Skinner v. Housatonic R.R., 55 Mass. (1848), where a father sued to recover for the loss of services of his deceased son. The Massachusetts court in *Carey* refused to recognize the wrongful death action at common law for the same reason that influenced English courts. Eight years before *Carey*, Massachusetts had passed a statute allowing wrongful death actions for between $500 and $5,000 to the families of deceased railway passengers whose death was caused by the negligence of the railroad. The deceased in *Carey* was an employee, not a passenger, and thus not covered by the statute, and the court did not wish to create its own wrongful death action in competition with the legislature's. State after state followed the opinion and logic of the *Carey* decision, with only Georgia willing to face the problems of policing and coordinating two different systems of wrongful death actions. See Shields v. Yonge, 15 Ga. 349 (1854).

Old habits died hard. It was only in 1972 that Moragne v. States Marine Lines, Inc., 398 U.S. 375 (1970) first allowed a non-statutory cause of action for wrongful death in admiralty. Ironically, Massachusetts quickly followed *Moragne* in Gaudette v. Webb, 284 N.E.2d 222, 229 (Mass. 1972), to overrule *Carey* and to recognize a common-law action for wrongful death, subject to many of the familiar statutory conditions:

> (a) requiring that damages recoverable for wrongful death be based upon the degree of the defendant's culpability; (b) prescribing the range of the damages recoverable against each defendant; (c) requiring that any action for wrongful death be brought by a personal representative on behalf of the designated categories of beneficiaries; and (d) requiring that the action be commenced within the specified period of time, as a limitation upon the remedy and not upon the right. We further hold that statutes limiting the period for bringing actions for death are to be construed in the same manner as the limitations contained in . . . the general statute of limitations, and that in appropriate cases they may be tolled by the various provisions of [the general statute].

It was this general statute of limitations and its tolling provisions that aided the infant plaintiffs in *Gaudette*.

One notable feature of the early wrongful death statutes was their stringent ceilings on the amount of damages permitted the surviving plaintiff. These ceilings were originally imposed in part because of the fear of the jury's passion and sympathy for the aggrieved plaintiff. The plaintiff whose action was by legislative grace could not complain of any attached conditions. Over time, these arguments have seemed less persuasive and the restrictions have steadily been removed. Ceilings in the wrongful death actions were found in the statutes of 22 states in 1893. By 1965 the number of states retaining such limitations had dropped to 12, and by 1974 the number had dwindled to 4. Today no state has any general limitation for damages in wrongful death actions, although a number of states retain special limitations for certain types of cases.

For an excellent overall account of the history of wrongful death see Malone, The Genesis of Wrongful Death, 17 Stan. L. Rev. 1043 (1965); see also Holdsworth, The Origin of the Rule in *Baker v. Bolton,* 32 Law Q. Rev. 431 (1916), a sustained attack on Baker v. Bolton written in anticipation of plaintiff's appeal to the House of Lords in Admiralty Commissioners v. S.S. Amerika.

b.   Measure of damages

The measure of damages in all wrongful death actions is determined by the language of each particular state statute. Basically most statutes fall into one of two camps: loss-to-survivors and loss-to-estate. Under a loss-to-survivors test, the defendant will be answerable in damages only if there is some beneficiary dependent upon the decedent for support. Under the loss-to-estate test, damages will be awarded against the defendant even if no one was dependent upon the decedent at the time of death. Most jurisdictions have adopted a loss-to-survivors test as the measure of damages.

The awarding of damages in wrongful death cases is fraught with many of the same difficulties in administration found in serious personal injury cases. To be sure, in the wrongful death context, no attention must be paid to either the decedent's pain and suffering or to medical expenses, but enormous controversy can exist over both the suffering of the survivors and the estimation of lost earnings, especially for children who have yet to assume any definable niche in life. Thus in Wycko v. Gnodtke, 105 N.W.2d 118 (Mich. 1960), the court allowed the parents of a reliable and trustworthy boy of 14 to recover $15,000 in damages, dismissing the objection that the parents were entitled to recover only for their pecuniary loss. The court noted the general progress in the social treatment of children since the passage of Lord Campbell's Act in 1846, but rejected "as prayed by appellant, the child-labor measure of the pecuniary loss suffered through the death of a minor child, namely, his probable wages less the cost of his keep." The court then allowed the plaintiff to recover under two separate heads of damage. First, on analogy to the costs of maintenance service and repairs for machinery, it allowed the parents damages for the "expenses of birth, of food, of clothing, of medicines, of instruction, of nurture and of shelter." Second, by treating the family as a functioning social unit, it allowed "the value of mutual society and protection, in a word, companionship."

Michigan law now provides: "[T]he court or jury may award damages as the court or jury shall consider fair and equitable, under all the circumstances including reasonable medical, hospital, funeral, and burial expenses for which the estate is liable; reasonable compensation for pain and suffering, while conscious, undergone by the deceased person during the period intervening between the time of injury and death; and damages for the loss of financial support and the loss of the society and companionship of the deceased." Mich. Comp. Laws Ann. §600.2922(6) (West 1992).

2. Survival of Personal Injury Actions

Before turning to actions for loss of consortium, it is necessary to mention one other feature of the common-law treatment of death in tort cases. From at least the fifteenth century, the common-law maxim actio personalis moritur cum persona provided that any tort action, including one for personal injuries or property damage, was extinguished by the death of either the plaintiff or the defendant. The right of action created by the defendant's wrong was treated as exclusively personal between the two original parties; as death severed that personal relationship, so too did it destroy the cause of action predicated upon it.

The abandonment of the early position came slowly, and it was only by degrees that various tort actions passed to the estate of either the plaintiff or the defendant, as the case may be. Today such survival of actions is well-nigh universal, except perhaps for the passage of actions concerning deceit or defamation, and even these actions pass in a few states. Under the typical survivor statute, compensation is allowed for the pain and suffering of the decedent before his death, an item of damages not covered under the wrongful death statutes proper. The subject of pain and suffering before death has been recently reviewed extensively in Leebron, Final Moments: Damages for Pain and Suffering Prior to Death, 64 N.Y.U. L. Rev. 256 (1989), where the author concludes that the primary justification for such awards must be deterrence and not compensation. Leebron then notes that, empirically, the variation in awards under this head of damage is exceptionally high and urges a greater level of judicial supervision to iron out the anomalies in this area.

3. Actions for Loss of Consortium

The historical development of the action for loss of consortium has taken very different lines. In England a persistent sense that all actions for loss of consortium were misconceived, and in an important case, Best v. Samuel Fox & Co. Ltd, [1952] A.C. 716, the House of Lords, with evident discomfort, refused to grant the action to the wife for her loss of the services and comfort of her husband. The American cases, however, universally vest the action for loss of consortium in the wife as well as the husband. The new era was ushered in by Hitaffer v. Argonee Co., 183 F.2d 811 (D.C. Cir. 1950), which has been universally followed in this country. See Restatement (Second) of Torts section 693(1), which provides that liability in these cases covers "the resulting loss of the society and services of the first spouse, including impairment of capacity for sexual intercourse, and for reasonable expense incurred by the second spouse in providing medical treatment." In a self-conscious break with the past, the court first argued that although the element of lost services was important in a consortium case, elements of "companionship, love, felicity and sexual relations" were of equal if not greater importance. It then rejected arguments that the wife's action should be barred on the ground that her injuries were too "indirect," too "remote," or too "consequential." If any of these arguments are good against the wife's claim, could they be maintained against the husband's action as well?

The more recent debate over the action for loss of consortium has now shifted from suits by the spouse to suits by children whose parents have been injured or killed. In this connection the argument for recovery essentially rests on the perceived justice of the case. Wrongful death actions are allowed to children in part because they have sustained injury from the interference by force of their advantageous relationships with their parents. The same type of relational loss, even with different extent, also exists when the parent is not killed but injured. If, the argument goes, one spouse may sue when the other is killed or injured, and children may sue (for wrongful death) when parents are killed, then children should also be able to sue when parents are injured.

On the opposite side of the question are the very substantial administrative costs that are entailed by the recognition of such actions. Although there is only one spouse, there may be many children (not to mention grandchildren and more distant relations), and, thus, severe difficulties in both estimating damages owed to each and coordinating the recovery of the injured party with that of the dependents. The leading case against the child's consortium action is Borer v. American Airlines, 563 P.2d 858, 860-861 (Cal. 1977), where the nine children of the injured party sought damages in their own right. Tobriner, J., rejected their claim for these reasons:

> Judicial recognition of a cause of action for loss of consortium, we believe, must be narrowly circumscribed. Loss of consortium is an intangible injury for which money damages do not afford an accurate measure or suitable recompense; recognition of a right to recover for such losses in the present context, moreover, may substantially increase the number of claims asserted in ordinary accident cases, the expense of settling or resolving such claims, and the ultimate liability of the defendants. Taking these considerations into account, we shall explain why we have concluded that the payment of damages to persons for the lost affection and society of a parent or child neither truly compensates for such loss nor justifies the social cost in attempting to do so. We perceive significant differences between the marital relationship and the parent-child relationship that support the limitation of a cause of action for loss of consortium to the marital situation; we shall therefore further elaborate our reasons for concluding that a child cannot maintain a cause of action for loss of parental consortium. In similar fashion we conclude in the companion case of Baxter v. Superior Court [563 P.2d 871 (Cal. 1977)] that a parent cannot maintain a cause of action for loss of a child's consortium.

More recent cases have been mixed. Thus, a large number of states have allowed children to bring actions for the loss of companionship of their parents. See, e.g., Berger v. Weber, 303 N.W.2d 424 (Mich. 1981). Similarly, these courts have also recognized an action in the parents for the loss of companionship of their children. Yet the *Berger* court, in Sizemore v. Smock, 422 N.W.2d 666 (Mich. 1988), held that Michigan "does not recognize a parent's action for the loss of a child's society and companionship, and that any decision to further extend a negligent tortfeasor's liability for consortium damages should be determined by the Legislature."

A somewhat different pattern emerged in Arizona, where the court now freely allows both children and parents to bring actions for loss of consortium. See Villareal v. Arizona, 774 P.2d 213 (Ariz. 1989). The Arizona rule, moreover, allows parents to recover for the loss of companionship of their adult children, even though the parents were not dependent upon those adult children for financial support. Howard Frank, M.D. P.C. v. Superior Court, 722 P.2d 955, 960 (Ariz. 1986). There the court stressed that the damage action should not be denied on "an archaic and outmoded pecuniary theory of parental rights" that misses the importance of companionship, love, and support. The court brushed aside the defendant's objections that with the new action an expanded class of plaintiffs will spawn increased litigation and insurance costs will increase. The danger of an increase in litigation has been raised as an objection in almost every instance where the courts have been asked to recognize a new cause of action. The short answer to this objection is that it is the court's responsibility to deal with suits on their merits, whether there be few suits or many. The rights of a new class of tort plaintiffs should be forthrightly judged without engaging in gloomy speculation as to where it will all end. Such fears have been likened to "the fabled cry of wolf," and have often proved groundless.

Nonetheless some limitations on the new actions for loss of consortium are invoked to control against the risk of double recovery. As a procedural requirement, the claim for loss of consortium must be joined with the underlying tort claim unless it can be shown that such joinder is not feasible. Ueland v. Reynolds Metals Co., 691 P.2d 190 (Wash. 1984).

At a substantive level, many courts have balked at the idea of extending actions for loss of consortium to unmarried couples who are living together. Butcher v. Superior Court, 188 Cal. Rptr. 503 (Cal. App. 1983), had allowed such an action on the grounds that anyone "who negligently causes a disabling injury to an adult may also reasonably expect in our contemporary society that the injured person may be cohabiting with another without the benefit of marriage." But that decision was disapproved outside of California in Weaver v. G. D. Searle & Co., 558 F. Supp. 720 (N.D. Ala. 1983), where the court noted that what may be right for California is wrong for the rest of the country. Subsequently, Butcher was explicitly rejected in California as well as in Elden v. Sheldon, 758 P.2d 582 (Cal. 1988), where the court stressed "the state's interest in promoting the responsibilities of marriage and the difficulty of assessing the emotional, sexual and financial relationship of cohabiting parties to determine whether their arrangement was the equivalent of marriage." In ordinary cases for loss of marital consortium, should the likelihood of divorce be taken into account when calculating damages?

F. PUNITIVE DAMAGES

Pacific Mutual Life Insurance Co. v. Haslip
499 U.S. 1 (1991)

JUSTICE BLACKMUN delivered the opinion of the Court.
This case is yet another that presents a challenge to a punitive damages award.

I

[The defendant-appellant issued group health and life insurance policies to the plaintiffs' employer. These policies were procured for the company by one Lemmie L. Ruffiin, Jr. Unbeknownst to the appellant, Ruffin did not remit payments under the policies to the respondents, but pocketed the money himself. When the appellant did not receive the money it canceled the coverage under the policy and sent notice to that effect to Ruffin and its own agent in Birmingham, but (or so the jury determined) no notice was sent to the individuals insured under the group policy. The plaintiffs incurred medical expenses for which coverage was then denied by the appellant, forcing them to pay their bills out of their own pockets. Respondents then brought suit against Pacific Mutual and Ruffin.]

II

. . . It was alleged that Ruffin collected premiums but failed to remit them to the insurers so that respondents' respective health insurance policies lapsed without their knowledge. Damages for fraud were claimed. The case against Pacific Mutual was submitted to the jury under a theory of respondeat superior.

Following the trial court's charge on liability, the jury was instructed that if it determined there was liability for fraud, it could award punitive damages. . . . Pacific Mutual made no objection on the ground of lack of specificity in the instructions and it did not propose a more particularized charge. No evidence was introduced as to Pacific Mutual's financial worth. The jury returned general verdicts for respondents against Pacific Mutual and Ruffin in the following amounts: [Haslip, $1,040,000; three other plaintiffs about $40,000]. Judgments were entered accordingly.

On Pacific Mutual's appeal, the Supreme Court of Alabama, by a divided vote, affirmed. 553 So. 2d 537 (1989). In addition to issues not now before us, the court ruled that, while punitive damages are not recoverable in Alabama for misrepresentation made innocently or by mistake, they are recoverable for deceit or willful fraud, and that on the evidence in this case a jury could not have concluded that Ruffin's misrepresentations were made either innocently or mistakenly. The majority then specifically upheld the punitive damages award. . . .

Pacific Mutual, but not Ruffin, then brought the case here. It challenged punitive damages in Alabama as the product of unbridled jury discretion and as violative of its due process rights. We stayed enforcement of the Haslip judgment, and then granted certiorari to review the punitive damages procedures and award in the light of the long-enduring debate about their propriety.[4]

III

This Court and individual Justices thereof on a number of occasions in recent years have expressed doubts about the constitutionality of certain punitive damages awards. [The Court then reviewed the cases, including Browning-Ferris Industries of Vermont, Inc. v. Kelco Disposal, Inc., 492 U.S. 257 (1989), where the Court had rejected a challenge to punitive damages brought on the theory that these damages were "excessive fines" under the Eighth Amendment, holding that this clause did not cover disputes between private parties. The Court in *Browning* recognized that the due process clause imposed limits on punitive awards actuated by bias or prejudice, but reserved the question of whether the excessive size of the award triggered due process concerns.]

IV

Two preliminary and overlapping due process arguments raised by Pacific Mutual deserve attention before we reach the principal issue in controversy. Did Ruffin act within the scope of his apparent authority as an agent of Pacific Mutual? If so, may Pacific Mutual be held responsible for Ruffin's fraud on a theory of *respondeat superior?*

Pacific Mutual was held responsible for the acts of Ruffin. [The Court held that the actions took place within the scope of employment given the general benefit that it derived from the sale of insurance policies. It was immaterial that the company did not authorize the fraud, and was in fact victimized by it, when Ruffin diverted the funds to his own use. The Court also noted that Pacific Mutual had received notice that "its agent Ruffin was engaged in a pattern of fraud identical to those perpetrated against respondents."]

Alabama's common-law rule is that a corporation is liable for both

---

4. Compare, e.g., Fay v. Parker, 53 N.H. 342, 382 (1873) ("The idea is wrong. It is a monstrous heresy. It is an unsightly and an unhealthy excrescence, deforming the symmetry of the body of the law."), with Luther v. Shaw, 157 Wis. 234, 238, 147 N.W. 18, 19-20 (1914) (Timlin, J., "Speaking for myself only in this paragraph. . . . The law giving exemplary damages is an outgrowth of the English love of liberty regulated by law. It tends to elevate the jury as a responsible instrument of government, discourage private reprisals, restrains the strong, influential, and unscrupulous, vindicates the right of the weak, and encourages recourse to and confidence in the courts of law by those wronged or oppressed by acts or practices not cognizable in or not sufficiently punished by the criminal law.")

compensatory and punitive damages for fraud of its employee effected within the scope of his employment. We cannot say that this does not rationally advance the State's interest in minimizing fraud. Alabama long has applied this rule in the insurance context, for it has determined that an insurer is more likely to prevent an agent's fraud if given sufficient financial incentive to do so.

Imposing exemplary damages on the corporation when its agent commits intentional fraud creates a strong incentive for vigilance by those in a position "to guard substantially against the evil to be prevented." Louis Pizitz Dry Goods Co. v. Yeldell, 274 U.S. 112, 116 (1927). If an insurer were liable for such damages only upon proof that it was at fault independently, it would have an incentive to minimize oversight of its agents. Imposing liability without independent fault deters fraud more than a less stringent rule. It therefore rationally advances the State's goal. We cannot say this is a violation of Fourteenth Amendment due process. . . .

We therefore readily conclude that Ruffin was acting as an employee of Pacific Mutual when he defrauded respondents, and that imposing liability upon Pacific Mutual for Ruffin's fraud under the doctrine of *respondeat superior* does not, on the facts here, violate Pacific Mutual's due process rights.

V

"Punitive damages have long been a part of traditional state tort law." Silkwood v. Kerr-McGee Corp., 464 U.S. 238, 255 (1984). Blackstone appears to have noted their use. 3 W. Blackstone, Commentaries 137-138. See also Wilkes v. Wood, 98 Eng. Rep. 489 (C.P. 1763) (The Lord Chief Justice validating exemplary damages as compensation, punishment, and deterrence). Among the first reported American cases are Genay v. Norris, 1 S.C.L. (1 Bay) 6 (1784), and Coryell v. Colbaugh, 1 N.J.L. 77 (1791).

Under the traditional common-law approach, the amount of the punitive award is initially determined by a jury instructed to consider the gravity of the wrong and the need to deter similar wrongful conduct. The jury's determination is then reviewed by trial and appellate courts to ensure that it is reasonable.

This Court more than once has approved the common-law method for assessing punitive awards. In Day v. Woodworth, 13 How. 363, 14 L.Ed. 181 (1852), a case decided before the adoption of the Fourteenth Amendment, Justice Grier, writing for a unanimous Court, observed: "It is a well-established principle of the common law, that in actions of trespass and all actions on the case for torts, a jury may inflict what are called exemplary, punitive, or vindictive damages upon a defendant, having in view the enormity of his offence rather than the measure of compensation to the plaintiff. We are aware that the propriety of this doctrine has been questioned by some writers; but if repeated judicial decisions for more than a century are to be received as the best exposition of what the law is, the question will not admit of argument. By the common as well as by statute law, men are often punished for aggravated misconduct or lawless acts, by means of a civil action, and the damages, inflicted by way of penalty or punishment, given to the party injured.

". . . . This has been always left to the discretion of the jury, as the degree of punishment to be thus inflicted must depend on the peculiar circumstances of each case." Id., at 371.

So far as we have been able to determine, every state and federal court that has considered the question has ruled that the common-law method for assessing punitive damages does not in itself violate due process. But see New Orleans, J. & G.N.R. Co. v. Hurst, 36 Miss. 660 (1859). In view of this consistent history, we cannot say that the common-law method for assessing punitive damages is so inherently unfair as to deny due process and be per se unconstitutional. "'If a thing has been practised for two hundred years by common consent, it will need a strong case for the Fourteenth Amendment to affect it.' " Sun Oil Co. v. Wortman, 486 U.S. 717, 730 (1988), quoting Jackman v. Rosenbaum Co., 260 U.S. 22, 31 (1922). As the Court in *Day v. Woodworth* made clear, the common-law method for assessing punitive damages was well established before the Fourteenth Amendment was enacted. Nothing in that Amendment's text or history indicates an intention on the part of its drafters to overturn the prevailing method.

This, however, is not the end of the matter. It would be just as inappropriate to say that, because punitive damages have been recognized for so long, their imposition is never unconstitutional. We note once again our concern about punitive damages that "run wild." Having said that, we conclude that our task today is to determine whether the Due Process Clause renders the punitive damages award in this case constitutionally unacceptable.

VI

One must concede that unlimited jury discretion — or unlimited judicial discretion for that matter — in the fixing of punitive damages may invite extreme results that jar one's constitutional sensibilities. We need not, and indeed we cannot, draw a mathematical bright line between the constitutionally acceptable and the constitutionally unacceptable that would fit every case. We can say, however, that general concerns of reasonableness and adequate guidance from the court when the case is tried to a jury properly enter into the constitutional calculus. With these concerns in mind, we review the constitutionality of the punitive damages awarded in this case.

We conclude that the punitive damages assessed by the jury against Pacific Mutual were not violative of the Due Process Clause of the Fourteenth Amendment. It is true, of course, that under Alabama law, as under the law of most States, punitive damages are imposed for purposes of retribution and deterrence. They have been described as quasi-criminal. But this in itself does not provide the answer. We move, then, to the points of specific attack.

1. We have carefully reviewed the instructions to the jury. By these instructions, the trial court expressly described for the jury the purpose of punitive damages, namely, "not to compensate the plaintiff for any injury" but "to punish the defendant" and "for the added purpose of protecting the public by [deterring] the defendant and others from doing such wrong in the future." Any evidence of Pacific Mutual's wealth was excluded from the trial in accord with Alabama law.

To be sure, the instructions gave the jury significant discretion in its determination of punitive damages. But that discretion was not unlimited. It was confined to deterrence and retribution, the state policy concerns sought to be advanced. And if punitive damages were to be awarded, the jury "must take into consideration the character and the degree of the wrong as shown by the evidence and necessity of preventing similar wrong." The instructions thus enlightened the jury as to the punitive damages' nature and purpose, identified the damages as punishment for civil wrongdoing of the kind involved, and explained that their imposition was not compulsory.

These instructions, we believe, reasonably accommodated Pacific Mutual's interest in rational decisionmaking and Alabama's interest in meaningful individualized assessment of appropriate deterrence and retribution. The discretion allowed under Alabama law in determining punitive damages is no greater than that pursued in many familiar areas of the law as, for example, deciding "the best interests of the child," or "reasonable care," or "due diligence," or appropriate compensation for pain and suffering or mental anguish.[9] As long as the discretion is exercised within reasonable constraints, due process is satisfied.

2. Before the trial in this case took place, the Supreme Court of Alabama had established post-trial procedures for scrutinizing punitive awards. In Hammond v. City of Gadsden, 493 So. 2d 1374 (Ala. 1986), it stated that trial courts are "to reflect in the record the reasons for interfering with a jury verdict, or refusing to do so, on grounds of exces-

---

9. The Alabama Legislature recently enacted a statute that places a $250,000 limit on punitive damages in most cases. See 1987 Ala. Acts, No. 87-185, §§1, 2, and 4. The legislation, however, became effective only on June 11, 1987, see §12, after the cause of action in the present case arose and the complaint was filed.

siveness of the damages." Among the factors deemed "appropriate for the trial court's consideration" are the "culpability of the defendant's conduct," the "desirability of discouraging others from similar conduct," the "impact upon the parties," and "other factors, such as the impact on innocent third parties." Ibid. The *Hammond* test ensures meaningful and adequate review by the trial court whenever a jury has fixed the punitive damages.

3. By its review of punitive awards, the Alabama Supreme Court provides an additional check on the jury's or trial court's discretion. It first undertakes a comparative analysis. It then applies the detailed substantive standards it has developed for evaluating punitive awards. In particular, it makes its review to ensure that the award does "not exceed an amount that will accomplish society's goals of punishment and deterrence." Green Oil Co. v. Hornsby, 539 So. 2d 218, 222 (Ala. 1989). This appellate review makes certain that the punitive damages are reasonable in their amount and rational in light of their purpose to punish what has occurred and to deter its repetition.

Also before its ruling in the present case, the Supreme Court of Alabama had elaborated and refined the *Hammond* criteria for determining whether a punitive award is reasonably related to the goals of deterrence and retribution. It was announced that the following could be taken into consideration in determining whether the award was excessive or inadequate: (a) whether there is a reasonable relationship between the punitive damages award and the harm likely to result from the defendant's conduct as well as the harm that actually has occurred; (b) the degree of reprehensibility of the defendant's conduct, the duration of that conduct, the defendant's awareness, any concealment, and the existence and frequency of similar past conduct; (c) the profitability to the defendant of the wrongful conduct and the desirability of removing that profit and of having the defendant also sustain a loss; (d) the "financial position" of the defendant; (e) all the costs of litigation; (f) the imposition of criminal sanctions on the defendant for its conduct, these to be taken in mitigation; and (g) the existence of other civil awards against the defendant for the same conduct, these also to be taken in mitigation.

The application of these standards, we conclude, imposes a sufficiently definite and meaningful constraint on the discretion of Alabama fact finders in awarding punitive damages. The Alabama Supreme Court's post-verdict review ensures that punitive damages awards are not grossly out of proportion to the severity of the offense and have some understandable relationship to compensatory damages. While punitive damages in Alabama may embrace such factors as the heinousness of the civil wrong, its effect upon the victim, the likelihood of its recurrence, and the extent of defendant's wrongful gain, the fact finder must be guided by more than the defendant's net worth. Alabama plaintiffs do not enjoy a windfall because they have the good fortune to have a defendant with a deep pocket.

These standards have real effect when applied by the Alabama Supreme Court to jury awards. And post-verdict review by the Alabama Supreme Court has resulted in reduction of punitive awards. The standards provide for a rational relationship in determining whether a particular award is greater than reasonably necessary to punish and deter. They surely are as specific as those adopted legislatively in Ohio Rev. Code Ann. §2307.80(B) (Supp. 1989) and in Mont. Code Ann. §27-1-221 (1989).[11]

Pacific Mutual thus had the benefit of the full panoply of Alabama's procedural protections. The jury was adequately instructed. The trial court conducted a post-verdict hearing that conformed with *Hammond*. The trial court specifically found the conduct in question "evidenced intentional malicious, gross, or oppressive fraud," and found the amount of the award to be reasonable in light of the importance of discouraging insurers from similar conduct. Pacific Mutual also received the benefit of appropriate review by the Supreme Court of Alabama. It applied the *Hammond* standards and approved the verdict thereunder. It brought to bear all relevant factors recited in *Hornsby*.

We are aware that the punitive damages award in this case is more than 4 times the amount of compensatory damages, is more than 200 times the out-of-pocket expenses of respondent Haslip, and, of course, is much in excess of the fine that could be imposed for insurance fraud under [Alabama law]. Imprisonment, however, could also be required of an individual in the criminal context. While the monetary comparisons are wide and, indeed, may be close to the line, the award here did not lack objective criteria. We conclude, after careful consideration, that in this case it does not cross the line into the area of constitutional impropriety. Accordingly, Pacific Mutual's due process challenge must be, and is, rejected.

The judgment of the Supreme Court of Alabama is affirmed.

It is so ordered.

Justice SOUTER took no part in the consideration or decision of this case.

Justice SCALIA, concurring in the judgment.

---

11. We have considered the arguments raised by Pacific Mutual and some of its amici as to the constitutional necessity of imposing a standard of proof of punitive damages higher than "preponderance of the evidence." There is much to be said in favor of a State's requiring, as many do, see, e.g., Ohio Rev. Code Ann. §2307.80 (1989), a standard of "clear and convincing evidence" or, even, "beyond a reasonable doubt," see Colo. Rev. Stat. §13-25-127(2) (Supp. 1979), as in the criminal context. We are not persuaded, however, that the Due Process Clause requires that much. We feel that the lesser standard prevailing in Alabama — "reasonably satisfied from the evidence" — when buttressed, as it is, by the procedural and substantive protections outline above, is constitutionally sufficient.

In Browning-Ferris Industries v. Kelco Disposal, Inc., 492 U.S. 257, (1989), we rejected the argument that the Eighth Amendment limits punitive damages awards, but left for "another day" the question whether "undue jury discretion to award punitive damages" violates the Due Process Clause of the Fourteenth Amendment, id., at 277. That day has come, the due process point has been thoroughly briefed and argued, but the Court chooses to decide only that the jury discretion in the present case was not undue. It says that Alabama's particular procedures (at least as applied here) are not so "unreasonable" as to "cross the line into the area of constitutional impropriety," ante, at 1046. This jury-like verdict provides no guidance as to whether any *other* procedures are sufficiently "reasonable," and thus perpetuates the uncertainty that our grant of certiorari in this case was intended to resolve.

I

Although both the majority and the dissenting opinions today concede that the common-law system for awarding punitive damages is firmly rooted in our history, both reject the proposition that this is dispositive for due process purposes. I disagree. In my view, it is not for the Members of this Court to decide from time to time whether a process approved by the legal traditions of our people is "due" process, nor do I believe such a rootless analysis to be dictated by our precedents. [Justice Scalia then concluded that the historical usage of the phrase "due process of law" never reached the award of punitive damages in ordinary tort cases.]

We have expended much ink upon the due-process implications of punitive damages, and the fact-specific nature of the Court's opinion guarantees that we and other courts will expend much more in the years to come. Since jury-assessed punitive damages are a part of our living tradition that dates back prior to 1868, I would end the suspense and categorically affirm their validity.

Justice KENNEDY, concurring in the judgment.

Historical acceptance of legal institutions serves to validate them not because history provides the most convenient rule of decision but because we have confidence that a long-accepted legal institution would not have survived if it rested upon procedures found to be either irrational or unfair. For this reason, Justice Scalia's historical approach to questions of procedural due process has much to commend it. I cannot say with the confidence maintained by Justice Scalia, however, that widespread adherence to a historical practice always forecloses further inquiry when a party challenges an ancient institution or procedure as violative of due process. But I agree that the judgment of history should govern the outcome in the case before us. Jury determination of punitive damages has such long and principled recognition as a central part of our system that no further evidence of its essential fairness or rationality ought to be deemed necessary. . . .

Justice O'CONNOR, dissenting.

Punitive damages are a powerful weapon. Imposed wisely and with restraint, they have the potential to advance legitimate state interests. Imposed indiscriminately, however, they have a devastating potential for harm. Regrettably, common-law procedures for awarding punitive damages fall into the latter category. States routinely authorize civil juries to impose punitive damages without providing them any meaningful instructions on how to do so. Rarely is a jury told anything more specific than "do what you think best."

In my view, such instructions are so fraught with uncertainty that they defy rational implementation. Instead, they encourage inconsistent and unpredictable results by inviting juries to rely on private beliefs and personal predilections. Juries are permitted to target unpopular defendants, penalize unorthodox or controversial views, and redistribute wealth. Multimillion dollar losses are inflicted on a whim. While I do not question the general legitimacy of punitive damages, I see a strong need to provide juries with standards to constrain their discretion so that they may exercise their power wisely, not capriciously or maliciously. The Constitution requires as much. . . .

I have no trouble concluding that Alabama's common-law scheme for imposing punitive damages is void for vagueness. . . .

NOTES

1. *The constitutionalization of punitive damages.* Even though it rejected defendant's challenges to a punitive damage award, *Haslip* has opened the door to constitutional challenges to each and every aspect of punitive damage awards. In TXO Production Corp. v. Alliance Resources Corp., — U.S. — , 113 S. Ct. 2711, 2721-2722 (1993), the Supreme Court refused to set aside a punitive damage award of $10,000,000 where the actual damages in the underlying slander of title action amounted to only $19,000, with Stevens, J., speaking for a plurality of the Court, noting that "both State Supreme Courts and this Court have eschewed an approach that concentrates entirely on the relationship between actual and punitive damages. It is appropriate to consider the magnitude of the *potential* harm that the defendant's conduct would have caused to its intended victim if the wrongful plan had succeeded, as well as the possible harm to other victims that might have resulted if similar future behavior were not deterred."

Yet the Supreme Court did apply its due process limitations in Honda Motor Co. Ltd v. Oberg, 114 S. Ct. 2331, 2340 (1994). Unlike the rules in all other states, Oregon's procedures in punitive damage cases required that the plaintiff show the customary elements for punitive damages outlined in *Haslip* by clear and convincing evidence, but prohibited judicial review of any jury award "unless the court can affirmatively say there is no evidence to support the jury." Stevens, J., found that the absence of standard judicial review for the excessiveness of punitive damages violated the due process norms set out in *Haslip*.

> Punitive damages pose an acute danger of the arbitrary deprivation of property. Jury instructions typically leave the jury with wide discretion in choosing amounts, and the presentation of evidence of a defendant's net worth creates the potential that juries will use their verdicts to express biases against big businesses, particularly those without strong local presences. Judicial review of the amount awarded was one of the few procedural safeguards which the common law provided against that danger. Oregon has removed that safeguard without providing any substitute procedure and without any indication that the danger of arbitrary awards has in any way subsided over time.

Other courts have generally found, however, that the standard state rules on punitive damages survive constitutional due process challenges. In Herman v. Sunshine Chemical Specialties, Inc., 627 A.2d 1081, 1086 (N.J. 1993), the court held *Haslip* did not upset the long-established New Jersey rule that allowed juries to take into account the wealth of defendants in punitive damage cases. And in Robertson Oil Co., Inc. v. Phillips Petroleum Co., 14 F.3d 373 (8th Cir. 1993), the court held that, as applied, the Arkansas "shock the conscience" standard also met due process requirements.

2. Punitive damages in asbestos cases. By far the largest number of punitive damage actions today arise in the context of asbestos litigation. The supporting evidence for these most notably is correspondence during the 1930s and 1940s among high officials in asbestos manufacturing, to keep from the public evidence of the harmful consequences of asbestos exposure. That evidence was held sufficient to support an award of punitive damages in Fischer v. Johns-Manville Corp., 512 A.2d 466, 476-478 (N.J. 1986), where Clifford, J., also addressed a number of arguments for rejecting the use of punitive damages in mass tort cases.

> [One] concern created by the time gap between exposure and litigation is that the corporate personnel who made the decisions at the time of the exposure are no longer with the defendant company, possibly no longer alive. From this fact it is argued that punitive damages are inappropriate because they will not punish the true wrongdoers. But as many courts have observed, this contention ignores the nature of a corporation as a separate legal entity. Although the responsible management personnel may escape punishment, the corporation itself will not. "It is agency at the time of the tortious act, not at the time of litigation, that determines the corporation's liability." *Moran v. Johns-Manville Sales Corp.*, 691

F.2d 811, 817 (6th Cir. 1982). We are reminded that a primary goal of punitive damages is general deterrence — that is, the deterrence of others from engaging in similar conduct. That purpose is, of course, well served regardless of changes in personnel within the offending corporation.

A related argument, which similarly ignores the legal nature of corporations, is that punitive damages unfairly punish innocent shareholders. This argument has been rejected repeatedly. It is the corporation, not the individual shareholders, that is recognized as an ongoing legal entity engaged in manufacturing and distributing products. True, payment of punitive damages claims will deplete corporate assets, which will possibly produce a reduction in net worth and thereby result in a reduction in the value of individual shares. But the same is true of compensatory damages. Both are possible legal consequences of the commission of harmful acts in the course of doing business. To the same extent that damages claims may affect shareholders adversely, so do profitable sales of harmful products redound to their benefit (at least temporarily). These are the risks and rewards that await investors. Also, we would not consider it harmful were shareholders to be encouraged by decisions such as this to give close scrutiny to corporate practices in making investment decisions. . . .

Defendant argues that the amount of compensatory damages assessed and to be assessed is so great that it will effectively serve the functions of punitive damages — that is, defendants are more than sufficiently punished and deterred. We are not at all satisfied, however, that compensatory damages effectively serve the same functions as punitive damages, even when they amount to staggering sums. Compensatory damages are often foreseeable as to amount, within certain limits difficult to reduce to a formula but nonetheless familiar to the liability insurance industry. Anticipation of these damages will allow potential defendants, aware of dangers of a product, to factor those anticipated damages into a cost-benefit analysis and to decide whether to market a particular product. The risk and amount of such damages can, and in some cases will, be reflected in the cost of a product, in which event the product will be marketed in its dangerous condition.

Without punitive damages a manufacturer who is aware of a dangerous feature of its product but nevertheless knowingly chooses to market it in that condition, willfully concealing from the public information regarding the dangers of the product, would be far better off than an innocent manufacturer who markets a product later discovered to be dangerous — this, because both will be subjected to the same compensatory damages, but the innocent manufacturer, unable to anticipate those damages, will not have incorporated the cost of those damages into the cost of the product. All else being equal, the law should not place the innocent manufacturer in a worse position than that of a knowing wrongdoer. Punitive damages tend to meet this need. . . .

Of greater concern to us is the possibility that asbestos defendants' assets may become so depleted by early awards that the defendants will no longer be in existence and able to pay compensatory damages to later plaintiffs. Again, it is difficult if not impossible to ascertain the additional impact of punitive damages as compared to the impact of mass compensatory damages alone. . . .

Accepting the possibility of punitive damage "overkill," we turn to means of addressing that problem. Because the problem is nationwide, several possible remedial steps can be effective only on a nationwide basis, and hence are beyond our reach. One such solution is the setting of a cap on total punitive damages against each defendant. Such a cap would be ineffective unless applied uniformly. To adopt such a cap in New Jersey would be to deprive our citizens of punitive damages without the concomitant benefit of assuring the availability of compensatory damages for later plaintiffs. This we decline to do.

As in *Fischer,* courts have generally rejected the argument that the large number of the lawsuits against a single defendant precludes the possibility of punitive damages. In Jackson v. Johns-Manville Sales Corp., 781 F.2d 394, 407 (5th Cir. 1986), the court held it was inappropriate to "shield the defendant from punitive damages by the sheer magnitude of its wrong." The court then noted the "less drastic" procedural steps available to the defendant under existing Mississippi law.

> Mississippi law already provides that the defendants could have introduced to the jury evidence of their asserted dire financial straits, and of the possibility that punitive damage awards might prevent other plaintiffs from recovering even compensatory damages. They could have attempted to convince the finder of fact that they did not need to be deterred, or that the effect of punitive damage awards would cripple their companies. They could have produced evidence of their contingent liability and then requested that the trial judge specifically instruct the jury that this evidence be taken into account in assessing the amount of punitive damages, if any. If the defendants had done so, the finder of fact could have assessed the merits of their contentions. Thereafter, the trial judge could have reviewed the propriety of the award, in light of the evidence supporting the defendants' contentions, on either a motion for judgment notwithstanding the verdict or a motion to remit the punitive damages. However, the defendants did not elect to follow the path which was available to them under existing law to bring their concerns about insolvency and the lack of need for deterrence to the attention first of the finder of fact and then to the judge.

In the post-*Haslip* period "the vast majority of courts that have addressed the issue have declined to strike punitive damage awards merely because they constituted repetitive punishment for the same conduct." Dunn v. Hovic, 1 F.3d 1371, 1385 (3d Cir. 1993).

3. Punitive damages: on the move. Even before *Haslip,* there had been an enormous expansion of punitive damage actions, of which only a few can be mentioned here.

In Gryc v. Dayton-Hudson Corp., 297 N.W.2d 727, 739 (Minn. 1980), the plaintiff, then 4 years old, was severely burned while clothed in pajamas made of a cotton flannelette manufactured by Riegel Textile Corp. The flannelette conformed to all applicable federal standards. The trial judge allowed the case to go to the jury on the strength of expert testimony that commercially available flame retardants, although nowhere in actual use, were nonetheless capable of preventing the burns in question. The jury awarded the plaintiff $750,000 in actual damages and $1,000,000 in punitive damages. The defendant's effort to set aside the award of punitive damages was rebuffed by the Minnesota Supreme Court on the ground that evidence in the record supported the inference that the statutory tests were known to be "unreliable" and had been "adopted as a result of industry influence, and therefore, served to protect the textile industry rather than the public." In addition, the court placed great weight on the fact that "in 1956 one of Riegel's top officials wrote in a memorandum, 'We are always sitting on somewhat of a powder keg as regards our flannelette being so inflammable.'"

Should compliance with customary and statutory standards be an absolute defense against punitive damages? Compliance with both statute and custom?

In Grimshaw v. Ford Motor Co., 174 Cal. Rptr. 348 (Cal. App. 1981), the jury awarded the plaintiff $125,000,000 in punitive damages against Ford. The trial judge reduced the award to $3,500,000, which was affirmed on appeal. The plaintiff sued on a crashworthiness theory, arguing that the design and location of the gas tank in the Ford Pinto made it extremely vulnerable to a rear-end collision and subsequent fire, facts known by Ford. The trial judge instructed the jury: " 'Malice' means a motive and willingness to vex, harass, annoy or injure another person. Malice may be inferred from acts and conduct, such as by showing that the defendant's conduct was wilful, intentional, and done in conscious disregard of its possible results." The court of appeals approved the instruction. In designing the Pinto, Ford had made a number of cost-benefit calculations that involved estimating the value of a human life. Does the making of *any* cost-benefit calculation itself support a reward for punitive damages? Any correct analysis? Should it make a difference if the changes proposed (such as a bladder inside the gas tank of the Pinto) had never been used commercially in cars sold at any price? If the Pinto had a rate of burn deaths or injuries no greater than that of other comparably priced and sized cars? For an exhaustive analysis of the case see Schwartz, The Myth of the Ford Pinto Case, 43 Rutgers L. Rev. 1013 (1991).

Other mass-produced products have also been involved in punitive damage cases. In O'Gilvie v. International Playtex, Inc., 821 F.2d 1438, 1446 (10th Cir. 1987), the jury awarded $10,000,000 in punitive damages to the plaintiff, whose wife had died of complications from toxic shock syndrome caused by her use of super-absorbent tampons. The trial judge reduced the punitive award to $1,350,000, and that award was sustained on appeal, the appellate court noting that its "review of the record reveals abundant evidence that Playtex deliberately disregarded studies and medical reports linking high-absorbency tampon fibers with increased risk of toxic shock at a time when other tampon manufacturers were responding to this information by modifying or withdrawing their high-absorbency products."

Similarly, in Tetuan v. A. H. Robins Co., 738 P.2d 1210 (Kan. 1987), the Kansas court upheld a punitive damages award against the defendant for the damage caused by its Dalkon Shield IUD, which resulted "in the complete removal of the plaintiff's uterus, Fallopian tubes, and ovaries." The court upheld a punitive damages award of $7,500,000 after an exhaustive review of the record, which indicated that A.H. Robins had engaged in "malicious silence" by concealing and suppressing information about the adverse consequences of the shield for some ten years before the plaintiff suffered as a result of using the shield. For a detailed account of the entire Dalkon Shield episode, see In re: Northern District of California, Dalkon Shield IUD Prods. Liab. Litigation, 693 F.2d 847 (9th Cir. 1982); M. Mintz, At Any Cost — Corporate Greed, Women, and the Dalkon Shield (1985).

4. *Legislative control of punitive damages.* The prospect that punitive damages could become almost a routine occurrence in products liability cases has spurred the movement toward legislative reform. Thus Fla. Stat. Ann. §768.73 provides:

> (1)(a) In any civil action based on negligence, strict liability, products liability, misconduct in commercial transactions, professional liability or breach of warranty, and involving willful, wanton, or gross misconduct, the judgment for the total amount of punitive damages awarded to a claimant may not exceed three times the amount of compensatory damages awarded to each person entitled thereto by the trier of fact, except as provided in paragraph (b). However, this subsection does not apply to any class action.
>
> (b) If any award for punitive damages exceeds the limitation specified in paragraph (a), the award is presumed to be excessive and the defendant is entitled to remittitur of the amount in excess of the limitation unless the claimant demonstrates to the court by clear and convincing evidence that the award is not excessive in light of the facts and circumstances which were presented to the trier of fact.
>
> (c) This subsection is not intended to prohibit an appropriate court from exercising its jurisdiction under §768.74 in determining the reasonableness of an award of punitive damages that is less than three times the amount of compensatory damages.
>
> (2) In any civil action, an award of punitive damages is payable as follows:
>
> (a) Sixty-five percent of the award is payable to the claimant.
>
> (b) If the cause of action was based on personal injury or wrongful death, 35 percent of the award is payable to the Public Medical Assistance Trust Fund; otherwise, 35 percent of the award is payable to the General Revenue Fund.

The limitations in the Florida statute have been justified on two grounds. First, it is claimed that the money should be paid to the state to reflect the quasi-criminal nature of the proceeding. Second, it is hoped (at least by the proponents of the regulation) that the diversion of part of the funds to the public treasury will diminish the incentive of plaintiffs to bring suit in the first place. Gordon v. State, 608 So. 2d 800, 801, 802 (Fla. 1992), upheld the statute against an attack that the payment of part of the award into the state treasury was both a taking of private property and a deprivation of property without due process of law. The takings case was dismissed as without merit "simply because he has no cognizable, protectable right to the recovery of punitive damages at all," given that the award of punitive damages is not done to vindicate private rights, but solely for reasons of public policy. The substantive due process claim was also easily brushed aside: "The statute under attack here bears a rational relationship to legitimate legislative objectives: to allot to the public weal a portion of damages designed to deter future harm to the public and to discourage punitive damage claims by making them less remunerative to the claimant and the claimant's attorney." The 1992 amendments to the 1986 statute reduced the state's share from 65 to 35 percent of the total award.

The Florida Supreme Court, however, was also "mindful" of *Haslip* in W. R. Grace & Co. v. Waters, 638 So. 2d 502 (Fla. 1994), when it modified its procedures in punitive damage cases to require a bifurcated trial. There Grimes, C.J., set out the revised procedures that, on motion of either party, required the jury to make its preliminary determination of liability for punitive damages at the initial stage of the trial, along with liability and compensatory damages, leaving the amount of punitive damages for determination at a second trial. This procedure was adopted to keep the jury from hearing either of defendant's wealth or of any prior punitive awards against it at the initial stage of the case, where it might prejudice the finding on liability. Similar procedures are now followed in about 14 states.

With *Gordon's* constitutional approach, contrast Kirk v. Denver Publishing Co., 818 P.2d 262, 269 (Colo. 1991), where the court struck a Colorado statute (6A Colo. Rev. Stat. §13-21-102(4) (1987)) which required one-third of any punitive damage award to be paid to the state on the ground that it was an unconstitutional taking of private property without just compensation. The court held that the exaction in question was neither a valid excise nor user tax, that it did not advance any deterrent goal, and that "the taking of a money judgment from the judgment creditor is substantially equivalent to taking the money itself." The same statute also limited punitive damages to an amount equal to actual damages unless there was some continuation of a knowing wrong during the pendency of the suit, in which case the damages could be trebled. Do these provisions amount to a taking of private property without just compensation? What about the abolition of all actions for punitive damages?

   5. *References.* There is exhaustive literature on every aspect of puni-

tive damages. Owen, Problems in Assessing Punitive Damages Against Manufacturers of Defective Products, 49 U. Chi. L. Rev. 1 (1982); Owen, Punitive Damages in Products Liability Litigation, 74 Mich. L. Rev. 1258 (1976); Abraham and Jeffries, Punitive Damages and the Rule of Law: The Role of Defendant's Wealth, 18 J. Legal Stud. 415 (1989); Ellis, Fairness and Efficiency in the Law of Punitive Damages, 56 S. Cal. L. Rev. 1 (1982). See also Symposium, 40 Ala. L. Rev. 687-1261 (1989), with articles by Chapman and Trebilcock, Cooter, Ellis, Elliot, Friedman, Grady, Huber, Priest, Owen, See, and Wheeler.

Chapter Eleven
Tort Immunities

A. INTRODUCTION

The materials in the previous ten chapters have examined tort actions largely with reference to substantive principles that govern defendant's liability for bodily injury or property damage. In order to complete our picture of the basic tort doctrine, one more piece must be added to the puzzle: the status of the defendant. Quite simply, the question is, when may a defendant gain an advantage — i.e., an immunity — in tort litigation not because of what he has done, but because of who he, she, or it is? Sometimes the benefits claimed are total immunity from suit. In others, the immunity claimed is partial (or, as is often said, "qualified"), so that a higher threshold — higher than proof of ordinary negligence — must be crossed before the plaintiff can successfully maintain suit.

There is a remarkable diversity in the nature and origin of immunity rules. Some of these rules are created at common law, some by statute, and some under the Constitution. In general, modern cases in all areas have shown an increased hostility to absolute immunity. Thus, many personal immunities, such as those that bar suits between spouses, between child and parent, or against charities, have been abandoned or are now in the process of contraction if not disintegration. Governmental and official immunities are both more problematic and more vital. With the continued expansion of government activity, litigation on these issues has surged to the fore; nonetheless, the ultimate shape of the judicial and legislative rules remains far from clear. In this chapter, we will examine both private and public immunities in light of their

939

historical development and their current position. Section B addresses domestic or intrafamily immunity, and covers suits between parent and child and between husband and wife. Section C turns to charitable immunity; Section D addresses the question of municipal immunity; and Section E addresses the question of sovereign immunity, with special reference to the liability of the United States under the Federal Tort Claims Act. Finally, Section F deals with official immunity, primarily under federal law.

B.   DOMESTIC OR INTRAFAMILY IMMUNITY

1.   Parent and Child

a.   Suits between parent and child

The rule that a minor child may not maintain a tort action against its father or mother apparently originated in the decision of the Mississippi Supreme Court in Hewlett v. George, Exr. of Ragsdale, 9 So. 885, 887 (Miss. 1891). The suit recognized that emancipated children could sue their parents as if they were strangers, but drew the line at suits between members of the nuclear family.

> [S]o long as the parent is under obligation to care for, guide and control, and the child is under reciprocal obligation to aid and comfort and obey, no such action as this can be maintained. The peace of society, and of the families composing society, and a sound public policy, designed to subserve the repose of families and the best interests of society, forbid to the minor child a right to appear in court in the assertion of a claim to civil redress for personal injuries suffered at the hands of the parent. The state, through its criminal laws, will give the minor child protection from parental violence and wrongdoing, and this is all the child can be heard to demand.

Most American courts followed Hewlett v. George until Dunlap v. Dunlap, 150 A. 905, 912-913 (N.H. 1930), which allowed an infant-employee to sue his father-employer for damages arising out of the employment relationship, for which the father had purchased liability insurance. Peaslee, C.J., said in part:

> It will be said that the father's act in taking out insurance against personal liability cannot create the liability where none existed before. The act which creates the liability, or more correctly, removes a barrier to the enforcement of a right, is the parent's removal of the element which theretofore impaired the right. Had he, instead of insuring, established

a trust fund of $10,000 to be applied solely to the liquidation of his liability to his son, the situation would have been in substance what it is here. The only infirmity in the liability is removed in each instance. In both cases the parties' interest and the family interest become for and not against a recovery.

In Levesque v. Levesque, 106 A.2d 563 (N.H. 1954), the court retreated from *Dunlap* when it refused to allow an unemancipated minor child injured in an automobile accident to sue his parent, by denying that "the existence of liability insurance should create a right of action where none would otherwise exist." *Levesque* was overturned 12 years later in Briere v. Briere, 224 A.2d 588, 590, 591 (N.H. 1966). The court noted that the "main reasons" urged by the defendant in support of the parent-child immunity were:

> (1) [T]he preservation of parental authority and family harmony; (2) depletion of the family exchequer; and (3) the danger of fraud and collusion. Analyzing these reasons in reverse order, we must agree that there is danger of fraud and collusion. However, this is true of suits between husband and wife, which we allow, between near relatives, and between host and guest, often intimate friends, all of which stand on the same footing as actions between strangers. Our court system, with its attorneys and juries, is experienced and reasonably well fitted to ferret out the chicanery which might exist in such cases. In short, we are unwilling to espouse the doctrine that the mere opportunity for fraud and collusion should be an insuperable barrier to an honest and meritorious action by a minor.

The court then argued that the depletion of the family exchequer was a reason of "no substantial weight," as the parent always has the power to cover the risk with insurance. It then turned to the impact of suit on parental authority.

> Parental authority does not appear to be in any real jeopardy in the circumstances before us. In fact, it is difficult, if not impossible, to perceive how such authority and family peace can be jeopardized more in an ordinary tort action for negligence by an unemancipated minor against a parent than by an action in contract or to protect property rights or for an assault — all of which are permitted in this state. To allow such a distinction as now exists between tort and other forms of action is indeed not only to perpetuate confusion and irreconcilable decisions, but to entrench a policy from which changing times have drained most of such vitality as it may have once possessed.

There is general agreement today that any blanket form of parental immunity is indefensible. There is some question, however, as to what should be done once that blanket immunity is removed. In Goller v. White, 122 N.W.2d 193, 198 (Wis. 1963), a case for negligent supervision, the court wrote:

After a careful review of the arguments for and against the parental-immunity rule in negligence cases, we are of the opinion that it ought to be abrogated except in these two situations: (1) Where the alleged negligent act involves an exercise of parental authority over the child; and (2) where the alleged negligent act involves an exercise of ordinary parental discretion with respect to the provision of food, clothing, housing, medical and dental services, and other care. Accordingly, the rule is abolished in personal-injury actions subject to these noted exceptions.

Goller in turn was explicitly rejected in Gibson v. Gibson, 479 P.2d 648, 653 (Cal. 1971), the court reasoning as follows:

In short, although a parent has the prerogative and the duty to exercise authority over his minor child, this prerogative must be exercised within reasonable limits. The standard to be applied is the traditional one of reasonableness, but viewed in light of the parental role. Thus, we think the proper test of a parent's conduct is this: what would an ordinarily prudent *parent* have done in similar circumstances?

We choose this approach over the *Goller*-type formula for several reasons. First, we think that the *Goller* view will inevitably result in the drawing of arbitrary distinctions about when particular parental conduct falls within or without the immunity guidelines. Second, we find intolerable the notion that if a parent can succeed in bringing himself within the "safety" of parental immunity, he may act negligently with impunity.

As a third approach, the New York Court of Appeals simply abolished the defense of intrafamilial immunity, without setting the appropriate scope of liability for parental negligence. Gelbman v. Gelbman, 245 N.E.2d 192 (N.Y. 1969). That approach was also taken in the Restatement (Second) of Torts, which in section 895G provides:

(1) A parent or child is not immune from tort liability to the other solely by reason of that relationship.

(2) Repudiation of a general tort immunity does not establish liability for an act or omission that, because of the parent-child relationship, is otherwise privileged or is not tortious.

The abrogation of tort immunity, consistent with the early New Hampshire cases, also has proved attractive in ordinary business contexts. Thus, in Dzenutis v. Dzenutis, 512 A.2d 130, 135 (Conn. 1986), the court concluded that "because of the general prevalence of liability insurance in the business activity setting, it is appropriate for us to recognize that in most instances family harmony will not be jeopardized by allowing suits between parents and children arising out of business activities conducted away from the home. . . ."

For the classic statement in defense of the *Dunlap* rule see McCurdy, Torts Between Persons in Domestic Relation, 43 Harv. L. Rev. 1030 (1930), an article published just days before *Dunlap* was handed down.

b. Third-party actions

The issue of parental immunity has proved to be of enormous difficulty in the context of third-party actions, especially after the liberalized rules of comparative negligence and contribution already canvassed in *American Motorcycle*, supra at 424. The central dilemma is this: if the parent cannot be subject to direct suit by the child, should a third party, if sued by the child, be allowed to bring an action for contribution from the parent? In Holodook v. Spencer, 324 N.E.2d 338 (N.Y. 1974), the New York Court of Appeals denied contribution where the claim against the parent was only for negligent supervision. "If the instant negligent supervision claims were allowed, it would be the rare parent who could not conceivably be called to account in the courts for his conduct toward his child, either by the child directly or by virtue of the procedures allowed by *Dole*," supra at 436, note 3, for contribution. *Holodook* in turn yielded to Nolechek v. Gesuale, 385 N.E.2d 1268, 1273 (N.Y. 1978), in which a minor was killed when he rode his motorcycle into a steel cable that defendants had suspended close to a public road. The defendants sought contribution and indemnity on the ground that the parents had negligently entrusted their son with a dangerous instrumentality, i.e., the motorcycle, even though he was blind in one eye and had not obtained an operator's license for the cycle. The court justified its distinction between negligent supervision and negligent entrustment of a dangerous instrumentality on the ground that negligent supervision "in general, creates no direct, unreasonable hazard to third parties" while negligent entrustment surely does on the ground that a "dangerous instrument in the hands of an infant child may foreseeably cause various types of harm: personal injury, property damage, or, as in this case, exposure to tort liability."

In principle the distinction between negligent entrustment and negligent supervision is infinitesimal where an infant plaintiff is injured when using a product manufactured by the defendant. In the seat belt cases, for example, the failure of parental supervision has adverse consequences both for the child and any responsible third party. Having the child sue the third party who in turn sues the parents incurs the cost of two separate lawsuits in order to facilitate a single partial recovery for the parent-child unit. Under comparative negligence and *Dole* contribution, it might be wise to resurrect imputed contributory negligence. The injured child recovers only part of the loss from the stranger whose action for indemnity or contribution is then barred. The conflict of interest between parent and child will be eliminated because the parent can now bring the child's suit without fear of being exposed to a third-party claim for contribution or indemnity. Parent and child can then allocate any recovery between pain and suffering for the child and medical expenses for the parent, in extreme cases, by litigation. The rules of imputation are used only in relation to strangers and not as between members of the family.

2. Husband and Wife

The common-law immunity between husband and wife had its common-law origins in the rule that the husband and wife were one person in law and hence could not be on opposite sides of any lawsuit for either personal injury or property damage. In some states the rule was so powerful that it barred actions for torts that occurred during the marriage even after the divorce or separation. See Phillips v. Barnet, 1 Q.B.D. 436 (1876).

The erosion of the strict common-law position came in stages. With the passage of the Married Women's Acts of the nineteenth century, suits between spouses were allowed for loss or damage to property: conversion, trespass to chattels, waste, damage to real property. But states found fresh and independent reasons of policy for preserving the immunity for personal injury actions. Such suits were regarded as a threat to the harmony of the marriage relationship, or were said to facilitate fraud against insurance companies. Some cases have even barred suits between husband and wife for wrongs that took place before the marriage, Greenberg v. Owens, 157 A.2d 689 (N.J. 1960), even when the action was commenced before the marriage. Spector v. Weisman, 40 F.2d 792 (D.C. Cir. 1930). Likewise, the immunity has been extended to cases in which separation, divorce, or death has ended the marriage relationship before the onset of the suit.

In recent years, the situation has undergone a rapid transformation in the courts. The Restatement (Second) of Torts §895F (1979) takes the view that the immunity should be abolished, and as of 1989 there are more than 40 states that have abolished the immunity, usually by judicial decision, and occasionally by statute, see, e.g., Va. Code Ann. §8.01-220.1 (Michie 1981). The passing of absolute immunity has brought forth a host of new variations. In some states the immunity has been lifted only for intentional torts, in others only in automobile cases, and in others it has been removed entirely. See generally Tobias, Interspousal Tort Immunity in America, 23 Ga. L. Rev. 359 (1989). Nonetheless, the problem of suits between spouses has still proved a concern for insurance companies, which have consistently tried to impose family exclusion provisions in their standardized policies. These exclusions have met with a mixed reception, being upheld in some jurisdictions, see Allstate Ins. Co. v. Boles, 481 N.E.2d 1096 (Ind. 1985), but struck down on grounds of public policy in others. Meyer v. State Farm Mut. Auto Ins. Co., 689 P.2d 585 (Colo. 1984).

C. CHARITABLE IMMUNITY

The common-law immunities for charitable institutions has also been in retreat. Charitable immunity appears to have originated in the English case of The Feoffees of Heriot's Hospital v. Ross, 12 Clark & Fin. 507, 8 Eng. Rep. 1508 (1846). There the court thought tort payments would constitute an improper diversion of trust funds from their original purpose, in defiance of the wishes of its grantor. *Heriot's Hospital* was overruled in England about 20 years later in Mersey Docks Trustees v. Gibbs, [1866] L.R. 1 H.L. 93, but it was given a new life in this country by the Massachusetts court in McDonald v. Massachusetts General Hospital, 120 Mass. 432, 436 (1876), and by the Maryland court in Perry v. House of Refuge, 63 Md. 20 (1885). In *McDonald,* the plaintiff's action for medical malpractice was rebuffed. "The liability of the defendant corporation can extend no further than this: if there has been no neglect on the part of those who administer the trust and control its management, and if due care has been used by them in the selection of their inferior agents, even if injury has occurred by the negligence of such agents, it cannot be made responsible. The funds intrusted to it are not to be diminished by such casualties. . . ."

The immunity of *McDonald* was applied outside the area of medical malpractice in Parks v. Northwestern University, 75 N.E. 991, 993 (Ill. 1905), where it barred a student from suing the university in negligence for injuries he received during his laboratory instruction:

> An institution of this character, doing charitable work of great benefit to the public without profit, and depending upon gifts, donations, legacies and bequests made by charitable persons for the successful accomplishment of its beneficial purposes, is not to be hampered in the acquisition of property and funds from those wishing to contribute and assist in the charitable work, by any doubt that might arise in the minds of such intending donors as to whether the funds supplied by them will be applied to the purposes for which they intended to devote them, or diverted to the entirely different purpose of satisfying judgments recovered against the donee because of the negligent acts of those employed to carry the beneficent purpose into execution.

In Piper v. Epstein, 62 N.E.2d 139, 144 (Ill. App. 1945), the court refused to abrogate the immunity rule in a malpractice action even though the defendant had procured liability insurance against the loss. That decision, however, was quickly repudiated in Wendt v. Servite Fathers, 76 N.E.2d 342, 349 (Ill. App. 1947), by holding that the decision of the Servite Fathers to procure liability insurance for schoolyard accidents constituted a waiver of their immunity defense, a position that was soon adopted by the Illinois Supreme Court in Moore v. Moyle, 92

N.E.2d 81, 86 (Ill. 1950), where the court concluded: "We are of the opinion that the exemption or immunity which has been afforded a charitable institution should go no further than to protect its trust funds from being taken to satisfy its liability for the tortious acts of its agents or servants." Fifteen years later, in Darling v. Charlestown Hospital, 211 N.E.2d 253, 260 (Ill. 1965), the court swept away the last remants of charitable immunity saying: "a doctrine which limits the liability of charitable corporations to the amount of liability insurance that they see fit to carry permits them to determine whether or not they will be liable for their torts and the amount of that liability, if any."

Darling represents the dominant rule in about 40 jurisdictions as of 1989, where the immunity has been abolished in its entirety, usually by common-law decision but occasionally by statute. For a leading common-law attack on the doctrine see President and Directors of Georgetown College v. Hughes, 130 F.2d 810 (D.C. Cir. 1942). For a statutory repeal, see, Conn. Gen. Stat. Ann. §52-557(d) (West Supp. 1994). In those jurisdictions where the immunity has been retained, moreover, it has been hedged about with limitations. In some cases the doctrine is applicable only to beneficiaries of the charities and not to strangers. In others it applies only when necessary to protect the charity against the depletion of its own assets. Even those states that retain partial immunity do not extend it to businesses run by charitable institutions, to cases in which there is negligence in the selection of the charity's servants, or to nuisance cases. The unmistakable trend today is toward the complete elimination of the doctrine, if not by common-law rule, then by legislation. For a convenient summary of the current rules see 6 Harper, James and Gray, Torts §29.17.

D.   MUNICIPAL CORPORATIONS

1.   At Common Law

We turn next to the special tort immunities accorded to municipal corporations. Until well into this century, the common law of virtually all American jurisdictions gave municipal corporations a special immunity from private tort actions. The reasons behind this judicial show of benevolence were in some instances similar to those offered on behalf of the immunities given to charitable institutions. The immunity of municipal corporations was justified as a means for preventing the diversion of public assets towards private gain; since municipalities received no profits from discharging their public duties, so too they should be insulated from economic loss. To these familiar arguments, three distinctive justifications were added. First, unlike the states of which they were mere subdivisions, municipal corporations were not full and complete legal persons, and therefore could not be held vicariously responsible for the wrongdoings of their servants. Second, municipal bodies could not be treated as fully voluntary actors since they were under public duties to provide a wide range of local services. Third, removing tort immunity would embroil the municipalities in endless wrangling and litigation that would impede their effective discharge of essential governmental functions. For a critical appraisal of these arguments see 6 Harper, James and Gray, Torts §29.3.

The basic immunity rule was early on subject to one important qualification. Beginning with Bailey v. City of New York, 3 Hill 531 (N.Y. 1842), almost all American jurisdictions extended municipal immunity only to "governmental" activities. For its "proprietary" functions, municipalities were treated like private corporations engaged in private business.

The governmental-proprietary distinction has been subjected to sustained scholarly criticism. See, e.g., Wells and Hellerstein, the Governmental-Proprietary Distinction in Constitutional Law, 66 Va. L. Rev. 1073 (1980). In Fuller and Casner, Municipal Tort Liability in Operation, 54 Harv. L. Rev. 437, 442-443 (1941), the authors said:

> After an enormous amount of litigation on what is a proprietary function or a governmental function, these may now be classified within broad limits: activities of fire prevention, police, education, and general government are governmental; municipal railways, airports, gas, water, and light systems are proprietary; activities involving streets, sidewalks, playgrounds, bridges, viaducts, and sewers are governmental in some jurisdictions and proprietary in others. Criteria for determination of these classes of functions are neither certain nor carefully followed by the courts. Attempts are often made to group them according to whether the functions are primarily of statewide or local concern. No such distinction exists in fact, and the attempt is rewarded only by arbitrary inclusions and exclusions within attempted classifications that fail to classify. Borderline cases cause unending trouble, especially when the complex interrelationships of the municipal functions make it difficult to charge a tort to any particular activity. There is also difficulty in obtaining agreement about what facts shall be sufficient as a basis for proprietary liability. For instance, "incidental" income may be substantial and yet leave an activity within the protection of governmental immunity, while another activity may be deemed proprietary without any monetary return at all.
>
> Thus the governmental-proprietary rule often produces legalistic distinctions that have only remote relationship to the fundamental considerations of municipal tort responsibility. It does not seem good policy to permit the chance that a school building may or may not be producing a rental income at the time to determine whether a victim may recover for his fall into a dark and unguarded basement stairway or elevator shaft. Instances like those found in Chicago could be multiplied. There the city

is liable for negligently driven vehicles of the library, water, and garbage disposal departments, but not for those concerned with health or police. Jurisdiction over streets by the city of Chicago opens the way to recovery for injuries from street defects, but the immunity rule applies when the Chicago Park District happens to have jurisdiction.

The case for abrogating the immunity of municipal corporations was forcefully set out by the Illinois court in Molitor v. Kaneland Community Unit District No. 302, 163 N.E.2d 89, 94-96 (Ill. 1959), a case in which the plaintiff schoolboy sued for injuries sustained from the negligence of the district's bus driver:

> We do not believe that in this present day and age, when public education constitutes one of the biggest businesses in the country, that school immunity can be justified on the protection-of-public-funds theory.
> In the first place, analysis of the theory shows that it is based on the idea that payment of damage claims is a diversion of educational funds to an improper purpose. As many writers have pointed out, the fallacy in this argument is that it assumes the very point which is sought to be proved, i.e., that payment of damage claims is not a proper purpose. "Logically, the 'No-fund' or 'trust fund' theory is without merit because it is of value only after a determination of what is a proper school expenditure. To predicate immunity upon the theory of a trust fund is merely to argue in a circle, since it assumes an answer to the very question at issue, to wit, what is an educational purpose? Many disagree with the 'no-fund' doctrine to the extent of ruling that the payment of funds for judgments resulting from accidents or injuries in schools is an educational purpose. Nor can it be properly argued that as a result of the abandonment of the common-law rule the district would be completely bankrupt. California, Tennessee, New York, Washington and other states have not been compelled to shut down their schools." Moreover, this argument is even more fallacious when viewed in the light of the Illinois School Code, which authorizes appropriations for "transportation purposes," authorizes issuance of bonds for the "payment of claims," and authorizes expenditures of school tax funds for liability insurance covering school bus operations. It seems to us that the payment of damage claims incurred as an adjunct to transportation is as much a "transportation purpose" and therefore a proper authorized purpose as are payments of other expenses involved in operating school buses. If tax funds can properly be spent to pay premiums on liability insurance, there seems to be no good reason why they cannot be spent to pay the liability itself in the absence of insurance.
> Neither are we impressed with defendant's plea that the abolition of immunity would create grave and unpredictable problems of school finance and administration. . . .
> Defendant strongly urges that if said immunity is to be abolished, it should be done by the legislature, not by this court. With this contention we must disagree. The doctrine of school district immunity was created by this court alone. Having found that doctrine to be unsound and unjust under present conditions, we consider that we have not only the power, but the duty, to abolish that immunity. "We closed our courtroom doors without legislative help, and we can likewise open them." Pierce v.

Yakima Valley Memorial Hospital Assn., 43 Wash. 2d 162, 260 P.2d 765, 774.

2. By Statute

The issue of municipal immunity proved, however, to be too volatile to remain exclusively in judicial hands. After *Molitor,* Illinois instituted in 1965 an elaborate statutory framework that continues to provide local governments extensive immunity from tort liability. Some significant sections of the total enactment is reprinted below.

Illinois Revised Statutes
(1994)

CHAPTER 85 — LOCAL GOVERNMENT

§2-102. PUNITIVE OR EXEMPLARY DAMAGES

Notwithstanding any other provision of law, a local public entity is not liable to pay punitive or exemplary damages in any action brought directly or indirectly against it by the injured party or a third party. In addition, no public official is liable to pay punitive or exemplary damages in any action arising out of an act or omission made by the public official while serving in an official executive, legislative, quasi-legislative or quasi-judicial capacity, brought directly or indirectly against him by the injured party or a third party.

§2-103. ADOPTION OR FAILURE TO ADOPT ENACTMENT — FAILURE TO ENFORCE LAW

A local public entity is not liable for an injury caused by adopting or failing to adopt an enactment or by failing to enforce any law.

§2-104. ISSUANCE, DENIAL, SUSPENSION OR REVOCATION OF PERMIT, ETC.

A local public entity is not liable for an injury caused by the issuance, denial, suspension or revocation of, or by the failure or refusal to issue, deny, suspend or revoke, any permit, license, certificate, approval, order or similar authorization where the entity or its employee is authorized by enactment to determine whether or not such authorization should be issued, denied, suspended or revoked.

§2-105.   Inspection of Property — Failure to Make or Negligent Inspection

A local public entity is not liable for injury caused by its failure to make an inspection, or by reason of making an inadequate or negligent inspection, of any property, other than its own, to determine whether the property complies with or violates any enactment or contains or constitutes a hazard to health or safety.

§2-106.   Oral promise or Misrepresentation

A local public entity is not liable for an injury caused by an oral promise or misrepresentation of its employee, whether or not such promise or misrepresentation is negligent or intentional.

§2-107.   Libel — Slander — Provision of Information

A local public entity is not liable for injury caused by any action of its employees that is libelous or slanderous or for the provision of information either orally, in writing, in a book or other form of library material.

§2-108.   Public Welfare Goods or Money — Granting or Failure to Grant

A local public entity is not liable for any injury caused by the granting, or failure to grant, public welfare goods or monies.

§2-109.   Acts or Omissions

A local public entity is not liable for an injury resulting from an act or omission of its employee where the employee is not liable.

§2-111.   Existing Defenses

Nothing contained herein shall operate to deprive any public entity of any defense heretofore existing and not described herein.

§2-201.   Determination of Policy or Exercise of Discretion

Except as otherwise provided by Statute, a public employee serving in a position involving the determination of policy or the exercise of discretion is not liable for an injury resulting from his act or omission in determining policy when acting in the exercise of such discretion even though abused.

§2-202. EXECUTION OR ENFORCEMENT OF LAW

A public employee is not liable for his act or omission in the execution or enforcement of any law unless such act or omission constitutes willful and wanton conduct. . . .

———————

Even these provisions do not capture the full extent of municipal immunity under the Code. Though paragraphs 2-201 and 2-202 are phrased as immunities for public employees, the statute also confers parallel immunities on public entities under §2-109. Whatever the liability, moreover, the Illinois statute authorizes the public entity to purchase liability insurance on its own behalf. §9-103.

The above list of statuory immunities, although long, has proved stable over time. It has, however, generated reams of litigation in borderline areas. To mention but one here, the statute does not exclude municipal liability in ordinary automobile actions. Yet even here the occasional ambiguity can arise in the interaction between ordinary tort principles, and, for example, the blanket protection afforded law enforcement provisions under paragraph 2-202. Thus in Aikens v. Morris, 583 N.E.2d 487 (Ill. 1991), the court refused to sanction any automatic immunity by a directed verdict for law enforcement activities under §2-202 when a police squad car, while transporting a prisoner, was involved in an ordinary intersection collision, since the officer's "negligent conduct was not shaped or affected in any manner by the nature of the duties in either enforcing or exececuting the law." But the immunity will be respected where a police car strikes a pedestrian while engaged in responding to an emergency, or in controlling a crowd, unless "wilful and wanton conduct" can be shown, a finding that could not be made as a matter of law when the officer sounds his siren and flashes his lights appropriately. Morris v. City of Chicago, 474 N.E.2d 1274 (Ill. App. 1985).

In addition to automobile accidents, other provisions of the statute set out detailed rules of liability where the local government operates and maintains property. Here as a general matter the "public entity has the duty to exercise ordinary care to maintain its property in a reasonably safe condition" and then only when it has had adequate notice of the dangerous condition to allow it "to have taken measures to remedy or protect" against the dangerous condition. §3-102. The statute then develops in great particularity the extent of responsibility that local governments have for maintaining public streets and signs (§3-104) and recreational areas (§3-106) and for supervising activities on its property (§3-108) and on its waterways (§3-110). Still other provisions make it abundantly clear that assumption of risk defenses are alive and well in connection with various "hazardous recreational activities" as regards both participants and spectators. §3-109. Entire articles of the code are devoted both to police and correctional institutions (Article IV), fire protection and rescue services (Article V), and medical, hospital, and public health (Article VI).

This comprehensive network of elaborate provisions goes far beyond any effort to spell out the traditional distinction between "governmental" and "proprietary" activities. Instead the ambition is to create detailed rules that govern all phases of local government activities. In this context, it should be noted that municipal liability is a subject of very powerful political pressures, for those citizens who may hope to obtain tort recovery against their local governments are the same persons whose tax dollars fund tort liability for others — including nontaxpaying persons outside the district — for any tort liability that is imposed. The statutes on municipal liability are accordingly more tightly drawn than the parallel rules that are applied in products liability cases, where the political dynamics are quite different given the dominance of in-state consumers and out-of-state manufacturers. It is quite impossible today to give any overall statement of the status of municipal liability, since the statutes in one state tend to diverge in important particulars from those found in others.

3.   Under the Constitution

This area is made more complicated still since it is clear that a vast body of constitutional tort law (beyond the scope of this book) has grown up that addresses the scope of both municipal and government liability. The key statutory provision is 42 U.S.C §1983, which provides in part as follows:

> Every person who, under color of any statute, ordinance, regulation, custom, or usage, of any State or Territory or the District of Columbia, subjects, or causes to be subjected, any citizen of the United States or other person within the jurisdiction thereof to the deprivation of any rights, privileges or immunities secured by the Constitution and laws, shall be liable to the party injured in an action at law, suit in equity, or other proper proceeding for redress.

For municipal governments, the critical case is Monell v. Department of Social Services of the City of New York, 436 U.S. 658, 694 (1978). *Monell* held that a municipal corporation was a "person" for the purposes of §1983, and then addressed its potential liability for constitutional torts committed by its employees, initially by rejecting the common-law rules of vicarious liability. "Instead, it is when execution of a government's policy or custom, whether made by its lawmakers or by those whose edicts or acts may fairly be said to represent official policy, inflicts the injury that the government as an entity is responsible under §1983." In Canton v. Harris, 489 U.S. 378, 388 (1989), the Court explored the scope of the policy or custom rule under §1983 when the local police department was sued for its "failure to train" its officials in the proper mode of giving medical care to suspects in custody. The Court refused to apply either ordinary negligence theories or general doctrines of vicarious liability. Instead it adhered to its original view that policy and custom controlled, and concluded "that the inadequacy of police training may serve as the basis for §1983 liability only where the failure to train amounts to deliberate indifference to the rights of persons with whom the police come into contact." For a comprehensive analysis of the entire situation that rejects *Monell*'s "policy and custom" line position in favor of the common-law approach see Kramer and Sykes, Municipal Liability under §1983: A Legal and Economic Analysis, 1987 Sup. Ct. Rev. 249.

Whatever the correct reading of *Monell*, it is now clear that liability under §1983 does not extend to state officials acting under color of state law, for in Will v. Michigan Department of State Police, 491 U.S. 58, (1989), the Supreme Court held by a five-to-four vote that states were not persons under that section. At a textual level, the Court followed the general rule that "in common usage, the term 'person' does not include the sovereign," [and] "statutes employing the [word] are ordinarily construed to exclude it." At a structural level, it held that any major redefinition in federal/state relations should be introduced in "unmistakably clear" language, not found in this statute. Should Congress amend §1983 to reverse *Will*?

Finally, in Lugar v. Edmonson Oil Co., 457 U.S. 922 (1982), the Supreme Court held that §1983 actions could be brought against private defendants who seized or attached assets in civil disputes pursuant to replevin statutes that were constitutionally infirm. The plaintiff did not have to show that the defendant had either "corrupted" or "usurped" public power, but did have to show that the deprivation of right "was caused by the exercise of some right or privilege created by the State," and that the private party "acted together with or . . . obtained significant aid from state officials."

In Wyatt v. Cole, 504 U.S. —, 112 S. Ct. 1827, 1833 (1992), the Court, speaking through O'Connor, J., extended its holding in *Lugar* by holding that the private parties were not entitled to any immunity, absolute or qualified, under §1983. The qualified immunity sought was that recognized generally for government officials under Harlow v. Fitzgerald, 457 U.S. 800 (1982), infra at page 966, which adopted an objective standard, unknown at common law, that protected all public officials whose actions did not violate any clearly established statutory or constitutional rights. The Court held that none of the reasons for creating a qualified immunity for public officials carried over to ordinary private persons who availed themselves of the state replevin powers. "[E]xtending *Harlow* qualified immunity to private parties would have no bearing on whether public officials are able to act forcefully and decisively in their jobs or on whether qualified applicants enter public service." The Court left for another day the possibility that a defendant could raise the weaker, subjective good faith defense that showed an absence of malice and/or the presence of probable cause for the seizure.

E.   SOVEREIGN IMMUNITY

The ability of private citizens to sue the sovereign is the subject of a long and complex history that can only be touched on here. One of the entrenched principles of the old English common law — embodied in the ancient maxim "the king can do no wrong" — was that no private citizen could sue the sovereign in his own court without his consent. That principle worked itself into the fabric of American law through the early decision of Chief Justice Marshall in Cohens v. Virginia, 19 U.S. 264 (1821), and received its classic expression by Justice Holmes in Kawananakoa v. Polyblank, 205 U.S. 349 (1907): "A sovereign is exempt from suit, not because of any formal conception or obsolete theory, but on the logical and practical ground that there can be no legal right as against the authority that makes the law on which the right depends." Until 1946 the right to maintain action against the United States was hedged about with various limitations and depended on the consent of the United States in individual cases. Then, in 1946, Congress passed the Federal Tort Claims Act, 28 U.S.C.A. §§2671 et seq. This statute was designed to allow recovery of damages against the federal government to those suffering harm from what, except for the traditional immunity, would be the tortious conduct of its employees. By no stretch of the imagination was this waiver an unqualified or universal submission to liability, for, as in the case of municipal liability, Congress created a complex structure with many statutory exceptions, all of which have been subjected to a constant stream of litigation. Some key provisions of the Federal Tort Claims Act follow:

> §2674. LIABILITY OF UNITED STATES.
> 1. The United States shall be liable, respecting the provisions of this title relating to tort claims, in the same manner and to the same extent as a private individual under like circumstances, but shall not be liable for interest prior to judgment or for punitive damages.

§2680. EXCEPTIONS.

The provisions of this chapter and section 1346(b) of this title shall not apply to —

(a) Any claim based upon an act or omission of an employee of the Government, exercising due care, in the execution of a statute or regulation, whether or not such statute or regulation be valid, or based upon the exercise or performance or the failure to exercise or perform a discretionary function or duty on the part of a federal agency or an employee of the Government, whether or not the discretion involved be abused.

(b) Any claim arising out of the loss, miscarriage, or negligent transmission of letters or postal matter. . . .

(h) Any claim arising out of assault, battery, false imprisonment, false arrest, malicious prosecution, abuse of process, libel, slander, misrepresentation, deceit, or interference with contract rights: *Provided,* That, with regard to acts or omissions of investigative or law enforcement officers of the United States Government, the provisions of this chapter and section 1346(b) of this title [28 U.S.C.] shall apply to any claim arising, on or after the date of the enactment of this proviso, out of assault, battery, false imprisonment, false arrest, abuse of process, or malicious prosecution. For the purpose of this subsection, "investigative or law enforcement officer" means any officer of the United States who is empowered by law to execute searches, to seize evidence, or to make arrests for violations of Federal law.

(i) Any claim for damages caused by the fiscal operations of the Treasury or by the regulation of the monetary system.

(j) Any claim arising out of the combatant activities of the military or naval forces, or the Coast Guard, during time of war.

See generally P. Schuck, Suing Government: Citizen Remedies for Official Wrongs (1983).

Berkovitz by Berkovitz v. United States
486 U.S. 531 (1988)

Justice MARSHALL delivered the opinion of the Court.

The question in this case is whether the discretionary function exception of the Federal Tort Claims Act (FTCA or Act) bars a suit based on the Government's licensing of an oral polio vaccine and on its subsequent approval of the release of a specific lot of that vaccine to the public.

I

On May 10, 1979, Kevan Berkovitz, then a 2-month-old infant, ingested a dose of Orimune, an oral polio vaccine manufactured by Lederle Laboratories. Within one month, he contracted a severe case of polio.

The disease left Berkovitz almost completely paralyzed and unable to breathe without the assistance of a respirator. The Communicable Disease Center, an agency of the Federal Government, determined that Berkovitz had contracted polio from the vaccine.

Berkovitz, joined by his parents as guardians, subsequently filed suit against the United States in Federal District Court.[1] The complaint alleged that the United States was liable for his injuries under the FTCA because the Division of Biologic Standards (DBS), then a part of the National Institutes of Health, had acted wrongfully in licensing Lederle Laboratories to produce Orimune and because the Bureau of Biologics of the Food and Drug Administration (FDA) had acted wrongfully in approving release to the public of the particular lot of vaccine containing Berkovitz's dose. According to petitioners, these actions violated federal law and policy regarding the inspection and approval of polio vaccines.

The Government moved to dismiss the suit for lack of subject-matter jurisdiction on the ground that the agency actions fell within the discretionary function exception of the FTCA. The District Court denied this motion, concluding that neither the licensing of Orimune nor the release of a specific lot of that vaccine to the public was a "discretionary function" within the meaning of the FTCA. . . .

A divided panel of the Court of Appeals reversed. 822 F.2d 1322 (CA3 1987). . . .

II

[The Court then set out the statutory provisions and continued.]

This exception, as we stated in our most recent opinion on the subject, "marks the boundary between Congress' willingness to impose tort liability upon the United States and its desire to protect certain governmental activities from exposure to suit by private individuals." *United States v. Varig Airlines,* 467 U.S. 797, 808 [1984].

The determination of whether the discretionary function exception bars a suit against the Government is guided by several established principles. This Court stated in *Varig* that "it is the nature of the conduct, rather than the status of the actor, that governs whether the discretionary function exception applies in a given case." *Id.,* at 813. In examining the nature of the challenged conduct, a court must first consider whether the action is a matter of choice for the acting employee. This inquiry is mandated by the language of the exception; conduct cannot be discretionary unless it involves an element of judgment or choice.

---

1. Petitioners also sued Lederle Laboratories in a separate civil action. That suit was settled before the instant case was filed.

See *Dalehite v. United States,* 346 U.S. 15, 34 (1953) (stating that the exception protects "the discretion of the executive or the administrator to act according to one's judgment of the best course"). Thus, the discretionary function exception will not apply when a federal statute, regulation, or policy specifically prescribes a course of action for an employee to follow. In this event, the employee has no rightful option but to adhere to the directive. And if the employee's conduct cannot appropriately be the product of judgment or choice, then there is no discretion in the conduct for the discretionary function exception to protect.

Moreover, assuming the challenged conduct involves an element of judgment, a court must determine whether that judgment is of the kind that the discretionary function exception was designed to shield. The basis for the discretionary function exception was Congress' desire to "prevent judicial 'second-guessing' of legislative and administrative decisions grounded in social, economic, and political policy through the medium of an action in tort." *United States v. Varig Airlines,* at 814. The exception, properly construed, therefore protects only governmental actions and decisions based on considerations of public policy. See *Dalehite v. United States,* at 36: ("Where there is room for policy judgment and decision there is discretion"). In sum, the discretionary function exception insulates the Government from liability if the action challenged in the case involves the permissible exercise of policy judgment.

This Court's decision in *Varig Airlines* illustrates these propositions. The two cases resolved in that decision were tort suits by the victims of airplane accidents who alleged that the Federal Aviation Administration (FAA) had acted negligently in certifying certain airplanes for operation. The Court characterized the suits as challenging the FAA's decision to certify the airplanes without first inspecting them and held that this decision was a discretionary act for which the Government was immune from liability. In reaching this result, the Court carefully reviewed the statutory and regulatory scheme governing the inspection and certification of airplanes. Congress had given the Secretary of Transportation broad authority to establish and implement a program for enforcing compliance with airplane safety standards. In the exercise of that authority, the FAA, as the Secretary's designee, had devised a system of "spot-checking" airplanes for compliance. This Court first held that the establishment of that system was a discretionary function within the meaning of the FTCA because it represented a policy determination as to how best to "accommodat[e] the goal of air transportation safety and the reality of finite agency resources." 467 U.S., at 820. The Court then stated that the discretionary function exception also protected "the acts of FAA employees in executing the 'spot-check' program" because under this program the employees "were specifically empowered to make policy judgments regarding the degree of confidence that might reasonably be placed in a given manufacturer, the need to maximize compliance with FAA regulations, and the efficient allocation of agency resources." *Ibid.* Thus, the Court held the challenged acts protected from liability because they were within the range of choice accorded by federal policy and law and were the results of policy determinations.[3]

In restating and clarifying the scope of the discretionary function exception, we intend specifically to reject the Government's argument, pressed both in this Court and the Court of Appeals, that the exception precludes liability for any and all acts arising out of the regulatory programs of federal agencies. That argument is rebutted first by the language of the exception, which protects "discretionary" functions, rather than "regulatory" functions. The significance of Congress' choice of language is supported by the legislative history. . . . The discretionary function exception applies only to conduct that involves the permissible exercise of policy judgment. The question in this case is whether the governmental activities challenged by petitioners are of this discretionary nature.

III

Petitioners' suit raises two broad claims. First, petitioners assert that the DBS violated a federal statute and accompanying regulations in issuing a license to Lederle Laboratories to produce Orimune. Second, petitioners argue that the Bureau of Biologics of the FDA violated federal regulations and policy in approving the release of the particular lot of Orimune that contained Kevan Berkovitz's dose. We examine each of these broad claims by reviewing the applicable regulatory scheme and petitioners' specific allegations of agency wrongdoing. . . .

A

Under federal law, a manufacturer must receive a product license prior to marketing a brand of live oral polio vaccine. . . .

[The Court then sets out in great detail the regulations governing the issue of licenses. The manufacturer must first select a proper seed

---

3. The decision in Indian Towing Co. v. United States, 360 U.S. 61 (1955), also illuminates the appropriate scope of the discretionary function exception. The plaintiff in that case sued the Government for failing to maintain a lighthouse in good working order. The Court stated that the initial decision to undertake and maintain lighthouse service was a discretionary judgment. See *id.,* at 69. The Court held, however, that the failure to maintain the lighthouse in good condition subjected the Government to suit under the FTCA. See *ibid.* The latter course of conduct did not involve any permissible exercise of policy judgment.

strain of virus and develop separate monopools, which are then combined into consumer-level products. These monopools are then extensively tested, and the manufacturer must submit both a sample of the finished product and the data from the tests performed. These are then evaluated under the public health act "to insure continued safety, purity and potency" of the vaccine.]

These statutory and regulatory provisions require the DBS, prior to issuing a product license, to receive all data the manufacturer is required to submit, examine the product, and make a determination that the product complies with safety standards.

Petitioners' first allegation with regard to the licensing of Orimune is that the DBS issued a product license without first receiving data that the manufacturer must submit showing how the product, at the various stages of the manufacturing process, matched up against regulatory safety standards. The discretionary function exception does not bar a cause of action based on this allegation. The statute and regulations described above require, as a precondition to licensing, that the DBS receive certain test data from the manufacturer relating to the product's compliance with regulatory standards. The DBS has no discretion to issue a license without first receiving the required test data; to do so would violate a specific statutory and regulatory directive. Accordingly, to the extent that petitioners' licensing claim is based on a decision of the DBS to issue a license without having received the required test data, the discretionary function exception imposes no bar.

Petitioners' other allegation regarding the licensing of Orimune is difficult to describe with precision. . . .

If petitioners aver that the DBS licensed Orimune either without determining whether the vaccine complied with regulatory standards or after determining that the vaccine failed to comply, the discretionary function exception does not bar the claim. Under the scheme governing the DBS's regulation of polio vaccines, the DBS may not issue a license except upon an examination of the product and a determination that the product complies with all regulatory standards. The agency has no discretion to deviate from this mandated procedure. . . .

If petitioners' claim is that the DBS made a determination that Orimune complied with regulatory standards, but that the determination was incorrect, the question of the applicability of the discretionary function exception requires a somewhat different analysis. In that event, the question turns on whether the manner and method of determining compliance with the safety standards at issue involves agency judgment of the kind protected by the discretionary function exception. . . . [The Court remanded this question to the District Court for further consideration of "whether agency officials appropriately exercise policy judgment in determining that a vaccine product complies with the relevant safety standards," if petitioners decided to pursue this claim.]

B

The regulatory scheme governing release of vaccine lots is distinct from that governing the issuance of licenses. The former set of regulations places an obligation on manufacturers to examine all vaccine lots prior to distribution to ensure that they comply with regulatory standards. These regulations, however, do not impose a corresponding duty on the Bureau of Biologics. Although the regulations empower the Bureau to examine any vaccine lot and prevent the distribution of a non-complying lot, they do not require the Bureau to take such action in all cases. The regulations generally allow the Bureau to determine the appropriate manner in which to regulate the release of vaccine lots, rather than mandating certain kinds of agency action. The regulatory scheme governing the release of vaccine lots is substantially similar in this respect to the scheme discussed in *United States v. Varig Airlines*.

Given this regulatory context, the discretionary function exception bars any claims that challenge the Bureau's formulation of policy as to the appropriate way in which to regulate the release of vaccine lots. . . .

The discretionary function exception, however, does not apply if the acts complained of do not involve the permissible exercise of policy discretion. Thus, if the Bureau's policy leaves no room for an official to exercise policy judgment in performing a given act, or if the act simply does not involve the exercise of such judgment, the discretionary function exception does not bar a claim that the act was negligent or wrongful. . . .

Viewed in light of these principles, petitioners' claim regarding the release of the vaccine lot from which Kevan Berkovitz received his dose survives the Government's motion to dismiss. Petitioners allege that, under the authority granted by the regulations, the Bureau of Biologics has adopted a policy of testing all vaccine lots for compliance with safety standards and preventing the distribution to the public of any lots that fail to comply. Petitioners further allege that notwithstanding this policy, which allegedly leaves no room for implementing officials to exercise independent policy judgment, employees of the Bureau knowingly approved the release of a lot that did not comply with safety standards. Thus, petitioners' complaint is directed at a governmental action that allegedly involved no policy discretion. Petitioners, of course, have not proved their factual allegations, but they are not required to do so on a motion to dismiss.

[Reversed and remanded.]

NOTES

1. Government regulation and administration under the FTCA. The enormous expansion in the underlying theories of tortious liability since 1946 have posed major challenges for courts construing the FTCA. In 1946, the most frequent form of tort action was for accidents on the public highways, i.e., situations in which it is easy to analogize the activities of the government to those of private parties. But matters are much more complex when the United States is sued for failing to discharge one of its many new regulatory or supervisory functions. Both *Berkovitz* and *Varig* increase the play in the joints by rejecting the government's categorical position that all regulatory activities fall within the discretionary function exception. Instead, both cases require the lower courts to examine on a case-by-case basis the details of complex regulatory schemes and the administrative practices they spawn.

The Supreme Court adhered to this basic position in United States v. Gaubert, 499 U.S. 315, 324 (1991), by allowing the discretionary function exception to protect the Federal Home Loan Bank Board (FHLBB) from charges of negligent supervision of a bank that it ran on a day-to-day basis. Plaintiff was the key shareholder and officer of the bank who had been forced to step aside from his management position and to post a $25,000,000 guarantee against future bank failures. His action against the FHLBB for the loss in value of his stock and for his liability failed, as the Court summarized the interaction between statutory authority and administrative behavior as follows:

> [I]f a regulation mandates particular conduct, and the employee obeys the direction, the Government will be protected because the action will be deemed in furtherance of the policies which led to the promulgation of the regulation. If the employee violates the mandatory regulation, there will be no shelter from liability because there is no room for choice and the action will be contrary to policy. On the other hand, if a regulation allows the employee discretion, the very existence of the regulation creates a strong presumption that a discretionary act authorized by the regulation involves consideration of the same policies which led to the promulgation of the regulations.

The restrictive slant of *Gaubert* is evident in C.R.S. by D.B.S. v. United States, 11 F.3d 791, 799 (8th Cir. 1993). The father-plaintiff contracted AIDS from a transfusion while in the National Guard, and the disease had been transmitted to his children when he married shortly thereafter. The court held that both the 1983 screening procedures adopted by the Military Blood Program Office, and its 1985 decision not to notify the plaintiff that he was at risk from the transfusion were protected by the discretionary function exception. The court held that "to remove discretion from government employees, a regulation must be mandatory and it must clearly and specifically define what the employees are supposed to do." The court then held that even though low-level government officials had carried out the screening and notification functions, a fair reading of the statutory scheme showed that they were not subject to any specific mandatory duty, and thus exercised a discretionary function under the Act.

Earlier cases also show the intense pressure that has been placed on the discretionary function line. In Lindgren v. United States, 665, F.2d 978 (9th Cir. 1982), the plaintiff, who was seriously injured while waterskiing on the Colorado River, alleged that the government was negligent first in artificially lowering the level of the river and second in failing to warn the plaintiff of the changes in the water level. The court affirmed the trial judge's ruling that any decision to raise or lower water levels fell within the discretionary function exception of the FTCA, but refused to conclude that this exception necessarily protected the government's failure to warn of the change in water level. Although the court thought it was too onerous to ask the government to issue a warning each time it changed the water level, it instructed the trial judge on remand to decide whether it was "not as administratively burdensome" to post a "one-time" warning to users that the water level in the river could change without notice.

The government claim of discretionary function also failed in Denham v. United States, 834 F.2d 518 (5th Cir. 1987), where the plaintiff sustained injuries that left him a quadriplegic when his head struck an abandoned concrete anchor that had originally held in place the buoys used to mark the permitted swimming area. Although the government had marked the swimming area with concrete blocks, it had "failed to ensure that they did not drift into an area where they would endanger swimmers." The court held that though the government had discretion to perform this "operational function," it "did not have the discretion to do so negligently."

In Prescott v. United States, 974 F.2d 696 (9th Cir. 1992), the Ninth Circuit sustained the decision of the trial judge to deny the government summary judgment under the discretionary function exception for injuries that allegedly resulted to its employees from the government's nuclear testing operations. The court held that the burden of proof with respect to the exception rested with the government, as it does with other affirmative defenses, and that summary judgment was inappropriate on "the particularized and fact-specific inquiries" under the exception.

The extensive military and civilian use of asbestos has also given rise to knotty questions under the discretionary function exception. In Gordon v. Lykes Bros. S.S. Co., Inc., 835 F.2d 96 (5th Cir. 1988), the court held that the discretionary function exception protected government decisions during World War II to build ships containing asbestos and not to establish a safety program to warn servicemen of its use. The government introduced "evidence showing that the use of asbestos was consistent both with the policy of building 'rapidly' and the existing standard design" as part of the overall war effort.

Finally, in Lively v. United States, 870 F.2d 296 (5th Cir. 1989), the Fifth Circuit held that the discretionary function exception protected the government against suits by longshoremen who were exposed to raw asbestos stockpiled by the General Services Administration, which failed to warn them of the risks. "The Secretaries of the Army, Navy and Interior base their decisions to stockpile a material on their determinations that the material is critical to the nation's industrial, military or naval needs." Why is the government systematically conferred discretion over matters of warning that are systematically denied to private suppliers and possessors of asbestos?

2. Misrepresentation. A second important exception to the basic waiver of sovereign immunity under the Federal Tort Claims Act applies to cases of "misrepresentation." One possible application of the section is to cases in which individual plaintiffs rely on statements made by the government to their financial detriment. In Neustadt v. United States, 366 U.S. 696 (1961), the Supreme Court barred the plaintiff's cause of action alleging that he had purchased his home for more than it was worth due to reliance on an appraisal made by a Federal Housing Administration official. *Neustadt* was sharply limited (if formally distinguished) in Block v. Neal, 460 U.S. 289, 297 (1983), where the misrepresentation exception did not protect a government official, here of the Farmers Home Administration, who "undertook to supervise construction" of plaintiff's house, an undertaking that was held to be "distinct from any duty to use due care in communicating information to respondent." Is the separation of the two duties consistent with *Neustadt*'s conclusion that the negligent misrepresentation exception applied when the government had breached its "duty to use due care in obtaining and communicating information upon which [the plaintiff] may reasonably be expected to rely in the conduct of his economic affairs"? The Court in *Block* stressed that the government's interpretation "would encourage the Government to shield itself completely from tort liability by adding misrepresentations to whatever otherwise actionable torts it commits."

The government did nonetheless obtain summary judgment on the merits in Moody v. United States, 774 F.2d 150 (6th Cir. 1985), because the applicable regulations made it clear that the inspections conducted in connection with loans issued by the Farmers Home Administration to rural residents were for the benefit of the "government rather than the borrower."

3. Assault and battery. In Sheridan v. United States, 487 U.S. 392, 403 (1988), an obviously intoxicated off-duty serviceman fired several rifle shots that injured the plaintiffs, who were riding in their automobiles. Everyone agreed that the assault and battery exception protected the government for the wrongs committed by the serviceman, but the Court refused to apply this exception to the plaintiffs' further claim that three naval corpsmen were negligent when, having discovered the serviceman "lying face down in a drunken stupor" with a loaded weapon, failed to take him into custody or to alert the appropriate officials that he was on the prowl. "If the Government has a duty to prevent a foreseeably dangerous individual from wandering about unattended, it would be odd to assume that Congress intended a breach of that duty to give rise to liability when the dangerous human instrument was merely negligent but not when he or she was malicious." The liability, therefore, was imposed wholly without regard to the question of whether the drunken serviceman was within or beyond the scope of his employment. See *Bushey,* supra at page 450.

4. *Injuries incident to military service.* One vitally important implied exception under the FTCA is for injuries "incident to military service." The exception was first announced in the critical case of Feres v. United States, 340 U.S. 135 (1950). In *Feres,* the decedent was killed by a fire in his barracks allegedly set by a defective heating unit. The plaintiff's negligence action was not caught by any of the explicit exceptions to the FTCA, including (j) (relating to combatant activities), but the Supreme Court barred suit under the FTCA for three distinct reasons: first, that the statute could not supply the remedy because it would make the obligations of a soldier turn upon the place where he is stationed, when a system of military law requires a uniform law for all personnel; second, that the threat of liability would undermine the discipline that commanding officers had over their troops; and, third, that the presence of a comprehensive system of veteran's benefits precluded the development of tort liability. What is the strength of these rationales in the instant case, when the government is sued for the failure to provide safe equipment for its barracks? Why is a uniform federal law more important in military matters than it is for other matters of nationwide regulation or administrative control? Why does not exception (j) provide the full measure of government immunity in this area?

5. *The genesis test.* Whatever its soundness, *Feres* was extended in Stencel Aero Engineering v. United States, 431 U.S. 666 (1977), where it was held that a manufacturer sued by a national guard officer on a products liability theory could not maintain an action for indemnity or contribution against the United States. Lower courts have grappled with the scope of *Stencel Aero.* In Romero by Romero v. United States, 954 F.2d 223, 225-226 (4th Cir. 1992), the plaintiff sued to recover damages from celebral palsy allegedly brought on by the medical malpractice of government physicians. The court allowed the suit to go forward, saying:

Although *Stencel* involved a derivative *claim,* some circuits have expanded the *Stencel* rationale to bar derivative *injury* where the dependent's injury had its "genesis in a service-related injury to a service member."

Genesis cases most notably have risen in the context of alleged government negligence in exposing service members to radiation or Agent Orange resulting in injury to the fetus or infant. These cases involved an injury to the service person with consequent genetic injury to the offspring. Recently the genesis test has been applied to situations similar to the facts presented here but with various results.

We are persuaded that the genesis analysis is inappropriate here. The genesis test was intended to address purely derivative injury — civilian injury to the service person. In our view the relevant inquiry in a genesis analysis is whether a service member was injured, not whether the negligent act occurred during active army service.

The court then held that the injuries to the plaintiff "breached an affirmative duty of care owed directly to him."

Feres was also extended in United States v. Johnson, 481 U.S. 681 (1987), where it barred a wrongful death action brought on behalf of a coast guard helicopter pilot allegedly killed during a rescue mission due to the negligence of FAA air controllers. By a vote of five to four, the Court, speaking through Justice Powell, rebuffed the plaintiff's argument that *Feres* did not apply because the government wrongs were committed by civilian and not military personnel, holding that the three reasons given in *Feres* made the veterans benefit system the exclusive source of remedy for all service-related injuries. The Court noted specifically that "military discipline involves not only obedience to orders, but more generally duty and loyalty to one's service and to one's country." A biting dissent by Justice Scalia attacked the special solicitude shown the military in this case, and hinted at the possibility that "Congress thought that *barring* recovery by servicemen might adversely affect military discipline," by demoralizing servicemen who know that civilian pilots could maintain negligence actions against the FAA.

Notwithstanding his dissent in *Johnson,* Justice Scalia held in United States v. Stanley, 483 U.S. 669 (1987), that *Feres* precluded the plaintiff from suing the government for a violation of his constitutional rights under Bivens v. Six Unknown Named Agents of Federal Bureau of Narcotics, 403 U.S. 388 (1971). In *Stanley* the plaintiff claimed that he had been secretly exposed to LSD while participating in a service program ostensibly designed to "test the effectiveness of protective clothing and equipment as defenses against chemical warfare." The Court held, however, that the same considerations which led to the *Feres* exception to the FTCA were if anything more powerful in the constitutional setting, given that Congress had acted pursuant to its powers to regulate the conduct of the land and naval forces, U.S. Const. Art. I, §8, cl. 14. It refused therefore to create a *Bivens*-like cause of action in the military sphere and denied the plaintiff's suit. Justice Brennan's dissent argued that the action should be allowed given the risks of official abuse that could flourish under a system of absolute immunity.

See generally Note: Making Intramilitary Tort Law More Civil: A Proposed Reform of the *Feres* Doctrine, 95 Yale L.J. 992 (1986).

F.   OFFICIAL IMMUNITY

Harlow v. Fitzgerald
457 U.S. 800 (1982)

POWELL, J. The issue in this case is the scope of the immunity available to the senior aides and advisers of the President of the United States in a suit for damages based upon their official acts.

I

In this suit for civil damages petitioners Bryce Harlow and Alexander Butterfield are alleged to have participated in a conspiracy to violate the constitutional and statutory rights of the respondent A. Ernest Fitzgerald. Respondent avers that petitioners entered the conspiracy in their capacities as senior White House aides to former President Richard M. Nixon. As the alleged conspiracy is the same as that involved in Nixon v. Fitzgerald, *ante,* the facts need not be repeated in detail.

[In January 1970 the plaintiff, A. Ernest Fitzgerald, lost his job as a management analyst with the Department of the Air Force, ostensibly as part of a departmental reorganization. His dismissal, however, attracted enormous public attention, for in November, 1968, during the waning days of the Johnson administration, Fitzgerald (to the evident embarrassment of his superiors) had testified before a congressional committee about a possible two-billion-dollar cost overrun in the procurement program for the C-5A transport plane. By the end of 1969 there was much public discussion about whether Fitzgerald would keep his old job, be assigned new responsibilities, or be fired. In response to the public pressures, President Nixon agreed to look closely into the matter. In the course of his deliberations Nixon consulted with, among others, Harlow, a presidential aide primarily in charge of congressional relations, and his co-petitioner Butterfield, a deputy assistant to the president and deputy chief of staff to H. R. Haldeman. Originally it appeared that Nixon wanted to reassign Fitzgerald to another job, perhaps in the Bureau of the Budget. That proposal, however, engendered strong opposition from his advisers, who stated that though Fitzgerald was admittedly "a top-notch cost expert," he received "very low marks in loyalty." Fitzgerald was therefore relieved of his former duties and, instead of being reassigned, was left to "bleed, for a while at least," without any job at all.

Fitzgerald then brought a complaint before the Civil Service Commission. After extensive and well-publicized hearings, the examiner determined that Fitzgerald's dismissal had violated the applicable civil service regulations for, far from being an economy measure as had been stated, it had been motivated by "reasons purely personal to" the president. The examiner also found that the dismissal was not in retaliation for the congressional testimony on the C-5A cost overruns, and then recommended that Fitzgerald be reappointed to his old position.

Shortly after the report was made public, Fitzgerald brought suit for damages in federal district court against eight named officials of the Defense Department and against various named and unnamed White House aides, including Harlow and Butterfield. Some eight years later he joined the president as a codefendant in the original suit. In the companion case of Fitzgerald v. Nixon, 457 U.S. 731 (1982), the Court held by a five-to-four vote that the president enjoyed absolute immunity from private suit. In the instant case, Harlow and Butterfield moved for summary judgment at the close of discovery, but the motion was denied because of a genuine issue of fact about their motives and conduct. The trial judge also held that neither petitioner was entitled to absolute immunity.]

. . . Never having determined the immunity available to the senior aides and advisers of the President of the United States, we granted certiorari. 452 U.S. 957 (1981).

II

As we reiterated today in Nixon v. Fitzgerald, 457 U.S. 731 (1982), our decisions consistently have held that government officials are entitled to some form of immunity from suits for damages. As recognized at common law, public officers require this protection to shield them from undue interference with their duties and from potentially disabling threats of liability. . . .

III

Petitioners argue that they are entitled to a blanket protection of absolute immunity as an incident of their offices as Presidential aides. In deciding this claim we do not write on an empty page. . . .

Having decided in *Butz* [v. Economou, 438 U.S. 478 (1978)] that members of the Cabinet ordinarily enjoy only qualified immunity from suit, we conclude today that it would be equally untenable to hold absolute immunity an incident of the office of every Presidential subordinate based in the White House. Members of the Cabinet are direct subordinates of the President, frequently with greater responsibilities, both to the President and to the Nation, than White House staff. The considerations that supported our decision in *Butz* apply with equal force to this case. It is no disparagement of the offices held by petitioners to hold that Presidential aides, like members of the Cabinet, generally are entitled only to a qualified immunity.

B

In disputing the controlling authority of *Butz* petitioners rely on the principles developed in Gravel v. United States, 408 U.S. 606 (1972). In *Gravel* we endorsed the view that "it is literally impossible . . . for Members of Congress to perform their legislative tasks without the help of aides and assistants" and that "the day-to-day work of such aides is so critical to the Members' performance that they must be treated as the latter's alter egos. . . ." Id., at 616-617. Having done so, we held the Speech and Debate Clause derivatively applicable to the "legislative acts" of a Senator's aide that would have been privileged if performed by the Senator himself. Id., at 621-622.

Petitioners contend that the rationale of *Gravel* mandates a similar "derivative" immunity for the chief aides of the President of the United States. Emphasizing that the President must delegate a large measure of authority to execute the duties of his office, they argue that recognition of derivative absolute immunity is made essential by all the considerations that support absolute immunity for the President himself.

Petitioners' argument is not without force. Ultimately, however, it sweeps too far. If the President's aides are derivatively immune because essential to the functioning of the Presidency, so should the members of the Cabinet — Presidential subordinates some of whose essential roles are acknowledged by the Constitution itself — be absolutely immune. Yet we implicitly rejected such derivative immunity in *Butz*. Moreover, in general our cases have followed a "functional" approach to immunity law. We have recognized that the judicial, prosecutorial, and legislative functions require absolute immunity. But this protection has extended no further than its justification would warrant. In *Gravel*, for example, we emphasized that Senators and their aides were absolutely immune only when performing "acts legislative in nature," and not when taking other acts even "in their official capacity." 408 U.S., at 625. Our cases involving judges and prosecutors have followed a similar line. The undifferentiated extension of absolute "derivative" immunity to the President's aides therefore could not be reconciled with the "functional" approach that has characterized the immunity decisions of this Court, indeed including *Gravel* itself.

C

Petitioners also assert an entitlement to immunity based on the "special functions" of White House aides. This form of argument accords with the analytical approach of our cases. For aides entrusted with discretionary authority in such sensitive areas as national security or foreign policy, absolute immunity might well be justified to protect the unhesitating performance of functions vital to the national interest. But a "special functions" rationale does not warrant a blanket recognition of absolute immunity for all Presidential aides in the performance of all their duties. This conclusion too follows from our decision in *Butz*, which establishes that an executive official's claim to absolute immunity must be justified by reference to the public interest in the special functions of his office, not the mere fact of high station.

Butz also identifies the location of the burden of proof. The burden of justifying absolute immunity rests on the official asserting the claim. 438 U.S., at 506. We have not of course had occasion to identify how a Presidential aide might carry this burden. But the general requisites are familiar in our cases. In order to establish entitlement to absolute immunity a Presidential aide first must show that the responsibilities of his office embraced a function so sensitive as to require a total shield from liability. He then must demonstrate that he was discharging the protected function when performing the act for which liability is asserted.

Applying these standards to the claims advanced by petitioners Harlow and Butterfield, we cannot conclude on the record before us that either has shown that "public policy requires [for any of the functions of his office] an exemption of [absolute] scope." *Butz*, supra, at 506. Nor, assuming that petitioners did have functions for which absolute immunity would be warranted, could we now conclude that the acts charged in this lawsuit — if taken at all — would lie within the protected area. We do not, however, foreclose the possibility that petitioners, on remand, could satisfy the standards properly applicable to their claims.

IV

Even if they cannot establish that their official functions require absolute immunity, petitioners assert that public policy at least mandates an application of the qualified immunity standard that would permit the defeat of insubstantial claims without resort to trial. We agree. . . .

B

Qualified or "good faith" immunity is an affirmative defense that must be pleaded by a defendant official. Gomez v. Toledo, 446 U.S. 635 (1980). Decisions of this Court have established that the "good faith" defense has both an "objective" and a "subjective" aspect. The objective element involves a presumptive knowledge of and respect for "basic, unquestioned constitutional rights." Wood v. Strickland, 420 U.S. 308, 320 (1975). The subjective component refers to "permissible intentions." Ibid. Characteristically the Court has defined these elements by identifying the circumstances in which qualified immunity would *not* be available. Referring both to the objective and subjective elements, we have held that qualified immunity would be defeated if an official "*knew or reasonably should have known* that the action he took within his sphere of official responsibility would violate the constitutional rights of the [plaintiff], *or* if he took the action *with malicious intention* to cause a deprivation of constitutional rights or other injury. . . ." Id., at 321-322 (emphasis added).

The subjective element of the good faith defense frequently has proved incompatible with our admonition in *Butz* that insubstantial claims should not proceed to trial. Rule 56 of the Federal Rules of Civil Procedure provides that disputed questions of fact ordinarily may not be decided on motions for summary judgment. And an official's subjective good faith has been considered to be a question of fact that some courts have regarded as inherently requiring resolution by a jury.

In the context of *Butz*'s attempted balancing of competing values, it now is clear that substantial costs attend the litigation of the subjective good faith of government officials. Not only are there the general costs of subjecting officials to the risks of trial — distraction of officials from their governmental duties, inhibition of discretionary action, and deterrence of able people from public service. There are special costs to "subjective" inquiries of this kind. Immunity generally is available only to officials performing discretionary functions. In contrast with the thought processes accompanying "ministerial" tasks, the judgments surrounding discretionary action almost inevitably are influenced by the decisionmaker's experiences, values, and emotions. These variables explain in part why questions of subjective intent so rarely can be decided by summary judgment. Yet they also frame a background in which there often is no clear end to the relevant evidence. Judicial inquiry into subjective motivation therefore may entail broad-ranging discovery and the deposing of numerous persons, including an official's professional colleagues. Inquiries of this kind can be peculiarly disruptive of effective government.

Consistently with the balance at which we aimed in *Butz*, we conclude today that bare allegations of malice should not suffice to subject government officials either to the costs of trial or to the burdens of broad-reaching discovery. We therefore hold that government officials performing discretionary functions generally are shielded from liability for civil damages insofar as their conduct does not violate clearly established statutory or constitutional rights of which a reasonable person would have known.

Reliance on the objective reasonableness of an official's conduct, as measured by reference to clearly established law, should avoid excessive disruption of government and permit the resolution of many insubstantial claims on summary judgment. On summary judgment, the judge appropriately may determine, not only the currently applicable law, but whether that law was clearly established at the time an action occurred. If the law at that time was not clearly established, an official could not reasonably be expected to anticipate subsequent legal developments, nor could he fairly be said to "know" that the law forbade conduct not previously identified as unlawful. Until this threshold immunity question is resolved, discovery should not be allowed. If the law was clearly established, the immunity defense ordinarily should fail, since a reasonably competent public official should know the law governing his conduct. Nevertheless, if the official pleading the defense claims extraordinary circumstances and can prove that he neither knew nor should have known of the relevant legal standard, the defense should be sustained. But again, the defense would turn primarily on objective factors.

By defining the limits of qualified immunity essentially in objective terms, we provide no license to lawless conduct. The public interest in deterrence of unlawful conduct and in compensation of victims remains protected by a test that focuses on the objective legal reasonableness of an official's acts. Where an official could be expected to know that certain conduct would violate statutory or constitutional rights, he should be made to hesitate and a person who suffers injury caused by such conduct may have a cause of action. But where an official's duties legitimately require action in which clearly established rights are not implicated, the public interest may be better served by action taken "with independence and without fear of consequences." Pierson v. Ray, 386 U.S. 547, 554 (1967).

C

In this case petitioners have asked us to hold that the respondent's pre-trial showings were insufficient to survive their motion for summary judgment. We think it appropriate, however, to remand the case to the District Court, for its reconsideration of this issue in light of this opinion. The trial court is more familiar with the record so far developed and also is better situated to make any such further findings as may be necessary.

V

The judgment of the Court of Appeals is vacated, and the case remanded for further action consistent with this opinion.

BRENNAN, J., with whom MARSHALL and BLACKMUN, JJ., join, concurring in the opinion of the Court. I agree with the substantive standard announced by the Court today, imposing liability when a public-official defendant "knew or should have known" of the constitutionally violative effect of his actions. . . . I write separately only to note that given this standard, it seems inescapable to me that some measure of discovery may sometimes be required to determine exactly what a public-official defendant did "know" at the time of his actions. . . . Of course, as the Court has already noted, summary judgment will be readily available to public-official defendants whenever the state of the law was so ambiguous at the time of the alleged violation that it could not have been "known" then, and thus liability could not ensue. In my view, summary judgment will also be readily available whenever the plaintiff cannot prove, as a threshold matter, that a violation of his constitutional rights actually occurred. I see no reason why discovery of defendants' "knowledge" should not be deferred by the trial judge pending decision of any motion of defendants for summary judgment on grounds such as these.

BRENNAN, WHITE, MARSHALL and BLACKMUN, JJ., concurring. We join the Court's opinion but, having dissented in Nixon v. Fitzgerald, we disassociate ourselves from any implication in the Court's opinion in the present case that Nixon v. Fitzgerald was correctly decided.

REHNQUIST, J., concurring. At such time as a majority of the Court is willing to re-examine our holding in Butz v. Economou, 438 U.S. 478 (1978), I shall join in that undertaking with alacrity. But until that time comes, I agree that the Court's opinion in this case properly disposes of the issues presented, and I therefore join it.

BURGER, C.J., dissenting. The Court today decides in Nixon v. Fitzgerald, what has been taken for granted for 190 years, that it is implicit in the Constitution that a President of the United States has absolute immunity from civil suits arising out of official acts as Chief Executive. I agree fully that absolute immunity for official acts of the President is, like Executive Privilege, "fundamental to the operation of Government and inextricably rooted in the separation of powers under the Constitution." United States v. Nixon, 418 U.S. 683, 708 (1974).

In this case the Court decides that senior aides of a President do not have derivative immunity from the President. I am at a loss, however, to reconcile this conclusion with our holding in Gravel v. United States, 408 U.S. 606 (1972). The Court reads Butz v. Economou, 438 U.S. 478 (1978), as resolving that question; I do not. *Butz* is clearly distinguishable.

NOTES

1. Absolute or qualified immunity? The question of official immunity has been litigated in a number of recent Supreme Court cases in which the court has veered uneasily between absolute and qualified immunity. Absolute immunity has generally been conferred on legislators, see Tenney v. Brandhove, 341 U.S. 367 (1951). It also extends to "judges, prosecutors, witnesses, and other persons acting 'under color of law' who perform official functions in the judicial process," including a police officer sued for damages for alleged perjured testimony that led to the plaintiff's false conviction. Briscoe v. LaHue, 460 U.S. 325 (1983). In addition, under the obvious influence of the *Feres* doctrine, the Supreme Court has extended absolute immunity to military officers who have been charged with violating the constitutional rights of military personnel by engaging in racial discrimination. Chappell v. Wallace, 462 U.S. 296 (1983).

Nonetheless, there are a clear number of cases in which only a qualified immunity has been extended to public officials. Scheuer v. Rhodes, 416 U.S. 232 (1974), supra at 63, note 4, restricted high state officials to a qualified immunity. That position was also adopted in Mitchell v. Forsyth, 472 U.S. 511 (1985), an action for invasion of privacy by a warrantless wiretap of a radical political group. The Court held that the attorney general, like cabinet officers, was only entitled to a qualified immunity, even when engaged in national security affairs. The Court adhered to the standard announced in *Harlow* that the "Attorney General will be entitled to immunity so long as his actions do not violate 'clearly established statutory or constitutional rights of which a reasonable person would have known,' " and pointedly concluded that in some cases the attorney general "should" be made to hesitate before invading individual constitutional rights. On an important procedural point, the Court held that the defendant was entitled to bring an immediate appeal if denied the qualified immunity by the trial judge, even in the absence of the final judgment ordinarily required under the federal rules of civil procedure, on the grounds that the immunity issue is "conceptually distinct" from the underlying merits of the claim, and that the immunity claim would be largely negated if upheld only after an extensive trial on the merits.

Subsequently, in Forrester v. White, 484 U.S. 219 (1988), the Court allowed a judge only a qualified immunity when it was alleged that in his administrative capacity he engaged in illegal sex discrimination in violation of the equal protection clause when he first demoted and then fired a female probation officer whom he had originally hired and promoted. The Court concluded that absolute immunity was "strong medicine" reserved only for those cases in which there was a "very great danger" that public officials would be deflected from performing their duties.

Overall pleas for absolute immunity have received a far cooler reception in recent years than they did in Barr v. Matteo, 360 U.S. 564 (1959), a defamation suit, which extended that immunity to high government officials acting within the "outer perimeter" of their official duties. Nonetheless, it is instructive to note briefly the classic defense of absolute immunity advanced by Hand, J., in Gregoire v. Biddle, 177 F.2d 579, 581 (2d Cir. 1949), an action for false arrest brought against the United States attorney general by a Frenchman who had been detained as a German alien during World War II, even after the Enemy Alien Hearing Board had ruled he was French:

> It does indeed go without saying that an official, who is in fact guilty of using his powers to vent his spleen upon others, or for any other personal motive not connected with the public good, should not escape liability for the injuries he may so cause; and, if it were possible in practice to confine such complaints to the guilty, it would be monstrous to deny recovery. The justification for doing so is that it is impossible to know whether the claim is well founded until the case has been tried, and that to subject all officials, the innocent as well as the guilty, to the burden of trial and to the inevitable danger of its outcome, would dampen the ardor of all but the most resolute, or the most irresponsible, in the unflinching discharge of their duties. . . . In this instance it has been thought in the end better to leave unredressed the wrongs done by dishonest officers than to subject those who try to do their duty to the constant dread of retaliation.

Has the Supreme Court fashioned adequate tests for deciding when a government official is entitled to obtain summary judgment under the qualified immunity rule? The point here is of intense practical importance when suits against the government join as codefendants former officials, who often find it necessary or desirable to retain private attorneys at their own expense.

2. *Presidential immunity.* As noted in *Harlow*, Nixon v. Fitzgerald recognized an absolute liability for the President. The scope of that immunity has been vigorously contested in the suit that Paula Jones brought

against President Clinton for forms of sexual misbehavior, personal and official misconduct that allegedly took place while Clinton was still governor of Arkansas in May 1991. Although the issue has yet to be resolved by any court, one central issue in that case is the extent to which Presidential immunity is available in civil suits for actions that took place *before* the president became president.

On this score three broad positions can be discerned. The first holds that the president is not above the law and must answer to all civil suits, whether for negligent driving, divorce, or sexual misconduct, like any other citizen. The distinctive position of the president within our constitutional system is taken into account by the protection that a trial judge can afford the president against excessive depositions and interrogatories and other procedural abuses.

The second position holds that the president, while liable for torts that occurred prior to public office, nonetheless is entitled to have these claims postponed until he is out of public office. The argument for this position is that it offers a good reconciliation between the demands of public office, and the rights of individual litigants to pursue their rights of action. The response is that justice delayed is often denied, for the passage of time results in the loss of evidence and the fraying of the memories of individual witnesses.

The third position is that the absolute immunity extends to all suits regardless of when the underlying occurrences took place to free the president of all distractions while in public office. The public debate seems to be most keenly centered on the first and second of these possibilities. Which is supported by the following passage (one among many) from *Nixon,* 457 U.S. at 748-750?

> Here a former President asserts his immunity from civil damages claims of two kinds. He stands named as a defendant in a direct action under the Constitution and in two statutory actions under federal laws of general applicability. In neither case has Congress taken express legislative action to subject the President to civil liability for officials acts.
>
> Applying the principles of our cases to claims of this kind we hold that petitioner, as a former President of the United States, is entitled to absolute immunity from damages liability predicated on his official acts. We consider this immunity a functionally mandated incident of the President's unique office, rooted in the constitutional tradition of the separation of powers and supported by our history. . . .
>
> [The constitutional] grant of authority establishes the President as the chief constitutional officer of the Executive Branch, entrusted with supervisory and policy responsibilities of utmost discretion and sensitivity. These include the enforcement of federal law — it is the President who is charged constitutionally to "take Care that the Laws be faithfully executed"; the conduct of foreign affairs — a realm in which this Court has recognized that "[i]t would be intolerable that courts, with the relevant information, should review and perhaps nullify actions of the Executive taken on information properly held secret"; and management of the Ex-

ecutive Branch — a task for which "imperative reasons requir[e] an unrestricted power [in the President] to remove the most important of his
subordinates in their most important duties.

Which of these considerations support limiting the immunity to public
acts committed while president? Which support extending some form
of immunity to all presidential acts? Note that the suit in *Nixon* was filed
in 1978, eight years after the actions complained of were taken, and
nearly four years after Nixon resigned the presidency.

   3. *The theory of official immunity.* The issues of government and official
immunity cover everything from mundane automobile accidents to the
highest and most sensitive decisions of state. The range of the doctrine
is revealed in the variety of tort claims against which it is interposed:
defamation, invasion of privacy, and false arrest — not to mention the
intentional torts of breaking and entering property and assault and
battery committed during the course of routine arrests and searches. It
is therefore appropriate to ask what substantive approach should be
taken to a question that has so divided commentators and the courts.

   The threshold question in all official immunity cases is, why should
any government official escape the ordinary rigors of the tort law, especially under a government "not of men, but of laws"? The usual answer
to that question has been framed in the language, if not of necessity,
then at least of utility. It is quite impossible for government to go forward if its officials are forever subject to damage suits whenever they
act to discharge their public functions. To be sure, all private parties
also face the possibility of suit, but public officials, unlike private officials, do not have the option of simply refusing to act at all; indeed,
they are often charged with acting in coercive ways. Police officers must
arrest, prosecutors must prosecute, and judges must try cases. Regulators must issue regulations and legions of government officials must
pass on thousands of requests for licenses, grants, assistance payments,
and the like. For officials making hundreds of decisions a year, the
situation could become intolerable if even a tiny fraction resulted in
suit, with the possible result that the able people most needed for public positions would be deterred from taking them or from acting in a
forceful fashion.

   The same concerns can be translated into economic terms. The nub
of the issue lies in the implicit imbalance in the incentives imposed on
public officials if left wholly unprotected by any immunity doctrine. Let
them make an incorrect decision and they will have to shoulder the
enormous costs of liability. Let their decisions be correct and there will
be enormous gains, which will be captured not by them, but by the
public at large. Why, therefore, should a public official take all the risks
for none of the gain? On the general problem of agency costs on which
this analysis rests see Jensen and Meckling, Theory of the Firm: Mana-

gerial Behavior, Agency Costs, and Ownership Structure, 3 J. Fin. Econ. 305 (1976).

One way to restore the possible balance would be to pay public officials enormous sums to compensate them for the great liability risks that they would be required to bear. Yet this alternative has its own perils. There are difficult financial questions to be answered concerning, for example, the level of salary required and whether private insurance markets will work for government officials. There are also the very heavy costs associated with the disruption of public services. The other way to restore the needed symmetry between official rewards and official burdens is to release the public official from liability, in whole or in part. In this way the system is brought into balance, since the official in question escapes capturing the full gain or bearing the full loss, albeit at the cost of individual redress for government wrongs.

On the general question of official immunity see Symposium, Civil Liability of Government Officials, 42 Law & Contemp. Probs. 1 (1978); Cass, Damage Suits Against Public Officers, 129 U. Pa. L. Rev. 1110 (1981).

The last piece of the puzzle concerns the interaction of official and governmental immunity. When the United States can obtain immunity under the discretionary function defense of the FTCA, should the individual official be immune as well? Conversely, should the discretionary function exception be broadened precisely because official immunity is so vital to government operations? When the government is immune under the *Feres* doctrine, should the government official be immune as well? See, e.g., Jaffee v. United States, 663 F.2d 1226 (3d Cir. 1981), where the absolute immunity was extended to commanding officers who, in 1953, had ordered the plaintiff soldier into the field without adequate protection when a nuclear device was exploded nearby. The court held that "the policy concerns expressed by the [Supreme] Court seem equally applicable to a case such as this where government officials are sued in their individual capacity for intentional torts."

Chapter Twelve
The Institution of Insurance

A. INTRODUCTION

In this chapter we leave our examination of the rules governing tortious liability for physical harm and turn our attention to the institutional framework for the defense, settlement, and litigation of tort claims. The focus of this inquiry is not on the rules of evidence or of civil procedure, which are covered in other courses in the curriculum. Nor is the focus on the "impact" of insurance on the formation of substantive tort doctrine, a matter raised most vividly in Chapter 11 on tort immunities. Instead, our subject is the institutional role of insurance companies in dealing with tort claims. Whatever the substantive principles of liability involved, it should be quite apparent that insurance companies play a dominant role in processing tort claims. Even where insurance coverage is not generally required, it is still carried by a large number of individuals and firms who prefer the constant stream of steady but limited payments to the remote possibility of a large, if not ruinous, economic loss. When damage to either person or property occurs, an insurance company is apt to be at the center of the controversy, since it is responsible both for the defense of the action and, within policy limits, for the satisfaction of any judgment entered against its insured.

In order to get some sense of how the tort system works in practice, it is necessary to understand the interaction of at least three actors — the accident victim, the insurance company, and the insured. The many and complex problems that arise in this three-party relationship are manifest in all kinds of tort actions. At one time, the issues of insurance coverage and defense were litigated largely in connection with automobile accidents. But in recent years, the major litigation to reach the courts have involved high-stakes disputes associated with products liability and toxic torts, both in individual and in mass tort contexts. The insurance litigation has changed its direction to follow the underlying litigation. Accordingly, the material in this chapter is divided up into two areas: coverage and bad faith litigation. The first examines some of the coverage disputes under the comprehensive general liability policy (CGL) and it begins with the modern disputes over coverage and exemption in such areas as pollution and products liability, and then offers a capsulized discussion of automobile liability insurance, still in the aggregate one of the largest lines of coverage. The second section of the chapter deals with the ancilliary obligations of the insured, the duty to defend and the duty to negotiate settlement in good faith, which have been staples in modern insurance litigation.

Before turning to these particulars it is useful to address briefly the connection between tort liability and insurance. The basic source of difficulty, which pervades every aspect of liability, is that the insurance contract between a defendant and its insurer must regulate the affairs not only as between those parties but also in relationship to the injured plaintiff whose rights against the insured are often satisfiable only from the proceeds of the insurance carrier.

The instabilities of this three-cornered game are well illustrated by two early twentieth century cases each of which rebuffed an attack on private insurance contracts. The first of these, Bain v. Atkins, 63 N.E. 414, 415 (Mass. 1902), involved a suit against an insurer who had written an indemnity policy on the insured which required it to pay a third party only to the extent that the insured was solvent. The contract was written to benefit the insured and insurer, but not the injured party. When the plaintiff was unable to collect from the bankrupt insured, he sued the carrier, but in vain:

> [The policy] contains no agreement that the insurance shall enure to the benefit of the person accidentally injured, and no language from which such an understanding or intention can be implied. Atkins was under no obligation to procure insurance for the benefit of the plaintiff, nor did any relation exist between the plaintiff and Atkins which could give the latter the right to procure insurance for the benefit of the plaintiff. The only correct statement of the situation is simply that the insurance was a matter wholly between the company and Atkins, in which the plaintiff had no legal or equitable interest, any more than in any other property belonging absolutely to Atkins.

The critical attack on *Bain*, which eventually bore fruit, was that public policy should prevent an insurer from hiding behind the insolvency of its insured, and that all indemnity contracts be read as creating vested rights that allowed third persons to recover against the insurer whether or not the insured was solvent. The impulse was therefore to increase the effectiveness of tort liability insurance in compensating strangers for losses. See Laube, The Social Vice of Accident Indemnity, 80 U. Pa. L. Rev. 189 (1930).

At the same time indemnity contracts were attacked from the opposite side, on the ground that these contracts should be wholly void as a matter of public policy. Here the focus is less on compensation of injuries after the fact and more on the deterrence of injury before the fact. In Breeden v. Frankfort Marine, Accident & Plate Glass Insurance Co., 119 S.W. 576, 608 (Mo. 1909), an injured worker sued his employer for personal injuries caused by the employer's negligence. The underlying suit was successful, and the question was whether the insurance indemnity contract was void against public policy on the ground that it encouraged sloth and indifference by employers who did not bear the financial sting of any adverse judgment. An exhaustive initial judgment by Woodson, J., upheld this contention, but it was reversed in a somewhat less exhaustive opinion which justified the use of indemnity contracts, by noting, among other things, that

> such insurance does not lessen the employer's liability or responsibility, but increases his means of meeting both; . . . that the existence of an indemnity fund does not directly or necessarily cause the master or carrier to relax his care and diligence to prevent injury to servants, passengers, or shippers; . . . that the employer, shipper, or passenger, instead of less security, has the added security of the vigilance, experience, and self-interest of the insurance company itself to prevent the use of negligent methods, negligently constructed or operated machines and appliances or other negligent exposure to injury; . . . [and] that there is no unvarying rule, of which judicial notice will be taken, that an indemnity against losses by negligence will, in and of itself, induce a master or carrier to omit the highest degree of care, and that (absent such rule) it does not logically follow that an indemnity contract is directly or incidentally repugnant to public policy.

For a detailed account of how tort liability meshes with liability insurance see Schwartz, The Ethics and the Economics of Tort Liability Insurance, 75 Cornell L. Rev. 313 (1990).

B.   THE SCOPE OF INSURANCE COVERAGE

1.   Modern Tort Litigation

Dimmitt Chevrolet, Inc. v. Southeastern Fidelity Insurance Corp.
636 So. 2d 700 (Fla. 1993)

PER CURIAM. This cause is before the Court on the following certified question of law from the United States Court of Appeals in Industrial

Indemnity Insurance Co. v. Crown Auto Dealerships, Inc., 935 F.2d 240 (11th Cir. 1991):

> WHETHER, AS A MATTER OF LAW, THE POLLUTION EXCLUSION CLAUSE CONTAINED IN THE COMPREHENSIVE GENERAL LIABILITY INSURANCE POLICY PRECLUDES COVERAGE TO ITS INSURED FOR LIABILITY FOR THE ENVIRONMENTAL CONTAMINATION THAT OCCURRED IN THIS CASE.

[Dimmitt Chevrolet operated two dealerships which sold the used crankcase oil generated by its business to Peak Oil Company from 1974 to 1979. From 1974 to 1979 Peak had recycled oil from Dimmitt and other sources for sale as used oil. In 1983 the Environmental Protection Agency determined that substantial pollution at Peak's worksite had resulted from Peak's storage of its waste sludge in unlined bins. In addition to its suit against Peak, the EPA designated Dimmitt as a potentially responsible party (PRP) under CERCLA because it had generated and transported hazardous materials to the Peak site. Dimmitt agreed to undertake remedial measures without conceding its liability under CERCLA.]

Appellee Southeastern Fidelity Insurance Corporation ("Southeastern") provided comprehensive general liability ("CGL") insurance coverage to Dimmitt from 1972 through 1980. The policy covered Dimmitt

> for all sums which the INSURED shall become legally obligated to pay as DAMAGES because of A. BODILY INJURY or B. PROPERTY DAMAGE to which this insurance applies, caused by an occurrence, and the Company shall have the right and duty to defend any suit against the INSURED seeking DAMAGES on account of such BODILY INJURY or PROPERTY DAMAGE, even if any of the allegations of the suit are groundless. . . .

An "occurrence", is defined by the policy as

> an accident including continuous or repeated exposure to conditions, which result in BODILY INJURY or PROPERTY DAMAGE neither expected nor intended from the standpoint of the INSURED. . . .

However, the policy excluded coverage for

> BODILY INJURY or PROPERTY DAMAGE arising out of the discharge, dispersal, release or escape of smoke, vapors, soot, fumes, acids, alkalis, toxic chemicals, liquids, or gases, waste materials . . . into or upon land, the atmosphere or any water course or body of water; but this exclusion does not apply if such discharge, dispersal, release or escape is sudden and accidental. . . .

In October 1988, Southeastern filed a declaratory judgment action against Dimmitt, seeking a declaration by the [federal] district court that Southeastern owed no duty to defend or indemnify Dimmitt under the CGL policy. Dimmitt filed a counterclaim seeking a contrary declaration. Both parties subsequently filed motions for summary judgment. The district court granted summary judgment in favor of Southeastern, reasoning that the pollution exclusion was not ambiguous and that the word "sudden" should be given a temporal meaning. Accordingly, the district court ruled that the pollution at the Peak site occurred over a period of years and therefore could not be considered "sudden." The district court subsequently denied without opinion Dimmitt's motion to alter or amend the judgment.

As noted by the [federal] court of appeals, Dimmitt Chevrolet, Inc. was not the actual cause of the pollution damage at issue. Its liability, however, is not in dispute in this case. The issue before us is whether Dimmitt's comprehensive liability insurance policy was intended to cover hazardous waste pollution under the circumstances set forth in the court of appeals' opinion. The question turns on the meaning of the term "sudden and accidental" within the pollution exclusion clause of Dimmitt's policy.

Dimmitt asserts that the term "sudden and accidental" is ambiguous because it is subject to multiple definitions. Thus, because ambiguous terms within an insurance policy should be construed in favor of the insured, the policy should be construed in Dimmitt's favor. Dimmitt argues that the word "sudden" does not have a temporal meaning and that the term was intentionally written so as to provide coverage for unexpected and unintended pollution discharge.

Southeastern Fidelity Insurance Corporation (Southeastern) contends that the clause excludes coverage for all pollution except when the discharge or dispersal of the pollutant occurs abruptly and accidentally. As such, Southeastern asserts that it had no duty to defend or indemnify Dimmitt because the pollution by the actual polluter, Peak Oil Company (Peak), was gradual and occurred over a period of several years.

Both sides also argue that the drafting history of pollution exclusion clauses favors their respective positions. In this regard, it should be noted that comprehensive general liability (CGL) policies are standard insurance policies developed by insurance industry trade associations, and these policies are the primary form of commercial insurance coverage obtained by businesses throughout the country. Before 1966, the standard CGL policy covered only property and personal injury damage that was caused by "accident." In 1966 the insurance industry switched to "occurrence-based" policies in which the term "occurrence" was defined as " 'an accident, including continuous or repeated exposure to conditions, which results in bodily injury or property damage neither expected nor intended from the standpoint of the insured.' " Beginning in 1970, the pollution exclusion clause at issue in this case was added to the standard policy. Finally, the policy was again changed in 1984 by the addition of what has been called an "absolute exclusion clause," which totally excludes coverage for pollution clean-up costs that arise from governmental directives. Kenneth S. Abraham, Environmental Liability Insurance Law 161 (1991).

Dimmitt argues that because many state insurance commissioners approved the 1970 addition of the pollution exclusion clause without ordering a reduction in premiums, this indicates that the clause did little more than clarify coverage. Southeastern counters by saying that the reason there was no premium reduction in 1970 was because there had been no premium increase when the coverage was expanded in 1966 to cover occurrences. Both parties also rely on conflicting statements made by insurance representatives who had appeared before state insurance commissions, as well as statements made by other insurance experts.

The policy language at issue here has been the subject of extensive litigation throughout the United States. There is substantial support for both parties' positions. On the one hand, the supreme courts of Colorado, Georgia, West Virginia, and Wisconsin have found the pollution exclusion clause to be ambiguous. In reaching their conclusions, these courts refer to the varying dictionary definitions of the word "sudden." They are also persuaded by the drafting history that the words "sudden and accidental" were intended to mean "unexpected and unintended."

On the other hand, the supreme courts of Massachusetts, Michigan, North Carolina, and Ohio have held that the word "sudden" has a temporal context. Therefore, when the word "sudden" is combined with the word "accidental," the clause means abrupt and unintended. A majority of federal courts of appeal appear to have adopted this view in construing policies in states in which the supreme court of that state has not yet set forth its position.

We are persuaded that the federal district judge properly construed Southeastern's pollution exclusion clause. The ordinary and common usage of the term "sudden" includes a temporal aspect with a sense of immediacy or abruptness. As stated by the court in Hybud Equipment Corp. v. Sphere Drake Insurance Co., 597 N.E.2d 1096, 1102 (Ohio 1992):

> As it is most commonly used, "sudden" means happening quickly, abruptly, or without prior notice. This is the plain and ordinary meaning of the word, and the context in which it is employed does not indicate that it should be given any other meaning.

Dimmitt points to dictionary definitions of "sudden" which also include the meaning of "happening or coming unexpectedly." Dictionaries are helpful insofar as they set forth the ordinary, usual meaning of words. However, as noted in New Castle County v. Hartford Accident & Indemnity Co., dictionaries are "imperfect yardsticks of ambiguity." 933 F.2d 1162 at 1193-94 (3d Cir. 1991). Our duty is to determine whether the word "sudden" is ambiguous in the context of the specific insurance policy at issue.

The use of the word "sudden" can connote a sense of the unexpected. However, rather than standing alone in the pollution exclusion clause, it is an integral part of the conjunctive phrase "sudden and accidental." The term accidental is generally understood to mean unexpected or unintended. Therefore, to construe sudden also to mean unintended and unexpected would render the words sudden and accidental entirely redundant.

As expressed in the pollution exclusion clause, the word sudden means abrupt and unexpected.

We reject Dimmitt's suggestion that the policy is ambiguous because the term accident is included both within the definition of occurrence and in the pollution exclusion provision.[6]

In the final analysis, we construe this policy to mean that (1) basic coverage arises from the occurrence of unintended damages, but (2) such damages as arise from the discharge of various pollutants are excluded from the basic coverage, except that (3) damages arising from the discharge of these pollutants will fall within the coverage of the policy where such discharge is sudden and accidental.

Because we conclude that the policy language is unambiguous, we find it inappropriate and unnecessary to consider the arguments pertaining to the drafting history of the pollution exclusion clause.

Applying the policy language to the facts of this case, we hold that the pollution damage was not within the scope of Southeastern's policy. The pollution took place over a period of many years and most of it occurred gradually. With respect to the pollution which resulted from oil spills and leaks at the site as well as from occasional runoff of contaminated rain water, we agree with the analysis of the federal district judge in this case when he said: These spills and leaks appear to be common place events which occurred in the course of daily business, and therefore cannot, as a matter of law, be classified as "sudden and accidental." That is, these "occasional accidental spills" are recurring events that took place in the usual course of recycling the oil. As one court observed: "contamination . . . by disposing of chemicals in the lagoon, or by annual careless spillage onto the ground surface cannot

6. Likewise, we also reject the dissenters' argument that the term "sudden and accidental" in the pollution exclusion clause should be given the same interpretation as certain courts have construed the term in boiler and machinery policies. The most obvious flaw in this argument is that it ascribes universal meaning to the phrase "sudden and accidental" regardless of the context of its use. Significantly, boiler and machinery policies provide coverage for damage that is sudden and accidental; Southeastern's pollution exclusion applies the phrase to the causative agent — the discharge. . . .

be sudden, or unexpected and accidental. . . ." American Mutual Liability Ins. v. Neville Chemical, 650 F. Supp. 929, 933 (W.D. Pa.1987).

We answer the certified question in the affirmative and return the record to the Eleventh Circuit.

It is so ordered.

MCDONALD, SHAW and KOGAN and HARDING, JJ. concur.

GRIMES, JUSTICE, concurring.

I originally concurred with the position of the dissenters in this case. I have now become convinced that I relied too much on what was said to be the drafting history of the pollution exclusion clause and perhaps subconsciously upon the social premise that I would rather have insurance companies cover these losses rather than parties such as Dimmitt who did not actually cause the pollution damage. In so doing, I departed from the basic rule of interpretation that language should be given its plain and ordinary meaning. Try as I will, I cannot wrench the words "sudden and accidental" to mean "gradual and accidental," which must be done in order to provide coverage in this case.

OVERTON, JUSTICE, dissenting.

I dissent. In my view, the majority: (1) ignores key factors in determining that the term "sudden and accidental," as used in comprehensive liability insurance policies, is not ambiguous; (2) fails to consider the facts in this record concerning the intent of the insurance industry in using that term and, consequently, is wrong on the merits; and (3) allows the insurance industry to grossly abuse the rehearing process in the presentation of its rehearing petition in this cause.

THE DEFINITION OF "SUDDEN AND ACCIDENTAL"

The majority's reasoning blatantly ignores evidence before this Court reflecting that the term "sudden and accidental" is ambiguous. The term "sudden and accidental" has been in use by the insurance industry in standard form insurance policies since before 1970. In those policies, "sudden and accidental" has been defined differently from the definition asserted in this case by Southeastern. For instance, in policies involving boilers and machinery, courts have uniformly found the term "sudden and accidental" to be defined as "unforeseen or unexpected" (the definition asserted by Dimmitt), as opposed to "instantaneous or abrupt" (the definition asserted by Southeastern). The law is clear and unrefuted on this point. . . .

In my view, the term "sudden and accidental" must be found to be ambiguous given that the term is, in fact, subject to more than one interpretation. Although the insurance industry asks that we find the term to be unambiguous, it is clear that the term can mean "unexpected and unintended," a definition not limited as to time of occurrence, in addition to Southeastern's asserted definition of "instantaneous or abrupt." This is especially true when considering the extreme divergence among the numerous jurisdictions considering this issue. As noted, even dictionaries cannot agree as to the primary and secondary meanings of the word "sudden." Notably, however, perhaps the most important illustration of this ambiguity is the definition that the insurance industry itself embraced in regulatory presentations. An examination of the pollution exclusion clause drafting history set forth below unquestionably supports the conclusion that the clause was included only to preclude coverage for intentionally caused pollution damage, not to preclude damage that was "unexpected and unintended."

THE DRAFTING HISTORY OF COMPREHENSIVE
GENERAL LIABILITY POLICIES AND THE POLLUTION
EXCLUSION CLAUSE

Comprehensive general liability (CGL) policies are standard insurance policies developed by insurance industry trade associations, and these policies are the primary form of commercial insurance coverage obtained by businesses throughout the country. CGL policies have been revised in pertinent part on three separate occasions: first in 1966, then again in the early 1970s and mid-1980s.[8] The pollution exclusion clause, the clause at issue in this proceeding, was included as a standard clause in CGL policies in the 1970s revision.

Before 1966, the standard comprehensive general liability policy covered only property and personal injury damage that was caused by "accident." The term "accident" was undefined in policies, and courts reached differing conclusions as to exactly what type of damage was covered. In defining the term "accident," most courts agreed that the term referred to damage caused by an unintentional or unexpected event. But some found that damage caused by gradual pollution was covered, while others did not.

To clarify this confusion, in 1966 the insurance industry switched from "accident-based" comprehensive general liability policies to "occurrence-based" policies. In the occurrence-based comprehensive general liability policy, the term "occurrence" was defined as " 'an accident, including continuous or repeated exposure to conditions, which results in bodily injury or property damage neither expected nor intended from the standpoint of the insured.' "

Statements by the insurance industry at that time indicate that the

8. In 1984 the industry proposed what has been called an "absolute pollution exclusion clause." The new clause completely eliminates the term "sudden and accidental" and totally excludes coverage for pollution clean-up costs that arise from governmental directives. Kenneth S. Abraham, Environmental Liability Insurance Law 161 (1991).

shift to an occurrence-based CGL policy was to "clarify the coverage provided by liability policies, and to avoid the confusion resulting from courts attempting to distinguish between accidental means and accidental results." Additionally, the shift was to clearly indicate that the term "occurrence" included damages caused by " 'exposure to conditions which may [have] continue[d] for an unmeasured period of time.' " . . .

On March 17, 1970, the industry again proposed to amend CGL policies to include the pollution exclusion clause at issue in Dimmitt. When the pollution exclusion clause was proposed, representatives of the industry indicated that the new clause was not designed to reduce coverage; instead, it was to ensure that insureds who recklessly and intentionally polluted or who failed to take reasonable precautions to prevent pollution would not be afforded coverage.

[The dissent then reviewed the statements in support of this position made by representatives of the insurance industry in various states.]

The drafting history of the pollution exclusion clause leads to the inescapable conclusion that the insurance industry was attempting to exclude from coverage those polluters who committed their acts intentionally. The record of representations by the insurance industry itself clearly support this conclusion. The addition of the pollution exclusion clause, specifically the term "sudden and accidental" was presented by the insurance industries to the regulators to mean that coverage would continue for those events that were "unexpected and unintended"; the clause's purpose was simply to make clear that intentionally committed pollution would not be covered.

BARKETT, C.J., and HARDING, J.,concur.

The Motion for Rehearing and Clarification, filed by Appellant, is hereby denied.

OVERTON, J., dissents with an opinion, in which BARKETT, C.J., and HARDING, J., concur.

NOTES

1. *The battle over the pollution coverage.* As *Dimmitt* indicates, state and federal courts have fought a battle royal over the scope of the insurer's responsibility for pollution since the advent of CERCLA in 1980. That struggle marks only one battle among many that continue to be fought. For an exhaustive decision on the CGL policy see the monster opinion in Morton International v. General Accident Insurance Co., 629 A.2d 831, 847, 876, 884 (N.J. 1993), which upheld coverage, both primary and excessive, when the insured had discharged mercury wastes into public waters for a period of some 40 years.

The insurers first argued that they were not liable for the costs of clean up under CERCLA because the CGL policy was limited to "all sums which the insured shall become legally obligated to pay *as damages.*" Stein, J., first conceded that a sizable minority of courts held that the words "as damages" "confines an insurer's duty of indemnity to judgment for traditional tort-liability money damages, and imposes no obligation to reimburse Morton for equitable remedies such as governmentally-mandated response costs intended to remediate environmental harm." See Continental Insurance Companies v. Northeastern Pharmaceutical & Chemical Co., 842 F.2d 977 (8th Cir. 1988), but it then sided with the majority of the court that came out four square for coverage, quoting the Washington Supreme Court in Boeing Co. v Aetna Casualty & Surety Co., 784 P.2d 507, 511-512 (Wash. 1990):

> If the state were to sue in court to recover in traditional "damages," including the state's costs incurred in cleaning up the contamination, for the injury to the ground water, defendant's obligation to defend against the law suit and to pay damages would be clear. It is merely fortuitous from the standpoint of either plaintiff or defendant that the state has chosen to have plaintiff remedy the contamination problem, rather than choosing to incur the costs of clean-up itself and then suing the plaintiff to recover those costs. The damages to the natural resources is simply measured in the cost to restore the water to its original state.

Turning next to the pollution exemption in the standard policy, the court agreed that the words "sudden and accidental" "connot[ed] an event that begins abruptly or without prior notice or warning," no matter what its duration. It then held, however, that the defendant was estopped from relying on the clause because in its presentations to the New Jersey insurance officials, it defended the incorporation of this exemption on the sole ground that

> Coverage for pollution or contamination is not provided in most cases under present policies because the damages can be said to be expected or intended and thus are excluded by the definition of occurrence. The above exclusion clarifies this situation so also to avoid any question of intent. Coverage is continued for pollution or contamination caused injuries when the pollution or contamination results from an accident.

Stein, J., then concluded that this memo fundamentally misstated the effect of the new pollution exemption clause, by treating it as merely duplicative of the basic coverage language, and justified the estoppel as follows:

> Had full disclosure been made, we would not hesitate to enforce the pollution-exclusion clause as written, resolving nuances inherent in the meaning of "sudden" on a case-by-case basis. Not only did the insurance industry fail to disclose the intended effect of this significant exclusionary clause, it knowingly misstated its intended effect in the industry's submis-

sion of the clause to the state Departments of Insurance. Having profited from that nondisclosure by maintaining pre-existing rates for substantially-reduced coverage, the industry justly should be required to bear the burden of its omission by providing coverage at a level consistent with its representations to regulatory authorities.

Should it make a difference if no individual insured was misled on the scope of coverage?

The last issue addressed in *Morton* concerned the insurer's liability for discharges committed by the prior owners of the Morton site. On that question Stein, J., held that the insurers were protected by the "neither expected nor intended from the standpoint of the insured" language found in the CGL.

> Without determining that such damage was intended, we find inescapable the conclusion that [substantial] damage . . . must have been anticipated by Morton's predecessors on the basis of their prolonged knowledge of and avoidance of compliance with complaints by regulatory officials that the company discharged unacceptable amounts of emissions including mercury compounds, into Berry's Creek.

Should *Morton International* be decided for the insurers if they realized only a competitive rate of return on the policies as written? See generally Ballard and Manus, Clearing Muddy Waters: Anatomy of the Comprehensive General Liability Pollution Exclusion, 75 Cornell L. Rev. 610 (1990); Note, The Pollution Exclusion Clause Through the Looking Glass, 74 Geo. L.J. 1237 (1986).

2. *Triggers for coverage under the CGL.* In one sense at least, *Dimmitt* puts the cart before the horse, by examining the scope of the pollution exemption when the "trigger" provision of the basic coverage is not in doubt. That trigger is not usually a source of difficulty in the ordinary case of traumatic injury, which like the "sudden and accidental" discharge, is contained within a single period. But even in this setting complications can develop. In Eljer Manufacturing Inc. v. Liberty Mutual Insurance Co., 972 F.2d 805, 809 (7th Cir. 1992), Eljer's United Brass Subsidiary marketed between 500,000 and 750,000 of its Qest plumbing system for home installation between 1979 and 1986. After installation, the system showed a tendency to leak and Eljer was forced to replace at least 17,000 units by breaking into walls. It was estimated that ultimately some five percent of all Qest systems would fail in circumstances that could provoke suit. Several hundred suits, including a number of class actions, were filed, claiming damages for both the Qest units that had failed and demanding that others be replaced before failure. Under the standard coverage provision, the defendant insurers claimed that "the physical injury to or destruction of tangible property which occurs during the policy period" was triggered only by those systems that had leaked before the defendants had terminated their cover-

age. Posner, J., rejected this "manifestation" approach and held that
the physical damage had occurred when the units were first installed —
when coverage was still in place.

> The central issue in the case — when if ever the incorporation of one
> product into another can be said to cause physical injury — pivots on a
> conflict between the connotations of the term "physical injury" and the
> objective of insurance. The central meaning of the term as it is used in
> everyday English — the image it would conjure up in the mind of a per-
> son unschooled in the subtleties of insurance law — is of harmful change
> in appearance, shape, composition, or some other physical dimension of
> the "injured" person or thing. If water leaks from a pipe and discolors a
> carpet or rots a beam, that is physical injury, perhaps beginning with
> the very earliest sign of rot — the initial contamination (an important
> question in asbestos cases . . .). The ticking time bomb, in contrast,
> does not injure the structure in which it is placed, in the sense of altering
> the structure in a harmful, or for that matter in any, way — until it ex-
> plodes. But these nice, physicalist, "realistic" (in the philosophical sense)
> distinctions have little to do with the objectives of parties to insurance
> contracts. The purpose of insurance is to spread risks and by spreading
> cancel them. . . . The last point at which a Qest plumbing system has an
> insurable risk of being defective and causing harm is when it is installed.
> When it starts to leak is too late; the risk has turned into a certainty and
> cannot be spread by being insured. [For Eljer] the pooling of the risks
> of the individual homeowners has produced a near certainty of a loss in
> excess of $100 million. . . . But we are told that Eljer has had no pri-
> mary liability coverage since the last Liberty policies expired at the end
> of 1988 and no excess coverage since the last Travelers policy expired at
> the end of 1986. . . .
>   . . . In these circumstances we should not be quick to assume that the
> standard general liability policy issued by the American insurance indus-
> try provides what to an outsider at any rate appears to be largely though
> not completely illusory coverage in an important class of cases.

Cudahy, J., dissented on the prosaic ground that "physical injury" in
the strictest sense of the term does not include the risk of future loss at
the time of installation, and that the risk-spreading function of insurance "does not extend to risks that were not bargained for ex ante."
Can the insurer protect itself from these kinds of losses by imposing
sharp limits on its primary or excessive coverage? If only one Qest
leaked, then the insurance trigger would be the time of the leak. Why
then does the time of the trigger change when thousands leak?

3. *The asbestos coverage dispute.* The identical trigger question under
the CGL arose in the asbestos coverage disputes that were extensively
litigated during the 1970s and 1980s. There the major question of contract interpretation was over *which* insurers or insureds must pay both
the indemnity (both by settlement and litigation) and the defense costs
of the underlying tort disputes. On this question the insurers were divided among themselves into two camps: one in support of the first
manifestation position and the other in support of proration of cover-

age from the period of initial exposure to first manifestation. The former position, adopted in Eagle-Picher Industries, Inc. v. Liberty Mutual Insurance Co., 682 F.2d 12 (1st Cir. 1982), tied the coverage to the moment at which the plaintiff manifested symptoms of an asbestos-related disease, and, as is the case with ordinary accidents, thus tied each tort dispute to a single insurance policy. The rival exposure position, adopted in Insurance Co. of North America v. Forty-Eight Insulations, Inc., 633 F.2d 1212 (6th Cir. 1980), modified, 657 F.2d 814 (6th Cir. 1981), prorated indemnity and defense coverage across the entire period from initial exposure to the defendant's product to the manifestation of disease, leaving the insured at risk for periods in which no coverage had been purchased or available coverage had been exhausted. Both sides to this dispute rejected the position that coverage was triggered solely at the time of initial exposure.

Both insurer positions eventually lost out to a third view propounded by the manufacturer-insureds that allowed the insured to *elect* to assign the loss to any policy in effect at the time of initial exposure, at first manifestation, or at any time in between. This "triple-trigger" view, championed in Keene v. INA, 667 F.2d 1034 (D.C. Cir. 1981), quickly became the industry benchmark for future settlement negotiations. As is the case with *Eljer,* the *Keene* position carries with it the risk of an enormous loss for a tiny premium. Thus any insurer that wrote coverage, say, for a month in 1970, could be held responsible for the full damages of all persons exposed before that date whose injuries were manifested thereafter, even though it received only a tiny premium to bear that enormous risk. Should the first manifestation position be rejected in asbestos cases because it renders the coverage illusory? Should the triple trigger be rejected on the grounds that it imposes heavy administrative burdens in the control and organization of the defense of a single insured that has multiple insurers for different policy periods? For a defense of the first manifestation position see Epstein, The Legal and Insurance Dynamics of Mass Tort Litigation, 13 J. Legal Stud. 475, 495-505 (1984); for a defense of *Keene*'s triple trigger see Note, Adjudicating Asbestos Insurance Liability: Alternatives to Contract Analysis, 97 Harv. L. Rev. 739 (1984). A copy of the CGL may be found in R. Keeton and A. Widiss, Insurance Law, Appendix J (1), 1243.

2. Automobile Insurance Coverage

a. The march to compulsory insurance

Notwithstanding the enormous coverage battles arising from mass tort litigation, much of the day to day business of insurance coverage still involves disputes arising out of automobile accidents. Unlike the commercial disputes, individual drivers have strong incentives not to take out any coverage at all. In fact most early insurance policies were in the form of indemnity policies of the sort upheld, as written, in Bain v. Atkins, 63 N.E. 414 (Mass. 1902), supra at 980. The broad dissatisfaction with indemnity policies led to a movement to require genuine protection to third parties injured by other drivers. Starting in the 1920s, many states passed so-called financial responsibility statutes that required individuals to show that they were financially able, within certain stated limits, to satisfy tort judgments against them. Since the mechanisms of enforcement were unclear, some states then passed security responsibility statutes that allowed a driver to renew a driving license only on a showing that assets were available within the stated limits to meet these tort claims.

These financial and security responsibility statutes did not require individuals to take out insurance, even though most did. Starting in the 1930s, a compulsory insurance movement picked up steam, which was promply challenged on constitutional grounds. These challenges were rebuffed as early as 1925 by the Massachusetts Supreme Judicial Court, which in Opinion of the Justices, 147 N.E. 681 (Mass. 1925), held that the general power to exclude automobiles from the public highways "includes the lesser power to grant the right to use public ways only upon the observance of prescribed conditions precedent." The court sanctioned this "extension of the police power into a new field" because the conditions imposed could not be "pronounced unreasonable" given the need to assure innocent persons full compensation for their accidents.

One major problem with the compulsory insurance laws concerns the treatment of those individuals whose risk profiles are so grim that no insurance company wishes to take the risk of insuring them. The usual answer to this problem has been to place those risky individuals in an "assigned risk" pool. All of the insurance companies that do business within the state are then required to insure some portion of the total pool, though at rates substantially above those charged to their regular customers. In California State Automobile Assn. Interinsurance Bureau v. Maloney, 341 U.S. 105 (1951), the Supreme Court upheld against various constitutional challenges those assigned risk provisions (here in the context of the California financial responsibility statutes), noting that the wisdom of those enactments was for the legislature to determine. Instead of requiring insurance companies to give coverage to risky drivers, would it be better to ban from the highway those drivers unable to obtain insurance coverage in the marketplace? See generally R. Keeton and A. Widiss, Insurance Law §4.10(b).

The strains on automobile insurance coverage remain evident today, as the powerful pressures from more frequent claims and larger verdicts and settlements continue to fuel the increase in the cost of automobile insurance. In an attempt to stem the tide of these increases California voters in 1989 narrowly approved by referendum Proposition 103, which extensively revised the way in which insurance companies did business in California. The initiative was described in these terms by the California Supreme Court in Calfarm Insurance Co v. Deukmejian, 771 P.2d 1247, 1250 (Cal. 1989).

> Insurance rates are to be immediately reduced to "at least 20 percent less" than those in effect on November 8, 1987 (approximately the date when the initiative was proposed, and one year prior to its enactment). (§18612.01, subd. (a).) All rate increases require the approval of the Insurance Commissioner, who may not approve rates which are "excessive, inadequate, unfairly discriminatory, or otherwise in violation of [the initiative]." (§1861.05) Prior to November 8, 1989, however, rates may be increased only if the commissioner finds "that an insurer is substantially threatened with insolvency." (§1861.01, subd. (b).) "Certain procedures are specified for hearing applications for rate approval." (§§1861.04-1861.10.)

The California Supreme Court upheld the basic structure of the initiative, but struck down, as a taking under the due process clause, the initiative's critical provision allowing a rate increase before November 1989 only upon a showing of a substantial threat of insolvency.

> The insolvency standard of subdivision (b) refers to the financial position of the company as a whole, not merely to the regulated lines of insurance. Many insurers do substantial business outside of California, or in lines of insurance within this state which are not regulated by Proposition 103. If an insurer had substantial net worth, or significant income from sources unregulated by Proposition 103, it might be able to sustain substantial and continuing losses on regulated insurance without danger of insolvency. In such a case the continued solvency of the insurer could not suffice to demonstrate that the regulated rate constitutes a fair return.
>
> The effect of section 1861.01, subdivision (b) is thus to bar safely solvent insurers from obtaining relief from "inadequate" rates until November 1989. Temporary rates which might be below a fair and reasonable level might compel insurers to return to their customers surpluses exacted through alleged excessive past rates. But the concept that rates may be set at less than a fair rate of return in order to compel the return of past surpluses is not one supported by precedent. "The just compensation safeguarded to the utility by the Fourteenth Amendment is a reasonable return on the value of the property used at the time that it is being used for the public service. . . . [T]he law does not require the company to give up for the benefit of future subscribers any part of its accumulations from past operations. Profits of the past cannot be used to sustain confiscatory rates for the future." . . .
>
> Proponents urge that the insolvency standard can be sustained as a temporary or emergency measure. They point out that temporary freezes while administrative machinery is set up are commonly approved, even if they lack any method whereby a seller can get relief. . . . [But h]ere we

have a law which mandates not maintenance of a rate set by the seller, but a reduction to at least 20 percent less than former rates. The risk that the rate set by the statute is confiscatory as to some insurers from its inception is high enough to require an adequate method for obtaining individualized relief.

The court then held that the insolvency provisions were "severable" from the rest of the initiative, and in effect authorized the commissioner of insurance to process individual applications of any company that claims the initiative's rate reductions are "confiscatory," an invitation that was promptly accepted by droves of insurance companies. Judicial decision thus allowed the insurance companies to charge higher rates if their applications were filed before the November 1989 deadline, subject to the risk that they should have to refund the overcharges if the commissioner found that the rates charged were excessive. After November 1989, higher rates could go into effect only with the prior approval of the commissioner. The ensuing rate hearings have been mired for years. For one account see Epstein, A Clash of Two Cultures: Will the Tort System Survive Automobile Insurance Reform?, 25 Val. U. L. Rev. 173 (1991).

b.   The standard provisions of the automobile insurance contract

i.   Omnibus clauses

An automobile insurance policy contains a number of important clauses. Perhaps the most important is the so-called omnibus clause that provides:

> The following are insureds [for tort liability] with respect to the owned automobile, (1) the named insured and any resident of the same household; (2) any other person using such automobile with the permission of the named insured, provided his actual operation or (if he is not operating) his actual use thereof is within the scope of such permission . . .

As drafted the clause provides the owner protection under circumstances in which he might be held vicariously liable. It also protects the owner from any liability that might be imposed upon him by operation of either the owner consent statutes or the family purpose doctrine. Its distinctive feature, however, is to protect the owner when his car is used with his permission by third parties, *whether or not* the owner himself is liable. It is a case of insurance beyond liability. In some cases the injured party seeks to reach the owner under an omnibus clause when the injury is caused by the negligence of someone who did not drive with the owner's permission, but only with the permission of, as is common, the owner's children who were prohibited from lending the car to third persons. In Hays v. County Mutual Insurance Co., 192 N.E.2d 855, 859 (Ill. 1963), Schaefer, J., adopted the general principle that the contract controls unless the state legislature overrides it for the benefit of third parties. He thus refused to read

> the requirement of permission out of the insurance contract on the ground that it is wholly purposeless, technical, and fortuitous. When the insured purchases extended coverage he seeks to protect those whom he allows to use his car from the risks of financial disaster as he would guard them against danger from mechanical defects. Ordinarily he has no interest in buying protection for those who use his car without permission. The insurer, on the other hand, limits the risk assumed by requiring permission, since usually the insured will use discretion in permitting others to use his car, if only as a matter of self-interest in avoiding damage to his property. As a matter of probability based on experience with policyholders as a group, we cannot say that the limitation to users who have the insured's permission carries no actuarial significance.

Schaefer's view of the situation was limited in the subsequent Illinois decision of Maryland Casualty Co. v. Iowa National Mutual Ins. Co., 297 N.E.2d 163, 168 (Ill. 1973), which took the position "that once the initial permission has been given by the named insured, coverage is fixed, barring theft or the like." U.S. Fidelity & Guaranty Co. v. McManus, 356 N.E.2d 78, 80 (Ill. 1976), subsequently held that once initial permission was given, the insurer was liable when other persons used the car without the permission (indeed, without the knowledge) of the original permittee. The court wrote: "We adhere to the view expressed in *Maryland Casualty* that where an insurer elects to include in its policy a broad provision extending liability coverage to persons operating or using a car with the permission of the owner, a further grant of permission from the initial permittee need not be shown in order to invoke the coverage."

The proper construction of the omnibus clause is often an issue whenever a driver who is given permission to use the car for one particular purpose decides to use it for quite another. In dealing with this problem, the court in Branch v. United States Fidelity & Guaranty Co., 198 F.2d 1007, 1009 (6th Cir. 1952), said:

> The construction and application of the omnibus clause in automobile liability insurance policies have been the subject of much litigation throughout the country. The Courts are divided in their holdings into three general groups: (1) the so-called strict rule, which denies coverage if the driver departs from the intended purposes of the owner; (2) the minor deviation rule holding that the policy covers the driver of the car if the deviation is slight; and (3) the so-called liberal rule which holds that the policy covers the driver although he deviates from the intended

purposes of the owner, if he originally obtained possession with the owner's permission.

In 6c J. Appleman, Insurance Law and Practice §4366 (1979), coverage of this third rule of construction is captioned: "Permission — Hell or High Water Rule."

ii. "Drive the other car" clauses

The so-called "drive the other car" clause gives the owner (and normally the owner's spouse) of an insured car liability coverage while driving another car. Such coverage is often subject to several limitations, but the most important coverage is in connection with the casual use of another car. See, e.g., Hochgurtel v. San Felippo, 253 N.W.2d 526 (Wis. 1977). This clause is often in tension with the omnibus clause, which makes coverage run with the vehicle, while the drive the other car clause makes it run with the driver. Where each insurance policy says that its liability is secondary to that contained in other policies, then the insured with two ostensible coverages might be left with no coverage at all. This conclusion has been stoutly resisted by the courts. See, e.g., American Automobile Insurance Co. v. Penn Mutual Indemnity Co., 161 F.2d 62 (3d Cir. 1947), where it was held that primary coverage lay with the drive the other car policy. The dispute is now resolved by the language of the standard automobile policy, under which the omnibus clause is treated as the primary policy. See generally I. Schermer, Automobile Liability Insurance §§17.02[3], 17.03 (2d rev. ed. 1989).

iii. Uninsured motorist coverage

Another of the common clauses found in automobile insurance contracts provides for the payment of benefits to an insured harmed by an uninsured motorist legally responsible for the accident. To guard against the possibility of collusion between the insured and the uninsured motorist, these clauses stipulate that the insurance company is bound by a judgment that the insured obtains against the uninsured motorist only with its approval. The coverage runs in favor of the insured, his immediate family, and any other person injured while occupying the insured's automobile.

"Within uninsured motorist insurance, third-party liability rights are implemented through a first-party insurance system." G. Schwartz, A Proposal for Tort Reform: Reformulating Uninsured Motorist Plans, 48 Ohio St. L.J. 419, 425 (1987). Accordingly, coverage extends to pain and suffering and punitive damages, even though these are not normally purchased in first-party settings. To avoid these anomalies and reduce premiums, Schwartz suggests that this coverage be configured along the lines of standard first-party policies, since any deterrent function is by the boards.

Under the uninsured motorist statutes, the underinsured motorist is treated as an uninsured motorist to the extent of the shortfall in coverage. See McDaniel v. State Farm Mutual Automobile Insurance Co., 139 S.E.2d 806 (Va. 1965). The problem of underinsurance has been also addressed explicitly in legislation, with a small handful of states mandating the coverage while in most states the coverage need merely be offered. See, e.g., Ariz. Rev. Stat. Ann. 20-259.01 (1994). Also see 3 A. Widiss, Uninsured and Underinsured Motorist Coverage ch. 32 (1985).

One oft-litigated problem the uninsured motorist provisions concerns the question of "stacking." Thus an insured may take out two or more insurance policies, each of which provides uninsurance coverage for an injured person, paid for by a separate premium. If the driver of the other car is uninsured, is the insured entitled to recover the full amount from each policy, both for general damages and particular medical expenses? In Descoteaux v. Liberty Mutual Insurance Co., 480 A.2d 14, 19 (N.H. 1984), the court allowed recovery of the full limits under both policies, even though both policies contained language (in a drive the other car clause) that purported to limit the plaintiff to the coverage of a single policy without specifying which. "Since the legislature created an option for additional coverage, it intended that those choosing to buy increased protection should receive its benefits." For a detailed examination of the many variations on this single theme see 3 A. Widiss, Uninsured and Underinsured Motorist Coverage ch. 35.3 (1985).

iv. Medical payments

Many policies offered today now make provision for the payment of medical expenses even before the resolution of any dispute about liability. Thus, one sort of clause now provides that the insurance company will pay, within the limits specified by the policy, "expenses incurred by the insured for such immediate medical and surgical relief to others as shall be imperative at the time of an accident involving an automobile insured hereunder and not due to war . . . " Courts have often been willing to place a liberal construction on the clause, noting that, in the words of the Illinois appellate court, "the basic purpose of medical pay provisions such as here involved is to make available a fund to assure prompt and adequate medical care when injury is incurred, to relieve the physical suffering of the insured and to relieve the insured of the anxiety of not knowing from what source the money to pay the bills is coming." Jackson v. County Mutual Insurance Co., 190 N.E.2d 490, 492 (Ill. App. 1963).

A second form of medical benefit is one which provides that the insurance company agrees to pay "all reasonable expenses incurred within one year from the date of accident for necessary medical, surgical, X-ray and dental services, including prosthetic devices and necessary ambulance, hospital, professional nursing and funeral services." Clauses of this sort contain explicit dollar limitations and benefit not only the insured and members of his immediate family, but also all persons in the insured's car with his permission whether or not the insured is found ultimately at fault. Accordingly, their introduction has been hailed as a first step toward a comprehensive no-fault system, and acknowledged as the forerunner of the medical payment provisions in some of the proposed automobile no-fault plans. See R. Keeton and J. O'Connell, Basic Protection for the Traffic Victim 273 (1965).

v.   Advance payments

Many insurance policies provide that the insurance company shall make advance payments, say, for emergency medical expenses, to the injured party before liability is determined. In the event that the insurance company is liable, the payments previously made are credited against the amount of recovery allowed. What provision should be made for these expenses if it turns out that the injured party is not entitled to anything from the insurance company? What procedure should be adopted if the injured party refuses to credit the amount of the advance payments against his total recovery? See Edwards v. Passarelli Bros., 221 N.E.2d 708 (Ohio 1966), where the court approved of a postjudgment motion for a credit against the amount of the plaintiff's award.

vi.   Misrepresentation and nondisclosure

An insurance company is entitled to set aside any policy that the insured has obtained through either misrepresentation or nondisclosure of a material fact. These rules are general to all insurance contracts, and were first introduced with marine insurance under the general rubric of good faith. Today they have contractual status as well, as the policies reserve to the insurer the right to rescind the policy if there has been misrepresentation or nondisclosure of a material fact. These contracts can usually be set aside if the applicant conceals the identity of all the owners of a vehicle, the driving history of the insured, the place where the car is garaged, or previous cancellations of coverage. See, e.g., Safeway Insurance Co. v. Duran, 393 N.E.2d 688 (Ill. App. 1979).

Judges have often invoked a number of doctrines to relieve injured parties of the harsh consequences of the misrepresentation rules, most notably waiver and estoppel. In a waiver the insurer expressly, or by its conduct impliedly, gives up a known privilege or power otherwise available under the policy. For an estoppel the insured changes his position in reliance upon representations, by word or conduct, of the insurance company to such an extent that it would be inequitable to permit the insurer to deny the truth of the representations.

vii.   Notice and cooperation

Two of the most typical clauses found in insurance contracts govern the questions of notice and cooperation. The typical notice clauses provide as follows:

> *Notice of accident.* When an accident occurs written notice shall be given by or on behalf of the insured to the company or any of its authorized agents as soon as practicable. Such notice shall contain particulars sufficient to identify the insured and also reasonably obtainable information respecting the time, place and circumstances of the accident, the names and addresses of the injured and of available witnesses.
>
> *Notice of claim or suit.* If claim is made or suit is brought against the insured, the insured shall immediately forward to the company every demand, notice, summons or other process received by him or his representative.

These clauses allow an insurance company adequate time to investigate the accident or claim in question. The most commonly litigated question under them is whether an insurance company must show actual prejudice to decline coverage or whether prejudice should be presumed from the fact of delay. The automatic rule avoids an expensive inquiry into causation, but at the price of allowing an insurer to avoid coverage for some inconsequential delay in notification by an insured. Is there anything to be said for (or against) a rule which holds that any failure to notify within 30 days shall be treated as immaterial, while any failure to notify after 30 days shall be treated as prejudicial?

The typical cooperation clause found in a standard insurance policy reads as follows:

> *Assistance and cooperation of the insured.* The insured shall cooperate with the company and, upon the company's request, shall attend hearings and trials and shall assist in effecting settlements, securing and giving evidence, obtaining the attendance of witnesses and in the conduct of suits. The insured shall not, except at his own cost, voluntarily make any payment, assume any obligation or incur any expense other than for such immediate medical and surgical relief to others as shall be imperative at the time of accident.

One common question under the cooperation clause is whether the insured has breached its terms by, for example, admitting liability either orally or in writing to the injured party, or fleeing the scene of an accident. A second question is the same question of prejudice that arises under the notice clause, which brings forth the same division of opinion on whether a minor breach by the insured excuses an insurer from all liability, with the more modern view being that substantial prejudice has to be shown. See M.F.A. Mutual Insurance Co. v. Cheek, 363 N.E.2d 809 (Ill. 1977), allowing coverage when an initial failure to notify was corrected in a "timely" fashion. The insured did still better in Billington v. Interinsurance Exch. of So. Cal., 456 P.2d 982, 987 (Cal. 1969), which held that "an insurer, in order to establish it was prejudiced by the failure of the insured to cooperate in his defense, must establish at the very least that if the cooperation clause had not been breached there was a substantial likelihood the trier of fact would have found in the insured's favor." The court then held that the failure of the insured to appear at a deposition to rebut charges that he was guilty of willful misconduct, raised by the plaintiff to overcome the contributory negligence and assumption of risk defenses, did not constitute the required prejudice. For a detailed discussion of all these clauses see R. Keeton and A. Widiss, Insurance Law §4.9.

C. AMBIGUITIES IN THE POSITION OF THE LIABILITY INSURER

The ordinary liability policy provides not only that the company will pay on behalf of the insured all sums the insured becomes legally obligated to pay for personal injury or property damage, but, perhaps equally important, it also provides: "the company shall defend any suit alleging such bodily injury or property damage — even if any of the allegations of the suit are groundless, false or fraudulent; but the company may make such investigation and settlement of any claim or suit as it deems expedient."

As a result, there are two key consequences: (1) The insurer obligates itself to handle the claim and to defend against it even when the risk of ultimate liability is low; (2) The insurer obtains control of both litigation and settlement. These two consequences underscore a principal practical benefit in having liability insurance — an experienced party is in charge of litigation, and bonds its performance by agreeing to pay damages in the event of an adverse consequence. Usually, however, the insurer will not take on the risk of infinite liability, but will impose limits on the amount of risk that it is willing to assume, such that the presence of insurance breaks the united front that a defendant might otherwise be able to present to a plaintiff. The major difficulties that ensue concern the scope of the duty to defend and the obligation to settle cases in good faith.

1.   The Duty to Defend

The insurance company frequently finds itself in an awkward position with respect to its desire to challenge its duty to defend the insured while simultaneously controlling litigation on behalf of the insured in the underlying tort suit. The problem can arise, for example, when the language of the complaint in the underlying action leaves it uncertain whether the case falls within one of the stated exclusions to the policy. Thus, in Maryland Casualty Co. v. Peppers, 355 N.E.2d 24, 28-29 (Ill. 1976), the insured, Peppers, shot Mims, a suspected burglar, and demanded protection under two policies, one issued by the St. Paul's Fire & Marine Insurance Company, and the other by Maryland Casualty. Each policy contained language that excluded from coverage harms that were intentionally inflicted by the insured. Two issues in the case are of concern here. The first was whether St. Paul owed a duty to defend the insured given that it was unclear whether the insured's case fell into the exception for intentional assaults. The second was whether St. Paul was estopped from denying coverage under this policy because it had simultaneously defended the insured and filed a suit for a declaratory judgment that it was not obligated to defend. Ryan, J., addressed these questions as follows:

> In determining whether the insurer owes a duty to the insured to defend an action brought against him, it is the general rule that the allegations of the complaint determine the duty. If the complaint alleges facts within the coverage of the policy or potentially within the coverage of the policy the duty to defend has been established. . . .
>
> This duty to defend extends to cases where the complaint alleges several causes of action or theories of recovery against an insured, one of which is within the coverage of a policy while the others may not be. . . . The trial court properly held that St. Paul was obligated to defend Peppers.
>
> The appellate court held that St. Paul, by undertaking the defense of Peppers in the Mims case, is estopped to deny coverage under the policy. . . .
>
> It is generally held that an insurer may be estopped from asserting a defense of noncoverage when the insurer undertakes the defense of an action against the insured. However, it is also the general rule that the undertaking must result in some prejudice to the insured. . . .

Whether an insured is prejudiced by an insurer's conduct in entering an appearance and assuming the defense of an action is a question of fact. Prejudice will not be conclusively presumed from the mere entry of appearance and assumption of the defense. . . . If, however, by the insurer's assumption of the defense the insured has been induced to surrender his right to control his own defense, he has suffered a prejudice which will support a finding that the insurer is estopped to deny policy coverage.

There is nothing in the record to establish that Peppers was not at all times represented by his own attorney, Massa, or that in reliance on the attorneys hired by St. Paul he was induced to surrender the right to conduct his own defense. The finding of the trial court that St. Paul was not estopped to deny coverage is not contrary to the manifest weight of the evidence.

In *Peppers,* what should be done if the tort plaintiff drops the action for unintentional harm (i.e., ordinary negligence), and proceeds solely on the count for intentional wrong? When the limits of the policy have been exhausted, does the insurer continue to owe a duty to defend in the absence of express language (contained only in more recent policies) that the duty to defend ceases when the limits of the policy are exhausted?

The scope of the defense obligation extends to all claims, not only valid or strong ones. In reversing the judgment below denying the duty to defend, Mikva, J., gave this explanation of the coverage provision in Continental Casualty Co. v. Cole, 809 F.2d 891, 898 (D.C. Cir. 1987).

The main purpose of the defense clause and the "groundless, false, and fraudulent allegations" language is to shift to the insurer the burden of defending against any and all attempts to assess liability against the insured which are based on covered activities. To follow the district court's reasoning would, in those instances in which an ultimate award of damages appears unlikely, place the insured in the difficult position of having to choose between two unappealing alternatives: pay for its own defense to protect against the possibility, no matter how remote, that damages might be awarded; or sit idle and do nothing in uneasy reliance on the insurer's promises that damages cannot possibly be awarded. The insured, who has paid for coverage, should not be required to make this choice.

When the insurer has wrongly refused to defend, and the insured has settled the case on its own account, it is then necessary to determine what damages the insured can recover from its own insurer. In American Motorists Ins. Co. v. Trane Co., 718 F.2d 842, 845 (7th Cir. 1983), the court affirmed a district court's order providing for "indemnification for covered claims and costs associated with defending" them. The court refused to require the insurance carrier to pay the full extent of the insured's damages where these exceeded the face value of the policy, noting that insurers "may refuse to defend suits and seek declaratory judgments without risking liability for the underlying suit's entire judgment — a risk so high as to coerce insurers to defend actions that they are not obligated to defend." With *Trane* contrast Johansen v. California State Auto. Assn. Inter-Ins. Bureau, 538 P.2d 744, 746 (Cal. 1975), where Tobriner, J., wrote: "California authorities establish that an insurer who fails to accept a reasonable settlement offer within policy limits because it believes that the policy does not provide coverage assumes the risk that it will be held liable for all damages resulting from such refusal, including damages in excess of applicable policy limits."

2.   The Obligation to Act in Good Faith

Crisci v. Security Insurance Co.
426 P.2d 173 (Cal. 1967)

PETERS, J. In an action against The Security Insurance Company of New Haven, Connecticut, the trial court awarded Rosina Crisci $91,000 (plus interest) because she suffered a judgment in a personal injury action after Security, her insurer, refused to settle the claim. Mrs. Crisci was also awarded $25,000 for mental suffering. Security has appealed.

June DiMare and her husband were tenants in an apartment building owned by Rosina Crisci. Mrs. DiMare was descending the apartment's outside wooden staircase when a tread gave way. She fell through the resulting opening up to her waist and was left hanging 15 feet above the ground. Mrs. DiMare suffered physical injuries and developed a very severe psychosis. In a suit brought against Mrs. Crisci the DiMares alleged that the step broke because Mrs. Crisci was negligent in inspecting and maintaining the stairs. They contended that Mrs. DiMare's mental condition was caused by the accident, and they asked for $400,000 as compensation for physical and mental injuries and medical expenses.

Mrs. Crisci had $10,000 of insurance coverage under a general liability policy issued by Security. The policy obligated Security to defend the suit against Mrs. Crisci and authorized the company to make any settlement it deemed expedient.[1] Security hired an experienced lawyer, Mr. Healy, to handle the case. Both he and defendant's claims manager believed that unless evidence was discovered showing that Mrs. DiMare had a prior mental illness, a jury would probably find that the accident precipitated Mrs. DiMare's psychosis. And both men believed that if

---

1. Mrs. Crisci's own attorney, Mr. Pardini, was consulted by the counsel for the insurance company, but Mr. Pardini did not direct or control either settlement negotiations or the defense of Mrs. DiMare's suit.

the jury felt that the fall triggered the psychosis, a verdict of not less than $100,000 would be returned.

An extensive search turned up no evidence that Mrs. DiMare had any prior mental abnormality. As a teenager Mrs. DiMare had been in a Washington mental hospital, but only to have an abortion. Both Mrs. DiMare and Mrs. Crisci found psychiatrists who would testify that the accident caused Mrs. DiMare's illness, and the insurance company knew of this testimony. Among those who felt the psychosis was not related to the accident were the doctors at the state mental hospital where Mrs. DiMare had been committed following the accident. All the psychiatrists agreed, however, that a psychosis could be triggered by a sudden fear of falling to one's death.

The exact chronology of settlement offers is not established by the record. However, by the time the DiMares' attorney reduced his settlement demands to $10,000, Security had doctors prepared to support its position and was only willing to pay $3,000 for Mrs. DiMare's physical injuries. Security was unwilling to pay one cent for the possibility of a plaintiff's verdict on the mental illness issue. This conclusion was based on the assumption that the jury would believe all of the defendant's psychiatric evidence and none of the plaintiff's. Security also rejected a $9,000 settlement demand at a time when Mrs. Crisci offered to pay $2,500 of the settlement.

A jury awarded Mrs. DiMare $100,000 and her husband $1,000. After an appeal the insurance company paid $10,000 of this amount, the amount of its policy. The DiMares then sought to collect the balance from Mrs. Crisci. A settlement was arranged by which the DiMares received $22,000, a 40 percent interest in Mrs. Crisci's claim to a particular piece of property, and an assignment of Mrs. Crisci's cause of action against Security. Mrs. Crisci, an immigrant widow of 70, became indigent. She worked as a babysitter, and her grandchildren paid her rent. The change in her financial condition was accompanied by a decline in physical health, hysteria, and suicide attempts. Mrs. Crisci then brought this action.

The liability of an insurer in excess of its policy limits for failure to accept a settlement offer within those limits was considered by this court in Comunale v. Traders & General Ins. Co., 328 P.2d 198. It was there reasoned that in every contract, including policies of insurance, there is an implied covenant of good faith and fair dealing that neither party will do anything which will injure the right of the other to receive the benefits of the agreement; that it is common knowledge that one of the usual methods by which an insured receives protection under a liability insurance policy is by settlement of claims without litigation; that the implied obligation of good faith and fair dealing requires the insurer to settle in an appropriate case although the express terms of the policy do not impose the duty; that in determining whether to settle the insurer must give the interests of the insured at least as much consideration as it gives to its own interests; and that when "there is great risk of a recovery beyond the policy limits so that the most reasonable manner of disposing of the claim is a settlement which can be made within those limits, a consideration in good faith of the insured's interest requires the insurer to settle the claim."

In determining whether an insurer has given consideration to the interests of the insured, the test is whether a prudent insurer without policy limits would have accepted the settlement offer. . . .

Several cases, in considering the liability of the insurer, contain language to the effect that bad faith is the equivalent of dishonesty, fraud, and concealment. Obviously a showing that the insurer has been guilty of actual dishonesty, fraud, or concealment is relevant to the determination whether it has given consideration to the insured's interest in considering a settlement offer within the policy limits. The language used in the cases, however, should not be understood as meaning that in the absence of evidence establishing actual dishonesty, fraud, or concealment no recovery may be had for a judgment in excess of the policy limits. Comunale v. Traders & General Ins. Co. makes it clear that liability based on an implied covenant exists whenever the insurer refuses to settle in an appropriate case and that liability may exist when the insurer unwarrantedly refuses an offered settlement where the most reasonable manner of disposing of the claim is by accepting the settlement. Liability is imposed not for a bad faith breach of the contract but for failure to meet the duty to accept reasonable settlements, a duty included within the implied covenant of good faith and fair dealing. Moreover, examination of the balance of [our prior] opinions makes it abundantly clear that recovery may be based on unwarranted rejection of a reasonable settlement offer and that the absence of evidence, circumstantial or direct, showing actual dishonesty, fraud, or concealment is not fatal to the cause of action.

Amicus curiae argues that, whenever an insurer receives an offer to settle within the policy limits and rejects it, the insurer should be liable in every case for the amount of any final judgment whether or not within the policy limits. As we have seen, the duty of the insurer to consider the insured's interest in settlement offers within the policy limits arises from an implied covenant in the contract, and ordinarily contract duties are strictly enforced and not subject to a standard of reasonableness. Obviously, it will always be in the insured's interest to settle within the policy limits when there is any danger, however slight, of a judgment in excess of those limits. Accordingly the rejection of a settlement within the limits where there is any danger of a judgment in excess of the limits can be justified, if at all, only on the basis of interests of the insurer, and, in light of the common knowledge that settlement is one of the usual methods by which an insured receives protection under a liability policy, it may not be unreasonable for an insured who purchases a policy with limits to believe that a sum of money equal to the limits is available and will be used so as to avoid liability on his part with regard to any covered accident. In view of such expectation an insurer should not be permitted to further its own interests by rejecting opportunities to settle within the policy limits unless it is also willing to absorb losses which may result from its failure to settle.

The proposed rule is a simple one to apply and avoids the burdens of a determination whether a settlement offer within the policy limits was reasonable. The proposed rule would also eliminate the danger that an insurer, faced with a settlement offer at or near the policy limits, will reject it and gamble with the insured's money to further its own interests. Moreover, it is not entirely clear that the proposed rule would place a burden on insurers substantially greater than that which is present under existing law. The size of the judgment recovered in the personal injury action when it exceeds the policy limits, although not conclusive, furnishes an inference that the value of the claim is the equivalent of the amount of the judgment and that acceptance of an offer within those limits was the most reasonable method of dealing with the claim.

Finally, and most important, there is more than a small amount of elementary justice in a rule that would require that, in this situation where the insurer's and insured's interests necessarily conflict, the insurer, which may reap the benefits of its determination not to settle, should also suffer the detriments of its decision. On the basis of these and other considerations, a number of commentators have urged that the insurer should be liable for any resulting judgment where it refuses to settle within the policy limits. . . .

We need not, however, here determine whether there might be some countervailing considerations precluding adoption of the proposed rule because, under Comunale v. Traders & General Ins. Co., and the cases following it, the evidence is clearly sufficient to support the determination that Security breached its duty to consider the interests of Mrs. Crisci in proposed settlements [owing to the inherent uncertainty in all psychiatric evidence].

The trial court found that defendant "knew that there was a considerable risk of substantial recovery beyond said policy limits" and that "the defendant did not give as much consideration to the financial interests of its said insured as it gave to its own interests." That is all that was required. The award of $91,000 must therefore be affirmed.

[The court then upheld a $25,000 verdict to Mrs. Crisci for mental suffering.]

Recovery of damages for mental suffering in the instant case does not mean that in every case of breach of contract the injured party may

recover such damages. Here the breach also constitutes a tort. Moreover, plaintiff did not seek by the contract involved here to obtain a
commercial advantage but to protect herself against the risks of accidental losses, including the mental distress which might follow from
the losses. Among the considerations in purchasing liability insurance,
as insurers are well aware, is the peace of mind and security it will provide in the event of an accidental loss, and recovery of damages for
mental suffering has been permitted for breach of contracts which directly concern the comfort, happiness or personal esteem of one of the
parties. . . .

It is not claimed that plaintiff's mental distress was not caused by
defendant's refusal to settle or that the damages awarded were excessive in the light of plaintiff's substantial suffering.

The judgment is affirmed.

NOTES

1. Conflicts of interest between insurer and insured. The opinion of the
California Court of Appeals in Merritt v. Reserve Insurance Co., 110
Cal. Rptr. 511, 519-520 (Cal. App. 1973), contains an excellent discussion of the possible conflicts of interest that can arise between insurer
and insured. The court there considered a case in which defendant had
a policy that provided only the minimum allowable coverage of $15,000
per injury and the plaintiff filed a tort action for $50,000 damage. More
generally, the basic problem for the two parties is that the insurance
company bears all the costs of litigation under the standard policy, even
though the insured may have to shoulder the bulk of the financial loss
if liability is established. If the insurance company looks only to its own
financial interest in the matter, then it will compare its costs of defense
with the $15,000 policy maximum, regardless of the size of the verdict.
Thus, if litigation costs $5,000, with a 50 percent chance of liability,
then the insurance company will refuse to settle for $15,000. That
$15,000 settlement is greater than its expected losses from fighting the
suit, which would equal $12,500 (the $5,000 in litigation expenses plus
$7,500 in damages, equal to the 50 percent chance of losing $15,000).

The prudential decision for the insurance company may, however,
have consequences ruinous for the insured. Settling the case for the
$15,000 policy limit completely insulates the insured from any possibil-
ity of liability. Litigating it at the insurer's expense exposes the insured
to a 50 percent chance of $35,000 in liability, an expected loss of
$17,500 for a risk-neutral insured.

Given this conflict, whose interest should prevail, the insurer's or the
insured's? One way to look at this question is to ask how the insurance
company would behave if its policy limits were in excess of the antici-

pated liability so that it bore all the loss no matter what course of action was followed. On the facts in *Merritt,* the company would choose to settle the case because the $15,000 payment is less than the anticipated liability of $30,000 ($5,000 in legal fees plus the 50 percent chance of having to pay $50,000). If so, then it has a duty to settle the case, The logic of the good faith action is to induce the insurer to act as though it bore the entire costs of all defense and indemnity costs.

The problem is more easily stated than solved, because eliminating the conflict of interest is both tricky and expensive so long as both parties want policies that contain explicit limitations on the underlying indemnity obligation. The court in *Merritt* made the following grim assessment of the possible avenues of escape:

> When an offer is made to settle a claim in excess of policy limits for an amount within policy limits, a genuine and immediate conflict of interest arises between carrier and assured. The normal legal remedy for conflicts in interest is separate representation for the conflicting interests. This remedy, however, possesses only a limited usefulness in the present situation, for while the assured can be advised, as he usually is, that he may employ separate counsel to look after his interests, separate representation usually amounts to nothing more than independent legal advice to the assured, since control of the litigation remains in the hands of the carrier. Control of the defense of the lawsuit cannot be split, and independent legal advice to the assured cannot force the carrier to accept a settlement offer it does not wish to accept. In this instance the normal legal remedy of separate representation is an inadequate solution to the conflict in interest.
>
> Nor can the liability of the assured be divided into separate segments, about which the carrier and the assured may make their separate evaluations and go their separate ways. Patently, the carrier cannot settle its share of the assured's liability and turn the assured adrift, exposed to a suit for excess liability financed by the carrier's settlement. Nor can the assured settle the claim for excess liability and abandon the carrier to defend a suit financed by the assured's settlement. For better or worse, like a married couple, assured and carrier must make the best of each other.
>
> Since the remedy of separate representation is inadequate, and since the remedy of a separate peace, or settlement, amounts to a betrayal of the obligations the parties have assumed under the contract, the courts have been forced to improvise in order to find a workable solution to the problem of conflict of interest. The current status of these efforts confirms the carrier in its control over the litigation, but requires the carrier to consider in good faith the interests of the assured equally with its own and evaluate settlement offers within policy limits as though it alone carried the entire risk of loss.

In dealing with bad faith actions, one approach is to include the insurer's cost of defense into the calculations, as those would be costs borne by the single owner. That approach was rejected, however, in Samson v. Transamerica Ins. Co., 636 P.2d 32, 46 (Cal. 1981), which held that "[t]he only permissible consideration in evaluating the reasonableness of the settlement offer becomes whether, in light of the victim's injuries and the probable liability of the insured, the ultimate judgment is likely to exceed the . . . offer." Does this amount to a rule that requires the insurer to attach greater interest to the condition of the insured than it does to itself?

See generally on these issues Syverud, The Duty to Settle, 76 Va. L. Rev. 1113 (1990); R. Keeton and A. Widiss, Insurance Law §7.8 (1988).

2. Basis of liability for bad faith claims. Crisci has generated enormous disputes over the proper standard of liability to apply to the insurance company's conduct in bad faith litigation. Although the term "bad faith" may suggest some overt dishonesty or malice on the part of the insured, many cases have refused to confine the liability so narrowly, perhaps because the control of dishonesty alone does not fully address the conflict of interest problem that plagues this area. *Crisci* itself points to a more expansive liability for insurers when it holds that "the test is whether a prudent insurer without policy limits would have accepted the settlement offer." Courts in other states have generally had a mixed reaction to this position. In some instances, they have followed *Crisci* in rejecting the position that "proof of malice or ill will is necessary to find a breach of the implied obligation of good faith and fair dealing." DeVries v. St. Paul Fire and Marine Insurance, 716 F.2d 939 (1st Cir. 1983) (New Hampshire law), which affirmed the soundness of the trial judge's instructions allowing the jury to find for the plaintiff if he proved by a preponderance of the evidence that the acts of the insurer "in investigating and adjusting the claim here amounted to a calculated and not inadvertent unreasonable denial of payment" in violation of "the contractual obligation of good faith and fair dealing." Is this a negligence standard? With *deVries* contrast Awrey v. Progressive Cas. Ins. Co., 728 F.2d 352, 357 (6th Cir. 1984) (Michigan law), which held that "it is not enough to show that the insurer 'ignored completely' and 'did not consider' the insured's position in order to prove bad faith on the part of the insurer. [Michigan law] requires a showing that the insured engaged in the 'conscious doing of wrong because of dishonest purpose or moral obliquity' for a finding of bad faith."

Should the terms of the insurance contract be allowed to specify the conditions for a bad faith action? Limit the damages? Bar the action altogether? Note in this context that the conflict of interest identified in *Crisci* and *Merritt* is a cost of doing business, but only one of many costs. The hard question is to decide whether the administrative inconveniences of a bad faith action are greater or lesser than those generated by the conflict itself.

3. Proper plaintiffs in bad faith actions. The plaintiff in *Crisci* was the defendant in the tort action who sued the insurance company for breach of its contractual obligations. One vital question in bad faith litigation is whether the *injured party* has the right to bring a direct action against the defendant's insurer for its unreasonable refusal to settle a claim. Actions of this sort were allowed in California Royal Globe Ins. Co. v. Superior Court, 592 P.2d 319 (Cal. 1979), as a private right of action under the Unfair Practices Act, contained in the state's insurance code. *Royal Globe* was followed in 2 states but, as of 1988, was apparently rejected in 17 others on the ground that the Unfair Practices Act created administrative remedies but not tort actions. In Moradi-Shalal v. Fireman's Fund Ins. Co., 758 P.2d 58 (Cal. 1988), the California Supreme Court overruled *Royal Globe* and joined the majority. In its exhaustive opinion, the court first noted that *Royal Globe* created an irresistible temptation for injured parties to maintain two actions for their injuries, one in tort and the other against the insurer directly under the Unfair Practices statute. The court then adopted the position of those who argued that "*Royal Globe,* and its allowance of a direct action against the insurer, may result in escalating insurance costs to the general public resulting from insurers' increased expenditures to fund coerced settlements, excessive jury awards and increased attorney fees."

4. The efficiency of bad faith actions. There is no evidence today that any insurer would agree to be bound by the bad faith rules as they have developed over the years since *Crisci.* Yet if the judicial right of action was to the benefit of the insured, the standard puzzle is why an insurance company would not agree to it voluntarily in exchange for a higher premium. One look at the subject concludes that the older view of the subject, which denied actions for bad faith, actually served the interests of the insured from an ex ante perspective, because these limits on coverage improved the bargaining position that the insurance company and the insured had against the plaintiff in the underlying lawsuit, by allowing the insurer to bargain hard without fear of retaliation if its tough strategy failed. Yet this gain to the insurer and the insured need not translate into a social benefit because it comes at the expense of the interest of the plaintiff whose search for the optimal level of tort recovery is frustrated by this device. Hence the bad faith action has been defended, less as a mode of protection of the insured, and more to protect the injured party. See, for the elaboration of this argument, Meurer, The Gains from Faith in an Unfaithful Agent: Settlement Conflicts between Defendants and Liability Insurers, 8 J. Law, Econ. & Org. 502 (1992).

The situation is still more complex, for there is some evidence that plaintiffs' lawyers use bad faith actions as a lever to extort settlements from the defendant in excess of the fair value of the settlement claim. "Practice manuals on settlement advise plaintiffs' lawyers to encourage settlement by fixing the claim above policy limits, and by sending a detailed demand letter to the insurer together with a request for a response in a brief period." Syverud, The Duty To Settle, 76 Va. L. Rev. 1113, 1169 n.146 (1990). As an example of a "set-up" letter, Syverud refers to Baton v. Transamerica Insurance Co., 584 F.2d 907 (9th Cir 1978), where the tort plaintiff offered to settle a case for the lower of $110,000 or the policy limits, but only if the offer were accepted within ten days.

5. *Excess insurance.* The question of whether an insurer is under a duty to settle a case within its policy limits has arisen with greater frequency in recent years in the context of excess insurance. Excess insurance usually covers catastrophic losses that are beyond the limits of the primary policy. Typically, the excess carrier insists that its insured have some approved primary coverage (why?), but there is ordinarily no direct contractual relationship between the primary and the excess carrier. When the primary carrier does not settle a case within policy limits, does it owe the same duties to the excess carrier as it would owe to the primary insured? Commercial Union Assur. v. Safeway Stores, 610 P.2d 1038, 1043 (Cal. 1980), held that an insured owed no obligation to settle a case in good faith for the benefit of an excess carrier. *Commercial Union* was confined to actions for breach of the *implied* covenant of good faith. "If an excess carrier wishes to insulate itself from liability for an insured's failure to accept what it deems to be a reasonable settlement offer, it may do so by appropriate language in the policy." Note also that some of the problems in this area can be avoided by having any two of the parties *pay* the third in order to assume all potential defense and indemnity obligations. At this point the remaining active party faces all the costs of indemnity and defense alone, and thus escapes the conflict of interest problem. The money received from the settling parties should be sufficient, moreover, to fund the additional liabilities. What obstacles lie in the path of these settlements? And which party should soldier on alone?

Chapter Thirteen
The No-Fault Systems

A. INTRODUCTION

This chapter examines the various "no-fault" systems to the tort system, some of which are in place and others which have merely been proposed.

The place to start is with workers' compensation, which has received relatively little attention in academic circles, notwithstanding its universal adoption and great practical importance. In recent years the study of workers' compensation has gained new urgency, for two reasons. First, the system itself has been subject to internal strains from expanded coverage, rising benefit levels, and, in some cases, widespread abuse. Workers' compensation is big business. In 1960, for example, employers spent $2 billion on the program, but these expenditures had risen to $35 billion in 1986. See 1 American Law Institute, Reporters' Study, Enterprise Responsibility for Personal Injury 106-107 (1991). Later estimates have that number increasing to $56 billion in 1990 and $62 billion in 1992, which is nearly one-half the total dollars that run through the tort system. See Schwartz, Waste, Fraud, and Abuse in Workers' Compensation: The Recent California Experience, 52 Md. L. Rev. 983, 984 (1993). Second, the system has served as the model for a number of contemporary no-fault systems of liability, including those for injuries arising out of the use of automobiles, the distribution of consumer products, or the provision of medical services. Each of these areas presents special and unique problems of its own, yet the workers' compensation laws, with their own history of no-fault liability, present us with the best precedent with which to compare possible no-fault schemes for other sorts of accidents.

A brief list of their common points is enough to show their close kinship. Both workers' compensation and modern no-fault systems provide compensation for individual injuries that would remain uncompensated as a matter of course at the common law; both make use of broad coverage formulas (arising out of employment or the use of an automobile, consumer product, or medical treatment, and so on); both contemplate sharp limitations on damages, with little or no recovery for pain and suffering; and both require coordination with the common-law tort rules retained after the adoption of the plan. The study of workers' compensation is today invaluable for what it tells us about how these problems might be approached.

B.   WORKERS' COMPENSATION

1.   Historical origins

The early history of workers' compensation laws is long and complex, and therefore is only briefly summarized here. Before 1837 there were no recorded cases in which an employee sought damages from an employer for a work-related injury. Then, with the English case of Priestly v. Fowler, 150 Eng. Rep. 1030 (Ex. 1837), and the leading American case of Farwell v. Boston & W.R.R., 45 Mass. (4 Met.) 49 (1842), workers began to sue employers on negligence theories for workplace accidents, only to be met with the famous trinity of common-law defenses: common employment, assumption of risk, and contributory negligence. See supra Chapter 4 at page 355. The resulting common-law development of industrial accident law was complex, and growing dissatisfaction with that complexity provoked two very different types of responses. The first was a private arrangement whereby the individual firms and the workers expressly contracted out of the common-law rules for industrial accidents, and frequently substituted in their place, not a total employer immunity from all responsibility, but a complex voluntary compensation system that in its particulars resembled the modern system of workers' compensation. See, e.g., Griffiths v. Earl of Dudley, 9 Q.B. 357 (1882); Clements v. London & N.E. Ry., [1894] 2 Q.B. 482. In addition, by the end of the nineteenth century explicit legislative intervention had modified the common-law rules of tort liability for industrial accidents. The first of these statutes — the Employer's Liability Act, 1880, 43 & 44 Vict. ch. 42 — eliminated the defense of common employment and also provided for the general liability of the employer to his workers on grounds of negligence; by judicial construction the Act was held to allow employers and employees to contract out of its provisions. See *Griffiths* and *Clements,* supra.

The English statute became the model for many state statutes on employment relations, see, e.g., Massachusetts Employer's Liability Act, 1887 Mass. Acts 566; California Employer's Liability Act, 1907 Cal. Stat. 119. At the federal level the common-law rules were also displaced by the Federal Employer's Liability Act, 35 Stat. 65 (1908), which applied to the employees of interstate common carriers, and which withstood constitutional challenge in the Second Employer's Liability Cases, 223 U.S. 1 (1912) after some earlier constitutional doubts. The FELA is still in effect today, as amended, 45 U.S.C. §§51-60 (1994), and has been the source of extensive litigation. See, e.g., Wilkerson v. McCarthy, supra at page 284.

For very different views on the early history see L. Friedman, A History of American Law ch. 14 (1973); Epstein, The Historical Origins and Economic Structure of the Workers' Compensation Act, 16 Ga. L. Rev. 775 (1982); Fischback, Liability Rules and Accident Prevention in the Workplace: Empirical Evidence from the Early Twentieth Century, 16 J. Legal Stud. 305 (1987); Posner, A Theory of Negligence, 1 J. Legal Stud. 29, 67-72 (1972); Schwartz, Tort Law and the Economy in Nineteenth-Century America: A Reinterpretation, 90 Yale L.J. 1717, 1768-1771 (1981); Schwartz, The Character of Early American Tort Law, 36 U.C.L.A. L. Rev. 641 (1989).

The passage of the various employer's liability acts was only one stage in the transformation of the law of industrial accidents. In England the 1880 statute was replaced by the first modern workers' compensation act in 1897, the Workmen's Compensation Act, 1897, 60 & 61 Vict. Ch. 37, which served as a blueprint for the American statutes. The first of the American workers' compensation statutes was passed by New York in 1910, 1910 N.Y. Laws 625, to implement the recommendations of the Wainwright Commission, which summarized its conclusions as follows:

> *First,* that the present system in New York rests on a basis that is economically unwise and unfair, and that in operation it is wasteful, uncertain and productive of antagonism between workmen and employers.
>
> *Second,* that it is satisfactory to none and tolerable only to those employers and workmen who practically disregard their legal rights and obligations, and fairly share the burden of accidents in industries.
>
> *Third,* that the evils of the system are most marked in hazardous employments, where the trade risk is high and serious accidents frequent.
>
> *Fourth,* that, as a matter of fact, workmen in the dangerous trades do not, and practically cannot, provide for themselves adequate accident insurance, and therefore, the burden of serious accidents falls on the workmen least able to bear it, and brings many of them and their families to want.

The legislation was immediately challenged in the courts on constitutional grounds and overturned by the New York Court of Appeals in the famous case of Ives v. South Buffalo Ry. Co., 94 N.E. 431, 436, 439-440, 449 (N.Y. 1911). In *Ives* the court gave an outline of the workers' compensation law that in broad outline is still accurate today.

> The statute, judged by our common-law standards, is plainly revolutionary. Its central and controlling feature is that every employer who is engaged in any of the classified industries shall be liable for any injury to a workman arising out of and in the course of the employment by "a necessary risk or danger of the employment or one inherent in the nature thereof, . . . provided that the employer shall not be liable in respect of any injury to the workman which is caused in whole or in part by the serious and willful misconduct of the workman." This rule of liability, stated in another form, is that the employer is responsible to the employee for every accident in the course of the employment, whether the employer is at fault or not, and whether the employee is at fault or not, except when the fault of the employee is so grave as to constitute serious and willful misconduct on his part. The radical character of this legislation is at once revealed by contrasting it with the rule of the common law, under which the employer is liable for injuries to his employee only when the employer is guilty of some act or acts of negligence which caused the occurrence out of which the injuries arise, and then only when the employee is shown to be free from any negligence which contributes to the occurrence.

The court then addressed the objections to the statute and concluded that it was constitutionally permissible to abolish the employer's "trinity" of common-law defenses in personal injury actions: the fellow servant doctrine (whereby the injured party could not recover from the employer for harm caused by the negligence of a fellow servant), assumption of risk, and contributory negligence. Yet in spite of the impressive economic and sociological brief made on behalf of the statute, the court struck it down as an impermissible exercise of the police power because it bore no relationship to the health, safety, or morals of employees. The court also found that the statutory imposition of "liability without fault" was an unconstitutional deprivation of property without due process of law:

> The right of property rests not upon philosophical or scientific speculations nor upon the commendable impulses of benevolence or charity, nor yet upon the dictates of natural justice. The right has its foundation in the fundamental law. That can be changed by the people, but not by legislatures. In a government like ours theories of public good or necessity are often so plausible or sound as to command popular approval, but courts are not permitted to forget that the law is the only chart by which the ship of state is to be guided. Law as used in this sense means the basic law and not the very act of legislation which deprives the citizen of his rights, privileges or property. Any other view would lead to the absurdity

that the Constitutions protect only those rights which the legislatures do not take away. If such economic and sociologic arguments as are here advanced in support of this statute can be allowed to subvert the fundamental idea of property, then there is no private right entirely safe, because there is no limitation upon the absolute discretion of legislatures, and the guarantees of the Constitution are a mere waste of words. . . . If the argument in support of this statute is sound we do not see why it cannot logically be carried much further. Poverty and misfortune from every cause are detrimental to the state. It would probably conduce to the welfare of all concerned if there could be a more equal distribution of wealth. Many persons have much more property than they can use to advantage and many more find it impossible to get the means for a comfortable existence. If the legislature can say to an employer, "you must compensate your employee for an injury not caused by you or by your fault," why can it not go further and say to the man of wealth, "you have more property than you need and your neighbor is so poor that he can barely subsist; in the interest of natural justice you must divide with your neighbor so that he and his dependents shall not become a charge upon the State?" The argument that the risk to an employee should be borne by the employer because it is inherent in the employment, may be economically sound, but it is at war with the legal principle that no employer can be compelled to assume a risk which is inseparable from the work of the employee, and which may exist in spite of a degree of care by the employer far greater than may be exacted by the most drastic law. If it is competent to impose upon an employer, who has omitted no legal duty and has committed no wrong, a liability based solely upon a legislative fiat that his business is inherently dangerous, it is equally competent to visit upon him a special tax for the support of hospitals and other charitable institutions, upon the theory that they are devoted largely to the alleviation of ills primarily due to his business. In its final and simple analysis that is taking the property of A and giving it to B, and that cannot be done under our Constitutions.

Cullen, C.J., echoed similar themes in his concurrence:

I know of no principle on which one can be compelled to indemnify another for loss unless it is based upon contractual obligation or fault. It might as well be argued in support of a law requiring a man to pay his neighbor's debts, that the common law requires each man to pay his own debts, and the statute in question was a mere modification of the common law so as to require each to pay his neighbor's debts.

This early setback was short-lived. Pursuant to a suggestion made by the court in *Ives*, the state passed a constitutional amendment that authorized passage of the workers' compensation statute. In New York Central R.R. v. White, 243 U.S. 188, 202-204, 208 (1916), the United States Supreme Court upheld the statute's constitutionality under federal law in a unanimous decision. In addition to the points raised in the *Ives* case, it was also argued that the employee's rights were unconstitutionally interfered with for injuries arising from the employer's fault; the limited compensation under the act deprived the employee of compensation commensurate with damages actually sustained. Justice Pitney responded as follows:

> Of course, we cannot ignore the question whether the new arrangement is arbitrary and unreasonable, from the standpoint of natural justice. Respecting this, it is important to be observed that the act applies only to disabling or fatal personal injuries received in the course of hazardous employment in gainful occupation. Reduced to its elements, the situation to be dealt with is this: Employer and employee, by mutual consent, engage in a common operation intended to be advantageous to both; the employee is to contribute his personal services, and for these is to receive wages, and ordinarily nothing more; the employer is to furnish plant, facilities, organization, capital, credit, is to control and manage the operation, paying the wages and other expenses, disposing of the product at such prices as he can obtain, taking all the profits, if any there be, and of necessity bearing the entire losses. In the nature of things, there is more or less of a probability that the employee may lose his life through some accidental injury arising out of the employment, leaving his widow or children deprived of their natural support or that he may sustain an injury not mortal but resulting in his total or partial disablement, temporary or permanent, with corresponding impairment of earning capacity. The physical suffering must be borne by the employee alone; the laws of nature prevent this from being evaded or shifted to another, and the statute makes no attempt to afford an equivalent in compensation. But, besides, there is the loss of earning power a loss of that which stands to the employee as his capital in trade. This is a loss arising out of the business, and, however it may be charged up, is an expense of the operation, as truly as the cost of repairing broken machinery or any other expense that ordinarily is paid by the employer. Who is to bear the charge? It is plain that, on grounds of natural justice, it is not unreasonable for the State, while relieving the employer from responsibility for damages measured by common-law standards and payable in cases where he or those for whose conduct he is answerable are found to be at fault, to require him to contribute a reasonable amount, and according to a reasonable and definite scale, by way of compensation for the loss of earning power incurred in the common enterprise, irrespective of the question of negligence, instead of leaving the entire loss to rest where it may chance to fall — that is, upon the injured employee or his dependents. Nor can it be deemed arbitrary and unreasonable, from the standpoint of the employee's interest, to supplant a system under which he assumed the entire risk of injury in ordinary cases, and in others had a right to recover an amount more or less speculative upon proving facts of negligence that often were difficult to prove, and substitute a system under which in all ordinary cases of accidental injury he is sure of a definite and easily ascertained compensation, not being obliged to assume the entire loss in any case but in all cases assuming any loss beyond the prescribed scale.
>
> Much emphasis is laid upon the criticism that the act creates liability without fault. This is sufficiently answered by what has been said, but we may add that liability without fault is not a novelty in the law. The common-law liability of the carrier, of the inn-keeper, of him who employed fire or other dangerous agency or harbored a mischievous animal, was

not dependent altogether upon questions of fault or negligence. Statutes imposing liability without fault have been sustained.

We conclude that the prescribed scheme of compulsory compensation is not repugnant to the provisions of the Fourteenth Amendment. . . .

What is the nature of the "bargain between workers and employers set by the workmen's compensation statutes"? If that bargain is to the benefit of all concerned, why must it be imposed by legislation?

The challenges to workers' compensation were not raised only on the constitutional level; as early as 1913, Professor Jeremiah Smith, Sequel to Workmen's Compensation Acts, 27 Harv. L. Rev. 235, 252, 363 (1913), argued that workers' compensation could not be justified on grounds of "justice and expediency."

It is argued that a part (at least) of the damage, happening to workmen in a business without fault on the part of any one, should be borne by the owner of the business, because the latter initiated the undertaking with a view to his own benefit, and because he will reap the net profit of the business if any should accrue. Indeed the assumption sometimes seems to be that the owner is to get all the benefits of the business, and that hence it would not be unjust to require him to bear all the risks encountered by the workmen and to make full compensation for the entire damage suffered by the workmen. The incorrectness of this assumption has been pointed out by Professor Mechem. The owner, or master, "in no proper sense gets all the benefits of the business." Ordinarily the master is not the only one who receives benefit. "Being employed may be just as great a benefit to the servant as the employment of him may be to his master." The employee generally takes none of the risks of the ultimate pecuniary success of the business. He usually "gets his pay, whether the business be successful or unsuccessful." But waiving these objections, and assuming that the workman may justly claim that the owner should be liable to partly compensate him for harm due to pure accident (nonculpable conduct) in carrying on the business, why has not an outsider (a member of the outside public, not participating in carrying on the undertaking) a claim for compensation, at least equal in justice to that of the workman, when he (the outsider) is damaged by pure accident in carrying on the undertaking?

The employee is himself a part of the undertaking. He has, in one sense, voluntarily participated in it; and is deriving benefit from it. Whereas outsiders have nothing to do with the undertaking. Frequently they "are exposed, without any choice on their side, to more or less risk of injury arising from what is done in the conduct of it by the owner or his servants." An outsider is not a participant in the business and "derives no direct benefit from its carrying on."

Why single out workmen employed in the undertaking and constitute them a specially protected class, while overlooking other persons whose claim stands on at least equal ground? . . .

Of what has heretofore been said this is the sum: The result reached in many cases under the Workmen's Compensation Acts is absolutely incongruous with the results reached under the modern common law as to various persons whose cases are not affected by these statutes. For this difference there is no satisfactory reason. . . .

One further clarification is in order before taking a closer look at the workers' compensation laws. "Liability without fault" has often been misconstrued to represent a belated triumph of the strict liability of the old common law. Thus, in *White*, for example, Justice Pitney grappled with cases of fire or mischievous animals, precisely because of the strict character of the rules that govern these cases. Likewise, Jeremiah Smith could say that "the rule of liability adopted by the statute (liability for damage irrespective of fault) is in direct conflict with the fundamental rule of the modern common law as to the ordinary requisites of a tort. In truth, the statute rejects the test prevailing in the courts in A.D. 1900, and comes much nearer to endorsing the test which used to prevail in A.D. 1400."

Yet the words "liability without fault" in the context of workers' compensation set up a new system for accident compensation that differs as much from common-law strict liability as it does from common-law negligence. In the first place, common-law strict liability, properly conceived, makes allowance for affirmative defenses based on plaintiff's conduct — recall the common-law trinity of defenses — that are expressly abolished or restricted by the workers' compensation statutes. A second difference is equally important. The modern workers' compensation law imposes upon employers liability for injuries, to use the time-honored phrase, "arising out of and in the course of employment." That test for compensation largely eliminates the requirement of a causal nexus between defendant's (particular) acts and the plaintiff's harm that is so central to the traditional common-law theory of strict liability. Thus, with common-law liability for damage caused by fire, the plaintiff must demonstrate that the defendant, or perhaps his guests or servants, set the fire in question. If the defendant is an "insurer" under this scheme, he is an insurer only for the consequences of his own acts, not for the plaintiff's harms attributable to an independent source. The workers' compensation scheme, however, focuses on the injuries to the worker. The emphasis is on where and when the worker suffered the harm by fire — it is of no importance whether or not the employer or a fellow employee set the fire. "Liability without fault" in the context of workers' compensation means not only liability without defendant's negligence, but also liability without the causal connection required under the strict liability rules.

We are now in a position to look more closely at the "arising out of and in the course of employment" language of the workers' compensation statutes. The formula is of vital importance in the administration of workers' compensation, as the thousands of cases that have litigated its outer limits testify. See for an exhaustive treatment of the subject 1, 1A, 1B & 1C A. Larson, Workmen's Compensation Law (1989, 1985, 1987, 1986). After evaluating the coverage formula, we will turn to two other distinctive features of workers' compensation laws: its rules for damages and its coordination with the common-law rules of tort.

2. The Scope of Coverage: "Arising out of and in the Course of Employment"

Matter of Richardson v. Fiedler
493 N.E.2d 228 (N.Y. 1986)

SIMONS, J.

Claimant's decedent, Norman Richardson, was employed by appellant, Fiedler Roofing, Inc. as a waterproofer and roofing mechanic. On January 20, 1981 he fell seven stories from the roof of a building near his jobsite sustaining head injuries which resulted in his death. Immediately before the accident, Richardson and a co-worker were at their work place on the roof waiting for material to arrive with no assigned work to do. While waiting, they moved some distance over the roof and across party walls to another part of the structure and removed some copper downspouts from the building to sell as salvage. While doing so, Richardson slipped on a patch of ice and fell to his death. Respondent Workers' Compensation Board affirmed a finding of the Administrative Law Judge that the accident occurred during the course of decedent's employment and that death was causally related to it and awarded benefits to decedent's five minor children. A divided Appellate Division affirmed the decision of the Board, and the employer and its insurer appeal. . . . They claim that the employer should not be required to pay benefits because decedent was actually engaged in a theft at the time of his accident, and thus his death resulted not from his work duties, but from "decedent's purely personal act of stealing copper downspouts."

To be compensable, an injury must arise out of and in the course of employment (Workers' Compensation Law §10). Activities which are purely personal pursuits are not within the scope of employment and compensation may not be recovered for injuries sustained while engaging in them. The test for determining whether specific activities are within the scope of employment or purely personal is whether the activities are both reasonable and sufficiently work related under the circumstances. It has been held that an employee directed to wait for a specified period of time until materials arrive, is not required to stand by idly but is free to engage in any reasonably related activity while waiting. Momentary deviation from the work routine for a customary and accepted purpose will not bar a claim for benefits. The determination of what is reasonable activity and what is unreasonable, and thus a deviation, is factual and the Board is afforded wide latitude in deciding whether the employee's conduct is disqualifying.

The Board found from the evidence in this case that it was common practice in the industry for roofers to remove copper downspouts and sell them for scrap. It further found that this employer not only knew of the practice but also frequently had been required to pay for or replace downspouts stolen by its employees. Despite this experience, the employer had never disciplined or discharged an employee for these thefts, and after it learned that decedent and his co-worker had been stealing downspouts on the day of the accident, it did not discipline or discharge the coemployee. Accordingly, the Board found that decedent's activities while waiting for necessary work materials to arrive did not constitute a deviation from, or an abandonment of, his employment and that the death arose out of and in the course of decedent's employment. These finding are supported by substantial evidence and thus are conclusive on the court.

Indeed, appellants do not now challenge the Appellate Division's finding that there was substantial evidence to support the award. They contend in this court, for the first time, that a claimant is excluded from compensation benefits, as a matter of law, if he is engaged in an illegal activity at the time of the accident. . . .

Appellants base their argument on policy grounds, urging that an employee who engages in illegal activity during his employment should not receive benefits. Appellants note that Workers' Compensation Law article 9, the disability benefits section, expressly precludes benefits for non-work-related injuries caused by a claimant's illegal acts and they contend that section 10 of the statute, the liability provision for work-related injuries, should be interpreted as containing a similar limitation.* The history and nature of these two clauses prove otherwise.

In 1913, the Bill of Rights of the 1894 New York State Constitution was amended to give the Legislature the power to enact workers' compensation legislation (*see,* 1894 NY Const, art I, §19) and the next year the Legislature did so. The resulting statute provided that employees were to be compensated on a "no-fault" basis, regardless of any negligence on their own part, for all injuries "arising out of and in the course of" their employment. To further the claimant's ability to establish his

---

*In 1981, when decedent died, Workers' Compensation Law §10 provided: "Every employer subject to this chapter shall in accordance with this chapter, except as otherwise provided in section twenty-five-a hereof, secure compensation to his employees and pay or provide compensation for their disability or death from injury arising out of and in the course of the employment without regard to fault as a cause of the injury, except that there shall be no liability for compensation under this chapter when the injury has been solely occasioned by intoxication of the injured employee while on duty; or by wilful intention of the injured employee to bring about the injury or death of himself or another."

right to benefits, the statute creates a presumption that the injuries are compensable. The statute was enacted for humanitarian purposes, framed, in the words of Chief Judge Cardozo, to insure that injured employees might "be saved from becoming one of the derelicts of society, a fragment of human wreckage." To further that purpose, we have held that the statutory obligation to compensate injuries sustained in the course of employment which are causally related to it does not depend on the equities of a particular case, nor may it be avoided because of the workers' fraud or wrongdoing: it is absolute.

The exceptions to this broad statutory liability are found in section 10, derived from the 1913 amendment to the Bill of Rights. They bar compensation when the injury has been occasioned solely by intoxication of the injured employee while on duty or by willful intention of the injured employee to bring about injury or death. Neither is applicable here.

[Simons, J., then notes that the disability provisions contain a prohibition against awarding benefits for illegal conduct that is not found in the sections dealing with work-related injuries.]

We have previously emphasized that the Workers' Compensation Law is remedial in nature and must be "construed liberally to accomplish the economic and humanitarian objects of the act." . . . It is one thing to disqualify a claimant for injuries he sustains during the course of an illegal activity pursued on his own time, an activity unknown to the employer and one which it cannot control. It is quite another to deprive dependents of benefits because the employee's death results from misconduct during the course of employment when the employer knows about the illegal activity and tolerates it.

Although the appellants' argument is based on moral grounds — the need to prevent parties from profiting from illegal acts — the suspicion is that the concern has more to do with dollars and cents than morality. The way for an employer to express dissatisfaction with its employees' acts and also avoid paying benefits for such claims, however, is not for the Board to disqualify innocent dependents but for the employer to make clear to its employees that illegal conduct on the job will not be tolerated.

Accordingly, the order of the Appellate Division should be affirmed, with costs.

TITONE, J. (dissenting). The majority holds that where an employer tolerates conduct blatantly in violation of the Penal Law, that conduct arises out of and in the course of employment within the meaning of Workers' Compensation Law §10. Because I find that holding totally unacceptable, I must dissent. . . .

On the merits, the majority reasons that intoxication and intentional self-infliction of injury are the only exceptions to the broad statutory liability imposed in Workers' Compensation Law §10. Such an analysis begs the very essence of the statute which endeavors to compensate workers for injuries, disabilities or deaths only "arising out of and in the course of employment." Thus, the threshold question to be decided in cases involving section 10, as here, is whether the employee's condition arose "out of and in the course of employment." . . . In my view, it did not.

There is no dispute that where, as in this case, an employee is instructed to wait for materials, he is not obliged to stand idly by. An employee may " 'indulge in any *reasonable* activity at that place, and if he does so the risk inherent in such activity is an incident of his employment.' "

If the prevailing word "reasonable" is to have any meaning at all, however, I cannot condone compensation for an injury sustained during the perpetration of a larceny. . . .

Moreover, that decedent's employer tolerated the criminal activity does not make him responsible for any injuries sustained during the larceny. The employer did not encourage the activity and certainly did not benefit from it. On the contrary, decedent's employer was put in a position of continually replacing downspouts. The decedent's conduct here does not even approach the equitable position of an employee who is injured while committing a relatively minor infraction which actually may further the employer's interest. More importantly, the employer is certainly empowered to waive its own rules by implied acquiescence in their habitual violation. Therefore, a violation of the employer's rules may not preclude compensation. The employer may not choose to ignore the mandates of the Penal Law, however, and the fact that a criminal statute is repeatedly violated cannot be construed as an implied permission on the part of the employer to allow such conduct.

NOTES

1. Injuries arising out of the course of employment. Richardson is one of literally thousands of cases that have probed the outer limits of coverage under the workers' compensation statutes. In a sense the unending stream of litigation under the statute creates a certain irony, for one of the major arguments against the common-law system of employer's liability based on negligence was that it unavoidably led to a high volume of case-by-case adjudication. The introduction of the compensation statute with its more generous coverage formula rendered easy many liability questions that were vexed at common law. But by expanding the boundaries of the compensable event outward, it has ushered in a new class of contested cases, of which injury during an employee's theft is only one. What result in *Richardson* if the employer had disciplined or discharged workers found to have stolen copper downspouts from the workplace? Does the majority view in *Richardson* suggest that any personal injury that takes place during work hours on the job site is compensable under the statute?

On this point contrast *Richardson* with Orsini v. Industrial Comm., 1509 N.E.2d 1005, 1009 (Ill. 1987), where the plaintiff mechanic, who used his employer's service bay to repair his own car, was injured because a missing transmission bin in his car caused the vehicle to lurch forward and pin Orsini's legs between the car and a workbench. The court, reversing a determination of the Industrial Commission, held that the accident was personal and noncompensable. It was not "a risk peculiar to the work or a risk to which the employee is exposed to a greater degree than the general public by reason of his employment." The court then explained its decision as follows:

> In the instant case, the risk of harm to Orsini was not increased by any condition of the employment premises. Unlike [other cases] cited by the appellee, where the harm to the employee came about as a result of a defect in the employer's premises, the injury here came about solely as a result of a defect in Orsini's own car — the missing retainer pin. It is undisputed that the malfunction on Orsini's car could have occurred anytime or anywhere, and only coincidentally occurred at the Wilmette Texaco service station. Nor is there any suggestion here that the tools provided by Wilmette Texaco and used by Orsini in repairing his car were in any way defective. Further, under the terms of his employment, Orsini was not required to work on his personal automobile during working hours, and Wilmette Texaco could just as well have permitted him to do nothing while he was waiting for the additional brake parts needed to complete the job he was performing for his employer.

2. Liability for acts of third parties. Workers' compensation statutes have universally expanded liability for attacks on workers by third persons while they are on the job — in fact a leading cause of death in the United States today. In Martinez v. Worker's Compensation Appeals Board, 544 P.2d 1350, 1352 (Cal. 1976), the injured worker had been hired to operate a beer stand at a fiesta operated by the Roman Catholic Church between the hours of noon and 4:30 P.M. While strolling through the fiesta with his family after work he heard reports that some teenagers had pilfered beer from the church's supplies. At 8:00 P.M. he encountered a group of boys with beer that he believed to be stolen and tried to grab it from them, at which point he was brutally beaten. The hearing examiner denied compensation because the injuries occurred after hours and because the employee had not been hired as a security guard. On appeal the court held that the plaintiff's injuries were covered by workers' compensation.

As a recognized authority in the compensation area has explained, "[i]t is too obvious for discussion that emergency efforts to save the employer's property from fire, theft, . . . or other hazards are within the course of employment. *The fact that the rescue effort takes place outside of working hours does not detract from its work-connected status.*" (1 Larson, Workmen's Compensation Law (1972) §28.11) Years ago, in an analogous situation, we held compensable a stable hand's injuries sustained during his attempt to rescue a child endangered by a horse on the employer's premises.

Similarly, in the present case, although petitioner may not have been employed to prevent theft of his employer's property, it was reasonably within the course of his employment that he might attempt to do so. As stated in a recent case, "Whether a particular activity be classified by the term's [sic] response to an emergency, rescue, personal comfort or convenience, recreation, exercise, courtesy, or common decency, the point is that the activity was reasonably to be contemplated because of its general nature as a normal human response in a particular situation or in some cases because of its being recognized as an acceptable practice in the particular place by custom. Human services cannot be employed without taking the whole package."

The court then held that since the employee had acted in good faith, he could not be treated as an "initial aggressor," not entitled to compensation under the statute, even if it turned out that the teenagers who assaulted him had not stolen the beer.

3. Acts of God under workers' compensation. Workers' compensation cases have also required a judicial reevaluation of the proper treatment of acts of God. In Electro-Voice, Inc. v. O'Dell, 519 S.W.2d 395 (Tenn. 1975), the claimant was awarded disability benefits when she suffered a violent allergic reaction after being stung by a bee while she was working on an assembly line. In demonstrating that the injury "arose out of" her employment, the claimant showed that the conditions in the plant "increased the risk or hazard" of suffering bee stings by proving that "bees often entered the walls of the building in the warm summer months and came out later in the year," and that the walls in the employer's building had been treated twice in the past two years in order to kill the bees that lived in them.

Electro-Voice adopted what is known as the "actual risk" test, whereby the claimant is allowed to recover only by showing that the employment increased (perhaps "materially") the risk of the harm beyond the levels to which an ordinary member of the public is exposed. This test, however, denies recovery in cases like Dawson v. A & H Mfg. Co., 463 A.2d 501 (R.I. 1983), where the claimant was stung by a bee while in the hallway of his employer's plant. The court noted that without proof of increased hazard, there was a "complete absence of evidence concerning the nexus between this employment and the bee sting. . . ."

Recovery in cases like *Dawson* is far more probable under the so-called "positional risk" theory adopted by a minority of jurisdictions.

This "but for" type test allows compensation if it turns out that the activities of the employer required the employee to be in a position to suffer the harm. This "positional risk" approach is gaining some ground. See, e.g., National Fire Ins. Co. v. Edwards, 263 S.E.2d 455, 456 (Ga. App. 1979), where the plaintiff, injured when a tornado struck the building in which he was working, was allowed recovery, the court noting that "for the injury to be compensable it is only necessary for the claimant to prove that his work brought him within range of the danger by requiring his presence in the locale when the peril struck, even though any other person present would have also been injured irrespective of his employment." See generally 1A A. Larson §§6-13.

4. Beyond accidents. The original compensation statutes tended to limit compensation to "personal injury by accident" where the last two words have often been read as limited to harms caused by a sudden and unexpected blow. One path to expansion has been to give accidental injuries a broad construction so that it is no longer necessary to establish a definite time, place, and cause. Thus in Johannesen v. New York City Department of Housing Preservation and Development, 636 N.E.2d 981, — (N.Y. 1994), the claimant suffered "two sudden and traumatic asthmatic attacks at work" when she had been exposed to high levels of secondhand smoke in a closed work environment. She had kept the position for ten years although her physicians had recommended a transfer. Bellacosa, J., held that the injuries were accidental because the exposures, from a common-sense point of view, had "an exacerbative and excessive quality. . . . Claimant worked in an office where the tools of her trade are papers, pens, files, computers and telephones. Cigarette smoke is surely not a natural by-product of the Department of Housing's activities and her employment role." For a defense of the broader reading of accident see 1B A. Larson §37.20.

In cases of this sort a constant level of stress and exposure can result not only in asthma attacks but in injuries as diverse as a bad back from lifting heavy weights to a heart attack that comes from stress on the job. In principle these cumulative trauma cases are as work related as a sudden injury, but the complications of proof they raise can be quite formidable as, for example, when a heart attack is suffered on the job by a worker who has arteriosclerotic heart disease. In Kostamo v. Marquette Iron Co., 274 N.W.2d 411, 415 (Mich. 1979), the court responded to the coverage challenge that these diseases create:

> The workers' compensation law does not provide compensation for a person afflicted by an illness or disease not caused or aggravated by his work or working conditions. Nor is a different result required because debility has progressed to the point where the worker cannot work without pain or injury. Accordingly, compensation cannot be awarded because the worker may suffer heart damage which would be work-related if he continued to work. Unless the work has accelerated or aggravated

the illness, disease or deterioration and, thus, contributed to it, or the
work, coupled with the illness, disease or deterioration, in fact causes an
injury, compensation is not payable.

Arteriosclerosis is an ordinary disease of life which is not caused by
work or aggravated by the stress of work. However, stress that would not
adversely affect a person who does not have arteriosclerosis may cause a
person who has that disease to have a heart attack.

The medical evidence necessary to establish that work aggravated,
accelerated, or precipitated a heart attack is, of course, expensive to
assemble and difficult to evaluate. Furthermore, the question of causation is, so the Michigan Supreme Court insisted, not exclusively one for
the medical evidence. In particular the court insisted that it was relevant for the Workers' Compensation Appeal Board to consider such
factors as the "[t]emporal proximity of the cardiac episodes to the work
experience, the hot and dusty conditions of employment, the repeated
return to work after each episode, and the mental stress" to which the
worker was subjected.

In recent years the matter of compensation in these exertion cases
has been regulated by statute. Thus the New Jersey statute (N.J. Stat.
Ann. §34:15-7.2.) (West 1993) provides:

> In any claim for compensation for injury or death from cardiovascular
> or cerebral vascular causes, the claimant shall prove by a preponderance
> of the credible evidence that the injury or death was produced by the
> work effort or strain involving a substantial condition, event or happen-
> ing in excess of the wear and tear of the claimant's daily living and in
> reasonable medical probability caused in a material degree the cardiovas-
> cular or cerebral vascular injury or death resulting therefrom.

However difficult the causation problem in heart attack and other
traumatic injury cases, it is even more difficult in the cumulative trauma
area, where there is no clear temporal division between the impact of
non-work-related and work-related causes. See, e.g., Pullman Kellogg v.
Workers' Compensation Appeals Board, 605 P.2d 422 (Cal. 1980),
where the California Supreme Court grappled with the apportionment
rules for cases of chronic bronchitis and emphysema as aggravated by
the claimant's heavy smoking over the entire length of the employment
period. The court concluded that under California statute "the board
must allow compensation not only for the disability resulting solely
from the employment, but also for that which results from the acceleration, aggravation, or 'lighting up' of a prior nondisabling disease." How
should the rule be applied in asbestos cases when smoking can increase
the risk of disease 30-fold?

5. *Drunkenness.* Although the workers' compensation statutes have
removed contributory negligence and assumption of risk from the catalogue of available defenses, they have not, as *Richardson* makes plain,

eliminated all defenses based on the employee's misconduct, since the employee's willful misconduct, drunkenness, and aggression may either bar or reduce recovery. Section 3600 of the California Labor Code, for example, parallels section 10 of the New York statute by denying compensation for an injury caused by the intoxication of the injured employee, for an injury that is intentionally self-inflicted, and "where the employee has willfully and deliberately caused his own death." Is there any reason why the drunkenness rule should apply only to injury and not to death?

More recent statutory innovations have specified with great particularity the levels of intoxication that offer a valid defense in a workers' compensation case. Thus, the Florida statute (Fla. Stat. Ann., §440.09(7b)) (West 1994) provides that

> If there was at the time of injury 0.08 percent or more by weight of alcohol in the employee's blood, or if the employee has a positive confirmation of a drug as defined in this act, it is presumed that the injury was occasioned primarily by the intoxication of, or the influence of the drug upon the employee. . . . However, if, before the accident, the employer had actual knowledge of and expressly acquiesced in the employee's presence at the workplace while under the influence of such drug or alcohol, the presumptions specified in this subsection do not apply.

6. Willful misconduct and willful disregard of safety rules. The workers' compensation statutes of about 20 states provide that the worker's recovery shall be barred or reduced on account of willful misconduct or willful disregard of safety regulations. When the conduct of the worker can be described only as negligent, even as grossly negligent, the claim for compensation has been allowed. Thus in Carter v. Koch Engineering, 735 P.2d 247 (Kan. App. 1987), compensation was allowed for a worker whose hand was crushed when he disregarded his employer's clear instructions to turn off his machine before dislodging the material that had jammed the equipment. "The evidence here was such that the factfinder was authorized to conclude that Carter had acted merely negligently, or even with gross negligence, but something short of intractably, without yielding to reason, obstinately or perversely."

7. Fraud and abuse on the system. The entire operation of the workers' compensation has been marked by large cost increases, which often speak of fraud and abuse. The most difficult area of compensation claims to administer has been in the area of mental distress claims that do not result in such discrete episodes as asthma or heart attacks. The so-called "mental-mental" stress claims were unrecognized before 1971, but have mushroomed under the broader construction given to compensable injuries under the various state laws. See generally 1B A. Larson §§42.23, 42.25(a). The difficult issues of proof in handling such claims have proved to be an open invitation to extensive fraud and abuse of the system, which seems to have been initiated not by disabled employees, but by an elaborate *institutional* network of fraud. A detailed account of the process as it operated in California is found in Schwartz, Waste, Fraud, and Abuse in Workers' Compensation: The Recent California Experience, 52 Md. L. Rev. 983 (1993). A short summary of the situation as it was in 1992 follows.

The process often begins when a "capper" approaches a worker, typically on the unemployment line, or outside plants that are laying off workers. The capper — who is paid some where between $150 and $450 per person on a piecework basis — tells the worker that if she comes with him she will be able to obtain compensation far in excess of unemployment benefits. A waiting car then whisks the worker away for interviews with lawyers and a barrage of medical tests that could easily cost $10,000 or $15,000, all of which under California law must be paid for by the employer, regardless of whether the claim is valid. Often this network of lawyers, physicians, cappers, and handlers seeks to persuade the employee that she suffered from various ailments in order to promote bogus claims or obtain more medical work. Often weak claims were settled for around $1,500 with some claims obviously bringing more. At its peak, Schwartz reports that the estimate for California was "that ten percent of all workers' compensation claims are fraudulent and that twenty-five percent of all employer payments are the result of either fraudulent claims or the deliberate padding of otherwise valid claims." Claim frequency is especially high in plants that have experienced extensive lay-offs or have otherwise closed down, and many small businesses treat these uncontrollable costs as reasons for leaving the state.

Without eliminating recovery for all these "mental-mental" stress claims, statutory reform has proved difficult. One direct line of attack was to require the worker to show that at least ten percent of the emotional distress was tied to "actual events" on the job, Cal. Lab. Code §3208.3(b) (West. Supp. 1993), a requirement that has been widely regarded as a joke by the bar and easily evaded in practice. California also has stepped up criminal prosecution for fraud; insurance companies have brought racketeering claims under RICO against certain workers' compensation mills, and a 1992 statute requires that all media advertisements soliciting workers' compensation claims contain notices that fraudulent claims are subject to criminal prosecution. Workers' Compensation Truth in Advertisement Act of 1992, Cal. Lab. Code §§5430-5434 (West Supp. 1993). These countermeasures have had some effect, but the ultimate picture is still uncertain. At present mountains of other reforms are pending before the California legislature.

Schwartz also draws some sobering conclusions from the ongoing episode: " 'Waste, fraud, and abuse' is certainly a political cliché; unfortunately, it is also an administrative reality." He then calls for a reexamination of the tort law generally to see how various doctrines, such as recovery for nervous shock, and the elimination of guest statutes, have performed in practice, but notes that no recent study of that sort has been undertaken. What implications does the California experience have for proposals to eliminate the work-related coverage rules in workers' compensation cases? See Henderson, Should Workmen's Compensation Be Extended to Nonoccupational Injuries?, 48 Tex. L. Rev. 117 (1969). For the expansion of federal disability programs, Medicare and Medicaid, national health care? Note that in California powerful market forces are also at work, as a new generation of Health-Care Organizations, patterned on the Health-Maintenence Organizations, are trying to gain a foothold into the compensation business over the strong opposition of the established lawyers and industrial-medicine physicians who run the current system. See Rhonda L. Rundle, *Mending Workers' Comp in California*, WALL STREET J., Aug. 17, 1994, at B1.

Wilson v. Workers' Compensation Appeals Board
545 P.2d 225 (Cal. 1976)

CLARK, J. Applicant seeks review of a Workers' Compensation Appeals Board decision vacating a referee's compensation award and holding that her injury did not arise "out of and in the course of the employment." (Lab. Code, §3600.) We affirm the board's order.

After driving her children to their school, applicant, a grade school teacher, sustained injury in an automobile accident driving to her school. Her car contained a small bag of thread spools for use in art class, materials graded at home the previous evening, and a few books, including her teaching manual.

The employing school district did not require instructors to commute in their personal cars. The school grounds were unitary and teachers did not travel elsewhere during the day. Public transportation was available and regularly used by at least one teacher. Since the class schedule did not include a specific period for planning lessons or grading papers, instructors commonly performed these duties at school outside class periods or at home in the evening. Teachers could complete class preparation at school but usually chose to work at home for their own convenience.

Although the school library contained a curriculum guide which, among other things, urged teachers to enliven lectures and to awaken pupil imagination with home-gathered sketches, charts, maps and other demonstrational materials, the school district did not require teachers to read the guide or to comply with its suggestions. Moreover, the district supplied adequate quantities of art materials for the children's use.

The board denied benefits after making the following principal findings: (1) applicant's home was not a second jobsite because her activities outside school hours were matters of personal choice, (2) only convenience motivated applicant's automobile trip, and (3) the "transportation of the work-related items was not a major part of the trip, nor even a significant alternative reason for the trip."

The "going and coming" rule provides that workers' compensation does not ordinarily compensate injuries sustained while the employee travels to or from work. In Hinojosa v. Workmen's Comp. Appeals Bd. 501 P.2d 1176 (Cal. 1976), this court stated that the going and coming rule makes noncompensable "the injury that occurs during a local commute enroute to a fixed place of business at fixed hours in the absence of special or extraordinary circumstances. The decisions have thereby excluded the ordinary, local commute that marks the daily transit of the mass of workers to and from their jobs; the employment, there, plays no special role in the requisites of portage except the normal need of the presence of the person for the performance of the work."

Applicant contends that, although the accident occurred during her regular commute, she is entitled to exemption from the going and coming rule because exceptional circumstances are established by her performing work at home the night before the accident and by her transporting work-related items — the graded materials and the spools — to class.

Work done at home may exempt an injury occurring during a regular commute from the going and coming rule if circumstances of the employment — and not mere dictates of convenience to the employee — make the home a second jobsite. . . . However, if work is performed at home for the employee's convenience, the commute does not constitute a business trip, since serving the employee's own convenience in selecting an off-premise place to work is a personal and not business purpose.

The record compels the board's determination that applicant's home did not constitute a second jobsite warranting exemption from the going and coming rule. The explicit job requirements demanded only that she report to the school grounds — nowhere else. Her employer's implicit requirement to work beyond classroom hours did not require labor at home. Teachers often worked after 3:15 in the school building unless their broad personal freedom vis-à-vis the nature and hours of class preparation led them home for the sake of convenience. There is no claim that facilities at school were not sufficient to permit completion of the preparatory chores.

That applicant's type of work regularly is performed at home must not disturb the board's determination. The contemporary professional frequently takes work home. There, the draftsman designs on a napkin, the businessman plans at breakfast, the lawyer labors in the evening. But this hearthside activity — while commendable — does not create a white-collar exception to the going and coming rule.

Because applicant performed work at home for her own convenience, transporting work-related materials to facilitate her work there was also for personal convenience, furnishing no basis for exception from the going and coming rule.

WRIGHT, C.J., and MCCOMB, SULLIVAN, and RICHARDSON, JJ., concur.

[Tobriner, J., joined by Mosk, J., dissented on the ground that the case fell into one of the "special" exceptions to the "going and coming" rule because the employee was expressly or implicitly "required or expected to furnish [her] own means of transportation to the job." The dissent relied on South v. Workmen's Comp. App. Bd., 447 P.2d 365 (Cal. 1968), where a social worker who was required to have his car at work in order to respond to emergencies and visit clients was awarded workers' compensation for injuries sustained en route to work. The dissent concluded that the petitioner should recover because she "provided a benefit to the school district by supplying additional teaching materials."]

NOTES

1. The "going and coming" rule. A great mass of litigation has helped establish the precise contours of the basic going and coming rule and the many exceptions to it. As a first approximation, the going and coming rule only bars recovery by those employees who, with fixed hours and places of employment, are injured while *off* the employer's premises. The rule itself is, however, subject to elaborate qualifications in most jurisdictions. Thus in another California case, Lewis v. Workers' Compensation Appeals Board, 542 P.2d 225 (Cal. 1975), the plaintiff recovered benefits in spite of the going and coming rule when she slipped and fell on a public street while walking from her employer's parking lot to her office. The court held that the ordinary commutation to work ended and her course of employment commenced the moment she entered the parking lot. Similarly, in Price v. Workers' Compensation Appeals Board, 693 P.2d 254 (Cal. 1984), the claimant was allowed to recover when he was hit by a passing motorist outside his employer's building before work while trying to change the oil in his car. The court relied on the rule of "liberal construction" to hold that the employee's commute had ended even if his work had not yet begun. The dissent stressed that "Price was injured *outside* the work premises, *before* working hours, while engaged in an act of *personal* convenience."

Another set of complications can arise when the employee has no single fixed place of work. Hinojosa v. Workmen's Compensation Appeals Board, 501 P.2d 1176 (Cal. 1972), involved a farm laborer whose employer owned several noncontiguous ranches. As a condition of his employment, the plaintiff was required to find transportation between worksites. He therefore arranged to be driven by a fellow worker, whom he paid $3.00 to cover his share of the operating expenses. The employee's accident occurred in a collision while he was being driven home from one of the employer's ranches. The court awarded compensation because the trips in question were "the extraordinary transits that vary from the norm because the employee requires a special, different transit, means of transit, or use of a car, for some particular reason of his own." Should compensation be awarded when the routine commute is over hazardous roads? When the employee is required to work long hours of overtime before returning home?

2. *Personal injuries while away from work.* Defining the course of employment often gives rise to intractable difficulties when the injury is suffered by an employee who is not on the employer's premises. Thus in Haugen v. State Accident Insurance Fund, 588 P.2d 77 (Or. App. 1978), the court refused compensation to a policeman injured while exercising at home to remain in good physical condition. The court rejected his claim that "police officers are in a special category because good physical conditioning is essential to their work," noting that the same is "required of a faller or topper employed in the forest products industry."

Liability for injuries off the premises was extended in Capizzi v. Southern District Reporters, 459 N.E.2d 847, 849 (N.Y. 1984). There the claimant, a court reporter, was injured when she slipped and fell while getting out of a hotel bathtub while out of town on a business trip. The traditional New York rule in this area allowed compensation only when the claimant was injured "while traveling on behalf of his employer." Nonetheless the court rejected its earlier cases and awarded compensation.

> Given the expanded theory of compensability with respect to injuries sustained by traveling employees involving incidents other than dressing or bathing, it is difficult to reconcile a compensation award to an employee who, when returning to her hotel after dinner, slipped and fell on a sidewalk with the denial of an award to a claimant in the present matter, who slipped and fell in a hotel bathtub in preparation for her return to her place of employment in New York City. Both employees sent by their employers on a business trip were removed from their normal environments, thereby increasing the risk of injury; and, as a result, were injured while engaged in "personal acts" attendant to their employment, although not participating in the actual duties of their employment.

What result if the hotel bathroom were safer than the claimant's bathroom at home?

3. Benefits Under the Workers' Compensation Statutes

It is most instructive to compare the common-law approach to tort damages with the workers' compensation approach to workers' benefits. The common-law damage rules impose no maximum limitation on recovery, and allow full recovery of lost earnings and medical expenses. Pain and suffering are everywhere treated as compensable. In contrast, all workers' compensation awards have a statutory base which is geared not to the severity of the claimant's injuries as such but only to its resulting "disability," that is, the degree to which it impairs the worker's earning capacity. The worker who is able to carry on without loss of income notwithstanding some physical impairment may be injured, but has not ordinarily sustained any compensable disability under the statutes.

Workers' compensation schemes also impose, albeit with wide variation, strict limitations on the amount of compensation recoverable from the employer. In all states the benefits payable to the employee are usually calculated in terms of the average weekly wage (AWW). The definition of the AWW provided under the New York Work. Comp. Law §14 (McKinney's 1992) is typical. That statute provides:

§14. WEEKLY WAGES BASIS OF COMPENSATION
Except as otherwise provided in this chapter, the average weekly wages of the injured employee at the time of the injury shall be taken as the basis upon which to compute compensation or death benefits, and shall be determined as follows:
1. If the injured employee shall have worked in the employment in which he was working at the time of the accident, whether for the same employer or not, during substantially the whole of the year immediately preceding his injury, his average annual earnings shall consist of three hundred times the average daily wage or salary for a six-day worker, and two hundred sixty times the average daily wage or salary for a five-day worker, which he shall have earned in such employment during the days when so employed;
2. If the injured employee shall not have worked in such employment during substantially the whole of such year, his average annual earnings, if a six-day worker, shall consist of three hundred times the average daily wage or salary, and, if a five-day worker, two hundred and sixty times the average daily wage or salary, which an employee of the same class working substantially the whole of such immediately preceding year in the same or in a similar employment in the same or a neighboring place shall have earned in such employment during the days when so employed.

The statute then provides that where neither of these methods is applicable, the AWW should be calculated by taking into account "the previous earnings of the injured employee and of other employees of the same or most similar class, working in the same or most similar employment." Cases in this class are subject to enormous difficulties, just as torts cases are, especially when injured workers have just started a new career, have changed jobs or locations, or have recently reentered the workforce. See 2 A. Larson, Workers' Compensation Law §60 (1989).

Under the workers' compensation laws, work-related injuries are then placed in one of four categories: temporary partial, temporary total, permanent partial, and permanent total. The disability is treated as temporary when it is believed that the employee, within some period set by statute, will be able to return to work with his capabilities undiminished by the accident. The disability is regarded as permanent when the employee's capacities remain impaired even after the recuperation period. Total and partial are more or less self-defining terms. Finally, the death cases receive separate treatment from the disability cases.

The statutes in every state set out in some detail the levels of compensation appropriate for the different categories of injuries. With permanent total benefits, for example, an initial calculation determines the weekly wage earned by the typical worker. Then, in most states the level of compensation is set at a figure equal to two-thirds that wage, although some states set benefits presumptively equal to 80 percent of spendable earnings. Thereafter, this individual weekly wage figure is subject to both statutory minimums and maximums. In California, for example, the figures run as follows. As of January 1993, the payments for temporary total benefits are set at two-thirds the worker's wage and two-thirds AWW. They run from a minimum of $126 to a maximum of $336, up from a $112 minimum and $224 maximum in 1987. The benefits run for the duration of the disability. The lowest state on the totem pole is Georgia whose compensation benefits are also set at two-thirds of the worker's wage, with a minimum of $25 (or full AWW if less) and a maximum of $250, where benefits run for only 400 weeks. Connecticut sets the standard for generosity at the high end, with benefits calculated at 150 percent of the workers' weekly wage, from a minimum of either $153.80 (20 percent of the maximum allowable) or 80 percent of the worker's wage, whichever is lower, up to a high of $769, for the duration of the disability. Similar calculations are made for permanent partial disabilities, although in some states the maximum figures allowable in these cases are lower than those permitted for permanent total disabilities. Finally, most states have special tables for death benefits. These award some multiple of the AWW wage, typically in the neighborhood of 400 or 500 weeks. For the detailed calculations see 4 A. Larson,

Tables 8 (permanent total), 9 (permanent partial), 10 (temporary total), and 16 (death benefits), as periodically updated.

The tables, of course, do not resolve all individual disputes over matters of fact, especially with setting the benefits for permanent disabilities, both partial and total. These benefits are, in general, measured by the expected loss in earning power attributable to the worker's medical impairment, up to some specified statutory maximum. For a broad class of undifferentiated injuries (e.g., backaches and occupational diseases), the calculation of benefits turns on a number of factors, each material but none decisive. One part of the picture is the medical condition itself, its amenability to improvement over time. A second part is whether the particular employee has engaged in useful employment after the injury. Where such employment is established, account must be taken of the wages earned in order to determine the diminution of earning capacity. Where, however, there is no further employment, it must be determined whether the employee is fit for any further employment and whether the employer has offered him work that is appropriate to his current condition. For an exhaustive summary of these rules see 2 A. Larson §57 (1989).

A full appreciation of the benefits systems created by the workers' compensation laws requires some brief discussion of "scheduled benefits." Whenever there is the loss or destruction of an organ or limb, the benefits awarded to the victim are not calculated anew in terms of wage loss attributable to the injury. Instead, reference is made to some schedule of damages either set out or authorized by statute. Here, not only is the nature of the disability (e.g., loss of sight in one eye, loss of leg below knee but above ankle) taken into account, but also the employee's occupation, age, and sometimes, as in California, number of dependents. Scheduled damages are not set out in dollar figures, but are typically expressed as some multiple of the AWW. Thus, the New York Workers' Compensation statute provides in section 15(3) (1993) as follows:

Member lost	Number of weeks' compensation	Member lost	Number of weeks' compensation
a. Arm	312	h. Great toe	38
b. Leg	288	i. Second finger	30
c. Hand	244	j. Third finger	25
d. Foot	205	k. Toe other than	
e. Eye	160	great toe	16
f. Thumb	75	l. Fourth finger	15
g. First finger	46		

The basic theme is embellished by setting an appropriate number of weeks for persons who suffer multiple disabilities, e.g., a loss of a hand plus loss of an eye. Thereafter further adjustments are made for moneys received from collateral sources, such as social security disability payments. See section 15(3)(v) of the New York statute.

Once the benefits have been calculated they belong to the worker, and are in no event tied to any actual wage loss. The worker who, by good fortune, can earn as much after the injury as before is, in effect, compensated for the extra effort needed to perform the job. When the evidence establishes an impairment in use, but not a total disability, statutory awards are reduced to reflect the degree of permanent partial disability suffered. Thus, for a 50 percent loss in the use of an arm, the claimant under section 15(3)(a) of the New York statute will be entitled to receive 166 weeks of compensation given that 312 weeks of benefits are awarded for permanent total disability. See, on scheduled benefits, 2 A. Larson, Workmen's Compensation Law §58 (1989).

4.   Exclusive Remedy

Beauchamp v. Dow Chemical Co.
398 N.W.2d 882 (Mich. 1986)

Levin, J. The questions presented are whether the exclusive remedy provision of the Workers' Disability Compensation Act bars an employee from commencing a civil action against his employer where the employee alleges (1) that the employer committed an intentional tort against the employee, and (2) that the employer breached its contract to provide a safe workplace.

I

Plaintiff Ronald Beauchamp was employed for two years as a research chemist by defendant Dow Chemical Company. He applied for workers' compensation benefits, alleging impairment of normal bodily functions caused by exposure to tordon, 2, 4-D, and 2, 4, 5-T ("agent orange").

Ronald Beauchamp and his wife, Karen, thereafter commenced this civil action against Dow. The complaint alleged that Ronald Beauchamp had been physically and mentally affected by exposure to "agent orange" and that Karen Beauchamp had suffered loss of consortium. The complaint further alleged that Dow intentionally misrepresented and fraudulently concealed the potential danger, that Dow intentionally assaulted Ronald Beauchamp, that Dow intentionally inflicted emotional distress, and that Dow breached its contract to provide safe working conditions. The circuit court granted summary judgment for Dow on all four counts on the basis that the complaint failed to state a claim on which relief could be granted. It does not appear that there had been any discovery.

The decision of the Court of Appeals, reversing in part and affirming in part, was "premised on . . . [its] understanding that an allegation of a 'true' intentional tort is not within the exclusive remedy provision of the [Workers' Disability Compensation Act]." A "true" intentional tort, as defined by the Court of Appeals, is one in which the injury, as well as the act, was intended. . . .

We conclude that the contract claim is barred by the exclusive remedy provision and remand for further proceedings on the intentional tort claims. . . .

IV

We conclude that actions for intentional torts are not barred. Before the workers' compensation act was enacted, employers were liable for intentional torts they committed against their employees. The workers' compensation act, as explained above, was a comprehensive restructuring of the mechanism for dealing with accidental injuries. The Legislature did not intend "that the exclusive remedy section of the act be construed to preclude a plaintiff's recovery for injuries suffered in an intentional tort. . . ."

The accident requirement assures that neither the employee nor the employer can use the workers' compensation act as a means of benefiting from their own intentional misconduct. Excluding recovery for self-inflicted injuries because self-inflicted injuries are not accidents is consistent with preventing employers from using the exclusive remedy provision of the act to shield them from civil suits for their intentional torts, because intentional torts are also not accidents. The employee will not be heard to claim his injury was an accident when the employee intentionally injured himself. Employers will not be heard to suggest that the exclusive remedy provision shields them from civil actions for intentional torts they commit against their employees. . . .

Dow has argued that the workers' compensation act embodies a quid pro quo, and the employer's quid is absolute immunity from liability other than that provided for in the workers' compensation act. Taken out of context, the language of the exclusivity provision lends apparent support to Dow's position: "The right to the recovery of benefits as provided in this act shall be the employee's exclusive remedy against the employer." Nevertheless, the legislative history indicates the quid pro quo concerned accidents; intentional torts by employers were never part of the bargain struck. . . .

Intentional misconduct would seem to be the type of behavior the Legislature would most want to deter and punish. Including intentional torts within the exclusivity provision would in that sense be counterproductive.

Because the Legislature intended to limit and diffuse liability for accidental injury by no means suggests the Legislature intended to limit and diffuse liability for intentional torts. Accidents are an inevitable part of industrial production; intentional torts by employers are not.

VI

Although a number of courts have agreed that the exclusivity provision of a workers' compensation act does not preclude employees from bringing intentional tort actions against their employers, the courts have not been able to agree on a definition of "intentional" in this context. Some courts have limited the recovery to so-called "true intentional torts," that is, when the employer truly intended the injury as well as the act. Other courts have relied on the standard in the Restatement of Torts, 2d, stating that when the employer intended the act that caused the injury and knew that the injury was substantially certain to occur from the act, the employer has committed an intentional tort. The substantial certainty test has apparently been extended by at least one state to cover substantial likelihood of injury. [Jones v. VIP Development Co., 472 N.E.2d 1046 (Ohio 1984).]

A

The Court of Appeals in the instant case declared, "In order to allege an intentional tort outside the act, the plaintiff must allege that the employer intended the injury itself and not merely the activity leading to the injury." A number of states have adopted a similar intentional tort test requiring an actual intent to injure.

B

The "substantial certainty" line of cases defines intentional tort more broadly. An intentional tort "is not . . . limited to consequences which are desired. If the actor knows that the consequences are certain, or substantially certain, to result from his act, and still goes ahead, he is treated by the law as if he had in fact desired to produce the result." It does not matter whether the employer wishes the injury would not occur or does not care whether it occurs. If the injury is substantially certain to occur as a consequence of actions the employer intended, the employer is deemed to have intended the injuries as well. The substantial certainty test tracks the Restatement definition of an intentional tort.

The distinction between the substantial certainty intentional tort test and the "true" intentional tort test can become important in cases such as *Griffin* [v. St. George's Inc, 589 S.W.2d 24 (Ark. 1979)], in which the facts were assumed, for the purpose of reviewing a trial court decision granting defendant's general demurrer, to be as follows: An employee was mangled when he fell into an auger. The employer had ordered the protective grate removed. The surface near the auger "sloped toward the opening . . . and, since there was usually grain lying upon this surface, one coming near the opening could easily slip . . . ." This violation of safety standards was extremely hazardous and the employer "recognized the substantial certainty that it would result in injury to an employee." Nevertheless, the employer placed Griffin "in direct danger of injury . . . in spite of the fact that it was substantially certain that an employee in Griffin's position would be injured by reason thereof." The court, using the true intentional tort test, concluded that the employer did not "desire to bring about the consequences of the act," and, as a result, the tort action was barred by the exclusivity provision of the workers' compensation statute. . . .

C

The recent *People v. Film Recovery Systems* case decided in Illinois adds a new perspective to the different intentional tort standards. The facts in the case were as follows: Film Recovery Systems went into the business of recovering silver from film negatives. This was done by placing the negatives into vats of cyanide. Hydrogen cyanide gas would bubble up from the vats and there was inadequate ventilation. The employer knew about the dangers. The labels on the chemicals being used contained adequate warnings; as a result, the employer hired only employees who could not speak or read English. The workers complained about the fumes daily. In 1981, an inspector had warned that the operation had outgrown the plant. The employer's response was to move the executive offices while tripling the size of the operations. Eventually one worker died and several others were seriously injured because of hydrogen cyanide poisoning. The corporate officers were convicted of involuntary manslaughter.

The facts in this case are a good example of the type of employer conduct that would seem to meet the substantial certainty as well as a substantial likelihood of harm standard. It is questionable, however, whether even this outrageous conduct would constitute a "true intentional tort." The employer did not desire to injure or kill the employees, even though the employer knew with a substantial certainty that his conduct would injure the employees.

D

. . . We adopt the substantial certainty standard. In an effort to avoid the misapplication of that test illustrated by the Ohio line of cases (see [Jones v. VIP Development Co.], we stress that substantial certainty should not be equated with substantial likelihood. The facts in *Serna* and *Film Recovery Systems* are examples of what would constitute substantial certainty.

VIII

The second issue presented is whether the exclusivity provision of the workers' compensation act precludes a common-law civil action by an employee who alleges that his employer breached a contractual promise to provide safe working conditions.

A claim that an injury is caused by failure to provide safe working conditions is essentially a recasting in contract form of a claim that the employee was injured by the employer's negligence. It is not even a recasting in contract form of an intentional tort. The workers' compensation act provides a quid pro quo for accidental injury. Limited but certain compensation for accidental injuries caused by unsafe working conditions has been substituted for the right to sue for accidental injuries caused by unsafe working conditions. Allowing a civil action as well as compensation for an injury caused by failure to provide safe working conditions would alter the balance struck by the legislation. . . .

Remanded to the circuit court for further proceedings consistent with this opinion. We do not retain jurisdiction.

NOTES

1. *Intentional wrongs by the employer.* In Jones v. VIP Development Co., 472 N.E.2d 1046, 1051 (Ohio 1984), disapproved of in *Beauchamp*, the court held that the broad Restatement definitions of intent defined the scope of the exception to the exclusive remedy rule.

> Thus, a specific intent to injure is not an essential element of an intentional tort where the actor proceeds despite a perceived threat of harm to others which is *substantially certain,* not merely likely to occur. It is this element of substantial certainty which distinguishes a merely negligent act from intentionally tortious conduct. Where a defendant acts despite his knowledge that the risk is appreciable, his conduct is negligent. Where the risk is great, his actions may be characterized as reckless or wanton, but not intentional. The actor must know or believe that harm is a substantially certain consequence of his act before an intent to injure will be inferred.

The court then applied this definition and allowed the plaintiff to maintain a tort action on the following facts:

> Plaintiff's complaint alleged that the defendant employer "intentionally, maliciously, willfully and wantonly" removed the safety cover from the discharge chute, thereby proximately causing the decedent's death. There was evidence to the effect that the employer knew that the cover was intended to protect employees from exactly the kind of injury that the decedent suffered, that the degree of risk posed to employees by the removal of the cover was extremely high, and that no warnings were issued to the employees concerning this risk.

As applied, *Jones* appears to convert every failure to warn case into an intentional tort, thereby gutting the exclusive remedy provision. The Ohio court retreated from that implication in its subsequent decision in Van Fossen v. Babcock & Wilcox Co., 522 N.E.2d 489 (Ohio 1988), where the court reinstated a summary judgment for the defendant entered by the trial judge. "To establish an intentional tort of an employer, proof beyond that required to prove negligence and beyond that to prove recklessness must be established." It then held that workers' compensation was the exclusive remedy when the plaintiff slipped and fell on some steps welded onto a piece of machinery by a co-worker, where the steps had not given rise to any concern for 20 years. But the court did not explicitly repudiate or overrule *Jones*.

The question of exclusive remedy has also surfaced in the asbestos litigation. In Millison v. E.I. du Pont de Nemours & Co., 501 A.2d 505, 514-515 (N.J. 1985), the court examined the relationship between knowledge and intent and concluded, "We must demand a virtual certainty." It therefore concluded that the plaintiffs' tort claims against their employer for "their initial work-related occupational diseases must fall. Although defendants' conduct clearly amounts to deliberately taking risks with employees' health, as we have observed heretofore the mere knowledge and appreciation of a risk — even the strong probability of a risk — will come up short of the substantial certainty needed to find an intentional wrong" that lies outside the exclusive remedy provision. The court did hold, however, that plaintiffs did have a good tort cause of action since they alleged that "in order to prevent employees from leaving the workforce, defendants fraudulently concealed from plaintiffs the fact that they were suffering from asbestos-related diseases, thereby delaying their treatment and aggravating their existing illnesses." For a similar result see Johns-Manville Product Corp. v. Superior Court of Contra Costa County (for Reba Rudkin), 612 P.2d 948 (Cal. 1980).

The exclusive remedy defense also failed to protect an employer against a claim of fraud. In Martin v. Lancaster Battery Co., Inc., 606

A.2d 444, 447-448 (Pa. 1992), the plaintiff, who suffered regular exposure to lead dust and fumes incident to his work in a battery factory, sued his employer for altering the results of medical examinations so as to conceal the high level of lead concentration in his blood. The receipt of that false information led the plaintiff to delay seeking medical treatment, resulting in an aggravation of preexisting injuries. The court held that the exclusive remedy provision afforded no protection against the tort action:

> We do not find the reasoning of the courts refusing to permit common law actions under these circumstances to be persuasive. The employee herein has alleged fraudulent misrepresentation on the part of his employer as causing the delay which aggravated a work-related injury. He is not seeking compensation for the work-related injury itself in this action. Clearly, when the Legislature enacted the Workmen's Compensation Act in this Commonwealth, it could not have intended to insulate employers from liability for the type of flagrant misconduct at issue herein by limiting liability to the coverage provided by the Workmen's Compensation Act. There is a difference between employers who tolerate workplace conditions that will result in a certain number of injuries or illnesses and those who *actively* mislead employees already suffering as the victims of workplace hazards, thereby precluding such employees from limiting their contact with the hazard and from receiving prompt medical attention and care.

How ought the apportionment of damages be made?

For the extensive literature on intentional torts see generally 2A A. Larson, Workmen's Compensation §68.13 (1988); King, The Exclusiveness of an Employee's Workers' Compensation Remedy Against His Employer, 55 Tenn. L. Rev. 405 (1988).

2. *Dual capacity.* A second important exception to the exclusive remedy provisions is the so-called dual capacity doctrine. In the landmark case of Duprey v. Shane, 249 P.2d 8, 15 (Cal. 1952), the defendant chiropractor mistreated his nurse when she came to him for treatment. The court held that the defendant was a "person other than the employer" and allowed her tort action against him in that capacity. "It is true that the law is opposed to the creation of a dual personality, where to do so is unrealistic and purely legalistic. But where, as here, it is perfectly apparent that the person involved — Dr. Shane — bore towards his employee two relationships — that of employer and that of a doctor — there should be no hesitancy in recognizing this fact as a fact."

In Bell v. Industrial Vangas, Inc., 637 P.2d 266, 273 (Cal. 1981), the court extended the dual capacity doctrine to allow the plaintiff, a route salesman, to sue his employer in its separate capacity as manufacturer when he was injured while delivering some flammable gas that his employer had manufactured. The court held an "extra" duty fell upon the employer in its role as supplier of the dangerous product, and thus subject to the strict requirements of California products liability law.

> The public policy goals underlying product liability doctrine should not be subverted by the mere fortuitous circumstance that the injured individual was an employee of the manufacturer whose product caused the injury. If the injured individual had not been an employee, he would have had a cause of action against the defendant. To deny Bell such a cause of action because he is an employee, gives the employer more protection than envisioned by the 1911 Act. In effect, the trial court rule would permit a manufacturer to test new products, utilizing his employees, and limit his liability from resulting injuries from a defective product to workers' compensation remedies. This is unsound social engineering grossly unfair to the worker. . . .

A biting dissent asked, "If an employer is to be held civilly liable to injured workers in the employer's capacity as a 'manufacturer,' what compelling reason can exist for denying similar liability for injuries attributable to the employer's other relationships including his status as 'landowner,' 'motor vehicle operator,' or 'cafeteria proprietor' "?

Bell has been superseded by statutory reforms that both raised compensation benefits across the board and narrowed the dual capacity doctrine. Thus Section 3602 of the California Labor Code was amended to buttress the exclusive remedy provision by explicitly declaring that "the fact that either the employee or the employer also occupied another or dual capacity prior to, or at the time of, the employee's industrial injury shall not permit" a tort action against the employer. The statute made exceptions for suits arising out of "willful physical assaults," workplace injuries "aggravated by the employer's fraudulent concealment of the existence of the injury," and cases in which defective products were manufactured by the employer and sold to an independent third party for valuable consideration, if thereafter used in the employer's business.

The New York Court of Appeals took a hostile view of the dual capacity doctrine in Billy v. Consolidated Machine Tool Corp., 412 N.E.2d 934, 939 (N.Y. 1980), where it wrote: "Having examined all of the pertinent precedent, we conclude that the 'dual capacity' doctrine as it has been applied to permit common-law suits against employers in their capacities as property owners or manufacturers of plant equipment is fundamentally unsound," because it undermines the basic structure of the original workers' compensation bargain. Quoting from earlier cases, it noted that "an employer remains an employer in his relations with his employees as to all matters arising from and connected with their employment. He may not be treated as a dual legal personality, 'a sort of Dr. Jekyll and Mr. Hyde.' "

After *Bell,* California took a more subdued view of the subject, refusing in Jones v. Kaiser Industries Corp., 737 P.2d 771 (Cal. 1987), to allow a widow whose husband, a policeman, was killed by an errant motorist, to sue his city-employer in tort for the negligent maintenance of city streets. "We discern no rational reason why it cannot be said that the city owes a duty as an employer to maintain safe streets for the benefit of the police officers who are required to work there. The fact that it owes the same duty to the public does not detract from this conclusion."

For a sustained criticism of the expansive version of the dual capacity test see 2A A. Larson §72.80 et seq.

3. Dual capacity in cumulative trauma cases. The dual capacity doctrine has received a novel twist in asbestos litigation. In Shelly v. Johns-Manville, 798 F.2d 93 (3d Cir. 1986), the plaintiffs, all employees of Johns-Manville, alleged that they were exposed to asbestos not only as workers but also "in and around their homes," "to and from their place of employment," and "outside work in the general atmosphere from ambient air." The court held that by its best guess the Pennsylvania courts would recognize that these separate exposures, entirely unrelated to their work as such, would permit the plaintiffs to escape from the exclusive remedy provision of the Pennsylvania compensation law. See Tatrai v. Presbyterian University Hospital, 439 A.2d 1162 (Pa. 1982). The court recognized that "plaintiffs may have a difficult time establishing a relationship between their injuries and their exposure away from the workplace to justify recovery," but held that problems of causation are properly raised at trial and are not relevant to the dual capacity issue as such. What rule of joint causation should be applied if each plaintiff was exposed to 1 percent of the total number of fibers outside the workplace and 99 percent within?

4. Tort actions against a third-party defendant. Employees have had almost uniform success in circumventing the exclusive remedy provision of the compensation laws by bringing tort actions against unrelated third parties. Whether that party was an automobile driver or a product manufacturer, the uniform view has been that strangers to the workers' compensation bargain are not entitled to benefit from it. See generally 2A A. Larson §71.00 (1989). Once that action is allowed, there is still the important question of how the tort actions against the third party should be integrated with the compensation system. One immediate source of conflict is, who is entitled to the money the employee recovers from the third party? If it is left to the employee, there is some form of double recovery. To avoid that possibility, most compensation systems allow the employer to recoup the compensation benefits to the extent of the recovery, in the form either of a lien against the employee's tort recovery or of a right of subrogation against the third party.

The matter becomes even more complex when the third party seeks contribution or indemnity from the employer who is protected against direct suit by the exclusive remedy provision. In the early case of Westchester Lighting Co. v. Westchester County Small Estates Corp., 15 N.E.2d 567, 569 (N.Y. 1938), the court allowed the action on a theory of implied indemnity based on the "independent obligation" of care that the employer owes the third party. Crane, C.J., argued in dissent that the indemnity had to violate the statute, "for it makes the employer liable indirectly in an amount which could not be recovered directly." In Crane's view, the third party's "recovery, if any, should be limited to the amount that the employer would have been obligated to pay under the Workers' Compensation Law."

Westchester Lighting was followed under the Federal Employees Compensation Act (FECA) in Lockheed Aircraft Corp. v. United States, 460 U.S. 190 (1983). There a civilian employee of the United States was killed when a C-5A transport, operated by the United States and manufactured by Lockheed, crashed outside of Saigon in April 1975. The employee sued Lockheed for its defective manufacture of the aircraft and Lockheed in turn sought indemnity from the United States, which argued that Lockheed's suit was barred by §8116(c) of the FECA. That section was modeled on the New York statute, which provided that liability under the statute is "exclusive . . . to the employee, his legal representative, spouse, dependents, next of kin [or] any other person otherwise entitled to recover tort damages against the United States." The Supreme Court held that the words "any other person" were not broad enough to encompass the third-party claim of Lockheed and allowed the action to go forward.

5. Breaking the eternal triangle. In addition to the system of "equitable apportionment" discussed above, other proposals have been made to simplify the relationship among the three parties. One alternative approach stipulates that in third-party actions the injured worker may recover only those damages that are in excess of the amounts paid or payable for such injury under the workers' compensation statutes. The employer would then remain liable in full under the workers' compensation statutes but would be denied any workers' compensation lien against the employee's (reduced) tort recovery against a third party. This plan also eliminates the need for any third-party indemnity actions against the employer. For a defense of this compensation setoff see Epstein, The Coordination of Workers' Compensation Benefits with Tort Damage Awards, 13 Forum 464 (1977).

C. NO-FAULT INSURANCE

1. Automobile No-Fault Insurance

The idea of extending workers' compensation principles to cover non-industrial accidents is almost as old as workers' compensation itself. Perhaps the earliest article advocating this extension is Ballantine, A Compensation Plan for Railway Accident Claims, 29 Harv. L. Rev. 705 (1916). There Professor Ballantine identifies the two elements that lie at the root of most modern no-fault proposals. The first, that liability, irrespective of negligence, "is founded upon conviction that the cost of transportation service should include the expense of insuring the passenger against all risks peculiar to the service for which he pays his fare." The second principle, that of a fixed and limited schedule of damages, "is founded upon the belief that exact money compensation for physical injury, now supposed to be determined by juries, is impossible, and that if companies are held as insurers and not as wrongdoers there is no reason why the entire risk involved in the transportation service should be borne by the transportation agency."

Although Ballantine envisioned his no-fault scheme for railway accidents, in fact his article established the basic pattern for the automobile no-fault proposals that followed a decade later. The first important proposal directed toward no-fault automobile insurance was the Columbia Plan, proposed in 1932. See Report of Committee to Study Compensation for Automobile Accidents (Columbia Reports) (1932). The Columbia Plan followed the tradition of tort law in that it contemplated a system of third-party insurance. Its basic coverage provision stated that "[e]very owner of a motor vehicle shall pay compensation for disability or death from personal injury caused by the operation of such motor vehicle, without regard to fault as a cause of the injury or death. . . ." The basic rule was then qualified by limited exceptions. One provided that persons who intentionally brought about their own injuries could not recover; another specified that liability did not extend to those who drove without the owner's permission, express or implied. At the time of its introduction, the plan was subject to considerable discussion and debate. It received serious study in Connecticut, New York, Virginia, and Wisconsin but was never adopted in any jurisdiction.

The Columbia Plan has had little direct influence on the next wave of no-fault automobile legislation, which reached its peak in the 1960s. These statutes all depend on first-party insurance mechanisms. The most influential defense of this system was R. Keeton and J. O'Connell, Basic Protection for the Accident Victim (1965), which also contains their version of a "Basic Protection Plan" for personal injuries, id. at 302. Judge Keeton later summarized the new wave of no-fault plans.

Keeton, Compensation Systems and Utah's No-Fault Statute
1973 Utah L. Rev. 383, 396-398

A COMPARISON OF SYSTEMS

In most no-fault plans, the no-fault coverage is primarily first-party insurance. That is, the claim for benefits will ordinarily be a claim, not involving any third party, against the injured person's own insurance company. Such a claim stands in contrast with the typical claim under liability insurance coverage in which there is a third party, the alleged tortfeasor, and in which the theory of the system is that benefits are being paid on his behalf under a form of insurance coverage initially designed to protect his assets. Even before no-fault plans were enacted, every state legislature in the United States had passed laws using automobile liability insurance to assure compensation to victims rather than simply to protect the assets of wrongdoers. But only with the advent of no-fault acts have legislatures chosen to assure compensation to virtually all traffic victims, using first party coverage for that purpose.

Another idea common to most no-fault systems and, to some extent, workmen's compensation is that benefits will be paid periodically as losses occur. In the tort-and-liability-insurance systems, on the other hand, it is customary for compensation to be determined by one fact-finding for both the past and the future, and to be paid in one lump sum. This lump-sum system remains in effect for the tort claims that are preserved under current no-fault acts, even though the no-fault benefits are paid periodically.

A further characteristic of many, though not all, no-fault laws places them in contrast with workmen's compensation. Benefits under no-fault laws are generally calculated on the basis of actual losses rather than by use of schedules of the type commonly used in workmen's compensation. Also, within the limits of the coverage, no-fault insurance generally comes nearer to reimbursing full loss than does workmen's compensation. In this last respect, workmen's compensation is currently under severe attack because it falls short of reimbursing the full loss of wages. Indeed, the development of no-fault automobile insurance may also hasten improvements in the system of compensation for work injuries.

The most distinctive feature of no-fault plans, and the most significant as well, is the partial tort exemption.* The other main feature is a concept that is as ancient as insurance itself. It is the concept that also

---

*Earlier in his article Professor Keeton distinguishes between the "partial-tort-exemption" statutes and the "add-on" laws. The former eliminate the tort actions for less serious injuries, while the add-on systems "merely add to the negligence system of reparation some kind of provision for no-fault insurance benefits." Neither system contemplates the complete replacement of all tort remedies by the no-fault system. — ED.

underlies life, health and accident, fire, and workmen's compensation insurance as well as the collision, comprehensive, and medical pay-ments coverages of automobile insurance policies. It is the concept that benefits depend simply upon whether the claimant has suffered a loss from an accident of a type within the insuring clause of the policy. One of the implications of this concept is that when the insuring clause makes no reference to fault or to fault-based liability, fault is irrele-vant to determining rights to compensation. It does not follow, how-ever, that fault is irrelevant in determining responsibility for paying premiums into the insurance system. That is a separate and distinct issue.

A corollary of the distinctive *partial* tort exemption of no-fault laws is that some victims — those with injuries of greater consequence — are entitled to claim compensation based on fault as well as no-fault com-pensation. No-fault laws differ from workmen's compensation laws in this respect. All of the no-fault laws thus far enacted preserve fault-based claims to some extent. Although the partial-tort exemption stat-utes draw the line between permitted and precluded tort actions at different points along the spectrum of severity of injury, they are alike in eliminating tort recoveries only for the injuries on the less serious side of the line and preserving them for injuries on the more serious side. Thus, all these laws are aimed at doing no less for any severely injured person than the fault-and-liability-insurance system does, and doing more for some — at least for those who would receive nothing under the tort system. In this respect, all of the partial-tort-exemption statutes make a contribution toward more equitable use of the re-sources committed to the automobile accident reparations system. That is, they redress to some extent the striking inequity of the tort-and-liability-insurance system, which is relatively generous to those with the least injuries and provides inadequately for those with more serious injuries. The inequity is condemned not only from a perspective out-side the fault system — the perspective of one who asks whether the resources committed to the reparations system are being used to achieve the fairest and best result possible — but also under the criteria of the fault system itself. The documented findings regarding the oper-ation of the fault-and-liability-insurance system in practice demonstrate that its practical performance is contrary to its own theory of equity. Surely most observers will agree, then, that the no-fault laws effect a distinct improvement in the reparations system to the extent that they correct the inequity of relatively poorer treatment for the more severely injured persons.

U.S. Department of Transportation, Motor Vehicle Crash Losses and Their Compensation in the United States
94-95, 128-129 (1971)

F. Summary of Findings

1.   Limited Scope of the Auto Accident Liability Reparations System

One major shortcoming of the auto accident liability system stems not from the way it performs but rather from its intended scope of operation, i.e., since only those who can prove that others were at fault while they were without fault in an accident have a legal right to recover their losses. Today, our society need not settle for a reparations system that deliberately excludes large numbers of victims from its protection or that gives clearly inadequate levels of protection to those who need it most. With only 45 percent of those killed or seriously injured in auto accidents benefiting in any way from the tort liability insurance system and one out of every ten of such victims receiving *nothing* from *any* system of reparations, the coverage of the present compensation mechanism is seriously deficient. . . .

3.   Cost Efficiency of the Auto Accident Liability Reparations System

The automobile accident tort liability insurance system would appear to possess the highly dubious distinction of having probably the highest cost/benefit ratio of any major compensation system currently in operation in this country. As has been shown, for every dollar of net benefits that it provides to victims, it consumes about a dollar. As it presently operates, the system absorbs vast amounts of resources, primarily in performing the functions of marketing insurance policies and settling claims. The measurable costs of these two functions alone approach in general magnitude all net benefits received by auto accident victims through the tort liability system. . . .

On the strength of these and other findings (relating to such matters as the length of time for settlement and the insurer losses in the automotive tort liability system), the DOT recommended the adoption of a privately operated first party system that provided some compensation benefits to all victims of accidents.

PART IV.   RECOMMENDATIONS FOR CHANGE

1.   Basic Reliance on First-Party Insurance

One of the important unmet needs apparent in the experience of the existing tort liability system is for a continuing, mutually confident and cooperative relationship between the insured and his insurer. Unlike the present system where the innocent victim must deal in an adversary relationship with a strange company, a "compensation" system in which the insured evaluates and chooses his own benefit source in advance of his loss would appear to offer many advantages. It would seem to be far more effective and satisfactory if the person injured in an accident could look to his own insurer for compensation just as is now true of homeowners or health and accident insurance where benefits are forthcoming as a matter of contract rather than of fault-finding and bargaining or suit. Such a "first-party" arrangement automatically places a greater importance on the quality of service to the victim, encouraging insurance companies to compete on this basis. Victims dealing with their own insurer would be less inclined to jeopardize that relationship by way of exaggerated or fraudulent claims than they are today when dealing with "somebody else's" company.

A basically first-party system would also enable the insurer to evaluate its risk in the broadest and fairest context, since it will know who it may have to compensate, the value and protective attributes of the vehicle they will be occupying, their driving habits, exposure and record, and their probable economic needs in the event of an accident. Unsafe, overpowered or delicately designed vehicles could begin to reflect their true costs in terms of their potential for causing and sustaining accident losses.

2. Availability of Benefits to All Accident Victims

A socially responsible auto accident reparations system should guarantee basic benefits to all accident victims, except, of course, those who willfully injure themselves or others. It should cover the economic losses associated with medical expenses, income loss, funeral expenses, required replacement services and property losses, at levels designed to prevent or effectively mitigate any serious economic dislocation for the individual victim or his dependents in all but the most catastrophic cases. Supplemental benefits should be available on a voluntary basis. At the same time, drivers should be given the choice not to insure themselves against minor losses, but instead to absorb them directly and, thereby, avoid the high administrative costs that the insurance institution incurs when handling minor claims.

American Bar Association, Special Committee on Automobile Insurance Legislation, Automobile No-Fault Insurance
13-17 (1978)*

WHY THE STATISTICAL STUDIES CRITICAL OF THE FAULT SYSTEM
ARE FATALLY FLAWED

. . . It is difficult to find any advocacy of changes in automobile insurance and accident compensation that does not mention the DOT's findings that:

---

*The preface to the report indicates that Professor Richard A. Posner was "primarily responsible" for its drafting.

Only 45% of all those killed or seriously injured in auto accidents bene-fited in any way under the tort liability system. . . .

Tort liability insurance would appear to cost in the neighborhood of $1.07 in total system expenses to deliver $1.00 in net benefits to vic-tims. . . .

Every one of these "findings" is seriously misleading, if not demon-strably incorrect. The first, that only 45 percent of those seriously in-jured in automobile accidents received any benefits under the tort liability system, is meaningless once it is recognized that tort liability is not intended as a system of insurance that can properly be evaluated under a criterion of comprehensiveness. Since not all accidents are the result of culpable fault solely on the part of the injurer, it is not surpris-ing that not all accident victims recover under the tort system. Indeed, if all did, that would be evidence that judges and juries had converted the tort system into an insurance scheme, contrary to its purposes. This illustrates the dilemma of tort liability, when evaluated as if it were an insurance system: if a low percentage of victims recover, this fact can be used as evidence that liability provides inadequate compensation; but if a high percentage recover, this fact can be used as evidence that liability has been converted into, and hence should be replaced by, explicit insurance.

The 45 percent figure is also misleading in ignoring the degree to which victims of automobile accidents obtain compensation outside of the tort system — from life, collision, disability, accident, medical, and other first-party insurance, and from wage-replacement sources such as sick leave and workers' compensation. When these sources of compen-sation are included, as DOT acknowledged, of those suffering serious injury or death in automobile accidents, "about 9 out of 10 recovered some losses." This is twice the percentage recovering in tort alone. It suggests that a combination of tort liability with voluntary first-party insurance and other sources of compensation provides compensation for almost all victims of automobile accidents. . . .

One of the most frequently cited statements in the DOT studies is that it costs about $1.07 in administrative expenses for each $1.00 in net benefits delivered to the accident victim. This may seem a high ratio of expense to pay-out — until it is remembered that a major benefit of tort liability which is not counted in the benefits received by victims is the reduction in the accident rate that is brought about by adherence to the standard of care established by the fault system. This effect of tort liability has not been adequately measured, nor its monetary equivalent computed, but to ignore it completely is to give a specious plausibility to DOT's statistical demonstration that the expenses of the system ex-ceed its benefits.

Furthermore, the policy implications of the ratio stressed by DOT are unclear once we look behind the summary figures. According to

DOT's own calculations, two-thirds of the $1.07 figure represent the insurance companies' internal administrative expense and, as we shall see elsewhere in this report, those expenses might actually be higher under no-fault. Moreover, some of the litigation expenses which constitute the remaining one-third of the expense of the automobile tort system will reappear under no-fault in the form of litigation over the first-party insurer's obligations to his insured.

Epstein, Automobile No-Fault Plans: A Second Look at First Principles
13 Creighton L. Rev. 769, 789-790 (1980)

[It is also important to examine the] soundness of the automobile no-fault plans when set in opposition to their nontort rival, the total abolition of the tort system without any substitute compulsory first party protection. In this connection the benefits of the no-liability system must be stressed. One of its great attractions is that it neatly avoids the troublesome question of how to make a collective determination of the level of payments for certain injuries, and the corresponding question of how to distribute the premium burden amongst those who will be conscripted to finance the system. To the contrary, it is a little noticed but important feature of most automobile no-fault plans that they achieve their universality of coverage by the *compulsory* purchase of the benefits in question, thereby committing all individuals to take a certain set of benefits in accordance with a predetermined set of coverage formulas. As I have in general a strong basic preference for voluntary markets, both on efficiency and liberty grounds, I think that there is much to be said for the system that allows individuals to choose the nature and type of benefits in light of their own estimation of the personal circumstances and needs. Those who wish to buy deep coverage with high deductibles should be allowed to do so, while those who want first dollar coverage with shallow protection should be free to do so as well. Those who want group coverage are free to explore that possibility. It may well be that the case is made for the abolition of all tort liability, but it does not follow that those same arguments require instituting compulsory first party insurance. The real quid pro quo for losing the benefits of being a tort plaintiff is being freed from the burden of being a tort defendant. It is *not* the surrender of a tort claim for the receipt of a set of benefits that are not requested, and which perhaps ill suit the needs of the party to which they are provided.

References. W. Blum and H. Kalven, Jr., Public Law Perspectives on a Private Law Problem — Auto Compensation Plans (1965); Blum and

Kalven, Ceilings, Costs, and Compulsion in Auto Compensation Legislation, 1973 Utah L. Rev. 341; Calabresi, Fault, Accidents and the Wonderful World of Blum and Kalven, 75 Yale L.J. 216 (1965); Blum and Kalven, The Empty Cabinet of Dr. Calabresi: Auto Accidents and General Deterrence, 34 U. Chi. L. Rev. 239 (1967); Franklin, Replacing the Negligence Lottery: Compensation and Selective Reimbursement, 53 Va. L. Rev. 774 (1967); Symposium: Alternative Compensation Schemes and Tort Theory, 73 Cal. L. Rev. 548 (1985); Trebilcock, Incentive Issues in the Design of "No-Fault" Compensation Systems, 39 U. Toronto L.J. 19 (1989).

Pinnick v. Cleary
271 N.E.2d 592 (Mass. 1971)

REARDON, J. [The plaintiff was injured in an automobile accident that he alleged was caused solely by the negligence of the defendant. His common-law tort action sought damages in excess of those allowed under the Massachusetts no-fault statute, ch. 670. The defendant interposed the statute as an affirmative defense to the plaintiff's cause of action, and the plaintiff then brought his bill in equity to the Massachusetts Supreme Judicial Court, alleging that the no-fault statute unconstitutionally deprived him of "his right to full recovery in tort."]

SUMMARY OF CHAPTER 670

. . . [W]e believe it advisable to summarize the basic structure of the statute. In so doing we will not attempt a comprehensive description of its scope and operation, for much of that, as we have indicated, is irrelevant for our present purposes. We wish rather at this juncture to draw attention first to the difference in the legal position of the injured party under c. 670 from his position at common law, and, secondly, to the practical consequences of the statute on him, taking into consideration the interaction of various forms of compulsory and optional insurance with c. 670.

[The court then gives an extensive account of the basic provisions of the statute, noting that] it appears that the statute affords the citizen the security of prompt and certain recovery to a fixed amount of the most salient elements of his out-of-pocket expenses and an increased flexibility in avoiding duplicate coverage, at double premiums, for the same expenses. In return for this he surrenders the possibly minimal damages for pain and suffering recoverable in cases not marked by serious economic loss or objective indicia of grave injury and the outside chance that through a generous settlement or a liberal award by a judge or jury in such a case he may be able to reap a monetary windfall out of his misfortune. . . .

The key concept embodied in c. 670 is that of personal injury protection insurance, which is required of all owners of motor vehicles registered in Massachusetts. Under this coverage, personal injury protection benefits are paid by the insurer, as the expenses they cover accrue, to the insured, members of his household, authorized operators or passengers of his motor vehicle including guest occupants, and any pedestrians struck by him, regardless of fault in the causation of the accident [up to $2,000.]

The plaintiff stresses that the residual tort action left after the payment of personal injury protection benefits is reduced in value inasmuch as the potential plaintiff must consider the extent to which legal fees will reduce his net recovery. However, legal fees are not a new burden imposed by c. 670; they have long been a factor to be considered in prosecuting any claim, including a tort action for personal injury instituted before the passage of c. 670.

The only limitation imposed by c. 670 on the potential plaintiff's prior right of recovery at common law is the elimination of damages for "pain and suffering, including mental suffering associated with . . . injury" except in certain specified categories of cases. Section 5 of c. 670 provides generally that the reasonable and necessary medical expenses incurred by a plaintiff in the treatment of his injuries must be over $500 to permit recovery for pain and suffering. However, recognizing that certain types of injuries could entail considerable pain and suffering which would warrant monetary compensation regardless of medical expense incurred, the Legislature provided by way of exception to the general rule that damages for pain and suffering could be sought in all cases involving five designated types of injuries. These are a fracture, injury causing death, injury consisting in whole or in part of loss of a body member, permanent and serious disfigurement, and injury resulting in loss of sight or hearing as elsewhere defined in the General Laws. The victim whose injury falls outside these categories and whose medical expenses are less than $500 cannot recover at all for pain and suffering. However, it is still possible for the person who desires to assure for himself recovery in excess of his out-of-pocket costs to do so. Just as he may elect a deductible if he has medical payments insurance to avoid duplicate recovery for medical expenses, so he may choose to keep both forms of insurance in full precisely to allow himself double recovery of these expenses.[6] Other forms of duplicate coverage are equally possible. It is true that the amount of excess he will receive

6. We recognize that certain policies of insurance exclude the possibility of double recovery.

thereby will bear no necessary relation to the value of his pain and suffering as arbitrarily set by a jury but, on the other hand, he is assured of some profit over out-of-pocket expenses in every motor vehicle accident. This certainty he was never afforded by his prior "right" to recovery for pain and suffering in a suitable case, which in order to be realized even in such a case had to be actively pursued at considerable expense.

The preceding discussion is not intended as a holding or ruling on any part of the statute, but only to permit a better understanding of that which follows.

NATURE OF RIGHTS AFFECTED

In approaching the numerous issues before us, it is advisable to dispose first of a contention which the plaintiff has argued vigorously and at some length, for if we accepted it, it would require a somewhat different approach to the attacks leveled at the statute than that we feel appropriate. The plaintiff claims that c. 670 has impaired a cause of action which is on a higher, more sacrosanct level than the "ordinary" common law cause of action. Two alternative reasons are advanced in support of this contention: first, that the tort action has the status of a "vested property right," and, second, that the function of the cause of action is to safeguard the fundamental "right of personal security and bodily integrity" which, although not mentioned in the Bill of Rights of the United States Constitution, is nonetheless protected by it. We find both grounds unpersuasive.

In arguing that the cause of action affected by c. 670 constitutes a vested property right, the plaintiff seems to ignore the distinction between a cause of action which has accrued and the expectation which every citizen has if a legal wrong should occur to find redress according to the rules of statutory and common law applicable at that time. The Legislature is admittedly restricted in the extent to which it can retroactively affect common law rights of redress which have already accrued. However, there is authority in abundance for the proposition that "[n]o person has a vested interest in any rule of law entitling him to insist that it shall remain unchanged for his benefit." New York Cent. R.R. v. White, 243 U.S. 188, 198. Munn v. Illinois, 94 U.S. 113, 134. And, as we shall demonstrate in more detail below, legislative actions based on this principle, prospectively modifying or abrogating common law causes of action, have been judicially upheld both in this Commonwealth and elsewhere on numerous occasions. The citizen may find that events occurring after passage of such a statute place him in a different position legally from that which he would have occupied had they occurred before passage of the statute. He has no cause, however, to complain solely because his rights are not now what they would have been before.

[The court then reviewed the administration of the tort law under the current system and, in the light of both the Department of Transportation Study and the Keeton-O'Connell studies, concluded that the legislation indeed bears a rational relationship to a legitimate legislative end.]

We conclude that the principles by which c. 670 should be judged are those generally applied when economic and social regulations enacted under the police power are attacked as a violation of due process and equal protection of the laws. The two grounds of attack although similar are sufficiently distinct to warrant separate treatment, to which we now proceed.

DUE PROCESS ISSUES

A.   APPLICABLE PRINCIPLES

We will deal first with the propriety of c. 670 under the due process clause. The overall test under this clause is whether the statute bears a reasonable relation to a permissible legislative objective. . . . In the application of this test, the statute is accorded a presumption of constitutionality, a corollary of which is that if a state of facts could exist which would justify the legislation, it must be presumed to have existed when the statute was passed.

In dealing with an alteration of the preexisting common law, we are guided also by cases which have dealt specifically with due process attacks on this kind of statute. Here we do not need to reach the difficult question of when the Legislature may abrogate a common law right of recovery without providing a substitute remedy. Such actions in other contexts have been sustained because it was felt that the Legislature was acting "to attain a permissible legislative object." Silver v. Silver, 280 U.S. 117, 122 ("guest statute," taking away right of gratuitous passenger in automobile to sue driver on account of mere negligence). Hanfgarn v. Mark, 274 N.Y. 22, appeal dismissed 302 U.S. 641 (abolition of actions for breach of promise, seduction, alienation of affections, and criminal conversation — no substantial Federal question presented on appeal to Supreme Court). We have never had the occasion to pass on comparable statutes enacted by our Legislature, although we have noted their existence and effect, and recognized generally the power of the Legislature to act in this regard.

In the instant case, however, the Legislature has not attempted to abolish the preexisting right of tort recovery and leave the automobile accident victim without redress. On the contrary, as was pointed out above, the statute has affected his substantive rights of recovery only in one respect and has simply altered his method of enforcing them in all others. Therefore, c. 670 may be judged by the stricter test which the plaintiff urges upon us and for which there is considerable authority in workmen's compensation cases: whether the statute provides an adequate and reasonable substitute for preexisting rights. New York Cent. R.R. v. White, 243 U.S. 188, 201 (New York workmen's compensation statute). The similarity between c. 670 and the workmen's compensation statutes, in the nature of their purposes and the means chosen to achieve them, also leads us to conclude that the reasonable and adequate substitute test is appropriate to apply here even if its application is not constitutionally required. We will, therefore, consider c. 670 in the light of a twofold test: the general test required by the due process clause of whether it bears a rational relation to a legitimate legislative objective, and the more particularized test for which the plaintiff argues — whether it provides a reasonable substitute for preexisting rights.

B. Does c. 670 Bear a Rational Relation to a Legitimate Legislative Objective?

[The court then concluded that the individual provisions of chapter 670 withstand challenges under the due process clause, and that the statute taken as a whole did not deprive the plaintiff of his rights under the equal protection clause.]

C. Does c. 670 Provide a Reasonable Substitution for Prior Rights?

[The court then relied heavily on New York Central R.R. v. White, supra at page 1027; which had sustained the workers' compensation bargain of broader coverage with smaller damages.]

It is immediately apparent that c. 670 alters prior legal rights to a much less drastic extent than did the act involved in the *White* case. However, the overall difference in status quo effected by c. 670 may be described in part in much the same terms as those used by the court in the *White* case.

In considering the effect of c. 670, we cannot view it from the point of view of plaintiffs and defendants, for these are not preexisting categories as are the employers and employees affected by a workmen's compensation act. Every driver is a potential plaintiff and, equally, a potential defendant. The desired effect of c. 670 on all motorists alike is initially to make available to them compulsory insurance at lower rates due to the savings to insurance companies in administrative expenses and total payments which are expected to follow from c. 670. If injury occurs on the road, motorists are assured of the probability of quick and efficient payment of the first $2,000 of defined losses incurred. In cases of accidents in which the motorist was not negligent, he avoids the uncertainty, delay and cost of a tort proceeding. He still retains the option of recovering more by litigation if he so wishes and the facts so warrant. Although c. 670 may also have the effect of depriving him of his damages for pain and suffering in such an instance, the exchange of rights involved with respect to the driver in an accident in which he was not negligent bears considerable resemblance to that effected by the statute in the *White* case with respect to employees.

This exchange of rights cannot be viewed in isolation, however, for non-negligent drivers are not a distinct class. To it must be added the effect of c. 670 on the driver in a case where he has been negligent or where negligence cannot be determined. In this situation, rather than no compensation for his own injuries, c. 670 accords him the same benefits he would have if he were non-negligent.[17] In addition, he is afforded immunity from liability to the extent other injured parties are eligible for benefits. And, just as his right to sue for pain and suffering is limited when he is non-negligent, so he is protected from comparable claims where he has been negligent. The effect of c. 670 on Massachusetts motorists thus is to provide benefits in return for affected rights at least as adequate as those provided to New York employers and employees in return for rights taken by the act in the *White* case.

It may be argued that c. 670 affects a second distinct class of persons, the pedestrian, and that the exchange of rights effected on this class must be considered separately from its effect on drivers. It is obvious, however, that all drivers are at some moment in time pedestrians. With this realization, the class of pedestrians as distinct from drivers is sharply reduced. Whether or not we define the class to include pedestrians who also drive, however, the effect of c. 670 on that class is no different from its effect on drivers. Pedestrians, too, may be negligent or non-negligent; they, too, are therefore afforded the certainty of prompt recovery of a limited amount and limited exemption from liability instead of the necessity of tort proceedings or no compensation at all and liability to an unlimited amount. The fact that the non-car

17. The day has long since passed when legal negligence in the automobile accident situation could be equated with moral culpability. The whole concept of negligence has in fact become something of a fiction, since in many cases fault cannot be meaningfully placed on any one of the parties more than on another. The new comparative negligence statute is a recognition of this inherent difficulty of assigning fault to one party only. The legally negligent driver is therefore morally as entitled to compensation as the other parties. It should be noted in addition that in defined cases where he is clearly culpable, the injured party is denied benefits under c. 670.

owner is not advantageously affected by lower insurance premiums by no means vitiates the adequacy of the exchange of rights as it operates on him. A similar analysis may be applied to any other nonmotorist who in a given instance happens to come within the scope of c. 670.

NOTES

1. *Constitutional issues.* Pinnick v. Cleary was the first major decision to uphold the constitutionality of automobile no-fault legislation. Similar statutes have also been upheld against constitutional attack, with the courts habitually relying a strong presumption in favor of the constitutionality of economic legislation, however unwise or even foolish it might be. See, e.g., Montgomery v. Daniels, 340 N.E.2d 444 (N.Y. 1975); Opinion of the Justices, 304 A.2d 881 (N.H. 1973). Where the no-fault schemes have been declared unconstitutional, courts have usually relied on the specific language of state constitutions and not on the general federal principles of the due process or equal protection clauses. Thus in Grace v. Howlett, 283 N.E.2d 474 (Ill. 1972), the Illinois Supreme Court struck down the state no-fault scheme as offending several state constitutional provisions, including one that required that no "special law" be passed when a "general law" could be made applicable. The court took pains to point out that this clause required the reviewing court to give greater scrutiny to legislation than would be called for under the federal equal protection clause. Likewise, the Florida court in Kluger v. White, 281 So. 2d 1 (Fla. 1973), sustained a challenge to the property no-fault provisions of the Florida law as violative of the state constitutional provisions guaranteeing that the courts "shall be open for redress of any injury." The clause was held applicable because the legislation did not provide any "reasonable alternative" remedy to protect the rights of individuals whose property was damaged or destroyed by the acts of another. Yet when the constitutionality of the personal injury provisions of the state no-fault law were challenged on general due process and equal protection grounds, the Florida court followed (without direct citation) the Massachusetts court and sustained the personal injury scheme in toto, except for that portion of the plan that allowed individuals to meet and cross the "tort threshold" with certain kinds of serious injuries, but not others.

2. *The varieties of the no-fault plan.* Although no-fault plans tend to share certain key features, most notably first-party compensation not based on fault, they differ among themselves on many important particulars that deal with limits, deductibles, options, the treatment of collateral sources, and the like. Thus, total benefits in New York can reach $50,000, subject to further limits on income loss and worker expenses,

which are payable to a level of $1,000 per month for a three-year pe-
riod. On the other hand, total benefits are sharply limited to $5,000 in
Connecticut. Kentucky provides for $10,000 in benefits, while Minne-
sota allows $20,000 for medical expenses and $10,000 for economic
losses. In some jurisdictions optional coverages may be purchased for
an additional premium. Pennsylvania, for example, allows optional
benefits of $100,000 for medical expenses, $2,500 per month to a maximum of $50,000 for lost income, and a $25,000 death benefit. This
bewildering array of plans resists any simple summarization or generalization, and the particulars in any event are often changed by legislation. For capsule summaries of the various auto no-fault plans see I.
Schermer, Automobile Liability Insurance ch. 14 (2d ed. 1994 rev.),
where it takes over 200 pages to outline the details of each plan presently in effect. See also 3 Harper, James and Gray, Torts §13.8 for a
selective summary of some key plan features.

   3. *Performance of the no-fault plans.* Given the wide range of no-fault
plans, it is very difficult to make any sensible assessment of how well
they have fared in practice. Overall, it seems, somewhat blandly, that
the dominant impression is that they have not done as well as their
supporters have hoped nor as badly as their detractors have feared. In
the political arena the massive push for automobile no-fault took place
in the early 1970s, and since then no new plans have been enacted,
although several have been repealed, and others (e.g., Florida, Massachusetts, and Pennsylvania) have undergone extensive reform since
their introduction. The system today is best described as one in steady-
state, with little current activity.

   On theoretical grounds, it has been argued that the adoption of a
no-fault system will increase accident levels by allowing careless drivers
to escape the consequences of their driving errors. Since each driver
knows that he may not be able to maintain a tort action for certain
injuries, more defensive driving may follow. But if the care substituted
is more costly than that which is no longer required, some net increase
in accidents should be expected. One systematic effort to trace this
argument is Elisabeth Landes, Insurance, Liability, and Accidents: A
Theoretical and Empirical Investigation of No-Fault Accidents, 25
J.L. & Econ. 49 (1982). This study concluded that for the years 1967 to
1976 "a medical expense threshold of $500 implies about a 4 percent
increase in fatal accident rates; a medical expense threshold of $1,500
implies an increase in fatal accidents of *more than 10 percent.*" Landes's
study adjusted the threshold dollar figure to take into account the differences in costs of medical services between states. In determining accident levels, she controlled for differences in age, race, and sex, as well
as for the reduction in driving levels attributable to gasoline prices. The
study did not, however, take expressly into account the major shifts in

tort liability (especially in products cases) that occurred over the same period, many of which allow recovery by careless drivers; nor did it control for the frequent changes in minimum drinking ages that also took place during the period. One further complication is that the passage of automobile no-fault insurance was accompanied by an insistence on compulsory *liability* insurance to motorists, which could have reduced the average quality of the drivers on the road. Is it ever possible to control for these factors? If not, how should states decide whether to adopt automobile no-fault insurance, or indeed any major institutional system, in the absence of accurate statistical information? For a reply to Landes see O'Connell and Levmore, A Reply to Landes: A Faulty Study of No-Fault's Effect on Fault, 48 Mo. L. Rev. 649 (1983).

The empirical evidence on the question is somewhat mixed. Thus Brown, Deterrence and No-Fault: The New Zealand Experience, 73 Cal. L. Rev. 976 (1985), which reports a steady decrease in the level of automobile fatalities after the introduction of the New Zealand accident compensation, adjusting for the number of registered vehicles and miles driven, but which could not take into account reductions in the speed limit and mandatory seat-belt and helmet laws. On the other hand, the evidence from Quebec suggested that bodily injuries increased by 26.3 percent, and fatalities by 6.8 percent, one year after the introduction of an extensive auto no-fault system, because of a reduction in care levels following the elimination of negligence liability. For a review of the evidence see Arlen, Compensation Systems and Efficient Deterrence, 52 Md. L. Rev. 1093, 1111-1115 (1993), arguing that the deterrent features of a tort liability system should not be ignored, and cannot be replicated by a scheme of direct government regulation.

4. *Litigation under automobile no-fault.* Unlike litigation under workers' compensation, the coverage disputes under automobile no-fault plans has been largely a humdrum affair. Representative of the disputes that fall on either side of the line are two Michigan cases. In Nickerson v. Citizens Mutual Ins. Co., 224 N.W.2d 896 (Mich. 1975), the plaintiff was walking in front of a stalled car that had been pushed to the side of the road when that car was struck from the rear by another vehicle. No-fault benefits were awarded even though plaintiff was not in strict physical contact with the vehicle when injured because he had been an occupant of the insured vehicle immediately prior to the injury. But in Dowdy v. Motorland Insurance Co, 293 N.W.2d 782, 783, 784 (Mich. App. 1980), the court denied coverage when a previously unloaded bundle of steel fell from its new perch and crushed the plaintiff's left ankle. The court affirmed a finding below "that the plaintiff did not sustain a bodily injury arising out of the ownership, maintenance or use of a parked vehicle within the meaning of the Michigan no-fault

statute. . . . Under the undisputed facts of the instant case, the plaintiff was not injured due to contact with any equipment permanently affixed to the vehicle, nor was the injury due to contact with property which was being lifted onto or lowered from the vehicle in the loading process."

See generally I. Schermer, Automobile Liability Insurance ch. 5 (2d ed. 1989).

5. The tort threshold. As of 1989 nine states — Arkansas, Delaware, Maryland, Oregon, Pennsylvania, South Carolina, South Dakota, Texas, and Virginia — were add-on states, in which the plaintiff's right to maintain a tort action was not limited by the adoption of the no-fault plan. In 16 other states, various thresholds were required before the tort action could be pursued. The various automobile no-fault provisions have different types of tort threshold. One type of threshold is simply monetary and provides that the injured party is entitled to enter the tort system so long as the medical costs of injury exceed the amount designated in the statute, which as of 1991 varied from a low of $400 in Connecticut to a high of $7,600 in Hawaii. Other states have what is known as a verbal threshold. In some states — Colorado, Georgia, Kansas, Kentucky, Minnesota, and Utah — permanent disfigurement is required. In others — Connecticut, Florida, and New Jersey — the verbal formula calls for permanent and significant disfigurement. New York requires significant disfigurement, while Massachusetts and North Carolina refer to "permanent and serious" disfigurement, and in Pennsylvania the requirement is more stringent still since "cosmetic disfigurement which is permanent, irreparable and severe" must be shown. See I. Schermer, Automobile Liability Insurance ch. 10 (2d ed. 1994 rev).

The choice of the type of tort threshold has an important effect on the overall operation of the no-fault system. Numerical thresholds act as magnets, and encourage parties (as with the workers' compensation system) to inflate their medical costs in order to obtain the keys to the tort kingdom. Verbal thresholds are much more immune from manipulation. Thus it appears that relatively few claims make it into the tort system over the strong verbal threshold that is found in New York, while in states like California that preserve the traditional tort system, many more personal injury cases make it into the tort system. As one measure of the difference, note that in 1989 for each 100 property damage claims there were 56 claims for bodily injury in California and only 11 in New York. For discussion of this and similar issues see O'Connell, Carroll, Horowitz, Abrahamse, Consumer Choice in the Auto Insurance Market, 52 Md. L. Rev. 1016 (1993). For an exhaustive survey of the evidence see S. Carroll, J. Kakalik, N. Pace and J. Adams, No-Fault Approaches to Compensating People Injured in Automobile Accidents (RAND 1991).

2. No-Fault Insurance for Medical and Product Injuries

The widespread adoption of automobile no-fault plans in the early 1970s spurred on proposals for the extension of no-fault plans into other areas of physical injury now governed by the tort law. Particular attention was paid to both medical malpractice and products liability as areas in which the stresses upon the tort system have been the greatest. Unlike automobile no-fault plans, these plans must all rely on the third-party coverage mechanisms that were originally championed by Ballantine for no-fault railway insurance. During the 1970s the break between the traditional tort law and its no-fault replacement was regarded as so significant that the initial case for a no-fault regime was put forward on an elective or voluntary basis. One such approach was described by O'Connell in Ending Insult to Injury: No-Fault Insurance for Products and Services 97 (1975):

> Any enterprise should be allowed to elect, if it chooses, to pay from then on for injuries it causes on a no-fault basis, thereby foreclosing claims based on fault or a defect. Under such an option, payment would be made regardless not only of lack of fault or defect on the payer's part but also, as under no-fault auto insurance and workers' compensation, regardless of any fault on the victim's part. In other words, elective no-fault liability would be true no-fault insurance, with the fault of neither the injurer nor the injured having a bearing on payment. The enterprise would be allowed to select all or, if it chose, just certain risks of personal injury it typically creates, for which it could agree to pay for out-of-pocket losses when injury results from those risks. To the extent — and only to the extent — a guarantee of no-fault payment exists at the time of the accident, as under no-fault auto or workers' compensation insurance, no claim based on fault or a defect would be allowed against the party electing to be covered under no-fault liability insurance.

The idea has met with little support, even by those in favor of automobile no-fault insurance. One objection is that it is difficult for a manufacturer of a product (especially a component product) to give notice to the ultimate user or consumer that it has elected coverage under the plan; and it is wholly impossible with bystander injuries. In addition, it is difficult to coordinate this new no-fault coverage with tort liability, workers' compensation, and first-party insurance. Most important, the plan has been attacked on the ground that without any concept of product defect, it is impossible to determine which injuries should be attributable to which products. Thus, Professor Blum has asked *who* should provide coverage when a worker wearing slippery shoes falls off a well-constructed ladder after drinking a few beers. Blum, Review of O'Connell's *Ending Insult to Injury*, 43 U. Chi. L. Rev. 217 (1975).

While proposals for no-fault coverage have largely disappeared in the products area they have had a more lasting influence in the area of medical and hospital malpractice. As before, the basic no-fault bargain is broader coverage and lower administrative expenses in exchange for reduced coverage awards. In dealing with these health-related injuries, the no-fault proposals have been made on both an elective and a mandatory basis. And, as before, the central question has been the revised and expanded definition of a compensable event.

Epstein, Medical Malpractice: The Case for Contract
1 Am. B. Found. Res. J. 87, 141-147 (1976)

MEDICAL NO-FAULT INSURANCE

There are reasons to believe that [this medical no-fault] program, even on a voluntary basis, will not produce the desired results, as the difficulties with the proposed no-fault system make the case against its adoption decisive. The first and perhaps most important problem raised by the no-fault system concerns the definition of the "compensable event." . . .

There is no sharp and clear distinction between harms attributable to the prior condition of the patient and those attributable to the care of treatment received while he was a patient. But the problem goes deeper than simple demarcation. . . Consider, for example, the kinds of determinations required when it is alleged that a physician has not availed himself of the appropriate diagnostic tests; take, for example, the "not giving" of the pressure test in Helling v. Carey [supra at page 225]. Do we award compensation or not? The answer to that question is not as important as the nature of the inquiry that it demands. To make the causal attribution between the patient's injury and the non-act of the defendant, we must decide what duty was incumbent upon the physician. Is it a simple case of "not doing" or is it a case of an omission or a failure to perform? If there is a duty to run the test, it seems that the harm can be attributed to the physician's failure to treat; that is, if the glaucoma could have been treated after detection. How do we decide the duty question? It is the same question raised by Helling v. Carey, and the general no-fault scheme can itself be faulted on the ground that it will require the new administrative board to set the appropriate standard of care for physicians. That is a question very close to if not indistinguishable from the one that must be decided by the courts today under the negligence rules for medical malpractice . . . The question of fault cannot be avoided. . . .

We must also consider the questions of multiple causation that are sure to recur when patients are seen or treated by more than one physician. What does the system require, for example, if the plaintiff in Helling v. Carey had several ophthalmologists, none of whom gave the pressure test for glaucoma? . . .

Ours is a tale with two morals. First, the inquiry into causation is never easy and is often bound up with the determination of fault in some sense of that term. Second, so long as there are limits to the scope of coverage there will always be the need for case-by-case adjudication at the border, no matter where that border has been set. Indeed, the crucial shift from medical malpractice to medical accident is apt to increase exponentially the administrative pressures in determining the boundaries of coverage. At common law, once the defendant establishes reasonable care there is no longer need to examine causal questions. The absence of negligence is a barrier against further inquiry. Yet with the proposed no-fault schemes, that proposition will no longer apply and there will be no threshold question which, if resolved in one direction, eliminates the causal inquiry in its entirety. Instead we will be forced to find "the" cause of harm in cases in which multiple causation will prove the rule, and we may well have to reverse the normal causal priorities by attaching legal responsibility to the physician's treatment rather than to the condition that necessitated that treatment in the first place. On these causal questions, the no-fault system will insure only that we are in the worst of all possible worlds. Fault will be excluded initially from the coverage section, so that *every* patient whose condition has deteriorated after he has seen a physician will have at least a colorable claim for compensation. Then fault will reappear in some attenuated form when the damages, if any, are determined in the case.

The interpretative difficulties with these broad coverage definitions have brought forth other efforts to deal with the definition of compensable event. Professors Havighurst and Tancredi, "Medical Adversity Insurance" — A No-Fault Approach to Medical Malpractice and Quality Assurance, The Milbank Memorial Fund Quarterly/Health and Society (Spring 1973), reprinted in 613 Ins. L.J. 69 (1974) and developed at greater length in Commission of Medical Professional Liability of the ABA, Designated Compensable Event System: A Feasibility Study (1979) proposed attacking this problem by drawing up a long list of designated compensable events (or DCEs) after extensive consultation with medical and surgical specialists. Supporters of the plan readily admit that the scheme in question requires an enormous front-end cost since it is necessary to define the list of compensable events not only for each procedure, but also for each separate specialist who is involved in the provision of medical or surgical care. Thus they recognize that it is not at all likely that a surgeon should be responsible for the same set of adverse occurrences as, for example, the hospital in which the operation takes place.

The exact criteria by which particular adverse effects are treated as compensable events escape any easy summarization. But, at the risk of some inaccuracy, it can be said that an event should be compensable if it satisfies two separate tests. First, the adverse consequence in question should be generally avoidable by the use of sound medical procedures. In effect, some version of the negligence standard is applied not to particular cases, as in ordinary malpractice litigation, but to broad classes of events, which are then compensated without regard to physician fault in the particular case. The second criterion seeks to make compensable the adverse consequences of pair procedures. Thus, if the associated adverse consequences of one course of treatment are compensable events, then there is additional reason to treat as compensable the adverse consequences associated with a substitute treatment, since no physician should have an incentive to use the inferior treatment to avoid liability.

The use of the DCE system has been criticized in P. Danzon, Medical Malpractice: Theory, Evidence and Public Policy 217-219 (1985). Danzon notes that in addition to the causation problems outlined above, the proposed no-fault system creates odd incentives for both doctor and patient. Thus, if it is unclear whether a certain adverse outcome is a DCE, the patient would argue that it is not a DCE only if her chances of recovering damages for medical malpractice were high. The physician would argue for no-fault coverage to limit liability when the negligence was palpable. The no-fault system also would have odd incentive effects on the physician's willingness to treat. "If physicians' no-fault insurance premiums were not experience-rated, incentives for injury avoidance would be reduced. But if they were experience-rated, as proposed under the DCE plan, or if the time costs of defending claims were high, then physicians would have incentives to avoid high-risk patients or high-risk procedures unless they could charge commensurately higher fees to cover the higher liability risk" — a prospect that might be limited by the ever-greater restrictions on physicians' fees imposed under both the Medicare and Medicaid programs.

Weiler, The Case for No-Fault Medical Liability
52 Md. L. Rev. 908, 919, 928-929, 931 (1993)

Under my no-fault liability proposal, patients would be entitled to compensation whenever they suffer a significant disability caused by their medical treatment — irrespective of whether the treatment was negligent. Compensation would be paid periodically for the actual financial losses — health care costs and lost earnings — that are not covered by either private or public insurance, and modest additional amounts would be paid to severely injured patients to help them adjust to their loss of enjoyment of life. The principal target of liability would not be the individual doctor but the *hospital* or other health care organization under whose auspices the patient had been treated; such enterprise-based liability would extend to all care rendered by doctors affiliated with the hospitals. Administration of this program would reside in a specialized and accessible tribunal that would utilize explicit criteria and specialists to decide what events are compensable and what payments are appropriate for nonmeasurable losses. . . .

Unquestionably it is harder to prove that medical treatment caused a patient's injury than to prove that a car caused injury to a driver or pedestrian, or that employment caused injury to a worker. Unlike the driver who gets into a car or the employee who goes to work, a patient who enters a hospital may already be suffering from an underlying illness which itself may be the cause of the eventual disability. . . . Indeed, it is evident that some of an injured patient's medical expenses and lost earnings must be attributable to her initial unhealthy condition and its treatment and expected recuperation. Determining whether medical treatment worsened the original condition — and estimating any corresponding financial loss — requires delicate judgments about what transpired inside the hospital, and how that treatment altered the path that the patient's condition would otherwise have been expected to follow.

The problem is more complex than simply identifying, factually, which losses — for example, which episodes of lost work and earnings — were caused by medical treatment. Equally difficult are the *conceptual* issues concerning which losses are properly attributable to a specialized program of liability for health care injuries. Doctors often undertake such traumatic medical procedures, for example, radical chemotherapy for cancer, because intervention is necessary to arrest and cure a disease that is even more life-threatening than the treatment. Consequently, in assessing liability it is not enough to decide that a particular disability episode was the consequence of — that it arose of and in the course of — medical treatment. The disability must fall outside the range of intended or expected consequences of the treatment. . . .

[Weiler then addresses the questions of missed diagnosis and other omissions.]

Our notion of causation must be broadened, therefore to include what might be called *policy* causation — what should have happened — as opposed to purely *factual* causation — what did or might have happened. If causation is so broad, however, we must ensure that a self-contained patient-compensation program does not eventually become a general social insurance for every disability or fatality that medical care did not prevent or cure. To prevent this, one must establish criteria specifying what *should* have happened, thereby distinguished the properly compensable cases from the noncompensable ones. The easy cases are those in which treatment was impossible. If a disease cannot be cured, it should be the responsibility of broad-based social insurance, public or private, to pay for the victim's losses from such diseases. This role should not be assigned to a patient-compensation program, which is supposed to saddle the health care system with only those costs of disabling injuries that are attributable to its own operations.

Suppose however, that the disease could have been cured if it had been treated by the top practitioner in one of the major teaching hospitals of the world. Under that *optimal care* standard, compensation should be available for any disability that could probably have been avoided by some doctor, somewhere. That would likely be a very expensive compensation program. To avoid going that far — by choosing to compensate only disabilities that would have been cured by the *reasonable care* expected from the average doctor in an actual practice setting — it is necessary to reinstate the fault principle as the basis for compensating at least this category of iatrogenic injuries.

NOTE

The Injured Infant Act. As of 1994 no state has yet decided to adopt any comprehensive medical no-fault insurance, although the matter is again under fresh consideration both in the United States and Canada. The no-fault approach has, however, been enacted into law for one class of injuries in the Virginia Birth-Related Neurological Injury Compensation Act, Va. Code Ann. §§38.2-5000-5001 (Michie Supp. 1989). Under the statute "a birth-related neurological injury" means

> injury to the brain or spinal cord of an infant caused by the deprivation of oxygen or mechanical injury occurring in the course of labor, delivery or resuscitation in the immediate post-delivery period in a hospital which renders the infant permanently nonambulatory, aphasic, incontinent, and in need of assistance in all phases of daily living.

The statute then specifies that participation in the program is elective with physicians and hospitals, who do not (it appears) have to notify their patients as to whether they have opted for the coverage. Once in the program, the statute specifies compensation formulas that closely track those under the workers' compensation statutes in their refusal to award damages for pain and suffering and in their limiting of lost future earnings to 50 percent of the average weekly wage. More notably, perhaps, is the funding mechanism of the statute, which imposes certain fixed charges on participating hospitals ($50 per delivery, with a maximum of $150,000 per year) and covered physicians ($5,000 per year), both of which are fixed by statute and which cannot be raised by administrative action in subsequent years. In addition the statute imposes a general tax on most physicians of $250 per year even if they do not participate in the fund. In the event that these charges are insufficient to cover the costs of running the program on a sound financial basis, the resulting shortfall is to be covered by a general levy placed on all insurance companies in the state, regardless of whether they sell medical malpractice coverage.

At the time of its passage, the Virginia statute raised concerns with respect to both its coverage and its financing provisions. On the former, it may well be difficult in practice to distinguish babies who are injured during delivery from those, for example, whose mothers took cocaine or other substances (legal or illegal), especially during early pregnancy. On the latter, there is a serious question as to whether it is appropriate to tax unrelated lines of insurance to solve the problem of affordability of coverage in the obstetrical area, given the distortions created in other sectors of the economy. For an attack on the statute on these grounds see Epstein, Market and Regulatory Approaches to Medical Malpractice: The Virginia Obstetrical No-Fault Statute, 74 Va. L. Rev. 1451 (1988); for a qualified defense of the statute see O'Connell, Pragmatic Constraints on Market Approaches: A Response to Professor Epstein, 74 Va. L. Rev. 1487 (1988).

In practice the major difficulty with the statute appears to hinge on the word "permanently." The difference between the benefits under the no-fault scheme and those under the tort law are so large that many lawyers who are faced with claims of this sort have chosen not to file for claims under the system at or shortly after the time of birth. By making that choice, the lawyers preserve the right to recover tort damages should the condition improve over time, since the statute of limitations does not run until the infant obtains his majority. And if the infant dies, or if the condition does become permanent, then it might still be possible to claim at least some compensation from the fund. The delay in filing claims makes it difficult for the state to anticipate the eventual payouts from the fund, which in turn has made it more difficult to set the appropriate levels of taxation. As of this writing, however, the statute has not been amended to eliminate the term "permanently" from the definition, or to shorten the time in which claims must be filed or tort actions brought.

D. THE NEW ZEALAND PLAN

The New Zealand Accident Compensation Act (as amended by the Accident Compensation Amendment (no. 2) Act 1973) is the most radical no-fault plan. Under it, virtually all actions for personal injuries or death have been abolished and their place taken by a comprehensive insurance scheme that awards benefits to all persons who suffer "personal injury by accident," where the words "by accident" were meant largely to exclude compensation for death or injury caused by sickness. The original outline and justifications for the plan were detailed in the Report of the Royal Commission of Inquiry, Compensation for Personal Injury in New Zealand, more commonly known as the Woodhouse Report, after the commission's chairman, Justice Owen Woodhouse. This section contains three parts: the first gives some excerpts from the Woodhouse Report; the second, some of the central provisions of the act; and the third, some of the important decisions of New Zealand's Accident Commission. For a convenient summary of the original Accident Compensation Act, which largely adopts the recommendation of the Woodhouse Report, see Harris, Accident Compensation in New Zealand: A Comprehensive Insurance System, 37 Mod. L. Rev. 361 (1974). See also Franklin, Personal Injury Accidents in New Zealand and the United States: Some Striking Similarities, 27 Stan. L. Rev. 653 (1975). For an exhaustive account of the New Zealand plan and the unsuccessful efforts to secure its introduction in Australia see G. Palmer, Compensation for Incapacity: A Study of Law and Social Change in New Zealand and Australia (1979). And for an account of the 1992 Amendments to the Act, see Miller, An Analysis and Critique of the 1992 Changes to New Zealand's Accident Compensation Scheme, 52 Md. L. Rev. 1070 (1993).

Report of the Royal Commission of Inquiry, Compensation for Personal Injury in New Zealand
19-22, 26, 113-114 (1967)

1. The Problem — One hundred thousand workers are injured in industrial accidents every year. By good fortune most escape with minor incapacities, but many are left with grievous personal problems. Directly or indirectly the cost to the nation for work injuries alone now approaches $50 million annually. . . .

The negligence action is a form of lottery. In the case of industrial accidents it provides inconsistent solutions for less than one victim in every hundred. The Workers' Compensation Act provides meagre compensation for workers, but only if their injury occurred at their work. The Social Security Act will assist with the pressing needs of those who remain, provided they can meet the means test. All others are left to fend for themselves.

Such a fragmented and capricious response to a social problem which cries out for co-ordinated and comprehensive treatment cannot be good enough. No economic reason justifies it. It is a situation which needs to be changed. This is the general theme of this report and the short summary of it which follows in the next 17 paragraphs.

2. Prevention, Rehabilitation, and Compensation — Injury arising from accident demands an attack on three fronts. The most important is obviously prevention. Next in importance is the obligation to rehabilitate the injured. Thirdly, there is the duty to compensate them for their losses. . . .

4. Five General Principles — We have made recommendations which recognize the inevitability of two fundamental principles —

First, no satisfactory system of injury insurance can be organized except on a basis of community responsibility;

Second, wisdom, logic, and justice all require that every citizen who is injured must be included, and equal losses must be given equal treatment. There must be comprehensive entitlement.

Moreover, always accepting the obvious need to produce something which the country can afford, it seemed necessary to lay down three further rules which, taken together with the two fundamental matters, would provide the framework for the new system. There must be complete rehabilitation. There must be real compensation — income-related benefits for income losses, payment throughout the whole period of incapacity, recognition of permanent bodily impairment as a loss in itself. And there must be administrative efficiency. The five guiding principles can be summarized as —

Community responsibility
Comprehensive entitlement
Complete rehabilitation
Real compensation
Administrative efficiency.

5. Community Responsibility — If the well-being of the work force is neglected, the economy must suffer injury. For this reason the nation has not merely a clear duty but also a vested interest in urging forward the physical and economic rehabilitation of every adult citizen whose activities bear upon the general welfare. This is the plain answer to any who might query the responsibility of the community in the matter. Of course, the injured worker himself has a moral claim, and further a more material claim based upon his earlier contribution, or his readiness to contribute to the national product. But the whole community has a very real stake in the matter. There is nothing new in this idea. It is something which for 30 years in New Zealand has been recognized for every citizen in the country in the area of medical and health services.

6. Injury, not Cause, is the Issue — Once the principle of community responsibility is recognized the principle of comprehensive entitlement follows automatically. Few would attempt to argue that injured workers

should be treated by society in different ways depending upon the cause of injury. Unless economic reasons demanded it the protection and remedy society might have to offer could not in justice be concentrated upon a single type of accident to the exclusion of others. With the admirable exception of the health services this has occurred in the past. There has been such concentration upon the risks faced by men during the working day that the considerable hazards they must face during the rest of each 24 hours (particularly on every road in the country) have been virtually disregarded. But workers do not change their status at 5 p.m., and if injured on the highway or at home they are the same men, and their needs and the country's need of them are unchanged.

7. The Self-employed and the Housewives — Exactly similar considerations clearly apply to every other gainfully employed person such as independent contractors and others who are self employed. The same considerations must apply, also, to the women in the population who as housewives make it possible for the productive work to be done. The need is for an integrated solution with comprehensive entitlement for every man and woman, and coverage in respect of every type of accident. This is the central recommendation of our Report.

8. Incentive — Incentive must be the driving purpose of any effective scheme. Incentive offered by effective rehabilitation to get well; incentive to return to work by leaving to each man a fair margin for independent effort; incentive which is not restricted by averaging benefits or begrudging help for long-term incapacities. Real compensation must be the aim, tailored to the severity of the injury and to the needs of citizens at all levels of employment and every normal level of income. By the avoidance of easy help for the minor problem the major effort can be made where it is really needed (and the few real passengers discouraged). By such means the system will be able to provide a thrust and purpose for each individual which will never justify the gibe of paternalism; instead it will be recognized as a return on personal investment.

9. The Cost — It will be asked, we do not doubt, whether we have kept in mind the need to balance the ideal with the practical. Even if the country were entirely free from current economic pressures, the money argument would weigh heavily upon an inquiry concerned, as this is, with systems of social insurance. The proposals we make for unifying and widening the scope of present arrangements must, of course, pass the economic test. And although difficulty has arisen from a dearth of statistical information, our proposals do this. In fact it seems that in overall terms the rationalization put forward avoids new large expenditures and yet permits at the same time greatly increased relief where it is needed most — for the losses which are greatest. That such a result is possible may seem surprising. The reason has been hidden in the past by its very simplicity. The great number of minor claims

have absorbed the great part of the funds at the expense of those whose injuries and needs have been most pressing. The various calculations are contained in Appendix 9. . . .

17. Sickness and Disease — It may be asked how incapacity arising from sickness and disease can be left aside. In logic there is no answer. A man overcome by ill health is no more able to work and no less afflicted than his neighbour hit by a car. In the industrial field certain diseases are included already. But logic on this occasion must give way to other considerations. First, it might be thought unwise to attempt one massive leap when two considered steps can be taken. Second, the urgent need is to co-ordinate the unrelated systems at present working in the injury field. Third, there is a virtual absence of the statistical signposting which alone can demonstrate the feasibility of the further move. And finally, the proposals now put forward for injury leave the way entirely open for sickness to follow whenever the relevant decision is taken.

18. Summary — On the basis of the principles outlined, the scheme proposed —

would provide immediate compensation without proof of fault for every injured person, regardless of his or her fault, and whether the accident occurred in the factory, on the highway, or in the home;

would entitle that person to compensation both for permanent physical disability and also for income losses on an income-related basis;

would provide for regular adjustment in the level of payment to accord with variations in the value of money;

would provide benefits, if necessary, for life, and in certain circumstances they would be commutable in whole or in part to lump sum payments;

would lift the present weekly maximum rate of compensation to $120 and thus safeguard the interests of persons on every normal level of income;

would be geared to urge forward their physical and vocational rehabilitation;

and in all these ways it would provide them with effective insurance for all the risks of the day. If the scheme can be said to have a single purpose it is 24-hour insurance for every member of the work force, and for the housewives who sustain them.

XVIII — CONTINGENCIES TO BE COVERED

289.   GENERAL PRINCIPLE

(a) The general basis for protection should be bodily injury by accident which is undesigned and unexpected so far as the person injured is concerned, but to the exclusion of incapacities arising from sickness or disease.

(b) No system of compensation or damages is able to avoid all the "hard" cases. In defining the area of protection the aim should be clarity and certainty and the avoidance of future dispute or disappointment.

(c) We recommend that, in general, protection should be afforded in respect of injury conditions which fall within the categories of external cause of injury classified as Numbers E800 to E999 in the International Classification of Diseases with the exception of categories E970 to E979 (suicide) and E985 (judicial execution) and perhaps some categories of therapeutic misadventure or late complications of therapeutic procedures (E950-E959).

(d) Incapacity arising from such injuries should be protected when the injury resulted from an unexpected or undesigned external cause, including exposure to the elements; or unusual and material physical strain or poisoning; or following upon some voluntary act in an emergency.   .

(e) On the other hand incapacities should be excluded which resulted from a condition of disease or sickness; or a sudden physiological change in the course of disease or sickness; or a physiological event occurring during activity which itself was normal and uneventful.

(f) Injury which has been deliberately self-inflicted should not be the subject of compensation.

(g) The issue of drawing a line between injury by accident and sickness or disease is a mixed question of law and medicine. The recommended approach to the matter by means of the International Classification of Diseases is a new one which may enable both professions to work more certainly at the boundary. We make the further recommendation, therefore, that a small group of medical and legal experts be appointed to study the question.

290. SICKNESS AND DISEASE

(a) It is possible to argue that if incapacity arising from accidental injury is to be the subject of comprehensive community insurance then interruption of work for reasons of sickness or unemployment, or other causes which cannot be guarded against should equally be included.

(b) We are able to understand the logic of the argument, but the proposal we now put forward is far-reaching and is designed to remedy a situation which at present is the subject of attention by unrelated processes which produce inconsistent and inadequate results. Moreover, there is a need for more statistical information in the area of sickness and disease before firm decisions could be taken as to the cost of a scheme which would embrace incapacities arising from these causes.

(c) Nevertheless certain industrial diseases are included within the scope of the present Workers' Compensation Act. For this practical reason we think they should remain within the protection to be afforded under the new scheme, but for work-connected injuries only, and upon the conditions at present laid down by the Workers' Compensation Act.

(d) In the past difficulties have arisen concerning damage to hearing as the result of repetitious noise. There is a good case for the inclusion of deafness within the scheme where the condition has resulted from noise. We recommend that deaf persons should have the advantage of a rebuttable presumption to the effect that the condition resulted from that cause. In the absence of evidence to the contrary the condition should then be regarded as an injury arising by accident.

Five years after the Woodhouse report, New Zealand passed the Accident Compensation Act of 1972 whose general provision supplied coverage for all persons "who suffer personal injury by accident." The definition of accident under the Act is generally decided from the point of view of the injured party, so that compensation is awarded to victims of intentional torts (including criminal assaults), as well as those who have been harmed in automobile accidents and product related injuries. Also covered under the statute are certain occupational diseases, including deafness. Otherwise disease and sickness as such are outside the scope of the statute. Given that decision, the most difficult question of coverage concerns medically related injuries, which include not only those for professional negligence but also for medical misadventure, whose definition has become a high art form under the statute.

Early on the 1972 Amendments to the original Accident Compensation Act simply extended coverage to "medical, surgical, dental or first aid misadventure," (§2(1)(a)(ii)) without further elaboration. The early case law on the subject then appeared to take the position that the adverse consequences of routine surgery or treatment should be treated as instances of medical misadventure compensable under the Act. In ACC v. Auckland Hospital Board, [1980] 2 N.Z.L.R. 748, 751, the court awarded damages to a claimant who became pregnant when a tubal ligation failed because the surgeon without negligence had been unable to close her fallopian tubes with his available forceps, since replaced with a more modern variety. The court found medical misadventure:

> It is in the nature of medical and surgical treatment that unexpected and abnormal consequences may follow to a greater or less degree depending upon the simplicity or sophistication of the treatment being undertaken. Where there is an unsatisfactory outcome of treatment which

can be classified as merely within the normal range of medical or surgical failure attendant upon even the most felicitous treatment, it could not be held to be a misadventure.

Similarly in MacDonald v. Accident Compensation Corp., [1985] 5 N.Z.A.R. 276, the plaintiff, who suffered a leaky bowel (a small but predictable risk) from a properly performed operation, was awarded compensation because the event had "turned out badly" and thus constituted a medical misadventure under the statute. For an account of recent developments see generally Gellhorn, Medical Malpractice Litigation (U.S.) — Medical Mishap Compensation (N.Z.), 73 Cornell L. Rev. 170 (1988).

Cases of this sort led in turn to the formulation of a two-page definition of the bad outcomes compensable in the context of medical treatment that raise all the difficulties found in connection with schemes for no-fault medical liability in this country. See Accident Rehabilitation and Compensation Insurance Act of 1992 No. 13, §1. That section first allows compensation for cases of "medical error," which in turn is defined to include both ordinary medical malpractice and "medical mishaps." A medical mishap in turn refers to "an adverse consequence of treatment by a registered health professional, properly given," that is both rare and severe.

The statute defines rare events as those adverse consequences that are likely to occur in less than one percent of the cases. It then goes on to exclude from the class of rare events those mishaps that occur in less than one percent of the cases in the general population, but which are likely to occur in more than one percent of the cases in a particular subclass of which the individual patient is a member, so long as the additional risks were disclosed to the patient or his guardian before treatment. In addition, the section also defines "severe " as adverse consequences that result in death or in 14 days of hospitalization or 28 days of total disability, or to persons otherwise entitled to receive "an independence allowance" (i.e. general supplemental benefits) under a general disability scheme.

The statute then excludes from coverage "normal" adverse reactions to treatment, cases where informed consent has not been obtained but where there is no physician negligence, cases of nonnegligent failures to diagnose disease or injury, and injuries that occur during clinical trials in which written consent for participation has been obtained. As with the American proposals, such as Weiler's, supra at page 1068, a substantial amount of negligence liability is thus brought back within the basic coverage scheme.

The administration of the New Zealand statute generally has had its ups and downs. While there is broad public support for the program in the abstract, the problem of cost containment has proved difficult to control. In 1988 the Commission's own report sought to explain the upsurge in cost by noting the increases in coverage had increased the time taken to resolve individual claims, and thus increased the number of older cases before the Commission. In 1981 these old cases accounted for $59,000,000 of a total of $127,000,000 in claims paid out (or about 47 percent of the total). By 1987 that total for old claims had risen to $153,000,000 of the $259,000,000 (or about 57 percent). The pie itself had more than doubled in size. See Law Commission, Personal Injury: Prevention and Recovery, Report No. 4, 16-22 (1988).

Politically a major political crisis was precipitated in December 1986 when an Order in Council imposed sharp premium increases on all class of participants, which averaged 192 percent for employers and 265 percent for self-employed enrollees. As is often the case with government programs, much of the concern was over the timing of the increase (it came just before Christmas), and with its large amount. In addition to the larger number of old claims, another reason for the high cost of the system was a shift in its internal accounting methods. Until 1982 the system was fully funded, which meant that the premiums collected in any single year were sufficient to supply all costs for claims arising in that year, including payments to be made in future years. In 1982 the system shifted to "pay as you go" financing, whereby only enough money was collected to pay the bills for that year, without reserving funds to pay the future claims associated with current accidents. By 1986 the accrued liabilities from past years became substantial enough to require the sudden and unexpected increase in premiums, and thus generated major administrative activity and political fallout. For a detailed account of the entire episode see Miller, The Future of New Zealand's Accident Compensation Scheme, 11 U. Haw. L. Rev. 1 (1989). For an analysis by New Zealand's National (or conservative) Minister of Labour, in charge of the program see W. F. Birch, Accident Compensation: A Fairer Scheme (1991). The sharp financial runups had taken place under the prior Labour government, which had been voted out of office in 1990. For an insider's account of the New Zealand experience see Palmer, New Zealand's Accident Compensation Scheme: Twenty Years On, 44 U. Toronto L. Rev. 223 (1994). What lessons does the New Zealand experience have in the United States context?

PART TWO
TORTS AGAINST
NONPHYSICAL INTERESTS

Chapter Fourteen
Defamation

A. INTRODUCTION

Of all the areas in the law of torts, defamation is perhaps the most difficult to organize and to understand. At one time defamation was, with only occasional statutory intervention, a common-law subject. Starting from the premise that an individual's reputation should be protected against false words that might hurt it, the common-law judges developed an elaborate set of rules to determine what statements were defamatory, when they were actionable, and what damages could be recovered for them.

The common law of defamation is still important today, but its universal supremacy has been effectively ended. The great transformation began with the epochal (no lesser word will do) Supreme Court decision in New York Times v. Sullivan, 376 U.S. 254 (1964). That case held that public officials could maintain actions in defamation only upon proof that the defendant's statement was made with "actual malice," defined by the Supreme Court to mean "with knowledge that it [the statement] was false or with reckless disregard of whether it was false or not." Malice in the sense of spite or ill-will harbored toward the plaintiff was rendered constitutionally irrelevant, at least in suits brought by public officials against media defendants. The actual malice rule was then extended to public figures in the important case of Curtis Publishing Co. v. Butts and Associated Press v. Walker, 388 U.S. 130 (1967). And the last of the great constitutional trilogy was Gertz v. Robert Welch, Inc., 418 U.S. 323 (1974), which in turn constitutionalized much of the law of defamation that relates to private plaintiffs, so that today each of the common-law rules (and any legislated variants) must be scrutinized under the First Amendment's guarantees of freedom of speech and of the press.

Today two key distinctions give shape to much of the law of defamation. Among plaintiffs the critical distinction is between public officials and public figures on the one hand, and ordinary private parties on the other. Among defendants the critical distinction is between media, both broadcast and print, and nonmedia defendants. The older common-law rules retain their dominance in cases brought by private plaintiffs against nonmedia defendants, for example, when an ex-employee claims to have been hurt by a false and malicious reference from the former employer. The new constitutional rules have their greatest sway when media defendants are charged with defamation by public officials or public figures. Likewise, a more limited form of constitutional protection, chiefly the requirement that negligence be proved, applies when private parties bring defamation actions against media defendants.

The constitutionalization of large portions of the law of defamation does not mark, however, the end of the traditional common-law inquiries. When public officials sue media defendants it is still necessary to determine whether the statements made were defamatory, whether they were true, and whether they caused damage to the plaintiff. A complex network of common-law issues therefore weaves its way through the modern constitutional fabric, so that the skilled defamation lawyer must be a master of two intersecting legal systems.

Despite the significant overlap between the common-law and constitutional inquiries, there are still powerful differences in basic orientation. Everyone agrees that the central task of the modern law of defamation is to reconcile the interest in reputation with the interest in freedom of speech. But no one thinks that the appropriate balance permits the complete protection of one interest to the exclusion of the other. The disagreement begins with the question of how the balance should be struck. Roughly speaking, the common law set its initial presumption in favor of reputation, while the Supreme Court has set its in favor of freedom of speech. As a result, defamation stands virtually alone in twentieth-century tort law. Every other major substantive area has expanded the plaintiff's right to recover, while in defamation the balance has shifted, and quite dramatically, in favor of the defendant.

The rapid changes in the law of defamation suggest two possible approaches to our subject matter. One would be to begin with New York Times v. Sullivan and the constitutional materials, working backwards to the common-law cases as the need arises. Such an approach has the virtue of placing us at the forefront of current controversy, but on balance it suffers from the greater handicap of requiring the student to form judgments about a most difficult area of law without the benefit of a (more or less) systematic presentation of its historical development, and without a sense of its special character and language. This chapter, for the sake of historical continuity and analytical clarity, begins at the beginning, dealing with the constitutional cases only after the substantive issues of defamation have been raised through the common-law cases. Our first concern, therefore, is with traditional issues, most of which retain some importance today: What is publication? What is defamation? What is the distinction between libel and slander, and why is it important? What is the basis of liability in defamation — strict liability, negligence, or intention to harm? What are general and special damages? What privileges are available to make defamatory statements in both the private and the public spheres, and are these privileges "absolute" or "defeasible"? Only after these issues are examined in detail is the constitutional material taken up, and then in its historical sequence. There is no neat division between the materials in different portions of the chapter, and the student may need to read them several times before they can be mastered.

B. PUBLICATION

Mims v. Metropolitan Life Insurance Co.
200 F.2d 800 (5th Cir. 1952)

STRUM, J. This is an action for libel brought by appellant against appellee, a corporation. The trial court entered summary judgment for defendant below on the ground, amongst others, that there was no publication of the alleged libel, from which judgment plaintiff appeals.

After about 32 years in the employ of defendant company as a branch manager and in other capacities, plaintiff was discharged. He suspected that the reason for this discharge was his refusal to contribute $1.00 to the campaign fund of Senator Taft of Ohio, as suggested in a chain letter sent by defendant's supervisor of agencies in New York to a group of local agency managers, one of whom in turn forwarded a copy to plaintiff. In February, 1950, plaintiff replied to the agent from whom he received the copy that he was not in sympathy with Senator Taft's policies, and declined to contribute.

When plaintiff's services were discontinued early in 1951, he wrote to his friend Senator Sparkman of Alabama, asking the latter to investigate the cause thereof. Pursuant to this request, and with plaintiff's knowledge and approval, Senator Sparkman directed a letter of inquiry to the defendant's president in New York, summarizing Senator Sparkman's understanding of the situation, and concluding: "I shall appreciate your attention to this matter and your giving me such information as you may care to give."

Defendant's president replied at length by letter, denying that plaintiff's discharge was in any way due to his refusal to contribute to the campaign fund, and stating in effect that it was due to inefficiency and to unsatisfactory production in the branch agencies of which plaintiff was manager from 1934 to 1951, so that it finally became necessary to discontinue plaintiff's services. The letter concludes that the only mistake made by defendant was in giving plaintiff so long an opportunity to make good, in the hope that he might improve. That letter is the basis of this suit. Plaintiff asserts that the statements therein are false, made with malice, and are therefore libelous and unprivileged.

The letter in question was dictated by the president of the defendant company to a company-employed stenographer, who wrote it. It was then mailed to Senator Sparkman in reply to his inquiry, and was received and read by him in Washington, D.C. Plaintiff relies on these circumstances as a sufficient publication to support an action for libel against the corporate defendant. It is not charged that the letter was seen by any other person.

Publication is essential to libel, and the publication must be made to one or more third parties. It is held in New York that dictation of a libelous letter by an individual to his own employee constitutes a sufficient publication in an action against the individual who dictated the letter, as in such circumstances the stenographer is a third party. Ostrowe v. Lee, 175 N.E. 505. . . .

But this is not such a case. Here, the letter was written by, and the action is against, a corporate defendant which can act only through its agents. Both the person who dictated the letter, and the stenographer who transcribed it, were employed by and acting for the corporation in the performance of a single corporate function, each supplying a component part thereof. When the letter was thus dictated and transcribed, it was not the act of two individuals acting separately. It was one corporate entity acting through two instrumentalities, neither of whom is a third party as respects the corporation, because each is acting as a part of the corporate entity in the performance of a single corporate act, the production of the letter, in the regular course of their duties.

This court has held that where the language complained of was communicated only by one corporate officer to another in the regular course of the corporation's business, such communication did not amount to a publication which would support an action for libel. Although there is one case to the contrary, the weight of authority in New York, where the letter in question was dictated and transcribed, is that mere dictation of libelous matter by a corporate officer or employee to a stenographer also employed by the corporation, in the regular course of the corporation's business, is not such a publication as will support an action for libel against the corporation itself, as in such circumstances the stenographer is not a third party. . . . This is not such a case as Kennedy v. James Butler, 156 N.E. 666, in which a corporate defendant communicated libelous matter to employees who had no part in producing the writing, thus exceeding the normal necessities of preparing the writing. If the language of this letter had been communicated to an employee of the corporation whose duties were unconnected with the process by which the letter was produced, such communication might be regarded as an actionable publication. But such is not the case here. Upon the authorities above cited, we hold that there was no sufficient publication of the letter in New York.

We have been directed to no decision squarely in point in the District of Columbia, as to whether writing the letter to Senator Sparkman, in the circumstances here involved, would constitute publication, although that jurisdiction follows the established general rule that it is essential to liability for either libel or slander that the defamatory language be communicated to some one other than the person defamed. It is the law of Alabama, however, which is the state of the forum in which this action was brought, and the state of which plaintiff is a citizen, that if the language complained of was uttered only to the complaining party or to his agent representing him in the matter discussed in the communication, it is not such a publication as will support an action for slander. Particularly is this true where the communication was solicited by the plaintiff or his agent. This rule prevails in many other jurisdictions, though there is authority to the contrary.

In making the inquiry above mentioned, Senator Sparkman was acting at the express request of plaintiff and with his approval — virtually as plaintiff's alter ego. Defendant's president replied to the person through whom the inquiry was thus made. The letter complained of having been solicited by plaintiff, through his representative Senator Sparkman, plaintiff thereby impliedly consented that defendant reply through the same representative. In contemplation of law it was a reply to the plaintiff himself. Without plaintiff's solicitation, the letter would not have been written. Upon the authorities above cited, we hold that there was no sufficient publication in the District of Columbia. The statements in the letter sued on do not exceed the scope of the inquiry so as to render the publication actionable because excessive, within the doctrine of Massee v. Williams, 6 Cir., 207 F. 222.

Plaintiff asserts that the language of the letter was uttered with malice, thus destroying the qualified privilege which would otherwise attend it. But we do not reach the matter of privilege or malice until publication has been established, which here has not been done.

Affirmed.

Rives, J., dissenting. There was publication, I think, in New York; and the evidence made a strong, if not compelling, case for the jury that there was also publication in Washington.

The fact that a corporation is an artificial entity, and therefore can act only through its agents, does not give it any added immunity for its torts. Corporate agents are just as much individual human beings as are the agents of natural persons. The same rules should apply to both. . . .

The controlling case in New York, it seems to me, should be Ostrowe v. Lee, 175 N.E. 505, where Judge Cardozo's opinion settled beyond dispute that publication results from dictation, where the stenographic notes have been transcribed. That case involved a stenographer employed by an individual, but there is nothing in Judge Cardozo's opinion to indicate that the rule would be different if the stenographer were employed by a corporation. . . .

It seems clear to me, however, that the matter did not concern merely the plaintiff but was of great public interest and that Senator Sparkman was properly acting not as a representative of the plaintiff, but in his capacity as a Senator of the United States. He was giving the defendant an opportunity to offer an explanation before referring the matter to the Senate Elections Subcommittee. Certainly the jury could have found that Senator Sparkman was not the plaintiff's alter ego. I therefore respectfully dissent.

NOTES

1. Publication, privilege, and the defamation triangle. The publication requirement has important structural significance for the law of defamation. Without this requirement it would be impossible in principle to distinguish defamation from ordinary cases of insult or deceit that might arise if the defendant uttered a false or abusive statement to the plaintiff directly. By introducing this publication requirement, moreover, it becomes clear that the tort of defamation protects only the interest in reputation, and not that of self-esteem. The publication requirement, moreover, accounts for much of the complexity of the tort of defamation, for it means that every defamation case involves at least three people — the plaintiff, defendant, and the third party to whom the statement was made. Indeed, in many cases defamation will involve more than this simple triangle, since it is possible to envision situations in which many defendants, including persons vicariously responsible for the actions of the speaker, defame many different persons to a large class of third parties, each of whom could stand in a different relation to both the plaintiff and the defendant.

In *Mims* could the plaintiff establish publication in an action against the defendant's president? If so, is the defendant corporation then vicariously liable?

How should *Mims* be decided under the Restatement (Second) of Torts, which provides:

§577. WHAT CONSTITUTES PUBLICATION
(1) Publication of defamatory matter is its communication intentionally or by a negligent act to one other than the person defamed.
(2) One who intentionally and unreasonably fails to remove defamatory matter that he knows to be exhibited on land or chattels in his possession or under his control is subject to liability for its continued publication.

Comment *e* to the section states:

The fact that the defamatory matter is communicated to an agent of the defamer does not prevent it from being a publication sufficient to constitute actionable defamation. The publication may be privileged, however, under the rule stated in §593. So too, the communication to a servant or agent of the person defamed is a publication although if the communication is in answer to a letter or a request from the other or his agent, the publication may not be actionable in defamation.

The Restatement position has generally been followed. See, e.g., Staples v. Bangor Hydro-Electric Co., 629 A.2d 601, 604 (Me. 1993), which concluded "that damage to one's reputation within the corporate community may be as devastating as that outside; and that the defense of qualified privilege provides adequate protection."

2. *Publication by default.* Section 577(2) is vividly illustrated by Heller v. Bianco, 244 P.2d 757, 758 (Cal. App. 1952). There the court stated the case thus: "Respondents were the proprietors of a public tavern and for the convenience of patrons maintained a toilet room for men on the wall of which there appeared on May 4, 1950, libelous matter indicating that appellant was an unchaste woman who indulged in illicit amatory ventures. The writer recommended that anyone interested should call a stated telephone number, which was the number of the telephone in appellant's home, and 'ask for Isabelle,' that being appellant's given name." Plaintiff was made aware of the writing by a telephone call from a stranger requesting a date. Her husband then phoned the bartender and said that he would give him thirty minutes to take the statement off the wall. The bartender replied that he was busy and alone and would do it when he got around to it. Plaintiff's husband, along with a policeman, then visited the tavern and found the writing still on the wall. The trial court nonsuited the plaintiff and the appellate court reversed, holding that knowingly permitting such matter to remain after a reasonable opportunity to remove it made the owner of the tavern guilty of a repub-

lication. Could a patron of the bar be charged with defamation if he saw the statement and did not remove it?

3. *Republication by plaintiff.* A particularly troublesome question arises when plaintiff himself shows the defamatory letter to others. Normally this is held to be a publication by the plaintiff himself. Sylvis v. Miller, 33 S.W. 921 (Tenn. 1896). Suppose, however, plaintiff is illiterate and asks another to read the letter to him. In Allen v. Wortham, 13 S.W. 73 (Ky. 1890), the court said that such exposure of the writing to a third person "was the proximate, and under the existing condition, inevitable, consequence of [defendant's] act of writing and sending, and he should therefore be held to have published it." When the defamatory letter was sent to plaintiff, who was blind and therefore showed it to another to have it read to him, the court held in Lane v. Schilling, 279 P. 267 (Or. 1929), that plaintiff had not himself published the libel. When the defamatory statement was shown only to the wife of the plaintiff, it was held, in Luick v. Driscoll, 41 N.E. 463 (Ind. App. 1895), to have been an adequate publication, although in Sesler v. Montgomery, 21 P. 185 (Cal. 1889), it was held not to have been.

4. *Compelled republication.* The issue of publication by the plaintiff has also assumed great importance in the context of employment recommendations. In Lewis v. Equitable Life Assur. Society, 389 N.W.2d 876, 888 (Minn. 1986), the defendant told the plaintiffs that they had been discharged for gross insubordination. This information was communicated by the plaintiffs to prospective employers in response to inquiries why they had left their previous employers. The court rejected the defendant's argument that the plaintiffs' defamation actions were barred by their own voluntary republication of the libel.

> The trend of modern authority persuades us that Minnesota law should recognize the doctrine of compelled self-publication. We acknowledge that recognition of this doctrine provides significant new basis for maintaining a cause of action for defamation and, as such, it should be cautiously applied. However, when properly applied, it need not substantially broaden the scope of liability for defamation. The doctrine of compelled self-publication does not more than hold the originator of the defamatory statement liable for damages caused by the statement where the originator knows, or should know, or circumstances whereby the defamed person has no reasonable means of avoiding publication of the statement or avoiding the resulting damages; in other words, in cases where the defamed person was compelled to publish the statement. In such circumstances, the damages are fairly viewed as the direct result of the originator's actions.

The court also imposed on plaintiffs a duty to mitigate damages, which was implemented by "requiring plaintiffs when they encounter a situation in which they are compelled to repeat a defamatory statement to take all reasonable steps to attempt to explain the true nature of the situation and to contradict the defamatory statement." Note that the defamation action in *Lewis* was paired with an action for wrongful discharge. The decision therefore could well put employers in a sharp dilemma. To dismiss without explanation opens them up to actions for wrongful dismissal. But to give the "for cause" explanation opens them up to defamation suits.

Lewis has not been well received in other jurisdictions. In DeLeon v. St. Joseph Hospital, Inc., 871 F.2d 1229, 1237 (4th Cir. 1989), the court, applying Maryland law, refused to apply the doctrine for the benefit of a physician who brought a defamation action against a hospital and its chief of surgery for statements that led to his denial of staff privileges. The plaintiff claimed that he would be forced to publish the negative decision of the hospital board in his search for other employment. Murnaghan, C.J., wrote that the doctrine was inadvisable because "otherwise, the theory of self-publication might visit liability for defamation on every Maryland employer each time a job applicant is rejected." The court also held that the action should be denied both because the reviews of plaintiff's work were prepared for internal use, and hence were not published to a "legally distinct third party," and because they were in any event subject to the ordinary qualified privilege.

5. *Republication privilege.* As a general rule the publication requirement in defamation cases makes good sense because a defendant normally has both knowledge of what is published and discretion over whether to make or withhold publication. In some contexts, however, neither of these assumptions holds true. A public library rarely knows the contents of its many holdings, and it could not refuse to check out a book that might contain some defamatory material. In order to protect these institutions against a myriad of law suits, "publication" receives a restrictive meaning. "Those who merely deliver or transmit defamatory material previously published by another will be considered to have published the material only if they knew, or had reason to know, that the material was defamatory. It is this rule that protects libraries and vendors of books, magazines and newspapers." Church of Scientology of Minnesota v. Minnesota State Medical Association Foundation, 264 N.W.2d 152, 156 (Minn. 1978).

6. *Mass publication.* At common law each communication of defamatory matter was a separate publication and therefore furnished the grounds for a separate cause of action. This rule has obviously required adjustment for mass publication of periodicals and books, and for broadcasts that are heard everywhere simultaneously. The so-called single publication rule now treats a mass publication as a single tortious act. However, difficult procedural and jurisdictional questions remain. For example, the statute of limitations for books has been fixed at the

time of initial publication. It is irrelevant that some buyers may read the defamation at a later date, or that other copies may be sold years after initial publication. See Gregoire v. G. P. Putnam's Sons, 81 N.E.2d 45 (N.Y. 1948). Today the publication question is controlled by Restatement (Second) of Torts §577A, which provides that "[a]ny one edition of a book or newspaper, or any one radio or television broadcast, exhibition of a motion picture or similar aggregate communication is a single publication" for which only one action in defamation may be maintained. Occasionally borderline cases arise, as in Advanced Training Systems v. Caswell Equipment Co., 352 N.W.2d 1, 7 (Minn. 1984), where the court refused to apply the single publication rule when the defendant distributed about 500-1000 copies of a technical bulletin to the trade over a three-year period, some copies of which contained false and defamatory comments about the plaintiff. The court held that the *Guidelines* book "was neither mass-produced nor mass-distributed" and hence not protected by the single publication rule.

The Restatement rule has been explicitly endorsed by the Supreme Court in Keeton v. Hustler Magazine, Inc., 465 U.S. 770, 777 (1984), a case involving the minimum "contacts" necessary to allow a state to assert its jurisdiction under the due process clause. In *Keeton* a resident of New York sued Hustler Magazine, incorporated in Ohio, in federal court in New Hampshire. Her sole purpose for bringing the suit there was to take advantage of New Hampshire's six-year statute of limitations, which had not yet run. Under the single publication rule, New Hampshire law allowed the plaintiff to recover for damage to her reputation not only in New Hampshire, but anywhere in the United States. Reversing the lower court, the Supreme Court held, first, that the regular circulation of the magazine in New Hampshire of from 10,000 to 15,000 copies established sufficient contacts for New Hampshire to assert its jurisdiction under the due process clause. Thereafter Rehnquist, J., praised the single publication rule as follows:

> New Hampshire also has a substantial interest in cooperating with other States, through the "single publication rule," to provide a forum for efficiently litigating all issues and damages arising out of libel in a unitary proceeding. The rule also reduces the potential serious drain of libel cases on judicial resources. It also serves to protect defendants from harassment resulting from multiple suits.

See generally Prosser, Interstate Publication, 51 Mich. L. Rev. 959 (1953), reprinted in Selected Topics of the Law of Torts 70 (1953).

C. FALSE OR DEFAMATORY STATEMENTS

Parmiter v. Coupland
151 Eng. Rep. 340, 342 (Ex. 1840)

PARKE, B.: A publication, without justification or lawful excuse, which is calculated to injure the reputation of another, by exposing him to hatred, contempt, or ridicule, is a libel.

American Law Institute, Restatement (Second) of Torts
(1977)

§559. DEFAMATORY COMMUNICATION DEFINED

A communication is defamatory if it tends so to harm the reputation of another as to lower him in the estimation of the community or to deter third persons from associating or dealing with him.

Draft Bill of the Faulks Committee on Defamation
(1976)

§1(1). Defamation shall consist of the publication to a third party of matter which in all the circumstances would be likely to affect a person adversely in the estimation of reasonable people generally.

Youssoupoff v. Metro-Goldwyn-Mayer Pictures
50 T.L.R. 581 (C.A. 1934)

SCRUTTON, L.J. An English company called Metro-Goldwyn-Mayer Pictures, Limited, which produces films circulated to the cinemas in this country, and which, according to its solicitor and chairman, is controlled by a firm of similar name in America, produced in this country a film which dealt with the alleged circumstances in which the influence of a man called Rasputin, an alleged monk, on the Czar and Czarina brought about the destruction of Russia. The film also dealt with the undoubted fact that Rasputin was ultimately murdered by persons who conceived him to be the evil genius of Russia.

In the course of that film a lady who had relations of affection with the person represented as the murderer was represented as having also had relations, which might be either relations of seduction or relations of rape, with the man Rasputin, a man of the worst possible character. When the film was produced in this country the plaintiff alleged that reasonable people would understand that she was the woman who was represented as having had these illicit relations. The plaintiff is a member of the Russian Royal House, Princess Irina Alexandrovna of Russia, and she was married after the incidents in question to a man who undoubtedly was one of the persons concerned in the killing of Rasputin. She issued a writ for libel against the English company. The English company declined to stop presenting the film. The action for libel proceeded. It was tried before one of the most experienced Judges on the Bench and a special jury, the constitutional tribunal for trying actions of libel, and, after several days' hearing, and after the jury had twice gone to see the film itself, they returned a verdict for the plaintiff with £25,000 damages.

The defendants now appeal from that verdict, and, as I understand the argument put before us by Sir William Jowitt and Mr. Wallington, for the defendants, it falls under three heads. First of all, they say that there was no evidence on which a jury, properly directed, could find that reasonable people would understand the Princess Natasha of the film to be Princess Irina, the plaintiff. That was the first point — the question of identification. Secondly, they say that if we are to take the Princess Natasha of the film to be identified with the Princess Irina, the plaintiff, there was no evidence on which a jury, reasonably directed, could find the film to be defamatory of the plaintiff. Thirdly, they say: "Assuming both of those points are decided against us, the damages were excessive. They were such as no jury, properly directed, could give in the circumstances of the case." . . .

[After an extensive discussion court disposed of the identification point as follows:] Therefore, on the first point, I come to the conclusion that we cannot possibly interfere with the verdict of the jury, who are the constitutional tribunal, when they think, as they obviously have thought that reasonable people, not all reasonable people but many reasonable people, would take the film representing Princess Natasha as also representing and referring to the plaintiff in the action, the Princess Irina. They would undoubtedly be helped to that by the defendants' own description of the film: "This concerns the destruction of an Empire brought about by the mad ambition of one man," obviously Rasputin. There is a list of eight principal characters given: "A few of the characters are still alive; the rest met with death by violence." Of the eight characters mentioned above the Czar, Czarina, Rasputin, the Czarevitch, and the Grand Duke Igor did meet death by violence. The rest are "still alive." The rest are Prince Chegodieff, Princess Natasha, and Dr. Remezov. Part of the defence in the action seems really to be: "It is quite true that the defendants said that this is a story of fact, but it is really all a fiction. We ought to have used, if we described it properly, the formula which is now put at the beginning of most novels: 'All circumstances in the novel are imaginary, and none of the characters are in real life.' " Of course, that would not have fitted in with the representation that it was really a representation of the relations of the Royal Family with Rasputin and the people who killed Rasputin. But the film is so far from the real facts in some cases, that one regrets that it was represented at all as being any genuine representation of the facts which had happened. However that may be on the first point, whether there was evidence on which the jury could reasonably find that a considerable number of reasonable people who saw the film would identify the Princess Natasha of the film with the Princess of Irina of Russia, I think that there was such evidence.

Now the second point is this, and it takes some courage to argue it, I think: suppose that the jury are right in treating Princess Irina, the plaintiff, as the Princess Natasha in real life, the film does not contain anything defamatory of her. There have been several formulae for describing what is defamation. The learned Judge at the trial uses the stock formula "calculated to bring into hatred, ridicule, or contempt," and because it has been clearly established some time ago that that is not exhaustive because there may be things which are defamatory which have nothing to do with hatred, ridicule, or contempt he adds the words "or causes them to be shunned or avoided." I, myself, have always preferred the language which Mr. Justice Cave used in Scott v. Sampson (8 Q.B.D. 491), a false statement about a man to his discredit. I think that satisfactorily expresses what has to be found. It has long been established that, with one modification, libel or no libel is for the jury, and the Court very rarely interferes with a finding by the jury that a particular statement is a libel or is no libel. The only exception is that it has been established with somewhat unfortunate results that a Judge may say: "No reasonable jury could possibly think this a libel, and consequently I will not ask the jury the question whether it is a libel or not." . . .

Fortunately, however, in this case we have not to deal with that exception because it is not suggested that the Judge in this case could have withdrawn the question of this libel from the jury on the point that it was not capable of a defamatory meaning. When you get the matter going to the jury it is extremely rare that the Court interferes with the finding of the jury whether a thing is libel or no libel. That has resulted from the action of Parliament in Mr. Fox's Libel Act in settling a dispute between Lord Mansfield and another eminent Judge as to the powers of the Judge in dealing with questions of libel. Lord Mansfield was of opinion that if a libel came before the Courts the Judge was to say whether it was a libel, and it was only for the jury to assess damages or to find guilty or not guilty on the direction. That was considered so contrary to the constitution with regard to juries that Parliament intervened and passed an Act, known as Mr. Fox's Libel Act, by which the matter was left to the jury. . . .

If libel alone is for the jury on those lines, why is it said that the jury in this case have come to a wrong decision? I desire to approach this argument seriously if I can, because I have great difficulty in approaching it seriously. I understand the principal thing argued by the defendants is this: "This procedure, as it contains some spoken words, is slander and not libel. Slanders are not as a rule actionable unless you prove special damage. No special damage was proved in this case. Consequently, the plaintiff must get within the exceptions in which slander is actionable without proof of special damage." One of those exceptions is the exception which is amplified in the Slander of Women Act, 1891 — namely, if the slander imports unchastity or adultery to a woman — and this is the argument as I understand it: "To say of a woman that she is raped does not impute unchastity." From that we get to this, which was solemnly put forward, that to say of a woman of good character that she has been ravished by a man of the worst possible character is not defamatory. That argument was solemnly presented to the jury, and I only wish the jury could have expressed, and that we could know, what they thought of it, because it seems to me to be one of the most legal arguments that were ever addressed to, I will not say a business body, but a sensible body.

That, really, as I understand it, is the argument upon which is based the contention that no reasonable jury could come to the conclusion that to say of a woman that she had been ravished by a man of very bad character when as a matter of fact she never saw the man at all and was never near him is not defamatory of the woman.

I really have no language to express my opinion of that argument. I therefore come, on the second point, to the view that there is no ground for interfering with the verdict of the jury (assuming the identification to stand, as I have assumed), that the words and the pictures in the film are defamatory of the lady whom they have found to be Princess Irina.

Then one comes to the third point, and that is the amount of damages. . . .

I find it quite impossible to say that the amount of damages here is such that no reasonable jury could have given it. There is the position of the plaintiff, a high position, although the Royal Family of Russia have fallen from their high position. There is the amount of publicity given by circulating the film through a large circle of cinemas to be seen at cheap prices by an enormous number of people. Apparently in this case there were performances for a week in more than 16, possibly 20, cinemas. Looking at all those matters, I come to the conclusion that, if the jury were properly directed, this Court cannot possibly interfere with the amount of the damages, even if any individual member of it, or all three members, had thought that if they had been on the jury they might have given a smaller sum. . . .

For these reasons, in my opinion, this appeal should be dismissed, with costs.

NOTES

1. Reputation in the eyes of which beholder? When defamatory statements have been made to a large number of persons, Scrutton, L.J., takes the position that the plaintiff's action can go forward as long as some significant fraction of the community has identified the plaintiff as the party defamed, and interprets the statement about the plaintiff as defamatory. One important issue concerns the identification of the relevant subclass of the population. There are three possibilities. The first is that it embraces persons drawn at random from the population. The second is that the defendant can identify that subgroup most sympathetic to its position. The third is that the plaintiff can identify that subgroup that is most sympathetic to her position. Before *Youssoupoff*, it appears that the English courts inclined to the second position, in the sense that words were regarded as defamatory only if they offended certain "right-minded" people. Thus, in Miller v. David, 9 L.R.C.P 118, 124 (1874), the plaintiff was fired from his job as a stonemason and apparently blacklisted in his trade after the defendant called him the "ringleader of the nine-hour system" who "had ruined a place by bringing about that system." The court refused to allow the action for defamation to go forward because it rejected as too "wide and general" the proposition that "a statement false and malicious made by one person in regard to another whereby that other might probably, under some circumstances, and at the hands of some persons, suffer damage, would, if the damage resulted in fact, support an action for defamation." As long as reasonable people as a group would not find the statement defamatory, the special audience — including fellow union workers or union members — to which it was directed was irrelevant.

In the United States today, however, the dominant view is that the plaintiff can prevail if plaintiff can point to any subgroup of the population that would find the statement defamatory. The key case is Peck v. Tribune Co., 214 U.S. 185, 189-190 (1909), in which an advertisement printed in the defendant's newspaper used the picture of the plaintiff, a nurse in real life, over the name of some other woman who had extolled the virtues of the malt whiskey promoted in the advertisement. Holmes, J., held, first, that the ad referred to the plaintiff, notwithstanding the incorrect name below the picture.

> The question, then, is whether the publication was a libel. It was held by the Circuit Court of Appeals not to be, or at most to entitle the plain-

tiff only to nominal damages, no special damage being alleged. It was pointed out that there was no general consensus of opinion that to drink whiskey is wrong or that to be a nurse is discreditable. It might have been added that very possibly giving a certificate and the use of one's portrait in aid of an advertisement would be regarded with irony, or a stronger feeling, only by a few. But it appears to us that such inquiries are beside the point. It may be that the action for libel is of little use, but while it is maintained it should be governed by the general principles of tort. If the advertisement obviously would hurt the plaintiff in the estimation of an important and respectable part of the community, liability is not a question of a majority vote.

  We know of no decision in which this matter is discussed upon principle. But obviously an unprivileged falsehood need not entail universal hatred to constitute a cause of action. No falsehood is thought about or even known by all the world. No conduct is hated by all. That it will be known by a large number and will lead an appreciable fraction of that number to regard the plaintiff with contempt is enough to do her practical harm.

Accordingly Holmes held that the question of defamation should have been left to the jury. The Restatement, following *Peck*, provides that a statement is defamatory only if it prejudices the plaintiff "in the eyes of a substantial and respectable minority" of the members of the community, but not if it simply offends "some individual or individuals with views sufficiently peculiar to regard as derogatory what the vast majority of persons regard as innocent." Restatement (Second) of Torts §559 comment *e*.

Illustration 3 of section 559 provides: "*A*, a member of a gang of hoodlums, writes to *B*, a fellow bandit, that *C*, a member of the gang, has reformed and is no longer to be trusted with the loot of the gang. *A* has not defamed *C*."

Is that result consistent with *Miller*? With *Peck*? Should the action be denied because there is no damage to reputation or because the illegality of the plaintiff's conduct defeats any prima facie case?

2. *Of and concerning the plaintiff. Youssoupoff* also raises the question of whether the defamatory statements are "of and concerning" the plaintiff when they do not refer to him by name. On this question the plaintiff typically bears the burden of proving that it does refer to him. At one time the law was quite rigorous and technical in its requirement that plaintiff plead, by what has usually been called the "colloquium," extraneous facts showing that the matter published referred to him; but that rule has generally been modified by both cases and statutes permitting plaintiff to allege in general terms that the matter published was "of and concerning" him.

In the modern context the question of "of and concerning" frequently arises with literary works in which authors take liberties in using real people as character models. Thus in Bindrim v. Mitchell, 155 Cal. Rptr. 29, 37 (Cal. App. 1979), the plaintiff, a licensed clinical psychologist, "used the so-called 'Nude Marathon' in group therapy as a means of helping people to shed their psychological inhibitions with the removal of their clothes." The defendant, an author, was given permission to attend the sessions, but only after she signed a written contract in which she agreed not to "disclose who has attended the workshop or what has transpired." Thereafter, in her novel "Touching," the defendant wrote about a similar nude encounter session in which the group leader, a Dr. Simon Herford, incorporating in the tale explicit vulgar language that the plaintiff had in fact not used. The jury rendered a verdict against Mitchell on a contract count and a libel count, and against her publisher on the libel count. On appeal the court rejected defendant's argument that the statements, even if defamatory, were not of and concerning the plaintiff.

> Appellants allege that the plaintiff failed to show he was identifiable as Simon Herford, relying on the fact that the character in "Touching" was described in the book as a "fat Santa Claus type with long white hair, white sideburns, a cherubic rosy face and rosy forearms," and that Bindrim was clean shaven and had short hair. . . . [T]he only differences between plaintiff and the Herford character in "Touching" were physical appearance and that Herford was a psychiatrist rather than psychologist. Otherwise, the character Simon Herford was very similar to the actual plaintiff. We cannot say . . . that no one who knew plaintiff Bindrim could reasonably identify him with the fictional character. Plaintiff was identified as Herford by several witnesses and plaintiff's own tape recordings of the marathon sessions show that the novel was based substantially on plaintiff's conduct in the nude marathon.

On the constitutional status of the "of and concerning" requirement see New York Times v. Sullivan, infra at page 1169. For a balanced discussion of the pros and cons of abolishing all liability for fiction see R. Posner, Law and Literature: A Misunderstood Relation 320-329 (1988).

3. *Group libel.* Yet another variation on this basic theme involves defamatory statements made about a group of which plaintiff is a member. Whether or not plaintiff succeeds in demonstrating a defamation "of and concerning" himself depends on the size of the group and on whether the defamatory comment speaks of all members of the group or merely of some. In general, recovery has been limited to cases in which the statement is made of all members of a small group. In Neiman-Marcus v. Lait, 13 F.R.D. 311 (S.D.N.Y. 1952), the defendants, in their book *U.S.A. Confidential,* charged that some models and saleswomen of the Neiman-Marcus store in Texas frequently served also as "call girls" and that most of the male salesmen were homosexuals. Suit was brought by 9 models (constituting the entire staff of models at the time of publication), by 15 salesmen out of a group of 25 at the time of publication, and by 30 saleswomen out of a group of 382. The defendants probably did not contest as to the 9 models, but moved to

dismiss as to the salesmen and saleswomen. The court denied the motion as to the salesmen, emphasizing that the group was small and that the characterization was of "most" of them; the court granted the motion to dismiss as to the saleswomen because of the size of the group, saying that "no reasonable man would take the writer seriously and conclude from the publication a reference to any individual saleswoman."

For much of this century there has been considerable concern over the calculated defamation of large groups such as Jews, Catholics, and blacks. Yet in these cases a defamation action has been consistently denied. Thus in Khalid Abdullah Tarig Al Mansour Faissal Fahd Al Talal v. Fanning, 506 F. Supp. 186, 187 (N.D. Cal. 1980), the plaintiff brought a class action on behalf of some 600 million Muslims, alleging that the film "Death of a Princess" was defamatory to all Muslims because "it depicts the public execution of a Saudi Arabian princess for adultery." The court denied the remedy, noting that "to permit an action to lie for the defamation of such a multitudinous group . . . would render meaningless the rights guaranteed by the First Amendment to explore issues of public import. Obviously, no member of a group that large has a tort remedy for damages, and independently of the group libel questions, there is a strong tradition against permitting the enjoining of defamation." This problem is carefully reviewed in Riesman, Democracy and Defamation: Control of Group Libel, 42 Colum. L. Rev. 727 (1942); Note, Statutory Prohibition of Group Defamation, 47 Colum. L. Rev. 595 (1947). See also Arcand v. Evening Call Pub. Co., 567 F.2d 1163 (1st Cir. 1977).

4. Defamation of character. Additional problems arise when the plaintiff is condemned not for committing some particular wrongful act but as having an immoral, unwholesome, or unattractive character. In Cooper v. Greeley, 1 Denio 347, 364-365 (N.Y. 1845), James Fenimore Cooper was held to have stated a cause of action for libel against Horace Greeley, who published the following statement in the New York *Tribune* about a libel suit that Cooper had proposed to bring against him and the newspaper: ". . . We have at all times stood ready to publish cheerfully any correction or contradiction he might choose to send us. He chooses to send none, but a suit for libel instead. So be it then — walk in Mr. Sheriff! There is one comfort to sustain us under this terrible dispensation. Mr. Cooper will have to bring his action to trial somewhere. He will not like to bring it in New York, for we are known here, nor in Otsego for he is known there."

The court construed the newspaper remark to mean that plaintiff had such a poor reputation in Otsego that he would not risk filing suit there. The defendants pleaded in justification that plaintiff had acquired in Otsego "the reputation of a proud, captious, censorious, arbitrary, dogmatical, malicious, illiberal, revengeful and litigious man, wherefore the said plaintiff was in bad repute in the said county of Otsego." The court allowed defendant's plea:

> This charge implies no particular act committed by the plaintiff. The defendants justify by averring the existence of the bad reputation, specifying in this plea the particular odious qualities which the plaintiff was reputed to possess, and averring that on that account he did not like to try his cause in that county. I think the plea is sufficient. I do not see in what other manner a justification could be interposed. In the nature of things, it would be impracticable for the defendants to spread upon paper the particular manifestations of pride, captiousness, malice, which go to form such a character, and to prove that his public reputation was the consequence of such conduct. Reputation is the estimate in which an individual is held by public fame in the place where he is known. And the existence of a good or bad reputation is, I think, a fact which may be directly put in issue.

Is it possible for a plaintiff to have so bad a reputation as to become "libel-proof"?

5. *Injurious falsehood.* Should a plaintiff be allowed to recover special damages for harm caused by false but *non*defamatory statements? In Cardiff v. Brooklyn Eagle, Inc., 75 N.Y.S.2d 222 (S. Ct. 1947), where defendant published an obituary of the living plaintiff, the court sustained a dismissal of the defamation action because the obituary did not expose the plaintiff to hatred, ridicule, or contempt. Had there been special damages, however, should the plaintiff have been allowed to recover, if not for defamation, then for a separate tort of injurious falsehood? As the large number of defamation suits that arise in commercial settings shows, defamation can be most devastating when it induces third parties not to do business with a plaintiff. The injury to the plaintiff is, of course, every bit as serious when the diversion of business is induced by injurious but nondefamatory falsehoods. This point is illustrated by Radcliffe v. Evans, [1892] 2 Q.B. 524. There, the defendant newspaper published of the plaintiff that he had ceased to carry on his business of engineer and boilermaker. The jury found specially that the words did not reflect on the plaintiff's character and were not libelous. Judgment for plaintiff was affirmed, however, Bowen, L.J., saying: "That an action will lie for written or oral falsehoods, not actionable per se nor even defamatory, where they are maliciously published, where they are calculated in the ordinary course of things to produce, and where they do produce, actual damage, is established law. Such an action is not one of libel or of slander, but an action on the case for damage wilfully and intentionally done without just occasion or excuse, analogous to an action for slander of title."

If defamation is actionable without proof of malice, is there any reason to require proof of malice in injurious falsehood cases? Should damages for emotional distress be allowed in injurious falsehood cases?

See Prosser, Injurious Falsehood: The Basis of Liability, 59 Colum. L. Rev. 425 (1959).

Burton v. Crowell Publishing Co.
82 F.2d 154 (2d Cir. 1936)

L. HAND, J. This appeal arises upon a judgment dismissing a complaint for libel upon the pleadings. The complaint alleged that the defendant had published an advertisement — annexed and incorporated by reference — made up of text and photographs; that one of the photographs was "susceptible of being regarded as representing plaintiff as guilty of indecent exposure and as being a person physically deformed and mentally perverted"; that some of the text, read with the offending photograph, was "susceptible of being regarded as falsely representing plaintiff as an utterer of salacious and obscene language"; and finally that "by reason of the premises plaintiff has been subjected to frequent and conspicuous ridicule, scandal, reproach, scorn, and indignity." The advertisement was of "Camel" cigarettes; the plaintiff was a widely known gentleman steeplechaser, and the text quoted him as declaring that "Camel" cigarettes "restored" him after "a crowded business day." Two photographs were inserted; the larger, a picture of the plaintiff in riding shirt and breeches, seated apparently outside a paddock with a cigarette in one hand and a cap and whip in the other. This contained the legend, "Get a lift with a Camel"; neither it, nor the photograph, is charged as part of the libel, except as the legend may be read upon the other and offending photograph. That represented him coming from a race to be weighed in; he is carrying his saddle in front of him with his right hand under the pommel and his left under the cantle; the line of the seat is about twelve inches below his waist. Over the pommel hangs a stirrup; over the seat at his middle a white girth falls loosely in such a way that it seems to be attached to the plaintiff and not to the saddle. So regarded, the photograph becomes grotesque, monstrous, and obscene; and the legends, which without undue violence can be made to match, reinforce the ribald interpretation. That is the libel. The answer alleged that the plaintiff had posed for the photographs and been paid for their use as an advertisement; a reply that they had never been shown to the plaintiff after they were taken. On this showing the judge held that the advertisement did not hold the plaintiff up to the hatred, ridicule, or contempt of fair-minded people and that in any event he consented to its use and might not complain.

We dismiss at once so much of the complaint as alleged that the advertisement might be read to say that the plaintiff was deformed, or that he had indecently exposed himself, or was making obscene jokes by means of the legends. Nobody could be fatuous enough to believe any of these things; everybody would at once see that it was the camera, and the camera alone, that had made the unfortunate mistake. If the advertisement is a libel it is such in spite of the fact that it asserts nothing whatever about the plaintiff, even by the remotest implications. It does not profess to depict him as he is; it does not exaggerate any part of his person so as to suggest that he is deformed; it is patently an optical illusion, and carries its correction on its face as much as though it were a verbal utterance which expressly declared that it was false. It would be hard for words so guarded to carry any sting, but the same is not true of caricatures, and this is an example; for, notwithstanding all we have just said, it exposed the plaintiff to overwhelming ridicule. The contrast between the drawn and serious face and the accompanying fantastic and lewd deformity was so extravagant that, though utterly unfair, it in fact made of the plaintiff a preposterously ridiculous spectacle; and the obvious mistake only added to the amusement. Had such a picture been deliberately produced, surely every right-minded person would agree that he would have had a genuine grievance; and the effect is the same whether it is deliberate or not. Such a caricature affects a man's reputation, if by that is meant his position in the minds of others; the association so established may be beyond repair; he may become known indefinitely as the absurd victim of this unhappy mischance. Literally, therefore, the injury falls within the accepted rubric; it exposes the sufferer to "ridicule" and "contempt." Nevertheless, we have not been able to find very much in the books that is in point, for although it has long been recognized that pictures may be libels, and in some cases they have been caricatures, in nearly all they have impugned the plaintiff at least by implication, directly or indirectly uttering some falsehood about him. . . .

The defendant answers that every libel must affect the plaintiff's character; but if by "character" is meant those moral qualities which the word ordinarily includes, the statement is certainly untrue, for there are many libels which do not affect the reputation of the victim in any such way. . . . [The court then indicated that it had been held libel to call a man insane, to say that a white man has Negro blood, to say a man is "too educated to earn his living," or is "desperately poor," or is a eunuch, or has an infectious disease other than venereal, or that he is illegitimate, or has near relatives who are criminals, or that he was mistaken for "Jack Ketch," or of a woman that she was served with process in a bathtub. It continued:] It is indeed not true that all ridicule . . . or all disagreeable comment . . . is actionable; a man must not be too thin-skinned or a self-important prig; but this advertisement was more than what only a morbid person would not laugh off; the mortification, however ill-deserved, was a very substantial grievance.

A more plausible challenge is that a libel must be something that can be true or false, since truth is always a defense. It would follow that if, as we agree, the picture was a mistake on its face and declared nothing about the plaintiff, it was not a libel. We have been able to find very little on the point. In Dunlop v. Dunlop Rubber Co. (1920), 1 Irish Ch. & Ld. Com. 280, 290-292, the picture represented the plaintiff in foppish clothes, and the opinion seems to rely merely upon the contempt which that alone might have aroused, but those who saw it might have taken it to imply that the plaintiff was in fact a fop. In Zbyszko v. New York American, 239 N.Y.S. 411, however, though the decision certainly went far, nobody could possibly have read the picture as asserting anything which was in fact untrue; it was the mere association of the plaintiff with a gorilla that was thought to lower him in others' esteem. Nevertheless, although the question is almost tabula rasa, it seems to us that in principle there should be no doubt. The gravamen of the wrong in defamation is not so much the injury to reputation, measured by the opinions of others, as the feelings, that is, the repulsion or the light esteem, which those opinions engender. We are sensitive to the charge of murder only because our fellows deprecate it in most forms; but a headhunter, or an aboriginal American Indian, or a gangster, would regard such an accusation as a distinction, and during the Great War an "ace," a man who had killed five others, was held in high regard. Usually it is difficult to arouse feelings without expressing an opinion, or asserting a fact; and the common law has so much regard for truth that it excuses the utterance of anything that is true. But it is non sequitur to argue that whenever truth is not a defense, there can be no libel; that would invert the proper approach to the whole subject. In all wrongs we must first ascertain whether the interest invaded is one which the law will protect at all; that is indeed especially important in defamation, for the common law did not recognize all injuries to reputation, especially when the utterance was oral. But the interest here is by hypothesis one which the law does protect; the plaintiff has been substantially enough ridiculed to be in a position to complain. The defendant must therefore find some excuse, and truth would be an excuse if it could be pleaded. The only reason why the law makes truth a defense is not because a libel must be false, but because the utterance of truth is in all circumstances an interest paramount to reputation; it is like a privileged communication, which is privileged only because the law prefers it conditionally to reputation. When there is no such counterprevailing interest, there is no excuse; and that is the situation here. In conclusion therefore we hold that because the picture taken with the legends was calculated to expose the plaintiff to more than trivial ridicule, it was prima facie actionable; that the fact that it did not assume to state a fact or an opinion is irrelevant; and that in consequence the publication is actionable.

Finally, the plaintiff's consent to the use of the photographs for which he posed as an advertisement was not a consent to the use of the offending photograph; he had no reason to anticipate that the lens would so distort his appearance. If the defendant wished to fix him with responsibility for whatever the camera might turn out, the result should have been shown him before publication. Possibly anyone who chooses to stir such a controversy in a court cannot have been very sensitive originally, but that is a consideration for the jury, which, if ever justified, is justified in actions for defamation.

Judgment reversed; cause remanded for trial.

NOTES

1. *Defamation and truth.* What is the proper relationship between defamation and truth? Under the standard view of the law it is said that the prima facie case in defamation does not require a showing that the statement published is false. Instead, it is enough that the defendant published defamatory matter about ("of and concerning") the plaintiff that tends to lower the estimation of plaintiff in the eyes of third parties to whom it is directed. Truth is then regarded as an absolute defense to the defamation so published, a statement tantamount to an assertion that a statement is defamatory only if it is false. See Restatement (Second) of Torts §581A.

In their desire to protect reputation, common-law courts often read statements quite closely, rejecting the defense where there have been small and seemingly insignificant factual errors in the defendant's statement. One of the classic cases on the degree of detail with which truth must be proved is Sharpe v. Stevenson, 34 N.C. 348, 348 (1851). The headnote of this case reads in part: "In an action of slander (under our statute) for charging that the plaintiff had criminal intercourse with one *A.* at a particular time and place, the defendant cannot justify by showing that she had such intercourse with *A.* at another time and place." That result was criticized in Courtney, Absurdities of the Law of Slander and Libel, 36 Am. L. Rev. 552, 563 (1902), where the author observed: "A criminal abandon in the drawing-room as completely destroys all claim to a reputation for chastity as a lascivious embrace in the bushes." For the modern treatment of truth see Moldea v. New York Times, infra at page 1107, Philadelphia Newspapers v. Hepps, 475 U.S. 767, infra at page 1208.

2. *Statements known to be false.* In *Burton* Hand, J., suggested that statements made could be defamatory but neither true nor false. Since he treated truth as a justification (instead of treating falsity as part of the plaintiff's case), he held the defendants liable because they could not

show these statements were true. Perhaps a better way to understand the situation in *Burton* is to recognize that the picture was false, but that everyone knew it as such. When a picture tends nonetheless to bring the plaintiff into hatred, ridicule, and contempt, should it be actionable in defamation? To that question, Hand, J., answered in the affirmative. Fifty years later in Hustler Magazine v. Falwell, 485 U.S. 46 (1988), supra at page 90, the Supreme Court by implication took a very different view of the scope of the tort of defamation. There, the vicious nature of the defendant's parody rendered it intrinsically unbelievable and therefore led the jury to deny the plaintiff's libel claim.

Falwell has been followed with enthusiasm in lower court decisions that have found *deliberate* parody is outside the scope of defamation on the ground that no one could believe it true. Thus in Dworkin v. Hustler Magazine, Inc., 867 F.2d 1188, 1191, 1193-1194 (9th Cir. 1989), the plaintiff, Andrea Dworkin, a prominent radical feminist was the target of a cartoon in Hustler magazine that "depicts two women engaged in a lesbian act of oral sex with the caption, 'You remind me so much of Andrea Dworkin, Edna. It's a dog-eat-dog world.' " In a subsequent issue "[o]ne photograph supposedly of a Jewish male, has a caption stating: 'While I'm teaching the little shiksa the joys of Yiddish, the Andrea Dworkin Fan Club begins some really *serious* suck-'n'-squat. Ready to give up the holy wafers for matzoh, yet, guys.' "

Hall, J., dispatched Dworkin's action for defamation on the ground that "*Hustler's* statements in this case are privileged opinion."

> An examination of a Hustler feature filed by appellants and amici Steinem and Brownmiller helps to illustrate this point. The work is entitled, "Hustler Interview: Gloria Steinem's Clit." This work contains a number of statements that by their terms can be read as statements of fact. Nevertheless, the article purports to be an interview of a body part, and therefore cannot be reasonably understood as making assertions of fact. By the same token, such phrases as "pus bloated walking sphincter," "wacko," or "bizarre paranoia" were not reasonably understood as attributions of physical or mental disease to the plaintiff in *Leidholt* [v. L.F.P. Inc., 860 F.2d 890, 894 (9th Cir. 1988)]. The statements about Dworkin contained in the Features are of the same ilk, and are not reasonably understood as statements of fact. Instead they are privileged opinion.
>
> Dworkin errs by limiting "opinion" to high-minded discourse. In this context, the word "opinion" is a label differentiating statements containing assertions of fact from those that do not. To differentiate among statements not of a factual nature would be at odds with fundamental principles of first amendment law, which seeks to facilitate the "search for truth" by encouraging "inhibited, robust, and wide open" public debate, *New York Times,* and is informed by the notion that "there is no such thing as a false idea." *Gertz.* We agree with counsel for Dworkin that this means that outrageous and outlandish statements are sometimes protected, but do not share their alarm over this prospect. . . . Ludicrous

statements are much less insidious and debilitating than falsities that bear the ring of truth. We have little doubt that the outrageous and the outlandish will be recognized for what they are.

Veeder, Freedom of Public Discussion
23 Harv. L. Rev. 413, 419-420 (1910)

The distinction is fundamental, then, between comment upon given facts and the direct assertion of facts. And the significance of the distinction is plain. If the facts are stated separately, and the comment appears as an inference drawn from those facts, any injustice that the imputation might occasion is practically negatived by reason of the fact that the reader has before him the grounds upon which the unfavorable inference is based. When the facts are truthfully stated, comment thereon, if unjust, will fall harmless, for the former furnish a ready antidote for the latter. The reader is then in a position to judge whether the critic has not by his unfairness or prejudice libelled himself rather than the object of his animadversion. But if a bare statement is made in terms of a fact, or if facts and comment are so intermingled that it is not clear what purports to be inference and what is claimed to be fact, the reader will naturally assume that the injurious statements are based upon adequate grounds known to the writer. In one case, the insufficiency of the facts to support the inference will lead fair-minded men to reject it; in the other, there is little, if any, room for the supposition that the injurious statement is other than a direct change of the fact, based upon grounds known to the writer, although not disclosed by him.

Moldea v. New York Times Co.
22 F.3d 310 (D.C. Cir. 1994)

Before: MIKVA, C.J., WALD and EDWARDS.

HARRY T. EDWARDS, CIRCUIT JUDGE. I often have been struck by Justice Stewart's concurring statement in Boys Markets, Inc. v. Retail Clerks Union, Local 770, 398 U.S. 235 (1970), a case in which the Court reconsidered and overruled an earlier decision. Justice Stewart remarked that, "[i]n these circumstances the temptation is strong to embark upon a lengthy personal apologia." This remark has special poignancy for me now, because it underscores the distress felt by a judge who, in grappling with a very difficult legal issue, concludes that he has made a mistake of judgment. Once discovered, confessing error is relatively easy. What is difficult is accepting the realization that, despite your best efforts, you may still fall prey to an error of judgment. Like Justice Stewart, I will take refuge in an aphorism of Justice Frankfurter: Wisdom too often never comes, and so one ought not to reject it merely because it comes late.

In Moldea v. New York Times Co., 15 F.3d 1137 (D.C. Cir. 1994) (*"Moldea (I)"*), this panel was faced with an appeal brought by author and investigative journalist Dan E. Moldea in connection with his defamation action against the New York Times Company, Inc. ("Times"). Moldea's lawsuit alleged that appellee libeled him in a book review (the "Times review" or "review") published in the New York Times Book Review, a supplement to the Sunday edition of its daily newspaper. The review stated that Moldea's book, Interference: How Organized Crime Influences Professional Football (*"Interference"*), was marred by "too much sloppy journalism," and offered a number of examples of the work's alleged journalistic shortcomings. The District Court granted summary judgment in favor of the Times, ruling that the review in question was not actionable as a matter of law because it consisted only of unverifiable statements of the reviewer's opinion, or of statements that no reasonable juror could find to be false. Moldea v. New York Times Co., 793 F. Supp. 335 (D.D.C. 1992). In a 2- 1 decision, the panel reversed on the ground that some of the review's characterizations of Moldea's book were potentially actionable because they were verifiable, and could not be held to be true as a matter of law.

After careful reconsideration, . . . we affirm the District Court's grant of summary judgment in favor of the Times.

I. BACKGROUND

The facts of this case are fully explained in *Moldea (I)*, so we need only briefly sketch them here. The instant case grows out of a highly negative review of *Interference* written by *New York Times* sportswriter Gerald Eskenazi, and published in the New York Times Book Review on September 3, 1989. Moldea contends that prior to the publication of this review he was a respected author and journalist, and that both he and his publisher anticipated that *Interference*, his fourth book, would be a success. Appellant alleges that the review's harsh critique of *Interference* destroyed the book's prospects for commercial success, and effectively ended his career as a writer as well, because he is now unable to interest other publishers in his work. Appellant also claims that, because of the review, he can no longer obtain bookings for lectures and other public appearances, activities which formerly provided him with significant income.

The plaintiff's suit for defamation focused on three statements in the review:

> But there is too much sloppy journalism to trust the bulk of this book's 512 pages — including its whopping 64 pages of footnotes.
>
> Mr. Moldea tells as well of Mr. Namath's "guaranteeing" a victory in Super Bowl III shortly after a sinister meeting in a bar with a member of the opposition, Lou Michaels, the Baltimore Colts' place-kicker. The truth is that the pair almost came to blows after they both had been drinking; and Mr. Namath's well-publicized "guarantee" came about quite innocently at a Miami Touchdown Club dinner when a fan asked him if he thought the Jets had a chance. "We'll win. I guarantee it," Mr. Namath replied.
>
> [Moldea] revives the discredited notion that Carroll Rosenbloom, the ornery owner of the Rams, who had a penchant for gambling, met foul play when he drowned in Florida 10 years ago.

II. DISCUSSION

A. THE IMPORTANCE OF CONTEXT

Moldea (I) noted that, "under the established case law, our analysis of this case is not altered by the fact that the challenged statements appeared in a 'book review' rather than in a hard news story." This statement is correct insofar as it suggests that there is no per se exemption from defamation for book reviews. Even the Times concedes this point in its Petition for Rehearing. A writer may not commit libel at will merely by labelling his work a "review." *Moldea (I)* is short-sighted, however, in failing to take account of the fact that the challenged statements were evaluations of a literary work which appeared in a forum in which readers expect to find such evaluations. As the Supreme Court has recognized, writers must be given some leeway to offer "rational interpretation" of ambiguous sources. See Masson v. The New Yorker Magazine, Inc., 501 U.S. 496 (1991). Thus, when a reviewer offers commentary that is tied to the work being reviewed, and that is a supportable interpretation of the author's work, that interpretation does not present a verifiable issue of fact that can be actionable in defamation.

The fundamental framework established in *Moldea (I)* for defamation actions is sound, and we do not modify it in this decision. As we stated in our initial opinion, the Supreme Court's decision in Milkovich v. Lorain Journal Co., 497 U.S. 1 (1990), and this court's decision in White v. Fraternal Order of Police, 909 F.2d 512 (D.C. Cir. 1990), make clear that there is no wholesale exemption from liability in defamation for statements of "opinion." Instead, statements of opinion can be actionable if they imply a provably false fact, or rely upon stated facts that are provably false.

In *Milkovich,* the Supreme Court rejected the argument that an accusation of perjury was nonactionable merely because it was offered as the writer's "opinion." In that case, a high school wrestling coach argued that an Ohio newspaper libeled him by printing a column which alleged that he had perjured himself in his testimony to a state court concerning his role in an altercation between his team and an opposing squad at a wrestling match. The column stated that: "Anyone who attended the meet . . . knows in his heart that Milkovich . . . lied at the hearing." Although the statements at issue in *Milkovich* appeared in an "opinion column" in a newspaper sports section, the Court found no relevance in this fact in reaching its decision, apparently because an accusation of perjury is not the sort of discourse that even arguably is the usual province of such columns. Sports columnists frequently offer intemperate denunciations of coaches' play-calling or strategy, and readers know this and presumably take such railings with a grain of salt; but an accusation of criminal conduct is a classic libel, and so *Milkovich* did not even pause to assess the effect that the column's context may have had on those who read it.

In *Moldea (I),* this court observed that *Milkovich* made no mention of the fact that the statements at issue in that case appeared in a sports column, and took that fact to mean that context was irrelevant in the instant case. We now recognize, however, as has the First Circuit, that *Milkovich* did not disavow the importance of context, but simply "discounted it in the circumstances of that case." Phantom Touring, Inc. v. Affiliated Publications, 953 F.2d 724, 729 n. 9 (1st Cir. 1992) . . . This conclusion is compelled by the logic of two Supreme Court cases expressly reaffirmed in *Milkovich,* and by the Court's decision in *Masson,* rendered the following term.

First, *Milkovich* reaffirmed the vitality of Greenbelt Cooperative Publishing Association v. Bresler, 398 U.S. 6 (1970), and Letter Carriers v. Austin, 418 U.S. 264 (1974). In *Bresler,* a real estate developer had engaged in negotiations with a city council for a zoning variance, while simultaneously negotiating with the city over other land that the city wished to purchase from him. A local newspaper account stated that some people had characterized the developer's tactics as "blackmail," and the developer sued for libel. The Court rejected the developer's argument that "blackmail" implied criminal activity, noting that "the word 'blackmail' in these circumstances was not slander when spoken. . . ." In *Letter Carriers,* the Court held that the use of the word "traitor" to define a "scab" in the context of a labor dispute could not be the basis for a defamation action. Both *Bresler* and *Letter Carriers* rely in large part on the notion that the speech at issue in each case was intended as hyperbole; however, this fact reinforces the importance of context, because it is in part the settings of the speech in question that makes their hyperbolic nature apparent, and which helps determine the way in which the intended audience will receive them. Thus, the "lusty and imaginative expression of the contempt felt by union members" for a "scab" may lawfully find hyperbolic expression during a strike, because the context assures that no reader could understand the epithet "traitor" to be a charge that the "scab" has committed the criminal offense of treason.

Second, *Masson,* handed down in the term following *Milkovich,* is further evidence that the Supreme Court has not abandoned the consideration of context in defamation actions. In *Masson,* the Court addressed the question whether a writer's alteration of quotations attributed to the subject of an interview could establish the "actual malice" required for a defamation suit by a public figure. *Masson* observed that whether quotations will be interpreted by readers as the actual statements of a speaker depends on context — for example, whether there is "an acknowledgment that the work is a so-called docudrama or historical fiction, or that it recreates conversations from memory, not from recordings. . . ."

In Ollman v. Evans, 750 F.2d 970, 983 (D.C. Cir. 1984), we recognized that courts have long "considered the influence that . . . well-established *genres* of writing will have on the average reader." Given that *Milkovich* was decided against the backdrop of this settled principle, and that it expressly reaffirmed two of the Court's key precedents in this area, we are, on reflection, convinced that *Moldea (I)* erred in assuming that *Milkovich* abandoned the principle of looking to the context in which speech appears. The Court's decision in *Masson* appears to confirm this interpretation of *Milkovich.* While *Milkovich* could be interpreted as we read it in our initial decision, we are unwilling to assume that the Court meant to sweep away so much settled law without a clearer indication that this was indeed its intent.

B. RELEVANCE OF THE BOOK REVIEW CONTEXT

In contrast to the situation in *Milkovich,* the instant case involves a context, a book review, in which the allegedly libelous statements were evaluations quintessentially of a type readers expect to find in that genre. The challenged statements in the Times review consist solely of the reviewer's comments on a literary work, and therefore must be judged with an eye toward readers' expectations and understandings of book reviews. This would not be the case if, for example, the review stated or implied that *Interference* was a badly written book because its author was a drug dealer. In that situation, this case would parallel *Milkovich:* the reviewer would simply be employing the medium of a book review as a vehicle for what would be a garden-variety libel, and the review would thus potentially be actionable.

There is a long and rich history in our cultural and legal traditions of affording reviewers latitude to comment on literary and other works. The statements at issue in the instant case are assessments of a book, rather than direct assaults on Moldea's character, reputation, or competence as a journalist. While a bad review necessarily has the effect of injuring an author's reputation to some extent — sometimes to a devastating extent, as Moldea alleges is true here — criticism's long and impressive pedigree persuades us that, while a critic's latitude is not unlimited, he or she must be given the constitutional "breathing space" appropriate to the genre. *New York Times Co. v. Sullivan.*

We believe that the Times has suggested the appropriate standard for evaluating critical reviews: "The proper analysis would make commentary actionable only when the interpretations are *unsupportable by reference to the written work.*" (emphasis added). This "supportable interpretation" standard provides that a critic's interpretation must be rationally supportable by reference to the actual text he or she is evaluating, and thus would not immunize situations analogous to that presented in *Milkovich,* in which a writer launches a personal attack, rather than interpreting a book. This standard also establishes boundaries even for textual interpretation. A critic's statement must be a rational assessment or account of something the reviewer can point to *in the text,* or *omitted from the text,* being critiqued. For instance, if the Times review stated that *Interference* was a terrible book because it asserted that African-Americans make poor football coaches, that reading would be "unsupportable by reference to the written work," because nothing in Moldea's book even hints at this notion. In such a case, the usual inquiries as to libel would apply: a jury could determine that the review falsely characterized *Interference,* thereby libeling its author by portraying him as a racist (assuming the other elements of the case could be proved).

Our decision to apply the "supportable interpretation" standard to book reviews finds strong support in analogous decisions of the Supreme Court, all decided or reaffirmed after *Milkovich.* . . .

Finally, *Masson* itself noted that: "The protection for rational interpretation serves First Amendment principles by allowing an author the interpretive license that is necessary when relying upon ambiguous sources." *Masson* concluded that in order to state a claim for defamation based upon the alteration of direct quotations, a plaintiff must show that the alterations resulted in "a material change in the meaning conveyed by the statement." . . . *Masson* . . . recognized that some materials by their very nature require interpretation, and that the First Amendment affords latitude to those engaged in that task. Reasonable minds can and do differ as to how to interpret a literary work. Accordingly, as *Masson* counsels, we must allow a degree of "interpretive license."

C.   APPLICATION OF THE "SUPPORTABLE INTERPRETATION"
STANDARD TO THE TIMES REVIEW

[The Court then determined that the review's charge of "sloppy journalism" rests on the errors it purported to identify in the book. It then applied the "supportable interpretation" standard to these assignments of error, in particular to the quotations about Rosenbloom and Namath.]

Moldea discusses Rosenbloom's drowning in pages 319 through 326 of his book, closing his account with quoted observations from several of Rosenbloom's friends, who speculate that he was murdered. *Interference* later reveals, on page 360, that Moldea has located previously unknown photographs, taken at Rosenbloom's autopsy, which make clear that he "died in a tragic accident and was not murdered." As we held in *Moldea (I)*, a reasonable jury could conclude that the Times review's characterization of *Interference*'s portrayal of Rosenbloom's death was false, and that the reviewer's account of the book creates the misleading impression that Moldea inadequately investigated this story. However, given that *Interference* does not reveal that Rosenbloom's death was accidental until 35 pages after giving undeniably titillating hints of homicide, we cannot hold that a reviewer could not reasonably suggest that Moldea sought to "revive" the notion that Rosenbloom was murdered in order to build suspense before disproving that theory.

[Turning to the Namath passage] *Moldea (I)* concluded that a reasonable jury could find that Moldea did not describe the meeting as a "sinister" rendezvous, but rather made clear that the meeting was "quite accidental and even confrontational." *Interference* at 197. Even applying the "supportable interpretation" standard, this review passage is close to the line. *Interference* not only states that the Namath-Michaels meeting was "accidental," but on the same page quotes Michaels as saying "What we talked about had no relationship to the game," and quotes another player present at the meeting as confirming that " 'nothing technical' about the game was discussed." *Interference* at 197. The Times' petition for rehearing argues only that the review's characterization is supported by the fact that *Interference*'s description of the Namath-Michaels meeting appears in a chapter of the book largely devoted to probing allegations that there was something "suspicious" about Super Bowl III.

We are troubled by the "sinister meeting" passage, but are constrained to conclude that it does not give rise to an actionable claim. The review offered at least six observations to support the charge of "sloppy journalism": the five challenged passages, plus the unchallenged claim that Moldea made several spelling errors. At least five of these observations could not be proved false at trial, either because they are true, are supported opinion, are reasonable interpretations, or are not challenged in this suit. Moldea is left with only the "sinister meeting" passage as a possible basis for his defamation claim, and this is a very weak basis indeed. For one thing, the "sinister meeting" passage is not defamatory on its face, but rather is simply one of the "interpretations" offered in support of the review's assessment of Moldea's book. Furthermore, even without the support of the "sinister meeting" passage, the review's assertion that *Interference* is marred by "too much sloppy journalism" is (as a legal matter) "substantially true," and so is not actionable in defamation.

As *Moldea (I)* noted, "substantial truth" is a defense to defamation. "Slight inaccuracies of expression are immaterial provided that the defamatory charge is true in substance." Liberty Lobby v. Dow Jones, 838 F.2d at 1296 (citing Restatement (Second) of Torts §581A cmt. *f* (1977)). The Supreme Court explained this defense in *Masson* by noting that: "Minor inaccuracies do not amount to falsity so long as the substance, the gist, the sting, of the libelous charge be justified."

Liberty Lobby v. Anderson, 746 F.2d 1563 (D.C. Cir. 1984), vacated on other grounds, 477 U.S. 242 (1986), rejected the defendants' claim that the plaintiffs in that case were "libel-proof" because "unchallenged portions of [defendants'] articles attribute[d] to the [plaintiffs] characteristics so much worse than those attributed in the challenged portions, that the latter could not conceivably do any incremental damage." Then-Judge Scalia observed that:

> The law, however, proceeds upon the optimistic premise that there is a little bit of good in all of us — or perhaps upon the pessimistic assumption that no matter how bad someone is, he can always be worse. It is shameful that Benedict Arnold was a traitor; but he was not a shoplifter to boot, and one should not be able to make that charge while knowing its falsity with impunity."

However, the opinion goes on to note that:

> There may be validity to the proposition that at some point the erroneous attribution of incremental evidence of a character flaw of a particular type which is in any event amply established by the facts is not derogatory. If, for example, an individual is said to have been convicted of 35 burglaries, when the correct number is 34, it is not likely that the statement is actionable. That is so, however, not because the object of the remarks is "libel-proof," but because, since the essentially derogatory implication of the statement ("he is an habitual burglar") is correct, he has not been libeled.

This latter point is dispositive of the instant case.

The disputed "sinister meeting" passage in the Times review is not inherently defamatory — i.e., it is not like calling Benedict Arnold a "traitor" and a "shoplifter," to cite the example used in *Anderson*.

Rather, the discussion of the "sinister meeting" is but one of several interpretations of the book offered to support the claim of "sloppy journalism." As such, it does not come within the compass of "incremental harm." Because the review relies principally on statements that are true, supported opinions or supportable interpretations to justify the "sloppy journalism" assessment, we are constrained to find that it is substantially true and therefore not actionable.

So ordered.

NOTES

1. Mitior sensus. As the decision in *Moldea* indicates, one recurrent question in the law of defamation concerns the rules of construction applicable to ambiguous statements. The issue is an old one at common law. At one time, in actions for slander, the maxim was: "Sensus verborum est duplex, mitis et asper, et verba semper sunt accipienda in mitiore sensu." (Loosely translated: "When words have two meanings, lenient and severe, they will always be construed in the more lenient sense.") "To take a few illustrations, it was solemnly held in one case that a 'coiner' *might* mean an officer in the Mint; in another, the expression 'forger' *might* conceivably import no more than the honourable industry of the metal-worker. . . ." J. Bower, Actionable Defamation 332 (1908). Bower then recounted the equally bizarre origins of this bizarre rule:

> This curious doctrine originated at a period in the history of the English law of defamation when the devices employed by the courts of common law to recover their lost jurisdiction over actions of slander had achieved an embarrassing success, and similarly artificial methods had to be resorted to in order to keep within manageable bounds the ever rising flood of this species of litigation. The fact that the doctrine was never applied to libel, the courts not being burdened overmuch with actions of this description, betrays the opportunism of its origin, and so also does the fact that, as soon as the practical necessity for its application ceased to exist, the rule, like all other expedients "ad hoc," disappeared utterly. . . .

Although shades of mitior sensus have occasionally surfaced in modern American cases, the dominant trend, as expressed in Chapski v. Copley Press, 442 N.E.2d 195, 199 (1982), holds that

> a written or oral statement is to be considered in context, with the words and the implications therefrom given their natural and obvious meaning; if, as so construed, the statement may reasonably be innocently interpreted or reasonably be interpreted as referring to someone other than the plaintiff, it cannot be actionable per se. This preliminary

> determination is properly a question of law to be resolved by the court in
> the first instance; whether the publication was in fact understood to be
> defamatory or to refer to the plaintiff is a question for the jury should
> the initial determination be resolved in favor of the plaintiff.

The formulation in *Chapski* has proved influential in subsequent
cases. In Nasr v. Connecticut Gen. Life Ins. Co., 632 F. Supp. 1024, 1028
(N.D. Ill. 1986), the court refused to dismiss the plaintiff's action when
the defendant insurance company called the plaintiff physician a
"quack." "To the ordinary person a reference to a physician as a quack
can have only one connotation. When that reference is followed by the
further statement that the physician has a 'racket going on' in his practice, the meaning becomes clear: the physician is not very capable and
he is placing financial or other considerations ahead of his medical
judgment." Elsewhere, in Kelly v. Schmidberger, 806 F.2d 44 (2d Cir.
1986), it was held that the assertion that the plaintiffs, two priests involved in a religious dispute, "have conveniently placed the property
belonging to the Archbishop Lefebvre and the Society in their own
names" could support a defamatory meaning, namely the illegal conversion or theft of trust property for their own advantage.

2. Newspaper headlines. The effort to give defamatory statements works
in favor of the writers of newspaper reviews. But no similar indulgence
is shown to false statements contained in newspaper headlines, even
when they are corrected by qualifications buried in the body of the
text. A headline may be libelous even though the full story sufficiently
explains it. The rule was justified in Sprouse v. Clay Communication,
Inc., 211 S.E.2d 674, 686 (W. Va. 1975), where the court wrote:

> Generally, where the headline is of normal size and does not lead to a
> conclusion totally unsupported by the body of the story, both story and
> headline are to be considered together for their total impression. How-
> ever, where oversized headlines are published which reasonably lead the
> average reader to an entirely different conclusion than [sic] the facts
> recited in the body of the story, and where the plaintiff can demonstrate
> that it was the intent of the publisher to use such misleading headlines
> to create a false impression on the normal reader, the headlines may
> be considered separately with regard to whether a known falsehood was
> published.

See also Restatement (Second) of Torts §563, comment *d,* which notes
that the "context" of a defamatory newspaper headline does not "ordinarily" include the text of the article itself. For analysis see R. Smolla,
Defamation §4.07 (1989).

3. Fact and opinion: political disputation. The elusive line between fact
and opinion remains as important today as it has ever been, for while a
plaintiff may recover for false statements of fact upon proof of actual
malice, statements of opinion are protected by an absolute privilege.

Given its importance, it is not surprising that the line has been tested not only in book reviews, but in other contexts as well. Ollman v. Evans, 750 F.2d 970 (D.C. Cir. 1984), arose out of an Evans and Novak column in November 1978, called "A Marxist Professor's Intentions," that protested the planned move of the plaintiff, a Marxist, to the Department of Government and Politics at the University of Maryland. The column first attacked Ollman for his willingness to use the classroom as a forum to promote "revolution" and labeled him "an outspoken proponent of Marxist ideas." It then recounted how he had finished last of sixteen candidates for the Caucus for a New Political Science and described Ollman's principal book, "Alienation: Marx's Concept of Man in Capitalist Society," as a "ponderous tome." Thereafter, in the passage specifically challenged as defamatory, the column said:

> Such pamphleteering is hooted at by one political scientist in a major eastern university, whose scholarship and reputation as a liberal are well known. "Ollman has no status within the profession, but is a pure and simple activist," he said. Would he say that publicly? No chance of it. Our Academic culture does not permit the raising of such questions.

Starr, J., proposed the following four-part test to elucidate the constitutional distinction between fact and opinion.

> First, we will analyze the common usage or meaning of the specific language of the challenged statement itself. Our analysis of the specific language under scrutiny will be aimed at determining whether the statement has a precise core of meaning for which a consensus of understanding exists or, conversely, whether the statement is indefinite and ambiguous. Readers are, in our judgment, considerably less likely to infer facts from an indefinite or ambiguous statement than one with a commonly understood meaning. Second, we will consider the statement's verifiability — is the statement capable of being objectively characterized as true or false? Insofar as a statement lacks a plausible method of verification, a reasonable reader will not believe that the statement has specific factual content. And, in the setting of litigation, the trier of fact obliged in a defamation action to assess the truth of an unverifiable statement will have considerable difficulty returning a verdict based upon anything but speculation. Third, moving from the challenged language itself, we will consider the full context of the statement — the entire article or column, for example — inasmuch as other, unchallenged language surrounding the allegedly defamatory statement will influence the average reader's readiness to infer that a particular statement has factual content. Finally, we will consider the broader context or setting in which the statement appears. Different types of writing have, as we shall more fully see, widely varying social conventions which signal to the reader the likelihood of a statement's being either fact or opinion.
>
> After deciding that a particular statement is opinion rather than fact, courts often undertake a second mode of analysis before wrapping the statement in the mantle of the First Amendment's opinion privilege. Relying upon the Restatement (Second) of Torts §566, the courts consider

whether the opinion implies the existence of undisclosed facts as the basis for the opinion. If the opinion implied factual assertions, courts have held that it should not receive the benefit of First Amendment protection as an opinion.

We have no quarrel with the purpose of section 566. . . .

The reasonable reader who peruses an Evans and Novak column on the editorial or Op-Ed page is fully aware that the statements found there are not "hard" news like those printed on the front page or elsewhere in the news sections of the newspaper. Readers expect that columnists will make strong statements, sometimes phrased in a polemical manner that would hardly be considered balanced or fair elsewhere in the newspaper. That proposition is inherent in the very notion of an "Op-Ed page."

Bork, J., then wrote a strong concurring opinion that voiced his concerns with the onslaught of new libel actions, but expressed his impatience with "such things as four-factor frameworks, three-pronged tests, and two-tiered analyses" and urged a return to "first principles." "A judge who refuses to see new threats to an established constitutional value, and hence provides a crabbed interpretation that robs a provision of its full, fair and reasonable meaning, fails in his judicial duty." He then concluded that the column should be protected because "a damage award would have a heavily inhibiting effect upon the journalism of opinion."

4. Fact and opinion: restaurant reviews. The distinction between fact and opinion has also surfaced in the mysterious world of restaurant reviews. In Mr. Chow of New York v. Ste. Jour Azur, S. A., 759 F.2d 219, 227-228 (2d Cir. 1985), the defendant restaurant guide published a review (in French, of course) that castigated the plaintiff's restaurant because, inter alia, "It is impossible to have the basic condiments . . . on the table," "the sweet and sour pork contained more dough . . . than meat," "the green peppers . . . remained still frozen on the plate," and the Peking Duck "was made up in only one dish (instead of the traditional three)." Among the grounds raised in defense of the review was that it contained statements of opinion and not of fact. The jury was unpersuaded and awarded the plaintiff $20,000 in actual damages and $5,000,000 in punitive damages, which were sustained by the trial judge. On appeal the court applied the analysis of fact and opinion adopted by Starr, J., in *Ollman* and held that the statements made constituted protected statements of opinion. As part of its remarks, it observed that

> Restaurant reviews are also [like the Evans and Novak column] the well recognized home of opinion and comment. Indeed, "by its very nature, an article commenting upon the quality of a restaurant or its food, like a review of a play or movie, constitutes the opinion of the reviewer." . . . The natural function of the review is to convey the critic's opinion of the restaurant reviewed: the food, the service, the decor, the atmosphere, and so forth. Such matters are to a large extent controlled by

personal tastes. The average reader approaches a review with the knowledge that it contains only one person's views of the establishment. And importantly, "[a]s is essential in aesthetic criticism . . . the object of the judgment is available to the critic's audience." Appellee does not cite a single case that has found a restaurant review libelous. Appellants and *amici* on the other hand cite numerous decisions that have refused to do so. Although the rationale of each of these decisions is different, they all recognize to some extent that reviews, although they may be unkind, are not normally a breeding ground for successful libel actions.

The court then held that the statement about the Peking Duck was an assertion of fact. "The statement is not metaphorical or hyperbolic; it clearly is laden with factual content." Plaintiff's victory on the point was, however, bittersweet, because the false statement about the Peking Duck was found protected by the actual malice rule, applicable because the restaurant was a public figure.

What if the condiments were always on the table, the sweet and sour pork was encased in a thin, delicate dough, and the green peppers were cooked to a turn? Does it make a difference that customers are free to patronize the restaurant if none will spend $30 or more for a dinner after reading that review?

5. *Defamatory meaning in the Supreme Court.* As *Moldea* indicates, for media publications at least, the question of defamatory meaning has to be evaluated in light of the Supreme Court standards, given the constitutional requirements of the First Amendment. In *Milkovich,* 497 U.S. at 21, the Court held that the charge of being a liar was not protected as opinion:

> We are not persuaded that, in addition to these protections, an additional separate constitutional privilege for "opinion" is required to ensure the freedom of expression guaranteed by the First Amendment. The dispositive question in the present case then becomes whether or not a reasonable factfinder could conclude that the statements in the [defendant's] column could imply an assertion that petitioner Milkovich perjured himself in a judicial proceeding. We believe that this question must be answered in the affirmative. . . . This is not the sort of loose, figurative or hyperbolic language which would negate the impression that the writer was seriously maintaining petitioner committed the crime of perjury. Nor does the general tenor of the article negate this impression.

The Court then noted that the truth of the statement could be determined by making a comparison between the materials contained in the story and those found in the transcript of the original hearing.

Its most notable foray into the area, Masson v. New York Magazine, 501 U.S. 496, 502-503, 512-513 (1991), arose out of a bitter suit brought by Jeffrey Masson, a psychoanalyst who had worked with Anna Freud in London and who was the subject of an extensive and unflattering profile by Janet Malcolm in New Yorker Magazine. The chief bone of contention was a statement in the profile in which Masson was alleged to have described himself as an "intellectual gigolo." As Kennedy, J., put the matter, the dispute arose because this statement and several others in the profile had been apparently fabricated by Malcom and falsely attributed to Masson.

> Malcolm quoted a description by petitioner of his relationship with Eissler [a psychiatrist] and Anna Freud as follows:
>
>> Then I met a rather attractive older graduate student and I had an affair with her. One day, she took me to some art event, and she was sorry afterward. She said, "Well, it is very nice sleeping with you in your room, but you're the kind of person who should never leave the room — you're just a social embarrassment anywhere else, though you do fine in your own room." And you know, in their way, if not in so many words, Eissler and Anna Freud told me the same thing. They like me well enough "in my own room." They loved to hear from me what creeps and dolts analysts are. I was like an intellectual gigolo — you get your pleasure from him, but you don't take him out in public. . . . *In the Freud Archives.*
>
> The tape recordings contain the substance of petitioner's reference to his graduate student friend, but no suggestion that Eissler or Anna Freud considered him, or that he considered himself, an "intellectual gigolo." Instead, petitioner said:
>
>> They felt, in a sense, I was a private asset but a public liability. . . . They liked me when I was alone in their living room, and I could talk and chat and tell them the truth about things and they would tell me. But that I was, in a sense, much too junior within the hierarchy of analysis, for these important training analysts to be caught dead with me.

Kennedy J. then held that the fabricated quotations could be regarded as both false and defamatory.

> A self-condemnatory quotation may carry more force than criticism by another. It is against self-interest to admit one's own criminal liability, arrogance, or lack of integrity, and so all the more easy to credit when it happens. This principle underlies the elemental rule of evidence which permits the introduction of admissions, despite their hearsay character, because we assume "that persons do not make statements which are damaging to themselves unless satisfied for good reason that they are true. . . .
> The work at issue here, however, as with much journalistic writing, provides the reader no clue that the quotations are being used as a rhetorical device or to paraphrase the speaker's actual statements. To the contrary, the work purports to be nonfiction, the result of numerous interviews. At least a trier of fact could so conclude. The work contains lengthy quotations attributed to petitioner, and neither Malcolm nor her publishers indicate to the reader that the quotations are anything but the reproduction of actual conversations. Further, the work was published in The New Yorker, a magazine which at the relevant time seemed to enjoy a reputation for scrupulous factual accuracy. These factors would, or at least could, lead a reader to take the quotations at face value. A defendant may be able to argue to the jury that quotations should be viewed by the reader as nonliteral or reconstructions, but we conclude that a

trier of fact in this case could find that the reasonable reader would understand the quotations to be nearly verbatim reports of statements made by the subject.

The *Masson* case appears to have been brought to closure eleven years after the publication of the original New Yorker story, as a jury found that two of her statements were false, one of which was defamatory, but that none had been uttered with the actual malice necessary for awarding damages. For an account of the subdued ending to an epic struggle see David Margolick, *Psychoanalyst Loses Libel Suit Against New Yorker Reporter,* N.Y. Times, November 3, 1994, at A1.

D. LIBEL AND SLANDER

1. The Common-Law Distinction

The common law traditionally drew a distinction between libel and slander. Historically, libel took place when the defendant's defamation was embodied in some permanent form, such as a book or a picture, or even a wax sculpture. Even public shadowing to prevent an individual from testifying against the defendant has been regarded as a form of libel because "[a]ctual pursuit and public surveillance of person and home are suggestive of criminality fatal to public esteem and productive of public contempt and ridicule." Schultz v. Frankfort Marine Accident & Plate Glass Insurance Co., 139 N.W. 386, 390 (Wis. 1913).

Slander, for its part, consists primarily of false spoken words. But it is also recognized that "the use of a mere transitory gesture commonly understood as a substitute for spoken words, such as a nod of the head, a wave of the hand, or a sign of the fingers, is slander rather than libel." Restatement (Second) of Torts §568 comment *d.* More generally, Restatement (Second) of Torts §568(3) provides: "The area of dissemination, the deliberate and premeditated character of its publication and the persistence of defamation are factors to be considered in determining whether a publication is a libel rather than a slander."

The basic idea behind the libel-slander distinction is that the permanence of libel made it a more dangerous form of misconduct. Accordingly, libels were ordinarily actionable per se without proof of special damages, while slander was generally actionable only upon proof of special damages (e.g., a lost business arrangement), except if the slander fell into one of four basic categories:

a. Loathsome diseases. The presumption of damage has been confined to diseases that are not merely contagious but also loathsome, such as plague, leprosy, and venereal disease, and therefore merit social ostracism. How should AIDS be classified?

b. Criminal conduct. Another type of statement treated as slanderous per se at common law is the imputation of criminal activities, the law's concern apparently being that such a statement might expose plaintiff to criminal prosecution. However, all charges of criminal misconduct are not slanderous per se. Most jurisdictions now insist that the crime involve "moral turpitude." See, e.g., Wooten v. Martin, 131 S.W. 783 (Ky. 1910). Other jurisdictions follow the English rule and require that the words charge an offense punishable by death or imprisonment.

If plaintiff is accused of conduct criminal under the law in the state where the allegations are made, but not criminal where the conduct was performed, are the statements slanderous per se? See Klumph v. Dunn, 66 Pa. 141 (1870), which opted for the "law of the country where the words are spoken," because it is by those laws that the reputation of the plaintiff is judged.

c. Imputation of unchastity. The older common law did not treat as slanderous per se words that imputed unchastity to a woman, but this was changed by statute in England in 1891, and similar legislation has been enacted in several states in the U.S. When the question has been raised in states without such statutes, some granted recovery on the theory that the charge of fornication was criminal under local laws, while others allowed the action regardless of whether there were imputations of criminal conduct. The first Restatement of Torts adopted the view that allegations of unchastity are slanderous per se, Restatement of Torts §574. The Restatement (Second) of Torts §574 now makes slanderous per se allegations of "serious sexual misconduct," which, as comment *c* now makes clear, applies to both men and women. How should false allegations of homosexuality be treated?

d. Slander of a person's trade or profession. This last category is probably the most important in litigation. The obvious illustrations are charges that a surgeon is a butcher, or a cashier has his hands in the till. More problematic are those statements reflecting adversely upon plaintiff's character by charging dishonesty, sloth, immorality, or drunkenness. In Lumby v. Allday, 148 Eng. Rep. 1434 (K.B. 1831), it was held that it was not slander per se to accuse a clerk working for a gas company of consorting with prostitutes since he might still be a perfectly competent clerk. Likewise, it was not slander per se to say of a stenographer that she did not pay her debts, Liebel v. Montgomery Ward & Co., 62 P.2d 667 (Mont. 1936). On the other hand, it was held slander per se to charge a clergyman with immorality, Haynes v. Robertson, 175 S.W. 290 (Mo. App. 1915), or to say of a teacher that he is insane, Wertz v. Lawrence, 179 P. 813 (Colo. 1919). Also slanderous per se are unprivileged charges of dishonesty or corruption against public officials.

Although the categories are generally clear, some difficult cases of classification can arise, especially where written and spoken words are linked together in a single chain of communication. Thus, when the defendant read aloud an anonymous letter defaming the plaintiff, the case was treated as one of libel and not slander. Forrester v. Tyrrell, 9 T.L.R. 257 (1893). Transmissions of telegraphic messages have also been held libels. See Peterson v. Western Union Telegraph Co., 74 N.W. 1022 (Minn. 1898). For the classic criticism of the distinction between libel and slander see Veeder, The History and Theory of the Law of Defamation, 3 Colum. L. Rev. 546, 571 et seq. (1903).

The main challenge to the distinction between libel and slander has come in the area of television and radio. In the early case of Hartman v. Winchell, 73 N.E.2d 30 (N.Y. 1947), the court held that reading a defamatory statement on the radio from a prepared manuscript should be treated as a libel because the wide dissemination of the broadcast could reach a "far-flung" audience larger than that attained by a newspaper. *Hartman* did not reach the question of how to treat radio broadcasts not reduced to writing; the Restatement (Second) of Torts §568A states the modern position that "[b]roadcasting of defamatory matter by means of radio or television is libel, whether or not it is read from a manuscript." The English Defamation Act, 15 & 16 Geo. VI and Eliz. II. ch. 66 §§1, 16 (1952), adopts the same rule. See also Theatres Act, 1968, ch. 54 §4, which treats the public performance of a play as "publication in permanent form," i.e., libel. Note too that the movies were governed by the law of libel in *Youssoupoff*, supra at page 1093.

2. Libel Per Quod and Libel Per Se

The elaborate distinction between libel per quod and libel per se at common law is a further complication in the law of libel that deserves special mention. In some instances the defendant libels the plaintiff by name, and in others the libel can be established only with reference to matters outside the publication, as when the defendant says, "The person who stole my money lives in the house next door." Here extrinsic evidence is needed to establish that the statement referred to the plaintiff. In other cases the identity of the plaintiff is undisputed, but extraneous facts are needed to establish the defamatory meaning.

The basic problem is nicely illustrated by two old New York cases. In Smith v. Smith, 142 N.E. 292 (N.Y. 1923), defendant had made the following statement in applying for a marriage license in 1921: "Number of marriage, 1; is applicant a divorced person, No." The plaintiff, however, alleged the following additional facts: That she and defendant had been married and were divorced in 1911, that the statement in the application therefore meant that defendant had never been married to plaintiff, and that during the time they lived together she had been his mistress. The court held in a memorandum opinion that with this amplification the complaint stated a cause of action. In Braun v. Armour & Co., 173 N.E. 845 (N.Y. 1930), defendant had issued an advertisement setting forth a list of dealers in its meat products, including plaintiff, stating: "These progressive dealers listed here sell Armour's Star Bacon in the new window-top carton." In the complaint plaintiff added that he was a dealer in kosher meat and that bacon was a non-kosher product. Again in a memorandum opinion the court held that the complaint stated a cause of action. The converse may also be true of extrinsic facts, since their context may render innocuous language that is otherwise defamatory.

The interaction between the rules on innuendo and those on libel and slander can be quite complex. The opening salvo was fired in Prosser, Libel Per Quod, 46 Va. L. Rev. 839 (1960), which suggested that in most states when libel has been established per quod, that is, by extrinsic evidence, then the plaintiff must show special damages, as in ordinary slander cases. An exception to this rule involves cases of words that, if spoken, would have been slanderous per se and therefore actionable without proof of special damages.

Prosser's reading of the cases was sharply challenged in Eldredge, The Spurious Role of Libel Per Quod, 79 Harv. L. Rev. 733 (1966), who argued that the majority of the states had retained the traditional rule that all libels, whether per se or per quod, were actionable without proof of special damages. The debate was carried on in the American Law Institute's discussions over revisions of the Restatement of Torts, with both Prosser and Eldredge participating. The revised Restatement adopted a compromise position that proof of special damages would be required only where the defendant was ignorant of the extrinsic facts that made his statements defamatory. This position was adopted in at least one case, Reed v. Melnick, 471 P.2d 178 (Mont. 1970). Recent cases, however, generally support the Eldredge position that all libels are actionable without proof of special damages. See, e.g., Hinsdale v. Orange County Publications, Inc., 217 N.E.2d 650 (N.Y. 1966), where the court reviews the confused line of New York decisions on the subject.

The Restatement (Second) §569 takes the traditional position that all libels are actionable without proof of special damages, on the ground that "[t]he principal justification urged for this minority position — that if the defendant did not himself know the extrinsic facts he would be held liable without fault — has now been eliminated by the current constitutional rule that the plaintiff must show fault on the part of the defendant regarding the defamatory character of the communication." Restatement (Second) of Torts §569 comment b. But see Gertz v. Robert Welch, Inc., infra at page 1196, on the question of whether "fault" must be shown in all defamation actions, even those with non-media defendants.

E.   BASIS OF LIABILITY: INTENTION, NEGLIGENCE, AND STRICT LIABILITY IN DEFAMATION

E. Hulton & Co. v. Jones
[1910] A.C. 20

[The defendant newspaper ran an article written by its Paris corre-
spondent that in part read as follows: " 'Whist! There is Artemus Jones
with a woman who is not his wife, who must be, you know — the other
thing!' whispers a fair neighbor of mine excitedly to her bosom friend's
ear. Really, is it not surprising how certain of our fellow-countrymen
behave when they come abroad? Who would suppose by his goings on,
that he is a church warden at Peckham?" Plaintiff was a lawyer named
Thomas Artemus Jones of North Wales; he was not a church warden,
nor did he reside at Peckham, but he had up to 1901 contributed
signed articles to defendant's newspaper. Defendant's contention that
they had never heard of plaintiff and had used the name Artemus Jones
as a fictitious name was accepted as true by plaintiff at the trial. Plaintiff
produced witnesses who said they had read the article and thought that
it referred to plaintiff. The trial judge charged the jury that the issue
was not what the writer had intended but how the statement would be
understood. At the trial plaintiff recovered a jury verdict of £1,750. The
court of appeal affirmed in a two-to-one decision and, on appeal, the
House of Lords affirmed.

The issue was perhaps most succinctly put during argument in the
House of Lords when defendant's counsel said: "The question is who
was meant," and Lord Loreburn asked: "Is it not rather who was hit?"
Counsel replied: "No. A man cannot be held responsible for remote
and improbable results of his actions."]

LOREBURN, L.C. My Lords, I think this appeal must be dismissed. A
question in regard to the law of libel has been raised which does not
seem to me to be entitled to the support of your Lordships. Libel is a
tortious act. What does the tort consist in? It consists in using language
which others knowing the circumstances would reasonably think to be
defamatory of the person complaining of and injured by it. A person
charged with libel cannot defend himself by shewing that he intended
in his own breast not to defame, or that he intended not to defame the
plaintiff, if in fact he did both. He has none the less imputed something
disgraceful and has none the less injured the plaintiff. A man in good
faith may publish a libel believing it to be true, and it may be found by
the jury that he acted in good faith believing it to be true, and reasonably believing it to be true, but that in fact the statement was false.
Under those circumstances he has no defence to the action, however
excellent his intention. If the intention of the writer be immaterial in
considering whether the matter written is defamatory, I do not see why

it need be relevant in considering whether it is defamatory of the plaintiff. The writing, according to the old form, must be malicious, and it must be of and concerning the plaintiff. Just as the defendant could not excuse himself from malice by proving that he wrote it in the most benevolent spirit, so he cannot shew that the libel was not of and concerning the plaintiff by proving that he never heard of the plaintiff. His intention in both respects equally is inferred from what he did. His remedy is to abstain from defamatory words. . . .

The damages are certainly heavy, but I think your Lordships ought to remember two things. The first is that the jury were entitled to think, in the absence of proof satisfactory to them (and they were the judges of it), that some ingredient of recklessness, or more than recklessness, entered into the writing and the publication of this article, especially as Mr. Jones, the plaintiff, had been employed on this very newspaper, and his name was well known in the paper and also well known in the district in which the paper circulated. In the second place the jury was entitled to say this kind of article is to be condemned. There is no tribunal more fitted to decide in regard to publications, especially publications in the newspaper Press, whether they bear a stamp and character which ought to enlist sympathy and to secure protection. If they think that the licence is not fairly used and that the tone and style of the libel is reprehensible and ought to be checked, it is for the jury to say so; and for my part, although I think the damages are certainly high, I am not prepared to advise your Lordships to interfere, especially as the Court of Appeal have not thought it right to interfere, with the verdict.

LORD SHAW . . . In the publication of matter of a libellous character, that is matter which would be libellous if applying to an actual person, the responsibility is as follows: In the first place there is responsibility for the words used being taken to signify that which readers would reasonably understand by them; in the second place there is responsibility also for the names used being taken to signify those whom the readers would reasonably understand by those names; and in the third place the same principle is applicable to persons unnamed but sufficiently indicated by designation or description.

NOTES

1. Strict liability and malicious intent. Even before *Hulton,* the common law regarded defamation as a tort of strict liability. Thus, in Bromage v. Prosser, 107 Eng. Rep. 1051, 1054 (K.B. 1825), Bayley, J., wrote:

> Malice in common acceptation means ill will against a person, but in its legal sense it means a wrongful act, done intentionally, without just

cause or excuse. If I give a perfect stranger a blow likely to produce death, I do it *of malice,* because I do it *intentionally* and without just cause or excuse. If I maim cattle, without knowing whose they are, if I poison a fishery, without knowing the owner, I do it *of malice,* because it is a wrongful act, and done intentionally.

Bromage then noted that actual malice in the sense of ill will was relevant where the defendant claimed a qualified privilege for the defamatory statement, see infra at 1144. Both *Bromage* and *Hulton* are followed today in the United States. "Actual malice, in the sense of spite or ill will, is presumed and need not be proved if the words are defamatory on their face." Tate v. Bradley, 837 F.2d 206 (5th Cir. 1988). Is there any reason why defamation should be a tort of strict liability if harms for physical injuries are governed by a principle of negligence?

Before *New York Times,* the commentators were divided on the merits of Hulton v. Jones. Jeremiah Smith pronounced it superior to all the alternatives. Smith, *Jones v. Hulton:* Three Conflicting Judicial Views as to a Question of Defamation, 60 U. Pa. L. Rev. 365 (1912); see also Morris, Inadvertent Newspaper Libel and Retraction, 32 Ill. L. Rev. 36 (1937), which favors the strict liability rule because it eliminates the need to prove the negligence that is present in most cases of this sort. The negligence position was taken, however, in Holdsworth, A Chapter of Accidents in the Law of Libel, 57 Law Q. Rev. 74 (1941); Note, 38 Harv. L. Rev. 1100 (1925). See also Prosser and Keeton, Torts, 810, where it is argued that the strict liability standard may be too demanding of publishers and that a better balance between innocent victims and innocent publishers is achieved by fashioning a negligence standard "coupled with a high standard of care and a presumption that defamatory publications are made negligently."

2. Basis of liability for publication. Under *Hulton,* must the defendant deliberately publish the defamatory statement? It seems widely agreed that the defendant will be liable only if the publication was intentional or at least negligent. Thus the Restatement of Torts §577 comment *n* excuses the defendant for "accidental" publications. That rule applies when *A* writes defamatory statements about *B* and they are stolen from a locked desk by a thief who reads or publishes them. Similarly if *A* sends a defamatory letter about *B* to *B* through the mail, the publication is regarded as accidental if a robber reads or publishes the stolen letter. Finally if *A* sends a defamatory letter to *B* marked "personal" which is opened and read by *B*'s secretary there is no publication, unless *A* knew of the secretary's practice. Note that even under a rule that imposed liability for all publications, even those not deliberately or negligently made, the defendant could escape responsibility in the above situations if the publication was made by some independent third person for whose acts the defendant is not responsible.

F.   DAMAGES

1.   Special Damages

"By 'actual damage' is meant what in the books is usually called 'special damage.' This latter expression is either meaningless or misleading." G. S. Bower, Actionable Defamation, Article 13, page 33, note p. (1908).

Terwilliger v. Wands
17 N.Y. 54 (1858)

[Action for slander. Plaintiff proved that defendant told La Fayette Wands that plaintiff was having continued sexual intercourse with one Mrs. Fuller and that he — plaintiff — would do all he could to keep Mr. Fuller in the penitentiary so that he could continue to enjoy Mrs. Fuller's favors. Plaintiff proved that defendant had said much the same things to one Neiper and that Neiper, a good friend of plaintiff's, had told plaintiff about this. Also, he proved that Neiper had told him that this information about plaintiff was spreading all over the county. As a result of learning this, plaintiff became very ill, both mentally and physically, had to have medical treatment, and could not do any work; subsequently his crops and business were neglected and he had to hire more help. A motion for nonsuit was sustained and affirmed in the intermediate appellate court below. Affirmed.]

STRONG, J. The words spoken by the defendant not being actionable of themselves, it was necessary in order to maintain the action to prove that they occasioned special damages to the plaintiff. The special damages must have been the natural, immediate and legal consequence of the words. . . . [The court first concluded that defendant was not responsible for a repetition of the words to plaintiff, and continued:]

But there is another ground upon which the judgment must be affirmed. The special damages relied upon are not of such a nature as will support the action. The action for slander is given by the law as a remedy for "injuries affecting a man's reputation or good name by malicious, scandalous and slanderous words, tending to his damage and derogation." (3 Bl. Com., 123.) It is injuries affecting the reputation only which are the subject of the action. In the case of slanderous words actionable per se, the law, from their natural and immediate tendency to produce injury, adjudges them to be injurious, though no special loss or damage can be proved. "But with regard to words that do not apparently and upon the face of them import such defamation as will of course be injurious, it is necessary that the plaintiff should aver some particular damage to have happened." (3 Bl. Com., 124.) As to what constitutes special damages, Starkie mentions the loss of a marriage, loss of hospitable gratuitous entertainment, preventing a servant or bailiff from getting a place, the loss of customers by a tradesman; and says that in general whenever a person is prevented by the slander from receiving that which would otherwise be conferred upon him, though gratuitously, it is sufficient. (1 Stark. on Sland., 195, 202.) In Olmsted v. Miller (1 Wend. 506), it was held that the refusal of civil entertainment at a public house was sufficient special damage. So in Williams v. Hill (19 Wend. 305), was the fact that the plaintiff was turned away from the house of her uncle and charged not to return until she had cleared up her character. So in Beach v. Ranney, was the circumstance that persons, who had been in the habit of doing so, refused longer to provide fuel, clothing, &c. These instances are sufficient to illustrate the kind of special damage that must result from defamatory words not otherwise actionable to make them so; they are damages produced by, or through, impairing the reputation.

It would be highly impolitic to hold all language, wounding the feelings and affecting unfavorably the health and ability to labor, of another, a ground of action; for that would be to make the right of action depend often upon whether the sensibilities of a person spoken of are easily excited or otherwise; his strength of mind to disregard abusive, insulting remarks concerning him; and his physical strength and ability to bear them. Words which would make hardly an impression on most persons, and would be thought by them, and should be by all, undeserving of notice, might be exceedingly painful to some, occasioning sickness and an interruption of ability to attend to their ordinary avocations. There must be some limit to liability for words not actionable per se, both as to the words and the kind of damages; and a clear and wise one has been fixed by the law. The words must be defamatory in their nature; and must in fact disparage the character; and this disparagement must be evidenced by some positive loss arising therefrom directly and legitimately as a fair and natural result. In this view of the law words which do not degrade the character do not injure it, and cannot occasion loss. . . . In the present case the words were defamatory, and the illness and physical prostration of the plaintiff may be assumed, so far as this part of the case is concerned, to have been actually produced by the slander, but this consequence was not, in a legal view, a natural, ordinary one, as it does not prove that the plaintiff's character was injured. The slander may not have been credited by or had the slightest influence upon any one unfavorable to the plaintiff; and it does not appear that any body believed it or treated the plaintiff any different from what they would otherwise have done on account of it. The cause was not adapted to produce the result which is claimed to be special damages. Such an effect may and sometimes does follow from such a cause but not ordinarily; and the rule of law was framed in reference to common and usual effects and not those which are accidental and occasional.

It is true that this element of the action for slander in the case of words not actionable of themselves — that the special damages must flow from impaired reputation — has been overlooked in several modern cases, and loss of health and consequent incapacity to attend to business held sufficient special damage. But these cases are a departure from principle and should not be followed. If such consequences were sufficient, it would not be necessary to allege in the complaint or prove that the words were spoken in the presence of a third person; if spoken directly to the plaintiff, in the presence of no one else, he might himself, under the recent law allowing parties to be witnesses, prove the words and the damages and be permitted to recover. . . .

Where there is no proof that the character has suffered from the words, if sickness results it must be attributed to apprehension of loss of character, and such fear of harm to character, with resulting sickness and bodily prostration, cannot be such special damage as the law requires for the action. The loss of character must be a substantive loss, one which has actually taken place.

NOTES

1. *Mental anguish as special damages.* Allsop v. Allsop, 157 Eng. Rep. 1292 (Ex. 1860), the leading English case, is in accord with *Terwilliger* in holding that neither mental nor physical illness constitutes special damage. The courts in *Terwilliger* and *Allsop* ignored allegations that the illness said to be caused by the slander prevented plaintiff from carrying out his normal business and household tasks. But in Underhill v. Welton, 32 Vt. 40 (1859), the court held that there was special damage when the illness resulted in "loss of time" and in the inability to perform "customary duties and labors."

Modern cases tend to allow for mental anguish that results from reading defamatory publications made available to third parties. See, e.g., Burnett v. National Enquirer, Inc., 193 Cal. Rptr. 206 (Cal. App. 1983), which sustained an award of $50,000 in actual damages for damages arising from the plaintiff's "loss of reputation, shame, mortification and injured feelings," that developed when she read a false article about her printed in the defendant's tabloid.

2. *Varieties of special damages.* Unlike those in *Terwilliger,* the allegations of special damages in many cases take on a more concrete form. Historically, defamation was closely associated with the intrigue of kings and generals. If the defendant falsely told the king that his chief minister had betrayed him, the special damages could be not only loss of position, but banishment and death. What if the charge of unchastity resulted in expulsion from a religious sect? Roberts v. Roberts, 122 Eng.

Rep. 874 (K.B. 1864), held, with evident discomfort, that there was no special damage. Suppose that a husband abandoned his wife when he heard the charge of unchastity? In Lynch v. Knight, 11 Eng. Rep. 854 (H.L.E. 1862), the court said that this was a proper ground of special damage, but denied recovery because the husband's action was not a "natural" result of the words spoken, a result that seems inconsistent with the expanded notions of proximate cause that have developed since 1862. For a decision holding that abandonment by the husband constitutes special damage see Felty v. Felty, 175 S.W. 643 (Ky. 1915); but see Beach v. Ranney, 2 Hill 309 (N.Y. 1842). A charge of unchastity resulting in the loss of a contemplated marriage was held to constitute special damage in Matthew v. Crass, Cro. Jac. 323 (1614).

Ellsworth v. Martindale-Hubbell Law Directory, Inc.
280 N.W. 879 (N.D. 1938)

[In this action for libel plaintiff alleged that defendant misstated his professional and financial rating in the code form that it uses in its directory. The directory itself is widely relied on by lawyers in many states and countries who have occasion to forward legal business. Plaintiff claimed that his rating in defendant's private key symbols was defamatory and that as a result his reputation was injured. In his pleadings he elaborately set forth the translation of this private key system, with which all members of his profession were presumably familiar. From 1907 through 1926, plaintiff's name was published in the directory with the rating "a v 5 g," of which "a" meant legal ability very high, "v," recommendations very high, "5," financial worth $10,000 to $20,000, and "g," promptness in paying bills very good. The defamation itself consisted of the following, appearing in the 1928 edition: "b w 5 f," of which "b" meant legal ability second class, "w," recommendations second class, "5," financial worth $10,000 to $20,000, and "f," promptness in paying bills fair. In the 1929 edition defendant left the rating of plaintiff blank, which plaintiff alleged meant that his rating was so low that it was not worthy of mention in the directory, although it appears that defendant had written a strong letter of protest after the 1928 edition.

When plaintiff's case was previously before the court, Ellsworth v. Martindale-Hubbell Law Directory, Inc., 268 N.W. 400 (N.D. 1936), it was held that the alleged defamation was not actionable per se and that plaintiff would have to allege and prove special damages to maintain his action. In an amended complaint plaintiff then offered allegations as to his professional income in 1928, the year prior to the alleged misstatements, and for the succeeding three years, during which his earnings were substantially lower, allegedly because of defendant's publication, to his damage of more than $2500. This is an appeal from an order overruling a demurrer to the amended complaint.]

NUESSLE, J. . . . The sole question on this appeal is as to whether this amended paragraph sufficiently sets forth the special damages claimed to have been suffered. The defendant contends that it does not. That it fails to set out the names of the clients lost by the plaintiff because of the publication of the alleged defamatory matter, and that it does not specify particularly the origin, character, and amount of the business the plaintiff has been deprived of because of its publication.

In substance, the amended complaint alleges that the plaintiff has been engaged in the practice of law for many years; that he has always borne a good reputation as a man and as a lawyer; that he has had a substantial law business that came to him largely from forwarders through a widely spread foreign territory; that he was personally unacquainted with such forwarders; that the defendant's publication in which the alleged defamatory matter was published, was circulated generally throughout such territory and among those who forwarded business to the plaintiff; that, as a consequence of the circulation of such matter and immediately following such publication and circulation, his practice decreased in the manner and to the extent as set out in that portion of the complaint quoted. . . .

While the rule with respect to the pleading of special damages is universally recognized, apparent contradictions have arisen in its application to particular states of fact. And nowhere is this application more difficult than in actions for defamation. Many cases may be found which actually or apparently sustain the defendant's contention as made in the instant case. An examination of these cases, however, discloses that they instance the application of a general rule to different states of fact but establish no accurate and definite standard of application. In any event, in the instant case, it seems to us that both right and reason are on the side of the plaintiff and that his amended complaint must be held sufficient. The statute declares that for every wrong there is a remedy. From the facts alleged it appears that unless the pleading be held good the plaintiff is remediless. He alleges that he had a fairly lucrative law business that came to him from foreign territory through forwarders with whom he was not and from the nature of things could not be personally acquainted; that such business came because of the personal and professional reputation and standing which he enjoyed; that because of the defamatory publication of which he complains, this reputation and standing was disparaged in the minds of those who sent business to him and consequently his business fell off. From the nature of the circumstances as disclosed by the pleading the plaintiff cannot describe the particular items of business which he has lost or give the names of particular individuals who would have become his clients had it not been for the publication. But he does show a diminution of his business and of the income therefrom by pleading what that business amounted to prior to the publication and what it was after the publication, and as a result thereof. As to whether he can make proof in support of the allegations contained in his pleading is another matter with which we are not now concerned. It seems to us that what was said by Bowen, L.J., in Ratcliffe v. Evans, [1892] 2 Q.B. 524 admirably states the reasoning which is applicable in such a case. (In that case the defendant had printed and published in his newspaper that the plaintiff had given up business and that his firm had ceased to exist. The plaintiff proved his business had fallen off and that his profits had diminished since the publication of the words, but gave no specific evidence of the loss of any particular customer or order. It was held the proof made was, in the special circumstances of the case, sufficient to sustain the action.) . . .

And in Odgers, Libel & Slander, 5th ed. at page 382, it is stated, citing Ratcliffe v. Evans, [1892] supra:

"But it is not always necessary for the plaintiff to call as his witnesses those who have ceased to deal with him. He may be able to show by his account-books or otherwise, a general diminution of business as distinct from the loss of particular known customers or promised orders. He has still to connect that diminution [sic] of business with the defendant's words. Such a connection may sometimes be established by the nature of the words themselves. Where the defendant has published a statement about the plaintiff's business, which is intended or reasonably calculated to produce, and in the ordinary course of things does produce, a general loss of business, evidence of such loss of business is admissible, and sufficient special damage to support the action, although the words are not actionable per se, and although no specific evidence is given at the trial of the loss of any particular customer or order by reason of such publication."

While, as we have hereinbefore stated, there are many cases that may be cited in support of the defendant's contention that the allegation as to special damages in the instant case is not sufficient, there also are many to be found, the reasoning of which sustains the sufficiency of the challenged pleading. . . . [Affirmed.]

MILLER, J. I dissent. . . .

A pleading should be liberally construed, but the allegations of such pleading disclose that no cause of action exists as a matter of law, and to hold otherwise is placing the defendant in the same position he would be were the statement libelous per se, i.e., it would be presuming that certain prospective clients had read the statement, understood its defamatory character and by reason thereof refused to send him business, to his pecuniary loss.

NOTES

1. Business losses as special damages. When a witness testifies that as a result of the slander he was dissuaded from dealing with plaintiff, special damage have clearly demonstrated. Storey v. Challends, 173 Eng. Rep. 475 (Ct 1837). Similarly loss of employment because of slander was early held to be special damage. Hartley v. Herring, 8 Term R. 130, 101 Eng. Rep. 1305 (Ct 1799). But loss of an election due to the slander was held not to be special damage in Field v. Colson, 20 S.W. 264 (Ky. 1892). Why?

The Restatement (Second) of Torts §575 comment *b* offers an account of special damages that reflects the decided cases:

> Thus, while a slander that has been so widely disseminated as to cause persons previously friendly to the plaintiff to refuse social intercourse with him is not of itself special harm, the loss of the material advantages of their hospitality is sufficient. Special harm may be a loss of presently existing advantage, as a discharge from employment. It may also be a failure to realize a reasonable expectation of gain, as the denial of employment which, but for the currency of the slander, the plaintiff would have received. It is not necessary that he be legally entitled to receive the benefits that are denied to him because of the slander. It is enough that the slander has disappointed his reasonable expectation of receiving a gratuity.

2. Proof of special damages. Plaintiff's attempt to establish special damages can raise sharp questions of fact if defendant claims that plaintiff's loss is caused not by defendant's defamatory statement but by some independent event. In Lawlor v. Gallagher President's Report, Inc., 394 F. Supp. 721 (S.D.N.Y. 1975), plaintiff brought an action against his former employer, Gulf + Western, some of its chief officers, and Gallagher's Report, a business news publication. The essence of his claim was that defendants had accused him of having "extracted" fees for the placement of executives with Gulf + Western. The court found the charges defamatory, but refused to allow plaintiff any damages for lost employment, saying that plaintiff's inability to get a job after his dismissal from Gulf + Western was substantially caused not by the defendant's defamatory statements but by Gulf + Western's "justified refusal" to recommend plaintiff to prospective employers. The court did, however, allow the plaintiff $45,000 in damages for loss of reputation and for pain and mental anguish.

The plaintiff in Calero v. Del Chemical Corp., 228 N.W.2d 737 (Wis. 1974), was, however, able to forge the causal link in his action against his former employer and another of its employees. The gist of the suit was that the defendants, after they had dismissed plaintiff, responded to inquiries from firms where plaintiff subsequently was employed or had applied for employment by stating that plaintiff had used company records to help start his own competing business. These reports made it difficult for the plaintiff to find or keep work. In one instance, the plaintiff was fired 15 minutes after his new employer had contacted the individual defendant to see if plaintiff should be given a promotion. Plaintiff ultimately moved to Arizona because his references were "too harmful to overcome." The Wisconsin Supreme Court upheld a verdict of $10,000 in compensatory damages and $9,000 in punitive damages.

2. General Damages

McCormick, Damages
§116, p. 422 (1935)

When "special" damage need not be shown, "general" damage may be recovered. That such damage has been suffered need not be proved by the plaintiff, for it is presumed; however, it is customary to make proof of some of the items. The elements of "general" damage are: (1) injury to reputation; (2) loss of business; (3) wounded feelings and bodily suffering resulting therefrom.

Faulk v. Aware, Inc.
231 N.Y.S.2d 270 (Sup. Ct. 1962)

[Aware, Inc., is a "membership corporation whose purpose is to combat communism in the entertainment and communication industries." John Henry Faulk, a popular radio and TV performer, brought a libel action against Aware, Inc., and Vincent Hartnett, its founder and president, for statements made by them and widely distributed charging him with communist sympathies and affiliations. The dramatic details of this case are recounted in two books, J. H. Faulk, Fear on Trial (1965), and L. Nizer, The Jury Returns 226-438 (1966).]

GELLER, J. In this libel action the jury rendered a verdict awarding compensatory damages of $1,000,000 against the three defendants and punitive damages of $1,250,000 each against defendants Aware, Inc., and Vincent Hartnett. . . .

The fact that the amounts awarded are very large does not necessarily render the verdict excessive as a matter of law. The question is whether there is a rational basis for the jury's awards in the evidence adduced and in the circumstances of this case. The court should not substitute its judgment for that of the jury, unless the amounts awarded are insupportable under any fair-minded view of the facts.

It has been said that the amount of damages in an action for libel is "peculiarly within the province of the jury" . . . ; that the actual damages "can rarely be computed" . . . ; and that "in the nature of things such proof is almost impossible". . . . In Lynch v. New York Times Co. (171 App. Div. 399, 401) the court pointed out: "In a libel case, more, perhaps, than in any other, the jury is generally considered to be the supreme arbiter on the question of damages. In actions for other torts there is generally to be found some standard by which the reasonableness of an award of damages may be tested, but it is seldom so in actions for libel and slander where the elements of wounded sensibilities and the loss of public esteem play a part."

However, since an award of damages always rests in the "sound discretion" of a jury, it is subject to court review. That discretion must be exercised in accordance with the applicable rules of law and on the basis of the evidence in the case.

The damages recoverable for a libel consist of two items:

(1) *Compensatory* damages, to compensate and make reparation in full for all the damage suffered by a plaintiff as the result and consequence thereof, so that a defamed person is entitled to be compensated for the injury to his reputation and standing publicly, privately and professionally; for his mental anguish and distress, his feeling of mortification and suffering, in his private as well as public life; and for loss of income or earnings.

(2) *Punitive* (exemplary) damages, which may be awarded in a jury's discretion in addition to compensatory damages only in certain actions of willful torts such as libel and assault, provided the jury finds malice on the part of a defendant or such reckless and wanton indifference to the rights of others as is deemed in law the equivalent of malice; punitive damages are authorized under the law as a penalty to punish such a defendant, to deter him from a repetition of the offense and to warn others of like mind from perpetrating similar wrongs.

We will consider each of these two types of awards separately, just as the jury was instructed to do in its deliberations and form of verdict.

I.   COMPENSATORY DAMAGES . . .

The principal item of damages was plaintiff's claim that he had been rendered unemployable in the television and radio industry as the direct result of the alleged libel and the concerted acts of the defendants, depriving him of the opportunity to realize his earning capacities in his profession. . . .

There was substantial testimony, which was uncontradicted, that prior to the alleged libel in February, 1956, plaintiff, in addition to his regular radio show, had appeared on a large number of television programs and had shown particular talent for that medium, being especially suited for the game, fun and quiz shows which were extremely popular during the period here involved. There also was uncontradicted testimony of an upward trend during this period in the television industry and in the income earned by television performers.

Plaintiff offered proof of his earning capacity through experts in the industry familiar with his achievements and abilities, among whom were Mark Goodson, David Susskind and Garry Moore, well-known producers of television shows.

It is well settled that a person wrongfully injured is entitled to recover for deprivation of future earning capacity, without limitation to his actual earnings preceding the injury; and that opinion testimony with regard to his potential earnings in that field by experts familiar with his capacities, is admissible.

. . . [Plaintiff's expert witnesses] testified that he would have earned between $150,000 and $500,000 annually, giving the reasons for their opinion. Defendants offered no proof in contradiction of plaintiff's experts.

The minimal figure of plaintiff's experts would represent damages of $900,000 for the six years involved. Assuming that the jury accepted that figure, they could take into consideration the other elements of injury to plaintiff's reputation and his mental anguish and distress in public and private life arising from the nature of the charge made against him, and find basis for arriving at compensatory damages in the sum of $1,000,000. . . .

Assessment of damages in such a matter is peculiarly within the province of a jury and, so long as it has a rational basis in the evidence, its verdict should not be disturbed.

The motions of all defendants to set aside the verdict with respect to compensatory damages are accordingly denied.

II. PUNITIVE DAMAGES . . .

Plaintiff's counsel in his summation asked the jury to bring in punitive damages of $1,000,000 each against the defendants. . . .

After deliberating for several hours, the jury submitted the following note, signed by the foreman: "The jury would like to have a clarification on the subject of awards for punitive damages — Is the jury allowed to award more than the amounts requested by the plaintiff?" . . .

About an hour later the jury returned and rendered its verdict, assessing punitive damages of $1,250,000 each against defendants Aware, Inc., and Vincent Hartnett.

There was substantial evidence from which the jury could find malice, intent to injure plaintiff pursuant to concerted plan and conspiracy, and reckless disregard of the rights of others on the part of both Hartnett and Aware, Inc. The jury could have determined that, as charged by plaintiff, the attack upon him was not an isolated transaction but was deliberately prepared to end his broadcasting career, to remove his opposition as an officer of AFTRA to the blacklisting practices which these defendants were directly interested in having continued, and to make an example of him.

The evidence revealed that Hartnett had increased considerably his earnings from his occupation as a paid "consultant" on alleged communist "infiltration" in the radio and television industry, and the jury could have determined that, with the aid of his associates in that purported undertaking, he had acted dictatorially and exerted pressure in blacklisting all categories of personnel in the industry, indiscriminately and without any reason being given to the persons whose livelihoods were thereby placed in jeopardy.

The jury could also have concluded from the evidence that Aware, Inc., was an instrumentality of the group which exerted pressure on the industry to induce the blacklisting of personnel; that it had interfered in and dominated AFTRA for many years; and that its practices indicated a reckless disregard of the rights of others and an abuse of the right of free speech and press.

Clearly, the jury's determination to impose substantial punitive damages against these two defendants was justified under such a view of the evidence and the circumstances of this case. The only question is as to the amount. Obviously, there can be no standard for measuring punitive damages. It is only when the award is clearly disproportionate to the offense that a jury's assessment is subject to review.

The full extent and nature of these defendant's designs, methods and practices, their impact throughout the radio and television industry, and their effect upon the livelihoods of many persons, can be properly assessed only by those cognizant of the entire record revealed during this long trial. . . .

In libel suits, of course, punitive damages have always been permitted in the discretion of the jury. The assessment of a penalty involves not only a consideration of the nature and degree of the offense, but the higher moral consideration that it may serve as a deterrent to antisocial practices where the public welfare is involved. The jury, representing the community, assesses such a penalty as, in its view, is adequate to stop the practices of defendants and others having similar designs.

Taking into consideration the fundamental issues of this case, the nature of the evidence, and the jury's undoubted conclusions and intentions, the court will not disturb its assessment of punitive damages, and the motions addressed to punitive damages on the ground of excessiveness are accordingly denied.

Faulk v. Aware, Inc.
244 N.Y.S.2d 259 (App. Div. 1963)

RABIN, J. . . . We are greatly concerned, however, with the size of the verdict — both as to compensatory and punitive damages. . . . We find the verdict to be grossly excessive and most unrealistic — even in the field of entertainment.

The plaintiff's prior earnings are an important factor in assessing the damage suffered when his earnings are cut off. His damage need not be limited to the level of his actual earnings at the time of the libel. His potential earnings may be taken into consideration when there is evidence to enable a jury to assess those potentialities. . . . In this case, the plaintiff's potential earnings were fixed by his witnesses in amounts ranging from $100,000.00 to $1,000,000.00 a year. The larger figure was arrived at by reference to the earnings of those who had reached the very top of the profession. We are mindful of the statement of our colleague, Mr. Justice Breitel, in the *Grayson* case where he said: "[I]n the case of persons of rare and special talents many are called but few are chosen." While the plaintiff's experts testified that the plaintiff would, without doubt, be among the "chosen," it seems that none of these experts, although in the entertainment field, was perceptive enough to contract for his services even though his earnings were never more than about $35,000.00 a year.

Those who testified to potential earnings of between $100,000.00 and $250,000.00 arrived at that estimate based upon what comparable performers were receiving. Yet they gave no explanation as to why the plaintiff's earnings were so comparatively low. In short, the testimony of the experts left plenty of room for speculation.

Upon that testimony, the jury was justified in its obvious conclusion that the plaintiff's prospects for advancement in his profession were extremely good and that his income would rise correspondingly. Despite that however, there is hardly enough justification for the finding of compensatory damages in the amount of $1,000,000.00, even making allowance for his mental pain and suffering. It is interesting to note that at current savings bank interest rates, his yearly income for life would exceed the best of his past earnings. We believe that the compensatory damages should be fixed at a figure no higher than $400,000.00.

We now consider the amount of punitive damages awarded. . . .

The jury awarded the sum of $1,250,000 against each of the two appellants. However, one was more culpable than the other. They should not be punished alike. While Aware was a willing participant in the publication of the libel, Hartnett was the chief actor. It was Hartnett, rather than Aware, who stood to gain or lose depending upon whether the plaintiff was to be permitted to resist his activities or be silenced. It was he who was the author of the objectionable pamphlet and it was he who put it in places where it would hurt the plaintiff the most. The assessment of punitive damages against him should be in a much greater amount than against Aware.

It is our considered opinion that the maximum sum that should have been awarded against Aware, by way of punitive damages, is $50,000.00, and as against Hartnett, who by far was the more guilty of the two, the sum of $100,000.00. . . .

Accordingly, the judgment should be reversed, on the law, on the facts and in the exercise of discretion, without costs and a new trial ordered unless the plaintiff consents to a reduction of the amount of compensatory damages to $400,000.00 and punitive damages as against Aware to the sum of $50,000.00 and as against Hartnett to the sum of $100,000.00, in which event the judgment as modified, should be affirmed, without costs.

NOTES

1. Justification for general damages. Awarding general damages in defamation cases has often been justified as a means of avoiding the administrative and evidentiary problems that arise out of the effort to prove special damages. The thought here is that a rough estimate is a better first approximation of the true state of affairs than the alternative presumption, which denies recovery altogether. This rationale, for example, was put forward in Tex Smith, The Harmonica Man, Inc. v. Godfrey, 102 N.Y.S.2d 251, 253 (Sup. Ct. 1951), where the defendant had made disparaging remarks about the plaintiff's ukuleles on both television and radio. The court noted that Godfrey's words could be taken as reflecting ill upon the plaintiff or its products. If the former, then damages could be recovered for slander per se. The court then continued:

> If the words are regarded purely as a reflection on the instruments, the same result would be reached. Here the words only become actionable if it is shown that damage followed upon their utterance. There was a time when such damage had to be specifically shown — the loss of a contract, a position, or the like. It is practicably impossible for one selling to the general public at retail or by mail order to show loss of particular sales. Under such circumstances those people were without remedy from the most groundless calumny. It is, however, now recognized that allegations and proof of a general loss of sales is sufficient, leaving it to the trier of the facts to determine whether the loss is properly to be attributed to the slander or not. The allegations of the complaint on this subject are sufficient by this standard.

Notwithstanding these arguments, general damages have been heavily criticized. One early argument is found in Courtney, Absurdities of the Law of Slander and Libel, 36 Am. L. Rev. 552 (1902), which insists that a "good character is seldom if ever injured by a false accusation of any kind." Note that the issues in a defamation case often parallel those found with toxic torts, since the plaintiff must show a causal connection between the defendant's false statements and plaintiff's loss or injury and thereafter quantify the level of the loss. See generally Anderson, Reputation, Compensation and Proof, 25 Wm. & Mary L. Rev. 747 (1984).

2. *Proof of general damages.* As the principal case well illustrates, it is rarely a simple matter to establish general damages in defamation cases. One especially difficult problem involves the relationship between general and special damages. Although it is difficult to find case authority for the proposition, it is generally said that in cases of oral defamation not slanderous per se, *once special damages are shown,* the jury may, if appropriate, award general damages as well. On this view the requirement of special damages would function much as the requirement of impact does in the emotional disturbance cases; and once special damages were shown, the case would be handled in the same way as if the words had been slanderous per se (i.e., damages for wounded feelings would be allowed). See 3 Restatement of Torts §575 comment *a*; McCormick, Damages 422 (1935). See also Developments in the Law: Defamation, 69 Harv. L. Rev. 875, 939-940 (1956), where the analogy to the impact rule is noted.

By the same token, the plaintiff who is entitled to collect for general damages may seek to collect for special damages as well. In Bishop v. New York Times, 135 N.E. 845 (N.Y. 1922), the court stated: "We are inclined to the view that a plaintiff is not compelled to rely upon a favorable presumption with which the law endows his cause of action but that he may prove if he can that he has been avoided and shunned by former friends and acquaintances as the direct and well-connected result of the libel." In Macy v. New York World-Telegram Corp., 141 N.E.2d 566, 569-570 (N.Y. 1957), the defendant newspaper falsely charged the plaintiff, a prominent civic figure and a Congressman running for reelection, with threatening to make public certain correspondence if plaintiff were not chosen as his party's senatorial nominee. On appeal the court vacated the plaintiff's jury award of $50,000 for general damages and granted the newspaper a new trial because the plaintiff had testified on his own behalf that he had been subject to personal attacks, expelled from his country club, and denied his seat in the House of Representatives. The court said that in some cases the plaintiff's own hearsay testimony might be sufficient to show the loss that followed from the libel, but it concluded that the "better practice would be to call as witnesses for plaintiff, subject to cross-examination, the persons who were supposed to have spoken or acted adversely to plaintiff and to demonstrate, if such demonstration be possible, a connection to the libel."

3. *Constitutional response.* The traditional common-law views on general and punitive damages have now been analyzed in a constitutional

context in Gertz v. Robert Welch, Inc., 418 U.S. 323 (1974), at page 1196 infra, and Dun & Bradstreet, Inc. v. Greenmoss Builders, 472 U.S. 749, at page 1206 infra.

3.   Other Remedies

a.   Injunctions

It has long been held that it is not proper to enjoin either slander or libel. Historically, the use of an equitable remedy was said to deprive defendants of the right to a jury trial when an "adequate" remedy at law was available. More recently, the justification of the rule has been placed squarely on the constitutional ground that the injunction would necessarily infringe on the freedom of speech protected under the First Amendment. See Near v. Minnesota, 283 U.S. 697 (1931). The classic article on the problem is Pound, Equitable Relief Against Defamation and Injuries to Personality, 29 Harv. L. Rev. 640 (1916). For a modern treatment see R. Smolla, Defamation §9.13[1][b].

b.   Retraction

A second remedy requires the defendant to retract the defamatory utterance, usually by publishing a withdrawal of the original charge in the same newspaper or broadcast that published the original libel. The "corrections" column in any newspaper is one convenient way to make retractions. At common law retraction was not considered a complete defense, but was only taken into account to mitigate damages. See, e.g., Webb v. Call Pub. Co., 180 N.W. 263 (Wis. 1920). The reason seems plain enough. The retraction does not restore the plaintiff to the position enjoyed before the initial libel was published. Even if the retraction is given broad publicity, it is highly likely that many people who read the original defamatory statement will not see the retraction. Or, the retraction itself may not erase lingering doubts that the original statement contained at least some grain of truth.

Recently many states have enacted retraction statutes that apply to media defendants, both print and broadcast. These statutes usually require that the defamed person first give the media defendant notice of the material he finds libelous and the opportunity to publish the retraction. Often the defendant will ask for information that shows the falsity of the published charges. Any retraction must be full and complete, since evasive apologies could confirm in the minds of readers that the defendant still believes in the truth of the original charges. The most common form of retraction statute limits the plaintiff to re-

covery of actual damages, and thus bars punitive damages. In some
states the protection goes further and limits the power of the plaintiff
to recover any form of special damages. For an exhaustive tabulation of
retraction statutes see R. Sack, Libel, Slander and Related Problems
§VII.2, 372 (1980). For a general account see R. Smolla, Law of Defamation §9.12 (1989).

c.   Reply statutes

In Miami Herald Publishing Co. v. Tornillo, 418 U.S. 241, 256-258
(1974), a unanimous Supreme Court struck down a Florida "right of
reply" statute which, in the words of the Court, "provides that if a candidate for nomination or election is assailed regarding his personal character or official record by any newspaper, the candidate has the right
to demand that the newspaper print, free of cost to the candidate, any
reply the candidate may make to the newspaper's charges. The reply
must appear in as conspicuous a place and in the same kind of type as
the charges which prompted the reply, provided it does not take up
more space than the charges. Failure to comply with the statute constitutes a first-degree misdemeanor."

As drafted the statute was not limited to defamatory statements. But
as drafted, the Court held that it was unconstitutional because it increased the costs of printing and distributing a newspaper. It did not,
however, rest solely on those economic considerations, but continued:

> Faced with the penalties that would accrue to any newspaper that pub-
> lished news or commentary arguably within the reach of the right-of-
> access statute, editors might well conclude that the safe course is to avoid
> controversy. Therefore, under the operation of the Florida statute, politi-
> cal and electoral coverage would be blunted or reduced. Government-
> enforced right of access inescapably "dampens the vigor and limits the
> variety of public debate," New York Times Co. v. Sullivan, ...
>
> Even if a newspaper would face no additional costs to comply with a
> compulsory access law and would not be forced to forgo publication of
> news or opinion by the inclusion of a reply, the Florida statute fails to
> clear the barriers of the First Amendment because of its intrusion into
> the function of editors. A newspaper is more than a passive receptacle or
> conduit for news, comment, and advertising. The choice of material to
> go into a newspaper, and the decisions made as to limitations on the
> size and content of the paper, and treatment of public issues and public
> officials — whether fair or unfair — constitute the exercise of editorial
> control and judgment. It has yet to be demonstrated how governmental
> regulation of this crucial process can be exercised consistent with First
> Amendment guarantees of a free press as they have evolved to this time.

See generally Barron, Access to the Press — A New First Amendment
Right, 80 Harv. L. Rev. 1641 (1967).

G. NONCONSTITUTIONAL DEFENSES

1. Privileges in the Private Sphere

Watt v. Longsdon
[1930] 1 K.B. 130

[Watt sued Longsdon for three separate defamatory publications. Plaintiff was the managing director at Casablanca, Morocco, of a British oil company of which the defendant was a director. At the time the various communications took place, the company was in the process of voluntary liquidation. In April 1928, Browne, who was the manager of the company in Casablanca, wrote a letter to the defendant in England at about the time the plaintiff left Casablanca for Lisbon and after his wife had returned to England. Browne's letter charged that plaintiff had left a liquor bill of £88, which Browne doubted would ever get paid, and related in detail how the plaintiff's maid had been plaintiff's mistress for several months. Browne expressed his surprise, "especially as she is an old woman, stone deaf, almost blind, with dyed hair!!!" but stated that the maid was able to give corroborating details. Browne's letter stated further that he was told by the servants that the plaintiff had had "orgies" with dancing girls, that he had designs on Browne's wife, and that plaintiff had shown himself to be "a blackguard, a thief, a liar and . . . lives exclusively to satisfy his own passions and lust." In a postscript, Browne suggested that it would probably be better not to show the plaintiff's wife the letter but that Mr. Singer, chairman of the board of directors of the company, should be told. In May 1928, defendant sent Browne's letter to Singer; and this is the first act of defamation complained of.

Defendant at the same time wrote Browne a letter in which he shared Browne's general view of the plaintiff and asked Browne to obtain sworn statements from his informants, offering to pay any bribes necessary to obtain such statements; the letter further said he thought it his duty to inform plaintiff's wife but that he would not do so until he had the sworn statements in his hand. This letter from the defendant to Browne was the second act of defamation complained of.

A few days later, without having received further confirmation of the statements in Browne's letter, the defendant showed it to plaintiff's wife, with the result that plaintiff and his wife separated and she began suit for divorce. The showing of Browne's letter to plaintiff's wife was the third act of defamation complained of.

Defendant did not justify the libels contained in the letters. Nevertheless, Horridge, J., gave judgment for the defendant, ruling that all three publications were privileged. The court of appeal reversed for the reasons indicated below.]

SCRUTTON, L.J. This case raises, amongst other matters, the extremely difficult question, equally important in its legal and social aspect, as to the circumstances, if any, in which a person will be justified in giving to one partner to a marriage information which that person honestly believes to be correct, but which is in fact untrue, about the matrimonial delinquencies of the other party to the marriage. . . .

By the law of England there are occasions on which a person may make defamatory statements about another which are untrue without incurring any legal liability for his statements. These occasions are called privileged occasions. A reason frequently given for this privilege is that the allegation that the speaker has "unlawfully and maliciously published," is displaced by proof that the speaker had either a duty or an interest to publish, and that this duty or interest confers the privilege. But communications made on these occasions may lose their privilege: (1.) they may exceed the privilege of the occasion by going beyond the limits of the duty or interest, or (2.) they may be published with express malice, so that the occasion is not being legitimately used, but abused. . . . The classical definition of "privileged occasions" is that of Parke B. in Toogood v. Spyring, a case where the tenant of a farm complained to the agent of the landlord, who had sent a workman to do repairs, that the workman had broken into the tenant's cellar, got drunk on the tenant's cider, and spoilt the work he was sent to do. The workman sued the tenant. Parke B. gave the explanation of privileged occasions in these words: "In general, an action lies for the malicious publication of statements which are false in fact, and injurious to the character of another (within the well-known limits as to verbal slander), and the law considers such publication as malicious, unless it is fairly made by a person in the discharge of some public or private duty, whether legal or moral, or in the conduct of his own affairs, in matters where his interest is concerned. In such cases, the occasion prevents the inference of malice, which the law draws from unauthorized communications, and affords a qualified defence depending upon the absence of actual malice. If fairly warranted by any reasonable occasion or exigency, and honestly made, such communications are protected for the common convenience and welfare of society; and the law has not restricted the right to make them within any narrow limits." It will be seen that the learned judge requires: (1.) a public or private duty to communicate, whether legal or moral; (2.) that the communication should be "fairly warranted by any reasonable occasion or exigency"; (3.) or a statement in the conduct of his own affairs where his interest is concerned. Parke B. had given several other definitions in slightly varying terms. For instance, in Cockayne v. Hodgkisson he

had directed the jury "Where the writer is acting on any duty, legal or
moral, towards the person to whom he writes, or where he has, by his
situation, to protect the interests of another, that which he writes under
such circumstances is a privileged communication." This adds to the
protection of his own interest spoken of in Toogood v. Spyring the
protection of the interests of another where the situation of the writer
requires him to protect those interests. This, I think, involves that his
"situation" imposes on him a legal or moral duty. The question whether
the occasion was privileged is for the judge, and so far as "duty" is concerned, the question is: Was there a duty, legal, moral, or social, to
communicate? As to legal duty, the judge should have no difficulty; the
judge should know the law; but as to moral or social duties of imperfect
obligation, the task is far more troublesome. The judge has no evidence
as to the view the community takes of moral or social duties. . . . Is the
judge merely to give his own view of moral and social duty, though he
thinks a considerable portion of the community hold a different opinion? Or is he to endeavour to ascertain what view "the great mass of
right-minded men" would take? It is not surprising that with such a
standard both judges and text-writers treat the matter as one of great
difficulty in which no definite line can be drawn. A conspicuous instance of the difficulties which arise when judges have to determine the
existence of duties, not legal, but moral or social, by the inner light of
their own conscience and judgment and knowledge of the world, is to
be found in the case of Coxhead v. Richards. A correct appreciation of
what was the difference of opinion in that case is, in my opinion, of
great importance in the decision of the present case. The short facts
were that Cass, the mate of a ship, wrote to Richards, an intimate friend
of his, a letter stating that on a voyage from the Channel to Wales,
which was going to continue to Eastern ports, the captain, Coxhead,
had by his drunkenness endangered the safety of the ship, and the lives
of the crew; and Cass asked Richards' advice what he should do in view
of the risk of repetition of this danger on the voyage to the East. Richards, after consulting "an Elder Brother of the Trinity House, and an
eminent shipowner," sent this letter to Ward, the owner of the ship.
Richards did not know Ward, and had no interest in the ship. The
owner dismissed the captain, who thereupon brought an action against
Richards. The judge at the trial directed the jury, if they should think
that the communication was strictly honest, and made solely in the execution of what he believed to be a duty, to find for the defendant. They
did so, while finding that the plea of justification failed. The plaintiff
then moved for a new trial, on which motion the Court after two hearings was equally divided. It is not very clear whether the judges differed
on a general principle, or on its application to the facts of the case. I
understand Tindal C.J. to have taken the view that if a man has information materially affecting the interests of another, and honestly commu-

nicates it to that other, he is protected, though he has no personal interest in the subject matter, and that his protection arises from "the various social duties by which men are bound to each other," and that it was the duty of the defendant to communicate this information to the owner. Erle J. appears to put the matter on "information given to protect damage from misconduct," "the importance of the information to the interest of the receiver," and says that a person having such information is justified in communicating it to the person interested, though the speaker did not stand in any relation to the recipient, and was a volunteer. He does not expressly refer to any social duty. On the other hand, Coltman and Cresswell JJ. both appear to me to hold that in such circumstances there was no moral duty, for that any tendency that way was counterbalanced by the moral duty not to slander your neighbour. . . .

[After considering various other English precedents, the court then summarized the occasions giving rise to a privileged communication as follows:] [E]ither (1.) a duty to communicate information believed to be true to a person who has a material interest in receiving the information, or (2.) an interest in the speaker to be protected by communicating information, if true, relevant to that interest, to a person honestly believed to have a duty to protect that interest, or (3.) a common interest in and reciprocal duty in respect of the subject matter of the communication between speaker and recipient. . . .

In my opinion Horridge J. went too far in holding that there could be a privileged occasion on the ground of interest in the recipient without any duty to communicate on the part of the person making the communication. But that does not settle the question, for it is necessary to consider, in the present case, whether there was, as to each communication, a duty to communicate, and an interest in the recipient.

First as to the communication between Longsdon and Singer, I think the case must proceed on the admission that at all material times Watt, Longsdon and Browne were in the employment of the same company, and the evidence afforded by the answer to the interrogatory put in by the plaintiff that Longsdon believed the statements in Browne's letter. In my view on these facts there was a duty, both from a moral and material point of view, on Longsdon to communicate the letter to Singer, the chairman of his company, who, apart from questions of present employment, might be asked by Watt for a testimonial to a future employer. Equally, I think Longsdon receiving the letter from Browne, might discuss the matter with him, and ask for further information, on the ground of a common interest in the affairs of the company, and to obtain further information for the chairman. I should therefore agree with the view of Horridge J. that these two occasions were privileged, though for different reasons. Horridge J. further held that there was no evidence of malice fit to be left to the jury, and, while

I think some of Longsdon's action and language in this respect was unfortunate, as the plaintiff has put in the answer that Longsdon believed the truth of the statements in Browne's and his own letter, like Lord Dunedin in Adam v. Ward, I should not try excess with too nice scales, and I do not dissent from his view as to malice. As to the communications to Singer and Browne, in my opinion the appeal should fail, but as both my brethren take the view that there was evidence of malice which should be left to the jury, there must, of course, be a new trial as to the claim based on these two publications.

The communication to Mrs. Watt stands on a different footing. I have no intention of writing an exhaustive treatise on the circumstances when a stranger or a friend should communicate to husband or wife information he receives as to the conduct of the other party to the marriage. I am clear that it is impossible to say he is always under a moral or social duty to do so; it is equally impossible to say he is never under such a duty. It must depend on the circumstances of each case, the nature of the information, and the relation of speaker and recipient. It cannot, on the one hand, be the duty even of a friend to communicate all the gossip the friend hears at men's clubs or women's bridge parties to one of the spouses affected. On the other hand, most men would hold that it was the moral duty of a doctor who attended his sister in law, and believed her to be suffering from a miscarriage, for which an absent husband could not be responsible, to communicate that fact to his wife and the husband. . . . If this is so, the decision must turn on the circumstances of each case, the judge being much influenced by the consideration that as a general rule it is not desirable for any one, even a mother in law, to interfere in the affairs of man and wife. Using the best judgment I can in this difficult matter, I have come to the conclusion that there was not a moral or social duty in Longsdon to make this communication to Mrs. Watt such as to make the occasion privileged, and that there must be a new trial so far as it relates to the claim for publication of a libel to Mrs. Watt. The communications to Singer and Browne being made on a privileged occasion, there must be a new trial of the issue as to malice defeating the privilege. There must also be a new trial of the complaint as to publication to Mrs. Watt, the occasion being held not to be privileged. The plaintiff must have the costs of this appeal; the costs of the first trial must abide the result of the second trial, the issues being separated.

GREER, L.J. . . . In my judgment no right minded man in the position of the defendant, a friend of the plaintiff and his wife, would have thought it right to communicate the horrible accusations contained in Mr. Browne's letter to the plaintiff's wife. The information came to Mr. Browne from a very doubtful source, and in my judgment no reasonably right-minded person could think it his duty, without obtaining some corroboration of the story, and without first communicating with the plaintiff, to pass on these outrageous charges of marital infidelity of a gross kind, and drunkenness and dishonesty to the plaintiff's wife. As regards the publication to the plaintiff's wife, the occasion was not privileged, and it is unnecessary to consider whether there was evidence of express malice. As regards the publication to the chairman of the company, who owned nearly all the shares, and to Mr. Browne, I think on the facts as pleaded there was between the defendant and the recipients of the letters a common interest which would make the occasion privileged, but I also think there is intrinsic evidence in the letter to Browne, and evidence in the hasty and unjustifiable communication to the plaintiff's wife, which would be sufficient to entitle the plaintiff to ask for a verdict on these publications on the ground of express malice.

The plaintiff's counsel put in as part of his case the defendant's answers to interrogatories 5 and 8, which were to the effect that the defendant believed all the matters alleged in Browne's letter, which he published to the plaintiff's wife and to Mr. Singer, to be true. It was suggested that this belief made it impossible to say that the publication was malicious. I do not agree with this view. Malice is a state of mind. . . . A man may believe in the truth of a defamatory statement, and yet when he publishes it be reckless whether his belief be well founded or not. His motive for publishing a libel on a privileged occasion may be an improper one, even though he believes the statement to be true. He may be moved by hatred or dislike, or a desire to injure the subject of the libel, and may be using the occasion for that purpose, and if he is doing so the publication will be maliciously made, even though he may believe the defamatory statements to be true. . . .

I think the defendant's conduct in disseminating the gross charges that he did to the plaintiff's wife, and to Mr. Singer, and repeating and to some extent adding to them in his letter to Mr. Browne, and his offer to provide funds for procuring the evidence of the two women in Casablanca, affords some evidence of malice which ought to have been left to the jury. It is not for us to weigh the evidence. It will be for the jury to decide whether they are satisfied that in publishing the libels the defendant was in fact giving effect to his malicious or otherwise improper feelings towards the plaintiff, and was not merely using the occasion for the protection of the interests of himself and his two correspondents.

NOTES

1. *When is a communication privileged?* It has long been widely recognized that the law is concerned with balancing interests in reputation with freedom of communication in areas thought to be socially useful. The problem is to identify private communications that deserve the

encouragement that comes from relaxing the rule of strict liability. To achieve that balance most courts and commentators, both in England and the United States, have closely followed the scheme suggested by Baron Parke in Toogood v. Spyring, 149 Eng. Rep. 1044 (Ex. 1834), discussed in Watt v. Longsdon, supra. Under this scheme the existence of privileged occasions depends on the interest of the speaker, the interest of the audience, or a common interest between the speaker and the audience. See Restatement of Torts §§594, 595, 596, following the basic rule.

The claim of privilege is recognized for character references of former servants and credit references for business professionals, where the defendant is replying to an inquiry. In Gardner v. Slade, 116 Eng. Rep. 1467, 1470 (Q.B. 1849), a case involving a domestic servant, Wightman, J., said: "It is quite a mistake to treat questions of this kind as if the law allowed a privilege only for the benefit of the giver of the character. It is of importance to the public that characters should be readily given. The servant who applies for the character, and the person who is to take him, are equally benefited. Indeed, there is no class to whom it is of so much importance that characters should be freely given as honest servants." In Smith v. Thomas, 2 Bing. N.C. 372 (1835), a case involving a credit reference, the court observed: "The publication is alleged to have taken place in the course of a confidential communication between one tradesman and another, as to the solvency of a third person, whom the inquirer was about to trust. If such communications are not protected by law from the danger of vexatious litigation in cases where they turn out to be incorrect in fact, the stability of men engaged in trade and commerce would be exposed to the greatest hazard, for no man would answer an inquiry as to the solvency of another."

A privilege arises when both the speaker and the audience have a strong common interest. In its simplest form it covers communications between an employer and an employee, such as a complaint from a servant to his superior, or the review of an employee's work by supervisory personnel. Kasachkoff v. City of New York, 485 N.Y.S.2d 992 (N.Y. App. 1985). It also attaches to statements made to an employee regarding the reasons for discharge, when that information is communicated to a prospective employer under the doctrine of compelled publication. See Lewis v. Equitable Life Assur. Soc., 389 N.W.2d 876 (Minn. 1986), supra at page 1090, note 4. In general, the litigation over employer references exploded during the 1980s, and by some estimates reached a third of the defamation suits filed. See Martha Middleton, *Employers Face Upsurge in Suits over Defamation*, NATIONAL LAW JOURNAL, May 4, 1987, at 1; Gregory Stricharchuk, *Fired Employees Turn the Reason for Dismissal into a Legal Weapon*, WALL ST. J., Oct. 2, 1986, at 33. Is there any way of preventing every discharge case from being turned into a defamation case?

The privilege has been extended to many intragroup situations such as churches, fraternal organizations, labor unions, and shareholders of a corporation. For a recent decision recognizing only a qualified privilege for statements concerning a teacher made to a faculty evaluation committee see Colson v. Stieg, 433 N.E.2d 246 (Ill. 1982).

2. *Credit reports.* The same view of privilege has been extended at common law to commercial credit agencies. Thus, in Shore v. Retailers Commercial Agency, 174 N.E.2d 376, 379 (Mass. 1961), Spaulding, J., wrote:

> We are of opinion that reports made by a mercantile agency to an interested subscriber should be conditionally privileged. Those about to engage in a commercial transaction like to know something about the persons with whom they are dealing. Often they are unable to get that information themselves and must obtain it through mercantile agencies. In furnishing such information the agencies are supplying a legitimate business need and ought to have the protection of the privilege. Without such protection few would undertake to furnish the information, and the cost would be high, if not prohibitive. For a good discussion of the reason supporting the privilege see Smith, Conditional Privilege for Mercantile Agencies, 14 Col. L. Rev. 187, 296, 306-310. We are not to be understood as holding that there is a privilege where information is published by the agency generally to subscribers having no particular interest in the report. Restatement: Torts, §595, comment *g.*

Shore reflects the majority view in the United States, with only Georgia and Idaho holding that no conditional privilege attaches to credit reports. For a listing of cases see Note, Protecting the Subjects of Credit Reports, 80 Yale L.J. 1035, 1050-1051, nn.85, 87 (1971). The leading authority against recognizing a privilege is Macintosh v. Dun, [1908] A.C. 390, 400 (P.C.). There the court noted that the credit business, like any business, was run "in the hope and expectation of making a profit," with heavy reliance on information from "gossip," "discharged servants," and "disloyal servants." The court concluded: "It is only right that those who engage in such a business, touching so closely very dangerous ground, should take the consequences if they overstep the law." Eight years later the House of Lords distinguished *Macintosh,* holding that a communication from a mutual credit agency that did not trade for profit and that acted simply as a clearinghouse for credit information among its 6,000 members, was privileged. London Assn. for Protection of Trade v. Greenlands, Ltd., [1916] 2 A.C. 15. This area of privilege has generally not been affected by *New York Times.* See Dun & Bradstreet, Inc. v. Greenmoss Builders, 472 U.S. 749 (1985), infra at page 1206, note 2.

3. *Volunteers.* As *Watt* indicates, one most troublesome problem arises when the defendant volunteered communication without a request. It would appear that one is not necessarily protected in speaking because

an inquiry has been made of him; nor is he necessarily denied protection because he volunteered the statement. Restatement (Second) of Torts §595(2)(a) notes that it is an "important factor" that "the publication is made in response to a request rather than volunteered by the publisher."

In "The Count Joannes" v. Bennett, 87 Mass. 169, 172 (1862), defendant had for several years been the pastor of the parents and daughter involved and was an intimate friend of the family. The defendant was persuaded by the father to write the daughter a letter urging her to call off her proposed marriage to plaintiff. While the court reversed plaintiff's judgment on other grounds, it held that the contents of the letter were not privileged, pointing out that the defendant, although he acted "from laudable motives in writing it," was no longer the daughter's pastor and was in no way related to her other than as a friend. The court said, in part: "It is obvious that if such communications could be protected merely on the ground that the party making them held friendly relations with those to whom they were written or spoken, a wide door would be left open by which indiscriminate aspersion of private character could escape with impunity. Indeed, it would rarely be difficult for a party to shelter himself from the consequences of uttering or publishing a slander or libel under a privilege which could be readily made to embrace almost every species of communication. The law does not tolerate any such license of speech or pen."

4. *When is the privilege lost? Watt* and similar cases only afford the defendant a qualified privilege that can be lost upon proof of malice. These defamation cases therefore involve three stages: the publication of the defamatory information, the privilege, and its possible abuse. That tripartite division of issue is reflected in the distribution of the burden of proof. The uniform rule is that once plaintiff has made out a prima facie case of defamation, the burden is on defendant to establish that the occasion was privileged; and once defendant has made out a prima facie privileged occasion, the burden is on plaintiff to establish abuse of the privilege. Similarly, the question of whether the occasion is privileged is exclusively a question of law for the court, whereas the question of whether the privilege has been abused is a question of fact for the jury.

In England, Clark v. Molyneux, [1877] 3 Q.B. 237, established the rule that plaintiff cannot override a qualified privilege simply by showing that defendant acted negligently. Instead, plaintiff must plead and prove that the statement was made with "actual malice" or "malice in fact," meaning that defendant either knew the statement to be false or "out of anger or some other wrong motive" made the statement "recklessly" without regard to whether it was true or false. Several American decisions have held, contrary to the English rule, that the defendant's qualified privilege is overcome by a showing of simple negligence. See, e.g., Toothaker v. Conant, 40 A. 331 (Me. 1898). The dominant position, however, has followed the English rule requiring that malice, not ordinary negligence, must be shown to defeat the privilege, thereby protecting the defendant who, though incompetent "honestly and in good faith" believed the offending statement to be true. Barry v. McCollom, 70 A. 1035 (Conn. 1908).

In addition, the privilege may be abused by an "unnecessary, unreasonable or excessive publication," Galvin v. New York, N.H. & H.R.R., 168 N.E.2d 262, 265 (Mass. 1960), where the burden of proof is placed on the plaintiff. See Restatement (Second) of Torts §600, which holds that the privilege is lost for "abuse" "if he (a) knows the matter to be false, or (b) acts in reckless disregard of its truth or falsity."

5. *Defamation in self-defense.* Still another form of conditional privilege arises "when the person making the publication reasonably believes that his interest in his own reputation has been unlawfully invaded by another person and that the defamatory matter that he publishes about the other is reasonably necessary to defend himself," — "including the statement that his accuser is an unmitigated liar." Restatement (Second) of Torts §594 comment *k*. The boundaries of this privilege are not clearly established and it gives rise to questions reminiscent of those raised in connection with self-defense against physical attack: How vigorous must the plaintiff's original aggression have been? Must the original attack have been defamatory? What if it was true or privileged? Again, how much verbal force may the defendant use in reply? Does the privilege extend to the defense of third parties? Further, there are strong overtones of a doctrine somewhat akin to assumption of risk or contributory negligence running through the cases in which plaintiff, having invited a reply, cannot complain when one is given.

6. *Consent.* An otherwise actionable defamatory statement may be privileged if the plaintiff has consented to its publication. Unlike the privileges discussed above, this resembles an absolute privilege and does not depend on the state of mind of defendant. Restatement (Second) of Torts §583. Yet there are some limits to this defense. Thus, plaintiff will not be held to have consented when, for example, he asks defendant for a recommendation and the letter that defendant sends turns out to be defamatory.

Is there consent if the plaintiff dares the defendant to utter defamatory words that are otherwise unprivileged? See Restatement (Second) of Torts §583 comment *e*, which gives the puzzling advice that the answer boils down to a question of fact. The Restatement also says that "one who agrees to submit his conduct to investigation, knowing that its results will be published, consents to the publication of honest findings of investigators."

3.   Privileges in the Public Sphere

a.   Legal Proceedings and Reports Thereon

Kennedy v. Cannon
182 A.2d 54 (Md. 1962)

SYBERT, J. This appeal questions whether the trial court erred in directing a verdict for the defendant, an attorney, in a suit for slander on the grounds that the allegedly slanderous statement was privileged as part of the defendant's duty as counsel to his client, and that no malice on the part of the defendant had been shown.

The appellee, Robert Powell Cannon (defendant below), was summoned to the Wicomico County jail in Salisbury at the request of Charles L. Humphreys, a Negro who had been arrested early that morning and charged with the rape of the appellant, Jane Linton Kennedy, a white, married woman. After conferring with the prisoner, appellee made a telephone call to Richard L. Moore, managing editor of the Salisbury Times, a daily newspaper published in Salisbury, with a circulation of about 23,000. He inquired concerning any information the newspaper might have received in regard to the charge against Humphreys and was informed by Mr. Moore that "we had talked to the authorities and had gotten a story together, and the story said that Humphreys had signed a statement admitting intercourse with the woman who was involved." Mr. Moore told the appellee that the information had been given by the State's Attorney. Thereupon, the appellee proceeded to tell Mr. Moore everything that Humphreys had related to him, including an assertion by Humphreys that Mrs. Kennedy had consented to the intercourse. When informed that it would be impossible to print matter of that type, and at such great length, appellee agreed, with some reluctance, to the publication as part of the news article of additional material quoting the appellee as to Humphreys' claim. The article which was published that afternoon included in the information furnished by the State's Attorney the identity of the appellant, the fact that she is a white woman, the fact that she had accused Humphreys, a Negro, of raping her, and a statement that Humphreys had signed an admission of the intercourse. The article then quoted appellee as having said, "He [Humphreys] emphatically denies the charge. He says that the woman submitted to his advances willingly."

As a result of the publication of the statement appellant alleged she suffered humiliation and harassment by annoying phone calls from unknown persons and eventually was forced to move with her family out of the community and the State. She instituted a suit against appellee alleging that the words spoken by him to the newspaper charged her with the crime of adultery, were slanderous per se under Art. 88, §1, Code (1957), and were not privileged.

The appellee admitted on the witness stand that the newspaper article correctly quoted his statement to the editor. He sought to justify its publication on the ground that the physical safety of his client required it. He stated he feared the possibility of a lynching if only the material released by the State's Attorney were published. Recalling a lynching which had occurred in Salisbury under similar circumstances some 25 years previously, he said he felt that the account should include a denial of the charge based upon his client's claim of consent by the woman. At the conclusion of the testimony before a jury, the trial court granted appellee's motion for a directed verdict, expressing the opinion that when the State had undertaken to publish a statement about the case damaging to his client, the appellee was justified and privileged in replying as he did. Appellant appeals from the judgment for costs entered in favor of appellee.

The question raised here is whether appellee's statement comes within the ambit of Code (1957), Art. 88, §1, supra (relating to slander), or whether a recovery by appellant is barred because the statement was privileged. Words of the nature involved here have been held to be slanderous per se. . . .

The privilege afforded an attorney in a judicial proceeding and its rationale are discussed in the leading case of Maulsby v. Reifsnider, 69 Md. 143 (1888), where this Court stated:

". . . All agree, that counsel are privileged and protected to a certain extent, at least, for defamatory words spoken *in a judicial proceeding*, and words thus spoken are not actionable, which would in themselves be actionable, if spoken elsewhere. He is obliged, in the discharge of a professional duty, to prosecute and defend the most important rights and interests, the life it may be, or the liberty or the property of his client, and it is absolutely essential to the administration of justice that he should be allowed the widest latitude in commenting on the character, the conduct and motives of parties and witnesses and other persons directly or remotely connected with the subject-matter in litigation. And to subject him to actions of slander by every one who may consider himself aggrieved, and to the costs and expenses of a harassing litigation, would be to fetter and restrain him in that open and fearless discharge of duty which he owes to his client, and which the demands of justice require. Not that the law means to say, that one, because he is counsel in the trial of a cause, has the right, abstractly considered, deliberately and maliciously to slander another, but it is the fear that if the rule were otherwise, actions without number might be brought against counsel who had not spoken falsely and maliciously. It is better therefore to make the rule of law so large that counsel acting bona fide in the discharge of duty, shall never be troubled, although by making it so large, others who have acted mala fide and maliciously, are included. The question whether words spoken by counsel were spoken maliciously or in good faith, are, and always will be, open questions, upon which opinion may differ, and counsel, however innocent, would be liable if not to judgments, to a vexatious and expensive litigation. The privilege thus recognized by law is not the privilege merely of counsel, but the privilege of clients, and the evil, if any, resulting from it must be endured for the sake of the greater good which is thereby secured. But this privilege is not an absolute and unqualified privilege, and cannot be extended beyond the reason and principles on which it is founded. . . ." (Emphasis added.)

[The Court went on to hold that the words, to be privileged, must also be relevant to the judicial proceedings in which they were spoken.]

The statement just quoted reflects the view of a majority of the jurisdictions in this country, although the semantics in this area of tort law have changed somewhat since the date of the *Maulsby* case. What was characterized in that case as a qualified privilege for communications, conditioned on their being pertinent or relevant to a judicial proceeding without regard to the motive of the speaker, is referred to by modern text writers and in case law as an absolute privilege. . . . This absolute immunity extends to the judge as well as to witnesses and parties to the litigation, for defamatory statements uttered in the course of a trial or contained in pleadings, affidavits, depositions, and other documents directly related to the case. . . . An absolute privilege is distinguished from a qualified privilege in that the former provides immunity regardless of the purpose or motive of the defendant, or the reasonableness of his conduct, while the latter is conditioned upon the absence of malice and is forfeited if it is abused. . . .

Appellee in this case contends that under the *Maulsby* case, his statement was absolutely privileged. It is not disputed that the statement was relevant to the criminal proceeding. The essential question to be answered is whether it was published in — that is, as part of — a "judicial proceeding."

The term "judicial proceeding" is broad enough to cover all steps in a criminal action, so that when Humphreys was arrested and charged with rape it would be a valid conclusion that the judicial proceeding had commenced. . . . However, this does not necessarily mean that every statement made by an attorney after the inception of a judicial proceeding will be privileged.

Appellee cites the oft quoted rule from 3 Restatement, Torts, §586:

"An attorney at law is absolutely privileged to publish false and defamatory matter of another in communications preliminary to a proposed judicial proceeding, or in the institution of, or during the course and as a part of a judicial proceeding in which he participates as counsel, if it has some relation thereto."

However, the extension of this absolute privilege to statements not made in the judicial proceeding itself is limited both by the comments on the rule of the Restatement itself, and by the decisions. The scope of the privilege is restricted to communications such as those made between an attorney and his client, or in the examination of witnesses by counsel, or in statements made by counsel to the court or jury. . . . Appellee cites no authorities which would extend the privilege beyond a communication to one actually involved in the proceeding, either as judge, attorney, party or witness. On the other hand, it has been held that such absolute privilege will not attach to counsel's extrajudicial publications, related to the litigation, which are made outside the purview of the judicial proceeding. . . . Nor will the attorney be privileged for actionable words spoken before persons in no way connected with the proceeding. [The court discusses several cases.]

All of the above cited cases make it obvious that aside from any question of ethics, an attorney who wishes to litigate his case in the press will do so at his own risk. We hold that appellee had no absolute privilege in regard to the statement made by him to the newspaper.

However, the argument is made (and the language of the trial court's opinion shows that it was persuasive there) that the forum had been chosen by the State's Attorney, and not by appellee, and that he had a right, perhaps even a duty to his client, to publish the statement in question. This argument raises indirectly the contention that because of the attorney-client relationship, at least a qualified privilege existed in the absence of a showing of malice or abuse of the privilege.

There may well be a qualified privilege based upon an attorney-client relationship which would justify an otherwise slanderous communication to certain other persons, to protect the rights of society or one to whom a legal or moral duty is owed. However, the communication *must be made in a proper manner and to proper parties only,* i.e., to parties having a corresponding interest or duty. . . . It may be conceded that appellee indeed had a duty to act upon the information he had gained as to the statement given by the State's Attorney to the newspaper, particularly in light of Humphreys' statement to him. However, the means he chose to fulfill that duty were not proper, nor did he release the communication to a party having a corresponding interest or duty in the matter; and it cannot be said that his action was within the scope of his professional acts as an attorney in a pending case. . . . Other steps more consonant with Canon 20, Canons of Professional Ethics, were open to appellee. He could have requested the transfer of Humphreys to the jail of another jurisdiction for safekeeping until trial. He could have sought to have the objectionable matter, contained in the proposed article, kept out of publication. Even if this attempt were unsuccessful, other tactics were possible to the attorney who eventually defended the case, e.g., a request for change of venue, voir dire examination of prospective jurors in regard to the article, and preservation of the question of the prejudicial effect of the article, for appellate review.

The solicitude of appellee for his client is understandable, and the initial act of the State's Attorney in releasing his statement to the press must be disapproved. Nevertheless, as we have stated, appellee's legal duty in no way justified the publication of his defamatory reply statement. To hold otherwise would open the door to the universally condemned "trial by press," a procedure forbidden to counsel and subversive of the fair and orderly conduct of judicial proceedings. . . .

We hold that as a matter of law appellee had neither an absolute nor a qualified privilege in regard to the defamatory statement. Since the words spoken were slanderous per se they required no proof of special damage and carried the implication of malice. However, even though appellee was not reasonably entitled to believe in the existence of privilege, since none existed at law under the circumstances of this case, the trier of facts, on retrial, may consider his testimony, if reoffered, that he acted in good faith and without malice, on the question of mitigation of damages. As was said in Brush-Moore Newsp. v. Pollitt:

". . . it is generally held that mitigation of damages is a partial defense to defamation, as tending to reduce both the general compensatory damages and to negative the express malice, or outrageous conduct, which is the basis for punitive damages. . . ."

For the reasons stated, the granting of a directed verdict for appellee was erroneous and the case should have been submitted to the jury.

NOTES

1. *Statements made in the course of government business.* The common-law courts have long recognized that an absolute privilege attaches to defamatory statements made in the course of government business as long as the matter published has some relation to the proceedings in question. Thus, the privilege extends without doubt to judges in the course of official business, to lawyers for conduct both preliminary to and in the course of judicial proceedings, and to parties to judicial proceedings. Restatement (Second) of Torts §§585-587.

The absolute privilege for statements made in the course of judicial proceedings was strongly affirmed in Barker v. Huang, 610 A.2d 1341, 1345-1346 (Del. 1992), where the plaintiff sought to create an exception for sham statements made in the course of litigation. Horsey, J., rejected the invitation: "To allow claims of defamation in the context of judicial proceedings to proceed to costly discovery in an attempt to ferret out facts purporting to show a sham nature to the litigation would largely defeat the purpose of the privilege. Moreover, sufficient sanctions already exist to deter and punish frivolous litigation. We therefore hold that no 'sham litigation' exception to the defense of absolute privilege exists under the law of Delaware."

2. *Quasi-government bodies.* The occasions to which an absolute privilege attach are of concern in an age of administrative agencies, quasi-judicial bodies, and special commissions. In Wiener v. Weintraub, 239 N.E.2d 540 (N.Y. 1968), the court held that an absolute privilege attached to complaints made before a bar association grievance committee. In Marino v. Wallace, 410 N.Y.S.2d 488 (N.Y. App. Div. 1978), reached the same result with regard to remarks at a Public Service Commission hearing, and in Park Knoll Associates v. Schmidt, 454 N.Y.S.2d 901 (1982), the absolute privilege was held to protect tenants, their tenants association, and its leaders, who presented grievances against their landlord to the State Division of Housing and Community Renewal. Finally, it has been extended "to include the information supplied by an employer on the 'fact-finding supplement' form of the employment security division of the state labor department," where the information provided is used for deciding questions of fact and law needed to process individual claims. Petyan v. Ellis, 510 A.2d 1337 (Conn. 1986).

Not all "official" statements receive the protection of this absolute privilege. In Ezekiel v. Jones Motor Co., Inc., 372 N.E.2d 1281, 1285 (Mass. 1978), the defendant's employee, when testifying before a joint management-union grievance board, falsely accused the plaintiff of stealing company property. The defendant's claim for absolute privilege was rejected by the court:

> While a witness at a judicial proceeding is free to make defamatory statements without fear of being sued by the defamed person, the witness is nevertheless subject to the control of the judge. If he or she gives false testimony, prosecution for perjury or punishment for contempt may be forthcoming. Such protections against false testimony simply do not exist at a labor grievance hearing such as the one which took place here. A witness at a grievance hearing need not give sworn testimony, nor is he subject to the control of a judge to limit his testimony to competent relevant and material evidence. A conditional privilege provides sufficient incentive for the witness to speak openly, but does not remove the safeguards against communications which are deliberately false.

States have also divided on the status of the privilege accorded to hospital peer review committees that evaluate — often in response to individual complaints — the performance of staff physicians. In Franklin v. Blank, 525 P.2d 945, 946 (N.M. Ct. App. 1974), the court held that both a letter written to initiate peer review and the peer review process at common law were subject to an absolute privilege. "The appropriate professional societies, by exercising peer review, can and do perform a great public service by exercising control over those persons in a position of public trust but nevertheless unfit to bear that responsibility." But in DiMiceli v. Klieger, 206 N.W.2d 184 (Wis. 1973), the court held that only a qualified privilege was available. Today most states have some specific statutes that supply some privilege for peer review proceedings. Thus Fla. Stat. Ann. §766.101 (West 1994) contains a complex statute whose main provision protects a peer review committee member, or health care provider who gives information to a peer review committee, when "the committee member or health care provider acts without intentional fraud." Further amendments limit the use in court of information presented to a peer reviw committee. In contrast Cal. Civ. Code §47(West 1994) extends the privilege to "any other official proceeding authorized by law," with unrelated exceptions. In Ascherman v. Natanson, 100 Cal. Rptr. 656 (Cal. App. 1972), the court interpreted this section as granting an absolute immunity for a proceeding "conducted in a manner similar to a judicial proceeding, including notice informal pleading and hearing."

3. *Criminal charges to public officials.* Many recent cases address the nature of privilege in the context of reports of criminal activities that private individuals make to police officers. As noted in *Kennedy,* the Restatement recognizes an absolute privilege for all communications "made preliminary to a proposed judicial proceeding," Restatement (Second) Torts §587, comment *b.* Some courts have followed that general rule see, e.g., Correllas v. Viveiros, 572 N.E.2d 7, 12 (Mass. 1991), granting an absolute privilege for statements made to the police in an investigation of a theft of $8,000 from a safe-deposit vault where both plaintiff and defendant worked. During the police investigation the defendant confessed to the theft of $4,000 and claimed the plaintiff had taken the rest. Defendant then testified at plaintiff's trial, at which the plaintiff was acquited. Plaintiff's ensuing defamation action was barred, with Nolan, J., writing:

> In contrast to these cases [of absolute privilege], there are many cases which held that the report of a crime is only conditionally privileged. In most of those cases, however, the defendant went to the police, or communicated with others, on their own initiative and published an accusation which might otherwise never have been known. . . . The key to understanding these cases lies in the fact that, when the defendants made the allegedly defamatory statements, no criminal action or judicial proceeding was then being contemplated or proposed. . . .
>
> An absolute privilege was appropriately applied in this case because police and prosecutors were contemplating a criminal action when the defendant made the allegedly defamatory statements. . . . [I]t was obvious that the defendant would either be a witness or one of the accused in the criminal case. By implicating the plaintiff, the defendant knew that she would have to repeat her accusations under oath, subjecting herself to possible perjury for any false testimony.

Similarly, in Miner v. Novotny, 498 A.2d 269, 275 (Md. 1985), the court was willing to recognize an absolute privilege to citizen complaints of police brutality made under oath: "Citizen complaints of such abuses, and the administrative disciplinary procedure which has been developed to investigate these complaints, serve a public function of vital importance by providing a mechanism through which abuses may be reported to the proper authorities, and the abusers held accountable." But in Caldor v. Bowden, 625 A.2d 959, 968 (Md. 1993), the same court followed *Correllas* and recognized only a qualified privilege for oral communications, not under oath, to the police. "Although we do not wish to discourage the reporting of criminal activities, we also do not wish to encourage harassment, or wasting of law enforcement resources, by investigations of false, maliciously made complaints."

b. Reports of Public Proceedings or Meetings

Brown & Williamson Tobacco Corp. v. Jacobson
713 F.2d 262 (7th Cir. 1983).

POSNER, CIRCUIT JUDGE.

This diversity suit brought by Brown & Williamson, the manufacturer of Viceroy cigarettes, charges CBS and Walter Jacobson with libel and other violations of Illinois law. Jacobson is a news commentator for WBBM-TV, a Chicago television station owned by CBS. The defendants moved to dismiss the complaint on a variety of grounds. Without writing an opinion the district court granted the motion "for the reasons set forth in defendants' memoranda," adding only: "to deny this motion would unduly restrict the freedom of the press and the right of a journalist to express opinions freely." Brown & Williamson appeals.

In 1975, Ted Bates, the advertising agency that had the Viceroy account, hired the Kennan market-research firm to help develop a new advertising strategy for Viceroy. Kennan submitted a report which stated that for "the younger smoker," "a cigarette, and the whole smoking process, is part of the illicit pleasure category. . . . In the young smoker's mind a cigarette falls into the same category with wine, beer, shaving, wearing a bra (or purposely not wearing one), declaration of independence and striving for self-identity. For the young starter, a cigarette is associated with introduction to sex life, with courtship, with smoking 'pot' and keeping late studying hours. . . ." The report recommended, therefore, the following pitches to "young smokers, starters": "Present the cigarette as part of the illicit pleasure category of products and activities. . . . To the best of your ability, (considering some legal constraints), relate the cigarette to 'pot', wine, beer, sex, etc. *Don't* communicate health or health-related points." Ted Bates forwarded the report to Brown & Williamson. According to the allegations of the complaint, which on this appeal we must accept as true, Brown &

Williamson rejected the "illicit pleasure strategy" proposed in the report, and fired Ted Bates primarily because of displeasure with the proposed strategy.

Years later the Federal Trade Commission conducted an investigation of cigarette advertising, and in May 1981 it published a report of its staff on the investigation. The FTC staff report discusses the Kennan report, correctly dates it to May 1975, and after quoting from it the passages we have quoted states that "B & W adopted many of the ideas contained in this report in the development of a Viceroy advertising campaign." In support of this assertion the staff report quotes an internal Brown & Williamson document on "Viceroy Strategy," dated 1976, which states, "The marketing efforts must cope with consumers' attitudes about smoking and health, either providing them a *rationale* for smoking a full flavor VICEROY or providing a means of *repressing* their concerns about smoking a full flavor VICEROY." The staff report then quotes a description of three advertising strategies. Although the description contains no reference to young smokers or to "starters," the staff report states: "B & W documents also show that it translated the advice [presumably from the Kennan report] on how to attract young 'starters' into an advertising campaign featuring young adults in situations that the vast majority of young people probably would experience and in situations demonstrating adherence to a 'free and easy, hedonistic lifestyle.' " The interior quotation is from another 1976 Brown & Williamson document on advertising strategy.

On November 4, 1981, a reporter for WBBM-TV called Brown & Williamson headquarters and was put in touch with a Mr. Humber in the corporate affairs department. The reporter told Mr. Humber that he was preparing a story on the tobacco industry for Walter Jacobson's "Perspective" program and asked him about the part of the FTC staff report that dealt with the Viceroy advertising strategy. Humber replied that Brown & Williamson had rejected the proposals in the Kennan report and had fired Ted Bates in part because of dissatisfaction with those proposals.

Walter Jacobson's "Perspective" on the tobacco industry was broadcast on November 11 and rebroadcast on November 12 and again on March 5, 1982. In the broadcast, Jacobson, after stating that "pushing cigarettes on television is prohibited," announces his theme: "Television is off limits to cigarettes and so the business, the killer business, has gone to the ad business in New York for help, to the slicksters on Madison Avenue with a billion dollars a year for bigger and better ways to sell cigarettes. Go for the youth of America, go get 'em guys. . . . Hook 'em while they are young, make 'em start now — just think how many cigarettes they'll be smoking when they grow up." Various examples of how cigarette marketing attempts "to addict the children to poison" are given. The last and longest concerns Viceroy.

The cigarette business insists, in fact, it will swear up and down in public, it is not selling cigarettes to children, that if children are smoking, which they are, more than ever before, it's not the fault of the cigarette business. "Who knows whose fault it is?" says the cigarette business. That's what Viceroy is saying, "Who knows whose fault it is that children are smoking? It's not ours."

Well, there is a confidential report on cigarette advertising in the files of the Federal Government right now, a Viceroy advertising, the Viceroy strategy for attracting young people, starters they are called, to smoking — "FOR THE YOUNG SMOKER. . . . A CIGARETTE FALLS INTO THE SAME CATEGORY WITH WINE, BEER, SHAVING OR WEARING A BRA. . . ." says the Viceroy strategy — "A DECLARATION OF INDEPENDENCE AND STRIVING FOR SELF-IDENTITY." Therefore, an attempt should be made, says Viceroy, to ". . . PRESENT THE CIGARETTE AS AN INITIATION INTO THE ADULT WORLD," to ". . . PRESENT THE CIGARETTE AS AN ILLICIT PLEASURE . . . A BASIC SYMBOL OF THE GROWING-UP, MATURING PROCESS." An attempt should be made, says the Viceroy slicksters, "TO RELATE THE CIGARETTE TO 'POT', WINE, BEER, SEX. DO NOT COMMUNICATE HEALTH OR HEALTH-RELATED POINTS." That's the strategy of the cigarette slicksters, the cigarette business which is insisting in public, "We are not selling cigarettes to children."

They're not slicksters, they're liars.

While Jacobson is speaking these lines the television screen is showing Viceroy ads published in print media in 1980. Each ad shows two packs of Viceroys alongside a golf club and ball. . . .

Under contemporary as under traditional Illinois law, Jacobson's broadcast is libelous per se. Accusing a cigarette company of what many people consider the immoral strategy of enticing children to smoke — enticing them by advertising that employs themes exploitive of adolescent vulnerability — is likely to harm the company. It may make it harder for the company to fend off hostile government regulation and may invite rejection of the company's product by angry parents who smoke but may not want their children to do so. These harms cannot easily be measured, but so long as some harm is highly likely the difficulty of measurement is an additional reason, under the modern functional approach of the Illinois courts, for finding libel per se rather than insisting on proof of special damage. . . .

The defendants also argue and the district court also found that the libel was privileged as a fair and accurate summary of the Federal Trade Commission staff's report on cigarette advertising. The parties agree as they must that Illinois recognizes a privilege for fair and accurate summaries of, or reports on, government proceedings and investigations. They agree that the privilege extends to a public FTC staff report on an investigation. But they disagree over whether Jacobson's summary of the FTC staff report was "fair," that is, whether the overall impression created by the summary was no more defamatory than that created by the original. See Restatement (Second) of Torts §611, Comment f (1977). Since this is a question of fact, and the case was dismissed on the pleadings, all we need decide is whether the fairness of the Jacobson summary emerges so incontrovertibly from a comparison of the FTC staff report with the broadcast that no rational jury considering these documents with the aid of whatever additional evidence Brown & Williamson might introduce could consider the summary unfair.

Although the FTC report (and the Kennan report from which it quotes) refers to the targets of the Viceroy advertising campaign as "young smokers" and "starters," not as children, the broadcast implies that the campaign is aimed at children; for after quoting from the Kennan report as quoted by the FTC staff, Jacobson comments: "That's the strategy of the cigarette slicksters, the cigarette business which is insisting in public, 'We are not selling cigarettes to children.' They're not slicksters, they're liars." Also, although the quotations in the broadcast are from the Kennan report rather than from any document written inside Brown & Williamson, and this is clearly indicated in the FTC staff report, the broadcast implies that they are quotations from Brown & Williamson. For example, Jacobson states that "an attempt should be made, says Viceroy" — and there follow quotations from the Kennan report without identification of the true source. This is misleading. True, the FTC staff report does state that Brown & Williamson "adopted many of the ideas in" the Kennan report, and does not say which these were. But its quotations from Brown & Williamson's "Viceroy Strategy" paper imply that they were the ideas of repressing any concerns about the health hazards of smoking and of attracting young smokers by an advertising campaign associating smoking with a "free and easy, hedonistic lifestyle"; there is no suggestion that Brown & Williamson adopted Kennan's specific proposal, quoted by Jacobson, "to relate the cigarette to 'pot', wine, beer, sex," or to "wearing a bra." Jacobson also deleted the qualification, "considering some legal constraints," and omitted mention of the fact that the Kennan report had been written six years before and that the advertising campaign which the FTC staff thought based in part on that report had been conducted five years before. The omission was misleading because the juxtaposition of the audio portion of the broadcast with current Viceroy advertising implied that Viceroy was continuing to employ the disreputable methods recommended by the Kennan report (though the connection between golf and a strategy of enticing children is obscure).

The fact that there are discrepancies between a libel and the government report on which it is based need not defeat the privilege of fair summary. Unless the report is published verbatim it is bound to convey a somewhat different impression from the original, no matter how carefully the publisher attempts to summarize or paraphrase or excerpt it fairly and accurately. An unfair summary in the present context is one that amplifies the libelous effect that publication of the government report verbatim would have on a reader who read it carefully — that carries a "greater sting." The FTC staff report conveys the following message: six years ago a market-research firm submitted to Brown & Williamson a set of rather lurid proposals for enticing young people to smoke cigarettes and Brown & Williamson adopted many of its ideas (though not necessarily the specific proposals quoted in the report) in an advertising campaign aimed at young smokers which it conducted the following year. The Jacobson broadcast conveys the following message: Brown & Williamson currently is advertising cigarettes in a manner designed to entice children to smoke by associating smoking with drinking, sex, marijuana, and other illicit pleasures of youth. So at least a rational jury might interpret the source and the summary, and if it did it would be entitled to conclude that the summary carried a greater sting and was therefore unfair.

[Reversed and remanded.]

NOTES

1. Brown & Williamson *on remand*. At trial *Brown & Williamson* recovered $3,000,000 in actual damages and $2,050,000 in punitives, of which $50,000 were against Jacobson personally and the rest against CBS. The trial judge reduced the compensatory damages to $1.00. On appeal compensatory damages were increased to $1,000,000 and the punitive damages award was preserved. Brown & Williamson Tobacco Corp. v. Jacobson, 827 F.2d 1119 (7th Cir. 1987).

2. *English origins of the fair reporting privilege*. In general the privilege of "record libel" — the traditional term for the fair report privilege — is accorded to persons who publish for the world at large statements that previously have been made as a matter of public record. In one famous early case, Stockdale v. Hansard, 112 Eng. Rep. 1112 (Q.B. 1839), the court held that a parliamentary report, even though published by Hansard at the direct request of Parliament, was not privileged. That decision was immediately overturned by legislation; see Parliamentary Papers Act, 1840, s. 4. It was not, however, until Wason v. Walter, 4 Q.B. 73 (1868), that the privilege was extended to proceedings of Parliament voluntarily republished by the press. This decision smacked of judicial legislation, since Parliament had twice previously refused to create a privilege for such reports. In his opinion Cockburn, C.J., noted that the privilege was well established with respect to judicial proceedings, and that it was "of paramount public and national importance that the proceedings of the houses of parliament shall be communicated to the public" in order that "confidence" be maintained in the

legislative process. Today in England the privilege extends not only to reports of parliamentary proceedings but to those of administrative bodies as well. Perera v. Peiris, [1949] A.C. 1 (P.C.).

3. Scope of the privilege in the United States. In this country the record libel privilege applies to reports of legislative, judicial, and administrative proceedings, and it was quickly extended to various functions performed by "quasi-public" bodies. Restatement (Second) of Torts §611 defines the privilege as follows:

> §611. REPORT OF OFFICIAL PROCEEDING OR PUBLIC MEETING
> The publication of defamatory matter concerning another in a report of an official action or proceeding or of a meeting open to the public that deals with a matter of public concern is privileged if the report is accurate and complete or a fair abridgment of the occurrence reported.

The record libel privilege at common law was in some respects closely circumscribed. The defendant's report was closely read to see if it was accurate in all respects; and the errors made were not excused even if the inaccuracy in reporting was unintentional or the result of a mistake. The justification for the strict rule requiring defendant at his peril to report accurately the results of legal proceedings was given by the Kansas court in Gobin v. Globe Publishing, 531 P.2d 76, 81-82 (Kan. 1975), where the defendant was accused of falsely reporting that the plaintiff had pleaded guilty to a charge of cruelty to animals.

> Reasons given for making a distinction in the law of libel applicable to reporting of judicial proceedings have included the fact that judicial proceedings are peculiarly susceptible to exact reporting; an account of that which transpired at trial is not contingent upon fallible or futile modes of investigation; court records are available and insofar as reports of in-progress proceedings are concerned, the threat of libel emanates only from incompetent reporting; moreover, because those participating in judicial proceedings enjoy an absolute immunity from suit for defamation, instances of defamation perpetrated by trial participants might well be compounded if reports of the proceedings enjoyed too protective a privilege.

However, this strict interpretation of the record libel privilege had been precluded by the Supreme Court's decision in *Gertz,* and the Kansas Supreme Court acknowledged that it was constrained henceforth to use a negligence standard in record libel cases. See Restatement (Second) of Torts §611 comment *b.*

While the common-law privilege is strict in one sense, it is liberal in quite another. Thus the privilege is absolute so long as the report is accurate, even if the speaker knows or believes that the statements reported are false. In Rosenberg v. Helinski, 616 A.2d 866, 873 (Md. 1992), Dr. Rosenberg, the defendant, a psychiatrist, testified in a divorce hearing that the plaintiff had abused his $2\frac{1}{2}$-year-old daughter. He repeated the substance of the charges on the courthouse steps before reporters. His claim for an absolute privilege was upheld , with Murphy, C.J., saying:

> Our early cases suggest that such a qualified privilege operates only when the report is fair, accurate and made without malice. . . The modern view discards the search for malice and requires simply the report be fair and substantially correct, or, in the language of the *Restatement,* "accurate and complete or a fair abridgment of the occurrence reported." Under the modern view, the privilege exists even if the reporter of defamatory statements made in court believes or knows them to be false; the privilege is abused only if the report fails the test of fairness and accuracy. . . .
>
> Any one of three theories may serve as a rationale for granting a privilege to such reports of events in court: (1) the agency rationale, by which the reporter as agent for an otherwise preoccupied public which could, if it possessed the time, energy or inclination, attend the proceeding; (2) the public supervision rationale, by which the reporter provides to the larger community data it needs to monitor government institutions; (3) or the public information rationale by which the reporter provides information affecting the greater public welfare.

The court then held that the privilege could be claimed not only by reporters but "to any person who makes an oral, written or printed report to pass on the information that is available to the general public."

Much litigation has also been directed to the requirement that the defendant's statement be a fair and accurate statement or abridgment of the official proceedings. Clearly, the report of a complex trial need not be exhaustive in all respects, but if a newspaper reports the derogatory portions of a judicial proceeding one day, "it may not, after reporting the derogatory parts, fail to publish the further proceedings that tend to vindicate the person defamed." Restatement (Second) of Torts §611 comment *f.* Several thorny aspects of the privilege concern the extent to which the statements made were based on public records and the completeness of any summary published by the defendant. In Bufalino v. Associated Press, 692 F.2d 266 (2d Cir. 1982), the court held that the privilege "should not be interpreted to protect unattributed, defamatory statements supported after-the-fact through a frantic search of official records."

C. Fair Comment: Artistic and Literary Criticism

At common law the privilege of fair comment extended to all matters that were in some sense in the public eye, and it is best understood as having allowed the defendant to express defamatory opinions on matters of public interest. The privilege extended to statements about public officials and candidates for public office, about educational, charitable, and religious institutions, about quasi-public institutions such as bar and medical associations, about events of public interest such as sporting games and contests, and about artistic, literary, and scientific matters generally. The cardinal distinction under the common-law privilege is that between fact and opinion; the defense of fair comment applied only to the latter. To be sure, a substantial minority of states (see Noel, Defamation of Public Officers and Candidates, 49 Colum. L. Rev. 875, 986-987 (1949)), held that the privilege applied to false statements of fact as well as to statements of opinion. For the best exposition of this position at common law, see Coleman v. MacLennan, 98 P. 281 (Kan. 1908). The majority of states that passed on the question, however, distinguished between fact and opinion and allowed the privilege of fair comment only for the latter. The leading decision was written by William Howard Taft, later President of the United States and Chief Justice of the United States Supreme Court, when he was a judge on the court of appeals. Post Publishing Company v. Hallman, 59 F. 530 (6th Cir. 1893).

The leading common-law decision on fair comment was Carr v. Hood, 170 Eng. Rep. 981, 983 (K.B. 1808), a libel action which involved some savage criticism of Sir John Carr's book "The Stranger in Ireland." Lord Ellenborough rebuffed the action as follows:

> Here the supposed libel has only attacked those works of which Sir John Carr is the avowed author; and one writer in exposing the follies and errors of another may make use of ridicule, however poignant. Ridicule is often the fittest weapon that can be employed for such a purpose. If the reputation or pecuniary interests of the person ridiculed suffer, it is damnum absque injuria. Where is the liberty of the press if an action can be maintained on such principles? Perhaps the plaintiff's *Tour through Scotland* is now unsaleable; but is he to be indemnified by receiving a compensation in damages from the person who may have opened the eyes of the public to the bad taste and inanity of his compositions? Who would have bought the works of Sir Robert Filmer after he had been refuted by Mr. Locke? but shall it be said that he might have sustained an action for defamation against that great philosopher, who was labouring to enlighten and ameliorate mankind? We really must not cramp observations upon authors and their works. They should be liable to criticism, to exposure, and even to ridicule, if their compositions be ridiculous; otherwise the first who writes a book on any subject will maintain a monopoly of sentiment and opinion respecting it. This would tend to the perpetuity of error. — Reflection on personal character is another thing. Shew me an attack on the moral character of this plaintiff, or any attack upon his character unconnected with his authorship, and I shall be as ready as any judge who ever sate here to protect him; but I cannot hear of malice on account of turning his works into ridicule.

Lord Ellenborough himself was taken for task for giving the privilege too narrow a scope in J. Spencer Bower, Actionable Defamation 383 (1908):

> Nothing could be more misleading than the above [opinion], which assumes not that honest comment is justified, because it is comment, but that the author is to be punished for "the bad taste and inanity of his compositions," as Cinna the poet was "torn" for his "bad verses," and that, if the positions be reversed, — if the author is "labouring to enlighten mankind," and the critic's compositions are inane, — the immunity would not exist; whereas the whole foundation, and the sole justification, of the protection is the freedom of *any* man, however worthless his observations may be, to criticize with the severity he pleases (provided that he does not stray beyond the assigned limits of comment into the region of personal imputation) the public conduct or the published work, however exalted or brilliant the rest of the world may deem it, of *any* other man. Sir Robert Filmer had the same right to criticize Locke, as Locke had to criticize him. The fact that one criticism may demolish the author, and another the critic himself, is utterly irrelevant to the question of the legal right.

The early decisions adhered to the distinction between criticisms of the book and the author, as even a glimmer of the pre-*New York Times* cases shows. Thus in Cherry v. Des Moines Leader, 86 N.W. 323, 323 (Iowa 1901), the court extended fair comment privilege to a vicious review of the plaintiff's three-sister vaudeville act, which described it as being performed by "strange creatures with painted faces and hideous mien." But in Triggs v. Sun Printing & Pub. Assn., 71 N.E. 739 (N.Y. 1904), the court let the jury decide whether comments about the private life of Professor Oscar Lovell Triggs of the English Department of the University of Chicago strayed into forbidden personal territory when they ridiculed his private life by stating, for example, "that he was unable to select a name for his baby until after a year of solemn deliberation." What happens to the public/private distinction after *New York Times*?

H.   CONSTITUTIONAL PRIVILEGES

1.   Public Officials and Public Figures

New York Times Co. v. Sullivan
376 U.S. 254 (1964)

BRENNAN, J. We are required in this case to determine for the first time the extent to which the constitutional protections for speech and press limit a State's power to award damages in a libel action brought by a public official against critics of his official conduct.

Respondent L. B. Sullivan is one of the three elected Commissioners of the City of Montgomery, Alabama. He testified that he was "Commissioner of Public Affairs and the duties are supervision of the Police Department, Fire Department, Department of Cemetery and Department of Scales." He brought this civil libel action against the four individual petitioners, who are Negroes and Alabama clergymen, and against petitioner the New York Times Company, a New York corporation which publishes the New York Times, a daily newspaper. A jury in the Circuit Court of Montgomery County awarded him damages of $500,000, the full amount claimed, against all the petitioners, and the Supreme Court of Alabama affirmed. 144 So. 2d 25.

Respondent's complaint alleged that he had been libeled by statements in a full-page advertisement that was carried in the New York Times on March 29, 1960. Entitled "Heed Their Rising Voices," the advertisements began by stating that "As the whole world knows by now, thousands of Southern Negro students are engaged in widespread non-violent demonstrations in positive affirmation of the right to live in human dignity as guaranteed by the U.S. Constitution and the Bill of Rights." It went on to charge that "in their efforts to uphold these guarantees, they are being met by an unprecedented wave of terror by those who would deny and negate that document which the whole world looks upon as setting the pattern for modern freedom. . . ." Succeeding paragraphs purported to illustrate the "wave of terror" by describing certain alleged events. The text concluded with an appeal for funds for three purposes: support of the student movement, "the struggle for the right-to-vote," and the legal defense of Dr. Martin Luther King, Jr., leader of the movement, against a perjury indictment then pending in Montgomery.

The text appeared over the names of 64 persons, many widely known for their activities in public affairs, religion, trade unions, and the performing arts. Below these names, and under a line reading "We in the south who are struggling daily for dignity and freedom warmly endorse this appeal," appeared the names of the four individual petitioners and of 16 other persons, all but two of whom were identified as clergymen in various Southern cities. The advertisment was signed at the bottom of the page by the "Committee to Defend Martin Luther King and the Struggle for Freedom in the South," and the officers of the Committee were listed.

Of the 10 paragraphs of text in the advertisement, the third and a portion of the sixth were the basis of respondent's claim of libel. They read as follows:

Third paragraph:

"In Montgomery, Alabama, after students sang 'My Country, 'Tis of Thee' on the State Capitol steps, their leaders were expelled from school, and truckloads of police armed with shotguns and tear-gas ringed the Alabama State College Campus. When the entire student body protested to state authorities by refusing to re-register, their dining hall was padlocked in an attempt to starve them into submission."

Sixth paragraph:

"Again and again the Southern violators have answered Dr. King's peaceful protests with intimidation and violence. They have bombed his home almost killing his wife and child. They have assaulted his person. They have arrested him seven times — for 'speeding,' 'loitering' and similar 'offenses.' And now they have charged him with 'perjury' — a *felony* under which they could imprison him for *ten years*. . . . "

Although neither of these statements mentions respondent by name, he contended that the word "police" in the third paragraph referred to him as the Montgomery Commissioner who supervised the Police Department, so that he was being accused of "ringing" the campus with police. He further claimed that the paragraph would be read as imputing to the police, and hence to him, the padlocking of the dining hall in order to starve the students into submission.[2] As to the sixth paragraph, he contended that since arrests are ordinarily made by the police, the statement "They have arrested [Dr. King] seven times" would be read as referring to him; he further contended that the "They" who did the arresting would be equated with the "They" who committed the other described acts and with the "Southern violators." Thus, he argued, the paragraph would be read as accusing the Montgomery police, and hence him, of answering Dr. King's protests with "intimidation and violence," bombing his home, assaulting his person, and charging him with perjury. Respondent and six other Montgomery residents testified that they read some or all of the statements as referring to him in his capacity as Commissioner.

It is uncontroverted that some of the statements contained in the two paragraphs were not accurate descriptions of events which occurred in Montgomery. Although Negro students staged a demonstration on the State Capitol steps, they sang the National Anthem and not "My Country, 'Tis of Thee." Although nine students were expelled by the State Board of Education, this was not for leading the demonstration at the Capitol, but for demanding service at a lunch counter in the Montgomery County Courthouse on another day. Not the entire student body, but most of it, had protested the expulsion, not by refusing to register, but by boycotting classes on a single day; virtually all the students did

2. Respondent did not consider the charge of expelling the students to be applicable to him, since "that responsibility rests with the State Department of Education."

register for the ensuing semester. The campus dining hall was not padlocked on any occasion, and the only students who may have been
barred from eating there were the few who had neither signed a prereg-
istration application nor requested temporary meal tickets. Although
the police were deployed near the campus in large numbers on three
occasions, they did not at any time "ring" the campus, and they were
not called to the campus in connection with the demonstration on the
State Capitol steps, as the third paragraph implied. Dr. King had not
been arrested seven times, but only four; and although he claimed to
have been assaulted some years earlier in connection with his arrest for
loitering outside a courtroom, one of the officers who made the arrest
denied that there was such an assault.

On the premise that the charges in the sixth paragraph could be
read as referring to him, respondent was allowed to prove that he had
not participated in the events described. Although Dr. King's home
had in fact been bombed twice when his wife and child were there,
both of these occasions antedated respondent's tenure as Commissioner, and the police were not only not implicated in the bombings,
but had made every effort to apprehend those who were. Three of Dr.
King's four arrests took place before respondent became Commissioner. Although Dr. King had in fact been indicted (he was subsequently acquitted) on two counts of perjury, each of which carried a
possible five-year sentence, respondent had nothing to do with procuring the indictment.

Respondent made no effort to prove that he suffered actual pecuniary loss as a result of the alleged libel. One of his witnesses, a former
employer, testified that if he had believed the statements, he doubted
whether he "would want to be associated with anybody who would be a
party to such things that are stated in that ad," and that he would not
re-employ respondent if he believed "that he allowed the Police Department to do the things that the paper said he did." But neither this
witness nor any of the others testified that he had actually believed the
statements in their supposed reference to respondent.

The cost of the advertisement was approximately $4800, and it was
published by the Times upon an order from a New York advertising
agency acting for the signatory Committee. The agency submitted the
advertisement with a letter from A. Philip Randolph, Chairman of
the Committee, certifying that the persons whose names appeared on
the advertisement had given their permission. Mr. Randolph was
known to the Times' Advertising Acceptability Department as a responsible person, and in accepting the letter as sufficient proof of authorization it followed its established practice. There was testimony that the
copy of the advertisement which accompanied the letter listed only the
64 names appearing under the text, and that the statement, "We in the
south . . . warmly endorse this appeal," and the list of names thereun-

der, which included those of the individual petitioners, were subsequently added when the first proof of the advertisement was received. Each of the individual petitioners testified that he had not authorized the use of his name, and that he had been unaware of its use until receipt of respondent's demand for a retraction. The manager of the Advertising Acceptability Department testified that he had approved the advertisement for publication because he knew nothing to cause him to believe that anything in it was false, and because it bore the endorsement of "a number of people who are well known and whose reputation" he "had no reason to question." Neither he nor anyone else at the Times made an effort to confirm the accuracy of the advertisement, either by checking it against recent Times news stories relating to some of the described events or by any other means.

Alabama law denies a public officer recovery of punitive damages in a libel action brought on account of a publication concerning his official conduct unless he first makes a written demand for a public retraction and the defendant fails or refuses to comply. Alabama Code, Tit. 7, §914. Respondent served such a demand upon each of the petitioners. None of the individual petitioners responded to the demand, primarily because each took the position that he had not authorized the use of his name on the advertisement and therefore had not published the statements that respondent alleged had libeled him. The Times did not publish a retraction in response to the demand, but wrote respondent a letter stating, among other things, that "we . . . are somewhat puzzled as to how you think the statements in any way reflect on you," and "you might, if you desire, let us know in what respect you claim that the statements in the advertisement reflect on you." Respondent filed this suit a few days later without answering the letter. [The Times did subsequently publish a retraction of the advertisement upon the demand of Governor John Patterson of Alabama, but only for him "as Governor of Alabama and Ex-Officio Chairman of the State Board of Education of Alabama." The Secretary of the Times testified that it made this individual retraction because the Alabama Governor could be seen as "the embodiment of the State of Alabama." Although the ad referred "to the action of the State authorities" he did not think that "any of the language in there referred to Mr. Sullivan."

[Justice Brennan then reviewed the instructions of the case given by the trial judge and approved by the Alabama Supreme Court. Under these instructions, the jury found the advertisement was found libelous per se, and hence actionable without proof of malice or special damages. The $500,000 award followed.]

Because of the importance of the constitutional issues involved, we granted the separate petitions for certiorari of the individual petitioners and of the Times. We reverse the judgment. We hold that the rule of law applied by the Alabama courts is constitutionally deficient for failure to provide the safeguards for freedom of speech and of the press that are required by the First and Fourteenth Amendments in a libel action brought by a public official against critics of his official conduct. We further hold that under the proper safeguards the evidence presented in this case is constitutionally insufficient to support the judgment for respondent.

[The Court first discussed two preliminary issues: whether there was state action and whether the defendant's statement, as an advertisement, was beyond the protection of the First Amendment. It decided that the common-law rule in Alabama was sufficient state action and that the statement was not a "commercial" advertisement but an "editorial" advertisement on an issue "of the highest public interest and concern." It continued:]

Under Alabama law as applied in this case, a publication is "libelous per se" if the words "tend to injure a person . . . in his reputation" or to "bring [him] into public contempt"; the trial court stated that the standard was met if the words are such as to "injure him in his public office, or impute misconduct to him in his office, or want of official integrity, or want of fidelity to a public trust. . . . " The jury must find that the words were published "of and concerning" the plaintiff, but where the plaintiff is a public official his place in the government hierarchy is sufficient evidence to support a finding that his reputation has been affected by statements that reflect upon the agency of which he is in charge. Once "libel per se" has been established, the defendant has no defense as to stated facts unless he can persuade the jury that they were true in all their particulars. . . . His privilege of "fair comment" for expressions of opinion depends on the truth of the facts upon which the comment is based. Unless he can discharge the burden of proving truth, general damages are presumed, and may be awarded without proof of pecuniary injury. A showing of actual malice is apparently a prerequisite to recovery of punitive damages, and the defendant may in any event forestall a punitive award by a retraction meeting the statutory requirements. Good motives and belief in truth do not negate an inference of malice, but are relevant only in mitigation of punitive damages if the jury chooses to accord them weight.

The question before us is whether this rule of liability, as applied to an action brought by a public official against critics of his official conduct, abridges the freedom of speech and of the press that is guaranteed by the First and Fourteenth Amendments.

Respondent relies heavily, as did the Alabama courts, on statements of this Court to the effect that the Constitution does not protect libelous publications. Those statements do not foreclose our inquiry here. None of the cases sustained the use of libel laws to impose sanctions upon expression critical of the official conduct of public officials. . . . In the only previous case that did present the question of constitutional

limitations upon the power to award damages for libel of a public official, the Court was equally divided and the question was not decided.
Schenectady Union Pub. Co. v. Sweeney, 316 U.S. 642. In deciding the
question now, we are compelled by neither precedent nor policy to give
any more weight to the epithet "libel" than we have to other "mere
labels" of state law. N.A.A.C.P. v. Button, 371 U.S. 415, 429. Like insur-
rection, contempt, advocacy of unlawful acts, breach of the peace, ob-
scenity, solicitation of legal business, and the various other formulae
for the representation of expression that have been challenged in this
Court, libel can claim no talismanic immunity from constitutional limitations. It must be measured by standards that satisfy the First Amendment.

The general proposition that freedom of expression upon public
questions is secured by the First Amendment has long been settled by
our decisions. . . .

Thus we consider this case against the background of a profound
national commitment to the principle that debate on public issues
should be uninhibited, robust, and wide-open, and that it may well include vehement, caustic, and sometimes unpleasantly sharp attacks on
government and public officials. The present advertisement, as an expression of grievance and protest on one of the major public issues of
our time, would seem clearly to qualify for the constitutional protection. The question is whether it forfeits that protection by the falsity of
some of its factual statements and by its alleged defamation of respondent.

Authoritative interpretations of the First Amendment guarantees
have consistently refused to recognize an exception for any test of
truth — whether administered by judges, juries, or administrative officials — and especially one that puts the burden of proving truth on the
speaker. The constitutional protection does not turn upon "the truth,
popularity, or social utility of the ideas and beliefs which are offered."
N.A.A.C.P. v. Button, 371 U.S. 415, 445. As Madison said, "Some degree
of abuse is inseparable from the proper use of everything; and in no
instance is this more than in that of the press." 4 Elliot's Debates on the
Federal Constitution (1876), p. 571. . . .

That erroneous statement is inevitable in free debate, and that it
must be protected if the freedoms of expression are to have the "breathing space" that they "need . . . to survive," N.A.A.C.P. v. Button, 371
U.S. 415, 433, was also recognized by the Court of Appeals for the District of Columbia Circuit in Sweeney v. Patterson, 128 F.2d 457, 458
(1942), cert. denied, 317 U.S. 678. . . .

Injury to official reputation affords no more warrant for repressing
speech that would otherwise be free than does factual error. Where
judicial officers are involved, this Court has held that concern for the
dignity and reputation of the courts does not justify the punishment as

criminal contempt of criticism of the judge or his decision. Bridges v. California, 314 U.S. 252. This is true even though the utterance contains "half-truths" and "misinformation." Such repression can be justified, if at all, only by a clear and present danger of the obstruction of justice. If judges are to be treated as "men of fortitude, able to thrive in a hardy climate," surely the same must be true of other government officials, such as elected city commissioners. Criticism of their official conduct does not lose its constitutional protection merely because it is effective criticism and hence diminishes their official reputations.

If neither factual error nor defamatory content suffices to remove the constitutional shield from criticism of official conduct, the combination of the two elements is no less inadequate. This is the lesson to be drawn from the great controversy over the Sedition Act of 1798, 1 Stat. 596, which first crystallized a national awareness of the central meaning of the First Amendment. See Levy, Legacy of Suppression (1960), at 258 et seq.; Smith, Freedom's Fetters (1956), at 426, 431, and passim. That statute made it a crime, punishable by a $5,000 fine and five years in prison, "if any person shall write, print, utter or publish . . . any false, scandalous and malicious writing or writings against the government of the United States, or either house of the Congress . . . , or the President . . . , with intent to defame . . . or to bring them, or either of them, into contempt or disrepute; or to excite against them, or either or any of them, the hatred of the good people of the United States." The Act allowed the defendant the defense of truth, and provided that the jury were to be judges both of the law and the facts. Despite these qualifications, the Act was vigorously condemned as unconstitutional in an attack joined in by Jefferson and Madison. In the famous Virginia Resolutions of 1798, the General Assembly of Virginia resolved that it "doth particularly protest against the palpable and alarming infractions of the Constitution, in the two late cases of the 'Alien and Sedition Acts,' passed at the last session of Congress. . . . [The Sedition Act] exercises . . . a power not delegated by the Constitution, but, on the contrary, expressly and positively forbidden by one of the amendments thereto — a power which, more than any other, ought to produce universal alarm, because it is levelled against the right of freely examining public characters and measures, and of free communication among the people thereon, which has ever been justly deemed the only effectual guardian of every other right." 4 Elliot's Debates, supra, pp. 553-554. Madison prepared the Report in support of the protest. His premise was that the Constitution created a form of government under which "The people, not the government, possess the absolute sovereignty." The structure of the government dispersed power in reflection of the people's distrust of concentrated power, and of power itself at all levels. This form of government was "altogether different" from the British form, under which the Crown was sovereign and the people were subjects. "Is it not natural and necessary, under such different circumstances," he asked, "that a different degree of freedom in the use of the press should be contemplated?" Id., pp. 569-570. Earlier, in a debate in the House of Representatives, Madison said: "If we advert to the nature of Republican Government, we shall find that the censorial power is in the people over the Government, and not in the Government over the people." 4 Annals of Congress, p. 934 (1794). Of the exercise of that power by the press, his Report said: "In every state, probably, in the union, the press has exerted a freedom in canvassing the merits and measures of public men, of every description, which has not been confined to the strict limits of the common law. On this footing the freedom of the press has stood; on this foundation it yet stands. . . ." 4 Elliot's Debates, supra, p. 570. The right of free public discussion of the stewardship of public officials was thus, in Madison's view, a fundamental principle of the American form of government.

Although the Sedition Act was never tested in this Court,[16] the attack upon its validity has carried the day in the court of history. Fines levied in its prosecution were repaid by Act of Congress on the ground that it was unconstitutional. See, e.g., Act of July 4, 1840, c. 45, 6 Stat. 802, accompanied by H.R. Rep. No. 86, 26th Cong., 1st Sess. (1840). Calhoun, reporting to the Senate on February 4, 1836, assumed that its invalidity was a matter "which no one now doubts." Report with Senate bill No. 122, 24th Cong., 1st Sess., p. 3. Jefferson, as President, pardoned those who had been convicted and sentenced under the Act and remitted their fines, stating: "I discharged every person under punishment or prosecution under the sedition law, because I considered, and now consider, that law to be a nullity, as absolute and as palpable as if Congress had ordered us to fall down and worship a golden image." Letter to Mrs. Adams, July 22, 1804, 4 Jefferson's Works (Washington ed.), pp. 555, 556. The invalidity of the Act has also been assumed by Justices of this Court. These views reflect a broad consensus that the Act, because of the restraint it imposed upon criticism of government and public officials, was inconsistent with the First Amendment.

There is no force in respondent's argument that the constitutional limitations implicit in the history of the Sedition Act apply only to Congress and not to the States. It is true that the First Amendment was originally addressed only to action by the Federal Government, and that Jefferson, for one, while denying the power of Congress "to control the freedom of the press," recognized such a power in the States. But this distinction was eliminated with the adoption of the Fourteenth Amendment and the application to the States of the First Amendment's restrictions. . . .

16. The Act expired by its terms in 1801.

What a State may not constitutionally bring about by means of a criminal statute is likewise beyond the reach of its civil law of libel. The fear of damage awards under a rule such as that invoked by the Alabama courts here may be markedly more inhibiting than the fear of prosecution under a criminal statute. Alabama, for example, has a criminal libel law which subjects to prosecution "any person who speaks, writes, or prints of and concerning another any accusation falsely and maliciously importing the commission by such person of a felony, or any other indictable offense involving moral turpitude," and which allows as punishment upon conviction a fine not exceeding $500 and a prison sentence of six months. Alabama Code, Tit. 14, §350. Presumably a person charged with violation of this statute enjoys ordinary criminal-law safeguards such as the requirements of an indictment and of proof beyond a reasonable doubt. These safeguards are not available to the defendant in a civil action. The judgment awarded in this case — without the need for any proof of actual pecuniary loss — was one thousand times greater than the maximum fine provided by the Alabama criminal statute, and one hundred times greater than that provided by the Sedition Act. And since there is no double-jeopardy limitation applicable to civil lawsuits, this is not the only judgment that may be awarded against petitioners for the same publication.[18] Whether or not a newspaper can survive a succession of such judgments, the pall of fear and timidity imposed upon those who would give voice to public criticism is an atmosphere in which the First Amendment freedoms cannot survive. Plainly the Alabama law of civil libel is "a form of regulation that creates hazards to protected freedoms markedly greater than those that attend reliance upon the criminal law." Bantam Books, Inc., v. Sullivan, 372 U.S. 58, 70.

The state rule of law is not saved by its allowance of the defense of truth. A defense for erroneous statements honestly made is no less essential here than was the requirement of proof of guilty knowledge which, in Smith v. California, 361 U.S. 147, we held indispensable to a valid conviction of a bookseller for possessing obscene writings for sale. . . . A rule compelling the critic of official conduct to guarantee the truth of all his factual assertions — and to do so on pain of libel judgments virtually unlimited in amount — leads to a comparable "self-censorship." Allowance of the defense of truth, with the burden of proving it on the defendant, does not mean that only false speech will be deterred. Even courts accepting this defense as an adequate safeguard have recognized the difficulties of adducing legal proofs that the al-

---

18. The Times states that four other libel suits based on the advertisements have been filed against it by others who have served as Montgomery City Commissioners and by the Governor of Alabama; that another $500,000 verdict has been awarded in the only one of these cases that has yet gone to trial; and that the damages sought in the other three total $2,000,000.

leged libel was true in all its factual particulars. . . . Under such a rule, would-be critics of official conduct may be deterred from voicing their criticism, even though it is believed to be true and even though it is in fact true, because of doubt whether it can be proved in court or fear of the expense of having to do so. They tend to make only statements which "steer far wider of the unlawful zone." The rule thus dampens the vigor and limits the variety of public debate. It is inconsistent with the First and Fourteenth Amendments.

The constitutional guarantees require, we think, a federal rule that prohibits a public official from recovering damages for a defamatory falsehood relating to his official conduct unless he proves that the statement was made with "actual malice" — that is, with knowledge that it was false or with reckless disregard of whether it was false or not. An oft-cited statement of a like rule, which has been adopted by a number of state courts, is found in the Kansas case of Coleman v. MacLennan, 98 P. 281 (Kan. 1908). . . .

Such a privilege for criticism of official conduct is appropriately analogous to the protection accorded a public official when *he* is sued for libel by a private citizen. In Barr v. Matteo, 360 U.S. 564, 575, this Court held the utterance of a federal official to be absolutely privileged if made "within the outer perimeter" of his duties. The States accord the same immunity to statements of their highest officers, although some differentiate their lesser officials and qualify the privilege they enjoy. But all hold that all officials are protected unless actual malice can be proved. The reason for the official privilege is said to be that the threat of damage suits would otherwise "inhibit the fearless, vigorous, and effective administration of policies of government" and "dampen the ardor of all but the most resolute, or the most irresponsible, in the unflinching discharge of their duties." Barr v. Matteo, supra, 360 U.S., at 571. Analogous considerations support the privilege for the citizen-critic of government. It is as much his duty to criticize as it is the official's duty to administer. . . . It would give public servants an unjustified preference over the public they serve, if critics of official conduct did not have a fair equivalent of the immunity granted to the officials themselves.

We conclude that such a privilege is required by the First and Fourteenth Amendments.

We hold today that the Constitution delimits a State's power to award damages for libel in actions brought by public officials against critics of their official conduct. Since this is such an action, the rule requiring proof of actual malice is applicable. While Alabama law apparently requires proof of actual malice for an award of punitive damages, where general damages are concerned malice is "presumed." Such a presumption is inconsistent with the federal rule. "The power to create presumptions is not a means of escape from constitutional restrictions,"

Bailey v. Alabama, 219 U.S. 219, 239; "the showing of malice required for the forfeiture of the privilege is not presumed but is a matter for proof by the plaintiff. . . ." Lawrence v. Fox, 97 N.W.2d 719, 725 (Mich. 1959). Since the trial judge did not instruct the jury to differentiate between general and punitive damages, it may be that the verdict was wholly an award of one or the other. But it is impossible to know, in view of the general verdict returned. Because of this uncertainty, the judgment must be reversed and the case remanded. . . .

Since respondent may seek a new trial, we deem that considerations of effective judicial administration require us to review the evidence in the present record to determine whether it could constitutionally support a judgment for respondent. This Court's duty is not limited to the elaboration of constitutional principles; we must also in proper cases review the evidence to make certain that those principles have been constitutionally applied. This is such a case, particularly since the question is one of alleged trespass across "the line between speech unconditionally guaranteed and speech which may legitimately be regulated." Speiser v. Randall, 357 U.S. 513, 525. In cases where that line must be drawn, the rule is that we "examine for ourselves the statements in issue and the circumstances under which they were made to see . . . whether they are of a character which the principles of the First Amendment, as adopted by the Due Process Clause of the Fourteenth Amendment, protect." . . .

Applying these standards, we consider that the proof presented to show actual malice lacks the convincing clarity which the constitutional standard demands, and hence that it would not constitutionally sustain the judgment for respondent under the proper rule of law. The case of the individual petitioners requires little discussion. Even assuming that they could constitutionally be found to have authorized the use of their names on the advertisement, there was no evidence whatever that they were aware of any erroneous statements or were in any way reckless in that regard. The judgment against them is thus without constitutional support.

As to the Times, we similarly conclude that the facts do not support a finding of actual malice. The statement by the Times' Secretary that, apart from the padlocking allegation, he thought the advertisement was "substantially correct," affords no constitutional warrant for the Alabama Supreme Court's conclusion that it was a "cavalier ignoring of the falsity of the advertisement [from which] the jury could not have but been impressed with the bad faith of The Times, and its maliciousness inferable therefrom." The statement does not indicate malice at the time of the publication; even if the advertisement was not "substantially correct" — although respondent's own proofs tend to show that it was — that opinion was at least a reasonable one, and there was no evidence to impeach the witness' good faith in holding it. The Times'

failure to retract upon respondent's demand, although it later retracted upon the demand of Governor Patterson, is likewise not adequate evidence of malice for constitutional purposes. Whether or not a
failure to retract may ever constitute such evidence, there are two reasons why it does not here. *First,* the letter written by the Times reflected
a reasonable doubt on its part as to whether the advertisement could
reasonably be taken to refer to respondent at all. *Second,* it was not a
final refusal, since it asked for an explanation on this point — a request
that respondent chose to ignore. Nor does the retraction upon the
demand of the Governor supply the necessary proof. It may be doubted
that a failure to retract which is not itself evidence of malice can retroactively become such by virtue of a retraction subsequently made to
another party. But in any event that did not happen here, since the
explanation given by the Times' Secretary for the distinction drawn
between the respondent and the Governor was a reasonable one, the
good faith of which was not impeached.

Finally, there is evidence that the Times published the advertisement
without checking its accuracy against the news stories in the Times' own
files. The mere presence of the stories in the files does not, of course,
establish that the Times "knew" the advertisement was false, since the
state of mind required for actual malice would have to be brought
home to the persons in the Times' organization having responsibility
for the publication of the advertisement. With respect to the failure of
those persons to make the check, the record shows that they relied
upon their knowledge of the good reputation of many of those whose
names were listed as sponsors of the advertisement, and upon the letter
from A. Philip Randolph, known to them as a responsible individual,
certifying that the use of the names was authorized. There was a testimony that the persons handling the advertisement saw nothing in it
that would render it unacceptable under the Times' policy of rejecting
advertisements containing "attacks of a personal character"; their failure to reject it on this ground was not unreasonable. We think the
evidence against the Times supports at most a finding of negligence in
failing to discover the misstatements, and is constitutionally insufficient
to show the recklessness that is required for a finding of actual
malice. . . .

We also think the evidence was constitutionally defective in another
respect: it was incapable of supporting the jury's finding that the allegedly libelous statements were made "of and concerning" respondent. Respondent relies on the words of the advertisement and the testimony of six witnesses to establish a connection between it and himself. . . .

There was no reference to respondent in the advertisement, either
by name or official position. A number of the allegedly libelous statements — the charges that the dining hall was padlocked and that Dr.

King's home was bombed, his person assaulted, and a perjury prosecution instituted against him — did not even concern the police; despite the ingenuity of the arguments which would attach this significance to the word "They," it is plain that these statements could not reasonably be read as accusing respondent of personal involvement in the acts in question. The statements upon which respondent principally relies as referring to him are the two allegations that did concern the police or police functions: that "truckloads of police . . . ringed the Alabama State College Campus" after the demonstration on the State Capitol steps, and that Dr. King had been "arrested . . . seven times." These statements were false only in that the police had been "deployed near" the campus but had not actually "ringed" it and had not gone there in connection with the State Capitol demonstration, and in that Dr. King had been arrested only four times. The ruling that these discrepancies between what was true and what was asserted were sufficient to injure respondent's reputation may itself raise constitutional problems, but we need not consider them here. Although the statements may be taken as referring to the police, they did not on their face make even an oblique reference to respondent as an individual. Support for the asserted reference must, therefore, be sought in the testimony of respondent's witnesses. But none of them suggested any basis for the belief that respondent himself was attacked in the advertisement beyond the bare fact that he was in overall charge of the Police Department and thus bore official responsibility for police conduct; to the extent that some of the witnesses thought respondent to have been charged with ordering or approving the conduct or otherwise being personally involved in it, they based this notion not on any statements in the advertisement, and not on any evidence that he had in fact been so involved, but solely on the unsupported assumption that, because of his official position, he must have been. . . .

The judgment of the Supreme Court of Alabama is reversed and the case is remanded to that court for further proceedings not inconsistent with this opinion.

Reversed and remanded.

BLACK, J., with whom DOUGLAS, J., joins, concurring. I concur in reversing this half-million-dollar judgment against the New York Times Company and the four individual defendants. In reversing the Court holds that "the Constitution delimits a State's power to award damages for libel in actions brought by public officials against critics of their official conduct." I base my vote to reverse on the belief that the First and Fourteenth Amendments not merely "delimit" a State's power to award damages to "public officials against critics of their official conduct" but completely prohibit a State from exercising such a power. The Court goes on to hold that a State can subject such critics to damages if "actual malice" can be proved against them. "Malice," even as defined by the Court, is an elusive, abstract concept, hard to prove and hard to disprove. The requirement that malice be proved provides at best an evanescent protection for the right critically to discuss public affairs and certainly does not measure up to the sturdy safeguard embodied in the First Amendment. Unlike the Court, therefore, I vote to reverse exclusively on the ground that the Times and the individual defendants had an absolute, unconditional right to publish in the Times advertisement their criticisms of the Montgomery agencies and officials. . . .

In my opinion the Federal Constitution has dealt with this deadly danger to the press in the only way possible without leaving the free press open to destruction — by granting the press an absolute immunity for criticism of the way public officials do their public duty. Compare Barr v. Matteo, 360 U.S. 564. Stopgap measures like those the Court adopts are in my judgment not enough. This record certainly does not indicate that any different verdict would have been rendered here whatever the Court had charged the jury about "malice," "truth," "good motives," "justifiable ends," or any other legal formulas which in theory would protect the press. Nor does the record indicate that any of these legalistic words would have caused the courts below to set aside or to reduce the half-million-dollar verdict in any amount.

. . . To punish the exercise of this right to discuss public affairs or to penalize it through libel judgments is to abridge or shut off discussion of the very kind most needed. This Nation, I suspect, can live in peace without libel suits based on public discussions of public affairs and public officials. But I doubt that a country can live in freedom where its people can be made to suffer physically or financially for criticizing their government, its actions, or its officials. An unconditional right to say what one pleases about public affairs is what I consider to be the minimum guarantee of the First Amendment.

I regret that the Court has stopped short of this holding indispensible to preserve our free press from destruction.

[The concurring opinion of Justice Goldberg has been omitted.]

NOTES

1. *The constitutionalization of the law of defamation.* New York Times v. Sullivan ushered in a new constitutional jurisprudence for all defamation cases brought by public officials against (to use the current expression) media defendants. In making its decision to override the common law, was the Court more swayed by the predicament of the New York Times or by the weaknesses of the common law of defamation? What are the narrowest grounds on which the case could have been decided for the New York Times? At common law was the

offending advertisement "of and concerning the plaintiff"? Could the Alabama Supreme Court justify a finding of actual malice because the Times insisted that the advertisement was substantially true and refused to retract it at the behest of the plaintiff, even though it did so at the behest of the governor? Should punitive damages be allowable without proof of actual damage? For an argument that Alabama misapplied the common law of defamation on all relevant issues see Epstein, Was *New York Times v. Sullivan* Wrong?, 53 U. Chi. L. Rev. 782 (1986).

2. *A jurisdictional escape.* In New York Times Co. v. Connor, 365 F.2d 567 (5th Cir. 1966), the court found that the plaintiff, Eugene "Bull" Connor, then one of Birmingham's city commissioners, had not made out actual malice against either the New York Times or Harrison Salisbury, then a staff member of the paper, who in April 1960 wrote an article entitled "Fear and Hatred Grip Birmingham." In a sense that finding was unnecessary because the court had previously held that under the due process clause Alabama did not have jurisdiction over the paper solely because it mailed papers to individual subscribers and local wholesalers in Alabama. In its view the "minimum contacts" for suit were not established because the defendant published in New York, had no agents or employees in Alabama, had paid stringers (part-time sources) a total of $415, and derived from Alabama sources "approximately 25/1000 to 46/1000 of 1% of the total Times advertising revenue." Was the same argument open to the Supreme Court in New York Times v. Sullivan? Note that in footnote 3 of *New York Times,* omitted above, Justice Brennan observed: "Approximately 394 copies of the edition of the Times containing the advertisement were circulated in Alabama. Of these, about 35 copies were distributed in Montgomery County. The total circulation of the Times for that day was approximately 650,000 copies." What result if Sullivan or Connor sued in New York state?

3. *The private conduct of public officials.* In Monitor Patriot Co. v. Roy, 401 U.S. 265 (1971), petitioner newspaper published a column characterizing senatorial candidate Roy as a "former small-time bootlegger." The jury found for respondent on the ground that the bootlegger charge was "in the private sector." The Court noted first that under *New York Times* "publications concerning candidates must be accorded at least as much protection under the First and Fourteenth Amendments as those concerning occupants of public office." It then rejected respondent's contentions that *New York Times* applies only to a candidate's "official conduct," meaning "conduct relevant to fitness for office" and that the public-private issue is one for the jury. The Court held "as a matter of constitutional law that a charge of criminal conduct, no matter how remote in time or place, can never be irrelevant to an official's or a candidate's fitness for office for purposes of the 'knowing falsehood or reckless disregard' rule of New York Times Co. v. Sullivan."

4. New York Times: collateral applications. In Linn v. Plant Guard Workers, 383 U.S. 53, 64-65 (1966), the issue before the Court was whether the elaborate statutory provisions of the National Labor Relations Act barred state law actions for libel, whether brought by unions, employers, or individual employees, for defamatory utterances made in the course of a labor dispute. The Court held that the national labor policy did not preclude all such defamation actions, and explained its position as follows:

> But it has been insisted that not only would the threat of state libel suits dampen the ardor of labor debate and truncate the free discussion envisioned by the Act, but that such suits might be used as weapons of economic coercion. Moreover, in view of the propensity of juries to award excessive damages for defamation, the availability of libel actions may pose a threat to the stability of labor unions and smaller employers. In order that the recognition of legitimate state interests does not interfere with effective administration of national policy the possibility of such consequences must be minimized. We therefore limit the availability of state remedies for libel to those instances in which the complainant can show that the defamatory statements were circulated with malice and caused him damage.
>
> The standards enunciated in New York Times Co. v. Sullivan are adopted by analogy, rather than under constitutional compulsion. We apply the malice test to effectuate the statutory design with respect to pre-emption. Construing the Act to permit recovery of damages in a state cause of action only for defamatory statements published with knowledge of their falsity or with reckless disregard of whether they were true or false guards against abuse of libel actions and unwarranted intrusion upon free discussion envisioned by the Act.

Similarly, in McDonald v. Smith, 472 U.S. 479 (1985), the Supreme Court held, by analogy to *New York Times,* that the right to petition the government for the redress of grievances did not generate an absolute privilege from the law of libel under the First Amendment. "The right to petition is guaranteed; the right to commit libel with impunity is not."

5. References. The literature on *New York Times* is extensive. For an enthusiastic interpretation of *New York Times* as an occasion "for dancing in the streets," see Kalven, The *New York Times* Case: A Note on "The Central Meaning of the First Amendment," 1964 Sup. Ct. Rev. 191; see also Brennan, The Supreme Court and the Meiklejohn Interpretation of the First Amendment, 79 Harv. L. Rev. 1 (1965). For more recent commentary see Symposium: New Perspectives in the Law of Defamation, 74 Cal. L. Rev. 3 (1986) (with contributions by Barrett, Bellah, Bezanson, Casper, Franklin, Post, Reston, Schauer, Shapiro, Skolnick, and Sunstein); Lewis, *New York Times v. Sullivan* Reconsidered: Time to Return to "The Central Meaning of the First Amendment," 83 Colum. L. Rev. 603 (1983); Smolla, Let the Author Beware: The Rejuvenation of the American Law of Libel, 132 U. Pa. L. Rev. 1 (1983).

Curtis Publishing Co. v. Butts and **Associated Press v. Walker**
388 U.S. 130 (1967)

[No. 37, Curtis Publishing Co. v. Butts, stemmed from an article published in petitioner's *Saturday Evening Post*. The article accused Butts, coach of the University of Georgia football team, of conspiring to fix a 1962 Georgia-Alabama game by giving to Paul Bryant, coach of the University of Alabama team, crucial information about Georgia's offensive strategy. The article concluded: "The chances are that Wally Butts will never help any football team again. . . . The investigation by university and Southeastern Conference officials is continuing; motion pictures of other games are being scrutinized; where it will end no one so far can say. But careers will be ruined, that is sure."

The article revealed that George Burnett, an Atlanta insurance salesman, had, because of "electronic error," overheard the phone conversation between the two coaches. Evidence at trial was directed to both the truth of the article and its preparation. Butts denied the charges and contended that his phone conversation with Bryant had been "general football talk." Expert witnesses supported Butts by analyzing the game itself and Burnett's notes of the conversation. The evidence also tended to show that the Post had "departed greatly from the standards of good investigation and reporting" and, according to Butts, amounted to "reckless and wanton conduct, in light of the devastating nature of the article's assertions."

The jury was instructed that in order to make out the defense of truth it was necessary to show that the libelous statements were substantially true. The jury was also instructed that it could award punitive damages if it found that the defendant had acted with actual malice. The jury returned a verdict for $60,000 in general damages and for $3,000,000 in punitive damages; the total was reduced by remittitur to $460,000. Shortly thereafter, the Supreme Court handed down its *New York Times* decision, which Curtis immediately brought to the attention of the trial court on a motion for a new trial. That motion was denied on two grounds — first, that *New York Times* was inapplicable because the plaintiff was not a public official and, second, that there was ample evidence from which a jury could have concluded that the article was published with reckless disregard for truth. The judgment of the trial court was affirmed on appeal. 351 F.2d 702 (5th Cir. 1965).

"No. 150, Associated Press v. Walker, arose out of the distribution of a news dispatch giving an eyewitness account of events on the campus of the University of Mississippi on the night of September 30, 1962, when a massive riot erupted because of federal efforts to enforce a court decree ordering the enrollment of a Negro, James Meredith, as a student in the University. The dispatch stated that respondent [Edwin] Walker, who was present on the campus, had taken command of the violent crowd and had personally led a charge against federal marshals sent there to effectuate the court's decree and to assist in preserving order. It also described Walker as encouraging rioters to use violence and giving them technical advice on combating the effects of tear gas.

"Walker was a private citizen at the time of the riot and publication. He had pursued a long and honorable career in the United States Army before resigning to engage in political activity, and had, in fact, been in command of the federal troops during the school segregation confrontation at Little Rock, Arkansas, in 1957. He was acutely interested in the issue of physical federal intervention, and had made a number of strong statements against such action which had received wide publicity. Walker had his own following, the 'Friends of Walker,' and could fairly be deemed a man of some political prominence."

Walker brought his libel action in a Texas state court, seeking a total of $2,000,000 in compensatory and punitive damages. Walker admitted his presence on the campus but claimed that he had "counseled restraint" to a group of students, had exercised no control over the crowd, and had not taken part in any charge against the federal marshals. There was also evidence of the negligence of the Associated Press in assigning an inexperienced reporter to cover the story and in failing to check minor discrepancies between an oral dispatch given the office and a later written dispatch. The jury awarded plaintiff $500,000 in compensatory and $300,000 in punitive damages, but the court refused to enter the award of punitive damages, concluding that there was at most evidence of negligence but not malice. Both sides appealed. The decision was affirmed by the Texas Civil Court of Appeals, 393 S.W.2d 671 (1965). The United States Supreme Court granted certiorari after the Supreme Court of Texas denied writ of error.

Four separate opinions were given by the Supreme Court; they are considerably condensed here.]

HARLAN, J. . . . We thus turn to a consideration, on the merits, of the constitutional claims raised by Curtis in *Butts* and by the Associated Press in *Walker*. Powerful arguments are brought to bear for the extension of the *New York Times* rule in both cases.

[Justice Harlan reviewed at length various leading precedents on free speech, and continued:]

In *New York Times* we were adjudicating in an area which lay close to seditious libel, and history dictated extreme caution in imposing liability. The plaintiff in that case was an official whose position in government was such "that the public [had] an independent interest in the qualifications and performance of the person who [held] it." Rosenblatt v. Baer, 383 U.S. 75, at 86. Such officials usually enjoy a privilege against libel actions for their utterances, see, e.g., Barr v. Matteo, 360 U.S. 564, and there were analogous considerations involved in *New York Times,* supra, at 282. Thus we invoked "the hypothesis that speech can rebut speech, propaganda will answer propaganda, free debate of ideas will result in the wisest governmental policies," Dennis v. United States, 341 U.S. 494, 503, and limited recovery to those cases where "calculated falsehood" placed the publisher "at odds with the premises of democratic government and with the orderly manner in which economic, social, or political change is to be effected." Garrison v. Louisiana, 379 U.S. 64, 75. That is to say, such officials were permitted to recover in libel only when they could prove that the publication involved was deliberately falsified, or published recklessly despite the publisher's awareness of probable falsity. Investigatory failures alone were held insufficient to satisfy this standard.

In the cases we decide today none of the particular considerations involved in *New York Times* is present. These actions cannot be analogized to prosecutions for seditious libel. Neither plaintiff has any position in government which would permit a recovery by him to be viewed as a vindication of governmental policy. Neither was entitled to a special privilege protecting his utterances against accountability in libel. We are prompted, therefore, to seek guidance from the rules of liability which prevail in our society with respect to compensation of persons injured by the improper performance of a legitimate activity by another. Under these rules, a departure from the kind of care society may expect from a reasonable man performing such activity leaves the actor open to a judicial shifting of loss. In defining these rules, and especially in formulating the standards for determining the degree of care to be expected in the circumstances, courts have consistently given much attention to the importance of defendants' activities. The courts have also, especially in libel cases, investigated the plaintiff's position to determine whether he has a legitimate call upon the court for protection in light of his prior activities and means of self-defense. We note that the public interest in the circulation of the materials here involved, and the publisher's interest in circulating them, is not less than that involved in *New York Times*. And both Butts and Walker commanded a substantial amount of independent public interest at the time of the publications; both, in our opinion, would have been labeled "public figures" under ordinary tort rules. Butts may have attained that status by position alone and Walker by his purposeful activity amounting to a thrusting of his personality into the "vortex" of an important public controversy, but both commanded sufficient continuing public interest and had sufficient access to the means of counterargument to be able to "expose through discussion the falsehood and fallacies" of the defamatory statements. Whitney v. California, 274 U.S. 357, 377 (Brandeis, J., dissenting).

These similarities and differences between libel actions involving persons who are public officials and libel actions involving those circumstanced as were Butts and Walker, viewed in light of the principles of liability which are of general applicability in our society, lead us to the conclusion that libel actions of the present kind cannot be left entirely to state libel laws, unlimited by any overriding constitutional safeguard, but that the rigorous federal requirements of *New York Times* are not the only appropriate accommodation of the conflicting interests at stake. We consider and would hold that a "public figure" who is not a public official may also recover damages for a defamatory falsehood whose substance makes substantial danger to reputation apparent, on a showing of highly unreasonable conduct constituting an extreme departure from the standards of investigation and reporting ordinarily adhered to by responsible publishers.

Nothing in this opinion is meant to affect the holdings in *New York Times* and its progeny, including our recent decision in Time, Inc. v. Hill.

Having set forth the standard by which we believe the constitutionality of the damage awards in these cases must be judged, we turn now, as the Court did in *New York Times,* to the question whether the evidence and findings below meet that standard. We find the standard satisfied in No. 37, *Butts,* and not satisfied by either the evidence or the findings in No. 150, *Walker.*

[Justice Harlan then reviewed the evidence in detail.]

We come finally to Curtis' contention that whether or not it can be required to compensate Butts for any injury it may have caused him, it cannot be subjected to an assessment for punitive damages limited only by the "enlightened conscience" of the community.

[Justice Harlan then examines defendants' challenge to the constitutionality of the punitive damages award and rejects it. His opinion concludes:]

The judgment of the Court of Appeals for the Fifth Circuit in No. 37 is affirmed. The judgment of the Texas Court of Civil Appeals in No. 150 is reversed and the case is remanded to that court for further proceedings not inconsistent with the opinions that have been filed herein by The Chief Justice, Justice Black, and Justice Brennan.

It is so ordered.

WARREN, C.J., concurring in the result. . . . To me, differentiation between "public figures" and "public officials" and adoption of separate standards of proof for each have no basis in law, logic, or First Amendment policy. Increasingly in this country, the distinctions between governmental and private sectors are blurred. Since the depression of the 1930's and World War II there has been a rapid fusion of economic and political power, a merging of science, industry, and government, and a high degree of interaction between the intellectual, governmental, and business worlds. Depression, war, international tensions, national and international markets, and the surging growth of science and technology have precipitated national and international problems that demand national and international solutions. While these trends and events have occasioned a consolidation of governmental power, power has also become much more organized in what we have commonly considered to be the private sector. In many situations, policy determinations which traditionally were channeled through formal political institutions are now originated and implemented through a complex array of boards, committees, commissions, corporations, and associations, some only loosely connected with the Government. This blending of positions and power has also occurred in the case of individuals so that many who do not hold public office at the moment are nevertheless intimately involved in the resolution of important public questions or, by reason of their fame, shape events in areas of concern to society at large.

Viewed in this context, then, it is plain that although they are not subject to the restraints of the political process, "public figures," like "public officials," often play an influential role in ordering society. And surely as a class these "public figures" have as ready access as "public officials" to mass media of communication, both to influence policy and to counter criticism of their views and activities. Our citizenry has a legitimate and substantial interest in the conduct of such persons, and freedom of the press to engage in uninhibited debate about their involvement in public issues and events is as crucial as it is in the case of "public officials." The fact that they are not amenable to the restraints of the political process only underscores the legitimate and substantial nature of the interest, since it means that public opinion may be the only instrument by which society can attempt to influence their conduct.

I therefore adhere to the *New York Times* standard in the case of "public figures" as well as "public officials." It is a manageable standard, readily stated and understood, which also balances to a proper degree the legitimate interests traditionally protected by the law of defamation. . . .

I have no difficulty in concluding that No. 150, Associated Press v. Walker, must be reversed since it is in a clear conflict with *New York Times.* . . .

But No. 37, Curtis Publishing Co. v. Butts, presents an entirely different situation. . . .

[The Chief Justice then discussed the failure of the defendants to raise at the trial any First Amendment defense and then noted that the decision of the Post to "change its image" in order to boost sagging sales and revenue supported the damage award, especially since the Post refused to investigate the matter further after Butts and his daughter stated that the story was absolutely untrue.]

I am satisfied that the evidence here discloses that degree of reckless disregard for the truth of which we spoke in *New York Times* and *Garri-*

son. Freedom of the press under the First Amendment does not include absolute license to destroy lives or careers.

[Justice Black, with whom Justice Douglas joined, concurred in the reversal of *Walker* and dissented from the affirmance of *Butts:*]

I think it is time for this Court to abandon New York Times Co. v. Sullivan and adopt the rule to the effect that the First Amendment was intended to leave the press free from the harassment of libel judgments.

[Mr. Justice Brennan, with whom Mr. Justice White joined, concurred in the reversal of *Walker* and dissented from the affirmance of *Butts*. He agreed with the Chief Justice that the evidence in *Butts* supported a jury award for the plaintiff under the *New York Times* rule.]

In No. 37, Curtis Publishing Co. v. Butts, insofar as The Chief Justice's opinion demonstrates that the evidence unmistakably would support a judgment for Butts under the *New York Times* standard, I agree. I would, however, remand for a new trial since the charge to the jury did not comport with that standard. . . .

NOTES

1. An embarrassment of constitutional standards? *Walker* and *Butts* extended the actual malice test of *New York Times* from public officials to public figures. Five members of the Court (Black and Douglas adopting for this purpose the Warren position) rejected the arguments put forward by Harlan, which would have allowed a public figure to override the constitutional defense by showing, in essence, the gross negligence of the defendant. The Harlan position was criticized in Kalven, The Reasonable Man and the First Amendment, 1967 Sup. Ct. Rev. 267, 299-300, as lacking in "constitutional dimensions."

> It makes at a constitutional level more discriminations than two centuries of tort law has worked out at the common-law level! If policies are to be weighed on scales this exquisite, surely it is the function of the legislature to do the weighing. Is the difference between "reckless disregard" of *Times* and the gross negligence of *Butts* and *Walker* a constitutional difference? . . .
>
> There is a kindred difficulty. The scheme rests to a surprising degree on sociological guesses lightly made. How free and robust is the New York press? How hardened are public officials to irresponsible publicity? Do they knowingly assume these risks? What are the relative possibilities for counterargument in the various situations? If we are to deal in conjectures and rough guesses of this sort about human behavior, is it not again the task of the legislature and not the Court to do the guessing? Or, at least, the business of the states?
>
> The more one contemplates the scheme the less secure it seems. It is a doubtful reading of *New York Times* to see it resting so heavily on a

concern with counterargument. Indeed the whole discussion of competition of ideas and counterargument seems to me misplaced in this
context. These are, to be sure, key principles when we are talking
about doctrines and ideas. Here, with Mr. Justice Brandeis, we look to
counterargument as the correct remedy for the mischief of false and
pernicious ideas and doctrine. And we grant an absolute privilege
to false doctrine. All this is well understood, widely shared, and invaluable.

But these notions sound only the faintest echo when we turn to false
statements of fact about individuals. For centuries it has been the experience of Anglo-American law that the truth never catches up with the lie,
and it is because it does not that there has been a law of defamation. I
simply do not see how the constitutional protection in this area can be
rested on the assurance that counterargument will take the sting out of
the falsehoods the law is thereby permitting. And if this premise is not
persuasive, the whole Harlan edifice tumbles.

Does Kalven's argument justify the extension of *New York Times* to
public figures, or the return to the common-law rules of fair comment
as they apply to both public officials and public figures?

2. *Actual malice.* In cases both of public officials and public figures,
the Supreme Court has strictly applied its standard that allows plaintiff
to recover only upon proof of actual malice. For example, in St. Amant
v. Thompson, 390 U.S. 727, 731-732 (1968), petitioner made a televised
political speech in which he charged respondent, a deputy sheriff, with
criminal conduct. The Supreme Court assumed that the charges were
defamatory and false and that respondent was a public official under
New York Times, but held that the evidence failed to support respondent's contention that petitioner had acted with reckless disregard of
the truth.

> It may be said that [the actual malice] test puts a premium on igno-
> rance, encourages the irresponsible publisher not to inquire, and per-
> mits the issue to be determined by the defendant's testimony that he
> published the statement in good faith and unaware of its probable falsity.
> Concededly the reckless disregard standard may permit recovery in fewer
> situations than would a rule that publishers must satisfy the standard of
> the reasonable man or the prudent publisher. But *New York Times* and
> succeeding cases have emphasized that the stake of the people in public
> business and the conduct of public officials is so great that neither the
> defense of truth nor the standard of ordinary care would protect against
> self-censorship and thus adequately implement First Amendment poli-
> cies. Neither lies nor false communications serve the ends of the First
> Amendment, and no one suggests their desirability or further prolifera-
> tion. But to insure the ascertainment and publication of the truth about
> public affairs, it is essential that the First Amendment protect some erro-
> neous publications as well as true ones. We adhere to this view and to the
> line which our cases have drawn between false communications which
> are protected and those which are not.
>
> The defendant in a defamation action brought by a public official can-
> not, however, automatically insure a favorable verdict by testifying that

he published with a belief that the statements were true. The finder of fact must determine whether the publication was indeed made in good faith. Professions of good faith will be unlikely to prove persuasive, for example, where a story is fabricated by the defendant, is the product of his imagination, or is based wholly on an unverified anonymous telephone call. Nor will they be likely to prevail when the publisher's allegations are so inherently improbable that only a reckless man would have put them in circulation. Likewise, recklessness may be found where there are obvious reasons to doubt the veracity of the informant or the accuracy of his reports.

3. Summary judgments under New York Times. One critical question under *New York Times* concerns the quantum of evidence that the plaintiff must present in order to survive a motion for summary judgment on the actual malice question. In Anderson v. Liberty Lobby, Inc., 477 U.S. 242, 254-255 (1986), Jack Anderson, the columnist, published three articles about the Liberty Lobby and its key officials that "portrayed the [plaintiffs] as neo-Nazi, anti-Semitic, racist, and fascist." All were public figures. In response to respondents' defamation suit, the defendant moved for summary judgment on the strength of affidavits by Anderson's key researcher that he had spent "substantial time" researching the articles. The precise issue in the case was whether "the clear-and-convincing-evidence requirement [of *New York Times*] must be considered by a court ruling on a motion for summary judgment." The Court, speaking through Justice White, held that it did:

> Just as the "convincing clarity" requirement is relevant in ruling on a motion for directed verdict, it is relevant in ruling on a motion for summary judgment. When determining if a genuine factual issue as to actual malice exists in a libel suit brought by a public figure, a trial judge must bear in mind the actual quantum and quality of proof necessary to support liability under *New York Times*. For example, there is no genuine issue if the evidence presented in the opposing affidavits is of insufficient caliber or quantity to allow a rational finder of fact to find actual malice by clear and convincing evidence. . . .
>
> Our holding that the clear-and-convincing standard of proof should be taken into account on summary judgment motions does not denigrate the role of the jury. It by no means authorizes trial on affidavits. Credibility determinations, the weighing of the evidence, and the drawing of legitimate inferences from the facts are jury functions, not those of a judge, whether he is ruling on a motion for summary judgment or for a directed verdict. The evidence of the non-movant is to be believed, and all justifiable inferences are to be drawn in his favor.

The Court then remanded the case to the trial judge to sort out the situation. Justice Brennan and Justice Rehnquist in separate dissents argued that the case should be left to the jury. In their view, the use of different standards for summary judgment would invade the province of the jury, induce trial judges to conduct exhaustive minitrials before

making their decision, and lead to confusion in the granting and denying of summary judgments.

4. *Discovery on mental state.* The issue of actual malice has injected into
many defamation cases the delicate question of the defendant's mental
state, an issue that was confronted less frequently under the common-
law privilege of fair comment. The modern rules of discovery, moreover, generally give the moving party broad latitude to "obtain discovery regarding any matter, not privileged, which is relevant to the subject
matter involved in the pending action, whether it relates to the claim
or defense" of any party to the litigation. Fed. R. Civ. P. 26(b)(1). In
Herbert v. Lando, 441 U.S. 153, 170 (1979), the defendant, an editor
of the television show "60 Minutes," urged the court to hold (as was
done in the Second Circuit below) that "when a member of the press is
alleged to have circulated damaging falsehoods and is sued for injury
to the plaintiff's reputation, the plaintiff is barred from inquiring into
the editorial process of those responsible for the publication, even
though the inquiry would produce evidence material to the proof of a
critical element of his cause of action." The Court rejected the claim,
in part for the following reasons:

> In the first place, it is plain enough that the suggested privilege for
> the editorial process would constitute a substantial interference with the
> ability of a defamation plaintiff to establish the ingredients of malice as
> required by *New York Times*. As respondents would have it, the defen-
> dant's reckless disregard of the truth, a critical element, could not be
> shown by direct evidence through inquiry into the thoughts, opinions
> and conclusions of the publisher but could be proved only by objective
> evidence from which the ultimate fact could be inferred. It may be that
> plaintiffs will rarely be successful in proving awareness of falsehood from
> the mouth of the defendant himself, but the relevance of answers to such
> inquiries, which the District Court recognized and the Court of Appeals
> did not deny, can hardly be doubted. To erect an impenetrable barrier
> to the plaintiff's use of such evidence on his side of the case is a matter
> of some substance, particularly when defendants themselves are prone to
> assert their good-faith belief in the truth of their publications, and libel
> plaintiffs are required to prove knowing or reckless falsehood with "con-
> vincing clarity."

Justice Brennan dissented in part: "I would hold, however that the
First Amendment requires predecisional communication among edi-
tors to be protected by an editorial privilege, but that this privilege must
yield if a public figure plaintiff is able to demonstrate to the prima
facie satisfaction of the trial judge that the libel in question constitutes
defamatory falsehood." Litigation in the case continued for some seven
more years, ending with a summary judgment for the defendant on the
actual malice question. See *Herbert v. Lando*, 781 F.2d 298 (2d Cir.
1986). On the Supreme Court decision see generally Franklin, Reflec-

tions on *Herbert v. Lando,* 31 Stan. L. Rev. 1035 (1979); Friedenthal, *Herbert v. Lando:* A Note on Discovery, 31 Stan. L. Rev. 1059 (1979).

5. *Public figures.* The identification of public officials under the *New York Times* rule is, in general, a straightforward affair. The determination of who counts as a public figure is, however, a far more difficult problem. To be sure, there are a host of simple cases: former public officials, professional athletes, entertainers, and celebrities of all sort and description are regarded as public figures (and here the ambiguity begins) most of the time and for most if not all purposes. Since *Butts* and *Walker,* the Supreme Court has frequently wrestled with this question. Thus, in Time, Inc. v. Firestone, 424 U.S. 448 (1976), the Supreme Court held that the wife of "the scion of one of America's wealthier industrial families" was not a public figure, even though she held a news conference during a sensational and messy divorce trial. The Supreme Court has also held that a research scientist who was awarded William Proxmire's "Golden Fleece" award was not a public figure, even though — as the award itself suggests — the plaintiff had been successful in getting federal grant support. Hutchinson v. Proxmire, 443 U.S. 111 (1979). In the companion case of Wolston v. Reader's Digest Assn., Inc., 443 U.S. 157 (1979), the plaintiff was listed in Reader's Digest as a Soviet agent along with (among others) Julius and Ethel Rosenberg and his uncle, Jack Soble. In fact, the plaintiff was not a Soviet agent, but had only refused to appear before a grand jury for questioning about his uncle. The Supreme Court, reversing the district court and court of appeals, held that the plaintiff was not a public figure because he was neither a person of general prominence nor had he "thrust himself to the forefront" of a particular public controversy simply because he had fled when pursued by the government. See also the discussion in *Gertz,* infra at page 1196.

The lower courts have also joined the chase. In Meeropol v. Nizer, 381 F. Supp. 29 (S.D.N.Y. 1974), Judge Tyler held that the two sons of Julius and Ethel Rosenberg were public figures, notwithstanding the fact that they "later may have renounced the public spotlight by changing their name to Meeropol," because "as children they were the subject of considerable public attention." In Perry v. Columbia Broadcasting System, Inc., 499 F.2d 797 (7th Cir. 1974), plaintiff, who as Stepin Fetchit was a leading black actor and movie star in the 1920s and '30s, was held to be a public figure. In other lower court decisions, land sale corporations, vice presidents of local school governments, undercover police informants, (some) well-known local attorneys, pet-shop owners, and horse trainers have successfully resisted defendants' characterizations as public figures.

On the other hand, large insurance companies, professional football players, navy officers during the Vietnam War, Johnny Carson, local mobsters, belly dancers, Nobel Prize winners, and debt collection agencies under public investigation have all been held public figures, at least on a "limited basis" for those aspects of their conduct subjected to public scrutiny and review. In Reuber v. Food Chemical News, Inc., 925 F.2d 703, 706, 708 (4th Cir. 1991), the plaintiff was a research scientist at the National Cancer Institue who "disseminated his own research and took other actions which created the misleading impression that the NCEI had reversed its official position that the pesticide malathion was a non-carcinogen." A letter from his supervisor rebuking his research and statements was published by the defendant. The Fourth Circuit held that the plaintiff was "a limited purpose" public figure because he had "injected" himself into the public arena by his previous publications on the problem.

See generally R. Smolla, The Law of Defamation §2 (1994); Schauer, Public Figures, 25 Wm. & Mary L. Rev. 905 (1984).

2. Private Parties

Gertz v. Robert Welch, Inc.
418 U.S. 323 (1974)

[Petitioner, a reputable attorney, was retained by the Nelson family to represent them in a civil action against Nuccio, a Chicago policeman who had previously been convicted of second-degree murder for the death of young Nelson. As counsel for the family, petitioner attended the coroner's inquest into Nelson's death and initiated actions for damages, but he neither discussed Officer Nuccio with the press nor played any part in the criminal proceeding.

Respondent published *American Opinion,* a periodical of the John Birch Society. As part of its campaign to warn America of a communist conspiracy to discredit local law enforcement agencies, respondent published an article entitled "Frame-Up: Richard Nuccio and the War On Police" that purported to show that Nuccio was innocent, that his prosecution was a communist "frame-up," and that petitioner was an "architect of the frame-up." The article also made various other false charges that Gertz was a communist and had engaged in communist activities. The managing editor of *American Opinion* had not independently investigated the article's charges but had relied on its author's "extensive research." The article was accompanied by a photograph of petitioner over the caption "Elmer Gertz of Red Guild harasses Nuccio."

Gertz filed a libel action in federal district court and won a jury verdict for $50,000. Concluding that the *New York Times* standard protects discussion of any public issue without regard to the status of the person defamed, the court entered judgment for the defendants notwithstanding the verdict. On appeal, that decision was affirmed, the Court of Appeals adding that petitioner had failed to show that respondent acted with actual malice as defined by *New York Times,* "mere proof of failure to investigate, without more" being insufficient to establish reckless disregard for the truth. 471 F.2d 801 (7th Cir. 1972). The Supreme Court reversed.]

POWELL, J. . . . The principal issue in this case is whether a newspaper or broadcaster that publishes defamatory falsehoods about an individual who is neither a public official nor a public figure may claim a constitutional privilege against liability for the injury inflicted by those statements. The Court considered this question on the rather different set of facts presented in Rosenbloom v. Metromedia, Inc., 403 U.S. 29 (1971). . . .

The eight Justices who participated in *Rosenbloom* announced their views in five separate opinions, none of which commanded more than three votes. The several statements not only reveal disagreement about the appropriate result in that case; they also reflect divergent traditions of thought about the general problem of reconciling the law of defamation with the First Amendment. One approach has been to extend the *New York Times* test to an expanding variety of situations. Another has been to vary the level of constitutional privilege for defamatory falsehood with the status of the person defamed. And a third view would grant to the press and broadcast media absolute immunity from liability for defamation. To place our holding in the proper context, we preface our discussion of this case with a review of the several *Rosenbloom* opinions and their antecedents.

In affirming the trial court's judgment in the instant case, the Court of Appeals relied on Mr. Justice Brennan's conclusion for the *Rosenbloom* plurality that "all discussion and communication involving matters of public or general concern," 403 U.S., at 44, warrant the protection from liability for defamation accorded by the rule originally enunciated in New York Times Co. v. Sullivan. . . .

[The Court then reviewed *New York Times, Butts,* and *Walker,* and continued:]

In his opinion for the plurality in Rosenbloom v. Metromedia, Inc., 403 U.S. 29 (1971), Mr. Justice Brennan took the *New York Times* privilege one step further. He concluded that its protection should extend to defamatory falsehoods relating to private persons if the statements concerned matters of general or public interest. He abjured the suggested distinction between public officials and public figures on the one hand and private individuals on the other. He focused instead on society's interest in learning about certain issues: "If a matter is a subject of public or general interest, it cannot suddenly become less so merely because a private individual is involved, or because in some sense the individual did not 'voluntarily' choose to become involved." Id., at 43.

Thus, under the plurality opinion, a private citizen involuntarily associated with a matter of general interest has no recourse for injury to his
reputation unless he can satisfy the demanding requirements of the
New York Times test.

[The Court then examined the other opinions in *Rosenbloom*.]

We begin with the common ground. Under the First Amendment
there is no such thing as a false idea. However pernicious an opinion
may seem, we depend for its correction not on the conscience of judges
and juries but on the competition of other ideas. But there is no constitutional value in false statements of fact. Neither the intentional lie nor
the careless error materially advances society's interest in "uninhibited,
robust, and wide-open" debate on public issues. They belong to that
category of utterances which "are no essential part of any exposition of
ideas, and are of such slight social value as a step to truth that any
benefit that may be derived from them is clearly outweighed by the
social interest in order and morality." Chaplinsky v. New Hampshire,
315 U.S. 568, 572 (1942).

[Powell, J., then reviewed the reasons why *New York Times* calls for
"breathing room" and the avoidance of self-censorship in order to promote open debate.]

The need to avoid self-censorship by the news media is, however, not
the only societal value at issue. If it were, this Court would have embraced long ago the view that publishers and broadcasters enjoy an
unconditional and indefeasible immunity from liability for defamation.
Such a rule would, indeed, obviate the fear that the prospect of civil
liability for injurious falsehood might dissuade a timorous press from
the effective exercise of First Amendment freedoms. Yet absolute protection for the communications media requires a total sacrifice of the
competing value served by the law of defamation.

The legitimate state interest underlying the law of libel is the compensation of individuals for the harm inflicted on them by defamatory
falsehood. We would not lightly require the State to abandon this purpose, for, as Mr. Justice Stewart has reminded us, the individual's right
to the protection of his own good name "reflects no more than our
basic concept of the essential dignity and worth of every human being — a concept at the root of any decent system of ordered liberty.
The protection of private personality, like the protection of life itself,
is left primarily to the individual States under the Ninth and Tenth
Amendments. But this does not mean that the right is entitled to any
less recognition by this Court as a basic of our constitutional system."
Rosenblatt v. Baer, 383 U.S. 75, 92 (1966) (concurring opinion).

Some tension necessarily exists between the need for a vigorous and
uninhibited press and the legitimate interest in redressing wrongful injury. . . . In our continuing effort to define the proper accommodation between these competing concerns, we have been especially

anxious to assure to the freedoms of speech and press that "breathing space" essential to their fruitful exercise. To that end this Court has extended a measure of strategic protection to defamatory falsehood.

The *New York Times* standard defines the level of constitutional protection appropriate to the context of defamation of a public person. Those who, by reason of the notoriety of their achievements or the vigor and success with which they seek the public's attention, are properly classed as public figures and those who hold governmental office may recover for injury to reputation only on clear and convincing proof that the defamatory falsehood was made with knowledge of its falsity or with reckless disregard for the truth. This standard administers an extremely powerful antidote to the inducement to media self-censorship of the common-law rule of strict liability for libel and slander. And it exacts a correspondingly high price from the victims of defamatory falsehood. Plainly many deserving plaintiffs, including some intentionally subjected to injury, will be unable to surmount the barrier of the *New York Times* test. Despite this substantial abridgment of the state law right to compensation for wrongful hurt to one's reputation, the Court has concluded that the protection of the *New York Times* privilege should be available to publishers and broadcasters of defamatory falsehood concerning public officials and public figures. We think that these decisions are correct, but we do not find their holdings justified solely by reference to the interest of the press and broadcast media in immunity from liability. Rather, we believe that the *New York Times* rule states an accommodation between this concern and the limited state interest present in the context of libel actions brought by public persons. For the reasons stated below, we conclude that the state interest in compensating injury to the reputation of private individuals requires that a different rule should obtain with respect to them.

Theoretically, of course, the balance between the needs of the press and the individual's claim to compensation for wrongful injury might be struck on a case-by-case basis. As Mr. Justice Harlan hypothesized, "it might seem, purely as an abstract matter, that the most utilitarian approach would be to scrutinize carefully every jury verdict in every libel case, in order to ascertain whether the final judgment leaves fully protected whatever First Amendment values transcend the legitimate state interest in protecting the particular plaintiff who prevailed." Rosenbloom v. Metromedia, Inc., 403 U.S., at 63. But this approach would lead to unpredictable results and uncertain expectations, and it could render our duty to supervise the lower courts unmanageable. Because an ad hoc resolution of the competing interests at stake in each particular case is not feasible, we must lay down broad rules of general application. Such rules necessarily treat alike various cases involving differences as well as similarities. Thus it is often true that not all of the considerations which justify adoption of a given rule will obtain in each particular case decided under its authority.

With that caveat we have no difficulty in distinguishing among defamation plaintiffs. The first remedy of any victim of defamation is self-help — using available opportunities to contradict the lie or correct the error and thereby to minimize its adverse impact on reputation. Public officials and public figures usually enjoy significantly greater access to the channels of effective communication and hence have a more realistic opportunity to counteract false statements than private individuals normally enjoy. Private individuals are therefore more vulnerable to injury, and the state interest in protecting them is correspondingly greater.

More important than the likelihood that private individuals will lack effective opportunities for rebuttal, there is a compelling normative consideration underlying the distinction between public and private defamation plaintiffs. An individual who decides to seek governmental office must accept certain necessary consequences of that involvement in public affairs. He runs the risk of closer public scrutiny than might otherwise be the case. And society's interest in the officers of government is not strictly limited to the formal discharge of official duties. As the Court pointed out in Garrison v. Louisiana, 379 U.S., at 77, the public's interest extends to "anything which might touch on an official's fitness for office. . . . Few personal attributes are more germane to fitness for office than dishonesty, malfeasance, or improper motivation, even though these characteristics may also affect the official's private character."

Those classed as public figures stand in a similar position. Hypothetically, it may be possible for someone to become a public figure through no purposeful action of his own, but the instances of truly involuntary public figures must be exceedingly rare. For the most part those who attain this status have assumed roles of especial prominence in the affairs of society. Some occupy positions of such persuasive power and influence that they are deemed public figures for all purposes. More commonly, those classed as public figures have thrust themselves to the forefront of particular public controversies in order to influence the resolution of the issues involved. In either event, they invite attention and comment.

Even if the foregoing generalities do not obtain in every instance, the communications media are entitled to act on the assumption that public officials and public figures have voluntarily exposed themselves to increased risk of injury from defamatory falsehood concerning them. No such assumption is justified with respect to a private individual. He has not accepted public office or assumed an "influential role in ordering society." Curtis Publishing Co. v. Butts, supra, at 164 (Warren, C.J., concurring in result). He has relinquished no part of his interest in the protection of his own good name, and consequently he has a more compelling call on the courts for redress of injury inflicted by defamatory falsehood. Thus, private individuals are not only more vulnerable to injury than public officials and public figures; they are also more deserving of recovery.

For these reasons we conclude that the States should retain substantial latitude in their efforts to enforce a legal remedy for defamatory falsehood injurious to the reputation of a private individual. The extension of the *New York Times* test proposed by the *Rosenbloom* plurality would abridge this legitimate state interest to a degree that we find unacceptable. And it would occasion the additional difficulty of forcing state and federal judges to decide on an ad hoc basis which publications address issues of "general or public interest" and which do not — to determine, in the words of Mr. Justice Marshall, "what information is relevant to self-government." Rosenbloom v. Metromedia, Inc., 403 U.S., at 79. We doubt the wisdom of committing this task to the conscience of judges. Nor does the Constitution require us to draw so thin a line between the drastic alternatives of the *New York Times* privilege and the common law of strict liability for defamatory error. The "public or general interest" test for determining the applicability of the *New York Times* standard to private defamation actions inadequately serves both of the competing values at stake. On the one hand, a private individual whose reputation is injured by defamatory falsehood that does concern an issue of public or general interest has no recourse unless he can meet the rigorous requirements of *New York Times*. This is true despite the factors that distinguish the state interest in compensating private individuals from the analogous interest involved in the context of public persons. On the other hand, a publisher or broadcaster of a defamatory error which a court deems unrelated to an issue of public or general interest may be held liable in damages even if it took every reasonable precaution to ensure the accuracy of its assertions. And liability may far exceed compensation for any actual injury to the plaintiff, for the jury may be permitted to presume damages without proof of loss and even to award punitive damages. . . .

We hold that, so long as they do not impose liability without fault, the States may define for themselves the appropriate standard of liability for a publisher or broadcaster of defamatory falsehood injurious to a private individual. This approach provides a more equitable boundary between the competing concerns involved here. It recognizes the strength of the legitimate state interest in compensating private individuals for wrongful injury to reputation, yet shields the press and broadcast media from the rigors of strict liability for defamation. At least this conclusion obtains where, as here, the substance of the defamatory statement "makes substantial danger to reputation apparent." This phrase places in perspective the conclusion we announce today. Our inquiry would involve considerations somewhat different from those discussed above if a State purported to condition civil liability on a factual misstatement whose content did not warn a reasonably prudent editor or broadcaster of its defamatory potential. Such a case is not now before us, and we intimate no view as to its proper resolution.

[The Court then stated that the state interest in the protection of reputation "extends no further than compensation for actual injury."] For the reasons stated below, we hold that the States may not permit recovery of presumed or punitive damages, at least when liability is not based on a showing of knowledge of falsity or reckless disregard for the truth.

The common law of defamation is an oddity of tort law, for it allows recovery of purportedly compensatory damages without evidence of actual loss. Under the traditional rules pertaining to actions for libel, the existence of injury is presumed from the fact of publication. Juries may award substantial sums as compensation for supposed damage to reputation without any proof that such harm actually occurred. The largely uncontrolled discretion of juries to award damages where there is no loss unnecessarily compounds the potential of any system of liability for defamatory falsehood to inhibit the vigorous exercise of First Amendment freedoms. Additionally, the doctrine of presumed damages invites juries to punish unpopular opinion rather than to compensate individuals for injury sustained by the publication of a false fact. More to the point, the States have no substantial interest in securing for plaintiffs such as this petitioner gratuitous awards of money damages far in excess of any actual injury.

We would not, of course, invalidate state law simply because we doubt its wisdom, but here we are attempting to reconcile state law with a competing interest grounded in the constitutional command of the First Amendment. It is therefore appropriate to require that state remedies for defamatory falsehood reach no farther than is necessary to protect the legitimate interest involved. It is necessary to restrict defamation plaintiffs who do not prove knowledge of falsity or reckless disregard for the truth to compensation for actual injury. We need not define "actual injury," as trial courts have wide experience in framing appropriate jury instructions in tort actions. Suffice it to say that actual injury is not limited to out-of-pocket loss. Indeed, the more customary types of actual harm inflicted by defamatory falsehood include impairment of reputation and standing in the community, personal humiliation, and mental anguish and suffering. Of course, juries must be limited by appropriate instructions, and all awards must be supported by competent evidence concerning the injury, although there need be no evidence which assigns an actual dollar value to the injury.

We also find no justification for allowing awards of punitive damages against publishers and broadcasters held liable under state-defined standards of liability for defamation. In most jurisdictions jury discretion over the amounts awarded is limited only by the gentle rule that they not be excessive. Consequently, juries assess punitive damages in wholly unpredictable amounts bearing no necessary relation to the actual harm caused. And they remain free to use their discretion selectively to punish expressions of unpopular views. Like the doctrine of presumed damages, jury discretion to award punitive damages unnecessarily exacerbates the danger of media self-censorship, but, unlike the former rule, punitive damages are wholly irrelevant to the state interest that justifies a negligence standard for private defamation actions. They are not compensation for injury. Instead, they are private fines levied by civil juries to punish reprehensible conduct and to deter its future occurrence. In short, the private defamation plaintiff who establishes liability under a less demanding standard than that stated by *New York Times* may recover only such damages as are sufficient to compensate him for actual injury.

[The Court then rejected respondent's argument that plaintiff was a public official or public figure. The petitioner was not a public official even though he appeared at the inquest or had once served on a city housing committee; nor was he a public official even though he was a lawyer and therefore an officer of the court. Likewise, his general activities in community and professional affairs did not give him any "general fame or notoriety in the community" sufficient to make him a public figure.

Justice Blackmun concurred for two reasons. First, he thought that the position taken by the Court gave the press sufficient protection against punitive damages. And second, although a supporter of the position of the *Rosenbloom* plurality, he voted with the Court to make a majority for the Court "to come to rest in the defamation area."

Justice Burger dissented, voting to reinstate the jury's verdict in favor of Gertz.

Justice Douglas dissented, for the reasons stated by Mr. Justice Black in *New York Times.*

Justice Brennan dissented, for the reasons stated in his *Rosenbloom* opinion.]

WHITE, J., dissenting. For some 200 years — from the very founding of the Nation — the law of defamation and right of the ordinary citizen to recover for false publication injurious to his reputation have been almost exclusively the business of state courts and legislatures. Under typical state defamation law, the defamed private citizen had to prove only a false publication that would subject him to hatred, contempt, or ridicule. Given such publication, general damage to reputation was presumed, while punitive damages required proof of additional facts. The law governing the defamation of private citizens remained untouched by the First Amendment because until relatively recently, the consistent view of the Court was that libelous words constitute a class of speech wholly unprotected by the First Amendment, subject only to limited exceptions carved out since 1964.

But now, using that Amendment as the chosen instrument, the Court, in a few printed pages, has federalized major aspects of libel law by declaring unconstitutional in important respects the prevailing defamation law in all or most of the 50 States. That result is accomplished by requiring the plaintiff in each and every defamation action to prove not only the defendant's culpability beyond his act of publishing defamatory material but also actual damage to reputation resulting from the publication. Moreover, punitive damages may not be recovered by showing malice in the traditional sense of ill will; knowing falsehood or reckless disregard of the truth will now be required.

[Justice White then reviewed the 1938 Restatement of Torts on defamation.]

The Court proceeds as though it were writing on tabula rasa and suggests that it must mediate between two unacceptable choices — on the one hand, the rigors of the *New York Times* rule which the Court thinks would give insufficient recognition to the interest of the private plaintiff, and, on the other hand, the prospect of imposing "liability without fault" on the press and others who are charged with defamatory utterances. Totally ignoring history and settled First Amendment law, the Court purports to arrive at an "equitable compromise," rejecting both what it considers faultless liability and *New York Times* malice, but insisting on some intermediate degree of fault. Of course, the Court necessarily discards the contrary judgment arrived at in the 50 States that the reputation interest of the private citizen is deserving of considerably more protection.

The Court evinces a deep-seated antipathy to "liability without fault." But this catch-phrase has no talismanic significance and is almost meaningless in this context where the Court appears to be addressing those libels and slanders that are defamatory on their face and where the publisher is no doubt aware from the nature of the material that it would be inherently damaging to reputation. He publishes notwithstanding, knowing that he will inflict injury. With this knowledge, he must intend to inflict that injury, his excuse being that he is privileged to do so — that he has published the truth. But as it turns out, what he has circulated to the public is a very damaging falsehood. Is he nevertheless "faultless"? Perhaps it can be said that the mistake about his defense was made in good faith, but the fact remains that it is he who launched the publication knowing that it could ruin a reputation.

In these circumstances, the law has heretofore put the risk of falsehood on the publisher where the victim is a private citizen and no grounds of special privilege are invoked. The Court would now shift this risk to the victim, even though he has done nothing to invite the calumny, is wholly innocent of fault, and is helpless to avoid his injury. I doubt that jurisprudential resistance to liability without fault is sufficient ground for employing the First Amendment to revolutionize the law of libel, and in my view, that body of legal rules poses no realistic threat to the press and its service to the public. The press today is vigorous and robust. To me, it is quite incredible to suggest that threats of libel suits from private citizens are causing the press to refrain from publishing the truth. I know of no hard facts to support that proposition, and the Court furnishes none.

The communications industry has increasingly become concentrated in a few powerful hands operating very lucrative businesses reaching across the Nation and into almost every home. Neither the industry as a whole nor its individual components are easily intimidated, and we are fortunate that they are not. Requiring them to pay for the occasional damage they do to private reputation will play no substantial part in their future performance or their existence.

In any event, if the Court's principal concern is to protect the communications industry from large libel judgments, it would appear that its new requirements with respect to general and punitive damages would be ample protection. Why it also feels compelled to escalate the threshold standard of liability I cannot fathom, particularly when this will eliminate in many instances the plaintiff's possibility of securing a judicial determination that the damaging publication was indeed false, whether or not he is entitled to recover money damages. Under the Court's new rules, the plaintiff must prove not only the defamatory statement but also some degree of fault accompanying it. The publication may be wholly false and the wrong to him unjustified, but his case will nevertheless be dismissed for failure to prove negligence or other fault on the part of the publisher. I find it unacceptable to distribute the risk in this manner and force the wholly innocent victim to bear the injury; for, as between the two, the defamer is the only culpable party. It is he who circulated a falsehood that he was not required to publish.

It is difficult for me to understand why the ordinary citizen should himself carry the risk of damage and suffer the injury in order to vindicate First Amendment values by protecting the press and others from liability for circulating false information. This is particularly true because such statements serve no purpose whatsoever in furthering the public interest or the search for truth but, on the contrary, may frustrate that search and at the same time inflict great injury on the defenseless individual. The owners of the press and the stockholders of the communications enterprises can much better bear the burden. And if they cannot, the public at large should somehow pay for what is essentially a public benefit derived at private expense.

[Mr. Justice White then attacked the Court for its rejection of the common-law rules on actual and punitive damages.]

NOTES

1. *The negligence principle under* Gertz. What are the contours of the negligence action under *Gertz?* Is the plaintiff entitled to rely on a principle of res ipsa loquitur, given that the defendant has exclusive access to the production of the story? Is there a presumption of negligence if a story is defamatory of the plaintiff on its face? Is compliance with standard reporting practices a defense against negligence actions?

Some sense of the height of the negligence barrier can be gleaned from the subsequent history of the *Gertz* litigation. On retrial, the jury awarded the plaintiff compensatory damages in the amount of $100,000 and punitive damages in the amount of $300,000, sums far in excess of those awarded in the original action. On appeal, in Gertz v. Robert Welch Inc., 680 F.2d 527 (7th Cir. 1982), both elements of the award were upheld over a number of objections that went (1) to the proof of actual malice, (2) to the ability of the plaintiff to relitigate the malice question, and (3) to the clarity of the instructions on both actual and punitive damages.

2. *Presumed damages after* Gertz. In Dun & Bradstreet v. Greenmoss Builders, 472 U.S. 749, 760-761 (1985), the defendant Dun & Bradstreet (D&B) issued a credit report on the plaintiff to several of its customers that stated that the firm had filed for voluntary bankruptcy. The report had been prepared by a 17-year-old high school student who had confused the bankruptcy petition of several of Greenmoss's former employees with the bankruptcy of the firm itself. The report therefore gave a highly inaccurate summary of the firm's financial position. When Greenmoss found out about the error, it asked D&B to send out an immediate correction and to give Greenmoss a list of the clients to whom the report had been sent. D&B promised only to look into the matter; a week later it sent to the five subscribers who had received the original report a correction letter, which noted the error in the earlier report, but did not give a complete appraisal of Greenmoss's actual financial position. When Greenmoss again protested that the notice was inaccurate, D&B refused to take any further steps. Greenmoss then brought a suit for defamation in Vermont State Court. At the trial D&B's employee testified that, although it was routine practice to verify information with the firm that was the subject of the report, no verification had been attempted in this particular case. The jury returned a verdict of $50,000 in presumed damages and $300,000 in punitive damages. The Vermont Supreme Court affirmed the judgment below not-

ing that *Gertz* was limited to media defendants, but did not include credit reporting firms.

The Supreme Court, speaking through Justice Powell, addressed two questions. First, whether the presumed and punitive damage rule in *Gertz* applied "where the defamatory statements do not involve matters of public concern." Second, whether these statements were of public concern.

On the first question, Powell first observed that private speech poses no threat to the "free and robust" debate of public issues or to questions of self-government, and continued:

> In *Gertz*, we found that the state interest in awarding presumed and punitive damages was not "substantial" in view of their effect on speech at the core of First Amendment concern. This interest, however, *is* "substantial" relative to the incidental effect these remedies may have on speech of significantly less constitutional interest. The rationale of the common-law rules has been the experience and judgment of history that "proof of actual damage will be impossible in a great many cases where, from the character of the defamatory words and the circumstances of publication, it is all but certain that serious harm has resulted in fact." W. Prosser, The Law of Torts, §112 p. 765 (4th ed. 1971). As a result, courts for centuries have allowed juries to presume that some damage occurred from many defamatory utterances and publications. Restatement of Torts §568, Comment *b*, p. 162 (1938) (noting that Hale announced that damages were to be presumed for libel as early as 1670). This rule furthers the state interest in providing remedies for defamation by ensuring that those remedies are effective. In light of the reduced constitutional value of speech involving no matters of public concern, we hold that the state interest adequately supports awards of presumed and punitive damages — even absent a showing of "actual malice."

The Court then held that the credit report was not directed to a public issue. "It was speech solely in the individual interest of the speaker and its specific business audience."

The Court was badly fractured on the question; only three justices (Powell, Rehnquist, and O'Connor) adopted this middle course. Two justices (Burger and White) concurred in the result. Thus, Justice White concluded a long opinion as follows: "The question before us is whether *Gertz* is to be applied in this case. For either of two reasons, I believe that it should not. First, I am unreconciled to the *Gertz* holding and believe that it should be overruled. Second, as Justice Powell indicates, the defamatory publication in this case does not deal with a matter of public importance." The dissent of the four remaining justices took exactly the opposite tack and urged that the speech involved in this case deserved explicit constitutional protection. "The credit reporting at issue here surely involves a subject matter of sufficient public concern to require the comprehensive protections of *Gertz*. Were this speech appropriately characterized as a matter of only private concern, moreover, the elimination of the *Gertz* restrictions on presumed and punitive damages would still violate basic First Amendment requirements." To what extent does the frequent mention of "matters of public concern" reintroduce the old *Rosenbloom* test?

3. State law responses to Gertz. *Gertz* does not bind the states to a negligence standard in defamation actions brought by private parties against media (or other) defendants; rather, the states are free to impose more stringent requirements on plaintiffs. It appears that well over forty states have at present chosen to follow the negligence standard of liability in cases that involve a suit by private figures against media defendants on issues of public concern, with only four states — Alaska, Colorado, Indiana, and New Jersey — requiring that the plaintiff prove actual malice. See R. Smolla, The Law of Defamation §§3.10-3.11. In addition, after *Dun & Bradstreet* the states may be able to return to a strict liability standard when private plaintiffs sue on matters of no public concern, although some states have decided to apply *Gertz* to nonmedia as well as media defendants. Jacron Sales Co. v. Sindorf, 350 A.2d 688 (Md. 1976). And Massachusetts, fearing "excessive and unbridled jury verdicts," has decided to abolish punitive damage actions after *Gertz* "in any defamation action, on any state of proof, whether based in negligence or reckless or wilful conduct." Stone v. Essex County Newspapers, Inc., 330 N.E.2d 161 (Mass. 1975).

As if to note the richness of the possibilities in this area, New York, in Chapadeau v. Utica Observer-Dispatch, Inc., 341 N.E.2d 569, 571 (N.Y. 1975), struck out on its own path to hold that "within the limits imposed by the Supreme Court where the content of the article is arguably within the sphere of legitimate public concern, which is reasonably related to matters warranting public exposition, the party defamed may recover; however, to warrant such recovery he must establish, by a preponderance of the evidence, that the publisher acted in a grossly irresponsible manner without due consideration for the standards of information gathering and dissemination ordinarily followed by responsible parties." It appears as though this unique standard will apply to both media and nonmedia defendants. Sheet Metal Works, Inc. v. Picarrazzi, 793 F. Supp. 1194 (N.D.N.Y. 1992).

Philadelphia Newspapers v. Hepps
475 U.S. 767 (1986)

O'CONNOR, J. This case requires us once more to "struggl[e] . . . to define the proper accommodation between the law of defamation and the freedoms of speech and press protected by the First Amendment." Gertz v. Robert Welch, Inc., 418 U.S. 323 (1974). In *Gertz,* the Court held that a private figure who brings a suit for defamation cannot recover without some showing that the media defendant was at fault in publishing the statements at issue. Id., at 347. Here, we hold that, at least where a newspaper publishes speech of public concern, a private-figure plaintiff cannot recover damages without also showing that the statements at issue are false.

I

Maurice S. Hepps is the principal stockholder of General Programming, Inc. (GPI), a corporation that franchises a chain of stores — known at the relevant time as "Thrifty" stores — selling beer, soft drinks, and snacks. Mr. Hepps, GPI, and a number of its franchisees are the appellees here. Appellant Philadelphia Newspapers, Inc. owns the Philadelphia Inquirer (Inquirer). The Inquirer published a series of articles, authorized by appellants William Ecenbarger and William Lambert, containing the statements at issue here. The general theme of the five articles, which appeared in the Inquirer between May 1975 and May 1976, was that appellees had links to organized crime and used some of those links to influence the State's governmental processes, both legislative and administrative. . . .

[The trial judge held that the plaintiff bore the burden of proving falsity, as distinguished from fault, but refused to issue any instructions on the question of whether plaintiff could draw any inference of falsity from the fact that the defendant relied on the Pennsylvania shield law, 42 Pa. Cons. Stat. §5942(a) (1982), which provides: "No person . . . employed by any newspaper of general circulation . . . or any radio or television station, or any magazine of general circulation, . . . shall be required to disclose the source of any information procured or obtained by such person, in any legal proceeding, trial or investigation before any government unit"]

Pursuant to Pennsylvania statute, the appellees here brought an appeal directly to the Pennsylvania Supreme Court. That court viewed *Gertz* as simply requiring the plaintiff to show fault in actions for defamation. It concluded that a showing of fault did not require a showing of falsity, held that to place the burden of showing truth on the defendant did not unconstitutionally inhibit free debate, and remanded the case for a new trial. We noted probable jurisdiction, and now reverse. . . .

II

[An extensive summary of *New York Times*, *Gertz*, and *Dun & Bradstreet* is omitted.]

One can discern in these decisions two forces that may reshape the common-law landscape to conform to the First Amendment. The first is whether the plaintiff is a public official or figure, or is instead a private figure. The second is whether the speech at issue is of public concern. When the speech is of public concern and the plaintiff is a public official or public figure, the Constitution clearly requires the plaintiff to surmount a much higher barrier before recovering damages from a media defendant than is raised by the common law. When the speech is of public concern but the plaintiff is a private figure, as in *Gertz*, the Constitution still supplants the standards of the common law, but the constitutional requirements are, in at least some of their range, less forbidding than when the plaintiff is a public figure and the speech is of public concern. When the speech is of exclusively private concern and the plaintiff is a private figure, as in *Dun & Bradstreet*, the constitutional requirements do not necessarily force any change in at least some of the features of the common-law landscape.

Our opinions to date have chiefly treated the necessary showings of fault rather than of falsity. Nonetheless, as one might expect given the language of the Court in *New York Times*, a public-figure plaintiff must show the falsity of the statements at issue in order to prevail on a suit for defamation. . . .

Here, as in *Gertz*, the plaintiff is a private figure and the newspaper articles are of public concern. In *Gertz*, as in *New York Times*, the common-law rule was superseded by a constitutional rule. We believe that the common law's rule on falsity — that the defendant must bear the burden of proving truth — must similarly fall here to a constitutional requirement that the plaintiff bear the burden of showing falsity, as well as fault, before recovering damages.

There will always be instances when the factfinding process will be unable to resolve conclusively whether the speech is true or false; it is in those cases that the burden of proof is dispositive. Under a rule forcing the plaintiff to bear the burden of showing falsity, there will be some cases in which plaintiffs cannot meet their burden despite the fact that the speech is in fact false. The plaintiff's suit will fail despite the fact that, in some abstract sense, the suit is meritorious. Similarly, under an alternative rule placing the burden of showing truth on defendants, there would be some cases in which defendants could not bear their burden despite the fact that the speech is in fact true. Those suits would succeed despite the fact that, in some abstract sense, those suits are unmeritorious. Under either rule, then, the outcome of the suit will sometimes be at variance with the outcome that we would desire if all speech were either demonstrably true or demonstrably false.

This dilemma stems from the fact that the allocation of the burden of proof will determine liability for some speech that is true and some that is false, but *all* of such speech is *unknowably* true or false. Because the burden of proof is the deciding factor only when the evidence is ambiguous, we cannot know how much of the speech affected by the allocation of the burden of proof is true and how much is false. In a case presenting a configuration of speech and plaintiff like the one we face here, and where the scales are in such an uncertain balance, we believe that the Constitution requires us to tip them in favor of protecting true speech. To ensure that true speech on matters of public concern is not deterred, we hold that the common-law presumption that defamatory speech is false cannot stand when a plaintiff seeks damages against a media defendant for speech of public concern. . . .

We recognize that requiring the plaintiff to show falsity will insulate from liability some speech that is false, but unprovably so. Nonetheless, the Court's previous decisions on the restrictions that the First Amendment places upon the common law of defamation firmly support our conclusion here with respect to the allocation of the burden of proof. In attempting to resolve related issues in the defamation context, the Court has affirmed that "[t]he First Amendment requires that we protect some falsehood in order to protect speech that matters." *Gertz*. . . . To provide " 'breathing space' " for true speech on matters of public concern, the Court has been willing to insulate even demonstrably false speech from liability, and has imposed additional requirements of fault upon the plaintiff in a suit for defamation. We therefore do not break new ground here in insulating speech that is not even demonstrably false.

We note that our decision adds only marginally to the burdens that the plaintiff must already bear as a result of our earlier decisions in the law of defamation. The plaintiff must show fault. A jury is obviously more likely to accept a plaintiff's contention that the defendant was at fault in publishing the statements at issue if convinced that the relevant statements were false. As a practical matter, then, evidence offered by plaintiffs on the publisher's fault in adequately investigating the truth of the published statements will generally encompass evidence of the falsity of the matters asserted.

We recognize that the plaintiff's burden in this case is weightier because of Pennsylvania's "shield" law, which allows employees of the media to refuse to divulge their sources. But we do not have before us here the question of the permissible reach of such laws. Indeed, we do not even know the precise reach of Pennsylvania's statute. The trial judge refused to give any instructions to the jury as to whether it could, or should, draw an inference adverse to the defendant from the defendant's decision to use the shield law rather than to present affirmative evidence of the truthfulness of some of the sources. That decision of the trial judge was not addressed by Pennsylvania's highest court, nor

was it appealed to this Court. In the situation before us, we are unconvinced that the State's shield law requires a different constitutional standard than would prevail in the absence of such a law.

For the reasons stated above, the judgment of the Pennsylvania Supreme Court is reversed, and the case is remanded for further proceedings not inconsistent with this opinion.

Justice BRENNAN, with whom Justice BLACKMUN joins, concurring. I
believe that where allegedly defamatory speech is of public concern,
the First Amendment requires that the plaintiff, whether public official,
public figure, or private individual, prove the statements at issue to be
false, and thus join the Court's opinion. I write separately only to note
that, while the Court reserves the question whether the rule it announces applies to non-media defendants, I adhere to my view that
such a distinction is "irreconcilable with the fundamental First Amendment principle that '[t]he inherent worth of . . . speech in terms of its
capacity for informing the public does not depend upon the identity of
the source, whether corporation, association, union, or individual.' "
Dun & Bradstreet, Inc. v. Greenmoss Builders, Inc. [supra] (Brennan,
J., dissenting).

Justice STEVENS, with whom The Chief Justice, Justice WHITE, and
Justice REHNQUIST join, dissenting. The issue the Court resolves today
will make a difference in only one category of cases — those in which a
private individual can prove that he was libeled by a defendant who was
at least negligent. For unless such a plaintiff can overcome the burden
imposed by Gertz v. Robert Welch, Inc., he cannot recover regardless
of how the burden of proof on the issue of truth or falsity is allocated.
By definition, therefore, the only litigants — and the only publishers —
who will benefit from today's decision are those who act negligently or
maliciously. . . .

I do not agree that our precedents require a private individual to
bear the risk that a defamatory statement — uttered either with a mind
toward assassinating his good name or with careless indifference to that
possibility — cannot be proven false. By attaching no weight to the
state's interest in protecting the private individual's good name, the
Court has reached a pernicious result.

To appreciate the thrust of the Court's holding, we must assume that
a private-figure libel plaintiff can prove that a story about him was published with "actual malice" — that is, without the publisher caring in
the slightest whether it was false or not. Indeed, in order to comprehend the full ramifications of today's decision, we should assume that
the publisher knew that it would be impossible for a court to verify or
discredit the story and that it was published for no other purpose than
to destroy the reputation of the plaintiff. Even if the plaintiff has overwhelming proof of malice — in both the common law sense and as the
term was used in New York Times Co. v. Sullivan — the Court today

seems to believe that the character assassin has a constitutional license to defame.

NOTES

1. Truth. The decision in *Hepps* is at sharp variance with the common-law treatment, which almost uniformly required the defendant to demonstrate the truth of his statements; since the plaintiff had to establish the invasion of a protected interest, the defendant had to show that the invasion was indeed justified. In fact, many common-law jurisdictions placed an additional obstacle in the path of a defendant who attempted to demonstrate truth by treating the unsuccessful assertion of the defense as a republication of the libel, entitling plaintiffs to additional damages. For an account of these rules see Corabi v. Curtis Publishing Co., 273 A.2d 899 (Pa. 1971).

Wholly apart from the Constitution, however, there are good reasons to question the common-law allocation of the burden of proof. One familiar argument is that plaintiff has better access to information concerning his own conduct and therefore is in an excellent position to rebut the charges against him. Alternatively, it could be justified on the ground that no one should be allowed to claim injury to good reputation when that reputation was undeserved in the first place.

How important is the allocation of the burden of proof on the question of truth in routine cases? When the Court holds that the private plaintiff must bear the burden of showing falsehood, does it refer to the original burden of producing evidence or to the ultimate burden of persuasion? If the Pennsylvania "shield law" received a broad construction, should the Court reconsider its opinion with either of these two burdens or with both? Is discovery possible, notwithstanding the shield law, on the authority of Herbert v. Lando?

2. Reform of defamation law. The initial reaction to *New York Times* was largely celebratory, not only for the boost that it gave to the civil rights movement, but also because of the implicit judgment that the actual malice rule could undo the litigation logjam in defamation cases. But starting in the 1970s and working through the 1980s, defamation suits resulted in mammoth struggles whose movements to and fro were avidly covered by the press. The expanded pace of civil litigation galvanized pressure for legislative action. During the 1980s, the *New York Times* actual malice rule came under attack from *both* sides. For the plaintiffs the chief grievance was that the actual malice rule allows a defendant to escape liability even when admittedly false statements worked substantial damage to reputation. One traditional function of the libel law — to provide official vindication to the plaintiff's reputation — is sidetracked by a motive-based privilege that prevents the plaintiff from setting the record straight. On the media side, the main concern is with the enormous cost and expense of defending a defamation action. Here, ironically, the actual malice rule may well be part of the problem. Although it reduces the number of cases that can be brought, it increases the uncertainty of the outcome and the size of any potential recovery in successful suits since proof of actual malice might easily justify claim for punitive damages, where damages may be both large and erratic. Litigation costs could easily escalate, as they did in the twin great cases of the 1980s, Sharon v. Time, Inc., 599 F. Supp. 538 (S.D.N.Y 1984), and Westmoreland v. CBS, 10 Media L. Rep. 2417 (S.D.N.Y. 1984).

Choosing a reform strategy was hardly easy even when everyone was displeased with the current regime. One extreme suggestion was to abolish all defamation actions by public officials and public figures. A more modest version of the same idea was to abolish punitive damages in all suits brought by public officials and public figures against media defendants. In this vein see also Lewis, *New York Times v. Sullivan* Reconsidered: Time to Return to "The Central Meaning of the First Amendment," 83 Colum. L. Rev. 603 (1983), advocating among other changes more frequent use of summary judgments, special verdicts, and a prohibition on recovery for mental anguish and punitive damages.

In the opposite direction, many scholars urged that the plaintiff be allowed to obtain a declaratory judgment on the question of truth or falsity without proof of actual malice, but only (under some versions of the proposal) by first waiving any right to damages. A declaratory judgment was achieved in a backhand manner in the *Sharon* case, where, in response to specific questions propounded by special verdicts, the jury decided both that Time's statements were wrong and that the error was not actuated by actual malice. What is the reputational effect of such a verdict on Time?

For various detailed proposals for reform see R. Adler, Reckless Disregard (1986); R. Bezanson, G. Cranberg, J. Soloski, Libel Law and the Press: Myth and Reality ch. 8 (1987); R. Smolla, The Law of Defamation §9.13[4] (1989).

Chapter Fifteen
Privacy

A. HISTORICAL BACKGROUND

Warren and Brandeis, The Right to Privacy
4 Harv. L. Rev. 193, 193-197 (1890)

That the individual shall have full protection in person and in property is a principle as old as the common law; but it has been found necessary from time to time to define anew the exact nature and extent of such protection. Political, social, and economic changes entail the recognition of new rights, and the common law, in its eternal youth, grows to meet the demands of society. Thus, in very early times, the law gave a remedy only for physical interference with life and property, for trespasses vi et armis. Then the "right to life" served only to protect the subject from battery in its various forms; liberty meant freedom from actual restraint; and the right to property secured to the individual his lands and his cattle. Later, there came a recognition of man's spiritual nature, of his feelings and his intellect. Gradually the scope of these legal rights broadened; and now the right to life has come to mean the right to enjoy life, — the right to be let alone; the right to liberty secures the exercise of extensive civil privileges; and the term "property" has grown to comprise every form of possession — intangible, as well as tangible.

Thus, with the recognition of the legal value of sensations, the protection against actual bodily injury was extended to prohibit mere attempts to do such injury; that is, the putting another in fear of such injury. From the action of battery grew that of assault. Much later there came a qualified protection of the individual against offensive noises

1215

and odors, against dust and smoke, and excessive vibration. The law of nuisance was developed. So regard for human emotions soon extended the scope of personal immunity beyond the body of the individual. His reputation, the standing among his fellow-men, was considered, and the law of slander and libel arose. Man's family relations became a part of the legal conception of his life, and the alienation of a wife's affections was held remediable. Occasionally the law halted, — as in its refusal to recognize the intrusion by seduction upon the honor of the family. But even here the demands of society were met. A mean fiction, the action per quod servitium amisit, was resorted to, and by allowing damages for injury to the parents' feelings, an adequate remedy was ordinarily afforded. Similar to the expansion of the right to life was the growth of the legal conception of property. From corporeal property arose the incorporeal rights issuing out of it; and then there opened the wide realm of intangible property, in the products and processes of the mind, as works of literature and art, goodwill, trade secrets, and trademarks.

This development of the law was inevitable. The intense intellectual and emotional life, and the heightening of sensations which came with the advance of civilization, made it clear to men that only a part of the pain, pleasure, and profit of life lay in physical things. Thoughts, emotions, and sensations demanded legal recognition, and the beautiful capacity for growth which characterizes the common law enabled the judges to afford the requisite protection, without the interposition of the legislature.

Recent inventions and business methods call attention to the next step which must be taken for the protection of the person, and for securing to the individual what Judge Cooley calls the right "to be let alone." Instantaneous photographs and newspaper enterprise have invaded the sacred precincts of private and domestic life; and numerous mechanical devices threaten to make good the prediction that "what is whispered in the closet shall be proclaimed from the house-tops." For years there has been a feeling that the law must afford some remedy for the unauthorized circulation of portraits of private persons; and the evil of the invasion of privacy by the newspapers, long keenly felt, has been but recently discussed by an able writer. The alleged facts of a somewhat notorious case brought before an inferior tribunal in New York a few months ago directly involved the consideration of the right of circulating portraits; and the question whether our law will recognize and protect the right to privacy in this and in other respects must soon come before our courts for consideration.

Of the desirability — indeed of the necessity — of some such protection, there can, it is believed, be no doubt. The press is overstepping in every direction the obvious bounds of propriety and decency. Gossip is no longer the resource of the idle and of the vicious, but has become a trade, which is pursued with industry as well as effrontery. To satisfy a prurient taste the details of sexual relations are spread broadcast in the columns of the daily papers. To occupy the indolent, column upon column is filled with idle gossip, which can only be procured by intrusion upon the domestic circle. The intensity and complexity of life, attendant upon advancing civilization, have rendered necessary some retreat from the world, and man, under the refining influence of culture, has become more sensitive to publicity, so that solitude and privacy have become more essential to the individual; but modern enterprise and invention have, through invasions upon his privacy, subjected him to mental pain and distress, far greater than could be inflicted by mere bodily injury. Nor is the harm wrought by such invasions confined to the suffering of those who may be made the subjects of journalistic or other enterprise. In this, as in other branches of commerce, the supply creates the demand. Each crop of unseemly gossip, thus harvested, becomes the seed of more, and, in direct proportion to its circulation, results in a lowering of social standards and of morality. Even gossip apparently harmless, when widely and persistently circulated, is potent for evil. It both belittles and perverts. It belittles by inverting the relative importance of things, thus dwarfing the thoughts and aspirations of a people. When personal gossip attains the dignity of print, and crowds the space available for matters of real interest to the community, what wonder that the ignorant and thoughtless mistake its relative importance. Easy of comprehension, appealing to that weak side of human nature which is never wholly cast down by the misfortunes and frailties of our neighbors, no one can be surprised that it usurps the place of interest in brains capable of other things. Triviality destroys at once robustness of thought and delicacy of feeling. No enthusiasm can flourish, no generous impulse can survive under its blighting influence.

It is our purpose to consider whether the existing law affords a principle which can properly be invoked to protect the privacy of the individual; and, if it does, what the nature and extent of such protection is.

Prosser, Privacy
48 Cal. L. Rev. 383, 383-384 (1960)

In the year 1890 Mrs. Samuel D. Warren, a young matron of Boston, which is a large city in Massachusetts, held at her home a series of social entertainments on an elaborate scale. She was the daughter of Senator Bayard of Delaware, and her husband was a wealthy young paper manufacturer, who only the year before had given up the practice of law to devote himself to an inherited business. Socially Mrs. Warren was among the élite; and the newspapers of Boston, and in particular the

Saturday Evening Gazette, which specialized in "blue blood" items, covered her parties in highly personal and embarrassing detail. It was the
era of "yellow journalism," when the press had begun to resort to ex-
cesses in the way of prying that have become more or less commonplace
today; and Boston was perhaps, of all of the cities in the country, the
one in which a lady and a gentleman kept their names and their personal affairs out of the papers. The matter came to a head when the
newspapers had a field day on the occasion of the wedding of a daughter, and Mr. Warren became annoyed. It was an annoyance for which
the press, the advertisers and the entertainment industry of America
were to pay dearly over the next seventy years.

Mr. Warren turned to his recent law partner, Louis D. Brandeis, who
was destined not to be unknown to history. The result was a noted
article, The Right to Privacy, in the Harvard Law Review, upon which
the two men collaborated. It has come to be regarded as the outstanding example of the influence of legal periodicals upon the American
law. In the Harvard Law School class of 1877 the two authors had stood
respectively second and first, and both of them were gifted with scholarship, imagination, and ability. Internal evidences of style, and the probabilities of the situation, suggest that the writing, and perhaps most of
the research, was done by Brandeis; but it was undoubtedly a joint effort, to which both men contributed their ideas.

The passages quoted from Warren and Brandeis are the introduction
to perhaps the most influential law review article ever published. After
setting out their basic premises, the authors attempt to isolate the common-law principle for invasion of privacy. They reject analogies to libel
and slander, noting that the tort is not concerned with plaintiff's reputation or "with the injury done to the individual in his external relations
to the community." They also reject the view that the tort is designed
to protect a person from "mere injury to feelings," noting that such
harm is compensable only if plaintiff establishes that he is the victim of
some "recognized" legal injury.

Their article then examines and rejects the view that plaintiff's right
to privacy can be predicated on a fiduciary or contract theory. These
theories apply when plaintiff and defendant have previously entered
into some consensual relationship, as when one party poses for a picture or lectures to students in a private hall. There the plaintiff can
argue that implicit in the special relationship between the parties is the
understanding that the picture taken or the information acquired will
be used only for limited purposes. But these consensual theories do not
explain how the right of privacy can be vindicated against a stranger
who, for example, takes, as "the latest advances in photographic art"

allow, the plaintiff's picture "surreptitiously," or who tape records a lecture from outside the hall.

In an effort to explain the "in rem" nature of the tort, the authors find the key analogy in the common law of copyright, which gives the owner control over access to his *unpublished* materials. "In every such case the individual is entitled to decide whether that which is his shall be given to the public." (Id. at 199.) Since under the better rule even writing of no literary value is protected as long as it is unpublished, they conclude: "The principle which protects personal writings and all other personal productions, not against theft and physical appropriation, but against publications in any form, is in reality not the principle of private property, but that of an inviolate personality." (Id. at 205.)

Having thus located the principle underlying the desired protection, the authors turn in conclusion to "limitations on this right to privacy" (id. at 214-219) and briefly touch on six points: It does not apply to oral communications in the absence of special damages; it inherits all the privileges of defamation, and in addition a privilege for matter "which is of public or general interest"; truth, however, is not a defense; malice in the sense of ill will is not required; and the right ceases upon voluntary publication.

Kalven, Privacy in the Tort Law — Were Warren and Brandeis Wrong?
31 Law & Contemp. Probs. 326, 330-331 (1966)

While the article is admirable in the care with which it specifies certain limitations on the new right, it makes it apparent at the birth of the right that there are certain major ambiguities. These are all points which haunt the tort today and to which we will return, but we would note here that there is no effort to specify what will constitute a prima facie case; no concern with how damages are to be measured; no concern, other than to dismiss actual malice, with what the basis of liability will be; and finally there is the projection of a generous set of privileges but no effort to assess whether they do not engulf the cause of action. And, of course, there is no hint that any but gentlemen will ever be moved to use the new remedy.

A decade after the publication of the Warren and Brandeis article, the right to privacy moved into the judicial arena in Roberson v. Rochester Folding Co., 64 N.E. 442, 443 (N.Y. 1902). There one of the defendants in this action, the Franklin Mills Company, purchased from the Rochester Folding Box Company 25,000 lithographic prints, which it circulated widely in "stores, warehouses, saloons, and other public places." The defendants had, without consent, reproduced on the prints a portrait of the plaintiff above which were printed the words "Flour of the Family," and below which in large capital letters were printed the words "Franklin Mills Flour." In the lower right-hand corner of the picture was printed the name of the defendant box company. As a result of the publication of these prints the plaintiff claimed that she had "been greatly humiliated by the scoffs and jeers of persons who have recognized her face and picture on this advertisement and her good name has been attacked, causing her great distress and suffering both in body and mind; that she was made sick and suffered a severe nervous shock, was confined to her bed and compelled to employ a physician, because of these facts."

The plaintiff's case reveals the two different sides to the action for privacy. One way to look at the case is as an action for restitution, whereby the plaintiff demands that the defendant disgorge the profits it obtained from the unauthorized use of her picture, a situation that does not differ in principle from an action for restitution for the unauthorized conversion of a physical asset. The second way to look at the case is as an action for the invasion of privacy, in which what is sought is compensation for anguish and loss of reputation derived from the attack on her reputation and good name. Here the tort is far closer to defamation. But Parker, J., had no patience with either form of a novel claim based on the refined theories of Warren and Brandeis:

> The so-called right of privacy is, as the phrase suggests, founded upon the claim that a man has the right to pass through this world, if he wills, without having his picture published, his business enterprises discussed, his successful experiments written up for the benefit of others, or his eccentricities commented upon either in handbills, circulars, catalogues, periodicals or newspapers, and, necessarily, that the things which may not be written and published of him must not be spoken of him by his neighbors, whether the comment be favorable or otherwise. While most persons would much prefer to have a good likeness of themselves appear in a responsible periodical or leading newspaper rather than upon an advertising card or sheet, the doctrine which the courts are asked to create for this case would apply as well to the one publication as to the other, for the principle which a court of equity is asked to assert in support of a recovery in this action is that the right of privacy exists and is enforceable in equity, and that the publication of that which purports to be a portrait of another person, even if obtained upon the street by an impertinent individual with a camera, will be restrained in equity on the ground that an individual has the right to prevent his features from becoming known to those outside of his circle of friends and acquaintances.
>
> If such a principle be incorporated into the body of the law through the instrumentality of a court of equity, the attempts to logically apply the principle will necessarily result, not only in a vast amount of litigation, but in litigation bordering upon the absurd, for the right of privacy, once established as a legal doctrine, cannot be confined to the restraint

of the publication of a likeness but must necessarily embrace as well the publication of a word-picture, a comment upon one's looks, conduct, domestic relations or habits. And were the right of privacy once legally asserted it would necessarily be held to include the same things if spoken instead of printed, for one, as well as the other, invades the right to be absolutely let alone. An insult would certainly be in violation of such a right and with many persons would more seriously wound the feelings than would the publication of their picture. And so we might add to the list of things that are spoken and done day by day which seriously offend the sensibilities of good people to which the principle which the plaintiff seeks to have imbedded in the doctrine of the law would seem to apply. I have gone only far enough to barely suggest the vast field of litigation which would necessarily be opened up should this court hold that privacy exists as a legal right enforceable in equity by injunction, and by damages where they seem necessary to give complete relief.

The legislative body could very well interfere and arbitrarily provide that no one should be permitted for his own selfish purpose to use the picture or the name of another for advertising purposes without his consent. In such event, no embarrassment would result to the general body of the law, for the rule would be applicable only to cases provided for by the statute. The courts, however, being without authority to legislate, are required to decide cases upon principle, and so are necessarily embarrassed by precedents created by an extreme, and, therefore, unjustifiable application of an old principle. . . .

The dissent of Gray, J. (joined by two others) took sharp issue:

[I]f it is to be permitted that the portraiture may be put to commercial, or other, uses for gain, by the publication of prints therefrom, then an act of invasion of the individual's privacy results, possibly more formidable and more painful in its consequences, than an actual bodily assault might be. Security of person is as necessary as the security of property; and for that complete personal security, which will result in the peaceful and wholesome enjoyment of one's privileges as a member of society, there should be afforded protection, not only against the scandalous portraiture and display of one's features and person, but against the display and use thereof for another's commercial purposes or gain.

Gray's dissent was quickly adopted in Pavesich v. New England Life Insurance Co., 50 S.E. 68 (Ga. 1905), another unauthorized advertisement case, and in Hinish v. Meier & Frank Co., 113 P.2d 438, 447 (Or. 1941), when the defendant signed plaintiff's name to a telegram urging a veto of certain legislation that would put the defendant out of business. Plaintiff sued because he feared that the telegram might cost him his job and pension with the federal government in light of a statutory prohibition against federal employee participation in political affairs. In allowing the cause of action, the Oregon Court emphatically rejected *Roberson*.

The opinion of the court in the *Roberson* case, after an exaggerated statement, as we view it, of what is claimed for the right of privacy, dwelt upon the absurd consequences which it was conceived would follow from acceptance of the doctrine. "The attempt to logically apply the principle," it was said, "will necessarily result not only in a vast amount of litigation but in litigation bordering on the absurd." It was not stated that the litigation then before the court was absurd. It may be doubted whether any court today would render the decision that the New York court did in that case. . . . When a legal principle is pushed to an absurdity, the principle is not abandoned, but the absurdity avoided. The courts are competent, we think, to deal with difficulties of the sort suggested, and case by case, through the traditional process of inclusion and exclusion, gradually to develop the fullness of the principle and its limitations. That there are difficulties may be conceded. . . .

Is *Hinish* closer to unlawful conversion or defamation?

By 1960 it was clear a large number of cases had recognized some form of the right of privacy, without articulating a clear structure for the tort. In order to lend some overall structure to the tort, without doing too much violence to the case law, the late Dean Prosser proposed a fourfold classification of the interests protected under the general rubric of privacy, which has exerted enormous influence over the subsequent law.

Prosser, Privacy
48 Cal. L. Rev. 383, 389, 407 (1960)

[The] law of privacy comprises four distinct kinds of invasion of four different interests of the plaintiff, which are tied together by the common name, but otherwise have almost nothing in common except that each represents an interference with the right of the plaintiff, in the phrase coined by Judge Cooley, "to be let alone." Without any attempt to exact definition, these four torts may be described as follows:

1. Intrusion upon the plaintiff's seclusion or solitude, or into his private affairs.
2. Public disclosure of embarrassing private facts about the plaintiff.
3. Publicity which places the plaintiff in a false light in the public eye.
4. Appropriation, for the defendant's advantage, of the plaintiff's name or likeness.

It should be obvious at once that these four types of invasion may be subject, in some respects at least, to different rules; and that when what is said as to any one of them is carried over to another, it may not be at all applicable, and confusion may follow. . . .

Judge Biggs has described the present state of the law of privacy as "still that of a haystack in a hurricane." Disarray there certainly is; but almost all of the confusion is due to a failure to separate and distinguish these four forms of invasion, and to realize that they call for different things. . . .

Taking them in order — intrusion, disclosure, false light, and appropriation — the first and second require the invasion of something secret, secluded or private pertaining to the plaintiff; the third and fourth do not. The second and third depend upon publicity, while the first does not, nor does the fourth, although it usually involves it. The third requires falsity or fiction; the other three do not. The fourth involves a use for the defendant's advantage, which is not true of the rest. . . .

Prosser's classification has been adopted by many courts, and it forms the basis for the treatment of the subject in the Restatement (Second) of Torts §652A-652L, of which Prosser was the original draftsman. Prosser's view has been attacked on the grounds that it is insufficiently supported by the cases and that it fails to recognize that the single interest at stake in all privacy cases is simply that of "human dignity." See Bloustein, Privacy as an Aspect of Human Dignity: An Answer to Dean Prosser, 39 N.Y.U. L. Rev. 962 (1964). See also Posner, The Right of Privacy, 12 Ga. L. Rev. 393 (1978); Epstein, Privacy, Property Rights, and Misrepresentations, 12 Ga. L. Rev. 455 (1978): Zimmerman, Requiem for a Heavyweight: a Farewell to Warren and Brandeis's Privacy Tort, 68 Cornell L. Rev. 291 (1983).

In this chapter we will adopt for purposes of exposition the classification proposed by Prosser, although we will consider the four torts in a different sequence. For reasons of historical development we will first take up the tort of commercial appropriation; second, public disclosure of embarrassing facts; third, publicity placing plaintiff in a "false light"; and fourth, intrusion upon plaintiff's seclusion.

B.   COMMERCIAL APPROPRIATION OF PLAINTIFF'S NAME OR LIKENESS, OR THE RIGHT OF PUBLICITY

American Law Institute, Restatement (Second) of the Law of Torts
(1976)

§652C.   APPROPRIATION OF NAME OR LIKENESS

One who appropriates to his own use or benefit the name or likeness of another is subject to liability to the other for invasion of his privacy.

Comment *b: How invaded.* The common form of invasion of privacy under the rule here stated is the appropriation and use of the plaintiff's name or likeness to advertise the defendant's business or product, or for some similar commercial purpose. Apart from statute, however, the rule stated is not limited to commercial appropriation. It applies also where the defendant makes use of the plaintiff's name or likeness for his own purposes and benefit, even though such use is not a commercial one, and even though the benefit sought to be obtained is not a pecuniary one. Statutes in some states have, however, limited the liability to commercial uses of name or likeness.

White v. Samsung Electronics America, Inc.
971 F.2d 1395 (9th Cir. 1992)

GOODWIN, SENIOR CIRCUIT JUDGE: This case involves a promotional "fame and fortune" dispute. In running a particular advertisement without Vanna White's permission, defendants Samsung Electronics America, Inc. (Samsung) and David Deutsch Associates, Inc. (Deutsch) attempted to capitalize on White's fame to enhance their fortune. White sued, alleging infringement of various intellectual property rights, but the district court granted summary judgment in favor of the defendants. We affirm in part, reverse in part, and remand.

Plaintiff Vanna White is the hostess of "Wheel of Fortune," one of the most popular game shows in television history. An estimated forty million people watch the program daily. Capitalizing on the fame which her participation in the show has bestowed on her, White markets her identity to various advertisers.

The dispute in this case arose out of a series of advertisements prepared for Samsung by Deutsch. The series ran in at least half a dozen publications with widespread, and in some cases national, circulation. Each of the advertisements in the series followed the same theme. Each depicted a current item from popular culture and a Samsung electronic product. Each was set in the twenty-first century and conveyed the message that the Samsung product would still be in use by that time. By hypothesizing outrageous future outcomes for the cultural items, the ads created humorous effects. For example, one lampooned current popular notions of an unhealthy diet by depicting a raw steak with the caption: "Revealed to be health food. 2010 A.D." Another depicted irreverent "news"-show host Morton Downey Jr. in front of an American flag with the caption: "Presidential candidate. 2008 A.D."

The advertisement which prompted the current dispute was for Samsung video-cassette recorders (VCRs). The ad depicted a robot, dressed in a wig, gown, and jewelry which Deutsch consciously selected to resemble White's hair and dress. The robot was posed next to a game board which is instantly recognizable as the Wheel of Fortune game show set, in a stance for which White is famous. The caption of the ad read: "Longest-running game show. 2012 A.D." Defendants referred to the ad as the "Vanna White" ad. Unlike the other celebrities used in the campaign, White neither consented to the ads nor was she paid.

Following the circulation of the robot ad, White sued Samsung and Deutsch in federal district court under: (1) California Civil Code §3344; (2) the California common law right of publicity; and (3) §43(a) of the Lanham Act, 15 U.S.C. §1125(a). The district court granted summary judgment against White on each of her claims. White now appeals.

I.   SECTION 3344

White first argues that the district court erred in rejecting her claim under section 3344. Section 3344(a) provides, in pertinent part, that "[a]ny person who knowingly uses another's name, voice, signature, photograph, or likeness, in any manner, . . . for purposes of advertising or selling, . . . without such person's prior consent . . . shall be liable for any damages sustained by the person or persons injured as a result thereof."

White argues that the Samsung advertisement used her "likeness" in contravention of section 3344. In Midler v. Ford Motor Co., 849 F.2d 460 (9th Cir. 1988), this court rejected Bette Midler's section 3344 claim concerning a Ford television commercial in which a Midler "sound-alike" sang a song which Midler had made famous. In rejecting Midler's claim, this court noted that "[t]he defendants did not use Midler's name or anything else whose use is prohibited by the statute. The voice they used was [another person's], not hers. The term 'likeness' refers to a visual image not a vocal imitation."

In this case, Samsung and Deutsch used a robot with mechanical features, and not, for example, a manikin molded to White's precise features. Without deciding for all purposes when a caricature or impressionistic resemblance might become a "likeness," we agree with the district court that the robot at issue here was not White's "likeness" within the meaning of section 3344. Accordingly, we affirm the court's dismissal of White's section 3344 claim.

II.   RIGHT OF PUBLICITY

White next argues that the district court erred in granting summary judgment to defendants on White's common law right of publicity claim. In Eastwood v. Superior Court, 198 Cal. Rptr. 342 (Cal. 1983), the California court of appeal stated that the common law right of publicity cause of action "may be pleaded by alleging (1) the defendant's use of the plaintiff's identity; (2) the appropriation of plaintiff's name or likeness to defendant's advantage, commercially or otherwise; (3) lack of consent; and (4) resulting injury." The district court dismissed White's claim for failure to satisfy *Eastwood*'s second prong, reasoning that defendants had not appropriated White's "name or likeness" with their robot ad. We agree that the robot ad did not make use of White's name or likeness. However, the common law right of publicity is not so confined.

The *Eastwood* court did not hold that the right of publicity cause of action could be pleaded only by alleging an appropriation of name or likeness. *Eastwood* involved an unauthorized use of photographs of Clint Eastwood and of his name. Accordingly, the *Eastwood* court had no occasion to consider the extent beyond the use of name or likeness to which the right of publicity reaches. That court held only that the right of publicity cause of action "may be" pleaded by alleging, inter alia, appropriation of name or likeness, not that the action may be pleaded only in those terms.

The "name or likeness" formulation referred to in *Eastwood* originated not as an element of the right of publicity cause of action, but as a description of the types of cases in which the cause of action had been recognized. The source of this formulation is Prosser, Privacy, 48 Cal. L. Rev. 383, 401-407 (1960), one of the earliest and most enduring articulations of the common law right of publicity cause of action. In looking at the case law to that point, Prosser recognized that right of publicity cases involved one of two basic factual scenarios: name appropriation, and picture or other likeness appropriation.

Even though Prosser focused on appropriations of name or likeness in discussing the right of publicity, he noted that "[i]t is not impossible that there might be appropriation of the plaintiff's identity, as by impersonation, without the use of either his name or his likeness, and that this would be an invasion of his right of privacy." At the time Prosser wrote, he noted however, that "[n]o such case appears to have arisen."

Since Prosser's early formulation, the case law has borne out his insight that the right of publicity is not limited to the appropriation of name or likeness. In Motschenbacher v. R.J. Reynolds Tobacco Co., 498 F.2d 821 (9th Cir. 1974), the defendant had used a photograph of the plaintiff's race car in a television commercial. Although the plaintiff appeared driving the car in the photograph, his features were not visible. Even though the defendant had not appropriated the plaintiff's name or likeness, this court held that the plaintiff's California right of publicity claim should reach the jury.

In *Midler*, this court held that, even though the defendants had not used Midler's name or likeness, Midler had stated a claim for violation of her California common law right of publicity because "the defendants . . . for their own profit in selling their product did appropriate part of her identity" by using a Midler sound-alike.

In Carson v. Here's Johnny Portable Toilets, Inc., 698 F.2d 831 (6th Cir. 1983), the defendant had marketed portable toilets under the brand name "Here's Johnny" — Johnny Carson's signature "Tonight Show" introduction — without Carson's permission. The district court had dismissed Carson's Michigan common law right of publicity claim because the defendants had not used Carson's "name or likeness." In reversing the district court, the sixth circuit found "the district court's conception of the right of publicity . . . too narrow" and held that the right was implicated because the defendant had appropriated Carson's identity by using, inter alia, the phrase "Here's Johnny."

These cases teach not only that the common law right of publicity reaches means of appropriation other than name or likeness, but that the specific means of appropriation are relevant only for determining whether the defendant has in fact appropriated the plaintiff's identity. The right of publicity does not require that appropriations of identity be accomplished through particular means to be actionable. It is noteworthy that the *Midler* and *Carson* defendants not only avoided using the plaintiff's name or likeness, but they also avoided appropriating the celebrity's voice, signature, and photograph. The photograph in *Motschenbacher* did include the plaintiff, but because the plaintiff was not visible the driver could have been an actor or dummy and the analysis in the case would have been the same.

Although the defendants in these cases avoided the most obvious means of appropriating the plaintiffs' identities, each of their actions directly implicated the commercial interests which the right of publicity is designed to protect. As the Carson court explained: "[t]he right of publicity has developed to protect the commercial interest of celebrities in their identities. The theory of the right is that a celebrity's identity can be valuable in the promotion of products, and the celebrity has an interest that may be protected from the unauthorized commercial exploitation of that identity. . . . If the celebrity's identity is commercially exploited, there has been an invasion of his right whether or not his "name or likeness" is used. It is not important how the defendant has appropriated the plaintiff's identity, but *whether* the defendant has done so. *Motschenbacher, Midler,* and *Carson* teach the impossibility of treating the right of publicity as guarding only against a laundry list of specific means of appropriating identity. A rule which says that the right of publicity can be infringed only through the use of nine different methods of appropriating identity merely challenges the clever advertising strategist to come up with the tenth.

Indeed, if we treated the means of appropriation as dispositive in our analysis of the right of publicity, we would not only weaken the right but effectively eviscerate it. The right would fail to protect those plaintiffs most in need of its protection. Advertisers use celebrities to promote their products. The more popular the celebrity, the greater the number of people who recognize her, and the greater the visibility for the product. The identities of the most popular celebrities are not only the most attractive for advertisers, but also the easiest to evoke without resorting to obvious means such as name, likeness, or voice.

Consider a hypothetical advertisement which depicts a mechanical robot with male features, an African-American complexion, and a bald head. The robot is wearing black hightop Air Jordan basketball sneakers, and a red basketball uniform with black trim, baggy shorts, and the number 23 (though not revealing "Bulls" or "Jordan" lettering). The ad depicts the robot dunking a basketball one-handed, stiff-armed, legs extended like open scissors, and tongue hanging out. Now envision that this ad is run on television during professional basketball games. Considered individually, the robot's physical attributes, its dress, and its stance tell us little. Taken together, they lead to the only conclusion that any sports viewer who has registered a discernible pulse in the past five years would reach: the ad is about Michael Jordan.

Viewed separately, the individual aspects of the advertisement in the present case say little. Viewed together, they leave little doubt about the celebrity the ad is meant to depict. The female-shaped robot is wearing a long gown, blond wig, and large jewelry. Vanna White dresses exactly like this at times, but so do many other women. The robot is in the process of turning a block letter on a game-board. Vanna White dresses like this while turning letters on a game-board but perhaps similarly attired Scrabble-playing women do this as well. The robot is standing on what looks to be the Wheel of Fortune game show set. Vanna White dresses like this, turns letters, and does this on the Wheel of Fortune game show. She is the only one. Indeed, defendants themselves referred to their ad as the "Vanna White" ad. We are not surprised.

Television and other media create marketable celebrity identity value. Considerable energy and ingenuity are expended by those who have achieved celebrity value to exploit it for profit. The law protects the celebrity's sole right to exploit this value whether the celebrity has achieved her fame out of rare ability, dumb luck, or a combination thereof. We decline Samsung and Deutch's invitation to permit the evisceration of the common law right of publicity through means as facile as those in this case. Because White has alleged facts showing that Samsung and Deutsch had appropriated her identity, the district court erred by rejecting, on summary judgment, White's common law right of publicity claim.

III.   THE LANHAM ACT

White's final argument is that the district court erred in denying her claim under §43(a) of the Lanham Act [for trademark infringement. The court upheld this dismissal because the plaintiff could not show the requisite "confusion or deception flowing from the violation" of the statute, where the protected mark is, in this instance, the plaintiff's persona.]

IV. THE PARODY DEFENSE

In defense, defendants cite a number of cases for the proposition that their robot ad constituted protected speech. The only cases they cite which are even remotely relevant to this case are Hustler Magazine v. Falwell [supra at page 90] and L.L. Bean, Inc. v. Drake Publishers, Inc., 811 F.2d 26 (1st Cir. 1987). Those cases involved parodies of advertisements run for the purpose of poking fun at Jerry Falwell and L.L. Bean, respectively. This case involves a true advertisement run for the purpose of selling Samsung VCRs. The ad's spoof of Vanna White and Wheel of Fortune is subservient and only tangentially related to the ad's primary message: "buy Samsung VCRs." Defendants' parody arguments are better addressed to non-commercial parodies. The difference between a "parody" and a "knock-off" is the difference between fun and profit.

V. CONCLUSION

In remanding this case, we hold only that White has pleaded claims which can go to the jury for its decision.

Affirmed in part, reversed in part and remanded.

[The dissenting opinion of Alarcon, J., is omitted. A petition for rehearing was denied, with three dissenting votes. 989 F.2d 1512 (9th Cir. 1993). Kozinski, J., wrote an impassioned dissent which began as follows:]

Saddam Hussein wants to keep advertisers from using his picture in unflattering contexts. Clint Eastwood doesn't want tabloids to write about him. Rudolf Valentino's heirs want to control his film biography. The Girl Scouts don't want their image soiled by association with certain activities. George Lucas wants to keep Strategic Defense Initiative fans from calling it "Star Wars." Pepsico doesn't want singers to use the word "Pepsi" in their songs. Guy Lombardo wants an exclusive property right to ads that show big bands playing on New Year's Eve. Uri Geller thinks he should be paid for ads showing psychics bending metal through telekinesis. Paul Prudhomme, that household name, thinks the same about ads featuring corpulent bearded chefs. And scads of copyright holders see purple when their creations are made fun of.

Something very dangerous is going on here. Private property, including intellectual property, is essential to our way of life. It provides an incentive for investment and innovation; it stimulates the flourishing of our culture; it protects the moral entitlements of people to the fruits of their labors. But reducing too much to private property can be bad medicine. Private land, for instance, is far more useful if separated from other private land by public streets, roads and highways. Public parks, utility rights-of- way and sewers reduce the amount of land in private hands, but vastly enhance the value of the property that remains.

So too it is with intellectual property. Overprotecting intellectual property is as harmful as underprotecting it. Creativity is impossible without a rich public domain. Nothing today, likely nothing since we tamed fire, is genuinely new: Culture, like science and technology, grows by accretion, each new creator building on the works of those who came before. Overprotection stifles the very creative forces it's supposed to nurture.

NOTE

Commercial exploitation of name or likeness. Starting with *Roberson* it was apparent that the right of publicity was in direct tension with the ordinary right of individuals to speak and comment on the affairs of the others. That tension was raised in a large number of cases in which the plaintiff's name or likeness was used in general newspaper stories that were included in commercial publication. Efforts to claim an invasion of the right of privacy in that context were decisively rebuffed in Tropeano v. Atlantic Monthly Co., 400 N.E.2d 847, 850, 851 (Mass. 1980). There the defendant published a picture of plaintiff in connection with its story "After the Sexual Revolution," without identifying her by name or discussing her. She claimed that publication violated her rights under Mass. Gen. L. ch. 214, §3A (1994), which provides that "[a]ny person whose name, portrait or picture is used within the commonwealth for advertising purposes or for the purposes of trade without his written consent . . . may recover damages for any injuries sustained by reason of such use." Hennessey, C.J., rejected her claim:

> The value of one's name, portrait or picture is not appropriated "when it is published for purposes other than taking advantage of his reputation, prestige, or other value associated with him, for purposes of publicity." See Restatement (Second) of Torts §652C, comment *d* (1977). Thus, the crucial distinction under G.L. c. 214, §3A, must be between situations in which the defendant makes an incidental use of the plaintiff's name, portrait or picture and those in which the defendant uses the plaintiff's name, portrait or picture deliberately to exploit its value for advertising or trade purposes. . . . Under the foregoing principles it is clear that the instant case is one of incidental use of the plaintiff's picture and

not an actionable appropriation of that picture for trade or advertising purposes. Here the photograph was published in connection with what is apparently a sociological commentary, and not as a means of soliciting sales or in association with an advertisement of any kind. The article or story involved, whether it be viewed as an effort to inform or entertain the readership, is a legitimate, noncommercial use. The fact that the defendant is engaged in the business of publishing the Atlantic Monthly magazine for profit does not by itself transform the incidental publication of the plaintiff's picture into an appropriation for advertising or trade purposes.

With *Tropeano* compare Anderson v. Fisher Broadcasting Co., 712 P.2d 803, 811-812 (Or. 1986). There a cameraman for the defendant TV station photographed the scene of an accident in which the plaintiff was injured. The plaintiff was "shown bleeding and in pain while receiving emergency medical treatment," and his face was recognizable from the picture. The shot was not used immediately by the network but some time later when, without plaintiff's consent, it was incorporated as part of a promotional spot designed to plug the station's special news report about a novel system for the dispatch of emergency care. The plaintiff sued for the appropriation of the picture for its commercial use. Linde, J., affirmed the summary judgment granted the defendant below, saying:

> Plaintiff in the present case concedes that KATU-TV would not be liable to him if it had included his picture in the ordinary news coverage of a traffic accident. He contends that the broadcaster became liable because instead it used the footage to draw audience attention to a later broadcast concerning emergency medical services, in which plaintiff's picture was not included. Does the distinction between "commercial" and "noncommercial" use of a person's name, likeness, or life history rest on a difference in the interest invaded by the publication or in the character of the publisher's motives and purposes? The reason should bear on the remedy.
>
> When actors, athletes or other performers object, not to a loss of anonymity, but to unauthorized exploitation of their valuable public identities, the remedy should reflect the wrongful appropriation of a "right to publicity" that has economic value to the plaintiff as well as to the defendant, rather than damages for psychic distress at a loss of "privacy." When a person who neither has nor wants a marketable public identity demands damages for unauthorized publicity, such a person may claim injury to noneconomic rather than an economic interest in his or her privacy; but it is not always obvious, as it is not in this case, why the loss of privacy is different when it occurs in a "commercial" rather than a "noncommercial" form of publication. If the plaintiff can show no psychic injury at all, for instance, an infant whose picture has been used in an advertisement for baby food rather than in a magazine or television report on child care, the answer must be that the advertiser, but not the reporter, has unjustly enriched himself by appropriating something for which he is expected to pay, an answer that begs the question.

Zacchini v. Scripps-Howard Broadcasting Co.
433 U.S. 562 (1977)

WHITE, J. Petitioner, Hugo Zacchini, is an entertainer. He performs a "human cannonball" act in which he is shot from a cannon into a net some 200 feet away. Each performance occupies some 15 seconds. In August and September 1972, petitioner was engaged to perform his act on a regular basis at the Geauga County Fair in Burton, Ohio. He performed in a fenced area, surrounded by grandstands, at the fair grounds. Members of the public attending the fair were not charged a separate admission fee to observe his act.

On August 30, a freelance reporter for Scripps-Howard Broadcasting Co., the operator of a television broadcasting station and respondent in this case, attended the fair. He carried a small movie camera. Petitioner noticed the reporter and asked him not to film the performance. The reporter did not do so on that day; but on the instructions of the producer of respondent's daily newscast, he returned the following day and videotaped the entire act. This film clip, approximately 15 seconds in length, was shown on the 11 o'clock news program that night, together with favorable commentary.[1]

Petitioner then brought this action for damages, alleging that he is "engaged in the entertainment business," that the act he performs is one "invented by his father and . . . performed only by his family for the last fifty years," that respondent "showed and commercialized the film of his act without his consent," and that such conduct was an "unlawful appropriation of plaintiff's professional property." Respondent answered and moved for summary judgment, which was granted by the trial court. . . .

[The Ohio Supreme Court also] gave judgment for respondent because, in the words of the syllabus: "A TV station has a privilege to report in its newscasts matters of legitimate public interest which would otherwise be protected by an individual's right of publicity, unless the actual intent of the TV station was to appropriate the benefit of the publicity for some non-privileged private use, or unless the actual intent was to injure the individual." Ibid.

We granted certiorari to consider an issue unresolved by this Court: whether the First and Fourteenth Amendments immunized respondent

---

1. The script of the commentary accompanying the film clip read as follows: "This . . . now . . . is the story of a *true spectator* sport . . . the sport of human cannonballing . . . in fact, the great *Zacchini* is about the only human cannonball around, these days . . . just happens that, *where* he is, is the Great Geauga County Fair, in Burton . . . and believe me, although it's not a *long* act, it's a thriller . . . and you really need to see it *in person*. . . to appreciate it. . . .!" (Emphasis in original.) App. 12.

from damages for its alleged infringement of petitioner's state-law "right of publicity." Insofar as the Ohio Supreme Court held that the First and Fourteenth Amendments of the United States Constitution required judgment for respondent, we reverse the judgment of that court.

[The Court first held that no independent state ground precluded the Supreme Court from reaching the federal constitutional issues raised by the case.]

The Ohio Supreme Court held that respondent is constitutionally privileged to include in its newscasts matters of public interest that would otherwise be protected by the right of publicity, absent an intent to injure or to appropriate for some nonprivileged purpose. If under this standard respondent had merely reported that petitioner was performing at the fair and described or commented on his act, with or without showing his picture on television, we would have a very different case. But petitioner is not contending that his appearance at the fair and his performance could not be reported by the press as newsworthy items. His complaint is that respondent filmed his entire act and displayed that film on television for the public to see and enjoy. This, he claimed, was an appropriation of his professional property. The Ohio Supreme Court agreed that petitioner had "a right of publicity" that gave him "personal control over commercial display and exploitation of his personality and the exercise of his talents." This right of "exclusive control over the publicity given to his performances" was said to be such a "valuable part of the benefit which may be attained by his talents and efforts" that it was entitled to legal protection. It was also observed, or at least expressly assumed, that petitioner had not abandoned his rights by performing under the circumstances present at the Geauga County Fair Grounds.

The Ohio Supreme Court nevertheless held that the challenged invasion was privileged, saying that the press "must be accorded broad latitude in its choice of how much it presents of each story or incident, and of the emphasis to be given to such presentation. No fixed standard which would bar the press from reporting or depicting either an entire occurrence or an entire discrete part of a public performance can be formulated which would not unduly restrict the 'breathing room' in reporting which freedom of the press requires." Under this view, respondent was thus constitutionally free to film and display petitioner's entire act.

[The Court then noted that Time, Inc. v. Hill, 385 U.S. 374 (1967), infra at page 1261, was a "false light" case, not a "right of publicity" case.]

The differences between these two torts are important. First, the State's interests in providing a cause of action in each instance are different. "The interest protected" in permitting recovery for placing the plaintiff in a false light "is clearly that of reputation, with the same overtones of mental distress as in defamation." Prosser, Privacy. By contrast, the State's interest in permitting a "right of publicity" is in protecting the proprietary interest of the individual in his act in part to encourage such entertainment. As we later note, the State's interest is closely analogous to the goals of patent and copyright law, focusing on the right of the individual to reap the reward of his endeavors and having little to do with protecting feelings or reputation. Second, the two torts differ in the degree to which they intrude on dissemination of information to the public. In "false light" cases the only way to protect the interests involved is to attempt to minimize publication of the damaging matter, while in "right of publicity" cases the only question is who gets to do the publishing. An entertainer such as petitioner usually has no objection to the widespread publication of his act as long as he gets the commercial benefit of such publication. Indeed, in the present case petitioner did not seek to enjoin the broadcast of his act; he simply sought compensation for the broadcast in the form of damages. . . .

Moreover, Time, Inc. v. Hill, *New York Times, Metromedia, Gertz,* and *Firestone* all involved the reporting of events; in none of them was there an attempt to broadcast or publish an entire act for which the performer ordinarily gets paid. It is evident, and there is no claim here to the contrary, that petitioner's state-law right of publicity would not serve to prevent respondent from reporting the newsworthy facts about petitioner's act. Wherever the line in particular situations is to be drawn between media reports that are protected and those that are not, we are quite sure that the First and Fourteenth Amendments do not immunize the media when they broadcast a performer's entire act without his consent. The Constitution no more prevents a State from requiring respondent to compensate petitioner for broadcasting his act on television than it would privilege respondent to film and broadcast a copyrighted dramatic work without liability to the copyright owner, or to film and broadcast a prize fight, or a baseball game, where the promoters or the participants had other plans for publicizing the event. There are ample reasons for reaching this conclusion.

The broadcast of a film of petitioner's entire act poses a substantial threat to the economic value of that performance. As the Ohio court recognized, this act is the product of petitioner's own talents and energy, the end result of much time, effort, and expense. Much of its economic value lies in the "right of exclusive control over the publicity given to his performance"; if the public can see the act free on television, it will be less willing to pay to see it at the fair. The effect of a public broadcast of the performance is similar to preventing petitioner from charging an admission fee. "The rationale for [protecting the right of publicity] is the straightforward one of preventing unjust enrichment by the theft of good will. No social purpose is served by having the defendant get free some aspect of the plaintiff that would have market value and for which he would normally pay." Kalven, Privacy in Tort Law — Were Warren and Brandeis Wrong?, 31 Law & Contemp. Prob. 326, 331 (1966). Moreover, the broadcast of petitioner's entire performance, unlike the unauthorized use of another's name for purposes of trade or the incidental use of a name or picture by the press, goes to the heart of petitioner's ability to earn a living as an entertainer. Thus, in this case, Ohio has recognized what may be the strongest case for a "right of publicity" — involving, not the appropriation of an entertainer's reputation to enhance the attractiveness of a commercial product, but the appropriation of the very activity by which the entertainer acquired his reputation in the first place.

Of course, Ohio's decision to protect petitioner's right of publicity here rests on more than a desire to compensate the performer for the time and effort invested in his act; the protection provides an economic incentive for him to make the investment required to produce a performance of interest to the public. This same consideration underlies the patent and copyright laws long enforced by this Court. As the Court stated in Mazer v. Stein, 347 U.S. 201, 219 (1954):

"The economic philosophy behind the clause empowering Congress to grant patents and copyrights is the conviction that encouragement of individual effort by personal gain is the best way to advance public welfare through the talents of authors and inventors in 'Science and useful Arts.' Sacrificial days devoted to such creative activities deserve rewards commensurate with the services rendered."

These laws perhaps regard the "reward to the owner [as] a secondary consideration," but they were "intended definitely to grant valuable, enforceable rights" in order to afford greater encouragement to the production of works of benefit to the public. The Constitution does not prevent Ohio from making a similar choice here in deciding to protect the entertainer's incentive in order to encourage the production of this type of work.

There is no doubt that entertainment, as well as news, enjoys First Amendment protection. It is also true that entertainment itself can be important news. Time Inc. v. Hill. But it is important to note that neither the public nor respondent will be deprived of the benefit of petitioner's performance as long as his commercial stake in his act is appropriately recognized. Petitioner does not seek to enjoin the broadcast of his performance; he simply wants to be paid for it. Nor do we think that a state-law damages remedy against respondent would represent a species of liability without fault contrary to the letter or spirit of Gertz v. Robert Welch, Inc., 418 U.S. 323 (1974). Respondent knew that petitioner objected to televising his act but nevertheless displayed the entire film.

We conclude that although the State of Ohio may as a matter of its own law privilege the press in the circumstances of this case, the First and Fourteenth Amendments do not require it to do so. Reversed.

POWELL, J. with whom BRENNAN and MARSHALL, JJ. join, dissenting. . . . The Court's holding that the station's ordinary news report may give rise to substantial liability has disturbing implications, for the decision could lead to a degree of media self-censorship. Hereafter, whenever a television news editor is unsure whether certain film footage received from a camera crew might be held to portray an "entire act," he may decline coverage — even of clearly newsworthy events — or confine the broadcast to watered-down verbal reporting, perhaps with an occasional still picture. The public is then the loser. This is hardly the kind of news reportage that the First Amendment is meant to foster.

In my view the First Amendment commands a different analytical starting point from the one selected by the Court. Rather than begin with a quantitative analysis of the performer's behavior — is this or is this not his entire act? — we should direct initial attention to the actions of the news media: what use did the station make of the film footage? When a film is used, as here, for a routine portion of a regular news program, I would hold that the First Amendment protects the station from a "right of publicity" or "appropriation" suit, absent a strong showing by the plaintiff that the news broadcast was a subterfuge or cover for private or commercial exploitation.

[The dissent of Justice Stevens is omitted.]

NOTE

A copyright alternative. It is important to note that Zacchini could not sue under the copyright law, because he had not, as the federal copyright law requires, "fixed" his act in some tangible medium of expression, as by filming it himself. The copyright law, however, normally permits the owner of the copyrighted material the exclusive right of its exploitation, subject solely to a "fair use" exception, "for purposes such as criticism, comment, news reporting, teaching (including multiple copies for classroom use), scholarship, and research," which are not regarded as infringements of copyright. See Copyright Act, 17 U.S.C.A. §107 (1977).

Is it possible that *Zacchini* should be decided on analogous "fair use" principles? If so, could the rebroadcast of the entire act be justified? Does it make a difference whether the broadcast is made to boost commercial ratings, or to expose chicanery on the part of the plaintiff? For a discussion of the copyright analogies see Note, Human Cannonballs and the First Amendment: *Zacchini v. Scripps-Howard Broadcasting Co.,* 30 Stan. L. Rev. 1185 (1978).

Factors Etc., Inc. v. Pro Arts, Inc.
579 F.2d 215 (2d Cir. 1978)

[The plaintiff in this action had received from Boxcars, Inc. — a corporation controlled by the late Elvis Presley and his business partner, Colonel Tom Parker — an exclusive license to commercially exploit the name and likeness of Elvis Presley. Factors Etc. had paid Boxcar $100,000 for the license against a guarantee of $150,000. Immediately upon learning of Presley's death, Pro Arts purchased the copyright of a Presley photograph from a staff reporter of the Atlanta (Georgia) Journal which it published on a poster three days after Presley's death. Above the picture were the words "IN MEMORY" and below it were the dates "1935-1977." Among the many purchasers of the posters was the New York codefendant, Stop and Shop Companies. When Factors Etc. learned of the Pro Arts poster, it demanded in writing that Pro Arts cease marketing the poster and threatened suit if it did not. Pro Arts responded by filing a declaratory judgment action in the Northern District of Ohio. Factors Etc. brought suit in the Southern District of New York. The issue on appeal was whether the district court had properly issued a preliminary injunction against Pro Arts.]

INGRAHAM, J. . . . The injunction restrained Pro Arts during the pendency of the action from manufacturing, selling or distributing (1) any more copies of the poster labeled "IN MEMORY . . . 1935-1977," (2) any other posters, reproductions or copies containing any likeness of Elvis Presley, and (3) utilizing for commercial profit in any manner or form the name or likeness of Elvis Presley. The order also denied Pro Arts' motion to dismiss, stay or transfer. Pro Arts has duly perfected this interlocutory appeal from the order. . . .

On appeal, Pro Arts alleges two errors of law on the part of the trial court. According to Pro Arts, the trial court erred first in concluding that the right of publicity could survive the death of the celebrity. Second, Pro Arts argues that even if the right did so survive, Pro Arts was privileged, as a matter of law, in printing and distributing its "memorial poster" of Presley, because the poster celebrated a newsworthy event.

The first issue, the duration of the so-called "right of publicity," is one of state law, more specifically the law of the State of New York. Because of the dearth of New York case law in this area, however, we have sought assistance from federal court decisions interpreting and applying New York law, as well as decisions from courts of other states.

[The court then relied on *Zacchini* and the excerpt from the Kalven article quoted therein to establish that the right of publicity is designed to protect the plaintiff's right of commercial exploitation and thus is sharply distinguishable from the other forms of privacy which, in contrast, are designed "to minimize the intrusion or publication" of damaging information.]

The State of New York provides a statutory right for the protection of a *living* person from commercial exploitation of his name and picture by others without his written consent. This statutory right, also called a "right of privacy," is predicated upon the classic right of privacy's theoretical basis which is to prevent injury to feelings. . . . In Haelan Laboratories, Inc. v. Topps Chewing Gum, Inc., 202 F.2d 866 (2d Cir.), we recognized that the right of publicity exists independent from the statutory right of privacy and that it can be validly transferred by its owner:

"We think that, in addition to and independent of that right of privacy (which in New York derives from statute), a man has a right in the publicity value of his photograph, i.e., the right to grant the exclusive privilege of publishing his picture, and that such a grant may validly be made 'in gross,' i.e., without an accompanying transfer of a business or of anything else. Whether it be labeled a 'property' right is immaterial; for here, as often elsewhere, the tag 'property' simply symbolizes the fact that courts enforce a claim which has pecuniary worth." Id. at 868.

Since the landmark *Haelan Laboratories, Inc.* case, several decisions by courts applying New York law have labeled the right of publicity as a valid transferable property right, as well as by recent decisions by courts applying the law of other states.

There can be no doubt that Elvis Presley assigned to Boxcar a valid property right, the exclusive authority to print, publish and distribute his name and likeness. In so doing, he carved out a separate intangible property right for himself, the right to a certain percentage of the royalties which would be realized by Boxcar upon exploitation of Presley's likeness and name. The identification of this exclusive right belonging to Boxcar as a transferable property right compels the conclusion that the right survives Presley's death. The death of Presley, who was merely the beneficiary of an income interest in Boxcar's exclusive right, should not in itself extinguish Boxcar's property right. Instead, the income interest, continually produced from Boxcar's exclusive right of commercial exploitation, should inure to Presley's estate at death like any other intangible property right. To hold that the right did not survive Presley's death, would be to grant competitors of Factors, such as Pro Arts, a windfall in the form of profits from the use of Presley's name and likeness. At the same time, the exclusive right purchased by Factors and the financial benefits accruing to the celebrity's heirs would be rendered virtually worthless. . . .

Pro Arts' final argument is that even if Factors possesses the exclusive right to distribute Presley memorabilia, this right does not prevent Pro Arts from publishing what it terms a "memorial poster" commemorating a newsworthy event. In support of this argument, Pro Arts cites Paulsen v. Personality Posters, Inc., 299 N.Y.S.2d 501 (Sup. Ct. 1968), a case arising out of the bogus presidential candidacy of the television comedian Pat Paulsen. Paulsen sued defendant for publishing and distributing a poster of Paulsen with the legend "FOR PRESIDENT." The court refused to enjoin sale of the poster because Paulsen's choice of the political arena for satire made him "newsworthy" in the First Amendment sense. We cannot accept Pro Arts' contention that the legend "IN MEMORY . . ." placed its poster in the same category as one picturing a presidential candidate, albeit a mock candidate. We hold, therefore, that Pro Arts' poster of Presley was not privileged as celebrating a newsworthy event. . . . Affirmed.

NOTES

1. Commercial life after death? The issue raised in the principle case received a very different treatment in Memphis Development Foundation v. Factors Etc., Inc., 616 F.2d 956, 958-960 (6th Cir. 1980). There the Development Foundation offered an eight-inch statuette of Elvis Presley to persons who contributed $25.00 to the Foundation. The Foundation then instituted a declaratory judgment action to establish that Factors' license did not preclude its distribution of the statue. Factors counterclaimed for damages and injunctive relief. In holding that the right of publicity did not survive the death of the actor, the court took issue with *Pro Arts* and examined some of the fundamental premises upon which the institutions of private property and a market economy rest.

> Recognition of a post-mortem right of publicity would vindicate two possible interests: the encouragement of effort and creativity, and the hopes and expectations of the decedent and those with whom he contracts that they are creating a valuable capital asset. Although fame and stardom may be ends in themselves, they are normally by-products of one's activities and personal attributes, as well as luck and promotion. The basic motivations are the desire to achieve success or excellence in a chosen field, the desire to contribute to the happiness or improvement of one's fellows and the desire to receive the psychic and financial rewards of achievement. As John Rawls has written, such needs come from the deep psychological fact that the individuals want the respect and good will of other persons and "enjoy the exercise of their realized capacities (their innate or trained abilities), and this enjoyment increases the more the capacity is realized, or the greater its complexity." . . .
> On the other hand, there are strong reasons for declining to recognize the inheritability of the right. A whole set of practical problems of judicial line-drawing would arise should the courts recognize such an inheritable right. How long would the "property" interest last? In perpetuity? For a term of years? Is the right of publicity taxable? At what point does the right collide with the right of free expression guaranteed by the First Amendment? Does the right apply to elected officials and military heroes whose fame was gained on the public payroll, as well as to movie stars,

singers and athletes? Does the right cover posters or engraved likenesses of, for example, Farrah Fawcett Majors or Mahatma Gandhi, kitchen utensils ("Revere Ware"), insurance ("John Hancock"), electric utilities ("Edison"), a football stadium ("RFK"), a pastry ("Napoleon"), or the innumerable urban subdivisions and apartment complexes named after famous people? Our legal system normally does not pass on to heirs other similar personal attributes even though the attributes may be shared during life by others or have some commercial value. Titles, offices and reputation are not inheritable. Neither are trust or distrust and friendship or enmity descendible. An employment contract during life does not create the right for heirs to take over the job. Fame falls in the same category as reputation; it is an attribute from which others may benefit but may not own.

The law of defamation, designed to protect against the destruction of reputation including the loss of earning capacity associated with it, provides an analogy. There is no right of action for defamation after death. See Restatement (Second) of Torts §560 (rev. ed. 1977). The two interests that support the inheritability of the right of publicity, namely, the "effort and creativity" and the "hopes and expectations" of the decedent, would also support an action for libel or slander for destruction of name and reputation after death. Neither of these reasons, however, is sufficient to overcome the common law policy terminating the action for defamation upon death. . . .

There is no indication that changing the traditional common law rule against allowing heirs the exclusive control of the commercial use of their ancestor's name will increase the efficiency or productivity of our economic system. It does not seem reasonable to expect that such a change would enlarge the stock or quality of the goods, services, artistic creativity, information, invention or entertainment available. Nor will it enhance the fairness of our political and economic system. It seems fairer and more efficient for the commercial, aesthetic, and political use of the name, memory and image of the famous to be open to all rather than to be monopolized by a few. An equal distribution of the opportunity to use the name of the dead seems preferable. The memory, name and pictures of famous individuals should be regarded as a common asset to be shared, an economic opportunity available in the free market system.

After the decision in *Memphis Development*, the Second Circuit passed upon the "esoteric question . . . concerning the deference a federal court exercising diversity jurisdiction should give to a rule by a court of appeals deciding the law of a state within its circuit" and held that it should be "conclusive." Factors Etc., Inc. v. Pro Arts, Inc., 652 F.2d 278 (2d Cir. 1981). On the descendibility question see generally Felcher and Rubin, Privacy, Publicity, and Portrayal of Real People by the Media, 88 Yale L.J. 1577 (1979).

2. Exploitation only after death? Factors, Etc., Inc. v. Pro Arts, Inc. left open the question of whether the right of publicity descended when not utilized during the lifetime of the original creator. That issue was answered in the negative by the California Appellate Court in its opinion in Lugosi v. Universal Pictures, 139 Cal. Rptr. 35 (Cal. App. 1977). There the decedent had not taken any steps while alive to exploit his famous Dracula image, developed in his movie roles for the defendant.

The defendant thereafter licensed a number of other businesses to make an impressive assortment of clothes, trinkets, and memorabilia that utilized the Dracula image. The California court refused to allow Lugosi's heirs to enjoin the sales. The decision is straightforward enough if the position taken in *Memphis Development* is followed. But what is the rationale for that decision if *Pro Arts* represents the correct view of the law?

C. PUBLIC DISCLOSURE OF EMBARRASSING PRIVATE FACTS

New York Civil Rights Law
§§50, 51 (McKinney 1994)

§50. RIGHT OF PRIVACY

A person, firm or corporation that uses for advertising purposes, or for the purposes of trade, the name, portrait or picture of any living person without having first obtained the written consent of such person, or if a minor of his or her parent or guardian, is guilty of a misdemeanor.

§51. ACTION FOR INJUNCTION AND FOR DAMAGES

Any person whose name, portrait or picture is used within this state for advertising purposes or for the purposes of trade without the written consent first obtained as above provided may maintain an equitable action in the supreme court of this state against the person, firm or corporation so using his name, portrait or picture, to prevent and restrain the use thereof; and may also sue and recover damages for any injuries sustained by reason of such use and if the defendant shall have knowingly used such person's name, portrait or picture in such manner as is forbidden or declared to be unlawful by the last section, the jury, in its discretion, may award exemplary damages. . . .

American Law Institute, Restatement (Second) of the Law of Torts
(1976)

§652D. PUBLICITY GIVEN TO PRIVATE LIFE

One who gives publicity to a matter concerning the private life of another is subject to liability to the other for invasion of his privacy, if the matter publicized is of a kind that

(a) would be highly offensive to a reasonable person, and
(b) is not of legitimate concern to the public.

Comment

a. Publicity. The form of invasion of the right of privacy covered in this Section depends upon publicity given to the private life of the individual. "Publicity," as it is used in this Section, differs from "publication," as that term is used in §577 in connection with liability for defamation. "Publication," in that sense, is a word of art, which includes any communication by the defendant to a third person. "Publicity," on the other hand, means that the matter is made public, by communicating it to the public at large, or to so many persons that the matter must be regarded as substantially certain to become one of public knowledge. The difference is not one of the means of communication, which may be oral, written, or by any other means. It is one of a communication which reaches, or is sure to reach, the public. . . .

b. Private life. The rule stated in this Section applies only to publicity given to matters concerning the private, as distinguished from the public, life of the individual. There is no liability when the defendant merely gives further publicity to information about the plaintiff which is already public. Thus there is no liability for giving publicity to facts about the plaintiff's life that are matters of public record, such as the date of his birth, the fact of his marriage, his military record, the fact that he is admitted to the practice of medicine or is licensed to drive a taxicab, or the pleadings which he has filed in a lawsuit. On the other hand, if the record is one not open to public inspection, as in the case of income tax returns, it is not public, and there is an invasion of privacy when it is made so.

Sidis v. F-R Publishing Corp.
113 F.2d 806 (2d Cir. 1940)

CLARK, J. William James Sidis was the unwilling subject of a brief biographical sketch and cartoon printed in the The New Yorker weekly magazine for August 14, 1937. Further references were made to him in the issue of December 25, 1937, and in a newspaper advertisement announcing the August 14 issue. He brought an action in the district court against the publisher, F-R Publishing Corporation. His complaint stated three "causes of action": The first alleged violation of his right of privacy as that right is recognized in California, Georgia, Kansas, Kentucky, and Missouri; the second charged infringement of the rights afforded him under §§50 and 51 of the N.Y. Civil Rights Law (Consol. Laws, c. 6); the third claimed malicious libel under the laws of Delaware, Florida, Illinois, Maine, Massachusetts, Nebraska, New Hampshire, Pennsylvania, and Rhode Island. Defendant's motion to dismiss the first two "causes of action" was granted, and plaintiff has filed an appeal from the order of dismissal. Since a majority of this court believe that order appealable, for reasons referred to below, we may consider the merits of the case.

William James Sidis was a famous child prodigy in 1910. His name and prowess were well known to newspaper readers of the period. At the age of eleven, he lectured to distinguished mathematicians on the subject of Four-Dimensional Bodies. When he was sixteen, he was graduated from Harvard College, amid considerable public attention. Since then, his name has appeared in the press only sporadically, and he has sought to live as unobtrusively as possible. Until the articles objected to appeared in The New Yorker, he had apparently succeeded in his endeavor to avoid the public gaze.

Among The New Yorker's features are brief biographical sketches of current and past personalities. In the latter department, which appears haphazardly under the title "Where Are They Now?" the article on Sidis was printed with a subtitle "April Fool." The author describes his subject's early accomplishments in mathematics and the wide-spread attention he received, then recounts his general breakdown and the revulsion which Sidis thereafter felt for his former life of fame and study. The unfortunate prodigy is traced over the years that followed, through his attempts to conceal his identity, through his chosen career as an insignificant clerk who would not need to employ unusual mathematical talents, and through the bizarre ways in which his genius flowered, as in his enthusiasm for collecting streetcar transfers and in his proficiency with an adding machine. The article closes with an account of an interview with Sidis at his present lodgings, "a hall bedroom of Boston's shabby south end." The untidiness of his room, his curious laugh, his manner of speech, and other personal habits are commented upon at length, as is his present interest in the lore of the Okamakammessett Indians. The subtitle is explained by the closing sentence, quoting Sidis as saying "with a grin" that it was strange, "but, you know, I was born on April Fool's Day." Accompanying the biography is a small cartoon showing the genius of eleven years lecturing to a group of astounded professors.

It is not contended that any of the matter printed is untrue. Nor is the manner of the author unfriendly; Sidis today is described as having "a certain childlike charm." But the article is merciless in its dissection of intimate details of its subject's personal life, and this in company with elaborate accounts of Sidis' passion for privacy and the pitiable lengths to which he has gone in order to avoid public scrutiny. The work possesses great reader interest, for it is both amusing and instructive; but it may be fairly described as a ruthless exposure of a once public character, who has since sought and has now been deprived of the seclusion of private life.

The article of December 25, 1937, was a biographical sketch of another former child prodigy, in the course of which William James Sidis and the recent account of him were mentioned. The advertisement published in the New York World-Telegram of August 13, 1937, read: "Out Today. Harvard Prodigy. Biography of the man who astonished Harvard at age 11. Where are they now? by J. L. Manley. Page 22. The New Yorker." . . .

All comment upon the right of privacy must stem from the famous article by Warren and Brandeis on The Right of [to] Privacy in 4 Harv. L. Rev. 193. [The court then quoted from those passages of the article set out supra at page 1215.]

Warren and Brandeis realized that the interest of the individual in privacy must inevitably conflict with the interest of the public in news. Certain public figures, they conceded, such as holders of public office, must sacrifice their privacy and expose at least part of their lives to public scrutiny as the price of the powers they attain. But even public figures were not to be stripped bare. "In general, then, the matters of which the publication should be repressed may be described as those which concern the private life, habits, acts, and relations of an individual, and have no legitimate connection with his fitness for a public office. . . . Some things all men alike are entitled to keep from popular curiosity, whether in public life or not, while others are only private because the persons concerned have not assumed a position which makes their doings legitimate matters of public investigation." Warren and Brandeis.

It must be conceded that under the strict standards suggested by these authors plaintiff's right of privacy has been invaded. Sidis today is neither politician, public administrator, nor statesman. Even if he were, some of the personal details revealed were of the sort that Warren and Brandeis believed "all men alike are entitled to keep from popular curiosity."

But despite eminent opinion to the contrary, we are not yet disposed to afford to all of the intimate details of private life an absolute immunity from the prying of the press. Everyone will agree that at some point the public interest in obtaining information becomes dominant over the individual's desire for privacy. Warren and Brandeis were willing to lift the veil somewhat in the case of public officers. We would go further, though we are not yet prepared to say how far. At least we would permit limited scrutiny of the "private" life of any person who has achieved, or has had thrust upon him, the questionable and indefinable status of a "public figure." . . .

William James Sidis was once a public figure. As a child prodigy, he excited both admiration and curiosity. Of him great deeds were expected. In 1910, he was a person about whom the newspapers might display a legitimate intellectual interest, in the sense meant by Warren and Brandeis, as distinguished from a trivial and unseemly curiosity. But the precise motives of the press we regard as unimportant. And even if Sidis had loathed public attention at that time, we think his uncommon achievements and personality would have made the attention permissible. Since then Sidis has cloaked himself in obscurity, but his subsequent history, containing as it did the answer to the question of whether or not he had fulfilled his early promise, was still a matter of public concern. The article in The New Yorker sketched the life of an unusual personality, and it possessed considerable popular news interest.

We express no comment on whether or not the news worthiness of the matter printed will always constitute a complete defense. Revelations may be so intimate and so unwarranted in view of the victim's position as to outrage the community's notions of decency. But when focused upon public characters, truthful comments upon dress, speech, habits, and the ordinary aspects of personality will usually not transgress this line. Regrettably or not, the misfortunes and frailties of neighbors and "public figures" are subjects of considerable interest and discussion to the rest of the population. And when such are the mores of the community, it would be unwise for a court to bar their expression in the newspapers, books, and magazines of the day.

Plaintiff in his first "cause of action" charged actual malice in the publication, and now claims that an order of dismissal was improper in the face of such an allegation. We cannot agree. If plaintiff's right of privacy was not invaded by the article, the existence of actual malice in its publication would not change that result. Unless made so by statute, a truthful and therefore non-libelous statement will not become libelous when uttered maliciously. A similar rule should prevail on invasions of the right of privacy. "Personal ill-will is not an ingredient of the offence, any more than in an ordinary case of trespass to person or to property." Warren and Brandeis. Nor does the malice give rise to an independent wrong based on an intentional invasion of the plaintiff's interest in mental and emotional tranquility. This interest, however real, is one not yet protected by law.

If the article appearing in the issue of August 14, 1937, does not furnish grounds for action, then it is clear that the brief and incidental reference to it contained in the article of December 25, 1937, is not actionable.

The second "cause of action" charged invasion of the rights conferred on plaintiff by §§50 and 51 of the N.Y. Civil Rights Law. Section 50 states that "A person, firm or corporation that uses for advertising purposes, or for the purposes of trade, the name, portrait or picture of any living person without having first obtained the written consent of such person, or if a minor of his or her parent or guardian, is guilty of a misdemeanor." Section 51 gives the injured person the right to an injunction and to damages.

Before passage of this statute, it had been held that no common law right of privacy existed in New York. Roberson v. Rochester Folding Box Co. . . . Any liability imposed upon defendant must therefore be derived solely from the statute, and not from general considerations as to the right of the individual to prevent publications of the intimate details of his private life. The statute forbids the use of a name or picture only when employed "for advertising purposes, or for the purposes of trade." In this context, it is clear that "for the purposes of trade" does not contemplate the publication of a newspaper, magazine, or book which imparts truthful news or other factual information to the public. Though a publisher sells a commodity, and expects to profit from the sale of his product, he is immune from the interdict of §§50 and 51 so long as he confines himself to the unembroidered dissemination of facts. Publishers and motion picture producers have occasionally been held to transgress that statute in New York, but in each case the factual presentation was embellished by some degree of fictionalization. . . . The New Yorker articles limit themselves to the unvarnished, unfictionalized truth.

The case as to the newspaper advertisement announcing the August 14 article is somewhat different, for it was undoubtedly inserted in the World-Telegram "for advertising purposes." But since it was to advertise the article on Sidis, and the article itself was unobjectionable, the advertisement shares the privilege enjoyed by the article. . . . Besides, the advertisement, quoted above, did not use the "name, portrait or picture" of the plaintiff. . . .

Affirmed.

NOTES

1. The painful truth. One of the most difficult questions in the law of defamation and privacy involves defendant's liability for truthful statements about the plaintiff's past that are of no immediate relevance to current issues and injure the plaintiff's reputation and peace of mind. One decision that reveals a very different mood from *Sidis* is Melvin v. Reid, 297 P. 91 (Cal. App. 1931). There the plaintiff was at one time a prostitute who had been tried for murder and acquitted. After her trial she reformed her character, married into respectable society, and gained the friendship of many persons who did not know of her past life. Several years after plaintiff's marriage, the defendants made and exhibited a film that told the true story of her past, using plaintiff's maiden name. Plaintiff sued for damages when she was scorned and abandoned by her friends, the film having exposed her to "obloquy, contempt, and ridicule, causing her grievous mental and physical suffering." After reviewing the law of privacy, the court sustained plaintiff's cause of action, concluding defendant's use of plaintiff's name after she had reformed "was not justified by any standard of morals or ethics known to us and was a direct invasion of her inalienable right, guaranteed to her by our Constitution, to pursue and obtain happiness. Whether we call this a right of privacy or give it any other name is immaterial. . . . "

A similar solicitude for privacy was shown in Briscoe v. Reader's Digest, 483 P.2d 34, 39-40 (Cal. 1971). Reader's Digest published a story entitled "The Big Business of Hijacking" which stated truthfully: "Typical of many beginners, Marvin Briscoe and [another man] stole a 'valuable-looking' truck in Danville, Ky., and then fought a gun battle with the local police, only to learn that they had hijacked four bowling-pin spotters." The story did not mention that the incident had occurred some 11 years earlier. In the interim the plaintiff had completely rehabilitated and led an honorable life. Upon publication of the article, plaintiff's 11-year-old daughter and his friends learned of the incident and thereafter "abandoned and scorned" him. Peters, J., held that the plaintiff had the right to a jury trial, saying:

> We have no doubt that reports of the facts of past crimes are newsworthy. Media publication of the circumstances under which crimes were committed in the past may prove educational in the same way that reports of current crimes do. The public has a strong interest in enforcing the law, and this interest is served by accumulating and disseminating data cataloguing the reasons men commit crimes, the methods they use, and the ways in which they are apprehended. Thus in an article on truck hijackings, Reader's Digest certainly had the right to report the *facts* of plaintiff's criminal act.
>
> However, identification of the *actor* in reports of long past crimes usually serves little independent public purpose. Once legal proceedings have terminated, and a suspect or offender has been released, identification of the individual will not usually aid the administration of justice. Identification will no longer serve to bring forth witnesses or obtain succor for victims. Unless the individual has reattracted the public eye to himself in some independent fashion, the only public "interest" that would usually be served is that of curiosity.
>
> There may be times, of course, when an event involving private citizens may be so unique as to capture the imagination of all. In such cases — e.g., the behavior of the passengers on the sinking Titanic, the heroism of Nathan Hale, the horror of the Saint Valentine's Day Massacre — purely private individuals may by an accident of history lose their privacy regarding that incident for all time. There need be no "reattraction" of the public eye because the public interest never wavered. An individual whose name is fixed in the public's memory, such as that of the political assassin, never becomes an anonymous member of the community again. But in each case it is for the trier of fact to determine whether the

individual's infamy is such that he has never left the public arena; we cannot do so as a matter of law.

Upon remand, Reader's Digest removed the case to federal court, whereupon it obtained a summary judgment. See Hill, Defamation and Privacy Under the First Amendment, 76 Colum. L. Rev. 1205, 1263 n.273 (1976).

2. *Painful present facts.* The judicial sentiment to protect individuals against revelations of past embarrassing facts does not carry over to facts about revelations of current details of a person's personal life. Thus the newsworthiness defense adumbrated in *Sidis* received a broad construction in Sipple v. Chronicle Publishing Co., 201 Cal. Rptr. 665 (Cal. App. 1984). There the plaintiff "grabbed or struck" the arm of Sarah Jane Moore as she attempted to shoot President Gerald Ford in September, 1975, possibly saving his life. Sipple received great publicity and was the subject of Herb Caen's column in the San Francisco Chronicle. The plaintiff alleged an invasion of privacy without consent

> by disclosing that plaintiff was homosexual in his personal and private sexual orientation; that said publications were highly offensive to plaintiff inasmuch as his parents, brothers and sisters learned for the first time of his homosexual orientation; and that as a consequence of disclosure of private facts about his life plaintiff was abandoned by his family, exposed to contempt and ridicule causing him great mental anguish, embarrassment and humiliation.

Caldecott, P.J., affirmed the trial court's grant of summary judgment to the defendant. He first noted that the facts published about the plaintiff were not private: Prior to the publication of the article plaintiff's "homosexual orientation and participation in gay community activities had been known by hundreds of people in a variety of cities, including New York, Dallas, Houston, San Diego, Los Angeles and San Francisco." In addition, plaintiff's "friendship with Harvey Milk, another prominent gay, was well known and publicized in gay newspapers." The court also held that the newsworthiness privilege applied.

> In the case at bench the publication of [Sipple's] homosexual orientation which had been already widely known by many people in a number of communities was not so offensive even at the time of the publication as to shock the community notions of decency. Moreover, and perhaps even more to the point, the record shows that the publications were not motivated by a morbid and sensational prying into [Sipple's] private life, but rather were prompted by legitimate political considerations, i.e., to dispel the false public opinion that gays were timid, weak and unheroic figures and to raise the equally important political question whether the President of the United States entertained a discriminatory attitude or bias against a minority group such as homosexuals.

Sipple then relied on Virgil v. Time, Inc., 527 F.2d 1122, 1128-1129 (9th Cir. 1975). *Virgil* stated:

> The privilege to publicize newsworthy matters is included in the definition of the tort set out in Restatement (Second) of Torts §652D. Liability may be imposed for an invasion of privacy only if "the matter publicized is of a kind which . . . is not of legitimate concern to the public." While the Restatement does not so emphasize, we are satisfied that this provision is one of constitutional dimension delimiting the scope of the tort and that the extent of the privilege thus is controlled by federal rather than state law.

On *Sidis* generally see Karafiol, The Right to Privacy and the *Sidis* Case, 12 Ga. L. Rev. 513 (1978).

3. Defamation and privacy. It is interesting to ask how *Briscoe, Melvin,* and *Sipple* fare as defamation cases. In each case plaintiff claims damage to reputation by defendant's publication, but the damage occurs not because of the widespread publicity, but only because the embarrassing information reached a few individuals with whom plaintiff maintained intimate association. A prima facie case of defamation is established and, given the facts of each case, truth is also established. It is as though truth is not an absolute defense in defamation actions, but is subject to an exception, patterned, as it were, on the statute of limitations, with respect to matters long since laid to rest. Does it make a difference if the plaintiffs in these cases had actually lied to members of their families about their present or past activities? How should the matter be resolved if a private party made direct private disclosures to the family and friends of either of these plaintiffs? If a private party threatened to make the disclosures unless his silence was purchased? And in all these cases, what role does the First Amendment play?

Cox Broadcasting Corp. v. Cohn
420 U.S. 469 (1975)

WHITE, J. . . . The issue before us in this case is whether consistently with the First and Fourteenth Amendments a State may extend a cause of action for damages for invasion of privacy caused by the publication of the name of a deceased rape victim which was publicly revealed in connection with the prosecution of the crime.

In August 1971, appellee's 17-year-old daughter was the victim of a rape and did not survive the incident. Six youths were soon indicted for murder and rape. Although there was substantial press coverage of the crime and of subsequent developments, the identity of the victim was not disclosed pending trial, perhaps because of Ga. Code Ann.

§26-9901 which makes it a misdemeanor to publish or broadcast the name or identity of a rape victim. In April 1972, some eight months later, the six defendants appeared in court. Five pled guilty to rape or attempted rape, the charge of murder having been dropped. The guilty pleas were accepted by the court, and the trial of the defendant pleading not guilty was set for a later date.

In the course of the proceedings that day, appellant Wassell, a reporter covering the incident for his employer, learned the name of the victim from an examination of the indictments which were made available for his inspection in the courtroom. That the name of the victim appears in the indictments and that the indictments were public records available for inspection are not disputed. Later that day, Wassell broadcast over the facilities of station WSB-TV, a television station owned by appellant Cox Broadcasting Corporation, a news report concerning the court proceedings. The report named the victim of the crime and was repeated the following day.

In May 1972, appellee brought an action for money damages against appellants, relying on §26-9901 and claiming that his right to privacy had been invaded by the television broadcasts giving the name of his deceased daughter. [Relying in part on *Briscoe,* the Georgia courts rejected Cox's claim of constitutional privilege and held that the plaintiff had stated a claim for invasion of privacy in the form of a tort of public disclosure of private facts, and further that it was a question for the jury whether the public disclosure of his daughter's name invaded his "zone of privacy."]

Georgia stoutly defends both §26-9901 and the State's common law privacy action challenged here. Her claims are not without force, for powerful arguments can be made, and have been made, that however it may be ultimately defined, there *is* a zone of privacy surrounding every individual, a zone within which the State may protect him from intrusion by the press, with all its attendant publicity. [The Court then referred to Warren and Brandeis; Prosser; Time, Inc. v. Hill; and Pavesich v. New England Life Insurance Co., a Georgia case.]

These are impressive credentials for a right of privacy, but we should recognize that we do not have at issue here an action for the invasion of privacy involving the appropriation of one's name or photograph, a physical or other tangible intrusion into a private area, or a publication of otherwise private information that is also false although perhaps not defamatory. The version of the privacy tort now before us — termed in Georgia "the tort of public disclosure," is that in which the plaintiff claims the right to be free from unwanted publicity about his private affairs, which, although wholly true, would be offensive to a person of ordinary sensibilities. Because the gravamen of the claimed injury is the publication of information, whether true or not, the dissemination of which is embarrassing or otherwise painful to an individual, it is here that claims of privacy most directly confront the constitutional free-doms of speech and press. The face-off is apparent, and the appellants urge upon us the broad holding that the press may not be made crimi-nally or civilly liable for publishing information that is neither false nor misleading but absolutely accurate, however damaging it may be to reputation or individual sensibilities.

It is true that in defamation actions, where the protected interest is personal reputation, the prevailing view is that truth is a defense; and the message of New York Times v. Sullivan, and like cases is that the defense of truth is constitutionally required where the subject of the publication is a public official or public figure. What is more, the de-famed public official or public figure must prove not only that the pub-lication is false but that it was knowingly so or was circulated with reckless disregard for its truth or falsity. Similarly, where the interest at issue is privacy rather than reputation and the right claimed is to be free from the publication of false or misleading information about one's affairs, the target of the publication must prove knowing or reck-less falsehood where the materials published, although assertedly pri-vate, are "matters of public interest." Time, Inc. v. Hill.

The Court has nevertheless carefully left open the question whether the First and Fourteenth Amendments require that truth be recognized as a defense in a defamation action brought by a private person as distinguished from a public official or public figure. Garrison [v. Louisi-ana] held that where criticism is of a public official and his conduct of public business, "the interest in private reputation is overborne by the larger public interest, secured by the Constitution, in the dissemination of truth," 379 U.S., at 72-73, but recognized that "different interests may be involved where purely private libels, totally unrelated to public affairs, are concerned; therefore, nothing we say today is to be taken as intimating any views as to the impact of the constitutional guarantees in the discrete area of purely private libels." Id., at 72 n. 8. In similar fashion, Time v. Hill expressly saved the question whether truthful pub-lication of very private matters unrelated to public affairs could be con-stitutionally proscribed.

Those precedents, as well as other considerations, counsel similar caution here. In this sphere of collision between claims of privacy and those of the free press, the interests on both sides are plainly rooted in the traditions and significant concerns of our society. Rather than ad-dress the broader question whether truthful publications may ever be subjected to civil or criminal liability consistently with the First and Fourteenth Amendments, or to put it another way, whether the State may ever define and protect an area of privacy free from unwanted publicity in the press, it is appropriate to focus on the narrower inter-face between press and privacy that this case presents, namely, whether the State may impose sanctions on the accurate publication of the name of a rape victim obtained from public records — more specifically, from judicial records which are maintained in connection with a public prosecution and which themselves are open to public inspection. We are convinced that the State may not do so.

In the first place, in a society in which each individual has but limited time and resources with which to observe at first hand the operations of his government, he relies necessarily upon the press to bring him in convenient form the facts of those operations. Great responsibility is accordingly placed upon the news media to report fully and accurately the proceedings of government, and official records and documents open to the public are the basic data of governmental operations. Without the information provided by the press most of us and many of our representatives would be unable to vote intelligently or to register opinions on the administration of government generally. With respect to judicial proceedings in particular, the function of the press serves to guarantee the fairness of trials and to bring to bear the beneficial effects of public scrutiny upon the administration of justice.

Appellee has claimed in this litigation that the efforts of the press have infringed his right to privacy by broadcasting to the world the fact that his daughter was a rape victim. The commission of crime, prosecutions resulting from it, and judicial proceedings arising from the prosecutions, however, are without question events of legitimate concern to the public and consequently fall within the responsibility of the press to report the operations of government.

The special protected nature of accurate reports of judicial proceedings has repeatedly been recognized. . . .

The developing law surrounding the tort of invasion of privacy recognizes a privilege in the press to report the events of judicial proceedings. The Warren and Brandeis article, supra, noted that the proposed new right would be limited in the same manner as actions for libel and slander where such a publication was a privileged communication: "the right to privacy is not invaded by any publication made in a court of justice . . . and (at least in many jurisdictions) reports of any such proceedings would in some measure be accorded a like privilege."

[The Restatement provides that there is no liability when the information in dispute is contained in public records.] Thus even the prevailing law of invasion of privacy generally recognizes that the interests in privacy fade when the information involved already appears on the public record. The conclusion is compelling when viewed in terms of the First and Fourteenth Amendments and in light of the public interest in a vigorous press. The Georgia cause of action for invasion of privacy through public disclosure of the name of a rape victim imposes sanctions on pure expression — the content of a publication — and not conduct or a combination of speech and nonspeech elements that might otherwise be open to regulation or prohibition. The publication of truthful information available on the public record contains none of the indicia of those limited categories of expression, such as "fighting" words, which "are no essential part of any exposition of ideas, and are of such slight social value as a step to truth that any benefit that may be derived from them is clearly outweighed by the social interest in order and morality." Chaplinsky v. New Hampshire, 315 U.S. 568, 572 (1942).

By placing the information in the public domain on official court records, the State must be presumed to have concluded that the public interest was thereby being served. Public records by their very nature are of interest to those concerned with the administration of government, and a public benefit is performed by the reporting of the true contents of the records by the media. The freedom of the press to publish that information appears to us to be of critical importance to our type of government in which the citizenry is the final judge of the proper conduct of public business. In preserving that form of government the First and Fourteenth Amendments command nothing less than that the States may not impose sanctions for the publication of truthful information contained in official court records open to public inspection.

We are reluctant to embark on a course that would make public records generally available to the media but forbid their publication if offensive to the sensibilities of the supposed reasonable man. Such a rule would make it very difficult for the press to inform their readers about the public business and yet stay within the law. The rule would invite timidity and self-censorship and very likely lead to the suppression of many items that would otherwise be put into print and that should be made available to the public. At the very least, the First and Fourteenth Amendments will not allow exposing the press to liability for truthfully publishing information released to the public in official court records. If there are privacy interests to be protected in judicial proceedings, the States must respond by means which avoid public documentation or other exposure of private information. Their political institutions must weigh the interests in privacy with the interests of the public to know and of the press to publish.[26] Once true information is disclosed in public court documents open to public inspection, the press cannot be sanctioned for publishing it. In this instance as in others reliance must rest upon the judgment of those who decide what to publish or broadcast.

Appellant Wassell based his televised report upon notes taken during the court proceedings and obtained the name of the victim from the indictments handed to him at his request during a recess in the hearing. Appellee has not contended that the name was obtained in an

---

26. We mean to imply nothing about any constitutional questions which might arise from a state policy not allowing access by the public and press to various kinds of official records, such as records of juvenile-court proceedings.

improper fashion or that it was not on an official court document open to public inspection. Under these circumstances, the protection of freedom of the press provided by the First and Fourteenth Amendments bars the State of Georgia from making appellants' broadcast the basis of civil liability.

Reversed.

[Justice Powell concurred separately in order to state his views solely on the meaning of Gertz v. Robert Welch, Inc., which, he believed, constitutionally required that truth be an absolute defense in defamation actions brought by either public or private persons. Justice Rehnquist dissented on the ground that there had been no final judgment in the case from which an appeal could be taken to the Supreme Court.]

NOTES

1. Privacy and the public record. What is left of *Reid* and *Briscoe* after *Cox Broadcasting?* How should the Supreme Court decide the questions left unanswered in footnote 26? What of the confidentiality of public records of adoption proceedings? Does the decision accord constitutional status to section 652D of the Restatement (Second)?

The clash between the First Amendment and privacy interests has also arisen in a number of Supreme Court cases since *Cox.* In Oklahoma Publishing Co. v. District Court, 430 U.S. 308, 311 (1977), the state court entered a pretrial order enjoining the publication of the name and picture of an 11-year-old boy charged with delinquency by second-degree murder. The Court held that *Cox* controlled and that the ban was in violation of the First Amendment. "No objection was made to the presence of the press in the courtroom or to the photographing of the juvenile as he left the courthouse. There is no evidence that petitioner acquired the information unlawfully or even without the State's implicit approval. The name and picture of the juvenile here were 'publicly revealed in connection with the prosecution of the crime,' much as the name of the rape victim in *Cox Broadcasting* was placed in the public domain." Could reporters have been excluded from the Court? See Globe Newspaper Co. v. Superior Court, 457 U.S. 596 (1982).

More recently in Florida Star v. B. J. F, 491 U.S 524, 533 (1989), the plaintiff B. J. F. (the original suit was filed with the plaintiff's full name, but the Florida court *sua sponte* revised the caption in order to protect her privacy interests) filed a report with the local sheriff's department that she had been robbed and raped. The Florida Star obtained this information lawfully and then, in violation of its own internal policy of not publishing the names of victims of sexual offenses, inadvertently published a short account of the rape in its "Police Reports" section. The plaintiff sued for violation of Florida Statute §794.03 (1987), rendering it unlawful to "print, publish, or broadcast . . . in any instrument of mass communication the name, address, or other identifying fact or information of the victim of any sexual offense. . . ." The jury awarded the plaintiff $75,000 in compensatory damages and $25,000 in punitive damages.

The Supreme Court threw out the jury awards for both compensatory and punitive damages. In reaching its conclusion, the Court refused to treat *Cox* as a dispositive precedent, noting that there the information was "taken from courthouse records that were open to public inspection," while here the information "comes from a police report prepared and disseminated at a time at which not only had no adversarial criminal proceedings begun, but no suspect had been identified." The Court then refused to adopt any categorical rule that said that it is (or is not) constitutionally protected to publish the name of a rape victim, but denied recovery on a more limited ground: "[I]f a newspaper lawfully obtains truthful information about a matter of public significance then state officials may not constitutionally punish publication of the information, absent a need to further a state interest of the highest order." The question of what should be done with unlawfully obtained information was again left unsettled.

Justice White's dissent stressed that as a result of publication "B. J. F. received harassing phone calls, required mental health counseling, was forced to move from her home, and was even threatened with being raped again." He then distinguished his earlier opinion in *Cox Broadcasting* by noting that in that case the state did not undertake any effort to keep the information confidential, while in this instance the state did seek to keep the information quiet.

Note that as a matter of practice over 90 percent of the newspapers in the country, according to one informal survey, do not publish the names of rape victims. See Alex S. Jones, *Rape Victim Is Still A Murky Issue for the Press,* N.Y. TIMES, June 25, 1989, §1, at 18. Does the general practice help the majority or the dissent?

The situation raised in *Cox* provoked two modifications of the New York privacy statute. In 1979 the legislature added a provision N.Y. Civ. Rights Law §50-b (Consol. 1994) that stated:

> The identity of any victim of a sex offense . . . shall be kept confidential. No report, paper, picture, photograph, court file or other documents, in the custody or possession of any public officer or employee, which identifies such a victim shall be made available for public inspection. No such public officer or employee shall disclose any portion of any police report, court file, or other document, which tends to identify such a victim except as provided in subdivision two of this section.

Subdivision 2 in turn allowed any person who wants to get that information to apply to court in order to show "good cause exists for disclosure to that person." Other interested parties are also given a chance to appear at the hearing. The statute indicates that any victim must give consent to any disclosure, and makes it clear that the right does not operate for the benefit of the person charged with the sexual offense. A 1991 amendment to the statute, N.Y. Civ. Rights Law §50-c then creates a private right of action for damages suffered to "any person" injured by the disclosure, and allows the court in its discretion to award reasonable attorney's fees to the prevailing plaintiff. The statute does not apply to disclosures made by private persons who have no access to public records.

2. *Private disclosure of past sexual transgressions.* Modern talk shows often feature candid disclosures of past actions that involve rape, incest, or other deviant or lurid sexual practices. In Anonsen v. Donahue, 857 S.W.2d 700, 706 (Tex. App. 1993), the Phil Donahue Show addressed the question of pregnancies resulting from rape. One guest, Miriam Booher, revealed in front of a nationwide audience how 16 or 17 years before her husband had raped her own 11-year-old daughter from a previous marriage. The incident was never reported to the police, and when her daughter's son was born, Booher raised him as her own child and her own daughter's half brother, when in fact he was her grandson. The names of the husband, daughter, and grandson were not mentioned on the air, but could be easily determined. From time to time during the broadcast the caption "Daughter Had Husband's Baby" flashed across the screen. The husband's, daughter's, and grandson's suit for invasion of privacy fell to a summary judgment based on the newsworthiness privilege, which was affirmed on appeal.

> [W]e are not without compassion for appellants, who certainly have been victimized by the tragic events revealed on the Donahue program. We are further mindful that the protection of Booher's right to reveal her story and her identify imposes additional emotional suffering upon appellants. Sensitive information which appellants have to some extent attempted to keep secret, has been given unwelcome publicity, causing them pain. Yet, we conclude that to allow a cause of action based upon Booher's truthful and undisguised account of her own and her family's experience is inconsistent with the first amendment. Freedom of speech would be severely compromised if discussions of matters of public interest were circumscribed in the manner advocated by appellants.

Is this result compelled by *Cox*? What result if Booher had agreed before going on the Donahue show not to reveal the identity of the parties? What should be done with information that is available from both public and private sources?

Haynes v. Alfred A. Knopf, Inc.
8 F.3d 1222 (7th Cir. 1993)

POSNER, CHIEF JUDGE. Luther Haynes and his wife, Dorothy Haynes nee Johnson, appeal from the dismissal on the defendants' motion for summary judgment of their suit against Nicholas Lemann, the author of a highly praised, best-selling book of social and political history called *The Promised Land: The Great Black Migration and How It Changed America* (1991), and Alfred A. Knopf, Inc., the book's publisher. The plaintiffs claim that the book libels Luther Haynes and invades both plaintiffs' right of privacy. Federal jurisdiction is based on diversity, and the common law of Illinois is agreed to govern the substantive issues. The appeal presents difficult issues at the intersection of tort law and freedom of the press.

Between 1940 and 1970, five million blacks moved from impoverished rural areas and, after sojourns of shorter or greater length in the poor black districts of the cities, moved to middle-class areas. Others, despite the ballyhooed efforts of the federal government, particularly between 1964 and 1972, to erase poverty and racial discrimination, remained mired in what has come to be called the "urban ghetto." *The Promised Land* is a history of the migration. It is not history as a professional historian, a demographer, or a social scientist would write it. Lemann is none of these. He is a journalist and has written a journalistic history, in which the focus is on individuals whether powerful or representative. In the former group are the politicians who invented, executed, or exploited the "Great Society" programs. In the latter are a handful of the actual migrants. Foremost among these is Ruby Lee Daniels. Her story is the spine of the book. We are introduced to her on page 7; we take leave of her on page 346, within a few pages of the end of the text of the book.

[Posner, J., then details the history of Daniel's life, starting from her early days during the 1940s as a sharecropper in Mississippi through her migration to Chicago where she met and married Luther Haynes. The story describes his descent from a well paid worker, a descent attributable to his drunkenness, adultery, temper, and irresponsibility throughout his marriage to Daniels. That marriage ended in divorce and thereafter Luther married another woman, Dorothy, with whom he lived a respectable life for 20 years. He now has a home, a steady job as a parking-lot attendant, and a position as deacon in his church.

Posner, J., first affirmed the dismissal of the defamation portions of the complaint on the ground that any deviations from the truth were too insubstantial to support an action for libel. He then addressed the privacy claims as follows.]

The branch of privacy law that the Hayneses invoke in their appeal is not concerned with, and is not a proper surrogate for legal doctrines that are concerned with, the accuracy of the private facts revealed. It is concerned with the propriety of stripping away the veil of privacy with which we cover the embarrassing, the shameful, the tabooed, truths about us. The revelations in the book are not about the intimate details of the Hayneses' life. They are about misconduct, in particular Luther's. (There is very little about Dorothy in the book, apart from the fact that she had had an affair with Luther while he was still married to Ruby and that they eventually became and have remained lawfully married.) The revelations are about his heavy drinking, his unstable employment, his adultery, his irresponsible and neglectful behavior toward his wife and children. So we must consider cases in which the right of privacy has been invoked as a shield against the revelation of previous misconduct.

[He then reviews *Melvin, Sidis,* and *Cox* and continues:]

The [Supreme] Court must believe that the First Amendment greatly circumscribes the right even of a private figure to obtain damages for the publication of newsworthy facts about him, even when they are facts of a kind that people want very much to conceal. To be identified in the newspaper as a rape victim is intensely embarrassing. And it is not invited embarrassment. No one asks to be raped; the plaintiff in Melvin v. Reid did not ask to be prosecuted for murder (remember, she was acquitted, though whether she actually was innocent is unknown); Sidis did not decide to be a prodigy; and Luther Haynes did not aspire to be a representative figure in the great black migration from the South to the North. People who do not desire the limelight and do not deliberately choose a way of life or course of conduct calculated to thrust them into it nevertheless have no legal right to extinguish it if the experiences that have befallen them are newsworthy, even if they would prefer that those experiences be kept private. The possibility of an involuntary loss of privacy is recognized in the modern formulations of this branch of the privacy tort, which require not only that the private facts publicized be such as would make a reasonable person deeply offended by such publicity but also that they be facts in which the public has no legitimate interest.

The two criteria, offensiveness and newsworthiness, are related. An individual, and more pertinently perhaps the community, is most offended by the publication of intimate personal facts when the community has no interest in them beyond the voyeuristic thrill of penetrating the wall of privacy that surrounds a stranger. The reader of a book about the black migration to the North would have no legitimate interest in the details of Luther Haynes's sex life; but no such details are disclosed. Such a reader does have a legitimate interest in the aspects of Luther's conduct that the book reveals. For one of Lemann's major themes is the transposition virtually intact of a sharecropper morality characterized by a family structure "matriarchal and elastic" and by an "extremely unstable" marriage bond to the slums of the northern cities, and the interaction, largely random and sometimes perverse, of that morality with governmental programs to alleviate poverty. Public aid policies discouraged Ruby and Luther from living together; public housing policies precipitated a marriage doomed to fail. No detail in the book claimed to invade the Hayneses' privacy is not germane to the story that the author wanted to tell, a story not only of legitimate but of transcendent public interest.

The Hayneses question whether the linkage between the author's theme and their private life really is organic. They point out that many social histories do not mention individuals at all, let alone by name. That is true. Much of social science, including social history, proceeds by abstraction, aggregation, and quantification rather than by case studies; the economist Robert Fogel has won a Nobel prize for his statistical studies of economic history, including, not wholly unrelated to the subject of Lemann's book, the history of Negro slavery in the United States. But it would be absurd to suggest that cliometric or other aggregative, impersonal methods of doing social history are the only proper way to go about it and presumptuous to claim even that they are the best way. Lemann's book has been praised to the skies by distinguished scholars, among them black scholars covering a large portion of the ideological spectrum — Henry Louis Gates Jr., William Julius Wilson, and Patricia Williams. Lemann's methodology places the individual case history at center stage. If he cannot tell the story of Ruby Daniels without waivers from every person who she thinks did her wrong, he cannot write this book.

Well, argue the Hayneses, at least Lemann could have changed their names. But the use of pseudonyms would not have gotten Lemann and Knopf off the legal hook. The details of the Hayneses' lives recounted in the book would identify them unmistakably to anyone who has known the Hayneses well for a long time (members of their families, for example), or who knew them before they got married; and no more is required for liability either in defamation law or in privacy law. Lemann would have had to change some, perhaps many, of the details. But then he would no longer have been writing history. He would have been writing fiction. The nonquantitative study of living persons would be abolished as a category of scholarship, to be replaced by the sociological novel. That is a genre with a distinguished history punctuated by famous names, such as Dickens, Zola, Stowe, Dreiser, Sinclair, Steinbeck, and Wolfe, but we do not think that the law of privacy makes it (or that the First Amendment would permit the law of privacy to make it) the exclusive format for a social history of living persons that tells their story rather than treating them as data points in a statistical study. . . .

The Promised Land does not afford the reader a titillating glimpse of tabooed activities. The tone is decorous and restrained. Painful though it is for the Hayneses to see a past they would rather forget brought into the public view, the public needs the information conveyed by the book, including the information about Luther and Dorothy Haynes, in order to evaluate the profound social and political questions that the book raises. Given the *Cox* decision, moreover, all the discreditable facts about the Hayneses that are contained in judicial records are beyond the power of tort law to conceal; and the disclosure of those facts alone would strip away the Hayneses' privacy as effectively as *The Promised Land* has done. (This case, it could be argued, has stripped them of their privacy, since their story is now part of a judicial record — the record of this case.) We do not think it is an answer that Lemann got his facts from Ruby Daniels rather than from judicial records. The courts got the facts from Ruby. We cannot see what difference it makes that Lemann went to the source.

Ordinarily the evaluation and comparison of offensiveness and newsworthiness would be, like other questions of the application of a legal standard to the facts of a particular case, matters for a jury, not for a judge on a motion for summary judgment. But summary judgment is properly granted to a defendant when on the basis of the evidence obtained in pretrial discovery no reasonable jury could render a verdict for the plaintiff, and that is the situation here. No modern cases decided after Cox, and precious few before, go as far as the plaintiffs would have us go in this case. . . .

Affirmed

D. FALSE LIGHT

American Law Institute, Restatement (Second) of the Law of Torts
(1976)

§652E. PUBLICITY PLACING PERSON IN FALSE LIGHT

One who gives publicity to a matter concerning another that places the other before the public in a false light is subject to liability to the other for invasion of his privacy, if

(a) The false light in which the other was placed would be highly offensive to a reasonable person, and

(b) The actor had knowledge of or acted in reckless disregard as to the falsity of the publicized matter and the false light in which the other would be placed.

Caveat:

The Institute takes no position as to whether there are any circumstances under which recovery can be obtained under this Section if the actor did not know of or act with reckless disregard as to the falsity of the matter publicized and the false light in which the other would be placed but was negligent in regard to these matters.

Comment:

b. Relation to defamation. The interest protected by this Section is the interest of the individual in not being made to appear before the public in an objectionable false light or false position, or in other words, otherwise than as he is. In many cases to which the rule stated here applies, the publicity given to the plaintiff is defamatory, so that he would have an action for libel or slander under the rules stated in Chapter 24. In such a case the action for invasion of privacy will afford an alternative or additional remedy, and the plaintiff can proceed upon either theory, or both, although he can have but one recovery for a single instance of publicity.

Time, Inc. v. Hill
385 U.S. 374 (1967)

Harold R. Medina, Jr., reargued the cause for appellant. With him on the briefs was Victor M. Earle III.

Richard M. Nixon reargued the cause and filed a brief for appellee.

Louis J. Lefkowitz, Attorney General, pro se. . . .

BRENNAN, J. . . . The question in this case is whether appellant, publisher of Life Magazine, was denied constitutional protections of speech and press by the application by the New York courts of §§50-51 of the New York Civil Rights Law to award appellee damages on allegations that Life falsely reported that a new play portrayed an experience suffered by appellee and his family.

[In September 1952, James Hill, his wife, and five Hill children were held hostage for 19 hours in their suburban Philadelphia home by three escaped convicts. The convicts released the Hill family untouched and unharmed, but the story made the front pages of the newspapers when the police, in a widely publicized encounter, subsequently killed two of the convicts and captured the third. Shortly after the incident, the Hills moved to Connecticut.

In 1955 *Life* magazine, owned by defendant Time, Inc., published an article entitled "True Crime Inspires Tense Play" that told of a new Broadway thriller, *The Desperate Hours*. The article said that the experience of the Hill family, which had first been brought to attention in

Joseph Hayes' novel *The Desperate Hours*, was now being "re-enacted" in
a new play based on the original book. The article said the play showed
that the family "rose in heroism" in its time of crisis. The article was
accompanied by pictures of scenes from the play, reenacted in the
Hill's suburban Philadelphia home. One showed a son being "roughed
up" by a "brutish convict"; another, the "darling daughter" biting the
hand of one of the convicts; and a third, of the father making a "brave
try" to save his family.

Hill brought his action in the New York State Supreme Court under
§§50 and 51 of the New York Civil Rights Law, [at page 1241 supra],
alleging that the article was intended to, and in fact did, give the public
the impression that the play was an accurate account of the experiences
of the Hill family. Hill also alleged that the defendant knew that its
article was "false and untrue." The defendant answered that the article
was "a subject of legitimate news interest," that it was "a subject of general interest and of value and concern to the public" at the time it was
published, and that it was "published in good faith without any malice
whatsoever. . . ." The trial judge denied defendant's motion to dismiss
on these grounds and the jury awarded plaintiff $50,000 in actual and
$25,000 in punitive damages. . . .

This decision was affirmed by the New York Court of Appeals, which
rested its judgment largely on its then-recent decision in Spahn v. Julian
Messner, Inc., 221 N.E.2d 543 (N.Y. 1966). In *Spahn* the plaintiff, a
famous left-handed baseball pitcher, was awarded a judgment because
defendant published an unauthorized "biography" of his life containing many "factual errors, distortions and fanciful passages" that
were included in the book solely to promote sales. The court observed
that Spahn would not have a cause of action if the biography were
substantially true, given that his baseball exploits had already brought
him to the attention of millions. It then held on the facts of the case
that defendant was not protected by the newsworthiness defense:

"But it is erroneous to confuse privacy with 'personality' or to assume
that privacy, though lost for a certain time or in a certain context, goes
forever unprotected. . . . Thus it may be appropriate to say that the
plaintiff here, Warren Spahn, is a public personality and that, insofar
as his professional career is involved, he is substantially without a right
to privacy. That is not to say, however, that his 'personality' may be
fictionalized and that, as fictionalized, it may be exploited for the defendants' commercial benefit through the medium of an unauthorized
biography."

The New York court also discussed whether plaintiff's cause of action
was barred by *New York Times* and, after noting that *Spahn* did not involve a public official, concluded: "The free speech which is encouraged and essential to the operation of a healthy government is

something quite different from an individual's attempt to enjoin the publication of a fictitious biography of him. No public interest is served by protecting the dissemination of the latter. We perceive no constitutional infirmities in this respect."

[With this groundwork established, Justice Brennan then continued:]

If this is meant to imply that proof of knowing or reckless falsity is not essential to a constitutional application of the statute in these cases, we disagree with the Court of Appeals. We hold that the constitutional protections for speech and press preclude the application of the New York statute to redress false reports of matters of public interest in the absence of proof that the defendant published the report with knowledge of its falsity or in reckless disregard of the truth.

The guarantees for speech and press are not the preserve of political expression or comment upon public affairs, essential as those are to healthy government. One need only pick up any newspaper or magazine to comprehend the vast range of published matter which exposes persons to public view, both private citizens and public officials. Exposure of the self to others in varying degrees is a concomitant of life in a civilized community. The risk of this exposure is an essential incident of life in a society which places a primary value on freedom of speech and of press. . . . We create a grave risk of serious impairment of the indispensable service of a free press in a free society if we saddle the press with the impossible burden of verifying to a certainty the facts associated in news articles with a person's name, picture or portrait, particularly as related to nondefamatory matter. Even negligence would be a most elusive standard, especially when the content of the speech itself affords no warning of prospective harm to another through falsity. A negligence test would place on the press the intolerable burden of guessing how a jury might assess the reasonableness of steps taken by it to verify the accuracy of every reference to a name, picture or portrait.

In this context, sanctions against either innocent or negligent misstatement would present a grave hazard of discouraging the press from exercising the constitutional guarantees. Those guarantees are not for the benefit of the press so much as for the benefit of all of us. A broadly defined freedom of the press assures the maintenance of our political system and an open society. Fear of large verdicts in damage suits for innocent or merely negligent misstatement, even fear of the expense involved in their defense, must inevitably cause publishers to "steer . . . wider of the unlawful zone," and thus "create the danger that the legitimate utterance will be penalized."

But the constitutional guarantees can tolerate sanctions against *calculated* falsehood without significant impairment of their essential function. We held in *New York Times* that calculated falsehood enjoyed no immunity in the case of alleged defamation of a public official concerning his official conduct. Similarly, calculated falsehood should enjoy no immunity in the situation here presented us. . . .

We find applicable here the standard of knowing or reckless falsehood, not through blind application of New York Times Co. v. Sullivan, relating solely to libel actions by public officials, but only upon consideration of the factors which arise in the particular context of the application of the New York statute in cases involving private individuals. This is neither a libel action by a private individual nor a statutory action by a public official. Therefore, although the First Amendment principles pronounced in *New York Times* guide our conclusion, we reach that conclusion only by applying these principles in this discrete context. It therefore serves no purpose to distinguish the facts here from those in *New York Times*. Were this a libel action, the distinction which has been suggested between the relative opportunities of the public official and the private individual to rebut defamatory charges might be germane. And the additional state interest in the protection of the individual against damage to his reputation would be involved. Moreover, a different test might be required in a statutory action by a public official, as opposed to a libel action by a public official or a statutory action by a private individual. Different considerations might arise concerning the degree of "waiver" of the protection the State might afford. But the question whether the same standard should be applicable both to persons voluntarily and involuntarily thrust into the public limelight is not here before us.

Turning to the facts of the present case, the proofs reasonably would support either a jury finding of innocent or merely negligent misstatement by Life, or a finding that Life portrayed the play as re-enactment of the Hill family's experience reckless of the truth or with actual knowledge that the portrayal was false. The relevant testimony is as follows.

[Justice Brennan then reviewed the evidence in great detail.]

The appellant argues that the statute should be declared unconstitutional on its face if construed by the New York courts to impose liability without proof of knowing or reckless falsity. Such a declaration would not be warranted even if it were entirely clear that this had previously been the view of the New York courts. The New York Court of Appeals, as the *Spahn* opinion demonstrates, has been assiduous in construing the statute to avoid invasion of the constitutional protections of speech and press. We, therefore, confidently expect that the New York courts will apply the statute consistently with the constitutional command. Any possible difference with us as to the thrust of the constitutional command is narrowly limited in this case to the failure of the trial judge to instruct the jury that a verdict of liability could be predicated only on a finding of knowing or reckless falsity in the publication of the Life article.

The judgment of the Court of Appeals is set aside and the case is remanded for further proceedings not inconsistent with this opinion.

It is so ordered.

[Justice Black, with whom Justice Douglas joined, concurred, but reiterated his interpretation of the First Amendment as expressed in New York Times v. Sullivan.]

DOUGLAS J., concurring. . . . The episode around which this book was written had been news of the day for some time. The most that can be said is that the novel, the play, and the magazine article revived that interest. A fictionalized treatment of the event is, in my view, as much in the public domain as would be a watercolor of the assassination of a public official. It seems to me irrelevant to talk of any right of privacy in this context. Here a private person is catapulted into the news by events over which he had no control. He and his activities are then in the public domain as fully as the matters at issue in New York Times Co. v. Sullivan, Such privacy as a person normally has ceases when his life has ceased to be private.

Once we narrow the ambit of the First Amendment, creative writing is imperiled and the "chilling effect" on free expression which we feared in Dombrowski v. Pfister, 380 U.S 479, 487, is almost sure to take place. That is, I fear, the result once we allow an exception for "knowing or reckless falsity.". . .

HARLAN, J., concurring in part and dissenting in part. While I find much with which I agree in the opinion of the Court, I am constrained to express my disagreement with its view of the proper standard of liability to be applied on remand. Were the jury on retrial to find negligent rather than, as the Court requires, reckless or knowing "fictionalization," I think that federal constitutional requirements would be met. . . .

[T]he distinction between the facts presented to us here and the situation at issue in the *New York Times* case and its progeny cast serious doubt on that grant of immunity and calls for a more limited "breathing space" than that granted in criticism of public officials.

First, we cannot avoid recognizing that we have entered an area where the "marketplace of ideas" does not function and where conclusions premised on the existence of that exchange are apt to be suspect. . . . [Falsehood] is more easily tolerated where public attention creates the strong likelihood of a competition among ideas. Here such competition is extremely unlikely for the scrutiny and discussion of the relationship of the Hill incident and the play is "occasioned by the particular charges in controversy" and the matter is not one in which the public has an "independent interest." It would be unreasonable to assume that Mr. Hill could find a forum for making a successful refutation of the Life material or that the public's interest in it would be sufficient for the truth to win out by comparison as it might in that area of discussion central to a free society. Thus the state interest in encouraging careful checking and preparation of published material is far stronger than in *New York Times*. The dangers of unchallengeable untruth are far too well documented to be summarily dismissed.

Second, there is a vast difference in the state interest in protecting individuals like Mr. Hill from irresponsibly prepared publicity and the state interest in similar protection for a public official. In *New York Times* we acknowledged public officials to be a breed from whom hardiness to exposure to charges, innuendoes, and criticisms might be demanded and who voluntarily assumed the risk of such things by entry into the public arena. But Mr. Hill came to public attention through an unfortunate circumstance not of his making rather than his voluntary actions and he can in no sense be considered to have "waived" any protection the State might justifiably afford him from irresponsible publicity. Not being inured to the vicissitudes of journalistic scrutiny such an individual is more easily injured and his means of self-defense are more limited. The public is less likely to view with normal skepticism what is written about him because it is not accustomed to seeing his name in the press and expects only a disinterested report.

The coincidence of these factors in this situation leads me to the view that a State should be free to hold the press to a duty of making a reasonable investigation of the underlying facts and limiting itself to "fair comment" on the materials so gathered.

Mr. Justice Fortas, with whom The Chief Justice and Mr. Justice Clark join, dissenting.

[Justice Fortas examined in detail the instructions given at the trial, comparing them to the standard set forth by the majority of the Court, and found that they were] close enough to this Court's insistence upon "knowing or reckless falsity" as to render a reversal arbitrary and unjustified. If the defendant *altered* or *changed* the true facts so that the article as published was a *fictionalized* version, this, in my judgment, was a knowing or reckless falsity. "Alteration" or "change" denotes a positive act — not a negligent or inadvertent happening. "Fictionalization" and "fiction" to the ordinary mind mean so departing from fact and reality as to be *deliberately* divorced from the fact — not merely in detail but in general and pervasive impact.

NOTES

1. *Time v. Hill and the New York privacy statute.* After the Supreme Court of the United States found a constitutional defect in the rule as applied in *Hill*, *Spahn* was appealed to the Supreme Court. The Court vacated the judgment and remanded it to the New York Court of Appeals for consideration in light of Time, Inc. v. Hill. On remand the

New York court affirmed the judgment for the plaintiff; it construed its statute to require "knowing" falsity and construed the record to support a finding of such "malice," 233 N.E.2d 840 (N.Y. 1967).

2. *Time v. Hill today.* The Supreme Court has not reconsidered in any detail the issues raised in Time v. Hill even though it might have done so in Cantrell v. Forest City Publishing Co., 419 U.S. 245, 250-251 (1974). There the Court upheld a verdict for plaintiff in a false light case after it satisfied itself that the trial judge had properly instructed the jury on plaintiff's burden of showing that defendant's story was written with knowledge of its falsity or with a reckless disregard of its truth. Given that plaintiff was a private person, *Cantrell* could have prompted a reexamination of Time v. Hill in the light of Gertz v. Welch. Since no objections were raised to the instructions below, the Court concluded that "this case presents no occasion to consider whether a State may constitutionally apply a more relaxed standard of liability for a publisher or broadcaster of false statements injurious to a private individual under a false-light theory of invasion of privacy, or whether the constitutional standard announced in Time, Inc. v. Hill applies to all false-light cases."

For their part, the lower courts have expressed hostility to false light actions. See, e.g., Machleder v. Diaz, 801 F.2d 46 (2d Cir. 1986), where the court upheld a summary judgment for the defendants, a CBS reporter and the television station, when they edited a "confrontational interview" wherein the plaintiff, an operator of a blending business that used toxic chemicals, was accused of illegally dumping them on lands owned by the Newark Housing Authority. CBS cut from the news report plaintiff's statement, "I don't want to be on television; I'm, sorry, I'm sorry," preferring his more hostile and incriminating statement, "Get that damn camera out of here." The court held that these tactics were not sufficient to make out a false light claim. "Any portrayal of plaintiff as intemperate and evasive could not be false since it was based on his own conduct which was accurately captured by the cameras." It also held that the action failed because the plaintiff did not show that the material broadcast was highly offensive. At trial the jury found for the plaintiff on the false light claim and the defendant on the defamation claim. Why?

See also Renwick v. News & Observer Publishing Co., 312 S.E.2d 405 (N.C. 1984), which totally repudiated as "constitutionally suspect" the false light tort as a matter of North Carolina common law. The same position has been urged after an exhaustive examination of the tort in Zimmerman, False Light Invasion of Privacy: The Light That Failed, 64 N.Y.U. L. Rev. 364 (1989). Those cases that have retained the false light tort have generally analyzed it in the same fashion as the law of defamation, see, e.g., White v. Fraternal Order of Police, 909 F.2d 512 (D.C. Cir. 1990). That trend is generally approved in Schwartz, Explaining and Justifying a Limited Tort of False Light Invasion of Privacy, 41 Case

W. Res. L. Rev. 885, 898 (1991), who then sorts out the connection between false light and defamation as follows:

> In a defamation action, the plaintiff complains that the defendant's statement has diminished his reputation; the statement's falsity comes in by showing that this diminution is not justified. In a false light action, the defendant's falsehood brings about a mismatch or conflict between the plaintiff's actual identity and his identity in the minds of others, a conflict that itself can be offensive or disorienting.

Can this distinction be maintained if the tort of defamation is defined as false statements that deter third parties from dealing with the plaintiff? As false statements that bring the plaintiff into "hatred, ridicule, or contempt?"

E. INTRUSION UPON SECLUSION

American Law Institute, Restatement (Second) of the Law of Torts
(1976)

§652B. INTRUSION UPON SECLUSION

One who intentionally intrudes, physically or otherwise, upon the solitude or seclusion of another, or his private affairs or concerns, is subject to liability to the other for invasion of his privacy, if the intrusion would be highly offensive to a reasonable person.

Nader v. General Motors
255 N.E.2d 765 (N.Y. 1970)

FULD, C. J. On this appeal, taken by permission of the Appellate Division on a certified question, we are called upon to determine the reach of the tort of invasion of privacy as it exists under the law of the District of Columbia.

The complaint, in this action by Ralph Nader, pleads four causes of action against the appellant, General Motors Corporation, and three other defendants allegedly acting as its agents. The first two causes of action charge an invasion of privacy, the third is predicated on the intentional infliction of severe emotional distress and the fourth on interference with the plaintiff's economic advantage. This appeal concerns only the legal sufficiency of the first two causes of action, which were upheld in the courts below as against the appellant's motion to dismiss.

The plaintiff, an author and lecturer on automotive safety, has, for some years, been an articulate and severe critic of General Motors' products from the standpoint of safety and design. According to the complaint — which, for present purposes, we must assume to be true — the appellant, having learned of the imminent publication of the plaintiff's book "Unsafe at any Speed," decided to conduct a campaign of intimidation against him in order to "suppress plaintiff's criticism of and prevent his disclosure of information" about its products. To that end, the appellant authorized and directed the other defendants to engage in a series of activities which, the plaintiff claims in his first two causes of action, violated his right to privacy.

Specifically, the plaintiff alleges that the appellant's agents (1) conducted a series of interviews with acquaintances of the plaintiff, "questioning them about, and casting aspersions upon [his] political, social . . . racial and religious views . . . ; his integrity; his sexual proclivities and inclinations; and his personal habits"; (2) kept him under surveillance in public places for an unreasonable length of time; (3) caused him to be accosted by girls for the purpose of entrapping him into illicit relationships; (4) made threatening, harassing and obnoxious telephone calls to him; (5) tapped his telephone and eavesdropped, by means of mechanical and electronic equipment, on his private conversations with others; and (6) conducted a "continuing" and harassing investigation of him. These charges are amplified in the plaintiff's bill of particulars, and those particulars are, of course, to be taken into account in considering the sufficiency of the challenged causes of action.

[The court then held that the applicable law was that of the District of Columbia, and that its court recognized the tort of invasion of privacy.] Thus, in the most recent of its cases on the subject, Pearson v. Dodd (410 F.2d 701), the Federal Court of Appeals for the District of Columbia declared (p. 704):

"We approve the extension of the tort of invasion of privacy to instances of *intrusion*, whether by physical trespass or not, into spheres from which an ordinary man in a plaintiff's position could reasonably expect that the particular defendant should be excluded." (Italics supplied.)

It is this form of invasion of privacy — initially termed "intrusion" by Dean Prosser in 1960 — on which the two challenged causes of action are predicated.

Quite obviously, some intrusions into one's private sphere are inevitable concomitants of life in an industrial and densely populated society, which the law does not seek to proscribe even if it were possible to do so. "The law does not provide a remedy for every annoyance that occurs in everyday life." However, the District of Columbia courts have held that the law should and does protect against certain types of intrusive conduct, and we must, therefore, determine whether the plaintiff's allegations are actionable as violations of the right to privacy under the law of that jurisdiction.

It should be emphasized that the mere gathering of information about a particular individual does not give rise to a cause of action under this theory. Privacy is invaded only if the information sought is of a confidential nature and the defendant's conduct was unreasonably intrusive. Just as a common-law copyright is lost when material is published, so, too, there can be no invasion of privacy where the information sought is open to public view or has been voluntarily revealed to others. In order to sustain a cause of action for invasion of privacy, therefore, the plaintiff must show that the appellant's conduct was truly "intrusive" and that it was designed to elicit information which would not be available through normal inquiry or observation.

The majority of the Appellate Division in the present case stated that *all of "[t]he activities complained of"* in the first two counts constituted actionable invasions of privacy under the law of the District of Columbia.[2] We do not agree with that sweeping determination. At most, only two of the activities charged to the appellant are, in our view, actionable as invasions of privacy under the law of the District of Columbia. However, since the first two counts include allegations which are sufficient to state a cause of action, we could — as the concurring opinion notes — merely affirm the order before us without further elaboration. To do so, though, would be a disservice both to the judge who will be called upon to try this case and to the litigants themselves. In other words, we deem it desirable, nay essential, that we go further and, for the guidance of the trial court and counsel, indicate the extent to which the plaintiff is entitled to rely on the various allegations in support of his privacy claim. . . .

Turning, then, to the particular acts charged in the complaint, we cannot find any basis for a claim of invasion of privacy, under District of Columbia law, in the allegations that the appellant, through its agents or employees, interviewed many persons who knew the plaintiff, asking questions about him and casting aspersions on his character. Although those inquiries may have uncovered information of a personal nature, it is difficult to see how they may be said to have invaded the plaintiff's privacy. Information about the plaintiff which was already known to others could hardly be regarded as private to the plaintiff.

---

2. "The activities complained of:" wrote the Appellate Division majority, "the shadowing, the indiscriminate interviewing of third persons about features of his intimate life, the wiretapping and eavesdropping, the prying into his bank accounts, taxes, the alleged accosting by young women and the receipt of threatening phone calls, all are within the purview of these cases." (31 A.D.2d, at p. 394.)

Presumably, the plaintiff had previously revealed the information to such other persons, and he would necessarily assume the risk that a friend or acquaintance in whom he had confided might breach the confidence. If, as alleged, the questions tended to disparage the plaintiff's character, his remedy would seem to be by way of an action for defamation, not for breach of his right to privacy.

Nor can we find any actionable invasion of privacy in the allegations that the appellant caused the plaintiff to be accosted by girls with illicit proposals, or that it was responsible for the making of a large number of threatening and harassing telephone calls to the plaintiff's home at odd hours. Neither of these activities, howsoever offensive and disturbing, involved intrusion for the purpose of gathering information of a private and confidential nature.

As already indicated, it is manifestly neither practical nor desirable for the law to provide a remedy against any and all activity which an individual might find annoying. On the other hand, where severe mental pain or anguish is inflicted through a deliberate and malicious campaign of harassment or intimidation, a remedy is available in the form of an action for the intentional infliction of emotional distress — the theory underlying the plaintiff's third cause of action. But the elements of such an action are decidedly different from those governing the tort of invasion of privacy, and just as we have carefully guarded against the use of the prima facie tort doctrine to circumvent the limitations relating to other established tort remedies we should be wary of any attempt to rely on the tort of invasion of privacy as a means of avoiding the more stringent pleading and proof requirements for an action for infliction of emotional distress.

Apart, however, from the foregoing allegations which we find inadequate to spell out a cause of action for invasion of privacy under District of Columbia law, the complaint contains allegations concerning other activities by the appellant or its agents which do satisfy the requirements for such a cause of action. The one which most clearly meets those requirements is the charge that the appellant and its codefendants engaged in unauthorized wiretapping and eavesdropping by mechanical and electronic means. The Court of Appeals in the *Pearson* case expressly recognized that such conduct constitutes a tortious intrusion and other jurisdictions have reached a similar conclusion. (See, e.g., Roach v. Harper, 105 S.E.2d 546 (W.Va. 1958)) In point of fact, the appellant does not dispute this, acknowledging that, to the extent the two challenged counts charge it with wiretapping and eavesdropping, an actionable invasion of privacy has been stated.

There are additional allegations that the appellant hired people to shadow the plaintiff and keep him under surveillance. In particular, he claims that, on one occasion, one of its agents followed him into a bank, getting sufficiently close to him to see the denomination of the bills he was withdrawing from his account. From what we have already said, it is manifest that the mere observation of the plaintiff in a public place does not amount to an invasion of his privacy. But, under certain circumstances, surveillance may be so "overzealous" as to render it actionable. Whether or not the surveillance in the present case falls into this latter category will depend on the nature of the proof. A person does not automatically make public everything he does merely by being in a public place, and the mere fact that Nader was in a bank did not give anyone the right to try to discover the amount of money he was withdrawing. On the other hand, if the plaintiff acted in such a way as to reveal that fact to any casual observer, then, it may not be said that the appellant intruded into his private sphere. In any event, though, it is enough for present purposes to say that the surveillance allegation is not insufficient as a matter of law. . . .

We would but add that the allegations concerning the interviewing of third persons, the accosting by girls and the annoying and threatening telephone calls, though insufficient to support a cause of action for invasion of privacy, are pertinent to the plaintiff's third cause of action — in which those allegations are reiterated — charging the intentional infliction of emotional distress. However, as already noted, it will be necessary for the plaintiff to meet the additional requirements prescribed by the law of the District of Columbia for the maintenance of a cause of action under that theory.

The order appealed from should be affirmed, with costs, and the question certified answered in the affirmative.

BREITEL, J., concurring in result. There is no doubt that the first and second causes of action are sufficient in alleging an invasion of privacy under what appears to be the applicable law in the District of Columbia. This should be the end of this court's proper concern with the pleadings, the only matter before the court being a motion to dismiss specified causes of action for insufficiency.

Thus it is not proper, it is submitted, for the court directly or indirectly to analyze particular allegations in the pleadings, once the causes of action are found sufficient, in order to determine whether they would alternatively sustain one cause of action or another, or whether evidence offered in support of the allegations is relevant only as to one rather than to another cause of action. Particularly, it is inappropriate to decide that several of the allegations as they now appear are referable only to the more restricted tort of intentional infliction of mental distress rather than to the common-law right of privacy upon which the first and second causes of action depend. The third cause of action is quite restricted. Thus many of the quite offensive acts charged will not be actionable unless plaintiff succeeds in the very difficult, if not impossible, task of showing that defendants' activities were designed, actually or virtually, to make plaintiff unhappy and not to uncover disgraceful information about him. The real issue in the volatile and developing law of privacy is whether a private person is entitled to be free of certain grave offensive intrusions unsupported by palpable social or economic excuse or justification. . . .

Accordingly, because of the prematurity of ruling on any other question but the sufficiency of the causes of action, I concur in result only.

Judges Scileppi, Bergan and Gibson concur with Chief Judge Fuld; Judge Breitel concurs in result in an opinion in which Judges Burke and Jasen concur.

Order affirmed, etc.

NOTES

1. *Unauthorized use.* Perhaps the easiest privacy claims arise when there is an unauthorized examination of the plaintiff's private papers and records. Thus in Birnbaum v. United States, 588 F.2d 319, 323 (2d Cir. 1978), the court held that the plaintiff stated a cause of action against the CIA when it covertly opened and read first-class mail sent between American citizens and the Soviet Union. The court noted that *Roberson,* supra at page 1219, did not foreclose the common-law developments in this area: "That the *Roberson* court rejected a privacy right in the context of an appropriation does not imply a rejection of a remedy for intrusion." It then agreed with the district court that "there is a claim for relief in New York against a private person for intrusion upon the privacy of another, and that such a claim includes the opening and reading of sealed mail." What privileges might be available to the CIA?

2. *Trespass by fraudulent entry.* The more difficult cases involve situations in which consent has been obtained to the initial intrusion. At its inception the tort of privacy developed as a gloss on the law of trespass to land, in cases where consent to entry was obtained by fraudulent means. In the early case of De May v. Roberts, 9 N.W. 146, 149 (Mich. 1881), this principle was extended to allow the plaintiff an action against an attending physician who brought a young unmarried man into the plaintiff's apartment when he delivered her baby. "In obtaining admission at such a time and under such circumstances without fully disclosing his true character, both parties were guilty of deceit, and the wrong thus done entitles the injured party to recover the damages afterwards sustained, from shame and mortification upon discovering the true character of the defendants."

The deceit motif was also powerful in Dietemann v. Time, Inc., 449 F.2d 245, 247-250 (9th Cir. 1971), where plaintiff, "a disabled veteran with little education, was engaged in the practice of healing with clay, minerals, and herbs — as practiced, simply quackery." As part of an effort to expose the practices of plaintiff and those like him, two of defendant's reporters for *Life* magazine, Mr. Ray and Mrs. Metcalf, hatched a scheme with the local district attorney's office which allowed the pair to gain entry into plaintiff's house by falsely representing that they had been sent by a friend for treatment. By means of concealed equipment, Mrs. Metcalf transmitted the conversations between herself and plaintiff to a parked car occupied by a *Life* employee and two government officials. Mr. Ray took secret pictures of plaintiff, later used in the Life story, including one of "plaintiff with his hand on the upper portion of Mrs. Metcalf's breast while he was looking at some gadgets and holding what appeared to be a wand in his right hand." Plaintiff was arrested for practicing medicine without a license some four weeks after the incident took place and, after the publication of the story, entered a plea of nolo contendere. He then recovered $1,000 for the invasion of privacy, and the verdict was affirmed on appeal. "The First Amendment has never been construed to accord newsmen immunity from torts or crimes committed during the course of newsgathering. The First Amendment is not a license to trespass, to steal, or to intrude by electronic means into the precincts of another's home or office."

3. *Privacy without trespass.* The tort of privacy, however, also extends to cases in which there is no entry onto the plaintiff's premises at all, as with the garden-variety cases of eavesdropping by an open window or overhearing conversations by means of a parabolic microphone. One possible line of argument takes the position "no physical invasion, no tort." See *Fontainebleau,* supra at page 692. The cases, however, have gone uniformly the other way. In Roach v. Harper, 105 S.E.2d 546 (W. Va. 1958), the court allowed an action for invasion of privacy when the defendant used a "hearing device" to overhear the plaintiff's private and confidential conversations in an apartment that he rented to her. *Roach* relied on earlier cases such as Rhodes v. Graham, 37 S.W.2d 46 (Ky. 1931), where phone conversations were overheard by means of a technical trespass, the tapping of a telephone line. Creating liability without trespass is best justified, perhaps, by asking whether the general security promoted by an expanded right works to the long-term advantage of all individuals governed by the newer rule. That conclusion perhaps may be advanced, empirically, by noting that the legal prohibition on all forms of snooping reduces the need for individuals to take elaborate precautions to fence themselves off from their neighbors.

The soundness of the privacy right against intrusion has not been sharply contested in the private law, but it has been the subject of enormous controversy in connection with the Fourth Amendment's guarantee against "unreasonable searches and seizures." See, e.g., Katz v. United States, 389 U.S. 347 (1967), which rejected the government's argument that its tap on a public telephone booth was not a search or seizure because the electronic device used "did not happen to penetrate the wall of the booth. . . . " The law of trespass does not limit the scope of the Fourth Amendment, but it is far from clear exactly how far the protection goes or why. The key question thus becomes whether the individual had a reasonable or legitimate expectation of privacy. Subsequent Fourth Amendment cases have retreated from the broad holding of *Katz*. For example, in Smith v. Maryland, 442 U.S. 735 (1979), the Court refused to apply *Katz* when the police, without a warrant, used a device known as a "pen register" to record the numbers dialed from a particular phone and the times they were dialed, because no conversations were recorded. Does the legitimate interest of privacy test allow a distinction between *Katz* and *Smith?*

4. *Receiving stolen information.* In Pearson v. Dodd, 410 F.2d 701, 703, 704-706, 708 (D.C. Cir. 1969), the facts were as follows:

> [O]n several occasions in June and July, 1965, two former employees of the plaintiff, at times with the assistance of two members of the plaintiff's staff, entered the plaintiff's office without authority and unbeknownst to him, removed numerous documents from his files, made copies of them, replaced the originals, and turned over the copies to the defendant Anderson, who was aware of the manner in which the copies had been obtained. The defendants Pearson and Anderson thereafter published articles containing information gleaned from these documents.

As the court of appeals observed:

> The columns complained of here gave appellants' version of appellee's relationship with certain lobbyists for foreign interests, and gave an interpretive biographical sketch of appellee's public career. They thus clearly bore on appellee's qualifications as a United States Senator, and as such amounted to a paradigm example of published speech not subject to suit for invasion of privacy.

Plaintiff brought an action for intrusion into his personal affairs. The court of appeals, while recognizing the tort existed in the District of Columbia, found that the appellants had not committed it.

> The question then becomes whether appellants Pearson and Anderson improperly intruded into the protected sphere of privacy of appellee Dodd in obtaining the information on which their columns were based. In determining this question, we may assume, without deciding, that appellee's employees and former employees did commit such an improper intrusion when they removed confidential files with the intent to show them to unauthorized outsiders.
>
> Although appellee's complaint charges that appellants aided and abetted in the removal of the documents, the undisputed facts, narrowed by the District Judge with the concurrence of counsel, established only that appellants received copies of the documents knowing that they had been removed without authorization. If we were to hold appellants liable for invasion of privacy on these facts, we would establish the proposition that

one who receives information from an intruder, knowing it has been obtained by improper intrusion, is guilty of a tort. In an untried and developing area of tort law, we are not prepared to go so far. A person approached by an eavesdropper with an offer to share in the information gathered through the eavesdropping would perhaps play the nobler part should he spurn the offer and shut his ears. However, it seems to us that at this point it would place too great a strain on human weakness to hold one liable in damages who merely succumbs to temptation and listens.

Of course, appellants did more than receive and peruse the copies of the documents taken from appellee's files; they published excerpts from them in the national press. But in analyzing a claimed breach of privacy, injuries from intrusion and injuries from publication should be kept clearly separate. Where there is intrusion, the intruder should generally be liable whatever the content of what he learns. An eavesdropper to the marital bedroom may hear marital intimacies, or he may hear statements of fact or opinion of legitimate interest to the public; for purposes of liability that should make no difference. On the other hand, where the claim is that private information concerning plaintiff has been published, the question of whether that information is genuinely private or is of public interest should not turn on the manner in which it has been obtained. Of course, both forms of invasion may be combined in the same case.

Here we have separately considered the nature of appellants' publications concerning appellee, and have found that the matter published was of obvious public interest. The publication was not itself an invasion of privacy. Since we have also concluded that appellants' role in obtaining the information did not make them liable to appellee for intrusion, their subsequent publication, itself no invasion of privacy, cannot reach back to render that role tortious.

The concurrence of Judge Tamm observed:

> Some legal scholars will see in the majority opinion — as distinguished from its actual holding — an ironic aspect. Conduct for which a law enforcement officer would be soundly castigated is, by the phraseology of the majority opinion, found tolerable; conduct which, if engaged in by government agents would lead to the suppression of evidence obtained by these means, is approved when used for the profit of the press. There is an anomaly lurking in this situation: the news media regard themselves as quasi-public institutions yet they demand immunity from the restraints which they vigorously demand be placed on government. That which is regarded as mortal taint on information secured by any illegal conduct of government would appear from the majority opinion to be permissible as a technique or modus operandi for the journalist.

Why is it impossible to treat the harm from publication as consequential damages aggravating the original tort? Could Anderson and Pearson have been sued under *Dietemann* for the damages caused by the publication in their columns if they or their agents had personally obtained the material in question?

Galella v. Onassis
487 F.2d 986 (2d Cir. 1973)

SMITH, J. Ronald Galella, a free-lance photographer, appeals from a summary judgment dismissing his complaint against three Secret Service agents for false arrest, malicious prosecution and interference with trade, the dismissal after trial of his identical complaint against Jacqueline Onassis and the grant of injunctive relief to defendant Onassis on her counterclaim and to the intervenor, the United States, on its intervening complaint and a third judgment retaxing transcript costs to plaintiff. In addition to numerous alleged procedural errors, Galella raises the First Amendment as an absolute shield against liability to any sanctions. The judgments dismissing the complaints are affirmed; the grant of injunctive relief is affirmed as herein modified. Taxation of costs against the plaintiff is affirmed in part, reversed in part.

Galella is a free-lance photographer specializing in the making and sale of photographs of well-known persons. Defendant Onassis is the widow of the late President, John F. Kennedy, mother of the two Kennedy children, John and Caroline, and is the wife of Aristotle Onassis, widely known shipping figure and reputed multimillionaire. John Walsh, James Kalafatis and John Connelly are U.S. Secret Service agents assigned to the duty of protecting the Kennedy children under 18 U.S.C. §3056, which provides for protection of the children of deceased presidents up to the age of 16.

Galella fancies himself as a "paparazzo" (literally a kind of annoying insect, perhaps roughly equivalent to the English "gadfly"). Paparazzi make themselves as visible to the public and obnoxious to their photographic subjects as possible to aid in the advertisement and wide sale of their works.

Some examples of Galella's conduct brought out at trial are illustrative. Galella took pictures of John Kennedy riding his bicycle in Central Park across the way from his home. He jumped out into the boy's path, causing the agents concern for John's safety. The agents' reaction and interrogation of Galella led to Galella's arrest and his action against the agents; Galella on other occasions interrupted Caroline at tennis, and invaded the children's private schools. At one time he came uncomfortably close in a power boat to Mrs. Onassis swimming. He often jumped and postured around while taking pictures of her party notably at a theater opening but also on numerous other occasions. He followed a practice of bribing apartment house, restaurant and nightclub doormen as well as romancing a family servant to keep him advised of the movements of the family.

After detention and arrest following complaint by the Secret Service agents protecting Mrs. Onassis' son and his acquittal in the state court, Galella filed suit in state court against the agents and Mrs. Onassis. Galella claimed that under orders from Mrs. Onassis, the three agents had falsely arrested and maliciously prosecuted him, and that this incident in addition to several others described in the complaint constituted an unlawful interference with his trade.

Mrs. Onassis answered denying any role in the arrest or any part in the claimed interference with his attempts to photograph her, and counterclaimed for damages and injunctive relief, charging that Galella had invaded her privacy, assaulted and battered her, intentionally inflicted emotional distress and engaged in a campaign of harassment.

The action was removed under 28 U.S.C. §1442(a) to the United States District Court. On a motion for summary judgment, Galella's claim against the Secret Service agents was dismissed, the court finding that the agents were acting within the scope of their authority and thus were immune from prosecution. At the same time, the government intervened requesting injunctive relief from the activities of Galella which obstructed the Secret Service's ability to protect Mrs. Onassis' children. Galella's motion to remand the case to state court, just prior to trial, was denied.

Certain incidents of photographic coverage by Galella, subsequent to an agreement among the parties for Galella not to so engage, resulted in the issuance of a temporary restraining order to prevent further harassment of Mrs. Onassis and the children. Galella was enjoined from "harassing, alarming, startling, tormenting, touching the person of the defendant . . . or her children . . . and from blocking their movements in the public places and thoroughfares, invading their immediate zone of privacy by means of physical movements, gestures or with photographic equipment and from performing any act reasonably calculated to place the lives and safety of the defendant . . . and her children in jeopardy." Within two months, Galella was charged with violation of the temporary restraining order; a new order was signed which required that the photographer keep 100 yards from the Onassis apartment and 50 yards from the person of the defendant and her children. Surveillance was also prohibited. . . .

After a six-week trial the court dismissed Galella's claim and granted relief to both the defendant and the intervenor. Galella was enjoined from (1) keeping the defendant and her children under surveillance or following any of them; (2) approaching within 100 yards of the home of defendant or her children, or within 100 yards of either child's school or within 75 yards of either child or 50 yards of defendant; (3) using the name, portrait or picture of defendant or her children for advertising; (4) attempting to communicate with defendant or her children except through her attorney.

[The court first found that the secret service agents were entitled to absolute immunity under the Barr v. Matteo doctrine. See supra at page 974.

Discrediting all of Galella's testimony the court found the photographer guilty of harassment, intentional infliction of emotional distress, assault and battery, commercial exploitation of defendant's personality, and invasion of privacy. Fully crediting defendant's testimony, the court found no liability on Galella's claim. Evidence offered by the defense showed that Galella had on occasion intentionally physically touched Mrs. Onassis and her daughter, caused fear of physical contact in his frenzied attempts to get their pictures, followed defendant and her children too closely in an automobile, endangered the safety of the children while they were swimming, water skiing and horseback riding. Galella cannot successfully challenge the court's finding of tortious conduct.

Finding that Galella had "insinuated himself into the very fabric of Mrs. Onassis' life . . ." the court framed its relief in part on the need to prevent further invasion of the defendant's privacy. Whether or not this accords with present New York law, there is no doubt that it is sustainable under New York's proscription of harassment.

Of course legitimate countervailing social needs may warrant some intrusion despite an individual's reasonable expectation of privacy and freedom from harassment. However the interference allowed may be no greater than that necessary to protect the overriding public interest. Mrs. Onassis was properly found to be a public figure and thus subject to news coverage. Nonetheless, Galella's action went far beyond the reasonable bounds of news gathering. When weighed against the de minimis public importance of the daily activities of the defendant, Galella's constant surveillance, his obtrusive and intruding presence, was unwarranted and unreasonable. If there were any doubt in our minds, Galella's inexcusable conduct toward defendant's minor children would resolve it.

Galella does not seriously dispute the court's finding of tortious conduct. Rather, he sets up the First Amendment as a wall of immunity protecting newsmen from any liability for their conduct while gathering news. There is no such scope to the First Amendment right. Crimes and torts committed in news gathering are not protected. There is no threat to a free press in requiring its agents to act within the law.

[The court then decided several further procedural points against Galella.]

Injunctive relief is appropriate. Galella has stated his intention to continue his coverage of defendant so long as she is newsworthy, and his continued harassment even while the temporary restraining orders were in effect indicate that no voluntary change in his technique can be expected. New York courts have found similar conduct sufficient to support a claim for injunctive relief.

The injunction, however, is broader than is required to protect the defendant. Relief must be tailored to protect Mrs. Onassis from the "paparazzo" attack which distinguishes Galella's behavior from that of other photographers; it should not unnecessarily infringe on reasonable efforts to "cover" defendant. Therefore, we modify the court's order to prohibit only (1) any approach within twenty-five (25) feet of defendant or any touching of the person of the defendant Jacqueline Onassis; (2) any blocking of her movement in public places and thoroughfares; (3) any act foreseeably or reasonably calculated to place the life and safety of defendant in jeopardy; and (4) any conduct which would reasonably be foreseen to harass, alarm or frighten the defendant.

Any further restriction on Galella's taking and selling pictures of defendant for news coverage is, however, improper and unwarranted by the evidence.

Likewise, we affirm the grant of injunctive relief to the government modified to prohibit any action interfering with Secret Service agents' protective duties. Galella thus may be enjoined from (a) entering the children's schools or play areas; (b) engaging in action calculated or reasonably foreseen to place the children's safety or well being in jeopardy, or which would threaten or create physical injury; (c) taking any action which could reasonably be foreseen to harass, alarm, or frighten the children; and (d) from approaching within thirty (30) feet of the children. . . .

As modified, the relief granted fully allows Galella the opportunity to photograph and report on Mrs. Onassis' public activities. Any prior restraint on news gathering is minuscule and fully supported by the findings.

Affirmed in part, reversed in part and remanded for modification of the judgment in accordance with this opinion. Costs on appeal to be taxed in favor of appellees.

TIMBERS, J., concurring in part and dissenting in part. With one exception, I concur in the judgment of the Court and in the able majority opinion of Judge Smith.

With the utmost deference to and respect for my colleagues, however, I am constrained to dissent from the judgment of the Court and the majority opinion to the extent that they modify the injunctive relief found necessary by the district court to protect Jacqueline Onassis and her children, Caroline B. and John F. Kennedy, Jr., from the continued predatory conduct of the self-proclaimed paparazzo Galella.

We start with what I take to be common ground that "a district court has broad discretion to enjoin possible future violations of law where past violations have been shown"; that "the court's determination [that permanent injunctive relief is required] should not be disturbed on appeal unless there has been a clear abuse of discretion"; and that "the party seeking to overturn the district court's exercise of discretion has the burden of showing that the court abused that discretion, and the burden necessarily is a heavy one." That certainly is the settled law in this Circuit. And it is the command of Fed. R. Civ. P. 52(a).

In the instant case, after a six week trial at which 25 witnesses testified, hundreds of exhibits were received and a 4,714 page record was compiled, Judge Cooper filed a careful, comprehensive 40 page opinion which meticulously sets forth detailed findings of fact and conclusions of law. As for the provisions of the injunction requiring Galella to keep certain distances away from Mrs. Onassis and her children (from the modification of which I dissent), Judge Cooper stated his reasons for these provisions as follows:

"For practical reasons, the injunction cannot be couched in terms of prohibitions upon Galella's leaping, blocking, taunting, grunting, hiding and the like. Nor have abstract concepts — harassing, endangering — proved workable. No effective relief seems possible without the fixing of proscribed distances.

"We must moreover make certain plaintiff keeps sufficiently far enough away to avoid problems as to compliance with the injunction and injurious disobedience. Disputes concerning his compliance may be frequent, thereby necessitating repeated application to the Court. Hence, the restraint must be clear, simple and effective so that Galella's substantial compliance cannot seriously be disputed unless a violation occurs.

"Of major importance in determining the scope of the relief to be afforded here is the attitude which Galella has demonstrated toward the process of this Court in the past. Galella blatantly violated our restraining orders of October 8 and December 2, 1971. He did so deliberately and in full knowledge of the fact of his violation. His deliberate disobedience to the subpoena and his attempts to obstruct justice with respect to Exhibit G, together with the perjury that infected his testimony, do not warrant mere token relief.

"In light of Galella's repeated misbehavior, it is clear that only a strong restraint — an injunction which will clearly protect Mrs. Onassis' rights and leave no room for quibbling about compliance and no room for evasion or circumvention — is appropriate in this case.

"As for the actual distance to be proscribed, we must bear in mind that plaintiff never moved to modify the distances heretofore imposed by our restraining order, even after the Court had clearly and explicitly invited him to do so if he could prove it was too harsh.

I have set forth the foregoing explanation by Judge Cooper of his reasons for the critical distance provisions of the injunction because they are weighty findings by the trial judge who had the benefit of seeing the parties before him and who obviously was in a better position than we to judge their demeanor. I feel very strongly that such findings should not be set aside or drastically modified by our Court unless they are clearly erroneous; and I do not understand the majority to suggest that they are.

But here is what the majority's modification of the critical distance provisions of the injunction has done:

Distances Galella is Required to Maintain	As Provided in District Court Injunction	As Modified by Court of Appeals Majority
From home of Mrs. Onassis and her children	100 yards	No restriction
From children's schools	100 yards	Restricted only from entering schools or play areas
From Mrs. Onassis personally	50 yards	25 feet and not to touch her
From children personally	75 yards	30 feet

In addition to modifying the distance restrictions of the injunction, the majority also has directed that Galella be prohibited from blocking Mrs. Onassis' movement in public places and thoroughfares; from any act "foreseeably or reasonably calculated" to place Mrs. Onassis' life and safety in jeopardy (and similarly with respect to her children); and from any conduct which would "reasonably be foreseen" to harass, alarm or frighten Mrs. Onassis (and similarly with respect to her children).

With deference, I believe the majority's modification of the injunction in the respects indicated above to be unwarranted and unworkable. Briefly summarized, the following are the reasons for my dissent from the modification of the injunction:

(1) The majority ignores the weighty findings of the district court. Without holding them clearly erroneous, Fed. R. Civ. P. 52(a), the majority simply sets them aside and substitutes its own perimeters for those carefully and wisely drawn by the district court.

(2) This results, for example, in a wholly unexplained and anomalous 84% reduction of the distance Galella is required to keep away from Mrs. Onassis (from 50 *yards* to 25 *feet*), and an equally implausible 87% reduction of the distance he is required to keep away from the children (from 75 *yards* to 30 *feet*).

(3) It further results in no restriction whatsoever against Galella's hovering at the entrance to the home of Mrs. Onassis and her children (where he has caused such agonizing humiliation in the past), or at the schools attended by the children — just so he does not physically enter their schools or play areas. This strikes me as an invitation for trouble.

(4) The majority, in substituting its own injunctive provisions for those of the district court, has couched its prohibitions in terms of conduct "*foreseeably or reasonably calculated*" to endanger the life or safety of Mrs. Onassis or her children, or conduct which would "*reasonably be foreseen*" to harass, alarm or frighten them (emphasis added). These are just the sort of abstract concepts which the district court found to be unworkable and ineffective. 353 F. Supp. at 237.

NOTE

Snooping and photographing and publishing. Since *Galella,* plaintiffs have had a very hard time winning cases for intrusion upon seclusion, even in cases that seem to invite application of the tort. Thus in Howell v. New York Post, Inc., 612 N.E.2d 699, 704-705 (N.Y. 1993), the plaintiff was a patient at the Four Winds Hospital, a private psychiatric hospital whose complaint (treated as true on appeal) alleged "that it was imperative to her recovery that the hospitalization remain a secret from all but her immediate family." A coresident at the facility was Hedda Nussbaum who had received massive publicity as the "adoptive" mother of 6-year-old Lisa Steinberg who had died of unrelenting child abuse. In September 1988, a photographer from the New York Post trespassed on the grounds and used a telephoto lens to take pictures of a group of patients that included Nussbaum and the plaintiff. That evening the medical director of Four Winds pleaded with the Post not to run the picture. But the next day it appeared, showing a happy and recuperating Nussbaum in the company of friends, next to a picture which showed her bruised and disfigured face at the time of her arrest. Beneath the picture was a caption which read: "The battered face above belongs to the Hedda Nussbaum people remember — the former live-in lover of Joel Steinberg. The serene woman in jeans at left is the same Hedda, strolling with a companion in the grounds of the upstate psychiatric center where her face and mind are healing from the terrible wounds Steinberg afflicted." The plaintiff's name was not used in the picture, but her identity was easily discernible.

Kaye, C.J., wrote for a unanimous court and rejected both the claim for intentional infliction of emotional distress and for an invasion of privacy. She noted first that the New York privacy statute covered only the use of the photograph in trade or advertising, neither of which was applicable here, and that the legislature had refused to expand its scope even though often requested to do so. Kaye, C.J., then noted that there was a real relationship between the public story and the inclusion of plaintiff in the picture, which blocked recognition of the privacy tort: "The visual impact would not have been the same had the Post cropped plaintiff out of the photograph, as she suggests was required. Thus, there is a real relationship between the article and the photograph of plaintiff," justifying the dismissal of the action." She then dispatched of *Galella* with equal speed:

> Courts have recognized that news-gathering methods may be tortious (see *Galella*), and, to the extent that a journalist engages in such atrocious, indecent and utterly despicable conduct as to meet the rigorous requirements of an intentional infliction of emotional distress claim, recovery may be available. The conduct alleged here, however — a trespass onto Four Winds' grounds — does not remotely approach the required standard. That plaintiff was photographed outdoors and from a distance diminishes her claim even further.

Is the gist of the complaint the taking of the picture or its use, or both combined? Has the newsworthiness privilege swallowed the basic tort of privacy in all cases save commercial appropriation? — a leading question, to be sure.

Chapter Sixteen
Misrepresentation

A. INTRODUCTION

All civil societies prohibit at least two forms of harmful conduct: aggression and deceit. In some cases the two are very much intertwined, for the man who feints before he attacks has combined both together in a single act. But most harms are accidental, yet even here some combination of force and misrepresentation may have brought that result about. Thus, a misrepresentation forms one link in the chain of causation when physical injuries are attributable to latent defects. By creating or maintaining the latent defect, the defendant has in effect misrepresented the condition of either his products or his premises, in consequence of which the plaintiff uses the product or premises in the wrong way and thus completes the causal chain. Because the plaintiff is mistaken, his intervening act does not insulate the defendant from legal responsibility. Elsewhere, misrepresentations may vitiate the plaintiff's consent to physical contact in cases of assault and battery. By way of extension of the basic principle, informed consent suits against physicians and duty to warn cases against product manufacturers concern, if not express misrepresentations, then inadequate disclosure in the face of a duty to speak. Likewise, misrepresentations play a critical role in the law of defamation, for with truth virtually an absolute defense, defamation typically covers false statements made by a defendant to a third party, to the discredit of the plaintiff.

In this chapter we consider the law of misrepresentation from a somewhat different vantage point — that of the plaintiff who claims *pecuniary* loss because he acted, to his detriment, on the faith of the defendant's misrepresentation. Typical situations include entering into a losing contract or making cash advances in reliance upon the defendant's false statements. Usually the plaintiff is required to show not only that he was misled by the defendant's misstatements, but also that the defendant knew that the statements were false, or at least was indifferent to their truth or falsity. Restatement (Second) of Torts §525 sets out the elements of common-law fraud as follows:

> One who fraudulently makes a misrepresentation of fact, opinion, intention or law for the purpose of inducing another to act or to refrain from action in reliance upon it, is subject to liability to the other in deceit for pecuniary loss caused to him by his justifiable reliance upon the misrepresentation.

The first section of the following materials is devoted to the law of fraud, and the second to the law of negligent misrepresentation.

B. FRAUD

Pasley v. Freeman
100 Eng. Rep. 450 (K.B. 1789)

[The plaintiffs were merchants who asked the defendant about the financial condition of John Christopher Falch before selling Falch a large amount of goods on credit. According to the plaintiff's allegations the defendant "did wrongfully and deceitfully encourage and persuade the said John Pasley and Edward, to sell and deliver to the said John Christopher Falch divers other goods, wares and merchandizes, to wit, 16 other bags of cochineal of great value, to wit, of the value of [about £2634] upon trust and credit; and did for that purpose then and there falsely, deceitfully, and fraudulently, assert and affirm to the said John Pasley and Edward, that the said John Christopher then and there was a person safely to be trusted and given credit in that respect." The plaintiffs further alleged that they sold the goods on credit, but that Falch, as the defendant had known all along, was a bad credit risk, wholly unable to pay for the goods; in fact he paid for no part of them. The action against the defendant was to recover from him the value of the goods sold and delivered to Falch. Verdict for the plaintiff.]

The Court took time to consider of this matter, and now delivered their opinions seriatim.

GROSE, J. Upon the face of this count in the declaration, no privity of contract is stated between the parties. No consideration arises to the defendant; and he is in no situation in which the law considers him in any trust, or in which it demands from him any account of the credit of Falch. He appears not to be interested in any transaction between the plaintiffs and Falch, nor to have colluded with them; but he knowingly asserted a falsehood, by saying that Falch might be safely entrusted with the goods, and given credit to, for the purpose of inducing the plaintiffs to trust him with them, by which the plaintiffs lost the value of the goods. Then this is an action against the defendant for making a false affirmation, or telling a lie, respecting the credit of a third person, with intent to deceive, by which the third person was damnified; and for the damages suffered, the plaintiffs contend that the defendant is answerable in an action upon the case. It is admitted, that the action is new in point of precedent: but it is insisted that the law recognises principles on which it may be supported. The principle on which it is contended to lie is, that wherever deceit or falsehood is practised to the detriment of another, the law will give redress. . . . When this was first argued at the Bar, on the motion for a new trial, I confess I thought it reasonable that the action should lie: but, on looking into the old books for cases in which the old action of deceit has been maintained upon the false affirmation of the defendant, I have changed my opinion. The cases on this head are brought together in Bro. tit. Deceit, pl. 29, & in Fitz. Abr. I have likewise looked into Danvers, Kitchins, and Comyns, and I have not met with any case of an action upon a false affirmation, except against a party to a contract, and where there is a promise, either express or implied, that the fact is true, which is misrepresented: and no other case has been cited at the Bar. Then if no such case has ever existed, it furnishes a strong objection against the action, which is brought for the first time for a supposed injury, which has been daily committed for centuries past; for I believe there has been no time when men have not been constantly damnified by the fraudulent misrepresentations of others: and if such an action would have lain, there certainly has been, and will be, a plentiful source of litigation, of which the public are not hitherto aware. A variety of cases may be put: suppose a man recommends an estate to another, as knowing it to be of greater value than it is; when the purchaser has bought it, he discovers the defect, and sells the estate for less than he gave; why may not an action be brought for the loss upon any principle that will support this action? And yet such an action has never been attempted. Or, suppose a person present at the sale of an horse asserts that he was his horse, and that he knows him to be sound and sure-footed, when in fact the horse is neither the one or the other; according to the principle contended for by the plaintiffs, an action lies against the person present as well as the seller; and the purchaser has two securities. And even in this very case, if the action lies, the plaintiffs will stand in a peculiarly fortunate predicament, for then they will have the responsibility both of Falch and the defendant. And they will be in a better situation than they would have been if, in the conversation that passed between them and the defendant, instead of asserting that Falch might safely be trusted, the defendant had said, "If he do not pay for the goods, I will:" for then undoubtedly an action would not have lain against the defendant. . . . The misrepresentation stated in the declaration is respecting the credit of Falch; the defendant asserted that the plaintiffs might safely give him credit: but credit to which a man is entitled is matter of judgment and opinion, on which different men might form different opinions, and upon which the plaintiffs might form their own; to mislead which no fact to prove the good credit of Falch is falsely asserted. It seems to me therefore that any assertion relative to credit, especially where the party making it has no interest, nor is in any collusion with the person respecting whose credit the assertion is made, is . . . not an assertion of a fact peculiarly in the knowledge of the defendant. Whether Falch deserved credit depended on the opinion of many; for credit exists on the good opinion of many. Respecting this, the plaintiffs might have inquired of others, who knew as much as the defendant; it was their fault that they did not, and they have suffered damage by their own laches. It was owing to their own gross negligence that they gave credence to the assertion of the defendant, without taking pains to satisfy themselves that that assertion was founded in fact, as in the case of Bayly v. Merrel. I am therefore of opinion, that this action is as novel in principle as it is in precedent, that it is against the principles to be collected from analogous cases, and consequently that it cannot be maintained.

BULLER, J. The foundation of this action is fraud and deceit in the defendant, and damage to the plaintiffs. And the question is, whether an action thus founded can be sustained in a Court of Law? Fraud without damage, or damage without fraud, gives no cause of action; but where these two concur, an action lies. But it is contended, that this was a bare naked lie; that, as no collusion with Falch is charged, it does not amount to a fraud: and, if there were any fraud, the nature of it is not stated. And it was supposed by the counsel who originally made the motion, that no action could be maintained, unless the defendant, who made this false assertion, had an interest in so doing. I agree that an action cannot be supported for telling a bare naked lie; but that I define to be, saying a thing which is false, knowing or not knowing it to be so, and without any design to injure, cheat, or deceive, another person. Every deceit comprehends a lie; but a deceit is more than a lie on account of the view with which it is practised, it's being coupled with some dealing, and the injury which it is calculated to occasion, and does occasion, to another person. Deceit is a very extensive head in the law; and it will be proper to take a short view of some of the cases which have existed on the subject, to see how far the Courts have gone, and what are the principles upon which they have decided. [Buller, J., then

reviewed the precedents and concluded that proof of collusion or conspiracy was not necessary to make out an action for deceit.] Some general arguments were urged at the Bar, to shew that mischiefs and
inconveniencies would arise if this action were sustained; for if a man,
who is asked a question respecting another's responsibility, hesitate, or
is silent, he blasts the character of the tradesman: and if he say that he
is insolvent, he may not be able to prove it. But let us see what is contended for: it is nothing less than that a man may assert that which he
knows to be false, and thereby do an everlasting injury to his neighbour,
and yet not be answerable for it. This is as repugnant to law as it is to
morality. Then it is said, that the plaintiffs had no right to ask the question of the defendant. But I do not agree in that; for the plaintiffs had
an interest in knowing what the credit of Falch was. It was not the inquiry of idle curiosity, but it was to govern a very extensive concern.
The defendant undoubtedly had his option to give an answer to the
question, or not: but if he gave none, or said he did not know, it is
impossible for any Court of Justice to adopt the possible inferences of
a suspicious mind as a ground for grave judgment. All that is required
of a person in the defendant's situation is, that he shall give no answer,
or that if he do, he shall answer according to the truth as far as he
knows. . . . If the answer import insolvency, it is not necessary that the
defendant should be able to prove that insolvency to a jury; for the law
protects a man in giving that answer, if he does it in confidence and
without malice. No action can be maintained against him for giving
such an answer unless express malice can be proved. From the circumstance of the law giving that protection, it seems to follow, as a necessary
consequence, that the law not only gives sanction to the question, but
requires that, if it be answered at all, it shall be answered honestly. . . .

ASHHURST, J. . . . For the gist of the action is the injury done to the
plaintiff, and not whether the defendant meant to be a gainer by it:
what is it to the plaintiff whether the defendant was or was not to gain
by it; the injury to him is the same. And it should seem that it ought
more emphatically to lie against him, as the malice is more diabolical,
if he had not the temptation of gain. For the same reason, it cannot be
necessary that the defendant should collude with one who has an interest. But if collusion were necessary, there seems all the reason in the
world to suppose both interest and collusion from the nature of the
act; for it is to be hoped that there is not to be found a disposition so
diabolical as to prompt any man to injure another without benefiting
himself. . . . Another argument which has been made use of is, that
this is a new case, and that there is no precedent of such an action.
Where cases are new in their principle, there I admit that it is necessary
to have recourse to legislative interposition in order to remedy the
grievance: but where the case is only new in the instance, and the only
question is upon the application of a principle recognized in the law to

such new case, it will be just as competent to Courts of Justice to apply the principle to any case which may arise two centuries hence as it was two centuries ago; if it were not, we ought to blot out of our law books one fourth part of the cases that are to be found in them. . . .

LORD KENYON, C.J. . . . There are many situations in life, and particularly in the commercial world, where a man cannot by any diligence inform himself of the degree of credit which ought to be given to the persons with whom he deals; in which cases he must apply to those whose sources of intelligence enable them to give that information. The law of prudence leads him to apply to them, and the law of morality ought to induce them to give the information required. In the case of Bulstrode the carrier might have weighed the goods himself: but in this case the plaintiffs had no means of knowing the state of Falch's credit but by an application to his neighbours. . . . Then it was contended here that the action cannot be maintained for telling a naked lie: but that proposition is to be taken sub modo. If, indeed, no injury is occasioned by the lie, it is not actionable: but if it be attended with a damage, it then becomes the subject of an action. As calling a woman a whore, if she sustain no damage by it, is not actionable; but if she loses her marriage by it, then she may recover satisfaction in damages. But in this case the two grounds of the action concur: here are both the damnum et injuria. The plaintiffs applied to the defendant telling him that they were going to deal with Falch, and desiring to be informed of his credit, when the defendant fraudulently, and knowing it to be otherwise, and with a design to deceive the plaintiffs, made the false affirmation which is stated on the record, by which they sustained a considerable damage. Then can a doubt be entertained for a moment but that this is injurious to the plaintiffs? If this be not an injury, I do not know how to define the word. Then as to the loss, this is stated in the declaration, and found by the verdict. Several of the words stated in this declaration, and particularly "fraudulenter," did not occur in several of the cases cited. It is admitted that the defendant's conduct was highly immoral, and detrimental to society. And I am of opinion that the action is maintainable on the grounds of deceit in the defendant, and injury and loss to the plaintiffs.

Rule for arresting the judgment discharged.

[Judgment affirmed.]

NOTES

1. The birth of an action. What would have been the impact upon commercial life if Pasley v. Freeman had been decided the other way? Would the dissent have allowed the action if the plaintiff had paid the defendant to acquire the information? Note that the early reception to *Pasley* was not always favorable. In Evans v. Bicknell, 31 Eng. Rep. 998, 1003 (Ch. 1801), Lord Eldon, stressing the difficulty of proof, said:

> So, as to the case of Pasley v. Freeman. It is almost improper at this day to say anything, having a tendency to shake it. . . . The doctrine laid down in that case is in practice and experience most dangerous. . . . [I]f the action is to be maintained in opposition to the positive denial of the Defendant against the stout assertion of a single witness, where the least deviation in the account of the conversation varies the whole, it will become necessary, in order to protect men from the consequences, that the Statute of Frauds (29 Ch. II c. 3) should be applied to that case.

2. *An action for deceit.* After *Pasley*, what is the proper scope of the action in deceit? The English courts, at least through the nineteenth century, hewed to a consistent line that the action for deceit requires, as its name suggests, proof of deliberate lying. Efforts were made from time to time to expand the potential scope of liability to reach a defendant guilty only of "legal fraud" or "fraud in law," i.e., circumstances in which the defendant makes a false statement of fact without having any reasonable grounds for believing that statement to be true — in practice a form of negligence liability. The debate over whether an action for deceit was proper for negligent misrepresentations came to a head in the famous case of Derry v. Peek, 14 App. Cas. 337, 374, 375-376 (H.L.E. 1889). The defendants were directors of a corporation who issued a prospectus in which they said that they had obtained by special act of Parliament "the right to use steam or mechanical motive power, instead of horses," to run their trams along public ways. They then claimed that this privilege would result in substantial financial advantage for the company. The plaintiff invested in shares of the company on the faith of the representations. After the investment was made it became clear that the Board of Trade could still prevent the company from using steam power. In fact, the board had consented to the use of steam and mechanical power, but only on limited portions of the company's tracks. The system built subject to this limitation was not profitable and, after the company wound up in liquidation, the plaintiff brought an action in deceit against the directors to recover the value of his original investment. The trial judge dismissed the plaintiff's cause of action, which was then allowed by the court of appeal. In Peek v. Derry, [1887] 37 Ch. 541, 566, Cotton, L.J., put the case for the plaintiff as follows:

> What, in my opinion, is a correct statement of the law is this — that where a man makes a statement to be acted upon by others which is false, and which is known by him to be false, or is made by him recklessly, or without care whether it is true or false — that is, without any reasonable ground for believing it to be true — he is liable in an action of deceit at the suit of anyone to whom it was addressed and who was materially induced by the misstatement to do an act to his prejudice.

The decision was reversed in the House of Lords. In the majority opinion Lord Herschell first took issue with Cotton's suggestion that negligence and recklessness are "convertible expressions." "To make a statement careless whether it be true or false, and therefore without any real belief in its truth, appears to me to be an essentially different thing from making, through want of care, a false statement, which is nevertheless honestly believed to be true." Later he summarized the law:

> I think the authorities establish the following propositions: First, in order to sustain an action of deceit, there must be proof of fraud, and nothing short of that will suffice. Secondly, fraud is proved when it is shewn that a false representation has been made (1) knowingly, or (2) without belief in its truth, or (3) recklessly, careless whether it be true or false. Although I have treated the second and third as distinct cases, I think the third is but an instance of the second, for one who makes a statement under such circumstances can have no real belief in the truth of what he states. To prevent a false statement being fraudulent, there must, I think, always be an honest belief in its truth. And this probably covers the whole ground, for one who knowingly alleges that which is false, has obviously no such honest belief. Thirdly, if fraud be proved, the motive of the person guilty of it is immaterial. It matters not that there was no intention to cheat or injure the person to whom the statement was made.

Elsewhere in his opinion Lord Herschell said:

> I can conceive of many cases where the fact that an alleged belief was destitute of all reasonable foundation would suffice of itself to convince the court that it was not really entertained, and that the representation was a fraudulent one. So, too, although means of knowledge are . . . a very different thing from knowledge, if I thought that a person making a false statement had shut his eyes to the facts, or purposely abstained from inquiring into them, I should hold that honest belief was absent and that he was just as fraudulent as if he had knowingly stated that which was false.

Lord Herschell then evaluated the evidence and concluded that charges of fraud could not be sustained. How might the case be argued the other way? He then expressed his misgivings about letting the defendant off scot-free:

> I have arrived with some reluctance at the conclusion to which I have felt myself compelled, for I think those who put before the public a prospectus to induce them to embark their money in a commercial enterprise ought to be vigilant to see that it contains such representations only as are in strict accordance with fact, and I should be very unwilling to give any countenance to the contrary idea. I think there is much to be said for the view that this moral duty ought to some extent to be converted into a legal obligation, and that the want of reasonable care to see

that statements, made under such circumstances, are true, should be made an actionable wrong. But this is not a matter fit for discussion on the present occasion. If it is to be done the legislature must intervene and expressly give a right of action in respect of such a departure from duty. It ought not, I think, to be done by straining the law, and holding that to be fraudulent which the tribunal feels cannot properly be so described. I think mischief is likely to result from blurring the distinction between carelessness and fraud, and equally holding a man fraudulent whether his acts can or cannot be justly so designated.

Parliament responded to the invitation with the Director's Liability Act, 1890, 53 & 54 Vict. ch. 64, which provides in part that a director or promoter of a corporation will be held liable for damages to purchasers of stocks and bonds unless the director or promoter can show that "he had reasonable ground to believe," and at all material times did believe his statements to be true. The statute also contained special rules governing the liability of directors for statements in the prospectus that reflected the opinion of experts in the venture or the state of the public record. What is the appropriate standard of liability in these cases?

3. *Securities fraud today.* The question of securities fraud is regulated extensively in this country by the Securities and Exchange Act of 1934, 15 U.S.C. §§78a-78kk (1994). Section 10(b), 15 U.S.C. §78j(b) (1994), of the statute provides that it shall be unlawful "To use or employ, in connection with the purchase or sale of any security . . . , any manipulative or deceptive device or contrivance in contravention of such rules and regulations as the Commission may prescribe as necessary or appropriate in the public interest or for the protection of investors." Pursuant to the statute, the SEC published Rule 10b-5, 17 C.F.R. §240.10b-5 (1993). It provides as follows:

EMPLOYMENT OF MANIPULATIVE AND DECEPTIVE DEVICES
It shall be unlawful for any person, directly or indirectly, by the use of any means or instrumentality of interstate commerce, or of the mails or of any facility of any national securities exchange,
(a) To employ any device, scheme, or artifice to defraud,
(b) To make any untrue statement of a material fact or to omit to state a material fact necessary in order to make the statements made, in the light of the circumstances under which they were made, not misleading, or
(c) To engage in any act, practice, or course of business which operates or would operate as a fraud or deceit upon any person,
in connection with the purchase or sale of any security.

In Ernst & Ernst v. Hochfelder, 425 U.S. 185, 199 (1976), the Supreme Court was asked to hold that negligent misrepresentations were actionable under the rule, on the ground that the effects of such misrepresentation were the same "regardless of whether the conduct is negligent or intentional." The Court rejected the invitation, noting that as a matter of ordinary English the commission's argument "simply ignores the use of the words 'manipulative,' 'device,' and 'contrivance' — terms that make unmistakable a Congressional intent to proscribe a type of conduct quite different from negligence. Use of the word 'manipulative' is especially significant. It is and was virtually a term of art when used in connection with securities markets. It connotes intentional or willful conduct designed to deceive or defraud investors by controlling or artificially affecting the price of securities." Even if the line between fraud and negligence is clear as a matter of language, should liability for misrepresentation be extended beyond deceit to cases of negligence? See infra at page 1315.

Edgington v. Fitzmaurice
29 Ch. 459 (1885)

[The plaintiff advanced £1500 for debentures of a society of which the defendants were directors and officers. In the circular distributed to raise the funds, the defendants announced that they had acquired a valuable property that was "subject to the half yearly payment of £500 in redemption of a mortgage of which £21,500 is outstanding." Elsewhere in the prospectus the defendants stated they would use the moneys raised "to complete . . . alterations and additions to the buildings, and to purchase their own horses and vans," and "to further develop the arrangements at present existing for the direct supply of cheap fish from the coast."

The statements in the prospectus were impeached on the following grounds:

1. That the prospectus was so framed as to lead to the belief that the debentures would be a charge on the property of the company.

2. That the prospectus omitted to refer to a second mortgage for £5000 to Messrs. Hores and Pattisson which had been made on the 10th of August, 1880.

3. That the prospectus stated that the property was subject to the half-yearly payment of £500 in redemption of the mortgage for £21,500, but omitted to state that on the 5th of April 1884, the whole balance of the mortgage that would then be due, namely, £18,000, might be at once called in.

4. That the real object of the issue of debentures was to pay off pressing liabilities of the company and not to complete the buildings or to purchase horses and vans or to develop the business of the company.

At trial, Denman, J., found for the plaintiffs. The defendants appealed.]

BOWEN, L.J. This is an action for deceit, in which the Plaintiff complains that he was induced to take certain debentures by the misrepresentations of the Defendants, and that he sustained damage thereby. The loss which the Plaintiff sustained is not disputed. In order to sustain his action he must first prove that there was a statement as to facts which was false; and secondly, that it was false to the knowledge of the Defendants, or that they made it not caring whether it was true or false. For it is immaterial whether they made the statement knowing it to be untrue, or recklessly, without caring whether it was true or not, because to make a statement recklessly for the purpose of influencing another person is dishonest. It is also clear that it is wholly immaterial with what object the lie is told. That is laid down in Lord Blackburn's judgment in Smith v. Chadwick [9 App. Cas. 187 (1884)], but it is material that the defendant should intend that it should be relied on by the person to whom he makes it. But, lastly, when you have proved that the statement was false, you must further shew that the plaintiff has acted upon it and has sustained damage by so doing: you must shew that the statement was either the sole cause of the plaintiff's act, or materially contributed to his so acting. So the law is laid down in Clarke v. Dickson [6 C.B. (N.S.) 453 (1859)], and that is the law which we have now to apply.

The alleged misrepresentations were three. First, it was said that the prospectus contained an implied allegation that the mortgage for £21,500 could not be called in at once, but was payable by instalments. I think that upon a fair construction of the prospectus it does so allege; and therefore that the prospectus must be taken to have contained an untrue statement on that point; but it does not appear to me clear that the statement was fraudulently made by the Defendants. It is therefore immaterial to consider whether the Plaintiff was induced to act as he did by that statement.

Secondly, it is said that the prospectus contains an implied allegation that there was no other mortgage affecting the property except the mortgage stated therein. I think there was such an implied allegation, but I think it is not brought home to the Defendants that it was made dishonestly; accordingly, although the Plaintiff may have been damnified by the weight which he gave to the allegation, he cannot rely on it in this action: for in an action of deceit the Plaintiff must prove dishonesty. Therefore if the case had rested on these two allegations alone, I think it would be too uncertain to entitle the Plaintiff to succeed.

But when we come to the third alleged misstatement I feel that the Plaintiff's case is made out. I mean the statement of the objects for which the money was to be raised. These were stated to be to complete the alterations and additions to the buildings, to purchase horses and vans, and to develope the supply of fish. A mere suggestion of possible purposes to which a portion of the money might be applied would not

have formed a basis for an action of deceit. There must be a misstatement of an existing fact: but the state of a man's mind is as much a fact
as the state of his digestion. It is true that it is very difficult to prove
what the state of a man's mind at a particular time is, but if it can be
ascertained it is as much a fact as anything else. A misrepresentation as
to the state of a man's mind is, therefore, a misstatement of fact. Having
applied as careful consideration to the evidence as I could, I have reluc-
tantly come to the conclusion that the true objects of the Defendants
in raising the money were not those stated in the circular. I will not go
through the evidence, but looking only to the cross-examination of the
Defendants, I am satisfied that the objects for which the loan was
wanted were misstated by the Defendants, I will not say knowingly, but
so recklessly as to be fraudulent in the eye of the law.

Then the question remains — Did this misstatement contribute to
induce the Plaintiff to advance his money. Mr. Davey's argument has
not convinced me that they did not. He contended that the Plaintiff
admits that he would not have taken the debentures unless he had
thought they would give him a charge on the property, and therefore
he was induced to take them by his own mistake, and the misstatement
in the circular was not material. But such misstatement was material if
it was actively present to his mind when he decided to advance his
money. The real question is, what was the state of the Plaintiff's mind,
and if his mind was disturbed by the misstatement of the Defendants,
and such disturbance was in part the cause of what he did, the mere
fact of his also making a mistake himself could make no difference. It
resolves itself into a mere question of fact. I have felt some difficulty
about the pleadings, because in the statement of claim this point is not
clearly put forward, and I had some doubt whether this contention as
to the third misstatement was not an afterthought. But the balance of
my judgment is weighed down by the probability of the case. What is
the first question which a man asks when he advances money? It is, what
is it wanted for? Therefore I think that the statement is material, and
that the Plaintiff would be unlike the rest of his race if he was not
influenced by the statement of the objects for which the loan was required. The learned Judge in the Court below came to the conclusion
that the misstatement did influence him, and I think he came to a right
conclusion.

NOTES

1. Causation in fraud cases. Will a defendant in a fraud case have a
good causal defense if the plaintiff had knowledge of the falsity at the
time the statement was made? If the plaintiff had the means to learn of
the falsity of the defendant's statements? Note that in the litigation of

fraud cases, the best defense is often a good offense. One tactic is for the defendant to show that the plaintiff, far from being deceived, is only a sore loser trying to recoup an unfortunate business investment out of the defendant's hide. Alternatively, the defendant might portray the plaintiff as fraudulent in his relations with third parties, say, persons for whom the plaintiff received a finder's fee for persuading them to invest with the defendant. As the web of interactions becomes more complex, so too does the litigation of the causation issue: far from an isolated remark, as in *Pasley*, or a single statement in a prospectus, as in *Edgington*, many fraud actions are preceeded by such a long course of dealings, some oral and some written, some formal and some informal, that the passage of time may render the statements ambiguous, or rip them out of context, making the reconstruction of the original sense a perilous and uncertain task.

2. *Materiality in fraud cases.* The proof of reliance in fraud cases presents the important issue of whether an objective or subjective standard of judgment should be used to determine whether the plaintiff's reliance was in fact "justifiable." One possible approach is to argue that the mere fact that a representation was relied on is proof of its materiality to the plaintiff. Nonetheless the cases, perhaps out of a fear of feigned suits, impose an additional requirement that the defendant's misrepresentation be of a "material" fact in order for the plaintiff's reliance to be justifiable. Under Restatement (Second) of Torts §538, a matter is regarded as material if one of two conditions is satisfied: "(a) a reasonable man would attach importance to its existence or nonexistence in determining his choice of action in the transaction in question, or (b) the maker of the representation knows or has reason to know that its recipient regards or is likely to regard the matter as important in determining his choice of action, although a reasonable man would not so regard it." The requirement is often construed as a jury control device. "The court may withdraw the case from the jury if the fact misrepresented is so obviously unimportant that the jury could not reasonably find that a reasonable man would have been influenced by it." Restatement (Second) of Torts §538 comment *e*. If a particular representation is regarded as material, should there be a presumption that the plaintiff in fact relied on it in a transaction?

The question of materiality and its relation to the issue of reliance has been much debated in cases arising under the securities law. In TSC Industries, Inc. v. Northway, Inc., 426 U.S. 438 (1976), the facts, much simplified, were as follows. National Corporation had acquired shares in a target corporation (TSC Industries) after the two companies had issued a joint proxy statement explaining the deal. The plaintiff (Northway, Inc.) was a shareholder in TSC which claimed that it had been misled into selling its shares by omissions from the proxy statement. One set of omissions had to do with the control that National already enjoyed over TSC. Thus the proxy statement did not mention that key officers of National had already assumed central managerial positions in TSC Industries. And it did not mention that under SEC rules National was regarded as TSC's "parent." The plaintiffs urged that these omissions were material because in their absence shareholders of TSC could have reasonably believed that their interests were adequately represented by the management of TSC. The proxy statement did disclose, however, that National owned 34 percent of TSC's shares and that five of TSC's ten directors were National's nominees. The Seventh Circuit nonetheless held that the omissions were material as a matter of law, using as its applicable test of materiality "all facts which a reasonable shareholder *might* consider important." The Supreme Court, concerned that this lax standard might lead to endless disclosures of trivial facts, reversed the case for a trial on the issue of materiality, stating the applicable standard as follows: "An omitted fact is material if there is a substantial likelihood that a reasonable shareholder would consider it important in deciding how to vote." Which standard better conforms to the Restatement's account of materiality? Is the same set of rules on materiality applicable to omissions as to positive misstatements?

In Basic Incorporated v. Levinson, 485 U.S. 224 (1988), the Supreme Court held that the definition of material in *TSC Industries* applied to actions brought under Rule 10b-5, governing actions for securities fraud. There the president of Basic made a public announcement that "management was unaware" of any reason for extensive trading in its stock, even though it had already been approached by a larger company seeking to acquire it. The court rejected Basic's argument that its statements were proper as long as there had been no "agreement-in-principle" for the acquisition. It wrote: "No particular event or factor short of closing the transaction need be either necessary or sufficient by itself to render merger discussions material." Rather, "materiality 'will depend at any given time upon a balancing of both the indicated probability that the event will occur and the anticipated magnitude of the event in the light of the totality of the company activities,' " which could include "board resolutions, instructions to investment bankers, and actual negotiations between principals or their intermediaries." The court then remanded the case for further consideration under its standard. What now?

3. Fraud on the market. In many cases it is difficult to trace the impact that specific misrepresentations by a defendant have on the decisions of individual market participants to buy and sell shares. Nonetheless, these misrepresentations can lead to some systematic errors in the pricing of stocks. The question then arises whether damages can be provided to persons who trade in the market in ignorance of the false statements of the defendants. Strictly construed, the traditional reliance element of the tort of deceit would block the action. In Basic, Inc. v. Levinson, supra note 2, the Supreme Court approved using the "fraud-on-the-market" theory in federal securities cases. Quoting from Peil v. Speiser, 806 F.2d 1154, 1160-1161 (3d Cir. 1986), it observed:

> The fraud on the market theory is based on the hypothesis that, in an open and developed securities market, the price of a company's stock is determined by the available material information regarding the company and its business. . . . Misleading statements will therefore defraud purchasers of stock even if the purchasers do not directly rely on the misstatements. . . . The causal connection between the defendants' fraud and the plaintiffs' purchase of stock in such a case is no less significant than in a case of direct reliance on misrepresentations.

Basic then held that the fraud-on-the-market theory was properly invoked to create a "rebuttable presumption of reliance." "Requiring proof of individualized reliance from each member of the proposed plaintiff class effectively would have prevented respondents from proceeding with a class action, since the individual issues then would have overwhelmed the common ones." It therefore concluded that although individual proof of reliance might be appropriate in the "face-to-face transactions contemplated by early fraud cases," it was inappropriate for transactions in mass markets.

Justice White dissented on the use of this theory. "But with no staff economists, no experts schooled in the 'efficient-capital-market hypothesis,' no ability to test the validity of empirical market studies, we are not well equipped to embrace novel constructions of a statute based on contemporary microeconomic theory." See generally Fischel, Use of Modern Finance Theory in Securities Fraud Cases, 38 Bus. Law. 1 (1982). On efficient markets generally see Gilson and Kraakman, The Mechanisms of Market Efficiency, 70 Va. L. Rev. 549 (1984).

4. Damages under a fraud-on-the-market theory. If the fraud-on-the-market theory is followed, how should damages be computed? Take a simple case in which a company places false statements in its prospectus in order to increase the price it can obtain for a new offering of its publicly traded stock. If a person both buys and sells shares in the firm before the fraud is unmasked, then ordinarily damages should not be allowed. The extra money paid to purchase shares is roughly offset by the extra money obtained on sale. But if an open-market purchase is made before the fraud is discovered, and the sale is made after the market breaks, then the downward adjustment in the share price (measurable, with difficulty, by statistical techniques) states the level of the damages suffered by these share purchasers.

Using the fraud-on-the-market theory still has its difficulties, however. As stated the theory makes it appear that all other market participants have suffered at the hands of the defendant. In many cases, however, large classes of ignorant buyers or sellers will *profit* incidentally from the defendant's fraud. Consider a person who owns stock in a company that launches a new issue of stock with fraudulent statements that inflate the value of both its new shares and the existing shares. The owner might dispose of the shares before the fraud is revealed, thereby obtaining a higher price than if the fraud had never been committed. The buyer of those shares will in turn suffer losses once the fraud has been revealed. The gains and losses of buyer and seller will roughly net out. Under the fraud-on-the-market theory, however, the buyer's losses will be charged to the issuer while the seller's gains will be ignored. The theory therefore may in effect overdeter fraud by overstating the *social* losses that it causes. One possible method is to set damages equal to the gains that the fraudulent defendant obtained from the fraud. Yet even these gains may be hard to measure, and, in some cases like *Basic*, appear to be nonexistent. On these damages problems see Fischel, id. at 16-17.

5. *Contributory negligence in fraud cases.* In Seeger v. Odell, 115 P.2d 977 (Cal. 1941), Traynor, J., noted: "Negligence on the part of the plaintiff in failing to discover the falsity of a statement is no defense when the misrepresentation was intentional rather than negligent." An explanation for that rule has been offered by Easterbrook, J., in Teamsters Local 282 Pension Trust Fund v. Angelos, 762 F.2d 522, 528 (7th Cir. 1985), where he held that the failure of a pension trustee to investigate did not relieve the defendant of liability for securities fraud.

> Securities law seeks to impose on issuers duties to disclose, the better to obviate the need for buyers to investigate. The buyer's investigation of things already known to the seller is a wasteful duplication of effort. If the securities laws worked perfectly there would be little need for investigation; sellers would disclose to the buyers and the market the information necessary for informed trading. Because some frauds will not be caught, and because people cannot interpret information flawlessly, this mechanism cannot work perfectly. This failure makes investigations by investors necessary and creates incentives for sellers to hire certifiers (such as auditors and investment bankers) to verify sellers' statements. But such investigations and other devices are distinctly second-best solutions to legal and practical problems, and we will not establish a legal rule under which investors must resort to the costly self-help approach of investigation on pain of losing the protection of the principal legal safeguard, the rule against fraud.
>
> This is just another way to state the common law rule that contributory negligence is not a defense to an intentional or reckless tort.

Vulcan Metals Co. v. Simmons Mfg. Co.
248 F. 853 (2d Cir. 1918)

[Simmons Manufacturing sold to Vulcan Manufacturing Co. all of its patents, tools, dies, and equipment for the manufacture of vacuum cleaners, together with all machines and parts then on hand. During the course of the negotiations for the sale, Simmons's agents made two sorts of representations to Albert Freeman, a promoter of the Vulcan Corporation. The first group of representations included "commendations of the cleanliness, economy, and efficiency of the machine"; that it was superior to rival methods of cleaning, such as "beating and brushing"; that it was so simple that a child of six could use it; that it was durable and long-lasting; and that it promised its users perfect satisfaction, if properly adjusted. The second class of representations was that the defendant "[c]ompany had not sold the machine, or made any attempt to sell it; that they had not shown it to any one; that it had never been on the market, and that no one outside the company officials and the men in the factory knew anything about it." Although 15,000 were on hand, the defendant's agent said "it would be a mistake for them to attempt to sell these along with their ordinary line, which was furniture."

The plaintiff's action for deceit alleged that the purchase was made on the strength of these representations, but that "the machines and patents were totally inefficient and unmarketable." The counterclaim was brought by Simmons on the notes that had been signed by Vulcan for part of the purchase price; Freeman had signed as a guarantor on the notes. The district court directed a verdict for Simmons on both the original action and the counterclaim, finding that Vulcan had not proved any actionable fraud. The record showed that the machines, when exploited by Vulcan, were of little value and that "their manufacture was discontinued by that company not very long after they had undertaken it." There was also evidence that defendant's agents had made several efforts to sell the machines, which had proved unsuccessful because the machines could not create the vacuum necessary for their operation.]

L. HAND, J. (after stating the facts as above). The first question is of the misrepresentations touching the quality and powers of the patented machine. These were general commendations, or, in so far as they included any specific facts, were not disproved; e.g., that the cleaner would produce 18 inches of vacuum with 25 pounds water pressure. They raise, therefore, the question of law how far general "puffing" or "dealers' talk" can be the basis of an action for deceit.

The conceded exception in such cases has generally rested upon the distinction between "opinion" and "fact"; but that distinction has not escaped the criticism it deserves. An opinion is a fact, and it may be a very relevant fact; the expression of an opinion is the assertion of a belief, and any rule which condones the expression of a consciously false opinion condones a consciously false statement of fact. When the parties are so situated that the buyer may reasonably rely upon the expression of the seller's opinion, it is no excuse to give a false one. And so it makes much difference whether the parties stand "on an

equality." For example, we should treat very differently the expressed
opinion of a chemist to a layman about the properties of a composition
from the same opinion between chemist and chemist, when the buyer
had full opportunity to examine. The reason of the rule lies, we think,
in this: There are some kinds of talk which no sensible man takes seriously, and if he does he suffers from his credulity. If we were all scrupulously honest, it would not be so; but, as it is, neither party usually
believes what the seller says about his own opinions, and each knows it.
Such statements, like the claims of campaign managers before election,
are rather designed to allay the suspicion which would attend their
absence than to be understood as having any relation to objective truth.
It is quite true that they induce a compliant temper in the buyer, but it
is by a much more subtle process than through the acceptance of his
claims for his wares.

So far as concerns statements of value, the rule is pretty well fixed
against the buyer. . . .

In the case at bar, since the buyer was allowed full opportunity to
examine the cleaner and to test it out, we put the parties upon an
equality. It seems to us that general statements as to what the cleaner
would do, even though consciously false, were not of a kind to be taken
literally by the buyer. As between manufacturer and customer, it may
not be so; but this was the case of taking over a business, after ample
chance to investigate. Such a buyer, who the seller rightly expects will
undertake an independent and adequate inquiry into the actual merits
of what he gets, has no right to treat as material in his determination
statements like these. The standard of honesty permitted by the rule
may not be the best; but, as Holmes, J., says in Deming v. Darling, 20
N.E. 107 (Mass. 1889), the chance that the higgling preparatory to a
bargain may be afterwards translated into assurances of quality may
perhaps be a set-off to the actual wrong allowed by the rule as it stands.
We therefore think that the District Court was right in disregarding all
these misrepresentations.

As respects the representation that the cleaners had never been put
upon the market or offered for sale, the rule does not apply; nor can
we agree that such representations could not have been material to
Freeman's decision to accept the contract. The actual test of experience in their sale might well be of critical consequence in his decision
to buy the business, and the jury would certainly have the right to accept his statement that his reliance upon these representations was determinative of his final decision. We believe that the facts as disclosed
by the depositions of the Western witnesses were sufficient to carry to
the jury the question whether those statements were false. It is quite
true, as the District Judge said, that the number of sales was small, perhaps not 60 in all; but they were scattered in various parts of the Mountain and Pacific States, and the jury might conclude that they were

enough to contradict the detailed statements of Simmons that the machines had been kept off the market altogether.

[The court then discussed whether this second misrepresentation was adequately retracted prior to the contract, and, after a rehearing, affirmed the judgment for Simmons.]

NOTES

1. Puffing. A broad latitude for puffing was recognized by Holmes, J., in Deming v. Darling, 20 N.E. 107, 108-109 (Mass. 1889). There plaintiff purchased a railroad bond from the defendant's agent. The agent had described the railroad mortgage as good security for the bond and had said that "the bond was of the very best and safest, and was an A No. 1 Bond." The jury was instructed to find for the defendant if the statement were made in good faith, but not if otherwise. On appeal from plaintiff's verdict, the defendant's exceptions to the instructions were upheld.

> It will be seen that the fundamental difference between the instructions given and those asked is that the former require good faith. The language of some cases certainly seems to suggest that bad faith might make a seller liable for what are known as seller's statements, apart from any other conduct by which the buyer is fraudulently induced to forbear inquiries. But this is a mistake. It is settled that the law does not exact good faith from a seller in those vague commendations of his wares which manifestly are open to difference of opinion, which do not imply untrue assertions concerning matters of direct observation, and as to which it always has been "understood, the world over that such statements are to be distrusted." Brown v. Castles, 11 Cush. 348, 350. Parker v. Moulton [114 Mass. 99 (1873)] also shows that the rule is not changed by the mere fact that the property is at a distance, and is not seen by the buyer. Moreover, in this case, market prices at least were easily accessible to the plaintiff.
>
> The defendant was known by the plaintiff's agent to stand in the position of a seller. If he went no further than to say that the bond was an A No. 1 bond, which we understand to mean simply that it was a first rate bond, or that the railroad was good security for the bonds, we are constrained to hold that he is not liable under the circumstances of this case, even if he made the statement in bad faith. The rule of law is hardly to be regretted, when it is considered how easily and insensibly words of hope or expectation are converted by an interested memory into statements of quality and value when the expectation has been disappointed.

Is the risk identified by Holmes present in the case at hand?

With *Deming* contrast Maxwell Ice Co. v. Brackett Shaw & Lunt Co., 116 A. 34, 36 (N.H. 1921), where the seller represented that a certain engine had sufficient power to meet the buyer's needs. The court held that the representations were not mere puff.

Representations by an expert on power to one not having equal knowledge as to the amount of energy which standard makes of motors and engines will develop, are not future promises, but are statements with reference to known facts based on tests and mathematical computations. Such representations differ materially from "sellers' talk" or mere opinions expressed to one having equal knowledge or equal opportunities for knowledge. In "the case of an expert stating to a non-expert his opinion on matters requiring peculiar skill or knowledge . . . it is difficult to see why a plaintiff (who acts reasonably in relying on the statement) may not recover against one who negligently volunteers an erroneous 'opinion,' intending the plaintiff to act upon it, and knowing that substantial loss is likely to follow if the 'opinion' proves incorrect. . . . Negligent misstatement exists just the same, whether it be due to carelessness in forming a belief or to carelessness in the mode of expressing one's belief."

2. *Misrepresentations of law.* At common law the dominant rule once provided that the action for deceit did not lie for misrepresentations of law. One motivation behind this general rule was doubtless the belief that propositions of law were generally matters of public record to which the plaintiff and defendant had equal access. Closely related was a second point, that the plaintiff could confirm those representations from an independent source if he desired. Nonetheless, the older rule has largely given way so that, especially in cases of "mixed" fact and law, suits for fraud may be routinely brought. In National Conversion Corp. v. Cedar Building Corp., 246 N.E.2d 351, 355 (N.Y. 1969), the plaintiff tenant entered into a five-year lease with the defendant after the landlord had represented in the lease that the demised premises were in an unrestricted zone and thus suitable for the plaintiff's business of converting restaurant garbage into fertilizer. The representations were false and the plaintiff was allowed to recover the rentals paid prior to the rescission as well as the costs of the installation and removal of the plaintiff's equipment. The court, per Breitel, J., specifically rejected the claim that the defendant's misrepresentations were not actionable:

Landlords also contend that only a misrepresentation of law rather than of fact is involved and, therefore, that fraud will not lie. There is no longer any doubt that the law has recognized, even in this State, a sharp distinction between a pure opinion of law which may not, except in unusual circumstances, base an action in tort, and a mixed statement of fact as to what the law is or whether it is applicable. In [Municipal Metallic Bed Mfg. Corp. v. Dobbs, 253 N.Y. 313, 316-318], it was held explicitly that a landlord's misrepresentation as to legality of use of demised premises would not, as to the tenant, be treated as an opinion of law, and that the tenant might rely on the contract representations of the landlord.

Most important it is that the law has outgrown the over-simple dichotomy between law and fact in the resolution of issues in deceit. It has been said that "a statement as to the law, like a statement as to anything else, may be intended and understood either as one of fact or one of opinion only, according to the circumstances of the case" (Prosser, [3d ed.] p. 741). The statements in this case, both before the execution of the lease, and in the body of the lease, exemplify ideally an instance in which the statements are not intended or understood merely as an expression of opinion. Landlords said they knew the premises were in an unrestricted district. This meant that they knew as a fact, that the zoning resolution did not restrict the use of the particular premises, and tenant so understood it. When coupled with the further fact that tenant's lawyer was persuaded not to verify the status of the premises on the landlords' representation, it is equally clear that tenant understood the statement to be one of fact, namely, what the zoning resolution provided by description, map, and requirements as to the area in question. The misrepresented fact, if it is at all necessary to find misrepresented facts, was what the zoning resolution contained by way of description, map, and requirements, hardly opinions as to the law albeit matters to be found in a law.

Swinton v. Whitinsville Savings Bank
42 N.E.2d 808 (Mass. 1942)

QUA, J. The declaration alleges that on or about September 12, 1938, the defendant sold the plaintiff a house in Newton to be occupied by the plaintiff and his family as a dwelling; that at the time of the sale the house "was infested with termites, an insect that is most dangerous and destructive to buildings"; that the defendant knew the house was so infested; that the plaintiff could not readily observe this condition upon inspection; that, "knowing the internal destruction that these insects were creating in said house," the defendant falsely and fraudulently concealed from the plaintiff its true condition; that the plaintiff at the time of his purchase had no knowledge of the termites, exercised due care thereafter, and learned of them about August 30, 1940; and that, because of the destruction that was being done and the dangerous condition that was being created by the termites, the plaintiff was put to great expense for repairs and for the installation of termite control in order to prevent the loss and destruction of said house.

There is no allegation of any false statement or representation, or of the uttering of a half truth which may be tantamount to a falsehood. There is no intimation that the defendant by any means prevented the plaintiff from acquiring information as to the condition of the house. There is nothing to show any fiduciary relation between the parties, or that the plaintiff stood in a position of confidence toward or dependence upon the defendant. So far as appears the parties made a business deal at arm's length. The charge is concealment and nothing more; and it is concealment in the simple sense of mere failure to reveal, with nothing to show any peculiar duty to speak. The characterization of the concealment as false and fraudulent of course adds nothing in the absence of further allegations of fact.

If this defendant is liable on this declaration every seller is liable who fails to disclose any nonapparent defect known to him in the subject of the sale which materially reduces its value and which the buyer fails to discover. Similarly it would seem that every buyer would be liable who fails to disclose any nonapparent virtue known to him in the subject of the purchase which materially enhances its value and of which the seller is ignorant. See Goodwin v. Agassiz, 186 N.E. 659 (Mass. 1933). The law has not yet, we believe, reached the point of imposing upon the frailties of human nature a standard so idealistic as this. That the particular case here stated by the plaintiff possesses a certain appeal to the moral sense is scarcely to be denied. Probably the reason is to be found in the facts that the infestation of buildings by termites has not been common in Massachusetts and constitutes a concealed risk against which buyers are off their guard. But the law cannot provide special rules for termites and can hardly attempt to determine liability according to the varying probabilities of the existence and discovery of different possible defects in the subjects of trade.

[Affirmed.]

NOTE

Latent defects: liability for nondisclosure by a seller? What result in the *Swinton* case if the defendant had said that the plaintiff was "sure to love his new house"? Could a demand for a high price be treated as an implicit representation that the house is worth the money that it costs? If the defendant had plastered over the parts of the woodwork where termites were present, could the action for concealment properly lie, even for Qua, J.? See Osborn v. Gene Teague Chevrolet Co., 459 P.2d 988 (Or. 1969), sustaining the plaintiff's verdict in a fraud case in which the defendant used car dealer had set back the odometer from 100,000 to 62,000 miles, even in the absence of any verbal misrepresentation.

Note that the conclusion reached in *Swinton* has been subject to attack in recent years. The Restatement (Second) of Torts §551 qualifies its general rule of nondisclosure with a long list of exceptions, the last of which requires disclosure of "facts basic to the transaction, if he [the defendant] knows that the other is about to enter into it under a mistake as to them, and that the other, because of the relationship between them, the customs of the trade or other objective circumstances, would reasonably expect a disclosure of those facts." The provision is then illustrated as follows: "*A* sells to *B* a dwelling house, without disclosing to *B* the fact that the house is riddled with termites. This is a fact basic to the transaction." What evidence of community norms might be relevant to the question of whether disclosure is required? If the standard contract for a home purchase contains an explicit warranty by the seller that a house is free of termites or other latent defects, is disclosure required when that contract is not used?

In reliance on Restatement (Second) §551, the duty to disclose has also been imposed with respect to conditions external to the property sold. In Strawn v. Canuso, 638 A.2d 141, 149, 150 (N.J. Super. A.D. 1994), the defendant developer and broker did not disclose that the new home they sold to plaintiff was located near a closed landfill site that contained many toxic substances. "The imposition of this duty comports with modern notions of justice, fair dealing and sound public policy of protecting home buyers in large developments who have limited bargaining power." The court also noted that an additional reason exists for imposing this duty.

> Even where no duty to speak exists, one who elects to speak must tell the truth when it is apparent that another may reasonably rely on the statements made. Here, the developer and broker chose to utilize the environment beyond the boundary lines of the developments to sell or enhance the saleability of the homes. The brochures and advertisements made the environment and off-site properties relevant to each sale by stating that the area was safe to go "hiking in the woods," that children could grow up in the "healthy, fresh, country air" and that country clubs and shopping malls were nearby. Having elected to use the off-site environment to induce sales, the seller and broker were obligated to disclose the existence of a landfill which could have a substantial negative impact upon the value of the homes and the quality of life in the area.

The court then rejected the defendants' claim that the plaintiffs were charged with constructive knowledge of the landfill because the condition was open and notorious, noting that "the doctrine of constructive knowledge cannot 'serve as a shield of protection from accountability for one who makes false representations to another's damage.' "

Laidlaw v. Organ
15 U.S. 178 (1817)

[The plaintiff Organ was a New Orleans merchant in the tobacco trade. He had learned from a friend that peace had been concluded between the British and American forces. Before the information had been made public, he had contracted to purchase a large order of tobacco from Laidlaw. Before the sale was completed the defendant Laidlaw had asked the plaintiff whether he knew any information that would affect the price of the tobacco; from the record it is unclear whether the plaintiff had made any reply, and if so, what he had said. When the peace was announced the price of tobacco advanced between 30 and 50 percent and Laidlaw, who had delivered the tobacco to Organ, repossessed it by force. Organ brought suit for damages for the loss of the tobacco. The key question in the case was whether their prior agreement, pursuant to which the tobacco was transferred, was vitiated by fraud or nondisclosure. The jury found that Organ was entitled to the tobacco, whereupon Laidlaw appealed. After extensive argument Marshall, C.J., issued a brief opinion.]

MARSHALL, C.J. The question in this case is, whether the intelligence of extrinsic circumstances, which might influence the price of the commodity, and which was exclusively within the knowledge of the vendee, ought to have been communicated by him to the vendor? The court is of opinion that he was not bound to communicate it. It would be difficult to circumscribe the contrary doctrine within proper limits, where the means of intelligence are equally accessible to both parties. But at the same time, each party must take care not to say or do any thing tending to impose upon the other. The court thinks that the absolute instruction of the judge was erroneous, and that the question, whether any imposition was practised by the vendee upon the vendor ought to have been submitted to the jury. For these reasons the judgment must be reversed, and the cause remanded to the district court of Louisiana, with directions to award a venire facias de novo [new trial].

NOTES

1. Latent virtue: liability for nondisclosure by a buyer? Unlike the latent defect cases, see *Swinton* supra, the nondisclosure of a material fact may be made by the buyer who happens to have superior information about the subject matter of the contract. The situation can occur in contexts far removed from the stock market. Thus, the proprietor of a second-hand music store may sell a Stradivarius violin for a trifling price to a violin expert who happens to wander into the premises. Generally, the buyer is under no duty to disclose, even though the price would surely be higher if the seller knew the violin's pedigree. See Restatement (Second) of Torts §551 comment *k*, illustration 6.

A similar problem can also arise in the purchase of land. Generally, the purchaser of farmland need not disclose that he is buying it because he believes that it contains oil. Similarly, the land developer who takes an option on farmland in order to assemble a large parcel of land from several buyers for a major real estate development is normally under no duty to disclose the purpose of his venture, and may even act in a manner calculated to persuade his seller that he is in fact only interested in farmland for its own sake. An explanation for the rule is offered in Guaranty Safe Deposit & Trust Co. v. Liebold, 56 A. 951, 953 (Pa. 1904), where the option in question had been procured by the trust company in order to provide a site for a steel mill. The court justified its judgment for the trust company as follows:

In this commercial age options are daily procured by those in possession of information from which they expect to profit, simply because those from whom the options are sought are ignorant of it. When the prospective seller knows as much as the prospective buyer, options can rarely, if ever, be procured, and the rule that counsel for appellant would have us apply would practically abolish them. The prospective buyer seeks an option instead of at once entering into a contract for the purchase of land, because, no matter what information he may possess exclusively, he is unwilling to act upon it until it becomes a certainty. In the meantime, on the contingency of its becoming so, he makes his contingent bargain to purchase. This is fair in law and in morals. If the appellee concealed anything it was his duty to disclose, or said anything to mislead or deceive the appellant, this rule, of course, would not apply; but they dealt at arm's length, as men always do under such circumstances, each trying to make what was supposed to be the best bargain for himself at the time.

The court then noted that its conclusion was especially apt because Liebold had increased the price for the land in response to a "rumor" that a large manufacturing company was contemplating setting up business in town.

2. *Insider trading.* The question of undisclosed information is also important in cases of the purchase of common stock by corporate insiders, typically directors, key officers, or major shareholders. In the famous case of Goodwin v. Agassiz, 186 N.E. 659, 661 (Mass. 1933), the defendants were directors of a corporation that purchased shares over the Boston Exchange from the plaintiff, himself an experienced trader who had kept records of his own transactions in the company stock. The plaintiff sought to rescind the sale or obtain other appropriate relief on the ground that the defendants did not disclose that they had received reports from a geologist which indicated that certain properties owned by the corporation might have valuable mineral deposits. The court rejected the defendant's contention that it had acted properly, but held in effect that the plaintiff was barred because he "made no inquiries of the defendant or of other officers of the company."

> Fiduciary obligations of directors ought not to be made so onerous that men of experience and ability will be deterred from accepting such office. Law in its sanctions is not coextensive with morality. It cannot take to put all parties to every contract on an equality as to knowledge, experience, skill and shrewdness. It cannot undertake to relieve against hard bargains made between competent parties without fraud. On the other hand, directors cannot rightly be allowed to indulge with impunity in practices which do violence to prevailing standards of upright business men. Therefore, where a director personally seeks a stockholder for the purpose of buying his shares without making disclosure of material facts within his peculiar knowledge and not within reach of the stockholder, the transaction will be closely scrutinized and relief may be granted in appropriate instances.

What might these instances be? Should the transaction in *Goodwin* be judged by the same rules applicable to latent defects in real estate?

There is today extensive regulation of insider trading under the current securities legislation, most of which requires that directors disclose before they trade on inside information. See, e.g., SEC v. Texas Gulf Sulfur Co. 401 F.2d 833 (2d Cir. 1968), another famous case involving mineral deposits. In *Goodwin* should it make a difference if there were other transactions between unrelated parties on the day that the plaintiff sold to the defendants? What should be done when a director trades on inside information in the exchanges, but the matching buyer cannot be found? Should the rule be different if the insider sells his shares or sells short because he has undisclosed information about the firm's incompetence? In principle, should it make a difference if the corporate charter generally permits insiders to trade over the organized exchange? There is a huge amount of literature on insider trading; see, e.g., Carlton and Fischel, The Regulation of Insider Trading, 35 Stan. L. Rev. 857 (1983).

3. An economic account of nondisclosure. As these materials make clear, the entire question of nondisclosure between the parties can always be clarified by an agreement between them. A purchaser can always ask a seller point blank if the premises are infested with termites; a seller can always ask a buyer if he thinks oil lies under his farmland or whether the land is to be used for industrial development. If the party so asked responds with a falsehood, the ordinary rules of fraud apply; and if he says that he chooses not to answer the question at all, the other party is on notice and can refuse to deal further. Within this environment the function of the law is to devise a set of rules that are applicable in those cases in which there are no explicit understandings. One notable effort to find a coherent set of principles to govern nondisclosure cases is found in Kronman, Mistake, Disclosure, Information, and the Law of Contracts, 7 J. Legal Stud. 1, 9 (1978), who argues:

> Where nondisclosure is permitted (or put differently, where the knowledgeable party's contract rights are enforced despite his failure to disclose a known mistake), the knowledge involved is typically the product of a costly search. A rule permitting nondisclosure is the only effective way of providing an incentive to invest in the production of such knowledge. By contrast, in the cases requiring disclosure, and in those excusing a unilaterally mistaken promisor because the other party knew or had reason to know of his error, the knowledgeable party's special information is typically not the fruit of a deliberate search. Although information of this sort is socially useful as well, a disclosure requirement will not cause a sharp reduction in the amount of such information which is actually produced. If one takes into account the investment costs incurred in the deliberate production of information, the two apparently divergent lines of cases described above may both be seen as conforming (roughly) to the principle of efficiency, which requires that the risk of a unilateral mistake be placed on the most effective risk-preventer.

Kronman then applies his analysis to most of the cases set out above. How good is the fit? Is expertise important even if there is a general duty to disclose? When that duty may be disclaimed by contract? In the case of insider trading, can it be argued that management will not undertake risky exploratory activities unless it can capture part of the gain by the purchase of shares?

Selman v. Shirley
91 P.2d 312 (Or. 1939)

[The plaintiffs purchased a parcel of real property from the defendants. The terms of the purchase called for a total price of $2,000, of which $500 was paid down in cash and the balance was due in annual installments of $200. Shortly after the sale was complete, the plaintiffs took possession of the property. After some $750 had been paid on the purchase price, they refused to make any additional payments on the ground that the defendant's fraud had induced the purchase and sale. The trial judge found that "the defendant, H. E. Shirley, knowingly and falsely represented to plaintiff that there was at least 4,000 cords of wood on said premises; that said representation was false and was made by defendant H. E. Shirley with the intention of inducing plaintiffs to purchase said premises; that the plaintiffs in purchasing said premises relied upon said representations."

The stated value of the wood was $0.50 per cord. There was also a finding that the defendants deliberately misrepresented to the plaintiffs that the land was well irrigated by a stream running through it. The court found ample support for these findings in the record, and then addressed the question of the proper remedy:]

ROSSMAN, J. As we have stated, the plaintiffs retained possession of the property after they discovered the fraud which had been practiced upon them. It has been many times stated by this court that a defrauded party is not required to rescind the contract in order to sue for deceit, and that if he affirms the contract he does not thereby waive his right to recover damages for the fraud which had been practiced upon him.

The plaintiffs argue that they are entitled to the benefit of their bargain which contemplated that they should have, not only 160 acres of land but also a growth of timber upon the land aggregating 4,000 cords and a good irrigating stream; and that the rule which measures their damages should be based upon that premise. The defendants contend that this court has rejected the benefit-of-the-bargain rule in favor of the rule which grants damages equal only to the out-of-pocket loss. The rule championed by the plantiffs would certainly be available if this action were based upon a warranty and were, therefore, contractual in nature. In support of their contentions that this court has rejected the benefit-of-the-bargain rule in fraud actions, the defendants cite [a number of Oregon decisions. The court then examines the cases in great detail and continues:]

It will be observed that in the three decisions just reviewed the defrauded party got the benefit of his bargain and that the out-of-pocket-loss rule was not employed. In one of them the out-of-pocket-loss rule was expressly rejected, the decision declaring that it is "applicable where property is exchanged." The fact that the defrauded party had sold the property and had, possibly, received for it more than he paid was deemed immaterial.

The rule which gives to the defrauded party the benefit of his bargain is favored by the textbook writers. The following is quoted from Williston on Contracts (rev. ed.) §1392:

"Not all courts allow the same damages to a buyer who has been induced to buy by fraudulent representations and sues for the deceit as to a buyer who sues for breach of warranty. The contrary view, confining the damages in deceit to the value of what the plaintiff parted with, less the value of what he received, has the support of the Supreme Court of the United States, and of some state courts. This also seems to be the law of England. At first sight it may seem that the latter rule is clearly and universally correct, confining as it does the plaintiff's recovery to a restitution of what he lost by entering into the transaction. The real explanation of the broader rule, at least in cases of sales of goods, seems to be that the defendant in deceit is not simply a fraudulent person; he is a warrantor of the truth of his statements. The injured person may, because of fraud, elect to rescind the transaction and claim restitution of what he has parted with, or he may demand that the representations be made good. Ordinary warranties where no fraud exists may be enforced by action of tort. The addition of the element of deceit cannot deprive the injured person of the rights which would be his if this element were lacking, and if the representation on which he relied were a warranty and nothing more. Nor is a strictness of pleading to be defended that denies to a plaintiff the relief that would be his if he omitted an allegation that the representation of the quality of goods, of which he complains, was fraudulent. A practical reason for the enforcement of the broader rule may be found in the fact that under the other rule a fraudulent person can in no event lose anything by his fraud. He runs the chance of making a profit if he successfully carries out his plan and is not afterward brought to account for it; and if he is brought to account, he at least will lose nothing by his misconduct. . . . Any universal statement, therefore, that the damages for fraudulent misrepresentation are the difference between the law governing sales of goods and that governing other transactions may explain some apparently inconsistent decisions."

Sedgwick on Damages (9th ed.), §1027, in stating the measure of damages where fraud is employed in the course of a sale of land, declares:

"In such actions, as in actions for fraud in the sale of chattels, it has usually been held that the measure of damages is the difference in value between the land as it would have been if as represented and as it actually was." . . .

However, the Restatement of the Law of Torts, §549, embraces the out-of-pocket-loss rule. We quote from it the following:

"The measure of damages which the recipient of a fraudulent misrepresentation is entitled to recover from its maker as damages under the rule stated in §525 is the pecuniary loss which results from the falsity of the matter misrepresented, including

(a) the difference between the value of the thing bought, sold or exchanged and its purchase price or the value of the thing exchanged for it,

(b) . . . ."

Williston on Contracts (rev. ed.), §1392, referring to the section of the Restatement just quoted, declares that it "adopts the minority rule." Professor Williston continues that under the maxim adopted by the Restatement, "if fraudulent representations constitute a warranty also, recovery may be had on that basis"; that is, the defrauded party obtains the benefit of his bargain. . . .

We come now to an effort to reconcile our decisions and to deduce a rule therefrom. First of all, it is evident that the party guilty of fraud is liable for such damages as naturally and proximately resulted from the fraud. This is the universal rule. Next, our decisions warrant the conclusions: (1) If the defrauded party is content with the recovery of only the amount that he actually lost, his damages will be measured under that rule; (2) if the fraudulent representation also amounted to a warranty, recovery may be had for loss of the bargain because a fraud accompanied by a broken promise should cost the wrongdoer as much as the latter alone; (3) where the circumstances disclosed by the proof are so vague as to cast virtually no light upon the value of the property had it conformed to the representations, the court will award damages equal only to the loss sustained; and (4) where the damages under the benefit-of-the-bargain rule are proved with sufficient certainty, that rule will be employed.

In the present instance, the plaintiffs are clearly the victims of a fraud. . . . We conclude that the plaintiffs are entitled to damages awarded upon the basis of 50 cents per cord for the difference between the represented 4,000 cords and the actual 200 cords. . . .

[The dissent of Belt, J., supported the rule that allowed the aggrieved party in a fraud action to claim only out-of-pocket damages, i.e., the difference between cash or the market value of the property transferred over the market value of the property received.]

NOTE

Remedies for deceit. As *Selman* indicates, there is a heavy overlap between the law of misrepresentation and the law of contract. In a sense, the result hardly could have been otherwise, given that misrepresentations are necessarily made to persons selected by the defendant or to persons who choose of their own volition to rely on them. This overlap becomes of great importance in selecting the proper remedy. Although a plaintiff may seek enforcement of the contract under a warranty or specific performance theory, when a contract for the sale of real property has been induced by fraud, he may also seek to rescind the contract and return to the status quo ante. Indeed, the general rule usually allows a party both to resist the performance of a contract in its executory stages and to rescind a contract already executed, even for the innocent misrepresentations of the other party. See, e.g., Derry v. Peek, 14 A.C. 337 (1889), where Lord Herschell said: "Where rescission is claimed it is only necessary to prove that there was misrepresentation; then, however honestly it may have been made, however free from blame the person who made it, the contract, having been obtained by misrepresentation, cannot stand." What is the functional difference between an action for rescission and an action for damages restricted to the difference between contract and market price?

Whatever its theoretical soundness, *Selman* represents the dominant rule. Restatement (Second) of Torts §549 now provides:

> §549. MEASURE OF DAMAGES FOR FRAUDULENT MISREPRESENTATION
>   (1) The recipient of a fraudulent misrepresentation is entitled to recover as damages in an action of deceit against the maker the pecuniary loss to him of which the misrepresentation is a legal cause, including
>   (a) the difference between the value of what he has received in the transaction and its purchase price or other value given for it; and
>   (b) pecuniary loss suffered otherwise as a consequence of the recipient's reliance upon the misrepresentation.
>   (2) The recipient of a fraudulent misrepresentation in a business transaction is also entitled to recover additional damages sufficient to give him the benefit of his contract with the maker, if these damages are proved with reasonable certainty.

The application of the proviso in section 549(a)(2) is illustrated by Fitzsimmons v. Chapman, 37 Mich. 139, 141 (1877). There the plaintiff paid $600 to a fund raised by the defendant in order to bring the manufacturing firm of Colby Brothers & Co. from Vermont to the plaintiff's home town in Michigan. The plaintiff paid the money into the fund because the defendant had fraudulently represented that Colby Brothers was in good financial shape and that bringing the company to town could increase the value of all the property therein, including the plaintiff's, by an amount far in excess of the cash payment needed to lure it from Vermont. The defendant also stated that he would contribute $2,000 to the effort, but contributed only property that he had overvalued at $1,600. Colby Brothers did move into town, but was in such poor financial shape that its presence did nothing to improve the local economy or to increase the value of plaintiff's real estate. In his action for fraud the plaintiff did not seek to recover the moneys paid over into the fund, but his loss of benefits stemming from the inferior performance of Colby's. The action was denied on the ground that "[s]uch benefits are purely speculative and imaginative" in light of the myriad ways in which the town might have prospered had Colby's been in strong financial shape. What result if Colby's had never come to town? If the plaintiff had sued to recover his contribution to the fund? The Restatement tracks the rule applied in normal contract cases, which awards reliance damages when expectation damages are too speculative to allow for precise calculation. See Security Store & Mfg. Co. v. American Railways Express Co., 51 S.W.2d 572 (Mo. App. 1932); C. Fried, Contract as Promise, 21-22 (1981).

C. NEGLIGENT MISREPRESENTATION

Ultramares Corporation v. Touche
174 N.E. 441 (N.Y. 1931)

CARDOZO, C.J. The action is in tort for damages suffered through the misrepresentations of accountants, the first cause of action being for misrepresentations that were merely negligent and the second for misrepresentations charged to have been fraudulent.

In January, 1924, the defendants, a firm of public accountants, were employed by Fred Stern & Co., Inc., to prepare and certify a balance sheet exhibiting the condition of its business as of December 31, 1923. They had been employed at the end of each of the three years preceding to render a like service. Fred Stern & Co., Inc., which was in substance Stern himself, was engaged in the importation and sale of rubber. To finance its operations, it required extensive credit and borrowed large sums of money from banks and other lenders. All this was known to the defendants. The defendants knew also that in the usual course of business the balance sheet when certified would be exhibited by the Stern Company to banks, creditors, stockholders, purchasers, or sellers, according to the needs of the occasion, as the basis of financial dealings. Accordingly, when the balance sheet was made up, the defendants supplied the Stern company with thirty-two copies certified with serial numbers as counterpart originals. Nothing was said as to the persons to whom these counterparts would be shown or the extent or number of the transactions in which they would be used. In particular there was no mention of the plaintiff, a corporation doing business chiefly as a factor, which till then had never made advances to the Stern Company, though it had sold it merchandise in small amounts. The range of the transactions in which a certificate of audit might be expected to play a part was as indefinite and wide as the possibilities of the business that was mirrored in the summary.

By February 26, 1924, the audit was finished and the balance sheet made up. It stated assets in the sum of $2,550,671.88 and liabilities other than capital and surplus in the sum of $1,479,956.62, thus showing a net worth of $1,070,715.26. Attached to the balance sheet was a certificate as follows:

TOUCHE, NIVEN & CO.
Public Accountants
Eighty Maiden Lane
New York

February 26, 1924

Certificate of Auditors

We have examined the accounts of Fred Stern & Co., Inc., for the year ending December 31, 1923, and hereby certify that the annexed balance sheet is in accordance therewith and with the information and explanations given us. We further certify that, subject to provision for federal taxes on income, the said statement, in our opinion, presents a true and correct view of the financial condition of Fred Stern & Co., Inc., as at December 31, 1923.

Touche, Niven & Co.
Public Accountants

[Cardozo, C.J., then noted that the accountant's statement was wrong in all material respects. As a matter of fact, Stern & Co. was insolvent at the time the balance sheet was prepared, and the defendant auditors had been taken in by false statements of income and expenses prepared by Stern's officers. After an extensive review of the evidence, Cardozo, C.J., concluded that a skilled auditor would have followed up various leads and detected the fraud perpetrated by Stern & Co.'s chief officers. On the faith of the balance sheet certified by the defendant, the plaintiff, as part of its factoring business, made various advances to Stern & Co. throughout most of 1924. Stern & Co. collapsed in January 1925, leaving the plaintiff with a host of unpaid loans, some of which were unsecured and others of which were inadequately secured. In November 1926, the plaintiffs sued the defendants for both negligence and fraud. The trial judge refused to allow the fraud count to go to the jury. The jury, however, found the defendant negligent and awarded the plaintiff some $187,500. The trial judge, who had reserved judgment on the sufficiency of the negligence claim, entered a judgment for the defendant on the ground that the plaintiff's claim for negligent misrepresentation did not state a cause of action. That decision was reversed by the appellate division. Cardozo, C.J., noted that the finding of negligence was supported by the evidence. "The reckoning was not wrong upon the evidence before us, if duty be assumed."]

We are brought to the question of duty, its origin and measure.

The defendants owed to their employer a duty imposed by law to make their certificate without fraud, and a duty growing out of contract to make it with the care and caution proper to their calling. Fraud includes the pretense of knowledge when knowledge there is none. To creditors and investors to whom the employer exhibited the certificate, the defendants owed a like duty to make it without fraud, since there was notice in the circumstances of its making that the employer did not intend to keep it to himself. A different question develops when we ask whether they owed a duty to these to make it without negligence. If liability for negligence exists, a thoughtless slip or blunder, the failure to detect a theft or forgery beneath the cover of deceptive entries, may expose accountants to a liability in an indeterminate amount for an indeterminate time to an indeterminate class. The hazards of a business conducted on these terms are so extreme as to enkindle doubt whether a flaw may not exist in the implication of a duty that exposes to these consequences. We put aside for the moment any statement in the certificate which involves the representation of a fact as true to the knowledge of the auditors. If such a statement was made, whether believed to be true or not, the defendants are liable for deceit in the event that it was false. The plaintiff does not need the invention of novel doctrine to help it out in such conditions. The case was submitted to the jury and the verdict was returned upon the theory that even in the absence of a misstatement of a fact there is a liability also for erroneous opinion. The expression of an opinion is to be subject to a warranty implied by law. What, then, is the warranty, as yet unformulated, to be? Is it merely that the opinion is honestly conceived and that the preliminary inquiry has been honestly pursued, that a halt has not been made without a genuine belief that the search has been reasonably adequate to bring disclosure of the truth? Or does it go farther and involve the assumption of a liability for any blunder or inattention that could fairly be spoken of as negligence if the controversy were one between accountant and employer for breach of a contract to render services for pay?

The assault upon the citadel of privity is proceeding in these days apace. How far the inroads shall extend is now a favorite subject of juridical discussion. . . . In the field of the law of contract there has been a gradual widening of the doctrine of Lawrence v. Fox (20 N. Y. 268), until today the beneficiary of a promise, clearly designated as such, is seldom left without a remedy (Seaver v. Ransom, 224 N. Y. 233, 238). Even in that field, however, the remedy is narrower where the beneficiaries of the promise are indeterminate or general. Something more must then appear than an intention that the promise shall redound to the benefit of the public or to that of a class of indefinite extension. The promise must be such as to "bespeak the assumption of a duty to make reparation directly to the individual members of the public if the benefit is lost" (Moch Co. v. Rensselaer Water Co). In the field of the law of torts a manufacturer who is negligent in the manufacture of a chattel in circumstances pointing to an unreasonable risk of serious bodily harm to those using it thereafter may be liable for negligence though privity is lacking between manufacturer and user (MacPherson v. Buick Motor Co., 217 N. Y. 382; American Law Institute, Restatement of the Law of Torts, §262). A force or instrument of harm having been launched with potentialities of danger manifest to the eye of prudence, the one who launches it is under a duty to keep it within bounds (Moch Co. v. Rensselaer Water Co., supra). Even so, the question is still open whether the potentialities of danger that will charge with liability are confined to harm to the person, or include injury to property. In either view, however, what is released or set in motion is a physical force. We are now asked to say that a like liability attaches to the circulation of a thought or a release of the explosive power resident in words.

Three cases in this court are said by the plaintiff to have committed us to the doctrine that words, written or oral, if negligently published with the expectation that the reader or listener will transmit them to another, will lay a basis for liability though privity be lacking. These are Glanzer v. Shepard (233 N. Y. 236); International Products Co. v. Erie R.R. Co. (244 N. Y. 331), and Doyle v. Chatham & Phenix Nat. Bank (253 N. Y. 369).

In Glanzer v. Shepard the seller of beans requested the defendants, public weighers, to make return of the weight and furnish the buyer with a copy. This the defendants did. Their return, which was made out in duplicate, one copy to the seller and the other to the buyer, recites that it was made by order of the former for the use of the latter. The buyer paid the seller on the faith of the certificate which turned out to be erroneous. We held that the weighers were liable at the suit of the buyer for the moneys overpaid. Here was something more than the rendition of a service in the expectation that the one who ordered the certificate would use it thereafter in the operations of his business as occasion might require. Here was a case where the transmission of the certificate to another was not merely one possibility among many, but the "end and aim of the transaction," as certain and immediate and deliberately willed as if a husband were to order a gown to be delivered to his wife, or a telegraph company, contracting with the sender of a message, were to telegraph it wrongly to the damage of the person expected to receive it. The intimacy of the resulting nexus is attested by the fact that after stating the case in terms of legal duty, we went on to point out that viewing it as a phase or extension of Lawrence v. Fox (supra), or Seaver v. Ransom (supra), we could reach the same result by stating it in terms of contract. The bond was so close as to approach that of privity, if not completely one with it. Not so in the case at hand. No one would be likely to urge that there was a contractual relation, or even one approaching it, at the root of any duty that was owing from the defendants now before us to the indeterminate class of persons who, presently or in the future, might deal with the Stern company in reliance on the audit. In a word, the service rendered by the defendant in Glanzer v. Shepard was primarily for the information of a third person, in effect, if not in name, a party to the contract, and only incidentally for that of the formal promisee. In the case at hand, the service was primarily for the benefit of the Stern company, a convenient instrumentality for use in the development of the business, and only incidentally or collaterally for the use of those to whom Stern and his associates might exhibit it thereafter. Foresight of these possibilities may charge with liability for fraud. The conclusion does not follow that it will charge with liability for negligence.

[A discussion of International Products Co. v. Erie R.R. Co. and Doyle v. Chatham & Phenix National Bank is omitted.]

From the foregoing analysis the conclusion is, we think, inevitable that nothing in our previous decisions commits us to a holding of liability for negligence in the circumstances of the case at hand, and that such liability, if recognized, will be an extension of the principle of those decisions to different conditions, even if more or less analogous. The question then is whether such an extension shall be made.

The extension, if made, will so expand the field of liability for negligent speech as to make it nearly, if not quite, coterminous with that of liability for fraud. Again and again, in decisions of this court, the bounds of this latter liability have been set up, with futility the fate of every endeavor to dislodge them. Scienter has been declared to be an indispensable element except where the representation has been put forward as true of one's own knowledge, or in circumstances where the expression of opinion was a dishonorable pretense. . . . Even an opinion, especially an opinion by an expert, may be found to be fraudulent if the grounds supporting it are so flimsy as to lead to the conclusion that there was no genuine belief back of it. Further than that this court has never gone. Directors of corporations have been acquitted of liability for deceit though they have been lax in investigation and negligent in speech (Reno v. Bull, 226 N.Y. 546, and cases there cited; Kountze v. Kennedy, 147 N.Y. 124). This has not meant, to be sure, that negligence may not be evidence from which a trier of the facts may draw an inference of fraud (Derry v. Peek, [L. R.] 14 A.C. 337) but merely that if that inference is rejected, or, in the light of all the circumstances, is found to be unreasonable, negligence alone is not a substitute for fraud. Many also are the cases that have distinguished between the willful or reckless representation essential to the maintenance at law of an action for deceit, and the misrepresentation, negligent or innocent, that will lay a sufficient basis for rescission in equity. If this action is well conceived, all these principles and distinctions, so nicely wrought and formulated, have been a waste of time and effort. They have even been a snare, entrapping litigants and lawyers into an abandonment of the true remedy lying ready to the call. The suitors thrown out of court because they proved negligence, and nothing else, in an action for deceit, might have ridden to triumphant victory if they had proved the self-same facts, but had given the wrong another label, and all this in a State where forms of action have been abolished. So to hold is near to saying that we have been paltering with justice. A word of caution or suggestion would have set the erring suitor right. Many pages of opinion were written by judges the most eminent, yet the word was never spoken. We may not speak it now. A change so revolutionary, if expedient, must be wrought by legislation. . . .

Liability for negligence if adjudged in this case will extend to many callings other than an auditor's. Lawyers who certify their opinion as to the validity of municipal or corporate bonds with knowledge that the opinion will be brought to the notice of the public, will become liable to the investors, if they have overlooked a statute or a decision, to the same extent as if the controversy were one between client and adviser. Title companies insuring titles to a tract of land, with knowledge that at an approaching auction the fact that they have insured will be stated to the bidders, will become liable to purchasers who may wish the benefit of a policy without payment of a premium. These illustrations may seem to be extreme, but they go little, if any, farther than we are invited to go now. Negligence, moreover, will have one standard when viewed in relation to the employer, and another and at times a stricter standard when viewed in relation to the public. Explanations that might seem plausible, omissions that might be reasonable, if the duty is confined to the employer, conducting a business that presumably at least is not a fraud upon his creditors, might wear another aspect if an independent duty to be suspicious even of one's principal is owing to investors. "Every one making a promise having the quality of a contract will be under a duty to the promisee by virtue of the promise, but under another duty, apart from contract, to an indefinite number of potential beneficiaries when performance has begun. The assumption of one relation will mean the involuntary assumption of a series of new relations, inescapably hooked together." (Moch Co. v. Rensselaer Water Co., supra.)

"The law does not spread its protection so far." (Robins Dry Dock & Repair Co. v. Flint, supra.)

Our holding does not emancipate accountants from the consequences of fraud. It does not relieve them if their audit has been so negligent as to justify a finding that they had no genuine belief in its adequacy, for this again is fraud. It does no more than say that if less than this is proved, if there has been neither reckless misstatement nor insincere profession of an opinion, but only honest blunder, the ensuing liability for negligence is one that is bounded by the contract, and is to be enforced between the parties by whom the contract has been made. We doubt whether the average business man receiving a certificate without paying for it and receiving it merely as one among a multitude of possible investors, would look for anything more.

(2) The second cause of action is yet to be considered.

The defendants certified as a fact, true to their own knowledge, that the balance sheet was in accordance with the books of account. If their statement was false, they are not to be exonerated because they believed it to be true. We think the triers of the facts might hold it to be false.

[The court then reviewed the evidence on the second cause of action and noted that accountants are to be judged by a strict standard of construction "when certifying to an agreement between the audit and the entries" as the defendants did here. The court also concluded that the defendants could not protect themselves against a charge that they did not detect the fictitious invoices "by invoking a practice known as that of testing and sampling," on the ground that it was "plainly insufficient" to determine whether there were in fact any accounts at all.]

We conclude, to sum up the situation, that in certifying to the correspondence between balance sheet and accounts the defendants made a statement as true to their own knowledge, when they had, as a jury might find, no knowledge on the subject. If that is so, they may also be found to have acted without information leading to a sincere or genuine belief when they certified to an opinion that the balance sheet faithfully reflected the condition of the business.

[The court then concluded that the defendants could not escape liability because they had "delegated the performance of this work to agents of their own selection."]

Upon the defendants' appeal as to the first cause of action, the judgment of the Appellate Division should be reversed, and that of the Trial Term affirmed, with costs in the Appellate Division and in this court.

Upon the plaintiff's appeal as to the second cause of action, the judgment of the Appellate Division and that of the Trial Term should be reversed, and a new trial granted, with costs to abide the event.

POUND, CRANE, LEHMAN, KELLOGG, O'BRIEN and HUBBS, JJ., concur.

Judgment accordingly.

NOTES

1. *Liability for negligent misrepresentation.* *Ultramares* is still the leading American common-law decision on liability for negligent misrepresentation. Does its use of the privity limitation make more sense than it does in the products liability cases? The waterworks cases? If the defendants had been told to mail a copy of their certified statement directly to the plaintiff for use in its lending operation, could the plaintiff have recovered in negligence? Does *Ultramares* stand for the proposition that only those who pay for the preparation of the report are entitled to maintain actions for damages if it is negligently prepared? Could the plaintiff recover under a third-party beneficiary theory?

In New York, *Ultramares* itself has been extensively reexamined in two important cases. In White v. Guarente, 372 N.E.2d 315, 318-319, (N.Y. 1977), the defendant Arthur Anderson & Co. had been retained to do financial and tax accounting for a limited partnership specializing in the trading and hedging of marketable securities. The general partners had withdrawn their own funds from the partnership in violation of the terms of the agreement. Andersen allegedly had failed to detect the breach through its own acts of professional negligence. The plaintiff's cause of action against the accountants was dismissed at first instance, but the cause of action was reinstated by the New York Court of Appeals:

> Citing Ultramares Corp. v. Touche and contending that plaintiff does not stand in privity with it, defendant Andersen maintains that plaintiff lacks capacity to sue and may not recover for these alleged acts of negligence. *Ultramares,* however, presented a noticeably different picture than that here, since there involved was an "indeterminate class of persons who, presently or in the future, might deal with the [debtor-promisee] in reliance on the audit". . . . Indeed, the import of *Ultramares* is its holding that an accountant need not respond in negligence to those in the extensive and indeterminable investing public-at-large.
>
> Here, the services of the accountant were not extended to a faceless or unresolved class of persons, but rather to a known group possessed of vested rights, marked by a definable limit and made up of certain components. The instant situation did not involve prospective limited partners, unknown at the time and who might be induced to join, but rather actual limited partners, fixed and determined. Here, accountant Andersen was retained to perform an audit and prepare the tax returns of Associates, known to be a limited partnership, and the accountant must have been aware that a limited partner would necessarily rely on or make use of the audit and tax returns of the partnership, or at least constituents of them, in order to properly prepare his or her own tax returns. This was within the contemplation of the parties to the accounting retainer. In such circumstances, assumption of the task of auditing and preparing the returns was the assumption of a duty to audit and prepare carefully for the benefit of those in the fixed, definable and contemplated group whose conduct was to be governed, since, given the contract and the relation, the

duty is imposed by law and it is not necessary to state the duty in terms of contract or privity. . . .

Could the limited partners be said to be in privity with the defendants, since they were hired to do the audit by the partnership?

More recently, in Credit Alliance Corp. v. Andersen & Co., 483 N.E.2d 110, 113, 118 (N.Y. 1985), the Court of Appeals examined two separate disputes in which disappointed lenders sought to hold accountants responsible for negligence. In *Credit Alliance,* Arthur Andersen & Co. prepared a consolidated financial audit for L. B. Smith, Inc. that was then used by Smith to obtain extensive loans from the plaintiff Credit Alliance. The complaint alleged that Andersen's audit was not performed in accordance with generally accepted accounting practices and it overstated "Smith's assets, net worth and general financial health," and that "Andersen knew, should have known or was on notice that the . . . . certified statements were being utilized by Smith to induce companies such as plaintiffs to make credit available to Smith." In the companion case of European American Bank & Trust (EAB) v. Strauhs & Kaye (S&K), EAB alleged that S&K had overstated the value of the inventory and accounts receivable of Majestic Electro Industries. On the strength of that audit EAB loaned certain funds to Majestic in order to finance its acquisition of other companies. The suit alleged that S&K "at all relevant times knew that EAB was Majestic Electro's principal lender, was familiar with the terms of the lending relationship, and was fully aware that EAB was relying on the financial statements and inventory valuations certified by S&K," and further that representatives of EAB and S&K were in constant and direct communication, both written and oral, with each other during the course of the lending negotiations.

After an exhaustive review of the earlier cases, the court concluded:

> Before accountants may be held liable in negligence to noncontractual parties who rely to their detriment on inaccurate financial reports, certain prerequisites must be satisfied: (1) the accountants must have been aware that the financial reports were to be used for a particular purpose or purposes; (2) in the furtherance of which a known party or parties was intended to rely; and (3) there must have been some conduct on the part of the accountants linking them to that party or parties, which evinces the accountants' understanding of that party or parties' reliance. While these criteria permit some flexibility in the application of the doctrine of privity to accountant's liability, they do not represent a departure from the principles articulated in *Ultramares, Glanzer* and *White,* but, rather, they are intended to preserve the wisdom and policy set forth therein.

Under this test, the court dismissed the action against Andersen in *Credit Alliance* because "no claim is made that Andersen was being employed to prepare the reports with the Smith loan in mind." But EAB's action was allowed against S&K because "S&K was well aware that a primary, if not the exclusive, *end and aim* of auditing its client, Majestic Electro, was to provide EAB with the financial information that it required."

Note that the Restatement (Second) of Torts §552 limits liability for negligent misrepresentation to, at most, persons who are members "of a limited group of persons for whose benefit and guidance" the information is supplied, provided that there is reliance on that information in that transaction, or "in a substantially similar transaction." Does the exception also reach *Ultramares?*

2. *From privity to foreseeability and back. Ultramares* received a chillier reception in Rosenblum v. Adler, 461 A.2d 138, 145, 149, 153 (N.J. 1983). There the defendant accounting firm of Touche Ross & Co. was charged with negligent misrepresentation because it failed to ferret out the fraud that Giant Stores Corporation had perpetrated against the plaintiffs, who, under a merger agreement, accepted worthless Giant stock in exchange for shares of their own private corporations. The trial judge dismissed the negligence count against Touche Ross & Co., but the New Jersey Supreme Court remanded for trial. The court first noted the conflict between Cardozo's opinions in *MacPherson* and *Ultramares,* and then insisted that privity should no more be a barrier in misrepresentation cases than in physical injury cases. Relying on section 552 of the Restatement, the court concluded: "Generally, within the outer limits fixed by the court as a matter of law, the reasonably foreseeable consequences of the negligent act define the duty and should be actionable."

The court then argued that the "auditor's function has expanded from that of a watchdog for management to an independent evaluator of the adequacy and fairness of financial statements issued by management to stockholders, creditors, and others," and concluded that auditors should be able to obtain insurance against the risks in question, and would in any event be induced to set "stricter standards" for conducting their work. It then continued:

> When the independent auditor furnishes an opinion with no limitation in the certificate as to whom the company may disseminate the financial statements, he has a duty to all those whom that auditor should reasonably foresee as recipients from the company of the statements for its proper business purposes, provided that the recipients rely on the statements pursuant to those business purposes. The principle that we have adopted applies by its terms only to those foreseeable users who receive the audited statements from the business entity for a proper business purpose to influence a business decision of the user, the audit having been made for that business entity. Thus, for example, an institutional investor or portfolio manager who does not obtain audited statements from the company would not come within the stated princi-

ple. Nor would stockholders who purchased the stock after a negligent audit be covered in the absence of demonstrating the necessary conditions precedent. Those and similar cases beyond the stated rule are not before us and we express no opinion with respect to such situations.

These expansionist tendencies of accountants' liability have been checked, at least in part, in the important California case of Bily v. Arthur Young & Co., 834 P.2d 745, 747, 762-767, 771-773 (Cal. 1992), an action which arose out of the demise of the Osborne Computer Corporation, whose short and eventful life lasted from 1980 to 1983. Osborne was the first company to offer a portable personal computer, which created a massive instant demand for its products, so that by the fall of 1982 it was shipping $10,000,000 in sales per month. Osborne then planned a public offering of its shares while it was working on its next generation of computers. In order to secure "bridge" financing to keep it in business until the offering had been completed, Osborne sold warrants to investors, which would allow them to buy large blocks of shares at favorable prices when the "going-public" transaction was completed. The funds from the warrants were used to secure letters of credit from the banks that made the interim loans. Osborne's second line of computers, however, contained some bugs, and IBM came out with its own line of personal computers in June 1983. The new rival destroyed Osborne's business, and Osborne filed for bankruptcy in September 1983. The purchasers of the warrants sued the accounting firm which had issued unqualified opinions on Osborne's balance sheets for 1981 and 1982 in accordance with Generally Accepted Accounting Practices. The complaint charged intentional concealment and negligent failure to discover defects in Osborne's statements. The plaintiff's experts identified about 40 weaknesses in Osborne's accounting procedures, and also claimed that there was one instance where "Arthur Young had actually discovered deviations from GAAP, but failed to disclose them as qualifications or corrections to its audit report," namely a failure to make allowances for customer rebates and customer returns of products. The jury exonerated defendant on the intentional fraud and negligent misrepresentation counts, but found for plaintiff on professional negligence, and awarded $4,300,000 in damages, equal to about 75 percent of plaintiff's investment.

After an exhaustive review of the case law, the court reversed the decision below. The court first rejected the "foreseeability" test of *Rosenblum* for three main reasons:

> (1) Given the secondary "watchdog" role of the auditor, the complexity of the professional opinions rendered in audit reports, and the difficult and potentially tenuous causal relationships between audit reports and economic losses from investment and credit decisions, if the auditor is

exposed to negligence claims from all foreseeable third parties, it faces a
potential liability far out of proportion to its fault.

(2) The generally more sophisticated class of plaintiffs in auditor liability
cases (e.g business lenders and investors) permits the effective use of
contract rather than tort liability to control and adjust the relevant risks
through "private ordering"; and

(3) The asserted advantages of more accurate auditing and more efficient
loss spreading (relied upon by those who advocate a pure foreseeability
approach) are unlikely to occur; indeed dislocations of resources, including increased expense and decreased availability of auditing services in
some sectors of the economy, are more probable consequences of expanded liability.

The court was, however, prepared to extend negligence liability under the Restatement (Second) §552 to a narrow class of persons, who,
although not clients, "are specifically intended beneficiaries of the
audit report who are known to the auditor and for whose benefit it
renders the audit report." These persons are entitled to recover for
negligent misrepresentations, but not for general negligence in the
manner in which the audits were conducted. The court refused to extend liability further because other persons desirous of protection "can
establish direct communication with an auditor and obtain a report for
their own direct use and benefit." In order to show that a particular
party falls within the class of intended beneficiaries, the court adopted

> an *objective standard* that looks to the specific circumstances (e.g. supplier-
> client engagement and the supplier's communications with the third
> party) to ascertain whether a supplier has undertaken to inform and
> guide a third party with respect to *an identified transaction or type of transac-
> tion.* If such a specific undertaking has been made, liability is imposed on
> the supplier. If, on the other hand, the supplier "merely knows of the
> ever-present possibility of repetition to anyone, and the possibility of ac-
> tion in reliance upon [the information] on the part of anyone to whom
> it may be repeated the supplier bears no legal responsibility.

Finally, the court reaffirmed the traditional view that the auditor is liable in tort for any intentional misrepresentation of the books to all
persons whom it knew, or could reasonably foresee, would rely on the
misrepresentation. In the case of a fraud on the public, the scope of
liability extends to every person who is actually misled by the fraud in
question.

On these standards the plaintiffs lost. Since they were not clients of
Arthur Young, they could not recover on a general negligence theory;
nor could they show that they were the victims of negligent misrepresentation or fraud, given the jury findings to the contrary. The dissent
of Kennard, J., stressed, first, that Arthur Young had printed up 100
copies of the report, which it gave to the corporation for general distribution, and, second, that under the traditional rule of liability, all per-

sons who reasonably and foreseeably rely on the negligent audit statements should be entitled to recover, which would insure that potential users of these reports will continue to have confidence in them.

3. *Contracting out of liability for negligent misrepresentation.* As *Bily* hints, it is not self-evident that negligent misrepresentation cases should be regarded as raising tort issues. In Hedley, Byrne & Co. Ltd. v. Heller & Partners Ltd., [1964] App. Cas. 465, 526 [H.L. 1963], Hedley, Byrne was a firm of advertising agents that had extended over £15,000 of credit to a firm called Easipower only after obtaining a credit report on Easipower from Heller. This report was alleged to have negligently overstated Easipower's creditworthiness. Lord Devlin in the House of Lords conducted an elaborate discussion in which he concluded that in principle it makes no difference "whether financial loss is caused through physical injury or whether it is caused directly."

> If irrespective of contract, a doctor negligently advises a patient that he can safely pursue his occupation and he cannot and the patient's health suffers and he loses his livelihood, the patient has a remedy. But if the doctor negligently advises him that he cannot safely pursue his occupation when in fact he can and he loses his livelihood, there is said to be no remedy. Unless, of course, the patient was a private patient and the doctor accepted half a guinea for his trouble: then the patient can recover all. I am bound to say, my Lords, that I think this to be nonsense. It is not the sort of nonsense that can arise even in the best system of law out of the need to draw nice distinctions between borderline cases. It arises, if it is the law, simply out of a refusal to make sense. The line is not drawn on any intelligible principle. It just happens to be the line which those who have been driven from the extreme assertion that negligent statements in the absence of contractual or fiduciary duty give no cause of action have in the course of their retreat so far reached.

After this general speech Lord Devlin nonetheless concluded that judgment had to be entered for the defendant on the strength of the disclaimer. "A man cannot be said voluntarily to be undertaking a responsibility if at the very moment when he is said to be accepting it he declares that in fact he is not."

Once disclaimers are regarded as effective, then the critical question is, what presumption should be made about liability for negligence in their absence? Professor Goldberg, Accountable Accountants: Is Third-Party Liability Necessary?, 17 J. Legal Stud. 295, 300-301 (1988), has defended the rule in *Ultramares* on the ground that the default rule should be one of no liability.

> If it turned out that it was appropriate that accountants should compensate third parties for their negligence, it would not be very difficult to have them assume the liability by contract rather than by having it imposed by tort. Third parties could receive explicit assurance in the form of a warranty, guarantee, bond, or a similar device. Even without

explicit liability, the negligent accounting firm would suffer the consequences of poor performance in the form of a decline in the value of its "brand name." Since it is probably true that accountants are not very good guarantors, I would guess that accountants would rarely agree to compensate third parties. But it is crucial to recognize that it is unnecessary for courts or legislatures to guess. It is sufficient for them to allow the parties to resolve the problem by contract.

Under Goldberg's approach is there any reason to distinguish between the positions of Andersen and S&K in *Credit Alliance?* For a defense of the expanded liability of accountants see Weiner, Common Law Liability of the Certified Public Accountant for Negligent Misrepresentation, 20 San Diego L. Rev. 233 (1983). See also Bishop, Negligent Misrepresentation Through Economists' Eyes, 96 Law Q. Rev. 360 (1980).

4. *Modern securities law and the indeterminate class.* The questions raised by *Ultramares* also come to the fore in modern securities law, where the potentially extensive liability for material nondisclosures as well as misstatements is a daily fact of life. One important question under the securities law concerns the class of persons who are entitled to sue for their financial losses. Section 10(b) of the Securities Exchange Act, supra at page 1293, proscribes fraud "in connection with the purchase or sale of securities," and in Blue Chip Stamps v. Manor Drug Stores, 421 U.S. 723, 747-748 (1975), the plaintiffs alleged that they did not purchase shares of the defendant's stock because the defendants had made false and misleading negative statements about its value. The Supreme Court held that only actual purchasers and sellers of stocks could sue under the section, for reasons which echoed those that moved Cardozo in *Ultramares.* The Court noted that the proposed rule would admit an enormous class of potential plaintiffs into court; would place heavy strains on the system of discovery; and would require the defendants to litigate against plaintiffs whose claims were wholly hypothetical. In explicit reliance on *Ultramares,* the Court then concluded as follows: "[W]hile much of the development of the law of deceit has been the elimination of artificial barriers to recovery on just claims, we are not the first court to express concern that the inexorable broadening of the class of plaintiffs who may sue in this area of the law will ultimately result in more harm than good." Does this passage answer Lord Devlin's contention that there is no sensible distinction between financial loss and physical injury cases? If both *Ultramares* and Goodwin v. Agassiz are sound law, is there any reason for a special regime of securities law?

Chapter Seventeen
Economic Harms

A. INTRODUCTION

This final chapter addresses when and how the law protects economic interests from interference by the actions of others. The protection of these economic interests is not a wholly new theme, for the broader issues have already been touched on in a number of earlier contexts. For example, the plaintiff's economic loss flowing from property damage or bodily injury is ordinarily recoverable in an action in tort, whether the underlying claim involves negligence, strict liability or some intentional wrong. Economic interests receive still more explicit protection when the plaintiff seeks a remedy for the misappropriation of a name or likeness by the defendant, a matter already covered in Chapter 15, or for the pecuniary losses attributable to misrepresentation, the subject of Chapter 16.

This chapter extends that analysis by considering three separate instances of economic harms to strangers. Section B examines the extent to which the law protects contractual relationships by providing a contracting party not only contractual remedies against the promisor, but also tort remedies against a third party who has induced, or threatens to induce, a breach of contract. Section C considers the nature of the protection afforded, not to existing contracts, but to advantageous relationships with third parties that the plaintiff hopes to maintain or enter into. The difference between the first and second classes is evident enough for, in the first, the plaintiff is normally entitled to some relief under an existing contract against another party while, in the second, the disappointed party has no contractual remedy against anybody. Section D explores the legal protection of valuable information at common law, with some discussion of the overlap between the common-law rules and the statutory systems that now regulate patents, copyrights, tradenames, and trademarks. This entire area of intellectual property continues to enjoy exponential legal growth.

In shaping the rule of liability, two great fears have driven the courts to narrow the scope of liability. The first fear, similar to that encountered with emotional distress and negligent misrepresentation, is that generalized protection of economic interests against any diminution in value will spawn endless lawsuits and create countless legal nightmares. The second fear, perhaps unique to this subject matter, is that the expansion of the law of "unfair competition" will destroy ordinary business competition and the social benefits it provides. Yet by the same token a complete withdrawal of legal protection could invite antisocial conduct that undermines the incentive to create and market new products. With tangible property, a clear prohibition against trespass is generally sufficient to protect the fruits of individual labor. But with intellectual property, that simple device is not available, so that more complex legal rules are required. As in so many other areas, the central task for judges is to balance these conflicting impulses. The complexity of the area, however, is so great that common-law remedies often prove insufficient, so that some brief note must be made of the statutory schemes from the labor and antitrust statutes, to patents, copyright, and tradename and trademark protection.

B. INDUCEMENT OF BREACH OF CONTRACT

Lumley v. Gye
118 Eng. Rep. 749 (K.B. 1853)

The 1st count of the declaration stated that plaintiff was lessee and manager of the Queen's Theatre, for performing operas for gain to him; and that he had contracted and agreed with Johanna Wagner to perform in the theatre for a certain time, with a condition, amongst others, that she should not sing nor use her talents elsewhere during the term without plaintiff's consent in writing: Yet defendant, knowing the premises, and maliciously intending to injure plaintiff as lessee and manager of the theatre, whilst the agreement with Wagner was in force, and before the expiration of the term, enticed and procured Wagner to refuse to perform: by means of which enticement and procurement of defendant, Wagner wrongfully refused to perform, and did not perform during the term.

Count 2, for enticing and procuring Johanna Wagner to continue to refuse to perform during the term, after the order of Vice Chancellor Parker, affirmed by Lord St. Leonards, restraining her from performing at a theatre of defendants.

Count 3. That Johanna Wagner had been and was hired by plaintiff to sing and perform at his theatre for a certain time, as the dramatic artiste of plaintiff, for reward to her, and had become and was such dramatic artiste of plaintiff at his theatre: Yet defendant, well knowing &c., maliciously enticed and procured her, then being such dramatic artiste, to depart from the said employment.

In each count special damage was alleged.

CROMPTON, J. . . . It was said, in support of the demurrer, that it did not appear in the declaration that the relation of master and servant ever subsisted between the plaintiff and Miss Wagner; that Miss Wagner was not averred, especially in the two first counts, to have entered upon the service of the plaintiff; and that the engagement of a theatrical performer, even if the performer has entered upon the duties, is not of such a nature as to make the performer a servant, within the rule of law which gives an action to the master for the wrongful enticing away of his servant. And it was laid down broadly, as a general proposition of law, that no action will lie for procuring a person to break a contract, although such procuring is with a malicious intention and causes great and immediate injury. And the law as to enticing servants was said to be contrary to the general rule and principle of law, and to be anomalous, and probably to have had its origin from the state of society when serfdom existed, and to be founded upon, or upon the equity of, the Statute of Labourers. It was said that it would be dangerous to hold that an action was maintainable for persuading a third party to break a contract, unless some boundary or limits could be pointed out; and that the remedy for enticing away servants was confined to cases where the relation of master and servant, in a strict sense, subsisted between the parties; and that, in all other cases of contract, the only remedy was against the party breaking the contract.

Whatever may have been the origin or foundation of the law as to enticing of servants, and whether it be, as contended by the plaintiff, an instance and branch of a wider rule, or whether it be, as contended by the defendant, an anomaly and an exception from the general rule of law on such subjects, it must now be considered clear law that a person who wrongfully and maliciously, or, which is the same thing, with notice, interrupts the relation subsisting between master and servant by procuring the servant to depart from the master's service, or by harbouring and keeping him as servant after he has quitted it and during the time stipulated for as the period of service, whereby the master is injured, commits a wrongful act for which he is responsible at law. I think that the rule applies wherever the wrongful interruption operates to prevent the service during the time for which the parties have contracted that the service shall continue: and I think that the relation of master and servant subsists, sufficiently for the purpose of such action, during the time for which there is in existence a binding contract of hiring and service between the parties; and I think that it is a fanciful and technical and unjust distinction to say that the not having actually entered into the service, or that the service not actually continuing, can make any difference. The wrong and injury are surely the same, whether the wrong doer entices away the gardener, who has hired himself for a year, the night before he is to go to his work, or after he has planted the first cabbage on the first morning of his service; and I should be sorry to support a distinction so unjust, and so repugnant to common sense, unless bound to do so by some rule or authority of law plainly shewing that such distinction exists. The proposition of the defendant, that there must be a service actually subsisting, seems to be inconsistent with the authorities that shew these actions to be maintainable for receiving or harbouring servants after they have left the actual service of the master. . . .

[Crompton, J., then reviewed earlier cases.]

. . . It appears to me that Miss Wagner had contracted to do work for the plaintiff within the meaning of this rule; and I think that, where a party has contracted to give his personal services for a certain time to another, the parties are in the relation of employer and employed, or master and servant, within the meaning of this rule. And I see no reason for narrowing such a rule; but I should rather, if necessary, apply such a remedy to a case "new in its instance, but" "not new in the reason and principle of it," that is, to a case where the wrong and damage are strictly analogous to the wrong and damage in a well recognised class of cases. In deciding this case on the narrower ground, I wish by no means to be considered as deciding that the larger ground taken by Mr. Cowling is not tenable, or as saying that in no case except that of master and servant is an action maintainable for *maliciously* inducing another to break a contract to the injury of the person with whom such contract has been made. It does not appear to me to be a sound answer, to say that the act in such cases is the act of the party who breaks the contract; for that reason would apply in the acknowledged case of master and servant. Nor is it an answer, to say that there is a remedy against the contractor, and that the party relies on the contract; for, besides that reason also applying to the case of master and servant, the action on the contract and the action against the malicious wrong-doer may be for a different matter; and the damages occasioned by such malicious injury might be calculated on a very different principle from the amount of the debt which might be the only sum recoverable on the contract. Suppose a trader, *with a malicious intent to ruin a rival trader,* goes to a banker or other party who owes money to his rival, and begs him not to pay the money which he owes him, and by that means ruins or greatly prejudices the party: I am by no means prepared to say that an action could not be maintained, and that damages, beyond the amount of the debt if the injury were less great, or much less than such amount if the injury were less serious, might not be recovered. . . . In this class of cases it must be assumed that it is the malicious act of the defendant, and that malicious act only, which causes the servant or contractor not to perform the work or contract which he would otherwise have done. The servant or contractor may be utterly unable to pay anything like the amount of the damage sustained entirely from the wrongful act of the defendant: and it would seem unjust, and contrary to the general principles of law, if such wrongdoer were not responsible for the damage caused by his wrongful and malicious act. . . .

Without however deciding any such more general question, I think that we are justified in applying the principle of action for enticing away servants to a case where the defendant *maliciously procures* a party, who is under a valid contract to give her exclusive personal services to the plaintiff for a specified period, to refuse to give such services *during the period for which she had so contracted,* whereby the plaintiff was injured.

I think, therefore, that our judgment should be for the plaintiff.

[The concurring opinions of Erle and Wightman, JJ., are omitted.]

COLERIDGE, J. . . . In order to maintain this action, one of two propositions must be maintained; either that an action will lie against any one by whose persuasions one party to a contract is induced to break it to the damage of the other party, or that the action, for seducing a servant from the master or persuading one who has contracted for service from entering into the employ, is of so wide application as to embrace the case of one in the position and profession of Johanna Wagner. After much consideration and enquiry I am of opinion that neither of these propositions is true; and they are both of them so important, and, if established by judicial decision, will lead to consequences so general, that, though I regret the necessity, I must not abstain from entering into remarks of some length in support of my view of the law.

It may simplify what I have to say, if I first state what are the conclusions which I seek to establish. They are these: that in respect of breach of contract the general rule of our law is to confine its remedies by action to the contracting parties, and to damages directly and proximately consequential on the act of him who is sued; that, as between master and servant, there is an admitted exception, that this exception dates from the Statute of Labourers, 23 Edw. III, and both on principle and according to authority is limited by it. If I am right in these positions, the conclusion will be for the defendant, because enough appears on this record to show, as to the first, that he, and, as to the second, that Johanna Wagner, is not within the limits so drawn.

First then, that the remedy for breach of contract is by the general rule of our law confined to the contracting parties. . . . There would be such a manifest absurdity in attempting to trace up the act of a free agent breaking a contract to all the advisers who may have influenced his mind, more or less honestly, more or less powerfully, and to make them responsible civilly for the consequences of what after all is his own act, and for the whole of the hurtful consequences of which the law makes him directly and fully responsible, that I believe it will never be contended for seriously. . . . Persuading with effect, or effectually or successfully persuading, may no doubt sometimes be actionable — as in trespass — even where it is used towards a free agent: the maxims qui facit per alium facit per se, and respondeat superior, are unquestionable; but, where they apply, the wrongful act done is properly charged to be the act of him who has procured it to be done. He is sued as a principal trespasser, and the damage, if proved, flows directly and immediately from his act, though it was the hand of another, and he a free agent, that was employed. But, when you apply the term of effectual persuasion to the breach of a contract, it has obviously a different meaning; the persuader has not broken and could not break the contract, for he had never entered into any; he cannot be sued upon the contract; and yet it is the breach of the contract only that is the cause of damage. Neither can it be said that in breaking the contract the contractor is the agent of him who procures him to do so; it is still his own act; he is principal in so doing, and is the only principal. This answer may seem technical; but it really goes to the root of the matter. It shows that the procurer has not done the hurtful act; what he has done is too remote from the damage to make him answerable for it. [After discussing certain precedents, Judge Coleridge continued:] None of this reasoning applies to the case of a breach of contract: if it does, I should be glad to know how any treatise on the law of contract could be complete without a chapter on this head, or how it happens that we have no decisions upon it. Certainly no subject could well be more fruitful or important; important contracts are more commonly broken with than without persuaders or procurers, and these often responsible persons when the principals may not be so. I am aware that with respect to an action on the case the argument primae impressionis is sometimes of no weight. If the circumstances under which the action would be brought have not before arisen, or are of rare occurrence, it will be of none, or only of inconsiderable weight; but, if the circumstances have been common, if there has been frequently occasion for the action, I apprehend it is important to find that the action has yet never been tried. Now we find a plentiful supply both of text and decision in the case of seduction of servants: and what inference does this lead to, contrasted with the silence of the books and the absence of decisions on the case of breach of ordinary contracts? . . . To draw a line between advice, persuasion, enticement and procurement is practically impossible in a court of justice; who shall say how much of a free agent's resolution flows from the interference of other minds, or the independent resolution of his own? This is a matter for the casuist rather than the jurist; still less is it for the juryman. Again, why draw the line between bad and good faith? If advice given mala fide, and loss sustained, entitle me to damages, why, though the advice be given honestly, but under wrong information, with a loss sustained, am I not entitled to them. According to all legal analogies, the bona fides of him who, by a conscious wilful act, directly injures me will not relieve him from the obligation to compensate me in damages for my loss. Again, where several persons happen to persuade to the same effect, and in the result the party persuaded acts upon the advice, how is it to be determined against whom the action may be brought, whether they are to be sued jointly or severally, in what proportions damages are to be recovered? . . .

I conclude then that this action cannot be maintained because: 1st. Merely to induce or procure a free contracting party to break his covenant, whether done maliciously or not, to the damage of another, for the reasons I have stated, is not actionable; 2d. That the law with regard to seduction of servants from their master's employ, in breach of their contract, is an exception, the origin of which is known, and that that exception does not reach the case of a theatrical performer. . . .

Judgment for plaintiff.

NOTES

1. Protection of contractual interests under Lumley v. Gye. Lumley v. Gye involved a personal services contract with a party of unique operatic skills. Subsequent decisions made it clear that the tort of inducement of breach was applicable to all types of contractual arrangements. In Bowen v. Hall, 6 Q.B.D. 333 (1881), the principle of Lumley v. Gye was applied to the contract of an employee brickmaker (albeit one who had knowledge of a secret glazing process) who was induced to breach a firm five-year contract of employment with the plaintiff. The court held that malice was the gist of the tort and then noted that though "mere persuasion" was not actionable, "if the persuasion be used for the indirect purpose of injuring the plaintiff, or of benefiting the defendant at the expense of the plaintiff, it is a malicious act." How does this definition of malice differ from the "notice" referred to by Crompton, J., in Lumley v. Gye? Shortly thereafter, in Temperton v. Russell, [1893] 1 Q.B. 715, inducement of breach of contract was held to reach interference with an ordinary contract for the sale of goods, here in the context of a labor dispute. On the early history and expansion of the action see

Note, Tortious Interference With Contractual Relations in the Nineteenth Century: The Transformation of Property, Contract, and Tort, 93 Harv. L. Rev. 1510 (1980).

Perhaps the most controversial application of the tort of inducement of breach of contract has stemmed from its use as a weapon of business in labor disputes. The leading case is Hitchman Coal & Coke Co. v. Mitchell, 245 U.S. 229 (1917). There the defendants were employees of the Mineworkers Union who had induced the miners at the plaintiff's mine to stay on the job after they had agreed to join the union. The miners' conduct was found in breach of their "yellow-dog" contract between the employer and the workers whereby the miners, working under a contract at will, agreed not to join a union while in the plaintiff's employ. The case drew a strong dissent by Brandeis, J. Note that the result in *Hitchman* was changed in the labor context first in 1932 by the Norris-LaGuardia Act, 29 U.S.C. §101 et seq. (1988 & Supp. 1993), which prohibited the enforcement of yellow-dog contracts in federal courts, 29 U.S.C. §103 (1988 & Supp. 1993), and thereafter in 1935 by the National Labor Relations Act, 29 U.S.C. §151 et seq. (1988 & Supp. 1993), which made it an "unfair labor practice" to discriminate against employees because of their participation in union activities. 29 U.S.C. §158. For an early defense of the statute see Magruder, A Half Century of Legal Influence upon the Development of Collective Bargaining, 50 Harv. L. Rev. 1071 (1937); for a defense of the common-law regime see Epstein, A Common Law for Labor Relations: A Critique of the New Deal Labor Legislation, 92 Yale L.J. 1357 (1983).

2. *Contracts covered by the tort.* In *Lumley* the plaintiff's contract afforded him an undeniable cause of action against Wagner. Should the defendant's inducement be actionable when there is some infirmity in the underlying contract? The tort in general will not lie when the underlying contract is void, as with gambling contracts in violation of public policy. Yet the tort action is available for inducing nonperformance of contracts with lesser infirmities. Thus there is ample authority that the defendant's conduct is actionable even if the contract between the plaintiff and the third party is voidable (say, because a child is underage) or unenforceable (say, because of the statute of limitations or the statute of frauds). See Restatement (Second) of Torts §766. It has also been said that the defendant's conduct is actionable even if the contract between the plaintiff and the defendant is terminable at the will of either party. See, e.g., Walker v. Cronin, 107 Mass. 555 (1871). That general statement is clearly true to the extent that one of the parties is induced to breach the contract in question: in *Walker,* the employee refused to return tools and materials to the employer upon leaving employment terminable at will. But it is highly unlikely that the doctrine applies with equal force when the employee's conduct is *not*

in breach of contract, as when he simply leaves the plaintiff for higher wages elsewhere.

3. Basis of liability for inducement of breach of contract. Today the Restatement (Second) of Torts §766 provides that "[o]ne who intentionally and improperly interferes with the performance of a contract" is subject to tortious liability such that "the actor must have knowledge of the contract with which he is interfering." §766 comment *i*. Liability for inducement thus stands on a different footing than liability for ordinary physical damage to person and property. One explanation for the current rule is offered in Epstein, Inducement of Breach of Contract as a Problem of Ostensible Ownership, 16 J. Legal Stud. 1, 24 (1987), where it is argued that the notice system here is closely analogous to that applied when, for example, a bailee sells the bailed goods to a third party. When the third party has knowledge of the original bailment arrangement, he is treated as a purchaser in bad faith from whom the true owner can recover the goods. When that third party is innocent, the claim of the true owner is often denied because the bailee looks like the "ostensible owner" to the rest of the world, so that the third party is a purchaser in good faith. "The tort of inducement of breach of contract is designed to protect contracts for the sale of labor by preventing others from subsequently acquiring that labor for themselves, once they know it has been committed to another. It is a restriction against double-dealing." Accordingly, the plaintiff may only maintain the action for inducement of breach of contract against one who *knows* of the existence of the contract, as Lumley v. Gye provides. With personal service contracts, moreover, actual notice is typically required, for although interests in land and certain valuable chattels (airplanes, cars) may be protected by recordation, ordinary labor contracts themselves cannot be recorded. When celebrities are involved, therefore, the best protection may be to publicly announce the signing of a contract in order to place the world on notice of the existence of the contract, without, however, revealing any confidential terms.

4. Privileges for inducement of breach of contract. The tort of inducement of breach has brought with it a broad, if undefined, set of privileges not dissimilar to those available to a defendant in a defamation action. Thus it has been said that the interference is privileged when it arises from a disinterested desire to protect the obligor, see Said v. Butt, [1920] 3 K.B. 497; or when done in order to further public morals, as in Brimelow v. Casson, [1924] 1 Ch. 302, where the plaintiff was alleged to have employed chorus girls on such unfavorable terms that they had to resort to immoral conduct, including in some instances prostitution, to earn enough money to live. See generally Restatement (Second) of Torts §767.

One privilege of great practical importance generally allows the officer or lawyer of a firm to advise the firm to breach an existing contract. The officer or lawyer is not treated as an independent third party acting for economic advantage, but as acting pursuant to a "confidential arrangement" between the parties. See, e.g., Imperial Ice Co. v. Rossier, 112 P.2d 631 (Cal. 1941).

5. *Conspiracy to induce breach of contract.* One of the important features of inducement of breach of contract is that it allows the plaintiff to recover generous tort damages against a third party, even if recovery under the contract is limited by the narrower rules of contract damages or by specific contractual provisions, such as those prohibiting the recovery of consequential or punitive damages. In order to make an end run around those contract limitations, injured promisees have sought to hold their own trading partners liable for entering into a conspiracy to induce breach of their own contract. That strategy proved successful in Wise v. Southern Pacific Co., 35 Cal. Rptr. 652 (Cal. App. 1963), but was in turn rebuffed in Applied Equipment v. Litton Saudi Arabia, 869 P.2d 454, 461 (Cal. 1994), where the plaintiff, who had been designated by the defendant as its purchasing agent on commission, sued the defendant for conspiracy to induce breach of its own contract when the defendant had gone directly to the third-party buyer in order to avoid paying the contractual commission. Lucas, C.J., denied the inducement claim for these reasons:

> The fundamental differences between contract and tort are obscured by the imposition of tort liability on a contracting party for conspiracy to interfere with contact. Whether or not a stranger to the contract induces its breach, the essential character of a contracting party's conduct remains the same — an unjustified failure or refusal to perform. In economic terms, the impact is identical — plaintiff has lost the benefit of a bargain and is entitled to recover compensation in the form of contract damages. In ethical terms, the mere entry of a stranger onto the scene does not render the contracting party's breach more socially or morally reprehensible. A party may breach a contract without any third party inducement because of personal, racial or ethnic animus, or for other nefarious or unethical reasons. In contrast a breach may be the product of naive or innocent misunderstanding or misperception created by the aggressive solicitation of an outsider. In any case, motivation is irrelevant. Regardless of the presence or absence of third party involvement, the contracting party has done nothing more opprobrious than to fall short in meeting a contractual commitment. Only contract damages are due.

Mosk, J., dissented, relying on earlier authority which held: "If it be an actionable wrong for a third person to interfere in a contract and induce one of the parties thereto to break it to the injury of the other, can it be said it is not equally a wrong for one of the parties to the contract to invite a third party to unite with him and aid him breaking the contract in such a way as possibly to escape liability in an action for nonperformance and, gaining his consent, to act together in consummating their agreement?" Motley, Green & Co. v. Detroit Steel & Spring Co. 161 F. 389, 397 (S.D.N.Y. 1908).

Suppose the agreement stipulates for double damages in the event that the defendant deliberately breaches a contract in order to join forces with a third party. More generally, is the dispute in *Applied Equipment* over the choice of a positive rule of law or a default rule of contract interpretation?

6. *Inducement of breach of contract: the theory of efficient breach.* As the dissent of Coleridge, J., indicates, there is no uniform acceptance of the tort of inducement of breach, at least when it does not involve means unlawful in themselves. One notable attack on the doctrine of Lumley v. Gye rests on the principle that the tort of inducement of breach of contract may be misplaced because breach of contract itself may create social wealth by increasing overall consumer satisfaction. See Perlman, Interference With Contract and Other Economic Expectancies: A Clash of Tort and Contract Doctrine, 49 U. Chi. L. Rev. 61 (1982).

Perlman's argument in essence hearkens back to Holmes's famous aphorism: "The only universal consequence of a legally binding promise is, that the law makes the promisor pay damages if the promised event does not come to pass." Holmes, The Common Law 301 (1881). In modern terms, it is said that breach of contract can be efficient whenever it allows the promisor to shift his resources to a higher-value use. The innocent party is left well off by an award of damages equal to the benefits provided under the contract; the promisor is left better off, having purchased his freedom; the net social welfare is therefore increased. The theory of "efficient breach" thus holds that a promisor should always be allowed to extricate himself unilaterally from a bargain if he is prepared to pay the proper social price. The argument concludes that inducement of breach of contract should not be a tort at all because it unduly complicates and undermines the incentives of contractual parties not to breach contracts when efficient to do so. The gist of Perlman's position, therefore, is that the action should be restricted to instances in which the defendant has used unlawful and independently tortious means, chiefly force or fraud, to induce the breach.

The soundness of the argument depends at least in part on the ability of the expectation measure of damages to leave a promisee indifferent between performance and breach. But if the contract damages do not reflect cash values, then the damage recovery, net of litigation costs, could well leave the innocent promisee worse off. See Epstein, supra note 3, at pages 37-40; Friedmann, The Efficient Breach Fallacy, 18 J. Legal Stud. 1 (1989), arguing in part that the costs of untangling expectation damages may well exceed the costs needed to negotiate a release from the original contract.

Note, too, that the model of expectation damages as the ideal contract remedy is not fully accepted in contract law. Specific performance is generally allowed in real estate transactions (and other cases involving "unique" goods) and, even with personal service contracts, a promisee may obtain an injunction that prevents the promisor from undertaking employment inconsistent with previous contractual obligations. Indeed, in Lumley v. Wagner, 42 Eng. Rep. 687, 693 (Ch. 1852), the companion case to Lumley v. Gye, Lumley was able to enjoin Wagner from singing elsewhere.

> Wherever this Court has not proper jurisdiction to enforce specific performance, it operates to bind men's consciences, as far as they can be bound, to a true and literal performance of their agreements; and it will not suffer them to depart from their contracts at their pleasure, leaving the party with whom they have contracted to the mere chance of any damages which a jury may give.. . . The effect, too, of the injunction in restraining J. Wagner from singing elsewhere may, in the event of an action being brought against her by the Plaintiff, prevent any such amount of vindictive damages being given against her as a jury might probably be inclined to give if she carried her talents and exercised them at the rival theatre: the injunction may also, as I have said, tend to the fulfilment of her engagement; though, in continuing the injunction, I disclaim doing indirectly what I cannot do directly.

Why no decree ordering Wagner to sing? What alternative account might be given of the tort? For the classical treatments of the subject see Sayre, Inducing Breach of Contract, 36 Harv. L. Rev. 663 (1923); Carpenter, Interference with Contract Relations, 41 Harv. L. Rev. 728 (1928). For another recent criticism of the tort see Dobbs, Tortious Interference With Contractual Relationships, 34 Ark. L. Rev. 335 (1980).

7. *The Texaco-Pennzoil fiasco.* The learned tort of inducement of breach of contract provided some high drama in connection with the takeover battle between Texaco and Pennzoil for Getty Oil. Much simplified, Getty and Pennzoil had reached an agreement in principle to sell the Getty shares to Pennzoil, when at the last moment Texaco topped the Pennzoil offer. Pennzoil's suit for inducement of breach of contract resulted in a verdict of $7.53 billion in actual damages and $2.5 billion in punitive damages. The jury award was upheld against a myriad of state law challenges in Texaco, Inc. v. Pennzoil, 729 S.W.2d 768 (Tex. App. 1987), and the case wound its way through the federal courts to the United States Supreme Court on exotic grounds of federal jurisdiction in Texaco, Inc. v. Pennzoil, 485 U.S. 994 (1988), until it settled for some $3 billion. For accounts of the case see T. Petzinger, Jr., Oil & Honor: The Texaco-Pennzoil Wars (1987); J. Shannon, Texaco and the $10 Billion Jury (1988); Epstein, The Pirates of Pennzoil, Regulation 18 (Nov./Dec. 1985).

C. INTERFERENCE WITH PROSPECTIVE ADVANTAGE

Tarleton v. M'Gawley
170 Eng. Rep. 153 (K.B. 1793)

This was a special action on the case. The declaration stated that the plaintiffs were possessed and owners of a certain ship called the *Tarleton*, which at the time of committing the grievance was lying at Calabar on the coast of Africa, under the command of Fairweather. That the ship had been fitted out at Liverpool with goods proper for trading with the natives of that coast for slaves and other goods. That also before the [sic] committing the grievance Fairweather had sent a smaller vessel called the *Bannister* with a crew on board, under the command of one Thomas Smith, and loaded with goods proper for trading with the natives, to another part of the said coast called Cameroon, to trade with the natives there. That while the last-mentioned ship was lying off Cameroon, a canoe with some natives on board came to the same for the purpose of establishing a trade, and went back to the shore, of which defendant had notice. And that he well knowing the premises, but contriving and maliciously intending to hinder and deter the natives from trading with the said Thomas Smith, for the benefit of the plaintiffs, with force and arms, fired from a certain ship called the *Othello*, of which he was master and commander, a certain cannon loaded with gunpowder and shot at the said canoe, and killed one of the natives on board the same. Whereby the natives of the said coast were deterred and hindered from trading with the said T. Smith for the benefit, &c. and plaintiffs lost their trade.

The plaintiffs called Thomas Smith, who proved the facts stated in the declaration; and further, that the defendant had declared the natives owed him a debt, and that he would not suffer any ship to trade with them until that was paid; in pursuance of which declaration he committed the act complained of by the plaintiffs. On his cross-examination he admitted that by the custom of that coast no Europeans can trade until a certain duty has been paid to the king of the country for his licence, and that no such duty had been paid, or licence obtained by the captain of the plaintiff's vessel.

Law, for the defendant, contended that the plaintiffs being engaged in a trade which by the law of that country was illicit, could not support an action for an interruption of such illicit commerce, and compared this case to an action brought for interrupting a plaintiff in his endeavours to smuggle goods into this country, or alarming the owner of a house which the plaintiff was about to break into. He also objected that this act of the defendant amounted to a felony, and therefore could not be made the ground of a civil action, but he did not lay much stress on this objection.

LORD KENYON. This action is brought by the plaintiffs to recover a satisfaction for a civil injury which they have sustained. The injury complained of is, that by the improper conduct of the defendant the natives were prevented from trading with the plaintiffs. The whole of the case is stated on the record, and if the parties desire it, the opinion of the Court may hereafter be taken whether it will support an action. I am of opinion it will. This case has been likened to cases which it does not at all resemble. It has been said that a person engaged in a trade violating the law of the country cannot support an action against another for hindering him in that illegal traffick. That I entirely accede to, but it does not apply to this case. This is a foreign law; the act of trading is not itself immoral, and a jus positivum is not binding on foreigners. The king of the country and not the defendant should have executed that law. Had this been an accidental thing, no action could have been maintained, but it is proved that the defendant had expressed an intention not to permit any to trade, until a debt due from the natives to himself was satisfied. If there was any Court in that country to which he could have applied for justice he might have done so, but he had no right to take the law into his own hands.

The plaintiffs had a verdict, and the parties agreed to refer the damages to arbitration.

Note. — In the beginning of the cause the plaintiffs' counsel proposed asking the witnesses whether some of the negroes did not assign their fear of the defendant as a reason for not trading with the plaintiffs, but Lord Kenyon said that no declaration of the negroes could be received in evidence.

NOTE

Prospective advantage and unlawful means. The protection afforded the plaintiff in *Tarleton* is both narrower and broader than that in Lumley v. Gye. It is narrower in that prospective advantage is protected only against interference by means that are unlawful in themselves, in this case the use of force against the natives. But it is broader in that it protects not only the promisee who may have actions against the promisor under an existing contract, but also the promisee who may have no action even though a contract exists (as in contracts terminable at will), and the party who was never able to form a contract in the first place. Why is there a need for a separate action by the plaintiff when the customers are protected by a wide array of tort actions? In evaluating the plaintiff's case in *Tarleton*, should it make a difference whether the customers suffer physical injury or only the loss of a bargain? Note that one frequent justification for the result in *Tarleton* is that the action by the trader helps vindicate the economic interests of potential customers who might be reluctant to incur heavy litigation costs to recover for small economic losses.

While the facts of *Tarleton* are both novel and dramatic, the principle of recovery that the case endorses has a long common-law lineage.

In Keeble v. Hickeringill, 103 Eng. Rep. 1127, 1128 (Q.B. 1706) (reported K.B. 1809), plaintiff used decoy ducks to attract wild fowl to his meadow for the purpose of capturing and selling them. Defendant repeatedly discharged guns nearby in order to drive away the ducks. He was successful and plaintiff sued. In affirming a verdict for plaintiff, Holt, C.J., said:

> if Mr. Hickeringill had set up another decoy on his own ground near the plaintiff, no action would lie because he had as much liberty to make and use a decoy as the plaintiff. . . . One schoolmaster sets up a new school to the damage of an antient school, and thereby the scholars are allured from the old school to come to his new. (The action was held there not to lie.) But suppose Mr. Hickeringill should lie in the way with his guns, and fright the boys from going to school, and their parents would not let them go thither; sure the schoolmaster might have an action for the loss of his scholars.

What other means unlawful in themselves are sufficient to support the plaintiff's action? In Evenson v. Spalding, 150 F. 517, 522 (9th Cir. 1907), the plaintiffs were Iowa manufacturers of high-class buggies and wagons who sold their product in the state of Washington through salesmen and agents. The defendants were employees of an association of Washington buggy manufacturers; they dogged the plaintiffs' salesmen whenever they tried to sell their wagons and buggies to local customers, usually on a public highway. The court recognized that the defendants had the right to compete with the plaintiffs for sales to local customers, but held that the defendants' conduct exceeded the permissible limits of competition with its own "policy of molestation," here "by breaking in on conversations, making false representations as to the nature of the appellees' goods . . . and other offensive acts."

People Express Airlines, Inc. v. Consolidated Rail Corp.
495 A.2d 107 (N.J. 1985)

HANDLER, J.

This appeal presents a question that has not previously been directly considered: whether a defendant's negligent conduct that interferes with a plaintiff's business resulting in purely economic losses, unaccompanied by property damage or personal injury, is compensable in tort. The appeal poses this issue in the context of the defendants' alleged negligence that caused a dangerous chemical to escape from a railway tank car, resulting in the evacuation from the surrounding area of persons whose safety and health were threatened. The plaintiff, a commercial airline, was forced to evacuate its premises and suffered an interruption of its business operations with resultant economic losses.

I

On July 22, 1981, a fire began in the Port Newark freight yard of defendant Consolidated Rail Corporation (Conrail) when ethylene oxide manufactured by defendant BASF Wyandotte Company (BASF) escaped from a tank car, punctured during a "coupling" operation with another rail car, and ignited. The tank car was owned by defendant Union Tank Car Company (Union Car) and was leased to defendant BASF.

The plaintiff asserted at oral argument that at least some of the defendants were aware from prior experiences that ethylene oxide is a highly volatile substance; further, that emergency response plans in case of an accident had been prepared. When the fire occurred that gave rise to this lawsuit, some of the defendants' consultants helped determine how much of the surrounding area to evacuate. The municipal authorities then evacuated the area within a one-mile radius surrounding the fire to lessen the risk to persons within the area should the burning tank car explode. The evacuation area included the adjacent North Terminal building of Newark International Airport, where plaintiff People Express Airlines' (People Express) business operations are based. Although the feared explosion never occurred, People Express employees were prohibited from using the North Terminal for twelve hours.

The plaintiff contends that it suffered business-interruption losses as a result of the evacuation. These losses consist of cancelled scheduled flights and lost reservations because employees were unable to answer the telephones to accept bookings; also, certain fixed operating expenses allocable to the evacuation time period were incurred and paid despite the fact that plaintiff's offices were closed. No physical damage to airline property and no personal injury occurred as a result of the fire.

According to People Express' original complaint, each defendant acted negligently and these acts of negligence proximately caused the plaintiff's harm. An amended complaint alleged additional counts of nuisance and strict liability based on the defendants' undertaking an abnormally dangerous activity, as well as defective manufacture or design of the tank car, causes of action with which we are not concerned here. . . .

II

The single characteristic that distinguishes parties in negligence suits whose claims for economic losses have been regularly denied by American and English courts from those who have recovered economic losses is, with respect to the successful claimants, the fortuitous occurrence of physical harm or property damage, however slight. It is well-accepted that a defendant who negligently injures a plaintiff or his property may be liable for all proximately caused harm, including economic losses. Nevertheless, a virtually per se rule barring recovery for economic loss unless the negligent conduct also caused physical harm has evolved throughout this century, based, in part, on Robins Dry Dock & Repair Co. v. Flint, 275 U.S. 303 (1927) and Cattle v. Stockton Waterworks Co., 10 Q.B. 453 (1875). This has occurred although neither case created a rule absolutely disallowing recovery in such circumstances. See, e.g., Stevenson v. East Ohio Gas Co., 73 N.E.2d 200 (Ohio Ct. App. 1946) (employee who was prohibited from working at his plant, which was closed due to conflagration begun by negligent rupture of stored liquified natural gas at nearby utility, could not recover lost wages); Byrd v. English, 43 S.E. 419 (Ga. 1903) (plaintiff who owned printing plant could not recover lost profits when defendant negligently damaged utility's electrical conduits that supplied power to the plant); see also Restatement (Second) of Torts §766C (1979) (positing rule of nonrecovery for purely economic losses absent physical harm). But see In re Kinsman Transit Co., 388 F.2d 821, 824 (2d Cir. 1968) (after rejecting an inflexible rule of nonrecovery, court applied traditional proximate cause analysis to claim for purely economic losses).

The reasons that have been advanced to explain the divergent results for litigants seeking economic losses are varied. Some courts have viewed the general rule against recovery as necessary to limit damages to reasonably foreseeable consequences of negligent conduct. This concern in a given case is often manifested as an issue of causation and has led to the requirement of physical harm as an element of proximate cause. In this context, the physical harm requirement functions as part of the definition of the causal relationship between the defendant's negligent act and the plaintiff's economic damages; it acts as a convenient clamp on otherwise boundless liability. The physical harm rule also reflects certain deep-seated concerns that underlie courts' denial of recovery for purely economic losses occasioned by a defendant's negligence. These concerns include the fear of fraudulent claims, mass litigation, and limitless liability, or liability out of proportion to the defendant's fault. . . .

Countervailing considerations of fairness and public policy have led courts to discard the requirement of physical harm as an element in defining proximate cause to overcome the problem of fraudulent or indefinite claims. See Dillon v. Legg, 441 P.2d 912 (Cal. 1968) (abandoning zone of danger rule in favor of a foreseeability test to determine whether the plaintiff may recover for mental distress arising from physical harm to another). . . .

The troublesome concern reflected in cases denying recovery for negligently-caused economic loss is the alleged potential for infinite liability, or liability out of all proportion to the defendant's fault. This objection is also not confined to negligently-caused economic injury. The same objection has been asserted and, ultimately, rejected by this Court and others in allowing recovery for other forms of negligent torts, see H. Rosenblum, Inc. v. Adler, 461 A.2d 138 (N.J. 1983), and in the creation of the doctrine of strict liability for defective products, see Feldman v. Lederle Laboratories, 479 A.2d 374 (N.J. 1984); Henningsen v. Bloomfield Motors, Inc., 161 A.2d 69 (N.J. 1960), and ultrahazardous activities, see Dep't of Envtl. Protection v. Ventron Corp., 468 A.2d 150 (N.J. 1983). The answer to the allegation of unchecked liability is not the judicial obstruction of a fairly grounded claim for redress. Rather, it must be a more sedulous application of traditional concepts of duty and proximate causation to the facts of each case.

It is understandable that courts, fearing that if even one deserving plaintiff suffering purely economic loss were allowed to recover, all such plaintiffs could recover, have anchored their rulings to the physical harm requirement. While the rationale is understandable, it supports only a limitation on, not a denial of, liability. The physical harm requirement capriciously showers compensation along the path of physical destruction, regardless of the status or circumstances of individual claimants. Purely economic losses are borne by innocent victims, who may not be able to absorb their losses. In the end, the challenge is to fashion a rule that limits liability but permits adjudication of meritorious claims. The asserted inability to fix chrystalline formulae for recovery on the differing facts of future cases simply does not justify the wholesale rejection of recovery in all cases.

Further, judicial reluctance to allow recovery for purely economic losses is discordant with contemporary tort doctrine. The torts process, like the law itself, is a human institution designed to accomplish certain social objectives. One objective is to ensure that innocent victims have avenues of legal redress, absent a contrary, overriding public policy. This reflects the overarching purpose of tort law: that wronged persons should be compensated for their injuries and that those responsible for the wrong should bear the cost of their tortious conduct.

Other policies underlie this fundamental purpose. Imposing liability on defendants for their negligent conduct discourages others from similar tortious behavior, fosters safer products to aid our daily tasks, vindicates reasonable conduct that has regard for the safety of others, and, ultimately, shifts the risk of loss and associated costs of dangerous activities to those who should be and are best able to bear them. Although these policies may be unevenly reflected or imperfectly articulated in any particular case, we strive to ensure that the application of negligence doctrine advances the fundamental purpose of tort law and does not unnecessarily or arbitrarily foreclose redress based on formalisms or technicalisms. Whatever the original common law justifications for the physical harm rule, contemporary tort and negligence doctrine allow — indeed, impel — a more thorough consideration and searching analysis of underlying policies to determine whether a particular defendant may be liable for a plaintiff's economic losses despite the absence of any attendant physical harm. . . .

A

Judicial discomfiture with the rule of nonrecovery for purely economic loss throughout the last several decades has led to numerous exceptions in the general rule. Although the rationalizations for these exceptions differ among courts and cases, two common threads run throughout the exceptions. The first is that the element of foreseeability emerges as a more appropriate analytical standard to determine the question of liability than a per se prohibitory rule. The second is that the extent to which the defendant knew or should have known the particular consequences of his negligence, including the economic loss of a particularly foreseeable plaintiff, is dispositive of the issues of duty and fault.

One group of exceptions is based on the "special relationship" between the tortfeasor and the individual or business deprived of economic expectations. Many of these cases are recognized as involving the tort of negligent misrepresentation, resulting in liability for specially foreseeable economic losses. Importantly, the cases do not involve a breach of contract claim between parties in privity; rather, they involve tort claims by innocent third parties who suffered purely economic losses at the hands of negligent defendants with whom no direct relationship existed. Courts have justified their finding of liability in these negligence cases based on notions of a special relationship between the negligent tortfeasors and the foreseeable plaintiffs who relied on the quality of defendants' work or services, to their detriment. The special relationship, in reality, is an expression of the courts' satisfaction that a duty of care existed because the plaintiffs were particularly foreseeable and the injury was proximately caused by the defendant's negligence. . . .

Courts have found it fair and just in all of these exceptional cases to impose liability on defendants who, by virtue of their special activities, professional training or other unique preparation for their work, had particular knowledge or reason to know that others, such as the intended beneficiaries of wills (e.g., Lucas v. Hamm, 364 P.2d 685 (Cal. 1961)) or the purchasers of stock who were expected to rely on the company's financial statement in the prospectus (e.g., H. Rosenblum, Inc. v. Adler), would be economically harmed by negligent conduct. In this group of cases, even though the particular plaintiff was not always foreseeable, the particular class of plaintiffs was foreseeable as was the particular type of injury.

A very solid exception allowing recovery for economic losses has also been created in cases akin to private actions for public nuisance. Where a plaintiff's business is based in part upon the exercise of a public right, the plaintiff has been able to recover purely economic losses caused by a defendant's negligence. See, e.g., Louisiana ex rel. Guste v. M/V Testbank, 752 F.2d 1019 (5th Cir. 1985) (en banc) (defendants responsible for ship collision held liable to all commercial fishermen, shrimpers, crabbers and oystermen for resulting pollution of Mississippi River); Union Oil Co. v. Oppen, 501 F.2d 558 (9th Cir. 1974) (fishermen making known commercial use of public waters may recover economic losses due to defendant's oil spill); Masonite Corp. v. Steede, 23 So. 2d 756 (Miss. 1945) (operator of fishing resort may recover lost profits due to pollution); . . .

Particular knowledge of the economic consequences has sufficed to establish duty and proximate cause in contexts other than those already considered. In Henry Clay v. Jersey City, 181 A.2d 545 (Ch. Div. 1962), aff'd, 200 A.2d 787 (A.D. 1964), for example, a lessee-manufacturer had to vacate the building in which its business was located because of the defendant city's negligent failure to maintain its sewer line while the line was repaired. While there was some property damage, the court treated the tenant's and owner's claims separately; the tenant's claims were purely economic, stemming from the loss of use of its property right, as in the instant case. Further, the city had had notice of the leak since 1957 and should have known about it even earlier. Duty, breach and proximate cause were found to exist; the plaintiff-tenant recovered lost profits and expenses incurred during the shut-down. See also J'Aire Corp. v. Gregory, 598 P.2d 60 (Cal. 1979).

These exceptions expose the hopeless artificiality of the per se rule against recovery for purely economic losses. When the plaintiffs are reasonably foreseeable, the injury is directly and proximately caused by defendant's negligence, and liability can be limited fairly, courts have endeavored to create exceptions to allow recovery. The scope and number of exceptions, while independently justified on various grounds, have nonetheless created lasting doubt as to the wisdom of the per se rule of nonrecovery for purely economic losses. Indeed, it has been fashionable for commentators to state that the rule has been giving way for nearly fifty years, although the cases have not always kept pace with the hypothesis. . . .

We hold therefore that a defendant owes a duty of care to take reasonable measures to avoid the risk of causing economic damages, aside from physical injury, to particular plaintiffs or plaintiffs comprising an identifiable class with respect to whom defendant knows or has reason to know are likely to suffer such damages from its conduct. A defendant failing to adhere to this duty of care may be found liable for such economic damages proximately caused by its breach of duty.

We stress that an identifiable class of plaintiffs is not simply a foreseeable class of plaintiffs. For example, members of the general public, or invitees such as sales and service persons at a particular plaintiff's business premises, or persons travelling on a highway near the scene of a negligently-caused accident, such as the one at bar, who are delayed in the conduct of their affairs and suffer varied economic losses, are certainly a foreseeable class of plaintiffs. Yet their presence within the area would be fortuitous, and the particular type of economic injury that could be suffered by such persons would be hopelessly unpredictable and not realistically foreseeable. Thus, the class itself would not be sufficiently ascertainable. An identifiable class of plaintiffs must be particularly foreseeable in terms of the type of persons or entities comprising the class, the certainty or predictability of their presence, the approximate numbers of those in the class, as well as the type of economic expectations disrupted.

We recognize that some cases will present circumstances that defy the categorization here devised to circumscribe a defendant's orbit of duty, limit otherwise boundless liability and define an identifiable class of plaintiffs that may recover. In these cases, the courts will be required to draw upon notions of fairness, common sense and morality to fix the line limiting liability as a matter of public policy, rather than an uncritical application of the principle of particular foreseeability.

B

Liability depends not only on the breach of a standard of care but also on a proximate causal relationship between the breach of the duty of care and resultant losses. The standard of particular foreseeability may be successfully employed to determine whether the economic injury was proximately caused, i.e., whether the particular harm that occurred is compensable, just as it informs the question whether a duty exists. . . .

We conclude therefore that a defendant who has breached his duty of care to avoid the risk of economic injury to particularly foreseeable plaintiffs may be held liable for actual economic losses that are proximately caused by its breach of duty. In this context, those economic losses are recoverable as damages when they are the natural and probable consequence of a defendant's negligence in the sense that they are reasonably to be anticipated in view of defendant's capacity to have foreseen that the particular plaintiff or identifiable class of plaintiffs is demonstrably within the risk created by defendant's negligence.

III

We are satisfied that our holding today is fully applicable to the facts that we have considered on this appeal. Plaintiff has set forth a cause of action under our decision, and it is entitled to have the matter proceed to a plenary trial. Among the facts that persuade us that a cause of action has been established is the close proximity of the North Terminal and People Express Airlines to the Conrail freight yard; the obvious nature of the plaintiff's operations and particular foreseeability of economic losses resulting from an accident and evacuation; the defendants' actual or constructive knowledge of the volatile properties of ethylene oxide; and the existence of an emergency response plan prepared by some of the defendants (alluded to in the course of oral argument), which apparently called for the nearby area to be evacuated to avoid the risk of harm in case of an explosion. We do not mean to suggest by our recitation of these facts that actual knowledge of the eventual economic losses is necessary to the cause of action; rather, particular foreseeability will suffice. The plaintiff still faces a difficult task in proving damages, particularly lost profits, to the degree of certainty required in other negligence cases. The trial court's examination of these proofs must be exacting to ensure that damages recovered are those reasonably to have been anticipated in view of the defendants' capacity to have foreseen that this particular plaintiff was within the risk created by their negligence.

We appreciate that there will arise many similar cases that cannot be resolved by our decision today. The cause of action we recognize, however, is one that most appropriately should be allowed to evolve on a case-by-case basis in the context of actual adjudications. We perceive no reason, however, why our decision today should be applied only prospectively. Our holdings are well grounded in traditional tort principles and flow from well-established exceptional cases that are philosophically compatible with this decision.

Accordingly, the judgment of the Appellate Division is modified, and, as modified, affirmed. The case is remanded for proceedings consistent with this opinion.

For modification and affirmance — Chief Justice WILENTZ, and Justices CLIFFORD, HANDLER, O'HERN, GARIBALDI and STEIN — 6.

For reversal — None.

NOTES

1. Tort recovery for economic loss. As the decision in *People Express* indicates, the common-law judges were historically reluctant to allow any recovery for pure economic losses attributable only to the defendant's negligence. Perhaps the leading case for this point of view was Byrd v. English, 43 S.E. 419, 420 (Ga. 1902), where the defendant's negligent excavation severed the power lines, owned by the electric company, that supplied the power that led to the plaintiff's plant. The plaintiff's cause of action was denied on grounds reminiscent of Winterbottom v. Wright, supra at page 730:

> According to this petition, the damage done by them was to the property of the Georgia Electric Light Company, which was under contract to furnish to the plaintiff electric power, and the resulting damage done to the plaintiff was that it was rendered impossible for that company to comply with its contract. If the plaintiff can recover of these defendants upon this cause of action, then a customer of his, who was injured by the delay occasioned by the stopping of his work, could also recover from them; and one who had been damaged through his delay could in turn hold them liable; and so on without limit to the number of persons who might recover on account of the injury done to the property of the company owning the conduits. To state such a proposition is to demonstrate its absurdity. The plaintiff is suing on account of an alleged tort by reason of which he was deprived of a supply of electric power with which to operate his printing establishment. What was his right to that power supply? Solely the right given him by virtue of his contract with the Georgia Electric Light Company, and with that contract the defendants are not even remotely connected. If, under the terms of his contract, he is precluded from recovering from the electric light company, that is a matter between themselves for which the defendants certainly can not be held responsible. They are, of course, liable to the company for any wrong that may have been done it, and the damages recoverable on that account might well be held to include any sums which the company was compelled to pay in damages to its customers; but the customers themselves can not go against the defendants to recover on their own account for the injury done the company.

Earlier cases developed the same theme. In Cattle v. Stockton Waterworks Co., 10 L.R.Q.B. 453, 457 (1875), the defendant waterworks company had constructed and maintained its pipes on the land of Knight in a negligent manner. The plaintiff had been hired for a fixed reward to build a tunnel on Knight's land and was required to incur increased costs when the water from the defendant's leaky pipes flooded his operations. Blackburn, J., was prepared to concede that Knight could have recovered damage for the increased cost of the completion if he had constructed the tunnel himself, but he denied recovery for those same costs at the insistence of the plaintiff. He argued that if the action was allowed "we should establish an authority for saying that, in such a case as that of Fletcher v. Rylands the defendant would be liable, not only to an action by the owner of the drowned mine, and by such of his workmen as had their tools or clothes destroyed, but also to an action by every workman and person employed in the mine, who in consequence of its stoppage made less wages than he otherwise would have done." He then distinguished Lumley v. Gye, noting that it was limited to "malicious" actions by the defendant. Does the point hold if "malice" in *Lumley* is coterminous with "notice"?

A narrow view of recovery for economic loss was also taken in Robins Dry Dock & Repair Co. v. Flint, 275 U.S. 303 (1927). There the plaintiffs hired a boat on a time charter with the third-party owner. The terms of the time charter called for the boat to be docked for maintenance and repair once every six months, with payments of money on the charter suspended until the boat was returned to service. While the boat was in the defendant's docks, the defendant negligently damaged the propeller, thereby causing the plaintiffs to lose the use of the boat for a two-week period while the necessary repairs were made. It was stipulated that the defendant took the boat in ignorance of the time charter or its terms. The accident took place in August 1917, shortly after the United States entered World War I, so the time charter offered the plaintiff highly favorable rates. In an earlier action arising out of the same incident, the plaintiff was not allowed to recover the lost value of the charter from the owner on a contract theory: the owner had discharged its obligation by selecting a competent independent contractor for the repairs, The Bjornefjord, 271 F. 282 (2d Cir. 1921). In the instant action the plaintiff was awarded recovery in tort by the Second Circuit, Flint v. Robins Dry Dock & Repair Co., 13 F.2d 3, 5 (2d Cir. 1926), with Mack, J., arguing as follows:

> Clearly, the result reached involves no injustice to respondent. Its liability for its tortious act is for the actual damage done to the combined interests in the ship. The measure of the total recovery is the market value of the loss of the use. If there had been no charter, the entire loss would have been sustained by the owner; therefore he could have recovered that amount himself. The wrongdoer has no interest in and should not benefit because of the contractual obligations of the shipowner to the charterer, or the absence of any liability of the owner to the charterer for respondent's negligence. This nonliability of the owner is neither a test nor a measure of the wrongdoer's liability, for, though the owner be not directly liable to the charterer, he may nevertheless be liable over to him as a trustee for so much of the recovery from the wrongdoer as exceeds his own personal loss.

Justice Holmes, writing for a unanimous Court, reversed the Second Circuit and dismissed the plaintiff's cause of action in Robins Dry Dock & Repair Co. v. Flint, 275 U.S. 303, 308-309:

The question is whether the respondents have an interest protected by the law against unintended injuries inflicted upon the vessel by third persons who know nothing of the charter. If they have, it must be worked out through their contract relations with the owners, not on the postulate that they have a right *in rem* against the ship.

Of course the contract of the petitioner with the owners imposed no immediate obligation upon the petitioner to third persons, as we already have said, and whether the petitioner performed it promptly or with negligent delay was the business of the owners and of nobody else. But as there was a tortious damage to a chattel it is sought to connect the claim of the respondents with that in some way. The damage was material to them only as it caused the delay in making the repairs, and that delay would be a wrong to no one except for the petitioner's contract with the owners. The injury to the propeller was no wrong to the respondents but only to those to whom it belonged. But suppose that the respondent's loss flowed directly from that source. Their loss arose only through their contract with the owners — and while intentionally to bring about a breach of contract may give rise to a cause of action, no authority need be cited to how that, as a general rule, at least, a tort to the person or property of one man does not make the tortfeasor liable to another merely because the injured person was under a contract with that other, unknown to the doer of the wrong. The law does not spread its protection so far.

Can Judge Mack's position be sustained if the contract between the charterer and the owner precludes recovery of lost profits attributable to the negligence of the owner? Can Justice Holmes's position be sustained if that contract allows expectation damages?

For sentiments similar to Holmes's see Weller & Co. v. Foot & Mouth Disease Research Institute, [1966] 1 Q.B. 569, 587, which refused to award the plaintiff cattle auctioneers their lost profits from the defendant research institute after viruses escaped from the defendant's operations and infected cattle in the region, leading the minister of agriculture to close down the local markets. Widgery, J., explained his position as follows:

> In the present case, the defendants' duty to take care to avoid the escape of the virus was due to the foreseeable fact that the virus might infect cattle in the neighbourhood and cause them to die. The duty of care is accordingly owed to the owners of cattle in the neighbourhood, but the plaintiffs are not owners of cattle and have no proprietary interest in anything which might conceivably be damaged by the virus if it escaped. Even if the plaintiffs have a proprietary interest in the premises known as Farnham market, these premises are not in jeopardy. In my judgment, therefore, the plaintiffs' claim in negligence fails even if the assumptions of fact most favourable to them are made.

With *Robins* and *Weller* also contrast J'Aire Corporation v. Gregory, 598 P.2d 60, 64 (Cal. 1979), where the plaintiff restaurant could not open for business because of the failure of the defendant contractor to complete work on the heating and air conditioning system on premises owned by a third party and leased in part to plaintiff. The question before the court was "whether a contractor who undertakes construction work pursuant to a contract with the owner of premises may be held liable in tort for business losses suffered by a lessee when the contractor negligently fails to complete the project with due diligence." The court answered the question in the affirmative for much the same reasons adopted in *People's Express.*

> [T]his court finds that respondent [defendant] had a duty to complete construction in a manner that would have avoided unnecessary injury to appellant's business, even though the construction contract was with the owner of a building rather than with appellant, the tenant. It is settled that a contractor owes a duty to avoid injury to the person or property of third parties. As appellant points out, injury to a tenant's business can often result in greater hardship than damage to a tenant's person or property. Where the risk of harm is foreseeable, as it was in the present case, the injury to the plaintiff's economic interests should not go uncompensated merely because it was unaccompanied by any injury to his person or property.

Should the tenant in *J'Aire* be limited to its action against its landlord? After *J'Aire,* should construction companies insert clauses in their standard contracts that either require landlords to obtain waivers from actual or prospective tenants against the construction company or that call on the landlord to indemnify the construction company for its expenses or losses? But that course of action is not open in cases such as *People's Express,* where the plaintiff and defendant are total strangers. If the release of dangerous chemicals is a strict liability action, then why require proof of negligence for recovery of economic loss in *People's Express?* And why adopt more stringent tests of foresight?

See generally Rabin, Tort Recovery for Negligently Inflicted Economic Loss: A Reassessment, 37 Stan. L. Rev. 1513 (1985).

2. An economic analysis of economic losses. Finding a theoretical justification for disallowing recovery for pure economic loss at common law has not been easy. Part of the problem is that ordinary tort doctrines do not account for the denial of recovery in any straightforward way. The defendant is by hypothesis negligent; the plaintiff's harm is typically foreseeable, even if the precise identity of the plaintiff is not; there are rarely any intervening acts or events sufficient to sever the causal connection; and typically there are no affirmative defenses based on plaintiff's misconduct. Why then the denial?

Apart from the obvious administrative concerns, the law and economics literature has offered two explanations for the dominant legal rule. Bishop, Economic Loss in Tort, 2 Oxford J. Legal Stud. 1 (1982), suggests that the economic losses to the plaintiffs do not represent social losses because whatever business is lost by the plaintiff is picked up by some rival firm whose "excess capacity" is available to satisfy the increased demand. The aggrieved plaintiff receives no compensation because there is no social loss, since the private loss to one producer is offset by an (approximately) equal gain to another.

That argument has been criticized on two separate grounds. First, some social loss always remains because the substitute performance is more costly than that originally contemplated: otherwise, the plaintiff could not have obtained the business in the first place. Second, the unprotected plaintiff will take measures to avoid losses that are far more costly than the substitute precautions open to the negligent defendant.

An alternative explanation, suggested in Rizzo, A Theory of Economic Loss in the Law of Torts, 11 J. Legal Stud. 281 (1982), is that the denial of the plaintiff's right is made in order to reduce the number of potential suits by "channelling" tort liability through a small class of plaintiffs, typically those who have suffered physical injury. The property owner who recovers losses can then reimburse the contractors and others for their increased costs of completion under contract, as may have been intimated, for example, in both Cattle v. Stockton Waterworks, supra, and Robins Dry Dock v. Flint, supra. Is there any reason to suppose that litigation costs will be reduced if disputes arise under the contract of indemnity between the owner and the third-party contractor?

D. UNFAIR COMPETITION

Mogul Steamship Co. v. McGregor, Gow, & Co.
23 Q.B.D. 598 (1889), affirmed [1892] A.C. 25

BOWEN, L.J. We are presented in this case with an apparent conflict or antinomy between two rights that are equally regarded by the law — the right of the plaintiffs to be protected in the legitimate exercise of their trade, and the right of the defendants to carry on their business as seems best to them, provided they commit no wrong to others. The plaintiffs complain that the defendants have crossed the line which the common law permits; and inasmuch as, for the purposes of the present case, we are to assume some possible damage to the plaintiffs, the real question to be decided is whether, on such an assumption, the defendants in the conduct of their commercial affairs have done anything that is unjustifiable in law. The defendants are a number of shipowners who formed themselves into a league or conference for the purpose of ultimately keeping in their own hands the control of the tea carriage from certain

Chinese ports, and for the purpose of driving the plaintiffs and other competitors from the field. In order to succeed in this object, and to discourage the plaintiffs' vessels from resorting to those ports, the defendants during the "tea harvest" of 1885 combined to offer to the local shippers very low freights, with a view of generally reducing or "smashing" rates, and thus rendering it unprofitable for the plaintiffs to send their ships thither. They offered, moreover, a rebate of 5 per cent. to all local shippers and agents who would deal exclusively with vessels belonging to the Conference, and any agent who broke the condition was to forfeit the entire rebate on all shipments made on behalf of any and every one of his principals during the whole year — a forfeiture of rebate or allowance which was denominated as "penal" by the plaintiffs' counsel. It must, however, be taken as established that the rebate was one which the defendants need never have allowed at all to their customers. It must also be taken that the defendants had no personal ill-will to the plaintiffs, nor any desire to harm them except such as is involved in the wish and intention to discourage by such measures the plaintiffs from sending rival vessels to such ports. . . . It is to be observed with regard to all these acts of which complaint is made that they were acts that in themselves could not be said to be illegal unless made so by the object with which, or the combination in the course of which, they were done; and that in reality what is complained of is the pursuing of trade competition to a length which the plaintiffs consider oppressive and prejudicial to themselves. We were invited by the plaintiffs' counsel to accept the position from which their argument started — that an action will lie if a man maliciously and wrongfully conducts himself so as to injure another in that other's trade. Obscurity resides in the language used to state this proposition. The terms "maliciously," "wrongfully," and "injure" are words all of which have accurate meanings, well known to the law, but which also have a popular and less precise signification, into which it is necessary to see that the argument does not imperceptibly slide. An intent to "injure" in strictness means more than an intent to harm. It connotes an intent to do wrongful harm. "Maliciously," in like manner, means and implies an intention to do an act which is wrongful, to the detriment of another. The term "wrongful" imports in its turn the infringement of some right. The ambiguous proposition to which we were invited by the plaintiffs' counsel still, therefore, leaves unsolved the question of what, as between the plaintiffs and defendants, are the rights of trade. For the purpose of clearness, I desire, as far as possible, to avoid terms in their popular use so slippery, and to translate them into less fallacious language wherever possible.

      . . . Now, intentionally to do that which is calculated in the ordinary course of events to damage, and which does, in fact, damage another in that other person's property or trade, is actionable if done without just cause or excuse. Such intentional action when done without just cause or excuse is what the law calls a malicious wrong . . . .

. . . The acts of the defendants which are complained of here were intentional and were also calculated, no doubt, to do the plaintiffs damage in their trade. But in order to see whether they were wrongful we have still to discuss the question whether they were done without any just cause or excuse. Such just cause or excuse the defendants on their side assert to be found in their own positive right (subject to certain limitations) to carry on their own trade freely in the mode and manner that best suits them, and which they think best calculated to secure their own advantage.

What, then, are the limitations which the law imposes on a trader in the conduct of his business as between himself and other traders? There seem to be no burdens or restrictions in law upon a trader which arise merely from the fact that he is a trader, and which are not equally laid on all other subjects of the Crown. His right to trade freely is a right which the law recognises and encourages, but it is one which places him at no special disadvantage as compared with others. No man, whether trader or not, can, however, justify damaging another in his commercial business by fraud or misrepresentation. Intimidation, obstruction, and molestation are forbidden; so is the intentional procurement of a violation of individual rights, contractual or other, assuming always that there is no just cause for it. The intentional driving away of customers by shew of violence: Tarleton v. M'Gawley; the obstruction of actors on stage by preconcerted hissing: Clifford v. Brandon [170 Eng. Rep. 1183 (N.P. 1809)]; Gregory v. Brunswick [134 Eng. Rep. 866 (C.P. 1843)]; the disturbance of wild fowl in decoys by the firing of guns: Carrington v. Taylor [103 Eng. Rep. 1126 (K.B. 1809)], and Keeble v. Hickeringill [103 Eng. Rep. 1127 (Q.B. 1706)]; the impeding or threatening servants or workmen: Garret v. Taylor [79 Eng. Rep. 485 (K.B. 1620)]; the inducing persons under personal contracts to break their contracts: Bowen v. Hall; Lumley v. Gye; all are instances of such forbidden acts. But the defendants have been guilty of none of these acts. They have done nothing more against the plaintiffs than pursue to the bitter end a war of competition waged in the interest of their own trade. To the argument that a competition so pursued ceases to have a just cause or excuse when there is ill-will or a personal intention to harm, it is sufficient to reply (as I have already pointed out) that there was here no personal intention to do any other or greater harm to the plaintiffs than such as was necessarily involved in the desire to attract to the defendants' ships the entire tea freights of the ports, a portion of which would otherwise have fallen to the plaintiffs' share. I can find no authority for the doctrine that such a commercial motive deprives of "just cause or excuse" acts done in the course of trade which would but for such a motive be justifiable. So to hold would be to convert into an illegal motive the instinct of self-advancement and self-protection, which is the very incentive to all trade. To say that a man is to trade freely, but that he is to stop short at any act which is calculated to harm other tradesmen, and which is designed to attract business to his own shop, would be a strange and impossible counsel of perfection. But we were told that competition ceases to be the lawful exercise of trade, and so to be a lawful excuse for what will harm another, if carried to a length which is not fair or reasonable. The offering of reduced rates by the defendants in the present case is said to have been "unfair." This seems to assume that, apart from fraud, intimidation, molestation, or obstruction, of some other personal right in rem or in personam, there is some natural standard of "fairness" or "reasonableness" (to be determined by the internal consciousness of judges and juries) beyond which competition ought not in law to go. There seems to be no authority, and I think, with submission, that there is no sufficient reason for such a proposition. It would impose a novel fetter upon trade. The defendants, we are told by the plaintiffs' counsel, might lawfully lower rates provided they did not lower them beyond a "fair freight," whatever that may mean. But where is it established that there is any such restriction upon commerce? And what is to be the definition of a "fair freight"? It is said that it ought to be a normal rate of freight, such as is reasonably remunerative to the shipowner. But over what period of time is the average of this reasonable remunerativeness to be calculated? All commercial men with capital are acquainted with the ordinary expedient of sowing one year a crop of apparently unfruitful prices, in order by driving competition away to reap a fuller harvest of profit in the future; and until the present argument at the bar it may be doubted whether shipowners or merchants were ever deemed to be bound by law to conform to some imaginary "normal" standard of freights or prices, or that Law Courts had a right to say to them in respect of their competitive tariffs, "Thus far shalt thou go and no further." To attempt to limit English competition in this way would probably be as hopeless an endeavour as the experiment of King Canute. . . .

It is urged, however, on the part of the plaintiffs, that even if the acts complained of would not be wrongful had they been committed by a single individual, they become actionable when they are the result of concerted action among several. In other words, the plaintiffs, it is contended, have been injured by an illegal conspiracy. Of the general proposition, that certain kinds of conduct not criminal in any one individual may become criminal if done by combination among several, there can be no doubt. The distinction is based on sound reason, for a combination may make oppressive or dangerous that which if it proceeded only from a single person would be otherwise, and the very fact of the combination may shew that the object is simply to do harm, and not to exercise one's own just rights. In the application of this undoubted principle it is necessary to be very careful not to press the doctrine of illegal conspiracy beyond that which is necessary for the protection of individuals or of the public; and it may be observed in passing that as a rule it is the damage wrongfully done, and not the conspiracy, that is the gist of actions on the case for conspiracy. But what is the definition of an illegal combination? It is an agreement by one or more to do an unlawful act, or to do a lawful act by unlawful means; and the question to be solved is whether there has been any such agreement here. Have the defendants combined to do an unlawful act? Have they combined to do a lawful act by unlawful means? A moment's consideration will be sufficient to shew that this new inquiry only drives us back to the circle of definitions and legal propositions which I have already traversed in the previous part of this judgment. The unlawful act agreed to, if any, between the defendants must have been the intentional doing of some act to the detriment of the plaintiffs' business without just cause or excuse. Whether there was any such justification or excuse for the defendants is the old question over again, which, so far as regards an individual trader, has been already solved. The only differentia that can exist must arise, if at all, out of the fact that the acts done are the joint acts of several capitalists, and not of one capitalist only. The next point is whether the means adopted were unlawful. The means adopted were competition carried to a bitter end. Whether such means were unlawful is in like manner nothing but the old discussion which I have gone through, and which is now revived under a second head of inquiry, except so far as a combination of capitalists differentiates the case of acts jointly done by them from similar acts done by a single man of capital. But I find it impossible myself to acquiesce in the view that the English law places any such restriction on the combination of capital as would be involved in the recognition of such a distinction. If so, one rich capitalist may innocently carry competition to a length which would become unlawful in the case of a syndicate with a joint capital no larger than his own, and one individual merchant may lawfully do that which a firm or a partnership may not. What limits, on such a theory, would be imposed by law on the competitive action of a joint-stock company limited, is a problem which might well puzzle a casuist. The truth is, that the combination of capital for purposes of trade and competition is a very different thing from such a combination of several persons against one, with a view to harm him, as falls under the head of an indictable conspiracy. There is no just cause or excuse in the latter class of cases. There is such a just cause or excuse in the former. . . . Would it be an indictable conspiracy to agree to drink up all the water from a common spring in a time of drought; to buy up by precon-

certed action all the provisions in a market or district in times of scarcity; to combine to purchase all the shares of a company against a
coming settling-day; or to agree to give away articles of trade gratis in
order to withdraw custom from a trader? May two itinerant match-ven-
dors combine to sell matches below their value in order by competition
to drive a third match-vendor from the street? . . .

In the result, I agree with Lord Coleridge, C.J., and differ, with regret, from the Master of the Rolls. The substance of my view is this, that
competition, however severe and egotistical, if unattended by circumstances of dishonesty, intimidation, molestation, or such illegalities as I
have above referred to, gives rise to no cause of action at common law.
I myself should deem it to be a misfortune if we were to attempt to
prescribe to the business world how honest and peaceable trade was to
be carried on in a case where no such illegal elements as I have mentioned exist, or were to adopt some standard of judicial "reasonableness," or of "normal" prices, or "fair freights," to which commercial
adventurers, otherwise innocent, were bound to conform.

In my opinion, accordingly, this appeal ought to be dismissed with
costs.

[FRY, L.J., issued an opinion concurring in the judgment of BOWEN,
L.J.

LORD ESHER, M.R., dissenting:]

It follows that the act of the defendants in lowering their freights far
beyond a lowering for any purpose of trade — that is to say, so low that
if they continued it they themselves could not carry on trade — was not
an act done in the exercise of their own free right of trade, but was an
act done evidently for the purpose of interfering with, i.e. with intent
to interfere with, the plaintiffs' right to a free course of trade, and was
therefore a wrongful act as against the plaintiffs' right; and as injury
ensued to the plaintiffs, they had also in respect of such act a right of
action against the defendants. The plaintiffs, in respect of that act,
would have had a right of action if it had been done by one defendant
only; they have it still more clearly when that act was done by several
defendants combined for that purpose. For these reasons I come to the
conclusion that the plaintiffs were entitled to judgment. The damages,
if that be the correct conclusion as to the right of action, are to be
ascertained. They are, in my opinion, the difference between the
freight of 25s., which the plaintiffs were forced to accept, and the
freight they would have obtained without other interference than a
legal fair competition in 1885, and damages at large for being prevented from endeavouring to earn freight from Hankow to England in
subsequent years, after taking into account the probability of using
their ships in some other trade. I am of opinion that the appeal should
be allowed.

NOTES

1. Predatory pricing. *Mogul* is one of the earliest cases on record in which the defendants have been sued for entering into a scheme of predatory pricing, i.e., a practice of selling below cost in the short run in the hope of obtaining monopoly gains later, after driving the competition from the market. In dealing with the legality of the practice, Bowen, L.J., did not concentrate on the social losses that predation might generate, or on the market power, if any, commanded, by the defendants, but treated the case as a private dispute in which the plaintiff could not show a violation of its individual rights, at least as Lord Bowen understood them. Is his opinion correct within his own framework? Should the result shift when the framework of analysis is changed to take into account asserted losses in social welfare?

This last question has spawned an enormous debate within the antitrust literature. The classic article on the subject is McGee, Predatory Price Cutting: the Standard Oil (N.J.) Case, 1 J.L. & Econ. 137 (1958), in which the author first concluded that merger and acquisition, but not predation, vaulted Standard Oil to its dominant market position, and then expressed doubt as to whether predatory practices could ever be effective in achieving a monopoly. Indeed the defendants' combination in *Mogul* broke up even before the legal issues were resolved on appeal. The recent debate on the subject dates from Areeda and Turner, Predatory Pricing and Related Practices Under Section 2 of the Sherman Act, 88 Harv. L. Rev. 697 (1975), which advocated, roughly speaking, a definition of predation that renders it illegal to sell a product below its marginal cost of production. For a critique of the modern theories of predation from an economic perspective see Easterbrook, Predatory Strategies and Counterstrategies, 48 U. Chi. L. Rev. 263 (1981), which concludes, consistent with *Mogul*, that "[t]he antitrust offense of predation should be forgotten." For a traditional torts analysis of the case reaching the same conclusion see Epstein, Intentional Harms, 4 J. Legal Stud. 391, 431 (1975), urging that only the intentional use of force or fraud needs some excuse or justification in the first place.

2. The English trilogy. *Mogul* is the first of three major cases decided around the turn of the century that attempted to define the limits of fair competition at common law. The other two cases were Allen v. Flood, [1898] A.C. 1, and Quinn v. Leathem, [1901] A.C. 495, both of which involved labor, not trade, disputes. In Allen v. Flood, the defendant Allen was a representative of the ironworkers union; the plaintiffs were members of the shipwrights union. Both the ironworkers and the shipwrights worked for the Glengall Iron Co. under contracts at will. Allen told Glengall that the ironworkers would walk off the job unless the shipwrights were dismissed. To keep the service of the ironworkers, Glengall dismissed the plaintiffs, who promptly sued. The case engendered an enormous controversy. The House of Lords rejected the recommendation of the majority of lower court judges especially empanelled to advise it and held that the plaintiffs had no cause of action. The headnote to the case places its central proposition in abstract form: "An act lawful in itself is not converted by a malicious or a bad motive into an unlawful act so as to make the doer of the act liable to a civil action." The connection between the abstract proposition and the law of trade disputes is revealed in the following excerpt from the lengthy opinion of Lord Herschell dismissing the plaintiff's claim:

> In Temperton v. Russell [[1893] 1 Q.B. 715, supra at page 1335], the further step was taken by the majority of the Court, A. L. Smith L.J. reserving his opinion on the point, of asserting that it was immaterial that the act induced was not the breach of a contract, but only the not entering into a contract, provided that the motive of desiring to injure the plaintiff, or to benefit the defendant at the expense of the plaintiff, was present. It seems to have been regarded as only a small step from the one decision to the other, and it was said that there seemed to be no good reason why, if an action lay for maliciously inducing a breach of contract, it should not equally lie for maliciously inducing a person not to enter into a contract. So far from thinking it a small step from the one decision to the other, I think there is a chasm between them. The reason for a distinction between the two cases appears to me to be this: that in the one case the act procured was the violation of a legal right, for which the person doing the act which injured the plaintiff could be sued as well as the person who procured it; whilst in the other case no legal right was violated by the person who did the act from which the plaintiff suffered: he would not be liable to be sued in respect of the act done, whilst the person who induced him to do the act would be liable to an action. . . .

In Quinn v. Leathem, [1901] A.C. 495, the last case in the trilogy, the plaintiff Leathem was a wholesale meat slaughterer. The defendant union demanded that he replace his current workers with union members paid at union wages. It refused to accept plaintiff's offer to pay his own workers union scale; it was, however, prepared to admit the fired workers as union members, but without any seniority. When the plaintiff refused to comply with the union's demands, the union (in what today is called a secondary boycott) warned the plaintiff's best customer, his brother-in-law Munce, that his own workers would be called off the job unless Munce purchased his meat elsewhere. When Munce yielded to the demand, the plaintiff sued the union, and his claim was upheld by the House of Lords. As stated in the headnote, the holding of the case was: "A combination of two or more, without justification or excuse, to injure a man in his trade by inducing his customers or servants to break their contracts with him or not to deal with him or continue in his employment is, if it results in damage to him, actionable."

Lord Halsbury disposed of Allen v. Flood (in which he had dissented) by taking a very narrow view of precedent, saying that "a case is only an authority for what it actually decides. I entirely deny that it can be quoted for a proposition that may seem to follow logically from it." Lord Shand distinguished the two cases in a single sentence. "In Allen v. Flood the purpose of the defendant was by the acts complained of to promote his own trade interest, which it was held he was entitled to do, although injurious to his competitors, whereas in the present case, while it was clear there was a combination, the purpose of the defendants was to injure the plaintiff in his trade as distinguished from the intention of legitimately advancing their own interests." Why was it not in the interests of the union to secure work for its own members? To enlarge its economic base by allowing Quinn's fired employees to join the union? Can Allen v. Flood be treated as a combination case? For criticism of *Quinn*, see C. Gregory, Labor and the Law ch. 2 (2d rev. ed. 1958). For a defense of *Quinn* and an attack on *Allen* as being both misconceived and misinterpreted see Petro, Unions and the Southern Courts: Part III — The Conspiracy and Tort Foundations of the Labor Injunction, 60 N.C. L. Rev. 544, 558-567 (1982).

In England the entire question of trade union power was removed from the common law by the Trade Disputes Act, 1906, 6 Ed. VII ch. 47. The key provisions of the Act: (a) made trade unions, as distinguished from their members, completely immune from liability in tort; (b) made the actions of individual persons done pursuant to agreement or combination actionable only to the extent that they would have been actionable if done without any such agreement or combination; and (c) abolished in the context of labor disputes the torts of inducement of breach of contract, interference with trade generally, and interference "with the right of some other person to dispose of his capital or his labour as he wills." Since that time there have been many revisions of the English labor law statutes, raising fierce controversy between the Conservative and Labor parties in England. For commentary see Rowley, Toward a Political Economy of British Labor Law, 51 U. Chi. L. Rev. 1135 (1984).

Both *Allen* and *Quinn* proved highly influential in the United States. For an approach congruent with *Quinn* see Plant v. Wood, 57 N.E. 1011 (Mass. 1900), in which the classic Holmes dissent relies on Allen v. Flood. *Allen* was also highly influential in National Protective Assn. v. Cumming, 63 N.E. 369 (N.Y. 1902). Is there any reason why unions should not be subject to the general common-law rules for trade disputes? Note that the American labor law has ousted many of the common-law rules but, unlike the British system, it has replaced them with a system of collective bargaining that is in turn subject to extensive administrative and judicial control, which includes detailed regulations of secondary boycotts.

3. *Malice in the trade cases.* The issue of malice raised in the English trilogy has from time to time been seized upon in unfair competition cases. The leading American authority is Tuttle v. Buck, 119 N.W. 946, 948 (Minn. 1909). There the plaintiff was a barber by trade and the defendant a banker. The plaintiff claimed that the defendant, acting out of sheer malice, sought to drive him out of the barbering business. In particular, the plaintiff alleged that the defendant had hired two barbers, afforded them rent-free use of a barber shop, and by "threats of his personal displeasure sought to persuade members of the general public not to frequent the plaintiff's business." The trial judge upheld the complaint on demurrer and the decision was affirmed on appeal. Elliott, J., writing for the court, held that the wholly malicious conduct of the defendant, if proved, overstepped the proper bounds of competition — only to express thereafter his personal doubts about the sufficiency of the plaintiff's factual allegations:

> To divert to one's self the customers of a business rival by the offer of goods at lower prices is in general a legitimate mode of serving one's own interest, and justifiable as fair competition. But when a man starts an opposition place of business, not for the sake of profit to himself, but regardless of loss to himself, and for the sole purpose of driving his competitor out of business, and with the intention of himself retiring upon the accomplishment of his malevolent purpose, he is guilty of a wanton wrong and an actionable tort. In such a case he would not be exercising his legal right, or doing an act which can be judged separately from the motive which actuated him. To call such conduct competition is a perversion of terms. It is simply the application of force without legal justification, which in its moral quality may be no better than highway robbery.
>
> Nevertheless, in the opinion of the writer this complaint is insufficient. It is not claimed that it states a cause of action for slander. No question of conspiracy or combination is involved. Stripped of the adjectives and the statement that what was done was for the sole purpose of injuring the plaintiff, and not for the purpose of serving a legitimate purpose of the defendant, the complaint states facts which in themselves amount only to an ordinary everyday business transaction. There is no allegation that the defendant was intentionally running the business at a financial loss to himself, or that after driving the plaintiff out of business the defendant closed up or intended to close up his shop. From all that appears from the complaint he may have opened the barber shop, energetically sought business from his acquaintances and the customers of the plaintiff, and as a result of his enterprise and command of capital obtained it, with the result that the plaintiff, from want of capital, acquaintance, or enterprise, was unable to stand the competition and was thus driven out of business.

As a general economic matter, how important are cases like Tuttle v. Buck? In particular, how well will any economic entity survive or prosper if motivated solely by malice instead of self-interest? Under *Tuttle,* can it be tortious to maliciously enforce a contract claim? Withdraw money from a bank? See generally Ames, How Far an Act May Be a Tort

Because of the Wrongful Motive of the Actor, 18 Harv. L. Rev. 411 (1905).

International News Service v. Associated Press
248 U.S. 215 (1918)

PITNEY, J. The parties are competitors in the gathering and distribution of news and its publication for profit in newspapers throughout the United States. The Associated Press, which was complainant in the District Court, is a cooperative organization, incorporated under the Membership Corporations Law of the State of New York, its members being individuals who are either proprietors or representatives of about 950 daily newspapers published in all parts of the United States. . . . Complainant gathers in all parts of the world, by means of various instrumentalities of its own, by exchange with its members, and by other appropriate means, news and intelligence of current and recent events of interest to newspaper readers and distributes it daily to its members for publication in their newspapers. The cost of the service, amounting approximately to $3,500,000 per annum, is assessed upon the members and becomes a part of their costs of operation, to be recouped, presumably with profit, through the publication of their several newspapers. . . .

Defendant is a corporation organized under the laws of the State of New Jersey, whose business is the gathering and selling of news to its customers and clients, consisting of newspapers published throughout the United States, under contracts by which they pay certain amounts at stated times for defendant's service. It has wide-spread news-gathering agencies; the cost of its operations amounts, it is said, to more than $2,000,000 per annum; and it serves about 400 newspapers located in the various cities of the United States and abroad, a few of which are represented, also, in the membership of the Associated Press.

The parties are in the keenest competition between themselves in the distribution of news throughout the United States; and so, as a rule, are the newspapers that they serve, in their several districts. . . .

The bill was filed to restrain the pirating of complainant's news by defendant in three ways: First, by bribing employees of newspapers published by complainant's members to furnish Associated Press news to defendant before publication, for transmission by telegraph and telephone to defendant's clients for publication by them; Second, by inducing Associated Press members to violate its by-laws and permit defendant to obtain news before publication; and Third, by copying news from bulletin boards and from early editions of complainant's newspapers and selling this, either bodily or after rewriting it, to defendant's customers.

The District Court, upon consideration of the bill and answer, with voluminous affidavits on both sides, granted a preliminary injunction under the first and second heads; but refused at that stage to restrain the systematic practice admittedly pursued by defendant, of taking news bodily from the bulletin boards and early editions of complainant's newspapers and selling it as its own. The court expressed itself as satisfied that this practice amounted to unfair trade, but as the legal question was one of first impression; it considered that the allowance of an injunction should await the outcome of an appeal. 240 F. 983, 996. Both parties having appealed, the Circuit Court of Appeals sustained the injunction order so far as it went, and upon complainant's appeal modified it and remanded the cause with directions to issue an injunction also against any bodily taking of the words or substance of complainant's news until its commercial value as news had passed away. 245 F. 244, 253. The present writ of certiorari was then allowed. 245 U.S. 644.

The only matter that has been argued before us is whether defendant may lawfully be restrained from appropriating news taken from bulletins issued by complainant or any of its members, or from newspapers published by them, for the purpose of selling it to defendant's clients. Complainant asserts that defendant's admitted course of conduct in this regard both violates complainant's property right in the news and constitutes unfair competition in business. And notwithstanding the case has proceeded only to the stage of preliminary injunction, we have deemed it proper to consider the underlying questions, since they go to the very merits of the action and are presented upon facts that are not in dispute. As presented in argument, these questions are: 1. Whether there is any property in news; 2. Whether, if there be property in news collected for the purpose of being published, it survives the instant of its publication in the first newspaper to which it is communicated by the news-gatherer; and 3. Whether defendant's admitted course of conduct in appropriating for commercial use matter taken from bulletins or early editions of Associated Press publications constitutes unfair competition in trade.

The federal jurisdiction was invoked because of diversity of citizenship, not upon the ground that the suit arose under the copyright or other laws of the United States. Complainant's news matter is not copyrighted. . . .

In considering the general question of property in news matter, it is necessary to recognize its dual character, distinguishing between the substance of the information and the particular form or collocation of words in which the writer has communicated it.

No doubt news articles often possess a literary quality, and are the subject of literary property at the common law; nor do we question that such an article, as a literary production, is the subject of copyright by the terms of the act as it now stands. . . .

But the news element — the information respecting current events contained in the literary production — is not the creation of the writer, but is a report of matters that ordinarily are publici juris; it is the history of the day. It is not to be supposed that the framers of the Constitution, when they empowered Congress "to promote the progress of science and useful arts, by securing for limited times to authors and inventors the exclusive right to their respective writings and discoveries" (Const., Art. I, §8, par. 8), intended to confer upon one who might happen to be the first to report a historic event the exclusive right for any period to spread the knowledge of it.

We need spend no time, however, upon the general question of property in news matter at common law, or the application of the copyright act, since it seems to us the case must turn upon the question of unfair competition in business. And, in our opinion, this does not depend upon any general right of property analogous to the common-law right of the proprietor of an unpublished work to prevent its publication without his consent; nor is it foreclosed by showing that the benefits of the copyright act have been waived. We are dealing here not with restrictions upon publication but with the very facilities and processes of publication. The peculiar value of news is in the spreading of it while it is fresh; and it is evident that a valuable property interest in the news, as news, cannot be maintained by keeping it secret. Besides, except for matters improperly disclosed, or published in breach of trust or confidence, or in violation of law, none of which is involved in this branch of the case, the news of current events may be regarded as common property. What we are concerned with is the business of making it known to the world, in which both parties to the present suit are engaged. That business consists in maintaining a prompt, sure, steady, and reliable service designed to place the daily events of the world at the breakfast table of the millions at a price that, while of trifling moment to each reader, is sufficient in the aggregate to afford compensation for the cost of gathering and distributing it, with the added profit so necessary as an incentive to effective action in the commercial world. The service thus performed for newspaper readers is not only innocent but extremely useful in itself, and indubitably constitutes a legitimate business. The parties are competitors in this field; and, on fundaumental principles, applicable here as elsewhere, when the rights or privileges of the one are liable to conflict with those of the other, each party is under a duty so to conduct its own business as not unnecessarily or unfairly to injure that of the other.

Obviously, the question of what is unfair competition in business must be determined with particular reference to the character and circumstances of the business. The question here is not so much the rights of either party as against the public but their rights as between themselves. And although we may and do assume that neither party has any remaining property interest as against the public in uncopyrighted news matter after the moment of its first publication, it by no means follows that there is no remaining property interest in it as between themselves. For, to both of them alike, news matter, however little susceptible of ownership or dominion in the absolute sense, is stock in trade, to be gathered at the cost of enterprise, organization, skill, labor, and money, and to be distributed and sold to those who will pay money for it, as for any other merchandise. Regarding the news, therefore, as but the material out of which both parties are seeking to make profits at the same time and in the same field, we hardly can fail to recognize that for this purpose, and as between them, it must be regarded as quasi property, irrespective of the rights of either as against the public. . . .

The question, whether one who has gathered general information or news at pains and expense for the purpose of subsequent publication through the press has such an interest in its publication as may be protected from interference, has been raised many times, although never, perhaps, in the precise form in which it is now presented. . . .

The peculiar features of the case arise from the fact that, while novelty and freshness form so important an element in the success of the business, the very processes of distribution and publication necessarily occupy a good deal of time. Complainant's service, as well as defendant's, is a daily service to daily newspapers; most of the foreign news reaches this country at the Atlantic seaboard, principally at the City of New York, and because of this, and of time differentials due to the earth's rotation, the distribution of news matter throughout the country is principally from east to west; and, since in speed the telegraph and telephone easily outstrip the rotation of the earth, it is a simple matter for defendant to take complainant's news from bulletins or early editions of complainant's members in the eastern cities and at the mere cost of telegraphic transmission cause it to be published in western papers issued at least as early as those served by complainant. Besides this, and irrespective of time differentials, irregularities in telegraphic transmission on different lines, and the normal consumption of time in printing and distributing the newspaper, result in permitting pirated news to be placed in the hands of defendant's readers sometimes simultaneously with the service of competing Associated Press papers, occasionally even earlier.

Defendant insists that when, with the sanction and approval of complainant, and as the result of the use of its news for the very purpose for which it is distributed, a portion of complainant's members communicate it to the general public by posting it upon bulletin boards so that all may read, or by issuing it to newspapers and distributing it indiscriminately, complainant no longer has the right to control the use to be made of it; that when it thus reaches the light of day it becomes the common possession of all to whom it is accessible; and that any purchaser of a newspaper has the right to communicate the intelligence which it contains to anybody and for any purpose, even for the purpose of selling it for profit to newspapers published for profit in competition with complainant's members.

The fault in the reasoning lies in applying as a test the right of the complainant as against the public, instead of considering the rights of complainant and defendant, competitors in business, as between themselves. The right of the purchaser of a single newspaper to spread knowledge of its contents gratuitously, for any legitimate purpose not unreasonably interfering with complainant's right to make merchandise of it, may be admitted; but to transmit that news for commercial use, in competition with complainant — which is what defendant has done and seeks to justify — is a very different matter. In doing this defendant, by its very act, admits that it is taking material that has been acquired by complainant as the result of organization and the expenditure of labor, skill, and money, and which is salable by complainant for money, and that defendant in appropriating it and selling it as its own is endeavoring to reap where it has not sown, and by disposing of it to newspapers that are competitors of complainant's members is appropriating to itself the harvest of those who have sown. Stripped of all disguises, the process amounts to an unauthorized interference with the normal operation of complainant's legitimate business precisely at the point where the profit is to be reaped, in order to divert a material portion of the profit from those who have earned it to those who have not; with special advantage to defendant in the competition because of the fact that it is not burdened with any part of the expense of gathering the news. The transaction speaks for itself, and a court of equity ought not to hesitate long in characterizing it as unfair competition in business.

. . . It is no answer to say that complainant spends its money for that which is too fugitive or evanescent to be the subject of property. That might, and for the purposes of the discussion we are assuming that it would, furnish an answer in a common-law controversy. But in a court of equity, where the question is one of unfair competition, if that which complainant has acquired fairly at substantial cost may be sold fairly at substantial profit, a competitor who is misappropriating it for the purpose of disposing of it to his own profit and to the disadvantage of complainant cannot be heard to say that it is too fugitive or evanescent to be regarded as property. It has all the attributes of property necessary for determining that a misappropriation of it by a competitor is unfair competition because contrary to good conscience.

The contention that the news is abandoned to the public for all purposes when published in the first newspaper is untenable. Abandonment is a question of intent, and the entire organization of the Associated Press negatives such a purpose. The cost of the service would be prohibitive if the reward were to be so limited. No single newspaper, no small group of newspapers, could sustain the expenditure. . . .

It is to be observed that the view we adopt does not result in giving to complainant the right to monopolize either the gathering or the distribution of the news, or, without complying with the copyright act, to prevent the reproduction of its news articles; but only postpones participation by complainant's competitor in the processes of distribution and reproduction of news that it has not gathered, and only to the extent necessary to prevent that competitor from reaping the fruits of complainant's efforts and expenditure, to the partial exclusion of complainant, and in violation of the principle that underlies the maxim sic utere tuo, etc.

It is said that the elements of unfair competition are lacking because there is no attempt by defendant to palm off its goods as those of the complainant, characteristic of the most familiar, if not the most typical, cases of unfair competition. But we cannot concede that the right to equitable relief is confined to that class of cases. In the present case the fraud upon complainant's rights is more direct and obvious. Regarding news matter as the mere material from which these two competing parties are endeavoring to make money, and treating it, therefore, as quasi property for the purposes of their business because they are both selling it as such, defendant's conduct differs from the ordinary case of unfair competition in trade principally in this that, instead of selling its own goods as those of complainant, it substitutes misappropriation in the place of misrepresentation, and sells complainant's goods as its own.

[The Court then brought its opinion to a close by considering: (1) whether plaintiff is barred in equity because it has "unclean hands," since it utilizes "tips" obtained from defendant's service, and concluded that this practice "is not shown to be such as to constitute an unconscientious or inequitable attitude . . . so as to fix upon complainant the taint of unclean hands"; (2) whether the injunction was too broad, and decided that although it may be subject to some criticism it should be left to the trial court to modify it if necessary at a later stage in the case.]

The decree of the Circuit Court of Appeals will be affirmed.

[Justice Holmes, in an opinion in which Justice McKenna concurred, would have limited relief to requiring defendant to give express credit to plaintiff for the news it took.]

BRANDEIS, J., dissenting. . . . News is a report of recent occurrences. The business of the news agency is to gather systematically knowledge of such occurrences of interest and to distribute reports thereof. The Associated Press contended that knowledge so acquired is property, because it costs money and labor to produce and because it has value for which those who have it not are ready to pay; that it remains property and is entitled to protection as long as it has commercial value as news; and that to protect it effectively the defendant must be enjoined from making, or causing to be made, any gainful use of it while it retains such value. An essential element of individual property is the legal right to exclude others from enjoying it. If the property is private, the right of exclusion may be absolute; if the property is affected with a public interest, the right of exclusion is qualified. But the fact that a product of the mind has cost its producer money and labor, and has a value for which others are willing to pay, is not sufficient to ensure to it this legal attribute of property. The general rule of law is, that the noblest of human productions — knowledge, truths ascertained, conceptions, and ideas — become, after voluntary communication to others, free as the air to common use. Upon these incorporeal productions the attribute of property is continued after such communication only in certain classes of cases where public policy has seemed to demand it. These exceptions are confined to productions which, in some degree, involve creation, invention, or discovery. But by no means all such are endowed with this attribute of property. The creations which are recognized as property by the common law are literary, dramatic, musical, and other artistic creations; and these have also protection under the copyright statutes. The inventions and discoveries upon which this attribute of property is conferred only by statute, are the few comprised within the patent law. There are also many other cases in which courts interfere to prevent curtailment of plaintiff's enjoyment of incorporeal productions; and in which the right to relief is often called a property right, but is such only in a special sense. In those cases, the plaintiff has no absolute right to the protection of his production; he has merely the qualified right to be protected as against the defendant's acts, because of the special relation in which the latter stands or the wrongful method or means employed in acquiring the knowledge or the manner in which it is used. Protection of this character is afforded where the suit is based upon breach of contract or of trust or upon unfair competition. . . .

Plaintiff further contended that defendant's practice constitutes unfair competition, because there is "appropriation without cost to itself of values created by" the plaintiff; and it is upon this ground that the decision of this court appears to be based. To appropriate and use for profit, knowledge and ideas produced by other men, without making compensation or even acknowledgment, may be inconsistent with a finer sense of propriety; but, with the exceptions indicated above, the law has heretofore sanctioned the practice. Thus it was held that one may ordinarily make and sell anything in any form, may copy with exactness that which another has produced, or may otherwise use his ideas without his consent and without the payment of compensation, and yet not inflict a legal injury; and that ordinarily one is at perfect liberty to find out, if he can by lawful means, trade secrets of another, however valuable, and then use the knowledge so acquired gainfully, although it cost the original owner much in effort and in money to collect or produce.

Such taking and gainful use of a product of another which, for reasons of public policy, the law has refused to endow with the attributes of property, does not become unlawful because the product happens to have been taken from a rival and is used in competition with him. The unfairness in competition which hitherto has been recognized by the law as a basis for relief, lay in the manner or means of conducting the business; and the manner or means held legally unfair, involves either fraud or force or the doing of acts otherwise prohibited by law. In the "passing off" cases (the typical and most common case of unfair competition), the wrong consists in fraudulently representing by word or act that defendant's goods are those of plaintiff. In the other cases, the diversion of trade was effected through physical or moral coercion, or by inducing breaches of contract or of trust or by enticing away employees. In some others, called cases of simulated competition, relief was granted because defendant's purpose was unlawful; namely, not competition but deliberate and wanton destruction of plaintiff's business. . . .

Nor is the use made by the International News Service of the information taken from papers or bulletins of Associated Press members legally objectionable by reason of the purpose for which it was employed. The acts here complained of were not done for the purpose of injuring the business of the Associated Press. Their purpose was not even to divert its trade, or to put it at a disadvantage by lessening defendant's necessary expenses. The purpose was merely to supply subscribers of the International News Service promptly with all available news. The suit is, as this court declares, in substance one brought for the benefit of the members of the Associated Press, who would be proper, and except for their number perhaps necessary, parties; and the plaintiff conducts the suit as representing their interest. It thus appears that the protection given by the injunction is not actually to the business of the complainant news agency; for this agency does not sell news nor seek to earn profits, but is a mere instrumentality by which 800 or more newspapers collect and distribute news. It is these papers severally which are protected; and the protection afforded is not from competition of the defendant, but from possible competition of one or more of the 400 other papers which receive the defendant's service. Furthermore, the protection to these Associated Press members consists merely in denying to other papers the right to use, as news, information which, by authority of all concerned, had theretofore been given to the public by some of those who joined in gathering it; and to which the law denies the attributes of property. There is in defendant's purpose nothing on which to base a claim for relief. . . .

[Justice Brandeis then argued that the complexity of the problem called for legislative and administrative solutions. He also pointed out, as an illustration of how the public interest might be affected, that British and French governments refused to give INS access to the war news from the front becuase of the German sympathies of its Hearst papers.]

Courts are ill-equipped to make the investigations which should precede a determination of the limitations which should be set upon any property right in news or of the circumstances under which news gathered by a private agency should be deemed affected with a public interest. Courts would be powerless to prescribe the detailed regulations essential to full enjoyment of the rights conferred or to introduce the machinery required for enforcement of such regulations. Considerations such as these should lead us to decline to establish a new rule of law in the effort to redress a newly-disclosed wrong, although the propriety of some remedy appears to be clear.

NOTE

The nature of intellectual property. Will the catalogue of tort actions ever close if common-law decisions can create novel property interests whenever one person tries to take advantage of the labor of another? Would the court have allowed the action if the INS had only serviced papers that were not in competition with papers serviced by the Associated Press? Would Brandeis, J., have remained in dissent if the Hearst papers had been allowed access to the front by the British authorities?

The lower courts have been divided about the soundness of *INS.* Learned Hand in particular was a staunch believer in limiting its reach. In Cheney Bros. v. Doris Silk Corp., 35 F.2d 279, 280 (2d Cir. 1929), the plaintiff was a silk manufacturer "which puts out each season many new patterns, designed to attract purchasers by their novelty and beauty." The expected life of any new pattern was generally about eight or nine months, and about 80 percent of the patterns marketed typically proved to have no consumer appeal. Design patents were costly to obtain, and copyright protection was then generally unavailable, probably as a matter of law. The question was whether the plaintiff was entitled to enjoin the defendant when it copied one of plaintiff's popular patterns and sold it at a price below the plaintiff's. Hand, J., relied on the argument of legislative deference to deny the plaintiff any relief:

> Of the cases on which the plaintiff relies, the chief is International News Service v. Associated Press. Although that concerned another subject-matter — printed news dispatches — we agree that, if it meant to lay down a general doctrine, it would cover this case; at least, the language of the majority opinion goes so far. We do not believe that it did. While

it is of course true that law ordinarily speaks in general terms, there are cases where the occasion is at once the justification for, and the limit of, what is decided. This appears to us such an instance; we think that no more was covered than situations substantially similar to those then at bar. The difficulties of understanding it otherwise are insuperable. We are to suppose that the court meant to create a sort of common-law patent or copyright for reasons of justice. Either would flagrantly conflict with the scheme which Congress has for more than a century devised to cover the subject-matter.

Qua patent, we should at least have to decide, as tabula rasa, whether the design or machine was new and required invention; further, we must ignore the Patent Office whose action has always been a condition upon the creation of this kind of property. Qua copyright, although it would be simpler to decide upon the merits, we should equally be obliged to dispense with the conditions imposed upon the creation of the right. Nor, if we went so far, should we know whether the property so recognized should be limited to the periods prescribed in the statutes, or should extend as long as the author's grievance. It appears to us incredible that the Supreme Court should have had in mind any such consequences. To exclude others from the enjoyment of a chattel is one thing; to prevent any imitation of it, to set up a monopoly in the plan of its structure, gives the author a power over his fellows vastly greater, a power which the Constitution allows only Congress to create.

The record piracy cases have also tested the limits of the doctrines of unfair competition. In Metropolitan Opera Association, Inc. v. Wagner-Nichols Recorder Corp., 101 N.Y.S.2d 483, aff'd, 107 N.Y.S.2d 795 (N.Y. App. Div. 1951), the defendant recorded the radio broadcasts of the Metropolitan Opera Company and then sold records. The court held this scheme to be unfair competition not only against Columbia Records, which had the exclusive right to make and sell recordings of the performances, but also against the Met. See also Capitol Records, Inc. v. Erickson, 82 Cal. Rptr. 798 (Cal. App. 1969), where *INS* was invoked to enjoin the unauthorized tape reproductions of the plaintiff's records even when the defendant disclosed that it had copied without permission and had refused to pay the appropriate royalties.

INS has also showed renewed vitality in a dispute over the creation and use of the Dow Jones Averages for financial futures. In Board of Trade of City of Chicago v. Dow Jones & Co., Inc., 456 N.E.2d 84, 90 (Ill. 1983), Dow Jones was allowed to enjoin the use of its index as the basis for a futures contract traded over the Chicago Board of Trade's exchanges:

> To hold that defendant has a proprietary interest in its indexes and averages which vests it with the exclusive right to license their use for trading in stock index futures contracts would not preclude plaintiff and others from marketing stock index futures contracts. The extent of the defendant's monopoly would be limited, for as defendant points out, there are an infinite number of stock market indexes which could be devised.

Should it matter that, before acting unilaterally, the Board of Trade in fact offered Dow Jones between $1 and $2 million per year for the use of its index? See also the parallel case of Standard & Poor's Corp. v. Commodity Exchange, Inc., 683 F.2d 704 (2d Cir. 1982), where a preliminary injunction was also granted. On the relationship between *INS* and the Dow Jones case see generally Baird, Common Law Intellectual Property and the Legacy of *International News Service v. Associated Press*, 50 U. Chi. L. Rev. 411 (1983).

INS did not help the plaintiffs in National Football League v. Governor of the State of Delaware, 435 F. Supp. 1372, 1378 (D. Del. 1977). There Delaware operated a state lottery "Scorecard" that allowed individuals to bet on the final scores of NFL games. The plaintiff's claim for relief under *INS* was based on the idea that the state should not reap where it did not sow. The court denied the injunction, limiting *INS* to cases of competing products:

> It is true that Delaware is thus making profits it would not make but for the existence of the NFL, but I find this difficult to distinguish from the multitude of charter bus companies who generate profit from servicing those of plaintiffs' fans who want to go to the stadium or, indeed, the sidewalk popcorn salesman who services the crowd as it surges towards the gate.
>
> While courts have recognized that one has the right to one's own harvest, this proposition has not been construed to preclude others from profiting from demands for collateral services generated by the success of one's business venture. . .

INS was also held inapplicable in United States Golf Association v. St. Andrews Systems, Data-Max, Inc., 749 F.2d 1028, 1038-1039 (3d Cir. 1984). There the defendant's computer calculated the handicap of an amateur golfer by using the formula developed by the U.S.G.A. as early as 1897 and modified several times in subsequent years. The association's claim for misappropriation under *INS* was, however, rebuffed on the ground that there was no "direct competition" between the parties.

> In *I.N.S.*, the Court based its conclusion in substantial part on the fact that I.N.S. was using information which A.P. had developed in direct competition with A.P. in its primary market, the sale of newspapers. I.N.S.'s activity, if not checked, could have destroyed A.P.'s incentive to create the information involved, and this would not only have harmed A.P. but also would have left the public without the information. . . .
>
> The competition in this case is indirect. The U.S.G.A. is not in the business of selling handicaps to golfers, but is primarily interested in the promotion of the game of golf, and in its own position in the governing body of amateur golf. The handicap formula was developed to further these two goals. A member of a golf club who obtains his handicap through his club does not pay for that service, and the U.S.G.A. is not directly affected by the number of official handicaps the clubs calculate each year or by the number of golfers who obtain handicaps.

Is Dow Jones in "direct competition" with the Chicago Board of Trade?

Ely-Norris Safe Co. v. Mosler Safe Co.
7 F.2d 603 (2d Cir. 1925)

Suit in equity by the Ely-Norris Safe Company against the Mosler Safe Company. From decree of dismissal, plaintiff appeals. Reversed.

The jurisdiction of the District Court depended upon diverse citizenship, and the suit was for unfair competition. The bill alleged that the plaintiff manufactured and sold safes under certain letters patent, which had as their distinctive feature an explosion chamber, designed for protection against burglars. Before the acts complained of, no one but the plaintiff had ever made or sold safes with such chambers, and, except for the defendant's infringement, the plaintiff has remained the only manufacturer and seller of such safes. By reason of the plaintiff's efforts the public has come to recognize the value of the explosion chamber and to wish to purchase safes containing them. Besides infringing the patent, the defendant has manufactured and sold safes without a chamber, but with a metal band around the door, in the same place where the plaintiff put the chamber, and has falsely told its customers that this band was employed to cover and close an explosion chamber. Customers have been thus led to buy safes upon the faith of the representation, who in fact wished to buy safes with explosion chambers, and would have done so, but for the deceit.

The bill prayed an injunction against selling safes with such metal bands, and against representing that any of its safes contained an explosion chamber. From the plaintiff's answers to interrogatories it appeared that all the defendant's safes bore the defendant's name and address, and were sold as its own. Furthermore, that the defendant never gave a customer reason to suppose that any safe sold by it was made by the plaintiff. . . .

HAND, J. (after stating the facts as above.) This case is not the same as that before Mr. Justice Bradley in New York & Rosendale Co. v. Coplay Cement Co. (C.C.) 44 F. 277 [1890]. The plaintiffs there manufactured cement at Rosendale, N.Y., but it did not appear that they were the only persons making cement at that place. There was no reason, therefore, to assume that a customer of the defendant, deceived as to the place of origin of the defendant's cement, and desiring to buy only such cement, would have bought of the plaintiffs. It resulted that the plaintiffs did not show any necessary loss of trade through the defendant's fraud upon its own customers. We agree that some of the language of the opinion goes further, but it was not necessary for the disposition of the case.

American Washboard Co. v. Saginaw Mfg. Co., 103 F. 281 (C.C.A. 6) [1900], was, however, a case in substance like that at bar, because there the plaintiff alleged that it had acquired the entire output of sheet aluminum suitable for washboards. It necessarily followed that the plaintiff had a practical monopoly of this metal for the articles in question, and from this it was a fair inference that any customer of the defendant, who was deceived into buying as an aluminum washboard one which was not such, was a presumptive customer of the plaintiff, who had therefore lost a bargain. This was held, however, not to constitute a private wrong, and so the bill was dismissed.

Furthermore, we do not agree with the plaintiff that cases like Federal Trade Commission v. Winsted Hosiery Co., 258 U.S. 483 [1922], and our decision in Royal Baking Powder Co. v. Federal Trade Commission, 281 F. 744 [1922], are in his favor. These arose under the Federal Trade Commission Act (Comp. St. §§8836a-8836k) where it is only necessary to show that the public interest has been affected. The defendant's customers in such cases had an undoubted grievance, and this was thought to be enough to justify the intervention of the Federal Trade Commission. It by no means follows from such decisions that a competing manufacturer has any cause of suit.

We must concede, therefore, that on the cases as they stand the law is with the defendant, and the especially high authority of the court which decided American Washboard Co. v. Saginaw Mfg. Co., supra, makes us hesitate to differ from their conclusion. Yet there is no part of the law which is more plastic than unfair competition, and what was not reckoned an actionable wrong 25 years ago may have become such today. We find it impossible to deny the strength of the plaintiff's case on the allegations of its bill. As we view it, the question is, as it always is in such cases, one of fact. Whilte a competitor may, generally speaking, take away all the customers of another that he can, there are means which he must not use. One of these is deceit. The false use of another's name as maker or source of his own goods is deceit, of which the false use of geographical or descriptive terms is only one example. But we conceive that,in the end the questions which arise are always two: Has the plaintiff in fact lost customers? And has he lost them by means which the law forbids? The false use of the plaintiff's name is only an instance in which each element is clearly shown.

In the case at bar the means are as plainly unlawful as in the usual case of palming off. It is as unlawful to lie about the quality of one's wares as about their maker; it equally subjects the seller to action by the buyer. Indeed, as to this the case of Federal Trade Commission v. Winsted Hosiery Co., supra, is flatly in point, if authority be needed. The reason, as we think, why such deceits have not been regarded as actionable by a competitor, depends only upon his inability to show any injury for which there is a known remedy. In an open market it is gener-

ally impossible to prove that a customer, whom the defendant has secured by falsely describing his goods, would have bought of the
plaintiff, if the defendant had been truthful. Without that, the plaintiff,
though aggrieved in company with other honest traders, cannot show
any ascertainable loss. He may not recover at law, and the equitable
remedy is concurrent. The law does not allow him to sue as a vicarious
avenger of the defendant's customers.

But, if it be true that the plaintiff has a monopoly of the kind of wares
concerned, and if to secure a customer the defendant must represent
his own as of that kind, it is a fair inference that the customer wants
those and those only. Had he not supposed that the defendant could
supply him, presumably he would have gone to the plaintiff, who alone
could. At least, if the plaintiff can prove that in fact he would, he shows
a direct loss, measured by his profits on the putative sale. If a tradesman
falsely foists on a customer a substitute for what the plaintiff alone can
supply, it can scarcely be that the plaintiff is without remedy, if he can
show that the customer would certainly have come to him, had the
truth been told.

Yet that is in substance the situation which this bill presents. It says
that the plaintiff alone could lawfully make such safes, and that the
defendant has sold others to customers who asked for the patented
kind. It can make no difference that the defendant sold them as its
own. The sale by hypothesis depended upon the structure of the safes,
not on their maker. To be satisfied, the customer must in fact have
gone to the plaintiff, or the defendant must have infringed. Had he
infringed, the plaintiff could have recovered his profit on the sale; had
the customer gone to him, he would have made that profit. Any possibilities that the customers might not have gone to the plaintiff, had they
been told the truth, are foreclosed by the allegation that the plaintiff in
fact lost the sales. It seems to us merely a corollary of Federal Trade
Commission v. Winsted Hosiery Co., supra, that, if this can be proved,
a private suit will lie.

Decree reversed.

Mosler Safe Co. v. Ely-Norris Safe Co.*
273 U.S. 132 (1926)

HOLMES, J. [after summarizing the facts]. At the hearing below all
attention seems to have been concentrated on the question passed
upon and the forcibly stated reasons that induced this Court of Appeals
to differ from that for the Sixth Circuit. But, upon a closer scrutiny of

*This is the same case, Ely-Norris Safe Co. v. Mosler Safe Co., on certiorari before the
United States Supreme Court. — ED.

the bill than seems to have been invited before, it does not present that broad and interesting issue. The bill alleges that the plaintiff has a patent for an explosion chamber as described and claimed in said Letters Patent; that it has the exclusive right to make and sell safes containing such an explosion chamber; that no other safes containing such an explosion chamber could be got in the United States before the defendant, as it is alleged, infringed the plaintiff's patent, for which alleged infringement a suit is pending. It then is alleged that the defendant is making and selling safes with a metal band around the door at substantially the same location as the explosion chamber of plaintiff's safes, and has represented to the public that the said metal band was employed to cover or close an explosion chamber by reason of which the public has been led to purchase defendant's said safes as and for safes containing an explosion chamber, such as is manufactured and sold by the plaintiff herein. It is alleged further that sometimes the defendant's safes have no explosion chamber under the band but are bought by those who want safes with a chamber and so the defendant has deprived the plaintiff of sales, competed unfairly and damaged the plaintiff's reputation. The plaintiff relies upon its patent suit for relief in respect of the sales of safes alleged to infringe its rights. It complains here only of false representations as to safes that do not infringe but that are sold as having explosion chambers although in fact they do not.

It is consistent with every allegation in the bill and the defendant in argument asserted it to be a fact, that there are other safes with explosion chambers beside that for which the plaintiff has a patent. The defendant is charged only with representing that its safes had an explosion chamber, which, so far as appears, it had a perfect right to do if the representation was true. If on the other hand the representation was false as it is alleged sometimes to have been, there is nothing to show that customers had they known the facts would have gone to the plaintiff rather than to other competitors in the market, or to lay a foundation for the claim for a loss of sales. The bill is so framed as to seem to invite the decision that was obtained from the Circuit Court of Appeals, but when scrutinized is seen to have so limited its statements as to exclude the right to complain.

Decree reversed.

NOTES

1. *Passing off.* Would the existence of a plaintiff's monopoly on all explosion chambers go to its ability to obtain an injunction? Damages? Both? How might damages be calculated if allowed?

In one sense, the plaintiff's case for passing off builds on the elements of ordinary misrepresentation already developed in Chapter 16

supra, and recognized in the context of unfair competition as early as
Mogul. Initially, the passing off action builds from the admitted proposition that a disappointed buyer has an action against the seller who has
passed off its own goods as the superior product of a rival. Yet in practice that action may not be brought because it is too costly for any
individual purchaser to mount an expensive suit in order to recover the
trifling losses that it has suffered from the defendant's misrepresentation. Even if that suit were brought, it would not vindicate the interests
of the rival in its product's reputation and good will. In a proper passing off suit, however, the plaintiff is not the purchaser, but the *competitor,* whose goods the defendant has palmed off as its own. With passing
off, the defendant has represented its own product to be better than it
really is by stating that it is the plaintiff's, or that it has desirable attributes associated with the plaintiff's product that it, in fact, lacks. The
substantive underpinnings of passing off are clear enough: the defendant's misrepresentation induces third parties to act to the detriment
of the plaintiff. Yet the basic misrepresentation theory that accounts for
passing off has far broader implications. Thus, if the defendant simply
overstates the reliability of its own product, it may induce consumers to
shift from the plaintiff's product; yet there is no passing off and no
confusion as to source. Should such actions nonetheless be allowed?
Disallowed because of their multiplicity? Does this example explain in
part a possible antifraud justification for the Federal Trade Commission? How effective are market mechanisms in counteracting systematic
fraud? See generally Posner, The Federal Trade Commission, 37 U.
Chi. L. Rev. 47 (1969).

2. *Product disparagement.* The opposite side of the coin from the wrong
of passing off is the tort of disparagement. With disparagement the
defendant asserts that the plaintiff's product is worse than it really is,
so as to induce consumers to purchase other products, including the
defendant's. See Tex Smith, The Harmonica Man v. Godfrey, supra
at page 1140. Disparagement is really a form of product defamation,
although many courts treat it as a distinct tort not governed by the
myriad of defamation rules such as those concerning innuendo or special damages. As the court noted in Dairy Stores, Inc. v. Sentinel Publishing Co., 516 A.2d 220, 224 (N.J. 1986):

> Although the two causes sometimes overlap, actions for defamation
> and product disparagement stem from different branches of tort law. A
> defamation action, which encompasses libel and slander, affords a rem-
> edy for damage to one's reputation. By comparison an action for product
> disparagement is an offshoot of the cause of action for interference with
> contractual relations, such as sales to a prospective buyer. The two causes
> may merge when a disparaging statement about a product reflects on the
> reputation of the business that made, distributed or sold it. If, for exam-
> ple, a statement about the poor quality of a product implies that the

seller is fraudulent, then the statement may be actionable under both theories.

Does a statement that a product is of poor quality suggest that the manufacturer is careless or incompetent? If so, then is there any principled distinction between the two torts at all? See generally Note, Corporate Defamation and Product Disparagement: Narrowing the Analogy in Personal Defamation, 75 Colum. L. Rev. 963 (1975).

3. *Trademark protection.* There is a close kinship between actions for unfair competition and those for violation of the Lanham Act, 15 U.S.C. §1051 et seq. (1988 & Supp. 1993), the trademark statute, the general intention of which is expressed in section 1127: "The intent of this Chapter is to regulate commerce within the control of Congress by making actionable the deceptive and misleading use of marks in such commerce, . . . [and] to protect persons engaged in such commerce against unfair competition. . . ." The statute provides protection for both common-law and statutory trademarks. The section also protects a diverse collection of marks, symbols, design elements, and characters that the public, or some relevant portion thereof, directly associates with the plaintiff or its product.

There has been a veritable explosion of recent cases that have tested the outer protection of trademark and tradename litigation. The classical suits involve actions to enjoin direct competitors. In Warner Bros., Inc. v. Gay Toys, Inc., 658 F.2d 76 (2d Cir. 1981), the court held that Warner Bros. was entitled to enjoin Gay Toys from the marketing of its "Dixie Racer," a 1969 Dodge Charger complete with a bright orange color, Confederate flag decal, numbers on the door, and the various symbols of "General Lee," all based on the popular television series, "The Dukes of Hazzard." As is common in such cases, the defendant had sought unsuccessfully to obtain a license from the plaintiff to market "Dukes of Hazzard" cars. Thereafter it had modified the features of an existing car to bear greater resemblance to the Dukes of Hazzard car, from which it still differed in certain respects. Notwithstanding the differences between the plaintiff's and defendant's products, the plaintiff was able to obtain a preliminary injunction against the defendant by marshaling a wide array of evidence to show that ordinary customers confused defendant's car with the original Dukes of Hazzard line: the defendant's Dixie Racer had sales far in excess of other cars in the same line; the dealers who sold the defendant's car sold it as "The Dukes of Hazzard Car"; and, as consumer surveys had determined, 80 percent of the children asked thought the Dixie Racer was the Dukes of Hazzard car. What evidence might be introduced to rebut the charge of trademark violation? Could the case have been treated as one of unfair competition at common law?

The question of automotive confusion can be raised with real as well as toy cars. In Esercizio v. Roberts, 944 F.2d 1235 (6th Cir. 1991), the defendant Roberts made kits and cars that duplicated the distinctive Ferrari exterior on its limited production models. Ferrari's "trade dress" claim with regard to its "unique and distinctive exterior shape" was upheld by the court which noted that the Ferrari exterior had obtained a powerful "secondary meaning" in the eyes of consumers. The court also held that the plaintiff established confusion from the similarity of the two marks, from the actual confusion reported by consumers, and from defendant's conscious decision to copy the plaintiff's design for its own commercial advantage. Finally, the court noted that the trademark protection was available in perpetuity even though the plaintiff had acquired a design patent for its exterior. It then relied on Application of Mogen David Wine Corp., 328 F.2d 925, 930 (Cust. & Pat. 1964):

> The protection accorded by the law of trademark and unfair competition is greater than that accorded by the law of patents because each is directed at a different purpose. The latter protects inventive activity which, after a term of years, is dedicated to the public domain. The former protects commercial activity, which, in our society, is essentially private.

4. *Noncompetitive use of trademarks.* While most trademark litigation takes place in commercial settings between rival sellers, trademark protection need not be so limited. In MGM-Pathé Communications v. Pink Panther Patrol, 774 F. Supp. 869, 875 (S.D.N.Y. 1991), the plaintiffs were the owner of the registered trademark THE PINK PANTHER, which applies to the popular series of films about its bumbling detective hero. It also lent its trademark to producers of a wide range of consumer and children's goods. The defendant was a gay rights defense organization that used the PINK PANTHER name in connection with an upside down pink triangle (used by the Nazis to mark homosexuals) as its symbol. Even though the defendant group sold no goods in competition with the plaintiffs', the court enjoined its use of the PINK PANTHER trademark on the ground that ordinary individuals could mistakenly assume that the owners of the trademark sponsored or otherwise supported the activities of the patrol.

> [A]lthough plaintiff and defendants are primarily engaged in different types of "commerce," the Patrol seeks public recognition for its name and mission in the news media, which is not so distant from plaintiff's field of entertainment. It is indeed entirely likely that a large percentage of the population of the United States might see and hear both plaintiff's and defendants' names during a single evening of nationwide television broadcasting, if a telecast of an MGM film should be followed by a newscast including reference to the Patrol's activities.

But tradename protection (and common-law misappropriation) were both denied in New Kids on the Block v. New America Pub. Inc., 971

F.2d 302, 308 (9th Cir. 1992). There two newspapers, USA Today and
The Star, ran popularity polls on (900) phone lines, asking callers to
say which of the (five) New Kids was the hottest (or coolest). Kozinski,
J., held that this use of their tradename was a protected *nominative* use
because there was no other conceivable way in which any newspaper
could otherwise refer to the group in order to get their readers' opinions about it. "It is no more reasonably possible, however, to refer to
the New Kids as an entity than it is to refer to the Chicago Bulls, Volks-
wagens or the Boston Marathon without using the trademark." The use
of the name was therefore adjudged fair because "[b]oth *The Star* and
USA Today reference the New Kids only to the extent necessary to identify them as the subject of the polls; they do not use the New Kids'
distinctive logo or anything else that isn't needed to make the an-
nouncements intelligible to readers. Finally, nothing in the announcement suggests joint sponsorship or endorsement by the New Kids."
Should it make a difference that the profits from the (900) calls are
donated to charity? That the New Kids have their own (900) numbers
for their fans to use? See generally Heald, Federal Intellectual Property
Law and the Economics of Preemption, 76 Iowa L. Rev. 959 (1991).

   5. Patents. Inventions have long received explicit statutory protection
under the patent system. The general substantive law requires that
there be a patentable subject matter, including "any new and useful
process, machine, manufacture, or composition of matter, or any new
and useful improvement thereof." Other requirements are originality,
novelty, and nonobviousness. See generally 35 U.S.C. §101 et seq.
(1988 & Supp. 1993). In addition, there are extensive procedural requirements for filing an application for a new patent with the patent
office. The application must be filed within one year of its public use
or publication, and it must contain "a written description of the invention, and of the manner and process of making and using it, in such
full, clear, concise, and exact terms as to enable any person skilled in
the art to which it pertains . . . to make and use the same," concluding
"with one or more claims particularly pointing out and distinctly claiming the subject matter which the applicant regards as his invention." 35
U.S.C. §112 (1988 & Supp. 1993) Why are the procedural elements for
the perfection of a patent so critical to the operation of the system?

   On the economic function of the patent system see Kitch, The Nature and Function of the Patent System, 20 J.L. & Econ. 265 (1977),
where it is argued that the system has two functions: prospect and reward. The reward function acts as a spur to invention by conferring an
exclusive monopoly. The prospect function (on analogy to the rule in
mining law that allows the party who discovers a vein of ore to have the
first crack at its exploitation) helps insure that certain "prospects" —
here new inventions — will be efficiently and sensibly developed by giving exclusive rights in the period between the time an invention is first

patented and the time it is first commercially exploited. One limitation of the prospect theory is that it tends to downplay the risk that the holder of a broad patent will seek to exploit it not through development but by licensing its use to other parties. A broad patent therefore has the undesirable effect of forcing people to "invent around" patented devices. See Grady and Alexander, Patent Law and Rent Dissipation, 78 Va. L. Rev. 305 (1992), with comments by Martin, Id. at 351, and Merges, Id. at 359. What is the relationship between a law of patents and a law of trade secrets? Why are both needed?

6. *Federal preemption of state unfair competition laws: unpatentable designs.* The questions of unfair competition in both *INS* and *Mosler Safe* were decided as a matter of general federal common law under the then-applicable doctrine of Swift v. Tyson, 41 U.S. 1 (1842). The further *federal* common-law development of the doctrine has been blocked by Erie R.R. Co. v. Tompkins, 304 U.S. 64 (1938), which held that there could be no "general" federal common law under the general diversity jurisdiction. *Erie* has not, however, eliminated the traditional tension over whether courts or legislatures should decide what protection is appropriate in unfair competition cases. To the contrary, it has added a second dimension to the question, for today unfair competition cases are state law matters, but only when federal copyright, patent, and trademark statutes do not preempt the creation of state law remedies. Here the fundamental text is Art. I, §8, cl. 8 of the United States Constitution, which provides that Congress shall have the power "[t]o promote the Progress of Science and useful Arts, by securing for limited times to Authors and Inventors the exclusive Right to their respective Writings and Discoveries."

One early foray into the preemption question was Sears, Roebuck & Co. v. Stiffel Co., 376 U.S. 225, 231-232 (1964). Sears, Roebuck marketed pole lamps that were substantially identical to those sold by Stiffel Corporation. Stiffel sought to enjoin Sears on the ground that its lamps were protected by a design patent, but this was rejected by the trial judge "for want of invention." The trial court held, however, that Stiffel was entitled to protection under the state law of unfair competition when Sears sold lamps identical to Stiffel's, even though there was no "palming off" or confusion as to source. The Supreme Court reversed, noting that patents, as a form of monopoly, should only be issued if the stringent conditions set out in the statute are satisfied. "To allow a State by use of its law of unfair competition to prevent the copying of an article which represents too slight an advance to be patented would be to permit the State to block off from the public something which federal law has said belongs to the public. The result would be that while federal law grants only 14 or 17 years' protection to genuine inventions, see 35 U.S.C. §§154, 173, States could allow perpetual protection to articles too lacking in novelty to merit any patent at all under federal constitutional standards."

Sears was recently applied in Bonito Boats, Inc. v. Thunder Craft Boats, Inc., 489 U.S. 141, 159-160 (1989), to strike down a state statute, Fla. Stat. §559.94 (1987), outlawing the use of the "plug molding" process, whereby one competitor uses the hull of a rival producer as the "plug" in order to create a mold that is then used to make identical hulls for its own use. No passing off or confusion was involved, but using the plug mold allowed a later competitor to produce a hull at low cost, an opportunity that had been denied the earlier entrant into the field. In a lower court case, Interpart Corp. v. Italia, 777 F.2d 678 (Fed. Cir. 1985), the court had held that the plug mold statute was not preempted because it only restricted the use of a single method to reproduce a hull shape; it did not, however, preclude "copying the product by hand, by using sophisticated machinery, or by any method other than the direct molding process. . . ." The Supreme Court rejected this argument and held that protection for the hull design was available only if the plug molding process was actually protected under the federal patent statutes.

> The Florida scheme offers [its] protection for an unlimited number of years to all boat hulls and their component parts, without regard to their ornamental or technological merit. Protection is available for subject matter for which patent protection has been denied or has expired, as well as for designs which have been freely revealed to the consuming public by their creators.
> . . . We think it clear that such protection conflicts with the federal policy "that all ideas in general circulation be dedicated to the common good unless they are protected by a valid patent."

Is the plaintiff trying to protect an "idea" or a prior investment in the labor needed to fashion the original hull design? Note that by not protecting the hull, it is now possible to buy fiberglass boats at a lower price than otherwise. Yet by the same token design innovations are less likely to occur once the plug mold statute is struck down. Should there be a patent protection against plug molding?

7. *Preemption of piracy and trade secrets. Sears* does not, however, imply that all state unfair competition laws have been preempted by federal statute. In Goldstein v. California, 412 U.S. 546, 569-570 (1973), the Supreme Court held that the defendant could be criminally convicted for record piracy under California's unfair competition law, even though the copying of recorded performances had no copyright protection under the then-applicable 1909 Copyright Act. *Sears* was treated as a case concerned with "mechanical configurations." "The application of state law in these cases to prevent the copying of articles which did

not meet the requirements for federal protection disturbed the careful balance which Congress had drawn and thereby necessarily gave way under the Supremacy Clause of the Constitution. No comparable conflict between state law and federal law arises in the case of recordings of musical performances. In regard to this category of 'Writings,' Congress has drawn no balance; rather, it has left the area unattended, and no reason exists why the State should not be free to act." What must be known to determine why Congress "occupied the field" in the design patent area but not in the copyright area?

Sears was also distinguished in Kewanee Oil Co. v. Bicron Corp., 416 U.S. 470, 483, 484 (1974), which held that the congressional power over patents did not preempt the power of a state to develop its own law of trade secrets. Trade secrets are often used to protect certain types of unpatentable materials (e.g., industrial "know-how"), but they may also extend to matters of doubtful patentability or even to matters for which patents may be granted. See generally Wexler v. Greenberg, 160 A.2d 430 (Pa. 1960). The Court in *Kewanee* first concluded that state law should govern with respect to nonpatentable materials. "Abolition of trade secret protection would, therefore, not result in increased disclosure to the public of discoveries in the area of nonpatentable subject matter. Also, it is hard to see how the public would be benefited by disclosure of customer lists or advertising campaigns; in fact, keeping such items secret encourages businesses to initiate new and individualized plans of operation, and constructive competition results." The Court next concluded that there was also no reason to deny trade secret protection even when patents might be obtainable. "Certainly the patent policy of encouraging invention is not disturbed by the existence of another form of incentive to invention. In this respect the two systems are not and never would be in conflict. Similarly, the policy that matter once in the public domain must remain in the public domain is not incompatible with the existence of trade secret protection. By definition a trade secret has not been placed in the public domain." Finally, the Court concluded that trade secret protection should also be extended to cases of clear patentability, on the ground that its denial might encourage private parties to adopt complex and costly security devices that could hamper innovation or, in the alternative, be driven to apply for a patent that they otherwise would not seek.

On the general question of preemption see Goldstein, *Kewanee Oil Co. v. Bicron Corp.*: Notes on a Closing Circle, 1974 Sup. Ct. Rev. 81. For the Supreme Court position on preemption see Aronson v. Quick Point Pencil Co., 440 U.S. 257 (1979), holding that licensing agreements under state law are not preempted by the federal patent law even if the underlying patent is found invalid.

8. Preemption under the copyright law. For the current legal position on preemption under the copyright laws see Copyrights, 17 U.S.C. §301

(1988 & Supp. 1993), governing works created as of January 1, 1978, which first preempts state law with respect to "works of authorship that are fixed in a tangible medium of expression" only to later provide that "[n]othing in this title annuls or limits any rights or remedies under the common law or statutes of any State with respect to (1) subject matter that does not come within the subject matter of copyright . . . including works of authorship not fixed in any tangible medium of expression, or . . . (3) activities violating legal or equitable rights that are not equivalent to any of the exclusive rights within the general scope of copyright." Does this statute afford any precision not afforded by common-law techniques? On the copyright law generally see Landes and Posner, An Economic Analysis of Copyright Law, 18 J. Legal Stud. 325 (1989).

Table of Cases

Table of Restatement Sections

RESTATEMENT (THIRD) OF TORTS
Tentative Draft No. 1 (1994)

Table of Secondary Authorities

Belli, The Use of Demonstrative Evidence in Achieving the More Adequate Award 33 (1952), 871

Bender, A Lawyer's Primer on Feminist Theory and Tort, 38 J. Legal Educ. 34 (1988), 568

Beven, T., Negligence in Law 45 (3d ed. 1908), 503

Bezanson, R., G. Cranberg, and J. Soloski, Libel Law and the Press: Myth and Reality ch. 8 (1987), 1214

Birch, W. F., Accident Compensation: A Fairer Scheme (1991), 1079

Bishop, Economic Loss in Tort, 2 Oxford J. Legal Stud. 1 (1982), 1354

————, Negligent Misrepresentation Through Economists' Eyes, 96 Law Q. Rev. 360 (1980), 1328

Blackstone, W., Commentaries, Vol. 3, p. 120 (1790), 67

Blum, Review of O'Connell's Ending Insult to Injury, 43 U. Chi. L. Rev. 217 (1975), 1065

Bohlen, Consent as Affecting Civil Liability for Breaches of the Peace, 24 Colum. L. Rev. 819; 79 U. Pa. L. Rev. 509; 17 Va. L. Rev. 374 (1924), 23

————, The Duty of a Landowner Towards Those Entering His Premises of Their Own Right, 69 U. Pa. L. Rev. 142 (1921), 587

————, Incomplete Privilege to Inflict Intentional Invasions of Interests of Property and Personalty, 39 Harv. L. Rev. 307 (1926), 60, 61

————, The Rule in *Rylands v. Fletcher* (pts. 1-3), 59 U. Pa. L. Rev. 298 (1911), 130

————, Studies in the Law of Torts 577 (1926), 26

————, Voluntary Assumption of Risk, 20 Harv. L. Rev. 14 (1906), 358

Bovbjerg, Sloan, and Blumstein, Valuing Life and Limb in Tort: Scheduling "Pain and Suffering," 83 Nw. L. Rev. 908 (1989), 872

Bower, J., Actionable Defamation (1908), 1115, 1169

Brennan, The Supreme Court and the Meiklejohn Interpretation of the First Amendment, 79 Harv. L. Rev. 1 (1965), 1185

Brickman, L., J. O'Connell and M. Horowitz, Rethinking Contingency Fees: A Proposal to Align the Contingency Fee System with its Policy Roots and Ethical Mandates (1994), 900

Broeder, Torts and Just Compensation: Some Personal Reflections, 17 Hastings L.J. 217 (1965), 63

Brown, Deterrence and No-Fault: The New Zealand Experience, 73 Cal. L. Rev. 976 (1985), 1063

————, Toward an Economic Theory of Liability, 2 J. Legal Stud. 323 (1973), 204, 324

Calabresi and Hirschoff, Toward a Test for Strict Liability in Torts, 81 Yale L.J. 1055 (1972), 206, 706

Calabresi and Melamed, Property Rules, Liability Rules and Inalienability: One View of the Cathedral, 85 Harv. L. Rev. 1089 (1972), 156, 716

Calfee and Craswell, Some Effects of Uncertainty on Compliance with Legal Standards, 70 Va. L. Rev. 965, n.36 (1984), 205

Carlton and Fischel, The Regulation of Insider Trading, 35 Stan. L. Rev. 857 (1983), 1310

Carpenter, Interference with Contract Relations, 41 Harv. L. Rev. 728 (1928), 1340

Carter and Palmer, Real Rates, Expected Rates, and Damage Awards, 20 J. Legal Stud. 439 (1991), 881

Clermont and Currivan, Improving on the Contingent Fee, 63 Cornell L. Rev. 529 (1978), 900

Coase, The Problem of Social Cost, 3 J.L. & Econ. 1 (1960), 338, 452, 690

Coleman, Efficiency, Utility and Wealth Maximization, 8 Hofstra L. Rev. 509 (1980), 691

Cooter, Towards a Market in Unmatured Tort Claims, 75 Va. L. Rev. 383 (1989), 906

Cooter and Ulen, An Economic Case for Comparative Negligence, 61 N.Y.U. L. Rev. 1067 (1986), 383

Jaffe, Damages for Personal Injury: The Impact of Insurance, 18 Law & Contemp. Probs. 219 (1953), 870

James, Assumption of Risk, 61 Yale L.J. 141 (1952), 364

———, Functions of Judge and Jury in Negligence Cases, 58 Yale L.J. 667 (1949), 277

———, Indemnity, Subrogation, and Contribution and the Efficient Distribution of Accident Losses, 21 NACCA L.J. 360 (1958), 458

———, Last Clear Chance — Transitional Doctrine, 47 Yale L.J. 704 (1938), 348

———, The Qualities of the Reasonable Man in Negligence Cases, 16 Mo. L. Rev. 1 (1951), 181

James, F., and G. Hazard, J. Leubsdorf, Civil Procedure 399 (4th ed. 1992), 890

Jensen and Meckling, Theory of the Firm: Managerial Behavior, Agency Costs, and Ownership Structure, 3 J. Fin. Econ. 305 (1976), 976

Johnsen, The Creation of Fetal Rights: Conflicts with Woman's Constitutional Rights to Liberty, Privacy, and Equal Protection, 95 Yale L.J. 599 (1986), 21

Jolowicz, The Right to Indemnity Between Master and Servant, [1958] Camb. L.J. 21, 458

Jones, Product Defects Causing Commercial Loss: The Ascendency of Contract over Tort, 44 U. Miami L. Rev. 731 (1990), 766

Kalven, The Dignity of the Civil Jury, 50 Va. L. Rev. 1055 (1964), 290

———, The New York Times Case: A Note on "the Central Meaning of the First Amendment," 1964 S. Ct. Rev. 191, 1185

———, Privacy in the Tort Law — Were Warren and Brandeis Wrong?, 31 Law & Contemp. Probs. 326 (1966), 1219

———, The Reasonable Man and the First Amendment, 1967 S. Ct. Rev. 267, 1191

———, Tort Law — Tort Watch, 34 A.T.L.J. 1 (1972), 760

Karafiol, The Right to Privacy and the *Sidis* Case, 12 Ga. L. Rev. 513 (1978), 1249

Karchmer, Informed Consent: A Plaintiff's Medical Malpractice "Wonder Drug," 31 Mo. L. Rev. 29 (1966), 235

Kaye, Probability Theory Meets Res Ipsa Loquitur, 77 Mich. L. Rev. 1456, 1465 (1979), 304

Kaye and Aicken, A Comment on Causal Apportionment, 13 J. Legal Stud. 191 (1984), 407

Keeton, Compensation Systems and Utah's No-Fault Statute, 1973 Utah L. Rev. 383, 1049

———, Conditional Fault in the Law of Torts, 72 Harv. L. Rev. 401 (1959), 60

———, Products Liability — Inadequacy of Information, 48 Tex. L. Rev. 398 (1970), 811

Keeton, R. and J. O'Connell, Basic Protection for the Traffic Victim 242 (1965), 161, 999

Keeton, R. and A. Widiss, Insurance Law (1988), 992, 993, 1010

Kessel, Transfused Blood, Serum Hepatitis, and The Coase Theorem, 17 J.L. & Econ. 265 (1974), 843

King, In Search of a Standard of Care for the Medical Profession: The "Accepted Practice" Formula, 28 Vand. L. Rev. 1213 (1975), 231

———, The Exclusiveness of an Employee's Workers' Compensation Remedy Against His Employer, 55 Tenn. L. Rev. 405 (1988), 1044

Kitch, The Nature and Function of the Patent System, 20 J.L. & Econ. 265 (1977), 1383

Klevorick and Rothschild, A Model of the Jury Decision Process, 8 J. Legal Stud. 141 (1979), 290

Komesar, Toward a General Theory of Personal Injury Loss, 3 J. Legal Stud. 457 (1974), 885

Kornhauser and Revesz, Settlements Under Joint and Several Liability, 68 N.Y.U. L. Rev. 427 (1993), 448

Kramer and Sykes, Municipal Liability Under §1983: A Legal and Economic Analysis, [1987] Sup. Ct. Rev. 249, 953

Kronman, Mistake, Disclosure, Information, and the Law of Contracts, 7 J. Legal Stud. 1 (1978), 1310

Index